PETERSON'S

COLLEGE & UNIVERSITY ALMANAC

A COMPACT GUIDE TO HIGHER EDUCATION

1999

PETERSON'S
Princeton, New Jersey

About Peterson's

Peterson's is the country's largest educational information/communications company, providing the academic, consumer, and professional communities with books, software, and online services in support of lifelong education access and career choice. Well-known references include Peterson's annual guides to private schools, summer programs, colleges and universities, graduate and professional programs, financial aid, international study, adult learning, and career guidance. Peterson's Web site at petersons.com is the only comprehensive—and most heavily traveled—education resource on the Internet. The site carries all of Peterson's fully searchable major databases and includes financial aid sources, test-prep help, job postings, direct inquiry and application features, and specially created Virtual Campuses for every accredited academic institution and summer program in the U.S. and Canada that offers in-depth narratives, announcements, and multimedia features.

Visit Peterson's Education Center on the Internet (World Wide Web) at www.petersons.com

Editorial inquiries concerning this book should be addressed to the editor at Peterson's, P.O. Box 2123, Princeton, New Jersey 08543-2123.

ISBN 0-7689-0035-2

Printed in Canada

10 9 8 7 6 5 4 3 2 1

Contents

A Guide to Good Four-Year Colleges

by Ernest L. Boyer, edited by Paul Boyer

When you think of college you probably imagine the cliché or Hollywood image: a campus filled with ivy-covered buildings, students socializing in the academic quad, or the faint sounds of a professor's voice coming from an open window. Despite this stereotypical picture of what college might look like on the surface, there is no single model of a "good college." Missions and circumstances vary greatly from one campus to another. Each four-year college and university has something different to offer its students. And with college costs rising, you want to be assured that you will get the best value out of the college investment. This makes choosing the right college even more difficult. It may help to know that despite all the differences among colleges, there are characteristics commonly shared by reputable schools that you should consider in your search.

Although these standards can be used to evaluate any college, you should narrow your list prior to the "test of quality" and put these questions to the schools on your final list. First consider other facts that may be important to you, such as location or size. As you work through the list, you will find that a great deal of this information can be uncovered by reading this book as well as the individual college's literature. But you will need to look further, to discuss these items with your guidance counselor, representatives from the colleges, and other advisers in order to come up with the most complete review of a particular school.

Some Common Measures of Quality

Every college should be guided by a clear and vital mission. It should understand its unique role in higher education and present itself honestly to prospective students through its literature and other information outlets. An institution cannot be all things to all people, so choices must be made and priorities assigned. What shows the strength of an institution is whether it has clearly defined its focus and, beyond that, whether it has successfully turned those goals into a living purpose for the campus. Of course, you also need to determine if the college's mission matches up with your own goals and values. At the very least, you need to know that you will be comfortable at a college and that it will deliver the type of educational experience you're seeking.

The quality of the undergraduate college is measured largely by the extent of its cooperation with high schools and by its willingness to smooth the transition of students into college. The way you are recruited by a college helps to shape your expectations of that college. A good college conducts its recruitment and selection with the best interests of the students in mind and should, therefore, try to learn more about you than simply your test scores and class rank.

Beyond the admissions process it is important for a college to continue to demonstrate commitment to you by taking steps to make you feel at home. The first few weeks on campus are a major rite of passage and may have a significant influence on your entire undergraduate experience. In short, you will want to determine whether the freshman year is viewed as something special and whether the college has a well-planned orientation program that addresses the particular concerns of the new student.

Since students need guidance throughout their entire education, a college of quality has a year-round program of academic advising and personal counseling, structured to serve all undergraduates, including part-time and commuting students. You will want to find out if the faculty is available to freshmen to talk about their disciplines and whether they give guidance to young students as they consider career choices. A college worthy of commendation works as hard at holding students as it does at getting them to the campus in the first place. You may wish to investigate a college's retention rate over the past five years and find out whether or not it offers guidance programs for students who are having trouble. These are all measures of a college's dedication to its students.

A Planned, Yet Flexible, Curriculum

At a good college, the academic major will broaden rather than restrict the perspective, presenting, in effect, an enriched major. An enriched major will answer three essential questions: What are the history and traditions of the field to be examined? What are the social and economic implications to be pursued? What are the ethical and moral issues within the specialty that need to be confronted? Rather than dividing the undergraduate experience into separate camps—general versus specialized education—the curriculum at a college of high quality will bring the two together. Therefore, it's important to determine if the college has a coherent general education sequence—an integrated core—rather than a more loosely connected distribution arrangement. This core academic program should provide not only for an integration of the separate academic principles but also for their application and relationship to life. All colleges impose requirements for graduation, including a set number of credits and some predetermined courses within a major. But within this set of general expectations, there is also room for flexibility. Increasingly, innovative colleges are recognizing the needs and skills of older students, encouraging individual learning, giving credit for experience, and helping students to craft their own unique majors. Students should not all have to march on to graduation in four years if they have interests, skills, and needs that are not acknowledged by a traditional degree program. New types of students are enrolling, and the location of learning has moved beyond the campus—to the home, the workplace, and around the world. In recognition of this trend, an effective college designs programs that meet new patterns and creates ways to both extend and encourage diversity on the campus.

The Classroom Climate

The undergraduate experience, at its best, also means encouraging students to be active rather than passive learners. In measuring the quality of a college, you should ask if the institution has a climate that encourages independent, self-directed study, where teaching is perceived as more than just lecturing. If a college encourages small discussion sessions in which students work together on group assignments, it may indicate dedication to the undergraduate curriculum. In addition, if undergraduate courses are taught by the most respected and most gifted teachers on campus, it speaks further to this commitment.

Indeed, the strength of the faculty plays a leading role in determining the quality of the undergraduate experience. Students and parents have become increasingly concerned with the balance of time that faculty members spend on research and publishing requirements versus lecturing or advising. To uncover how an institution views this balance, you should ask if good teaching is valued equally with research and if it is an important criterion for tenure and promotion. It's important to know if the college recognizes that some faculty members are great teachers, others great researchers, and still others a blend of both. The central qualities that make for successful teaching are the ones that can be simply stated: command of the material to be taught, a contagious enthusiasm for the play of ideas, optimism about the potential of one's students, and sensitivity, integrity, and warmth as a human being. At a good college, this combination is present in the classroom.

Devoting Resources to Learning

An institution of high quality is one that supports its mission of learning both financially and philosophically. In doing so, a college should allot ample funds to its library and other educational resources. In terms of its use, you should determine if the library is more than just a study hall and if students are encouraged to spend at least as much time with library resources as they spend in classes. These resources should primarily serve the interests of undergraduate research and not be dominated by narrow scholarly interests of faculty members or graduate students. In addition, computers offer great potential for learning on campus. Some colleges now require that you purchase a computer before coming to campus. Others make terminals available to all students in common areas. Particularly if you are looking to advance in computer-related fields, or if you are inclined toward furthering your computer skills, you will want to know if campus terminals are linked to wider networks (including the Internet) and if the college connects technology, the library, and the classroom, letting each resource do what it does best and encouraging students to engage in creative, independent learning.

The Campus Culture

A college campus is also a community. A high-quality college will work to make the time spent outside of the classroom as meaningful as the time spent in class. The high-quality college sees academic and nonacademic functions as related and arranges events ranging from lecture series and concerts to sports and student organizations to reinforce the curriculum. These campuswide activities, intended for both faculty and students, should encourage community, sustain college traditions, and stimulate both social and cultural interaction. Because much learning occurs outside the classroom, it is important to know how accessible faculty members are to their students—not only through office hours but also elsewhere on the campus, at social or extracurricular functions. In this setting, the academic campus transcends the classroom and is viewed as a place for learning. Beyond the structured programs, the campus culture extends into the residence halls and other social areas on campus. Residential living can be one of the most chaotic parts of campus life, yet it has the potential of being one of the most rewarding. It is a good idea to find out if residence halls also promote a sense of community through organized activities and informal learning.

A Final Word of Advice

In the end, a high-quality college is concerned about outcomes. It asks questions about student development that go beyond the evaluation of skill. But a good college will avoid measuring that which matters least and will focus on the need for students to think clearly, to be well informed, to integrate their knowledge, and to apply what they have learned.

The impact of college extends beyond graduation, and a college of quality will provide placement guidance to its students and follow their careers. These students will be well equipped to put their work in context and adequately prepared to move from one intellectual challenge to another. The undergraduate experience will also have prepared students to see beyond the narrow boundaries of their own interests and discover global connections. The college succeeds as its graduates are inspired by a larger vision, using their newfound knowledge to form values and advance the common good.

When you make your college contacts and campus visits, you now know what questions to ask and what to look for in order to make an informed decision. In doing so, however, you should always take into account your specific goals and you'll find that some colleges will immediately fall from your list. In the end, the important thing to remember is that a college of high quality is one that will prepare you for a productive career but will also offer you values and principles that you can apply beyond graduation day.

Using This Book

In the preceding article, "A Guide to Good Four-Year Colleges," you were presented with several points to consider when evaluating the quality of a particular college. There are other factors to consider, in addition, that don't necessarily point to the overall quality of the education you might receive but that heavily influence your final choice. Among the many criteria you might use are the location, size, cost, entrance selectivity, or diversity of an institution. Rather than flipping through the hundreds of pages in this guide to find the perfect college, you might first consider other means of narrowing your search. By answering some of the following types of questions: "What part of the country do you want to be in?" "Do you prefer an urban or rural setting?" or "Are you looking for a small, intimate environment or a college with a large student body?" you will be able to develop a personalized list of criteria. By compiling that list of questions and answers, you will soon arrive at a list of things that you'll need to research for each college under consideration.

This guide's easy-to-use college profiles are designed to provide you with the data you'll need to single out colleges for "the final list." In addition to using resources such as this one, don't underestimate the guidance of your parents, high school counselor, friends, and alumni of the institutions you are considering. Be sure to carefully review the college's viewbook and recruiting literature and make use of the campus visit, especially as a screening tool for your narrowed list.

Considering Your Options

If you have a very specific idea of what you want out of a college education, you will have an easier time compiling your list of prospective colleges. By considering some of the following criteria, you will soon find that your initial list of perhaps fifty colleges has been narrowed to a more reasonable number.

1. **Location**. For some students, staying close to home might be a priority. Or, venturing all the way across the country might be something you've always wanted to do and college seems like the perfect time to do it. Likewise, you may know that city life is not for you; therefore, you would like to limit your search to suburban or

even rural colleges. Whatever the reason, the location of a college often plays a key role in the college selection process.

2. **Entrance Difficulty**. Many students will look to a college's entrance difficulty as an indication of whether or not they will be admitted. For instance, if you have an excellent academic record, you might wish to primarily consider those colleges that are highly selective. Although entrance difficulty does not necessarily translate into quality of education, it does often indicate whether a college is highly sought-after.
3. **Education Costs**. As the price tag for higher education continues to rise, cost becomes an increasingly important factor when selecting a college. Certainly it is necessary to consider your family's resources when choosing a list of schools to which you might apply. On the other hand, avoid eliminating colleges that you might otherwise consider based solely on cost. You may be able to obtain the necessary financial aid to allow you to enroll in your higher-priced college of choice.
4. **Most Popular Recent Majors**. Despite all of the other factors that might influence your selection, one of the most important is whether a college offers a program in your academic area of interest. Or, conversely, if you have not selected a program at the onset, you will want to find a college with a broad enough selection to satisfy your eventual choice.

Beyond these major factors, you will undoubtedly uncover other criteria that will strongly influence your choice of where to attend college. Questions about a particular institution's size, the diversity of its student body, or special academic programs or services may weigh heavily in the decision process. The straightforward format of the College Profiles makes it easy to gather the facts on all of these points and more, providing you with the answers you need to make the most informed choice. The following paragraph describes in detail the data that are contained within these features.

How Hard Is It to Get In?

The five levels of entrance difficulty, as defined below, are based on the percentage of applicants who were accepted for fall 1997 freshman admission (or, in the case of upper-level schools, for entering-class admission) and on the high school class rank and standardized test scores of the accepted freshmen who actually enrolled in fall 1997. The colleges were asked to select the level that most closely corresponds to their entrance difficulty, according to the guidelines below, to assist prospective students in assessing their chances for admission.

The five levels of entrance difficulty are as follows:

1. **Most difficult:** More than 75% of the freshmen were in the top 10% of their high school class and scored over 1250 on the SAT I (verbal and mathematical combined) or over 29 on the ACT (composite); about 30% or fewer of the applicants were accepted.
2. **Very difficult:** More than 50% of the freshmen were in the top 10% of their high school class and scored over 1150 on the SAT I or over 26 on the ACT; about 60% or fewer of the applicants were accepted.
3. **Moderately difficult:** More than 75% of the freshmen were in the top half of their high school class and scored over 900 on the SAT I or over 18 on the ACT; about 85% or fewer of the applicants were accepted.
4. **Minimally difficult:** Most freshmen were not in the top half of their high school class and scored somewhat below 900 on the SAT I or below 19 on the ACT; up to 95% of the applicants were accepted.
5. **Noncompetitive:** Virtually all applicants were accepted regardless of high school rank or test scores.

Profile Highlights

Setting: Designated as urban (located within a major city), suburban (a residential area within commuting distance of a major city), small town (a small but compactly settled area not within commuting distance of a major city), or rural (a remote and sparsely populated area).

Total enrollment: The number of matriculated undergraduate and (if applicable) graduate students, both full-time and part-time, as of fall 1997.

Student/faculty ratio: The school's estimate of the ratio of matriculated undergraduate students to faculty members teaching undergraduate courses.

Application Deadline: Deadlines and dates for notification of acceptance or rejection are given either as specific dates or as rolling and continuous. Rolling means that applications are processed as they are received, and qualified students are accepted as long as there are openings. Continuous notification means that applicants are notified of acceptance or rejection as applications are processed up until the date indicated or the actual beginning of classes.

Freshmen: Figures are given for the percentage of applicants who were accepted.

Housing: Indicates whether on-campus housing is available.

Costs: *Tuition* is the average basic tuition for an academic year is presented as a dollar amount. *Room & board* is the average yearly room and board costs are presented as a dollar amount.

Undergraduates: Percentages of undergraduates who are women, part-time students, 25 or older, Native American (Indian, Eskimo, Polynesian), Hispanic, African American, and Asian American are given.

Most popular recent majors: The most popular majors of the 1997 graduating class.

Average class size: The average class size for required undergraduate courses.

Advanced Placement: Credit toward a degree awarded for acceptable scores on some or all College Board Advanced Placement tests.

Accelerated degree program: Students may earn a bachelor's degree in three academic years.

Self-designed majors: Students may design their own program of study based on individual interests.

Honors program: Unusually challenging academic program for superior students.

Summer session for credit: Summer courses through which students may make up degree work or accelerate their program.

Part-time degree programs: Students may earn a degree without having to attend classes full-time; part-time degree programs may be offered for students attending regular-session classes (daytime) or evening, weekend, or summer classes.

External degree programs: Students may earn a degree through a program that (1) requires no more than 25% of the degree credit to be earned through campus-located instruction, (2) grants credit for documented extra-institutional and experiential learning, and (3) emphasizes off-campus self-directed study.

Adult/continuing education programs: Courses offered for nontraditional students who are currently working or are returning to formal education.

Cooperative (co-op) education programs: Formal arrangement with off-campus employers allowing students to combine work and study in order to gain degree-related experience, usually extending the time required to complete a degree.

Internships: College-arranged work experience for which students earn academic credit.

Contact: The name, title, mailing address, Web site, and telephone number of the person to contact for further information are given at the end of the profile. Toll-free telephone numbers may also be included. The admission office fax number and e-mail address may be provided.

The Colleges and Universities in This Guide

The profiles of the colleges and universities include all four-year colleges in the United States that appear in *Peterson's Guide to Four-Year Colleges 1999.* The term "four-year college" is the commonly used designation for institutions that grant the baccalaureate, since four years is the normal duration of the traditional undergraduate curriculum. However, some bachelor's programs may be completed in three years, others require five years, and, of course, part-time programs may take a considerably longer period. Also included are upper-level institutions that award the baccalaureate but require that entering students have at least two years of previous college-level credit and thus normally require an additional two years to complete a degree program.

Accreditation

To be included in this guide, an institution must have full accreditation or candidate-for-accreditation (preaccreditation) status granted by an institutional or specialized accrediting body recognized by the U.S. Department of Education or the Council on Postsecondary Accreditation. Recognized institutional accrediting bodies, which consider each institution as a whole, are the following: the six regional associations of schools and colleges (Middle States, New England, North Central, Northwest, Southern, and Western), each of which is responsible for a specified portion of the United States and its territories; the Accrediting Association of Bible Colleges (AABC); the Accrediting Council for Independent Colleges and Schools (ACICS); the Accrediting Commission of Career Schools/Colleges of Technology (ACCSCT); The Distance Education and Training Council (DETC); and the Transnational Association of Christian Schools (TRACS). Program registration by the New York State Board of Regents is considered to be the equivalent of institutional accreditation, since the Board requires that all programs offered by an institution meet its standards before recognition is granted. A Canadian institution must be chartered and authorized to grant degrees by the provincial government, affiliated with a chartered institution, or accredited by a recognized U.S. accrediting body. This guide also includes institutions outside the United States, the U.S. territories, and Canada that are accredited by recognized U.S. accrediting bodies. There are recognized specialized accrediting bodies in more than forty different fields, each of which is authorized to accredit specific programs in its particular field. This can serve as the equivalent of institutional accreditation for specialized institutions that offer programs in one field only (schools of art, music, optometry, theology, etc.). For a full explanation of the accrediting process and complete information on recognized accrediting bodies, the reader should refer to *Peterson's Directory of College and University Administrators* (formerly *Peterson's Register of Higher Education).*

Research Procedures

The data contained in the college indexes and college profiles were collected between fall 1997 and spring 1998 through Peterson's Annual Survey of Undergraduate Institutions. Surveys were sent to the colleges and universities that meet the criteria for inclusion outlined above. All data that appear in this edition have been submitted by officials (usually admission and financial aid officers, registrars, or institutional research personnel) at the schools themselves. In addition, the great majority of institutions that submitted data were contacted directly by Peterson's editorial and research staff to verify unusual figures, resolve discrepancies, and obtain additional data. All usable information received in time for publication has been included. The omission of any particular item from an index or profile listing signifies that the item is either not applicable to that institution or that data were not available. Because of the comprehensive editorial review that takes place in our offices and because all material comes directly from college officials, we have every reason to believe that the information presented in this guide is accurate. However, students should check with a specific college or university at the time of application to verify such figures as tuition and fees, which may have changed since the publication of this volume.

For Further Information

If you would like in-depth information about the colleges of your choice, refer to Peterson's Web site at http://www.petersons.com.

A Guide to Financing a College Education

by Don M. Betterton, Director of Undergraduate Aid,
Princeton University

Given the lifelong benefit of a college degree (college graduates are projected to earn in a lifetime an average of $600,000 more than those with only a high school diploma), higher education is a very worthwhile investment. However, it is also an expensive one made even harder to manage by cost increases that have outpaced both inflation and gains in family income. This reality of higher education economics means that parental concern about how to pay college costs is a dilemma that shows no sign of getting easier.

Because of the high cost involved (even the most inexpensive four-year education at a public institution costs about $10,000 a year), good information about college budgets and strategies for reducing the "sticker price" is essential. In the following chapter you will learn valuable information about the four main sources of aid—federal, state, college, and private. Before you learn about the various programs, however, it will be helpful if you have an overview of how the college financial aid system operates and what long-range financing strategies are available.

Financial Aid

Financial aid refers to money that is awarded to a student, usually in a "package" that consists of a scholarship (also called grant or gift aid), a student loan, and a campus job.

College Costs and Qualifying for Need-Based Aid

The starting point for organizing a plan to pay for your college education is making a good estimate of the yearly cost. The profiles give you an estimate of tuition, but there are other costs to consider. *Peterson's College Money Handbook* is an excellent resource to make this first step of determining total costs easy for you.

The next step is to evaluate whether or not you are likely to qualify for financial aid based on need. This step is critical, since more than 90 percent of the yearly total of $55 billion in student aid is awarded only after a determination is made that the family lacks sufficient financial resources to pay the full cost of college on its own. To judge your chance of receiving need-based aid, it is necessary to estimate an Expected Family Contribution (EFC) according to a government formula known as the Federal Methodology, also found in the *College Money Handbook*.

Applying for Need-Based Aid

Because the federal government provides about 75 percent of all aid awarded, the application and need evaluation process is controlled by Congress and the U.S. Department of Education. The application used is the Free Application for Federal Student Aid (FAFSA). The FAFSA is your "passport" to receiving your share of the billions of dollars awarded annually in need-based aid. If you think you might qualify for aid, pick up a FAFSA from the high school guidance office after mid-November 1998. The form will ask for 1998 financial data and it should be filed after January 1, 1999, in time to meet the earliest college or state scholarship deadline. Within two to four weeks after you submit the form, you will receive a summary of the FAFSA information, which is called the Student Aid Report (SAR). The SAR will give you an estimated expected family contribution and will also allow you to make corrections to the data you submitted.

Students can apply for 1999–2000 federal student aid over the Internet using the interactive FAFSA on the Web. The 1999–2000 FAFSA and an interactive renewal application will be available in December 1998. FAFSA on the Web can be accessed at http://www.fafsa.ed.gov/ with Netscape Navigator 3.0 or higher. It can be used with any computer, including Macintosh and UNIX.

Many colleges feel that the federal aid system (FAFSA and FM) does not collect or evaluate information thoroughly enough to be used to award their institutional funds. These colleges have made an arrangement with the College Scholarship Service, a branch of the College Board, to establish a separate application system to meet their needs. The application is called the Financial Aid PROFILE, and the means of need determination is known as the Institutional Methodology (IM). (When used, the PROFILE is always in addition to the FAFSA; it does not replace it.) If you apply for financial aid at one of the approximately 400 colleges that use PROFILE, the admission material will state that the PROFILE is required in addition to the FAFSA. You should read the information carefully and file the PROFILE to meet the earliest deadline among the colleges involved. Before you can receive the PROFILE form, however, you must register, providing enough basic information so the PROFILE package can be designed specifically for you. Also, while the FAFSA is free, there is a charge for the PROFILE.

Many colleges provide the option to apply for early-decision admission. If you apply for this before January 1, which is prior to when FAFSA can be is used, follow the college's instructions. Many colleges use either PROFILE or their own application form for early-decision candidates.

Awarding Aid

About the same time you receive the SAR, the colleges you list will receive the FAFSA information so they can calculate a financial aid award in a package that typically includes aid from at least one of the major sources—federal, state, college, or private. In addition, the award will probably consist of a combination of scholarship or grant, loan, and campus job. These last two pieces—loan and job—are called self-help aid because they require effort on the part of the student. Scholarships or grants are outright gifts that have no such obligation.

When you receive an award letter from a college, it is important that you understand each part of the package so that you can determine your true costs. For example: How much is gift aid? What are the interest rate and repayment terms of the student loan? How many hours per week does the campus job require? There should be an enclosure with the award letter that answers these kinds of questions. If not, make a list of your questions and call or visit the financial aid office.

Once you understand the terms of each item in the award letter, you should turn your attention to the "bottom line"—how much you will have to pay for each college to which you are admitted. In addition to understanding the aid award, you must have a good estimate of the college budget so that you can accurately calculate how much you and your family will have to contribute (often an aid package does not cover the entire need). If you think that what the college expects you and your family to pay is too high, you should contact the college's financial aid office and ask whether additional aid is available. Many colleges, private high-cost colleges in particular, have a service perspective—they are willing to work with families to help make education at their colleges affordable. If there is still a gap between the expected contribution and what you feel you can pay from income and savings, you are left with two choices. One option is to attend a college where paying your share of the bill will not be a problem. (This assumes that an affordable option was included on the original list of colleges, a wise admission application strategy.) The second is to look into an alternate method of financing, including loans and tuition payment plans. A loan can bring the yearly cost down to a manageable level by spreading payments over a number of years. A tuition payment plan is essentially a short-term loan and allows you to pay the cost over ten to twelve months. It is an option for families who have the resources available but need help with managing their cash-flow.

Aid Not Based on Need

Whether or not you qualify for a need-based award, it is always worthwhile to look into merit, or non-need, scholarships from sources such as foundations, agencies, religious groups, and service organizations. If you aren't eligible for need-based aid, merit scholarships are the only form of gift aid available. If you later qualify for a need-based award, a merit scholarship can be quite helpful in providing additional resources when the aid does not fully cover the costs. Even if the college meets 100 percent of need, a merit scholarship can benefit the student by reducing the self-help (loan and job) portion of an award.

In searching for outside merit-based scholarships, keep in mind that there are relatively few awards (compared to those that are need-based) and most of them are highly competitive. Use the following checklist when investigating merit scholarships.

- Take advantage of any scholarships for which you are automatically eligible based on employer benefits, military service, association or church membership, other affiliations, or student or parent attributes (ethnic background, nationality, etc.). Company or union tuition remissions are the most common examples of these awards.
- Look for other awards for which you might be eligible based on the characteristics and affiliations indicated above, but where there is a selection process and an application is required. Computerized searches are available on the Internet. Scholarship directories, such as *Peterson's Scholarships, Grants & Prizes,* which details some 2,000 scholarship programs, are useful resources and can be found in bookstores, high school guidance offices, or public libraries.
- Look into national scholarship competitions. High school guidance counselors usually know about these scholarships. Examples of these awards are the National Merit Scholarship, Coca Cola Scholarship, Aid Association for Lutherans, Westinghouse Science Talent Search, and the U.S. Senate Youth Program. *Winning Money for College* (Peterson's, 4th ed., 1997) provides detailed profiles of fifty of the most lucrative and prestigious competitions open to high school students.
- ROTC (Reserve Officers' Training Corps) scholarships are offered by the Army, Navy, Air Force, and Marine Corps. A full ROTC scholarship can cover virtually all tuition, fees, and textbook costs. Acceptance of an ROTC scholarship entails a commitment to take a military science course and to serve for a specific number of years as an officer in the sponsoring branch of the service. ROTC is not available at every college. Competition is heavy, and preference may be given to students in certain fields of study, such as nursing, engineering, science, or business. Contact an armed services recruiter or a high school guidance counselor for further information.

- Investigate community scholarships. The high school guidance counselor usually has a list of these awards, and announcements are published in the town newspaper. Most common are awards given by service organizations such as the American Legion, Rotary International, and the local women's club.
- If you are strong academically (for example, a National Merit Commended Scholar or better) or are very talented in fields such as athletics or performing/creative arts, you may want to consider colleges that offer their own merit awards to gifted students they wish to enroll.

In addition to merit scholarships, there are loan and job opportunities for students who do not qualify for need-based aid. Some of the organizations that sponsor scholarships—for example, the Air Force Aid Society—also provide loans.

Work opportunities during the academic year are another type of assistance that is not restricted to aid recipients. Many colleges, after assigning jobs to students on aid, will open campus positions to all students looking for work. In addition, there are usually off-campus employment opportunities available to everyone.

Financing Your College Education

In this section, "financing" means arranging for the use of resources to pay balances due to the college over and above payments from the primary sources of aid—scholarships, student loans, and jobs. Financing strategies are important because the high cost of a college education today often requires you, whether you receive aid or not, to think about stretching the payment for college beyond the four-year period of enrollment. For high-cost colleges, it is not unreasonable to think about a 10-4-10 plan: ten years of saving; four years of paying college bills out of current income, savings, and borrowing; and ten years to repay a loan.

Savings

Although saving for college is always a good idea, many families are unclear about its advantages. Families do not save for two reasons. First, after expenses have been covered, many families do not have much money to set aside. An affordable but regular savings plan through a payroll deduction is usually the answer to the problem of spending your entire paycheck every month.

The second reason that saving for college is not a high priority is the belief that the financial aid system penalizes a family by lowering aid eligibility. The Federal Methodology of need determination is very kind to savers. In fact, savings are ignored completely for those who earn less than $50,000.

A sensible savings plan is important because of the financial advantage of saving compared to borrowing. The amount of money students borrow for college is now greater than the amount they receive in grants and scholarships. With loans becoming so widespread, savings should be carefully considered as an alternative to borrowing. Your incentive for saving is that a dollar saved is a dollar not borrowed.

Borrowing

Once you've calculated your "bottom-line" parental contribution and determined that the amount is not affordable out of your current income and assets, the most likely alternative is borrowing. First determine if you are eligible for a Subsidized FFEL Stafford or Direct Loan. Because no interest is due while a student attends college, these are the most favorable loans. If you are not eligible, look into the Unsubsidized Stafford or Direct Loan, which does not require a needs test but where the interest is due each year. The freshman year limit (either Subsidized or Unsubsidized) is $2625.

After you have taken out the maximum amount of student loans, the next step is to look into parental loans. The federal government's parent loan program is called PLUS and is the standard against which other loans are judged. A local bank that participates in the PLUS can give you a schedule of monthly repayments per $1000 borrowed. Use this repayment figure to compare other parental loans available through commercial lenders (including home equity loans), state programs, or colleges themselves. Choose the one that offers the best terms after all up-front costs, tax advantages, and the amount of monthly payments are considered.

Creditworthiness

If you will be borrowing to pay for your college education, making sure you qualify for a loan is critical. For the most part, that means your credit record must be free of default or delinquency. You can check your credit history with a credit bureau and clean up any adverse information that appears.

Making Financial Aid Work for You

This overview is intended to provide you with a road map to help you think about financing strategies and navigate through the complexities of the financial aid process. For further information about the process, consult *Peterson's College Money Handbook*. Use the parental contribution tables in conjunction with the college cost worksheet to estimate need eligibility. If there is any chance you could qualify for aid, complete the FAFSA (and PROFILE if required). At the same time look into merit scholarships. Finally, check out the terms of PLUS and parental loan options. The key is to understand the financial aid system and to follow the best path for you. The result of good information and good planning should be that you will receive your fair share of the billions of dollars available each year and that the cost of college will not prevent you from attending.

Federal Financial Aid Programs

There are a number of sources of financial aid available to students: the federal government, state governments, private lenders, foundations and private agencies, and the institutions themselves. In addition, there are three different forms of aid: grants, earnings, and loans.

The federal government is the single largest source of financial aid for students. The U.S. Department of Education's student financial aid programs will make more than $47 billion available to about 8.1 million students. There are two federal grant programs—the Federal Pell Grant and the Federal Supplemental Educational Opportunity Grant (FSEOG); three loan programs—the Federal Perkins Loan, the William D. Ford Federal Direct Loans, and the Federal Family Education (FFEL) Loan (Stafford Loan); and a work program that helps colleges provide jobs for students, the Federal Work-Study Program (FWS).

The two grants, Federal Work-Study, Federal Perkins Loan, and two other loan programs—the Subsidized Federal Direct Loan and the Subsidized Federal Stafford Loan—are awarded to students with demonstrated financial need. Interest on the loans is paid by the government during the time the student is in school. For the Federal Unsubsidized Direct Loan and Federal Unsubsidized Stafford Loan, the interest begins to accrue as soon as the money is received. There is also a parental loan (PLUS) available under the Direct or Stafford programs.

Federal Pell Grant

The Federal Pell Grant is the largest grant program; almost 4 million students receive awards annually. This grant is intended to be the base, or starting point, of assistance for lower-income families. Eligibility for a Federal Pell Grant depends on the Expected Family Contribution (EFC). The amount you receive will depend on your EFC, the cost of education at the college or university you will attend, and whether you attend full-time or part-time. The highest award depends on how much the program is funded. The maximum for 1998–99 was $3000.

Federal Supplemental Educational Opportunity Grant (FSEOG)

As its name implies, the Federal Supplemental Educational Opportunity Grant (FSEOG) provides additional need-based federal grant money to supplement the Federal Pell Grant. Each participating college is given funds to award to especially needy students. The maximum award is $4000 per year, but the amount you receive depends on the college's policy, the availability of FSEOG funds, the total cost of education, and the amount of other aid awarded.

Federal Work-Study (FWS)

This program provides jobs for students who need financial aid for their educational expenses. The salary is paid by funds from the federal government and the college (or the employer). You work on an hourly basis in jobs on or off campus and must be paid at least the federal minimum wage. You may earn only up to the amount awarded, which depends on the calculated financial need and the total amount of money available to the college.

Federal Perkins Loan

This loan is a low-interest (5 percent) loan for students with exceptional financial need. Federal Perkins Loans are made through the college's financial aid office. That is, the college is the lender. Students may borrow a maximum of $3000 per year for up to five years of undergraduate study. They may take up to ten years to repay the loan, beginning nine months after they graduate, leave school, or drop below half-time status. No interest accrues while they are in school, and, under certain conditions (e.g., they teach in low-income areas, work in law enforcement, are full-time nurses or medical technicians, serve as Peace Corps or VISTA volunteers, etc.), some or all of the loan can be canceled or payments deferred.

FFEL Stafford Loan

An FFEL Stafford Loan may be borrowed from a participating commercial lender such as a bank, credit union, or savings and loan association. The interest rate varies annually, up to a maximum of 8.25 percent. If you qualify for a need-based, subsidized FFEL Stafford Loan, the interest is paid by the federal government while you are enrolled in school. There is also an unsubsidized FFEL Stafford Loan not based on need for which you are eligible regardless of your family income.

The maximum amount dependent students may borrow in any one year is $2625 for freshmen, $3500 for sophomores, and $5500 for juniors and seniors, with a maximum of $23,000 for the total undergraduate program. The maximum amount independent students can borrow is $6625 for freshmen (no more than $2625 in subsidized Stafford Loans),

$7500 for sophomores (no more than $3500 in subsidized Stafford Loans), and $10,500 for juniors and seniors (no more than $5500 in subsidized Stafford Loans). Borrowers must pay a 4 percent fee, which is deducted from the loan proceeds.

To apply for an FFEL Stafford Loan, you must first complete a FAFSA to determine eligibility for a subsidized loan, then a separate loan application that is submitted to a lender. The financial aid office can help in selecting a lender, or you can contact your state department of higher education to find a participating lender.

If you qualify for a subsidized FFEL Stafford Loan, you do not have to pay interest while in school. For an unsubsidized FFEL Stafford Loan, you will be responsible for paying the interest from the time the loan is established. However, some lenders will permit borrowers to delay making payments and will add the interest to the loan. Once the repayment period starts, borrowers of both subsidized and unsubsidized FFEL Stafford Loans will have to pay a combination of interest and principal monthly for up to a ten-year period.

PLUS

PLUS is a loan for parents of dependent students. There is no needs test to qualify, and the loans are made by participating lenders. The loan has a variable interest rate that cannot exceed 9 percent. There is no specific yearly limit; parents can borrow up to the cost of education less other financial aid received. Repayment begins sixty days after the money is advanced. A 4 percent fee is subtracted from the proceeds. Parent borrowers must generally have a good credit record to qualify for PLUS.

PLUS is processed under either the Direct or Stafford system, depending on the type of loan program for which the college has contracted.

Federal Direct Student Loans

The Federal Direct Student Loan is a relatively new program that is basically the same as the FFEL Stafford Loan. The difference is that the U.S. Department of Education is the lender rather than a bank. Not all colleges participate in this program, and if your college does not, you can still apply for an FFEL Stafford Loan.

Many of the terms of the Federal Direct Student Loan are similar to those of the FFEL Stafford Loan. In particular, the interest rate, loan maximums, deferments, and cancellation benefits are the same. However, under the terms of the Federal Direct Student Loan, students have a choice of repayment plans. They may choose either a fixed monthly payment for ten years; a different fixed monthly payment for twelve to thirty years at a rate that varies with the loan balance; or a variable monthly payment for up to twenty-five years that is based on a percentage of income. Students cannot receive both a Federal Direct Student Loan and an FFEL Stafford Loan for the same period of time but may receive both in different enrollment periods.

Americorps

Americorps is a program for a limited number of students. Participants work in a public or private nonprofit agency providing service to the community in one of four priority areas: education, human services, the environment, and public safety. In exchange, they earn a stipend between $7400 and $14,800 a year for living expenses and up to $4725 for up to two years to apply toward college expenses. Students can work either before, during, or after they go to college and can use the funds to pay either current educational expenses or repay federal student loans. Speak to a college financial aid officer for more details about this program and any other new initiatives available to students.

Returning to School: A Guide for Adult Students

by Sandra Cook, Ph.D., Director, University Advising Center, San Diego State University

Many adults think about returning to school for a long time without taking any action. One purpose of this article is to help the "thinkers" finally make some decisions by examining what is keeping them from action. Another purpose is to describe not only some of the difficulties and obstacles that adult students may face when returning to school but also tactics for coping with them.

If you have been thinking about going back to college, believing you are the only person your age contemplating college, you should know that approximately six million adult students are currently enrolled in higher education institutions. This number represents 45 percent of total higher education enrollments. And the majority of adult students are enrolled at two-year colleges.

There are many reasons why adult students choose to attend a two-year college. Studies have shown that the three most important criteria that adult students consider when choosing a college are location, cost, and availability of the major or program desired. Most two-year colleges are public institutions that serve a geographic district, making them readily accessible to the community. Costs at most two-year colleges are far less than at other types of higher education institutions. For many students who plan to pursue a bachelor's degree, completing their first two years of college at a community college is an affordable means to that end. If you are interested in an academic program that will transfer to a four-year institution, most two-year colleges offer the "general education" courses that compose most freshman and sophomore years. If you are interested in a vocational or technical program, two-year colleges excel in providing this type of training.

Uncertainty, Choice, and Support

There are three different "stages" in the process of adults returning to school. The first stage is uncertainty. Do I really want to go back to school? What will my friends or family think? Can I compete with those 18-year-old whiz kids? Am I too old? The second stage is choice. Once the decision to return has been made, you must choose where you will attend. There are many criteria to use in making this decision. The third stage is support. You have just added another role to your already-too-busy life. There are, however, strategies that will help you accomplish your goals—perhaps not without struggle but with grace and humor. Let's look at each of these stages.

Uncertainty

Why are you thinking about returning to school? Is it to:

- fulfill a dream that had to be delayed?
- become more educationally well rounded?
- fill an intellectual void in your life?

These reasons focus on *personal growth*.
If you are returning to school to:

- meet people and make friends
- attain and enjoy higher social status and prestige among friends, relatives, and associates
- understand/study a cultural heritage, or
- have a medium in which to exchange ideas,

you are interested in *social and cultural opportunities*.
If you are like most adult students, you want to:

- qualify for a new occupation
- enter or reenter the job market
- increase earnings potential, or
- qualify for a more challenging position in the same field of work.

You are seeking *career growth*.

Understanding the reasons why you want to go back to school is an important step in setting your educational goals and will help you to establish some criteria in selecting a college. However, don't delay your decision because you haven't been able to clearly define your motives. Many times these aren't clear until you have already begun the process, and they may change as you move through your college experience.

Assuming that you agree that additional education will be of benefit to you, what is it that keeps you from returning to school? You may have a litany of excuses running through your mind:

- I don't have time.
- I can't afford it.
- I'm too old to learn.
- My friends will think I'm crazy.
- The teachers will be younger than me.

- My family can't survive without me to take care of them every minute.
- I'll be X years old when I finish.
- I'm afraid.
- I don't know what to expect.

And that is just what these are—excuses. You can make school, like anything else in your life, a priority or not. If you really want to return, you can. The more you understand your motivation for returning to school and the more you understand what excuses are keeping you from taking action, the easier your task will be.

If you think you don't have time: The best way to decide how attending class and studying can fit into your schedule is to keep track of what you do with your time each day for several weeks. Completing a standard time-management grid (each day is plotted out by the half hour) is helpful for visualizing how your time is spent. For each 3-credit-hour class you take, you will need to find 3 hours for class plus 6 to 9 hours for reading-studying-library time. This study time should be spaced evenly throughout the week, not loaded up on one day. It is not possible to learn or retain the material that way. When you examine your grid, see where there are activities that could be replaced with school and study time. You may decide to give up your bowling league or some time in front of the TV. Try not to give up sleeping, and don't cut out every moment of free time. There are also a number of smaller ways to divert time to school. Here are some suggestions that have come from adults who have returned to school:

- Enroll in a time-management workshop. It helps you rethink how you use your time.
- Don't think you have to take more than one course at a time. You may eventually want to work up to taking more, but consider starting with one. (It's more than you're taking now!)
- If you have a family, start assigning those household chores that you usually do to them—and don't redo what they do.
- Use your lunch hour or commuting time for reading.

If you think you can't afford it: As mentioned earlier, two-year colleges are extremely affordable. If you cannot afford the tuition, look into the various financial aid options. Most federal and state funds are available to full- and part-time students. Loans are also available. While many people prefer not to accumulate a debt for school, these same people will think nothing of taking out a loan to buy a car. After five or six years, which is the better investment? Adult students who work should look into whether their company has a tuition-reimbursement policy. There are also an increasing number of private scholarships, available through foundations, service organizations, and clubs, that are focused on adult learners. Your public library and a college financial aid adviser are two excellent sources for reference materials regarding financial aid.

If you think you are too old to learn: This is pure myth. A number of studies have shown that adult learners perform as well as or better than traditional-age students.

If you are afraid your friends will think you're crazy: Who cares? Maybe they will, maybe they won't. Usually they will admire your courage and be just a little jealous of your ambition (although they'll never tell you that). Follow your dreams, not theirs.

If you are concerned because the teachers or students will be younger than you: Don't be. The age differences that may be apparent in other settings evaporate in the classroom. If anything, an adult in the classroom strikes fear into the hearts of some 18-year-olds because adults have been known to be prepared, ask questions, be truly motivated, and be there to learn!

If you think your family will have a difficult time surviving while you are in school: If you have done everything for them up to now, they might struggle. Consider this an opportunity to help them become independent, more self-sufficient people. Your family can only make you feel guilty if you let them. You are not abandoning them; you are becoming an educational role model. When you are happy and working toward your goals, everyone benefits. Admittedly, it sometimes takes time for them to realize this. For single parents there are schools that have begun to offer support groups, child care, and cooperative babysitting.

If you're appalled at the thought of being X years old when you graduate in Y years: How old will you be in Y years if you don't go back to school?

If you are afraid or don't know what to expect: Know that these are natural feelings when one encounters any new situation. Adult students find that their fears usually dissipate once they begin classes. Fear of trying is usually the biggest roadblock to the reentry process.

No doubt you have dreamed up a few more reasons for not making the decision to return to school. Keep in mind that what you are doing is making up excuses, and you are using these excuses to release you from the obligation to make a decision about your life. The thought of returning to college can be scary. Anytime anyone ventures into unknown territory there is a risk, but taking risks is a necessary component of personal and professional growth. It is your life, and you alone are responsible for making the decisions that determine its course. Education is an investment in your future.

Choice

Once you have decided to go back to school, your next task is to decide where to go. If your educational goals are well defined (e.g., you want to pursue a degree in order to change careers), then your task is a bit easier. But even if your educational goals are still evolving, don't deter your return. Many students who enter higher education with a specific major in mind change that major at least once.

Most students who attend a public two-year college choose the community college in the district in which they live. This is generally the closest and least expensive option if the school offers the programs you want. If you are planning to begin your education at a two-year college and then transfer to a four-year school, there are distinct advantages to choosing your four-year school early. Many community and four-year colleges have "articulation" agreements that designate what credits from the two-year school will transfer to the four-year college and how. Some four-year institutions accept an associate degree as equivalent to the freshman and sophomore years regardless of the courses you have taken. Some four-year schools accept two-year college work only on a course-by-course basis. If you can identify which school you will transfer to, you can know in advance exactly how your two-year credits will apply. This can prevent an unexpected loss of credit or time. You can use the strategies outlined below not only to help you choose your two-year college but also to help you identify early which four-year school you will transfer to.

Each institution of higher education is distinctive. Your goal in choosing a college is to come up with the best student-institution fit—matching your needs with the offerings and characteristics of the school. The first step in choosing a college is to determine what criteria are most important to you in attaining your educational goals. Location, cost, and program availability are the three main factors that influenced an adult student's college choice. In considering location, don't forget that some colleges have conveniently located branch campuses. In considering cost, remember to explore your financial aid options before ruling out an institution because of its tuition. Program availability should include not only the major in which you are interested but also whether classes in that major are available when you can take them.

Some additional considerations beyond location, cost, and programs are:

- Does the school have a commitment to adult students and offer appropriate services such as child care, tutoring, and advising?
- Are classes offered when you can take them?
- Are there academic options for adults such as credit for life or work experience, credit by examination (including CLEP and PEP), credit for military service, or accelerated programs?
- Is the faculty sensitive to the needs of adult learners?

Once you determine which criteria are vital in your choice of an institution, you can begin to narrow your choices. There are myriad ways for you to locate the information you desire. This guide and others, including *Peterson's Guide to Four-Year Colleges,* are excellent sources of information. Many urban newspapers publish a "School Guide" several times a year in which colleges and universities advertise to an adult student market. In addition, schools themselves publish catalogs, class schedules, and promotional materials that contain much of the information you need, and they are yours for the asking. Many colleges sponsor information sessions and open houses that allow you to visit the campus and ask questions. An appointment with an adviser is a good way to assess the fit between you and the institution. Be sure to bring your questions with you to your interview.

Support

Once you have made the decision to return to school and have chosen the institution that best meets your needs, take some additional steps to ensure your success during your crucial first semester. Take advantage of institutional support and build some social support systems of your own. Here are some ways of doing just that:

- Plan to participate in any orientation programs. These serve the threefold purpose of providing you with a great deal of important information, familiarizing you with the campus and its facilities, and giving you the opportunity to meet and begin networking with other students.
- Take steps to deal with any academic weaknesses. Take mathematics and writing placement tests if you have reason to believe you may need some extra help in these areas. It is not uncommon for adult students to need a math refresher course or a program to help alleviate math anxiety. Ignoring a weakness won't make it go away.

- Look into adult reentry programs. Many institutions offer study-skills, textbook-reading, test-taking, and time-management workshops to help adult students.
- Build new support networks by joining an adult student organization, making a point of meeting other adult students through workshops, or actively seeking out a "study buddy" in each class—that invaluable friend who shares and understands your experience.
- You can incorporate your new status as "student" into your family life. Doing your homework with your children at a designated "homework time" is a valuable family activity and reinforces the importance of education.
- Make sure you take a reasonable course load in your first semester. It is far better to have some extra time on your hands and succeed magnificently than to spend the entire semester on the brink of a breakdown. Also, whenever possible, try to focus your first courses not only on requirements but also in areas of personal interest.
- Faculty, advisers, and student affairs personnel are there to help you during difficult times—let them.

After completing your first semester, you will probably look back in wonder at why you thought going back to school was so imposing. Certainly it's not without its occasional exasperations. But, as with life, keeping things in perspective and maintaining your sense of humor make the difference between just coping and succeeding brilliantly.

PROFILES

This section contains quick-reference profiles of colleges and universities, covering such items as background information, entrance difficulty, academic programs, and contact information. The data in each of these profiles, collected from fall 1997 to spring 1998, come solely from Peterson's Annual Survey of Undergraduate Institutions, which was sent to deans or admissions officers at each institution. The profiles are organized by state and then alphabetically within those states by the official names of the institutions.

ALABAMA

ALABAMA AGRICULTURAL AND MECHANICAL UNIVERSITY
NORMAL, ALABAMA

General State-supported, university, coed **Entrance** Minimally difficult **Setting** 2,001-acre suburban campus **Total enrollment** 5,094 **Student/faculty ratio** 12:1 **Application deadline** Rolling **Freshmen** 65% were admitted **Housing** Yes **Expenses** Tuition $2168; Room & Board $2678 **Undergraduates** 52% women, 8% part-time, 7% 25 or older, 0.2% Native American, 0.3% Hispanic, 89% black, 1% Asian American or Pacific Islander **Most popular recent majors** Elementary education; biology; business statistics **Academic program** Average class size 30, advanced placement, accelerated degree program, tutorials, honors program, summer session, adult/continuing education programs, internships **Contact** Mr. Antonio Boyle, Director of Admissions, Alabama Agricultural and Mechanical University, PO Box 908, Normal, AL 35762. Telephone: 256-851-5245 or toll-free 800-553-0816. Fax: 256-851-9747. E-mail: jheyward@asnaam.aamu.edu. Web site: http://www.aamu.edu/.

ALABAMA STATE UNIVERSITY
MONTGOMERY, ALABAMA

General State-supported, comprehensive, coed **Entrance** Minimally difficult **Setting** 114-acre urban campus **Total enrollment** 5,273 **Student/faculty ratio** 16:1 **Application deadline** 8/26 **Housing** Yes **Expenses** Tuition $2030; Room & Board $3300 **Undergraduates** 56% women, 11% part-time, 8% 25 or older, 0.04% Native American, 0.2% Hispanic, 92% black, 0.1% Asian American or Pacific Islander **Most popular recent majors** Business administration; liberal arts and studies; education **Academic program** Average class size 35, advanced placement, accelerated degree program, tutorials, honors program, summer session, adult/continuing education programs, internships **Contact** Mr. Billy Brooks, Director of Admissions and Recruitment, Alabama State University, 915 South Jackson Street, Montgomery, AL 36101-0271. Telephone: 334-229-4291 or toll-free 800-253-5037. Fax: 334-229-4984. E-mail: dcrump@asunet.alasu.edu. Web site: http://www.alasu.edu/.

ATHENS STATE COLLEGE
ATHENS, ALABAMA

General State-supported, upper-level, coed **Entrance** Noncompetitive **Setting** 45-acre small town campus **Total enrollment** 2,671 **Student/faculty ratio** 30:1 **Application deadline** Rolling **Freshmen** 100% were admitted **Housing** Yes **Expenses** Tuition $1845; Room only $825 **Undergraduates** 63% women, 50% part-time, 68% 25 or older **Most popular recent majors** Education; business administration; computer science **Academic program** Advanced placement, tutorials, summer session, adult/continuing education programs **Contact** Ms. Necedah Henderson, Coordinator of Admissions, Athens State College, 300 North Beaty Street, Athens, AL 35611-1902. Telephone: 205-233-8217 or toll-free 800-522-0272 (in-state). Fax: 205-233-8164. Web site: http://www.athens.edu.

AUBURN UNIVERSITY
AUBURN, ALABAMA

General State-supported, university, coed **Entrance** Moderately difficult **Setting** 1,875-acre small town campus **Total enrollment** 21,505 **Student/faculty ratio** 16:1 **Application deadline** 9/1 **Freshmen** 86% were admitted **Housing** Yes **Expenses** Tuition $2610; Room only $1905 **Undergraduates** 48% women, 8% part-time, 8% 25 or older, 1% Native American, 1% Hispanic, 6% black, 1% Asian American or Pacific Islander **Most popular recent majors** Psychology; business administration; civil engineering **Academic program** English as a second language, advanced placement, accelerated degree program, honors program, summer session, adult/continuing education programs, internships **Contact** Dr. James P. Golson, Assistant Vice President of Enrollment Management, Auburn University, 202 Mary Martin Hall, Auburn University, AL 36849-0001. Telephone: 334-844-4080 or toll-free 800-AUBURN9 (in-state). E-mail: admissions@mail.auburn.edu. Web site: http://www.auburn.edu/.

AUBURN UNIVERSITY MONTGOMERY
MONTGOMERY, ALABAMA

General State-supported, comprehensive, coed **Entrance** Moderately difficult **Setting** 500-acre suburban campus **Total enrollment** 5,526 **Student/faculty ratio** 16:1 **Application deadline** 9/1 **Freshmen** 81% were admitted **Housing** Yes **Expenses** Tuition $2289; Room only $1830 **Undergraduates** 62% women, 29% part-time, 31% 25 or older, 0.3% Native American, 1% Hispanic, 31% black, 1% Asian American or Pacific Islander **Most popular recent majors** Elementary education; nursing; secondary education **Academic program** Average class size 28, English as a second language, advanced placement, accelerated degree program, self-designed majors, tutorials, honors program, summer session, adult/continuing education programs, internships **Contact** Ms. Tina Higbe, Coordinator, Admissions, Auburn University Montgomery, PO Box 244023, Montgomery, AL 36124-4023. Telephone: 334-244-3621 or toll-free 800-227-2649 (in-state). Fax: 334-244-3795. E-mail: auminfo@mickey.aum.edu. Web site: http://www.aum.edu/.

BIRMINGHAM-SOUTHERN COLLEGE
BIRMINGHAM, ALABAMA

General Independent Methodist, comprehensive, coed **Entrance** Moderately difficult **Setting** 185-acre urban campus **Total enrollment** 1,531 **Student/faculty ratio** 12:1 **Application deadline** 5/1 **Freshmen** 96% were admitted **Housing** Yes **Expenses** Tuition $13,960; Room & Board $5200 **Undergraduates** 58% women, 11% part-time, 17% 25 or older, 0.3% Native American, 0.1% Hispanic, 13% black, 4% Asian American or Pacific Islander **Most popular recent majors** Business administration; biology; English **Academic program** Average class size 22, English as a second language, advanced placement, accelerated degree program, self-designed majors, tutorials, honors program, summer session, adult/continuing education programs, internships **Contact** Ms. DeeDee Barnes Bruns, Dean of Admission and Financial Aid, Birmingham-Southern College, 900 Arkadelphia Road, Birmingham, AL 35254. Telephone: 205-226-4696 or toll-free 800-523-5793. Fax: 205-226-3074. E-mail: admissions@bsc.edu. Web site: http://www.bsc.edu/.

CONCORDIA COLLEGE
SELMA, ALABAMA

General Independent Lutheran, 4-year, coed **Entrance** Noncompetitive **Setting** 22-acre small town campus **Total enrollment** 525 **Application deadline** 9/2 **Housing** Yes **Expenses** Tuition $4600; Room & Board $2600 **Undergraduates** 71% women, 15% part-time, 40% 25 or older **Most popular recent majors** Elementary education; early childhood education; business administration **Academic program** Summer session, adult/continuing education programs **Contact** Ms. Gwendolyn Moore, Director of Admissions, Concordia College, 1804 Green Street, PO Box 1329, Selma, AL 36701. Telephone: 334-874-7143. Fax: 334-874-3728.

FAULKNER UNIVERSITY
MONTGOMERY, ALABAMA

General Independent, comprehensive, coed, affiliated with Church of Christ **Entrance** Moderately difficult **Setting** 75-acre urban campus **Total enrollment** 2,420 **Student/faculty ratio** 19:1 **Application deadline** Rolling **Freshmen** 75% were admitted **Housing** Yes **Expenses** Tuition $6980; Room & Board $3700 **Undergraduates** 60% women, 32% part-time, 42% 25 or older, 0.3% Native American, 1% Hispanic, 31% black, 1% Asian American or Pacific Islander **Most popular recent majors** Business administration; elementary education; biblical studies **Academic program** Accelerated degree program, tutorials, summer session, adult/continuing education programs, internships **Contact** Mr. Keith Mock, Director of Admissions, Faulkner University, 5345 Atlanta Highway, Montgomery, AL 36109-3398. Telephone: 334-260-6200 or toll-free 800-879-9816. Fax: 334-260-6137. Web site: http://www.faulkner.edu/.

HUNTINGDON COLLEGE
MONTGOMERY, ALABAMA

General Independent United Methodist, 4-year, coed **Entrance** Moderately difficult **Setting** 58-acre suburban campus **Total enrollment** 673 **Student/faculty ratio** 12:1 **Application deadline** Rolling **Freshmen** 75% were admitted **Housing** Yes **Expenses** Tuition $11,230; Room & Board $5000 **Undergraduates** 59% women, 9% part-time, 9% 25 or older, 1% Native American, 0.3% Hispanic, 6% black, 1% Asian American or Pacific Islander **Most popular recent majors** Business administration; history; psychology **Academic program** Average class size 14, advanced placement, accelerated degree program, self-designed majors, tutorials, honors program, summer session, adult/continuing education programs, internships **Contact** Ms. Suellen Ofe, Vice President for Enrollment Management, Huntingdon College, 1500 East Fairview Avenue, Montgomery, AL 36106-2148. Telephone: 334-833-4515 or toll-free 800-763-0313. Fax: 334-833-4347. Web site: http://www.huntingdon.edu/.

INTERNATIONAL BIBLE COLLEGE
FLORENCE, ALABAMA

General Independent, 4-year, coed, affiliated with Church of Christ **Entrance** Noncompetitive **Setting** 46-acre small town campus **Total enrollment** 143 **Application deadline** Rolling **Housing** Yes **Expenses** Tuition $5220; Room only $1200 **Undergraduates** 26% women, 47% part-time, 68% 25 or older, 0% Native American, 0% Hispanic, 12% black, 0% Asian American or Pacific Islander **Academic program** Accelerated degree program, tutorials, summer session, adult/continuing education programs, internships **Contact** Mr. Jim Collins, Director of Enrollment Services, International Bible College, PO Box IBC, Florence, AL 35630. Telephone: 205-766-6610 ext. 26 or toll-free 800-367-3565. E-mail: jdcollinsadm@juno.com.

JACKSONVILLE STATE UNIVERSITY
JACKSONVILLE, ALABAMA

General State-supported, comprehensive, coed **Entrance** Minimally difficult **Setting** 345-acre

Jacksonville State University *(continued)*

small town campus **Total enrollment** 7,619 **Student/faculty ratio** 23:1 **Application deadline** Rolling **Housing** Yes **Expenses** Tuition $2060; Room & Board $2980 **Undergraduates** 56% women, 18% part-time, 14% 25 or older, 1% Native American, 1% Hispanic, 16% black, 1% Asian American or Pacific Islander **Academic program** Average class size 25, English as a second language, advanced placement, accelerated degree program, tutorials, honors program, summer session, adult/continuing education programs, internships **Contact** Dr. Jerry D. Smith, Dean of Admissions and Records, Jacksonville State University, 700 Pelham Road North, Jacksonville, AL 36265-9982. Telephone: 205-782-5400 or toll-free 800-231-5291. Fax: 256-782-5291. E-mail: jsmith@jsucc.edu. Web site: http://www.jsu.edu/.

JUDSON COLLEGE
MARION, ALABAMA

General Independent Baptist, 4-year, women only **Entrance** Moderately difficult **Setting** 80-acre rural campus **Total enrollment** 305 **Student/faculty ratio** 11:1 **Application deadline** Rolling **Housing** Yes **Expenses** Tuition $6700; Room & Board $4150 **Undergraduates** 10% 25 or older, 0.3% Native American, 1% Hispanic, 14% black, 1% Asian American or Pacific Islander **Most popular recent majors** Psychology; biology; elementary education **Academic program** Average class size 30, advanced placement, accelerated degree program, self-designed majors, tutorials, honors program, summer session, adult/continuing education programs, internships **Contact** Mrs. Charlotte Clements, Director of Admissions, Judson College, PO Box 120, Marion, AL 36756. Telephone: 334-683-5110 or toll-free 800-447-9472. Fax: 334-683-5158. E-mail: admissions@future.judson.edu. Web site: http://www.home.judson.edu/.

MILES COLLEGE
BIRMINGHAM, ALABAMA

General Independent Christian Methodist Episcopal, 4-year, coed **Contact** Ms. Brenda Grant-Smith, Director of Admissions and Recruitment, Miles College, PO Box 3800, Birmingham, AL 35208. Telephone: 205-929-1657.

OAKWOOD COLLEGE
HUNTSVILLE, ALABAMA

General Independent Seventh-day Adventist, 4-year, coed **Contact** Mr. Robert Edwards, Director of Enrollment Management, Oakwood College, Oakwood Road, NW, Huntsville, AL 35810. Telephone: 205-726-7354 or toll-free 800-824-5312 (in-state).

SAMFORD UNIVERSITY
BIRMINGHAM, ALABAMA

General Independent Baptist, university, coed **Entrance** Moderately difficult **Setting** 280-acre suburban campus **Total enrollment** 4,485 **Student/faculty ratio** 14:1 **Application deadline** Rolling **Freshmen** 91% were admitted **Housing** Yes **Expenses** Tuition $9432; Room & Board $4396 **Undergraduates** 62% women, 9% part-time, 11% 25 or older **Most popular recent majors** Liberal arts and studies; business administration **Academic program** Advanced placement, accelerated degree program, self-designed majors, honors program, summer session, adult/continuing education programs, internships **Contact** Mr. Phil Kimrey, Dean of Admissions and Financial Aid, Samford University, 800 Lakeshore Drive, Samford Hall, Birmingham, AL 35229-0002. Telephone: 205-870-2901 or toll-free 800-888-7218. Fax: 205-870-2171. E-mail: seberry@vm.samford.edu. Web site: http://www.samford.edu/.

SOUTHEAST COLLEGE OF TECHNOLOGY
MOBILE, ALABAMA

Contact Southeast College of Technology, 828 Downtowner Loop West, Mobile, AL 36609-5404. Telephone: 334-343-8200.

SOUTHEASTERN BIBLE COLLEGE
BIRMINGHAM, ALABAMA

Contact Mrs. Jean Judge, Registrar, Southeastern Bible College, 3001 Highway 280 East, Birmingham, AL 35243-4181. Telephone: 205-969-0880 ext. 208.

SOUTHERN CHRISTIAN UNIVERSITY
MONTGOMERY, ALABAMA

General Independent, comprehensive, coed, affiliated with Church of Christ **Entrance** Minimally difficult **Setting** 9-acre urban campus **Total enrollment** 240 **Student/faculty ratio** 6:1 **Application deadline** Rolling **Housing** No **Expenses** Tuition $7026 **Undergraduates** 90% 25 or older, 0% Native American, 1% Hispanic, 10% black, 8% Asian American or Pacific Islander **Contact** Mr. Mac Adkins, Director of Admissions, Southern Christian University, 1200 Taylor Road, Montgomery, AL 36117. Telephone: 334-277-2277 ext. 228 or toll-free 800-351-4040. E-mail: scuniversity@mindspring.com. Web site: http://www.southernchristian.edu/.

SPRING HILL COLLEGE
MOBILE, ALABAMA

General Independent Roman Catholic (Jesuit), comprehensive, coed **Entrance** Moderately difficult **Setting** 500-acre suburban campus **Total enrollment** 1,745 **Student/faculty ratio** 15:1 **Application deadline** Rolling **Freshmen** 85% were admitted **Housing** Yes **Expenses** Tuition $13,860; Room & Board $4980 **Undergraduates** 12% 25 or older **Most popular recent majors** Psychology; public relations; business administration **Academic program** English as a second language, advanced placement, accelerated degree program, self-designed majors, honors program, summer session, adult/continuing education programs, internships **Contact** Mr. Steven Pochard, Dean of Enrollment Management, Spring Hill College, 4000 Dauphin Street, Mobile, AL 36608-1791. Telephone: 334-380-3030 or toll-free 800-SHC-6704. Fax: 334-460-2186. E-mail: admit@shc.edu. Web site: http://www.shc.edu/.

STILLMAN COLLEGE
TUSCALOOSA, ALABAMA

General Independent, 4-year, coed, affiliated with Presbyterian Church (U.S.A.) **Contact** Mr. Mason Bonner, Enrollment Management Coordinator, Stillman College, PO Drawer 1430, Tuscaloosa, AL 35403-9990. Telephone: 205-366-8817 or toll-free 800-523-6331 (in-state), 800-841-5722 (out-of-state). Fax: 205-366-8996.

TALLADEGA COLLEGE
TALLADEGA, ALABAMA

General Independent, 4-year, coed **Entrance** Minimally difficult **Setting** 130-acre small town campus **Total enrollment** 650 **Student/faculty ratio** 14:1 **Application deadline** 4/1 **Freshmen** 40% were admitted **Housing** Yes **Expenses** Tuition $5949; Room & Board $2964 **Undergraduates** 64% women, 3% part-time, 7% 25 or older, 0.2% Hispanic, 99% black **Most popular recent majors** Biology; business administration; psychology **Academic program** Average class size 36, tutorials, adult/continuing education programs **Contact** Mr. Johnny Byrd, Associate Dean of Enrollment Management, Talladega College, 627 West Battle Street, Talladega, AL 35160. Telephone: 205-761-6341 or toll-free 800-633-2440 (out-of-state). Fax: 205-362-2268.

TROY STATE UNIVERSITY
TROY, ALABAMA

General State-supported, comprehensive, coed **Entrance** Moderately difficult **Setting** 500-acre small town campus **Total enrollment** 6,468 **Student/faculty ratio** 22:1 **Application deadline** Rolling **Freshmen** 79% were admitted **Housing** Yes **Expenses** Tuition $2250; Room & Board $3480 **Undergraduates** 59% women, 19% part-time, 1% Native American, 1% Hispanic, 19% black, 1% Asian American or Pacific Islander **Most popular recent majors** Education; business administration; nursing **Academic program** Advanced placement, accelerated degree program, self-designed majors, honors program, summer session, adult/continuing education programs, internships **Contact** Mr. James Hutto, Dean of Enrollment Services, Troy State University, University Avenue, Troy, AL 36082. Telephone: 334-670-3175 or toll-free 800-551-9716 (in-state). Fax: 334-670-3815. Web site: http://www.troyst.edu/.

TROY STATE UNIVERSITY DOTHAN
DOTHAN, ALABAMA

General State-supported, comprehensive, coed **Entrance** Minimally difficult **Setting** 250-acre small town campus **Total enrollment** 2,102 **Student/faculty ratio** 21:1 **Application deadline** Rolling **Freshmen** 74% were admitted **Housing** No **Expenses** Tuition $2229 **Undergraduates** 60% women, 48% part-time, 85% 25 or older, 1% Native American, 1% Hispanic, 14% black, 1% Asian American or Pacific Islander **Most popular recent majors** Business administration; education; psychology **Academic program** Advanced placement, accelerated degree program, summer session, internships **Contact** Mr. Bob Willis, Director of Admissions, Troy State University Dothan, PO Box 8368, Dothan, AL 36304-0368. Telephone: 334-983-6556 ext. 231. Fax: 334-983-6322. E-mail: bwillis@tsud.edu. Web site: http://www.tsud.edu/.

TROY STATE UNIVERSITY MONTGOMERY
MONTGOMERY, ALABAMA

General State-supported, comprehensive, coed **Entrance** Noncompetitive **Setting** 6-acre urban campus **Total enrollment** 3,349 **Student/faculty ratio** 21:1 **Application deadline** Rolling **Housing** No **Expenses** Tuition $2085 **Undergraduates** 58% women, 74% part-time, 61% 25 or older, 0.4% Native American, 1% Hispanic, 36% black, 1% Asian American or Pacific Islander **Academic program** Advanced placement, accelerated degree program, self-designed majors, honors program, summer session, adult/continuing education programs **Contact** Mr. Frank Hrabe, Director of Enrollment Management, Troy State University Montgomery, PO Drawer 4419, Montgomery, AL 36103-4419. Telephone: 334-241-9506 or toll-free 800-355-TSUM. Web site: http://www.tsum.edu/.

TUSKEGEE UNIVERSITY
TUSKEGEE, ALABAMA

General Independent, comprehensive, coed **Entrance** Moderately difficult **Setting** 4,390-acre

Tuskegee University *(continued)*

small town campus **Total enrollment** 3,023 **Student/faculty ratio** 12:1 **Application deadline** 4/15 **Freshmen** 73% were admitted **Housing** Yes **Expenses** Tuition $8662; Room & Board $4104 **Undergraduates** 60% women, 5% part-time, 1% 25 or older, 3% Native American, 0% Hispanic, 95% black, 0.04% Asian American or Pacific Islander **Most popular recent majors** Electrical/electronics engineering; business administration; (pre)veterinary studies **Academic program** English as a second language, honors program, summer session, internships **Contact** Ms. Carolyn Tippett, Acting Director of Admissions, Tuskegee University, Carnegie Hall, Tuskegee, AL 36088. Telephone: 334-727-8500.

▶ **For more information, see page 530.**

THE UNIVERSITY OF ALABAMA
TUSCALOOSA, ALABAMA

General State-supported, university, coed **Entrance** Moderately difficult **Setting** 1,000-acre suburban campus **Total enrollment** 18,324 **Student/faculty ratio** 17:1 **Application deadline** 6/1 **Freshmen** 81% were admitted **Housing** Yes **Expenses** Tuition $2594; Room & Board $3610 **Undergraduates** 52% women, 11% part-time, 13% 25 or older, 1% Native American, 1% Hispanic, 13% black, 1% Asian American or Pacific Islander **Most popular recent majors** Business marketing and marketing management; psychology; nursing **Academic program** Average class size 31, English as a second language, advanced placement, accelerated degree program, self-designed majors, tutorials, honors program, summer session, adult/continuing education programs, internships **Contact** Mr. Tom Davis, Acting Director of Admissions, The University of Alabama, Tuscaloosa, AL 35487. Telephone: 205-348-5666 or toll-free 800-933-BAMA. Fax: 205-348-9046. Web site: http://www.ua.edu/.

THE UNIVERSITY OF ALABAMA AT BIRMINGHAM
BIRMINGHAM, ALABAMA

General State-supported, university, coed **Entrance** Moderately difficult **Setting** 265-acre urban campus **Total enrollment** 14,933 **Student/faculty ratio** 19:1 **Application deadline** 8/1 **Freshmen** 90% were admitted **Housing** Yes **Expenses** Tuition $2850; Room only $3090 **Undergraduates** 56% women, 34% part-time, 34% 25 or older, 0.3% Native American, 1% Hispanic, 26% black, 2% Asian American or Pacific Islander **Most popular recent majors** Nursing; psychology; biology **Academic program** Advanced placement, self-designed majors, tutorials, honors program, summer session, adult/continuing education programs, internships **Contact** Ms. Wendy Troxel, Director of Admissions, The University of Alabama at Birmingham, Office of Undergraduate Admissions, 1400 University Boulevard, Birmingham, AL 35294-1150. Telephone: 205-934-8221 or toll-free 800-421-8743 (in-state). Fax: 205-975-7114. E-mail: uabadmit@undergradadmit.uab.edu. Web site: http://www.uab.edu/.

THE UNIVERSITY OF ALABAMA IN HUNTSVILLE
HUNTSVILLE, ALABAMA

General State-supported, university, coed **Entrance** Moderately difficult **Setting** 376-acre suburban campus **Total enrollment** 6,464 **Student/faculty ratio** 10:1 **Application deadline** 8/15 **Freshmen** 85% were admitted **Housing** Yes **Expenses** Tuition $2832; Room & Board $3700 **Undergraduates** 51% women, 35% part-time, 33% 25 or older, 2% Native American, 2% Hispanic, 14% black, 4% Asian American or Pacific Islander **Most popular recent majors** Nursing; electrical/electronics engineering; mechanical engineering **Academic program** Average class size 32, English as a second language, advanced placement, accelerated degree program, honors program, summer session, adult/continuing education programs, internships **Contact** Ms. Sabrina Williams, Associate Director of Admissions, The University of Alabama in Huntsville, Enrollment Services, Huntsville, AL 35899. Telephone: 205-890-6070 or toll-free 800-UAH-CALL. Fax: 205-890-6073. E-mail: admitme@emial.uah.edu. Web site: http://www.uah.edu/.

UNIVERSITY OF MOBILE
MOBILE, ALABAMA

General Independent Southern Baptist, comprehensive, coed **Entrance** Moderately difficult **Setting** 830-acre suburban campus **Total enrollment** 2,117 **Student/faculty ratio** 17:1 **Application deadline** Rolling **Freshmen** 87% were admitted **Housing** Yes **Expenses** Tuition $7260; Room & Board $4080 **Undergraduates** 60% women, 23% part-time, 30% 25 or older, 1% Native American, 0% Hispanic, 16% black, 0% Asian American or Pacific Islander **Most popular recent majors** Nursing; elementary education **Academic program** Average class size 35, advanced placement, accelerated degree program, honors program, summer session, adult/continuing education programs, internships **Contact** Mrs. Kim Leousis, Director of Admissions, University of Mobile, PO Box 13220, Mobile, AL 36663-0220. Telephone: 334-675-5990 ext. 290 or toll-free 800-946-7267. Fax: 334-675-6329. E-mail: adminfo@umobile.edu. Web site: http://www.umobile.edu/.

UNIVERSITY OF MONTEVALLO
MONTEVALLO, ALABAMA

General State-supported, comprehensive, coed **Entrance** Moderately difficult **Setting** 106-acre small town campus **Total enrollment** 3,125 **Student/faculty ratio** 19:1 **Application deadline** 8/1 **Freshmen** 76% were admitted **Housing** Yes **Expenses** Tuition $3180; Room & Board $3116 **Undergraduates** 68% women, 10% part-time, 11% 25 or older, 0.4% Native American, 0.3% Hispanic, 12% black, 0.3% Asian American or Pacific Islander **Most popular recent majors** Elementary education; speech-language pathology/audiology; mass communications **Academic program** Advanced placement, honors program, summer session, internships **Contact** Mr. Robert A. Doyle, Director of Admissions, University of Montevallo, Station 6001, Montevallo, AL 35115. Telephone: 205-665-6030. E-mail: admissions@um.montevallo.edu. Web site: http://www.montevallo.edu/.

UNIVERSITY OF NORTH ALABAMA
FLORENCE, ALABAMA

General State-supported, comprehensive, coed **Entrance** Minimally difficult **Setting** 125-acre urban campus **Total enrollment** 5,575 **Student/faculty ratio** 22:1 **Application deadline** Rolling **Freshmen** 87% were admitted **Housing** Yes **Expenses** Tuition $2184; Room & Board $3260 **Undergraduates** 57% women, 15% part-time, 23% 25 or older, 2% Native American, 1% Hispanic, 8% black, 1% Asian American or Pacific Islander **Most popular recent majors** Nursing; secondary education; elementary education **Academic program** English as a second language, advanced placement, accelerated degree program, tutorials, summer session, adult/continuing education programs, internships **Contact** Mrs. Kim Mauldin, Director of Admissions, University of North Alabama, University Station, Florence, AL 35632-0001. Telephone: 205-765-4680 or toll-free 800-TALKUNA. Fax: 256-765-4329. E-mail: admis1@unanov.una.edu. Web site: http://www.una.edu/.

UNIVERSITY OF SOUTH ALABAMA
MOBILE, ALABAMA

General State-supported, university, coed **Contact** Ms. Catherine P. King, Director of Admissions, University of South Alabama, 307 University Boulevard, Mobile, AL 36688-0002. Telephone: 334-460-6141 or toll-free 800-872-5247. Fax: 334-460-7023. E-mail: admiss@jaguarl.usouthal.edu. Web site: http://www.usouthal.edu/.

THE UNIVERSITY OF WEST ALABAMA
LIVINGSTON, ALABAMA

General State-supported, comprehensive, coed **Entrance** Minimally difficult **Setting** 595-acre small town campus **Total enrollment** 2,068 **Student/faculty ratio** 19:1 **Application deadline** Rolling **Housing** Yes **Expenses** Tuition $2568; Room & Board $3003 **Undergraduates** 53% women, 8% part-time, 22% 25 or older, 1% Native American, 1% Hispanic, 34% black, 0.2% Asian American or Pacific Islander **Most popular recent majors** Elementary education; business administration; physical education **Academic program** Advanced placement, accelerated degree program, honors program, summer session, internships **Contact** Dr. Ervin L. Wood, Dean of Students, The University of West Alabama, Livingston, AL 35470. Telephone: 205-652-9661 ext. 352 or toll-free 800-621-7742 (in-state), 800-621-8044 (out-of-state). Web site: http://www.westal.edu/.

ALASKA

ALASKA BIBLE COLLEGE
GLENNALLEN, ALASKA

General Independent nondenominational, 4-year, coed **Entrance** Minimally difficult **Setting** 80-acre rural campus **Total enrollment** 43 **Student/faculty ratio** 8:1 **Application deadline** 8/1 **Housing** Yes **Expenses** Tuition $3790; Room & Board $3570 **Undergraduates** 44% women, 15% part-time, 38% 25 or older, 9% Native American **Most popular recent majors** Religious education; pastoral counseling **Academic program** Average class size 15, advanced placement, self-designed majors, internships **Contact** Mrs. Karen Pregizer, Admissions Officer, Alaska Bible College, Box 289, Glennallen, AK 99588-0289. Telephone: 907-822-3201 or toll-free 800-478-7884. Fax: 907-822-5027. E-mail: akbibcol@alaska.net.

ALASKA PACIFIC UNIVERSITY
ANCHORAGE, ALASKA

General Independent, comprehensive, coed **Entrance** Minimally difficult **Setting** 170-acre suburban campus **Total enrollment** 563 **Student/faculty ratio** 9:1 **Application deadline** 2/1 **Freshmen** 100% were admitted **Housing** Yes **Expenses** Tuition $9296; Room & Board $5700 **Undergraduates** 59% women, 34% part-time, 56% 25 or older, 11% Native American, 4% Hispanic, 5% black, 3% Asian American or Pacific Islander **Most popular recent majors** Environmental science; business administration; elementary educa-

Alaska Pacific University *(continued)*

tion **Academic program** Average class size 13, advanced placement, accelerated degree program, self-designed majors, tutorials, summer session, adult/continuing education programs, internships **Contact** Ms. Johanna Walker, Admissions Counselor, Alaska Pacific University, 4101 University Drive, Anchorage, AK 99508-4672. Telephone: 907-564-8248 or toll-free 800-252-7528. Fax: 907-564-8317. E-mail: apu@corecom.net. Web site: http://www.corecom.net/apu.

SHELDON JACKSON COLLEGE
SITKA, ALASKA

General Independent, 4-year, coed, affiliated with Presbyterian Church (U.S.A.) **Entrance** Noncompetitive **Setting** 320-acre small town campus **Total enrollment** 192 **Application deadline** Rolling **Freshmen** 100% were admitted **Housing** Yes **Expenses** Tuition $7100; Room & Board $4800 **Undergraduates** 48% women, 16% part-time, 68% 25 or older, 20% Native American, 2% Hispanic, 3% black, 1% Asian American or Pacific Islander **Most popular recent majors** Natural resources management; fish/game management; education **Academic program** Average class size 10, advanced placement, self-designed majors, tutorials, internships **Contact** Mr. John Schafer, Dean of Enrollment, Sheldon Jackson College, 801 Lincoln Street, Sitka, AK 99835-7699. Telephone: 907-747-5221 or toll-free 800-478-5220 (in-state), 800-544-2231 (out-of-state). Fax: 907-747-5212. E-mail: sombrozak@juno.com. Web site: http://www.sj-alaska.edu/.

UNIVERSITY OF ALASKA ANCHORAGE
ANCHORAGE, ALASKA

General State-supported, comprehensive, coed **Entrance** Noncompetitive **Setting** 428-acre urban campus **Total enrollment** 14,765 **Student/faculty ratio** 29:1 **Application deadline** Rolling **Housing** Yes **Expenses** Tuition $2466; Room & Board $6591 **Undergraduates** 63% women, 36% part-time, 62% 25 or older, 6% Native American, 4% Hispanic, 5% black, 4% Asian American or Pacific Islander **Most popular recent majors** Accounting; elementary education; psychology **Academic program** Advanced placement, self-designed majors, tutorials, summer session, adult/continuing education programs, internships **Contact** Ms. Linda Berg Smith, Associate Vice Chancellor for Student Affairs, University of Alaska Anchorage, Administration Building, Room 176, Anchorage, AK 99508-8060. Telephone: 907-786-4712. Fax: 907-786-4888. Web site: http://www.uaa.alaska.edu/.

UNIVERSITY OF ALASKA FAIRBANKS
FAIRBANKS, ALASKA

General State-supported, university, coed **Entrance** Moderately difficult **Setting** 2,250-acre small town campus **Total enrollment** 7,686 **Student/faculty ratio** 15:1 **Application deadline** 8/1 **Freshmen** 79% were admitted **Housing** Yes **Expenses** Tuition $2410; Room & Board $3690 **Undergraduates** 57% 25 or older **Most popular recent majors** Education; business administration; accounting **Academic program** Advanced placement, accelerated degree program, self-designed majors, tutorials, honors program, summer session, adult/continuing education programs **Contact** Ms. Nancy Dix, Admissions Counselor, University of Alaska Fairbanks, Signers' Hall, Room 215, Fairbanks, AK 99775-7480. Telephone: 907-474-7822 or toll-free 800-478-1UAF (in-state). Fax: 907-474-5379. E-mail: fyapply@aurora.alaska.edu. Web site: http://www.uaf.edu/.

UNIVERSITY OF ALASKA SOUTHEAST
JUNEAU, ALASKA

General State-supported, comprehensive, coed **Entrance** Noncompetitive **Setting** 198-acre small town campus **Total enrollment** 1,803 **Student/faculty ratio** 15:1 **Application deadline** Rolling **Freshmen** 72% were admitted **Housing** Yes **Expenses** Tuition $2164; Room only $2570 **Undergraduates** 56% 25 or older **Most popular recent majors** Education; business administration **Academic program** Average class size 20, advanced placement, self-designed majors, tutorials, summer session, adult/continuing education programs, internships **Contact** Mr. Greg Wagner, Director of Admissions, University of Alaska Southeast, 11120 Glacier Highway, Juneau, AK 99801-8625. Telephone: 907-465-6239. Fax: 907-465-6365. E-mail: jyuas@acadi.alaska.edu. Web site: http://www.jun.alaska.edu/.

ARIZONA

AL COLLINS GRAPHIC DESIGN SCHOOL
TEMPE, ARIZONA

Contact Al Collins Graphic Design School, 1140 South Priest Drive, Tempe, AZ 85281-5206. Telephone: 602-966-3000. Web site: http://www.alcollins.com.

AMERICAN INDIAN COLLEGE OF THE ASSEMBLIES OF GOD, INC.
PHOENIX, ARIZONA

General Independent, 4-year, coed, affiliated with Assemblies of God **Entrance** Minimally difficult

Setting 10-acre urban campus **Total enrollment** 106 **Application deadline** 8/15 **Freshmen** 64% were admitted **Housing** Yes **Expenses** Tuition $3280; Room & Board $3150 **Undergraduates** 36% 25 or older **Academic program** Internships **Contact** Ms. Ruth Collins, Admissions Coordinator, American Indian College of the Assemblies of God, Inc., 10020 North Fifteenth Avenue, Phoenix, AZ 85021-2199. Telephone: 602-944-3335 ext. 232 or toll-free 800-933-3828. Web site: http://www.amerindcol.edu/.

ARIZONA BIBLE COLLEGE
PHOENIX, ARIZONA

General Independent religious, 4-year, coed **Entrance** Minimally difficult **Setting** 7-acre urban campus **Total enrollment** 130 **Student/faculty ratio** 11:1 **Application deadline** 8/5 **Freshmen** 83% were admitted **Housing** Yes **Expenses** Tuition $5886; Room & Board $4128 **Undergraduates** 39% 25 or older **Academic program** Summer session, adult/continuing education programs, internships **Contact** Ms. Beth DeHart, Admissions Counselor, Arizona Bible College, 1718 West Maryland Avenue, Phoenix, AZ 85015-1701. Telephone: 602-242-6400. Fax: 602-242-1992. E-mail: mail@abc.edu.

ARIZONA STATE UNIVERSITY
TEMPE, ARIZONA

General State-supported, university, coed **Entrance** Moderately difficult **Setting** 814-acre suburban campus **Total enrollment** 44,255 **Student/faculty ratio** 17:1 **Application deadline** Rolling **Freshmen** 79% were admitted **Housing** Yes **Expenses** Tuition $2059; Room & Board $4500 **Undergraduates** 51% women, 20% part-time, 25% 25 or older, 2% Native American, 11% Hispanic, 3% black, 5% Asian American or Pacific Islander **Most popular recent majors** Elementary education; psychology **Academic program** English as a second language, advanced placement, accelerated degree program, honors program, summer session, adult/continuing education programs, internships **Contact** Mr. Timothy J. Desch, Director of Undergraduate Admissions, Arizona State University, Box 870112, Tempe, AZ 85287-0112. Telephone: 602-965-7788. E-mail: ugradadm@asuvm.inre.asau.edu. Web site: http://www.asu.edu/.

ARIZONA STATE UNIVERSITY EAST
MESA, ARIZONA

General State-supported, university, coed **Entrance** Moderately difficult **Setting** 600-acre small town campus **Total enrollment** 1,052 **Application deadline** Rolling **Housing** Yes **Expenses** Tuition $2059; Room & Board $5400 **Academic program** Advanced placement, accelerated degree program, self-designed majors, honors program, internships **Contact** Ms. Vira Thorne, Director of Enrollment Management, Arizona State University East, 6001 South Power Road, Mesa, AZ 85206-0903. Telephone: 602-727-1041. Fax: 602-727-1008. Web site: http://www.east.asu.edu.

ARIZONA STATE UNIVERSITY WEST
PHOENIX, ARIZONA

General State-supported, upper-level, coed **Entrance** Moderately difficult **Setting** 300-acre urban campus **Total enrollment** 4,807 **Student/faculty ratio** 17:1 **Application deadline** Rolling **Freshmen** 92% were admitted **Housing** No **Expenses** Tuition $2059 **Undergraduates** 68% women, 49% part-time, 61% 25 or older, 2% Native American, 13% Hispanic, 3% black, 3% Asian American or Pacific Islander **Most popular recent majors** Criminal justice/law enforcement administration; accounting; mass communications **Academic program** Self-designed majors, tutorials, honors program, summer session, adult/continuing education programs, internships **Contact** Mr. Tom Cabot, Director of Enrollment Services/Registrar, Arizona State University West, 4701 West Thunderbird Road, PO Box 37100, Phoenix, AZ 85069-7100. Telephone: 602-543-8123. Web site: http://www.west.asu.edu/.

CAD INSTITUTE
See University of Advancing Computer Technology

DEVRY INSTITUTE OF TECHNOLOGY
PHOENIX, ARIZONA

General Proprietary, 4-year, coed **Entrance** Minimally difficult **Setting** 18-acre urban campus **Total enrollment** 3,252 **Student/faculty ratio** 28:1 **Application deadline** Rolling **Freshmen** 71% were admitted **Housing** No **Expenses** Tuition $7308 **Undergraduates** 22% women, 20% part-time, 41% 25 or older, 4% Native American, 12% Hispanic, 5% black, 6% Asian American or Pacific Islander **Most popular recent majors** Electrical/electronic engineering technology; information sciences/systems **Academic program** Advanced placement, summer session, adult/continuing education programs **Contact** Mr. Kim Galetti, Director of Admissions, DeVry Institute of Technology, 2149 West Dunlap Avenue, Phoenix, AZ 85021-2995. Telephone: 602-870-9201 ext. 451 or toll-free 800-528-0250 (out-of-state). E-mail: webadmin@devry-phx.edu. Web site: http://www.devry-phx.edu/.

EMBRY-RIDDLE AERONAUTICAL UNIVERSITY
PRESCOTT, ARIZONA

General Independent, 4-year, coed **Entrance** Moderately difficult **Setting** 547-acre small town campus **Total enrollment** 1,512 **Student/faculty ratio** 17:1 **Application deadline** Rolling **Freshmen** 87% were admitted **Housing** Yes **Expenses** Tuition $9920; Room & Board $4950 **Undergraduates** 17% women, 7% part-time, 12% 25 or older, 1% Native American, 5% Hispanic, 1% black, 6% Asian American or Pacific Islander **Most popular recent majors** Aircraft pilot (professional); aerospace engineering; aviation/airway science **Academic program** Average class size 26, advanced placement, tutorials, summer session, adult/continuing education programs, internships **Contact** Mr. Terry E. Whittum, Director of Enrollment Management, Embry-Riddle Aeronautical University, 3200 Willow Creek Road, Prescott, AZ 86301-3720. Telephone: 520-708-3858 or toll-free 800-888-3728. Fax: 520-708-6606. E-mail: admit@pr.erau.edu. Web site: http://www.pr.erau.edu/.

GRAND CANYON UNIVERSITY
PHOENIX, ARIZONA

General Independent Southern Baptist, comprehensive, coed **Entrance** Moderately difficult **Setting** 90-acre suburban campus **Total enrollment** 2,245 **Student/faculty ratio** 17:1 **Application deadline** 8/15 **Freshmen** 83% were admitted **Housing** Yes **Expenses** Tuition $7526; Room & Board $3740 **Undergraduates** 64% women, 8% part-time, 29% 25 or older, 2% Native American, 6% Hispanic, 4% black, 2% Asian American or Pacific Islander **Most popular recent majors** Elementary education; nursing; psychology **Academic program** Average class size 24, English as a second language, advanced placement, accelerated degree program, tutorials, honors program, summer session, adult/continuing education programs, internships **Contact** Mr. Carl Tichenor, Director of Admissions, Grand Canyon University, 3300 W Camelback Road, PO Box 11097, Phoenix, AZ 86017-3030. Telephone: 602-589-2855. Fax: 602-589-2580. E-mail: admiss@grand-canyon.edu. Web site: http://www.grand-canyon.edu/.

INTERNATIONAL BAPTIST COLLEGE
TEMPE, ARIZONA

General Independent Baptist, comprehensive, coed **Entrance** Difficulty N/R **Setting** 12-acre suburban campus **Total enrollment** 37 **Housing** Yes **Expenses** Tuition $3540; Room & Board $2600 **Undergraduates** 15% 25 or older, 6% Hispanic, 9% black **Academic program** Average class size 8 **Contact** Dr. Stanley Bushey, Administrative Services Director, International Baptist College, 2150 East Southern Avenue, Tempe, AZ 85282. Telephone: 602-838-7070 or toll-free 800-422-4858. Fax: 602-838-5432.

METROPOLITAN COLLEGE OF COURT REPORTING
PHOENIX, ARIZONA

Contact Metropolitan College of Court Reporting, 4640 East Elwood Street, Suite 12, Phoenix, AZ 85040. Telephone: 602-955-5900.

NORTHERN ARIZONA UNIVERSITY
FLAGSTAFF, ARIZONA

General State-supported, university, coed **Entrance** Moderately difficult **Setting** 730-acre small town campus **Total enrollment** 19,618 **Student/faculty ratio** 22:1 **Application deadline** 7/15 **Freshmen** 82% were admitted **Housing** Yes **Expenses** Tuition $2080; Room & Board $3500 **Undergraduates** 27% 25 or older, 7% Native American, 9% Hispanic, 1% black, 2% Asian American or Pacific Islander **Most popular recent majors** Business administration; education; psychology **Academic program** English as a second language, advanced placement, accelerated degree program, tutorials, honors program, summer session, internships **Contact** Ms. Molly Munger, Director of Admissions, Northern Arizona University, PO Box 4084, Flagstaff, AZ 86011. Telephone: 520-523-5511 or toll-free 800-345-1987 (in-state), 888-MORE-NAU (out-of-state). Fax: 520-523-6023. E-mail: undergraduate.admissions@nau.edu. Web site: http://www.nau.edu/.

PRESCOTT COLLEGE
PRESCOTT, ARIZONA

General Independent, comprehensive, coed **Entrance** Moderately difficult **Setting** Small town campus **Total enrollment** 921 **Application deadline** 2/1 **Freshmen** 68% were admitted **Housing** No **Expenses** Tuition $11,783 **Undergraduates** 17% 25 or older, 1% Native American, 1% Hispanic, 0.4% black, 2% Asian American or Pacific Islander **Most popular recent majors** Environmental science; interdisciplinary studies; humanities **Academic program** Accelerated degree program, self-designed majors, tutorials, summer session, adult/continuing education programs, internships **Contact** Director of RDP Admissions, Prescott College, 220 Grove Avenue, Prescott, AZ 86301-2990. Telephone: 520-776-5180 or toll-free 800-628-6364 (out-of-state). Fax: 520-776-5252. E-mail: applypc@aztec.asu.edu. Web site: http://www.prescott.edu/.

SOUTHWESTERN COLLEGE
PHOENIX, ARIZONA

Contact Mrs. Nancy Jones, Admissions Counselor, Southwestern College, 2625 East Cactus Road, Phoenix, AZ 85032-7097. Telephone: 602-992-6101.

UNIVERSITY OF ADVANCING COMPUTER TECHNOLOGY
TEMPE, ARIZONA

General Proprietary, 4-year, coed **Entrance** Difficulty N/R **Setting** Urban campus **Total enrollment** 850 **Housing** No **Academic program** Accelerated degree program **Contact** Mr. Dominic Pistillo, President, University of Advancing Computer Technology, 2625 West Baseline Road, Tempe, AZ 85283-1042. Telephone: 602-383-8228 or toll-free 800-658-5744 (out-of-state). Fax: 602-383-8222. E-mail: admissions@uact.edu. Web site: http://www.uact.edu/.

THE UNIVERSITY OF ARIZONA
TUCSON, ARIZONA

General State-supported, university, coed **Entrance** Moderately difficult **Setting** 351-acre urban campus **Total enrollment** 33,737 **Student/faculty ratio** 18:1 **Application deadline** 4/1 **Freshmen** 85% were admitted **Housing** Yes **Expenses** Tuition $2058; Room & Board $4930 **Undergraduates** 52% women, 15% part-time, 19% 25 or older, 2% Native American, 15% Hispanic, 3% black, 5% Asian American or Pacific Islander **Most popular recent majors** Psychology; political science; finance **Academic program** English as a second language, advanced placement, self-designed majors, tutorials, honors program, summer session, adult/continuing education programs, internships **Contact** Ms. Lori Goldman, Director of Admissions, The University of Arizona, PO Box 210040, Tucson, AZ 85721-0040. Telephone: 520-621-3237. Fax: 520-621-9799. E-mail: appinfo@arizona.edu. Web site: http://www.arizona.edu/.

UNIVERSITY OF PHOENIX
PHOENIX, ARIZONA

General Proprietary, comprehensive, coed **Entrance** Noncompetitive **Setting** Urban campus **Total enrollment** 41,467 **Student/faculty ratio** 6:1 **Application deadline** Rolling **Housing** No **Expenses** Tuition $5352 **Undergraduates** 55% women, 86% 25 or older, 1% Native American, 13% Hispanic, 13% black, 7% Asian American or Pacific Islander **Most popular recent majors** Business administration; accounting; information sciences/systems **Academic program** Advanced placement, accelerated degree program, adult/continuing education programs **Contact** Ms. Nina Omelchenko, Vice President of University Services, University of Phoenix, 4615 East Elwood St, PO Box 52069, Phoenix, AZ 85072-2069. Telephone: 602-966-9577 ext. 1712. Web site: http://www.uophx.edu/.

WESTERN INTERNATIONAL UNIVERSITY
PHOENIX, ARIZONA

General Proprietary, comprehensive, coed **Entrance** Moderately difficult **Setting** 4-acre urban campus **Total enrollment** 1,436 **Student/faculty ratio** 15:1 **Application deadline** Rolling **Housing** No **Expenses** Tuition $6400 **Undergraduates** 90% 25 or older, 1% Native American, 8% Hispanic, 4% black, 0.4% Asian American or Pacific Islander **Most popular recent majors** Information sciences/systems; business administration; accounting **Academic program** Average class size 15, English as a second language, advanced placement, accelerated degree program, honors program, summer session, adult/continuing education programs **Contact** Ms. Jo Arney, Director of Student Services, Western International University, 9215 North Black Canyon Highway, Phoenix, AZ 85021-2718. Telephone: 602-943-2311 ext. 139. Web site: http://www.wintu.edu/.

ARKANSAS

ARKANSAS BAPTIST COLLEGE
LITTLE ROCK, ARKANSAS

Contact Mrs. Annie Hightower, Registrar, Arkansas Baptist College, 1600 Bishop Street, Little Rock, AR 72202-6067. Telephone: 501-374-7856 ext. 19.

ARKANSAS STATE UNIVERSITY
JONESBORO, ARKANSAS

General State-supported, comprehensive, coed **Entrance** Moderately difficult **Setting** 900-acre small town campus **Total enrollment** 10,012 **Student/faculty ratio** 18:1 **Application deadline** 8/12 **Freshmen** 79% were admitted **Housing** Yes **Expenses** Tuition $2280; Room & Board $2840 **Undergraduates** 56% women, 18% part-time, 24% 25 or older, 0.2% Native American, 1% Hispanic, 10% black, 1% Asian American or Pacific Islander **Most popular recent majors** Accounting; early childhood education; business administration **Academic program** Average class size 35, English as a second language, advanced placement, accelerated degree program, honors program, summer

Arkansas State University *(continued)*

session, internships **Contact** Ms. Paula James, Director of Admissions, Arkansas State University, PO Box 1630, Jonesboro, AR 72401. Telephone: 870-972-3024 or toll-free 800-382-3030 (in-state), 800-643-0080 (out-of-state). Fax: 870-972-3843. E-mail: admissions@chickasaw.astate.edu. Web site: http://www.astate.edu/.

ARKANSAS TECH UNIVERSITY
RUSSELLVILLE, ARKANSAS

General State-supported, comprehensive, coed **Entrance** Minimally difficult **Setting** 517-acre small town campus **Total enrollment** 4,238 **Student/faculty ratio** 18:1 **Application deadline** 9/15 **Housing** Yes **Expenses** Tuition $2126; Room & Board $2676 **Undergraduates** 53% women, 19% part-time, 24% 25 or older, 1% Native American, 1% Hispanic, 3% black, 1% Asian American or Pacific Islander **Most popular recent majors** Elementary education; business administration; agricultural business **Academic program** Average class size 25, English as a second language, advanced placement, accelerated degree program, tutorials, honors program, summer session, adult/continuing education programs, internships **Contact** Mr. Harold Cornett, Director of Admissions, Arkansas Tech University, Alumni House, Russellville, AR 72801-2222. Telephone: 501-968-0343 or toll-free 800-582-6953 (in-state). Fax: 501-964-0522. E-mail: adrf@atuvm.atu.edu. Web site: http://www.atu.edu/.

CENTRAL BAPTIST COLLEGE
CONWAY, ARKANSAS

General Independent Baptist, 4-year, coed **Entrance** Minimally difficult **Setting** 11-acre small town campus **Total enrollment** 333 **Student/faculty ratio** 20:1 **Application deadline** 8/15 **Housing** Yes **Expenses** Tuition $4550; Room & Board $3222 **Undergraduates** 47% women, 7% part-time, 12% 25 or older, 0% Native American, 1% Hispanic, 6% black, 0% Asian American or Pacific Islander **Most popular recent majors** Biblical studies; music; religious education **Academic program** Advanced placement, summer session, internships **Contact** Mr. Gary McAllister, Registrar, Central Baptist College, 1501 College Avenue, Conway, AR 72032-6470. Telephone: 501-329-6872 ext. 106 or toll-free 800-205-6872.

HARDING UNIVERSITY
SEARCY, ARKANSAS

General Independent, comprehensive, coed, affiliated with Church of Christ **Entrance** Very difficult **Setting** 200-acre small town campus **Total enrollment** 3,754 **Student/faculty ratio** 17:1 **Application deadline** 7/1 **Freshmen** 60% were admitted **Housing** Yes **Expenses** Tuition $7712; Room & Board $3986 **Undergraduates** 56% women, 6% part-time, 7% 25 or older, 1% Native American, 1% Hispanic, 4% black, 1% Asian American or Pacific Islander **Most popular recent majors** Business administration; elementary education; mass communications **Academic program** Average class size 34, English as a second language, advanced placement, accelerated degree program, self-designed majors, tutorials, honors program, summer session, adult/continuing education programs, internships **Contact** Mr. Mike Williams, Assistant Vice President of Admissions, Harding University, Box 11255, Searcy, AR 72149-0001. Telephone: 501-279-4407 or toll-free 800-477-4407. Fax: 501-279-4865. E-mail: admissions@harding.edu. Web site: http://www.harding.edu/.

HENDERSON STATE UNIVERSITY
ARKADELPHIA, ARKANSAS

General State-supported, comprehensive, coed **Entrance** Moderately difficult **Setting** 135-acre small town campus **Total enrollment** 3,773 **Student/faculty ratio** 18:1 **Application deadline** Rolling **Freshmen** 93% were admitted **Housing** Yes **Expenses** Tuition $2166; Room & Board $2856 **Undergraduates** 57% women, 13% part-time, 17% 25 or older, 1% Native American, 1% Hispanic, 15% black, 1% Asian American or Pacific Islander **Most popular recent majors** Elementary education; business administration **Academic program** Average class size 30, advanced placement, honors program, summer session, internships **Contact** Ms. Vikita Hardwrick, Director of University Relations/Admissions, Henderson State University, 1100 Henderson Street, PO Box 7560, Arkadelphia, AR 71999-0001. Telephone: 870-230-5028 or toll-free 800-228-7333 (in-state). Fax: 870-230-5144. E-mail: hardwrv@oaks.hsu.edu. Web site: http://www.hsu.edu/.

HENDRIX COLLEGE
CONWAY, ARKANSAS

General Independent United Methodist, 4-year, coed **Entrance** Very difficult **Setting** 158-acre suburban campus **Total enrollment** 1,034 **Student/faculty ratio** 12:1 **Application deadline** Rolling **Freshmen** 89% were admitted **Housing** Yes **Expenses** Tuition $10,408; Room & Board $4000 **Undergraduates** 55% women, 1% part-time, 1% 25 or older, 0% Native American, 1% Hispanic, 6% black, 3% Asian American or Pacific Islander **Most popular recent majors** Biology; psychology; economics **Academic program** Average class size 24, advanced placement, self-designed majors, tutorials, honors program, internships **Contact** Mr. Rock Jones, Vice President for Enrollment, Hendrix College, 1600 Washington Avenue, Conway, AR

72032. Telephone: 501-450-1362 or toll-free 800-277-9017. Fax: 501-450-3843. E-mail: adm@hendrix.edu. Web site: http://www.hendrix.edu/.

JOHN BROWN UNIVERSITY
SILOAM SPRINGS, ARKANSAS

General Independent nondenominational, comprehensive, coed **Entrance** Moderately difficult **Setting** 200-acre small town campus **Total enrollment** 1,403 **Student/faculty ratio** 16:1 **Application deadline** 3/1 **Freshmen** 71% were admitted **Housing** Yes **Expenses** Tuition $9802; Room & Board $4478 **Undergraduates** 56% women, 4% part-time, 24% 25 or older, 1% Native American, 1% Hispanic, 1% black, 1% Asian American or Pacific Islander **Most popular recent majors** Business administration; elementary education; engineering **Academic program** Average class size 30, English as a second language, advanced placement, tutorials, honors program, adult/continuing education programs, internships **Contact** Ms. Karyn Byrne, Application Coordinator, John Brown University, 2000 West University Street, Siloam Springs, AR 72761-2121. Telephone: 501-524-7121 or toll-free 800-634-6969. Fax: 501-524-4196. E-mail: jbuinfo@acc.jbu.edu. Web site: http://www.jbu.edu/.

LYON COLLEGE
BATESVILLE, ARKANSAS

General Independent Presbyterian, 4-year, coed **Entrance** Very difficult **Setting** 136-acre small town campus **Total enrollment** 511 **Student/faculty ratio** 11:1 **Application deadline** Rolling **Freshmen** 53% were admitted **Housing** Yes **Expenses** Tuition $9880; Room & Board $4418 **Undergraduates** 54% women, 14% part-time, 13% 25 or older, 1% Native American, 1% Hispanic, 4% black, 2% Asian American or Pacific Islander **Most popular recent majors** Biology; psychology; English **Academic program** Average class size 20, advanced placement, self-designed majors, tutorials, summer session, adult/continuing education programs **Contact** Ms. Kristine Penix, Director of Admissions, Lyon College, PO Box 2317, Batesville, AR 72503-2317. Telephone: 870-698-4250 or toll-free 800-423-2542. Fax: 870-698-4622. E-mail: admissions@lyon.edu. Web site: http://www.lyon.edu/.

OUACHITA BAPTIST UNIVERSITY
ARKADELPHIA, ARKANSAS

General Independent Baptist, 4-year, coed **Entrance** Moderately difficult **Setting** 60-acre small town campus **Total enrollment** 1,619 **Student/faculty ratio** 12:1 **Application deadline** 8/15 **Freshmen** 81% were admitted **Housing** Yes **Expenses** Tuition $8090; Room & Board $3040 **Undergraduates** 52% women, 5% part-time, 6% 25 or older, 0.4% Native American, 0.4% Hispanic, 3% black, 0.4% Asian American or Pacific Islander **Most popular recent majors** Education; business administration; religious studies **Academic program** English as a second language, advanced placement, accelerated degree program, tutorials, honors program, summer session, internships **Contact** Mr. Randy Garner, Director of Admissions Counseling, Ouachita Baptist University, 410 Ouachita Street, Arkadelphia, AR 71998-0001. Telephone: 870-245-5110 or toll-free 800-342-5628 (in-state). Fax: 870-245-5500. E-mail: jonesj@sigma.obu.edu. Web site: http://www.obu.edu/.

PHILANDER SMITH COLLEGE
LITTLE ROCK, ARKANSAS

General Independent United Methodist, 4-year, coed **Entrance** Noncompetitive **Setting** 20-acre urban campus **Total enrollment** 848 **Student/faculty ratio** 16:1 **Application deadline** Rolling **Freshmen** 100% were admitted **Housing** Yes **Expenses** Tuition $3336; Room & Board $2746 **Undergraduates** 67% women, 22% part-time, 37% 25 or older, 0% Native American, 0% Hispanic, 97% black, 0% Asian American or Pacific Islander **Most popular recent majors** Business administration; mathematics; biology **Academic program** Average class size 15, tutorials, summer session, internships **Contact** Mrs. Arnella Hayes, Admission Officer, Philander Smith College, 812 West 13th Street, Little Rock, AR 72202-3799. Telephone: 501-370-5310 or toll-free 800-446-6772. Fax: 501-370-5225. E-mail: admarnella@philander.edu.

SOUTHERN ARKANSAS UNIVERSITY–MAGNOLIA
MAGNOLIA, ARKANSAS

General State-supported, comprehensive, coed **Entrance** Minimally difficult **Setting** 781-acre small town campus **Total enrollment** 2,676 **Student/faculty ratio** 18:1 **Application deadline** 8/15 **Freshmen** 91% were admitted **Housing** Yes **Expenses** Tuition $1896; Room & Board $2530 **Undergraduates** 54% women, 10% part-time, 20% 25 or older, 0.4% Native American, 1% Hispanic, 21% black, 0.4% Asian American or Pacific Islander **Most popular recent majors** Business; elementary education; physical education **Academic program** Average class size 30, advanced placement, accelerated degree program, tutorials, summer session, adult/continuing education programs, internships **Contact** Mr. James E. Whittington, Director of Admissions, Southern Arkansas University-Magnolia, 100 East University, Magnolia, AR 71753. Telephone: 870-235-4040.

Southern Arkansas University–Magnolia *(continued)*

Fax: 870-235-5005. E-mail: adsonny@saumag.edu. Web site: http://www.saumag.edu/.

UNIVERSITY OF ARKANSAS
FAYETTEVILLE, ARKANSAS

General State-supported, university, coed **Entrance** Moderately difficult **Setting** 420-acre small town campus **Total enrollment** 14,322 **Student/faculty ratio** 14:1 **Application deadline** 8/15 **Freshmen** 91% were admitted **Housing** Yes **Expenses** Tuition $2661; Room & Board $3867 **Undergraduates** 48% women, 12% part-time, 16% 25 or older, 2% Native American, 1% Hispanic, 6% black, 3% Asian American or Pacific Islander **Most popular recent majors** Business marketing and marketing management; finance; accounting **Academic program** English as a second language, advanced placement, honors program, summer session, internships **Contact** Ms. Maribeth Lynes, Director of Undergraduate Recruitment, University of Arkansas, 200 Silas H. Hunt Hall, Fayetteville, AR 72701-1201. Telephone: 501-575-5346 or toll-free 800-377-8632. Fax: 501-575-7515. E-mail: uafadmis@comp.uark.edu. Web site: http://www.uark.edu/.

▶ **For more information, see page 532.**

UNIVERSITY OF ARKANSAS AT LITTLE ROCK
LITTLE ROCK, ARKANSAS

General State-supported, university, coed **Entrance** Minimally difficult **Setting** 150-acre urban campus **Total enrollment** 10,959 **Student/faculty ratio** 15:1 **Application deadline** Rolling **Freshmen** 67% were admitted **Housing** Yes **Expenses** Tuition $3026; Room only $2500 **Undergraduates** 35% 25 or older **Most popular recent majors** Psychology; biology; liberal arts and studies **Academic program** English as a second language, advanced placement, accelerated degree program, self-designed majors, honors program, summer session, adult/continuing education programs, internships **Contact** Office of Admissions and Records, University of Arkansas at Little Rock, 2801 South University Avenue, Little Rock, AR 72204-1099. Telephone: 501-569-3127 or toll-free 800-482-8892 (in-state). Fax: 501-569-8915. E-mail: dspine@ualr.edu. Web site: http://www.ualr.edu/.

UNIVERSITY OF ARKANSAS AT MONTICELLO
MONTICELLO, ARKANSAS

General State-supported, comprehensive, coed **Contact** Mrs. JoBeth Johnson, Director of Admissions, University of Arkansas at Monticello, Monticello, AR 71656. Telephone: 501-460-1026. Fax: 870-460-1321. Web site: http://www.uamont.edu/.

UNIVERSITY OF ARKANSAS AT PINE BLUFF
PINE BLUFF, ARKANSAS

General State-supported, comprehensive, coed **Contact** Ms. Kwurly M. Floyd, Director of Admissions and Academic Records, University of Arkansas at Pine Bluff, UAPB Box 17, 1200 University Drive, Pine Bluff, AR 71601-2799. Telephone: 501-543-8487.

UNIVERSITY OF ARKANSAS FOR MEDICAL SCIENCES
LITTLE ROCK, ARKANSAS

General State-supported, university, coed **Entrance** Very difficult **Setting** 5-acre urban campus **Total enrollment** 1,624 **Housing** Yes **Expenses** Tuition $2204; Room only $1377 **Undergraduates** 54% 25 or older, 0.2% Native American, 1% Hispanic, 14% black, 2% Asian American or Pacific Islander **Most Popular Recent Major** Nursing **Contact** Mr. Paul Carter, Assistant to the Vice Chancellor for Academic Affairs, University of Arkansas for Medical Sciences, 4301 West Markham-Slot 601, Little Rock, AR 72205-7199. Telephone: 501-686-5454. Web site: http://www.uams.edu/.

UNIVERSITY OF CENTRAL ARKANSAS
CONWAY, ARKANSAS

General State-supported, comprehensive, coed **Entrance** Moderately difficult **Setting** 285-acre small town campus **Total enrollment** 8,938 **Student/faculty ratio** 18:1 **Application deadline** Rolling **Freshmen** 77% were admitted **Housing** Yes **Expenses** Tuition $2692; Room & Board $2920 **Undergraduates** 61% women, 10% part-time, 17% 25 or older, 1% Native American, 1% Hispanic, 12% black, 1% Asian American or Pacific Islander **Most popular recent majors** Physical therapy; (pre)medicine; education **Academic program** Average class size 35, English as a second language, advanced placement, accelerated degree program, tutorials, honors program, summer session, internships **Contact** Mr. Joe F. Darling, Director of Admissions, University of Central Arkansas, 201 Donaghey Avenue, Conway, AR 72035-0001. Telephone: 501-450-5145 or toll-free 800-243-8245 (in-state). Fax: 501-450-5228. E-mail: admisson@ecom.uca.edu. Web site: http://www.uca.edu/.

UNIVERSITY OF THE OZARKS
CLARKSVILLE, ARKANSAS

General Independent Presbyterian, 4-year, coed **Entrance** Moderately difficult **Setting** 56-acre small town campus **Total enrollment** 534 **Student/faculty ratio** 13:1 **Application deadline** 8/15 **Freshmen** 84% were admitted **Housing** Yes **Expenses** Tuition $7390; Room & Board $3600 **Undergraduates** 8% 25 or older, 1% Native American, 1% Hispanic, 1% black, 1% Asian American or Pacific Islander **Most popular recent majors** Business administration; elementary education; secondary education **Academic program** Average class size 25, advanced placement, tutorials, summer session, internships **Contact** Mr. James D. Decker, Director of Admissions, University of the Ozarks, 415 North College Avenue, Clarksville, AR 72830-2880. Telephone: 501-979-1209 or toll-free 800-264-8636. Fax: 501-979-1355. E-mail: admiss@ozarks.edu. Web site: http://www.ozarks.edu/.

WILLIAMS BAPTIST COLLEGE
WALNUT RIDGE, ARKANSAS

General Independent Southern Baptist, 4-year, coed **Entrance** Minimally difficult **Setting** 186-acre rural campus **Total enrollment** 708 **Student/faculty ratio** 10:1 **Application deadline** Rolling **Freshmen** 79% were admitted **Housing** Yes **Expenses** Tuition $5260; Room & Board $2922 **Undergraduates** 53% women, 30% part-time, 22% 25 or older, 0.4% Native American, 0% Hispanic, 2% black, 0.1% Asian American or Pacific Islander **Most popular recent majors** Elementary education; business administration; psychology **Academic program** Average class size 22, English as a second language, advanced placement, self-designed majors, tutorials, honors program, summer session, adult/continuing education programs, internships **Contact** Ms. Angela Flippo, Director of Admissions, Williams Baptist College, 60 West Fulbright Avenue, Walnut Ridge, AR 72476. Telephone: 870-886-6741 ext. 127. E-mail: admissions@wbclab.wbcoll.edu. Web site: http://wbc2.wbcoll.edu/.

CALIFORNIA

ACADEMY OF ART COLLEGE
SAN FRANCISCO, CALIFORNIA

General Proprietary, comprehensive, coed **Entrance** Noncompetitive **Setting** 3-acre urban campus **Total enrollment** 4,976 **Application deadline** Rolling **Freshmen** 100% were admitted **Housing** Yes **Expenses** Tuition $14,910; Room only $6500 **Undergraduates** 41% women, 35% part-time, 27% 25 or older, 1% Native American, 9% Hispanic, 4% black, 17% Asian American or Pacific Islander **Most popular recent majors** Graphic design/commercial art/illustration; interior design **Academic program** English as a second language, tutorials, summer session, adult/continuing education programs, internships **Contact** Mr. Ron Bunn, Director of Admissions, Academy of Art College, 79 New Montgomery Street, San Francisco, CA 94105-3410. Telephone: 415-263-4127 or toll-free 800-544-ARTS. Fax: 415-263-4130. Web site: http://www.academyart.edu/.

THE ADVERTISING ARTS COLLEGE
SAN DIEGO, CALIFORNIA

General Proprietary, 4-year, coed **Contact** Ms. Tracy Myers, Vice President and Director of Admissions, The Advertising Arts College, 10025 Mesa Rim Road, San Diego, CA 92121. Telephone: 619-546-0602. E-mail: info.@taac.edu. Web site: http://www.taac.edu/.

THE AMERICAN COLLEGE
See American InterContinental University

AMERICAN INTERCONTINENTAL UNIVERSITY
LOS ANGELES, CALIFORNIA

General Proprietary, comprehensive, coed **Entrance** Noncompetitive **Setting** Urban campus **Total enrollment** 500 **Student/faculty ratio** 10:1 **Application deadline** Rolling **Housing** Yes **Expenses** Tuition $11,250; Room only $4185 **Undergraduates** 3% 25 or older **Academic program** English as a second language, accelerated degree program, summer session, internships **Contact** Ms. Laurie Nalepa, Director of Admissions, American InterContinental University, 1651 Westwood Boulevard, Los Angeles, CA 90024-5603. Telephone: 310-470-2000 ext. 32 or toll-free 800-333-2652 (out-of-state). Fax: 310-477-8640.

ANTIOCH SOUTHERN CALIFORNIA/LOS ANGELES
MARINA DEL REY, CALIFORNIA

General Independent, upper-level, coed **Entrance** Moderately difficult **Setting** 1-acre urban campus **Total enrollment** 474 **Student/faculty ratio** 6:1 **Application deadline** 8/8 **Freshmen** 78% were admitted **Housing** No **Expenses** Tuition $9600 **Undergraduates** 80% women, 59% part-time, 93% 25 or older, 3% Native American, 6% Hispanic, 15% black, 2% Asian American or Pacific Islander **Academic program** Average class

Antioch Southern California/Los Angeles *(continued)*

size 8, advanced placement, accelerated degree program, self-designed majors, tutorials, summer session, adult/continuing education programs, internships **Contact** Dr. MeHee Hyun, Director of Admissions, Antioch Southern California/Los Angeles, 13274 Fiji Way, Marina del Rey, CA 90292-7090. Telephone: 310-578-1080 or toll-free 800-7AN-TIOC. Fax: 310-822-4824. E-mail: mehee_hyun@antiochla.edu. Web site: http://www.antiochla.edu/.

ANTIOCH SOUTHERN CALIFORNIA/SANTA BARBARA
SANTA BARBARA, CALIFORNIA

General Independent, upper-level, coed **Entrance** Minimally difficult **Setting** Small town campus **Total enrollment** 222 **Application deadline** Rolling **Freshmen** 100% were admitted **Housing** No **Expenses** Tuition $8850 **Undergraduates** 62% women, 47% part-time, 95% 25 or older, 3% Native American, 9% Hispanic, 4% black, 3% Asian American or Pacific Islander **Academic program** Average class size 15, accelerated degree program, self-designed majors, tutorials, summer session, adult/continuing education programs, internships **Contact** Mrs. Carol Flores, Admissions Officer, Antioch Southern California/Santa Barbara, 801 Garden Street, Santa Barbara, CA 93101-1580. Telephone: 805-962-8179 ext. 113. Fax: 805-962-4786. E-mail: cflores@antiochsb.edu.

ARMSTRONG UNIVERSITY
OAKLAND, CALIFORNIA

General Independent, comprehensive, coed **Entrance** Moderately difficult **Setting** Urban campus **Total enrollment** 156 **Student/faculty ratio** 3:1 **Application deadline** Rolling **Freshmen** 52% were admitted **Housing** No **Expenses** Tuition $6060 **Undergraduates** 45% 25 or older **Most popular recent majors** International business; business administration; finance **Academic program** Average class size 5, English as a second language, advanced placement, accelerated degree program, tutorials, summer session **Contact** Office of Admissions, Armstrong University, 1608 Webster Street, Oakland, CA 94612. Telephone: 510-835-7900 ext. 10. Fax: 510-835-8935. E-mail: info@armstrong-u.edu. Web site: http://www.armstrong-u.edu/.

ART CENTER COLLEGE OF DESIGN
PASADENA, CALIFORNIA

General Independent, comprehensive, coed **Entrance** Very difficult **Setting** 175-acre suburban campus **Total enrollment** 1,433 **Student/faculty ratio** 5:1 **Application deadline** Rolling **Freshmen** 61% were admitted **Housing** No **Expenses** Tuition $17,180 **Undergraduates** 38% women, 47% 25 or older, 1% Native American, 9% Hispanic, 1% black, 26% Asian American or Pacific Islander **Most popular recent majors** Graphic design/commercial art/illustration; industrial design; photography **Academic program** Average class size 20, advanced placement, accelerated degree program, tutorials, summer session, adult/continuing education programs **Contact** Ms. Kit Baron, Vice President, Student Services, Art Center College of Design, 1700 Lida Street, Pasadena, CA 91103-1999. Telephone: 626-396-2373. Fax: 626-795-0578. Web site: http://www.artcenter.edu/.

ART INSTITUTE OF SOUTHERN CALIFORNIA
LAGUNA BEACH, CALIFORNIA

General Independent, 4-year, coed **Entrance** Moderately difficult **Setting** 9-acre small town campus **Total enrollment** 196 **Student/faculty ratio** 5:1 **Application deadline** Rolling **Freshmen** 73% were admitted **Housing** No **Expenses** Tuition $10,900 **Undergraduates** 39% women, 18% part-time, 30% 25 or older, 1% Native American, 13% Hispanic, 2% black, 9% Asian American or Pacific Islander **Most Popular Recent Major** Art **Academic program** Average class size 12, advanced placement, tutorials, summer session, adult/continuing education programs, internships **Contact** Mr. Anthony Padilla, Director of Admissions, Art Institute of Southern California, 2222 Laguna Canyon Road, Laguna Beach, CA 92651-1136. Telephone: 714-376-6000 ext. 232 or toll-free 800-255-0762. Fax: 714-376-6009. Web site: http://www.aisc.edu/.

ART INSTITUTES INTERNATIONAL AT SAN FRANCISCO
SAN FRANCISCO, CALIFORNIA

General Independent, 4-year, coed **Contact** Mr. Joe Herschelle, Director of Admissions, Art Institutes International at San Francisco, 101 Jessie Street, San Francisco, CA 94105-3507. Telephone: 415-974-6666. Fax: 415-863-6344.

AZUSA PACIFIC UNIVERSITY
AZUSA, CALIFORNIA

General Independent nondenominational, comprehensive, coed **Entrance** Moderately difficult **Setting** 60-acre small town campus **Total enrollment** 5,069 **Student/faculty ratio** 15:1 **Application deadline** 7/15 **Freshmen** 85% were admitted **Housing** Yes **Expenses** Tuition $13,947; Room & Board $4482 **Undergraduates** 63%

women, 7% part-time, 1% Native American, 12% Hispanic, 4% black, 7% Asian American or Pacific Islander **Most popular recent majors** Liberal arts and studies; business administration; nursing **Academic program** English as a second language, advanced placement, accelerated degree program, honors program, summer session, adult/continuing education programs, internships **Contact** Mrs. Deana Porterfield, Dean of Admissions, Azusa Pacific University, 901 East Alosta Avenue, PO Box 7000, Azusa, CA 91702-7000. Telephone: 626-812-3016 or toll-free 800-TALK-APU. E-mail: admissions@apu.edu. Web site: http://www.apu.edu/.

BETHANY COLLEGE OF THE ASSEMBLIES OF GOD
SCOTTS VALLEY, CALIFORNIA

General Independent, comprehensive, coed, affiliated with Assemblies of God **Entrance** Minimally difficult **Setting** 40-acre small town campus **Total enrollment** 590 **Student/faculty ratio** 20:1 **Application deadline** 7/1 **Housing** Yes **Expenses** Tuition $8670; Room & Board $4190 **Undergraduates** 57% women, 24% part-time, 48% 25 or older, 1% Native American, 10% Hispanic, 3% black, 4% Asian American or Pacific Islander **Most popular recent majors** Divinity/ministry; education; psychology **Academic program** Advanced placement, summer session, adult/continuing education programs, internships **Contact** Ms. Cheri Logan, Admissions Coordinator, Bethany College of the Assemblies of God, 800 Bethany Drive, Scotts Valley, CA 95066-2820. Telephone: 408-438-3800 ext. 1400 or toll-free 800-843-9410. Fax: 408-438-4517. E-mail: info@bethany.edu. Web site: http://www.bethany.edu/.

BIOLA UNIVERSITY
LA MIRADA, CALIFORNIA

General Independent interdenominational, university, coed **Entrance** Moderately difficult **Setting** 95-acre suburban campus **Total enrollment** 3,257 **Student/faculty ratio** 17:1 **Application deadline** 6/1 **Freshmen** 88% were admitted **Housing** Yes **Expenses** Tuition $14,286; Room & Board $4902 **Undergraduates** 60% women, 7% part-time, 1% Native American, 7% Hispanic, 4% black, 12% Asian American or Pacific Islander **Most popular recent majors** Business administration; mass communications; psychology **Academic program** English as a second language, advanced placement, accelerated degree program, tutorials, honors program, summer session, adult/continuing education programs, internships **Contact** Mr. Greg Vaughan, Director of Enrollment Management, Biola University, 13800 Biola Avenue, La Mirada, CA 90639-0001. Telephone: 562-903-4727 or toll-free 800-652-4652. Fax: 562-903-4709. E-mail: admissions@biola.edu. Web site: http://www.biola.edu/.

BROOKS INSTITUTE OF PHOTOGRAPHY
SANTA BARBARA, CALIFORNIA

General Proprietary, comprehensive, coed **Entrance** Moderately difficult **Setting** 25-acre suburban campus **Total enrollment** 363 **Student/faculty ratio** 13:1 **Application deadline** Rolling **Freshmen** 89% were admitted **Housing** No **Expenses** Tuition $14,550 **Undergraduates** 32% women, 53% 25 or older, 0.3% Native American, 4% Hispanic, 1% black, 2% Asian American or Pacific Islander **Academic program** Average class size 21, advanced placement, accelerated degree program, adult/continuing education programs, internships **Contact** Ms. Inge B. Kautzmann, Director of Admissions, Brooks Institute of Photography, 801 Alston Road, Santa Barbara, CA 93108-2399. Telephone: 805-966-3888 ext. 217. Fax: 805-564-1475. E-mail: admissions@brooks.edu. Web site: http://www.brooks.edu/.

CALIFORNIA BAPTIST COLLEGE
RIVERSIDE, CALIFORNIA

General Independent Southern Baptist, comprehensive, coed **Entrance** Moderately difficult **Setting** 75-acre suburban campus **Total enrollment** 2,009 **Student/faculty ratio** 16:1 **Application deadline** Rolling **Freshmen** 70% were admitted **Housing** Yes **Expenses** Tuition $8520; Room & Board $4594 **Undergraduates** 58% women, 14% part-time, 27% 25 or older, 1% Native American, 6% Hispanic, 4% black, 1% Asian American or Pacific Islander **Most popular recent majors** Business administration; psychology; education **Academic program** Average class size 16, English as a second language, advanced placement, accelerated degree program, tutorials, honors program, summer session, adult/continuing education programs, internships **Contact** Ms. Keri Overstreet, Director of Recruitment, California Baptist College, 8432 Magnolia Avenue, Riverside, CA 92504-3206. Telephone: 909-343-4212 or toll-free 800-782-3382. Fax: 909-351-1808. Web site: http://www.calbaptist.edu/.

CALIFORNIA COLLEGE FOR HEALTH SCIENCES
NATIONAL CITY, CALIFORNIA

General Proprietary, comprehensive, coed **Entrance** Noncompetitive **Setting** 2-acre urban campus **Total enrollment** 7,500 **Application deadline** Rolling **Housing** No **Undergraduates** 85% 25 or older **Most popular recent majors** Respiratory therapy; health science; health services ad-

California College for Health Sciences *(continued)*

ministration **Academic program** Accelerated degree program, internships **Contact** Ms. Marita Gubbe, Registrar, Director of Admissions and Records, California College for Health Sciences, 222 West 24th Street, National City, CA 91950-6605. Telephone: 619-477-4800 ext. 320 or toll-free 800-221-7374 (out-of-state). Fax: 619-477-4360. Web site: http://www.cchs.edu/.

CALIFORNIA COLLEGE OF ARTS AND CRAFTS

SAN FRANCISCO, CALIFORNIA

General Independent, comprehensive, coed **Entrance** Moderately difficult **Setting** 4-acre urban campus **Total enrollment** 1,073 **Application deadline** Rolling **Freshmen** 62% were admitted **Housing** Yes **Expenses** Tuition $15,950; Room & Board $4894 **Undergraduates** 59% women, 12% part-time, 44% 25 or older, 1% Native American, 8% Hispanic, 2% black, 14% Asian American or Pacific Islander **Most popular recent majors** Graphic design/commercial art/illustration; architecture; drawing **Academic program** Average class size 15, advanced placement, self-designed majors, summer session, internships **Contact** Ms. Sheri Sivin McKenzie, Director of Enrollment Services, California College of Arts and Crafts, 450 Irwin St. at 16th and Wisconsin, San Francisco, CA 94107. Telephone: 415-703-9523 or toll-free 800-447-1ART. Fax: 415-703-9539. E-mail: enroll@ccac-art.edu. Web site: http://www.ccac-art.edu/.

▶ **For more information, see page 399.**

CALIFORNIA INSTITUTE OF INTEGRAL STUDIES

SAN FRANCISCO, CALIFORNIA

Contact California Institute of Integral Studies, 9 Peter Yorke Way, San Francisco, CA 94109. Telephone: 415-674-5500. Fax: 415-674-5555.

CALIFORNIA INSTITUTE OF TECHNOLOGY

PASADENA, CALIFORNIA

General Independent, university, coed **Entrance** Most difficult **Setting** 124-acre suburban campus **Total enrollment** 1,925 **Student/faculty ratio** 3:1 **Application deadline** 1/1 **Freshmen** 23% were admitted **Housing** Yes **Expenses** Tuition $18,816; Room & Board $5700 **Undergraduates** 27% women, 0% 25 or older, 0.2% Native American, 4% Hispanic, 1% black, 27% Asian American or Pacific Islander **Most popular recent majors** Engineering; physics; biology **Academic program** Average class size 13, English as a second language, self-designed majors, tutorials, internships **Contact** Ms. Charlene Liebau, Director of Admissions, California Institute of Technology, 1200 East California Boulevard, Pasadena, CA 91125-0001. Telephone: 626-395-6341 or toll-free 800-568-8324. Fax: 626-683-3026. E-mail: ugadmissions@caltech.edu. Web site: http://www.caltech.edu/.

CALIFORNIA INSTITUTE OF THE ARTS

VALENCIA, CALIFORNIA

General Independent, comprehensive, coed **Entrance** Very difficult **Setting** 60-acre suburban campus **Total enrollment** 1,140 **Student/faculty ratio** 8:1 **Application deadline** 2/1 **Freshmen** 40% were admitted **Housing** Yes **Expenses** Tuition $18,185; Room only $2800 **Undergraduates** 40% women, 2% part-time, 15% 25 or older, 1% Native American, 8% Hispanic, 5% black, 8% Asian American or Pacific Islander **Academic program** English as a second language, advanced placement, self-designed majors, tutorials, honors program, internships **Contact** Mr. Kenneth Young, Director of Admissions, California Institute of the Arts, 24700 McBean Parkway, Valencia, CA 91355-2340. Telephone: 805-253-7863 or toll-free 800-292-ARTS (in-state), 800-545-ARTS (out-of-state). E-mail: admiss@muse.calarts.edu. Web site: http://www.calarts.edu/.

CALIFORNIA LUTHERAN UNIVERSITY

THOUSAND OAKS, CALIFORNIA

General Independent Lutheran, comprehensive, coed **Entrance** Moderately difficult **Setting** 290-acre suburban campus **Total enrollment** 2,590 **Student/faculty ratio** 13:1 **Application deadline** 6/1 **Freshmen** 81% were admitted **Housing** Yes **Expenses** Tuition $15,415; Room & Board $5985 **Undergraduates** 54% women, 19% part-time, 32% 25 or older, 1% Native American, 13% Hispanic, 3% black, 5% Asian American or Pacific Islander **Most popular recent majors** Business administration; liberal arts and studies; (pre)medicine **Academic program** Advanced placement, accelerated degree program, self-designed majors, tutorials, summer session, adult/continuing education programs, internships **Contact** Mr. Marc D. Meredith, Director of Admission, California Lutheran University, 60 West Olsen Road, Thousand Oaks, CA 91360-2787. Telephone: 805-493-3135. Fax: 805-493-3114. E-mail: cluadm@clunet.edu. Web site: http://www.clunet.edu/.

CALIFORNIA MARITIME ACADEMY

VALLEJO, CALIFORNIA

General State-supported, 4-year, coed **Entrance** Moderately difficult **Setting** 67-acre suburban campus **Total enrollment** 390 **Student/faculty ratio** 14:1 **Application deadline** 7/1 **Freshmen** 70% were admitted **Housing** Yes **Expenses** Tuition $3812; Room & Board $4920 **Undergraduates** 31% 25 or older **Academic program** Advanced placement, tutorials, summer session, internships **Contact** Mr. Aaron Martin, Director of Enrollment Management, California Maritime Academy, PO Box 1392, Vallejo, CA 94590-0644. Telephone: 707-648-4222 or toll-free 800-561-1945. Fax: 707-648-4204. E-mail: enroll@prop.csum.edu.

CALIFORNIA POLYTECHNIC STATE UNIVERSITY, SAN LUIS OBISPO

SAN LUIS OBISPO, CALIFORNIA

General State-supported, comprehensive, coed **Entrance** Moderately difficult **Setting** 6,000-acre small town campus **Total enrollment** 16,735 **Student/faculty ratio** 19:1 **Application deadline** 11/30 **Freshmen** 32% were admitted **Housing** Yes **Expenses** Tuition $2231; Room & Board $5553 **Undergraduates** 43% women, 8% part-time, 14% 25 or older, 2% Native American, 14% Hispanic, 2% black, 12% Asian American or Pacific Islander **Most popular recent majors** Business administration; agricultural business; mechanical engineering **Academic program** Average class size 40, English as a second language, advanced placement, summer session, internships **Contact** Mr. James Maraviglia, Director of Admissions and Evaluations, California Polytechnic State University, San Luis Obispo, San Luis Obispo, CA 93407. Telephone: 805-756-2311. E-mail: admprosp@polymail.calpoly.edu. Web site: http://www.calpoly.edu/.

CALIFORNIA STATE POLYTECHNIC UNIVERSITY, POMONA

POMONA, CALIFORNIA

General State-supported, comprehensive, coed **Entrance** Moderately difficult **Setting** 1,400-acre urban campus **Total enrollment** 17,246 **Student/faculty ratio** 19:1 **Application deadline** Rolling **Freshmen** 70% were admitted **Housing** Yes **Expenses** Tuition $1923; Room & Board $5300 **Undergraduates** 42% women, 22% part-time, 24% 25 or older, 1% Native American, 22% Hispanic, 4% black, 34% Asian American or Pacific Islander **Most popular recent majors** Information sciences/systems; electrical/electronics engineering; business marketing and marketing management **Academic program** English as a second language, advanced placement, accelerated degree program, summer session, adult/continuing education programs, internships **Contact** Ms. Rose M. Smith, Director of Admissions, California State Polytechnic University, Pomona, 3801 West Temple Avenue, Pomona, CA 91768-2557. Telephone: 909-869-2000 ext. 3423. Fax: 909-869-4529. E-mail: cppadmit@csupomona.edu. Web site: http://www.csupomona.edu/.

▶ **For more information, see page 400.**

CALIFORNIA STATE UNIVERSITY, BAKERSFIELD

BAKERSFIELD, CALIFORNIA

General State-supported, comprehensive, coed **Entrance** Moderately difficult **Setting** 575-acre urban campus **Total enrollment** 5,717 **Student/faculty ratio** 19:1 **Application deadline** 9/23 **Freshmen** 69% were admitted **Housing** Yes **Expenses** Tuition $1965; Room & Board $4185 **Undergraduates** 37% 25 or older, 2% Native American, 28% Hispanic, 7% black, 8% Asian American or Pacific Islander **Most popular recent majors** Liberal arts and studies; business administration; nursing **Academic program** English as a second language, advanced placement, accelerated degree program, self-designed majors, honors program, summer session, adult/continuing education programs, internships **Contact** Dr. Homer S. Montalvo, Associate Dean of Admissions and Records, California State University, Bakersfield, 9001 Stockdale Highway, Bakersfield, CA 93311-1099. Telephone: 805-664-2160. Web site: http://www.csubak.edu/.

CALIFORNIA STATE UNIVERSITY, CHICO

CHICO, CALIFORNIA

General State-supported, comprehensive, coed **Entrance** Moderately difficult **Setting** 119-acre small town campus **Total enrollment** 14,247 **Student/faculty ratio** 20:1 **Application deadline** Rolling **Freshmen** 83% were admitted **Housing** Yes **Expenses** Tuition $2075; Room & Board $5129 **Undergraduates** 53% women, 9% part-time, 20% 25 or older, 2% Native American, 10% Hispanic, 2% black, 4% Asian American or Pacific Islander **Most popular recent majors** Business administration; liberal arts and studies; psychology **Academic program** Average class size 22, English as a second language, advanced placement, self-designed majors, honors program, summer session, adult/continuing education programs, internships **Contact** Ms. Linda MacMichael, Director of Admissions, California State University, Chico, 400 West First Street, Chico, CA 95929-0722. Telephone: 530-898-4428 or toll-free 800-542-4426. Fax: 530-898-6456. E-mail: info@oavax.csuchico.edu. Web site: http://www.csuchico.edu/.

CALIFORNIA STATE UNIVERSITY, DOMINGUEZ HILLS

CARSON, CALIFORNIA

General State-supported, comprehensive, coed **Entrance** Moderately difficult **Setting** 350-acre

California State University, Dominguez Hills *(continued)*

urban campus **Total enrollment** 12,378 **Application deadline** Rolling **Freshmen** 53% were admitted **Housing** Yes **Expenses** Tuition $1821; Room only $3066 **Undergraduates** 70% women, 42% part-time, 58% 25 or older, 1% Native American, 29% Hispanic, 28% black, 7% Asian American or Pacific Islander **Most Popular Recent Major** Business administration **Academic program** English as a second language, advanced placement, self-designed majors, honors program, summer session, adult/continuing education programs, internships **Contact** Information Center, California State University, Dominguez Hills, 1000 East Victoria Street, Carson, CA 90747-0001. Telephone: 310-516-3696. Web site: http://www.csudh.edu/.

CALIFORNIA STATE UNIVERSITY, FRESNO

FRESNO, CALIFORNIA

General State-supported, comprehensive, coed **Entrance** Moderately difficult **Setting** 1,410-acre urban campus **Total enrollment** 18,113 **Student/faculty ratio** 18:1 **Application deadline** 5/15 **Freshmen** 72% were admitted **Housing** Yes **Expenses** Tuition $1806; Room & Board $5610 **Undergraduates** 54% women, 15% part-time, 29% 25 or older, 1% Native American, 28% Hispanic, 6% black, 12% Asian American or Pacific Islander **Most popular recent majors** Business administration; elementary education; criminology **Academic program** English as a second language, advanced placement, accelerated degree program, self-designed majors, summer session, adult/continuing education programs, internships **Contact** Mr. Joseph Marshall, Associate Vice President of Enrollment Services, California State University, Fresno, 5241 North Maple Avenue, Fresno, CA 93740. Telephone: 209-278-2261. Fax: 209-278-4812. E-mail: donna_mills@csufresno.edu. Web site: http://www.csufresno.edu/.

CALIFORNIA STATE UNIVERSITY, FULLERTON

FULLERTON, CALIFORNIA

General State-supported, comprehensive, coed **Entrance** Moderately difficult **Setting** 225-acre suburban campus **Total enrollment** 24,906 **Student/faculty ratio** 22:1 **Application deadline** Rolling **Freshmen** 77% were admitted **Housing** Yes **Expenses** Tuition $1947; Room only $3662 **Undergraduates** 57% women, 30% part-time, 29% 25 or older, 1% Native American, 22% Hispanic, 3% black, 24% Asian American or Pacific Islander **Most popular recent majors** Mass communications; finance; developmental/child psychology **Academic program** English as a second language, advanced placement, accelerated degree program, self-designed majors, honors program, summer session, adult/continuing education programs, internships **Contact** Ms. Nancy J. Dority, Admissions Director, California State University, Fullerton, PO Box 34080, Fullerton, CA 92834-9480. Telephone: 714-278-2370.

CALIFORNIA STATE UNIVERSITY, HAYWARD

HAYWARD, CALIFORNIA

General State-supported, comprehensive, coed **Entrance** Moderately difficult **Setting** 343-acre suburban campus **Total enrollment** 12,863 **Application deadline** 9/9 **Freshmen** 62% were admitted **Housing** Yes **Expenses** Tuition $1827; Room only $3230 **Undergraduates** 63% women, 27% part-time, 35% 25 or older **Most popular recent majors** Business administration; liberal arts and studies; computer science **Academic program** English as a second language, advanced placement, accelerated degree program, self-designed majors, tutorials, honors program, summer session, adult/continuing education programs, internships **Contact** Ms. Susan Lakis, Associate Director of Admissions, California State University, Hayward, 25800 Carlos Bee Boulevard, Hayward, CA 94542-3035. Telephone: 510-885-3248. Fax: 510-885-3816. E-mail: adminfo@csuhayward.edu. Web site: http://www.csuhayward.edu/.

CALIFORNIA STATE UNIVERSITY, LONG BEACH

LONG BEACH, CALIFORNIA

General State-supported, comprehensive, coed **Entrance** Moderately difficult **Setting** 320-acre suburban campus **Total enrollment** 27,809 **Student/faculty ratio** 20:1 **Application deadline** 11/30 **Freshmen** 82% were admitted **Housing** Yes **Expenses** Tuition $1846; Room & Board $5200 **Undergraduates** 56% women, 26% part-time, 33% 25 or older, 1% Native American, 21% Hispanic, 8% black, 25% Asian American or Pacific Islander **Most popular recent majors** Psychology; liberal arts and studies; art **Academic program** English as a second language, advanced placement, self-designed majors, tutorials, honors program, summer session, adult/continuing education programs, internships **Contact** Mr. Thomas Enders, Director of Enrollment Services, California State University, Long Beach, 1250 Bellflower Boulevard, Long Beach, CA 90840-0119. Telephone: 562-985-4641.

CALIFORNIA STATE UNIVERSITY, LOS ANGELES

LOS ANGELES, CALIFORNIA

General State-supported, comprehensive, coed **Entrance** Moderately difficult **Setting** 173-acre

urban campus **Total enrollment** 19,160 **Student/faculty ratio** 19:1 **Application deadline** 6/15 **Freshmen** 55% were admitted **Housing** Yes **Expenses** Tuition $1757; Room only $2915 **Undergraduates** 40% 25 or older, 0.5% Native American, 45% Hispanic, 9% black, 24% Asian American or Pacific Islander **Most popular recent majors** Child care/development; accounting; psychology **Academic program** English as a second language, advanced placement, accelerated degree program, self-designed majors, honors program, summer session, adult/continuing education programs, internships **Contact** Mr. George Bachmann, Associate Director of Admissions and University Outreach, California State University, Los Angeles, 5151 State University Drive, Los Angeles, CA 90032-8530. Telephone: 213-343-3131. E-mail: jslanin@calstatela.edu.

CALIFORNIA STATE UNIVERSITY, NORTHRIDGE

NORTHRIDGE, CALIFORNIA

General State-supported, comprehensive, coed **Entrance** Moderately difficult **Setting** 353-acre urban campus **Total enrollment** 27,653 **Application deadline** 11/30 **Freshmen** 77% were admitted **Housing** Yes **Expenses** Tuition $1980; Room only $4190 **Undergraduates** 31% 25 or older, 1% Native American, 23% Hispanic, 9% black, 15% Asian American or Pacific Islander **Most popular recent majors** Business administration; psychology; liberal arts and studies **Academic program** English as a second language, advanced placement, accelerated degree program, self-designed majors, honors program, summer session, adult/continuing education programs **Contact** Ms. Mary Baxton, Associate Director of Admissions and Records, California State University, Northridge, 18111 Nordhoff Street, Northridge, CA 91330. Telephone: 818-677-3777. Fax: 818-677-3766. Web site: http://www.csun.edu/.

CALIFORNIA STATE UNIVERSITY, SACRAMENTO

SACRAMENTO, CALIFORNIA

General State-supported, comprehensive, coed **Entrance** Moderately difficult **Setting** 288-acre urban campus **Total enrollment** 23,481 **Application deadline** Rolling **Freshmen** 65% were admitted **Housing** Yes **Expenses** Tuition $1982; Room & Board $5100 **Undergraduates** 35% 25 or older **Most popular recent majors** Business administration; liberal arts and studies; engineering **Academic program** Average class size 30, English as a second language, advanced placement, self-designed majors, tutorials, summer session, internships **Contact** Ms. Doris Tormes, Director of University Outreach Services, California State University, Sacramento, 6000 J Street, Sacramento, CA 95819-6048. Telephone: 916-278-7362 or toll-free 800-722-4748 (in-state). E-mail: glasmirel@csus.edu.

CALIFORNIA STATE UNIVERSITY, SAN BERNARDINO

SAN BERNARDINO, CALIFORNIA

General State-supported, comprehensive, coed **Entrance** Moderately difficult **Setting** 430-acre suburban campus **Total enrollment** 13,280 **Student/faculty ratio** 19:1 **Application deadline** Rolling **Housing** Yes **Expenses** Tuition $1896; Room & Board $4174 **Undergraduates** 62% women, 20% part-time, 38% 25 or older, 1% Native American, 25% Hispanic, 10% black, 9% Asian American or Pacific Islander **Most popular recent majors** Business administration; humanities; social sciences **Academic program** English as a second language, advanced placement, self-designed majors, honors program, summer session, adult/continuing education programs **Contact** Ms. Cynthia Shum, Admissions Counselor, California State University, San Bernardino, 5500 University Parkway, San Bernardino, CA 92407-2397. Telephone: 909-880-5212. Web site: http://www.csusb.edu/.

CALIFORNIA STATE UNIVERSITY, SAN MARCOS

SAN MARCOS, CALIFORNIA

General State-supported, comprehensive, coed **Entrance** Moderately difficult **Setting** 302-acre suburban campus **Total enrollment** 4,678 **Application deadline** Rolling **Freshmen** 79% were admitted **Housing** Yes **Expenses** Tuition $1720; Room only $3114 **Undergraduates** 64% women, 35% part-time, 52% 25 or older **Most popular recent majors** Business administration; liberal arts and studies; psychology **Academic program** Advanced placement, self-designed majors, honors program, summer session, internships **Contact** Ms. Terrie Rodriguez, Director of Admissions, California State University, San Marcos, San Marcos, CA 92096. Telephone: 760-750-4848. Fax: 760-750-3285. E-mail: how_apply@mailhost1.csusm.edu. Web site: http://www.csusm.edu/.

CALIFORNIA STATE UNIVERSITY, STANISLAUS

TURLOCK, CALIFORNIA

General State-supported, comprehensive, coed **Entrance** Moderately difficult **Setting** 220-acre small town campus **Total enrollment** 6,213 **Student/faculty ratio** 18:1 **Application deadline** 7/31 **Freshmen** 95% were admitted **Housing** Yes **Expenses** Tuition $1915; Room & Board $5461

California State University, Stanislaus *(continued)*

Undergraduates 63% women, 34% part-time, 38% 25 or older, 2% Native American, 23% Hispanic, 4% black, 9% Asian American or Pacific Islander **Most popular recent majors** Liberal arts and studies; business administration; psychology **Academic program** English as a second language, advanced placement, accelerated degree program, self-designed majors, tutorials, honors program, summer session, adult/continuing education programs, internships **Contact** Admissions Office, California State University, Stanislaus, 801 West Monte Vista Avenue, Turlock, CA 95382. Telephone: 209-667-3070 or toll-free 800-300-7420 (in-state). Fax: 209-667-3333. E-mail: outreach@toto.csustan.edu. Web site: http://www.csutan.edu/.

CHAPMAN UNIVERSITY
ORANGE, CALIFORNIA

General Independent, comprehensive, coed, affiliated with Christian Church (Disciples of Christ) **Entrance** Moderately difficult **Setting** 40-acre suburban campus **Total enrollment** 3,806 **Student/faculty ratio** 11:1 **Application deadline** 3/1 **Freshmen** 77% were admitted **Housing** Yes **Expenses** Tuition $18,750; Room & Board $6806 **Undergraduates** 56% women, 13% part-time, 20% 25 or older, 1% Native American, 13% Hispanic, 4% black, 9% Asian American or Pacific Islander **Most popular recent majors** Mass communications; business administration; liberal arts and studies **Academic program** English as a second language, advanced placement, accelerated degree program, self-designed majors, tutorials, honors program, summer session, adult/continuing education programs, internships **Contact** Ms. Saskia Knight, Dean and Vice President of Enrollment, Chapman University, 333 North Glassell Street, Orange, CA 92866. Telephone: 714-997-6982 or toll-free 800-578-CHAP. Fax: 714-997-6713. E-mail: low@chapman.edu. Web site: http://www.chapman.edu/.

CHARLES R. DREW UNIVERSITY OF MEDICINE AND SCIENCE
LOS ANGELES, CALIFORNIA

General Independent, comprehensive, coed **Entrance** Moderately difficult **Total enrollment** 635 **Application deadline** 2/28 **Freshmen** 20% were admitted **Expenses** Tuition $6850 **Contact** Ms. Mala Sharma, Director of Enrollment Services, Charles R. Drew University of Medicine and Science, 1621 East 120th Street, Los Angeles, CA 90059. Telephone: 213-563-4832.

CHRISTIAN HERITAGE COLLEGE
EL CAJON, CALIFORNIA

General Independent nondenominational, 4-year, coed **Entrance** Moderately difficult **Setting** 32-acre suburban campus **Total enrollment** 617 **Student/faculty ratio** 14:1 **Application deadline** 8/1 **Housing** Yes **Expenses** Tuition $10,240; Room & Board $4500 **Undergraduates** 60% women, 18% part-time, 52% 25 or older, 0.5% Native American, 11% Hispanic, 9% black, 3% Asian American or Pacific Islander **Most popular recent majors** Business administration; psychology; elementary education **Academic program** Average class size 25, English as a second language, advanced placement, self-designed majors, tutorials, summer session, adult/continuing education programs, internships **Contact** Mr. Paul Berry, Vice President of Enrollment Management/Registrar, Christian Heritage College, 2100 Greenfield Drive, El Cajon, CA 92019-1157. Telephone: 619-441-2200 or toll-free 800-676-2242. Fax: 619-440-0209. E-mail: chcadm@adm.christianheritage.edu. Web site: http://www.christianheritage.edu/.

CLAREMONT MCKENNA COLLEGE
CLAREMONT, CALIFORNIA

General Independent, 4-year, coed **Entrance** Very difficult **Setting** 50-acre small town campus **Total enrollment** 979 **Student/faculty ratio** 9:1 **Application deadline** 1/15 **Freshmen** 32% were admitted **Housing** Yes **Expenses** Tuition $19,020; Room & Board $6720 **Undergraduates** 44% women, 0.2% part-time, 0.2% 25 or older, 0.2% Native American, 13% Hispanic, 3% black, 20% Asian American or Pacific Islander **Most popular recent majors** Economics; political science; psychology **Academic program** Average class size 20, advanced placement, accelerated degree program, self-designed majors, tutorials, honors program, internships **Contact** Mr. Richard C. Vos, Vice President/Dean of Admission and Financial Aid, Claremont McKenna College, 500 East 9th Street, Claremont, CA 91711. Telephone: 909-621-8088. E-mail: admission@mckenna.edu. Web site: http://www.mckenna.edu/.

▶ **For more information, see page 411.**

COGSWELL POLYTECHNICAL COLLEGE
SUNNYVALE, CALIFORNIA

General Independent, 4-year, coed **Entrance** Moderately difficult **Setting** 2-acre suburban campus **Total enrollment** 482 **Student/faculty ratio** 10:1 **Application deadline** Rolling **Freshmen** 97% were admitted **Housing** No **Expenses** Tuition $7840 **Undergraduates** 49% 25 or older, 1% Native American, 5% Hispanic, 2% black, 16%

Asian American or Pacific Islander **Most popular recent majors** Computer graphics; electrical/electronic engineering technology **Academic program** Average class size 14, advanced placement, accelerated degree program, tutorials, honors program, summer session, adult/continuing education programs, internships **Contact** Mr. Paul A. Schreivogel, Dean of Recruitment and Marketing, Cogswell Polytechnical College, 1175 Bordeaux Drive, Sunnyvale, CA 94089-1299. Telephone: 408-541-0100 ext. 112 or toll-free 800-264-7955. Fax: 408-747-0764. E-mail: admin@cogswell.edu. Web site: http://www.cogswell.edu/.

COLEMAN COLLEGE
LA MESA, CALIFORNIA

General Independent, comprehensive, coed **Entrance** Moderately difficult **Setting** Suburban campus **Total enrollment** 1,071 **Application deadline** Rolling **Housing** No **Expenses** Tuition $9000 **Undergraduates** 68% 25 or older, 0.2% Native American, 7% Hispanic, 7% black, 11% Asian American or Pacific Islander **Most popular recent majors** Computer/information sciences; computer engineering technology; secretarial science **Academic program** Accelerated degree program, summer session **Contact** Admissions Department, Coleman College, 7380 Parkway Drive, La Mesa, CA 91942-1532. Telephone: 619-465-3990. Fax: 619-465-0162. E-mail: jschafer@cts.com. Web site: http://www.coleman.edu/.

COLLEGE OF NOTRE DAME
BELMONT, CALIFORNIA

General Independent Roman Catholic, comprehensive, coed **Entrance** Moderately difficult **Setting** 80-acre suburban campus **Total enrollment** 1,782 **Student/faculty ratio** 10:1 **Application deadline** 6/1 **Freshmen** 82% were admitted **Housing** Yes **Expenses** Tuition $14,976; Room & Board $6500 **Undergraduates** 70% women, 37% part-time, 48% 25 or older, 0.3% Native American, 15% Hispanic, 6% black, 13% Asian American or Pacific Islander **Most popular recent majors** Business administration; psychology; liberal arts and studies **Academic program** Average class size 15, English as a second language, advanced placement, accelerated degree program, self-designed majors, tutorials, summer session, adult/continuing education programs, internships **Contact** Dr. Gregory Smith, Director of Admission, College of Notre Dame, 1500 Ralston Avenue, Belmont, CA 94002-1997. Telephone: 650-508-3607 or toll-free 800-263-0545 (in-state). Fax: 650-508-3426. E-mail: admiss@cnd.edu. Web site: http://www.cnd.edu/.

COLUMBIA COLLEGE–HOLLYWOOD
TARZANA, CALIFORNIA

General Independent, 4-year, coed **Entrance** Minimally difficult **Setting** 1-acre urban campus **Total enrollment** 250 **Application deadline** Rolling **Housing** No **Expenses** Tuition $6705 **Undergraduates** 35% 25 or older **Academic program** Accelerated degree program, summer session, adult/continuing education programs **Contact** Ms. Lilly Kemenes, Registration, Columbia College–Hollywood, 18618 Oxnard Street, Tarzana, CA 91356. Telephone: 818-345-8414. Fax: 818-345-9053.

CONCORDIA UNIVERSITY
IRVINE, CALIFORNIA

General Independent, comprehensive, coed, affiliated with Lutheran Church–Missouri Synod **Entrance** Moderately difficult **Setting** 70-acre suburban campus **Total enrollment** 1,063 **Student/faculty ratio** 18:1 **Application deadline** Rolling **Freshmen** 80% were admitted **Housing** Yes **Expenses** Tuition $14,550; Room & Board $5380 **Undergraduates** 62% women, 3% part-time, 7% 25 or older, 0.4% Native American, 8% Hispanic, 4% black, 6% Asian American or Pacific Islander **Most popular recent majors** Business administration; religious studies; education **Academic program** Average class size 20, English as a second language, advanced placement, self-designed majors, honors program, summer session, adult/continuing education programs, internships **Contact** Mr. W. Stan Meyer, Dean of Enrollment Services, Concordia University, 1530 Concordia West, Irvine, CA 92612-3299. Telephone: 714-854-8002 ext. 108 or toll-free 800-229-1200. Fax: 949-854-6894. Web site: http://www.cui.edu/.

DESIGN INSTITUTE OF SAN DIEGO
SAN DIEGO, CALIFORNIA

General Proprietary, 4-year, coed **Entrance** Noncompetitive **Setting** Urban campus **Total enrollment** 253 **Student/faculty ratio** 11:1 **Application deadline** Rolling **Housing** No **Expenses** Tuition $9200 **Undergraduates** 70% 25 or older **Academic program** Internships **Contact** Ms. Paula Parrish, Director of Admissions, Design Institute of San Diego, 8555 Commerce Avenue, San Diego, CA 92121-2685. Telephone: 619-566-1200 or toll-free 800-619-4DESIGN (out-of-state). Fax: 619-566-2711.

DEVRY INSTITUTE OF TECHNOLOGY
LONG BEACH, CALIFORNIA

General Proprietary, 4-year, coed **Entrance** Minimally difficult **Setting** Urban campus **Total en-**

DeVry Institute of Technology *(continued)*

rollment 1,814 **Student/faculty ratio** 20:1 **Application deadline** Rolling **Freshmen** 75% were admitted **Housing** No **Expenses** Tuition $7308 **Undergraduates** 27% women, 22% part-time, 47% 25 or older, 1% Native American, 25% Hispanic, 18% black, 24% Asian American or Pacific Islander **Most popular recent majors** Information sciences/systems; electrical/electronic engineering technology; telecommunications **Academic program** Advanced placement, summer session **Contact** Ms. Elaine Francisco, Director of Admissions, DeVry Institute of Technology, 3880 Kilroy Airport Way, Long Beach, CA 90806. Telephone: 562-427-4162. Web site: http://www.devry.edu/long/htm/.

DEVRY INSTITUTE OF TECHNOLOGY
POMONA, CALIFORNIA

General Proprietary, 4-year, coed **Entrance** Minimally difficult **Setting** 15-acre urban campus **Total enrollment** 3,307 **Student/faculty ratio** 23:1 **Application deadline** Rolling **Freshmen** 74% were admitted **Housing** No **Expenses** Tuition $7308 **Undergraduates** 24% women, 26% part-time, 65% 25 or older, 1% Native American, 30% Hispanic, 10% black, 24% Asian American or Pacific Islander **Most popular recent majors** Telecommunications; information sciences/systems; electrical/electronic engineering technology **Academic program** Advanced placement, accelerated degree program, summer session, adult/continuing education programs **Contact** Mr. Keith Paridy, Director of Admissions, DeVry Institute of Technology, 901 Corporate Center Drive, Pomona, CA 91768-2642. Telephone: 909-622-9800 or toll-free 800-243-3660 (in-state). Web site: http://www.pom.devry.edu/.

DOMINICAN COLLEGE OF SAN RAFAEL
SAN RAFAEL, CALIFORNIA

General Independent, comprehensive, coed **Entrance** Moderately difficult **Setting** 80-acre suburban campus **Total enrollment** 1,465 **Student/faculty ratio** 12:1 **Application deadline** Rolling **Freshmen** 88% were admitted **Housing** Yes **Expenses** Tuition $15,424; Room & Board $6968 **Undergraduates** 79% women, 40% part-time, 57% 25 or older, 1% Native American, 10% Hispanic, 6% black, 12% Asian American or Pacific Islander **Most popular recent majors** Nursing; psychology; business administration **Academic program** English as a second language, advanced placement, self-designed majors, tutorials, honors program, summer session, adult/continuing education programs, internships **Contact** Mr. Allen Gallaway, Director of Freshman Admissions, Dominican College of San Rafael, 50 Acacia Avenue, San Rafael, CA 94901-2298. Telephone: 415-485-3204 or toll-free 800-788-3522. Fax: 415-485-3214. E-mail: enroll@dominican.edu. Web site: http://www.dominican.edu/.

DOMINICAN SCHOOL OF PHILOSOPHY AND THEOLOGY
BERKELEY, CALIFORNIA

General Independent Roman Catholic, upper-level, coed **Entrance** Moderately difficult **Setting** Urban campus **Total enrollment** 75 **Application deadline** Rolling **Freshmen** 89% were admitted **Housing** Yes **Expenses** Tuition $7130 **Undergraduates** 100% 25 or older **Academic program** Tutorials **Contact** Ms. Teresa O'Rourke, Dean of Student Affairs and Admissions, Dominican School of Philosophy and Theology, 2401 Ridge Road, Berkeley, CA 94709-1295. Telephone: 510-883-2073.

EMMANUEL BIBLE COLLEGE
PASADENA, CALIFORNIA

General Independent, 4-year, affiliated with Church of the Nazarene **Contact** Mr. Yeghia Babikian, Director, Emmanuel Bible College, 1605 East Elizabeth Street, Pasadena, CA 91104. Telephone: 626-791-2575.

FRESNO PACIFIC UNIVERSITY
FRESNO, CALIFORNIA

General Independent, comprehensive, coed, affiliated with Mennonite Brethren Church **Entrance** Moderately difficult **Setting** 42-acre suburban campus **Total enrollment** 1,546 **Student/faculty ratio** 13:1 **Application deadline** Rolling **Freshmen** 78% were admitted **Housing** Yes **Expenses** Tuition $11,936; Room & Board $4100 **Undergraduates** 64% women, 7% part-time, 32% 25 or older, 2% Native American, 15% Hispanic, 3% black, 3% Asian American or Pacific Islander **Most popular recent majors** Business administration; liberal arts and studies; social sciences **Academic program** English as a second language, advanced placement, self-designed majors, summer session, adult/continuing education programs, internships **Contact** Mr. Cary Templeton, Director of Admissions, Fresno Pacific University, 1717 South Chestnut Avenue, Fresno, CA 93702-4709. Telephone: 209-453-2030 or toll-free 800-660-6089 (in-state). Fax: 209-453-2007. E-mail: ugradmiss@fresno.edu. Web site: http://www.fresno.edu/.

GOLDEN GATE UNIVERSITY
SAN FRANCISCO, CALIFORNIA

General Independent, university, coed **Entrance** Moderately difficult **Setting** Urban campus **Total enrollment** 5,646 **Application deadline** Rolling **Freshmen** 44% were admitted **Housing** No **Expenses** Tuition $8472 **Undergraduates** 59% women, 70% part-time, 0.5% Native American, 8% Hispanic, 8% black, 16% Asian American or Pacific Islander **Most popular recent majors** Business administration; human resources management; accounting **Academic program** English as a second language, advanced placement, accelerated degree program, summer session, adult/continuing education programs, internships **Contact** Enrollment Services, Golden Gate University, 536 Mission Street, San Francisco, CA 94105-2968. Telephone: 415-442-7800 or toll-free 800-448-4968. Fax: 415-442-7807. E-mail: info@ggu.edu. Web site: http://www.ggu.edu/.

▶ **For more information, see page 442.**

HARVEY MUDD COLLEGE
CLAREMONT, CALIFORNIA

General Independent, comprehensive, coed **Entrance** Most difficult **Setting** 33-acre suburban campus **Total enrollment** 657 **Student/faculty ratio** 8:1 **Application deadline** 1/15 **Freshmen** 43% were admitted **Housing** Yes **Expenses** Tuition $20,325; Room & Board $7521 **Undergraduates** 24% women, 1% 25 or older, 1% Native American, 4% Hispanic, 0.3% black, 21% Asian American or Pacific Islander **Most popular recent majors** Engineering; computer science; chemistry **Academic program** Advanced placement, self-designed majors, tutorials, internships **Contact** Ms. Patricia Coleman, Dean of Admission, Harvey Mudd College, 301 East 12th Street, Claremont, CA 91711-5994. Telephone: 909-621-8011. Fax: 909-621-8360. E-mail: admission@hmc.edu. Web site: http://www.hmc.edu/.

HOLY NAMES COLLEGE
OAKLAND, CALIFORNIA

General Independent Roman Catholic, comprehensive, coed **Entrance** Moderately difficult **Setting** 60-acre urban campus **Total enrollment** 861 **Student/faculty ratio** 6:1 **Application deadline** 8/1 **Freshmen** 93% were admitted **Housing** Yes **Expenses** Tuition $13,870; Room & Board $5790 **Undergraduates** 82% women, 61% part-time, 21% 25 or older, 1% Native American, 11% Hispanic, 30% black, 9% Asian American or Pacific Islander **Most popular recent majors** Business administration; nursing; psychology **Academic program** English as a second language, advanced placement, accelerated degree program, self-designed majors, honors program, summer session, adult/continuing education programs, internships **Contact** Ms. Jo Ann Berridge, Dean of Undergraduate Admissions, Holy Names College, 3500 Mountain Boulevard, Oakland, CA 94619-1699. Telephone: 510-436-1321 or toll-free 800-430-1321. Fax: 510-436-1325. E-mail: admissions@admin.hnc.edu. Web site: http://www.hnc.edu/.

HOPE INTERNATIONAL UNIVERSITY
FULLERTON, CALIFORNIA

General Independent, comprehensive, coed, affiliated with Christian Churches and Churches of Christ **Entrance** Moderately difficult **Setting** 16-acre suburban campus **Total enrollment** 1,022 **Student/faculty ratio** 16:1 **Application deadline** 7/1 **Housing** Yes **Expenses** Tuition $9190; Room & Board $3619 **Undergraduates** 55% women, 18% part-time, 36% 25 or older, 1% Native American, 12% Hispanic, 6% black, 5% Asian American or Pacific Islander **Most popular recent majors** Business administration; general studies; biblical studies **Academic program** English as a second language, advanced placement, accelerated degree program, self-designed majors, honors program, summer session, adult/continuing education programs, internships **Contact** Admissions Office, Hope International University, 2500 East Nutwood Avenue, Fullerton, CA 92831-3138. Telephone: 714-879-3901 or toll-free 800-762-1294. Fax: 714-526-0231. E-mail: twinston@hiu.edu. Web site: http://www.hiu.edu/.

HUMBOLDT STATE UNIVERSITY
ARCATA, CALIFORNIA

General State-supported, comprehensive, coed **Entrance** Moderately difficult **Setting** 161-acre rural campus **Total enrollment** 7,492 **Student/faculty ratio** 18:1 **Application deadline** 11/30 **Freshmen** 77% were admitted **Housing** Yes **Expenses** Tuition $1926; Room & Board $5194 **Undergraduates** 52% women, 9% part-time, 26% 25 or older, 3% Native American, 9% Hispanic, 2% black, 3% Asian American or Pacific Islander **Most popular recent majors** Biology; psychology; elementary education **Academic program** English as a second language, advanced placement, self-designed majors, tutorials, honors program, summer session, adult/continuing education programs, internships **Contact** Mr. Jeffery Savage, Office of Admissions and School Relations, Humboldt State University, Arcata, CA 95521-8299. Telephone: 707-826-4402. Fax: 707-826-6194. E-mail: hsuinfo@laurel.humboldt.edu. Web site: http://www.humboldt.edu/.

HUMPHREYS COLLEGE
STOCKTON, CALIFORNIA

General Independent, comprehensive, coed **Entrance** Noncompetitive **Setting** 10-acre suburban campus **Total enrollment** 721 **Student/**

Humphreys College *(continued)*

faculty ratio 11:1 **Application deadline** Rolling **Housing** Yes **Expenses** Tuition $6258; Room & Board $4660 **Undergraduates** 70% 25 or older **Most popular recent majors** Court reporting; paralegal/legal assistant; business administration **Academic program** Average class size 15, advanced placement, accelerated degree program, self-designed majors, tutorials, summer session, adult/continuing education programs, internships **Contact** Ms. Wilma Okamoto Vaughn, Dean of Administration, Humphreys College, 6650 Inglewood Avenue, Stockton, CA 95207-3896. Telephone: 209-478-0800. Fax: 209-478-8721.

HURON INTERNATIONAL UNIVERSITY
SAN DIEGO, CALIFORNIA

Contact Huron International University, 2801 Camino Del Rio South, Suite 201, San Diego, CA 92108-3801. Telephone: 619-298-9040. Fax: 619-298-9056.

INSTITUTE OF COMPUTER TECHNOLOGY
LOS ANGELES, CALIFORNIA

General Proprietary, 4-year, coed **Entrance** Noncompetitive **Setting** Urban campus **Total enrollment** 231 **Housing** No **Expenses** Tuition $7165 **Undergraduates** 94% 25 or older, 1% Native American, 32% Hispanic, 8% black, 28% Asian American or Pacific Islander **Academic program** Advanced placement, internships **Contact** Mr. Bud Hutchins, Director of Admissions, Institute of Computer Technology, 3200 Wilshire Boulevard, # 400, Los Angeles, CA 90010-1308. Telephone: 213-838-8300. Web site: http://www.ictcollege.edu/.

INTERIOR DESIGNERS INSTITUTE
NEWPORT BEACH, CALIFORNIA

Contact Interior Designers Institute, 1061 Camelback Road, Newport Beach, CA 92660. Telephone: 714-675-4451.

JOHN F. KENNEDY UNIVERSITY
ORINDA, CALIFORNIA

General Independent, comprehensive, coed **Contact** Admissions and Records Office, John F. Kennedy University, 12 Altarinda Road, Orinda, CA 94563-2689. Telephone: 510-258-2213. Fax: 925-254-6964.

LA SIERRA UNIVERSITY
RIVERSIDE, CALIFORNIA

General Independent Seventh-day Adventist, comprehensive, coed **Entrance** Minimally difficult **Setting** 630-acre suburban campus **Total enrollment** 1,466 **Student/faculty ratio** 13:1 **Application deadline** Rolling **Housing** Yes **Expenses** Tuition $14,025; Room & Board $4065 **Undergraduates** 50% women, 9% part-time, 14% 25 or older, 1% Native American, 19% Hispanic, 7% black, 22% Asian American or Pacific Islander **Most popular recent majors** Business administration; biology; elementary education **Academic program** Average class size 20, English as a second language, advanced placement, accelerated degree program, self-designed majors, tutorials, honors program, summer session, adult/continuing education programs, internships **Contact** Dr. Tom Smith, Vice President for Enrollment Services, La Sierra University, 4700 Pierce Street, Riverside, CA 92515. Telephone: 909-785-2432 or toll-free 800-874-5587. Fax: 909-785-2901. E-mail: ivy@polaris.lasierra.edu. Web site: http://www.lasierra.edu/.

LEE COLLEGE AT THE UNIVERSITY OF JUDAISM
See University of Judaism

LIFE BIBLE COLLEGE
SAN DIMAS, CALIFORNIA

General Independent, 4-year, coed, affiliated with International Church of the Foursquare Gospel **Entrance** Minimally difficult **Setting** 9-acre suburban campus **Total enrollment** 424 **Student/faculty ratio** 14:1 **Application deadline** 7/15 **Freshmen** 63% were admitted **Housing** Yes **Expenses** Tuition $4880; Room & Board $3000 **Undergraduates** 47% women, 22% part-time, 25% 25 or older, 0.5% Native American, 9% Hispanic, 2% black, 6% Asian American or Pacific Islander **Academic program** Average class size 32, advanced placement, summer session, internships **Contact** Ms. Linda Hibdon, Admissions Director, LIFE Bible College, 1100 Covina Boulevard, San Dimas, CA 91773-3298. Telephone: 909-599-5433 ext. 303 or toll-free 800-356-0001. Fax: 909-599-6690. E-mail: adm@lifebible.edu. Web site: http://www.lifebible.edu/.

LINCOLN UNIVERSITY
SAN FRANCISCO, CALIFORNIA

Contact Ms. Vivian Xu, Admissions Officer, Lincoln University, 281 Masonic Avenue, San Francisco, CA 94118-4498. Telephone: 415-221-1212 ext. 115. Fax: 415-387-9730.

LOMA LINDA UNIVERSITY
LOMA LINDA, CALIFORNIA

General Independent Seventh-day Adventist, university, coed **Entrance** Difficulty N/R **Setting**

Small town campus **Total enrollment** 3,400 **Student/faculty ratio** 15:1 **Housing** Yes **Expenses** Tuition $10,530; Room only $1890 **Undergraduates** 52% 25 or older, 1% Native American, 15% Hispanic, 5% black, 25% Asian American or Pacific Islander **Academic program** English as a second language **Contact** Dr. Tony Valenzuela, Director of Marketing, Loma Linda University, Loma Linda, CA 92350. Telephone: 909-824-4792. Web site: http://www.llu.edu/.

LOUISE SALINGER ACADEMY OF FASHION

See Art Institutes International at San Francisco

LOYOLA MARYMOUNT UNIVERSITY

LOS ANGELES, CALIFORNIA

General Independent Roman Catholic, comprehensive, coed **Entrance** Moderately difficult **Setting** 128-acre suburban campus **Total enrollment** 6,721 **Student/faculty ratio** 14:1 **Application deadline** 2/1 **Freshmen** 70% were admitted **Housing** Yes **Expenses** Tuition $16,495; Room & Board $6736 **Undergraduates** 8% 25 or older **Most popular recent majors** Business administration; mass communications; psychology **Academic program** Average class size 20, advanced placement, accelerated degree program, self-designed majors, tutorials, honors program, summer session, adult/continuing education programs, internships **Contact** Mr. Matthew X. Fissinger, Director of Admissions, Loyola Marymount University, 7900 Loyola Boulevard, Los Angeles, CA 90045-8350. Telephone: 310-338-2750 or toll-free 800-LMU-INFO. Fax: 310-338-2797. E-mail: admissns@lmumail.lmu.edu. Web site: http://www.lmu.edu/.

▶ **For more information, see page 459.**

THE MASTER'S COLLEGE AND SEMINARY

SANTA CLARITA, CALIFORNIA

General Independent nondenominational, comprehensive, coed **Entrance** Moderately difficult **Setting** 110-acre suburban campus **Total enrollment** 1,198 **Student/faculty ratio** 16:1 **Application deadline** 3/6 **Freshmen** 82% were admitted **Housing** Yes **Expenses** Tuition $12,180; Room & Board $4798 **Undergraduates** 52% women, 6% part-time, 9% 25 or older, 1% Native American, 5% Hispanic, 3% black, 5% Asian American or Pacific Islander **Most popular recent majors** Biblical studies; liberal arts and studies; business administration **Academic program** Advanced placement, accelerated degree program, tutorials, summer session, adult/continuing education programs, internships **Contact** Mr. Yaphet Peterson, Director of Enrollment, The Master's College and Seminary, 21726 Placerita Canyon Road, Santa Clarita, CA 91321-1200. Telephone: 805-259-3540 ext. 368 or toll-free 800-568-6248. Fax: 805-254-1998. E-mail: enrollment@masters.edu. Web site: http://www.masters.edu/.

MENLO COLLEGE

ATHERTON, CALIFORNIA

General Independent, 4-year, coed **Entrance** Minimally difficult **Setting** 45-acre small town campus **Total enrollment** 522 **Student/faculty ratio** 10:1 **Application deadline** Rolling **Freshmen** 93% were admitted **Housing** Yes **Expenses** Tuition $16,280; Room & Board $6800 **Undergraduates** 39% women, 2% part-time, 22% 25 or older, 1% Native American, 9% Hispanic, 7% black, 13% Asian American or Pacific Islander **Most popular recent majors** Business administration; mass communications **Academic program** Average class size 20, English as a second language, advanced placement, accelerated degree program, self-designed majors, tutorials, honors program, summer session, adult/continuing education programs, internships **Contact** Ms. Terri Bouska, Director of Admissions, Menlo College, 1000 El Camino Real, Atherton, CA 94027-4301. Telephone: 650-833-3305 or toll-free 800-556-3656. Fax: 650-617-2395. E-mail: admissions@menlo.edu. Web site: http://www.menlo.edu/.

MILLS COLLEGE

OAKLAND, CALIFORNIA

General Independent, comprehensive, women only **Entrance** Moderately difficult **Setting** 135-acre urban campus **Total enrollment** 1,115 **Student/faculty ratio** 12:1 **Application deadline** Rolling **Freshmen** 82% were admitted **Housing** Yes **Expenses** Tuition $16,522; Room & Board $6800 **Undergraduates** 6% part-time, 1% Native American, 7% Hispanic, 8% black, 11% Asian American or Pacific Islander **Most popular recent majors** English; psychology; mass communications **Academic program** English as a second language, advanced placement, accelerated degree program, self-designed majors, tutorials, adult/continuing education programs, internships **Contact** Ms. Avis E. Hinkson, Dean of Admission, Mills College, 5000 MacArthur Boulevard, Oakland, CA 94613-1000. Telephone: 510-430-2135 or toll-free 800-87-MILLS. Fax: 510-430-3314. E-mail: admission@mills.edu. Web site: http://www.mills.edu/.

▶ **For more information, see page 473.**

MONTEREY INSTITUTE OF INTERNATIONAL STUDIES

MONTEREY, CALIFORNIA

General Independent, upper-level, coed **Entrance** Moderately difficult **Setting** 5-acre small

Monterey Institute of International Studies *(continued)*

town campus **Total enrollment** 778 **Application deadline** 8/1 **Freshmen** 79% were admitted **Housing** No **Expenses** Tuition $18,250 **Undergraduates** 25% 25 or older **Academic program** Average class size 25, English as a second language, honors program, summer session, internships **Contact** Ms. Debbie Bigelow, Admissions Officer, Monterey Institute of International Studies, 425 Van Buren Street, Monterey, CA 93940-2691. Telephone: 408-647-4124 or toll-free 800-824-7235 (in-state). Fax: 408-647-6405. E-mail: admit@miis.edu. Web site: http://www.miis.edu/.

MOUNT ST. MARY'S COLLEGE
LOS ANGELES, CALIFORNIA

General Independent Roman Catholic, comprehensive, primarily women **Entrance** Moderately difficult **Setting** 71-acre suburban campus **Total enrollment** 1,984 **Student/faculty ratio** 14:1 **Application deadline** Rolling **Housing** Yes **Expenses** Tuition $15,216; Room & Board $5338 **Undergraduates** 94% women, 36% part-time, 40% 25 or older, 1% Native American, 35% Hispanic, 10% black, 21% Asian American or Pacific Islander **Most popular recent majors** Nursing; liberal arts and studies; business administration **Academic program** Advanced placement, accelerated degree program, self-designed majors, tutorials, honors program, summer session, adult/continuing education programs, internships **Contact** Ms. Katy Murphy, Executive Director of Admissions and Financial Aid, Mount St. Mary's College, 12001 Chalon Road, Los Angeles, CA 90049-1599. Telephone: 310-954-4252 or toll-free 800-999-9893. E-mail: info@msmc.la.edu. Web site: http://www.msmc.la.edu/.

MUSICIANS INSTITUTE
HOLLYWOOD, CALIFORNIA

General Proprietary, 4-year, coed **Contact** Mr. Steve Lunn, Admissions Representative, Musicians Institute, 1655 North McCadden Place, Hollywood, CA 90028. Telephone: 213-462-1384 ext. 156 or toll-free 800-255-PLAY.

THE NATIONAL HISPANIC UNIVERSITY
SAN JOSE, CALIFORNIA

General Independent, 4-year, coed **Contact** Ms. Leticia Vallejo, Director of Admissions, The National Hispanic University, 14271 Story Road, San Jose, CA 95127-3823. Telephone: 408-254-6900 ext. 17.

NATIONAL UNIVERSITY
LA JOLLA, CALIFORNIA

General Independent, comprehensive, coed **Entrance** Noncompetitive **Setting** 15-acre urban campus **Total enrollment** 13,397 **Application deadline** Rolling **Housing** No **Expenses** Tuition $6975 **Undergraduates** 86% 25 or older **Most popular recent majors** Business administration; computer science; psychology **Academic program** English as a second language, advanced placement, accelerated degree program, summer session, adult/continuing education programs **Contact** Admission Department, National University, 11255 North Torrey Pines Road, La Jolla, CA 92037-1011. Telephone: 619-563-7100 or toll-free 800-628-8648 (out-of-state). Fax: 619-563-7395. Web site: http://www.nu.edu/.

NEW COLLEGE OF CALIFORNIA
SAN FRANCISCO, CALIFORNIA

General Independent, comprehensive, coed **Entrance** Noncompetitive **Setting** Urban campus **Total enrollment** 641 **Application deadline** Rolling **Housing** No **Expenses** Tuition $8376 **Undergraduates** 50% 25 or older **Academic program** English as a second language, advanced placement, accelerated degree program, self-designed majors, tutorials, internships **Contact** Ms. Sheryl Kaskowitz, Undergraduate Admissions Coordinator, New College of California, 50 Fell Street, San Francisco, CA 94102-5206. Telephone: 415-437-3460 or toll-free 888-437-3460. Fax: 415-865-2636. E-mail: cmesposito@ncgate.newcollege.edu. Web site: http://www.newcollege.edu/.

NEWSCHOOL OF ARCHITECTURE
SAN DIEGO, CALIFORNIA

General Proprietary, comprehensive, coed **Contact** Ms. Katie Gent, Director of Admissions, Newschool of Architecture, 1249 F Street, San Diego, CA 92101-6634. Telephone: 619-235-4100 ext. 112. E-mail: nsa1249@aol.com. Web site: http://www.adnc.com/web/nsa/.

NORTHROP-RICE AVIATION INSTITUTE OF TECHNOLOGY
INGLEWOOD, CALIFORNIA

General Proprietary, comprehensive, primarily men **Contact** Mr. Bill Robinson, Director of Admissions, Northrop-Rice Aviation Institute of Technology, 8911 Aviation Boulevard, Inglewood, CA 90301-2904. Telephone: 310-337-4444 or toll-free 800-597-8690.

OCCIDENTAL COLLEGE
LOS ANGELES, CALIFORNIA

General Independent, comprehensive, coed **Entrance** Very difficult **Setting** 136-acre urban campus **Total enrollment** 1,580 **Student/faculty ratio** 11:1 **Application deadline** 1/15 **Freshmen** 77% were admitted **Housing** Yes **Expenses** Tuition $19,957; Room & Board $5890 **Undergraduates** 56% women, 2% part-time, 3% 25 or older, 1% Native American, 18% Hispanic, 6% black, 19% Asian American or Pacific Islander **Most popular recent majors** Psychology; comparative literature; biology **Academic program** Advanced placement, accelerated degree program, self-designed majors, tutorials, honors program, summer session, internships **Contact** Mr. Mark Hatch, Director of Admissions, Occidental College, 1600 Campus Road, Los Angeles, CA 90041-3392. Telephone: 213-259-2700 or toll-free 800-825-5262. Fax: 213-341-4875. E-mail: admission@oxy.edu. Web site: http://www.oxy.edu/.

OTIS COLLEGE OF ART AND DESIGN
LOS ANGELES, CALIFORNIA

General Independent, comprehensive, coed **Entrance** Moderately difficult **Setting** 5-acre urban campus **Total enrollment** 726 **Application deadline** Rolling **Freshmen** 67% were admitted **Housing** No **Expenses** Tuition $16,300 **Undergraduates** 59% women, 1% part-time, 30% 25 or older, 1% Native American, 16% Hispanic, 4% black, 25% Asian American or Pacific Islander **Academic program** Average class size 25, English as a second language, advanced placement, self-designed majors, tutorials, summer session, adult/continuing education programs, internships **Contact** Mr. Michael Fuller, Director of Admissions, Otis College of Art and Design, 9045 Lincoln Boulevard, Los Angeles, CA 90045-9785. Telephone: 310-665-6800 or toll-free 800-527-OTIS. Fax: 310-665-6805. E-mail: otisart@otisart.edu. Web site: http://www.primenet.com/~otisart/.

▶ **For more information, see page 490.**

PACIFIC CHRISTIAN COLLEGE
See Hope International University

PACIFIC OAKS COLLEGE
PASADENA, CALIFORNIA

General Independent, upper-level, coed **Contact** Ms. Marsha Franker, Director of Admissions, Pacific Oaks College, 5 Westmoreland Place, Pasadena, CA 91103. Telephone: 818-397-1349.

PACIFIC STATES UNIVERSITY
LOS ANGELES, CALIFORNIA

General Independent, comprehensive, coed **Entrance** Minimally difficult **Setting** 1-acre urban campus **Total enrollment** 75 **Application deadline** 6/15 **Freshmen** 54% were admitted **Housing** No **Expenses** Tuition $7455 **Undergraduates** 80% 25 or older, 0% Native American, 0% Hispanic, 0% black, 100% Asian American or Pacific Islander **Academic program** English as a second language, accelerated degree program, self-designed majors, tutorials, summer session, adult/continuing education programs **Contact** Ms. Jill Currey, Admissions Officer, Pacific States University, 1516 South Western Avenue, Los Angeles, CA 90006. Telephone: 213-731-2383. Web site: http://www.psuca.edu/.

PACIFIC UNION COLLEGE
ANGWIN, CALIFORNIA

General Independent Seventh-day Adventist, comprehensive, coed **Entrance** Moderately difficult **Setting** 200-acre rural campus **Total enrollment** 1,570 **Student/faculty ratio** 12:1 **Application deadline** Rolling **Freshmen** 67% were admitted **Housing** Yes **Expenses** Tuition $14,055; Room & Board $4305 **Undergraduates** 54% women, 10% part-time, 17% 25 or older, 1% Native American, 9% Hispanic, 3% black, 14% Asian American or Pacific Islander **Most popular recent majors** Nursing; business administration; behavioral sciences **Academic program** English as a second language, advanced placement, accelerated degree program, self-designed majors, honors program, summer session, adult/continuing education programs, internships **Contact** Mr. Al Trace, Director of Enrollment Services, Pacific Union College, Angwin, CA 94508. Telephone: 707-965-6336 or toll-free 800-862-7080 (in-state), 800-358-9180 (out-of-state). Web site: http://www.puc.edu/.

PATTEN COLLEGE
OAKLAND, CALIFORNIA

General Independent interdenominational, 4-year, coed **Entrance** Noncompetitive **Setting** 5-acre urban campus **Total enrollment** 714 **Student/faculty ratio** 13:1 **Application deadline** 7/31 **Freshmen** 91% were admitted **Housing** Yes **Expenses** Tuition $7008; Room only $2350 **Undergraduates** 36% women, 71% part-time, 59% 25 or older, 0% Native American, 9% Hispanic, 17% black, 11% Asian American or Pacific Islander **Most popular recent majors** Pastoral counseling; liberal arts and studies; business administration **Academic program** Average class size 15, advanced placement, accelerated degree program, tutorials,

Patten College *(continued)*

honors program, summer session, adult/continuing education programs, internships **Contact** Mr. Mike Mann, Director of Admissions, Patten College, 2433 Coolidge Avenue, Oakland, CA 94601-2699. Telephone: 510-533-8300 ext. 265. Fax: 510-534-8564.

PEPPERDINE UNIVERSITY
MALIBU, CALIFORNIA

General Independent, university, coed, affiliated with Church of Christ **Entrance** Very difficult **Setting** 830-acre small town campus **Total enrollment** 7,804 **Student/faculty ratio** 13:1 **Application deadline** 1/15 **Freshmen** 54% were admitted **Housing** Yes **Expenses** Tuition $21,170; Room & Board $6980 **Undergraduates** 4% 25 or older **Most popular recent majors** Business administration; communications; international relations **Academic program** Average class size 17, English as a second language, advanced placement, accelerated degree program, self-designed majors, tutorials, honors program, summer session, internships **Contact** Mr. Paul A. Long, Dean of Admission, Pepperdine University, 24255 Pacific Coast Highway, Malibu, CA 90263-0001. Telephone: 310-456-4392. Fax: 310-456-4861. E-mail: admission-seaver@pepperdine.edu. Web site: http://www.pepperdine.edu/.

PITZER COLLEGE
CLAREMONT, CALIFORNIA

General Independent, 4-year, coed **Entrance** Very difficult **Setting** 35-acre suburban campus **Total enrollment** 871 **Student/faculty ratio** 9:1 **Application deadline** 2/1 **Freshmen** 62% were admitted **Housing** Yes **Expenses** Tuition $21,880; Room & Board $6694 **Undergraduates** 59% women, 7% part-time, 11% 25 or older, 1% Native American, 13% Hispanic, 5% black, 10% Asian American or Pacific Islander **Most popular recent majors** Psychology; sociology; anthropology **Academic program** English as a second language, advanced placement, self-designed majors, tutorials, honors program, adult/continuing education programs, internships **Contact** Dr. Arnaldo Rodriguez, Vice President for Admission and Financial Aid, Pitzer College, 1050 North Mills Avenue, Claremont, CA 91711-6101. Telephone: 909-621-8129 or toll-free 800-748-9371 (in-state), 800-749-9371 (out-of-state). Fax: 909-621-8770. E-mail: admission@email.pitzer.edu. Web site: http://www.pitzer.edu/.

POINT LOMA NAZARENE UNIVERSITY
SAN DIEGO, CALIFORNIA

General Independent Nazarene, comprehensive, coed **Entrance** Moderately difficult **Setting** 88-acre suburban campus **Total enrollment** 2,358 **Student/faculty ratio** 15:1 **Application deadline** 3/1 **Freshmen** 88% were admitted **Housing** Yes **Expenses** Tuition $12,650; Room & Board $5220 **Undergraduates** 61% women, 7% part-time, 9% 25 or older, 1% Native American, 7% Hispanic, 2% black, 3% Asian American or Pacific Islander **Most popular recent majors** Liberal arts and studies; business administration; nursing **Academic program** Average class size 25, English as a second language, advanced placement, accelerated degree program, tutorials, honors program, summer session, internships **Contact** Executive Director for Enrollment Services, Point Loma Nazarene University, 3900 Lomaland Drive, San Diego, CA 92106-2899. Telephone: 619-849-2225. Fax: 619-849-2579. E-mail: cnlsr3ad@ptloma.edu. Web site: http://www.ptloma.edu/.

POMONA COLLEGE
CLAREMONT, CALIFORNIA

General Independent, 4-year, coed **Entrance** Most difficult **Setting** 140-acre suburban campus **Total enrollment** 1,421 **Student/faculty ratio** 9:1 **Application deadline** 1/1 **Freshmen** 32% were admitted **Housing** Yes **Expenses** Tuition $20,680; Room & Board $8180 **Undergraduates** 48% women, 1% 25 or older, 0.3% Native American, 9% Hispanic, 4% black, 22% Asian American or Pacific Islander **Most popular recent majors** Psychology; economics; English **Academic program** Advanced placement, self-designed majors, internships **Contact** Mr. Bruce Poch, Dean of Admissions, Pomona College, 333 North College Way, Claremont, CA 91711. Telephone: 909-621-8134. Fax: 909-621-8403. E-mail: admissions@pomona.edu. Web site: http://www.pomona.edu/.

ST. JOHN'S SEMINARY COLLEGE
CAMARILLO, CALIFORNIA

General Independent Roman Catholic, 4-year, men only **Contact** Rev. Gary Landry CM, Director of Admissions, St. John's Seminary College, 5118 Seminary Road, Camarillo, CA 93012-2599. Telephone: 805-482-4697 ext. 206. Fax: 805-987-5097.

SAINT MARY'S COLLEGE OF CALIFORNIA
MORAGA, CALIFORNIA

General Independent Roman Catholic, comprehensive, coed **Entrance** Moderately difficult **Setting** 440-acre suburban campus **Total enrollment** 4,238 **Student/faculty ratio** 14:1 **Application deadline** 2/1 **Freshmen** 84% were admitted **Housing** Yes **Expenses** Tuition $15,998; Room & Board $7119 **Undergraduates** 59% women, 6% part-time, 5% 25 or older, 1% Native

American, 14% Hispanic, 5% black, 10% Asian American or Pacific Islander **Most popular recent majors** Business administration; psychology; mass communications **Academic program** Average class size 20, English as a second language, advanced placement, self-designed majors, tutorials, honors program, adult/continuing education programs, internships **Contact** Ms. Dorothy Benjamin, Director of Admissions, Saint Mary's College of California, PO Box 4800, Moraga, CA 94575-4800. Telephone: 510-631-4224 or toll-free 800-800-4SMC. Fax: 925-376-7193. E-mail: smcadmit@stmarys-ca.edu. Web site: http://www.stmarys-ca.edu/.

SAMUEL MERRITT COLLEGE

OAKLAND, CALIFORNIA

General Independent, comprehensive, coed **Entrance** Moderately difficult **Setting** 1-acre urban campus **Total enrollment** 723 **Student/faculty ratio** 7:1 **Application deadline** Rolling **Freshmen** 63% were admitted **Housing** Yes **Expenses** Tuition $14,625; Room only $3330 **Undergraduates** 88% women, 7% part-time, 55% 25 or older, 2% Native American, 7% Hispanic, 10% black, 19% Asian American or Pacific Islander **Academic program** Advanced placement, accelerated degree program, tutorials, summer session, internships **Contact** Mr. John Garten-Shuman, Director of Admissions, Samuel Merritt College, 370 Hawthorne Avenue, Oakland, CA 94609-3108. Telephone: 510-869-6727 or toll-free 800-607-MERRITT. Fax: 510-869-6525. E-mail: jgartenshuman@compuserve.com. Web site: http://www.samuelmerritt.edu/.

SAN DIEGO STATE UNIVERSITY

SAN DIEGO, CALIFORNIA

General State-supported, university, coed **Entrance** Moderately difficult **Setting** 300-acre urban campus **Total enrollment** 29,898 **Student/faculty ratio** 13:1 **Application deadline** 11/15 **Freshmen** 80% were admitted **Housing** Yes **Expenses** Tuition $1854; Room & Board $6730 **Undergraduates** 55% women, 23% part-time, 25% 25 or older, 1% Native American, 20% Hispanic, 6% black, 15% Asian American or Pacific Islander **Most popular recent majors** Business administration; psychology; biology **Academic program** English as a second language, advanced placement, accelerated degree program, self-designed majors, tutorials, honors program, summer session, adult/continuing education programs, internships **Contact** Admissions and Records Office, San Diego State University, 5500 Campanile Drive, San Diego, CA 92182. Telephone: 619-594-6871. Web site: http://www.sdsu.edu/.

SAN FRANCISCO ART INSTITUTE

SAN FRANCISCO, CALIFORNIA

General Independent, comprehensive, coed **Entrance** Moderately difficult **Setting** 3-acre urban campus **Total enrollment** 680 **Student/faculty ratio** 9:1 **Application deadline** 9/1 **Housing** No **Expenses** Tuition $17,400 **Undergraduates** 53% women, 13% part-time, 38% 25 or older, 1% Native American, 9% Hispanic, 3% black, 6% Asian American or Pacific Islander **Most popular recent majors** Drawing; photography; film studies **Academic program** Average class size 20, English as a second language, advanced placement, tutorials, summer session, adult/continuing education programs, internships **Contact** Mr. Tim Robison, Vice President of Enrollment Services, San Francisco Art Institute, 800 Chestnut Street, San Francisco, CA 94133. Telephone: 415-771-7020 or toll-free 800-345-SFAI. E-mail: admissions@cdmweb.sfai.edu. Web site: http://www.sfai.edu/.

SAN FRANCISCO CONSERVATORY OF MUSIC

SAN FRANCISCO, CALIFORNIA

General Independent, comprehensive, coed **Entrance** Moderately difficult **Setting** 2-acre urban campus **Total enrollment** 261 **Student/faculty ratio** 7:1 **Application deadline** 3/1 **Freshmen** 53% were admitted **Housing** No **Expenses** Tuition $16,550 **Undergraduates** 53% women, 5% part-time, 18% 25 or older, 0% Native American, 6% Hispanic, 4% black, 19% Asian American or Pacific Islander **Most popular recent majors** Music (piano and organ performance); music (voice and choral/opera performance); stringed instruments **Academic program** Average class size 10, English as a second language, advanced placement, accelerated degree program **Contact** Ms. Joan Gordon, Admissions Officer, San Francisco Conservatory of Music, 1201 Ortega Street, San Francisco, CA 94122-4411. Telephone: 415-759-3431. Fax: 415-759-3499. E-mail: jgordon@sirius.com. Web site: http://www.sfcm.edu/.

SAN FRANCISCO STATE UNIVERSITY

SAN FRANCISCO, CALIFORNIA

General State-supported, comprehensive, coed **Entrance** Moderately difficult **Setting** 90-acre urban campus **Total enrollment** 27,420 **Student/faculty ratio** 21:1 **Application deadline** 11/30 **Freshmen** 72% were admitted **Housing** Yes **Expenses** Tuition $1982; Room & Board $5935 **Undergraduates** 58% women, 30% part-time, 34% 25 or older, 1% Native American, 12% Hispanic, 7% black, 33% Asian American or Pacific Islander **Most popular recent majors** Accounting; lib-

San Francisco State University *(continued)*

eral arts and studies; business administration **Academic program** English as a second language, advanced placement, accelerated degree program, self-designed majors, honors program, summer session, adult/continuing education programs **Contact** Ms. Patricia Wade, Admissions Officer, San Francisco State University, 1600 Holloway Avenue, San Francisco, CA 94132-1722. Telephone: 415-338-2037. E-mail: ugadmit@apollo.sfsu.edu. Web site: http://www.sfsu.edu/.

SAN JOSE CHRISTIAN COLLEGE
SAN JOSE, CALIFORNIA

General Independent nondenominational, 4-year, coed **Entrance** Noncompetitive **Setting** 9-acre urban campus **Total enrollment** 744 **Student/faculty ratio** 12:1 **Application deadline** 8/1 **Housing** Yes **Expenses** Tuition $7014; Room & Board $3564 **Undergraduates** 63% 25 or older **Most popular recent majors** Biblical studies; pastoral counseling; education **Academic program** English as a second language, advanced placement, summer session, internships **Contact** Mr. Jim Jessup, Director of Enrollment, San Jose Christian College, PO Box 1090, San Jose, CA 95108. Telephone: 408-293-9058 or toll-free 800-355-7522. Fax: 408-293-7352. Web site: http://www.sjchristiancol.edu/.

SAN JOSE STATE UNIVERSITY
SAN JOSE, CALIFORNIA

General State-supported, comprehensive, coed **Entrance** Moderately difficult **Setting** 104-acre urban campus **Total enrollment** 26,897 **Student/faculty ratio** 16:1 **Application deadline** Rolling **Freshmen** 77% were admitted **Housing** Yes **Expenses** Tuition $2017; Room & Board $5306 **Undergraduates** 52% women, 31% part-time, 39% 25 or older, 1% Native American, 15% Hispanic, 5% black, 28% Asian American or Pacific Islander **Most popular recent majors** Accounting; business marketing and marketing management; art **Academic program** Average class size 37, English as a second language, advanced placement, accelerated degree program, self-designed majors, honors program, summer session, adult/continuing education programs, internships **Contact** Mr. John Bradbury, Interim Director of Admissions, San Jose State University, One Washington Square, San Jose, CA 95192-0001. Telephone: 408-924-2000. Fax: 408-924-2050. Web site: http://www.sjsu.edu/.

SANTA CLARA UNIVERSITY
SANTA CLARA, CALIFORNIA

General Independent Roman Catholic (Jesuit), comprehensive, coed **Entrance** Moderately difficult **Setting** 104-acre suburban campus **Total enrollment** 7,946 **Student/faculty ratio** 10:1 **Application deadline** 1/15 **Freshmen** 66% were admitted **Housing** Yes **Expenses** Tuition $16,635; Room & Board $7026 **Undergraduates** 54% women, 3% part-time, 5% 25 or older, 1% Native American, 14% Hispanic, 3% black, 20% Asian American or Pacific Islander **Most popular recent majors** Finance; psychology; political science **Academic program** Average class size 30, advanced placement, self-designed majors, tutorials, honors program, summer session, adult/continuing education programs, internships **Contact** Sr. Annette Schmeling, Director of Undergraduate Admissions, Santa Clara University, 500 El Camino Real, Santa Clara, CA 95053-0001. Telephone: 408-554-4700. Fax: 408-554-5255. E-mail: ugadmissions@scu.edu. Web site: http://www.scu.edu/.

SCRIPPS COLLEGE
CLAREMONT, CALIFORNIA

General Independent, 4-year, women only **Entrance** Very difficult **Setting** 30-acre suburban campus **Total enrollment** 734 **Student/faculty ratio** 11:1 **Application deadline** 2/1 **Freshmen** 70% were admitted **Housing** Yes **Expenses** Tuition $19,480; Room & Board $7750 **Undergraduates** 2% part-time, 3% 25 or older, 1% Native American, 7% Hispanic, 3% black, 16% Asian American or Pacific Islander **Most popular recent majors** Psychology; biology; international relations **Academic program** Average class size 16, English as a second language, advanced placement, self-designed majors, tutorials, honors program, internships **Contact** Ms. Patricia F. Goldsmith, Dean of Admission and Financial Aid, Scripps College, 1030 Columbia Avenue, Claremont, CA 91711-3948. Telephone: 909-621-8149 or toll-free 800-770-1333. Fax: 909-621-8323. E-mail: admofc@ad.scrippscol.edu. Web site: http://www.ScrippsCol.edu/.

SHASTA BIBLE COLLEGE
REDDING, CALIFORNIA

General Independent nondenominational, 4-year **Contact** Mr. George Gunn, Director of Admissions, Shasta Bible College, 2980 Hartnell Avenue, Redding, CA 96002. Telephone: 916-221-4275.

SIMPSON COLLEGE AND GRADUATE SCHOOL
REDDING, CALIFORNIA

General Independent, comprehensive, coed, affiliated with The Christian and Missionary Alliance **Entrance** Moderately difficult **Setting** 60-acre suburban campus **Total enrollment** 1,248

Student/faculty ratio 14:1 **Application deadline** Rolling **Freshmen** 72% were admitted **Housing** Yes **Expenses** Tuition $9110; Room & Board $3900 **Undergraduates** 65% women, 2% part-time, 0.4% Native American, 4% Hispanic, 0.4% black, 4% Asian American or Pacific Islander **Most popular recent majors** Elementary education; business administration; psychology **Academic program** Average class size 26, English as a second language, advanced placement, accelerated degree program, self-designed majors, tutorials, summer session, adult/continuing education programs, internships **Contact** Mrs. Beth Spencer, Administrative Assistant to Vice President for Enrollment, Simpson College and Graduate School, 2211 College View Drive, Redding, CA 96003-8606. Telephone: 530-224-5606 ext. 2602 or toll-free 800-598-2493. Fax: 530-224-5608. E-mail: admissions@simpsonca.edu. Web site: http://www.simpsonca.edu/.

SONOMA STATE UNIVERSITY
ROHNERT PARK, CALIFORNIA

General State-supported, comprehensive, coed **Entrance** Moderately difficult **Setting** 220-acre small town campus **Total enrollment** 7,050 **Student/faculty ratio** 19:1 **Application deadline** 1/31 **Housing** Yes **Expenses** Tuition $2130; Room & Board $5769 **Undergraduates** 63% women, 17% part-time, 28% 25 or older, 1% Native American, 10% Hispanic, 3% black, 5% Asian American or Pacific Islander **Most popular recent majors** Business administration; psychology; liberal arts and studies **Academic program** Average class size 36, English as a second language, advanced placement, self-designed majors, tutorials, honors program, summer session, adult/continuing education programs, internships **Contact** Ms. Sarah Boldt, Data Coordinator, Sonoma State University, 1801 East Cotati Avenue, Rohnert Park, CA 94928-3609. Telephone: 707-664-2322. E-mail: admitme@sonoma.edu. Web site: http://www.sonoma.edu/.

SOUTHERN CALIFORNIA COLLEGE
COSTA MESA, CALIFORNIA

General Independent, comprehensive, coed, affiliated with Assemblies of God **Entrance** Moderately difficult **Setting** 38-acre suburban campus **Total enrollment** 1,312 **Student/faculty ratio** 16:1 **Application deadline** Rolling **Housing** Yes **Expenses** Tuition $11,848; Room & Board $4860 **Undergraduates** 58% women, 9% part-time, 22% 25 or older, 1% Native American, 11% Hispanic, 5% black, 3% Asian American or Pacific Islander **Most popular recent majors** Business administration; interdisciplinary studies; religious studies **Academic program** Average class size 25, advanced placement, accelerated degree program, summer session, adult/continuing education programs, internships **Contact** Mr. Virgil Zeigler, Associate Director of Admissions, Southern California College, 55 Fair Drive, Costa Mesa, CA 92626-6597. Telephone: 714-556-3610 ext. 219 or toll-free 800-722-6279. Fax: 714-668-6194. E-mail: admissions@sccu.edu. Web site: http://www.sccu.edu/.

SOUTHERN CALIFORNIA INSTITUTE OF ARCHITECTURE
LOS ANGELES, CALIFORNIA

General Independent, comprehensive, coed **Entrance** Moderately difficult **Setting** Urban campus **Total enrollment** 430 **Student/faculty ratio** 15:1 **Application deadline** Rolling **Freshmen** 65% were admitted **Housing** No **Expenses** Tuition $14,990 **Undergraduates** 42% 25 or older **Academic program** English as a second language, advanced placement, summer session, internships **Contact** Ms. Debra Abel, Director of Admissions, Southern California Institute of Architecture, 5454 Beethoven Street, Los Angeles, CA 90066-7017. Telephone: 310-574-1123. Fax: 310-829-7518. E-mail: admissions@sciarc.edu.

STANFORD UNIVERSITY
STANFORD, CALIFORNIA

General Independent, university, coed **Entrance** Most difficult **Setting** 8,180-acre suburban campus **Total enrollment** 16,496 **Student/faculty ratio** 10:1 **Application deadline** 12/15 **Freshmen** 15% were admitted **Housing** Yes **Expenses** Tuition $21,389; Room & Board $7560 **Undergraduates** 50% women, 1% Native American, 10% Hispanic, 7% black, 22% Asian American or Pacific Islander **Most popular recent majors** Engineering; economics **Academic program** English as a second language, advanced placement, accelerated degree program, self-designed majors, tutorials, honors program, summer session, adult/continuing education programs, internships **Contact** Mr. John Bunnell, Associate Dean of Admissions, Stanford University, Stanford, CA 94305-9991. Telephone: 650-723-2091. Fax: 650-725-2846. E-mail: undergrad.admissions@forsythe.stanford.edu. Web site: http://www.stanford.edu/.

THOMAS AQUINAS COLLEGE
SANTA PAULA, CALIFORNIA

General Independent Roman Catholic, 4-year, coed **Entrance** Very difficult **Setting** 170-acre rural campus **Total enrollment** 219 **Student/faculty ratio** 9:1 **Application deadline** Rolling **Freshmen** 84% were admitted **Housing** Yes **Expenses** Tuition $14,900; Room & Board $4300

Thomas Aquinas College *(continued)*

Undergraduates 42% women, 10% 25 or older **Academic program** Average class size 15 **Contact** Mr. Thomas J. Susanka Jr., Director of Admissions, Thomas Aquinas College, 10000 North Ojai Road, Santa Paula, CA 93060-9980. Telephone: 805-525-4417 ext. 361 or toll-free 800-634-9797. Fax: 805-525-0620. E-mail: admissions@thomasquinas.edu. Web site: http://www.ewtn.com/tac/.

UNITED STATES INTERNATIONAL UNIVERSITY

SAN DIEGO, CALIFORNIA

General Independent, university, coed **Entrance** Moderately difficult **Setting** 200-acre suburban campus **Total enrollment** 1,331 **Application deadline** Rolling **Freshmen** 71% were admitted **Housing** Yes **Expenses** Tuition $11,745; Room & Board $4800 **Undergraduates** 55% women, 9% part-time, 25% 25 or older, 1% Native American, 15% Hispanic, 4% black, 5% Asian American or Pacific Islander **Most popular recent majors** International business; psychology **Academic program** English as a second language, advanced placement, accelerated degree program, honors program, summer session, adult/continuing education programs, internships **Contact** Ms. Susan Topham, Assistant Director of Admissions, United States International University, 10455 Pomerado Road, San Diego, CA 92131-1799. Telephone: 619-635-4772. Fax: 619-635-4739. E-mail: admissions@usiu.edu. Web site: http://www.usiu.edu/.

UNIVERSITY OF CALIFORNIA, BERKELEY

BERKELEY, CALIFORNIA

General State-supported, university, coed **Entrance** Very difficult **Setting** 1,232-acre urban campus **Student/faculty ratio** 17:1 **Application deadline** 11/30 **Freshmen** 31% were admitted **Housing** Yes **Expenses** Tuition $4355; Room & Board $7657 **Most popular recent majors** Molecular biology; English; psychology **Academic program** Advanced placement, accelerated degree program, self-designed majors, tutorials, honors program, summer session, adult/continuing education programs, internships **Contact** Pre-Admission Advising, Office of Undergraduate Admission and Relations With Schools, University of California, Berkeley, Berkeley, CA 94720-1500. Telephone: 510-642-3175. Fax: 510-642-7333. E-mail: ouars@uclink.berkeley.edu. Web site: http://www.berkeley.edu/.

UNIVERSITY OF CALIFORNIA, DAVIS

DAVIS, CALIFORNIA

General State-supported, university, coed **Entrance** Very difficult **Setting** 5,993-acre suburban campus **Total enrollment** 24,551 **Student/faculty ratio** 14:1 **Application deadline** 11/30 **Freshmen** 70% were admitted **Housing** Yes **Expenses** Tuition $4332; Room & Board $6050 **Undergraduates** 54% women, 12% part-time, 8% 25 or older, 1% Native American, 10% Hispanic, 3% black, 35% Asian American or Pacific Islander **Most popular recent majors** Psychology; biology; international relations **Academic program** English as a second language, advanced placement, self-designed majors, tutorials, honors program, summer session, adult/continuing education programs, internships **Contact** Dr. Gary Tudor, Director of Undergraduate Admissions, University of California, Davis, Davis, CA 95616. Telephone: 530-752-2971. E-mail: thinkucd@ucdavis.edu. Web site: http://www.ucdavis.edu/.

UNIVERSITY OF CALIFORNIA, IRVINE

IRVINE, CALIFORNIA

General State-supported, university, coed **Contact** Ms. Susan Wilbur, Director of Admissions, University of California, Irvine, Irvine, CA 92697. Telephone: 714-824-6703. E-mail: oars@uci.edu. Web site: http://www.uci.edu/.

UNIVERSITY OF CALIFORNIA, LOS ANGELES

LOS ANGELES, CALIFORNIA

General State-supported, university, coed **Entrance** Very difficult **Setting** 419-acre urban campus **Total enrollment** 35,558 **Student/faculty ratio** 19:1 **Application deadline** 11/30 **Freshmen** 36% were admitted **Housing** Yes **Expenses** Tuition $4050; Room & Board $6490 **Undergraduates** 53% women, 6% part-time, 9% 25 or older, 1% Native American, 16% Hispanic, 6% black, 38% Asian American or Pacific Islander **Most popular recent majors** Biology; psychology; economics **Academic program** English as a second language, advanced placement, self-designed majors, honors program, summer session, adult/continuing education programs, internships **Contact** Dr. Rae Lee Siporin, Director of Undergraduate Admissions, University of California, Los Angeles, 405 Hilgard Avenue, Los Angeles, CA 90095. Telephone: 310-825-3101. E-mail: ugadm@saonet.ucla.edu. Web site: http://www.ucla.edu/.

UNIVERSITY OF CALIFORNIA, RIVERSIDE

RIVERSIDE, CALIFORNIA

General State-supported, university, coed **Entrance** Very difficult **Setting** 1,200-acre urban campus **Total enrollment** 9,850 **Student/faculty ratio** 18:1 **Application deadline** 11/30 **Freshmen** 84% were admitted **Housing** Yes **Expenses** Tuition $4126; Room & Board $6209 **Undergraduates** 53% women, 5% part-time, 9% 25 or older, 1% Native American, 19% Hispanic, 5% black, 41% Asian American or Pacific Islander **Most popular recent majors** Business administration; biology; psychology **Academic program** English as a second language, advanced placement, accelerated degree program, self-designed majors, tutorials, honors program, summer session, adult/continuing education programs, internships **Contact** Ms. Laurie Nelson, Associate Admissions Officer, University of California, Riverside, 900 University Avenue, Riverside, CA 92521-0102. Telephone: 909-787-3411. Fax: 909-787-6344. E-mail: discover@pop.ucr.edu. Web site: http://www.ucr.edu/.

UNIVERSITY OF CALIFORNIA, SAN DIEGO

LA JOLLA, CALIFORNIA

General State-supported, university, coed **Entrance** Very difficult **Setting** 1,976-acre suburban campus **Total enrollment** 18,667 **Student/faculty ratio** 19:1 **Application deadline** 11/30 **Freshmen** 53% were admitted **Housing** Yes **Expenses** Tuition $4200; Room & Board $6682 **Undergraduates** 51% women, 8% 25 or older, 1% Native American, 11% Hispanic, 2% black, 35% Asian American or Pacific Islander **Most popular recent majors** Biology; psychology; engineering **Academic program** English as a second language, advanced placement, accelerated degree program, self-designed majors, tutorials, honors program, summer session, adult/continuing education programs, internships **Contact** Mr. Tim Johnston, Associate Director of Admissions and Outreach, University of California, San Diego, 9500 Gilman Drive, 0337, La Jolla, CA 92093-0337. Telephone: 619-534-4831. E-mail: admissionsinfo@ucsd.edu. Web site: http://www.infopath.ucsd.edu/.

UNIVERSITY OF CALIFORNIA, SANTA BARBARA

SANTA BARBARA, CALIFORNIA

General State-supported, university, coed **Entrance** Very difficult **Setting** 989-acre suburban campus **Total enrollment** 18,940 **Student/faculty ratio** 19:1 **Application deadline** 11/30 **Freshmen** 72% were admitted **Housing** Yes **Expenses** Tuition $4098; Room & Board $6407 **Undergraduates** 6% 25 or older, 1% Native American, 13% Hispanic, 3% black, 16% Asian American or Pacific Islander **Most popular recent majors** Business economics; biology; psychology **Academic program** English as a second language, advanced placement, accelerated degree program, self-designed majors, honors program, summer session, internships **Contact** Mr. William Villa, Director of Admissions/Relations with Schools, University of California, Santa Barbara, Santa Barbara, CA 93106. Telephone: 805-893-2485. E-mail: appinfo@sa.ucsb.edu. Web site: http://www.ucsb.edu/.

UNIVERSITY OF CALIFORNIA, SANTA CRUZ

SANTA CRUZ, CALIFORNIA

General State-supported, university, coed **Entrance** Very difficult **Setting** 2,000-acre small town campus **Total enrollment** 10,638 **Student/faculty ratio** 19:1 **Application deadline** 11/30 **Freshmen** 83% were admitted **Housing** Yes **Expenses** Tuition $4181; Room & Board $6690 **Undergraduates** 60% women, 2% part-time, 10% 25 or older, 1% Native American, 14% Hispanic, 2% black, 13% Asian American or Pacific Islander **Most popular recent majors** Biology; psychology; literature **Academic program** Average class size 20, advanced placement, self-designed majors, tutorials, honors program, summer session, internships **Contact** Mr. Michael McCawley, Associate Director, Evaluations and Processing, University of California, Santa Cruz, Admissions Office, Cook House, Santa Cruz, CA 95064. Telephone: 408-459-2131. Fax: 408-459-4452. E-mail: admissions@cats.ucsc.edu. Web site: http://www.ucsc.edu/.

UNIVERSITY OF JUDAISM

BEL AIR, CALIFORNIA

General Independent Jewish, comprehensive, coed **Entrance** Moderately difficult **Setting** 28-acre suburban campus **Total enrollment** 189 **Student/faculty ratio** 9:1 **Application deadline** 1/31 **Freshmen** 79% were admitted **Housing** Yes **Expenses** Tuition $14,400; Room & Board $7290 **Undergraduates** 62% women, 1% part-time, 12% 25 or older, 1% Native American, 1% Hispanic, 3% black **Most popular recent majors** Psychology; literature; Judaic studies **Academic program** Advanced placement, accelerated degree program, self-designed majors, honors program, adult/continuing education programs, internships **Contact** Mr. Richard Scaffidi, Director of Undergraduate Admissions, University of Judaism, 15600 Mulholland Drive, Bel Air, CA 90077-1599. Telephone: 310-476-9777 ext. 250 or toll-free 888-853-6763. Fax: 310-471-3657. E-mail: admissions@uj.edu. Web site: http://www.uj.edu.

UNIVERSITY OF LA VERNE

LA VERNE, CALIFORNIA

General Independent, university, coed **Entrance** Moderately difficult **Setting** 26-acre suburban campus **Total enrollment** 6,026 **Applica-**

University of La Verne *(continued)*

tion deadline 2/1 **Freshmen** 80% were admitted **Housing** Yes **Expenses** Tuition $15,160; Room & Board $5080 **Undergraduates** 59% women, 48% part-time, 65% 25 or older, 1% Native American, 25% Hispanic, 13% black, 7% Asian American or Pacific Islander **Most popular recent majors** Business administration; mass communications; physical education **Academic program** Average class size 20, English as a second language, advanced placement, accelerated degree program, self-designed majors, tutorials, honors program, summer session, adult/continuing education programs, internships **Contact** Director of Admissions, University of La Verne, 1950 Third Street, La Verne, CA 91750-4443. Telephone: 909-593-3511 or toll-free 800-876-4858. Fax: 909-593-0965. E-mail: laup@ulavacs.ulaverne.edu. Web site: http://www.ulaverne.edu/.

UNIVERSITY OF REDLANDS

REDLANDS, CALIFORNIA

General Independent, comprehensive, coed **Entrance** Moderately difficult **Setting** 140-acre small town campus **Total enrollment** 1,490 **Student/faculty ratio** 12:1 **Application deadline** 3/1 **Freshmen** 83% were admitted **Housing** Yes **Expenses** Tuition $18,545; Room & Board $7096 **Undergraduates** 55% women, 2% part-time, 1% 25 or older, 2% Native American, 13% Hispanic, 3% black, 8% Asian American or Pacific Islander **Most popular recent majors** Liberal arts and studies; social sciences; business administration **Academic program** Average class size 12, English as a second language, advanced placement, self-designed majors, tutorials, honors program, adult/continuing education programs, internships **Contact** Mr. Paul Driscoll, Dean of Admissions, University of Redlands, PO Box 3080, Redlands, CA 92373-0999. Telephone: 909-335-4074 or toll-free 800-455-5064. Fax: 909-335-4089. E-mail: adkwolf@uor.edu. Web site: http://www.uor.edu/.

UNIVERSITY OF SAN DIEGO

SAN DIEGO, CALIFORNIA

General Independent Roman Catholic, university, coed **Entrance** Moderately difficult **Setting** 180-acre urban campus **Total enrollment** 6,694 **Student/faculty ratio** 18:1 **Application deadline** 1/15 **Freshmen** 70% were admitted **Housing** Yes **Expenses** Tuition $15,780; Room & Board $6970 **Undergraduates** 57% women, 4% part-time, 9% 25 or older, 1% Native American, 15% Hispanic, 2% black, 8% Asian American or Pacific Islander **Most popular recent majors** Business administration; political science; psychology **Academic program** Average class size 22, advanced placement, tutorials, honors program, summer session, adult/continuing education programs, internships **Contact** Mr. Warren Muller, Director of Undergraduate Admissions, University of San Diego, 5998 Alcala Park, San Diego, CA 92110-2492. Telephone: 619-260-4506. E-mail: vmuller@acusd.edu. Web site: http://www.acusd.edu/.

UNIVERSITY OF SAN FRANCISCO

SAN FRANCISCO, CALIFORNIA

General Independent Roman Catholic (Jesuit), university, coed **Entrance** Moderately difficult **Setting** 55-acre urban campus **Total enrollment** 7,975 **Student/faculty ratio** 15:1 **Application deadline** 2/1 **Freshmen** 76% were admitted **Housing** Yes **Expenses** Tuition $15,950; Room & Board $7260 **Undergraduates** 63% women, 5% part-time, 13% 25 or older, 0.5% Native American, 10% Hispanic, 5% black, 21% Asian American or Pacific Islander **Most popular recent majors** Nursing; mass communications; psychology **Academic program** Average class size 28, English as a second language, advanced placement, accelerated degree program, self-designed majors, honors program, summer session, adult/continuing education programs, internships **Contact** Mr. William Henley, Director of Admissions, University of San Francisco, 2130 Fulton Street, San Francisco, CA 94117-1080. Telephone: 415-422-6563 or toll-free 800-CALL USF (out-of-state). Fax: 415-422-2217. E-mail: admissions@usfca.edu. Web site: http://www.usfca.edu/.

UNIVERSITY OF SOUTHERN CALIFORNIA

LOS ANGELES, CALIFORNIA

General Independent, university, coed **Entrance** Very difficult **Setting** 155-acre urban campus **Total enrollment** 28,342 **Student/faculty ratio** 14:1 **Application deadline** 1/31 **Freshmen** 46% were admitted **Housing** Yes **Expenses** Tuition $20,480; Room & Board $6748 **Undergraduates** 49% women, 6% part-time, 11% 25 or older, 1% Native American, 14% Hispanic, 6% black, 23% Asian American or Pacific Islander **Most popular recent majors** Business administration; mass communications; political science **Academic program** English as a second language, advanced placement, accelerated degree program, self-designed majors, tutorials, honors program, summer session, internships **Contact** Mr. Duncan Murdoch, Director of Admissions, University of Southern California, University Park Campus, Los Angeles, CA 90089. Telephone: 213-740-1111. Fax: 213-740-6364. Web site: http://www.usc.edu/.

UNIVERSITY OF THE PACIFIC
STOCKTON, CALIFORNIA

General Independent, university, coed **Entrance** Moderately difficult **Setting** 175-acre suburban campus **Total enrollment** 5,585 **Application deadline** 2/15 **Freshmen** 84% were admitted **Housing** Yes **Expenses** Tuition $19,365; Room & Board $5770 **Undergraduates** 57% women, 5% part-time, 5% 25 or older, 1% Native American, 10% Hispanic, 3% black, 24% Asian American or Pacific Islander **Most popular recent majors** Liberal arts and studies; pharmacy; business administration **Academic program** Average class size 25, English as a second language, advanced placement, accelerated degree program, self-designed majors, tutorials, honors program, summer session, adult/continuing education programs, internships **Contact** Ms. Janet Dial, Associate Dean of Admissions, University of the Pacific, 3601 Pacific Avenue, Stockton, CA 95211-0197. Telephone: 209-946-2211 or toll-free 800-959-2867. Fax: 209-946-2413. E-mail: admissions@uop.edu. Web site: http://www.uop.edu/.

UNIVERSITY OF WEST LOS ANGELES
INGLEWOOD, CALIFORNIA

General Independent, upper-level, coed **Entrance** Minimally difficult **Setting** 2-acre suburban campus **Total enrollment** 133 **Student/faculty ratio** 12:1 **Application deadline** Rolling **Housing** No **Expenses** Tuition $6030 **Undergraduates** 71% women, 90% 25 or older **Academic program** Adult/continuing education programs, internships **Contact** Mr. Joel Abend, Director of Admissions, University of West Los Angeles, 1155 West Arbor Vitae Street, Inglewood, CA 90301-2902. Telephone: 310-342-5200 ext. 287. Fax: 310-313-2124.

WESTMONT COLLEGE
SANTA BARBARA, CALIFORNIA

General Independent interdenominational, 4-year, coed **Entrance** Moderately difficult **Setting** 133-acre suburban campus **Total enrollment** 1,263 **Student/faculty ratio** 14:1 **Application deadline** 3/1 **Freshmen** 77% were admitted **Housing** Yes **Expenses** Tuition $17,998; Room & Board $6048 **Undergraduates** 61% women, 0.1% part-time, 2% 25 or older, 1% Native American, 6% Hispanic, 1% black, 4% Asian American or Pacific Islander **Most popular recent majors** Business economics; English; biology **Academic program** Average class size 25, advanced placement, accelerated degree program, self-designed majors, tutorials, honors program, summer session, internships **Contact** Mr. David Morley, Dean of Admissions, Westmont College, 955 La Paz Road, Santa Barbara, CA 93108-1099. Telephone: 805-565-6200 ext. 6003 or toll-free 800-777-9011 (out-of-state). Fax: 805-565-6234. E-mail: admissions@westmont.edu. Web site: http://www.westmont.edu/.

WHITTIER COLLEGE
WHITTIER, CALIFORNIA

General Independent, comprehensive, coed **Entrance** Moderately difficult **Setting** 95-acre suburban campus **Total enrollment** 2,104 **Student/faculty ratio** 13:1 **Application deadline** Rolling **Freshmen** 87% were admitted **Housing** Yes **Expenses** Tuition $18,634; Room & Board $6232 **Undergraduates** 56% women, 3% part-time, 7% 25 or older, 1% Native American, 30% Hispanic, 6% black, 10% Asian American or Pacific Islander **Most popular recent majors** Business administration; English; biology **Academic program** Advanced placement, accelerated degree program, self-designed majors, tutorials, summer session, adult/continuing education programs, internships **Contact** Mr. Doug Locker, Director of Admission, Whittier College, 13406 E Philadelphia Street, PO Box 634, Whittier, CA 90608-0634. Telephone: 562-907-4238. Fax: 562-907-4870. E-mail: admission@whittier.edu. Web site: http://www.whittier.edu/.

WOODBURY UNIVERSITY
BURBANK, CALIFORNIA

General Independent, comprehensive, coed **Entrance** Moderately difficult **Setting** 23-acre suburban campus **Total enrollment** 1,049 **Student/faculty ratio** 6:1 **Application deadline** Rolling **Freshmen** 78% were admitted **Housing** Yes **Expenses** Tuition $15,170; Room & Board $5685 **Undergraduates** 53% women, 28% part-time, 36% 25 or older, 1% Native American, 28% Hispanic, 8% black, 20% Asian American or Pacific Islander **Most popular recent majors** Business administration; architecture; interior design **Academic program** Average class size 16, English as a second language, advanced placement, accelerated degree program, tutorials, summer session, adult/continuing education programs, internships **Contact** Mr. Patrick N. Contrades, Director of Admission, Woodbury University, 7500 Glenoaks Boulevard, Burbank, CA 91510. Telephone: 818-767-0888 or toll-free 800-784-9663. Fax: 818-504-9320. E-mail: admissions@vaxb.woodbury.edu. Web site: http://www.woodburyu.edu/.

▶ **For more information, see page 558.**

YESHIVA OHR ELCHONON CHABAD/WEST COAST TALMUDICAL SEMINARY
LOS ANGELES, CALIFORNIA

General Independent Jewish, 4-year, men only **Contact** Rabbi Joseph Schneerson, Director of

Yeshiva Ohr Elchonon Chabad/West Coast Talmudical Seminary *(continued)*

Student Financial Aid, Yeshiva Ohr Elchonon Chabad/West Coast Talmudical Seminary, 7215 Waring Avenue, Los Angeles, CA 90046-7660. Telephone: 213-937-3763.

COLORADO

ADAMS STATE COLLEGE
ALAMOSA, COLORADO

General State-supported, comprehensive, coed **Entrance** Moderately difficult **Setting** 90-acre small town campus **Total enrollment** 2,331 **Student/faculty ratio** 18:1 **Application deadline** 8/1 **Freshmen** 88% were admitted **Housing** Yes **Expenses** Tuition $1956; Room & Board $4424 **Undergraduates** 24% 25 or older, 1% Native American, 27% Hispanic, 2% black, 1% Asian American or Pacific Islander **Most popular recent majors** Biology; business administration; education **Academic program** Average class size 45, advanced placement, accelerated degree program, self-designed majors, tutorials, summer session, adult/continuing education programs **Contact** Mr. Gary C. Pierson, Director of Admissions, Adams State College, 208 Edgemont Boulevard, Alamosa, CO 81102. Telephone: 719-587-7712 or toll-free 800-824-6494. Fax: 719-587-7522. E-mail: ascadmit@adams.edu. Web site: http://www.adams.edu/.

COLORADO CHRISTIAN UNIVERSITY
LAKEWOOD, COLORADO

General Independent interdenominational, comprehensive, coed **Entrance** Moderately difficult **Setting** 26-acre suburban campus **Total enrollment** 1,910 **Student/faculty ratio** 17:1 **Application deadline** 8/15 **Freshmen** 80% were admitted **Housing** Yes **Expenses** Tuition $10,010; Room & Board $4560 **Undergraduates** 51% women, 17% part-time, 53% 25 or older, 1% Native American, 4% Hispanic, 6% black, 2% Asian American or Pacific Islander **Most popular recent majors** Business administration; information sciences/systems; elementary education **Academic program** Average class size 25, advanced placement, accelerated degree program, self-designed majors, tutorials, honors program, summer session, adult/continuing education programs, internships **Contact** Ms. Rebecca Leavenworth, Admissions Office Manager, Colorado Christian University, 180 South Garrison Street, Lakewood, CO 80226-7499. Telephone: 303-202-0100 ext. 165 or toll-free 800-44-FAITH. Fax: 303-238-2191. E-mail: admissions@ccu.edu. Web site: http://www.ccu.edu/.

THE COLORADO COLLEGE
COLORADO SPRINGS, COLORADO

General Independent, comprehensive, coed **Entrance** Very difficult **Setting** 90-acre suburban campus **Total enrollment** 2,041 **Student/faculty ratio** 11:1 **Application deadline** 1/15 **Freshmen** 53% were admitted **Housing** Yes **Expenses** Tuition $19,980; Room & Board $5100 **Undergraduates** 54% women, 1% 25 or older, 1% Native American, 5% Hispanic, 2% black, 3% Asian American or Pacific Islander **Most popular recent majors** English; biology; economics **Academic program** English as a second language, advanced placement, self-designed majors, tutorials, honors program, summer session **Contact** Mr. Terrance K. Swenson, Dean of Admission and Financial Aid, The Colorado College, 14 East Cache La Poudre, Colorado Springs, CO 80903-3294. Telephone: 719-389-6344 or toll-free 800-542-7214. Fax: 719-389-6816. E-mail: admission@cc.colorado.edu. Web site: http://www.cc.colorado.edu/.

THE COLORADO INSTITUTE OF ART
DENVER, COLORADO

General Proprietary, 4-year, coed **Entrance** Minimally difficult **Setting** Urban campus **Total enrollment** 1,694 **Student/faculty ratio** 20:1 **Application deadline** Rolling **Freshmen** 99% were admitted **Housing** Yes **Expenses** Tuition $10,260; Room & Board $5490 **Undergraduates** 39% women, 8% part-time, 28% 25 or older, 1% Native American, 6% Hispanic, 3% black, 3% Asian American or Pacific Islander **Academic program** Advanced placement, adult/continuing education programs **Contact** Ms. Barbara Browning, Vice President and Director of Admissions, The Colorado Institute of Art, 200 East Ninth Avenue, Denver, CO 80203-2903. Telephone: 303-837-0825 ext. 520 or toll-free 800-275-2420. Fax: 303-860-8520 ext. 549. Web site: http://www.aii.edu/.

COLORADO SCHOOL OF MINES
GOLDEN, COLORADO

General State-supported, university, coed **Entrance** Very difficult **Setting** 373-acre small town campus **Total enrollment** 3,199 **Student/faculty ratio** 16:1 **Application deadline** 6/1 **Freshmen** 78% were admitted **Housing** Yes **Expenses** Tuition $5013; Room & Board $4730 **Undergraduates** 24% women, 3% part-time, 2% 25 or older, 1% Native American, 7% Hispanic, 2% black, 5% Asian American or Pacific Islander **Most popular recent majors** Engineering; chemical engineering; computer science **Academic pro-**

gram English as a second language, advanced placement, accelerated degree program, honors program, summer session, adult/continuing education programs **Contact** Mr. William Young, Director of Enrollment Management, Colorado School of Mines, 1500 Illinois Street, Golden, CO 80401-1869. Telephone: 303-273-3227 or toll-free 800-446-9488 (out-of-state). Fax: 303-273-3509. E-mail: admit@mines.edu. Web site: http://www.mines.edu/.

COLORADO STATE UNIVERSITY
FORT COLLINS, COLORADO

General State-supported, university, coed **Entrance** Moderately difficult **Setting** 666-acre urban campus **Total enrollment** 22,344 **Student/faculty ratio** 20:1 **Application deadline** 7/1 **Freshmen** 78% were admitted **Housing** Yes **Expenses** Tuition $3083; Room & Board $5050 **Undergraduates** 51% women, 12% part-time, 16% 25 or older, 1% Native American, 5% Hispanic, 1% black, 3% Asian American or Pacific Islander **Most popular recent majors** Business administration; liberal arts and studies; exercise sciences **Academic program** English as a second language, advanced placement, accelerated degree program, self-designed majors, tutorials, honors program, summer session, adult/continuing education programs, internships **Contact** Ms. Mary Ontiveros, Director of Admissions, Colorado State University, Spruce Hall, Fort Collins, CO 80523-0015. Telephone: 970-491-6909. Fax: 970-491-7799. E-mail: admissions@vines.colostate.edu. Web site: http://www.colostate.edu/.

COLORADO TECHNICAL UNIVERSITY
COLORADO SPRINGS, COLORADO

General Proprietary, comprehensive, coed **Entrance** Moderately difficult **Setting** 14-acre suburban campus **Total enrollment** 1,793 **Student/faculty ratio** 14:1 **Application deadline** Rolling **Freshmen** 85% were admitted **Housing** No **Expenses** Tuition $6838 **Undergraduates** 71% 25 or older **Most popular recent majors** Computer science; electrical/electronic engineering technology; electrical/electronics engineering **Academic program** Average class size 26, advanced placement, accelerated degree program, tutorials, honors program, summer session, adult/continuing education programs, internships **Contact** Mr. Ron Begora, Admissions Manager, Colorado Technical University, 4435 North Chestnut Street, Colorado Springs, CO 80907-3896. Telephone: 719-598-0200. E-mail: cotechcs@iex.net.

COLORADO TECHNICAL UNIVERSITY DENVER CAMPUS
GREENWOOD VILLAGE, COLORADO

Contact Colorado Technical University Denver Campus, 5775 Denver Tech Center Boulevard, Greenwood Village, CO 80111. Telephone: 303-706-0400.

COMMONWEALTH INTERNATIONAL COLLEGE
DENVER, COLORADO

Contact Commonwealth International College, Uinta Way, Building 1433, Denver, CO 80220. Telephone: 303-426-1000. Fax: 303-426-0641.

DENVER INSTITUTE OF TECHNOLOGY
See Westwood College of Technology

DENVER TECHNICAL COLLEGE
DENVER, COLORADO

General Proprietary, comprehensive, coed **Entrance** Moderately difficult **Setting** 1-acre urban campus **Total enrollment** 1,407 **Application deadline** Rolling **Housing** No **Undergraduates** 41% women, 60% 25 or older, 1% Native American, 5% Hispanic, 9% black, 3% Asian American or Pacific Islander **Academic program** Accelerated degree program, tutorials, honors program, summer session, adult/continuing education programs, internships **Contact** Mr. David Phillips, Director of Admissions, Denver Technical College, 925 South Niagara Street, Denver, CO 80224-1658. Telephone: 303-329-3000. E-mail: dphillips@dtc.edu. Web site: http://www.dtc.edu/.

DENVER TECHNICAL COLLEGE AT COLORADO SPRINGS
COLORADO SPRINGS, COLORADO

General Proprietary, 4-year, coed **Entrance** Noncompetitive **Setting** 3-acre urban campus **Total enrollment** 463 **Student/faculty ratio** 11:1 **Application deadline** 9/15 **Freshmen** 97% were admitted **Housing** No **Expenses** Tuition $8400 **Undergraduates** 74% 25 or older **Most popular recent majors** Computer maintenance technology; electrocardiograph technology; pharmacy technician/assistant **Academic program** Tutorials, summer session, adult/continuing education programs, internships **Contact** Ms. Katherine Benner, Director of Admissions, Denver Technical College at Colorado Springs, 225 South Union Boulevard, Colorado Springs, CO 80910. Telephone: 719-632-3000 ext. 107. Fax: 719-632-1909. Web site: http://www.dtc.edu/.

FORT LEWIS COLLEGE
DURANGO, COLORADO

General State-supported, 4-year, coed **Entrance** Moderately difficult **Setting** 350-acre small town campus **Total enrollment** 4,440 **Student/faculty ratio** 20:1 **Application deadline** 6/15 **Freshmen** 90% were admitted **Housing** Yes **Expenses** Tuition $2084; Room & Board $4236 **Undergraduates** 47% women, 8% part-time, 20% 25 or older, 13% Native American, 5% Hispanic, 1% black, 1% Asian American or Pacific Islander **Most popular recent majors** Business administration; humanities; English **Academic program** Average class size 20, English as a second language, advanced placement, accelerated degree program, self-designed majors, tutorials, honors program, summer session, adult/continuing education programs, internships **Contact** Mr. Harlan Steinle, Vice President of Admission, Fort Lewis College, 1000 Rim Drive, Durango, CO 81301-3999. Telephone: 970-247-7184. Fax: 970-247-7179. E-mail: steinle_h@fortlewis.edu. Web site: http://www.fortlewis.edu/.

INTERNATIONAL UNIVERSITY
ENGLEWOOD, COLORADO

General Independent, upper-level, coed **Entrance** Noncompetitive **Total enrollment** 58 **Student/faculty ratio** 25:1 **Application deadline** Rolling **Freshmen** 100% were admitted **Housing** No **Expenses** Tuition $3650 **Undergraduates** 71% women, 100% 25 or older **Academic program** Accelerated degree program, summer session, adult/continuing education programs **Contact** Admissions, International University, 9697 East Mineral Avenue, PO Box 6512, Englewood, CO 80155-6512. Telephone: 303-784-8045 or toll-free 800-777-6463. Fax: 303-784-8547. E-mail: info@international.edu. Web site: http://www.international.edu/.

MESA STATE COLLEGE
GRAND JUNCTION, COLORADO

General State-supported, comprehensive, coed **Entrance** Minimally difficult **Setting** 42-acre small town campus **Total enrollment** 4,703 **Student/faculty ratio** 20:1 **Application deadline** 8/15 **Freshmen** 92% were admitted **Housing** Yes **Expenses** Tuition $1986; Room & Board $4538 **Undergraduates** 55% women, 19% part-time, 32% 25 or older, 1% Native American, 7% Hispanic, 1% black, 1% Asian American or Pacific Islander **Most popular recent majors** Business administration; liberal arts and studies; nursing **Academic program** English as a second language, advanced placement, accelerated degree program, self-designed majors, honors program, summer session, adult/continuing education programs, internships **Contact** Mr. Michael Poll, Associate Director of Admissions, Mesa State College, PO Box 2647, Grand Junction, CO 81502-2647. Telephone: 970-248-1083 or toll-free 800-982-MESA (in-state). Fax: 970-248-1973. E-mail: stone@wpogate.mesa.colorado.edu. Web site: http://www.mesastate.edu/.

METROPOLITAN STATE COLLEGE OF DENVER
DENVER, COLORADO

General State-supported, 4-year, coed **Entrance** Minimally difficult **Setting** 175-acre urban campus **Total enrollment** 17,343 **Student/faculty ratio** 18:1 **Application deadline** 8/1 **Housing** No **Expenses** Tuition $1976 **Undergraduates** 56% women, 43% part-time, 46% 25 or older, 1% Native American, 12% Hispanic, 6% black, 4% Asian American or Pacific Islander **Most popular recent majors** Criminal justice/law enforcement administration; behavioral sciences; accounting **Academic program** Advanced placement, accelerated degree program, self-designed majors, honors program, summer session, adult/continuing education programs, internships **Contact** Mr. Paul Cesare, Assistant Director, Metropolitan State College of Denver, PO Box 173362-Campus Box 16, Denver, CO 80217-3362. Telephone: 303-556-3994. Fax: 303-556-6345. Web site: http://www.mscd.edu/.

THE NAROPA INSTITUTE
BOULDER, COLORADO

General Independent, comprehensive, coed **Entrance** Moderately difficult **Setting** 4-acre urban campus **Total enrollment** 825 **Application deadline** Rolling **Housing** No **Expenses** Tuition $11,358 **Undergraduates** 60% women, 20% part-time, 69% 25 or older, 1% Native American, 2% Hispanic, 1% black, 4% Asian American or Pacific Islander **Most popular recent majors** Psychology; environmental science; theater arts/drama **Academic program** Average class size 13, advanced placement, self-designed majors, tutorials, summer session, adult/continuing education programs, internships **Contact** Ms. Donna McIntyre, Admissions Counselor, The Naropa Institute, 2130 Arapahoe Avenue, Boulder, CO 80302-6697. Telephone: 303-546-3555. Fax: 303-444-0410. E-mail: inquiry@naropa.edu. Web site: http://www.naropa.edu/.

NATIONAL AMERICAN UNIVERSITY
COLORADO SPRINGS, COLORADO

General Proprietary, 4-year, coed **Entrance** Noncompetitive **Setting** 1-acre suburban campus **To-**

tal enrollment 350 **Student/faculty ratio** 13:1 **Application deadline** Rolling **Housing** No **Expenses** Tuition $8235 **Undergraduates** 98% 25 or older **Most popular recent majors** Business administration; accounting; information sciences/systems **Academic program** English as a second language, accelerated degree program, tutorials, summer session, adult/continuing education programs, internships **Contact** Mr. Nathan Larson, Director of Admissions, National American University, 2577 North Chelton Road, Colorado Springs, CO 80909. Telephone: 719-471-4205. Fax: 719-471-4751.

NATIONAL AMERICAN UNIVERSITY
DENVER, COLORADO

General Proprietary, 4-year, coed **Contact** Ms. Leigh Ann Sutherland, Director of Admissions, National American University, 1325 South Colorado Blvd, Suite 100, Denver, CO 80222. Telephone: 303-758-6700.

NAZARENE BIBLE COLLEGE
COLORADO SPRINGS, COLORADO

General Independent, 4-year, coed, affiliated with Church of the Nazarene **Entrance** Noncompetitive **Setting** 64-acre urban campus **Total enrollment** 350 **Student/faculty ratio** 14:1 **Application deadline** 8/31 **Housing** No **Expenses** Tuition $5055 **Undergraduates** 31% women, 45% part-time, 82% 25 or older, 1% Native American, 3% Hispanic, 4% black, 2% Asian American or Pacific Islander **Most Popular Recent Major** Biblical studies **Academic program** Summer session, internships **Contact** Rev. J. Fred Shepard, Director of Admissions/Public Relations, Nazarene Bible College, 1111 Academy Park Loop, Colorado Springs, CO 80916. Telephone: 719-596-5110 ext. 167 or toll-free 800-873-3873 (out-of-state). Fax: 719-550-9437.

REGIS UNIVERSITY
DENVER, COLORADO

General Independent Roman Catholic (Jesuit), comprehensive, coed **Entrance** Moderately difficult **Setting** 90-acre suburban campus **Total enrollment** 1,178 **Student/faculty ratio** 16:1 **Application deadline** 8/15 **Freshmen** 82% were admitted **Housing** Yes **Expenses** Tuition $14,970; Room & Board $5900 **Undergraduates** 55% women, 4% part-time, 10% 25 or older, 1% Native American, 9% Hispanic, 2% black, 3% Asian American or Pacific Islander **Most popular recent majors** Nursing; business administration; psychology **Academic program** Average class size 30, advanced placement, accelerated degree program, self-designed majors, tutorials, honors program, summer session, adult/continuing education programs, internships **Contact** Ms. Penny Dempsey St. John, Director of Admissions, Regis University, 3333 Regis Boulevard, Denver, CO 80221-1099. Telephone: 303-458-4900 or toll-free 800-388-2366. Fax: 303-964-5534. E-mail: regisadm@regis.edu.

ROCKY MOUNTAIN COLLEGE OF ART & DESIGN
DENVER, COLORADO

General Proprietary, 4-year, coed **Entrance** Moderately difficult **Setting** 1-acre urban campus **Total enrollment** 388 **Application deadline** Rolling **Freshmen** 94% were admitted **Housing** No **Expenses** Tuition $9727 **Undergraduates** 48% women, 19% part-time, 35% 25 or older, 1% Native American, 4% Hispanic, 2% black, 2% Asian American or Pacific Islander **Most popular recent majors** Graphic design/commercial art/illustration; drawing **Academic program** Average class size 18, advanced placement, summer session, internships **Contact** Ms. Amy Williams, Assistant Director of Admissions, Rocky Mountain College of Art & Design, 6875 East Evans Avenue, Denver, CO 80224-2329. Telephone: 303-753-6046 or toll-free 800-888-ARTS. Fax: 303-759-4970. E-mail: admit@rmcad.edu.

TEIKYO LORETTO HEIGHTS UNIVERSITY
DENVER, COLORADO

Contact Teikyo Loretto Heights University, 3001 South Federal Boulevard, Denver, CO 80236-2711. Telephone: 303-937-4200.

UNITED STATES AIR FORCE ACADEMY
COLORADO SPRINGS, COLORADO

General Federally supported, 4-year, coed **Entrance** Most difficult **Setting** 18,000-acre suburban campus **Total enrollment** 4,096 **Student/faculty ratio** 7:1 **Application deadline** 1/31 **Freshmen** 15% were admitted **Housing** Yes **Expenses** Tuition $0 **Undergraduates** 16% women, 0% 25 or older, 1% Native American, 7% Hispanic, 5% black, 4% Asian American or Pacific Islander **Academic program** Average class size 17, English as a second language, advanced placement, self-designed majors, tutorials, summer session, internships **Contact** Mr. Rolland Stoneman, Associate Director of Admissions/Selections, United States Air Force Academy, HQ USAFA/RR 2304 Cadet Drive, Suite 200, USAF Academy, CO 80840-5025. Telephone: 719-333-2520 or toll-free 800-443-9266. Fax: 719-333-3012. E-mail: rrmail.rr@usafa.af.mil. Web site: http://www.usafa.af.mil/.

UNIVERSITY OF COLORADO AT BOULDER
BOULDER, COLORADO

General State-supported, university, coed **Entrance** Moderately difficult **Setting** 600-acre suburban campus **Total enrollment** 25,109 **Student/faculty ratio** 14:1 **Application deadline** 2/15 **Freshmen** 83% were admitted **Housing** Yes **Expenses** Tuition $2939; Room & Board $4566 **Undergraduates** 48% women, 9% part-time, 10% 25 or older, 1% Native American, 6% Hispanic, 2% black, 6% Asian American or Pacific Islander **Most popular recent majors** Psychology; biology; English **Academic program** English as a second language, advanced placement, accelerated degree program, self-designed majors, tutorials, honors program, summer session, adult/continuing education programs, internships **Contact** Admission Counselor, University of Colorado at Boulder, Campus Box 30, Boulder, CO 80309-0030. Telephone: 303-492-6301. Fax: 303-492-7115. E-mail: apply@colorado.edu. Web site: http://www.colorado.edu/.

UNIVERSITY OF COLORADO AT COLORADO SPRINGS
COLORADO SPRINGS, COLORADO

General State-supported, comprehensive, coed **Entrance** Moderately difficult **Setting** 400-acre suburban campus **Total enrollment** 6,440 **Student/faculty ratio** 14:1 **Application deadline** 7/1 **Freshmen** 77% were admitted **Housing** Yes **Expenses** Tuition $2558; Room & Board $4790 **Undergraduates** 60% women, 34% part-time, 35% 25 or older, 2% Native American, 8% Hispanic, 4% black, 5% Asian American or Pacific Islander **Most popular recent majors** Business administration; communications; psychology **Academic program** Average class size 25, advanced placement, accelerated degree program, summer session, adult/continuing education programs, internships **Contact** Mr. James Tidwell, Assistant Admissions Director, University of Colorado at Colorado Springs, PO Box 7150, Colorado Springs, CO 80933-7150. Telephone: 719-262-3383 or toll-free 800-990-8227. E-mail: admrec@mail.uccs.edu. Web site: http://www.uccs.edu/.

UNIVERSITY OF COLORADO AT DENVER
DENVER, COLORADO

General State-supported, university, coed **Entrance** Moderately difficult **Setting** 171-acre urban campus **Total enrollment** 13,092 **Application deadline** 7/22 **Freshmen** 76% were admitted **Housing** No **Expenses** Tuition $2204 **Undergraduates** 53% women, 37% part-time, 47% 25 or older, 1% Native American, 10% Hispanic, 4% black, 8% Asian American or Pacific Islander **Most popular recent majors** Business administration; psychology; biology **Academic program** Advanced placement, self-designed majors, tutorials, honors program, summer session, adult/continuing education programs, internships **Contact** Ms. Alice Holman, Associate Director of Admissions, University of Colorado at Denver, PO Box 173364, Campus Box 167, Denver, CO 80217-3364. Telephone: 303-556-2275. Fax: 303-556-4838. E-mail: admissions@castle.cudenver.edu. Web site: http://www.cudenver.edu/.

UNIVERSITY OF COLORADO HEALTH SCIENCES CENTER
DENVER, COLORADO

General State-supported, upper-level, coed **Entrance** Moderately difficult **Setting** 40-acre urban campus **Total enrollment** 1,662 **Freshmen** 30% were admitted **Housing** No **Expenses** Tuition $3079 **Most popular recent majors** Pharmacy; nursing **Academic program** Advanced placement, summer session, adult/continuing education programs, internships **Contact** Dr. David P. Sorenson, Director of Admissions, University of Colorado Health Sciences Center, 4200 East Ninth Avenue, Denver, CO 80262. Telephone: 303-315-7676. Fax: 303-315-3358. E-mail: stuserv@mongo.uchsc.edu. Web site: http://www.uchsc.edu/.

UNIVERSITY OF DENVER
DENVER, COLORADO

General Independent, university, coed **Entrance** Moderately difficult **Setting** 125-acre suburban campus **Total enrollment** 8,667 **Student/faculty ratio** 13:1 **Application deadline** Rolling **Freshmen** 84% were admitted **Housing** Yes **Expenses** Tuition $17,886; Room & Board $5743 **Undergraduates** 58% women, 14% part-time, 7% 25 or older, 1% Native American, 6% Hispanic, 4% black, 5% Asian American or Pacific Islander **Most popular recent majors** Biology; communications; business marketing and marketing management **Academic program** Average class size 20, English as a second language, advanced placement, accelerated degree program, self-designed majors, tutorials, honors program, summer session, adult/continuing education programs, internships **Contact** Mr. Morris Price, Associate Dean of Admission, University of Denver, University Park, Denver, CO 80208. Telephone: 303-871-3373 or toll-free 800-525-9495 (out-of-state). Fax: 303-871-3301. E-mail: admission@du.edu. Web site: http://www.du.edu/.

UNIVERSITY OF NORTHERN COLORADO
GREELEY, COLORADO

General State-supported, university, coed **Entrance** Moderately difficult **Setting** 240-acre suburban campus **Total enrollment** 11,860 **Student/faculty ratio** 21:1 **Application deadline** Rolling **Freshmen** 80% were admitted **Housing** Yes **Expenses** Tuition $2578; Room & Board $4420 **Undergraduates** 59% women, 7% part-time, 11% 25 or older, 1% Native American, 7% Hispanic, 3% black, 4% Asian American or Pacific Islander **Most popular recent majors** Business administration; physical education; social sciences **Academic program** Average class size 42, English as a second language, advanced placement, accelerated degree program, self-designed majors, honors program, summer session, adult/continuing education programs, internships **Contact** Mr. Gary O. Gullickson, Director of Admissions, University of Northern Colorado, Greeley, CO 80639. Telephone: 970-351-2881. E-mail: unc@mail.univnorthco.edu. Web site: http://www.univnorthco.edu/.

UNIVERSITY OF SOUTHERN COLORADO
PUEBLO, COLORADO

General State-supported, comprehensive, coed **Entrance** Moderately difficult **Setting** 275-acre suburban campus **Total enrollment** 5,066 **Student/faculty ratio** 17:1 **Application deadline** Rolling **Freshmen** 85% were admitted **Housing** Yes **Expenses** Tuition $2191; Room & Board $4508 **Undergraduates** 55% women, 16% part-time, 36% 25 or older **Most popular recent majors** Business administration; mass communications; biology **Academic program** Average class size 50, English as a second language, advanced placement, accelerated degree program, tutorials, honors program, summer session, adult/continuing education programs, internships **Contact** Ms. Christie Kangas, Director of Admissions, University of Southern Colorado, 2200 Bonforte Boulevard, Pueblo, CO 81001-4901. Telephone: 719-549-2461 or toll-free 800-872-4769. Fax: 719-549-2419. E-mail: info@uscolo.edu. Web site: http://www.uscolo.edu/.

WESTERN STATE COLLEGE OF COLORADO
GUNNISON, COLORADO

General State-supported, 4-year, coed **Entrance** Moderately difficult **Setting** 381-acre small town campus **Total enrollment** 2,517 **Student/faculty ratio** 20:1 **Application deadline** Rolling **Freshmen** 86% were admitted **Housing** Yes **Expenses** Tuition $2152; Room & Board $4790 **Undergraduates** 41% women, 7% part-time, 14% 25 or older, 1% Native American, 4% Hispanic, 1% black, 2% Asian American or Pacific Islander **Most popular recent majors** Business administration; exercise sciences; sociology **Academic program** Advanced placement, accelerated degree program, self-designed majors, honors program, summer session, adult/continuing education programs, internships **Contact** Ms. Sara Axelson, Director of Admissions, Western State College of Colorado, 600 North Adams Street, Gunnison, CO 81231. Telephone: 970-943-2119 or toll-free 800-876-5309. Fax: 970-943-7069. E-mail: saxelson@western.edu. Web site: http://www.western.edu/.

WESTWOOD COLLEGE OF TECHNOLOGY
DENVER, COLORADO

General Proprietary, 4-year, coed **Entrance** Moderately difficult **Setting** 11-acre suburban campus **Total enrollment** 950 **Student/faculty ratio** 20:1 **Application deadline** Rolling **Freshmen** 92% were admitted **Housing** No **Expenses** Tuition $8000 **Undergraduates** 33% 25 or older **Academic program** Advanced placement, accelerated degree program, tutorials, summer session, internships **Contact** Mr. Richard A. Rodman, Director of Admissions, Westwood College of Technology, 7350 North Broadway, Denver, CO 80221-3653. Telephone: 303-650-5050 ext. 360 or toll-free 800-992-5050. Fax: 303-426-1832. Web site: http://www.westwood.tec.co.us/.

YESHIVA TORAS CHAIM TALMUDICAL SEMINARY
DENVER, COLORADO

Contact Rabbi Israel Kagan, Dean, Yeshiva Toras Chaim Talmudical Seminary, 1400 Quitman Street, Denver, CO 80204-1415. Telephone: 303-629-8200. Fax: 303-623-5949.

CONNECTICUT

ALBERTUS MAGNUS COLLEGE
NEW HAVEN, CONNECTICUT

General Independent Roman Catholic, comprehensive, coed **Entrance** Moderately difficult **Setting** 55-acre suburban campus **Total enrollment** 1,549 **Student/faculty ratio** 13:1 **Application deadline** Rolling **Freshmen** 93% were admitted **Housing** Yes **Expenses** Tuition $17,262; Room & Board $7636 **Undergraduates** 65% women, 13% part-time, 71% 25 or older, 0.2% Native American, 5% Hispanic, 15% black, 1% Asian American or Pacific Islander **Most popular recent majors** Business economics; psychology; sociology **Academic program** English as a second language, advanced placement, accelerated degree program, self-designed majors, tutorials, honors program, summer session, adult/continuing education programs, internships **Contact** Ms. Allison Rowett-Sewell, Assistant Director of Admissions,

Albertus Magnus College *(continued)*

Albertus Magnus College, 700 Prospect Street, New Haven, CT 06511-1189. Telephone: 203-773-8501 or toll-free 800-578-9160. Fax: 203-785-8652. E-mail: admissions@albertus.edu. Web site: http://www.albertus.edu/.

BETH BENJAMIN ACADEMY OF CONNECTICUT
STAMFORD, CONNECTICUT

Contact Rabbi David Mayer, Director of Admissions, Beth Benjamin Academy of Connecticut, 132 Prospect Street, Stamford, CT 06901-1202. Telephone: 203-325-4351.

CENTRAL CONNECTICUT STATE UNIVERSITY
NEW BRITAIN, CONNECTICUT

General State-supported, comprehensive, coed **Entrance** Moderately difficult **Setting** 294-acre suburban campus **Total enrollment** 11,625 **Student/faculty ratio** 17:1 **Application deadline** 5/1 **Freshmen** 69% were admitted **Housing** Yes **Expenses** Tuition $3614; Room & Board $5300 **Undergraduates** 52% women, 27% part-time, 31% 25 or older, 0.4% Native American, 5% Hispanic, 7% black, 2% Asian American or Pacific Islander **Most popular recent majors** Elementary education; accounting; psychology **Academic program** English as a second language, advanced placement, self-designed majors, tutorials, honors program, summer session, adult/continuing education programs, internships **Contact** Ms. Barbara Lukas, Interim Director of Admissions, Central Connecticut State University, 1615 Stanley Street, New Britain, CT 06050-4010. Telephone: 860-832-2278 or toll-free 800-755-2278 (out-of-state). Fax: 860-832-2522. E-mail: admissions@ccsu.edu. Web site: http://www.ccsu.edu/.

CHARTER OAK STATE COLLEGE
NEWINGTON, CONNECTICUT

General State-supported, 4-year, coed **Entrance** Noncompetitive **Setting** Small town campus **Total enrollment** 1,232 **Housing** No **Undergraduates** 99% 25 or older, 0.2% Native American, 4% Hispanic, 5% black, 1% Asian American or Pacific Islander **Academic program** Advanced placement, accelerated degree program, self-designed majors **Contact** Mr. Paul Morganti, Director of Admissions, Charter Oak State College, 66 Cedar Street, Newington, CT 06111-2646. Telephone: 860-666-4595 ext. 25. E-mail: pmorganti@commnet.edu. Web site: http://www.cosc.edu/.

CONNECTICUT COLLEGE
NEW LONDON, CONNECTICUT

General Independent, comprehensive, coed **Entrance** Very difficult **Setting** 702-acre suburban campus **Total enrollment** 1,857 **Student/faculty ratio** 11:1 **Application deadline** 1/15 **Freshmen** 40% were admitted **Housing** Yes **Expenses** Tuition $28,475 **Undergraduates** 57% women, 4% part-time, 3% 25 or older, 0.1% Native American, 3% Hispanic, 5% black, 3% Asian American or Pacific Islander **Most popular recent majors** Psychology; English; biology **Academic program** Advanced placement, accelerated degree program, self-designed majors, tutorials, honors program, summer session, adult/continuing education programs, internships **Contact** Mr. Lee A. Coffin, Dean of Admissions, Connecticut College, 270 Mohegan Avenue, New London, CT 06320-4196. Telephone: 860-439-2202. Fax: 860-439-4301. E-mail: admit@conncoll.edu. Web site: http://www.camel.conncoll.edu/.

EASTERN CONNECTICUT STATE UNIVERSITY
WILLIMANTIC, CONNECTICUT

General State-supported, comprehensive, coed **Entrance** Moderately difficult **Setting** 178-acre small town campus **Total enrollment** 4,632 **Student/faculty ratio** 17:1 **Application deadline** 5/1 **Freshmen** 82% were admitted **Housing** Yes **Expenses** Tuition $3838; Room & Board $5048 **Undergraduates** 58% women, 23% part-time, 26% 25 or older, 1% Native American, 4% Hispanic, 7% black, 1% Asian American or Pacific Islander **Most Popular Recent Major** Business administration **Academic program** Advanced placement, self-designed majors, tutorials, honors program, summer session, adult/continuing education programs, internships **Contact** Ms. Kimberly Crone, Director of Admissions and Enrollment Management, Eastern Connecticut State University, 83 Windham Street, Willimantic, CT 06226-2295. Telephone: 860-465-5286. E-mail: admissions@ecsu.ctstateu.edu. Web site: http://www.ecsu.ctstate.edu/.

FAIRFIELD UNIVERSITY
FAIRFIELD, CONNECTICUT

General Independent Roman Catholic (Jesuit), comprehensive, coed **Entrance** Moderately difficult **Setting** 200-acre suburban campus **Total enrollment** 5,179 **Student/faculty ratio** 13:1 **Application deadline** 2/1 **Freshmen** 68% were admitted **Housing** Yes **Expenses** Tuition $18,310; Room & Board $7024 **Undergraduates** 51% women, 14% part-time, 1% 25 or older, 0.2% Native American, 3% Hispanic, 3% black, 3% Asian

American or Pacific Islander **Most popular recent majors** English; psychology; nursing **Academic program** Average class size 24, advanced placement, tutorials, honors program, summer session, adult/continuing education programs, internships **Contact** Ms. Mary Spiegel, Director of Admission, Fairfield University, 1073 North Benson Road, Fairfield, CT 06430-5195. Telephone: 203-254-4100. Fax: 203-254-4199. E-mail: admis@fair1.fairfield.edu. Web site: http://www.fairfield.edu/.

HARTFORD COLLEGE FOR WOMEN
HARTFORD, CONNECTICUT

General Independent, 4-year, women only **Entrance** Moderately difficult **Setting** 13-acre suburban campus **Total enrollment** 187 **Student/faculty ratio** 8:1 **Application deadline** Rolling **Housing** Yes **Expenses** Tuition $14,415; Room & Board $7060 **Undergraduates** 44% 25 or older, 19% Hispanic, 20% black, 11% Asian American or Pacific Islander **Most popular recent majors** Liberal arts and studies; law and legal studies; women's studies **Academic program** Average class size 15, English as a second language, advanced placement, accelerated degree program, self-designed majors, tutorials, honors program, summer session, adult/continuing education programs, internships **Contact** Ms. Gwendolyn Gardner, Director of Admissions, Hartford College for Women, 1265 Asylum Avenue, Hartford, CT 06105-2299. Telephone: 860-768-5600 or toll-free 800-582-6118. Fax: 860-233-5493. E-mail: ggardner@uhavax.hartford.edu.

HOLY APOSTLES COLLEGE AND SEMINARY
CROMWELL, CONNECTICUT

General Independent Roman Catholic, comprehensive, coed **Contact** Rev. Raymond Halliwell MSA, Director of Admissions, Holy Apostles College and Seminary, 33 Prospect Hill Road, Cromwell, CT 06416-2005. Telephone: 860-632-3030 or toll-free 800-330-7272. Fax: 860-632-0176. Web site: http://www.novavista.com/holyapostles/.

LYME ACADEMY OF FINE ARTS
OLD LYME, CONNECTICUT

General Independent, 4-year, coed **Entrance** Moderately difficult **Setting** 3-acre small town campus **Total enrollment** 80 **Application deadline** Rolling **Freshmen** 86% were admitted **Housing** No **Expenses** Tuition $8690 **Undergraduates** 46% women, 28% part-time, 50% 25 or older, 1% Native American, 6% Hispanic, 0% black, 1% Asian American or Pacific Islander **Most Popular Recent Major** Drawing **Academic program** Average class size 16, summer session **Contact** Mrs. Marnie-Ann Balaski, Admissions/Student Services, Lyme Academy of Fine Arts, 84 Lyme Street, Old Lyme, CT 06371. Telephone: 860-434-5232 ext. 104. Fax: 860-434-8725.

PAIER COLLEGE OF ART, INC.
HAMDEN, CONNECTICUT

General Proprietary, 4-year, coed **Entrance** Minimally difficult **Setting** 3-acre suburban campus **Total enrollment** 261 **Student/faculty ratio** 7:1 **Application deadline** Rolling **Freshmen** 84% were admitted **Housing** No **Expenses** Tuition $10,595 **Undergraduates** 45% women, 36% part-time, 40% 25 or older, 0% Native American, 2% Hispanic, 2% black, 2% Asian American or Pacific Islander **Most popular recent majors** Graphic design/commercial art/illustration; interior design; photography **Academic program** Average class size 12, advanced placement, tutorials, summer session **Contact** Ms. Lynn Pascale, Secretary to Admissions, Paier College of Art, Inc., 20 Gorham Avenue, Hamden, CT 06514-3902. Telephone: 203-287-3031. E-mail: info@www.paierart.com. Web site: http://www.paierart.com/.

QUINNIPIAC COLLEGE
HAMDEN, CONNECTICUT

General Independent, comprehensive, coed **Entrance** Moderately difficult **Setting** 200-acre suburban campus **Total enrollment** 5,571 **Student/faculty ratio** 15:1 **Application deadline** 2/15 **Freshmen** 62% were admitted **Housing** Yes **Expenses** Tuition $14,880; Room & Board $7190 **Undergraduates** 66% women, 8% part-time, 10% 25 or older, 0.2% Native American, 3% Hispanic, 3% black, 2% Asian American or Pacific Islander **Most popular recent majors** Physical therapy; accounting; occupational therapy **Academic program** Average class size 25, advanced placement, self-designed majors, tutorials, honors program, summer session, adult/continuing education programs, internships **Contact** Ms. Joan Isaac-Mohr, Vice President and Dean of Admissions, Quinnipiac College, 275 Mount Carmel Avenue, Hamden, CT 06518-1904. Telephone: 203-281-8600 or toll-free 800-462-1944 (out-of-state). Fax: 203-281-8906. E-mail: admissions@quinnipiac.edu. Web site: http://www.quinnipiac.edu/.

SACRED HEART UNIVERSITY
FAIRFIELD, CONNECTICUT

General Independent Roman Catholic, comprehensive, coed **Entrance** Moderately difficult **Setting** 56-acre suburban campus **Total enrollment** 5,900 **Student/faculty ratio** 14:1 **Application deadline** 4/15 **Freshmen** 87% were admitted **Housing** Yes **Expenses** Tuition $13,475; Room

Sacred Heart University *(continued)*

& Board $6570 **Undergraduates** 7% 25 or older **Most popular recent majors** Business administration; mass communications; psychology **Academic program** English as a second language, advanced placement, accelerated degree program, tutorials, honors program, summer session, adult/continuing education programs, internships **Contact** Ms. Karen N. Pagliuco, Dean of Undergraduate Admissions, Sacred Heart University, 5151 Park Avenue, Fairfield, CT 06432-1000. Telephone: 203-371-7880. Fax: 203-371-7889. E-mail: enroll@sacredheart.edu.

SAINT JOSEPH COLLEGE
WEST HARTFORD, CONNECTICUT

General Independent Roman Catholic, comprehensive, primarily women **Entrance** Moderately difficult **Setting** 84-acre suburban campus **Total enrollment** 1,938 **Student/faculty ratio** 12:1 **Application deadline** 5/1 **Freshmen** 83% were admitted **Housing** Yes **Expenses** Tuition $14,490; Room & Board $5725 **Undergraduates** 99% women, 34% part-time, 17% 25 or older, 0.2% Native American, 5% Hispanic, 9% black, 3% Asian American or Pacific Islander **Most popular recent majors** Nursing; social work; special education **Academic program** Average class size 15, English as a second language, advanced placement, accelerated degree program, self-designed majors, honors program, summer session, adult/continuing education programs, internships **Contact** Ms. Alice Brown, Coordinator of Admissions, Saint Joseph College, 1678 Asylum Avenue, West Hartford, CT 06117-2700. Telephone: 860-232-4571 ext. 384 or toll-free 800-285-6565. Fax: 860-233-5695. E-mail: admissions@mercy.sjc.edu. Web site: http://www.sjc.edu/.

SOUTHERN CONNECTICUT STATE UNIVERSITY
NEW HAVEN, CONNECTICUT

General State-supported, comprehensive, coed **Entrance** Moderately difficult **Setting** 168-acre urban campus **Total enrollment** 11,395 **Student/faculty ratio** 11:1 **Application deadline** 7/1 **Freshmen** 75% were admitted **Housing** Yes **Expenses** Tuition $3568; Room & Board $5366 **Undergraduates** 57% women, 27% part-time, 23% 25 or older, 0.2% Native American, 5% Hispanic, 11% black, 2% Asian American or Pacific Islander **Most popular recent majors** Communications; psychology; sociology **Academic program** Average class size 28, advanced placement, accelerated degree program, self-designed majors, tutorials, honors program, summer session, adult/continuing education programs, internships **Contact** Ms. Paula Kennedy, Associate Director of Admissions, Southern Connecticut State University, Admissions House, New Haven, CT 06515-1202. Telephone: 203-392-5651. Fax: 203-392-5727. E-mail: adminfo@scsu.ctstateu.edu. Web site: http://www.scsu.ctstate.edu/.

► **For more information, see page 517.**

TEIKYO POST UNIVERSITY
WATERBURY, CONNECTICUT

General Independent, 4-year, coed **Entrance** Minimally difficult **Setting** 70-acre suburban campus **Total enrollment** 1,334 **Application deadline** Rolling **Freshmen** 85% were admitted **Housing** Yes **Expenses** Tuition $12,260; Room & Board $5600 **Undergraduates** 63% women, 56% part-time, 54% 25 or older, 0.4% Native American, 3% Hispanic, 7% black, 1% Asian American or Pacific Islander **Most Popular Recent Major** Business administration **Academic program** Average class size 16, English as a second language, advanced placement, accelerated degree program, self-designed majors, tutorials, honors program, summer session, adult/continuing education programs, internships **Contact** Mr. Scott Ouellette, Senior Assistant Director of Admissions, Teikyo Post University, 800 Country Club Road, Waterbury, CT 06723-2540. Telephone: 203-596-4520 or toll-free 800-345-2562. Fax: 203-756-5810. E-mail: tpuadmiss@teikyopost.edu. Web site: http://teikyopost.edu/.

TRINITY COLLEGE
HARTFORD, CONNECTICUT

General Independent, comprehensive, coed **Entrance** Very difficult **Setting** 100-acre urban campus **Total enrollment** 2,215 **Student/faculty ratio** 10:1 **Application deadline** 1/15 **Freshmen** 43% were admitted **Housing** Yes **Expenses** Tuition $22,470; Room & Board $6320 **Undergraduates** 47% women, 9% part-time, 8% 25 or older, 0.2% Native American, 4% Hispanic, 5% black, 5% Asian American or Pacific Islander **Most popular recent majors** English; political science; economics **Academic program** Average class size 19, advanced placement, accelerated degree program, self-designed majors, tutorials, honors program, summer session, adult/continuing education programs, internships **Contact** Mr. Larry Dow, Director of Admissions, Trinity College, 300 Summit Street, Hartford, CT 06106-3100. Telephone: 860-297-2180. Fax: 860-297-2287. E-mail: admissions.office@trincoll.edu. Web site: http://www.trincoll.edu/.

UNITED STATES COAST GUARD ACADEMY
NEW LONDON, CONNECTICUT

General Federally supported, 4-year, coed **Entrance** Very difficult **Setting** 110-acre suburban campus **Total enrollment** 830 **Student/faculty ratio** 7:1 **Application deadline** 12/15 **Freshmen** 9% were admitted **Housing** Yes **Expenses** Tuition $0 **Undergraduates** 28% women, 0% 25 or older, 1% Native American, 6% Hispanic, 4% black, 5% Asian American or Pacific Islander **Most popular recent majors** Naval architecture/ marine engineering; business administration; marine science **Academic program** English as a second language, tutorials, honors program, summer session **Contact** Capt. R. W. Thorne, Director of Admissions, United States Coast Guard Academy, 15 Mohegan Avenue, New London, CT 06320-4195. Telephone: 860-444-8500. Fax: 860-444-8289. E-mail: uscgatr@dcseq.uscga.edu. Web site: http://www.cga.edu/.

UNIVERSITY OF BRIDGEPORT

BRIDGEPORT, CONNECTICUT

General Independent, comprehensive, coed **Entrance** Moderately difficult **Setting** 86-acre urban campus **Total enrollment** 2,427 **Student/ faculty ratio** 10:1 **Application deadline** 4/1 **Freshmen** 84% were admitted **Housing** Yes **Expenses** Tuition $13,644; Room & Board $6810 **Undergraduates** 53% women, 25% part-time, 33% 25 or older, 0.2% Native American, 8% Hispanic, 15% black, 5% Asian American or Pacific Islander **Most popular recent majors** Liberal arts and studies; dental hygiene; business administration **Academic program** Average class size 15, English as a second language, advanced placement, accelerated degree program, self-designed majors, tutorials, honors program, summer session, adult/continuing education programs, internships **Contact** Mr. Joseph Marrone, Director of Unvergraduate Admissions, University of Bridgeport, 380 University Avenue, Bridgeport, CT 06601. Telephone: 203-576-4552 or toll-free 800-EXCEL-UB (in-state), 800-243-9496 (out-of-state). Fax: 203-576-4941. E-mail: admit@cse.bridgeport.edu. Web site: http://www.bridgeport.edu/.

► **For more information, see page 533.**

UNIVERSITY OF CONNECTICUT

STORRS, CONNECTICUT

General State-supported, university, coed **Entrance** Moderately difficult **Setting** 4,212-acre rural campus **Total enrollment** 18,205 **Student/ faculty ratio** 14:1 **Application deadline** 3/1 **Freshmen** 70% were admitted **Housing** Yes **Expenses** Tuition $5242; Room & Board $5462 **Undergraduates** 52% women, 6% part-time, 9% 25 or older, 0.3% Native American, 4% Hispanic, 4% black, 6% Asian American or Pacific Islander **Most popular recent majors** Psychology; individual/ family development **Academic program** English as a second language, advanced placement, accelerated degree program, self-designed majors, honors program, summer session, adult/continuing education programs, internships **Contact** Mr. Brian Usher, Associate Director of Admissions, University of Connecticut, 2131 Hillside Road, U-88, Storrs, CT 06269-3088. Telephone: 860-486-3137. Fax: 860-486-1476. E-mail: beahusky@uconnvm.uconn.edu. Web site: http://www.uconn.edu/.

UNIVERSITY OF HARTFORD

WEST HARTFORD, CONNECTICUT

General Independent, comprehensive, coed **Entrance** Moderately difficult **Setting** 320-acre suburban campus **Total enrollment** 7,089 **Student/ faculty ratio** 13:1 **Application deadline** Rolling **Freshmen** 78% were admitted **Housing** Yes **Expenses** Tuition $18,224; Room & Board $7200 **Undergraduates** 52% women, 18% part-time, 16% 25 or older, 0.1% Native American, 3% Hispanic, 6% black, 2% Asian American or Pacific Islander **Academic program** English as a second language, advanced placement, self-designed majors, honors program, summer session, adult/continuing education programs, internships **Contact** Mr. Richard Zeiser, Dean of Admissions, University of Hartford, 200 Bloomfield Avenue, West Hartford, CT 06117-1599. Telephone: 860-768-4296 or toll-free 800-947-4303. Fax: 860-768-4961. E-mail: admission@uhavax.hartford.edu. Web site: http://www.hartford.edu/.

UNIVERSITY OF NEW HAVEN

WEST HAVEN, CONNECTICUT

General Independent, university, coed **Entrance** Moderately difficult **Setting** 78-acre suburban campus **Total enrollment** 4,976 **Student/ faculty ratio** 11:1 **Application deadline** 9/1 **Freshmen** 85% were admitted **Housing** Yes **Expenses** Tuition $13,100; Room & Board $5700 **Undergraduates** 1% Native American, 4% Hispanic, 6% black, 2% Asian American or Pacific Islander **Most popular recent majors** Business administration; mechanical engineering; criminal justice/law enforcement administration **Academic program** English as a second language, advanced placement, self-designed majors, honors program, adult/continuing education programs, internships **Contact** Mr. Patrick Quinn, Director of Admissions, University of New Haven, 300 Orange Avenue, West Haven, CT 06516-1916. Telephone: 203-932-7088 or toll-free 800-DIAL-UNH (out-of-state). Web site: http://www.newhaven.edu/.

► **For more information, see page 539.**

WESLEYAN UNIVERSITY

MIDDLETOWN, CONNECTICUT

General Independent, university, coed **Entrance** Most difficult **Setting** 120-acre small town

Wesleyan University *(continued)*

campus **Total enrollment** 3,335 **Student/faculty ratio** 11:1 **Application deadline** 1/1 **Freshmen** 33% were admitted **Housing** Yes **Expenses** Tuition $22,980; Room & Board $6210 **Undergraduates** 52% women, 0.04% part-time, 1% 25 or older, 0.1% Native American, 6% Hispanic, 8% black, 9% Asian American or Pacific Islander **Most popular recent majors** English; political science; history **Academic program** English as a second language, advanced placement, accelerated degree program, self-designed majors, tutorials, adult/continuing education programs, internships **Contact** Ms. Barbara-Jan Wilson, Dean of Admissions and Financial Aid, Wesleyan University, 70 Wyllys Avenue, Middletown, CT 06459-0265. Telephone: 860-685-3000. Fax: 860-685-3001. E-mail: admissions@wesleyan.edu. Web site: http://www.wesleyan.edu/.

WESTERN CONNECTICUT STATE UNIVERSITY

DANBURY, CONNECTICUT

General State-supported, comprehensive, coed **Contact** Mr. Patrick Quinn, Director of Admissions, Western Connecticut State University, 181 White Street, Danbury, CT 06810-6885. Telephone: 203-837-9000.

YALE UNIVERSITY

NEW HAVEN, CONNECTICUT

General Independent, university, coed **Entrance** Most difficult **Setting** 200-acre urban campus **Total enrollment** 11,059 **Application deadline** 12/31 **Freshmen** 18% were admitted **Housing** Yes **Expenses** Tuition $23,100; Room & Board $6850 **Undergraduates** 49% women, 1% part-time, 1% 25 or older, 1% Native American, 6% Hispanic, 7% black, 16% Asian American or Pacific Islander **Most popular recent majors** Biology; history; economics **Academic program** English as a second language, advanced placement, accelerated degree program, self-designed majors, tutorials, honors program, summer session **Contact** Admissions Director, Yale University, PO Box 208234, New Haven, CT 06520-8324. Telephone: 203-432-9300. Fax: 203-432-9392. E-mail: undergraduate.admissions@yale.edu. Web site: http://www.yale.edu/.

DELAWARE

DELAWARE STATE UNIVERSITY

DOVER, DELAWARE

General State-supported, comprehensive, coed **Entrance** Moderately difficult **Setting** 400-acre small town campus **Total enrollment** 3,320 **Student/faculty ratio** 14:1 **Application deadline** 6/1 **Freshmen** 51% were admitted **Housing** Yes **Expenses** Tuition $2970; Room & Board $4862 **Undergraduates** 57% women, 21% part-time, 25% 25 or older **Most popular recent majors** Business administration; education; nursing **Academic program** English as a second language, advanced placement, accelerated degree program, self-designed majors, honors program, summer session, adult/continuing education programs, internships **Contact** Mr. Jethro C. Williams, Director of Admissions, Delaware State University, 1200 North DuPont Highway, Dover, DE 19901-2277. Telephone: 302-739-4917. Fax: 302-739-5309. Web site: http://www.dsu.edu/.

GOLDEY-BEACOM COLLEGE

WILMINGTON, DELAWARE

General Independent, comprehensive, coed **Entrance** Moderately difficult **Setting** 27-acre suburban campus **Total enrollment** 1,650 **Student/faculty ratio** 23:1 **Application deadline** Rolling **Freshmen** 77% were admitted **Housing** Yes **Expenses** Tuition $7200; Room only $3290 **Undergraduates** 43% 25 or older **Most popular recent majors** Business administration; accounting; information sciences/systems **Academic program** Average class size 28, advanced placement, accelerated degree program, tutorials, honors program, summer session, internships **Contact** Mr. Kevin McIntyre, Director of Admissions, Goldey-Beacom College, 4701 Limestone Road, Wilmington, DE 19808-1999. Telephone: 302-998-8814 ext. 266 or toll-free 800-833-4877. Fax: 302-996-5408. E-mail: mcintyrk@goldey.gbc.edu. Web site: http://www.goldey.gbc.edu/.

UNIVERSITY OF DELAWARE

NEWARK, DELAWARE

General State-related, university, coed **Entrance** Moderately difficult **Setting** 1,000-acre small town campus **Total enrollment** 18,230 **Student/faculty ratio** 15:1 **Application deadline** 3/1 **Freshmen** 65% were admitted **Housing** Yes **Expenses** Tuition $4574; Room & Board $4770 **Undergraduates** 7% 25 or older **Most popular recent majors** Elementary education; nursing; psychology **Academic program** English as a second language, advanced placement, accelerated degree program, self-designed majors, tutorials, honors program, summer session, adult/continuing education programs, internships **Contact** Mr. Fred Siegel, Associate Provost, Enrollment Services, University of Delaware, Newark, DE 19716. Telephone: 302-831-8123. Fax: 302-831-6905. E-mail: admissions@udel.edu. Web site: http://www.udel.edu/.

WESLEY COLLEGE
DOVER, DELAWARE

General Independent United Methodist, comprehensive, coed **Entrance** Moderately difficult **Setting** 20-acre small town campus **Total enrollment** 1,249 **Student/faculty ratio** 19:1 **Application deadline** Rolling **Freshmen** 88% were admitted **Housing** Yes **Expenses** Tuition $11,709; Room & Board $5019 **Undergraduates** 53% women, 28% part-time, 13% 25 or older, 0.3% Native American, 1% Hispanic, 16% black, 2% Asian American or Pacific Islander **Most Popular Recent Majors** Business administration; accounting; elementary education **Academic program** Average class size 19, English as a second language, advanced placement, accelerated degree program, tutorials, summer session, adult/continuing education programs, internships **Contact** Mr. Brian D. Best, Director of Admissions, Wesley College, 120 North State Street, Dover, DE 19901-3875. Telephone: 302-736-2428 or toll-free 800-937-5398 (out-of-state). Fax: 302-736-2301. E-mail: admissions@mail.wesley.edu. Web site: http://www.wesley.edu/.

WILMINGTON COLLEGE
NEW CASTLE, DELAWARE

General Independent, comprehensive, coed **Entrance** Noncompetitive **Setting** 13-acre suburban campus **Total enrollment** 4,155 **Student/faculty ratio** 22:1 **Application deadline** Rolling **Housing** No **Expenses** Tuition $5750 **Undergraduates** 60% 25 or older **Academic program** Accelerated degree program, tutorials, summer session, adult/continuing education programs, internships **Contact** Ms. Joanne Ciofettelli, Assistant Director of Admissions, Wilmington College, 320 DuPont Highway, New Castle, DE 19720-6491. Telephone: 302-328-9407 ext. 104. Fax: 302-328-5902.

DISTRICT OF COLUMBIA

AMERICAN UNIVERSITY
WASHINGTON, DISTRICT OF COLUMBIA

General Independent Methodist, university, coed **Entrance** Moderately difficult **Setting** 77-acre suburban campus **Total enrollment** 10,710 **Student/faculty ratio** 14:1 **Application deadline** 2/1 **Freshmen** 79% were admitted **Housing** Yes **Expenses** Tuition $18,555; Room & Board $7250 **Undergraduates** 59% women, 9% part-time, 7% 25 or older, 0.4% Native American, 6% Hispanic, 8% black, 4% Asian American or Pacific Islander **Most popular recent majors** International relations; mass communications; political science **Academic program** Average class size 31, English as a second language, advanced placement, self-designed majors, honors program, summer session, adult/continuing education programs, internships **Contact** Mr. Stephen Pultz, Director of Admissions, American University, 4400 Massachusetts Avenue, NW, Washington, DC 20016-8001. Telephone: 202-885-6000. Fax: 202-885-6014. E-mail: afa@american.edu. Web site: http://www.american.edu/.

THE CATHOLIC UNIVERSITY OF AMERICA
WASHINGTON, DISTRICT OF COLUMBIA

General Independent, university, coed, affiliated with Roman Catholic Church **Entrance** Moderately difficult **Setting** 144-acre urban campus **Total enrollment** 5,616 **Student/faculty ratio** 10:1 **Application deadline** 2/15 **Freshmen** 69% were admitted **Housing** Yes **Expenses** Tuition $17,110; Room & Board $7036 **Undergraduates** 55% women, 9% part-time, 14% 25 or older, 0.4% Native American, 5% Hispanic, 11% black, 5% Asian American or Pacific Islander **Most popular recent majors** Architecture; engineering; political science **Academic program** English as a second language, advanced placement, accelerated degree program, self-designed majors, tutorials, honors program, summer session, adult/continuing education programs, internships **Contact** Ms. Katherine S. Lafrance, Dean of Admissions and Financial Aid, The Catholic University of America, Cardinal Station Post Office, Washington, DC 20064. Telephone: 202-319-5305 or toll-free 800-673-2772 (out-of-state). Fax: 202-319-6533. E-mail: cua-admissions@cua.edu. Web site: http://www.cua.edu/.

▶ **For more information, see page 406.**

THE CORCORAN SCHOOL OF ART
WASHINGTON, DISTRICT OF COLUMBIA

General Independent, 4-year, coed **Entrance** Moderately difficult **Setting** 7-acre urban campus **Total enrollment** 380 **Application deadline** Rolling **Freshmen** 54% were admitted **Housing** No **Expenses** Tuition $12,800 **Undergraduates** 56% women, 2% part-time, 28% 25 or older, 1% Native American, 7% Hispanic, 8% black, 9% Asian American or Pacific Islander **Most popular recent majors** Art; graphic design/commercial art/illustration; photography **Academic program** Advanced placement, tutorials, summer session, adult/continuing education programs, internships **Contact** Mr. Raheel Masood, Director of Admissions, The Corcoran School of Art, 500 17th Street, NW, Washington, DC 20006-4804. Telephone: 202-639-1811. E-mail: admofc@aol.com. Web site: http://www.corcoran.edu/.

GALLAUDET UNIVERSITY
WASHINGTON, DISTRICT OF COLUMBIA

General Independent, university, coed **Entrance** Moderately difficult **Setting** 99-acre urban campus **Total enrollment** 1,697 **Application deadline** 5/15 **Freshmen** 75% were admitted **Housing** Yes **Expenses** Tuition $6283; Room & Board $6709 **Undergraduates** 20% 25 or older, 1% Native American, 6% Hispanic, 11% black, 4% Asian American or Pacific Islander **Most Popular Recent Majors** Psychology; business administration; biology **Academic program** English as a second language, advanced placement, accelerated degree program, honors program, summer session, adult/continuing education programs, internships **Contact** Ms. Deborah E. DeStefano, Director of Admissions, Gallaudet University, 800 Florida Avenue, NE, Washington, DC 20002-3625. Telephone: 202-651-5750 or toll-free 800-995-0550 (out-of-state). Fax: 202-651-5774. E-mail: admissions@gallua.gallaudet.edu. Web site: http://www.gallaudet.edu/.

GEORGETOWN UNIVERSITY
WASHINGTON, DISTRICT OF COLUMBIA

General Independent Roman Catholic (Jesuit), university, coed **Entrance** Most difficult **Setting** 110-acre urban campus **Total enrollment** 12,532 **Student/faculty ratio** 11:1 **Application deadline** 1/10 **Freshmen** 21% were admitted **Housing** Yes **Expenses** Tuition $21,405; Room & Board $8091 **Undergraduates** 53% women, 3% part-time, 5% 25 or older, 0.3% Native American, 6% Hispanic, 6% black, 8% Asian American or Pacific Islander **Most popular recent majors** International relations; finance; political science **Academic program** Average class size 34, English as a second language, advanced placement, self-designed majors, tutorials, honors program, summer session, adult/continuing education programs, internships **Contact** Mr. Charles A. Deacon, Dean of Undergraduate Admissions, Georgetown University, 37th and O Street, NW, Washington, DC 20057. Telephone: 202-687-3600. Fax: 202-687-5084. E-mail: guadmiss@gunet.georgetown.edu. Web site: http://www.georgetown.edu/.

THE GEORGE WASHINGTON UNIVERSITY
WASHINGTON, DISTRICT OF COLUMBIA

General Independent, university, coed **Entrance** Very difficult **Setting** 36-acre urban campus **Total enrollment** 19,356 **Student/faculty ratio** 14:1 **Application deadline** 2/1 **Freshmen** 49% were admitted **Housing** Yes **Expenses** Tuition $21,360; Room & Board $7325 **Undergraduates** 54% women, 7% part-time, 7% 25 or older, 0.4% Native American, 4% Hispanic, 7% black, 10% Asian American or Pacific Islander **Most popular recent majors** International relations; biology; psychology **Academic program** Average class size 27, English as a second language, advanced placement, accelerated degree program, self-designed majors, tutorials, honors program, summer session, adult/continuing education programs, internships **Contact** Dr. Kathryn M. Napper, Director of Admission, The George Washington University, Office of Undergraduate Admissions, Washington, DC 20052. Telephone: 202-994-6040 or toll-free 800-447-3765. E-mail: gwadm@gwis2.circ.gwu.edu. Web site: http://www.gwu.edu/index.html.

HOWARD UNIVERSITY
WASHINGTON, DISTRICT OF COLUMBIA

General Independent, university, coed **Entrance** Moderately difficult **Setting** 242-acre urban campus **Total enrollment** 10,438 **Application deadline** 4/1 **Freshmen** 59% were admitted **Housing** Yes **Expenses** Tuition $8985; Room & Board $4162 **Undergraduates** 18% 25 or older **Most popular recent majors** Political science; psychology; radio/television broadcasting **Academic program** Advanced placement, tutorials, honors program, summer session, adult/continuing education programs, internships **Contact** Mr. Avon Dennis, Director of Admissions, Howard University, 2400 Sixth Street, NW, Washington, DC 20059-0002. Telephone: 202-806-2750.

MOUNT VERNON COLLEGE
WASHINGTON, DISTRICT OF COLUMBIA

General Independent, comprehensive, women only **Contact** Ms. Susan Knight, Director of Admissions, Mount Vernon College, 2100 Foxhall Road, NW, Washington, DC 20007. Telephone: 202-625-4682 or toll-free 800-682-4636 (out-of-state). Web site: http://www.mvc.edu/.

POTOMAC COLLEGE
WASHINGTON, DISTRICT OF COLUMBIA

General Proprietary, 4-year, coed **Entrance** Noncompetitive **Setting** Urban campus **Total enrollment** 248 **Application deadline** Rolling **Housing** No **Expenses** Tuition $7290 **Undergraduates** 62% women, 36% part-time, 98% 25 or older, 0% Native American, 3% Hispanic, 45% black, 2% Asian American or Pacific Islander **Most Popular Recent Major** Computer management **Academic program** Average class size 10, advanced placement, accelerated degree program, tutorials, summer session, adult/continuing education programs, internships **Contact** Office of Admissions, Potomac College, PO Box 40398, Washington, DC

20016-0398. Telephone: 202-686-0876 or toll-free 888-686-0876. Fax: 202-686-0818.

SOUTHEASTERN UNIVERSITY

WASHINGTON, DISTRICT OF COLUMBIA

General Independent, comprehensive, coed **Entrance** Noncompetitive **Setting** 1-acre urban campus **Total enrollment** 806 **Application deadline** Rolling **Housing** No **Expenses** Tuition $5900 **Undergraduates** 50% 25 or older **Most popular recent majors** Business administration; accounting **Academic program** Average class size 18, English as a second language, advanced placement, accelerated degree program, tutorials, honors program, summer session, adult/continuing education programs, internships **Contact** Mr. Jack Flinter, Director of Admissions, Southeastern University, 501 I Street, SW, Washington, DC 20024-2788. Telephone: 202-265-5343 ext. 211. Fax: 202-488-8162. E-mail: jackf@admin.seu.edu. Web site: http://www.seu.edu/.

STRAYER UNIVERSITY

WASHINGTON, DISTRICT OF COLUMBIA

General Proprietary, comprehensive, coed **Entrance** Minimally difficult **Setting** Urban campus **Total enrollment** 9,419 **Student/faculty ratio** 20:1 **Application deadline** Rolling **Housing** No **Expenses** Tuition $8100 **Undergraduates** 59% women, 70% part-time, 80% 25 or older, 0.4% Native American, 5% Hispanic, 41% black, 5% Asian American or Pacific Islander **Most popular recent majors** Information sciences/systems; business administration; accounting **Academic program** Average class size 30, advanced placement, accelerated degree program, summer session, adult/continuing education programs, internships **Contact** Mr. Michael Williams, Campus Coordinator, Strayer University, 1025 15th Street, NW, Washington, DC 20005. Telephone: 202-408-2400. Fax: 202-289-1831. E-mail: mw@net.strayer.edu. Web site: http://www.strayer.edu/.

TRINITY COLLEGE

WASHINGTON, DISTRICT OF COLUMBIA

General Independent Roman Catholic, comprehensive, women only **Entrance** Moderately difficult **Setting** 26-acre urban campus **Total enrollment** 1,489 **Application deadline** 3/1 **Housing** Yes **Expenses** Tuition $12,490; Room & Board $3530 **Undergraduates** 52% part-time, 49% 25 or older, 0.5% Native American, 6% Hispanic, 51% black, 3% Asian American or Pacific Islander **Most popular recent majors** Business administration; political science; psychology **Academic program** Average class size 17, English as a second language, advanced placement, accelerated degree program, self-designed majors, tutorials, summer session, adult/continuing education programs, internships **Contact** Ms. Margaret Artley, Director of Admissions, Trinity College, 125 Michigan Avenue, NE, Washington, DC 20017-1094. Telephone: 202-884-9400. Fax: 202-884-9229. Web site: http://www.consortium.org/~trinity/.

UNIVERSITY OF THE DISTRICT OF COLUMBIA

WASHINGTON, DISTRICT OF COLUMBIA

General District-supported, comprehensive, coed **Entrance** Noncompetitive **Setting** 28-acre urban campus **Total enrollment** 4,754 **Application deadline** 8/1 **Housing** No **Expenses** Tuition $2360 **Undergraduates** 56% 25 or older **Academic program** English as a second language, accelerated degree program, honors program, summer session, adult/continuing education programs, internships **Contact** Dr. Laverne Blagmon-Earl, Director of Admissions, University of the District of Columbia, 4200 Connecticut Avenue, NW, Washington, DC 20008-1175. Telephone: 202-274-5153.

FLORIDA

BARRY UNIVERSITY

MIAMI SHORES, FLORIDA

General Independent Roman Catholic, comprehensive, coed **Entrance** Moderately difficult **Setting** 122-acre suburban campus **Total enrollment** 6,899 **Student/faculty ratio** 11:1 **Application deadline** Rolling **Freshmen** 49% were admitted **Housing** Yes **Expenses** Tuition $13,550; Room & Board $5850 **Undergraduates** 66% women, 62% part-time, 61% 25 or older, 0.2% Native American, 33% Hispanic, 14% black, 1% Asian American or Pacific Islander **Most popular recent majors** Nursing; education; biology **Academic program** Average class size 17, English as a second language, advanced placement, accelerated degree program, tutorials, honors program, summer session, adult/continuing education programs, internships **Contact** Mr. David Poole, Director of Admissions, Barry University, 11300 Northeast Second Avenue, Miami Shores, FL 33161-6695. Telephone: 305-899-3114 or toll-free 800-695-2279. Fax: 305-899-2971. E-mail: admissions@jeanne.barry.edu. Web site: http://www.barry.edu/.

BETHUNE-COOKMAN COLLEGE

DAYTONA BEACH, FLORIDA

General Independent Methodist, 4-year, coed **Entrance** Minimally difficult **Setting** 60-acre urban

Bethune-Cookman College *(continued)*

campus **Total enrollment** 2,523 **Student/faculty ratio** 17:1 **Application deadline** 7/30 **Freshmen** 72% were admitted **Housing** Yes **Expenses** Tuition $8047; Room & Board $4984 **Undergraduates** 57% women, 7% part-time, 14% 25 or older, 1% Hispanic, 94% black, 0.1% Asian American or Pacific Islander **Most popular recent majors** Business administration; elementary education; criminal justice/law enforcement administration **Academic program** Average class size 25, advanced placement, accelerated degree program, honors program, summer session, adult/continuing education programs, internships **Contact** Mr. William Byrd, Assistant Vice President for Enrollment Management, Bethune-Cookman College, 640 Dr. Mary McLeod Bethune Blvd, Daytona Beach, FL 32114-3099. Telephone: 904-255-1401 ext. 333 or toll-free 800-448-0228. Fax: 904-257-5338. E-mail: wilsonf8@cookman.edu. Web site: http://www.bethune.cookman.edu/.

CARIBBEAN CENTER FOR ADVANCED STUDIES/MIAMI INSTITUTE OF PSYCHOLOGY
MIAMI, FLORIDA

General Independent, upper-level, coed **Entrance** Difficulty N/R **Setting** 2-acre urban campus **Total enrollment** 600 **Application deadline** Rolling **Freshmen** 100% were admitted **Housing** No **Expenses** Tuition $5934 **Undergraduates** 70% 25 or older **Academic program** Average class size 6, advanced placement, summer session, adult/continuing education programs **Contact** Ms. Zoraida Seguinot, Recruitment and Outreach, Caribbean Center for Advanced Studies/Miami Institute of Psychology, 8180 NW 36th Street, 2nd Floor, Miami, FL 33166-6653. Telephone: 305-593-1223 ext. 136 or toll-free 800-672-3246. E-mail: zsequinot@mip.edu.

CLEARWATER CHRISTIAN COLLEGE
CLEARWATER, FLORIDA

General Independent nondenominational, 4-year, coed **Entrance** Minimally difficult **Setting** 50-acre suburban campus **Total enrollment** 603 **Student/faculty ratio** 17:1 **Application deadline** 7/15 **Freshmen** 96% were admitted **Housing** Yes **Expenses** Tuition $7580; Room & Board $3500 **Undergraduates** 53% women, 4% part-time, 0.2% Native American, 4% Hispanic, 3% black, 0.3% Asian American or Pacific Islander **Academic program** Advanced placement, summer session, internships **Contact** Mr. Benjamin J. Puckett, Director of Admissions, Clearwater Christian College, 3400 Gulf-to-Bay Boulevard, Clearwater, FL 33759-4595. Telephone: 813-726-1153 ext. 222 or toll-free 800-348-4463. Fax: 813-726-8597. E-mail: admissions@clearwater.edu. Web site: http://www.clearwater.edu/.

ECKERD COLLEGE
ST. PETERSBURG, FLORIDA

General Independent Presbyterian, 4-year, coed **Entrance** Moderately difficult **Setting** 267-acre suburban campus **Total enrollment** 1,443 **Student/faculty ratio** 14:1 **Application deadline** Rolling **Freshmen** 76% were admitted **Housing** Yes **Expenses** Tuition $17,130; Room & Board $4660 **Undergraduates** 57% women, 1% part-time, 5% 25 or older, 0.3% Native American, 3% Hispanic, 3% black, 1% Asian American or Pacific Islander **Most popular recent majors** Marine biology; international business; business administration **Academic program** Average class size 25, English as a second language, advanced placement, accelerated degree program, self-designed majors, tutorials, honors program, summer session, adult/continuing education programs, internships **Contact** Dr. Richard R. Hallin, Dean of Admissions, Eckerd College, 4200 54th Avenue South, St. Petersburg, FL 33711. Telephone: 813-864-8331 or toll-free 800-456-9009. Fax: 813-866-2304. E-mail: admissions@eckerd.edu. Web site: http://www.eckerd.edu/.

EDWARD WATERS COLLEGE
JACKSONVILLE, FLORIDA

General Independent African Methodist Episcopal, 4-year, coed **Entrance** Noncompetitive **Setting** 20-acre urban campus **Total enrollment** 516 **Student/faculty ratio** 13:1 **Application deadline** Rolling **Housing** Yes **Expenses** Tuition $5760; Room & Board $4300 **Most Popular Recent Major** Business administration **Academic program** Self-designed majors, tutorials, honors program, summer session, adult/continuing education programs, internships **Contact** Mr. Richard F. Pride, Edward Waters College, 1658 Kings Road, Jacksonville, FL 32209-6199. Telephone: 904-366-2715.

EMBRY-RIDDLE AERONAUTICAL UNIVERSITY
DAYTONA BEACH, FLORIDA

General Independent, comprehensive, coed **Entrance** Moderately difficult **Setting** 164-acre urban campus **Total enrollment** 4,586 **Student/faculty ratio** 17:1 **Application deadline** 3/1 **Freshmen** 85% were admitted **Housing** Yes **Expenses** Tuition $9890; Room & Board $4600 **Undergraduates** 14% women, 10% part-time, 16% 25 or older, 0.4% Native American, 7% Hispanic, 5% black, 3% Asian American or Pacific Islander

Most popular recent majors Aircraft pilot (professional); aviation/airway science; aerospace engineering **Academic program** Average class size 28, English as a second language, advanced placement, tutorials, summer session, adult/continuing education programs, internships **Contact** Ms. Carol Cotman Hogan, Director of Admissions, Embry-Riddle Aeronautical University, 600 South Clyde Morris Boulevard, Daytona Beach, FL 32114-3900. Telephone: 904-226-6112 or toll-free 800-222-ERAU. Fax: 904-226-7070. E-mail: admit@db.erau.edu. Web site: http://www.db.erau.edu/.

► **For more information, see page 429.**

EMBRY-RIDDLE AERONAUTICAL UNIVERSITY, EXTENDED CAMPUS
DAYTONA BEACH, FLORIDA

General Independent, comprehensive, coed **Entrance** Minimally difficult **Total enrollment** 6,623 **Application deadline** Rolling **Housing** No **Expenses** Tuition $1590 **Undergraduates** 1% Native American, 6% Hispanic, 7% black, 3% Asian American or Pacific Islander **Most popular recent majors** Aviation/airway science; business administration; aviation management **Academic program** Average class size 10, advanced placement, adult/continuing education programs **Contact** Mrs. Pam Thomas, Director of Admissions, Records and Registration, Embry-Riddle Aeronautical University, Extended Campus, 600 South Clyde Morris Boulevard, Daytona Beach, FL 32114-3900. Telephone: 904-226-7610 or toll-free 800-522-6787. Fax: 904-226-6984. E-mail: ecinfo@ec.db.erau.edu. Web site: http://ec.db.erau.edu/.

FLAGLER COLLEGE
ST. AUGUSTINE, FLORIDA

General Independent, 4-year, coed **Entrance** Moderately difficult **Setting** 36-acre small town campus **Total enrollment** 1,655 **Student/faculty ratio** 21:1 **Application deadline** 3/1 **Freshmen** 47% were admitted **Housing** Yes **Expenses** Tuition $5950; Room & Board $3680 **Undergraduates** 63% women, 2% part-time, 7% 25 or older, 0.2% Native American, 3% Hispanic, 1% black, 0.5% Asian American or Pacific Islander **Most popular recent majors** Elementary education; business administration; mass communications **Academic program** Average class size 24, advanced placement, tutorials, summer session, internships **Contact** Mr. Marc G. Williar, Director of Admissions, Flagler College, PO Box 1027, St. Augustine, FL 32085-1027. Telephone: 904-829-6481 ext. 220 or toll-free 800-304-4208. Fax: 904-826-0094. E-mail: admiss@flagler.edu. Web site: http://www.flagler.edu/.

FLORIDA AGRICULTURAL AND MECHANICAL UNIVERSITY
TALLAHASSEE, FLORIDA

General State-supported, university, coed **Entrance** Moderately difficult **Setting** 419-acre urban campus **Total enrollment** 10,991 **Student/faculty ratio** 16:1 **Application deadline** 5/1 **Housing** Yes **Expenses** Tuition $2105; Room & Board $3198 **Undergraduates** 56% women, 14% part-time, 18% 25 or older **Most popular recent majors** Education; pharmacy; business administration **Academic program** Average class size 23, advanced placement, accelerated degree program, honors program, summer session, adult/continuing education programs, internships **Contact** Ms. Barbara R. Cox, Director of Admissions, Florida Agricultural and Mechanical University, Office of Admissions, Tallahassee, FL 32307. Telephone: 850-599-3796. Fax: 850-561-2428. E-mail: bcox@ns1.famu.edu. Web site: http://www.famu.edu/.

FLORIDA ATLANTIC UNIVERSITY
BOCA RATON, FLORIDA

General State-supported, university, coed **Entrance** Moderately difficult **Setting** 850-acre suburban campus **Total enrollment** 18,823 **Student/faculty ratio** 15:1 **Application deadline** Rolling **Freshmen** 70% were admitted **Housing** Yes **Expenses** Tuition $2022; Room & Board $4680 **Undergraduates** 59% women, 43% part-time, 55% 25 or older, 0.4% Native American, 11% Hispanic, 13% black, 4% Asian American or Pacific Islander **Most popular recent majors** Elementary education; biology; accounting **Academic program** English as a second language, advanced placement, accelerated degree program, self-designed majors, honors program, summer session, adult/continuing education programs, internships **Contact** Mr. Richard Griffin, Director of Admissions, Florida Atlantic University, 777 Glades Road, PO Box 3091, Boca Raton, FL 33431-0991. Telephone: 561-297-3040 ext. 3031 or toll-free 800-299-4FAU. Fax: 561-297-2758. Web site: http://www.fau.edu/.

FLORIDA BAPTIST THEOLOGICAL COLLEGE
GRACEVILLE, FLORIDA

General Independent Southern Baptist, 4-year, coed **Entrance** Noncompetitive **Setting** 150-acre small town campus **Total enrollment** 486 **Application deadline** Rolling **Freshmen** 100% were admitted **Housing** Yes **Expenses** Tuition $2934; Room only $1500 **Undergraduates** 28% women, 13% part-time, 41% 25 or older, 0.2% Native American, 2% Hispanic, 3% black, 0.4% Asian American or Pacific Islander **Most popular recent majors**

Florida Baptist Theological College *(continued)*

Theology; religious education; sacred music **Academic program** Advanced placement, accelerated degree program, summer session, adult/continuing education programs, internships **Contact** Mr. O. Lavan Wilson, Director of Admissions, Florida Baptist Theological College, PO Box 1306, Graceville, FL 32440-3306. Telephone: 850-263-3261 ext. 462 or toll-free 800-328-2660. Fax: 850-263-7506. Web site: http://www.fbtc.edu/.

FLORIDA CHRISTIAN COLLEGE
KISSIMMEE, FLORIDA

General Independent, 4-year, coed, affiliated with Christian Churches and Churches of Christ **Entrance** Minimally difficult **Setting** 40-acre small town campus **Total enrollment** 179 **Student/faculty ratio** 14:1 **Application deadline** 7/15 **Housing** Yes **Expenses** Tuition $5174; Room only $1240 **Undergraduates** 49% women, 19% part-time, 27% 25 or older, 0% Native American, 2% Hispanic, 2% black, 1% Asian American or Pacific Islander **Academic program** Advanced placement, summer session, adult/continuing education programs, internships **Contact** Mr. Terry Davis, Admissions Director, Florida Christian College, 1011 Bill Beck Boulevard, Kissimmee, FL 34744-5301. Telephone: 407-847-8966 ext. 364. Fax: 407-847-3925.

FLORIDA COLLEGE
TEMPLE TERRACE, FLORIDA

General Independent, 4-year, coed **Entrance** Moderately difficult **Setting** 95-acre small town campus **Total enrollment** 396 **Student/faculty ratio** 12:1 **Application deadline** 8/1 **Housing** Yes **Expenses** Tuition $6390; Room & Board $3690 **Undergraduates** 52% women, 1% part-time, 3% 25 or older, 1% Native American, 4% Hispanic, 3% black, 1% Asian American or Pacific Islander **Academic program** Advanced placement, tutorials **Contact** Mrs. Mari Smith, Admissions Officer, Florida College, 119 North Glen Arven Avenue, Temple Terrace, FL 33617. Telephone: 813-988-5131 ext. 6716 or toll-free 800-326-7655. Fax: 813-899-6772. E-mail: admissions@flcoll.edu. Web site: http://www.flcoll.edu/.

FLORIDA GULF COAST UNIVERSITY
FORT MYERS, FLORIDA

General State-supported, comprehensive, coed **Entrance** Difficulty N/R **Setting** 765-acre suburban campus **Total enrollment** 2,601 **Freshmen** 57% were admitted **Housing** Yes **Expenses** Tuition $1656; Room only $3200 **Undergraduates** 72% women, 50% part-time, 62% 25 or older, 0.3% Native American, 7% Hispanic, 4% black, 2% Asian American or Pacific Islander **Academic program** Advanced placement, accelerated degree program, tutorials, honors program, summer session, adult/continuing education programs, internships **Contact** Ms. Michele Yovanovich, Florida Gulf Coast University, 10501 FGCU Boulevard South, Fort Myers, FL 33965-6565. Telephone: 941-590-7878 or toll-free 888-889-1015. Fax: 941-590-7894. Web site: http://www.fgcu.edu/.

FLORIDA INSTITUTE OF TECHNOLOGY
MELBOURNE, FLORIDA

General Independent, university, coed **Entrance** Moderately difficult **Setting** 175-acre small town campus **Total enrollment** 4,135 **Student/faculty ratio** 12:1 **Application deadline** Rolling **Freshmen** 85% were admitted **Housing** Yes **Expenses** Tuition $15,550; Room & Board $4640 **Undergraduates** 32% women, 8% part-time, 13% 25 or older, 0.2% Native American, 6% Hispanic, 4% black, 2% Asian American or Pacific Islander **Most popular recent majors** Aircraft pilot (professional); business administration; electrical/electronics engineering **Academic program** Average class size 14, English as a second language, advanced placement, accelerated degree program, tutorials, summer session, adult/continuing education programs, internships **Contact** Ms. Judi Marino, Director of Undergraduate Admissions, Florida Institute of Technology, 150 West University Boulevard, Melbourne, FL 32901-6975. Telephone: 407-674-8030 or toll-free 800-348-4636 (in-state), 800-888-4348 (out-of-state). Fax: 407-723-9468. E-mail: admissions@fit.edu. Web site: http://www.fit.edu/.

▶ **For more information, see page 437.**

FLORIDA INTERNATIONAL UNIVERSITY
MIAMI, FLORIDA

General State-supported, university, coed **Entrance** Moderately difficult **Setting** 573-acre urban campus **Total enrollment** 30,012 **Student/faculty ratio** 14:1 **Application deadline** Rolling **Freshmen** 75% were admitted **Housing** Yes **Expenses** Tuition $2035; Room & Board $7378 **Undergraduates** 56% women, 44% part-time, 32% 25 or older, 0.1% Native American, 53% Hispanic, 15% black, 3% Asian American or Pacific Islander **Most popular recent majors** Psychology; biology; accounting **Academic program** English as a second language, advanced placement, accelerated degree program, tutorials, honors program, summer session, adult/continuing education programs, internships **Contact** Ms. Carmen Brown, Director of Admissions, Florida International University, University Park, Miami, FL 33199. Telephone: 305-348-3675. Fax: 305-348-3648. E-mail: admiss@servms.fiu.edu. Web site: http://www.fiu.edu/.

FLORIDA MEMORIAL COLLEGE
MIAMI, FLORIDA

General Independent, 4-year, coed, affiliated with Baptist Church **Contact** Mrs. Peggy Kelley, Director of Admissions and International Student Advisor, Florida Memorial College, 15800 NW 42nd Avenue, Miami, FL 33054. Telephone: 305-626-3750 or toll-free 800-822-1362.

FLORIDA METROPOLITAN UNIVERSITY–FORT LAUDERDALE COLLEGE
FORT LAUDERDALE, FLORIDA

General Proprietary, comprehensive, coed **Entrance** Minimally difficult **Setting** Suburban campus **Total enrollment** 500 **Student/faculty ratio** 20:1 **Application deadline** Rolling **Housing** No **Expenses** Tuition $5835 **Undergraduates** 25% 25 or older **Most popular recent majors** Accounting; paralegal/legal assistant; computer programming **Academic program** English as a second language, advanced placement, accelerated degree program, tutorials, summer session, adult/continuing education programs, internships **Contact** Mr. Tony Wallace, Director of Admissions, Florida Metropolitan University–Fort Lauderdale College, 1040 Bayview Drive, Fort Lauderdale, FL 33304-2522. Telephone: 954-568-1600 or toll-free 800-468-0168. Fax: 954-568-2008.

FLORIDA METROPOLITAN UNIVERSITY–ORLANDO COLLEGE, MELBOURNE
MELBOURNE, FLORIDA

General Proprietary, 4-year, coed **Contact** Ms. Teresa Stinson-Kumar, Director of Admissions, Florida Metropolitan University–Orlando College, Melbourne, 2401 North Harbor City Boulevard, Melbourne, FL 32935-6657. Telephone: 407-253-2929. Fax: 407-255-2017.

FLORIDA METROPOLITAN UNIVERSITY–ORLANDO COLLEGE, NORTH
ORLANDO, FLORIDA

General Proprietary, comprehensive, coed **Contact** Ms. Shana Dyer, Director of Admissions, Florida Metropolitan University–Orlando College, North, 5421 Diplomat Circle, Orlando, FL 32810-5674. Telephone: 407-628-5870 ext. 12 or toll-free 800-628-5870. Fax: 407-628-2616.

FLORIDA METROPOLITAN UNIVERSITY–ORLANDO COLLEGE, SOUTH
ORLANDO, FLORIDA

Contact Florida Metropolitan University–Orlando College, South, 2411 Sand Lake Road, Orlando, FL 32809. Telephone: 407-851-2525. Fax: 407-851-1477.

FLORIDA METROPOLITAN UNIVERSITY–TAMPA COLLEGE
TAMPA, FLORIDA

General Proprietary, comprehensive, coed **Entrance** Minimally difficult **Setting** 4-acre urban campus **Total enrollment** 981 **Student/faculty ratio** 30:1 **Application deadline** Rolling **Freshmen** 87% were admitted **Housing** No **Expenses** Tuition $5475 **Undergraduates** 64% women, 46% 25 or older **Most popular recent majors** Business administration; business marketing and marketing management; accounting **Academic program** English as a second language, advanced placement, accelerated degree program, self-designed majors, summer session, adult/continuing education programs, internships **Contact** Mr. Foster Thomas, Admissions Coordinator, Florida Metropolitan University–Tampa College, 3319 West Hillsborough Avenue, Tampa, FL 33614-5899. Telephone: 813-879-6000. Fax: 813-871-2483.

FLORIDA METROPOLITAN UNIVERSITY–TAMPA COLLEGE, BRANDON
TAMPA, FLORIDA

General Proprietary, comprehensive **Contact** Admissions, Florida Metropolitan University–Tampa College, Brandon, 3924 Coconut Palm Drive, Tampa, FL 33619. Telephone: 813-621-0041.

FLORIDA METROPOLITAN UNIVERSITY–TAMPA COLLEGE, LAKELAND
LAKELAND, FLORIDA

General Proprietary, comprehensive, coed **Entrance** Minimally difficult **Setting** Suburban campus **Total enrollment** 536 **Freshmen** 95% were admitted **Housing** No **Expenses** Tuition $5220 **Undergraduates** 56% 25 or older **Most popular recent majors** Paralegal/legal assistant; computer science; accounting **Academic program** Advanced placement, tutorials, summer session, adult/continuing education programs, internships **Contact** Ms. Diana Simmons, Director of Admissions, Florida Metropolitan University–Tampa College, Lakeland, 995 East Memorial Boulevard, Suite 110, Lakeland, FL 33801. Telephone: 941-686-1444. Fax: 941-688-9881.

FLORIDA METROPOLITAN UNIVERSITY–TAMPA COLLEGE, PINELLAS
CLEARWATER, FLORIDA

General Proprietary, comprehensive, coed **Entrance** Minimally difficult **Setting** 3-acre urban campus **Total enrollment** 929 **Student/faculty ratio** 26:1 **Application deadline** Rolling **Freshmen** 94% were admitted **Housing** No **Expenses** Tuition $5835 **Undergraduates** 61% women, 21% part-time, 88% 25 or older, 1% Native American, 6% Hispanic, 10% black, 5% Asian American or Pacific Islander **Most popular recent majors** Business; accounting **Academic program** Average class size 28, advanced placement, accelerated degree program, tutorials, honors program, summer session, adult/continuing education programs, internships **Contact** Mr. Wayne Childers, Director of Admissions, Florida Metropolitan University–Tampa College, Pinellas, 2471 McMullen Booth Road, Suite 200, Clearwater, FL 33759. Telephone: 813-725-2688 ext. 702. Fax: 813-796-3722. E-mail: wchilder@cci.edu.

FLORIDA SOUTHERN COLLEGE
LAKELAND, FLORIDA

General Independent, comprehensive, coed, affiliated with United Methodist Church **Entrance** Moderately difficult **Setting** 100-acre suburban campus **Total enrollment** 1,775 **Student/faculty ratio** 17:1 **Application deadline** 8/1 **Freshmen** 76% were admitted **Housing** Yes **Expenses** Tuition $10,604; Room & Board $5430 **Undergraduates** 59% women, 4% part-time, 5% 25 or older, 0.2% Native American, 4% Hispanic, 5% black, 1% Asian American or Pacific Islander **Most popular recent majors** Business administration; education; biology **Academic program** Average class size 27, English as a second language, advanced placement, summer session, adult/continuing education programs, internships **Contact** Mr. Peter Freyberg, Director of Admissions, Florida Southern College, 111 Lake Hollingsworth Drive, Lakeland, FL 33801-5698. Telephone: 941-680-3912 or toll-free 800-274-4131. Fax: 941-680-4120. E-mail: fscadm@cris.com. Web site: http://www.flsouthern.edu/.

FLORIDA STATE UNIVERSITY
TALLAHASSEE, FLORIDA

General State-supported, university, coed **Entrance** Very difficult **Setting** 456-acre suburban campus **Total enrollment** 30,401 **Application deadline** 3/2 **Freshmen** 72% were admitted **Housing** Yes **Expenses** Tuition $1988; Room & Board $4570 **Undergraduates** 55% women, 11% part-time, 13% 25 or older, 0.4% Native American, 7% Hispanic, 12% black, 2% Asian American or Pacific Islander **Most popular recent majors** Biology; criminology; psychology **Academic program** English as a second language, advanced placement, accelerated degree program, tutorials, honors program, summer session, adult/continuing education programs, internships **Contact** Office of Admissions, Florida State University, Tallahassee, FL 32306-2400. Telephone: 850-644-6200. Fax: 850-644-0197. E-mail: admissions@admin.fsu.edu. Web site: http://www.fsu.edu/.

THE HARID CONSERVATORY
BOCA RATON, FLORIDA

General Independent, comprehensive, coed **Entrance** Most difficult **Setting** 5-acre suburban campus **Total enrollment** 61 **Student/faculty ratio** 2:1 **Application deadline** 3/31 **Housing** No **Expenses** Tuition $0 **Undergraduates** 44% women, 4% 25 or older **Academic program** Average class size 15, English as a second language, advanced placement, tutorials **Contact** Ms. Chantal Prosperi, Administrative Assistant/Admissions, The Harid Conservatory, 2285 Potomac Road, Boca Raton, FL 33431-5518. Telephone: 561-997-2677 ext. 62. Fax: 561-997-8920.

HOBE SOUND BIBLE COLLEGE
HOBE SOUND, FLORIDA

General Independent nondenominational, 4-year, coed **Entrance** Noncompetitive **Setting** 84-acre small town campus **Total enrollment** 113 **Student/faculty ratio** 7:1 **Application deadline** Rolling **Freshmen** 94% were admitted **Housing** Yes **Expenses** Tuition $4140; Room & Board $2850 **Undergraduates** 56% women, 17% part-time, 13% 25 or older, 1% Native American, 0% Hispanic, 0% black, 0% Asian American or Pacific Islander **Most popular recent majors** Divinity/ministry; elementary education; biblical studies **Academic program** Average class size 20, English as a second language, advanced placement, summer session, internships **Contact** Mrs. Ann French, Director of Admissions, Hobe Sound Bible College, PO Box 1065, Hobe Sound, FL 33475-1065. Telephone: 561-546-5534 ext. 415 or toll-free 800-881-5534. Fax: 561-545-1422. E-mail: hsbcuwin@aol.com.

INTERNATIONAL ACADEMY OF MERCHANDISING & DESIGN, INC.
TAMPA, FLORIDA

General Proprietary, 4-year, coed **Entrance** Noncompetitive **Setting** 1-acre urban campus **Total enrollment** 500 **Student/faculty ratio** 12:1 **Application deadline** Rolling **Housing** No **Expenses** Tuition $10,785 **Undergraduates** 60% 25 or older **Most Popular Recent Major** Interior design **Academic program** Advanced placement, accelerated degree program, summer session, adult/continuing education programs, internships **Contact** Mr. F. Michael Santoro, President, International Academy of Merchandising & Design, Inc., 5225 Memorial Highway, Tampa, FL 33634-7350. Telephone: 813-881-0007 or toll-free 800-ACADEMY. Fax: 813-881-0008. Web site: http://www.academy.edu/.

INTERNATIONAL COLLEGE
NAPLES, FLORIDA

General Independent, 4-year, coed **Entrance** Minimally difficult **Setting** Suburban campus **Total enrollment** 592 **Student/faculty ratio** 15:1 **Application deadline** Rolling **Freshmen** 69% were admitted **Housing** No **Expenses** Tuition $7770 **Undergraduates** 77% women, 55% part-time, 77% 25 or older, 2% Native American, 7% Hispanic, 12% black, 1% Asian American or Pacific Islander **Academic program** Average class size 18, English as a second language, advanced placement, accelerated degree program, tutorials, summer session, adult/continuing education programs, internships **Contact** Ms. Bunty Cantwell, Director of Enrollment Management, International College, 2654 Tamiami Trail East, Naples, FL 34112. Telephone: 941-774-4700 or toll-free 800-466-8017. Fax: 941-774-4593. E-mail: admit@naples.net. Web site: http://www.internationalcollege.edu/.

ITT TECHNICAL INSTITUTE
MAITLAND, FLORIDA

Contact Mr. Dan Canfield, Director of Recruitment, ITT Technical Institute, 2600 Lake Lucien Drive, Suite 140, Maitland, FL 32751-7234. Telephone: 407-660-2900.

JACKSONVILLE UNIVERSITY
JACKSONVILLE, FLORIDA

General Independent, comprehensive, coed **Entrance** Moderately difficult **Setting** 260-acre suburban campus **Total enrollment** 2,157 **Student/faculty ratio** 14:1 **Application deadline** Rolling **Freshmen** 64% were admitted **Housing** Yes **Expenses** Tuition $13,900; Room & Board $4900 **Undergraduates** 54% women, 23% part-time, 32% 25 or older, 1% Native American, 4% Hispanic, 10% black, 3% Asian American or Pacific Islander **Most popular recent majors** Business administration; nursing; biology **Academic program** English as a second language, advanced placement, accelerated degree program, self-designed majors, tutorials, honors program, summer session, adult/continuing education programs, internships **Contact** Dr. Susan Hallenbeck, Director of Admissions, Jacksonville University, 2800 University Boulevard North, Jacksonville, FL 32211-3394. Telephone: 904-745-7000 or toll-free 800-225-2027. Fax: 904-745-7012. E-mail: admissions@junix.ju.edu. Web site: http://www.ju.edu/.

JOHNSON & WALES UNIVERSITY
NORTH MIAMI, FLORIDA

General Independent, 4-year, coed **Entrance** Minimally difficult **Setting** 8-acre suburban campus **Total enrollment** 1,054 **Student/faculty ratio** 22:1 **Application deadline** Rolling **Freshmen** 79% were admitted **Housing** Yes **Expenses** Tuition $15,855; Room only $3930 **Undergraduates** 40% women, 7% part-time, 36% 25 or older, 1% Native American, 22% Hispanic, 26% black, 2% Asian American or Pacific Islander **Most Popular Recent Major** Culinary arts **Academic program** English as a second language, advanced placement, accelerated degree program, tutorials, honors program, summer session, internships **Contact** Mr. Jeff Greenip, Director of Admissions, Johnson & Wales University, 1701 Northeast 127th Street, North Miami, FL 33181. Telephone: 305-892-7002 or toll-free 800-232-2433. Fax: 305-892-7030. E-mail: admissions@jwu.edu. Web site: http://www.jwu.edu/.

JONES COLLEGE
JACKSONVILLE, FLORIDA

General Independent, 4-year, coed **Contact** Mr. Barry Darden, Director of Development, Jones College, 5353 Arlington Expressway, Jacksonville, FL 32211-5540. Telephone: 904-743-1122 ext. 115. E-mail: bdarden@jones.edu. Web site: http://www.jones.edu/.

LYNN UNIVERSITY
BOCA RATON, FLORIDA

General Independent, comprehensive, coed **Entrance** Minimally difficult **Setting** 123-acre suburban campus **Total enrollment** 1,782 **Application deadline** 8/15 **Freshmen** 77% were admitted **Housing** Yes **Expenses** Tuition $17,200; Room & Board $6250 **Undergraduates** 55% women, 32% part-time, 24% 25 or older, 0.1% Native American, 5% Hispanic, 5% black, 1% Asian American or Pacific Islander **Most popular recent majors** Hotel and restaurant management; international business; business administration **Academic program** English as a second language, advanced placement, honors program, summer session, adult/continuing education programs, internships **Contact** Mr. James P. Sullivan, Director of Admissions, Lynn University, 3601 North Military Trail, Boca Raton, FL 33431-5598. Telephone: 561-994-0770 ext. 157 or toll-free 800-

Lynn University *(continued)*

544-8035 (out-of-state). Fax: 561-241-3552. E-mail: admission@lynn.edu. Web site: http://www.lynn.edu/.

► **For more information, see page 463.**

NEW COLLEGE OF THE UNIVERSITY OF SOUTH FLORIDA
SARASOTA, FLORIDA

General State-supported, 4-year, coed **Entrance** Very difficult **Setting** 140-acre suburban campus **Total enrollment** 604 **Student/faculty ratio** 11:1 **Application deadline** Rolling **Freshmen** 62% were admitted **Housing** Yes **Expenses** Tuition $2287; Room & Board $4117 **Undergraduates** 57% women, 5% 25 or older, 0% Native American, 7% Hispanic, 3% black, 5% Asian American or Pacific Islander **Most popular recent majors** Biology; psychology; literature **Academic program** Accelerated degree program, self-designed majors, tutorials, honors program, internships **Contact** Ms. Kathleen Killion, Director of Admissions, New College of the University of South Florida, 5700 North Tamiami Trail, Sarasota, FL 34243-2197. Telephone: 941-359-4269. Fax: 941-359-4435. E-mail: ncadmissions@virtu.sar.usf.edu. Web site: http://www.newcollege.usf.edu/.

NEW WORLD SCHOOL OF THE ARTS
MIAMI, FLORIDA

General State-supported, 4-year, coed **Entrance** Most difficult **Setting** 5-acre urban campus **Total enrollment** 359 **Student/faculty ratio** 4:1 **Freshmen** 48% were admitted **Housing** No **Expenses** Tuition $1478 **Undergraduates** 10% 25 or older, 44% Hispanic, 11% black, 5% Asian American or Pacific Islander **Academic program** Average class size 25, English as a second language, advanced placement, tutorials, honors program, summer session, internships **Contact** Ms. Lourdes Werner, Director of Student Services, New World School of the Arts, 300 NE 2nd Avenue, Miami, FL 33132. Telephone: 305-237-3135. E-mail: nwsapost.robs@mdcc.edu. Web site: http://www.mdcc.edu/nwsa/.

NORTHWOOD UNIVERSITY, FLORIDA CAMPUS
WEST PALM BEACH, FLORIDA

General Independent, 4-year, coed **Entrance** Moderately difficult **Setting** 90-acre suburban campus **Total enrollment** 902 **Application deadline** Rolling **Freshmen** 79% were admitted **Housing** Yes **Expenses** Tuition $10,874; Room & Board $6013 **Undergraduates** 42% women, 21% part-time, 7% 25 or older, 0% Native American, 6% Hispanic, 8% black, 2% Asian American or Pacific Islander **Most popular recent majors** Business administration; computer management; accounting **Academic program** English as a second language, advanced placement, accelerated degree program, tutorials, honors program, summer session, adult/continuing education programs, internships **Contact** Mr. John M. Letvinchuck, Director of Admissions, Northwood University, Florida Campus, 2600 North Military Trail, West Palm Beach, FL 33409-2911. Telephone: 561-478-5500 or toll-free 800-458-8325. Fax: 561-640-3328. E-mail: fladmit@northwood.edu. Web site: http://www.northwood.edu/.

NOVA SOUTHEASTERN UNIVERSITY
FORT LAUDERDALE, FLORIDA

General Independent, university, coed **Entrance** Moderately difficult **Setting** 232-acre suburban campus **Total enrollment** 15,782 **Student/faculty ratio** 11:1 **Application deadline** Rolling **Housing** Yes **Expenses** Tuition $10,570; Room & Board $5797 **Undergraduates** 70% women, 30% part-time, 69% 25 or older, 0.3% Native American, 19% Hispanic, 17% black, 2% Asian American or Pacific Islander **Most Popular Recent Major** Business administration **Academic program** Average class size 15, advanced placement, accelerated degree program, summer session, adult/continuing education programs, internships **Contact** Dr. Jean Lewis, Director of Undergraduate Admissions, Nova Southeastern University, 3301 College Avenue, Fort Lauderdale, FL 33314-7721. Telephone: 954-262-8000 or toll-free 800-541-6682. E-mail: ncsinfo@polaris.acast.nova.edu. Web site: http://www.nova.edu/.

► **For more information, see page 489.**

PALM BEACH ATLANTIC COLLEGE
WEST PALM BEACH, FLORIDA

General Independent nondenominational, comprehensive, coed **Entrance** Moderately difficult **Setting** 25-acre urban campus **Total enrollment** 1,932 **Student/faculty ratio** 16:1 **Application deadline** 8/1 **Housing** Yes **Expenses** Tuition $9900; Room & Board $4638 **Undergraduates** 22% 25 or older **Most popular recent majors** Business administration; education; psychology **Academic program** Advanced placement, tutorials, honors program, summer session, adult/continuing education programs, internships **Contact** Mr. Buck James, Dean of Enrollment Services, Palm Beach Atlantic College, 901 South Flagler Dr, PO Box 24708, West Palm Beach, FL 33416-4708. Telephone: 561-803-2100 or toll-free 800-238-3998. E-mail: admit@pbac.edu. Web site: http://www.pbac.edu/.

PHILLIPS JUNIOR COLLEGE OF BUSINESS

See Florida Metropolitan University–Orlando College, Melbourne

RINGLING SCHOOL OF ART AND DESIGN

SARASOTA, FLORIDA

General Independent, 4-year, coed **Entrance** Moderately difficult **Setting** 35-acre urban campus **Total enrollment** 850 **Student/faculty ratio** 13:1 **Application deadline** Rolling **Freshmen** 60% were admitted **Housing** Yes **Expenses** Tuition $13,250; Room & Board $6692 **Undergraduates** 25% 25 or older, 1% Native American, 9% Hispanic, 1% black **Most Popular Recent Major** Graphic design/commercial art/ illustration **Academic program** Advanced placement, internships **Contact** Mr. James Dean, Dean of Admissions, Ringling School of Art and Design, 2700 North Tamiami Trail, Sarasota, FL 34234-5895. Telephone: 941-351-5100 or toll-free 800-255-7695. Fax: 941-359-7517. E-mail: admissions@rsad.edu. Web site: http://www.rsad.edu/.

ROLLINS COLLEGE

WINTER PARK, FLORIDA

General Independent, comprehensive, coed **Entrance** Very difficult **Setting** 67-acre suburban campus **Total enrollment** 2,166 **Student/faculty ratio** 12:1 **Application deadline** 2/15 **Freshmen** 70% were admitted **Housing** Yes **Expenses** Tuition $20,010; Room & Board $6340 **Undergraduates** 59% women, 1% part-time, 2% 25 or older, 0.5% Native American, 8% Hispanic, 3% black, 3% Asian American or Pacific Islander **Most popular recent majors** Psychology; economics; English **Academic program** Advanced placement, accelerated degree program, self-designed majors, tutorials, honors program, adult/ continuing education programs, internships **Contact** Mr. David Erdmann, Dean of Admissions and Student Financial Planning, Rollins College, 1000 Holt Avenue, Winter Park, FL 32789-4499. Telephone: 407-646-2161. Fax: 407-646-2600. E-mail: admissions@rollins.edu. Web site: http://www.rollins.edu/.

ST. JOHN VIANNEY COLLEGE SEMINARY

MIAMI, FLORIDA

General Independent Roman Catholic, 4-year, primarily men **Entrance** Moderately difficult **Setting** 33-acre urban campus **Total enrollment** 47 **Student/faculty ratio** 3:1 **Application deadline** Rolling **Freshmen** 100% were admitted **Housing** Yes **Expenses** Tuition $7000; Room & Board $4000 **Undergraduates** 7% women, 2% part-time, 45% 25 or older, 0% Native American, 40% Hispanic, 11% black, 4% Asian American or Pacific Islander **Academic program** Average class size 12, English as a second language, advanced placement, tutorials **Contact** Dr. Zoila L. Diaz, Academic Dean, St. John Vianney College Seminary, 2900 Southwest 87th Avenue, Miami, FL 33165-3244. Telephone: 305-223-4561 ext. 13. E-mail: academic@sjvcs.edu.

SAINT LEO COLLEGE

SAINT LEO, FLORIDA

General Independent Roman Catholic, comprehensive, coed **Entrance** Moderately difficult **Setting** 170-acre rural campus **Total enrollment** 1,675 **Student/faculty ratio** 15:1 **Application deadline** 3/1 **Freshmen** 84% were admitted **Housing** Yes **Expenses** Tuition $10,996; Room & Board $5240 **Undergraduates** 56% women, 37% part-time, 51% 25 or older, 0.4% Native American, 6% Hispanic, 5% black, 1% Asian American or Pacific Islander **Most popular recent majors** Business administration; education; criminology **Academic program** Advanced placement, accelerated degree program, honors program, summer session, adult/continuing education programs, internships **Contact** Mr. Gary Bracken, Dean of Admissions and Financial Aid, Saint Leo College, PO Box 6665 MC 2008, Saint Leo, FL 33574-2008. Telephone: 352-588-8283 or toll-free 800-334-5532 (in-state), 800-247-6559 (out-of-state). Fax: 352-588-8257. E-mail: admissns@saintleo.edu. Web site: http://www.saintleo.edu/.

ST. THOMAS UNIVERSITY

MIAMI, FLORIDA

General Independent Roman Catholic, comprehensive, coed **Entrance** Moderately difficult **Setting** 140-acre suburban campus **Total enrollment** 2,203 **Student/faculty ratio** 15:1 **Application deadline** Rolling **Freshmen** 71% were admitted **Housing** Yes **Expenses** Tuition $11,840; Room & Board $4000 **Undergraduates** 56% women, 26% part-time, 37% 25 or older, 0.2% Native American, 50% Hispanic, 19% black, 0.4% Asian American or Pacific Islander **Most popular recent majors** Elementary education; business administration; psychology **Academic program** English as a second language, advanced placement, tutorials, honors program, summer session, adult/continuing education programs, internships **Contact** Mr. David Pezzino, Admissions Counselor, St. Thomas University, 16400 Northwest 32nd Avenue, Miami, FL 33054-6459. Telephone: 305-628-6546 or toll-free 800-367-9006 (in-state), 800-367-9010 (out-of-state). Fax: 305-628-6591. E-mail: cwillems@stu.edu. Web site: http://www.stu.edu/.

► **For more information, see page 509.**

SCHILLER INTERNATIONAL UNIVERSITY
DUNEDIN, FLORIDA

General Independent, comprehensive, coed **Entrance** Noncompetitive **Setting** Suburban campus **Total enrollment** 248 **Application deadline** Rolling **Freshmen** 85% were admitted **Housing** Yes **Expenses** Tuition $11,750; Room & Board $4700 **Undergraduates** 13% 25 or older **Most popular recent majors** International business; hotel and restaurant management; travel-tourism management **Academic program** English as a second language, advanced placement, accelerated degree program, self-designed majors, tutorials, summer session, adult/continuing education programs, internships **Contact** Mr. Christoph Leibrecht, Director of Admissions, Schiller International University, 453 Edgewater Drive, Dunedin, FL 34698-7532. Telephone: 813-736-5082 or toll-free 800-336-4133. Fax: 813-734-0359. E-mail: study@schiller.edu.

SOUTHEASTERN COLLEGE OF THE ASSEMBLIES OF GOD
LAKELAND, FLORIDA

General Independent, 4-year, coed, affiliated with Assemblies of God **Entrance** Minimally difficult **Setting** 62-acre small town campus **Total enrollment** 1,069 **Student/faculty ratio** 20:1 **Application deadline** 8/1 **Housing** Yes **Expenses** Tuition $4999; Room & Board $3274 **Undergraduates** 49% women, 5% part-time, 15% 25 or older, 0.5% Native American, 8% Hispanic, 4% black, 1% Asian American or Pacific Islander **Most popular recent majors** Religious studies; education; psychology **Academic program** Average class size 55, advanced placement, accelerated degree program, summer session, internships **Contact** Ms. Sandy Markharn, Admissions Secretary, Southeastern College of the Assemblies of God, 1000 Longfellow Boulevard, Lakeland, FL 33801-6099. Telephone: 941-667-5011. Fax: 941-667-5200. E-mail: rmshelto@secollege.edu. Web site: http://www.secollege.edu/.

STETSON UNIVERSITY
DELAND, FLORIDA

General Independent, comprehensive, coed **Entrance** Moderately difficult **Setting** 162-acre small town campus **Total enrollment** 2,857 **Student/faculty ratio** 12:1 **Application deadline** 3/1 **Freshmen** 88% were admitted **Housing** Yes **Expenses** Tuition $15,765; Room & Board $4655 **Undergraduates** 57% women, 4% part-time, 12% 25 or older, 0.4% Native American, 5% Hispanic, 4% black, 2% Asian American or Pacific Islander **Most popular recent majors** Business administration; education; psychology **Academic program** Advanced placement, accelerated degree program, self-designed majors, honors program, summer session, adult/continuing education programs, internships **Contact** Ms. Mary Napier, Dean of Admissions, Stetson University, 421 North Woodland Boulevard, DeLand, FL 32720-3781. Telephone: 904-822-7100 or toll-free 800-688-0101. Fax: 904-822-8832. E-mail: admissions@stetson.edu. Web site: http://www.stetson.edu/.

TALMUDIC COLLEGE OF FLORIDA
MIAMI BEACH, FLORIDA

Contact Mr. David Faigen, Executive Director, Talmudic College of Florida, 4014 Chase Avenue, Miami Beach, FL 33139. Telephone: 305-534-7050.

TRINITY BAPTIST COLLEGE
JACKSONVILLE, FLORIDA

General Independent Baptist, 4-year, coed **Entrance** Moderately difficult **Setting** 6-acre urban campus **Total enrollment** 309 **Student/faculty ratio** 10:1 **Application deadline** Rolling **Freshmen** 66% were admitted **Housing** Yes **Expenses** Tuition $3698; Room & Board $2800 **Undergraduates** 39% women, 12% part-time, 30% 25 or older, 0.3% Native American, 3% Hispanic, 4% black, 4% Asian American or Pacific Islander **Most popular recent majors** Biblical studies; education; secretarial science **Academic program** Average class size 30, advanced placement, accelerated degree program, summer session, adult/continuing education programs, internships **Contact** Mrs. Shirley F. Hartman, Director of Admissions, Trinity Baptist College, 426 South McDuff Avenue, Jacksonville, FL 32254. Telephone: 904-384-2206 ext. 115 or toll-free 800-786-2206 (out-of-state). Fax: 904-387-4440. E-mail: trinity@tbc.edu. Web site: http://www.tbc.edu/.

TRINITY COLLEGE OF FLORIDA
NEW PORT RICHEY, FLORIDA

General Independent nondenominational, 4-year, coed **Entrance** Minimally difficult **Setting** 20-acre small town campus **Total enrollment** 211 **Student/faculty ratio** 12:1 **Application deadline** Rolling **Housing** Yes **Expenses** Tuition $3470; Room & Board $2400 **Undergraduates** 34% 25 or older, 0.5% Native American, 5% Hispanic, 11% black, 2% Asian American or Pacific Islander **Most popular recent majors** Biblical studies; pastoral counseling **Academic program** English as a second language, advanced placement, tutorials, summer session, internships **Contact** Mr. John-Paul Perea, Admissions Counselor, Trinity College of Florida, 2430 Trinity Oaks Boulevard, New Port Richey, FL 34655. Telephone: 813-376-6911 ext. 1112. Fax: 813-376-0781. E-mail: trinityc@gte.net.

TRINITY INTERNATIONAL UNIVERSITY, SOUTH FLORIDA CAMPUS
MIAMI, FLORIDA

General Independent nondenominational, comprehensive, coed **Contact** Mr. Liam Gillen, Director of Enrollment Services, Trinity International University, South Florida Campus, PO Box 019674, Miami, FL 33101-9674. Telephone: 305-577-4600 ext. 135 or toll-free 800-288-1138 (out-of-state).

UNIVERSITY OF CENTRAL FLORIDA
ORLANDO, FLORIDA

General State-supported, university, coed **Entrance** Moderately difficult **Setting** 1,445-acre suburban campus **Total enrollment** 28,685 **Student/faculty ratio** 16:1 **Application deadline** 7/15 **Freshmen** 66% were admitted **Housing** Yes **Expenses** Tuition $2025; Room & Board $4370 **Undergraduates** 54% women, 31% part-time, 30% 25 or older, 1% Native American, 10% Hispanic, 7% black, 5% Asian American or Pacific Islander **Most popular recent majors** Psychology; elementary education; liberal arts and studies **Academic program** Average class size 30, English as a second language, advanced placement, accelerated degree program, self-designed majors, honors program, summer session, adult/continuing education programs, internships **Contact** Ms. Susan J. McKinnon, Director of Admissions, University of Central Florida, PO Box 160111, Orlando, FL 32816. Telephone: 407-823-3000. Fax: 407-823-3419. E-mail: admissio@pegasus.cc.ucf.edu. Web site: http://www.ucf.edu/.

▶ **For more information, see page 534.**

UNIVERSITY OF FLORIDA
GAINESVILLE, FLORIDA

General State-supported, university, coed **Entrance** Very difficult **Setting** 2,000-acre suburban campus **Total enrollment** 41,713 **Student/faculty ratio** 17:1 **Application deadline** 1/30 **Housing** Yes **Expenses** Tuition $1930; Room & Board $4610 **Undergraduates** 50% women, 8% part-time, 22% 25 or older, 0.3% Native American, 10% Hispanic, 7% black, 6% Asian American or Pacific Islander **Most popular recent majors** Psychology; finance; English **Academic program** English as a second language, advanced placement, accelerated degree program, self-designed majors, tutorials, honors program, summer session, adult/continuing education programs, internships **Contact** Office of Admissions, University of Florida, PO Box 114000, Gainesville, FL 32611-4000. Telephone: 352-392-1365. Web site: http://www.ufl.edu/.

UNIVERSITY OF MIAMI
CORAL GABLES, FLORIDA

General Independent, university, coed **Entrance** Moderately difficult **Setting** 260-acre suburban campus **Total enrollment** 13,651 **Student/faculty ratio** 13:1 **Application deadline** 3/1 **Freshmen** 57% were admitted **Housing** Yes **Expenses** Tuition $19,512; Room & Board $7352 **Undergraduates** 54% women, 8% part-time, 12% 25 or older, 0.2% Native American, 29% Hispanic, 11% black, 5% Asian American or Pacific Islander **Most popular recent majors** Psychology; biology; business marketing and marketing management **Academic program** English as a second language, advanced placement, accelerated degree program, self-designed majors, tutorials, honors program, summer session, adult/continuing education programs, internships **Contact** Mr. Edward M. Gillis, Associate Dean of Enrollments, University of Miami, PO Box 248025, Coral Gables, FL 33146. Telephone: 305-284-4323. Fax: 305-284-2507. E-mail: admission@admiss.msmail.miami.edu. Web site: http://www.miami.edu/.

UNIVERSITY OF NORTH FLORIDA
JACKSONVILLE, FLORIDA

General State-supported, comprehensive, coed **Entrance** Very difficult **Setting** 1,300-acre urban campus **Total enrollment** 11,389 **Student/faculty ratio** 15:1 **Application deadline** Rolling **Freshmen** 70% were admitted **Housing** Yes **Expenses** Tuition $2006; Room & Board $3492 **Undergraduates** 59% women, 43% part-time, 45% 25 or older, 0.4% Native American, 4% Hispanic, 9% black, 5% Asian American or Pacific Islander **Most popular recent majors** Elementary education; psychology; health science **Academic program** Advanced placement, accelerated degree program, tutorials, honors program, summer session, adult/continuing education programs, internships **Contact** Ms. Deborah M. Kaye, Enrollment Services and Admissions, University of North Florida, 4567 St Johns Bluff Road South, Jacksonville, FL 32224-2645. Telephone: 904-620-2624. Fax: 904-620-2414. E-mail: osprey@unfivm.unf.edu. Web site: http://www.unf.edu/.

UNIVERSITY OF SOUTH FLORIDA
TAMPA, FLORIDA

General State-supported, university, coed **Entrance** Moderately difficult **Setting** 1,913-acre urban campus **Total enrollment** 34,036 **Student/faculty ratio** 16:1 **Application deadline** 5/1 **Freshmen** 66% were admitted **Housing** Yes **Ex-**

University of South Florida *(continued)*

penses Tuition $2086; Room & Board $4596 **Undergraduates** 57% women, 36% part-time, 38% 25 or older, 0.4% Native American, 9% Hispanic, 10% black, 5% Asian American or Pacific Islander **Most popular recent majors** Business administration; education; psychology **Academic program** Average class size 36, English as a second language, advanced placement, accelerated degree program, self-designed majors, honors program, summer session, adult/continuing education programs, internships **Contact** Dr. Mark Rubinstein, Director of Admissions, University of South Florida, 4202 East Fowler Avenue, Tampa, FL 33620-6900. Telephone: 813-974-3350. Fax: 813-974-9689. E-mail: bullseye@admin.usf.edu. Web site: http://www.usf.edu/.

UNIVERSITY OF SOUTH FLORIDA, NEW COLLEGE

See New College of the University of South Florida

THE UNIVERSITY OF TAMPA
TAMPA, FLORIDA

General Independent, comprehensive, coed **Entrance** Moderately difficult **Setting** 70-acre urban campus **Total enrollment** 2,896 **Student/faculty ratio** 15:1 **Application deadline** Rolling **Freshmen** 93% were admitted **Housing** Yes **Expenses** Tuition $14,652; Room & Board $4780 **Undergraduates** 60% women, 21% part-time, 29% 25 or older, 1% Native American, 9% Hispanic, 7% black, 2% Asian American or Pacific Islander **Most popular recent majors** Mass communications; nursing; business administration **Academic program** English as a second language, advanced placement, tutorials, honors program, summer session, adult/continuing education programs, internships **Contact** Ms. Edesa Scarborough, Director of Admissions, The University of Tampa, 401 West Kennedy Boulevard, Tampa, FL 33606-1480. Telephone: 813-253-6211 or toll-free 800-733-4773. Fax: 813-254-4955. E-mail: admissions@alpha.utampa.edu. Web site: http://www.utampa.edu/.

▶ **For more information, see page 540.**

UNIVERSITY OF WEST FLORIDA
PENSACOLA, FLORIDA

General State-supported, comprehensive, coed **Entrance** Moderately difficult **Setting** 1,000-acre suburban campus **Total enrollment** 8,038 **Student/faculty ratio** 27:1 **Application deadline** 6/30 **Freshmen** 89% were admitted **Housing** Yes **Expenses** Tuition $1985; Room only $2144 **Undergraduates** 59% women, 32% part-time, 44% 25 or older, 1% Native American, 4% Hispanic, 8% black, 4% Asian American or Pacific Islander **Most popular recent majors** Accounting; elementary education; business administration **Academic program** English as a second language, advanced placement, honors program, summer session, internships **Contact** Ms. Susie Neeley, Director of Admissions, University of West Florida, 11000 University Parkway, Pensacola, FL 32514-5750. Telephone: 850-474-2230. Fax: 850-474-2096. E-mail: sneeley@uwf.edu. Web site: http://www.uwf.edu/.

WARNER SOUTHERN COLLEGE
LAKE WALES, FLORIDA

General Independent, 4-year, coed, affiliated with Church of God **Entrance** Minimally difficult **Setting** 320-acre rural campus **Total enrollment** 646 **Student/faculty ratio** 14:1 **Application deadline** Rolling **Freshmen** 53% were admitted **Housing** Yes **Expenses** Tuition $8220; Room & Board $3969 **Undergraduates** 57% women, 9% part-time, 55% 25 or older, 1% Native American, 6% Hispanic, 14% black, 1% Asian American or Pacific Islander **Most popular recent majors** Business administration; elementary education; (pre)theology **Academic program** Advanced placement, accelerated degree program, tutorials, summer session, adult/continuing education programs, internships **Contact** Ms. Karen Steverson, Director of Admissions, Warner Southern College, 5301 US Highway 27 South, Lake Wales, FL 33853-8725. Telephone: 941-638-7212 ext. 7208. Web site: http://www.warner.edu/.

WEBBER COLLEGE
BABSON PARK, FLORIDA

General Independent, comprehensive, coed **Entrance** Moderately difficult **Setting** 110-acre small town campus **Total enrollment** 433 **Student/faculty ratio** 15:1 **Application deadline** Rolling **Freshmen** 71% were admitted **Housing** Yes **Expenses** Tuition $7390; Room & Board $3300 **Undergraduates** 26% 25 or older **Most popular recent majors** Business administration; business marketing and marketing management; hotel and restaurant management **Academic program** Advanced placement, accelerated degree program, tutorials, summer session, adult/continuing education programs, internships **Contact** Mr. Mike Mattison, Director of Admissions, Webber College, PO Box 96, Babson Park, FL 33827-0096. Telephone: 941-638-2910. Fax: 941-638-2823. E-mail: warriors@interserv.com. Web site: http://www.webber.edu/.

▶ **For more information, see page 548.**

GEORGIA

AGNES SCOTT COLLEGE
DECATUR, GEORGIA

General Independent, comprehensive, women only, affiliated with Presbyterian Church (U.S.A.) **Entrance** Very difficult **Setting** 100-acre urban campus **Total enrollment** 773 **Student/faculty ratio** 9:1 **Application deadline** 3/1 **Freshmen** 77% were admitted **Housing** Yes **Expenses** Tuition $14,960; Room & Board $6230 **Undergraduates** 3% part-time, 12% 25 or older, 0.1% Native American, 3% Hispanic, 16% black, 5% Asian American or Pacific Islander **Most popular recent majors** English; psychology; biology **Academic program** Average class size 20, advanced placement, accelerated degree program, self-designed majors, tutorials, summer session, adult/continuing education programs, internships **Contact** Ms. Stephanie Balmer, Director of Admission, Agnes Scott College, 141 East College Avenue, Decatur, GA 30030-3797. Telephone: 404-638-6285 or toll-free 800-868-8602. Fax: 404-471-6414. E-mail: admission@agnesscott.edu. Web site: http://www.agnesscott.edu/.

ALBANY STATE UNIVERSITY
ALBANY, GEORGIA

General State-supported, comprehensive, coed **Entrance** Minimally difficult **Setting** 144-acre urban campus **Total enrollment** 3,226 **Student/faculty ratio** 20:1 **Application deadline** 7/1 **Freshmen** 60% were admitted **Housing** Yes **Expenses** Tuition $2124; Room & Board $3225 **Undergraduates** 64% women, 12% part-time, 15% 25 or older, 0.2% Native American, 0.3% Hispanic, 94% black, 0.1% Asian American or Pacific Islander **Academic program** Average class size 25, advanced placement, tutorials, honors program, summer session, adult/continuing education programs, internships **Contact** Mrs. Patricia Price, Assistant Director of Admissions, Albany State University, 504 College Drive, Albany, GA 31705-2717. Telephone: 912-430-4646 or toll-free 800-822-RAMS (in-state). Fax: 912-430-3936. E-mail: kcaldwell@rams.alsnet.peachnet.edu. Web site: http://www.alsnet.peachnet.edu/.

THE AMERICAN COLLEGE
See American InterContinental University

AMERICAN INTERCONTINENTAL UNIVERSITY
ATLANTA, GEORGIA

General Proprietary, comprehensive, coed **Entrance** Noncompetitive **Setting** Urban campus **Total enrollment** 1,016 **Student/faculty ratio** 12:1 **Application deadline** Rolling **Housing** Yes **Expenses** Tuition $10,300; Room only $4050 **Undergraduates** 8% 25 or older **Academic program** English as a second language, accelerated degree program, summer session, adult/continuing education programs, internships **Contact** Ms. Suzanne McBride, Vice President and Director of Admissions, American InterContinental University, 3330 Peachtree Road, NE, Atlanta, GA 30326-1019. Telephone: 404-231-9000 or toll-free 800-255-6839 (out-of-state). Fax: 404-231-1062. E-mail: acatl@ix.netcom.com.

ARMSTRONG ATLANTIC STATE UNIVERSITY
SAVANNAH, GEORGIA

General State-supported, comprehensive, coed **Entrance** Minimally difficult **Setting** 250-acre suburban campus **Total enrollment** 5,696 **Student/faculty ratio** 18:1 **Application deadline** 8/15 **Freshmen** 78% were admitted **Housing** Yes **Expenses** Tuition $1962; Room & Board $4116 **Undergraduates** 69% women, 35% part-time, 45% 25 or older, 0.3% Native American, 2% Hispanic, 23% black, 2% Asian American or Pacific Islander **Most popular recent majors** Education; nursing; criminal justice/law enforcement administration **Academic program** Average class size 18, advanced placement, accelerated degree program, tutorials, honors program, summer session, adult/continuing education programs, internships **Contact** Ms. Melanie Mirande, Assistant Director of Recruitment, Armstrong Atlantic State University, 11935 Abercorn Street, Savannah, GA 31419-1997. Telephone: 912-925-5275 or toll-free 800-633-2349. Fax: 912-921-5462. E-mail: cynthia_buskey@mailgate.armstrong.edu. Web site: http://www.armstrong.edu/.

ATLANTA CHRISTIAN COLLEGE
EAST POINT, GEORGIA

General Independent Christian, 4-year, coed **Entrance** Minimally difficult **Setting** 52-acre suburban campus **Total enrollment** 301 **Application deadline** 8/1 **Freshmen** 72% were admitted **Housing** Yes **Expenses** Tuition $6426; Room & Board $3170 **Undergraduates** 52% women, 7% part-time, 30% 25 or older, 0% Native American, 0.3% Hispanic, 19% black, 1% Asian American or Pacific Islander **Most popular recent majors** Biblical studies; humanities; early childhood education **Academic program** Advanced placement, tutorials, summer session, internships **Contact** Mr. Keith Wagner, Director of Admissions, Atlanta Christian College, 2605 Ben Hill Road, East Point, GA 30344-1999. Telephone: 404-761-8861. E-mail: chargers777@juno.com. Web site: http://www.acc.edu/.

ATLANTA COLLEGE OF ART
ATLANTA, GEORGIA

General Independent, 4-year, coed **Entrance** Moderately difficult **Setting** 6-acre urban campus **Total enrollment** 420 **Student/faculty ratio** 11:1 **Application deadline** Rolling **Housing** Yes **Expenses** Tuition $12,250; Room only $3750 **Undergraduates** 47% women, 9% part-time, 1% Native American, 2% Hispanic, 18% black, 8% Asian American or Pacific Islander **Most popular recent majors** Graphic design/commercial art/illustration; drawing; photography **Academic program** English as a second language, advanced placement, self-designed majors, summer session, adult/continuing education programs, internships **Contact** Ms. Carol Lee Conchar, Director of Enrollment Management, Atlanta College of Art, 1280 Peachtree Street, NE, Atlanta, GA 30309-3582. Telephone: 404-733-5101 or toll-free 800-832-2104. Fax: 404-733-5107. E-mail: acainfo@woodruff-arts.org. Web site: http://www.aca.edu/.

AUGUSTA STATE UNIVERSITY
AUGUSTA, GEORGIA

General State-supported, comprehensive, coed **Entrance** Minimally difficult **Setting** 72-acre urban campus **Total enrollment** 5,479 **Student/faculty ratio** 17:1 **Application deadline** 7/24 **Freshmen** 77% were admitted **Housing** No **Expenses** Tuition $1926 **Undergraduates** 64% women, 33% part-time, 43% 25 or older, 0.4% Native American, 2% Hispanic, 28% black, 3% Asian American or Pacific Islander **Most popular recent majors** Nursing; early childhood education; psychology **Academic program** Advanced placement, honors program, summer session, adult/continuing education programs, internships **Contact** Ms. Carol Giardina, Acting Director of Admissions, Augusta State University, 2500 Walton Way, Augusta, GA 30904-2200. Telephone: 706-737-1632. Fax: 706-667-4355. E-mail: admissions@ac.edu. Web site: http://www.aug.edu/.

BERRY COLLEGE
MOUNT BERRY, GEORGIA

General Independent, comprehensive, coed **Entrance** Moderately difficult **Setting** 28,000-acre small town campus **Total enrollment** 2,070 **Student/faculty ratio** 15:1 **Application deadline** Rolling **Freshmen** 69% were admitted **Housing** Yes **Expenses** Tuition $10,210; Room & Board $4536 **Undergraduates** 62% women, 2% part-time, 4% 25 or older, 0.2% Native American, 1% Hispanic, 2% black, 1% Asian American or Pacific Islander **Most popular recent majors** Early childhood education; psychology; communications **Academic program** Advanced placement, accelerated degree program, self-designed majors, honors program, summer session, adult/continuing education programs, internships **Contact** Mr. George Gaddie, Dean of Admissions, Berry College, PO Box 490 159, Mount Berry, GA 30149-0159. Telephone: 706-236-2215 or toll-free 800-237-7942. Fax: 706-290-2178. E-mail: admissions@berry.edu. Web site: http://www.berry.edu/.

BEULAH HEIGHTS BIBLE COLLEGE
ATLANTA, GEORGIA

General Independent religious, 4-year, coed **Entrance** Noncompetitive **Setting** 7-acre urban campus **Total enrollment** 454 **Student/faculty ratio** 20:1 **Application deadline** Rolling **Freshmen** 83% were admitted **Housing** Yes **Expenses** Tuition $3620; Room only $1500 **Undergraduates** 54% women, 48% part-time, 94% 25 or older, 0% Native American, 0% Hispanic, 70% black, 0.4% Asian American or Pacific Islander **Most Popular Recent Major** Biblical studies **Academic program** Average class size 45, advanced placement, accelerated degree program, summer session, adult/continuing education programs, internships **Contact** Dr. James B. Keiller, Vice President and Dean of Academic Affairs, Beulah Heights Bible College, 892 Berne Street, SE, PO Box 18145, Atlanta, GA 30316. Telephone: 404-627-2681 ext. 102 or toll-free 888-777-BHBC. Fax: 404-627-0702. E-mail: cjkjr@aol.com. Web site: http://users.aol.com/cjkjr/beulah.htm.

BRENAU UNIVERSITY
GAINESVILLE, GEORGIA

General Independent, comprehensive, primarily women **Entrance** Moderately difficult **Setting** 57-acre small town campus **Total enrollment** 2,366 **Student/faculty ratio** 15:1 **Application deadline** Rolling **Freshmen** 77% were admitted **Housing** Yes **Expenses** Tuition $10,740; Room & Board $6610 **Undergraduates** 85% women, 26% part-time, 22% 25 or older, 0.1% Native American, 1% Hispanic, 20% black, 1% Asian American or Pacific Islander **Most popular recent majors** Education; business administration; nursing **Academic program** English as a second language, advanced placement, accelerated degree program, self-designed majors, honors program, summer session, internships **Contact** Dr. John D. Upchurch, Director of Admissions, Brenau University, One Centennial Circle, Gainesville, GA 30501-3697. Telephone: 770-534-6100 or toll-free 800-252-5119 (out-of-state). Fax: 770-534-6114. E-mail: upchurch@lib.brenau.edu. Web site: http://www.brenau.edu/.

BREWTON-PARKER COLLEGE
MT. VERNON, GEORGIA

General Independent Southern Baptist, 4-year, coed **Entrance** Noncompetitive **Setting** 280-acre rural campus **Total enrollment** 1,652 **Student/faculty ratio** 16:1 **Application deadline** Rolling **Housing** Yes **Expenses** Tuition $5760; Room & Board $2670 **Undergraduates** 35% 25 or older, 0.1% Native American, 1% Hispanic, 21% black, 0.5% Asian American or Pacific Islander **Most Popular Recent Majors** Business administration; education; religious studies **Academic program** English as a second language, advanced placement, tutorials, honors program, summer session, adult/continuing education programs, internships **Contact** Mrs. Jill O'Neal, Director of Admissions, Brewton-Parker College, Highway 280, Mt. Vernon, GA 30445-0197. Telephone: 912-583-3268 or toll-free 800-342-1087. Fax: 912-583-4498. Web site: http://www.bpc.edu/.

CLARK ATLANTA UNIVERSITY
ATLANTA, GEORGIA

General Independent United Methodist, university, coed **Entrance** Moderately difficult **Setting** 113-acre urban campus **Total enrollment** 5,912 **Student/faculty ratio** 16:1 **Application deadline** 3/1 **Housing** Yes **Expenses** Tuition $9348; Room & Board $5600 **Undergraduates** 70% women, 7% part-time, 2% 25 or older, 0.04% Native American, 0.02% Hispanic, 99% black, 0.1% Asian American or Pacific Islander **Most popular recent majors** Mass communications; business administration; psychology **Academic program** Average class size 25, English as a second language, advanced placement, accelerated degree program, tutorials, honors program, summer session, adult/continuing education programs, internships **Contact** Office of Admissions, Clark Atlanta University, 223 James P. Brawley Dr, SW, Atlanta, GA 30314. Telephone: 404-880-8784 ext. 6650 or toll-free 800-688-3228. Fax: 404-880-6174. Web site: http://www.cau.edu/.

CLAYTON COLLEGE & STATE UNIVERSITY
MORROW, GEORGIA

General State-supported, 4-year, coed **Entrance** Minimally difficult **Setting** 163-acre suburban campus **Total enrollment** 4,713 **Student/faculty ratio** 17:1 **Application deadline** 7/15 **Housing** No **Expenses** Tuition $2168 **Undergraduates** 65% women, 55% part-time, 49% 25 or older, 0.3% Native American, 2% Hispanic, 29% black, 2% Asian American or Pacific Islander **Most popular recent majors** Business administration; nursing; dental hygiene **Academic program** Average class size 25, advanced placement, self-designed majors, tutorials, honors program, summer session, adult/continuing education programs, internships **Contact** Ms. Carol S. Montgomery, Admissions, Clayton College & State University, 5900 North Lee Street, Morrow, GA 30260-0285. Telephone: 770-961-3500. Fax: 770-961-3752. E-mail: csc-info@ce.clayton.peachnet.edu. Web site: http://www.clayton.edu/.

COLUMBUS STATE UNIVERSITY
COLUMBUS, GEORGIA

General State-supported, comprehensive, coed **Entrance** Minimally difficult **Setting** 132-acre suburban campus **Total enrollment** 5,405 **Student/faculty ratio** 24:1 **Application deadline** 9/3 **Freshmen** 69% were admitted **Housing** Yes **Expenses** Tuition $2463; Room & Board $3825 **Undergraduates** 36% 25 or older **Most popular recent majors** Liberal arts and studies; criminal justice/law enforcement administration; elementary education **Academic program** Advanced placement, accelerated degree program, tutorials, summer session, adult/continuing education programs, internships **Contact** Ms. Kim Padgett, Admission Counselor, Columbus State University, 4225 University Avenue, Columbus, GA 31907-5645. Telephone: 706-568-2035. Fax: 706-568-2462.

COVENANT COLLEGE
LOOKOUT MOUNTAIN, GEORGIA

General Independent, comprehensive, coed, affiliated with Presbyterian Church in America **Entrance** Moderately difficult **Setting** 250-acre suburban campus **Total enrollment** 945 **Student/faculty ratio** 15:1 **Application deadline** Rolling **Freshmen** 83% were admitted **Housing** Yes **Expenses** Tuition $12,900; Room & Board $4120 **Undergraduates** 52% women, 2% part-time, 1% 25 or older, 0.5% Native American, 1% Hispanic, 3% black, 1% Asian American or Pacific Islander **Most popular recent majors** Elementary education; business administration; history **Academic program** Average class size 25, advanced placement, accelerated degree program, tutorials, honors program, summer session, internships **Contact** Mr. Joe Stephens, Director of Admissions, Covenant College, 14049 Scenic Highway, Lookout Mountain, GA 30750. Telephone: 706-820-1560 ext. 1643 or toll-free 800-926-8362. E-mail: admissions@covenant.edu. Web site: http://www.covenant.edu/.

DEVRY INSTITUTE OF TECHNOLOGY
DECATUR, GEORGIA

General Proprietary, 4-year, coed **Entrance** Minimally difficult **Setting** 21-acre suburban campus

DeVry Institute of Technology *(continued)*

Total enrollment 2,889 **Student/faculty ratio** 18:1 **Application deadline** Rolling **Freshmen** 67% were admitted **Housing** No **Expenses** Tuition $7308 **Undergraduates** 35% women, 20% part-time, 49% 25 or older, 1% Native American, 2% Hispanic, 65% black, 3% Asian American or Pacific Islander **Most popular recent majors** Information sciences/systems; electrical/electronic engineering technology **Academic program** Advanced placement, accelerated degree program, summer session, adult/continuing education programs **Contact** Mr. George Ollennu, Director of Admissions, DeVry Institute of Technology, 250 North Arcadia Avenue, Decatur, GA 30030-2198. Telephone: 404-292-2645 ext. 430 or toll-free 800-221-4771 (out-of-state). E-mail: dwalters@admin.atl.devry.edu. Web site: http://www.atl.devry.edu/.

EMMANUEL COLLEGE
FRANKLIN SPRINGS, GEORGIA

General Independent, 4-year, coed, affiliated with Pentecostal Holiness Church **Entrance** Minimally difficult **Setting** 90-acre rural campus **Total enrollment** 810 **Student/faculty ratio** 15:1 **Application deadline** 8/1 **Freshmen** 70% were admitted **Housing** Yes **Expenses** Tuition $6060; Room & Board $3420 **Undergraduates** 58% women, 9% part-time, 20% 25 or older, 0.4% Hispanic, 9% black, 0.1% Asian American or Pacific Islander **Most popular recent majors** Biblical studies; early childhood education; business administration **Academic program** Average class size 35, advanced placement, summer session, internships **Contact** Mr. Tim Harrison, Director of Admissions, Emmanuel College, PO Box 129, Franklin Springs, GA 30639-0129. Telephone: 706-245-7226 ext. 2722 or toll-free 800-860-8800 (in-state). E-mail: admissions@emmanuel-college.edu. Web site: http://www.emmanuel-college.edu/.

EMORY UNIVERSITY
ATLANTA, GEORGIA

General Independent Methodist, university, coed **Entrance** Most difficult **Setting** 631-acre suburban campus **Total enrollment** 11,109 **Student/faculty ratio** 10:1 **Application deadline** 1/15 **Freshmen** 46% were admitted **Housing** Yes **Expenses** Tuition $21,120; Room & Board $6800 **Undergraduates** 55% women, 4% part-time, 0% 25 or older, 0.2% Native American, 3% Hispanic, 10% black, 14% Asian American or Pacific Islander **Most popular recent majors** Psychology; biology; political science **Academic program** Average class size 35, advanced placement, accelerated degree program, tutorials, honors program, summer session, internships **Contact** Mr. Daniel C. Walls, Dean of Admission, Emory University, Boisfeuillet Jones Center–Office of Admissions, Atlanta, GA 30322-1100. Telephone: 404-727-6036 or toll-free 800-727-6036. E-mail: admiss@unix.cc.emory.edu. Web site: http://www.emory.edu/.

FORT VALLEY STATE UNIVERSITY
FORT VALLEY, GEORGIA

General State-supported, comprehensive, coed **Entrance** Minimally difficult **Setting** 1,307-acre small town campus **Total enrollment** 2,804 **Student/faculty ratio** 18:1 **Application deadline** 9/1 **Housing** Yes **Expenses** Tuition $2157; Room & Board $3075 **Academic program** Advanced placement, tutorials, honors program, summer session, adult/continuing education programs, internships **Contact** Ms. Harriet Steele, Interim Dean of Admissions and Enrollment Management, Fort Valley State University, 1005 State University Drive, Fort Valley, GA 31030-3298. Telephone: 912-825-6313.

GEORGIA BAPTIST COLLEGE OF NURSING
ATLANTA, GEORGIA

General Independent Baptist, 4-year, women only **Entrance** Moderately difficult **Setting** 20-acre urban campus **Total enrollment** 345 **Student/faculty ratio** 10:1 **Application deadline** 4/15 **Housing** Yes **Expenses** Tuition $9521; Room only $1845 **Undergraduates** 8% part-time, 30% 25 or older, 1% Hispanic, 12% black, 2% Asian American or Pacific Islander **Academic program** Average class size 18, advanced placement, tutorials, summer session **Contact** Mrs. Connie G. Simpson, Director of Enrollment Services, Georgia Baptist College of Nursing, 274 Boulevard, NE, Atlanta, GA 30312. Telephone: 404-265-4800. E-mail: gbcnadm@mindspring.com.

GEORGIA COLLEGE AND STATE UNIVERSITY
MILLEDGEVILLE, GEORGIA

General State-supported, comprehensive, coed **Entrance** Moderately difficult **Setting** 666-acre small town campus **Total enrollment** 5,512 **Application deadline** Rolling **Freshmen** 97% were admitted **Housing** Yes **Expenses** Tuition $2064; Room & Board $4203 **Undergraduates** 0.2% Native American, 1% Hispanic, 17% black, 1% Asian American or Pacific Islander **Most popular recent majors** Nursing; early childhood education; accounting **Academic program** Advanced placement, accelerated degree program, self-designed majors, honors program, summer session, adult/continuing education programs, internships **Contact** Ms. Maryllis Wolfgang, Director of Admissions, Georgia College and State University, CPO

Box 023, Milledgeville, GA 31061. Telephone: 912-445-6285 or toll-free 800-342-0471 (in-state). Fax: 912-445-1914. E-mail: gcsu@mail.gac.peachnet.edu. Web site: http://www.gac.peachnet.edu/.

GEORGIA INSTITUTE OF TECHNOLOGY
ATLANTA, GEORGIA

General State-supported, university, coed **Entrance** Very difficult **Setting** 360-acre urban campus **Student/faculty ratio** 14:1 **Application deadline** 1/15 **Freshmen** 61% were admitted **Housing** Yes **Expenses** Tuition $2901; Room & Board $5031 **Undergraduates** 6% 25 or older **Most popular recent majors** Industrial engineering; electrical/electronics engineering; business administration **Academic program** English as a second language, advanced placement, accelerated degree program, self-designed majors, tutorials, honors program, summer session, internships **Contact** Ms. Deborah Smith, Director of Admissions, Georgia Institute of Technology, 225 North Avenue, NW, Atlanta, GA 30332-0320. Telephone: 404-894-4154. Fax: 404-853-9163. E-mail: admissions@success.gatech.edu. Web site: http://www.gatech.edu/.

GEORGIA SOUTHERN UNIVERSITY
STATESBORO, GEORGIA

General State-supported, comprehensive, coed **Entrance** Moderately difficult **Setting** 601-acre small town campus **Total enrollment** 13,963 **Student/faculty ratio** 20:1 **Application deadline** 7/1 **Housing** Yes **Expenses** Tuition $2256; Room & Board $3465 **Undergraduates** 53% women, 8% part-time, 12% 25 or older **Most popular recent majors** Early childhood education; business marketing and marketing management; finance **Academic program** Average class size 30, English as a second language, advanced placement, honors program, summer session, adult/continuing education programs, internships **Contact** Dr. Dale Wasson, Director of Admissions, Georgia Southern University, GSU PO Box 8024, Statesboro, GA 30460. Telephone: 912-681-5531. Fax: 912-681-5635. E-mail: admissions@gasou.edu. Web site: http://www.gasou.edu/.

GEORGIA SOUTHWESTERN STATE UNIVERSITY
AMERICUS, GEORGIA

General State-supported, comprehensive, coed **Entrance** Moderately difficult **Setting** 187-acre small town campus **Total enrollment** 2,414 **Student/faculty ratio** 15:1 **Application deadline** Rolling **Freshmen** 78% were admitted **Housing** Yes **Expenses** Tuition $2145; Room & Board $3222 **Undergraduates** 63% women, 21% part-time, 24% 25 or older, 0.4% Native American, 0.4% Hispanic, 28% black, 1% Asian American or Pacific Islander **Most popular recent majors** Education; business administration; computer science **Academic program** Average class size 22, English as a second language, advanced placement, tutorials, honors program, summer session, adult/continuing education programs, internships **Contact** Mr. Gary Fallis, Director of Admissions, Georgia Southwestern State University, 800 Wheatley Street, Americus, GA 31709-4693. Telephone: 912-928-1273 or toll-free 800-338-0082. Fax: 912-931-2983. E-mail: gswadm@canes.gsw.peachnet.edu. Web site: http://gswrs6k1.gsw.peachnet.edu/.

GEORGIA STATE UNIVERSITY
ATLANTA, GEORGIA

General State-supported, university, coed **Entrance** Moderately difficult **Setting** 24-acre urban campus **Total enrollment** 24,276 **Student/faculty ratio** 14:1 **Application deadline** 5/1 **Housing** Yes **Expenses** Tuition $2673; Room only $3789 **Undergraduates** 61% women, 41% part-time, 58% 25 or older, 0.3% Native American, 3% Hispanic, 30% black, 8% Asian American or Pacific Islander **Most popular recent majors** Business administration; mathematics; accounting **Academic program** English as a second language, advanced placement, accelerated degree program, self-designed majors, tutorials, honors program, summer session, adult/continuing education programs, internships **Contact** Mr. Rob Sheinkopf, Dean of Admissions and Acting Dean for Enrollment Services, Georgia State University, University Plaza, Atlanta, GA 30303-3083. Telephone: 404-651-2365. Web site: http://www.gsu.edu/.

KENNESAW STATE UNIVERSITY
KENNESAW, GEORGIA

General State-supported, comprehensive, coed **Entrance** Moderately difficult **Setting** 186-acre suburban campus **Total enrollment** 13,108 **Student/faculty ratio** 27:1 **Application deadline** 7/17 **Freshmen** 86% were admitted **Housing** No **Expenses** Tuition $2013 **Undergraduates** 42% 25 or older **Academic program** Average class size 27, advanced placement, honors program, summer session, adult/continuing education programs, internships **Contact** Ms. Angela Evans, Admissions Counselor, Kennesaw State University, 1000 Chastain Road, Kennesaw, GA 30144-5591. Telephone: 770-423-6300 ext. 2001. Fax: 770-423-6541. E-mail: ksuadmit@ksumail.kennesaw.edu. Web site: http://www.kennesaw.edu/.

LAGRANGE COLLEGE
LAGRANGE, GEORGIA

General Independent United Methodist, comprehensive, coed **Entrance** Moderately difficult **Setting** 120-acre small town campus **Total enrollment** 973 **Student/faculty ratio** 11:1 **Application deadline** 8/15 **Freshmen** 76% were admitted **Housing** Yes **Expenses** Tuition $9726; Room & Board $4275 **Undergraduates** 35% 25 or older **Academic program** English as a second language, advanced placement, tutorials, summer session, adult/continuing education programs, internships **Contact** Mr. Andrew Geeter, Director of Admission, LaGrange College, 601 Broad Street, LaGrange, GA 30240-2999. Telephone: 706-812-7260. E-mail: p.dodson@mentor.lgc.peachnet.edu. Web site: http://www.lgc.peachnet.edu/.

▶ **For more information, see page 456.**

LIFE UNIVERSITY
MARIETTA, GEORGIA

Contact Life University, 1269 Barclay Circle, Marietta, GA 30060-2903. Telephone: 770-426-2600.

LUTHER RICE BIBLE COLLEGE AND SEMINARY
LITHONIA, GEORGIA

General Independent Baptist, comprehensive, coed **Entrance** Noncompetitive **Setting** 5-acre urban campus **Total enrollment** 1,300 **Student/faculty ratio** 18:1 **Application deadline** Rolling **Housing** No **Expenses** Tuition $2512 **Undergraduates** 88% 25 or older **Academic program** Adult/continuing education programs **Contact** Dr. Dennis Dieringer, Director of Admissions and Records, Luther Rice Bible College and Seminary, 3038 Evans Mill Road, Lithonia, GA 30038-2418. Telephone: 770-484-1204 or toll-free 800-442-1577. E-mail: 70420.1270@compuserve.com.

MEDICAL COLLEGE OF GEORGIA
AUGUSTA, GEORGIA

General State-supported, university, coed **Entrance** Moderately difficult **Setting** 100-acre urban campus **Total enrollment** 2,020 **Application deadline** Rolling **Housing** Yes **Expenses** Tuition $2526; Room only $1176 **Undergraduates** 81% women, 8% part-time, 27% 25 or older, 0.1% Native American, 2% Hispanic, 13% black, 4% Asian American or Pacific Islander **Most popular recent majors** Nursing; occupational therapy; physician assistant **Contact** Ms. Elizabeth Griffin, Director of Academic Admissions, Medical College of Georgia, 1120 Fifteenth Street, Augusta, GA 30912-1003. Telephone: 706-721-2725. Fax: 706-721-3461. E-mail: underadm@mail.mcg.edu. Web site: http://www.mcg.edu/.

MERCER UNIVERSITY
MACON, GEORGIA

General Independent Baptist, comprehensive, coed **Entrance** Moderately difficult **Setting** 130-acre suburban campus **Total enrollment** 6,801 **Student/faculty ratio** 17:1 **Application deadline** Rolling **Freshmen** 85% were admitted **Housing** Yes **Expenses** Tuition $14,656; Room & Board $4882 **Undergraduates** 64% women, 19% part-time, 32% 25 or older, 0.4% Native American, 1% Hispanic, 20% black, 3% Asian American or Pacific Islander **Most popular recent majors** Early childhood education; business administration; human services **Academic program** English as a second language, advanced placement, self-designed majors, tutorials, summer session, adult/continuing education programs, internships **Contact** Mr. J. Timothy Copeland, Director of Admission, Mercer University, 1400 Coleman Avenue, Macon, GA 31207-0003. Telephone: 912-752-2650 or toll-free 800-342-0841 (in-state), 800-637-2378 (out-of-state). Fax: 912-752-2828. E-mail: admissions@mercer.edu. Web site: http://www.mercer.edu/.

MERCER UNIVERSITY, CECIL B. DAY CAMPUS
ATLANTA, GEORGIA

General Independent Baptist, upper-level, coed **Entrance** Moderately difficult **Setting** 400-acre suburban campus **Total enrollment** 2,001 **Student/faculty ratio** 15:1 **Application deadline** Rolling **Freshmen** 76% were admitted **Housing** No **Expenses** Tuition $9300 **Undergraduates** 75% 25 or older **Most popular recent majors** Business administration; accounting **Academic program** English as a second language, advanced placement, tutorials, summer session, adult/continuing education programs **Contact** Ms. Argy Russell, Director of Undergraduate Admissions, Mercer University, Cecil B. Day Campus, 3001 Mercer University Drive, Atlanta, GA 30341-4155. Telephone: 770-986-3134 or toll-free 800-694-2284. Fax: 770-986-3135. E-mail: atlinfo@mercer.edu. Web site: http://www.mercer.edu/.

MOREHOUSE COLLEGE
ATLANTA, GEORGIA

General Independent, 4-year, men only **Entrance** Moderately difficult **Setting** 61-acre urban campus **Total enrollment** 3,000 **Student/faculty ratio** 15:1 **Application deadline** 2/15 **Freshmen** 69% were admitted **Housing** Yes **Expenses** Tuition $9724; Room & Board $6214 **Un-**

dergraduates 5% part-time, 6% 25 or older, 0.1% Hispanic, 99% black, 0.2% Asian American or Pacific Islander **Most popular recent majors** Business administration; psychology; biology **Academic program** Advanced placement, tutorials, honors program, summer session, internships **Contact** Mr. André Pattillo, Director of Admissions, Morehouse College, 630 Westview Drive, SW, Atlanta, GA 30314. Telephone: 404-215-2632 or toll-free 800-851-1254. Fax: 404-659-6536. E-mail: apattillo@morehouse.edu.

MORRIS BROWN COLLEGE
ATLANTA, GEORGIA

General Independent, 4-year, coed, affiliated with African Methodist Episcopal Church **Entrance** Minimally difficult **Setting** 21-acre urban campus **Total enrollment** 2,093 **Student/faculty ratio** 13:1 **Application deadline** 6/30 **Freshmen** 47% were admitted **Housing** Yes **Expenses** Tuition $8233; Room & Board $4750 **Undergraduates** 59% women, 2% part-time, 11% 25 or older, 0% Native American, 0.2% Hispanic, 96% black, 0.2% Asian American or Pacific Islander **Most popular recent majors** Early childhood education; accounting; business administration **Academic program** Average class size 20, English as a second language, accelerated degree program, tutorials, honors program, adult/continuing education programs, internships **Contact** Ms. Vorrey Billips, Director of Admissions/Recruitment, Morris Brown College, 643 Martin Luther King Jr Drive, NW, Atlanta, GA 30314-4140. Telephone: 404-220-0152. Fax: 404-220-0267. Web site: http://www.morrisbrown.edu/.

NORTH GEORGIA COLLEGE & STATE UNIVERSITY
DAHLONEGA, GEORGIA

General State-supported, comprehensive, coed **Entrance** Moderately difficult **Setting** 140-acre small town campus **Total enrollment** 3,344 **Student/faculty ratio** 16:1 **Application deadline** 7/15 **Freshmen** 81% were admitted **Housing** Yes **Expenses** Tuition $2052; Room & Board $3219 **Most popular recent majors** Criminal justice/law enforcement administration; education; business administration **Academic program** Average class size 35, advanced placement, honors program, summer session, internships **Contact** Mr. Bill Smith, Director of Recruitment, North Georgia College & State University, Admissions Center, Dahlonega, GA 30533. Telephone: 706-864-1800 or toll-free 800-498-9581. Fax: 706-864-1478. E-mail: tdavis@nugget.ngc.peachnet.edu. Web site: http://www.ngc.peachnet.edu/.

► **For more information, see page 486.**

OGLETHORPE UNIVERSITY
ATLANTA, GEORGIA

General Independent, comprehensive, coed **Entrance** Very difficult **Setting** 118-acre suburban campus **Total enrollment** 1,230 **Student/faculty ratio** 12:1 **Application deadline** 8/1 **Freshmen** 81% were admitted **Housing** Yes **Expenses** Tuition $15,920; Room & Board $4990 **Undergraduates** 64% women, 18% part-time, 6% 25 or older, 0.2% Native American, 3% Hispanic, 9% black, 4% Asian American or Pacific Islander **Most popular recent majors** Business administration; psychology; English **Academic program** Average class size 20, English as a second language, advanced placement, accelerated degree program, self-designed majors, tutorials, honors program, summer session, adult/continuing education programs, internships **Contact** Mr. Dennis T. Matthews, Associate Dean for Enrollment Management, Oglethorpe University, 4484 Peachtree Road, NE, Atlanta, GA 30319-2797. Telephone: 404-364-8307 or toll-free 800-428-4484. Fax: 404-364-8500. E-mail: admission@oglethrope.edu. Web site: http://www.oglethorpe.edu/.

PAINE COLLEGE
AUGUSTA, GEORGIA

General Independent Methodist, 4-year, coed **Entrance** Minimally difficult **Setting** 54-acre urban campus **Total enrollment** 857 **Student/faculty ratio** 13:1 **Application deadline** 8/1 **Freshmen** 86% were admitted **Housing** Yes **Expenses** Tuition $6910; Room & Board $3070 **Undergraduates** 20% 25 or older **Most popular recent majors** Business administration; sociology; psychology **Academic program** Advanced placement, accelerated degree program, tutorials, honors program, summer session, internships **Contact** Mrs. Ellen C. King, Director of Admission, Paine College, 1235 15th Street, Augusta, GA 30901-3182. Telephone: 706-821-8320 or toll-free 800-476-7703. Fax: 706-821-8293. E-mail: ek@mail.paine.edu.

PIEDMONT COLLEGE
DEMOREST, GEORGIA

General Independent, comprehensive, coed, affiliated with Congregational Christian Church **Entrance** Moderately difficult **Setting** 300-acre rural campus **Total enrollment** 1,587 **Student/faculty ratio** 9:1 **Application deadline** Rolling **Freshmen** 66% were admitted **Housing** Yes **Expenses** Tuition $8200; Room & Board $3930 **Undergraduates** 61% women, 20% part-time, 30% 25 or older **Most popular recent majors** Business administration; early childhood education; psychology **Academic program** Average class size

Piedmont College *(continued)*

18, advanced placement, accelerated degree program, tutorials, honors program, summer session, adult/continuing education programs, internships **Contact** Mr. James Clement, Director of Admissions, Piedmont College, PO Box 10, Demorest, GA 30535-0010. Telephone: 706-776-0103 ext. 183 or toll-free 800-277-7020. Fax: 706-776-6635. E-mail: admit@piedmont.edu. Web site: http://www.piedmont.edu/.

REINHARDT COLLEGE

WALESKA, GEORGIA

General Independent, 4-year, coed, affiliated with United Methodist Church **Entrance** Moderately difficult **Setting** 600-acre rural campus **Total enrollment** 1,071 **Student/faculty ratio** 18:1 **Application deadline** Rolling **Freshmen** 65% were admitted **Housing** Yes **Expenses** Tuition $6210; Room & Board $4263 **Undergraduates** 61% women, 20% part-time, 31% 25 or older, 0% Native American, 1% Hispanic, 3% black, 1% Asian American or Pacific Islander **Most popular recent majors** Liberal arts and studies; business administration; biological and physical sciences **Academic program** Average class size 18, advanced placement, tutorials, honors program, summer session, adult/continuing education programs, internships **Contact** Ms. Jodi Johnson, Director of Admissions, Reinhardt College, 7300 Reinhardt College Circle, Waleska, GA 30183-0128. Telephone: 770-720-5526. Fax: 770-720-5602. E-mail: admissions@mail.reinhardt.edu. Web site: http://www.reinhardt.edu/.

SAVANNAH COLLEGE OF ART AND DESIGN

SAVANNAH, GEORGIA

General Independent, comprehensive, coed **Entrance** Moderately difficult **Setting** Urban campus **Total enrollment** 3,464 **Student/faculty ratio** 15:1 **Application deadline** Rolling **Freshmen** 75% were admitted **Housing** Yes **Expenses** Tuition $13,500; Room & Board $6375 **Undergraduates** 41% women, 11% part-time, 8% 25 or older, 0.1% Native American, 3% Hispanic, 6% black, 2% Asian American or Pacific Islander **Most popular recent majors** Graphic design/commercial art/illustration; computer graphics; architecture **Academic program** Average class size 20, English as a second language, advanced placement, tutorials, summer session, internships **Contact** Ms. Dianne Taylor, Vice President of Admissions, Savannah College of Art and Design, 342 Bull Street, PO Box 3146, Savannah, GA 31402-3146. Telephone: 912-238-2483 or toll-free 800-869-SCAD. Fax: 912-238-2436. E-mail: admissions@scad.edu. Web site: http://www.scad.edu/.

▶ **For more information, see page 510.**

SAVANNAH STATE UNIVERSITY

SAVANNAH, GEORGIA

General State-supported, comprehensive, coed **Entrance** Minimally difficult **Setting** 165-acre suburban campus **Total enrollment** 2,745 **Application deadline** 9/1 **Housing** Yes **Expenses** Tuition $2226; Room & Board $3495 **Undergraduates** 59% women, 12% part-time, 9% 25 or older, 0.2% Native American, 0.5% Hispanic, 92% black, 0.2% Asian American or Pacific Islander **Academic program** Advanced placement, accelerated degree program, tutorials, summer session, adult/continuing education programs, internships **Contact** Dr. Roy A. Jackson, Director of Admissions, Savannah State University, PO Box 20209, Savannah, GA 31404. Telephone: 912-356-2181 or toll-free 800-788-0478. Fax: 912-356-2256.

SHORTER COLLEGE

ROME, GEORGIA

General Independent Baptist, 4-year, coed **Entrance** Moderately difficult **Setting** 155-acre small town campus **Total enrollment** 1,639 **Student/faculty ratio** 13:1 **Application deadline** Rolling **Housing** Yes **Expenses** Tuition $8260; Room & Board $4250 **Undergraduates** 10% 25 or older, 0.3% Native American, 1% Hispanic, 10% black, 1% Asian American or Pacific Islander **Most popular recent majors** Biology; early childhood education; business administration **Academic program** Average class size 25, advanced placement, accelerated degree program, self-designed majors, tutorials, honors program, summer session, adult/continuing education programs, internships **Contact** Ms. Wendy Sutton, Director of Admissions, Shorter College, 315 Shorter Avenue, Rome, GA 30165-4298. Telephone: 706-233-7319 or toll-free 800-868-6980. Fax: 706-236-1515. E-mail: admissions@shorter.edu. Web site: http://www.shorter.edu/.

▶ **For more information, see page 514.**

SOUTH COLLEGE

SAVANNAH, GEORGIA

General Proprietary, 4-year, coed **Entrance** Minimally difficult **Setting** 5-acre suburban campus **Total enrollment** 439 **Student/faculty ratio** 14:1 **Application deadline** Rolling **Housing** No **Expenses** Tuition $6310 **Undergraduates** 82% women, 24% part-time, 49% 25 or older, 0% Native American, 3% Hispanic, 45% black, 1% Asian American or Pacific Islander **Most popular recent majors** Medical assistant; paralegal/legal assistant; business administration **Academic program** Average class size 18, tutorials, summer session, adult/continuing education programs, internships **Contact** Mr. Robin Manning, Director of Admissions, South College, 709 Mall Boulevard, Savannah, GA 31406-4881. Telephone: 912-691-6000. Fax: 912-691-6070. E-mail: southcollege@southcollege.edu. Web site: http://www.southcollege.edu/.

SOUTHERN COLLEGE OF TECHNOLOGY

See Southern Polytechnic State University

SOUTHERN POLYTECHNIC STATE UNIVERSITY

MARIETTA, GEORGIA

General State-supported, comprehensive, coed **Entrance** Moderately difficult **Setting** 200-acre suburban campus **Total enrollment** 3,918 **Student/faculty ratio** 18:1 **Application deadline** 7/15 **Freshmen** 80% were admitted **Housing** Yes **Expenses** Tuition $1998; Room & Board $3450 **Undergraduates** 17% women, 37% part-time, 42% 25 or older, 0.3% Native American, 2% Hispanic, 18% black, 5% Asian American or Pacific Islander **Most popular recent majors** Electrical/electronic engineering technology; civil engineering technology; industrial technology **Academic program** Average class size 25, advanced placement, accelerated degree program, summer session, adult/continuing education programs **Contact** Mrs. Virginia A. Head, Director of Admissions, Southern Polytechnic State University, South Marietta Parkway, Marietta, GA 30060-2896. Telephone: 770-528-7281 or toll-free 800-635-3204. E-mail: vhead@sct.edu. Web site: http://www.spsu.edu/.

SPELMAN COLLEGE

ATLANTA, GEORGIA

General Independent, 4-year, women only **Entrance** Very difficult **Setting** 32-acre urban campus **Total enrollment** 1,937 **Student/faculty ratio** 14:1 **Application deadline** 2/1 **Freshmen** 50% were admitted **Housing** Yes **Expenses** Tuition $10,095; Room & Board $6370 **Undergraduates** 5% part-time, 4% 25 or older, 0% Native American, 0.2% Hispanic, 96% black, 0.1% Asian American or Pacific Islander **Most popular recent majors** Psychology; economics; English **Academic program** Advanced placement, accelerated degree program, self-designed majors, tutorials, honors program, adult/continuing education programs, internships **Contact** Ms. Victoria Valle, Director of Admissions and Orientation Services, Spelman College, 350 Spelman Lane, SW, Atlanta, GA 30314-4399. Telephone: 404-681-3643 ext. 2188 or toll-free 800-982-2411 (out-of-state). Fax: 404-215-7788. E-mail: admiss@spelman.edu. Web site: http://www.spelman.edu/.

STATE UNIVERSITY OF WEST GEORGIA

CARROLLTON, GEORGIA

General State-supported, comprehensive, coed **Entrance** Minimally difficult **Setting** 400-acre small town campus **Total enrollment** 8,422 **Student/faculty ratio** 16:1 **Application deadline** Rolling **Freshmen** 62% were admitted **Housing** Yes **Expenses** Tuition $2088; Room & Board $3399 **Undergraduates** 61% women, 19% part-time, 18% 25 or older, 0.2% Native American, 1% Hispanic, 18% black, 1% Asian American or Pacific Islander **Most popular recent majors** Early childhood education; nursing; psychology **Academic program** English as a second language, advanced placement, accelerated degree program, honors program, summer session, adult/continuing education programs, internships **Contact** Dr. Robert Johnson, Director of Admissions, State University of West Georgia, 1600 Maple Street, Carrollton, GA 30118. Telephone: 770-836-6416. Fax: 770-836-6720. E-mail: rjohnson@westga.edu. Web site: http://www.westga.edu/.

THOMAS COLLEGE

THOMASVILLE, GEORGIA

General Independent, 4-year, coed **Entrance** Noncompetitive **Setting** 24-acre small town campus **Total enrollment** 706 **Student/faculty ratio** 14:1 **Application deadline** Rolling **Freshmen** 100% were admitted **Housing** No **Expenses** Tuition $5340 **Undergraduates** 67% women, 22% part-time, 44% 25 or older, 1% Native American, 1% Hispanic, 26% black, 0.3% Asian American or Pacific Islander **Academic program** English as a second language, advanced placement, accelerated degree program, tutorials, honors program, summer session, adult/continuing education programs, internships **Contact** Ms. Darla Glass, Registrar, Thomas College, 1501 Millpond Road, Thomasville, GA 31792-7499. Telephone: 912-226-1621 ext. 122 or toll-free 800-538-9784. Web site: http://www.thomascollege.edu/.

TOCCOA FALLS COLLEGE

TOCCOA FALLS, GEORGIA

General Independent interdenominational, comprehensive, coed **Entrance** Moderately difficult **Setting** 1,100-acre small town campus **Total enrollment** 1,032 **Student/faculty ratio** 18:1 **Application deadline** Rolling **Freshmen** 36% were admitted **Housing** Yes **Expenses** Tuition $7525; Room & Board $3708 **Undergraduates** 1% Hispanic, 3% black, 4% Asian American or Pacific Islander **Most popular recent majors** Early childhood education; mass communications; pastoral counseling **Academic program** Average class size 35, advanced placement, accelerated degree pro-

Toccoa Falls College *(continued)*

gram, self-designed majors, tutorials, summer session, adult/continuing education programs, internships **Contact** Mr. Paul Worley, Assistant Director of Enrollment Management, Toccoa Falls College, Office of Admissions, Toccoa Falls, GA 30598-1000. Telephone: 706-886-6831 ext. 5380 or toll-free 800-868-3257. Fax: 706-886-6412 ext. 5380. E-mail: admissions@toccoafalls.edu. Web site: http://www.toccoafalls.edu/.

UNIVERSITY OF GEORGIA
ATHENS, GEORGIA

General State-supported, university, coed **Entrance** Moderately difficult **Setting** 1,289-acre suburban campus **Total enrollment** 29,693 **Application deadline** 2/1 **Freshmen** 73% were admitted **Housing** Yes **Expenses** Tuition $2838; Room & Board $4323 **Undergraduates** 54% women, 10% part-time, 8% 25 or older, 0.1% Native American, 1% Hispanic, 7% black, 3% Asian American or Pacific Islander **Most popular recent majors** English; accounting; political science **Academic program** Average class size 32, English as a second language, advanced placement, accelerated degree program, self-designed majors, tutorials, honors program, summer session, adult/continuing education programs, internships **Contact** Dr. John Albright, Associate Director of Admissions, University of Georgia, Athens, GA 30602. Telephone: 706-542-3000. E-mail: undergrad@admissions.uga.edu. Web site: http://www.uga.edu/.

VALDOSTA STATE UNIVERSITY
VALDOSTA, GEORGIA

General State-supported, university, coed **Entrance** Moderately difficult **Setting** 168-acre small town campus **Total enrollment** 9,779 **Student/faculty ratio** 23:1 **Application deadline** Rolling **Freshmen** 71% were admitted **Housing** Yes **Expenses** Tuition $1974; Room & Board $3465 **Undergraduates** 21% 25 or older, 0.3% Native American, 1% Hispanic, 23% black, 1% Asian American or Pacific Islander **Most popular recent majors** Biology; business administration; early childhood education **Academic program** English as a second language, advanced placement, accelerated degree program, tutorials, honors program, summer session, adult/continuing education programs, internships **Contact** Mr. Walter Peacock, Director of Admissions, Valdosta State University, 1500 North Patterson Street, Valdosta, GA 31698. Telephone: 912-333-5791 or toll-free 800-618-1878. Fax: 912-333-5482. E-mail: btillman@valdosta.edu. Web site: http://www.valdosta.edu/.

WESLEYAN COLLEGE
MACON, GEORGIA

General Independent United Methodist, comprehensive, women only **Entrance** Moderately difficult **Setting** 200-acre suburban campus **Total enrollment** 478 **Student/faculty ratio** 9:1 **Application deadline** Rolling **Freshmen** 70% were admitted **Housing** Yes **Expenses** Tuition $14,200; Room & Board $5300 **Undergraduates** 7% part-time, 14% 25 or older, 0.4% Native American, 4% Hispanic, 22% black, 4% Asian American or Pacific Islander **Most popular recent majors** Psychology; English; early childhood education **Academic program** Average class size 20, advanced placement, accelerated degree program, self-designed majors, tutorials, honors program, summer session, adult/continuing education programs, internships **Contact** Ms. Lynne Henderson, Director of Admissions, Wesleyan College, 4760 Forsyth Road, Macon, GA 31210-4462. Telephone: 912-757-5206 or toll-free 800-447-6610. Fax: 912-757-4030. E-mail: admissions@post.wesleyan-college.edu. Web site: http://www.wesleyan-college.edu/.

WEST GEORGIA COLLEGE
See State University of West Georgia

HAWAII

BRIGHAM YOUNG UNIVERSITY–HAWAII CAMPUS
LAIE, OAHU, HAWAII

General Independent Latter-day Saints, 4-year, coed **Entrance** Moderately difficult **Setting** 60-acre small town campus **Total enrollment** 2,294 **Student/faculty ratio** 21:1 **Application deadline** 3/31 **Freshmen** 33% were admitted **Housing** Yes **Expenses** Tuition $2665; Room & Board $4900 **Undergraduates** 62% women, 6% part-time, 28% 25 or older, 0.3% Native American, 1% Hispanic, 0.3% black, 21% Asian American or Pacific Islander **Most popular recent majors** Business administration; accounting; education **Academic program** Average class size 25, English as a second language, advanced placement, accelerated degree program, honors program, summer session, adult/continuing education programs, internships **Contact** Dr. David Settle, Assistant Dean for Admissions and Records, Brigham Young University–Hawaii Campus, 55-220 Kulanui Street, Laie, Oahu, HI 96762-1294. Telephone: 808-293-3738. Web site: http://byuh.edu/.

CHAMINADE UNIVERSITY OF HONOLULU
HONOLULU, HAWAII

General Independent Roman Catholic, comprehensive, coed **Entrance** Moderately difficult **Setting** 62-acre urban campus **Total enrollment** 2,613 **Application deadline** Rolling **Freshmen** 75% were admitted **Housing** Yes **Expenses** Tuition $10,900; Room & Board $5200 **Undergraduates** 53% women, 50% part-time, 51% 25 or older, 1% Native American, 7% Hispanic, 16% black, 31% Asian American or Pacific Islander **Most Popular Recent Majors** Criminal justice/law enforcement administration; biology; behavioral sciences **Academic program** English as a second language, advanced placement, honors program, summer session, adult/continuing education programs, internships **Contact** Office of Admissions, Chaminade University of Honolulu, 3140 Waialae Avenue, Honolulu, HI 96816-1578. Telephone: 808-735-4735 or toll-free 800-735-3733 (out-of-state). Fax: 808-739-4647. E-mail: cuhadmin@lava.net. Web site: http://www.chaminade.edu/.

▶ **For more information, see page 408.**

HAWAII PACIFIC UNIVERSITY
HONOLULU, HAWAII

General Independent, comprehensive, coed **Entrance** Moderately difficult **Setting** 135-acre urban campus **Total enrollment** 8,390 **Student/faculty ratio** 20:1 **Application deadline** Rolling **Freshmen** 78% were admitted **Housing** Yes **Expenses** Tuition $7500; Room & Board $7800 **Undergraduates** 52% women, 42% part-time, 35% 25 or older, 1% Native American, 5% Hispanic, 9% black, 25% Asian American or Pacific Islander **Most popular recent majors** Business administration; computer science; travel-tourism management **Academic program** Average class size 22, English as a second language, advanced placement, accelerated degree program, self-designed majors, tutorials, honors program, summer session, adult/continuing education programs, internships **Contact** Mr. Scott Stensrud, Director of Admissions, Hawaii Pacific University, 1164 Bishop Street, Honolulu, HI 96813-2785. Telephone: 808-544-0238 or toll-free 800-669-4724 (out-of-state). Fax: 808-544-1136. E-mail: admissions@hpu.edu. Web site: http://www.hpu.edu/.

▶ **For more information, see page 448.**

INTERNATIONAL COLLEGE AND GRADUATE SCHOOL
HONOLULU, HAWAII

General Independent interdenominational, upper-level **Contact** Mr. Jon Rawlings, Director of Admissions, International College and Graduate School, 20 Dowsett Avenue, Honolulu, HI 96817. Telephone: 808-595-4247. Fax: 808-595-4779. E-mail: icgs@pixie.com. Web site: http://www.pixie.com/icga.

UNIVERSITY OF HAWAII AT HILO
HILO, HAWAII

General State-supported, 4-year, coed **Entrance** Moderately difficult **Setting** 115-acre small town campus **Total enrollment** 2,462 **Student/faculty ratio** 13:1 **Application deadline** 5/15 **Freshmen** 71% were admitted **Housing** Yes **Expenses** Tuition $2186; Room & Board $4810 **Undergraduates** 59% women, 16% part-time, 37% 25 or older, 1% Native American, 2% Hispanic, 1% black, 57% Asian American or Pacific Islander **Most popular recent majors** Business administration; psychology **Academic program** Average class size 22, English as a second language, advanced placement, self-designed majors, tutorials, honors program, summer session, internships **Contact** Mr. James Cromwell, UH Student Services Specialist III, University of Hawaii at Hilo, 200 West Kawili Street, Hilo, HI 96720-4091. Telephone: 808-974-7414 or toll-free 800-897-4456. E-mail: uhhao@hawaii.edu. Web site: http://www.uhh.hawaii.edu/.

UNIVERSITY OF HAWAII AT MANOA
HONOLULU, HAWAII

General State-supported, university, coed **Entrance** Moderately difficult **Setting** 300-acre urban campus **Total enrollment** 17,356 **Student/faculty ratio** 14:1 **Application deadline** 5/1 **Freshmen** 69% were admitted **Housing** Yes **Expenses** Tuition $2950; Room & Board $4740 **Undergraduates** 54% women, 16% part-time, 19% 25 or older, 0.2% Native American, 1% Hispanic, 1% black, 77% Asian American or Pacific Islander **Most popular recent majors** Psychology; business administration; civil engineering **Academic program** Average class size 25, English as a second language, advanced placement, self-designed majors, tutorials, honors program, summer session, adult/continuing education programs, internships **Contact** Dr. David Robb, Director of Admissions and Records, University of Hawaii at Manoa, 2600 Campus Road, Room 001, Honolulu, HI 96822. Telephone: 808-956-8975 or toll-free 800-823-9771 (in-state). Web site: http://www.hawaii.edu/admrec/.

UNIVERSITY OF HAWAII–WEST OAHU
PEARL CITY, HAWAII

General State-supported, upper-level, coed **Contact** Ms. Stella Ho-McGinnes, Dean of Student Services, University of Hawaii–West Oahu, 96-043

University of Hawaii–West Oahu *(continued)*

Ala Ike, Pearl City, HI 96782-3366. Telephone: 808-453-6565. E-mail: okazaki@uhwoa.uhwo.hawaii.edu.

IDAHO

ALBERTSON COLLEGE OF IDAHO
CALDWELL, IDAHO

General Independent, 4-year, coed **Entrance** Moderately difficult **Setting** 43-acre small town campus **Total enrollment** 671 **Student/faculty ratio** 11:1 **Application deadline** 6/1 **Freshmen** 87% were admitted **Housing** Yes **Expenses** Tuition $15,335; Room & Board $3675 **Undergraduates** 53% women, 3% part-time, 1% Native American, 4% Hispanic, 1% black, 4% Asian American or Pacific Islander **Most popular recent majors** Business administration; biology; elementary education **Academic program** Average class size 16, English as a second language, advanced placement, accelerated degree program, self-designed majors, tutorials, honors program, adult/continuing education programs, internships **Contact** Mr. Dennis P. Bergvall, Dean of Admissions, Albertson College of Idaho, 2112 Cleveland Boulevard, Caldwell, ID 83605-4494. Telephone: 208-459-5305 or toll-free 800-AC-IDAHO. Fax: 208-454-2077. E-mail: admissio@acofi.edu. Web site: http://www.acofi.edu/.

BOISE BIBLE COLLEGE
BOISE, IDAHO

General Independent nondenominational, 4-year, coed **Entrance** Minimally difficult **Setting** 17-acre suburban campus **Total enrollment** 106 **Student/faculty ratio** 9:1 **Application deadline** Rolling **Freshmen** 100% were admitted **Housing** Yes **Expenses** Tuition $4400; Room & Board $3424 **Undergraduates** 35% women, 12% part-time, 19% 25 or older, 0% Native American, 2% Hispanic, 3% black, 0% Asian American or Pacific Islander **Most popular recent majors** Divinity/ministry; biblical studies; sacred music **Academic program** Average class size 30, advanced placement, internships **Contact** Mr. Randy Bourn, Director of Admissions, Boise Bible College, 8695 Marigold Street, Boise, ID 83714-1220. Telephone: 208-376-7731 or toll-free 800-893-7755. Fax: 208-376-7743.

BOISE STATE UNIVERSITY
BOISE, IDAHO

General State-supported, comprehensive, coed **Entrance** Minimally difficult **Setting** 130-acre urban campus **Total enrollment** 15,433 **Student/faculty ratio** 17:1 **Application deadline** 7/23 **Freshmen** 87% were admitted **Housing** Yes **Expenses** Tuition $2294; Room & Board $3264 **Undergraduates** 57% women, 32% part-time, 41% 25 or older, 1% Native American, 5% Hispanic, 1% black, 2% Asian American or Pacific Islander **Most popular recent majors** Elementary education; accounting; business marketing and marketing management **Academic program** Average class size 40, English as a second language, advanced placement, self-designed majors, honors program, summer session, adult/continuing education programs, internships **Contact** Mr. Stephen Spafford, Dean of Admissions, Boise State University, 1910 University Drive, Boise, ID 83725-0399. Telephone: 208-385-1177 or toll-free 800-632-6586 (in-state), 800-824-7017 (out-of-state). E-mail: mwheeler@bsu.idbsu.edu. Web site: http://www.idbsu.edu/.

IDAHO STATE UNIVERSITY
POCATELLO, IDAHO

General State-supported, university, coed **Entrance** Minimally difficult **Setting** 735-acre small town campus **Total enrollment** 11,886 **Student/faculty ratio** 17:1 **Application deadline** 8/1 **Freshmen** 87% were admitted **Housing** Yes **Expenses** Tuition $1984; Room & Board $3580 **Undergraduates** 57% women, 22% part-time, 35% 25 or older, 2% Native American, 3% Hispanic, 1% black, 1% Asian American or Pacific Islander **Most popular recent majors** Elementary education; secondary education; biology **Academic program** English as a second language, advanced placement, self-designed majors, honors program, summer session, adult/continuing education programs, internships **Contact** Ms. Bessie Katsilometes, Director of Academic Services, Idaho State University, PO Box 8054, Pocatello, ID 83209. Telephone: 208-236-3277. Fax: 208-236-4314. E-mail: echamike@isu.edu. Web site: http://www.isu.edu/.

▶ **For more information, see page 451.**

LEWIS-CLARK STATE COLLEGE
LEWISTON, IDAHO

General State-supported, 4-year, coed **Entrance** Minimally difficult **Setting** 44-acre rural campus **Total enrollment** 2,981 **Student/faculty ratio** 15:1 **Application deadline** Rolling **Freshmen** 85% were admitted **Housing** Yes **Expenses** Tuition $1868; Room & Board $3400 **Undergraduates** 60% women, 22% part-time, 38% 25 or older, 5% Native American, 1% Hispanic, 1% black, 1% Asian American or Pacific Islander **Most popular recent majors** Elementary education; business administration; nursing **Academic program** English as a second language, advanced placement, accelerated degree program, self-designed majors, tutorials, honors program, summer session, adult/continuing education programs, internships **Contact** Mr. Steve Bussolini, Director of Admissions, Lewis-Clark State College, 500 Eighth Avenue, Lewiston, ID 83501-2698. Telephone: 208-799-2210 or toll-free 800-933-LCSC. Fax: 208-799-2063. E-mail: sbussoli@lcsc.edu. Web site: http://www.lcsc.edu/.

NORTHWEST NAZARENE COLLEGE
NAMPA, IDAHO

General Independent, comprehensive, coed, affiliated with Church of the Nazarene **Entrance** Moderately difficult **Setting** 85-acre small town campus **Total enrollment** 1,774 **Student/faculty ratio** 13:1 **Application deadline** 9/19 **Freshmen** 46% were admitted **Housing** Yes **Expenses** Tuition $12,456; Room & Board $3519 **Undergraduates** 56% women, 2% part-time, 7% 25 or older, 1% Native American, 2% Hispanic, 1% black, 2% Asian American or Pacific Islander **Most popular recent majors** Elementary education; business administration; social sciences **Academic program** Average class size 21, advanced placement, accelerated degree program, self-designed majors, tutorials, honors program, summer session, internships **Contact** Ms. Stacey Henrickson, Director of Admissions, Northwest Nazarene College, 623 Holly Street, Nampa, ID 83686-5897. Telephone: 208-467-8950 or toll-free 800-NNC-4-YOU. Fax: 208-467-8645. E-mail: bwswanson@exodus.nnc.edu. Web site: http://www.nnc.edu/.

UNIVERSITY OF IDAHO
MOSCOW, IDAHO

General State-supported, university, coed **Entrance** Moderately difficult **Setting** 1,450-acre small town campus **Total enrollment** 11,027 **Student/faculty ratio** 17:1 **Application deadline** 8/1 **Housing** Yes **Expenses** Tuition $1942; Room & Board $3824 **Undergraduates** 45% women, 9% part-time, 21% 25 or older, 1% Native American, 2% Hispanic, 1% black, 2% Asian American or Pacific Islander **Most popular recent majors** Elementary education; accounting; secondary education **Academic program** Average class size 28, English as a second language, advanced placement, accelerated degree program, self-designed majors, honors program, summer session, adult/continuing education programs, internships **Contact** Mr. Dan Davenport, Director of Admissions, University of Idaho, Moscow, ID 83844-4140. Telephone: 208-885-6326. Fax: 208-885-5752. E-mail: admappl@uidaho.edu. Web site: http://www.uidaho.edu/.

ILLINOIS

AMERICAN CONSERVATORY OF MUSIC
CHICAGO, ILLINOIS

General Independent, comprehensive, coed **Entrance** Moderately difficult **Setting** Urban campus **Total enrollment** 73 **Student/faculty ratio** 4:1 **Application deadline** Rolling **Housing** No **Expenses** Tuition $9600 **Undergraduates** 71% 25 or older **Most popular recent majors** Music (piano and organ performance); music (voice and choral/opera performance) **Academic program** Average class size 10, English as a second language, advanced placement, accelerated degree program, tutorials, summer session, adult/continuing education programs, internships **Contact** Ms. Mary Ellen Newsom, Registrar, American Conservatory of Music, 36 South Wabash Avenue, Suite 800, Chicago, IL 60603-2901. Telephone: 312-263-4161. Fax: 312-263-5832.

THE ART INSTITUTE OF ILLINOIS
See The Illinois Institute of Art

AUGUSTANA COLLEGE
ROCK ISLAND, ILLINOIS

General Independent, 4-year, coed, affiliated with Evangelical Lutheran Church in America **Entrance** Moderately difficult **Setting** 115-acre suburban campus **Total enrollment** 2,277 **Student/faculty ratio** 13:1 **Application deadline** 4/1 **Freshmen** 81% were admitted **Housing** Yes **Expenses** Tuition $15,300; Room & Board $4689 **Undergraduates** 59% women, 1% part-time, 2% 25 or older, 0.2% Native American, 2% Hispanic, 3% black, 3% Asian American or Pacific Islander **Most popular recent majors** Biology; business administration; English **Academic program** Advanced placement, accelerated degree program, tutorials, honors program, summer session, internships **Contact** Mr. Martin Sauer, Director of Admissions, Augustana College, 639 38th Street, Rock Island, IL 61201-2296. Telephone: 309-794-7341 or toll-free 800-798-8100. Fax: 309-794-7431. E-mail: admissions@augustana.edu. Web site: http://www.augustana.edu/.

AURORA UNIVERSITY
AURORA, ILLINOIS

General Independent, comprehensive, coed **Entrance** Moderately difficult **Setting** 26-acre suburban campus **Total enrollment** 2,121 **Application deadline** Rolling **Housing** Yes **Expenses** Tuition $11,310; Room & Board $4320 **Undergraduates** 59% women, 25% part-time, 42% 25 or older, 1% Native American, 7% Hispanic, 13%

Aurora University *(continued)*

black, 4% Asian American or Pacific Islander **Most popular recent majors** Nursing; elementary education; social work **Academic program** Average class size 28, advanced placement, accelerated degree program, self-designed majors, honors program, summer session, adult/continuing education programs, internships **Contact** Dean of Admissions, Aurora University, 347 South Gladstone Avenue, Aurora, IL 60506-4892. Telephone: 630-896-1975 or toll-free 800-742-5281. Fax: 630-844-5535. E-mail: admissions@admin.aurora.edu. Web site: http://www.aurora.edu/.

BARAT COLLEGE
LAKE FOREST, ILLINOIS

General Independent Roman Catholic, comprehensive, coed **Entrance** Moderately difficult **Setting** 30-acre suburban campus **Total enrollment** 749 **Application deadline** Rolling **Freshmen** 92% were admitted **Housing** Yes **Expenses** Tuition $12,570; Room & Board $4966 **Undergraduates** 77% women, 29% part-time, 41% 25 or older, 0.4% Native American, 7% Hispanic, 9% black, 4% Asian American or Pacific Islander **Most popular recent majors** Business administration; psychology; education **Academic program** English as a second language, advanced placement, accelerated degree program, self-designed majors, tutorials, summer session, adult/continuing education programs, internships **Contact** Mr. Douglas Schacke, Dean of Admission and Financial Aid, Barat College, 700 East Westleigh Road, Lake Forest, IL 60045-3297. Telephone: 847-295-4260. Fax: 847-604-6300.

BENEDICTINE UNIVERSITY
LISLE, ILLINOIS

General Independent Roman Catholic, comprehensive, coed **Entrance** Moderately difficult **Setting** 108-acre suburban campus **Total enrollment** 2,709 **Student/faculty ratio** 16:1 **Application deadline** Rolling **Freshmen** 87% were admitted **Housing** Yes **Expenses** Tuition $12,330; Room & Board $4610 **Undergraduates** 57% women, 22% part-time, 24% 25 or older, 0.1% Native American, 5% Hispanic, 6% black, 12% Asian American or Pacific Islander **Most popular recent majors** Biology; education; business economics **Academic program** English as a second language, advanced placement, accelerated degree program, tutorials, honors program, summer session, adult/continuing education programs, internships **Contact** Mr. Michael Rodewald, Undergraduate Admissions Office, Benedictine University, 5700 College Road, Lisle, IL 60532-0900. Telephone: 630-829-6300 or toll-free 800-829-6300. Fax: 630-960-1126. E-mail: admit@eagle.ibc.edu. Web site: http://www.ben.edu/.

▶ **For more information, see page 395.**

BLACKBURN COLLEGE
CARLINVILLE, ILLINOIS

General Independent Presbyterian, 4-year, coed **Entrance** Moderately difficult **Setting** 80-acre small town campus **Total enrollment** 557 **Student/faculty ratio** 15:1 **Application deadline** Rolling **Freshmen** 68% were admitted **Housing** Yes **Expenses** Tuition $7880; Room & Board $3240 **Undergraduates** 50% women, 5% part-time, 6% 25 or older **Most popular recent majors** Business administration; elementary education; biology **Academic program** Advanced placement, accelerated degree program, self-designed majors, honors program, internships **Contact** Mr. John Malin, Director of Admissions, Blackburn College, 700 College Avenue, Carlinville, IL 62626-1498. Telephone: 217-854-3231 ext. 4252 or toll-free 800-233-3550. Fax: 217-854-3713.

BLESSING-RIEMAN COLLEGE OF NURSING
QUINCY, ILLINOIS

General Independent, 4-year, primarily women **Entrance** Moderately difficult **Setting** 1-acre small town campus **Total enrollment** 132 **Application deadline** Rolling **Freshmen** 63% were admitted **Housing** Yes **Expenses** Tuition $9200; Room & Board $4230 **Undergraduates** 91% women, 14% part-time, 27% 25 or older, 0% Native American, 1% Hispanic, 3% black, 1% Asian American or Pacific Islander **Academic program** Advanced placement, summer session, adult/continuing education programs, internships **Contact** Ms. Linda Riggs Mayfield, Director of Enrollment Management/Registrar, Blessing-Rieman College of Nursing, Broadway at 11th Street, POB 7005, Quincy, IL 62305-7005. Telephone: 217-228-5520 ext. 6992 or toll-free 800-877-9140. Fax: 217-223-6400. E-mail: bradmiss@moses.culver.edu. Web site: http://www.rsa.lib.il.us/bles/homepg.html.

BRADLEY UNIVERSITY
PEORIA, ILLINOIS

General Independent, comprehensive, coed **Entrance** Moderately difficult **Setting** 65-acre urban campus **Total enrollment** 5,861 **Student/faculty ratio** 14:1 **Application deadline** Rolling **Freshmen** 89% were admitted **Housing** Yes **Expenses** Tuition $12,690; Room & Board $4690 **Undergraduates** 53% women, 11% part-time, 11% 25 or older, 0.2% Native American, 2% Hispanic, 5% black, 2% Asian American or Pacific Islander **Most popular recent majors** Communications;

psychology; accounting **Academic program** Advanced placement, accelerated degree program, self-designed majors, tutorials, honors program, summer session, adult/continuing education programs, internships **Contact** Ms. Nickie Roberson, Director of Admissions, Bradley University, 1501 West Bradley Avenue, Peoria, IL 61625-0002. Telephone: 309-677-1000 or toll-free 800-447-6460. E-mail: admissions@bradley.edu. Web site: http://www.bradley.edu/.

CHICAGO STATE UNIVERSITY

CHICAGO, ILLINOIS

General State-supported, comprehensive, coed **Contact** Ms. Annie Epps, Director of Admissions, Chicago State University, 95th Street at King Drive, Chicago, IL 60628. Telephone: 773-995-2513.

COLLEGE OF ST. FRANCIS

See University of St. Francis

COLUMBIA COLLEGE

CHICAGO, ILLINOIS

General Independent, comprehensive, coed **Entrance** Noncompetitive **Setting** Urban campus **Total enrollment** 8,473 **Student/faculty ratio** 7:1 **Application deadline** Rolling **Freshmen** 90% were admitted **Housing** Yes **Expenses** Tuition $8618; Room only $4523 **Undergraduates** 48% women, 26% part-time, 28% 25 or older, 0.5% Native American, 11% Hispanic, 20% black, 4% Asian American or Pacific Islander **Most popular recent majors** Film/video production; art; radio/television broadcasting **Academic program** Average class size 15, English as a second language, advanced placement, self-designed majors, tutorials, summer session, adult/continuing education programs, internships **Contact** Mr. Terry Miller, Director of Admissions and Recruitment, Columbia College, 600 South Michigan Avenue, Chicago, IL 60605-1997. Telephone: 312-663-1600 ext. 7133. E-mail: admissions@mail.colum.edu. Web site: http://www.colum.edu/.

CONCORDIA UNIVERSITY

RIVER FOREST, ILLINOIS

General Independent, comprehensive, coed, affiliated with Lutheran Church–Missouri Synod **Entrance** Moderately difficult **Setting** 40-acre suburban campus **Total enrollment** 1,860 **Student/faculty ratio** 17:1 **Application deadline** Rolling **Freshmen** 54% were admitted **Housing** Yes **Expenses** Tuition $11,987; Room & Board $5024 **Undergraduates** 68% women, 15% part-time, 20% 25 or older, 0% Native American, 4% Hispanic, 7% black, 3% Asian American or Pacific Islander **Most popular recent majors** Education; nursing; psychology **Academic program** Average class size 25, advanced placement, accelerated degree program, honors program, summer session, adult/continuing education programs, internships **Contact** Mr. Kurt R. Schick, Director of Undergraduate Admission, Concordia University, 7400 Augusta Street, River Forest, IL 60305-1499. Telephone: 708-209-3100 or toll-free 800-285-2668. Fax: 708-209-3176. E-mail: crfadmis@crf.cuis.edu. Web site: http://www.curf.edu/.

DEPAUL UNIVERSITY

CHICAGO, ILLINOIS

General Independent Roman Catholic, university, coed **Entrance** Moderately difficult **Setting** 36-acre urban campus **Total enrollment** 17,804 **Student/faculty ratio** 16:1 **Application deadline** 8/15 **Freshmen** 80% were admitted **Housing** Yes **Expenses** Tuition $13,490; Room & Board $5841 **Undergraduates** 61% women, 34% part-time, 45% 25 or older, 0.4% Native American, 12% Hispanic, 12% black, 8% Asian American or Pacific Islander **Most popular recent majors** Accounting; finance; mass communications **Academic program** English as a second language, advanced placement, accelerated degree program, self-designed majors, tutorials, honors program, summer session, adult/continuing education programs, internships **Contact** Mr. Ray Kennelley, Dean of Admission, DePaul University, 1 East Jackson Boulevard, Chicago, IL 60604-2287. Telephone: 312-362-8300 or toll-free 800-4DE-PAUL (out-of-state). Fax: 312-362-3322. E-mail: admitdpu@wppost.depaul.edu. Web site: http://www.depaul.edu/.

DEVRY INSTITUTE OF TECHNOLOGY

ADDISON, ILLINOIS

General Proprietary, 4-year, coed **Entrance** Minimally difficult **Setting** 14-acre suburban campus **Total enrollment** 3,712 **Student/faculty ratio** 30:1 **Application deadline** Rolling **Freshmen** 76% were admitted **Housing** No **Expenses** Tuition $7308 **Undergraduates** 22% women, 40% part-time, 44% 25 or older, 0.5% Native American, 6% Hispanic, 9% black, 9% Asian American or Pacific Islander **Most popular recent majors** Information sciences/systems; electrical/electronic engineering technology **Academic program** Advanced placement, accelerated degree program, summer session, adult/continuing education programs **Contact** Ms. Tash Uray, Director of Admissions, DeVry Institute of Technology, 1221 North Swift Road, Addison, IL 60101-6106. Telephone: 630-953-2000 or toll-free 800-346-5420 (out-of-state). Web site: http://www.devry.com/.

DEVRY INSTITUTE OF TECHNOLOGY
CHICAGO, ILLINOIS

General Proprietary, 4-year, coed **Entrance** Minimally difficult **Setting** 17-acre urban campus **Total enrollment** 3,492 **Student/faculty ratio** 20:1 **Application deadline** Rolling **Freshmen** 83% were admitted **Housing** No **Expenses** Tuition $7308 **Undergraduates** 32% women, 37% part-time, 45% 25 or older, 1% Native American, 22% Hispanic, 33% black, 14% Asian American or Pacific Islander **Most popular recent majors** Information sciences/systems; electrical/electronic engineering technology **Academic program** English as a second language, advanced placement, accelerated degree program, summer session, adult/continuing education programs **Contact** Mr. Hamed Shibly, Director of Admissions, DeVry Institute of Technology, 3300 North Campbell Avenue, Chicago, IL 60618-5994. Telephone: 773-929-6550 or toll-free 800-383-3879 (out-of-state). E-mail: gkroepel@chi.devry.edu. Web site: http://www.chi.devry.edu/.

DR. WILLIAM M. SCHOLL COLLEGE OF PODIATRIC MEDICINE
CHICAGO, ILLINOIS

General Independent, upper-level, coed **Entrance** Moderately difficult **Setting** Urban campus **Total enrollment** 373 **Application deadline** 4/1 **Housing** No **Expenses** Tuition $19,310 **Undergraduates** 64% 25 or older **Academic program** Honors program, adult/continuing education programs **Contact** Dr. Howard M. Bers, Associate Dean for Student Affairs, Dr. William M. Scholl College of Podiatric Medicine, 1001 North Dearborn Street, Chicago, IL 60610-2856. Telephone: 312-280-2940 or toll-free 800-843-3059 (out-of-state). Fax: 312-280-2997. E-mail: admiss@scholl.edu. Web site: http://www.scholl.edu/.

DOMINICAN UNIVERSITY
RIVER FOREST, ILLINOIS

General Independent Roman Catholic, comprehensive, coed **Entrance** Moderately difficult **Setting** 30-acre suburban campus **Total enrollment** 1,800 **Student/faculty ratio** 12:1 **Application deadline** Rolling **Freshmen** 86% were admitted **Housing** Yes **Expenses** Tuition $13,700; Room & Board $4880 **Undergraduates** 72% women, 19% part-time, 20% 25 or older, 0.1% Native American, 12% Hispanic, 5% black, 2% Asian American or Pacific Islander **Most popular recent majors** Business administration; accounting; psychology **Academic program** Average class size 15, English as a second language, advanced placement, accelerated degree program, self-designed majors, tutorials, honors program, summer session, adult/continuing education programs, internships **Contact** Ms. Hildegarde Schmidt, Dean of Admissions and Financial Aid, Dominican University, 7900 West Division Street, River Forest, IL 60305-1099. Telephone: 708-524-6800 or toll-free 800-828-8475. Fax: 708-366-5360. E-mail: domadmis@email.dom.edu. Web site: http://www.dom.edu/.

EASTERN ILLINOIS UNIVERSITY
CHARLESTON, ILLINOIS

General State-supported, comprehensive, coed **Entrance** Moderately difficult **Setting** 320-acre small town campus **Total enrollment** 11,777 **Student/faculty ratio** 15:1 **Application deadline** Rolling **Freshmen** 75% were admitted **Housing** Yes **Expenses** Tuition $3112; Room & Board $3919 **Undergraduates** 58% women, 9% part-time, 10% 25 or older, 0.2% Native American, 1% Hispanic, 5% black, 1% Asian American or Pacific Islander **Most popular recent majors** Elementary education; psychology; speech/rhetorical studies **Academic program** Average class size 35, English as a second language, advanced placement, tutorials, honors program, summer session, adult/continuing education programs, internships **Contact** Mr. Dale W. Wolf, Director of Admissions, Eastern Illinois University, 600 Lincoln Avenue, Charleston, IL 61920-3099. Telephone: 217-581-2223 or toll-free 800-252-5711. Fax: 217-581-7060. E-mail: admissns@eiu.edu. Web site: http://www.eiu.edu/.

▶ **For more information, see page 426.**

EAST-WEST UNIVERSITY
CHICAGO, ILLINOIS

General Independent, 4-year, coed **Entrance** Minimally difficult **Setting** Urban campus **Total enrollment** 584 **Application deadline** Rolling **Freshmen** 94% were admitted **Housing** No **Expenses** Tuition $6960 **Undergraduates** 56% women, 2% part-time, 34% 25 or older **Most popular recent majors** Business administration; electrical/electronic engineering technology; computer science **Academic program** Summer session **Contact** Mr. George Carbart, Director of Admissions, East-West University, 816 South Michigan Avenue, Chicago, IL 60605-2103. Telephone: 312-939-0111. Fax: 312-939-0083.

ELMHURST COLLEGE
ELMHURST, ILLINOIS

General Independent, 4-year, coed, affiliated with United Church of Christ **Entrance** Moderately difficult **Setting** 38-acre suburban campus **Total enrollment** 2,842 **Student/faculty ratio** 14:1 **Application deadline** 7/15 **Freshmen** 72% were admitted **Housing** Yes **Expenses** Tuition $11,900; Room & Board $5000 **Undergraduates** 64% women, 27% part-time, 36% 25 or older, 0.3% Native American, 5% Hispanic, 5% black, 2% Asian American or Pacific Islander **Most popular recent majors** Business administration; elementary education; psychology **Academic program** Average class size 25, advanced placement, accelerated degree program, tutorials, honors program, summer session, adult/continuing education programs, internships **Contact** Mr. Stephen Mueller, Director of Freshman Admission, Elmhurst College, 190 Prospect Avenue, Elmhurst, IL 60126-3296. Telephone: 630-617-3068 or toll-free 800-697-1871 (out-of-state). Fax: 630-617-5501. E-mail: admit@elmhurst.edu. Web site: http://www.elmhurst.edu/.

EUREKA COLLEGE
EUREKA, ILLINOIS

General Independent, 4-year, coed, affiliated with Christian Church (Disciples of Christ) **Entrance** Moderately difficult **Setting** 112-acre small town campus **Total enrollment** 511 **Student/faculty ratio** 12:1 **Application deadline** Rolling **Freshmen** 76% were admitted **Housing** Yes **Expenses** Tuition $13,950; Room & Board $4400 **Undergraduates** 6% 25 or older **Most popular recent majors** Education; business administration; athletic training/sports medicine **Academic program** Average class size 20, advanced placement, self-designed majors, tutorials, honors program, internships **Contact** Mr. Kurt R. Krile, Dean of Admissions and Financial Aid, Eureka College, 300 East College Avenue, Eureka, IL 61530-0128. Telephone: 309-467-6350 or toll-free 888-4-EUREKA. Fax: 309-467-6576. E-mail: admissions@eureka.edu. Web site: http://www.eureka.edu/.

FINCH UNIVERSITY OF HEALTH SCIENCES/ THE CHICAGO MEDICAL SCHOOL
NORTH CHICAGO, ILLINOIS

General Independent, upper-level, coed **Entrance** Minimally difficult **Setting** 50-acre suburban campus **Total enrollment** 1,428 **Student/faculty ratio** 3:1 **Application deadline** 8/15 **Freshmen** 20% were admitted **Housing** No **Expenses** Tuition $11,342 **Undergraduates** 69% women, 11% part-time, 46% 25 or older, 1% Native American, 2% Hispanic, 0% black, 8% Asian American or Pacific Islander **Academic program** Average class size 40, advanced placement, tutorials, summer session, adult/continuing education programs, internships **Contact** Ms. Kristine A. Jones, Director of Admissions and Records, Finch University of Health Sciences/The Chicago Medical School, 3333 Green Bay Road, North Chicago, IL 60064-3095. Telephone: 847-578-3204. Fax: 847-578-3284.

GOVERNORS STATE UNIVERSITY
UNIVERSITY PARK, ILLINOIS

General State-supported, upper-level, coed **Entrance** Minimally difficult **Setting** 750-acre suburban campus **Total enrollment** 6,200 **Student/faculty ratio** 16:1 **Application deadline** 7/15 **Housing** No **Expenses** Tuition $2278 **Undergraduates** 55% 25 or older, 0.3% Native American, 4% Hispanic, 25% black, 1% Asian American or Pacific Islander **Most popular recent majors** Business administration; elementary education; nursing **Academic program** Advanced placement, self-designed majors, honors program, summer session, adult/continuing education programs, internships **Contact** Mr. Michael Toney, Director of Admissions, Governors State University, University Park, IL 60466. Telephone: 708-534-4490. Fax: 708-534-1640. Web site: http://www.govst.edu/.

GREENVILLE COLLEGE
GREENVILLE, ILLINOIS

General Independent Free Methodist, 4-year, coed **Entrance** Moderately difficult **Setting** 12-acre small town campus **Total enrollment** 955 **Student/faculty ratio** 16:1 **Application deadline** Rolling **Freshmen** 74% were admitted **Housing** Yes **Expenses** Tuition $12,586; Room & Board $4850 **Undergraduates** 56% women, 1% part-time, 20% 25 or older, 1% Native American, 2% Hispanic, 4% black, 2% Asian American or Pacific Islander **Most popular recent majors** Education; business administration; biology **Academic program** Average class size 40, English as a second language, advanced placement, accelerated degree program, self-designed majors, tutorials, honors program, summer session, adult/continuing education programs, internships **Contact** Mr. Randy Comfort, Dean of Admissions, Greenville College, 315 East College, PO Box 159, Greenville, IL 62246-0159. Telephone: 618-664-2800 ext. 4401 or toll-free 800-248-2288 (in-state), 800-345-4440 (out-of-state). Fax: 618-664-9841. E-mail: admissions@greenville.edu. Web site: http://www.greenville.edu/.

HARRINGTON INSTITUTE OF INTERIOR DESIGN
CHICAGO, ILLINOIS

General Proprietary, 4-year, coed **Entrance** Noncompetitive **Setting** Urban campus **Total enrollment** 384 **Student/faculty ratio** 11:1 **Application deadline** Rolling **Housing** No **Expenses** Tuition $10,466 **Undergraduates** 86% women, 40% part-time, 64% 25 or older, 0% Native American, 5% Hispanic, 9% black, 5% Asian American or Pacific Islander **Academic program** English as a

Harrington Institute of Interior Design *(continued)*

second language, adult/continuing education programs, internships **Contact** Ms. Wendy Davidson, Director of Admissions, Harrington Institute of Interior Design, 410 South Michigan Avenue, Chicago, IL 60605-1496. Telephone: 312-939-4975. Fax: 312-939-8005. E-mail: harringtoninstitute@interiordesign.edu. Web site: http://www.interiordesign.edu/.

HEBREW THEOLOGICAL COLLEGE

COORDINATE WITH ANNE M. BLITSTEIN TEACHERS INSTITUTE OF THE HEBREW THEOLOGICAL COLLEGE

SKOKIE, ILLINOIS

General Independent Jewish, 4-year, men only, coordinate with Anne M. Blitstein Teachers Institute of the Hebrew Theological College **Entrance** Moderately difficult **Setting** 13-acre suburban campus **Application deadline** Rolling **Housing** Yes **Expenses** Tuition $6500 **Academic program** Advanced placement, accelerated degree program, tutorials, summer session, internships **Contact** Office of Admissions, Hebrew Theological College, 7135 North Carpenter Road, Skokie, IL 60077-3263. Telephone: 847-982-2500. Web site: http://www.htcnet.edu/.

ILLINOIS COLLEGE

JACKSONVILLE, ILLINOIS

General Independent interdenominational, 4-year, coed **Entrance** Moderately difficult **Setting** 62-acre small town campus **Total enrollment** 909 **Student/faculty ratio** 15:1 **Application deadline** 8/15 **Freshmen** 84% were admitted **Housing** Yes **Expenses** Tuition $9500; Room & Board $4200 **Undergraduates** 58% women, 2% part-time, 4% 25 or older, 0.2% Native American, 0.4% Hispanic, 2% black, 1% Asian American or Pacific Islander **Most popular recent majors** Business administration; biology; education **Academic program** Advanced placement, accelerated degree program, tutorials, summer session, internships **Contact** Mr. Gale Vaughn, Director of Enrollment, Illinois College, 1101 West College Avenue, Jacksonville, IL 62650-2299. Telephone: 217-245-3030 or toll-free 888-595-3030. Fax: 217-245-3034. E-mail: admissions@hilltop.ic.edu. Web site: http://www.ic.edu/.

THE ILLINOIS INSTITUTE OF ART

CHICAGO, ILLINOIS

General Proprietary, 4-year, coed **Entrance** Minimally difficult **Setting** Urban campus **Total enrollment** 600 **Application deadline** Rolling **Freshmen** 95% were admitted **Housing** No **Expenses** Tuition $9984 **Undergraduates** 30% 25 or older **Most popular recent majors** Computer graphics; fashion design/illustration; graphic design/commercial art/illustration **Academic program** Advanced placement, accelerated degree program, summer session, adult/continuing education programs, internships **Contact** Ms. Janis Anton, Director of Admissions, The Illinois Institute of Art, 350 North Orleans, Chicago, IL 60654. Telephone: 312-280-3500 ext. 132. Fax: 312-280-3528. Web site: http://www.aii.edu/.

ILLINOIS INSTITUTE OF TECHNOLOGY

CHICAGO, ILLINOIS

General Independent, university, coed **Entrance** Very difficult **Setting** 120-acre urban campus **Total enrollment** 6,100 **Student/faculty ratio** 11:1 **Application deadline** Rolling **Freshmen** 68% were admitted **Housing** Yes **Expenses** Tuition $16,620; Room & Board $4940 **Undergraduates** 21% women, 19% part-time, 29% 25 or older, 0.2% Native American, 8% Hispanic, 10% black, 13% Asian American or Pacific Islander **Most popular recent majors** Electrical/electronics engineering; mechanical engineering; architecture **Academic program** English as a second language, advanced placement, accelerated degree program, tutorials, summer session, internships **Contact** Dr. Carole L. Snow, Dean of Admission, Illinois Institute of Technology, 10 West 33rd Street PH101, Chicago, IL 60616-3793. Telephone: 312-567-3025 or toll-free 800-448-2329 (out-of-state). Fax: 312-567-6939. E-mail: admission@vax1.ais.iit.edu. Web site: http://www.iit.edu/.

ILLINOIS STATE UNIVERSITY

NORMAL, ILLINOIS

General State-supported, university, coed **Entrance** Moderately difficult **Setting** 850-acre urban campus **Total enrollment** 20,331 **Student/faculty ratio** 20:1 **Application deadline** 5/1 **Freshmen** 79% were admitted **Housing** Yes **Expenses** Tuition $4123; Room & Board $3975 **Undergraduates** 57% women, 8% part-time, 11% 25 or older, 0.4% Native American, 2% Hispanic, 8% black, 2% Asian American or Pacific Islander **Most popular recent majors** Elementary education; business; management information systems/business data processing **Academic program** Average class size 47, English as a second language, advanced placement, accelerated degree program, self-designed majors, tutorials, honors program, summer session, internships **Contact** Mr. Steve Adams, Director of Admissions, Illinois State University, Campus Box 2200, Normal, IL 61790-2200. Telephone: 309-438-2181 or toll-free 800-

366-2478 (in-state). Fax: 309-438-3932. E-mail: pawutz@rs6000.cmp.ilstu.edu. Web site: http://www.ilstu.edu/.

ILLINOIS WESLEYAN UNIVERSITY
BLOOMINGTON, ILLINOIS

General Independent, 4-year, coed **Entrance** Very difficult **Setting** 70-acre suburban campus **Total enrollment** 2,021 **Student/faculty ratio** 13:1 **Application deadline** Rolling **Freshmen** 60% were admitted **Housing** Yes **Expenses** Tuition $18,376; Room & Board $4824 **Undergraduates** 53% women, 0.4% part-time, 1% 25 or older, 0.1% Native American, 2% Hispanic, 4% black, 4% Asian American or Pacific Islander **Most popular recent majors** Business administration; biology; English **Academic program** Advanced placement, accelerated degree program, self-designed majors, honors program, summer session, internships **Contact** Mr. James R. Ruoti, Dean of Admissions, Illinois Wesleyan University, PO Box 2900, Bloomington, IL 61702-2900. Telephone: 309-556-3031 or toll-free 800-332-2498. Fax: 309-556-3411. E-mail: iwuadmit@titan.iwu.edu. Web site: http://www.iwu.edu/.

INTERNATIONAL ACADEMY OF MERCHANDISING & DESIGN, LTD.
CHICAGO, ILLINOIS

General Proprietary, 4-year, coed **Entrance** Minimally difficult **Setting** Urban campus **Total enrollment** 815 **Student/faculty ratio** 15:1 **Application deadline** Rolling **Housing** No **Expenses** Tuition $9900 **Undergraduates** 47% 25 or older, 0% Native American, 14% Hispanic, 25% black, 6% Asian American or Pacific Islander **Most popular recent majors** Fashion merchandising; fashion design/illustration; interior design **Academic program** Advanced placement, summer session, adult/continuing education programs, internships **Contact** Mr. Raymond Sokohl, Director of Admissions, International Academy of Merchandising & Design, Ltd., One North State Street, Suite 400, Chicago, IL 60602-9736. Telephone: 312-541-3900 or toll-free 800-ACADEMY (out-of-state). Fax: 312-828-9405. Web site: http://www.iamd.edu/.

JUDSON COLLEGE
ELGIN, ILLINOIS

General Independent Baptist, 4-year, coed **Entrance** Moderately difficult **Setting** 80-acre suburban campus **Total enrollment** 993 **Student/faculty ratio** 15:1 **Application deadline** 8/15 **Freshmen** 90% were admitted **Housing** Yes **Expenses** Tuition $12,310; Room & Board $4910 **Undergraduates** 62% women, 16% part-time, 18% 25 or older, 0.1% Native American, 4% Hispanic, 3% black, 2% Asian American or Pacific Islander **Most popular recent majors** Education; business administration; graphic design/commercial art/illustration **Academic program** Average class size 25, English as a second language, advanced placement, accelerated degree program, self-designed majors, tutorials, honors program, summer session, adult/continuing education programs, internships **Contact** Mr. Brad Hughes, Director of Admissions, Judson College, 1151 North State Street, Elgin, IL 60123-1498. Telephone: 847-695-2500 ext. 2310 or toll-free 800-879-5376. Fax: 847-695-0216. E-mail: admission@mail.judson-il.edu. Web site: http://www.judson-il.edu/.

▶ **For more information, see page 453.**

KENDALL COLLEGE
EVANSTON, ILLINOIS

General Independent United Methodist, 4-year, coed **Entrance** Moderately difficult **Setting** 1-acre suburban campus **Total enrollment** 493 **Student/faculty ratio** 15:1 **Application deadline** Rolling **Housing** Yes **Expenses** Tuition $10,128; Room & Board $5091 **Undergraduates** 44% women, 25% part-time, 45% 25 or older, 0.4% Native American, 8% Hispanic, 14% black, 3% Asian American or Pacific Islander **Most popular recent majors** Culinary arts; early childhood education; business administration **Academic program** Advanced placement, self-designed majors, tutorials, summer session, internships **Contact** Ms. Jennifer McDermott, Director of Admissions, Kendall College, 2408 Orrington Avenue, Evanston, IL 60201-2899. Telephone: 847-866-1304. Fax: 847-866-1320. Web site: http://www.kendall.edu/.

KNOX COLLEGE
GALESBURG, ILLINOIS

General Independent, 4-year, coed **Entrance** Very difficult **Setting** 75-acre small town campus **Total enrollment** 1,195 **Student/faculty ratio** 12:1 **Application deadline** 2/15 **Freshmen** 79% were admitted **Housing** Yes **Expenses** Tuition $19,074; Room & Board $5076 **Undergraduates** 55% women, 1% part-time, 1% 25 or older, 0.4% Native American, 4% Hispanic, 4% black, 5% Asian American or Pacific Islander **Most popular recent majors** Biology; creative writing; psychology **Academic program** Average class size 16, English as a second language, advanced placement, self-designed majors, tutorials, honors program, internships **Contact** Mr. Paul Steenis, Director of Admissions, Knox College, Admissions Office, Box K-148, Galesburg, IL 61401. Telephone: 309-341-7100 or toll-free 800-678-KNOX. Fax: 309-341-7070. E-mail: admission@knox.edu. Web site: http://www.knox.edu/.

LAKE FOREST COLLEGE
LAKE FOREST, ILLINOIS

General Independent, comprehensive, coed **Entrance** Very difficult **Setting** 110-acre suburban campus **Total enrollment** 1,190 **Student/faculty ratio** 11:1 **Application deadline** 3/1 **Freshmen** 78% were admitted **Housing** Yes **Expenses** Tuition $19,560; Room & Board $4550 **Undergraduates** 55% women, 1% part-time, 2% 25 or older, 0.3% Native American, 4% Hispanic, 7% black, 4% Asian American or Pacific Islander **Most popular recent majors** Psychology; English; business economics **Academic program** Average class size 19, English as a second language, advanced placement, accelerated degree program, self-designed majors, tutorials, honors program, summer session, adult/continuing education programs, internships **Contact** Mr. William G. Motzer Jr., Director of Admissions, Lake Forest College, 555 North Sheridan Road, Lake Forest, IL 60045-2399. Telephone: 847-735-5000 or toll-free 800-828-4751. Fax: 847-735-6271. E-mail: motzer@lfc.edu. Web site: http://www.lfc.edu/.

LAKEVIEW COLLEGE OF NURSING
DANVILLE, ILLINOIS

General Independent, upper-level, coed **Entrance** Moderately difficult **Setting** Small town campus **Total enrollment** 108 **Application deadline** Rolling **Freshmen** 100% were admitted **Housing** No **Expenses** Tuition $7099 **Undergraduates** 94% women, 41% part-time, 51% 25 or older, 0% Native American, 2% Hispanic, 5% black, 1% Asian American or Pacific Islander **Academic program** Summer session **Contact** Mr. Tom Dequimpaul, Director of Student Services, Lakeview College of Nursing, 812 North Logan Avenue, Danville, IL 61832. Telephone: 217-443-5238. Fax: 217-431-4015.

LEWIS UNIVERSITY
ROMEOVILLE, ILLINOIS

General Independent, comprehensive, coed, affiliated with Roman Catholic Church **Entrance** Moderately difficult **Setting** 600-acre small town campus **Total enrollment** 3,977 **Student/faculty ratio** 17:1 **Application deadline** Rolling **Freshmen** 85% were admitted **Housing** Yes **Expenses** Tuition $13,024; Room & Board $5500 **Undergraduates** 54% women, 36% part-time, 46% 25 or older, 0.3% Native American, 6% Hispanic, 14% black, 3% Asian American or Pacific Islander **Most popular recent majors** Nursing; business administration; criminal justice/law enforcement administration **Academic program** Average class size 25, advanced placement, accelerated degree program, self-designed majors, tutorials, summer session, adult/continuing education programs, internships **Contact** Ms. Karen Calloway, Assistant Director of Admissions, Lewis University, Route 53, Romeoville, IL 60446. Telephone: 815-838-0500 ext. 5237. Fax: 815-838-9456.

LINCOLN CHRISTIAN COLLEGE
LINCOLN, ILLINOIS

General Independent, 4-year, coed, affiliated with Christian Churches and Churches of Christ **Entrance** Moderately difficult **Setting** 227-acre small town campus **Total enrollment** 625 **Student/faculty ratio** 15:1 **Application deadline** Rolling **Freshmen** 82% were admitted **Housing** Yes **Expenses** Tuition $6324; Room & Board $3800 **Undergraduates** 54% women, 18% part-time, 21% 25 or older, 1% Native American, 2% Hispanic, 3% black, 0.3% Asian American or Pacific Islander **Most popular recent majors** Divinity/ministry; religious education; elementary education **Academic program** Advanced placement, summer session, adult/continuing education programs, internships **Contact** Ms. Patsy Wilson, Assistant Director of Admissions, Lincoln Christian College, 100 Campus View Drive, Lincoln, IL 62656-2167. Telephone: 217-732-3168 ext. 2218 or toll-free 888-522-5228. Fax: 217-732-5914. E-mail: coladmis@lccs.edu. Web site: http://www.lccs.edu/.

LOYOLA UNIVERSITY CHICAGO
CHICAGO, ILLINOIS

General Independent Roman Catholic (Jesuit), university, coed **Entrance** Moderately difficult **Setting** 105-acre urban campus **Total enrollment** 13,604 **Student/faculty ratio** 13:1 **Application deadline** 4/1 **Freshmen** 89% were admitted **Housing** Yes **Expenses** Tuition $16,054; Room & Board $6380 **Undergraduates** 63% women, 25% part-time, 6% 25 or older, 0.2% Native American, 8% Hispanic, 8% black, 13% Asian American or Pacific Islander **Most popular recent majors** Psychology; biology; nursing **Academic program** Average class size 24, English as a second language, advanced placement, accelerated degree program, honors program, summer session, adult/continuing education programs, internships **Contact** Mr. Edward Moore, Director of Admissions, Loyola University Chicago, 820 North Michigan Avenue, Chicago, IL 60611-2196. Telephone: 312-915-6500 or toll-free 800-262-2373. E-mail: admission@luc.edu. Web site: http://www.luc.edu/.

▶ **For more information, see page 460.**

MACMURRAY COLLEGE
JACKSONVILLE, ILLINOIS

General Independent United Methodist, 4-year, coed **Entrance** Moderately difficult **Setting** 60-

acre small town campus **Total enrollment** 647 **Student/faculty ratio** 12:1 **Application deadline** 7/15 **Freshmen** 77% were admitted **Housing** Yes **Expenses** Tuition $11,820; Room & Board $4210 **Undergraduates** 56% women, 7% part-time, 14% 25 or older, 0.5% Native American, 3% Hispanic, 7% black, 0.2% Asian American or Pacific Islander **Most popular recent majors** Special education; nursing; business administration **Academic program** Average class size 20, advanced placement, tutorials, honors program, summer session, internships **Contact** Mrs. Lori A. Hall, Dean of Enrollment, MacMurray College, 447 East College Avenue, Jacksonville, IL 62650. Telephone: 217-479-7056 or toll-free 800-252-7485 (in-state). Fax: 217-245-0405. E-mail: admiss@mac.edu. Web site: http://www.mac.edu/.

MCKENDREE COLLEGE
LEBANON, ILLINOIS

General Independent, 4-year, coed, affiliated with United Methodist Church **Entrance** Moderately difficult **Setting** 80-acre small town campus **Total enrollment** 1,848 **Student/faculty ratio** 13:1 **Application deadline** Rolling **Freshmen** 70% were admitted **Housing** Yes **Expenses** Tuition $10,400; Room & Board $4600 **Undergraduates** 61% women, 35% part-time, 48% 25 or older, 0.4% Native American, 1% Hispanic, 9% black, 1% Asian American or Pacific Islander **Most popular recent majors** Business administration; nursing; elementary education **Academic program** Average class size 20, English as a second language, advanced placement, accelerated degree program, self-designed majors, tutorials, honors program, summer session, internships **Contact** Mrs. Sue Cordon, Dean of Admissions, McKendree College, 701 College Road, Lebanon, IL 62254-1299. Telephone: 618-537-4481 ext. 6830 or toll-free 800-232-7228 (in-state). Fax: 618-537-6259.

MENNONITE COLLEGE OF NURSING
BLOOMINGTON, ILLINOIS

General Independent interdenominational, upper-level, coed **Entrance** Moderately difficult **Setting** 2-acre urban campus **Total enrollment** 220 **Student/faculty ratio** 8:1 **Application deadline** Rolling **Freshmen** 49% were admitted **Housing** Yes **Expenses** Tuition $9364; Room & Board $2680 **Undergraduates** 90% women, 7% part-time, 31% 25 or older, 0% Native American, 2% Hispanic, 3% black, 3% Asian American or Pacific Islander **Academic program** Average class size 25, advanced placement, tutorials, summer session **Contact** Mrs. Mary Ann Watkins, Director of Admissions and Financial Aid, Mennonite College of Nursing, 804 North East Street, Bloomington, IL 61701. Telephone: 309-829-0718. Fax: 309-829-0789. Web site: http://www.mcon.edu/.

MILLIKIN UNIVERSITY
DECATUR, ILLINOIS

General Independent, 4-year, coed, affiliated with Presbyterian Church (U.S.A.) **Entrance** Moderately difficult **Setting** 70-acre suburban campus **Total enrollment** 1,997 **Student/faculty ratio** 15:1 **Application deadline** Rolling **Freshmen** 86% were admitted **Housing** Yes **Expenses** Tuition $14,138; Room & Board $5070 **Undergraduates** 56% women, 3% part-time, 5% 25 or older, 0.2% Native American, 1% Hispanic, 8% black, 2% Asian American or Pacific Islander **Most popular recent majors** Biology; nursing; elementary education **Academic program** Average class size 22, advanced placement, self-designed majors, tutorials, honors program, summer session, adult/continuing education programs, internships **Contact** Mr. Lin Stoner, Dean of Admission, Millikin University, 1184 West Main Street, Decatur, IL 62522. Telephone: 217-424-6210 or toll-free 800-373-7733. Fax: 217-425-4669. E-mail: admis@mail.millikin.edu. Web site: http://www.millikin.edu/.

MONMOUTH COLLEGE
MONMOUTH, ILLINOIS

General Independent, 4-year, coed, affiliated with Presbyterian Church **Entrance** Moderately difficult **Setting** 40-acre suburban campus **Total enrollment** 1,044 **Student/faculty ratio** 14:1 **Application deadline** 5/1 **Freshmen** 78% were admitted **Housing** Yes **Expenses** Tuition $15,120; Room & Board $4410 **Undergraduates** 60% women, 0.2% part-time, 4% 25 or older, 0.4% Native American, 2% Hispanic, 3% black, 1% Asian American or Pacific Islander **Most popular recent majors** Business administration; education; biology **Academic program** Average class size 22, advanced placement, self-designed majors, honors program, summer session, internships **Contact** Mrs. Marybeth Kemp, Director of Admission, Monmouth College, 700 East Broadway, Monmouth, IL 61462-1998. Telephone: 309-457-2131 or toll-free 800-747-2687. Fax: 309-457-2141. E-mail: admit@monm.edu. Web site: http://www.monm.edu/.

MOODY BIBLE INSTITUTE
CHICAGO, ILLINOIS

General Independent nondenominational, comprehensive, coed **Entrance** Moderately difficult **Setting** 25-acre urban campus **Total enrollment** 1,404 **Student/faculty ratio** 18:1 **Application deadline** 3/1 **Freshmen** 56% were admitted **Housing** Yes **Expenses** Tuition $830; Room & Board $4480 **Undergraduates** 43% women, 4% part-time, 20% 25 or older, 0.2% Native American, 3% Hispanic, 2% black, 3% Asian American or Pa-

Moody Bible Institute *(continued)*

cific Islander **Most Popular Recent Major** Biblical studies **Academic program** Advanced placement, summer session, adult/continuing education programs, internships **Contact** Ms. Susan Esau, Application Coordinator, Moody Bible Institute, 820 North LaSalle Boulevard, Chicago, IL 60610. Telephone: 312-329-4266 or toll-free 800-967-4MBI. Fax: 312-329-8987. E-mail: admissions@moody.edu. Web site: http://www.moody.edu/.

NAES COLLEGE
CHICAGO, ILLINOIS

General Independent, 4-year, coed **Contact** Ms. Christine Redcloud, Registrar, NAES College, 2838 West Peterson Avenue, Chicago, IL 60659-3813. Telephone: 773-761-5000. Fax: 773-761-3808.

THE NATIONAL COLLEGE OF CHIROPRACTIC
LOMBARD, ILLINOIS

General Independent, upper-level, coed **Entrance** Moderately difficult **Setting** 32-acre suburban campus **Total enrollment** 1,012 **Student/faculty ratio** 9:1 **Application deadline** Rolling **Housing** Yes **Expenses** Tuition $10,500; Room only $2470 **Undergraduates** 60% 25 or older, 0.1% Native American, 1% Hispanic, 2% black, 6% Asian American or Pacific Islander **Academic program** Tutorials, summer session, adult/continuing education programs, internships **Contact** Ms. Julie Talarico, Director of Admissions, The National College of Chiropractic, 200 East Roosevelt Road, Lombard, IL 60148-4583. Telephone: 630-889-6572 or toll-free 800-826-6285.

NATIONAL-LOUIS UNIVERSITY
EVANSTON, ILLINOIS

General Independent, university, coed **Contact** Mr. Randall Berd, Director of Student Enrollment, National-Louis University, 1000 Capitol Drive, Wheeling, IL 60090. Telephone: 847-465-0575 ext. 5151 or toll-free 800-624-8521 (in-state), 800-443-5522 (out-of-state). Web site: http://www.nlu.nl.edu/.

NORTH CENTRAL COLLEGE
NAPERVILLE, ILLINOIS

General Independent United Methodist, comprehensive, coed **Entrance** Moderately difficult **Setting** 56-acre suburban campus **Total enrollment** 2,709 **Student/faculty ratio** 9:1 **Application deadline** Rolling **Freshmen** 82% were admitted **Housing** Yes **Expenses** Tuition $13,845; Room & Board $5070 **Undergraduates** 57% women, 18% part-time, 20% 25 or older, 0.04% Native American, 3% Hispanic, 5% black, 3% Asian American or Pacific Islander **Most popular recent majors** Business administration; psychology; mass communications **Academic program** Average class size 19, English as a second language, advanced placement, accelerated degree program, self-designed majors, tutorials, honors program, summer session, adult/continuing education programs, internships **Contact** Ms. Marguerite Waters, Dean of Admission, North Central College, 30 North Brainard Street, PO Box 3063, Naperville, IL 60566-7063. Telephone: 630-637-5802 or toll-free 800-411-1861. E-mail: ncadm@noctrl.edu. Web site: http://www.noctrl.edu/.

NORTHEASTERN ILLINOIS UNIVERSITY
CHICAGO, ILLINOIS

General State-supported, comprehensive, coed **Entrance** Minimally difficult **Setting** 67-acre urban campus **Total enrollment** 10,224 **Student/faculty ratio** 16:1 **Application deadline** 7/1 **Freshmen** 70% were admitted **Housing** No **Expenses** Tuition $2,470 **Undergraduates** 42% 25 or older, 0.2% Native American, 25% Hispanic, 13% black, 12% Asian American or Pacific Islander **Most popular recent majors** Accounting; elementary education **Academic program** Average class size 40, English as a second language, advanced placement, self-designed majors, tutorials, honors program, summer session, adult/continuing education programs **Contact** Ms. Miriam Rivera, Director of Admissions and Records, Northeastern Illinois University, 5500 North St Louis Avenue, Chicago, IL 60625-4699. Telephone: 773-794-2853. Fax: 773-794-6243. Web site: http://www.neiu.edu/.

NORTHERN ILLINOIS UNIVERSITY
DE KALB, ILLINOIS

General State-supported, university, coed **Entrance** Moderately difficult **Setting** 589-acre small town campus **Total enrollment** 22,082 **Student/faculty ratio** 17:1 **Application deadline** 8/1 **Freshmen** 72% were admitted **Housing** Yes **Expenses** Tuition $3837; Room & Board $4000 **Undergraduates** 54% women, 12% part-time, 16% 25 or older, 0.3% Native American, 6% Hispanic, 11% black, 7% Asian American or Pacific Islander **Most popular recent majors** Mass communications; education; accounting **Academic program** Advanced placement, accelerated degree program, self-designed majors, honors program, summer session, adult/continuing education programs, internships **Contact** Dr. Robert Burk, Director of Admissions, Northern Illinois University, De Kalb, IL 60115-2854. Telephone: 815-753-0446 or toll-free 800-892-3050 (in-state). E-mail: admission-info@niu.edu. Web site: http://www.niu.edu/.

NORTH PARK UNIVERSITY
CHICAGO, ILLINOIS

General Independent, comprehensive, coed, affiliated with Evangelical Covenant Church **Entrance** Moderately difficult **Setting** 30-acre urban campus **Total enrollment** 2,004 **Student/faculty ratio** 16:1 **Application deadline** Rolling **Freshmen** 85% were admitted **Housing** Yes **Expenses** Tuition $14,690; Room & Board $4820 **Undergraduates** 61% women, 23% part-time, 26% 25 or older, 0.4% Native American, 8% Hispanic, 8% black, 8% Asian American or Pacific Islander **Most popular recent majors** Business administration; nursing; psychology **Academic program** English as a second language, advanced placement, accelerated degree program, self-designed majors, tutorials, honors program, summer session, adult/continuing education programs, internships **Contact** Office of Admissions, North Park University, 3225 West Foster Avenue, Chicago, IL 60625-4895. Telephone: 773-244-5500 or toll-free 800-888-NPC8. Fax: 773-583-0858. E-mail: afao@northpark.edu. Web site: http://www.northpark.edu/.

NORTHWESTERN UNIVERSITY
EVANSTON, ILLINOIS

General Independent, university, coed **Entrance** Most difficult **Setting** 231-acre suburban campus **Total enrollment** 15,487 **Student/faculty ratio** 9:1 **Application deadline** 1/1 **Freshmen** 29% were admitted **Housing** Yes **Expenses** Tuition $22,458; Room & Board $6675 **Undergraduates** 52% women, 1% part-time, 1% 25 or older, 0.3% Native American, 3% Hispanic, 6% black, 17% Asian American or Pacific Islander **Most popular recent majors** Economics; political science; engineering **Academic program** Advanced placement, accelerated degree program, self-designed majors, tutorials, honors program, summer session, adult/continuing education programs, internships **Contact** Ms. Carol Lunkenheimer, Director of Admissions, Northwestern University, 1801 Hinman Avenue, Evanston, IL 60208. Telephone: 847-491-7271. E-mail: ug-admission@nwu.edu. Web site: http://www.nwu.edu/.

OLIVET NAZARENE UNIVERSITY
KANKAKEE, ILLINOIS

General Independent, comprehensive, coed, affiliated with Church of the Nazarene **Entrance** Moderately difficult **Setting** 168-acre small town campus **Total enrollment** 2,285 **Student/faculty ratio** 17:1 **Application deadline** 8/1 **Freshmen** 92% were admitted **Housing** Yes **Expenses** Tuition $10,838; Room & Board $4560 **Undergraduates** 58% women, 17% part-time, 10% 25 or older, 0.2% Native American, 1% Hispanic, 8% black, 1% Asian American or Pacific Islander **Most popular recent majors** Elementary education; nursing; psychology **Academic program** Advanced placement, accelerated degree program, self-designed majors, summer session, adult/continuing education programs, internships **Contact** Rev. John Mongerson, Director of Admissions, Olivet Nazarene University, PO Box 592, Kankakee, IL 60901-0592. Telephone: 815-939-5203. E-mail: admissions@olivet.edu. Web site: http://www.olivet.edu/.

PRINCIPIA COLLEGE
ELSAH, ILLINOIS

General Independent Christian Science, 4-year, coed **Entrance** Moderately difficult **Setting** 2,800-acre rural campus **Total enrollment** 552 **Student/faculty ratio** 7:1 **Application deadline** 4/1 **Freshmen** 88% were admitted **Housing** Yes **Expenses** Tuition $14,751; Room & Board $5586 **Undergraduates** 53% women, 3% part-time, 4% 25 or older, 0.2% Native American, 2% Hispanic, 1% black, 1% Asian American or Pacific Islander **Most popular recent majors** Business administration; mass communications; biology **Academic program** Average class size 15, English as a second language, advanced placement, accelerated degree program, self-designed majors, honors program, adult/continuing education programs, internships **Contact** Ms. Ashley Beeman, Administrative Assistant, Principia College, One Maybeck Place, Elsah, IL 62028-9799. Telephone: 618-374-5181 or toll-free 800-277-4648 Ext. 2802. Fax: 618-374-4000. E-mail: collegeadmissions@prin.edu. Web site: http://www.prin.edu/.

QUINCY UNIVERSITY
QUINCY, ILLINOIS

General Independent Roman Catholic, comprehensive, coed **Entrance** Moderately difficult **Setting** 75-acre small town campus **Total enrollment** 1,149 **Student/faculty ratio** 12:1 **Application deadline** Rolling **Freshmen** 76% were admitted **Housing** Yes **Expenses** Tuition $12,410; Room & Board $4420 **Undergraduates** 52% women, 4% part-time, 9% 25 or older, 0.3% Native American, 1% Hispanic, 6% black, 2% Asian American or Pacific Islander **Most popular recent majors** Elementary education; mass communications; psychology **Academic program** Advanced placement, accelerated degree program, self-designed majors, tutorials, honors program, summer session, adult/continuing education programs, internships **Contact** Mr. Jeff Van Camp, Director of Admissions, Quincy University, 1800 College Avenue, Quincy, IL 62301-2699. Telephone: 217-222-8020 ext. 5215 or toll-free 800-

Quincy University *(continued)*

688-4295. Fax: 217-228-5479. E-mail: admissions@quincy.edu. Web site: http://www.quincy.edu/.

ROBERT MORRIS COLLEGE
CHICAGO, ILLINOIS

General Independent, 4-year, coed **Entrance** Minimally difficult **Setting** Urban campus **Total enrollment** 3,581 **Student/faculty ratio** 20:1 **Application deadline** Rolling **Freshmen** 63% were admitted **Housing** No **Expenses** Tuition $10,500 **Undergraduates** 76% women, 6% part-time, 38% 25 or older, 1% Native American, 22% Hispanic, 43% black, 3% Asian American or Pacific Islander **Most popular recent majors** Accounting; business administration; secretarial science **Academic program** Advanced placement, accelerated degree program, tutorials, honors program, summer session, adult/continuing education programs, internships **Contact** Mr. Vince Norton, Vice President of Enrollment Services, Robert Morris College, 180 North LaSalle Street, Chicago, IL 60601-2592. Telephone: 312-836-4639 or toll-free 800-225-1520. Fax: 312-836-9020. E-mail: enroll@rmcil.edu. Web site: http://www.rmcil.edu/.

ROCKFORD COLLEGE
ROCKFORD, ILLINOIS

General Independent, comprehensive, coed **Entrance** Moderately difficult **Setting** 130-acre suburban campus **Total enrollment** 1,264 **Student/faculty ratio** 9:1 **Application deadline** Rolling **Freshmen** 77% were admitted **Housing** Yes **Expenses** Tuition $14,750; Room & Board $4800 **Undergraduates** 69% women, 26% part-time, 41% 25 or older, 1% Native American, 4% Hispanic, 8% black, 2% Asian American or Pacific Islander **Most popular recent majors** Education; business administration; psychology **Academic program** Average class size 15, English as a second language, advanced placement, self-designed majors, tutorials, honors program, summer session, adult/continuing education programs, internships **Contact** Mr. Paul Hartzog, Associate Director of Admission, Rockford College, 5050 East State Street, Rockford, IL 61108-2393. Telephone: 815-226-4050 or toll-free 800-892-2984. Fax: 815-226-4119. E-mail: admission@rockford.edu. Web site: http://www.rockford.edu/.

ROOSEVELT UNIVERSITY
CHICAGO, ILLINOIS

General Independent, comprehensive, coed **Entrance** Moderately difficult **Setting** Urban campus **Total enrollment** 6,605 **Student/faculty ratio** 13:1 **Application deadline** 8/15 **Freshmen** 92% were admitted **Housing** Yes **Expenses** Tuition $11,030; Room & Board $5500 **Undergraduates** 61% women, 64% part-time, 72% 25 or older, 0.3% Native American, 10% Hispanic, 25% black, 4% Asian American or Pacific Islander **Most popular recent majors** Accounting; social sciences; psychology **Academic program** English as a second language, advanced placement, accelerated degree program, self-designed majors, honors program, summer session, adult/continuing education programs, internships **Contact** Admission Counselors, Roosevelt University, Office of Admissions, Chicago, IL 60605-1394. Telephone: 312-341-3515. E-mail: dessimm@admvsbk.roosevelt.edu. Web site: http://www.roosevelt.edu/.

ROSARY COLLEGE
See Dominican University

RUSH UNIVERSITY
CHICAGO, ILLINOIS

General Independent, upper-level, coed **Entrance** Moderately difficult **Setting** 35-acre urban campus **Total enrollment** 1,460 **Student/faculty ratio** 6:1 **Application deadline** Rolling **Freshmen** 65% were admitted **Housing** Yes **Expenses** Tuition $10,665; Room only $5094 **Undergraduates** 86% women, 10% part-time, 53% 25 or older, 0% Native American, 7% Hispanic, 12% black, 17% Asian American or Pacific Islander **Contact** Ms. Phyllis Peterson, Director of College Admission Services, Rush University, 600 South Paulina, Chicago, IL 60612-3878. Telephone: 312-942-7100. Fax: 312-942-2219. Web site: http://www.univ.rush.edu/univ/.

SAINT ANTHONY COLLEGE OF NURSING
ROCKFORD, ILLINOIS

General Independent Roman Catholic, upper-level, coed **Contact** Ms. Cathy Mueller, Student Services Assistant, Saint Anthony College of Nursing, 5658 East State Street, Rockford, IL 61108-2468. Telephone: 815-395-5089.

SAINT FRANCIS MEDICAL CENTER COLLEGE OF NURSING
PEORIA, ILLINOIS

General Independent Roman Catholic, upper-level, coed **Entrance** Moderately difficult **Setting** Urban campus **Total enrollment** 155 **Application deadline** Rolling **Housing** Yes **Expenses** Tuition $8548; Room only $1600 **Undergraduates** 50% 25 or older, 1% Native American, 1% Hispanic, 3% black, 3% Asian American or Pacific Islander **Academic program** Advanced placement, summer session **Contact** Mrs. Janice

Farquharson, Director of Admissions and Registrar, Saint Francis Medical Center College of Nursing, 511 Greenleaf Street, Peoria, IL 61603-3783. Telephone: 309-655-2596. Web site: http://www.iaonline.com/sfmc/home.htm/.

ST. JOHN'S COLLEGE
SPRINGFIELD, ILLINOIS

General Independent Roman Catholic, upper-level, coed **Entrance** Moderately difficult **Setting** Urban campus **Total enrollment** 99 **Student/faculty ratio** 6:1 **Freshmen** 90% were admitted **Housing** No **Expenses** Tuition $6991 **Undergraduates** 92% women, 1% part-time, 31% 25 or older, 0% Native American, 0% Hispanic, 2% black, 1% Asian American or Pacific Islander **Academic program** Average class size 45 **Contact** Ms. Nancy Cobetto, Student Development Officer, St. John's College, 421 North Ninth Street, Springfield, IL 62702-5317. Telephone: 217-525-5628.

SAINT JOSEPH COLLEGE OF NURSING
See University of St. Francis

SAINT XAVIER UNIVERSITY
CHICAGO, ILLINOIS

General Independent Roman Catholic, comprehensive, coed **Entrance** Moderately difficult **Setting** 55-acre urban campus **Total enrollment** 3,719 **Student/faculty ratio** 16:1 **Application deadline** 8/1 **Freshmen** 80% were admitted **Housing** Yes **Expenses** Tuition $12,560; Room & Board $5184 **Undergraduates** 72% women, 37% part-time, 38% 25 or older, 0.1% Native American, 11% Hispanic, 15% black, 2% Asian American or Pacific Islander **Most popular recent majors** Business administration; nursing; education **Academic program** Average class size 20, advanced placement, self-designed majors, summer session, adult/continuing education programs, internships **Contact** Sr. Evelyn McKenna, Director of Admissions, Saint Xavier University, 3700 West 103rd Street, Chicago, IL 60655-3105. Telephone: 773-298-3050 or toll-free 800-462-9288 (in-state). Fax: 773-298-3076 ext. 3050. E-mail: admissions@sxu.edu. Web site: http://www.sxu.edu/.

SCHOOL OF THE ART INSTITUTE OF CHICAGO
CHICAGO, ILLINOIS

General Independent, comprehensive, coed **Entrance** Moderately difficult **Setting** 1-acre urban campus **Total enrollment** 2,228 **Student/faculty ratio** 12:1 **Application deadline** Rolling **Freshmen** 73% were admitted **Housing** Yes **Expenses** Tuition $17,160; Room only $5150 **Undergraduates** 60% women, 12% part-time, 21% 25 or older, 1% Native American, 6% Hispanic, 5% black, 7% Asian American or Pacific Islander **Academic program** English as a second language, advanced placement, self-designed majors, tutorials, summer session, internships **Contact** Director of Admissions, School of the Art Institute of Chicago, 37 South Wabash, Chicago, IL 60603-3103. Telephone: 312-899-5219 or toll-free 800-232-SAIC. Fax: 312-263-0141. E-mail: admiss@artic.edu. Web site: http://www.artic.edu/saic/saichome.html/.

SHIMER COLLEGE
WAUKEGAN, ILLINOIS

General Independent, 4-year, coed **Entrance** Moderately difficult **Setting** 3-acre suburban campus **Total enrollment** 112 **Student/faculty ratio** 7:1 **Application deadline** 8/10 **Freshmen** 100% were admitted **Housing** Yes **Expenses** Tuition $13,850; Room only $1745 **Undergraduates** 58% women, 4% part-time, 30% 25 or older, 4% Hispanic, 5% black, 2% Asian American or Pacific Islander **Most popular recent majors** Humanities; social sciences; natural sciences **Academic program** Average class size 8, accelerated degree program, self-designed majors, tutorials, summer session, adult/continuing education programs, internships **Contact** Mr. Marc Hoffman, Assistant Director of Admissions, Shimer College, PO Box 500, Waukegan, IL 60079-0500. Telephone: 847-249-7174 or toll-free 800-215-7173. Fax: 847-249-7171. Web site: http://www.shimer.edu/.

▶ **For more information, see page 513.**

SOUTHERN ILLINOIS UNIVERSITY AT CARBONDALE
CARBONDALE, ILLINOIS

General State-supported, university, coed **Entrance** Moderately difficult **Setting** 1,128-acre small town campus **Total enrollment** 21,908 **Student/faculty ratio** 18:1 **Application deadline** Rolling **Freshmen** 73% were admitted **Housing** Yes **Expenses** Tuition $3420; Room & Board $3649 **Undergraduates** 43% women, 11% part-time, 20% 25 or older, 0.5% Native American, 3% Hispanic, 15% black, 2% Asian American or Pacific Islander **Most popular recent majors** Trade and industrial education; industrial technology; aviation management **Academic program** English as a second language, advanced placement, accelerated degree program, tutorials, honors program, summer session, adult/continuing education programs, internships **Contact** Mr. Thomas McGinnis, Associate Director of Admissions, Southern Illinois University at Carbondale, Mail Code 6806, Carbondale, IL 62901-6806. Telephone: 618-

Southern Illinois University at Carbondale *(continued)*

536-4405. Fax: 618-453-3250. E-mail: Admrec@siu.edu. Web site: http://www.siu.edu/cwis.

SOUTHERN ILLINOIS UNIVERSITY AT EDWARDSVILLE

EDWARDSVILLE, ILLINOIS

General State-supported, comprehensive, coed **Entrance** Moderately difficult **Setting** 2,660-acre suburban campus **Total enrollment** 11,207 **Student/faculty ratio** 15:1 **Application deadline** 8/4 **Freshmen** 86% were admitted **Housing** Yes **Expenses** Tuition $2665; Room & Board $4066 **Undergraduates** 58% women, 23% part-time, 28% 25 or older, 0.4% Native American, 1% Hispanic, 12% black, 2% Asian American or Pacific Islander **Most popular recent majors** Nursing; business administration; elementary education **Academic program** Average class size 21, English as a second language, advanced placement, accelerated degree program, honors program, summer session, adult/continuing education programs, internships **Contact** Mr. Gene Magac, Director of School and College Relations, Southern Illinois University at Edwardsville, Edwardsville, IL 62026-0001. Telephone: 618-692-3705 or toll-free 800-447-SIUE (in-state). Fax: 618-692-2081. E-mail: admis@siue.edu. Web site: http://www.siue.edu/.

TELSHE YESHIVA–CHICAGO

CHICAGO, ILLINOIS

Contact Rabbi Avrohom C. Levin, Rosh Hayeshiva, Telshe Yeshiva–Chicago, 3535 West Foster Avenue, Chicago, IL 60625-5598. Telephone: 773-463-7738.

TRINITY CHRISTIAN COLLEGE

PALOS HEIGHTS, ILLINOIS

General Independent interdenominational, 4-year, coed **Entrance** Moderately difficult **Setting** 53-acre suburban campus **Total enrollment** 618 **Student/faculty ratio** 12:1 **Application deadline** 8/15 **Freshmen** 89% were admitted **Housing** Yes **Expenses** Tuition $12,290; Room & Board $4830 **Undergraduates** 65% women, 4% part-time, 8% 25 or older, 1% Native American, 2% Hispanic, 5% black, 1% Asian American or Pacific Islander **Most popular recent majors** Nursing; elementary education; business administration **Academic program** Average class size 26, advanced placement, tutorials, honors program, adult/continuing education programs, internships **Contact** Mr. Peter Hamstra, Dean of Admissions, Trinity Christian College, 6601 West College Drive, Palos Heights, IL 60463-0929. Telephone: 708-239-4709 or toll-free 800-748-0085. Fax: 708-239-3995. E-mail: admissions@trnty.edu. Web site: http://www.trnty.edu/.

TRINITY COLLEGE OF NURSING

MOLINE, ILLINOIS

Contact Trinity College of Nursing, 501 10th Avenue, Moline, IL 61265. Telephone: 309-757-2910.

TRINITY INTERNATIONAL UNIVERSITY

DEERFIELD, ILLINOIS

General Independent, university, coed, affiliated with Evangelical Free Church of America **Entrance** Moderately difficult **Setting** 108-acre suburban campus **Total enrollment** 2,571 **Student/faculty ratio** 17:1 **Application deadline** Rolling **Housing** Yes **Expenses** Tuition $12,630; Room & Board $4630 **Undergraduates** 52% women, 11% part-time, 26% 25 or older, 1% Native American, 4% Hispanic, 11% black, 2% Asian American or Pacific Islander **Most popular recent majors** Education; divinity/ministry; business administration **Academic program** Average class size 30, advanced placement, honors program, summer session, adult/continuing education programs, internships **Contact** Mr. Brian Medaglia, Dean of Undergraduate Admissions, Trinity International University, 2065 Half Day Road, Deerfield, IL 60015-1284. Telephone: 847-317-7000 or toll-free 800-822-3225 (out-of-state). Fax: 847-317-7081. E-mail: tcdadm@tiu.edu. Web site: http://www.tiu.edu/.

UNIVERSITY OF CHICAGO

CHICAGO, ILLINOIS

General Independent, university, coed **Entrance** Most difficult **Setting** 203-acre urban campus **Total enrollment** 11,849 **Student/faculty ratio** 6:1 **Application deadline** 1/1 **Freshmen** 62% were admitted **Housing** Yes **Expenses** Tuition $22,476; Room & Board $7604 **Undergraduates** 47% women, 1% part-time, 1% 25 or older, 0.1% Native American, 5% Hispanic, 4% black, 25% Asian American or Pacific Islander **Most popular recent majors** Economics; biology; English **Academic program** Average class size 25, advanced placement, accelerated degree program, self-designed majors, tutorials, summer session, adult/continuing education programs, internships **Contact** Mr. Theodore O'Neill, Dean of Admissions, University of Chicago, 5801 Ellis Avenue, Chicago, IL 60637-1513. Telephone: 773-702-8650. Fax: 773-702-4199. E-mail: collegeadmissions@uchicago.edu. Web site: http://www.uchicago.edu/.

UNIVERSITY OF ILLINOIS AT CHICAGO

CHICAGO, ILLINOIS

General State-supported, university, coed **Entrance** Moderately difficult **Setting** 200-acre urban campus **Total enrollment** 24,578 **Student/faculty ratio** 13:1 **Application deadline** 2/28 **Freshmen** 62% were admitted **Housing** Yes **Expenses** Tuition $3898; Room & Board $5526 **Undergraduates** 54% women, 14% part-time, 17% 25 or older, 0.3% Native American, 17% Hispanic, 10% black, 21% Asian American or Pacific Islander **Most popular recent majors** Psychology; accounting; nursing **Academic program** English as a second language, advanced placement, accelerated degree program, self-designed majors, honors program, summer session, adult/continuing education programs, internships **Contact** Ms. Marge Gockel, Associate Director for Undergraduate Admissions, University of Illinois at Chicago, 601 South Morgan Street, Chicago, IL 60607-7128. Telephone: 312-996-4350. E-mail: cgadmit@uicvmc.aiss.uic.edu. Web site: http://www.uic.edu/.

UNIVERSITY OF ILLINOIS AT SPRINGFIELD

SPRINGFIELD, ILLINOIS

General State-supported, upper-level, coed **Entrance** Minimally difficult **Setting** 746-acre suburban campus **Total enrollment** 4,463 **Student/faculty ratio** 14:1 **Application deadline** Rolling **Freshmen** 94% were admitted **Housing** Yes **Expenses** Tuition $2789 **Undergraduates** 64% women, 50% part-time, 63% 25 or older, 0.4% Native American, 1% Hispanic, 7% black, 1% Asian American or Pacific Islander **Most popular recent majors** Business administration; psychology; criminal justice/law enforcement administration **Academic program** Self-designed majors, tutorials, summer session, adult/continuing education programs, internships **Contact** Office of Enrollment Services, University of Illinois at Springfield, PO Box 19243, Springfield, IL 62794-9243. Telephone: 217-786-6626 or toll-free 800-252-8533 (in-state). Fax: 217-206-7188. Web site: http://www.uis.edu/.

UNIVERSITY OF ILLINOIS AT URBANA–CHAMPAIGN

URBANA, ILLINOIS

General State-supported, university, coed **Entrance** Very difficult **Setting** 1,470-acre small town campus **Total enrollment** 36,019 **Student/faculty ratio** 16:1 **Application deadline** 1/1 **Freshmen** 68% were admitted **Housing** Yes **Expenses** Tuition $4120; Room & Board $5078 **Undergraduates** 47% women, 2% part-time, 3% 25 or older, 0.2% Native American, 5% Hispanic, 7% black, 13% Asian American or Pacific Islander **Most popular recent majors** Biology; electrical/electronics engineering; psychology **Academic program** Average class size 31, advanced placement, accelerated degree program, self-designed majors, tutorials, honors program, summer session, internships **Contact** Ms. Tammy Bouseman, Assistant Director of Admissions, University of Illinois at Urbana–Champaign, 901 West Illinois, Urbana, IL 61801. Telephone: 217-333-0302. E-mail: undergrad@admissions.uiuc.edu. Web site: http://www.uiuc.edu/.

UNIVERSITY OF ST. FRANCIS

JOLIET, ILLINOIS

General Independent Roman Catholic, comprehensive, coed **Entrance** Moderately difficult **Setting** 16-acre suburban campus **Total enrollment** 4,333 **Application deadline** 7/1 **Freshmen** 84% were admitted **Housing** Yes **Expenses** Tuition $11,950; Room & Board $4740 **Undergraduates** 84% women, 72% part-time, 37% 25 or older, 0.2% Native American, 2% Hispanic, 2% black, 1% Asian American or Pacific Islander **Most popular recent majors** Business administration; mass communications; elementary education **Academic program** Average class size 20, advanced placement, accelerated degree program, tutorials, summer session, adult/continuing education programs, internships **Contact** Mr. Vic Davolt, Director of Admissions, University of St. Francis, 500 North Wilcox Street, Joliet, IL 60435-6188. Telephone: 815-740-3400 or toll-free 800-735-7500. Fax: 815-740-4285. E-mail: csfinfo@stfrancis.edu. Web site: http://www.stfrancis.edu/.

VANDERCOOK COLLEGE OF MUSIC

CHICAGO, ILLINOIS

General Independent, comprehensive, coed **Entrance** Moderately difficult **Setting** 1-acre urban campus **Total enrollment** 173 **Student/faculty ratio** 6:1 **Application deadline** Rolling **Housing** Yes **Expenses** Tuition $10,350; Room & Board $5000 **Undergraduates** 16% 25 or older **Academic program** Average class size 20, advanced placement, summer session, adult/continuing education programs, internships **Contact** Mr. George Pierard, Director of Admissions, VanderCook College of Music, 3140 South Federal, Chicago, IL 60616-3886. Telephone: 312-225-6288 or toll-free 800-448-2655. Fax: 312-225-5211. E-mail: vcmusic@mcs.com. Web site: http://www.mcs.com/~vcmusic/.

WESTERN ILLINOIS UNIVERSITY

MACOMB, ILLINOIS

General State-supported, comprehensive, coed **Entrance** Moderately difficult **Setting** 1,050-acre

Western Illinois University *(continued)*

small town campus **Total enrollment** 12,200 **Student/faculty ratio** 15:1 **Application deadline** 8/10 **Freshmen** 70% were admitted **Housing** Yes **Expenses** Tuition $3,037; Room & Board $3838 **Undergraduates** 51% women, 15% part-time, 20% 25 or older, 0.3% Native American, 3% Hispanic, 7% black, 1% Asian American or Pacific Islander **Most popular recent majors** Criminal justice/law enforcement administration; liberal arts and studies; elementary education **Academic program** English as a second language, advanced placement, self-designed majors, tutorials, honors program, summer session, adult/continuing education programs, internships **Contact** Ms. Karen Helmers, Director of Admissions, Western Illinois University, 1 University Circle, 115 Sherman Hall, Macomb, IL 61455-1390. Telephone: 309-298-3157. Fax: 309-298-3111. E-mail: karen_helmers@wiu.edu. Web site: http://www.wiu.edu/.

► **For more information, see page 552.**

WEST SUBURBAN COLLEGE OF NURSING

OAK PARK, ILLINOIS

General Independent, 4-year, coed **Entrance** Moderately difficult **Setting** 10-acre suburban campus **Total enrollment** 152 **Application deadline** Rolling **Freshmen** 81% were admitted **Housing** Yes **Expenses** Tuition $12,442; Room & Board $5024 **Undergraduates** 95% women, 34% part-time **Academic program** Average class size 17, advanced placement, tutorials, summer session, adult/continuing education programs **Contact** Mr. Edward Pryor, Director of Admission, West Suburban College of Nursing, Erie at Austin, Oak Park, IL 60302. Telephone: 708-763-6530. Fax: 708-763-1531.

WHEATON COLLEGE

WHEATON, ILLINOIS

General Independent nondenominational, comprehensive, coed **Entrance** Very difficult **Setting** 80-acre suburban campus **Total enrollment** 2,725 **Student/faculty ratio** 15:1 **Application deadline** 1/15 **Freshmen** 55% were admitted **Housing** Yes **Expenses** Tuition $13,780; Room & Board $4740 **Undergraduates** 51% women, 1% part-time, 2% 25 or older, 1% Native American, 3% Hispanic, 2% black, 5% Asian American or Pacific Islander **Most popular recent majors** Literature; biblical studies; music **Academic program** Average class size 28, advanced placement, self-designed majors, summer session, internships **Contact** Mr. Dan Crabtree, Director of Admissions, Wheaton College, 501 East College Avenue, Wheaton, IL 60187-5593. Telephone: 630-752-5011 or toll-free 800-222-2419 (out-of-state). Fax: 630-752-5285. E-mail: admissions@wheaton.edu. Web site: http://www.wheaton.edu/.

INDIANA

ANDERSON UNIVERSITY

ANDERSON, INDIANA

General Independent, comprehensive, coed, affiliated with Church of God **Entrance** Moderately difficult **Setting** 100-acre suburban campus **Total enrollment** 2,165 **Student/faculty ratio** 13:1 **Application deadline** 8/25 **Freshmen** 77% were admitted **Housing** Yes **Expenses** Tuition $13,360; Room & Board $4330 **Undergraduates** 60% women, 10% part-time, 15% 25 or older, 1% Native American, 1% Hispanic, 4% black, 0.4% Asian American or Pacific Islander **Most popular recent majors** Elementary education; social work; business administration **Academic program** Average class size 27, advanced placement, accelerated degree program, self-designed majors, tutorials, summer session, adult/continuing education programs, internships **Contact** Mr. Jim King, Director of Admissions, Anderson University, 1100 East Fifth Street, Anderson, IN 46012-3495. Telephone: 765-641-4080 or toll-free 800-421-3014 (in-state), 800-428-6414 (out-of-state). Fax: 765-641-3851. E-mail: info@anderson.edu. Web site: http://www.anderson.edu/.

► **For more information, see page 390.**

BALL STATE UNIVERSITY

MUNCIE, INDIANA

General State-supported, university, coed **Entrance** Moderately difficult **Setting** 955-acre suburban campus **Total enrollment** 19,419 **Student/faculty ratio** 17:1 **Application deadline** Rolling **Freshmen** 92% were admitted **Housing** Yes **Expenses** Tuition $3414; Room & Board $4120 **Undergraduates** 11% 25 or older, 0.4% Native American, 1% Hispanic, 6% black, 1% Asian American or Pacific Islander **Most popular recent majors** Elementary education; liberal arts and studies; journalism **Academic program** English as a second language, advanced placement, accelerated degree program, tutorials, honors program, summer session, adult/continuing education programs, internships **Contact** Dr. Lawrence Waters, Dean of Admissions and Financial Aid, Ball State University, Office of Admissions, Muncie, IN 47306-1099. Telephone: 765-285-8300 or toll-free 800-482-4BSU. Fax: 765-285-1632. E-mail: askus@wp.bsu.edu. Web site: http://www.bsu.edu/.

BETHEL COLLEGE
MISHAWAKA, INDIANA

General Independent, comprehensive, coed, affiliated with Missionary Church **Entrance** Moderately difficult **Setting** 70-acre suburban campus **Total enrollment** 1,526 **Student/faculty ratio** 18:1 **Application deadline** 8/1 **Freshmen** 85% were admitted **Housing** Yes **Expenses** Tuition $11,500; Room & Board $3700 **Undergraduates** 66% women, 30% part-time, 41% 25 or older, 0.1% Native American, 1% Hispanic, 12% black, 1% Asian American or Pacific Islander **Most popular recent majors** Elementary education; nursing; psychology **Academic program** Average class size 30, advanced placement, accelerated degree program, honors program, summer session, adult/continuing education programs, internships **Contact** Mr. Steve Matteson, Dean of Admissions, Bethel College, 1001 West McKinley Avenue, Mishawaka, IN 46545-5591. Telephone: 219-257-3339 ext. 319 or toll-free 800-422-4101. Fax: 219-257-3326. E-mail: admissions@bethel-in.edu. Web site: http://www.bethel-in.edu/.

BUTLER UNIVERSITY
INDIANAPOLIS, INDIANA

General Independent, comprehensive, coed **Entrance** Moderately difficult **Setting** 290-acre urban campus **Total enrollment** 3,911 **Student/faculty ratio** 11:1 **Application deadline** 8/15 **Freshmen** 87% were admitted **Housing** Yes **Expenses** Tuition $15,690; Room & Board $5430 **Undergraduates** 62% women, 3% part-time, 4% 25 or older, 0.3% Native American, 1% Hispanic, 4% black, 2% Asian American or Pacific Islander **Most popular recent majors** Pharmacy; elementary education; secondary education **Academic program** Average class size 26, English as a second language, advanced placement, accelerated degree program, tutorials, honors program, summer session, adult/continuing education programs, internships **Contact** Ms. Carroll Davis, Director of Admissions, Butler University, 4600 Sunset Avenue, Indianapolis, IN 46208-3485. Telephone: 317-940-8100 or toll-free 888-940-8100. Fax: 317-940-8150. E-mail: admission@butler.edu. Web site: http://www.butler.edu/.

CALUMET COLLEGE OF SAINT JOSEPH
WHITING, INDIANA

General Independent Roman Catholic, 4-year, coed **Entrance** Minimally difficult **Setting** 260-acre suburban campus **Total enrollment** 966 **Student/faculty ratio** 15:1 **Application deadline** Rolling **Housing** No **Expenses** Tuition $6293 **Undergraduates** 68% women, 55% part-time, 72% 25 or older, 1% Native American, 15% Hispanic, 26% black, 0.4% Asian American or Pacific Islander **Most popular recent majors** Business administration; accounting; information sciences/systems **Academic program** Accelerated degree program, self-designed majors, tutorials, honors program, summer session, adult/continuing education programs, internships **Contact** Mr. Kevin Gober, Director of Admissions, Calumet College of Saint Joseph, 2400 New York Avenue, Whiting, IN 46394-2195. Telephone: 219-473-4215. Fax: 219-473-4259. Web site: http://www.ccsj.edu/.

DEPAUW UNIVERSITY
GREENCASTLE, INDIANA

General Independent, 4-year, coed, affiliated with United Methodist Church **Entrance** Moderately difficult **Setting** 175-acre small town campus **Total enrollment** 2,334 **Student/faculty ratio** 12:1 **Application deadline** 2/15 **Freshmen** 88% were admitted **Housing** Yes **Expenses** Tuition $17,050; Room & Board $5616 **Undergraduates** 55% women, 1% part-time, 1% 25 or older, 0.3% Native American, 3% Hispanic, 6% black, 2% Asian American or Pacific Islander **Most popular recent majors** Mass communications; economics; English composition **Academic program** Average class size 23, English as a second language, advanced placement, self-designed majors, tutorials, honors program, internships **Contact** Mr. Larry West, Director of Admission, DePauw University, 101 East Seminary Street, Greencastle, IN 46135. Telephone: 765-658-4006 or toll-free 800-447-2495. Fax: 765-658-4007. E-mail: admissions@depauw.edu. Web site: http://www.depauw.edu/.

EARLHAM COLLEGE
RICHMOND, INDIANA

General Independent, 4-year, coed, affiliated with Society of Friends **Entrance** Moderately difficult **Setting** 800-acre small town campus **Total enrollment** 1,025 **Student/faculty ratio** 11:1 **Application deadline** 2/15 **Freshmen** 80% were admitted **Housing** Yes **Expenses** Tuition $18,618; Room & Board $4544 **Undergraduates** 58% women, 2% part-time, 0% 25 or older, 0.5% Native American, 1% Hispanic, 6% black, 3% Asian American or Pacific Islander **Most popular recent majors** Biology; English; psychology **Academic program** Average class size 22, advanced placement, accelerated degree program, self-designed majors, tutorials, internships **Contact** Ms. Nancy Sinex, Dean of Admissions, Earlham College, 801 National Road West, Richmond, IN 47374. Telephone: 765-983-1600 or toll-free 800-327-5426. Fax: 765-983-1560. E-mail: admission@earlham.edu. Web site: http://www.earlham.edu/.

► **For more information, see page 424.**

FRANKLIN COLLEGE OF INDIANA
FRANKLIN, INDIANA

General Independent, 4-year, coed, affiliated with American Baptist Churches in the U.S.A. **Entrance** Moderately difficult **Setting** 74-acre small town campus **Total enrollment** 917 **Student/faculty ratio** 13:1 **Application deadline** 8/1 **Freshmen** 88% were admitted **Housing** Yes **Expenses** Tuition $12,360; Room & Board $4080 **Undergraduates** 53% women, 3% part-time, 2% 25 or older **Most popular recent majors** Journalism; education; biology **Academic program** Average class size 18, advanced placement, accelerated degree program, tutorials, summer session, internships **Contact** Mr. Bruce Stephen Richards, Dean of Admissions and Financial Aid, Franklin College of Indiana, 501 East Monroe Street, Franklin, IN 46131-2598. Telephone: 317-738-8062 or toll-free 800-852-0232. Fax: 317-738-8274. E-mail: admissions@franklincoll.edu. Web site: http://www.franklincoll.edu/.

GOSHEN COLLEGE
GOSHEN, INDIANA

General Independent Mennonite, 4-year, coed **Entrance** Moderately difficult **Setting** 135-acre small town campus **Total enrollment** 1,016 **Student/faculty ratio** 13:1 **Application deadline** Rolling **Freshmen** 77% were admitted **Housing** Yes **Expenses** Tuition $11,450; Room & Board $4000 **Undergraduates** 58% women, 18% 25 or older, 0.5% Native American, 4% Hispanic, 2% black, 1% Asian American or Pacific Islander **Most popular recent majors** Business administration; nursing; elementary education **Academic program** Average class size 31, English as a second language, advanced placement, accelerated degree program, self-designed majors, tutorials, honors program, summer session, adult/continuing education programs, internships **Contact** Ms. Martha Lehman, Director of Admissions, Goshen College, 1700 South Main Street, Goshen, IN 46526-4794. Telephone: 219-535-7535 or toll-free 800-348-7422. Fax: 219-535-7609. E-mail: admissions@goshen.edu. Web site: http://www.goshen.edu/.

GRACE COLLEGE
WINONA LAKE, INDIANA

General Independent, comprehensive, coed, affiliated with Fellowship of Grace Brethren Churches **Entrance** Moderately difficult **Setting** 160-acre small town campus **Total enrollment** 800 **Application deadline** 8/1 **Freshmen** 88% were admitted **Housing** Yes **Expenses** Tuition $9820; Room & Board $4282 **Undergraduates** 53% women, 10% part-time, 5% 25 or older, 0.3% Native American, 1% Hispanic, 2% black, 1% Asian American or Pacific Islander **Most popular recent majors** Elementary education; psychology; business administration **Academic program** Average class size 30, advanced placement, accelerated degree program, summer session, internships **Contact** Mr. Ron Henry, Dean of Enrollment, Grace College, 200 Seminary Drive, Winona Lake, IN 46590-1294. Telephone: 219-372-5128 or toll-free 800-845-2930 (in-state), 800-54 GRACE (out-of-state). Fax: 219-372-5265. E-mail: rhenry@grace.edu. Web site: http://www.grace.edu/.

▶ **For more information, see page 445.**

HANOVER COLLEGE
HANOVER, INDIANA

General Independent Presbyterian, 4-year, coed **Entrance** Moderately difficult **Setting** 630-acre rural campus **Total enrollment** 1,092 **Student/faculty ratio** 11:1 **Application deadline** 3/1 **Freshmen** 86% were admitted **Housing** Yes **Expenses** Tuition $10,085; Room & Board $4275 **Undergraduates** 53% women, 1% part-time, 0.2% 25 or older, 0.1% Native American, 1% Hispanic, 1% black, 1% Asian American or Pacific Islander **Most popular recent majors** Business administration; psychology; biology **Academic program** Average class size 16, advanced placement, accelerated degree program, tutorials, honors program, internships **Contact** Mr. Kenneth Moyer Jr., Dean of Admissions, Hanover College, Box 108, Hanover, IN 47243-0108. Telephone: 812-866-7021 or toll-free 800-213-2178. Fax: 812-866-7098. E-mail: admissions@hanover.edu. Web site: http://www.hanover.edu/.

HUNTINGTON COLLEGE
HUNTINGTON, INDIANA

General Independent, comprehensive, coed, affiliated with Church of the United Brethren in Christ **Entrance** Moderately difficult **Setting** 200-acre small town campus **Total enrollment** 814 **Student/faculty ratio** 14:1 **Application deadline** 8/15 **Freshmen** 91% were admitted **Housing** Yes **Expenses** Tuition $12,800; Room & Board $4770 **Undergraduates** 57% women, 7% part-time, 15% 25 or older **Most popular recent majors** Elementary education; business administration; theology **Academic program** English as a second language, advanced placement, accelerated degree program, self-designed majors, tutorials, summer session, adult/continuing education programs, internships **Contact** Mr. Jeff Berggren, Dean of Enrollment, Huntington College, 2303 College Avenue, Huntington, IN 46750-1299. Telephone: 219-359-4000 ext. 4016 or toll-free 800-642-6493. Fax: 219-356-9448. E-mail: admissions@huntington.edu. Web site: http://www.@huntington.edu/.

INDIANA INSTITUTE OF TECHNOLOGY
FORT WAYNE, INDIANA

General Independent, 4-year, coed **Entrance** Moderately difficult **Setting** 25-acre urban campus **Total enrollment** 1,400 **Application deadline** 8/1 **Freshmen** 89% were admitted **Housing** Yes **Expenses** Tuition $11,500; Room & Board $4430 **Undergraduates** 5% 25 or older, 0% Native American, 2% Hispanic, 19% black, 2% Asian American or Pacific Islander **Most popular recent majors** Business administration; accounting **Academic program** English as a second language, advanced placement, tutorials, summer session, adult/continuing education programs, internships **Contact** Mrs. Diane L. Maldeney, Registrar, Indiana Institute of Technology, 1600 East Washington Boulevard, Fort Wayne, IN 46803-1297. Telephone: 219-422-5561 ext. 265 or toll-free 800-937-2448 (in-state). Fax: 219-422-7696. E-mail: lange@indtech.edu. Web site: http://www.indtech.edu/.

INDIANA STATE UNIVERSITY
TERRE HAUTE, INDIANA

General State-supported, university, coed **Entrance** Moderately difficult **Setting** 91-acre suburban campus **Total enrollment** 10,784 **Student/faculty ratio** 15:1 **Application deadline** 8/15 **Freshmen** 88% were admitted **Housing** Yes **Expenses** Tuition $3196; Room & Board $4143 **Undergraduates** 17% 25 or older, 0.4% Native American, 1% Hispanic, 9% black, 1% Asian American or Pacific Islander **Most popular recent majors** Elementary education; criminology; nursing **Academic program** Average class size 25, English as a second language, advanced placement, accelerated degree program, tutorials, honors program, summer session, adult/continuing education programs, internships **Contact** Ms. Leah Bell, Director of Admissions, Indiana State University, Terre Haute, IN 47809-1401. Telephone: 812-237-2121 or toll-free 800-742-0891. Fax: 812-237-8023. E-mail: admisu@amber.indstate.edu. Web site: http://www-isu.indstate.edu/.

INDIANA UNIVERSITY BLOOMINGTON
BLOOMINGTON, INDIANA

General State-supported, university, coed **Entrance** Moderately difficult **Setting** 1,878-acre small town campus **Total enrollment** 34,937 **Student/faculty ratio** 17:1 **Application deadline** 2/15 **Freshmen** 84% were admitted **Housing** Yes **Expenses** Tuition $3929; Room & Board $4900 **Undergraduates** 54% women, 6% part-time, 6% 25 or older, 0.3% Native American, 2% Hispanic, 4% black, 3% Asian American or Pacific Islander **Academic program** English as a second language, advanced placement, accelerated degree program, self-designed majors, tutorials, honors program, summer session, adult/continuing education programs, internships **Contact** Ms. Mary Ellen Anderson, Acting Director of Admissions, Indiana University Bloomington, 300 North Jordan Avenue, Bloomington, IN 47405. Telephone: 812-855-0661. E-mail: iuadmit@indiana.edu. Web site: http://www.indiana.edu/.

INDIANA UNIVERSITY EAST
RICHMOND, INDIANA

General State-supported, 4-year, coed **Entrance** Noncompetitive **Setting** 194-acre small town campus **Total enrollment** 2,309 **Student/faculty ratio** 12:1 **Application deadline** Rolling **Housing** No **Expenses** Tuition $2849 **Undergraduates** 72% women, 54% part-time, 34% 25 or older, 0.3% Native American, 0.5% Hispanic, 3% black, 0.3% Asian American or Pacific Islander **Most popular recent majors** Business administration; education; nursing **Academic program** Advanced placement, tutorials, summer session, adult/continuing education programs, internships **Contact** Ms. Susanna Tanner, Admissions Counselor, Indiana University East, 2325 Chester Boulevard, Richmond, IN 47374-1289. Telephone: 765-973-8415 or toll-free 800-959-3278. Fax: 765-973-8288. E-mail: musmith@indiana.edu. Web site: http://www.iue.indiana.edu/.

INDIANA UNIVERSITY KOKOMO
KOKOMO, INDIANA

General State-supported, comprehensive, coed **Entrance** Minimally difficult **Setting** 54-acre small town campus **Total enrollment** 2,927 **Student/faculty ratio** 16:1 **Application deadline** 8/1 **Housing** No **Expenses** Tuition $2890 **Undergraduates** 73% women, 55% part-time, 31% 25 or older, 1% Native American, 1% Hispanic, 3% black, 1% Asian American or Pacific Islander **Most Popular Recent Major** Nursing **Academic program** English as a second language, advanced placement, tutorials, honors program, summer session, adult/continuing education programs, internships **Contact** Mr. Darren Bush, Admissions Director, Indiana University Kokomo, PO Box 9003, Kokomo, IN 46904-9003. Telephone: 765-455-9217. Fax: 765-455-9537. E-mail: iukadmis@iukfs1.indiana.edu. Web site: http://www.iuk.indiana.edu/.

INDIANA UNIVERSITY NORTHWEST
GARY, INDIANA

General State-supported, comprehensive, coed **Entrance** Minimally difficult **Setting** 38-acre urban campus **Total enrollment** 5,256 **Student/**

Indiana University Northwest *(continued)*

faculty ratio 14:1 **Application deadline** 8/1 **Freshmen** 56% were admitted **Housing** No **Expenses** Tuition $2895 **Undergraduates** 71% women, 44% part-time, 30% 25 or older, 0.2% Native American, 9% Hispanic, 24% black, 1% Asian American or Pacific Islander **Most popular recent majors** Business administration; accounting; nursing **Academic program** Advanced placement, accelerated degree program, honors program, summer session, adult/continuing education programs, internships **Contact** Mr. William Lee, Director of Admissions, Indiana University Northwest, 3400 Broadway, Gary, IN 46408-1197. Telephone: 219-980-6991 or toll-free 800-437-5409. Fax: 219-981-4219. E-mail: wlee@unhaw1.iun.indiana.edu. Web site: http://www.iun.indiana.edu/.

INDIANA UNIVERSITY–PURDUE UNIVERSITY FORT WAYNE

FORT WAYNE, INDIANA

General State-supported, comprehensive, coed **Entrance** Minimally difficult **Setting** 412-acre urban campus **Total enrollment** 10,749 **Student/faculty ratio** 20:1 **Application deadline** 8/1 **Freshmen** 99% were admitted **Housing** No **Expenses** Tuition $3321 **Undergraduates** 44% 25 or older **Most popular recent majors** Business administration; education; engineering **Academic program** Average class size 23, advanced placement, self-designed majors, honors program, summer session, adult/continuing education programs, internships **Contact** Ms. Carol Isaacs, Interim Director of Admissions, Indiana University-Purdue University Fort Wayne, 2101 Coliseum Boulevard East, Fort Wayne, IN 46805-1499. Telephone: 219-481-6147. Web site: http://www.ipfw.edu.

INDIANA UNIVERSITY–PURDUE UNIVERSITY INDIANAPOLIS

INDIANAPOLIS, INDIANA

General State-supported, university, coed **Entrance** Moderately difficult **Setting** 511-acre urban campus **Total enrollment** 27,036 **Application deadline** Rolling **Freshmen** 94% were admitted **Housing** Yes **Expenses** Tuition $3441; Room & Board $3216 **Undergraduates** 60% women, 45% part-time, 25% 25 or older, 0.3% Native American, 1% Hispanic, 11% black, 2% Asian American or Pacific Islander **Most popular recent majors** Nursing; business **Academic program** English as a second language, advanced placement, accelerated degree program, tutorials, honors program, summer session, adult/continuing education programs, internships **Contact** Dr. Alan Crist, Director of Admissions, Indiana University-Purdue University Indianapolis, Cavanaugh Hall Room 129, Indianapolis, IN 46202-5143. Telephone: 317-274-4591. Fax: 317-278-1862. E-mail: apply@iupui.edu. Web site: http://www.iupui.edu/.

INDIANA UNIVERSITY SOUTH BEND

SOUTH BEND, INDIANA

General State-supported, comprehensive, coed **Entrance** Moderately difficult **Setting** 73-acre suburban campus **Total enrollment** 7,169 **Student/faculty ratio** 13:1 **Application deadline** 7/1 **Freshmen** 91% were admitted **Housing** No **Expenses** Tuition $2985 **Undergraduates** 65% women, 45% part-time, 27% 25 or older, 0.3% Native American, 2% Hispanic, 6% black, 1% Asian American or Pacific Islander **Most popular recent majors** Business; education; liberal arts and studies **Academic program** English as a second language, accelerated degree program, honors program, summer session, adult/continuing education programs **Contact** Mr. Esker E. Ligon, Director of Admissions, Indiana University South Bend, 1700 Mishawaka Avenue, PO Box 7111, South Bend, IN 46634-7111. Telephone: 219-237-IUSB. Fax: 219-237-4834.

INDIANA UNIVERSITY SOUTHEAST

NEW ALBANY, INDIANA

General State-supported, comprehensive, coed **Entrance** Minimally difficult **Setting** 177-acre suburban campus **Total enrollment** 5,520 **Student/faculty ratio** 14:1 **Application deadline** 8/1 **Freshmen** 100% were admitted **Housing** No **Expenses** Tuition $2847 **Undergraduates** 63% women, 46% part-time, 26% 25 or older, 0.2% Native American, 1% Hispanic, 3% black, 0.5% Asian American or Pacific Islander **Academic program** Advanced placement, accelerated degree program, self-designed majors, tutorials, summer session, adult/continuing education programs, internships **Contact** Mr. David B. Campbell, Director of Admissions, Indiana University Southeast, 4201 Grant Line Road, New Albany, IN 47150-6405. Telephone: 812-941-2212 or toll-free 800-852-8835. E-mail: admissions@ius.indiana.edu. Web site: http://ius.indiana.edu/.

INDIANA WESLEYAN UNIVERSITY

MARION, INDIANA

General Independent Wesleyan, comprehensive, coed **Entrance** Moderately difficult **Setting** 132-acre small town campus **Total enrollment** 6,057 **Student/faculty ratio** 16:1 **Application deadline** Rolling **Freshmen** 71% were admitted **Housing** Yes **Expenses** Tuition $11,204; Room & Board $4310 **Undergraduates** 65% women, 10% part-time, 14% 25 or older, 1% Native American, 1% Hispanic, 8% black, 1% Asian American or Pacific Islander **Most popular recent majors** Nursing; divinity/ministry; elementary education **Academic program** Advanced placement, accelerated degree program, self-designed majors, honors program, summer session, adult/continuing education programs, internships **Contact** Ms. Gaytha Holloway, Director of Admissions, Indiana Wesleyan University, 4201 South Washington Street, Marion, IN 46953-4999. Telephone: 765-677-2138 or toll-free 800-332-6901. Fax: 765-677-2333. E-mail: admissions@indwes.edu.

MANCHESTER COLLEGE
NORTH MANCHESTER, INDIANA

General Independent, comprehensive, coed, affiliated with Church of the Brethren **Entrance** Moderately difficult **Setting** 125-acre small town campus **Total enrollment** 1,067 **Student/faculty ratio** 14:1 **Application deadline** Rolling **Freshmen** 83% were admitted **Housing** Yes **Expenses** Tuition $12,660; Room & Board $4550 **Undergraduates** 49% women, 3% part-time, 3% 25 or older, 0.4% Native American, 2% Hispanic, 3% black, 1% Asian American or Pacific Islander **Most popular recent majors** Accounting; education; social work **Academic program** Average class size 21, advanced placement, accelerated degree program, self-designed majors, tutorials, honors program, summer session, internships **Contact** Ms. Jolane Rohr, Director of Admissions, Manchester College, 604 College Avenue, North Manchester, IN 46962-1225. Telephone: 219-982-5055 or toll-free 800-852-3648. Fax: 219-982-5043. E-mail: admitinfo@manchester.edu. Web site: http://www.manchester.edu/.

MARIAN COLLEGE
INDIANAPOLIS, INDIANA

General Independent Roman Catholic, 4-year, coed **Entrance** Moderately difficult **Setting** 114-acre urban campus **Total enrollment** 1,418 **Student/faculty ratio** 12:1 **Application deadline** 8/15 **Freshmen** 85% were admitted **Housing** Yes **Expenses** Tuition $13,406; Room & Board $4644 **Undergraduates** 73% women, 36% part-time, 38% 25 or older, 0.2% Native American, 1% Hispanic, 12% black, 1% Asian American or Pacific Islander **Most popular recent majors** Nursing; business administration; education **Academic program** Average class size 25, English as a second language, advanced placement, accelerated degree program, tutorials, honors program, summer session, adult/continuing education programs, internships **Contact** Dr. Brent Smith, Dean for Enrollment Management and Admissions, Marian College, 3200 Cold Spring Road, Indianapolis, IN 46222-1997. Telephone: 317-955-6300 or toll-free 800-772-7264 (in-state). Web site: http://www.marian.edu/.

MARTIN UNIVERSITY
INDIANAPOLIS, INDIANA

General Independent, comprehensive, coed **Entrance** Noncompetitive **Setting** 5-acre urban campus **Total enrollment** 596 **Student/faculty ratio** 11:1 **Application deadline** Rolling **Housing** No **Expenses** Tuition $8370 **Undergraduates** 76% women, 39% part-time, 80% 25 or older **Most popular recent majors** Business administration; alcohol/drug abuse counseling **Academic program** English as a second language, advanced placement, accelerated degree program, self-designed majors, honors program, summer session, adult/continuing education programs, internships **Contact** Ms. Brenda Shaheed, Director of Admissions, Martin University, 2171 Avondale Place, PO Box 18567, Indianapolis, IN 46218-3867. Telephone: 317-543-3237. Fax: 317-543-3257.

OAKLAND CITY UNIVERSITY
OAKLAND CITY, INDIANA

General Independent General Baptist, comprehensive, coed **Contact** Mr. H. B. Harris, Director of Admissions, Oakland City University, 143 North Lucretia Street, Oakland City, IN 47660-1099. Telephone: 812-749-1222 or toll-free 800-737-5125. Fax: 812-749-1233.

PURDUE UNIVERSITY
WEST LAFAYETTE, INDIANA

General State-supported, university, coed **Entrance** Moderately difficult **Setting** 1,579-acre suburban campus **Total enrollment** 35,715 **Student/faculty ratio** 14:1 **Application deadline** Rolling **Freshmen** 89% were admitted **Housing** Yes **Expenses** Tuition $3368; Room & Board $4800 **Undergraduates** 43% women, 5% part-time, 7% 25 or older, 1% Native American, 2% Hispanic, 4% black, 4% Asian American or Pacific Islander **Most popular recent majors** Electrical/electronics engineering; communications; civil engineering **Academic program** Advanced placement, accelerated degree program, self-designed majors, tutorials, honors program, summer session, adult/continuing education programs, internships **Contact** Director of Admissions, Purdue University, Schleman Hall, West Lafayette, IN 47907-1080. Telephone: 765-494-4600. Fax: 765-494-0544. E-mail: admissions@adms.purdue.edu. Web site: http://www.purdue.edu/.

PURDUE UNIVERSITY CALUMET
HAMMOND, INDIANA

General State-supported, comprehensive, coed **Entrance** Noncompetitive **Setting** 167-acre urban campus **Total enrollment** 9,974 **Student/faculty ratio** 29:1 **Application deadline** Rolling **Housing** No **Expenses** Tuition $3088 **Undergraduates** 47% 25 or older **Most popular recent majors** Engineering; nursing; business administration **Academic program** Advanced placement, honors program, summer session, adult/continuing education programs, internships **Contact** Mr. Paul McGuinness, Director of Admissions, Purdue University Calumet, 173rd and Woodmar Avenue, Hammond, IN 46323-2094. Telephone: 219-989-2289 or toll-free 800-228-0799 Ext. 2400 (in-state). Fax: 219-989-2775. E-mail: williamf@calumet.purdue.edu. Web site: http://www.calumet.purdue.edu/.

PURDUE UNIVERSITY NORTH CENTRAL
WESTVILLE, INDIANA

General State-supported, comprehensive, coed **Entrance** Noncompetitive **Setting** 264-acre rural campus **Total enrollment** 3,369 **Student/faculty ratio** 14:1 **Application deadline** 8/6 **Freshmen** 93% were admitted **Housing** No **Expenses** Tuition $2979 **Undergraduates** 61% women, 48% part-time, 52% 25 or older **Most popular recent majors** Business administration; nursing; liberal arts and studies **Academic program** Average class size 23, advanced placement, self-designed majors, tutorials, honors program, summer session, adult/continuing education programs, internships **Contact** Ms. Cathy Buckman, Director of Admissions, Purdue University North Central, 1401 South US Highway 421, Westville, IN 46391-9528. Telephone: 219-785-5458 or toll-free 800-872-1231 (in-state). Fax: 219-785-5538. E-mail: cbuckman@purduenc.edu. Web site: http://www.purduenc.edu/.

ROSE-HULMAN INSTITUTE OF TECHNOLOGY
TERRE HAUTE, INDIANA

General Independent, comprehensive, coed **Entrance** Very difficult **Setting** 130-acre rural campus **Total enrollment** 1,757 **Student/faculty ratio** 11:1 **Application deadline** Rolling **Freshmen** 68% were admitted **Housing** Yes **Expenses** Tuition $18,105; Room & Board $5300 **Undergraduates** 15% women, 0% 25 or older, 1% Native American, 1% Hispanic, 1% black, 2% Asian American or Pacific Islander **Most popular recent majors** Mechanical engineering; electrical/electronics engineering; chemical engineering **Academic program** Average class size 25, advanced placement, tutorials, honors program, summer session, adult/continuing education programs, internships **Contact** Mr. Charles G. Howard, Dean of Admissions, Rose-Hulman Institute of Technology, 5500 Wabash Avenue, Terre Haute, IN 47803-3920. Telephone: 812-877-8213 or toll-free 800-248-7448 (in-state). Fax: 812-877-8941. E-mail: admis.ofc@rose-hulman.edu. Web site: http://www.Rose-Hulman.edu/.

SAINT FRANCIS COLLEGE
See University of Saint Francis

SAINT JOSEPH'S COLLEGE
RENSSELAER, INDIANA

General Independent Roman Catholic, comprehensive, coed **Entrance** Moderately difficult **Setting** 340-acre small town campus **Total enrollment** 927 **Student/faculty ratio** 15:1 **Application deadline** Rolling **Freshmen** 82% were admitted **Housing** Yes **Expenses** Tuition $12,950; Room & Board $4780 **Undergraduates** 55% women, 13% part-time, 13% 25 or older, 1% Native American, 3% Hispanic, 5% black, 0.2% Asian American or Pacific Islander **Most popular recent majors** Business administration; elementary education; psychology **Academic program** Average class size 18, advanced placement, accelerated degree program, self-designed majors, tutorials, honors program, summer session, internships **Contact** Mr. Frank P. Bevec, Director of Admissions, Saint Joseph's College, PO Box 890, Rensselaer, IN 47978-0850. Telephone: 219-866-6170 or toll-free 800-447-8781 (out-of-state). Fax: 219-866-6122. E-mail: admissions@saintjoe.edu. Web site: http://www.saintjoe.edu/.

SAINT MARY-OF-THE-WOODS COLLEGE
SAINT MARY-OF-THE-WOODS, INDIANA

General Independent Roman Catholic, comprehensive, women only **Contact** Ms. Marcia DeAngelo, Director of Admission, Saint Mary-of-the-Woods College, Guerin Hall, Saint Mary-of-the-Woods, IN 47876. Telephone: 812-535-5106 or toll-free 800-926-SMWC. Fax: 812-535-5215. E-mail: adms@woods.smwc.edu. Web site: http://www.woods.smwc.edu/.

SAINT MARY'S COLLEGE
NOTRE DAME, INDIANA

General Independent Roman Catholic, 4-year, women only **Entrance** Moderately difficult **Setting** 275-acre suburban campus **Total enrollment** 1,347 **Student/faculty ratio** 11:1 **Application deadline** 3/1 **Freshmen** 84% were admitted **Housing** Yes **Expenses** Tuition $15,652; Room & Board $5197 **Undergraduates** 1% part-time, 1% 25 or older, 0.4% Native American, 4% Hispanic, 1% black, 1% Asian American or Pacific Islander **Most popular recent majors** Business administration; mass communications; nursing **Academic program** Advanced placement, accelerated degree program, self-designed majors, tutorials, internships **Contact** Ms. Mary Pat Nolan, Director of Admissions, Saint Mary's College, Notre Dame, IN 46556. Telephone: 219-284-4587. E-mail: admission@saintmarys.edu. Web site: http://www.saintmarys.edu/.

TAYLOR UNIVERSITY
UPLAND, INDIANA

General Independent interdenominational, 4-year, coed **Entrance** Very difficult **Setting** 250-acre rural campus **Total enrollment** 1,884 **Student/faculty ratio** 18:1 **Application deadline** Rolling **Freshmen** 69% were admitted **Housing** Yes **Expenses** Tuition $13,484; Room & Board $4410 **Undergraduates** 53% women, 1% part-time, 1% 25 or older, 0.4% Native American, 1% Hispanic, 1% black, 1% Asian American or Pacific Islander **Most popular recent majors** Business administration; elementary education; psychology **Academic program** Average class size 25, advanced placement, accelerated degree program, self-designed majors, tutorials, honors program, summer session, internships **Contact** Mr. Stephen R. Mortland, Director of Admissions, Taylor University, 500 West Reade Avenue, Upland, IN 46989-1001. Telephone: 765-998-5134 or toll-free 800-882-3456. Fax: 765-998-4925. E-mail: admissions_u@tayloru.edu. Web site: http://www.tayloru.edu/.

TAYLOR UNIVERSITY, FORT WAYNE CAMPUS
FORT WAYNE, INDIANA

General Independent interdenominational, 4-year, coed **Entrance** Moderately difficult **Setting** 32-acre suburban campus **Total enrollment** 406 **Student/faculty ratio** 11:1 **Application deadline** Rolling **Freshmen** 78% were admitted **Housing** Yes **Expenses** Tuition $12,085; Room & Board $4150 **Undergraduates** 58% women, 19% part-time, 0% Native American, 2% Hispanic, 7% black, 0.5% Asian American or Pacific Islander **Most popular recent majors** Divinity/ministry; elementary education; psychology **Academic program** Average class size 14, advanced placement, accelerated degree program, self-designed majors, tutorials, summer session, internships **Contact** Mr. Leo Gonot, Director of Admissions, Taylor University, Fort Wayne Campus, 1025 West Rudisill Boulevard, Fort Wayne, IN 46807-2197. Telephone: 219-456-2111 ext. 2274 or toll-free 800-233-3922. Fax: 219-456-2119. E-mail: admissions_f@tayloru.edu. Web site: http://www.tayloru.edu/.

TRI-STATE UNIVERSITY
ANGOLA, INDIANA

General Independent, 4-year, coed **Entrance** Moderately difficult **Setting** 400-acre small town campus **Total enrollment** 1,116 **Student/faculty ratio** 16:1 **Application deadline** 6/1 **Freshmen** 82% were admitted **Housing** Yes **Expenses** Tuition $11,900; Room & Board $4850 **Undergraduates** 29% women, 8% part-time, 11% 25 or older, 0.4% Native American, 1% Hispanic, 3% black, 1% Asian American or Pacific Islander **Most popular recent majors** Mechanical engineering; electrical/electronics engineering; elementary education **Academic program** Average class size 25, English as a second language, advanced placement, self-designed majors, tutorials, summer session, adult/continuing education programs, internships **Contact** Mr. Kim Bryan, Director of Admissions, Tri-State University, 1 University Avenue, Angola, IN 46703-1764. Telephone: 219-665-4139 or toll-free 800-347-4TSU. Fax: 219-665-4292. E-mail: admit@alpha.tristate.edu. Web site: http://www.tristate.edu/.

UNIVERSITY OF EVANSVILLE
EVANSVILLE, INDIANA

General Independent, comprehensive, coed, affiliated with United Methodist Church **Entrance** Moderately difficult **Setting** 75-acre suburban campus **Total enrollment** 3,023 **Student/faculty ratio** 13:1 **Application deadline** 2/15 **Freshmen** 87% were admitted **Housing** Yes **Expenses** Tuition $13,880; Room & Board $4900 **Undergraduates** 58% women, 6% part-time, 11% 25 or older, 0.3% Native American, 1% Hispanic, 3% black, 1% Asian American or Pacific Islander **Most popular recent majors** Accounting; electrical/electronics engineering; elementary education **Academic program** English as a second language, advanced placement, tutorials, honors program, summer session, adult/continuing education programs, internships **Contact** Ms. Jennifer Garner, Director of Undergraduate Admission, University of Evansville, 1800 Lincoln Avenue, Evansville, IN 47722-0002. Telephone: 812-479-2468 or toll-free 800-992-5877 (in-state), 800-423-8633 (out-of-state). Fax: 812-474-4076. E-mail: admission@evansville.edu. Web site: http://www.evansville.edu/.

UNIVERSITY OF INDIANAPOLIS
INDIANAPOLIS, INDIANA

General Independent, comprehensive, coed, affiliated with United Methodist Church **Entrance**

University of Indianapolis *(continued)*

Moderately difficult **Setting** 60-acre suburban campus **Total enrollment** 3,829 **Student/faculty ratio** 11:1 **Application deadline** 8/15 **Housing** Yes **Expenses** Tuition $12,990; Room & Board $4550 **Undergraduates** 67% women, 41% part-time, 0.5% Native American, 1% Hispanic, 7% black, 1% Asian American or Pacific Islander **Most popular recent majors** Nursing; physical therapy assistant; business administration **Academic program** Average class size 20, English as a second language, advanced placement, self-designed majors, tutorials, honors program, summer session, adult/continuing education programs, internships **Contact** Mr. Mark T. Weigand, Director of Admissions, University of Indianapolis, 1400 East Hanna Avenue, Indianapolis, IN 46227-3697. Telephone: 317-788-3216 or toll-free 800-232-8634. Fax: 317-788-3300. E-mail: admissions@gandlf.uindy.edu. Web site: http://www.uindy.edu/.

UNIVERSITY OF NOTRE DAME
NOTRE DAME, INDIANA

General Independent Roman Catholic, university, coed **Entrance** Most difficult **Setting** 1,250-acre suburban campus **Total enrollment** 10,275 **Student/faculty ratio** 12:1 **Application deadline** 1/9 **Freshmen** 40% were admitted **Housing** Yes **Expenses** Tuition $19,947; Room & Board $5060 **Undergraduates** 45% women, 0.4% part-time, 1% 25 or older, 0.5% Native American, 7% Hispanic, 3% black, 4% Asian American or Pacific Islander **Most popular recent majors** Accounting; political science; finance **Academic program** English as a second language, advanced placement, accelerated degree program, tutorials, honors program, summer session **Contact** Mr. Daniel J. Saracino, Assistant Provost for Enrollment, University of Notre Dame, University of Notre Dame, Admissions Office, Notre Dame, IN 46556-5612. Telephone: 219-631-7505. Fax: 219-631-8865. E-mail: admissions.admissio.1@nd.edu. Web site: http://www.nd.edu/.

UNIVERSITY OF SAINT FRANCIS
FORT WAYNE, INDIANA

General Independent Roman Catholic, comprehensive, coed **Entrance** Moderately difficult **Setting** 73-acre suburban campus **Total enrollment** 1,005 **Student/faculty ratio** 19:1 **Application deadline** Rolling **Freshmen** 90% were admitted **Housing** Yes **Expenses** Tuition $10,710; Room & Board $4270 **Undergraduates** 65% women, 23% part-time, 34% 25 or older, 1% Native American, 2% Hispanic, 6% black, 1% Asian American or Pacific Islander **Most popular recent majors** Nursing; education; business administration **Academic program** Advanced placement, tutorials, honors program, summer session, adult/continuing education programs, internships **Contact** Mr. Scott Flanagan, Assistant Vice President for Enrollment Services, University of Saint Francis, 2701 Spring Street, Fort Wayne, IN 46808-3994. Telephone: 219-434-3264 or toll-free 800-729-4732. E-mail: admiss@sfc.edu. Web site: http://www.sfc.edu/.

UNIVERSITY OF SOUTHERN INDIANA
EVANSVILLE, INDIANA

General State-supported, comprehensive, coed **Entrance** Noncompetitive **Setting** 300-acre suburban campus **Total enrollment** 8,300 **Student/faculty ratio** 18:1 **Application deadline** 8/15 **Freshmen** 93% were admitted **Housing** Yes **Expenses** Tuition $2650; Room only $2020 **Undergraduates** 60% women, 24% part-time, 26% 25 or older, 0.3% Native American, 1% Hispanic, 3% black, 1% Asian American or Pacific Islander **Most popular recent majors** Elementary education; business administration **Academic program** Average class size 24, advanced placement, summer session, adult/continuing education programs, internships **Contact** Mr. Michael Oligmueller, Director of Admissions, University of Southern Indiana, 8600 University Boulevard, Evansville, IN 47712-3590. Telephone: 812-464-1765 or toll-free 800-467-1965. Fax: 812-465-7154. E-mail: enroll.ucs@smtp.usi.edu. Web site: http://www.usi.edu/.

VALPARAISO UNIVERSITY
VALPARAISO, INDIANA

General Independent, comprehensive, coed, affiliated with Lutheran Church **Entrance** Moderately difficult **Setting** 310-acre small town campus **Total enrollment** 3,603 **Student/faculty ratio** 14:1 **Application deadline** Rolling **Freshmen** 84% were admitted **Housing** Yes **Expenses** Tuition $15,060; Room & Board $3930 **Undergraduates** 55% women, 6% part-time, 19% 25 or older, 1% Native American, 3% Hispanic, 4% black, 1% Asian American or Pacific Islander **Most popular recent majors** Nursing; business administration; elementary education **Academic program** Average class size 25, English as a second language, advanced placement, accelerated degree program, self-designed majors, honors program, summer session, adult/continuing education programs, internships **Contact** Ms. Karen Foust, Director of Admissions, Valparaiso University, 651 South College Avenue, Valparaiso, IN 46383-6493. Telephone: 219-464-5011 or toll-free 888-GO-VALPO (out-of-state). Fax: 219-464-6898. E-mail: undergrad_admissions@valpo.edu. Web site: http://www.valpo.edu/.

▶ **For more information, see page 543.**

WABASH COLLEGE
CRAWFORDSVILLE, INDIANA

General Independent, 4-year, men only **Entrance** Moderately difficult **Setting** 50-acre small town campus **Total enrollment** 793 **Student/faculty ratio** 10:1 **Application deadline** 3/1 **Freshmen** 77% were admitted **Housing** Yes **Expenses** Tuition $15,700; Room & Board $4780 **Undergraduates** 1% 25 or older, 1% Native American, 5% Hispanic, 4% black, 3% Asian American or Pacific Islander **Most popular recent majors** English; psychology; history **Academic program** Advanced placement, accelerated degree program, self-designed majors, tutorials, internships **Contact** Mr. Steve Klein, Director of Admissions, Wabash College, PO Box 362, Crawfordsville, IN 47933-0352. Telephone: 765-361-6225 or toll-free 800-345-5385. Fax: 765-361-6437. E-mail: admissions@wabash.edu. Web site: http://www.wabash.edu/.

IOWA

ALLEN COLLEGE
WATERLOO, IOWA

General Independent, 4-year, coed **Entrance** Moderately difficult **Setting** 20-acre suburban campus **Total enrollment** 219 **Student/faculty ratio** 14:1 **Freshmen** 59% were admitted **Housing** No **Expenses** Tuition $6830 **Undergraduates** 93% women, 27% part-time, 33% 25 or older, 0.5% Native American, 1% Hispanic, 1% black, 0.5% Asian American or Pacific Islander **Academic program** Average class size 45, advanced placement, tutorials, summer session **Contact** Ms. Lois Hagedorn, Student Services, Allen College, 1825 Logan Avenue, Waterloo, IA 50703. Telephone: 319-235-3649. Fax: 319-235-5280.

BRIAR CLIFF COLLEGE
SIOUX CITY, IOWA

General Independent Roman Catholic, 4-year, coed **Entrance** Moderately difficult **Setting** 70-acre suburban campus **Total enrollment** 1,011 **Student/faculty ratio** 14:1 **Application deadline** Rolling **Freshmen** 83% were admitted **Housing** Yes **Expenses** Tuition $11,880; Room & Board $4180 **Undergraduates** 68% women, 33% part-time, 35% 25 or older, 1% Native American, 2% Hispanic, 1% black, 1% Asian American or Pacific Islander **Most popular recent majors** Business administration; nursing; elementary education **Academic program** English as a second language, advanced placement, accelerated degree program, self-designed majors, tutorials, summer session, adult/continuing education programs, internships **Contact** Ms. Laurie Grothaus, Director of Admissions, Briar Cliff College, 3303 Rebecca Street, Sioux City, IA 51104-2100. Telephone: 712-279-5200 ext. 1628 or toll-free 800-662-3303. Fax: 712-279-5410. E-mail: admissions@briar-cliff.edu. Web site: http://www.briar-cliff.edu/.

BUENA VISTA UNIVERSITY
STORM LAKE, IOWA

General Independent, comprehensive, coed, affiliated with Presbyterian Church (U.S.A.) **Entrance** Moderately difficult **Setting** 60-acre small town campus **Total enrollment** 2,693 **Application deadline** Rolling **Freshmen** 91% were admitted **Housing** Yes **Expenses** Tuition $14,848; Room & Board $4375 **Undergraduates** 60% women, 14% part-time, 6% 25 or older, 0.2% Native American, 0.5% Hispanic, 1% black, 2% Asian American or Pacific Islander **Most popular recent majors** Business administration; education; biological and physical sciences **Academic program** Average class size 25, English as a second language, advanced placement, self-designed majors, tutorials, honors program, summer session, adult/continuing education programs, internships **Contact** Mr. Mike Frantz, Director of Admissions, Buena Vista University, 610 West Fourth Street, Storm Lake, IA 50588. Telephone: 712-749-2235 or toll-free 800-383-9600. Fax: 712-749-2037. E-mail: admissions@bvu.edu. Web site: http://www.bvu.edu/.

CENTRAL COLLEGE
PELLA, IOWA

General Independent, 4-year, coed, affiliated with Reformed Church in America **Entrance** Moderately difficult **Setting** 133-acre small town campus **Total enrollment** 1,120 **Student/faculty ratio** 11:1 **Application deadline** Rolling **Freshmen** 89% were admitted **Housing** Yes **Expenses** Tuition $12,802; Room & Board $4350 **Undergraduates** 59% women, 2% part-time, 1% 25 or older, 0% Native American, 2% Hispanic, 1% black, 1% Asian American or Pacific Islander **Most popular recent majors** Business administration; elementary education; general studies **Academic program** Average class size 20, English as a second language, advanced placement, self-designed majors, tutorials, honors program, summer session, internships **Contact** Mr. John Olsen, Dean of Admission and Student Financial Planning, Central College, 812 University Street, Pella, IA 50219-1999. Telephone: 515-628-7600 or toll-free 800-458-5503. Fax: 515-628-5316. E-mail: admissions@central.edu. Web site: http://www.central.edu/.

CLARKE COLLEGE
DUBUQUE, IOWA

General Independent Roman Catholic, comprehensive, coed **Entrance** Moderately difficult **Setting** 55-acre urban campus **Total enrollment** 1,160 **Student/faculty ratio** 13:1 **Application deadline** Rolling **Freshmen** 85% were admitted **Housing** Yes **Expenses** Tuition $12,439; Room & Board $4555 **Undergraduates** 68% women, 29% part-time, 34% 25 or older, 0.5% Native American, 3% Hispanic, 2% black, 0.4% Asian American or Pacific Islander **Most popular recent majors** Physical therapy; nursing; business administration **Academic program** Average class size 25, English as a second language, advanced placement, self-designed majors, honors program, summer session, adult/continuing education programs, internships **Contact** Mr. John Foley, Director of Admissions, Clarke College, 1550 Clarke Drive, Dubuque, IA 52001-3198. Telephone: 319-588-6316 or toll-free 800-383-2345. Fax: 319-588-6789. E-mail: admissions@keller.clarke.edu. Web site: http://www.clarke.edu/.

COE COLLEGE
CEDAR RAPIDS, IOWA

General Independent, comprehensive, coed, affiliated with Presbyterian Church **Entrance** Moderately difficult **Setting** 55-acre urban campus **Total enrollment** 1,318 **Student/faculty ratio** 12:1 **Application deadline** 3/1 **Freshmen** 84% were admitted **Housing** Yes **Expenses** Tuition $16,320; Room & Board $4570 **Undergraduates** 54% women, 15% part-time, 7% 25 or older, 0% Native American, 2% Hispanic, 2% black, 1% Asian American or Pacific Islander **Most popular recent majors** Business administration; psychology; biology **Academic program** Average class size 15, English as a second language, advanced placement, accelerated degree program, self-designed majors, tutorials, honors program, summer session, adult/continuing education programs, internships **Contact** Mr. Dennis Trotter, Vice President of Admission and Financial Aid, Coe College, 1220 1st Avenue, NE, Cedar Rapids, IA 52402-5070. Telephone: 319-399-8500 or toll-free 800-332-8404. Fax: 319-399-8816. E-mail: admission@coe.edu. Web site: http://www.coe.edu/.

CORNELL COLLEGE
MOUNT VERNON, IOWA

General Independent Methodist, 4-year, coed **Entrance** Moderately difficult **Setting** 129-acre small town campus **Total enrollment** 1,079 **Student/faculty ratio** 13:1 **Application deadline** 3/1 **Freshmen** 81% were admitted **Housing** Yes **Expenses** Tuition $17,840; Room & Board $4850 **Undergraduates** 58% women, 1% part-time, 1% 25 or older, 1% Native American, 3% Hispanic, 2% black, 1% Asian American or Pacific Islander **Most popular recent majors** Psychology; English; biology **Academic program** Average class size 16, English as a second language, advanced placement, accelerated degree program, self-designed majors, tutorials, adult/continuing education programs, internships **Contact** Ms. Florence Hines, Dean of Admission and Financial Assistance, Cornell College, 600 First Street West, Mount Vernon, IA 52314-1098. Telephone: 319-895-4215 or toll-free 800-747-1112. Fax: 319-895-4492. E-mail: admissions@cornell-iowa.edu. Web site: http://www.cornell-iowa.edu/.

DIVINE WORD COLLEGE
EPWORTH, IOWA

General Independent Roman Catholic, 4-year, primarily men **Entrance** Minimally difficult **Setting** 28-acre rural campus **Total enrollment** 111 **Student/faculty ratio** 4:1 **Application deadline** 7/15 **Freshmen** 50% were admitted **Housing** Yes **Expenses** Tuition $8000; Room & Board $1600 **Undergraduates** 2% women, 1% part-time, 53% 25 or older **Most Popular Recent Major** Philosophy **Academic program** Average class size 9, English as a second language, advanced placement **Contact** Br. Dennis Newton SVD, Vice President of Recruitment/Director of Admissions, Divine Word College, 102 Jacoby Drive SW, Epworth, IA 52045-0380. Telephone: 319-876-3332 or toll-free 800-553-3321. Fax: 319-876-3407.

DORDT COLLEGE
SIOUX CENTER, IOWA

General Independent Christian Reformed, comprehensive, coed **Entrance** Moderately difficult **Setting** 65-acre small town campus **Total enrollment** 1,301 **Student/faculty ratio** 15:1 **Application deadline** 8/1 **Freshmen** 90% were admitted **Housing** Yes **Expenses** Tuition $11,450; Room & Board $3030 **Undergraduates** 50% women, 1% part-time, 5% 25 or older, 0.1% Native American, 0.3% Hispanic, 0.2% black, 0.3% Asian American or Pacific Islander **Most popular recent majors** Education; business administration; engineering **Academic program** Average class size 40, English as a second language, advanced placement, self-designed majors, tutorials, internships **Contact** Mr. Quentin Van Essen, Executive Director of Admissions, Dordt College, 498 4th Avenue, NE, Sioux Center, IA 51250-1697. Telephone: 712-722-6080 or toll-free 800-343-6738. Fax: 712-722-1967. E-mail: admissions@dordt.edu. Web site: http://www.dordt.edu/.

DRAKE UNIVERSITY
DES MOINES, IOWA

General Independent, university, coed **Entrance** Moderately difficult **Setting** 120-acre suburban campus **Total enrollment** 5,184 **Student/faculty ratio** 12:1 **Application deadline** Rolling **Freshmen** 93% were admitted **Housing** Yes **Expenses** Tuition $15,200; Room & Board $4970 **Undergraduates** 61% women, 12% part-time, 12% 25 or older, 0.3% Native American, 2% Hispanic, 4% black, 5% Asian American or Pacific Islander **Most popular recent majors** Pharmacy; advertising; business marketing and marketing management **Academic program** English as a second language, advanced placement, self-designed majors, honors program, summer session, internships **Contact** Mr. Thomas F. Willoughby, Dean of Admission, Drake University, 2507 University Avenue, Des Moines, IA 50311-4516. Telephone: 515-271-3181 or toll-free 800-44DRAKE. Fax: 515-271-2831. E-mail: admitinfo@acad.drake.edu. Web site: http://www.drake.edu/.

EMMAUS BIBLE COLLEGE
DUBUQUE, IOWA

General Independent nondenominational, 4-year, coed **Entrance** Noncompetitive **Setting** 22-acre small town campus **Total enrollment** 260 **Student/faculty ratio** 16:1 **Application deadline** 8/1 **Housing** Yes **Expenses** Tuition $2870; Room & Board $4580 **Undergraduates** 52% women, 4% part-time, 10% 25 or older, 0% Native American, 4% Hispanic, 2% black, 2% Asian American or Pacific Islander **Academic program** Advanced placement, tutorials, internships **Contact** Miss Nancy Ferguson, Registrar, Emmaus Bible College, 2570 Asbury Road, Dubuque, IA 52001-3097. Telephone: 319-588-8000 ext. 122 or toll-free 800-397-2425. Fax: 319-588-1216.

FAITH BAPTIST BIBLE COLLEGE AND THEOLOGICAL SEMINARY
ANKENY, IOWA

General Independent, comprehensive, coed, affiliated with General Association of Regular Baptist Churches **Entrance** Minimally difficult **Setting** 52-acre small town campus **Total enrollment** 375 **Student/faculty ratio** 20:1 **Application deadline** 8/1 **Freshmen** 88% were admitted **Housing** Yes **Expenses** Tuition $6694; Room & Board $3276 **Undergraduates** 55% women, 11% part-time, 8% 25 or older, 0.3% Native American, 2% Hispanic, 0.3% black, 0% Asian American or Pacific Islander **Most popular recent majors** Elementary education; pastoral counseling; biblical studies **Academic program** Advanced placement, summer session, adult/continuing education programs, internships **Contact** Mr. Tim Nilius, Vice President of Enrollment and Constituent Services, Faith Baptist Bible College and Theological Seminary, 1900 Northwest 4th Street, Ankeny, IA 50021-2152. Telephone: 515-964-0601 ext. 238 or toll-free 888-324-8448. Fax: 515-964-1638. E-mail: fbblenroll@aol.com.

GRACELAND COLLEGE
LAMONI, IOWA

General Independent Reorganized Latter Day Saints, comprehensive, coed **Entrance** Moderately difficult **Setting** 169-acre small town campus **Total enrollment** 1,260 **Student/faculty ratio** 15:1 **Application deadline** 5/1 **Freshmen** 63% were admitted **Housing** Yes **Expenses** Tuition $10,860; Room & Board $3620 **Undergraduates** 17% 25 or older **Most popular recent majors** Nursing; business administration; education **Academic program** Average class size 28, English as a second language, advanced placement, self-designed majors, tutorials, honors program, summer session, adult/continuing education programs, internships **Contact** Ms. Bonita A. Booth, Dean of Admissions, Graceland College, 700 College Avenue, Lamoni, IA 50140. Telephone: 515-784-5118 or toll-free 800-346-9208. Fax: 515-784-5480. E-mail: admissions@graceland.edu. Web site: http://www.graceland.edu/.

GRAND VIEW COLLEGE
DES MOINES, IOWA

General Independent, 4-year, coed, affiliated with Evangelical Lutheran Church in America **Entrance** Noncompetitive **Setting** 25-acre urban campus **Total enrollment** 1,433 **Student/faculty ratio** 13:1 **Application deadline** Rolling **Freshmen** 85% were admitted **Housing** Yes **Expenses** Tuition $11,410; Room & Board $3775 **Undergraduates** 42% 25 or older, 0.4% Native American, 1% Hispanic, 4% black, 3% Asian American or Pacific Islander **Most popular recent majors** Business administration; nursing; education **Academic program** Average class size 21, English as a second language, advanced placement, accelerated degree program, self-designed majors, tutorials, honors program, summer session, internships **Contact** Mr. Brian R. Bowman, Director of Admissions, Grand View College, 1200 Grandview Avenue, Des Moines, IA 50316-1599. Telephone: 515-263-2810 ext. 2808 or toll-free 800-444-6083. Fax: 515-263-2974. E-mail: admiss@gvc.edu. Web site: http://www.gvc.edu/.

GRINNELL COLLEGE
GRINNELL, IOWA

General Independent, 4-year, coed **Entrance** Very difficult **Setting** 95-acre small town campus **Total**

Grinnell College *(continued)*

enrollment 1,363 **Student/faculty ratio** 10:1 **Application deadline** 2/1 **Freshmen** 69% were admitted **Housing** Yes **Expenses** Tuition $17,568; Room & Board $5152 **Undergraduates** 56% women, 0.1% part-time, 1% 25 or older, 1% Native American, 4% Hispanic, 3% black, 4% Asian American or Pacific Islander **Most Popular Recent Majors** Biology; English; history **Academic program** Advanced placement, accelerated degree program, self-designed majors, tutorials, internships **Contact** Mr. Vincent Cuseo, Director of Admission, Grinnell College, PO Box 805, Grinnell, IA 50112-0807. Telephone: 515-269-3600 or toll-free 800-247-0113. Fax: 515-269-4600. E-mail: askgrin@admin.grin.edu. Web site: http://www.grin.edu/.

HAMILTON TECHNICAL COLLEGE

DAVENPORT, IOWA

General Proprietary, 4-year, coed **Entrance** Noncompetitive **Setting** Urban campus **Student/faculty ratio** 20:1 **Application deadline** Rolling **Housing** No **Expenses** Tuition $5400 **Academic program** Accelerated degree program **Contact** Ms. Greta Bierman, Director of Admissions, Hamilton Technical College, 1011 East 53rd Street, Davenport, IA 52807-2653. Telephone: 319-386-3570. Fax: 319-386-6756.

IOWA STATE UNIVERSITY OF SCIENCE AND TECHNOLOGY

AMES, IOWA

General State-supported, university, coed **Entrance** Moderately difficult **Setting** 1,788-acre suburban campus **Total enrollment** 25,384 **Student/faculty ratio** 13:1 **Application deadline** 8/21 **Freshmen** 91% were admitted **Housing** Yes **Expenses** Tuition $2766; Room & Board $3647 **Undergraduates** 43% women, 9% part-time, 13% 25 or older, 0.3% Native American, 1% Hispanic, 3% black, 2% Asian American or Pacific Islander **Most popular recent majors** Elementary education; mechanical engineering; civil engineering **Academic program** English as a second language, advanced placement, accelerated degree program, self-designed majors, tutorials, honors program, summer session, adult/continuing education programs, internships **Contact** Mr. Phil Caffrey, Associate Director for Freshman Admissions, Iowa State University of Science and Technology, Ames, IA 50011-2010. Telephone: 515-294-5836 or toll-free 800-262-3810. Fax: 515-294-2592. E-mail: admissions@iastate.edu. Web site: http://www.iastate.edu/.

IOWA WESLEYAN COLLEGE

MOUNT PLEASANT, IOWA

General Independent United Methodist, 4-year, coed **Entrance** Moderately difficult **Setting** 60-acre small town campus **Total enrollment** 804 **Student/faculty ratio** 12:1 **Application deadline** 8/15 **Freshmen** 82% were admitted **Housing** Yes **Expenses** Tuition $12,220; Room & Board $4090 **Undergraduates** 66% women, 47% part-time, 47% 25 or older, 0.2% Native American, 1% Hispanic, 6% black, 2% Asian American or Pacific Islander **Most popular recent majors** Business administration; nursing; elementary education **Academic program** Average class size 22, English as a second language, advanced placement, self-designed majors, tutorials, summer session, adult/continuing education programs, internships **Contact** Mr. Donald Hapward, Director of Admissions, Iowa Wesleyan College, 601 North Main Street, Mount Pleasant, IA 52641-1398. Telephone: 319-385-6231 or toll-free 800-582-2383. Fax: 319-385-6296. E-mail: admitrwl@iwc.edu. Web site: http://www.iwc.edu/.

LORAS COLLEGE

DUBUQUE, IOWA

General Independent Roman Catholic, comprehensive, coed **Entrance** Moderately difficult **Setting** 60-acre suburban campus **Total enrollment** 1,776 **Student/faculty ratio** 13:1 **Application deadline** Rolling **Freshmen** 81% were admitted **Housing** Yes **Expenses** Tuition $13,750; Room & Board $5005 **Undergraduates** 53% women, 9% part-time, 2% 25 or older **Most popular recent majors** Business administration; social sciences; education **Academic program** English as a second language, advanced placement, accelerated degree program, self-designed majors, tutorials, honors program, summer session, adult/continuing education programs, internships **Contact** Ms. Joan Williams, Assistant Director of Admissions, Loras College, 1450 Alta Vista, Dubuque, IA 52004-0178. Telephone: 319-588-7236 or toll-free 800-24-LORAS. Fax: 319-588-7964. E-mail: adms@loras.edu. Web site: http://www.loras.edu/.

LUTHER COLLEGE

DECORAH, IOWA

General Independent, 4-year, coed, affiliated with Evangelical Lutheran Church in America **Entrance** Moderately difficult **Setting** 800-acre small town campus **Total enrollment** 2,400 **Student/faculty ratio** 13:1 **Application deadline** 6/1 **Freshmen** 92% were admitted **Housing** Yes **Expenses** Tuition $15,630; Room & Board $3700 **Undergraduates** 60% women, 3% part-time, 3%

25 or older, 0.2% Native American, 1% Hispanic, 1% black, 1% Asian American or Pacific Islander **Most popular recent majors** Biology; business administration; elementary education **Academic program** Average class size 28, advanced placement, self-designed majors, tutorials, honors program, summer session, internships **Contact** Dr. David Sallee, Vice President for Enrollment Management, Luther College, 700 College Drive, Decorah, IA 52101-1045. Telephone: 319-387-1287 or toll-free 800-458-8437. Fax: 319-387-2159. E-mail: admissions@luther.edu. Web site: http://www.luther.edu/luther.htm.

▶ **For more information, see page 462.**

MAHARISHI UNIVERSITY OF MANAGEMENT
FAIRFIELD, IOWA

General Independent, university, coed **Entrance** Moderately difficult **Setting** 262-acre small town campus **Total enrollment** 1,422 **Student/faculty ratio** 11:1 **Application deadline** 8/1 **Freshmen** 74% were admitted **Housing** Yes **Expenses** Tuition $14,670; Room & Board $4960 **Undergraduates** 47% women, 4% part-time, 28% 25 or older, 0.5% Native American, 0.5% Hispanic, 0.5% black, 0.4% Asian American or Pacific Islander **Most popular recent majors** Business administration; literature; art **Academic program** Average class size 60, English as a second language, advanced placement, self-designed majors, tutorials, honors program, adult/continuing education programs, internships **Contact** Mr. Brad Mylett, Director of Admissions, Maharishi University of Management, 1000 North 4th Street, Fairfield, IA 53557. Telephone: 515-472-1110. Fax: 515-472-1179. E-mail: admissions@mum.edu. Web site: http://www.miu.edu/.

MARYCREST INTERNATIONAL UNIVERSITY
DAVENPORT, IOWA

General Independent, comprehensive, coed **Entrance** Moderately difficult **Setting** 30-acre urban campus **Total enrollment** 769 **Student/faculty ratio** 11:1 **Application deadline** Rolling **Freshmen** 74% were admitted **Housing** Yes **Expenses** Tuition $11,998; Room & Board $4686 **Undergraduates** 65% women, 27% part-time, 53% 25 or older, 0.2% Native American, 4% Hispanic, 8% black, 2% Asian American or Pacific Islander **Most popular recent majors** Business administration; nursing; elementary education **Academic program** Average class size 18, English as a second language, self-designed majors, tutorials, summer session, adult/continuing education programs, internships **Contact** Mr. Mark Anderson, Assistant Director of Admission, Marycrest International University, 1607 West 12th Street, Davenport, IA 82804-4906. Telephone: 319-326-9431 or toll-free 800-728-9705 ext. 2225. Fax: 319-327-9620. E-mail: mfarber@acc.mcrest.edu. Web site: http://www.mcrest.edu/.

MORNINGSIDE COLLEGE
SIOUX CITY, IOWA

General Independent United Methodist, comprehensive, coed **Entrance** Moderately difficult **Setting** 41-acre suburban campus **Total enrollment** 1,166 **Student/faculty ratio** 14:1 **Application deadline** Rolling **Freshmen** 85% were admitted **Housing** Yes **Expenses** Tuition $12,306; Room & Board $4390 **Undergraduates** 58% women, 9% part-time, 8% 25 or older, 0.5% Native American, 0.2% Hispanic, 2% black, 1% Asian American or Pacific Islander **Most popular recent majors** Business administration; education; biology **Academic program** Average class size 20, English as a second language, advanced placement, accelerated degree program, self-designed majors, tutorials, honors program, summer session, adult/continuing education programs, internships **Contact** Ms. Lora Vander Zwaag, Director of Admissions, Morningside College, 1501 Morningside Avenue, Sioux City, IA 51106-1751. Telephone: 712-274-5111 or toll-free 800-831-0806. E-mail: mscadm@alpha.morningside.edu. Web site: http://www.morningside.edu/.

MOUNT MERCY COLLEGE
CEDAR RAPIDS, IOWA

General Independent Roman Catholic, 4-year, coed **Entrance** Moderately difficult **Setting** 36-acre suburban campus **Total enrollment** 1,200 **Student/faculty ratio** 11:1 **Application deadline** 8/15 **Freshmen** 87% were admitted **Housing** Yes **Expenses** Tuition $11,860; Room & Board $3945 **Undergraduates** 73% women, 43% part-time, 38% 25 or older, 0.2% Native American, 1% Hispanic, 1% black, 1% Asian American or Pacific Islander **Most popular recent majors** Business administration; elementary education; nursing **Academic program** Advanced placement, accelerated degree program, self-designed majors, tutorials, honors program, summer session, adult/continuing education programs, internships **Contact** Dr. Alex Popovics, Vice President for Enrollment Management, Mount Mercy College, 1330 Elmhurst Drive, NE, Cedar Rapids, IA 52402-4797. Telephone: 319-363-8213 ext. 1221 or toll-free 800-248-4504. Fax: 319-363-5270. E-mail: admission@mmc.mtmercy.edu. Web site: http://www.mtmary.edu/.

MOUNT ST. CLARE COLLEGE
CLINTON, IOWA

General Independent Roman Catholic, 4-year, coed **Entrance** Minimally difficult **Setting** 24-

Mount St. Clare College *(continued)*

acre small town campus **Total enrollment** 579 **Student/faculty ratio** 12:1 **Application deadline** 8/15 **Housing** Yes **Expenses** Tuition $11,640; Room & Board $4020 **Undergraduates** 59% women, 17% part-time, 43% 25 or older **Most popular recent majors** Liberal arts and studies; education; business administration **Academic program** Average class size 20, English as a second language, advanced placement, self-designed majors, tutorials, honors program, summer session, adult/continuing education programs, internships **Contact** Ms. Waunita M. Sullivan, Director of Enrollment, Mount St. Clare College, 400 North Bluff Boulevard, PO Box 2967, Clinton, IA 52733-2967. Telephone: 319-242-4153 ext. 427 or toll-free 800-242-4153. Fax: 319-242-2003. E-mail: admiffnf@clare.edu. Web site: http://www.clare.edu/.

NORTHWESTERN COLLEGE
ORANGE CITY, IOWA

General Independent, 4-year, coed, affiliated with Reformed Church in America **Entrance** Moderately difficult **Setting** 45-acre rural campus **Total enrollment** 1,177 **Student/faculty ratio** 16:1 **Application deadline** Rolling **Freshmen** 93% were admitted **Housing** Yes **Expenses** Tuition $11,300; Room & Board $3300 **Undergraduates** 59% women, 2% part-time, 3% 25 or older, 0.2% Native American, 1% Hispanic, 0.3% black, 0.3% Asian American or Pacific Islander **Most popular recent majors** Business administration; elementary education; biology **Academic program** Average class size 40, English as a second language, advanced placement, accelerated degree program, self-designed majors, tutorials, honors program, summer session, internships **Contact** Mr. Ronald K. DeJong, Director of Admissions, Northwestern College, 101 College Lane, Orange City, IA 51041-1996. Telephone: 712-737-7000 or toll-free 800-747-4757 (in-state). Fax: 712-737-7164. E-mail: markb@nwciowa.edu. Web site: http://www.nwciowa.edu/.

PALMER COLLEGE OF CHIROPRACTIC
DAVENPORT, IOWA

General Independent, comprehensive, coed **Entrance** Moderately difficult **Setting** 3-acre urban campus **Total enrollment** 1,818 **Student/faculty ratio** 14:1 **Application deadline** Rolling **Housing** No **Expenses** Tuition $14,520 **Undergraduates** 62% 25 or older **Academic program** Summer session, internships **Contact** Mr. Gary Mohr, Director of Institutional Advancement, Palmer College of Chiropractic, 1000 Brady Street, Davenport, IA 52803-5287. Telephone: 319-326-9626 or toll-free 800-722-3648. Fax: 319-326-8414. E-mail: pcadmit@palmer.edu.

ST. AMBROSE UNIVERSITY
DAVENPORT, IOWA

General Independent Roman Catholic, comprehensive, coed **Entrance** Moderately difficult **Setting** 11-acre urban campus **Total enrollment** 2,776 **Student/faculty ratio** 16:1 **Application deadline** Rolling **Freshmen** 85% were admitted **Housing** Yes **Expenses** Tuition $12,850; Room & Board $4810 **Undergraduates** 58% women, 24% part-time, 21% 25 or older **Most popular recent majors** Business administration; biology; mass communications **Academic program** Advanced placement, accelerated degree program, self-designed majors, tutorials, summer session, adult/continuing education programs, internships **Contact** Mr. Patrick O O'Connor, Dean of Admissions, St. Ambrose University, 518 West Locust Street, Davenport, IA 52803-2898. Telephone: 319-333-6300 or toll-free 800-383-2627. Fax: 319-383-8791.

▶ **For more information, see page 503.**

SIMPSON COLLEGE
INDIANOLA, IOWA

General Independent United Methodist, 4-year, coed **Entrance** Moderately difficult **Setting** 63-acre small town campus **Total enrollment** 1,958 **Student/faculty ratio** 14:1 **Application deadline** Rolling **Freshmen** 87% were admitted **Housing** Yes **Expenses** Tuition $13,095; Room & Board $4290 **Undergraduates** 55% women, 32% part-time, 30% 25 or older, 1% Native American, 1% Hispanic, 1% black, 1% Asian American or Pacific Islander **Most popular recent majors** Business administration; accounting; biology **Academic program** Average class size 25, advanced placement, accelerated degree program, self-designed majors, tutorials, honors program, summer session, adult/continuing education programs, internships **Contact** Mr. John Kellogg, Vice President of Enrollment and Planning, Simpson College, 701 North C Street, Indianola, IA 50125-1297. Telephone: 515-961-1624 or toll-free 800-362-2454. Fax: 515-961-1498. E-mail: admiss@simpson.edu. Web site: http://www.simpson.edu/.

▶ **For more information, see page 515.**

TEIKYO MARYCREST UNIVERSITY
See Marycrest International University

UNIVERSITY OF DUBUQUE
DUBUQUE, IOWA

General Independent Presbyterian, comprehensive, coed **Entrance** Moderately difficult **Setting**

56-acre suburban campus **Total enrollment** 999 **Student/faculty ratio** 14:1 **Application deadline** Rolling **Housing** Yes **Expenses** Tuition $12,640; Room & Board $4340 **Undergraduates** 42% women, 15% part-time, 20% 25 or older, 0.4% Native American, 0.4% Hispanic, 1% black, 0.1% Asian American or Pacific Islander **Most popular recent majors** Education; aviation management; environmental science **Academic program** Average class size 20, English as a second language, advanced placement, accelerated degree program, self-designed majors, tutorials, summer session, adult/continuing education programs, internships **Contact** Mr. Clifford D. Bunting, Dean of Admissions and Records, University of Dubuque, 2000 University Avenue, Dubuque, IA 52001-5050. Telephone: 319-589-3200 ext. 3270 or toll-free 800-722-5583 (in-state). Fax: 319-589-3690. E-mail: admssns@univ.dbq.edu. Web site: http://www.dbq.edu/.

THE UNIVERSITY OF IOWA
IOWA CITY, IOWA

General State-supported, university, coed **Entrance** Moderately difficult **Setting** 1,900-acre small town campus **Total enrollment** 28,409 **Student/faculty ratio** 16:1 **Application deadline** 5/15 **Freshmen** 84% were admitted **Housing** Yes **Expenses** Tuition $2760; Room & Board $4046 **Undergraduates** 54% women, 14% part-time, 12% 25 or older, 0.4% Native American, 2% Hispanic, 2% black, 4% Asian American or Pacific Islander **Most popular recent majors** Psychology; English; finance **Academic program** English as a second language, advanced placement, accelerated degree program, self-designed majors, tutorials, honors program, summer session, adult/continuing education programs, internships **Contact** Mr. Michael Barron, Director of Admissions, The University of Iowa, 107 Calvin Hall, Iowa City, IA 52242. Telephone: 319-335-3847 or toll-free 800-553-4692. Fax: 319-335-1535. E-mail: admissions@uiowa.edu. Web site: http://www.uiowa.edu/.

UNIVERSITY OF NORTHERN IOWA
CEDAR FALLS, IOWA

General State-supported, comprehensive, coed **Entrance** Moderately difficult **Setting** 940-acre small town campus **Total enrollment** 13,503 **Student/faculty ratio** 17:1 **Application deadline** Rolling **Freshmen** 84% were admitted **Housing** Yes **Expenses** Tuition $2752; Room & Board $3452 **Undergraduates** 58% women, 12% part-time, 6% 25 or older, 0.2% Native American, 1% Hispanic, 2% black, 1% Asian American or Pacific Islander **Most popular recent majors** Elementary education; accounting; biology **Academic program** Average class size 54, English as a second language, advanced placement, accelerated degree program, self-designed majors, summer session, adult/continuing education programs, internships **Contact** Mr. Clark Elmer, Director of Enrollment Management and Admissions, University of Northern Iowa, 1222 West 27th Street, Cedar Falls, IA 50614. Telephone: 319-273-2281 or toll-free 800-772-2037. Fax: 319-273-2885. E-mail: admissions@uni.edu. Web site: http://www.uni.edu/.

UNIVERSITY OF OSTEOPATHIC MEDICINE AND HEALTH SCIENCES
DES MOINES, IOWA

General Independent, upper-level, coed **Entrance** Most difficult **Setting** 20-acre urban campus **Total enrollment** 1,155 **Student/faculty ratio** 20:1 **Application deadline** Rolling **Freshmen** 10% were admitted **Housing** No **Expenses** Tuition $12,070 **Undergraduates** 59% women, 50% 25 or older, 2% Native American, 3% Hispanic, 2% black, 3% Asian American or Pacific Islander **Academic program** Advanced placement, internships **Contact** Dr. Dennis Bates, Director of Admissions, University of Osteopathic Medicine and Health Sciences, 3200 Grand Avenue, Des Moines, IA 50312-4104. Telephone: 515-271-1450. Fax: 515-271-1578. E-mail: pchamber@uomhs.edu. Web site: http://www.uomhs.edu/.

UPPER IOWA UNIVERSITY
FAYETTE, IOWA

General Independent, comprehensive, coed **Entrance** Moderately difficult **Setting** 80-acre rural campus **Total enrollment** 4,109 **Student/faculty ratio** 18:1 **Application deadline** Rolling **Freshmen** 74% were admitted **Housing** Yes **Expenses** Tuition $9750; Room & Board $3770 **Undergraduates** 56% women, 50% part-time, 8% 25 or older, 0.4% Native American, 2% Hispanic, 8% black, 2% Asian American or Pacific Islander **Most popular recent majors** Business administration; biology; education **Academic program** Advanced placement, accelerated degree program, self-designed majors, tutorials, summer session, adult/continuing education programs, internships **Contact** Mr. Kent McElvania, Vice President for Enrollment Management, Upper Iowa University, Box 1859, Fayette, IA 52142-1857. Telephone: 319-425-5281 or toll-free 800-553-4150. Fax: 319-425-5277. E-mail: admission@uiu.edu. Web site: http://www.uiu.edu/.

WARTBURG COLLEGE
WAVERLY, IOWA

General Independent Lutheran, 4-year, coed **Entrance** Moderately difficult **Setting** 118-acre small town campus **Total enrollment** 1,528 **Student/faculty ratio** 15:1 **Application deadline** Rolling

Wartburg College *(continued)*

Housing Yes **Expenses** Tuition $13,610; Room & Board $4010 **Undergraduates** 58% women, 8% part-time, 4% 25 or older, 0.2% Native American, 1% Hispanic, 6% black, 1% Asian American or Pacific Islander **Most popular recent majors** Biology; business administration; elementary education **Academic program** Average class size 28, English as a second language, advanced placement, accelerated degree program, self-designed majors, tutorials, honors program, summer session, internships **Contact** Mr. Doug Bowman, Director of Admissions, Wartburg College, 222 Ninth Street, NW, PO Box 1003, Waverly, IA 50677-1003. Telephone: 319-352-8264 or toll-free 800-772-2085. Fax: 319-352-8579. E-mail: admissions@wartburg.edu. Web site: http://www.wartburg.edu/.

WILLIAM PENN COLLEGE
OSKALOOSA, IOWA

General Independent, 4-year, coed, affiliated with Society of Friends **Entrance** Moderately difficult **Setting** 40-acre rural campus **Total enrollment** 770 **Freshmen** 92% were admitted **Housing** Yes **Expenses** Tuition $11,490; Room & Board $4110 **Undergraduates** 46% women, 9% part-time, 25% 25 or older **Most popular recent majors** Elementary education; physical education; accounting **Academic program** English as a second language, advanced placement, accelerated degree program, self-designed majors, tutorials, summer session, adult/continuing education programs, internships **Contact** Mr. Eric Otto, Director of Admissions, William Penn College, 201 Trueblood Avenue, Oskaloosa, IA 52577-1799. Telephone: 515-673-1012 ext. 2081 or toll-free 800-779-7366. Fax: 515-673-1396. E-mail: ottoe@wmpenn.edu. Web site: http://www.wmpenn.edu/.

KANSAS

BAKER UNIVERSITY
BALDWIN CITY, KANSAS

General Independent United Methodist, comprehensive, coed **Entrance** Moderately difficult **Setting** 26-acre small town campus **Total enrollment** 796 **Student/faculty ratio** 11:1 **Application deadline** Rolling **Freshmen** 83% were admitted **Housing** Yes **Expenses** Tuition $10,900; Room & Board $4600 **Undergraduates** 53% women, 1% part-time, 1% 25 or older, 1% Native American, 3% Hispanic, 4% black, 1% Asian American or Pacific Islander **Most popular recent majors** Business administration; psychology **Academic program** Average class size 20, English as a second language, advanced placement, accelerated degree program, tutorials, honors program, summer session, adult/continuing education programs, internships **Contact** Mr. Jody Johnson, Vice President for Enrollment Management, Baker University, Box 65, Baldwin City, KS 66006-0065. Telephone: 785-594-6451 ext. 541 or toll-free 800-873-4282. Fax: 785-594-6721. E-mail: adm_constant@george.bakeru.edu. Web site: http://www.bakeru.edu/.

BARCLAY COLLEGE
HAVILAND, KANSAS

General Independent, 4-year, coed, affiliated with Society of Friends **Entrance** Minimally difficult **Setting** 13-acre rural campus **Total enrollment** 133 **Student/faculty ratio** 13:1 **Application deadline** 9/1 **Housing** Yes **Expenses** Tuition $5000; Room & Board $2900 **Undergraduates** 49% women, 12% part-time, 28% 25 or older, 1% Native American, 3% Hispanic, 3% black, 3% Asian American or Pacific Islander **Most popular recent majors** Business administration; divinity/ministry; pastoral counseling **Academic program** Average class size 15, advanced placement, accelerated degree program, self-designed majors, tutorials, internships **Contact** Ms. Deborah Durham, Director of Admissions, Barclay College, PO Box 288, Haviland, KS 67059-0288. Telephone: 316-862-5252 ext. 41 or toll-free 800-862-0226. Fax: 316-862-5403.

BENEDICTINE COLLEGE
ATCHISON, KANSAS

General Independent Roman Catholic, comprehensive, coed **Entrance** Moderately difficult **Setting** 225-acre small town campus **Total enrollment** 915 **Student/faculty ratio** 12:1 **Application deadline** 8/15 **Freshmen** 98% were admitted **Housing** Yes **Expenses** Tuition $11,750; Room & Board $4620 **Undergraduates** 47% women, 11% part-time, 12% 25 or older, 0.3% Native American, 5% Hispanic, 5% black, 2% Asian American or Pacific Islander **Most popular recent majors** Business administration; elementary education; biology **Academic program** Average class size 22, English as a second language, advanced placement, accelerated degree program, self-designed majors, tutorials, honors program, summer session, internships **Contact** Ms. Kelly Vowels, Dean of Enrollment Management, Benedictine College, 1020 North 2nd Street, Atchison, KS 66002-1499. Telephone: 913-367-5340 ext. 2475. E-mail: mail@benedictine.edu. Web site: http://www.benedictine.edu/.

BETHANY COLLEGE
LINDSBORG, KANSAS

General Independent Lutheran, 4-year, coed **Entrance** Moderately difficult **Setting** 80-acre small town campus **Total enrollment** 667 **Student/faculty ratio** 13:1 **Application deadline** Rolling **Freshmen** 63% were admitted **Housing** Yes **Expenses** Tuition $11,390; Room & Board $3535 **Undergraduates** 47% women, 4% part-time, 12% 25 or older **Most popular recent majors** Business economics; education; psychology **Academic program** Advanced placement, accelerated degree program, self-designed majors, tutorials, summer session, internships **Contact** Ms. Karli Grant, Dean of Admissions and Financial Aid, Bethany College, 421 North First Street, Lindsborg, KS 67456-1897. Telephone: 785-227-3311 ext. 8108 or toll-free 800-826-2281. Fax: 785-649-3217. E-mail: admissions@bethany.bethanylb.edu. Web site: http://www.bethanylb.edu/.

BETHEL COLLEGE
NORTH NEWTON, KANSAS

General Independent, 4-year, coed, affiliated with General Conference Mennonite Church **Entrance** Moderately difficult **Setting** 60-acre small town campus **Total enrollment** 610 **Student/faculty ratio** 12:1 **Application deadline** 8/15 **Freshmen** 92% were admitted **Housing** Yes **Expenses** Tuition $10,330; Room & Board $4200 **Undergraduates** 57% women, 13% part-time, 17% 25 or older, 0.5% Native American, 4% Hispanic, 3% black, 3% Asian American or Pacific Islander **Most popular recent majors** Nursing; education; business administration **Academic program** Average class size 16, advanced placement, accelerated degree program, self-designed majors, tutorials, summer session, internships **Contact** Mr. Michael Lamb, Director of Admissions, Bethel College, 300 East 27th Street, North Newton, KS 67117. Telephone: 316-283-2500 ext. 230 or toll-free 800-522-1887. Fax: 316-284-5286. E-mail: admissions@bethelks.edu. Web site: http://www.bethelks.edu/.

EMPORIA STATE UNIVERSITY
EMPORIA, KANSAS

General State-supported, comprehensive, coed **Entrance** Noncompetitive **Setting** 207-acre small town campus **Total enrollment** 5,320 **Student/faculty ratio** 18:1 **Application deadline** Rolling **Freshmen** 100% were admitted **Housing** Yes **Expenses** Tuition $1982; Room & Board $3560 **Undergraduates** 59% women, 11% part-time, 18% 25 or older, 0.4% Native American, 3% Hispanic, 3% black, 1% Asian American or Pacific Islander **Most popular recent majors** Elementary education; business administration; sociology **Academic program** Average class size 35, English as a second language, advanced placement, accelerated degree program, self-designed majors, tutorials, honors program, summer session, adult/continuing education programs, internships **Contact** Mr. Karl Kandt, Coordinator of Student Recruitment, Emporia State University, 1200 Commercial Street, Emporia, KS 66801-5087. Telephone: 316-341-5465 or toll-free 800-896-7544. E-mail: ugadmiss@esumail.emporia.edu. Web site: http://www.emporia.edu/.

FORT HAYS STATE UNIVERSITY
HAYS, KANSAS

General State-supported, comprehensive, coed **Entrance** Noncompetitive **Setting** 200-acre small town campus **Total enrollment** 5,616 **Student/faculty ratio** 17:1 **Application deadline** Rolling **Freshmen** 100% were admitted **Housing** Yes **Expenses** Tuition $1992; Room & Board $3400 **Undergraduates** 36% 25 or older, 0.3% Native American, 2% Hispanic, 1% black, 1% Asian American or Pacific Islander **Most popular recent majors** Elementary education; physical education; nursing **Academic program** Advanced placement, summer session, adult/continuing education programs, internships **Contact** Mr. Joey Linn, Director of Admissions, Fort Hays State University, 600 Park Street, Hays, KS 67601-4099. Telephone: 785-628-4222 or toll-free 800-432-0248 (in-state). Fax: 785-628-4014. E-mail: tigers@fhsu.edu. Web site: http://www.fhsu.edu/.

FRIENDS UNIVERSITY
WICHITA, KANSAS

General Independent, comprehensive, coed **Entrance** Moderately difficult **Setting** 45-acre urban campus **Total enrollment** 2,729 **Application deadline** Rolling **Freshmen** 99% were admitted **Housing** Yes **Expenses** Tuition $9975; Room & Board $3250 **Undergraduates** 0.3% 25 or older **Most popular recent majors** Business administration; psychology; education **Academic program** Average class size 30, advanced placement, accelerated degree program, self-designed majors, tutorials, honors program, summer session, adult/continuing education programs, internships **Contact** Mr. Tony Meyers, Director of Admissions, Friends University, 2100 West University Street, Wichita, KS 67213. Telephone: 316-295-5100 or toll-free 800-577-2233. Fax: 316-262-5027. E-mail: tonym@friends.edu. Web site: http://www.friends.edu/.

KANSAS NEWMAN COLLEGE
WICHITA, KANSAS

General Independent Roman Catholic, comprehensive, coed **Contact** Mr. Thomas C. Green, Dean of Enrollment Management, Kansas Newman College, 3100 McCormick Avenue, Wichita, KS 67213-

Kansas Newman College *(continued)*

2084. Telephone: 316-942-4291 ext. 144 or toll-free 800-736-7585 (out-of-state). Fax: 316-942-4483.

KANSAS STATE UNIVERSITY
MANHATTAN, KANSAS

General State-supported, university, coed **Entrance** Noncompetitive **Setting** 668-acre suburban campus **Total enrollment** 20,306 **Student/faculty ratio** 15:1 **Application deadline** Rolling **Freshmen** 66% were admitted **Housing** Yes **Expenses** Tuition $2467; Room & Board $3640 **Undergraduates** 47% women, 14% part-time, 12% 25 or older, 1% Native American, 2% Hispanic, 3% black, 2% Asian American or Pacific Islander **Most popular recent majors** Journalism; animal sciences; elementary education **Academic program** English as a second language, advanced placement, accelerated degree program, honors program, summer session, adult/continuing education programs, internships **Contact** Mr. Larry Moeder, Interim Director of Admissions, Kansas State University, Anderson Hall, Room 1, Manhattan, KS 66506. Telephone: 785-532-6250 or toll-free 800-432-8270 (in-state). E-mail: kstate@ksu.edu. Web site: http://www.ksu.edu/.

KANSAS WESLEYAN UNIVERSITY
SALINA, KANSAS

General Independent United Methodist, comprehensive, coed **Entrance** Moderately difficult **Setting** 28-acre urban campus **Total enrollment** 688 **Student/faculty ratio** 15:1 **Application deadline** Rolling **Housing** Yes **Expenses** Tuition $10,400; Room & Board $3700 **Undergraduates** 61% women, 14% part-time, 34% 25 or older, 1% Native American, 3% Hispanic, 8% black, 3% Asian American or Pacific Islander **Most popular recent majors** Education; business administration; nursing **Academic program** Average class size 22, English as a second language, advanced placement, accelerated degree program, self-designed majors, tutorials, honors program, summer session, adult/continuing education programs, internships **Contact** Mr. Jeffery D. Miller, Office Manager-Admissions, Kansas Wesleyan University, 100 East Claflin, Salina, KS 67401-6196. Telephone: 785-827-5541 ext. 1283 or toll-free 800-874-1154. Fax: 785-827-0927. E-mail: admissions@diamond.kwu.edu. Web site: http://www.kwu.edu/.

MANHATTAN CHRISTIAN COLLEGE
MANHATTAN, KANSAS

General Independent, 4-year, coed, affiliated with Christian Churches and Churches of Christ **Entrance** Minimally difficult **Setting** 10-acre small town campus **Total enrollment** 317 **Student/faculty ratio** 14:1 **Application deadline** Rolling **Freshmen** 92% were admitted **Housing** Yes **Expenses** Tuition $6036; Room & Board $3126 **Undergraduates** 51% women, 28% part-time, 8% 25 or older, 1% Native American, 2% Hispanic, 3% black, 0% Asian American or Pacific Islander **Most popular recent majors** Religious education; divinity/ministry **Academic program** Advanced placement, self-designed majors, summer session, internships **Contact** Mr. John Poulson, Vice President of Admissions, Manhattan Christian College, 1415 Anderson, Manhattan, KS 66502-4081. Telephone: 785-539-3571 ext. 30. Fax: 785-539-0832. Web site: http://www.mccks.edu/.

MCPHERSON COLLEGE
MCPHERSON, KANSAS

General Independent, 4-year, coed, affiliated with Church of the Brethren **Entrance** Moderately difficult **Setting** 26-acre small town campus **Total enrollment** 513 **Student/faculty ratio** 12:1 **Application deadline** Rolling **Freshmen** 78% were admitted **Housing** Yes **Expenses** Tuition $9970; Room & Board $3930 **Undergraduates** 47% women, 14% part-time, 13% 25 or older, 1% Native American, 5% Hispanic, 6% black, 1% Asian American or Pacific Islander **Most popular recent majors** Business administration; elementary education; accounting **Academic program** Advanced placement, self-designed majors, tutorials, summer session, adult/continuing education programs, internships **Contact** Mrs. Anne M. Kirchner, Director of Admission, McPherson College, 1600 East Euclid, PO Box 1402, McPherson, KS 67460-1402. Telephone: 316-241-0731 ext. 1270 or toll-free 800-365-7402. Fax: 316-241-8443 ext. 1270. E-mail: madm@acck.edu. Web site: http://www.mcpherson.edu/.

MIDAMERICA NAZARENE UNIVERSITY
OLATHE, KANSAS

General Independent, comprehensive, coed, affiliated with Church of the Nazarene **Entrance** Minimally difficult **Setting** 112-acre suburban campus **Total enrollment** 1,400 **Student/faculty ratio** 17:1 **Application deadline** 8/1 **Freshmen** 90% were admitted **Housing** Yes **Expenses** Tuition $10,022; Room & Board $4810 **Undergraduates** 57% women, 9% part-time, 23% 25 or older, 1% Native American, 2% Hispanic, 5% black, 2% Asian American or Pacific Islander **Most popular recent majors** Human resources management; elementary education; nursing **Academic program** English as a second language, advanced placement, accelerated degree program, summer session, adult/continuing education programs, internships **Contact** Mr. Dennis Troyer, Admissions Counselor, MidAmerica Nazarene University, 2030

East College Way, Olathe, KS 66062-1899. Telephone: 913-782-3750 ext. 481 or toll-free 800-800-8887. Fax: 913-791-3481. E-mail: admissions@mnu.edu. Web site: http://www.mnu.edu/.

OTTAWA UNIVERSITY

OTTAWA, KANSAS

General Independent American Baptist, comprehensive, coed **Entrance** Moderately difficult **Setting** 60-acre small town campus **Total enrollment** 521 **Student/faculty ratio** 17:1 **Application deadline** Rolling **Freshmen** 62% were admitted **Housing** Yes **Expenses** Tuition $9010; Room & Board $3920 **Undergraduates** 42% women, 2% part-time, 13% 25 or older, 2% Native American, 2% Hispanic, 10% black, 1% Asian American or Pacific Islander **Most popular recent majors** Elementary education; business administration; biology **Academic program** Average class size 30, English as a second language, advanced placement, accelerated degree program, self-designed majors, tutorials, summer session, internships **Contact** Mr. Tim Albers, Director of Admissions, Ottawa University, 1001 South Cedar, Ottawa, KS 66067-3399. Telephone: 785-242-5200 ext. 5558 or toll-free 800-755-5200. Fax: 785-242-7429. E-mail: wwwadmiss@ott.edu.

PITTSBURG STATE UNIVERSITY

PITTSBURG, KANSAS

General State-supported, comprehensive, coed **Entrance** Noncompetitive **Setting** 233-acre small town campus **Total enrollment** 6,355 **Student/faculty ratio** 18:1 **Application deadline** Rolling **Housing** Yes **Expenses** Tuition $2016; Room & Board $3396 **Undergraduates** 19% 25 or older **Most popular recent majors** Business administration; elementary education; engineering technology **Academic program** English as a second language, advanced placement, self-designed majors, tutorials, honors program, summer session, adult/continuing education programs, internships **Contact** Ms. Ange Peterson, Director of Admissions and Retention, Pittsburg State University, 1701 South Broadway, Pittsburg, KS 66762-5880. Telephone: 316-235-4252 or toll-free 800-854-7488. Fax: 316-235-4080. E-mail: psuadmit@pittstate.edu. Web site: http://pittstate.edu/.

SAINT MARY COLLEGE

LEAVENWORTH, KANSAS

General Independent Roman Catholic, comprehensive, coed **Entrance** Moderately difficult **Setting** 240-acre small town campus **Total enrollment** 555 **Student/faculty ratio** 8:1 **Application deadline** Rolling **Housing** Yes **Expenses** Tuition $10,350; Room & Board $4300 **Undergraduates** 73% women, 33% part-time, 18% 25 or older, 1% Native American, 3% Hispanic, 17% black, 3% Asian American or Pacific Islander **Most popular recent majors** Business administration; elementary education **Academic program** English as a second language, advanced placement, self-designed majors, honors program, summer session, adult/continuing education programs, internships **Contact** Mr. John Wilbur, Director of Admissions, Saint Mary College, 4100 South Fourth Street Trafficway, Leavenworth, KS 66048-5082. Telephone: 913-682-5151 ext. 6118 or toll-free 800-758-6140 (out-of-state). E-mail: admiss@hub.smcks.edu. Web site: http://www.smcks.edu/.

SOUTHWESTERN COLLEGE

WINFIELD, KANSAS

General Independent United Methodist, comprehensive, coed **Entrance** Moderately difficult **Setting** 70-acre small town campus **Total enrollment** 826 **Student/faculty ratio** 13:1 **Application deadline** 8/1 **Freshmen** 94% were admitted **Housing** Yes **Expenses** Tuition $9260; Room & Board $3840 **Undergraduates** 53% women, 32% part-time, 41% 25 or older, 1% Native American, 2% Hispanic, 5% black, 1% Asian American or Pacific Islander **Most popular recent majors** Biology; nursing; elementary education **Academic program** Average class size 20, English as a second language, advanced placement, self-designed majors, tutorials, honors program, summer session, adult/continuing education programs, internships **Contact** Ms. Brenda D. Hicks, Director of Admission, Southwestern College, 100 College Street, Winfield, KS 67156-2499. Telephone: 316-221-8236 or toll-free 800-846-1543. Fax: 316-221-8344 ext. 236. E-mail: scadmit@jinx.sckans.edu. Web site: http://www.sckans.edu/.

STERLING COLLEGE

STERLING, KANSAS

General Independent Presbyterian, 4-year, coed **Entrance** Minimally difficult **Setting** 46-acre small town campus **Total enrollment** 457 **Student/faculty ratio** 15:1 **Application deadline** Rolling **Freshmen** 70% were admitted **Housing** Yes **Expenses** Tuition $10,076; Room & Board $4104 **Undergraduates** 48% women, 4% part-time, 4% 25 or older, 1% Native American, 4% Hispanic, 5% black, 0.4% Asian American or Pacific Islander **Most popular recent majors** Education; business administration; behavioral sciences **Academic program** Advanced placement, self-designed majors, honors program, summer session, internships **Contact** Mr. Dennis W. Dutton, Director of Admissions, Sterling College, PO Box 98, Sterling, KS 67579-0098. Telephone: 316-278-4364 or toll-free 800-346-1017. Fax: 316-278-

Sterling College *(continued)*

3690. E-mail: admissions@acc.stercolks.edu. Web site: http://www.stercolks.edu/.

TABOR COLLEGE
HILLSBORO, KANSAS

General Independent Mennonite Brethren, 4-year, coed **Entrance** Moderately difficult **Setting** 26-acre small town campus **Total enrollment** 516 **Application deadline** Rolling **Freshmen** 67% were admitted **Housing** Yes **Expenses** Tuition $10,560; Room & Board $4000 **Undergraduates** 48% women, 15% part-time, 48% 25 or older, 1% Native American, 3% Hispanic, 4% black, 1% Asian American or Pacific Islander **Most popular recent majors** Business administration; social sciences; elementary education **Academic program** Average class size 27, advanced placement, self-designed majors, tutorials, honors program, summer session, adult/continuing education programs, internships **Contact** Mr. Glenn Lygrisse, Vice President for Enrollment Management, Tabor College, 400 South Jefferson, Hillsboro, KS 67063. Telephone: 316-947-3121 ext. 1723 or toll-free 800-822-6799. Fax: 316-947-2607. E-mail: admissions@tcnet.tabor.edu. Web site: http://www.tabor.edu/.

UNIVERSITY OF KANSAS
LAWRENCE, KANSAS

General State-supported, university, coed **Entrance** Moderately difficult **Setting** 1,000-acre suburban campus **Total enrollment** 27,567 **Student/faculty ratio** 15:1 **Application deadline** 4/1 **Freshmen** 61% were admitted **Housing** Yes **Expenses** Tuition $2385; Room & Board $3736 **Undergraduates** 51% women, 10% part-time, 11% 25 or older, 1% Native American, 2% Hispanic, 3% black, 3% Asian American or Pacific Islander **Most popular recent majors** Business; biology; journalism **Academic program** English as a second language, advanced placement, accelerated degree program, self-designed majors, tutorials, honors program, summer session, adult/continuing education programs, internships **Contact** Mr. Alan Cerveny, Director of Admissions, University of Kansas, 126 Strong Hall, Lawrence, KS 66045-1910. Telephone: 785-864-3911 or toll-free 888-686-7323 (out-of-state). Fax: 785-864-5006. E-mail: be.a.jayhawk@st37.eds.ukans.edu. Web site: http://www.ukans.edu/.

WASHBURN UNIVERSITY OF TOPEKA
TOPEKA, KANSAS

General City-supported, comprehensive, coed **Entrance** Noncompetitive **Setting** 160-acre urban campus **Total enrollment** 6,281 **Student/faculty ratio** 18:1 **Application deadline** 8/1 **Freshmen** 98% were admitted **Housing** Yes **Expenses** Tuition $3150; Room & Board $3300 **Undergraduates** 61% women, 42% part-time, 50% 25 or older **Most popular recent majors** Business administration; education; mass communications **Academic program** English as a second language, advanced placement, self-designed majors, tutorials, honors program, summer session, adult/continuing education programs, internships **Contact** Mr. Greg Gomez, Director of Admission, Washburn University of Topeka, Topeka, KS 66621. Telephone: 785-231-1010 ext. 1293 or toll-free 800-332-0291 (in-state). Fax: 785-231-1089. E-mail: zzgomez@acc.washburn.edu. Web site: http://www.wuacc.edu/.

WICHITA STATE UNIVERSITY
WICHITA, KANSAS

General State-supported, university, coed **Entrance** Noncompetitive **Setting** 335-acre urban campus **Total enrollment** 14,061 **Student/faculty ratio** 15:1 **Application deadline** Rolling **Freshmen** 76% were admitted **Housing** Yes **Expenses** Tuition $1986; Room & Board $3760 **Undergraduates** 56% women, 41% part-time, 40% 25 or older, 1% Native American, 4% Hispanic, 6% black, 6% Asian American or Pacific Islander **Most Popular Recent Major** Business administration **Academic program** Average class size 23, English as a second language, advanced placement, accelerated degree program, self-designed majors, tutorials, honors program, summer session, adult/continuing education programs, internships **Contact** Ms. Christine Schneikart-Luebbe, Director of Admissions, Wichita State University, 1845 North Fairmount, Wichita, KS 67260. Telephone: 316-978-3085 or toll-free 800-362-2594. Fax: 316-978-3795. E-mail: wsuadmis@twsuvm.uc.twsu.edu. Web site: http://www.twsu.edu/.

KENTUCKY

ALICE LLOYD COLLEGE
PIPPA PASSES, KENTUCKY

General Independent, 4-year, coed **Entrance** Moderately difficult **Setting** 175-acre rural campus **Total enrollment** 501 **Student/faculty ratio** 18:1 **Application deadline** 8/1 **Freshmen** 63% were admitted **Housing** Yes **Expenses** Tuition $360; Room & Board $2680 **Undergraduates** 50% women, 3% part-time, 10% 25 or older, 0% Native American, 0.2% Hispanic, 1% black, 1% Asian American or Pacific Islander **Most popular recent majors** Elementary education; biology **Academic program** Average class size 30, advanced placement, tutorials **Contact** Mr. Billy C. Melton, Director of Admissions, Alice Lloyd College, 100 Purpose Road, Pippa Passes, KY 41844. Telephone: 606-368-2101 ext. 4404. Fax: 606-368-2125.

ASBURY COLLEGE
WILMORE, KENTUCKY

General Independent nondenominational, 4-year, coed **Entrance** Moderately difficult **Setting** 400-acre small town campus **Total enrollment** 1,258 **Student/faculty ratio** 14:1 **Application deadline** Rolling **Freshmen** 89% were admitted **Housing** Yes **Expenses** Tuition $12,020; Room & Board $3390 **Undergraduates** 57% women, 3% part-time, 6% 25 or older, 0.4% Native American, 1% Hispanic, 1% black, 1% Asian American or Pacific Islander **Academic program** Average class size 30, advanced placement, tutorials, summer session, internships **Contact** Mr. Stan F. Wiggam, Dean of Admissions, Asbury College, 1 Macklem Drive, Wilmore, KY 40390. Telephone: 606-858-3511 ext. 2142 or toll-free 800-888-1818. Fax: 606-858-3921. E-mail: admissions@asbury.edu. Web site: http://www.asbury.edu/.

BELLARMINE COLLEGE
LOUISVILLE, KENTUCKY

General Independent Roman Catholic, comprehensive, coed **Entrance** Moderately difficult **Setting** 120-acre suburban campus **Total enrollment** 2,678 **Student/faculty ratio** 14:1 **Application deadline** 8/15 **Freshmen** 94% were admitted **Housing** Yes **Expenses** Tuition $10,970; Room & Board $3580 **Undergraduates** 25% 25 or older **Most popular recent majors** Business administration; accounting; nursing **Academic program** Advanced placement, accelerated degree program, self-designed majors, honors program, summer session, adult/continuing education programs, internships **Contact** Mr. Timothy A. Sturgeon, Dean of Admissions, Bellarmine College, 2001 Newburg Road, Louisville, KY 40205-0671. Telephone: 502-452-8131 or toll-free 800-274-4723. Fax: 502-452-8002. Web site: http://www.bellarmine.edu/.

BEREA COLLEGE
BEREA, KENTUCKY

General Independent, 4-year, coed **Entrance** Moderately difficult **Setting** 140-acre small town campus **Total enrollment** 1,464 **Student/faculty ratio** 12:1 **Application deadline** 4/15 **Freshmen** 35% were admitted **Housing** Yes **Expenses** Tuition $195; Room & Board $3330 **Undergraduates** 58% women, 0.4% part-time, 7% 25 or older **Most popular recent majors** Business administration; child care/development; nursing **Academic program** Advanced placement, self-designed majors, summer session, internships **Contact** Mr. Joe Bagnoli, Director of Admissions, Berea College, CPO 2344, Berea, KY 40404. Telephone: 606-986-9341 ext. 5083 or toll-free 800-326-5948. E-mail: admissions@berea.edu. Web site: http://www.berea.edu/.

BRESCIA COLLEGE
OWENSBORO, KENTUCKY

General Independent Roman Catholic, comprehensive, coed **Entrance** Moderately difficult **Setting** 6-acre urban campus **Total enrollment** 663 **Student/faculty ratio** 15:1 **Application deadline** Rolling **Freshmen** 80% were admitted **Housing** Yes **Expenses** Tuition $8648; Room & Board $3594 **Undergraduates** 64% women, 23% part-time, 55% 25 or older, 1% Native American, 1% Hispanic, 3% black, 0% Asian American or Pacific Islander **Most popular recent majors** Education; business administration; social work **Academic program** English as a second language, advanced placement, accelerated degree program, self-designed majors, tutorials, honors program, summer session, adult/continuing education programs, internships **Contact** Mr. Rick Eber, Director of Admissions, Brescia College, 717 Frederica Street, Owensboro, KY 42301-3023. Telephone: 502-686-4241 ext. 241 or toll-free 800-264-1234. Fax: 502-686-4266. E-mail: ricke@brescia.edu. Web site: http://brescia.edu/.

CAMPBELLSVILLE UNIVERSITY
CAMPBELLSVILLE, KENTUCKY

General Independent, comprehensive, coed, affiliated with Kentucky Baptist Convention **Entrance** Moderately difficult **Setting** 70-acre small town campus **Total enrollment** 1,521 **Student/faculty ratio** 16:1 **Application deadline** Rolling **Freshmen** 82% were admitted **Housing** Yes **Expenses** Tuition $7302; Room & Board $3440 **Undergraduates** 54% women, 9% part-time, 20% 25 or older, 0.1% Native American, 1% Hispanic, 3% black, 0.3% Asian American or Pacific Islander **Most popular recent majors** Elementary education; business administration; social sciences **Academic program** English as a second language, advanced placement, accelerated degree program, honors program, summer session, adult/continuing education programs, internships **Contact** Mr. R. Trent Argo, Director of Admissions, Campbellsville University, 1 University Drive, Campbellsville, KY 42718-2799. Telephone: 502-789-5220 or toll-free 800-264-6014. Fax: 502-789-5071. E-mail: admissions@campbellsvil.edu. Web site: http://www.campbellsvil.edu/.

CENTRE COLLEGE
DANVILLE, KENTUCKY

General Independent, 4-year, coed **Entrance** Very difficult **Setting** 100-acre small town campus **Total enrollment** 1,001 **Student/faculty ratio** 11:1 **Application deadline** 3/1 **Freshmen** 85% were admitted **Housing** Yes **Expenses** Tuition $14,600; Room & Board $4800 **Undergraduates** 49% women, 0.3% part-time, 1% 25 or older, 0.1% Native American, 0.4% Hispanic, 2% black, 0.5% Asian American or Pacific Islander **Most Popular Recent Major** English **Academic program** Average class size 17, English as a second language, advanced placement, self-designed majors, tutorials, internships **Contact** Dr. Thomas B. Martin, Dean of Enrollment Management, Centre College, 600 West Walnut Street, Danville, KY 40422-1394. Telephone: 606-238-5350 or toll-free 800-423-6236. Fax: 606-238-5373. E-mail: admission@centre.edu. Web site: http://www.centre.edu/.

CLEAR CREEK BAPTIST BIBLE COLLEGE
PINEVILLE, KENTUCKY

General Independent Southern Baptist, 4-year, primarily men **Entrance** Noncompetitive **Setting** 700-acre rural campus **Total enrollment** 170 **Student/faculty ratio** 12:1 **Application deadline** 7/15 **Freshmen** 83% were admitted **Housing** Yes **Expenses** Tuition $2370; Room & Board $2480 **Undergraduates** 90% 25 or older **Academic program** Tutorials, summer session **Contact** Mr. Jayson Barnett, Director of Admissions, Clear Creek Baptist Bible College, 300 Clear Creek Road, Pineville, KY 40977-9754. Telephone: 606-337-3196 ext. 103.

CUMBERLAND COLLEGE
WILLIAMSBURG, KENTUCKY

General Independent Kentucky Baptist, comprehensive, coed **Entrance** Moderately difficult **Setting** 30-acre rural campus **Total enrollment** 1,698 **Student/faculty ratio** 17:1 **Application deadline** Rolling **Freshmen** 66% were admitted **Housing** Yes **Expenses** Tuition $8430; Room & Board $3776 **Undergraduates** 54% women, 3% part-time, 8% 25 or older, 0.3% Native American, 0.4% Hispanic, 3% black, 0.3% Asian American or Pacific Islander **Most popular recent majors** Biology; psychology; education **Academic program** Average class size 25, English as a second language, advanced placement, accelerated degree program, self-designed majors, tutorials, honors program, summer session, adult/continuing education programs, internships **Contact** Mrs. Erica Harris, Coordinator of Admissions, Cumberland College, 6178 College Station Drive, Williamsburg, KY 40769-1372. Telephone: 606-539-4241 or toll-free 800-343-1609. Fax: 606-539-4303. E-mail: admiss@cc.cumber.edu. Web site: http://www.cc.cumber.edu/.

EASTERN KENTUCKY UNIVERSITY
RICHMOND, KENTUCKY

General State-supported, comprehensive, coed **Entrance** Noncompetitive **Setting** 500-acre small town campus **Total enrollment** 15,424 **Student/faculty ratio** 23:1 **Application deadline** Rolling **Freshmen** 95% were admitted **Housing** Yes **Expenses** Tuition $2060; Room & Board $3240 **Undergraduates** 29% 25 or older **Most Popular Recent Major** Nursing **Academic program** English as a second language, advanced placement, accelerated degree program, self-designed majors, honors program, summer session, adult/continuing education programs, internships **Contact** Mr. James L. Grigsby, Director of Admissions, Eastern Kentucky University, Richmond, KY 40475-3101. Telephone: 606-622-2106 or toll-free 800-262-7493 (in-state). Web site: http://www.eku.edu.

GEORGETOWN COLLEGE
GEORGETOWN, KENTUCKY

General Independent, comprehensive, coed, affiliated with Baptist Church **Entrance** Moderately difficult **Setting** 110-acre suburban campus **Total enrollment** 1,626 **Student/faculty ratio** 13:1 **Application deadline** 7/1 **Freshmen** 89% were admitted **Housing** Yes **Expenses** Tuition $10,190; Room & Board $4180 **Undergraduates** 57% women, 2% part-time, 1% 25 or older, 0.2% Native American, 0.5% Hispanic, 2% black, 0.1% Asian American or Pacific Islander **Most popular recent majors** Biology; education; psychology **Academic program** Average class size 25, advanced placement, accelerated degree program, self-designed majors, tutorials, summer session, internships **Contact** Mr. Michael Konopski, Director of Admissions, Georgetown College, 400 East College Street, Georgetown, KY 40324-1696. Telephone: 502-863-8009 or toll-free 800-788-9985. Fax: 502-868-8891. E-mail: admissions@gtc.georgetown.ky.us. Web site: http://www.gtc.georgetown.ky.us/.

KENTUCKY CHRISTIAN COLLEGE
GRAYSON, KENTUCKY

General Independent, 4-year, coed, affiliated with Christian Churches and Churches of Christ **Entrance** Moderately difficult **Setting** 124-acre rural campus **Total enrollment** 523 **Student/faculty ratio** 15:1 **Application deadline** 8/1 **Freshmen** 84% were admitted **Housing** Yes **Expenses** Tuition $5984; Room & Board $3764 **Undergradu-**

ates 54% women, 10% 25 or older, 0.4% Native American, 1% Hispanic, 1% black, 0% Asian American or Pacific Islander **Most popular recent majors** Pastoral counseling; elementary education; business administration **Academic program** Average class size 30, advanced placement, summer session, internships **Contact** Mrs. Sandra Deakins, Director of Admissions, Kentucky Christian College, 100 Academic Parkway, Grayson, KY 41143-2205. Telephone: 606-474-3266 or toll-free 800-522-3181. Fax: 606-474-3155. E-mail: ad80382@kcc.edu. Web site: http://www.kcc.edu/.

KENTUCKY MOUNTAIN BIBLE COLLEGE
VANCLEVE, KENTUCKY

General Independent interdenominational, 4-year, coed **Entrance** Minimally difficult **Setting** 35-acre rural campus **Total enrollment** 69 **Student/faculty ratio** 4:1 **Application deadline** Rolling **Freshmen** 72% were admitted **Housing** Yes **Expenses** Tuition $3515; Room & Board $2830 **Undergraduates** 46% women, 14% part-time, 23% 25 or older **Academic program** Average class size 15, advanced placement, adult/continuing education programs, internships **Contact** Mr. James Nelson, Director of Recruiting, Kentucky Mountain Bible College, PO Box 10, Vancleve, KY 41385. Telephone: 606-666-5000 ext. 221 or toll-free 800-879-KMBC. Fax: 606-666-7744. E-mail: kmbc@kmbc.edu. Web site: http://www.kmbc.edu/.

KENTUCKY STATE UNIVERSITY
FRANKFORT, KENTUCKY

General State-related, comprehensive, coed **Entrance** Minimally difficult **Setting** 485-acre small town campus **Total enrollment** 2,288 **Student/faculty ratio** 15:1 **Application deadline** Rolling **Housing** Yes **Expenses** Tuition $2050; Room & Board $3190 **Undergraduates** 58% women, 21% part-time, 33% 25 or older, 0.2% Native American, 0.4% Hispanic, 52% black, 1% Asian American or Pacific Islander **Most popular recent majors** Nursing; business administration **Academic program** English as a second language, advanced placement, accelerated degree program, self-designed majors, tutorials, honors program, summer session, adult/continuing education programs, internships **Contact** Ms. Laronistine Dyson, Associate Director of Admissions, Kentucky State University, East Main Street, Dept. PG-92, Frankfort, KY 40601. Telephone: 502-227-6000 or toll-free 800-633-9415 (in-state), 800-325-1716 (out-of-state). E-mail: ldyson@gwmail.kysu.edu.

KENTUCKY WESLEYAN COLLEGE
OWENSBORO, KENTUCKY

General Independent Methodist, 4-year, coed **Entrance** Moderately difficult **Setting** 52-acre suburban campus **Total enrollment** 777 **Student/faculty ratio** 11:1 **Application deadline** Rolling **Freshmen** 85% were admitted **Housing** Yes **Expenses** Tuition $9730; Room & Board $4630 **Undergraduates** 12% 25 or older, 0% Native American, 0% Hispanic, 6% black, 0% Asian American or Pacific Islander **Most popular recent majors** Biology; business administration; accounting **Academic program** Average class size 20, advanced placement, self-designed majors, tutorials, summer session, adult/continuing education programs, internships **Contact** Mr. Scott Schaeffer, Dean of Admission, Kentucky Wesleyan College, 3000 Frederica Street, PO Box 1039, Owensboro, KY 42302-1039. Telephone: 502-926-3111 ext. 145 or toll-free 800-999-0592. Fax: 502-926-3196. E-mail: admission@kwc.edu. Web site: http://www.kwc.edu/.

▶ **For more information, see page 454.**

LEXINGTON BAPTIST COLLEGE
LEXINGTON, KENTUCKY

General Independent, 4-year, coed, affiliated with Baptist Church **Entrance** Noncompetitive **Setting** 24-acre urban campus **Total enrollment** 105 **Student/faculty ratio** 8:1 **Application deadline** Rolling **Housing** Yes **Expenses** Tuition $3200; Room & Board $3772 **Undergraduates** 13% 25 or older, 0% Native American, 1% Hispanic, 6% black, 0% Asian American or Pacific Islander **Academic program** Average class size 15, English as a second language, advanced placement, tutorials, summer session, adult/continuing education programs, internships **Contact** Mr. Robert B. Traeger, Director of Admissions and Records, Lexington Baptist College, 147 Walton Avenue, Lexington, KY 40508. Telephone: 606-252-1130. Fax: 606-252-5649. E-mail: lexbapcol@aol.com.

LINDSEY WILSON COLLEGE
COLUMBIA, KENTUCKY

General Independent United Methodist, comprehensive, coed **Entrance** Minimally difficult **Setting** 40-acre rural campus **Total enrollment** 1,425 **Student/faculty ratio** 20:1 **Application deadline** Rolling **Freshmen** 74% were admitted **Housing** Yes **Expenses** Tuition $8760; Room & Board $4400 **Undergraduates** 17% 25 or older **Most popular recent majors** Business administration; elementary education; human services **Academic program** English as a second language, advanced placement, accelerated degree program, self-designed majors, tutorials, summer session, adult/continuing education programs, internships **Contact** Mr. Kevin A. Thompson, Vice President for Enrollment Management, Lindsey Wilson College, 210 Lindsey Wilson Street, Columbia, KY 42728-

Lindsey Wilson College *(continued)*

1298. Telephone: 502-384-8100 or toll-free 800-264-0138. Fax: 502-384-8200.

MID-CONTINENT BAPTIST BIBLE COLLEGE
MAYFIELD, KENTUCKY

General Independent, 4-year, coed, affiliated with Baptist Church **Entrance** Noncompetitive **Setting** 60-acre small town campus **Total enrollment** 172 **Student/faculty ratio** 8:1 **Application deadline** Rolling **Freshmen** 100% were admitted **Housing** Yes **Expenses** Tuition $2490; Room & Board $2532 **Undergraduates** 39% women, 34% part-time, 57% 25 or older, 0% Native American, 0% Hispanic, 5% black, 0% Asian American or Pacific Islander **Academic program** English as a second language, summer session **Contact** Mr. Jerry Muniz, Dean of Students, Mid-Continent Baptist Bible College, 99 Powell Road East, Mayfield, KY 42066. Telephone: 502-247-8521 ext. 19 or toll-free 800-232-4662. Fax: 502-247-3115. E-mail: mcollege@apex.net. Web site: http://www.mcbc.edu/.

MIDWAY COLLEGE
MIDWAY, KENTUCKY

General Independent, 4-year, women only, affiliated with Christian Church (Disciples of Christ) **Entrance** Minimally difficult **Setting** 105-acre small town campus **Total enrollment** 1,021 **Student/faculty ratio** 14:1 **Application deadline** Rolling **Housing** Yes **Expenses** Tuition $8160; Room & Board $4500 **Undergraduates** 45% part-time, 40% 25 or older, 0.3% Native American, 0.5% Hispanic, 4% black **Most popular recent majors** Nursing; equestrian studies; biology **Academic program** Average class size 20, advanced placement, accelerated degree program, self-designed majors, tutorials, summer session, adult/continuing education programs, internships **Contact** Mrs. Karen Britt Statler, Dean of Admissions and Financial Aid, Midway College, 512 East Stephens Street, Midway, KY 40347-1120. Telephone: 606-846-5346 or toll-free 800-755-0031. Fax: 606-846-5823. E-mail: admissions@midway.edu. Web site: http://www.midway.edu/.

MOREHEAD STATE UNIVERSITY
MOREHEAD, KENTUCKY

General State-supported, comprehensive, coed **Entrance** Minimally difficult **Setting** 809-acre small town campus **Total enrollment** 8,200 **Student/faculty ratio** 20:1 **Application deadline** Rolling **Freshmen** 84% were admitted **Housing** Yes **Expenses** Tuition $2150; Room & Board $3200 **Undergraduates** 59% women, 11% part-time, 24% 25 or older, 0.2% Native American, 0.3% Hispanic, 4% black, 0.3% Asian American or Pacific Islander **Most Popular Recent Major** Elementary education **Academic program** English as a second language, advanced placement, accelerated degree program, self-designed majors, honors program, summer session, adult/continuing education programs, internships **Contact** Director of Admissions, Morehead State University, University Boulevard, Morehead, KY 40351. Telephone: 606-783-2000 or toll-free 800-262-7474 (in-state), 800-354-2090 (out-of-state). Fax: 606-783-2678. E-mail: sa.barker@morehead-st.edu. Web site: http://www.morehead-st.edu/.

MURRAY STATE UNIVERSITY
MURRAY, KENTUCKY

General State-supported, comprehensive, coed **Entrance** Moderately difficult **Setting** 238-acre small town campus **Total enrollment** 8,811 **Student/faculty ratio** 16:1 **Application deadline** Rolling **Freshmen** 69% were admitted **Housing** Yes **Expenses** Tuition $2300; Room & Board $3560 **Undergraduates** 56% women, 14% part-time, 22% 25 or older **Most Popular Recent Major** Business administration **Academic program** Average class size 30, English as a second language, advanced placement, accelerated degree program, honors program, summer session, adult/continuing education programs, internships **Contact** Mrs. Kristi Jackson, Admission Clerk, Murray State University, PO Box 9, Murray, KY 42071-0009. Telephone: 502-762-3035 or toll-free 800-272-4678. Fax: 502-762-3050. E-mail: p.bryan@murraystate.edu.. Web site: http://www.murraystate.edu/.

NORTHERN KENTUCKY UNIVERSITY
HIGHLAND HEIGHTS, KENTUCKY

General State-supported, comprehensive, coed **Entrance** Noncompetitive **Setting** 300-acre suburban campus **Total enrollment** 11,763 **Student/faculty ratio** 17:1 **Application deadline** Rolling **Freshmen** 100% were admitted **Housing** Yes **Expenses** Tuition $2120; Room & Board $3439 **Undergraduates** 59% women, 27% part-time, 31% 25 or older, 0.3% Native American, 0.4% Hispanic, 3% black, 1% Asian American or Pacific Islander **Most popular recent majors** Education; nursing; psychology **Academic program** Average class size 26, advanced placement, honors program, summer session, internships **Contact** Mrs. Debbie Poweleit, Associate Director of Admissions, Northern Kentucky University, Administrative Center 400, Highland Heights, KY 41099-7010. Telephone: 606-572-5220 ext. 5154 or toll-free 800-637-9948. E-mail: admitnku@nku.edu. Web site: http://www.nku.edu/.

▶ **For more information, see page 485.**

PATHOLOGY AND CYTOLOGY LABORATORIES, INC.
LEXINGTON, KENTUCKY

Contact Pathology and Cytology Laboratories, Inc., 290 Big Run Road, Lexington, KY 40503. Telephone: 606-278-9513.

PIKEVILLE COLLEGE
PIKEVILLE, KENTUCKY

General Independent, comprehensive, coed, affiliated with Presbyterian Church (U.S.A.) **Entrance** Noncompetitive **Setting** 25-acre small town campus **Total enrollment** 771 **Student/faculty ratio** 15:1 **Application deadline** 8/20 **Freshmen** 66% were admitted **Housing** Yes **Expenses** Tuition $7000; Room & Board $3100 **Undergraduates** 69% women, 8% part-time, 25% 25 or older **Most popular recent majors** Education; business administration; nursing **Academic program** Average class size 22, advanced placement, accelerated degree program, summer session, internships **Contact** Dr. John Sanders, Associate Dean of Admissions and Financial Aid, Pikeville College, Sycamore Street, Pikeville, KY 41501. Telephone: 606-432-9322. Fax: 606-432-9328. Web site: http://www.pc.edu/.

SPALDING UNIVERSITY
LOUISVILLE, KENTUCKY

General Independent, comprehensive, coed, affiliated with Roman Catholic Church **Entrance** Moderately difficult **Setting** 5-acre urban campus **Total enrollment** 1,563 **Student/faculty ratio** 17:1 **Application deadline** 8/15 **Freshmen** 74% were admitted **Housing** Yes **Expenses** Tuition $10,396; Room & Board $2990 **Undergraduates** 81% women, 29% part-time, 43% 25 or older, 0.2% Native American, 1% Hispanic, 13% black, 1% Asian American or Pacific Islander **Most popular recent majors** Nursing; business administration; education **Academic program** English as a second language, advanced placement, tutorials, summer session, adult/continuing education programs, internships **Contact** Ms. Dorothy G. Allen, Director of Admission, Spalding University, 851 South Fourth Street, Louisville, KY 40203-2188. Telephone: 502-585-7111 ext. 225 or toll-free 800-896-8941. Fax: 502-585-7158. E-mail: admissions@spalding30.win.net. Web site: http://www.spalding.edu/.

SULLIVAN COLLEGE
LOUISVILLE, KENTUCKY

General Proprietary, comprehensive, coed **Entrance** Minimally difficult **Setting** 10-acre suburban campus **Total enrollment** 2,481 **Student/faculty ratio** 20:1 **Application deadline** Rolling **Housing** Yes **Expenses** Tuition $8904; Room only $2700 **Undergraduates** 50% 25 or older **Most popular recent majors** Business administration; culinary arts; paralegal/legal assistant **Academic program** Accelerated degree program, summer session, adult/continuing education programs, internships **Contact** Mr. Greg Cawthon, Director of Admissions, Sullivan College, 3101 Bardstown Road, Louisville, KY 40205. Telephone: 502-456-6504 ext. 330 or toll-free 800-844-1354 (in-state). Fax: 502-454-4880. E-mail: tfd@corp.sullivan.edu.

THOMAS MORE COLLEGE
CRESTVIEW HILLS, KENTUCKY

General Independent Roman Catholic, comprehensive, coed **Entrance** Moderately difficult **Setting** 100-acre suburban campus **Total enrollment** 1,402 **Student/faculty ratio** 12:1 **Application deadline** 8/15 **Freshmen** 81% were admitted **Housing** Yes **Expenses** Tuition $11,250; Room & Board $4500 **Undergraduates** 36% 25 or older, 1% Native American, 1% Hispanic, 3% black, 1% Asian American or Pacific Islander **Most popular recent majors** Business administration; biology; information sciences/systems **Academic program** Advanced placement, accelerated degree program, self-designed majors, tutorials, honors program, summer session, adult/continuing education programs, internships **Contact** Mr. Robert A. McDermott, Director of Admissions, Thomas More College, 333 Thomas More Parkway, Crestview Hills, KY 41017-3495. Telephone: 606-344-3332 or toll-free 800-825-4557. Fax: 606-344-3638. E-mail: cantralk@thomasmore.edu. Web site: http://www.thomasmore.edu/.

TRANSYLVANIA UNIVERSITY
LEXINGTON, KENTUCKY

General Independent, 4-year, coed, affiliated with Christian Church (Disciples of Christ) **Entrance** Very difficult **Setting** 35-acre urban campus **Total enrollment** 1,027 **Student/faculty ratio** 14:1 **Application deadline** 3/1 **Freshmen** 93% were admitted **Housing** Yes **Expenses** Tuition $13,260; Room & Board $4990 **Undergraduates** 57% women, 0.4% part-time, 1% 25 or older, 0.1% Native American, 0.5% Hispanic, 2% black, 4% Asian American or Pacific Islander **Most popular recent majors** Business administration; biology; psychology **Academic program** Average class size 25, advanced placement, self-designed majors, summer session, internships **Contact** Mr. John O. Gaines, Director of Admissions, Transylvania University, 300 North Broadway, Lexington, KY 40508-1797. Telephone: 606-233-8242 or toll-free 800-872-6798. Fax: 606-233-8797. E-mail: admissions@mail.transy.edu. Web site: http://www.transy.edu/.

UNION COLLEGE
BARBOURVILLE, KENTUCKY

General Independent United Methodist, comprehensive, coed **Entrance** Moderately difficult **Setting** 110-acre small town campus **Total enrollment** 1,016 **Student/faculty ratio** 13:1 **Application deadline** 8/15 **Housing** Yes **Expenses** Tuition $9340; Room & Board $3120 **Undergraduates** 51% women, 13% part-time, 21% 25 or older, 0.3% Native American, 2% Hispanic, 6% black, 0.3% Asian American or Pacific Islander **Most popular recent majors** Education; business administration; sociology **Academic program** Average class size 16, advanced placement, accelerated degree program, tutorials, honors program, summer session, internships **Contact** Mrs. Lisa Jordan-Payne, Dean of Admissions, Union College, 310 College Street, Barbourville, KY 40906-1499. Telephone: 606-546-1220 or toll-free 800-489-8646. Fax: 606-546-1667. E-mail: enroll@unionky.edu. Web site: http://www.unionky.edu/.

UNIVERSITY OF KENTUCKY
LEXINGTON, KENTUCKY

General State-supported, university, coed **Entrance** Moderately difficult **Setting** 682-acre urban campus **Total enrollment** 23,540 **Student/faculty ratio** 16:1 **Application deadline** 6/1 **Freshmen** 78% were admitted **Housing** Yes **Expenses** Tuition $2736; Room & Board $3388 **Undergraduates** 51% women, 11% part-time, 16% 25 or older, 0.3% Native American, 1% Hispanic, 5% black, 2% Asian American or Pacific Islander **Most popular recent majors** Psychology; accounting; business marketing and marketing management **Academic program** English as a second language, advanced placement, accelerated degree program, self-designed majors, honors program, summer session, adult/continuing education programs, internships **Contact** Mr. Randy Mills, Senior Associate Director of Admissions, University of Kentucky, Lexington, KY 40506-0032. Telephone: 606-257-2000 or toll-free 800-432-0967 (in-state). Web site: http://www.uky.edu/.

UNIVERSITY OF LOUISVILLE
LOUISVILLE, KENTUCKY

General State-supported, university, coed **Entrance** Moderately difficult **Setting** 169-acre urban campus **Total enrollment** 20,283 **Student/faculty ratio** 15:1 **Application deadline** Rolling **Freshmen** 62% were admitted **Housing** Yes **Expenses** Tuition $2630; Room & Board $4982 **Undergraduates** 53% women, 28% part-time, 33% 25 or older, 0.3% Native American, 1% Hispanic, 14% black, 3% Asian American or Pacific Islander **Most popular recent majors** Psychology; accounting **Academic program** English as a second language, advanced placement, accelerated degree program, self-designed majors, honors program, summer session, adult/continuing education programs, internships **Contact** Ms. Jenny Sawyer, Executive Director for Admissions, University of Louisville, 2211 South Brook, Louisville, KY 40208. Telephone: 502-852-6531 or toll-free 800-334-8635 (out-of-state). Fax: 502-852-4776 ext. 6531. E-mail: admitme@ulkyvm.louisville.edu. Web site: http://www.louisville.edu/.

WESTERN KENTUCKY UNIVERSITY
BOWLING GREEN, KENTUCKY

General State-supported, comprehensive, coed **Entrance** Moderately difficult **Setting** 223-acre suburban campus **Total enrollment** 14,543 **Application deadline** 8/1 **Freshmen** 99% were admitted **Housing** Yes **Expenses** Tuition $2140; Room & Board $2700 **Undergraduates** 58% women, 18% part-time, 21% 25 or older, 0.3% Native American, 1% Hispanic, 7% black, 1% Asian American or Pacific Islander **Most popular recent majors** Elementary education; psychology; nursing **Academic program** English as a second language, advanced placement, accelerated degree program, self-designed majors, honors program, summer session, adult/continuing education programs, internships **Contact** Dr. Cheryl C. Chambless, Director of Admissions, Western Kentucky University, Potter Hall, Bowling Green, KY 42101-3576. Telephone: 502-745-5422 or toll-free 800-452-3095 (in-state). Fax: 502-745-6133. E-mail: admission@wku.edu. Web site: http://www.wku.edu/.

LOUISIANA

AMERICAN COLLEGE OF PREHOSPITAL MEDICINE
NEW ORLEANS, LOUISIANA

General Proprietary, 4-year, coed **Entrance** Noncompetitive **Total enrollment** 120 **Student/faculty ratio** 3:1 **Application deadline** Rolling **Expenses** Tuition $2707 **Undergraduates** 90% 25 or older **Contact** Dr. Richard A. Clinchy, Chairman/CEO, American College of Prehospital Medicine, 365 Canal Street, Suite 2300, New Orleans, LA 70130-1135. Telephone: 504-561-6543 or toll-free 800-735-2276. E-mail: acpmceo@aol.com. Web site: http://www.acpm.edu/.

CENTENARY COLLEGE OF LOUISIANA
SHREVEPORT, LOUISIANA

General Independent United Methodist, comprehensive, coed **Entrance** Moderately difficult **Set-**

ting 65-acre suburban campus **Total enrollment** 986 **Student/faculty ratio** 11:1 **Application deadline** 3/1 **Freshmen** 85% were admitted **Housing** Yes **Expenses** Tuition $11,400; Room & Board $3900 **Undergraduates** 56% women, 3% part-time, 0.4% Native American, 1% Hispanic, 6% black, 2% Asian American or Pacific Islander **Most popular recent majors** Business administration; biology; psychology **Academic program** Advanced placement, accelerated degree program, self-designed majors, tutorials, honors program, summer session, adult/continuing education programs, internships **Contact** Mr. Joel R. Wincowski, Dean of Enrollment Management, Centenary College of Louisiana, 2911 Centenary Blvd, PO Box 41188, Shreveport, LA 71134-1188. Telephone: 318-869-5131. E-mail: tcrowley@beta.centenary.edu. Web site: http://alpha.centenary.edu/.

DILLARD UNIVERSITY

NEW ORLEANS, LOUISIANA

General Independent interdenominational, 4-year, coed **Contact** Mr. Darrin Q. Rankin, Director, Enrollment Management and Admissions, Dillard University, 2601 Gentilly Boulevard, New Orleans, LA 70122-3097. Telephone: 504-286-4670. Fax: 504-286-4895.

GRAMBLING STATE UNIVERSITY

GRAMBLING, LOUISIANA

General State-supported, comprehensive, coed **Contact** Mr. Martin Lemelle, Head Recruiter/Admission Officer, Grambling State University, PO Box 607, Grambling, LA 71245. Telephone: 318-274-3395. Fax: 318-274-6172. E-mail: bingamann@medgar.gram.edu.

GRANTHAM COLLEGE OF ENGINEERING

SLIDELL, LOUISIANA

General Proprietary, 4-year, coed **Entrance** Noncompetitive **Setting** Small town campus **Total enrollment** 2,300 **Application deadline** Rolling **Housing** No **Expenses** Tuition $3800 **Undergraduates** 96% 25 or older **Most popular recent majors** Electrical/electronic engineering technology; computer engineering technology; computer science **Academic program** Advanced placement, accelerated degree program, honors program, adult/continuing education programs **Contact** Mrs. Maria Adcock, Director of Student Services, Grantham College of Engineering, PO Box 5700, Slidell, LA 70460-6815. Telephone: 504-649-4191 or toll-free 800-955-2527. Fax: 504-649-4183. E-mail: gce@grantham.edu. Web site: http://www.grantham.edu/.

LOUISIANA COLLEGE

PINEVILLE, LOUISIANA

General Independent Southern Baptist, 4-year, coed **Entrance** Moderately difficult **Setting** 81-acre small town campus **Total enrollment** 925 **Student/faculty ratio** 15:1 **Application deadline** 8/1 **Freshmen** 85% were admitted **Housing** Yes **Expenses** Tuition $6763; Room & Board $3036 **Undergraduates** 60% women, 8% part-time, 22% 25 or older, 1% Native American, 2% Hispanic, 6% black, 1% Asian American or Pacific Islander **Most popular recent majors** Business administration; nursing; education **Academic program** Average class size 25, advanced placement, accelerated degree program, self-designed majors, tutorials, honors program, summer session, adult/continuing education programs, internships **Contact** Ms. Karin Gregorczyk, Director of Admissions, Louisiana College, Box 560, Pineville, LA 71359-0001. Telephone: 318-487-7259 or toll-free 800-487-1906. Fax: 318-487-7550. E-mail: admissions@andria.lacollege.edu. Web site: http://www.lacollege.edu/.

LOUISIANA STATE UNIVERSITY AND AGRICULTURAL AND MECHANICAL COLLEGE

BATON ROUGE, LOUISIANA

General State-supported, university, coed **Entrance** Moderately difficult **Setting** 2,000-acre urban campus **Total enrollment** 28,066 **Student/faculty ratio** 23:1 **Application deadline** 6/1 **Freshmen** 79% were admitted **Housing** Yes **Expenses** Tuition $2711; Room & Board $3772 **Undergraduates** 51% women, 10% part-time, 15% 25 or older, 0.4% Native American, 3% Hispanic, 9% black, 4% Asian American or Pacific Islander **Most popular recent majors** Liberal arts and studies; psychology; accounting **Academic program** Average class size 29, English as a second language, advanced placement, accelerated degree program, self-designed majors, honors program, summer session, adult/continuing education programs, internships **Contact** Dr. Lisa B. Harris, Dean of Admissions, Louisiana State University and Agricultural and Mechanical College, Baton Rouge, LA 70803-3103. Telephone: 504-388-1175. Fax: 504-388-4433. E-mail: mmoorez@lsu.edu. Web site: http://www.lsu.edu/.

LOUISIANA STATE UNIVERSITY IN SHREVEPORT

SHREVEPORT, LOUISIANA

General State-supported, comprehensive, coed **Entrance** Noncompetitive **Setting** 200-acre urban campus **Total enrollment** 4,259 **Student/faculty ratio** 18:1 **Application deadline** 8/5

Louisiana State University in Shreveport *(continued)*

Freshmen 100% were admitted **Housing** Yes **Expenses** Tuition $2230; Room & Board $6095 **Undergraduates** 58% women, 38% part-time, 24% 25 or older, 0.5% Native American, 2% Hispanic, 16% black, 2% Asian American or Pacific Islander **Most popular recent majors** Psychology; elementary education; accounting **Academic program** Average class size 30, advanced placement, accelerated degree program, self-designed majors, tutorials, honors program, summer session, adult/continuing education programs, internships **Contact** Assistant Director of Admissions and Records, Louisiana State University in Shreveport, One University Place, Shreveport, LA 71115-2399. Telephone: 318-797-5057 or toll-free 800-229-5957 (in-state). Fax: 318-797-5286. E-mail: admissions@pilot.lsus.edu. Web site: http://www.lsus.edu/.

LOUISIANA STATE UNIVERSITY MEDICAL CENTER

NEW ORLEANS, LOUISIANA

General State-supported, university, coed **Entrance** Very difficult **Setting** Urban campus **Total enrollment** 2,566 **Housing** Yes **Expenses** Room only $2268 **Undergraduates** 24% 25 or older, 0.2% Native American, 4% Hispanic, 7% black, 6% Asian American or Pacific Islander **Academic program** Advanced placement, summer session **Contact** Mr. Edmund A. Vidacovich, Registrar, Louisiana State University Medical Center, 433 Bolivar Street, New Orleans, LA 70112-2223. Telephone: 504-568-4829. Web site: http://www.lsumc.edu/.

LOUISIANA TECH UNIVERSITY

RUSTON, LOUISIANA

General State-supported, university, coed **Entrance** Moderately difficult **Setting** 247-acre small town campus **Total enrollment** 9,500 **Student/faculty ratio** 26:1 **Application deadline** Rolling **Freshmen** 98% were admitted **Housing** Yes **Expenses** Tuition $2567; Room & Board $2805 **Undergraduates** 47% women, 16% part-time, 19% 25 or older, 0.4% Native American, 1% Hispanic, 13% black, 1% Asian American or Pacific Islander **Most popular recent majors** Nursing; sociology; elementary education **Academic program** English as a second language, advanced placement, tutorials, honors program, summer session, adult/continuing education programs, internships **Contact** Mrs. Jan B. Albritton, Director of Admissions, Louisiana Tech University, PO Box 3168, Ruston, LA 71272. Telephone: 318-257-3036. E-mail: usjba@latech.edu. Web site: http://www.latech.edu/.

LOYOLA UNIVERSITY NEW ORLEANS

NEW ORLEANS, LOUISIANA

General Independent Roman Catholic (Jesuit), comprehensive, coed **Entrance** Moderately difficult **Setting** 26-acre urban campus **Total enrollment** 5,079 **Student/faculty ratio** 12:1 **Application deadline** Rolling **Freshmen** 91% were admitted **Housing** Yes **Expenses** Tuition $13,354; Room & Board $5830 **Undergraduates** 62% women, 20% part-time, 9% 25 or older, 1% Native American, 10% Hispanic, 14% black, 3% Asian American or Pacific Islander **Most popular recent majors** Communications; psychology; accounting **Academic program** Average class size 23, English as a second language, advanced placement, accelerated degree program, self-designed majors, tutorials, honors program, summer session, adult/continuing education programs, internships **Contact** Ms. Debbie Stieffel, Director of Admissions, Loyola University New Orleans, 6363 Saint Charles Avenue, Box 18, New Orleans, LA 70118-6195. Telephone: 504-865-3240 or toll-free 800-4-LOYOLA. Fax: 504-865-3383. E-mail: admit@loyno.edu. Web site: http://www.loyno.edu/.

▶ **For more information, see page 461.**

MCNEESE STATE UNIVERSITY

LAKE CHARLES, LOUISIANA

General State-supported, comprehensive, coed **Entrance** Noncompetitive **Setting** 580-acre suburban campus **Total enrollment** 8,117 **Student/faculty ratio** 26:1 **Application deadline** 7/15 **Housing** Yes **Expenses** Tuition $2012; Room & Board $2310 **Undergraduates** 58% women, 19% part-time, 32% 25 or older, 1% Native American, 1% Hispanic, 17% black, 1% Asian American or Pacific Islander **Most popular recent majors** Business administration; education; nursing **Academic program** English as a second language, advanced placement, accelerated degree program, summer session, adult/continuing education programs, internships **Contact** Ms. Kathy Bond, Admissions Counselor, McNeese State University, PO Box 92495, Lake Charles, LA 70609-2495. Telephone: 318-475-5148 or toll-free 800-622-3352. E-mail: kbond@mcneese.edu. Web site: http://www.mcneese.edu/.

NEW ORLEANS BAPTIST THEOLOGICAL SEMINARY

NEW ORLEANS, LOUISIANA

General Independent Southern Baptist, comprehensive, coed **Contact** Dr. Paul E. Gregoire Jr., Registrar/Director of Admissions, New Orleans Baptist Theological Seminary, 3939 Gentilly Boulevard, New Orleans, LA 70126-4858. Telephone: 504-282-4455 ext. 3632 or toll-free 800-662-8701.

NICHOLLS STATE UNIVERSITY
THIBODAUX, LOUISIANA

General State-supported, comprehensive, coed **Entrance** Noncompetitive **Setting** 210-acre small town campus **Total enrollment** 7,173 **Student/faculty ratio** 18:1 **Application deadline** Rolling **Freshmen** 92% were admitted **Housing** Yes **Expenses** Tuition $2507; Room & Board $2720 **Undergraduates** 62% women, 19% part-time, 31% 25 or older, 2% Native American, 1% Hispanic, 16% black, 1% Asian American or Pacific Islander **Most popular recent majors** Liberal arts and studies; nursing; elementary education **Academic program** Average class size 30, English as a second language, advanced placement, accelerated degree program, tutorials, summer session, adult/continuing education programs, internships **Contact** Mrs. Becky L. Durocher, Director of Admissions, Nicholls State University, PO Box 2004-NSU, Thibodaux, LA 70310. Telephone: 504-448-4507. Fax: 504-448-4929. E-mail: nicholls@server.nich.edu. Web site: http://server.nich.edu/.

NORTHEAST LOUISIANA UNIVERSITY
MONROE, LOUISIANA

General State-supported, comprehensive, coed **Entrance** Noncompetitive **Setting** 238-acre urban campus **Total enrollment** 10,942 **Student/faculty ratio** 19:1 **Application deadline** Rolling **Freshmen** 92% were admitted **Housing** Yes **Expenses** Tuition $1952; Room only $1140 **Undergraduates** 61% women, 15% part-time, 28% 25 or older, 0.4% Native American, 1% Hispanic, 23% black, 3% Asian American or Pacific Islander **Most popular recent majors** Pharmacy; liberal arts and studies; nursing **Academic program** English as a second language, advanced placement, accelerated degree program, honors program, summer session, internships **Contact** Mr. Don Weems, Director of Admissions, Northeast Louisiana University, Monroe, LA 71209-1115. Telephone: 318-342-5252 or toll-free 800-372-5127. Fax: 318-342-5274. E-mail: reweems@alpha.nlu.edu. Web site: http://www.nlu.edu/.

NORTHWESTERN STATE UNIVERSITY OF LOUISIANA
NATCHITOCHES, LOUISIANA

General State-supported, comprehensive, coed **Entrance** Noncompetitive **Setting** 1,000-acre small town campus **Total enrollment** 8,873 **Student/faculty ratio** 26:1 **Application deadline** Rolling **Freshmen** 100% were admitted **Housing** Yes **Expenses** Tuition $2177; Room & Board $2416 **Undergraduates** 65% women, 23% part-time, 30% 25 or older, 2% Native American, 2% Hispanic, 23% black, 1% Asian American or Pacific Islander **Most popular recent majors** Nursing; business administration; education **Academic program** Average class size 33, advanced placement, honors program, summer session, adult/continuing education programs, internships **Contact** Mr. Chris Maggio, Director of Recruiting and Admissions, Northwestern State University of Louisiana, Natchitoches, LA 71497. Telephone: 318-357-4503 or toll-free 800-426-3754 (in-state), 800-327-1903 (out-of-state). E-mail: admissions@alpha.nsula.edu. Web site: http://www.NSULA.edu/.

OUR LADY OF HOLY CROSS COLLEGE
NEW ORLEANS, LOUISIANA

General Independent Roman Catholic, comprehensive, coed **Entrance** Minimally difficult **Setting** 40-acre suburban campus **Total enrollment** 1,300 **Student/faculty ratio** 23:1 **Application deadline** Rolling **Freshmen** 57% were admitted **Housing** No **Expenses** Tuition $5580 **Undergraduates** 77% women, 44% part-time, 52% 25 or older, 1% Native American, 5% Hispanic, 14% black, 2% Asian American or Pacific Islander **Most popular recent majors** Nursing; business education; education **Academic program** Advanced placement, summer session, adult/continuing education programs, internships **Contact** Ms. Kristine Hatfield, Director of Student Affairs and Admissions, Our Lady of Holy Cross College, 4123 Woodland Drive, New Orleans, LA 70131-7399. Telephone: 504-394-7744 ext. 185 or toll-free 800-259-7744 ext. 175. Fax: 504-391-2421.

SAINT JOSEPH SEMINARY COLLEGE
SAINT BENEDICT, LOUISIANA

Contact Mr. Thomas A. Siegrist, Registrar/Director of Admissions, Saint Joseph Seminary College, Saint Benedict, LA 70457. Telephone: 504-892-1800 ext. 29.

SOUTHEASTERN LOUISIANA UNIVERSITY
HAMMOND, LOUISIANA

General State-supported, comprehensive, coed **Entrance** Noncompetitive **Setting** 375-acre small town campus **Total enrollment** 15,241 **Application deadline** 7/15 **Housing** Yes **Expenses** Tuition $2155; Room & Board $2400 **Undergraduates** 60% women, 15% part-time, 23% 25 or older, 1% Native American, 1% Hispanic, 10% black, 1% Asian American or Pacific Islander **Most popular recent majors** Business administration; education; nursing **Academic program** Advanced placement, self-designed majors, honors program, summer session, adult/continuing education programs, internships **Contact** Ms. Pat

Southeastern Louisiana University *(continued)*

Duplessis, University Admissions Analyst, Southeastern Louisiana University, SLU 752, Hammond, LA 70402. Telephone: 504-549-2066 or toll-free 800-222-7358 (in-state). Fax: 504-549-5095. E-mail: ssoutullo@selu.edu. Web site: http://www.selu.edu/.

SOUTHERN UNIVERSITY AND AGRICULTURAL AND MECHANICAL COLLEGE

BATON ROUGE, LOUISIANA

General State-supported, comprehensive, coed **Entrance** Noncompetitive **Setting** 964-acre suburban campus **Total enrollment** 9,815 **Student/faculty ratio** 18:1 **Application deadline** 7/1 **Freshmen** 84% were admitted **Housing** Yes **Expenses** Tuition $2068; Room & Board $3270 **Undergraduates** 58% women, 8% part-time, 18% 25 or older, 0.01% Native American, 0.1% Hispanic, 96% black, 1% Asian American or Pacific Islander **Academic program** Average class size 30, self-designed majors, honors program, summer session, adult/continuing education programs, internships **Contact** Mr. Wayne Broomfield, Director of Admissions, Southern University and Agricultural and Mechanical College, Baton Rouge, LA 70813. Telephone: 504-771-2430.

SOUTHERN UNIVERSITY AT NEW ORLEANS

NEW ORLEANS, LOUISIANA

Contact Dr. Melvin Hodges, Registrar/Director of Admissions, Southern University at New Orleans, 6400 Press Drive, New Orleans, LA 70126-1009. Telephone: 504-286-5314.

TULANE UNIVERSITY

NEW ORLEANS, LOUISIANA

General Independent, university, coed **Entrance** Very difficult **Setting** 110-acre urban campus **Total enrollment** 10,921 **Student/faculty ratio** 10:1 **Application deadline** 1/15 **Freshmen** 76% were admitted **Housing** Yes **Expenses** Tuition $22,720; Room & Board $6600 **Undergraduates** 52% women, 22% part-time, 15% 25 or older, 0.4% Native American, 5% Hispanic, 9% black, 5% Asian American or Pacific Islander **Most popular recent majors** Biology; English; psychology **Academic program** English as a second language, advanced placement, accelerated degree program, self-designed majors, tutorials, honors program, summer session, adult/continuing education programs, internships **Contact** Mr. Richard Whiteside, Dean of Admission and Enrollment Management, Tulane University, 6823 St Charles Avenue, New Orleans, LA 70118-5669. Telephone: 504-865-5731 or toll-free 800-873-9283. Fax: 504-862-8715. E-mail: undergrad.admission@tulane.edu. Web site: http://www.tulane.edu/.

▶ **For more information, see page 529.**

UNIVERSITY OF NEW ORLEANS

NEW ORLEANS, LOUISIANA

General State-supported, university, coed **Entrance** Moderately difficult **Setting** 345-acre urban campus **Total enrollment** 15,833 **Student/faculty ratio** 17:1 **Application deadline** 8/19 **Freshmen** 88% were admitted **Housing** Yes **Expenses** Tuition $2512; Room & Board $3150 **Undergraduates** 57% women, 31% part-time, 30% 25 or older, 0.4% Native American, 6% Hispanic, 19% black, 4% Asian American or Pacific Islander **Most popular recent majors** General studies; elementary education; accounting **Academic program** English as a second language, advanced placement, self-designed majors, honors program, summer session, adult/continuing education programs, internships **Contact** Ms. Roslyn Sheley, Director of Admissions, University of New Orleans, Lake Front, New Orleans, LA 70145. Telephone: 504-280-6595 or toll-free 800-256-5866 (in-state). Fax: 504-280-5522. E-mail: admission@uno.edu. Web site: http://www.uno.edu/.

UNIVERSITY OF SOUTHWESTERN LOUISIANA

LAFAYETTE, LOUISIANA

General State-supported, university, coed **Entrance** Noncompetitive **Setting** 1,375-acre urban campus **Total enrollment** 17,020 **Student/faculty ratio** 23:1 **Application deadline** Rolling **Housing** Yes **Expenses** Tuition $1947; Room & Board $2592 **Undergraduates** 56% women, 17% part-time, 22% 25 or older, 0.5% Native American, 1% Hispanic, 20% black, 1% Asian American or Pacific Islander **Academic program** English as a second language, advanced placement, accelerated degree program, self-designed majors, tutorials, honors program, summer session, adult/continuing education programs, internships **Contact** Mr. Leroy Broussard Jr., Director of Admissions, University of Southwestern Louisiana, PO Drawer 41210, Lafayette, LA 70504. Telephone: 318-482-6473. E-mail: admissions@usl.edu. Web site: http://www.usl.edu/.

XAVIER UNIVERSITY OF LOUISIANA

NEW ORLEANS, LOUISIANA

General Independent Roman Catholic, comprehensive, coed **Entrance** Moderately difficult **Setting** 23-acre urban campus **Total enrollment**

3,506 **Student/faculty ratio** 15:1 **Application deadline** 3/1 **Freshmen** 92% were admitted **Housing** Yes **Expenses** Tuition $8215; Room & Board $4700 **Undergraduates** 71% women, 2% part-time, 17% 25 or older, 0.03% Native American, 0.5% Hispanic, 94% black, 1% Asian American or Pacific Islander **Most Popular Recent Majors** Biology; business administration; psychology **Academic program** Average class size 29, advanced placement, accelerated degree program, tutorials, honors program, summer session, adult/continuing education programs, internships **Contact** Mr. Winston Brown, Dean of Admissions, Xavier University of Louisiana, 7325 Palmetto Street, New Orleans, LA 70125. Telephone: 504-483-7388. E-mail: apply@xula.edu. Web site: http://www.xula.edu/.

MAINE

BATES COLLEGE
LEWISTON, MAINE

General Independent, 4-year, coed **Entrance** Most difficult **Setting** 109-acre suburban campus **Total enrollment** 1,611 **Student/faculty ratio** 11:1 **Application deadline** 1/15 **Freshmen** 34% were admitted **Housing** Yes **Expenses** Tuition $28,650 **Undergraduates** 53% women, 1% 25 or older, 0.1% Native American, 2% Hispanic, 2% black, 5% Asian American or Pacific Islander **Most popular recent majors** Biology; psychology; English **Academic program** Advanced placement, accelerated degree program, self-designed majors, tutorials, honors program, summer session, internships **Contact** Mr. Wylie L. Mitchell, Dean of Admissions, Bates College, 23 Campus Avenue, Lewiston, ME 04240-6028. Telephone: 207-786-6000. Fax: 207-786-6025. E-mail: admissions@bates.edu. Web site: http://www.bates.edu/.

BOWDOIN COLLEGE
BRUNSWICK, MAINE

General Independent, 4-year, coed **Entrance** Most difficult **Setting** 110-acre small town campus **Total enrollment** 1,605 **Student/faculty ratio** 11:1 **Application deadline** 1/1 **Freshmen** 34% were admitted **Housing** Yes **Expenses** Tuition $22,905; Room & Board $6115 **Undergraduates** 50% women, 0.2% part-time, 0.3% Native American, 3% Hispanic, 2% black, 8% Asian American or Pacific Islander **Most popular recent majors** Political science; biology; history **Academic program** Average class size 17, advanced placement, accelerated degree program, self-designed majors, tutorials **Contact** Dr. Richard E. Steele, Dean of Admissions, Bowdoin College, 5000 College Station, Brunswick, ME 04011-2546. Telephone: 207-725-3190. Fax: 207-725-3003. E-mail: admissions-lit@polar.bowdoin.edu. Web site: http://www.bowdoin.edu/.

COLBY COLLEGE
WATERVILLE, MAINE

General Independent, 4-year, coed **Entrance** Most difficult **Setting** 714-acre small town campus **Total enrollment** 1,753 **Student/faculty ratio** 11:1 **Application deadline** 1/15 **Freshmen** 34% were admitted **Housing** Yes **Expenses** Tuition $29,190 **Undergraduates** 53% women, 0% 25 or older, 0.2% Native American, 3% Hispanic, 2% black, 6% Asian American or Pacific Islander **Most popular recent majors** Biology; English; political science **Academic program** English as a second language, advanced placement, self-designed majors, tutorials, honors program, internships **Contact** Mr. Parker J. Beverage, Dean of Admissions and Financial Aid, Colby College, Mayflower Hill, Waterville, ME 04901-8840. Telephone: 207-872-3168 or toll-free 800-723-3032. Fax: 207-872-3474. E-mail: admissions@colby.edu. Web site: http://www.colby.edu/.

COLLEGE OF THE ATLANTIC
BAR HARBOR, MAINE

General Independent, comprehensive, coed **Entrance** Very difficult **Setting** 25-acre small town campus **Total enrollment** 289 **Student/faculty ratio** 9:1 **Application deadline** 3/1 **Freshmen** 58% were admitted **Housing** Yes **Expenses** Tuition $18,151; Room & Board $5300 **Undergraduates** 73% women, 3% part-time, 14% 25 or older, 0% Native American, 1% Hispanic, 0% black, 0.3% Asian American or Pacific Islander **Most popular recent majors** Environmental science; public policy analysis **Academic program** Average class size 16, advanced placement, accelerated degree program, self-designed majors, tutorials, internships **Contact** Mr. Steve Thomas, Director of Admission and Student Services, College of the Atlantic, 105 Eden Street, Bar Harbor, ME 04609-1198. Telephone: 207-288-5015 ext. 233 or toll-free 800-528-0025. Fax: 207-288-4126. E-mail: inquiry@ecology.coa.edu. Web site: http://www.coa.edu/.

HUSSON COLLEGE
BANGOR, MAINE

General Independent, comprehensive, coed **Entrance** Moderately difficult **Setting** 170-acre suburban campus **Total enrollment** 1,263 **Student/faculty ratio** 21:1 **Application deadline** 9/1 **Freshmen** 82% were admitted **Housing** Yes **Expenses** Tuition $8800; Room & Board $4740 **Un-**

Husson College *(continued)*

dergraduates 22% 25 or older, 1% Native American, 1% Hispanic, 1% black, 2% Asian American or Pacific Islander **Most popular recent majors** Business administration; accounting; nursing **Academic program** Average class size 40, English as a second language, advanced placement, tutorials, honors program, summer session, adult/continuing education programs, internships **Contact** Mrs. Jane Goodwin, Director of Admissions, Husson College, One College Circle, Bangor, ME 04401-2999. Telephone: 207-941-7100 or toll-free 800-4-HUSSON. Fax: 207-941-7935. E-mail: admit@husson.edu. Web site: http://www.husson.edu/.

MAINE COLLEGE OF ART
PORTLAND, MAINE

General Independent, comprehensive, coed **Entrance** Moderately difficult **Setting** Urban campus **Total enrollment** 313 **Student/faculty ratio** 10:1 **Application deadline** Rolling **Freshmen** 77% were admitted **Housing** Yes **Expenses** Tuition $15,005; Room & Board $5794 **Undergraduates** 55% women, 8% part-time, 24% 25 or older **Most popular recent majors** Ceramic arts; graphic design/commercial art/illustration; painting **Academic program** Average class size 20, advanced placement, self-designed majors, tutorials, summer session, adult/continuing education programs, internships **Contact** Ms. Alicia Mills, Administrative Assistant, Maine College of Art, 97 Spring Street, Portland, ME 04101-3987. Telephone: 207-775-3052 or toll-free 800-639-4808. Fax: 207-772-5069. E-mail: admissions@meca.edu. Web site: http://www.meca.edu/.

MAINE MARITIME ACADEMY
CASTINE, MAINE

General State-supported, comprehensive, coed **Entrance** Moderately difficult **Setting** 35-acre small town campus **Total enrollment** 701 **Student/faculty ratio** 10:1 **Application deadline** 7/1 **Freshmen** 76% were admitted **Housing** Yes **Expenses** Tuition $4656; Room & Board $5022 **Undergraduates** 13% women, 8% 25 or older **Most popular recent majors** Naval architecture/marine engineering; maritime science **Academic program** Average class size 25, advanced placement, tutorials, adult/continuing education programs, internships **Contact** Mr. Jeffrey C. Wright, Director of Admissions, Maine Maritime Academy, Pleasant Street, Castine, ME 04420. Telephone: 207-326-2215 or toll-free 800-464-6565 (in-state), 800-227-8465 (out-of-state). Fax: 207-326-2515. Web site: http://www.mainemaritime.edu/.

▶ **For more information, see page 464.**

SAINT JOSEPH'S COLLEGE
STANDISH, MAINE

General Independent, comprehensive, coed, affiliated with Roman Catholic Church **Entrance** Moderately difficult **Setting** 330-acre small town campus **Total enrollment** 5,040 **Application deadline** Rolling **Housing** Yes **Expenses** Tuition $11,710; Room & Board $5530 **Undergraduates** 82% women, 80% part-time, 65% 25 or older, 0.1% Native American, 0.2% Hispanic, 1% black, 1% Asian American or Pacific Islander **Most popular recent majors** Nursing; business administration; elementary education **Academic program** Average class size 22, advanced placement, accelerated degree program, tutorials, honors program, summer session, adult/continuing education programs, internships **Contact** Ms. Mary Bishop, Director of Admissions, Saint Joseph's College, 278 Whites Bridge Road, Standish, ME 04084-5263. Telephone: 207-893-7746 or toll-free 800-338-7057. Fax: 207-893-7862. E-mail: admissions@sjcme.edu. Web site: http://www.sjcme.edu/.

THOMAS COLLEGE
WATERVILLE, MAINE

General Independent, comprehensive, coed **Entrance** Minimally difficult **Setting** 70-acre small town campus **Total enrollment** 905 **Student/faculty ratio** 18:1 **Application deadline** Rolling **Housing** Yes **Expenses** Tuition $11,725; Room & Board $5175 **Undergraduates** 59% women, 33% part-time, 36% 25 or older, 0.4% Native American, 0.3% Hispanic, 1% black, 1% Asian American or Pacific Islander **Most popular recent majors** Accounting; business administration; business marketing and marketing management **Academic program** Average class size 22, advanced placement, summer session, adult/continuing education programs, internships **Contact** Mr. Robert Callahan, Director of Admissions, Thomas College, 180 West River Road, Waterville, ME 04901-5097. Telephone: 207-873-0771 or toll-free 800-339-7001. Fax: 207-877-0114. E-mail: admiss@host2.thomas.edu. Web site: http://www.thomas.edu/.

UNITY COLLEGE
UNITY, MAINE

General Independent, 4-year, coed **Entrance** Moderately difficult **Setting** 205-acre rural campus **Total enrollment** 523 **Student/faculty ratio** 14:1 **Application deadline** Rolling **Housing** Yes **Expenses** Tuition $11,200; Room & Board $5200 **Undergraduates** 27% women, 1% part-time, 3% 25 or older, 0% Native American, 0.2% Hispanic, 0.2% black, 0% Asian American or Pacific Islander **Academic program** English as a second language, advanced placement, accelerated degree program, self-designed majors, tutorials, honors program, summer session, internships **Contact** Dr. John M. B. Craig, Vice President and Dean for Admissions, Unity College, PO Box 532, Unity, ME 04988-0532. Telephone: 207-948-3131 ext. 222. Fax: 207-948-6277. Web site: http://www.unity.edu/.

UNIVERSITY OF MAINE

ORONO, MAINE

General State-supported, university, coed **Entrance** Moderately difficult **Setting** 3,298-acre small town campus **Total enrollment** 8,917 **Student/faculty ratio** 14:1 **Application deadline** Rolling **Freshmen** 75% were admitted **Housing** Yes **Expenses** Tuition $4344; Room & Board $4906 **Undergraduates** 47% women, 12% part-time, 21% 25 or older **Most popular recent majors** Business administration; elementary education; nursing **Academic program** Average class size 25, English as a second language, advanced placement, accelerated degree program, honors program, summer session, adult/continuing education programs, internships **Contact** Mr. Sherman A. Rosser Jr., Director of Admissions, University of Maine, 5713 Chadbourne Hall, Orono, ME 04469-5713. Telephone: 207-581-1561. Fax: 207-581-1213. E-mail: um_admit@maine.maine.edu. Web site: http://www.ume.maine.edu/.

UNIVERSITY OF MAINE AT AUGUSTA

AUGUSTA, MAINE

General State-supported, 4-year, coed **Entrance** Noncompetitive **Setting** 165-acre small town campus **Total enrollment** 5,248 **Student/faculty ratio** 22:1 **Application deadline** Rolling **Housing** No **Expenses** Tuition $3255 **Undergraduates** 76% women, 67% part-time, 60% 25 or older, 3% Native American, 0.3% Hispanic, 0.3% black, 0.2% Asian American or Pacific Islander **Most popular recent majors** Business administration; nursing; social sciences **Academic program** Advanced placement, honors program, summer session, adult/continuing education programs, internships **Contact** Mr. William Clark Ketcham, Director of Enrollment Services, University of Maine at Augusta, 46 University Drive, Augusta, ME 04330-9410. Telephone: 207-621-3185 or toll-free 800-696-6000 ext. 3185 (in-state). Fax: 207-621-3116. E-mail: umaar@maine.maine.edu. Web site: http://www.uma.maine.edu/.

UNIVERSITY OF MAINE AT FARMINGTON

FARMINGTON, MAINE

General State-supported, 4-year, coed **Entrance** Moderately difficult **Setting** 50-acre small town campus **Total enrollment** 2,337 **Student/faculty ratio** 15:1 **Application deadline** 4/15 **Housing** Yes **Expenses** Tuition $3520; Room & Board $4406 **Undergraduates** 67% women, 12% part-time, 20% 25 or older, 1% Native American, 0.1% Hispanic, 0.3% black, 1% Asian American or Pacific Islander **Most popular recent majors** Interdisciplinary studies; elementary education; mental health/rehabilitation **Academic program** Average class size 30, advanced placement, accelerated degree program, self-designed majors, tutorials, honors program, summer session, internships **Contact** Mr. James G. Collins, Associate Director of Admissions, University of Maine at Farmington, 102 Main Street, Farmington, ME 04938-1994. Telephone: 207-778-7050. Fax: 207-778-8182. E-mail: umfadmit@maine.maine.edu. Web site: http://www.umf.maine.edu/.

UNIVERSITY OF MAINE AT FORT KENT

FORT KENT, MAINE

General State-supported, 4-year, coed **Entrance** Moderately difficult **Setting** 52-acre rural campus **Total enrollment** 690 **Student/faculty ratio** 12:1 **Application deadline** Rolling **Freshmen** 96% were admitted **Housing** Yes **Expenses** Tuition $3140; Room & Board $3800 **Undergraduates** 43% 25 or older, 1% Native American, 0.4% Hispanic, 0.4% black, 1% Asian American or Pacific Islander **Most popular recent majors** Nursing; education; social sciences **Academic program** Average class size 20, advanced placement, self-designed majors, honors program, summer session, internships **Contact** Mr. Jerald R. Nadeau, Director of Admissions, University of Maine at Fort Kent, 25 Pleasant Street, Fort Kent, ME 04743-1292. Telephone: 207-834-7600 or toll-free 888-TRY-UMFK. Fax: 207-834-7609. E-mail: umfkadm@maine.maine.edu. Web site: http://www.umfk.maine.edu/.

UNIVERSITY OF MAINE AT MACHIAS

MACHIAS, MAINE

General State-supported, 4-year, coed **Entrance** Moderately difficult **Setting** 42-acre rural campus **Total enrollment** 884 **Student/faculty ratio** 16:1 **Application deadline** Rolling **Freshmen** 83% were admitted **Housing** Yes **Expenses** Tuition $3225; Room & Board $4075 **Undergraduates** 61% women, 26% part-time, 37% 25 or older, 4% Native American, 0.5% Hispanic, 0.5% black, 1% Asian American or Pacific Islander **Most popular recent majors** Environmental science; elementary education; behavioral sciences **Academic program** Advanced placement, accelerated degree program, self-designed majors, honors program, summer session, adult/continuing education programs, internships **Contact** Mr. David Baldwin, Director of Admissions, University of Maine at Machias, 9 O'Brien Avenue, Machias, ME

University of Maine at Machias *(continued)*

04654-1321. Telephone: 207-255-1318 or toll-free 888-GOTOUMM. Fax: 207-255-1363. E-mail: admissions@acad.umm.maine.edu. Web site: http://www.umm.maine.edu/.

UNIVERSITY OF MAINE AT PRESQUE ISLE
PRESQUE ISLE, MAINE

General State-supported, 4-year, coed **Entrance** Minimally difficult **Setting** 150-acre small town campus **Total enrollment** 1,413 **Student/faculty ratio** 18:1 **Application deadline** Rolling **Freshmen** 88% were admitted **Housing** Yes **Expenses** Tuition $3210; Room & Board $3918 **Undergraduates** 60% women, 14% part-time, 33% 25 or older, 3% Native American, 0.2% Hispanic, 1% black, 1% Asian American or Pacific Islander **Most popular recent majors** Education; liberal arts and studies; business administration **Academic program** Average class size 20, advanced placement, accelerated degree program, self-designed majors, honors program, summer session, adult/continuing education programs, internships **Contact** Mr. Michael Sullivan, Admissions Representative, University of Maine at Presque Isle, 181 Main Street, Presque Isle, ME 04769-2888. Telephone: 207-768-9534. Fax: 207-768-9608. E-mail: infoumpi@polaris.umpi.maine.edu. Web site: http://www.umpi.maine.edu/.

UNIVERSITY OF NEW ENGLAND
BIDDEFORD, MAINE

General Independent, comprehensive, coed **Entrance** Moderately difficult **Setting** 410-acre small town campus **Total enrollment** 2,478 **Student/faculty ratio** 19:1 **Application deadline** Rolling **Freshmen** 81% were admitted **Housing** Yes **Expenses** Tuition $14,830; Room & Board $5820 **Undergraduates** 75% women, 13% part-time, 11% 25 or older **Most popular recent majors** Occupational therapy; physical therapy; nursing **Academic program** Average class size 25, English as a second language, advanced placement, accelerated degree program, self-designed majors, summer session, adult/continuing education programs, internships **Contact** Ms. Patricia Cribby, Dean of Admissions, University of New England, Hills Beach Road, Biddeford, ME 04005-9526. Telephone: 207-283-0171 ext. 2240 or toll-free 800-477-4UNE. E-mail: msinkowicz@mailbox.une.edu. Web site: http://www.une.edu/.

UNIVERSITY OF SOUTHERN MAINE
PORTLAND, MAINE

General State-supported, comprehensive, coed **Entrance** Moderately difficult **Setting** 143-acre suburban campus **Total enrollment** 10,236 **Student/faculty ratio** 14:1 **Application deadline** Rolling **Freshmen** 78% were admitted **Housing** Yes **Expenses** Tuition $3938; Room & Board $4646 **Undergraduates** 61% women, 44% part-time, 60% 25 or older **Most popular recent majors** Nursing; business administration; English **Academic program** Average class size 25, English as a second language, advanced placement, self-designed majors, tutorials, honors program, summer session, adult/continuing education programs, internships **Contact** Ms. Debbie Jordan, Director of Admissions, University of Southern Maine, 37 College Avenue, Gorham, ME 04038. Telephone: 207-780-5670 or toll-free 800-800-4USM. Fax: 207-780-5640. E-mail: usmadm@maine.maine.edu. Web site: http://www.usm.maine.edu/.

WESTBROOK COLLEGE
See University of New England

MARYLAND

BALTIMORE HEBREW UNIVERSITY
BALTIMORE, MARYLAND

General Independent, comprehensive, coed **Entrance** Moderately difficult **Setting** 2-acre urban campus **Total enrollment** 277 **Student/faculty ratio** 12:1 **Application deadline** Rolling **Housing** No **Expenses** Tuition $4030 **Undergraduates** 90% 25 or older **Most Popular Recent Major** Judaic studies **Academic program** Average class size 10, advanced placement, accelerated degree program, tutorials, honors program, summer session, adult/continuing education programs **Contact** Dr. George Berlin, Dean, Baltimore Hebrew University, 5800 Park Heights Avenue, Baltimore, MD 21215-3996. Telephone: 410-578-6912 or toll-free 888-248-7420. Fax: 410-578-6940. E-mail: bhu@bhu.edu.

BOWIE STATE UNIVERSITY
BOWIE, MARYLAND

General State-supported, comprehensive, coed **Entrance** Minimally difficult **Setting** 312-acre small town campus **Total enrollment** 5,167 **Student/faculty ratio** 18:1 **Application deadline** 4/1 **Freshmen** 34% were admitted **Housing** Yes **Expenses** Tuition $3357; Room & Board $4253 **Undergraduates** 64% women, 29% part-time, 34% 25 or older, 0.3% Native American, 1% Hispanic, 84% black, 2% Asian American or Pacific Islander **Most popular recent majors** Business administration; elementary education; psychology **Academic program** Advanced placement, accelerated degree program, tutorials, honors program, summer session, adult/continuing education programs, internships **Contact** Ms. Hope Ransom, Coordinator of Undergraduate Enrollment, Bowie State University, 14000 Jericho Park Road, Bowie, MD 20715. Telephone: 301-464-6563. Fax: 301-464-7521. E-mail: hope.ransom@bowiestate.edu. Web site: http://www.bowiestate.edu/.

▶ **For more information, see page 397.**

CAPITOL COLLEGE
LAUREL, MARYLAND

General Independent, comprehensive, coed **Entrance** Minimally difficult **Setting** 52-acre suburban campus **Total enrollment** 739 **Student/faculty ratio** 14:1 **Application deadline** Rolling **Freshmen** 94% were admitted **Housing** Yes **Expenses** Tuition $10,112; Room only $3040 **Undergraduates** 18% women, 47% part-time, 46% 25 or older, 0.2% Native American, 3% Hispanic, 34% black, 6% Asian American or Pacific Islander **Most popular recent majors** Electrical/electronic engineering technology; electrical/electronics engineering; computer engineering **Academic program** English as a second language, advanced placement, accelerated degree program, summer session, adult/continuing education programs **Contact** Mr. Anthony G. Miller, Director of Admissions, Capitol College, 11301 Springfield Road, Laurel, MD 20708-9759. Telephone: 301-953-3200 or toll-free 800-950-1992. E-mail: admissions@capitol-college.edu. Web site: http://www.capitol-college.edu/.

▶ **For more information, see page 403.**

COLLEGE OF NOTRE DAME OF MARYLAND
BALTIMORE, MARYLAND

General Independent Roman Catholic, comprehensive, women only **Entrance** Moderately difficult **Setting** 58-acre suburban campus **Total enrollment** 3,100 **Student/faculty ratio** 15:1 **Application deadline** 2/15 **Freshmen** 80% were admitted **Housing** Yes **Expenses** Tuition $14,086; Room & Board $6130 **Undergraduates** 72% part-time, 0.3% Native American, 2% Hispanic, 17% black, 2% Asian American or Pacific Islander **Most popular recent majors** Business administration; education; mass communications **Academic program** English as a second language, advanced placement, accelerated degree program, self-designed majors, tutorials, honors program, summer session, adult/continuing education programs, internships **Contact** Mrs. Karen Stakem Hornig, Director of Admissions, College of Notre Dame of Maryland, 4701 North Charles Street, Baltimore, MD 21210-2476. Telephone: 410-532-5330 or toll-free 800-435-0200 (in-state), 800-435-0300 (out-of-state). Fax: 410-532-6287. E-mail: admiss@ndm.edu. Web site: http://www.ndm.edu/.

COLUMBIA UNION COLLEGE
TAKOMA PARK, MARYLAND

General Independent Seventh-day Adventist, 4-year, coed **Entrance** Minimally difficult **Setting** 19-acre suburban campus **Total enrollment** 1,212 **Application deadline** 8/1 **Freshmen** 89% were admitted **Housing** Yes **Expenses** Tuition $11,790; Room & Board $4150 **Undergraduates** 61% women, 48% part-time, 36% 25 or older, 0.2% Native American, 7% Hispanic, 42% black, 6% Asian American or Pacific Islander **Most popular recent majors** Nursing; psychology; business administration **Academic program** English as a second language, advanced placement, self-designed majors, summer session, adult/continuing education programs, internships **Contact** Ms. Cindy Carreno, Director of Admissions, Columbia Union College, 7600 Flower Avenue, Takoma Park, MD 20912-7794. Telephone: 301-891-4080 or toll-free 800-492-1715 (in-state), 800-835-4212 (out-of-state). Fax: 301-891-4230.

COPPIN STATE COLLEGE
BALTIMORE, MARYLAND

General State-supported, comprehensive, coed **Entrance** Moderately difficult **Setting** 33-acre urban campus **Total enrollment** 3,540 **Student/faculty ratio** 17:1 **Application deadline** 7/15 **Housing** Yes **Expenses** Tuition $3624; Room & Board $4884 **Undergraduates** 73% women, 27% part-time, 50% 25 or older, 0.5% Native American, 0.4% Hispanic, 95% black, 0.2% Asian American or Pacific Islander **Most popular recent majors** Business administration; nursing; psychology **Academic program** Average class size 20, English as a second language, advanced placement, tutorials, honors program, summer session, adult/continuing education programs, internships **Contact** Mr. Allen Mosley, Director of Admissions, Coppin State College, 2500 West North Avenue, Baltimore, MD 21216-3698. Telephone: 410-383-5990 or toll-free 800-635-3674. Fax: 410-333-7094. E-mail: amosley@coe.coppin.umd.edu. Web site: http://coeacl.coppin.umd.edu/.

FROSTBURG STATE UNIVERSITY
FROSTBURG, MARYLAND

General State-supported, comprehensive, coed **Entrance** Moderately difficult **Setting** 260-acre small town campus **Total enrollment** 5,199 **Student/faculty ratio** 17:1 **Application deadline** Rolling **Freshmen** 76% were admitted **Housing** Yes **Expenses** Tuition $3544; Room & Board

Frostburg State University *(continued)*

$4786 **Undergraduates** 52% women, 7% part-time, 14% 25 or older, 0.5% Native American, 1% Hispanic, 9% black, 1% Asian American or Pacific Islander **Most popular recent majors** Education; business administration; criminal justice studies **Academic program** Advanced placement, accelerated degree program, tutorials, honors program, summer session, adult/continuing education programs, internships **Contact** Mr. Edgerton Deuel II, Director of Admissions, Frostburg State University, 101 Braddock Road, Frostburg, MD 21532-1099. Telephone: 301-687-4201. Fax: 301-687-7074. E-mail: fsuadmissions@fra00fsu.umd.edu.

GOUCHER COLLEGE
BALTIMORE, MARYLAND

General Independent, comprehensive, coed **Entrance** Moderately difficult **Setting** 287-acre suburban campus **Total enrollment** 1,382 **Student/faculty ratio** 11:1 **Application deadline** 2/1 **Freshmen** 78% were admitted **Housing** Yes **Expenses** Tuition $18,525; Room & Board $6925 **Undergraduates** 74% women, 3% part-time, 5% 25 or older, 0.1% Native American, 3% Hispanic, 8% black, 4% Asian American or Pacific Islander **Most popular recent majors** Biology; management science; psychology **Academic program** Average class size 19, advanced placement, accelerated degree program, self-designed majors, tutorials, honors program, summer session, adult/continuing education programs, internships **Contact** Mr. Carlton E. Surbeck III, Director of Admissions, Goucher College, 1021 Dulaney Valley Road, Baltimore, MD 21204-2794. Telephone: 410-337-6100 or toll-free 800-GOUCHER. Fax: 410-337-6123. E-mail: admission@goucher.edu. Web site: http://www.goucher.edu/.

▶ **For more information, see page 444.**

GRIGGS UNIVERSITY
SILVER SPRING, MARYLAND

General Independent Seventh-day Adventist, 4-year, coed **Entrance** Minimally difficult **Setting** Suburban campus **Total enrollment** 370 **Application deadline** Rolling **Housing** No **Expenses** Tuition $4560 **Most popular recent majors** Religious studies; theology **Academic program** Accelerated degree program, summer session, adult/continuing education programs, internships **Contact** Ms. Eva Michel, Enrollment Officer, Griggs University, PO Box 4437, Silver Spring, MD 20914-4437. Telephone: 301-680-6593 or toll-free 800-394-4769 (in-state). Fax: 301-680-6577. E-mail: 74617.74@compuserve.com.

HARVEST CHRISTIAN COLLEGE
CAMP SPRINGS, MARYLAND

Contact Harvest Christian College, 4700 Auth Place, Suite 550, Camp Springs, MD 20746. Telephone: 301-423-2772.

HOOD COLLEGE
FREDERICK, MARYLAND

General Independent, comprehensive, primarily women, affiliated with United Church of Christ **Entrance** Moderately difficult **Setting** 50-acre suburban campus **Total enrollment** 1,856 **Student/faculty ratio** 10:1 **Application deadline** 3/1 **Freshmen** 77% were admitted **Housing** Yes **Expenses** Tuition $16,418; Room & Board $6592 **Undergraduates** 34% 25 or older, 4% Hispanic, 9% black, 2% Asian American or Pacific Islander **Most popular recent majors** Business administration; education; biology **Academic program** Average class size 15, English as a second language, advanced placement, accelerated degree program, self-designed majors, tutorials, honors program, summer session, adult/continuing education programs, internships **Contact** Ms. Kerry Durgin, Director of Admissions, Hood College, 401 Rosemont Avenue, Frederick, MD 21701-8575. Telephone: 301-696-3400 or toll-free 800-922-1599. E-mail: admissions@nimue.hood.edu. Web site: http://www.hood.edu.

JOHNS HOPKINS UNIVERSITY
BALTIMORE, MARYLAND

General Independent, university, coed **Entrance** Most difficult **Setting** 140-acre urban campus **Total enrollment** 5,022 **Student/faculty ratio** 10:1 **Application deadline** 1/1 **Freshmen** 41% were admitted **Housing** Yes **Expenses** Tuition $21,700; Room & Board $7355 **Undergraduates** 40% women, 1% part-time, 0% 25 or older, 0.1% Native American, 3% Hispanic, 6% black, 21% Asian American or Pacific Islander **Most popular recent majors** Biology; bioengineering; international relations **Academic program** English as a second language, advanced placement, accelerated degree program, self-designed majors, tutorials, honors program, summer session, adult/continuing education programs, internships **Contact** Mr. Paul White, Director of Undergraduate Admissions, Johns Hopkins University, 3400 North Charles Street, Baltimore, MD 21218-2699. Telephone: 410-516-8171. Fax: 410-516-6025. E-mail: gotojhu@jhu.edu. Web site: http://www.jhu.edu/.

LOYOLA COLLEGE
BALTIMORE, MARYLAND

General Independent Roman Catholic (Jesuit), comprehensive, coed **Entrance** Moderately difficult **Setting** 89-acre urban campus **Total enrollment** 6,241 **Student/faculty ratio** 14:1 **Application deadline** 1/15 **Freshmen** 70% were admitted **Housing** Yes **Expenses** Tuition $16,560; Room & Board $7240 **Undergraduates** 55% women, 2% part-time, 2% 25 or older, 0.2% Native American, 2% Hispanic, 5% black, 2% Asian American or Pacific Islander **Most popular recent majors** Business administration; psychology; communications **Academic program** Average class size 25, advanced placement, tutorials, honors program, summer session, internships **Contact** Mr. William Bossemeyer, Director of Admissions, Loyola College, 4501 North Charles Street, Baltimore, MD 21210-2699. Telephone: 410-617-2000 ext. 2252 or toll-free 800-221-9107 Ext. 2252 (in-state). Fax: 410-617-2176. Web site: http://www.loyola.edu/.

MAPLE SPRINGS BAPTIST BIBLE COLLEGE AND SEMINARY

CAPITOL HEIGHTS, MARYLAND

General Independent Baptist, comprehensive **Entrance** Minimally difficult **Setting** 1-acre suburban campus **Total enrollment** 152 **Student/faculty ratio** 10:1 **Application deadline** Rolling **Freshmen** 100% were admitted **Housing** No **Expenses** Tuition $1970 **Undergraduates** 51% women, 97% part-time, 90% 25 or older, 100% black **Academic program** Average class size 10, accelerated degree program, adult/continuing education programs, internships **Contact** Ms. Mazie Murphy, Assistant Director of Admissions and Records, Maple Springs Baptist Bible College and Seminary, 4130 Belt Road, Capitol Heights, MD 20743. Telephone: 301-736-3631. Fax: 301-735-6507.

MARYLAND INSTITUTE, COLLEGE OF ART

BALTIMORE, MARYLAND

General Independent, comprehensive, coed **Entrance** Very difficult **Setting** 12-acre urban campus **Total enrollment** 1,143 **Student/faculty ratio** 6:1 **Application deadline** 2/1 **Freshmen** 50% were admitted **Housing** Yes **Expenses** Tuition $16,760; Room & Board $5200 **Undergraduates** 8% 25 or older, 0.4% Native American, 4% Hispanic, 5% black, 6% Asian American or Pacific Islander **Most popular recent majors** Art; graphic design/commercial art/illustration; painting **Academic program** Advanced placement, accelerated degree program, self-designed majors, tutorials, summer session, adult/continuing education programs, internships **Contact** Ms. Theresa Lynch Bedoya, Dean of Admissions and Financial Aid, Maryland Institute, College of Art, 1300 Mount Royal Avenue, Baltimore, MD 21217-4192. Telephone: 410-225-2294. Fax: 410-225-2337. E-mail: admissions@mica.edu. Web site: http://www.mica.edu/.

MORGAN STATE UNIVERSITY

BALTIMORE, MARYLAND

General State-supported, university, coed **Entrance** Moderately difficult **Setting** 140-acre urban campus **Total enrollment** 6,299 **Student/faculty ratio** 18:1 **Application deadline** Rolling **Freshmen** 55% were admitted **Housing** Yes **Expenses** Tuition $3412; Room & Board $5090 **Undergraduates** 27% 25 or older **Most popular recent majors** Electrical/electronics engineering; accounting; biology **Academic program** Advanced placement, accelerated degree program, tutorials, honors program, summer session, adult/continuing education programs, internships **Contact** Ms. Chelseia Harold-Miller, Director of Admission and Recruitment, Morgan State University, 1700 East Cold Spring Lane, Baltimore, MD 21251. Telephone: 410-319-3000 or toll-free 800-332-6674. E-mail: tjenness@moac.morgan.edu. Web site: http://www.morgan.edu/.

MOUNT SAINT MARY'S COLLEGE AND SEMINARY

EMMITSBURG, MARYLAND

General Independent Roman Catholic, comprehensive, coed **Entrance** Moderately difficult **Setting** 1,400-acre rural campus **Total enrollment** 1,798 **Student/faculty ratio** 15:1 **Application deadline** 3/1 **Freshmen** 82% were admitted **Housing** Yes **Expenses** Tuition $15,650; Room & Board $6450 **Undergraduates** 54% women, 10% part-time, 8% 25 or older, 0.2% Native American, 2% Hispanic, 5% black, 2% Asian American or Pacific Islander **Most popular recent majors** Business administration; accounting; elementary education **Academic program** Average class size 20, English as a second language, advanced placement, self-designed majors, tutorials, honors program, summer session, adult/continuing education programs, internships **Contact** Mr. Stephen Neitz, Director of Admissions, Mount Saint Mary's College and Seminary, 16300 Old Emmitsburg Road, Emmitsburg, MD 21727-7799. Telephone: 301-447-5214 or toll-free 800-448-4347. E-mail: admissions@msmary.edu. Web site: http://www.msmary.edu/.

NER ISRAEL RABBINICAL COLLEGE

BALTIMORE, MARYLAND

Contact Rabbi Berel Weisbord, Dean of Admissions, Ner Israel Rabbinical College, Mount Wilson Lane, Baltimore, MD 21208. Telephone: 410-484-7200.

PEABODY CONSERVATORY OF MUSIC OF THE JOHNS HOPKINS UNIVERSITY
BALTIMORE, MARYLAND

General Independent, comprehensive, coed **Entrance** Very difficult **Setting** Urban campus **Total enrollment** 617 **Student/faculty ratio** 3:1 **Application deadline** 12/15 **Freshmen** 53% were admitted **Housing** Yes **Expenses** Tuition $19,925; Room & Board $7340 **Undergraduates** 56% women, 2% part-time, 6% 25 or older, 3% Hispanic, 3% black, 13% Asian American or Pacific Islander **Most popular recent majors** Stringed instruments; music (piano and organ performance); music (voice and choral/opera performance) **Academic program** Average class size 15, English as a second language, advanced placement, accelerated degree program, tutorials, honors program, summer session, internships **Contact** Mr. David Lane, Director of Admissions, Peabody Conservatory of Music of The Johns Hopkins University, 1 East Mount Vernon Place, Baltimore, MD 21202-2397. Telephone: 410-659-8110 or toll-free 800-368-2521 (out-of-state). Web site: http://www.peabody.jhu.edu/.

ST. JOHN'S COLLEGE
ANNAPOLIS, MARYLAND

General Independent, comprehensive, coed **Entrance** Moderately difficult **Setting** 36-acre small town campus **Total enrollment** 534 **Student/faculty ratio** 8:1 **Application deadline** Rolling **Freshmen** 85% were admitted **Housing** Yes **Expenses** Tuition $21,180; Room & Board $6010 **Undergraduates** 42% women, 0.4% part-time, 4% 25 or older, 1% Native American, 5% Hispanic, 1% black, 2% Asian American or Pacific Islander **Academic program** Average class size 16, tutorials **Contact** Mr. John Christensen, Director of Admissions, St. John's College, PO Box 2800, Annapolis, MD 21404. Telephone: 410-263-2371 ext. 222 or toll-free 800-727-9238. E-mail: admissions@sjca.edu. Web site: http://www.sjca.edu/.

ST. MARY'S COLLEGE OF MARYLAND
ST. MARY'S CITY, MARYLAND

General State-supported, 4-year, coed **Entrance** Very difficult **Setting** 275-acre rural campus **Total enrollment** 1,682 **Student/faculty ratio** 14:1 **Application deadline** 1/15 **Freshmen** 61% were admitted **Housing** Yes **Expenses** Tuition $6875; Room & Board $5645 **Undergraduates** 58% women, 4% part-time, 7% 25 or older, 0.3% Native American, 2% Hispanic, 9% black, 4% Asian American or Pacific Islander **Most popular recent majors** Biology; psychology; economics **Academic program** Average class size 19, advanced placement, self-designed majors, tutorials, honors program, summer session, adult/continuing education programs, internships **Contact** Mr. Richard J. Edgar, Director of Admissions, St. Mary's College of Maryland, Admissions Office, St. Mary's City, MD 20686. Telephone: 301-862-0292 or toll-free 800-492-7181. Fax: 301-862-0906. E-mail: admissions@honors.smcm.edu. Web site: http://www.smcm.edu/.

▶ **For more information, see page 506.**

ST. MARY'S SEMINARY AND UNIVERSITY
BALTIMORE, MARYLAND

General Independent Roman Catholic, upper-level, coed **Entrance** Difficulty N/R **Setting** Urban campus **Total enrollment** 250 **Application deadline** Rolling **Housing** Yes **Expenses** Tuition $9235; Room & Board $7200 **Undergraduates** 80% 25 or older **Contact** Rev. Thomas J. Burke, Formation Coordinator, St. Mary's Seminary and University, 5400 Roland Avenue, Baltimore, MD 21210-1994. Telephone: 410-864-4000.

SALISBURY STATE UNIVERSITY
SALISBURY, MARYLAND

General State-supported, comprehensive, coed **Entrance** Moderately difficult **Setting** 140-acre small town campus **Total enrollment** 6,022 **Student/faculty ratio** 15:1 **Application deadline** 3/1 **Freshmen** 59% were admitted **Housing** Yes **Expenses** Tuition $3842; Room & Board $5140 **Undergraduates** 57% women, 10% part-time, 17% 25 or older, 0.3% Native American, 1% Hispanic, 8% black, 1% Asian American or Pacific Islander **Most popular recent majors** Elementary education; business administration; biology **Academic program** English as a second language, advanced placement, accelerated degree program, self-designed majors, tutorials, honors program, summer session, adult/continuing education programs, internships **Contact** Mrs. Jane H. Dané, Dean of Admissions, Salisbury State University, 1101 Camden Avenue, Salisbury, MD 21801-6837. Telephone: 410-543-6161. E-mail: d3adadm@ssa.ssu.umd.edu. Web site: http://www.ssu.edu/.

SOJOURNER-DOUGLASS COLLEGE
BALTIMORE, MARYLAND

General Independent, 4-year, coed **Contact** Ms. Diana Samuels, Manager, Office of Admissions, Sojourner-Douglass College, 500 North Caroline Street, Baltimore, MD 21205-1814. Telephone: 410-276-0306 ext. 249. Fax: 410-675-1810.

TOWSON UNIVERSITY
TOWSON, MARYLAND

General State-supported, comprehensive, coed **Entrance** Moderately difficult **Setting** 321-acre

suburban campus **Total enrollment** 15,524 **Student/faculty ratio** 16:1 **Application deadline** 5/1 **Freshmen** 64% were admitted **Housing** Yes **Expenses** Tuition $4120; Room & Board $5044 **Undergraduates** 60% women, 16% part-time, 18% 25 or older, 0.3% Native American, 2% Hispanic, 10% black, 3% Asian American or Pacific Islander **Most popular recent majors** Mass communications; business administration; elementary education **Academic program** English as a second language, advanced placement, accelerated degree program, self-designed majors, tutorials, honors program, summer session, adult/continuing education programs, internships **Contact** Ms. Angel Jackson, Director of Admissions, Towson University, 8000 York Road, Towson, MD 21252-0001. Telephone: 410-830-3333 or toll-free 888-4TOWSON. Fax: 410-830-3030. E-mail: admissions@towson.edu. Web site: http://www.towson.edu/.

▶ **For more information, see page 528.**

UNITED STATES NAVAL ACADEMY
ANNAPOLIS, MARYLAND

General Federally supported, 4-year, coed **Entrance** Very difficult **Setting** 329-acre small town campus **Total enrollment** 3,994 **Student/faculty ratio** 7:1 **Application deadline** 2/28 **Freshmen** 17% were admitted **Housing** Yes **Expenses** Tuition $0 **Undergraduates** 16% women, 1% 25 or older, 1% Native American, 7% Hispanic, 7% black, 4% Asian American or Pacific Islander **Most popular recent majors** Political science; aerospace engineering; oceanography **Academic program** Average class size 20, English as a second language, advanced placement, tutorials, honors program, summer session **Contact** Col. David A. Vetter, Dean of Admissions, United States Naval Academy, 117 Decatur Road, Annapolis, MD 21402-5000. Telephone: 410-293-4361 or toll-free 800-638-9156. Fax: 410-293-4348. Web site: http://www.nadn.navy.mil/.

UNIVERSITY OF BALTIMORE
BALTIMORE, MARYLAND

General State-supported, upper-level, coed **Entrance** Noncompetitive **Setting** 49-acre urban campus **Total enrollment** 4,609 **Student/faculty ratio** 16:1 **Application deadline** Rolling **Freshmen** 89% were admitted **Housing** No **Expenses** Tuition $3804 **Undergraduates** 54% women, 57% part-time, 72% 25 or older, 3% Native American, 1% Hispanic, 25% black, 3% Asian American or Pacific Islander **Most popular recent majors** Business administration; criminal justice/law enforcement administration; interdisciplinary studies **Academic program** Advanced placement, self-designed majors, honors program, summer session, adult/continuing education programs, internships **Contact** Ms. Julia Pitman, Associate Director of Admissions, University of Baltimore, 1420 North Charles Street, Baltimore, MD 21201-5779. Telephone: 410-837-4777. Fax: 410-837-4793. E-mail: admissions@ubmail.ubalt.edu. Web site: http://www.ubalt.edu/.

UNIVERSITY OF MARYLAND, BALTIMORE COUNTY
BALTIMORE, MARYLAND

General State-supported, university, coed **Entrance** Moderately difficult **Setting** 500-acre suburban campus **Total enrollment** 9,863 **Student/faculty ratio** 14:1 **Application deadline** Rolling **Freshmen** 65% were admitted **Housing** Yes **Expenses** Tuition $4570; Room & Board $4998 **Undergraduates** 52% women, 22% part-time, 25% 25 or older, 1% Native American, 2% Hispanic, 16% black, 14% Asian American or Pacific Islander **Most popular recent majors** Psychology; information sciences/systems; computer science **Academic program** English as a second language, advanced placement, self-designed majors, tutorials, honors program, summer session, adult/continuing education programs, internships **Contact** Ms. Rachael Hendrickson, Director of Admissions, University of Maryland, Baltimore County, 1000 Hilltop Circle, Baltimore, MD 21250-5398. Telephone: 410-455-1300 or toll-free 800-862-2402. Fax: 410-455-1094. E-mail: admissions@umbc.edu. Web site: http://www.umbc.edu/.

▶ **For more information, see page 535.**

UNIVERSITY OF MARYLAND, COLLEGE PARK
COLLEGE PARK, MARYLAND

General State-supported, university, coed **Entrance** Moderately difficult **Setting** 3,773-acre suburban campus **Total enrollment** 32,711 **Student/faculty ratio** 13:1 **Application deadline** 2/15 **Freshmen** 65% were admitted **Housing** Yes **Expenses** Tuition $4460; Room & Board $5667 **Undergraduates** 48% women, 11% part-time, 15% 25 or older, 0.3% Native American, 5% Hispanic, 14% black, 14% Asian American or Pacific Islander **Most popular recent majors** Criminology; psychology; accounting **Academic program** Average class size 20, English as a second language, advanced placement, accelerated degree program, self-designed majors, tutorials, honors program, summer session, adult/continuing education programs, internships **Contact** Ms. Shannon Gundy, Assistant Director of Admissions, University of Maryland, College Park, College Park, MD 20742-5235. Telephone: 301-374-8385 or toll-free

University of Maryland, College Park *(continued)*

800-422-5867. Fax: 301-314-9693. E-mail: um-admit@uga.umd.edu. Web site: http://www.umcp.umd.edu/.

► **For more information, see page 536.**

UNIVERSITY OF MARYLAND EASTERN SHORE
PRINCESS ANNE, MARYLAND

General State-supported, university, coed **Entrance** Moderately difficult **Setting** 700-acre rural campus **Total enrollment** 3,204 **Application deadline** Rolling **Freshmen** 70% were admitted **Housing** Yes **Expenses** Tuition $3240; Room & Board $4330 **Undergraduates** 13% 25 or older, 0.1% Native American, 1% Hispanic, 77% black, 1% Asian American or Pacific Islander **Academic program** Advanced placement, accelerated degree program, self-designed majors, tutorials, honors program, summer session, adult/continuing education programs, internships **Contact** Dr. Rochell Peoples, Assistant V.P. of Student Affairs/Enrollment Management, University of Maryland Eastern Shore, Princess Anne, MD 21853-1299. Telephone: 410-651-6410. Fax: 410-651-7922. Web site: http://www.umes.umd.edu/.

UNIVERSITY OF MARYLAND UNIVERSITY COLLEGE
COLLEGE PARK, MARYLAND

General State-supported, comprehensive, coed **Entrance** Noncompetitive **Setting** Suburban campus **Total enrollment** 13,786 **Application deadline** Rolling **Housing** No **Expenses** Tuition $5490 **Undergraduates** 56% women, 88% part-time, 86% 25 or older, 0.05% Native American, 3% Hispanic, 27% black, 7% Asian American or Pacific Islander **Most popular recent majors** Business administration; computer/information sciences; information sciences/systems **Academic program** Advanced placement, accelerated degree program, summer session, adult/continuing education programs **Contact** Ms. Anne Rahill, Technical Director of Admissions and Information, University of Maryland University College, University Boulevard at Adelphi Road, College Park, MD 20742-1600. Telephone: 301-985-7930 or toll-free 800-888-UMUC (in-state). Fax: 301-985-7678. Web site: http://www.umuc.edu/.

VILLA JULIE COLLEGE
STEVENSON, MARYLAND

General Independent, comprehensive, coed **Entrance** Moderately difficult **Setting** 60-acre suburban campus **Total enrollment** 1,951 **Student/faculty ratio** 13:1 **Application deadline** 7/15 **Housing** Yes **Expenses** Tuition $9240; Room only $3350 **Undergraduates** 75% women, 29% part-time, 37% 25 or older, 0.2% Native American, 1% Hispanic, 12% black, 2% Asian American or Pacific Islander **Most popular recent majors** Nursing; information sciences/systems; paralegal/legal assistant **Academic program** Average class size 18, English as a second language, advanced placement, self-designed majors, tutorials, honors program, summer session, adult/continuing education programs, internships **Contact** Mr. Mark Hergan, Director of Admissions, Villa Julie College, Green Spring Valley Road, Stevenson, MD 21153. Telephone: 410-486-7001. E-mail: admissions@vjc.edu. Web site: http://www.vjc.edu/.

WASHINGTON BIBLE COLLEGE
LANHAM, MARYLAND

General Independent nondenominational, 4-year, coed **Entrance** Moderately difficult **Setting** 63-acre suburban campus **Total enrollment** 366 **Student/faculty ratio** 12:1 **Application deadline** Rolling **Housing** Yes **Expenses** Tuition $5220; Room & Board $3990 **Undergraduates** 41% women, 60% part-time, 66% 25 or older, 1% Native American, 1% Hispanic, 48% black, 6% Asian American or Pacific Islander **Academic program** English as a second language, advanced placement, accelerated degree program, summer session, adult/continuing education programs, internships **Contact** Mr. Brad Bergeron, Director of Admissions, Washington Bible College, 6511 Princess Garden Parkway, Lanham, MD 20706-3599. Telephone: 301-552-1400 ext. 213 or toll-free 800-787-0256. Fax: 301-552-2775. E-mail: admiss@bible.edu. Web site: http://www.bible.edu/.

WASHINGTON COLLEGE
CHESTERTOWN, MARYLAND

General Independent, comprehensive, coed **Entrance** Moderately difficult **Setting** 120-acre small town campus **Total enrollment** 1,152 **Student/faculty ratio** 12:1 **Application deadline** 2/15 **Freshmen** 88% were admitted **Housing** Yes **Expenses** Tuition $18,250; Room & Board $5740 **Undergraduates** 56% women, 1% part-time, 2% 25 or older, 0.4% Native American, 1% Hispanic, 5% black, 2% Asian American or Pacific Islander **Most popular recent majors** English; psychology; business administration **Academic program** Average class size 14, English as a second language, advanced placement, self-designed majors, tutorials, internships **Contact** Mr. Kevin Coveney, Vice President for Admissions, Washington College, 300 Washington Avenue, Chestertown, MD 21620-1197. Telephone: 410-778-7700 or toll-free 800-422-1782. Fax: 410-778-

7287. E-mail: admissions_office@washcoll.edu. Web site: http://www.washcoll.edu/.

▶ **For more information, see page 546.**

WESTERN MARYLAND COLLEGE
WESTMINSTER, MARYLAND

General Independent, comprehensive, coed **Entrance** Moderately difficult **Setting** 160-acre small town campus **Total enrollment** 2,785 **Student/faculty ratio** 13:1 **Application deadline** 3/15 **Freshmen** 83% were admitted **Housing** Yes **Expenses** Tuition $17,730; Room & Board $5350 **Undergraduates** 55% women, 1% part-time, 5% 25 or older, 0.2% Native American, 2% Hispanic, 5% black, 2% Asian American or Pacific Islander **Most popular recent majors** Sociology; communications; biology **Academic program** Average class size 19, advanced placement, self-designed majors, tutorials, honors program, summer session, adult/continuing education programs, internships **Contact** Ms. M. Martha O'Connell, Dean of Admissions, Western Maryland College, 2 College Hill, Westminster, MD 21157-4390. Telephone: 410-857-2230 or toll-free 800-638-5005. Fax: 410-857-2729. E-mail: admissio@ns1.wmc.car.md.us. Web site: http://www.wmdc.edu/.

▶ **For more information, see page 553.**

MASSACHUSETTS

AMERICAN INTERNATIONAL COLLEGE
SPRINGFIELD, MASSACHUSETTS

General Independent, comprehensive, coed **Entrance** Moderately difficult **Setting** 58-acre urban campus **Total enrollment** 1,889 **Student/faculty ratio** 15:1 **Application deadline** Rolling **Freshmen** 81% were admitted **Housing** Yes **Expenses** Tuition $11,244; Room & Board $5692 **Undergraduates** 57% women, 15% part-time, 25% 25 or older, 0.4% Native American, 6% Hispanic, 17% black, 3% Asian American or Pacific Islander **Most popular recent majors** Criminal justice/law enforcement administration; accounting; nursing **Academic program** Average class size 25, English as a second language, advanced placement, accelerated degree program, tutorials, honors program, summer session, adult/continuing education programs, internships **Contact** Mr. Peter J. Miller, Dean of Admissions, American International College, 1000 State Street, Springfield, MA 01109-3189. Telephone: 413-747-6201 or toll-free 800-242-3142. Fax: 413-737-2803. E-mail: inquiry@www.aic.edu. Web site: http://www.aic.edu/.

AMHERST COLLEGE
AMHERST, MASSACHUSETTS

General Independent, 4-year, coed **Entrance** Most difficult **Setting** 964-acre small town campus **Total enrollment** 1,642 **Student/faculty ratio** 9:1 **Application deadline** 12/31 **Freshmen** 20% were admitted **Housing** Yes **Expenses** Tuition $23,027; Room & Board $6080 **Undergraduates** 47% women, 1% 25 or older, 0.3% Native American, 8% Hispanic, 6% black, 12% Asian American or Pacific Islander **Most popular recent majors** English; economics; biology **Academic program** Self-designed majors, tutorials, honors program **Contact** Ms. Jane E. Reynolds, Dean of Admission, Amherst College, PO Box 5000, Box 2231, Amherst, MA 01002. Telephone: 413-542-2328. Fax: 413-542-2040. E-mail: admissions@amherst.edu. Web site: http://www.amherst.edu/.

▶ **For more information, see page 389.**

ANNA MARIA COLLEGE
PAXTON, MASSACHUSETTS

General Independent Roman Catholic, comprehensive, coed **Entrance** Moderately difficult **Setting** 180-acre rural campus **Total enrollment** 1,668 **Student/faculty ratio** 15:1 **Application deadline** Rolling **Freshmen** 88% were admitted **Housing** Yes **Expenses** Tuition $12,240; Room & Board $5256 **Undergraduates** 60% women, 49% part-time, 0.5% Native American, 1% Hispanic, 1% black, 1% Asian American or Pacific Islander **Most popular recent majors** Criminal justice/law enforcement administration; business administration; elementary education **Academic program** English as a second language, advanced placement, accelerated degree program, self-designed majors, tutorials, summer session, adult/continuing education programs, internships **Contact** Ms. Christine L. Soverow, Director of Admissions, Anna Maria College, Box, Paxton, MA 01612. Telephone: 508-849-3360. E-mail: admissions@amc.anna-maria.edu. Web site: http://www.anna-maria.edu/.

ART INSTITUTE OF BOSTON
BOSTON, MASSACHUSETTS

General Independent, 4-year, coed **Entrance** Moderately difficult **Setting** Urban campus **Total enrollment** 447 **Student/faculty ratio** 13:1 **Application deadline** Rolling **Freshmen** 84% were admitted **Housing** Yes **Expenses** Tuition $11,770; Room & Board $7100 **Undergraduates** 51% women, 14% part-time, 20% 25 or older, 0% Native American, 2% Hispanic, 2% black, 2% Asian American or Pacific Islander **Most popular recent majors** Graphic design/commercial art/illustration; photography **Academic program** Av-

Art Institute of Boston *(continued)*

erage class size 14, English as a second language, advanced placement, self-designed majors, tutorials, honors program, summer session, adult/continuing education programs, internships **Contact** Ms. Diana Arcadipone, Dean of Admissions, Art Institute of Boston, 700 Beacon Street, Boston, MA 02215-2598. Telephone: 617-262-1223 ext. 304 or toll-free 800-773-0494 (in-state). Fax: 617-437-1226. E-mail: admissions@aiboston.edu. Web site: http://www.aiboston.edu/.

ASSUMPTION COLLEGE
WORCESTER, MASSACHUSETTS

General Independent Roman Catholic, comprehensive, coed **Entrance** Moderately difficult **Setting** 145-acre urban campus **Total enrollment** 2,592 **Student/faculty ratio** 14:1 **Application deadline** 3/1 **Freshmen** 81% were admitted **Housing** Yes **Expenses** Tuition $15,595; Room & Board $6400 **Undergraduates** 63% women, 20% part-time, 2% 25 or older, 0% Native American, 1% Hispanic, 0.2% black, 1% Asian American or Pacific Islander **Most popular recent majors** Rehabilitation therapy; psychology; English **Academic program** Average class size 27, English as a second language, advanced placement, self-designed majors, summer session, adult/continuing education programs, internships **Contact** Ms. Kathleen Murphy, Co-Director of Admissions, Assumption College, 500 Salisbury Street, PO Box 15005, Worcester, MA 01615-0005. Telephone: 508-767-7285 or toll-free 888-882-7786. Fax: 508-799-4412. E-mail: admis@assumption.edu. Web site: http://www.assumption.edu/.

ATLANTIC UNION COLLEGE
SOUTH LANCASTER, MASSACHUSETTS

General Independent Seventh-day Adventist, comprehensive, coed **Entrance** Moderately difficult **Setting** 314-acre small town campus **Total enrollment** 722 **Student/faculty ratio** 11:1 **Application deadline** 8/1 **Housing** Yes **Expenses** Tuition $12,000; Room & Board $3900 **Most popular recent majors** Elementary education; business administration; nursing **Academic program** English as a second language, advanced placement, tutorials, honors program, summer session, adult/continuing education programs, internships **Contact** Ms. Julie Lee, Associate Director for Enrollment Management, Atlantic Union College, PO Box 1000, South Lancaster, MA 01561-1000. Telephone: 978-368-2255 or toll-free 800-282-2030. Fax: 978-368-2015. E-mail: enroll@math.atlanticuc.edu. Web site: http://www.atlanticuc.edu/.

BABSON COLLEGE
WELLESLEY, MASSACHUSETTS

General Independent, comprehensive, coed **Entrance** Very difficult **Setting** 450-acre suburban campus **Total enrollment** 3,336 **Student/faculty ratio** 11:1 **Application deadline** 2/1 **Freshmen** 49% were admitted **Housing** Yes **Expenses** Tuition $20,365; Room & Board $8100 **Undergraduates** 2% 25 or older, 0.2% Native American, 5% Hispanic, 2% black, 6% Asian American or Pacific Islander **Most popular recent majors** Finance; business administration; business marketing and marketing management **Academic program** Average class size 26, advanced placement, accelerated degree program, self-designed majors, tutorials, honors program, summer session, internships **Contact** Dr. Charles Nolan, Dean of Undergraduate Admission, Babson College, Office of Undergraduate Admission, Mustard Hall, Babson Park, MA 02157-0310. Telephone: 781-239-5522 or toll-free 800-488-3696. Fax: 781-239-4006. E-mail: ugradadmission@babson.edu. Web site: http://www.babson.edu/.

BAY PATH COLLEGE
LONGMEADOW, MASSACHUSETTS

General Independent, 4-year, women only **Entrance** Moderately difficult **Setting** 44-acre suburban campus **Total enrollment** 614 **Student/faculty ratio** 12:1 **Application deadline** Rolling **Freshmen** 82% were admitted **Housing** Yes **Expenses** Tuition $11,800; Room & Board $6470 **Undergraduates** 31% part-time, 39% 25 or older, 5% Hispanic, 5% black, 1% Asian American or Pacific Islander **Most popular recent majors** Psychology; business; law and legal studies **Academic program** Average class size 25, English as a second language, advanced placement, self-designed majors, tutorials, honors program, summer session, adult/continuing education programs, internships **Contact** Mr. William F. Campanella, Associate Dean of Enrollment Services, Bay Path College, 588 Longmeadow Street, Longmeadow, MA 01106-2292. Telephone: 413-567-0621 ext. 335 or toll-free 800-782-7284. Fax: 413-567-0501. E-mail: admiss@baypath.edu. Web site: http://www.baypath.edu/.

► **For more information, see page 393.**

BECKER COLLEGE–LEICESTER CAMPUS
LEICESTER, MASSACHUSETTS

General Independent, 4-year, coed **Entrance** Minimally difficult **Setting** 75-acre small town campus **Total enrollment** 400 **Application deadline** Rolling **Housing** Yes **Expenses** Tuition $10,130; Room & Board $4890 **Undergraduates** 77% women, 6% part-time, 14% 25 or older, 0.3%

Native American, 4% Hispanic, 5% black, 0% Asian American or Pacific Islander **Most Popular Recent Major** Veterinary technology **Academic program** Average class size 25, advanced placement, self-designed majors, summer session, adult/continuing education programs, internships **Contact** Mr. Brian Davis, Dean of Admissions, Becker College-Leicester Campus, 61 Sever Street, Worcester, MA 01615. Telephone: 508-791-9241 ext. 245. Fax: 508-892-0330. E-mail: admissions@go.becker.edu. Web site: http://www.becker.edu/.

BECKER COLLEGE–WORCESTER CAMPUS
WORCESTER, MASSACHUSETTS

General Independent, 4-year, coed **Entrance** Minimally difficult **Setting** Urban campus **Total enrollment** 618 **Student/faculty ratio** 15:1 **Application deadline** Rolling **Freshmen** 73% were admitted **Housing** Yes **Expenses** Tuition $10,130; Room & Board $4890 **Undergraduates** 77% women, 20% part-time, 14% 25 or older **Most popular recent majors** Physical therapy assistant; nursing; criminal justice/law enforcement administration **Academic program** Average class size 25, English as a second language, advanced placement, summer session, adult/continuing education programs, internships **Contact** Mr. Brian Davis, Dean of Admissions, Becker College-Worcester Campus, 61 Sever Street, Worcester, MA 01615-0071. Telephone: 508-791-9241 ext. 245. Fax: 508-831-7505. E-mail: admissions@go.becker.edu. Web site: http://www.becker.edu/.

BENTLEY COLLEGE
WALTHAM, MASSACHUSETTS

General Independent, comprehensive, coed **Entrance** Moderately difficult **Setting** 110-acre suburban campus **Total enrollment** 5,946 **Student/faculty ratio** 18:1 **Application deadline** 2/15 **Housing** Yes **Expenses** Tuition $16,495; Room & Board $6755 **Undergraduates** 45% women, 23% part-time, 20% 25 or older, 0.1% Native American, 3% Hispanic, 3% black, 7% Asian American or Pacific Islander **Most popular recent majors** Accounting; finance; business marketing and marketing management **Academic program** Average class size 30, English as a second language, advanced placement, accelerated degree program, self-designed majors, honors program, summer session, adult/continuing education programs, internships **Contact** Ms. JoAnn McKenna, Director of Admissions, Bentley College, 175 Forest Street, Waltham, MA 02154-4705. Telephone: 781-891-2244 or toll-free 800-523-2354 (out-of-state). Fax: 781-891-3414. E-mail: moreinfo@bentley.edu. Web site: http://www.bentley.edu/.

BERKLEE COLLEGE OF MUSIC
BOSTON, MASSACHUSETTS

General Independent, 4-year, coed **Entrance** Moderately difficult **Setting** Urban campus **Total enrollment** 2,933 **Student/faculty ratio** 9:1 **Application deadline** Rolling **Freshmen** 73% were admitted **Housing** Yes **Expenses** Tuition $15,100; Room & Board $7890 **Undergraduates** 22% women, 10% part-time, 15% 25 or older, 0.2% Native American, 3% Hispanic, 3% black, 2% Asian American or Pacific Islander **Academic program** English as a second language, advanced placement, accelerated degree program, self-designed majors, summer session **Contact** Ms. Yvette Agan, Director of Admissions, Berklee College of Music, 1140 Boyleston Street, Boston, MA 02215-3693. Telephone: 617-266-1400 ext. 2367 or toll-free 800-421-0084. Fax: 617-747-2047. E-mail: admissions@berklee.edu. Web site: http://www.berklee.edu/.

BOSTON ARCHITECTURAL CENTER
BOSTON, MASSACHUSETTS

General Independent, comprehensive, coed **Entrance** Noncompetitive **Setting** Urban campus **Total enrollment** 854 **Student/faculty ratio** 6:1 **Application deadline** Rolling **Freshmen** 90% were admitted **Housing** No **Expenses** Tuition $5691 **Undergraduates** 24% women, 16% part-time, 67% 25 or older, 1% Native American, 3% Hispanic, 1% black, 2% Asian American or Pacific Islander **Academic program** Average class size 18, advanced placement, tutorials, summer session, adult/continuing education programs, internships **Contact** Ms. Kristen Keefe, Associate Director of Admission, Boston Architectural Center, 320 Newbury Street, Boston, MA 02115-2795. Telephone: 617-536-3170 ext. 256. Fax: 617-536-5829. E-mail: admission@the-bac.edu. Web site: http://www.the-bac.edu/.

BOSTON COLLEGE
CHESTNUT HILL, MASSACHUSETTS

General Independent Roman Catholic (Jesuit), university, coed **Entrance** Very difficult **Setting** 240-acre suburban campus **Total enrollment** 13,640 **Student/faculty ratio** 15:1 **Application deadline** 1/15 **Freshmen** 39% were admitted **Housing** Yes **Expenses** Tuition $20,292; Room & Board $7770 **Undergraduates** 53% women, 0.3% Native American, 5% Hispanic, 4% black, 8% Asian American or Pacific Islander **Most popular recent majors** English; finance; psychology **Academic program** Advanced placement, accelerated degree program, self-designed majors, tutorials, honors program, summer session, adult/continuing education programs, internships **Contact** Mr. John L. Mahoney Jr., Director of

Boston College *(continued)*

Undergraduate Admission, Boston College, 140 Commonwealth Avenue, Devlin Hall 208, Chestnut Hill, MA 02167-3809. Telephone: 617-552-3100 or toll-free 800-360-2522. Fax: 617-552-0798. E-mail: ugadmis@bc.edu. Web site: http://www.bc.edu/.

BOSTON CONSERVATORY
BOSTON, MASSACHUSETTS

General Independent, comprehensive, coed **Entrance** Moderately difficult **Setting** Urban campus **Total enrollment** 501 **Student/faculty ratio** 10:1 **Application deadline** Rolling **Freshmen** 47% were admitted **Housing** Yes **Expenses** Tuition $15,925; Room & Board $7150 **Undergraduates** 73% women, 2% part-time, 1% Native American, 2% Hispanic, 4% black, 3% Asian American or Pacific Islander **Most popular recent majors** Music; theater arts/drama; dance **Academic program** English as a second language, advanced placement, summer session, adult/continuing education programs **Contact** Mr. Richard Wallace, Director of Enrollment, Boston Conservatory, 8 The Fenway, Boston, MA 02215. Telephone: 617-912-9115. Fax: 617-536-3176.

BOSTON UNIVERSITY
BOSTON, MASSACHUSETTS

General Independent, university, coed **Entrance** Very difficult **Setting** 132-acre urban campus **Total enrollment** 29,387 **Student/faculty ratio** 13:1 **Application deadline** 1/15 **Freshmen** 55% were admitted **Housing** Yes **Expenses** Tuition $23,148; Room & Board $7870 **Undergraduates** 57% women, 4% part-time, 6% 25 or older, 0.2% Native American, 5% Hispanic, 3% black, 11% Asian American or Pacific Islander **Most popular recent majors** Social sciences; business administration; mass communications **Academic program** English as a second language, advanced placement, accelerated degree program, self-designed majors, tutorials, honors program, summer session, adult/continuing education programs, internships **Contact** Ms. Kelly Walter, Senior Associate Director of Admissions, Boston University, 121 Bay State Road, Boston, MA 02215. Telephone: 617-353-2300. Fax: 617-353-9695. E-mail: admissions@bu.edu. Web site: http://www.bu.edu/.

BRADFORD COLLEGE
HAVERHILL, MASSACHUSETTS

General Independent, 4-year, coed **Entrance** Moderately difficult **Setting** 80-acre suburban campus **Total enrollment** 586 **Student/faculty ratio** 12:1 **Application deadline** Rolling **Freshmen** 2% were admitted **Housing** Yes **Expenses** Tuition $16,315; Room & Board $6720 **Undergraduates** 63% women, 4% part-time, 11% 25 or older, 0.3% Native American, 4% Hispanic, 5% black, 2% Asian American or Pacific Islander **Most popular recent majors** Psychology; art; business marketing and marketing management **Academic program** English as a second language, advanced placement, accelerated degree program, self-designed majors, tutorials, honors program, summer session, adult/continuing education programs, internships **Contact** Mr. James M. Abbuhl, Vice President for Enrollment Management, Bradford College, 320 South Main Street, Haverhill, MA 01835-7393. Telephone: 978-372-7161 ext. 5282 or toll-free 800-336-6448. Fax: 978-521-0480. E-mail: admission@bnet.bradford.edu. Web site: http://www.Bradford.edu/.

BRANDEIS UNIVERSITY
WALTHAM, MASSACHUSETTS

General Independent, university, coed **Entrance** Very difficult **Setting** 235-acre suburban campus **Total enrollment** 4,276 **Student/faculty ratio** 10:1 **Application deadline** 2/1 **Freshmen** 55% were admitted **Housing** Yes **Expenses** Tuition $22,851; Room & Board $6970 **Undergraduates** 56% women, 0.1% part-time, 2% 25 or older, 0.2% Native American, 3% Hispanic, 3% black, 9% Asian American or Pacific Islander **Most popular recent majors** Psychology; economics; biology **Academic program** Average class size 17, English as a second language, advanced placement, accelerated degree program, self-designed majors, tutorials, honors program, summer session, adult/continuing education programs, internships **Contact** Mr. Michael Kalafatas, Director of Admissions, Brandeis University, 415 South Street, Waltham, MA 02254-9110. Telephone: 781-736-3500 or toll-free 800-622-0622 (out-of-state). Fax: 781-736-3536. E-mail: sendinfo@brandeis.edu. Web site: http://www.brandeis.edu/.

BRIDGEWATER STATE COLLEGE
BRIDGEWATER, MASSACHUSETTS

General State-supported, comprehensive, coed **Entrance** Moderately difficult **Setting** 235-acre suburban campus **Total enrollment** 8,926 **Student/faculty ratio** 19:1 **Application deadline** 3/1 **Freshmen** 69% were admitted **Housing** Yes **Expenses** Tuition $3324; Room & Board $4343 **Undergraduates** 60% women, 17% part-time, 21% 25 or older, 0.4% Native American, 1% Hispanic, 3% black, 1% Asian American or Pacific Islander **Most popular recent majors** Business administration; physical education; psychology **Academic program** Average class size 30, English as a second language, advanced placement, self-designed majors, tutorials, honors program, summer session, adult/continuing education programs, internships **Contact** Mr. James F. Plotner Jr., Associate Dean of Academic Admissions, Bridgewater State College, Admission Office, Bridgewater, MA 02325-0001. Telephone: 508-697-1237 or toll-free 800-698-2006. Fax: 508-697-1746. E-mail: admission@bridgew.edu. Web site: http://www.bridgew.edu/.

CAMBRIDGE COLLEGE
CAMBRIDGE, MASSACHUSETTS

General Independent, comprehensive, coed **Entrance** Minimally difficult **Total enrollment** 1,679 **Student/faculty ratio** 17:1 **Application deadline** Rolling **Housing** No **Expenses** Tuition $7620 **Contact** Ms. Joy King, Associate Director of Enrollment Services, Cambridge College, 1000 Massachusetts Avenue, Cambridge, MA 02138-5304. Telephone: 617-868-1000 or toll-free 800-877-4723. Fax: 617-349-3545. E-mail: enroll@idea.cambridge.edu. Web site: http:// www.cambridge.edu/.

CLARK UNIVERSITY
WORCESTER, MASSACHUSETTS

General Independent, university, coed **Entrance** Moderately difficult **Setting** 50-acre urban campus **Total enrollment** 3,083 **Student/faculty ratio** 11:1 **Application deadline** 2/1 **Freshmen** 77% were admitted **Housing** Yes **Expenses** Tuition $20,940; Room & Board $4250 **Undergraduates** 59% women, 6% part-time, 26% 25 or older, 0.2% Native American, 3% Hispanic, 3% black, 5% Asian American or Pacific Islander **Most popular recent majors** Psychology; political science; business administration **Academic program** English as a second language, advanced placement, accelerated degree program, self-designed majors, tutorials, honors program, summer session, adult/continuing education programs, internships **Contact** Mr. Harold M. Wingood, Dean of Admissions, Clark University, 950 Main Street, Worcester, MA 01610-1477. Telephone: 508-793-7431 or toll-free 800-GO-CLARK (out-of-state). Fax: 508-793-8821. E-mail: admissions@clarku.edu. Web site: http://www.clarku.edu/.

COLLEGE OF OUR LADY OF THE ELMS
CHICOPEE, MASSACHUSETTS

General Independent Roman Catholic, comprehensive, coed **Entrance** Moderately difficult **Setting** 32-acre suburban campus **Total enrollment** 1,098 **Student/faculty ratio** 12:1 **Application deadline** Rolling **Freshmen** 93% were admitted **Housing** Yes **Expenses** Tuition $13,450; Room & Board $5000 **Undergraduates** 28% 25 or older **Most popular recent majors** Nursing; social work; education **Academic program** English as a second language, advanced placement, accelerated degree program, self-designed majors, tutorials, honors program, summer session, adult/continuing education programs, internships **Contact** Ms. Cori L. Nevers, Director of Admission, College of Our Lady of the Elms, 291 Springfield Street, Chicopee, MA 01013-2839. Telephone: 413-592-3189 ext. 350 or toll-free 800-255-ELMS. Fax: 413-594-2781. E-mail: admissions@elms.edu. Web site: http://www.elms.edu/.

COLLEGE OF THE HOLY CROSS
WORCESTER, MASSACHUSETTS

General Independent Roman Catholic (Jesuit), 4-year, coed **Entrance** Very difficult **Setting** 174-acre suburban campus **Total enrollment** 2,730 **Student/faculty ratio** 13:1 **Application deadline** 1/15 **Freshmen** 50% were admitted **Housing** Yes **Expenses** Tuition $22,005; Room & Board $7100 **Undergraduates** 53% women, 0% 25 or older, 0.1% Native American, 3% Hispanic, 3% black, 3% Asian American or Pacific Islander **Most popular recent majors** English; psychology; economics **Academic program** Average class size 30, advanced placement, accelerated degree program, self-designed majors, tutorials, honors program, internships **Contact** Ms. Ann Bowe McDermott, Director of Admissions, College of the Holy Cross, 1 College Street, Worcester, MA 01610-2395. Telephone: 508-793-2443 or toll-free 800-442-2421. Fax: 508-793-3888. E-mail: admissions@holycross.edu. Web site: http://www.holycross.edu/.

CURRY COLLEGE
MILTON, MASSACHUSETTS

General Independent, comprehensive, coed **Entrance** Moderately difficult **Setting** 120-acre suburban campus **Total enrollment** 1,909 **Student/faculty ratio** 12:1 **Application deadline** 4/1 **Freshmen** 83% were admitted **Housing** Yes **Expenses** Tuition $15,700; Room & Board $5815 **Undergraduates** 54% women, 31% part-time, 13% 25 or older, 0.3% Native American, 2% Hispanic, 4% black, 1% Asian American or Pacific Islander **Most popular recent majors** Business administration; mass communications; nursing **Academic program** Advanced placement, accelerated degree program, self-designed majors, tutorials, honors program, summer session, adult/continuing education programs, internships **Contact** Ms. Janet Cromie Kelly, Dean of Admissions and Financial Aid, Curry College, 1071 Blue Hill Avenue, Milton, MA 02186-9984. Telephone: 617-333-2210 or toll-free 800-669-0686. Fax: 617-

Curry College *(continued)*

333-6860. E-mail: curryadm@curry.edu. Web site: http://www.curry.edu:8080/.

EASTERN NAZARENE COLLEGE
QUINCY, MASSACHUSETTS

General Independent, comprehensive, coed, affiliated with Church of the Nazarene **Entrance** Moderately difficult **Setting** 15-acre suburban campus **Total enrollment** 1,508 **Student/faculty ratio** 12:1 **Application deadline** Rolling **Housing** Yes **Expenses** Tuition $11,440; Room & Board $3975 **Undergraduates** 57% women, 1% part-time, 7% 25 or older **Most popular recent majors** Business administration; education; psychology **Academic program** Average class size 45, English as a second language, advanced placement, accelerated degree program, tutorials, summer session, adult/continuing education programs, internships **Contact** Mr. Keith Conant, Director of Admissions, Eastern Nazarene College, 23 East Elm Avenue, Quincy, MA 02170-2999. Telephone: 617-745-3868. Fax: 617-745-3490. E-mail: admissions@enc.edu. Web site: http://www.enc.edu/.

ELMS COLLEGE
See College of Our Lady of the Elms

EMERSON COLLEGE
BOSTON, MASSACHUSETTS

General Independent, comprehensive, coed **Entrance** Moderately difficult **Setting** Urban campus **Total enrollment** 3,885 **Student/faculty ratio** 17:1 **Application deadline** 2/1 **Freshmen** 60% were admitted **Housing** Yes **Expenses** Tuition $17,826; Room & Board $8250 **Undergraduates** 58% women, 19% part-time, 8% 25 or older, 0.3% Native American, 3% Hispanic, 3% black, 2% Asian American or Pacific Islander **Most popular recent majors** Mass communications; theater arts/drama; public relations **Academic program** Average class size 35, advanced placement, self-designed majors, tutorials, honors program, summer session, adult/continuing education programs, internships **Contact** Ms. Sara Ramirez, Acting Director of Admission, Emerson College, 100 Beacon Street, Boston, MA 02116-1511. Telephone: 617-824-8600. Fax: 617-824-8609. E-mail: admission@emerson.edu. Web site: http://www.emerson.edu/admiss/.

▶ **For more information, see page 430.**

EMMANUEL COLLEGE
BOSTON, MASSACHUSETTS

General Independent Roman Catholic, comprehensive, women only **Entrance** Moderately difficult **Setting** 16-acre urban campus **Total enrollment** 1,552 **Student/faculty ratio** 12:1 **Application deadline** Rolling **Freshmen** 84% were admitted **Housing** Yes **Expenses** Tuition $14,550; Room & Board $6785 **Undergraduates** 46% part-time, 66% 25 or older, 0.2% Native American, 4% Hispanic, 9% black, 3% Asian American or Pacific Islander **Most popular recent majors** Interdisciplinary studies; biology; art **Academic program** English as a second language, advanced placement, accelerated degree program, self-designed majors, honors program, summer session, adult/continuing education programs, internships **Contact** Ms. Meg Miller, Director of Admissions, Emmanuel College, 400 The Fenway, Boston, MA 02115. Telephone: 617-735-9715. Fax: 617-735-9801. E-mail: enroll@emmanuel.edu. Web site: http://www.emmanuel.edu/.

ENDICOTT COLLEGE
BEVERLY, MASSACHUSETTS

General Independent, comprehensive, coed **Entrance** Moderately difficult **Setting** 150-acre suburban campus **Total enrollment** 1,270 **Student/faculty ratio** 12:1 **Application deadline** Rolling **Freshmen** 83% were admitted **Housing** Yes **Expenses** Tuition $14,040; Room & Board $7160 **Undergraduates** 23% 25 or older, 0.5% Native American, 3% Hispanic, 1% black, 1% Asian American or Pacific Islander **Most popular recent majors** Nursing; psychology; physical therapy assistant **Academic program** English as a second language, advanced placement, self-designed majors, tutorials, honors program, summer session, adult/continuing education programs, internships **Contact** Mr. Thomas J. Redman, Vice President of Admissions and Financial Aid, Endicott College, 376 Hale Street, Beverly, MA 01915-2096. Telephone: 978-921-1000 or toll-free 800-325-1114 (out-of-state). Fax: 978-927-0084. E-mail: admissio@endicott.edu. Web site: http://www.endicott.edu/.

FITCHBURG STATE COLLEGE
FITCHBURG, MASSACHUSETTS

General State-supported, comprehensive, coed **Entrance** Moderately difficult **Setting** 45-acre small town campus **Total enrollment** 5,847 **Student/faculty ratio** 12:1 **Application deadline** Rolling **Freshmen** 72% were admitted **Housing** Yes **Expenses** Tuition $3346; Room & Board $4410 **Undergraduates** 57% women, 19% part-time, 18% 25 or older **Most Popular Recent Major** Business administration **Academic program** Average class size 20, advanced placement, accelerated degree program, self-designed majors, honors program, summer session, adult/continuing education programs, internships **Contact** Mr. James Dupont, Director of Admissions, Fitchburg

State College, 160 Pearl Street, Fitchburg, MA 01420-2697. Telephone: 978-665-3144 or toll-free 800-705-9692. Fax: 978-665-4540. E-mail: admissions@fsc.edu. Web site: http://www.fsc.edu/.

▶ **For more information, see page 435.**

FRAMINGHAM STATE COLLEGE
FRAMINGHAM, MASSACHUSETTS

General State-supported, comprehensive, coed **Entrance** Moderately difficult **Setting** 73-acre suburban campus **Total enrollment** 5,315 **Application deadline** 3/15 **Freshmen** 70% were admitted **Housing** Yes **Expenses** Tuition $3150; Room & Board $3944 **Undergraduates** 65% women, 19% part-time, 20% 25 or older, 0.5% Native American, 3% Hispanic, 3% black, 2% Asian American or Pacific Islander **Most popular recent majors** Business administration; psychology; elementary education **Academic program** Average class size 23, English as a second language, advanced placement, self-designed majors, honors program, summer session, adult/continuing education programs, internships **Contact** Dr. Philip M. Dooher, Dean of Admissions and Enrollment Services, Framingham State College, 100 State Street, PO Box 9101, Framingham, MA 01701-9101. Telephone: 508-626-4500. Fax: 508-626-4017. E-mail: admiss@frc.mass.edu. Web site: http://www.framingham.edu/.

GORDON COLLEGE
WENHAM, MASSACHUSETTS

General Independent nondenominational, comprehensive, coed **Entrance** Moderately difficult **Setting** 500-acre small town campus **Total enrollment** 1,375 **Student/faculty ratio** 18:1 **Application deadline** Rolling **Freshmen** 79% were admitted **Housing** Yes **Expenses** Tuition $15,760; Room & Board $4950 **Undergraduates** 65% women, 2% part-time, 3% 25 or older, 0.2% Native American, 2% Hispanic, 1% black, 2% Asian American or Pacific Islander **Most popular recent majors** English; psychology; biblical studies **Academic program** Average class size 31, advanced placement, self-designed majors, tutorials, honors program, internships **Contact** Mrs. Pamela B. Lazarakis, Dean of Admissions, Gordon College, 255 Grapevine Road, Wenham, MA 01984-1899. Telephone: 978-927-2300 ext. 4217 or toll-free 800-343-1379. Fax: 978-524-3704. E-mail: admissions@hope.gordonc.edu. Web site: http://www.gordonc.edu/.

HAMPSHIRE COLLEGE
AMHERST, MASSACHUSETTS

General Independent, 4-year, coed **Entrance** Moderately difficult **Setting** 800-acre rural campus **Total enrollment** 1,152 **Student/faculty ratio** 12:1 **Application deadline** 2/1 **Freshmen** 66% were admitted **Housing** Yes **Expenses** Tuition $23,780; Room & Board $6225 **Undergraduates** 57% women, 3% 25 or older, 0.3% Native American, 3% Hispanic, 4% black, 4% Asian American or Pacific Islander **Most popular recent majors** Art; theater arts/drama; creative writing **Academic program** Average class size 17, advanced placement, self-designed majors, internships **Contact** Ms. Audrey Smith, Director of Admissions, Hampshire College, 839 West Street, Amherst, MA 01002. Telephone: 413-582-5471. Fax: 413-582-5631. E-mail: admissions@hampshire.edu. Web site: http://www.hampshire.edu/.

HARVARD UNIVERSITY
CAMBRIDGE, MASSACHUSETTS

General Independent, university, coed **Entrance** Most difficult **Setting** 380-acre urban campus **Total enrollment** 17,425 **Student/faculty ratio** 8:1 **Application deadline** 1/1 **Freshmen** 13% were admitted **Housing** Yes **Expenses** Tuition $22,802; Room & Board $7278 **Undergraduates** 1% 25 or older, 1% Native American, 8% Hispanic, 8% black, 18% Asian American or Pacific Islander **Most popular recent majors** Economics; biology; political science **Academic program** English as a second language, advanced placement, accelerated degree program, self-designed majors, tutorials, honors program, summer session, adult/continuing education programs **Contact** Office of Admissions and Financial Aid, Harvard University, Byerly Hall, 8 Garden Street, Cambridge, MA 02138. Telephone: 617-495-1551. E-mail: college@harvard.edu. Web site: http://www.fas.harvard.edu/.

HEBREW COLLEGE
BROOKLINE, MASSACHUSETTS

General Independent Jewish, comprehensive, coed **Entrance** Noncompetitive **Setting** 3-acre suburban campus **Application deadline** 4/15 **Housing** No **Expenses** Tuition $10,590 **Academic program** Tutorials, summer session, adult/continuing education programs, internships **Contact** Mrs. Norma Frankel, Registrar, Hebrew College, 43 Hawes Street, Brookline, MA 02146-5495. Telephone: 617-278-4944. Fax: 617-734-9769. E-mail: nfrankel@lynx.neu.edu. Web site: http://www.hebrewcollege.edu.

HELLENIC COLLEGE
BROOKLINE, MASSACHUSETTS

General Independent Greek Orthodox, 4-year, coed **Entrance** Minimally difficult **Setting** 52-acre suburban campus **Total enrollment** 172 **Stu-**

Hellenic College *(continued)*

dent/faculty ratio 6:1 **Application deadline** Rolling **Freshmen** 63% were admitted **Housing** Yes **Expenses** Tuition $7815; Room & Board $5900 **Undergraduates** 38% women, 14% 25 or older, 0% Native American, 2% Hispanic, 0% black, 0% Asian American or Pacific Islander **Most Popular Recent Majors** Religious studies; elementary education; individual/family development **Academic program** Average class size 20, advanced placement, tutorials, summer session, internships **Contact** Dr. John Klentos, Director of Admissions and Records, Hellenic College, 50 Goddard Avenue, Brookline, MA 02146-7496. Telephone: 617-731-3500 ext. 260. Fax: 617-232-7819. E-mail: admissions@hchc.edu. Web site: http://www.hchc.edu/.

LASELL COLLEGE
NEWTON, MASSACHUSETTS

General Independent, 4-year, coed **Entrance** Moderately difficult **Setting** 50-acre suburban campus **Total enrollment** 638 **Student/faculty ratio** 10:1 **Application deadline** Rolling **Housing** Yes **Expenses** Tuition $14,500; Room & Board $7200 **Undergraduates** 100% women, 18% part-time, 24% 25 or older, 0% Native American, 5% Hispanic, 8% black, 4% Asian American or Pacific Islander **Most popular recent majors** Education; fashion merchandising; physical therapy **Academic program** Average class size 14, English as a second language, advanced placement, self-designed majors, tutorials, honors program, internships **Contact** Mr. David Eddy, Director of Admission, Lasell College, 1844 Commonwealth Avenue, Newton, MA 02166-2709. Telephone: 617-243-2225 or toll-free 888-LASELL-4. Fax: 617-796-4343. E-mail: info@lasell.edu. Web site: http://www.lasell.edu.

LESLEY COLLEGE
CAMBRIDGE, MASSACHUSETTS

General Independent, comprehensive, women only **Entrance** Moderately difficult **Setting** 5-acre urban campus **Total enrollment** 6,128 **Student/faculty ratio** 14:1 **Application deadline** 3/15 **Freshmen** 84% were admitted **Housing** Yes **Expenses** Tuition $14,606; Room & Board $6700 **Undergraduates** 28% part-time, 50% 25 or older, 0.3% Native American, 4% Hispanic, 6% black, 2% Asian American or Pacific Islander **Most popular recent majors** Education; human services; business administration **Academic program** Average class size 16, English as a second language, advanced placement, summer session, adult/continuing education programs, internships **Contact** Ms. Jane A. Raley, Director of Women's College Admissions, Lesley College, 29 Everett Street, Cambridge, MA 02138-2790. Telephone: 617-349-8800 or toll-free 800-999-1959 ext. 8800. Fax: 617-349-8150. E-mail: ugadm@mail.lesley.edu. Web site: http://www.lesley.edu/.

MASSACHUSETTS COLLEGE OF ART
BOSTON, MASSACHUSETTS

General State-supported, comprehensive, coed **Entrance** Very difficult **Setting** 5-acre urban campus **Total enrollment** 2,289 **Student/faculty ratio** 12:1 **Application deadline** 3/1 **Freshmen** 47% were admitted **Housing** Yes **Expenses** Tuition $3964; Room & Board $6348 **Undergraduates** 59% women, 16% part-time, 29% 25 or older, 0.1% Native American, 3% Hispanic, 2% black, 4% Asian American or Pacific Islander **Most popular recent majors** Painting; graphic design/commercial art/illustration **Academic program** Average class size 22, advanced placement, self-designed majors, summer session, internships **Contact** Ms. Kay Ransdell, Dean of Admissions, Massachusetts College of Art, 621 Huntington Avenue, Boston, MA 02115-5882. Telephone: 617-232-1555 ext. 235. Fax: 617-739-9744. E-mail: admissions@massart.edu.

MASSACHUSETTS COLLEGE OF LIBERAL ARTS
NORTH ADAMS, MASSACHUSETTS

General State-supported, comprehensive, coed **Entrance** Moderately difficult **Setting** 80-acre small town campus **Total enrollment** 1,679 **Student/faculty ratio** 14:1 **Application deadline** Rolling **Freshmen** 68% were admitted **Housing** Yes **Expenses** Tuition $3437; Room & Board $4840 **Undergraduates** 59% women, 17% part-time, 24% 25 or older, 0.3% Native American, 1% Hispanic, 3% black, 1% Asian American or Pacific Islander **Most popular recent majors** Business administration; English; sociology **Academic program** Average class size 22, advanced placement, self-designed majors, tutorials, honors program, summer session, internships **Contact** Ms. Denise Richardello, Dean of Enrollment Management, Massachusetts College of Liberal Arts, 375 Church Street, North Adams, MA 01247-4100. Telephone: 413-662-5410 ext. 5416 or toll-free 800-292-6632 (in-state). Fax: 413-662-5179. E-mail: admissions@mcla.mass.edu. Web site: http://www.mcla.mass.edu/.

MASSACHUSETTS COLLEGE OF PHARMACY AND ALLIED HEALTH SCIENCES
BOSTON, MASSACHUSETTS

General Independent, university, coed **Entrance** Moderately difficult **Setting** 2-acre urban campus **Total enrollment** 1,666 **Student/**

faculty ratio 14:1 **Application deadline** 3/1 **Freshmen** 59% were admitted **Housing** Yes **Expenses** Tuition $14,508; Room & Board $7500 **Undergraduates** 63% women, 20% part-time, 1% Native American, 2% Hispanic, 5% black, 29% Asian American or Pacific Islander **Most popular recent majors** Pharmacy; nursing; nuclear medical technology **Academic program** English as a second language, advanced placement, tutorials, summer session, adult/continuing education programs, internships **Contact** Mr. Joseph M. Hemmings, Director of Admission, Massachusetts College of Pharmacy and Allied Health Sciences, 179 Longwood Avenue, Boston, MA 02115-5896. Telephone: 617-732-2850 ext. 2791 or toll-free 800-225-5506 (out-of-state). Fax: 617-732-2801. Web site: http://www.mcp.edu/.

MASSACHUSETTS INSTITUTE OF TECHNOLOGY
CAMBRIDGE, MASSACHUSETTS

General Independent, university, coed **Entrance** Most difficult **Setting** 154-acre urban campus **Total enrollment** 9,880 **Student/faculty ratio** 5:1 **Application deadline** 1/1 **Freshmen** 25% were admitted **Housing** Yes **Expenses** Tuition $23,100; Room & Board $5610 **Undergraduates** 40% women, 1% part-time, 1% 25 or older, 1% Native American, 10% Hispanic, 6% black, 28% Asian American or Pacific Islander **Most popular recent majors** Electrical/electronics engineering; computer science; mechanical engineering **Academic program** English as a second language, advanced placement, accelerated degree program, self-designed majors, tutorials, summer session, internships **Contact** Ms. Marilee Jones, Dean of Admissions, Massachusetts Institute of Technology, 77 Massachusetts Avenue, Cambridge, MA 02139-4307. Telephone: 617-253-4791. Fax: 617-258-8304. E-mail: mitfrosh@mit.edu. Web site: http://web.mit.edu/.

MASSACHUSETTS MARITIME ACADEMY
BUZZARDS BAY, MASSACHUSETTS

General State-supported, 4-year, coed **Entrance** Moderately difficult **Setting** 55-acre small town campus **Total enrollment** 750 **Student/faculty ratio** 14:1 **Application deadline** Rolling **Freshmen** 82% were admitted **Housing** Yes **Expenses** Tuition $3023; Room & Board $3960 **Undergraduates** 9% 25 or older **Most Popular Recent Major** Naval architecture/marine engineering **Academic program** Advanced placement, tutorials, adult/continuing education programs, internships **Contact** Cmdr. Keith D. Rabine, Dean of Enrollment Services, Massachusetts Maritime Academy, 101 Academy Drive, Buzzards Bay, MA 02532-1803. Telephone: 508-830-5000 or toll-free 800-544-3411. Fax: 508-830-5077. E-mail: mmadmit@bridge.mma.mass.edu. Web site: http://www.mma.mass.edu/.

MERRIMACK COLLEGE
NORTH ANDOVER, MASSACHUSETTS

General Independent Roman Catholic, comprehensive, coed **Entrance** Moderately difficult **Setting** 220-acre small town campus **Total enrollment** 2,732 **Student/faculty ratio** 14:1 **Application deadline** 3/1 **Freshmen** 80% were admitted **Housing** Yes **Expenses** Tuition $15,110; Room & Board $7200 **Undergraduates** 50% women, 23% part-time, 3% 25 or older **Most popular recent majors** Business administration; psychology; biology **Academic program** Average class size 20, English as a second language, advanced placement, self-designed majors, honors program, summer session, adult/continuing education programs, internships **Contact** Ms. MaryLou Retelle, Dean of Admissions and Financial Aid, Merrimack College, 315 Turnpike Street, North Andover, MA 01845-5800. Telephone: 978-837-5100 ext. 5120. Fax: 978-837-5222. E-mail: admissions@merrimack.edu. Web site: http://www.merrimack.edu/.

MONTSERRAT COLLEGE OF ART
BEVERLY, MASSACHUSETTS

General Independent, 4-year, coed **Entrance** Moderately difficult **Setting** 10-acre suburban campus **Total enrollment** 333 **Application deadline** 7/15 **Housing** Yes **Expenses** Tuition $11,680; Room only $3300 **Undergraduates** 50% women, 8% part-time, 20% 25 or older, 1% Native American, 2% Hispanic, 2% black, 3% Asian American or Pacific Islander **Most popular recent majors** Drawing; graphic design/commercial art/illustration **Academic program** Average class size 20, English as a second language, advanced placement, self-designed majors, honors program, summer session, adult/continuing education programs, internships **Contact** Mr. Stephen M. Negron, Director of Recruitment, Montserrat College of Art, 23 Essex Street, Box 26, Beverly, MA 01915. Telephone: 978-921-4242 ext. 1153 or toll-free 800-836-0487. Fax: 978-922-4268. E-mail: admiss@montserrat.edu. Web site: http://www.montserrat.edu/.

MOUNT HOLYOKE COLLEGE
SOUTH HADLEY, MASSACHUSETTS

General Independent, 4-year, women only **Entrance** Very difficult **Setting** 800-acre small town campus **Total enrollment** 1,860 **Student/faculty ratio** 10:1 **Application deadline** 1/15 **Freshmen** 61% were admitted **Housing** Yes **Ex-**

Mount Holyoke College *(continued)*

penses Tuition $22,340; Room & Board $6525 **Undergraduates** 3% part-time, 5% 25 or older, 1% Native American, 5% Hispanic, 4% black, 8% Asian American or Pacific Islander **Most Popular Recent Majors** English; psychology; biology **Academic program** Advanced placement, accelerated degree program, self-designed majors, tutorials, honors program, adult/continuing education programs, internships **Contact** Ms. Anita Smith, Director of Admission, Mount Holyoke College, 50 College Street, South Hadley, MA 01075-1414. Telephone: 413-538-2023. Fax: 413-538-2409. E-mail: admissions@mtholyoke.edu. Web site: http://www.mtholyoke.edu/.

NEW ENGLAND COLLEGE OF OPTOMETRY
BOSTON, MASSACHUSETTS

General Independent, upper-level, coed **Contact** Mr. Lawrence W. Shattuck, Director of Student Recruitment, New England College of Optometry, 424 Beacon Street, Boston, MA 02115-1100. Telephone: 617-236-6210 or toll-free 800-824-5526.

NEW ENGLAND CONSERVATORY OF MUSIC
BOSTON, MASSACHUSETTS

General Independent, comprehensive, coed **Entrance** Very difficult **Setting** Urban campus **Total enrollment** 800 **Student/faculty ratio** 4:1 **Application deadline** 1/2 **Freshmen** 41% were admitted **Housing** Yes **Expenses** Tuition $18,000; Room & Board $8375 **Undergraduates** 50% women, 9% part-time, 6% 25 or older, 0.3% Native American, 3% Hispanic, 5% black, 9% Asian American or Pacific Islander **Most popular recent majors** Music (voice and choral/opera performance); music (piano and organ performance); stringed instruments **Academic program** Average class size 20, English as a second language, advanced placement, summer session, adult/continuing education programs, internships **Contact** Ms. Allison T. Ball, Dean of Enrollment Services, New England Conservatory of Music, 290 Huntington Avenue, Boston, MA 02115-5000. Telephone: 617-262-1120 ext. 430. Fax: 617-262-0500. Web site: http://copernicus.bbn.com/nec/.

THE NEW ENGLAND SCHOOL OF ART AND DESIGN AT SUFFOLK UNIVERSITY
See Suffolk University

NICHOLS COLLEGE
DUDLEY, MASSACHUSETTS

General Independent, comprehensive, coed **Entrance** Moderately difficult **Setting** 210-acre rural campus **Total enrollment** 1,542 **Student/faculty ratio** 22:1 **Application deadline** Rolling **Freshmen** 84% were admitted **Housing** Yes **Expenses** Tuition $11,325; Room & Board $6400 **Undergraduates** 49% women, 46% part-time, 0.2% Native American, 2% Hispanic, 2% black, 1% Asian American or Pacific Islander **Most popular recent majors** Business administration; accounting; business marketing and marketing management **Academic program** Average class size 23, advanced placement, summer session, adult/continuing education programs, internships **Contact** Ms. Louise Sisley, Records Assistant, Nichols College, PO Box 5000, Dudley, MA 01571. Telephone: 508-943-2055 ext. 2275 or toll-free 800-470-3379. Fax: 508-943-9885. E-mail: admissions@nichols.edu. Web site: http://www.nichols.edu/.

NORTH ADAMS STATE COLLEGE
See Massachusetts College of Liberal Arts

NORTHEASTERN UNIVERSITY
BOSTON, MASSACHUSETTS

General Independent, university, coed **Entrance** Moderately difficult **Setting** 57-acre urban campus **Total enrollment** 24,325 **Student/faculty ratio** 11:1 **Application deadline** Rolling **Freshmen** 70% were admitted **Housing** Yes **Expenses** Tuition $16,511; Room & Board $8265 **Undergraduates** 50% women, 39% part-time, 7% 25 or older, 0.3% Native American, 2% Hispanic, 5% black, 5% Asian American or Pacific Islander **Most popular recent majors** Criminal justice/law enforcement administration; nursing; physical therapy **Academic program** English as a second language, advanced placement, accelerated degree program, self-designed majors, tutorials, honors program, summer session, adult/continuing education programs, internships **Contact** Mr. Alan Kines, Dean of Admissions, Northeastern University, 360 Huntington Avenue, Boston, MA 02115-5096. Telephone: 617-373-2200. Fax: 617-373-8780. E-mail: admissions@neu.edu. Web site: http://www.neu.edu/.

► **For more information, see page 484.**

PINE MANOR COLLEGE
CHESTNUT HILL, MASSACHUSETTS

General Independent, comprehensive, women only **Entrance** Moderately difficult **Setting** 79-acre suburban campus **Total enrollment** 324 **Application deadline** Rolling **Freshmen** 88% were admitted **Housing** Yes **Expenses** Tuition $10,700; Room & Board $6900 **Undergraduates** 9% part-time, 5% 25 or older, 0.3% Native American, 7% Hispanic, 14% black, 4% Asian American or Pacific Islander **Most Popular Recent Major** Business administration **Academic program** Average class size 10, English as a second language, advanced placement, accelerated degree program, self-designed majors, tutorials, honors program, summer session, adult/continuing education programs, internships **Contact** Ms. Nerida Vargas, Associate Director of Admissions, Pine Manor College, 400 Heath Street, Chestnut Hill, MA 02167-2332. Telephone: 617-731-7105 or toll-free 800-762-1357. Fax: 617-731-7199. E-mail: admission@pmc.edu. Web site: http://www.pmc.edu/.

RADCLIFFE COLLEGE

See Harvard University

REGIS COLLEGE

WESTON, MASSACHUSETTS

General Independent Roman Catholic, comprehensive, women only **Entrance** Moderately difficult **Setting** 168-acre small town campus **Total enrollment** 1,336 **Student/faculty ratio** 10:1 **Application deadline** Rolling **Freshmen** 87% were admitted **Housing** Yes **Expenses** Tuition $15,250; Room & Board $6900 **Undergraduates** 12% 25 or older, 0.1% Native American, 4% Hispanic, 3% black, 4% Asian American or Pacific Islander **Most popular recent majors** English; mass communications; art **Academic program** English as a second language, advanced placement, self-designed majors, tutorials, honors program, summer session, adult/continuing education programs, internships **Contact** Ms. Valerie L. Brown-McGuire, Associate Director of Admission, Regis College, 235 Wellesley Street, Weston, MA 09193-1571. Telephone: 781-768-7100 or toll-free 800-456-1820. Fax: 781-768-8339. E-mail: admission@regiscollege.edu/. Web site: http://www.regiscollege.edu/.

SAINT JOHN'S SEMINARY COLLEGE OF LIBERAL ARTS

BRIGHTON, MASSACHUSETTS

General Independent Roman Catholic, 4-year, men only **Entrance** Minimally difficult **Setting** 70-acre urban campus **Total enrollment** 37 **Student/faculty ratio** 4:1 **Application deadline** 8/1 **Freshmen** 50% were admitted **Housing** Yes **Expenses** Tuition $5400; Room & Board $2600 **Undergraduates** 25% 25 or older **Academic program** Average class size 10, English as a second language, self-designed majors, tutorials **Contact** Rev. Robert W. Flagg, Dean of the College, Saint John's Seminary College of Liberal Arts, 197 Foster Street, Brighton, MA 02135-4644. Telephone: 617-746-5460.

SALEM STATE COLLEGE

SALEM, MASSACHUSETTS

Contact Mr. Nate Bryant, Director of Admissions, Salem State College, 352 Lafayette Street, Salem, MA 01970-5353. Telephone: 508-741-6200. Fax: 978-542-6126.

SCHOOL OF THE MUSEUM OF FINE ARTS

BOSTON, MASSACHUSETTS

General Independent, comprehensive, coed **Entrance** Moderately difficult **Setting** 14-acre urban campus **Total enrollment** 1,133 **Student/faculty ratio** 10:1 **Application deadline** Rolling **Housing** No **Expenses** Tuition $15,890 **Undergraduates** 63% women, 48% part-time, 37% 25 or older, 0.1% Native American, 2% Hispanic, 1% black, 5% Asian American or Pacific Islander **Academic program** Self-designed majors, tutorials, summer session, adult/continuing education programs **Contact** Mr. John A. Williamson, Director of Enrollment and Student Services, School of the Museum of Fine Arts, 230 The Fenway, Boston, MA 02115. Telephone: 617-369-3626 or toll-free 800-643-6078 (in-state). Fax: 617-369-3679. E-mail: info@smfa.edu. Web site: http://www.smfa.edu/.

SIMMONS COLLEGE

BOSTON, MASSACHUSETTS

General Independent, comprehensive, women only **Entrance** Moderately difficult **Setting** 12-acre urban campus **Total enrollment** 3,494 **Student/faculty ratio** 10:1 **Application deadline** 2/1 **Freshmen** 68% were admitted **Housing** Yes **Expenses** Tuition $18,564; Room & Board $7228 **Undergraduates** 16% part-time, 18% 25 or older, 0.2% Native American, 3% Hispanic, 7% black, 6% Asian American or Pacific Islander **Most popular recent majors** Nursing; physical therapy; psychology **Academic program** Average class size 16, English as a second language, advanced placement, accelerated degree program, self-designed majors, tutorials, honors program, summer session, adult/continuing education programs, internships **Contact** Ms. Lisa Mayer, Dean of Enrollment Services, Simmons College, 300 The Fenway, Boston, MA 02115. Telephone: 617-521-2051 or toll-free 800-345-8468 (out-of-state). Fax: 617-521-3199. E-mail: yadm@vmsvax.simmons.edu. Web site: http://www.simmons.edu/.

SIMON'S ROCK COLLEGE OF BARD

GREAT BARRINGTON, MASSACHUSETTS

General Independent, 4-year, coed **Entrance** Very difficult **Setting** 275-acre rural campus **Total enrollment** 331 **Student/faculty ratio** 9:1 **Application deadline** 6/15 **Freshmen** 61% were ad-

Simon's Rock College of Bard *(continued)*

mitted **Housing** Yes **Expenses** Tuition $21,550; Room & Board $6100 **Undergraduates** 56% women, 0.3% part-time, 0% 25 or older, 0.3% Native American, 2% Hispanic, 3% black, 6% Asian American or Pacific Islander **Academic program** Average class size 15, self-designed majors, tutorials, adult/continuing education programs, internships **Contact** Ms. Mary King Austin, Director of Admissions, Simon's Rock College of Bard, 84 Alford Road, Great Barrington, MA 01230-9702. Telephone: 413-528-0771 ext. 317 or toll-free 800-235-7186. Fax: 413-528-7334. E-mail: admit@simons-rock.edu. Web site: http://www.simons-rock.edu/.

SMITH COLLEGE
NORTHAMPTON, MASSACHUSETTS

General Independent, comprehensive, women only **Entrance** Very difficult **Setting** 125-acre urban campus **Total enrollment** 3,199 **Student/faculty ratio** 10:1 **Application deadline** 1/15 **Freshmen** 56% were admitted **Housing** Yes **Expenses** Tuition $21,512; Room & Board $7250 **Undergraduates** 3% part-time, 9% 25 or older, 1% Native American, 3% Hispanic, 4% black, 10% Asian American or Pacific Islander **Most popular recent majors** Political science; psychology; English **Academic program** Advanced placement, accelerated degree program, self-designed majors, tutorials, honors program, adult/continuing education programs, internships **Contact** Ms. Nanci Tessier, Director of Admissions, Smith College, 7 College Lane, Northampton, MA 01063. Telephone: 413-585-2500. Fax: 413-585-2527. E-mail: admission@smith.edu. Web site: http://www.smith.edu/.

SPRINGFIELD COLLEGE
SPRINGFIELD, MASSACHUSETTS

General Independent, comprehensive, coed **Entrance** Moderately difficult **Setting** 167-acre suburban campus **Total enrollment** 2,490 **Student/faculty ratio** 15:1 **Application deadline** 4/1 **Freshmen** 58% were admitted **Housing** Yes **Expenses** Tuition $14,825; Room & Board $5018 **Undergraduates** 2% Hispanic, 4% black, 1% Asian American or Pacific Islander **Academic program** English as a second language, advanced placement, accelerated degree program, honors program, summer session, adult/continuing education programs, internships **Contact** Ms. Mary DeAngelo, Interim Director of Admissions, Springfield College, 263 Alden Street, Springfield, MA 01109-3797. Telephone: 413-748-3136 or toll-free 800-343-1257 (out-of-state). Fax: 413-748-3694. E-mail: admissions@spfldcol.edu. Web site: http://www.spfldcol.edu/.

► **For more information, see page 520.**

STONEHILL COLLEGE
EASTON, MASSACHUSETTS

General Independent Roman Catholic, 4-year, coed **Entrance** Moderately difficult **Setting** 375-acre suburban campus **Total enrollment** 2,715 **Student/faculty ratio** 11:1 **Application deadline** 2/1 **Freshmen** 57% were admitted **Housing** Yes **Expenses** Tuition $15,730; Room & Board $7350 **Undergraduates** 58% women, 15% part-time, 1% 25 or older, 0.1% Native American, 1% Hispanic, 2% black, 2% Asian American or Pacific Islander **Most popular recent majors** Psychology; education; biology **Academic program** Average class size 24, advanced placement, self-designed majors, honors program, summer session, adult/continuing education programs, internships **Contact** Mr. Brian P. Murphy, Dean of Admissions and Enrollment, Stonehill College, 320 Washington Street, Easton, MA 02357-5610. Telephone: 508-565-1373. Fax: 508-565-1500. E-mail: admissions@stonehill.edu. Web site: http://www.stonehill.edu/.

SUFFOLK UNIVERSITY
BOSTON, MASSACHUSETTS

General Independent, comprehensive, coed **Entrance** Moderately difficult **Setting** 2-acre urban campus **Total enrollment** 6,290 **Student/faculty ratio** 12:1 **Application deadline** Rolling **Freshmen** 77% were admitted **Housing** Yes **Expenses** Tuition $12,920; Room & Board $8350 **Undergraduates** 57% women, 20% part-time, 30% 25 or older, 0.3% Native American, 4% Hispanic, 6% black, 6% Asian American or Pacific Islander **Most popular recent majors** Sociology; finance; accounting **Academic program** English as a second language, advanced placement, accelerated degree program, tutorials, honors program, summer session, adult/continuing education programs, internships **Contact** Ms. Kathleen Lynch, Director of Undergraduate Admission, Suffolk University, 8 Ashburton Place, Boston, MA 02108-2770. Telephone: 617-573-8460 or toll-free 800-6-SUFFOLK. Fax: 617-742-4291. E-mail: admission@admin.suffolk.edu. Web site: http://www.suffolk.edu/.

► **For more information, see page 525.**

TUFTS UNIVERSITY
MEDFORD, MASSACHUSETTS

General Independent, university, coed **Entrance** Most difficult **Setting** 150-acre suburban campus **Total enrollment** 8,742 **Student/faculty ratio** 13:1 **Application deadline** 1/1 **Freshmen** 32% were admitted **Housing** Yes **Expenses** Tuition $22,811; Room & Board $6804 **Undergraduates** 52% women, 0.3% part-time,

0.2% Native American, 5% Hispanic, 5% black, 14% Asian American or Pacific Islander **Most popular recent majors** Biology; international relations; English **Academic program** Average class size 25, English as a second language, advanced placement, self-designed majors, tutorials, honors program, summer session, adult/continuing education programs, internships **Contact** Mr. David D. Cuttino, Dean of Undergraduate Admissions, Tufts University, Medford, MA 02155. Telephone: 617-627-3170. Fax: 617-627-3860. E-mail: uadmiss_inquiry@infonet.tufts.edu. Web site: http://www.tufts.edu/.

UNIVERSITY OF MASSACHUSETTS AMHERST

AMHERST, MASSACHUSETTS

General State-supported, university, coed **Entrance** Moderately difficult **Setting** 1,463-acre small town campus **Total enrollment** 24,884 **Student/faculty ratio** 18:1 **Application deadline** 2/1 **Freshmen** 73% were admitted **Housing** Yes **Expenses** Tuition $5572; Room & Board $4520 **Undergraduates** 49% women, 6% part-time, 7% 25 or older, 0.4% Native American, 4% Hispanic, 5% black, 6% Asian American or Pacific Islander **Most popular recent majors** Psychology; hospitality management; communications **Academic program** Average class size 46, English as a second language, advanced placement, self-designed majors, tutorials, honors program, summer session, adult/continuing education programs, internships **Contact** Ms. Arlene Cash, Director of Undergraduate Admissions, University of Massachusetts Amherst, University Admissions Center, Amherst, MA 01003-0120. Telephone: 413-545-0222. Fax: 413-545-4312. E-mail: amh.admis@umassp.edu. Web site: http://www.umass.edu/.

UNIVERSITY OF MASSACHUSETTS BOSTON

BOSTON, MASSACHUSETTS

General State-supported, university, coed **Entrance** Moderately difficult **Setting** 177-acre urban campus **Total enrollment** 12,828 **Student/faculty ratio** 16:1 **Application deadline** 3/1 **Freshmen** 54% were admitted **Housing** No **Expenses** Tuition $4297 **Undergraduates** 55% women, 33% part-time, 53% 25 or older, 0.3% Native American, 5% Hispanic, 13% black, 9% Asian American or Pacific Islander **Most popular recent majors** Business administration; nursing; psychology **Academic program** Average class size 25, English as a second language, advanced placement, accelerated degree program, self-designed majors, tutorials, honors program, summer session, adult/continuing education programs, internships **Contact** Office of Admissions Information Service, University of Massachusetts Boston, 100 Morrissey Boulevard, Boston, MA 02125-3393. Telephone: 617-287-6000. E-mail: bos.admiss@umassp.edu. Web site: http://www.umb.edu/.

UNIVERSITY OF MASSACHUSETTS DARTMOUTH

NORTH DARTMOUTH, MASSACHUSETTS

General State-supported, comprehensive, coed **Entrance** Moderately difficult **Setting** 710-acre suburban campus **Total enrollment** 6,366 **Student/faculty ratio** 14:1 **Application deadline** Rolling **Freshmen** 68% were admitted **Housing** Yes **Expenses** Tuition $4254; Room & Board $4828 **Undergraduates** 54% women, 15% part-time, 16% 25 or older, 1% Native American, 2% Hispanic, 5% black, 2% Asian American or Pacific Islander **Most popular recent majors** Psychology; nursing; business administration **Academic program** English as a second language, advanced placement, self-designed majors, tutorials, honors program, summer session, adult/continuing education programs, internships **Contact** Mr. Steven Briggs, Director of Admissions, University of Massachusetts Dartmouth, 285 Old Westport Road, North Dartmouth, MA 02747-2300. Telephone: 508-999-8606. Fax: 508-999-8755. E-mail: admissions@umassd.edu. Web site: http://www.umassd.edu/.

▶ **For more information, see page 537.**

UNIVERSITY OF MASSACHUSETTS LOWELL

LOWELL, MASSACHUSETTS

General State-supported, university, coed **Entrance** Moderately difficult **Setting** 100-acre urban campus **Total enrollment** 12,322 **Application deadline** Rolling **Freshmen** 81% were admitted **Housing** Yes **Expenses** Tuition $4422; Room & Board $4580 **Undergraduates** 39% women, 22% part-time, 30% 25 or older, 0.2% Native American, 3% Hispanic, 2% black, 5% Asian American or Pacific Islander **Most popular recent majors** Business administration; criminal justice/law enforcement administration; electrical/electronics engineering **Academic program** Advanced placement, accelerated degree program, honors program, summer session, adult/continuing education programs, internships **Contact** Ms. Rayanne Lapierre, Assistant Director of Admissions, University of Massachusetts Lowell, 1 University Avenue, Lowell, MA 01854-2881. Telephone: 978-934-3944 or toll-free 800-410-4607. Fax: 978-934-3086. Web site: http://www.uml.edu/.

WELLESLEY COLLEGE

WELLESLEY, MASSACHUSETTS

General Independent, 4-year, women only **Entrance** Most difficult **Setting** 500-acre suburban

Wellesley College *(continued)*

campus **Total enrollment** 2,283 **Student/faculty ratio** 9:1 **Application deadline** 1/15 **Freshmen** 44% were admitted **Housing** Yes **Expenses** Tuition $21,660; Room & Board $6670 **Undergraduates** 3% part-time, 3% 25 or older, 1% Native American, 7% Hispanic, 7% black, 23% Asian American or Pacific Islander **Most popular recent majors** Psychology; economics; English **Academic program** Advanced placement, accelerated degree program, self-designed majors, honors program, adult/continuing education programs, internships **Contact** Ms. Janet Lavin Rapelye, Dean of Admission, Wellesley College, 106 Central Street, Wellesley, MA 02181. Telephone: 781-283-2270. Fax: 781-283-3678. E-mail: admission@wellesley.edu. Web site: http://www.wellesley.edu/.

WENTWORTH INSTITUTE OF TECHNOLOGY
BOSTON, MASSACHUSETTS

General Independent, 4-year, coed **Entrance** Moderately difficult **Setting** 35-acre urban campus **Total enrollment** 3,094 **Student/faculty ratio** 18:1 **Application deadline** Rolling **Freshmen** 77% were admitted **Housing** Yes **Expenses** Tuition $11,500; Room & Board $6200 **Undergraduates** 14% women, 23% part-time, 14% 25 or older, 0.4% Native American, 3% Hispanic, 8% black, 7% Asian American or Pacific Islander **Most popular recent majors** Electrical/electronic engineering technology; architectural engineering technology; mechanical engineering technology **Academic program** English as a second language, advanced placement, accelerated degree program, summer session **Contact** Ms. Melinda Mitchell, Director of Admissions, Wentworth Institute of Technology, 550 Huntington Avenue, Boston, MA 02115-5998. Telephone: 617-989-4003 or toll-free 800-556-0610. Fax: 617-989-4010. E-mail: admissions@wit.edu. Web site: http://www.wit.edu/.

► **For more information, see page 550.**

WESTERN NEW ENGLAND COLLEGE
SPRINGFIELD, MASSACHUSETTS

General Independent, comprehensive, coed **Entrance** Moderately difficult **Setting** 185-acre suburban campus **Total enrollment** 4,738 **Student/faculty ratio** 17:1 **Application deadline** Rolling **Freshmen** 76% were admitted **Housing** Yes **Expenses** Tuition $11,448; Room & Board $6120 **Undergraduates** 37% women, 37% part-time, 36% 25 or older, 0.3% Native American, 2% Hispanic, 3% black, 2% Asian American or Pacific Islander **Most popular recent majors** Business administration; accounting; criminal justice/law enforcement administration **Academic program** Average class size 20, advanced placement, self-designed majors, tutorials, honors program, summer session, adult/continuing education programs, internships **Contact** Dr. Charles R. Pollock, Dean of Enrollment Management, Western New England College, 1215 Wilbraham Road, Springfield, MA 01119-2654. Telephone: 413-782-1321 or toll-free 800-325-1122. Fax: 413-782-1777. E-mail: ugradmis@wnec.edu. Web site: http://www.wnec.edu/.

► **For more information, see page 555.**

WESTFIELD STATE COLLEGE
WESTFIELD, MASSACHUSETTS

General State-supported, comprehensive, coed **Entrance** Moderately difficult **Setting** 227-acre small town campus **Total enrollment** 4,937 **Student/faculty ratio** 19:1 **Application deadline** 3/1 **Freshmen** 61% were admitted **Housing** Yes **Expenses** Tuition $3094; Room & Board $4441 **Undergraduates** 51% women, 12% part-time, 4% 25 or older, 0.2% Native American, 2% Hispanic, 3% black, 1% Asian American or Pacific Islander **Most popular recent majors** Criminal justice/law enforcement administration; psychology; elementary education **Academic program** Average class size 30, advanced placement, accelerated degree program, tutorials, honors program, summer session, adult/continuing education programs, internships **Contact** Ms. Michelle Mattie, Director of Admission and Financial Aid, Westfield State College, Western Avenue, Westfield, MA 01086. Telephone: 413-572-5218 or toll-free 800-322-8401 (in-state). E-mail: admission@wsc.mass.edu.

WHEATON COLLEGE
NORTON, MASSACHUSETTS

General Independent, 4-year, coed **Entrance** Moderately difficult **Setting** 385-acre small town campus **Total enrollment** 1,443 **Student/faculty ratio** 13:1 **Application deadline** 2/1 **Freshmen** 73% were admitted **Housing** Yes **Expenses** Tuition $20,820; Room & Board $6470 **Undergraduates** 67% women, 1% part-time, 1% 25 or older, 1% Native American, 3% Hispanic, 3% black, 4% Asian American or Pacific Islander **Most popular recent majors** Psychology; English; sociology **Academic program** Average class size 19, advanced placement, accelerated degree program, self-designed majors, tutorials, honors program, adult/continuing education programs, internships **Contact** Ms. Lynne M. Stack, Director of Admission, Wheaton College, East Main Street, Norton, MA 02766. Telephone: 508-285-8251 or toll-free 800-394-6003. Fax: 508-285-8271. E-mail: admission@wheatonma.edu. Web site: http://www.wheatonma.edu/.

WHEELOCK COLLEGE
BOSTON, MASSACHUSETTS

General Independent, comprehensive, primarily women **Entrance** Moderately difficult **Setting** 5-acre urban campus **Total enrollment** 1,308 **Student/faculty ratio** 11:1 **Application deadline** 2/15 **Freshmen** 78% were admitted **Housing** Yes **Expenses** Tuition $15,520; Room & Board $6000 **Undergraduates** 95% women, 2% part-time, 8% 25 or older, 0.1% Native American, 2% Hispanic, 7% black, 2% Asian American or Pacific Islander **Most popular recent majors** Education; social work; child care/development **Academic program** Advanced placement, honors program, internships **Contact** Ms. Lynne E. Dailey, Dean of Admissions, Wheelock College, 200 The Riverway, Boston, MA 02215. Telephone: 617-734-5200 ext. 204 or toll-free 800-734-5212 (out-of-state). Fax: 617-566-7369. E-mail: undergrad@wheelock.edu. Web site: http://www.wheelock.edu/.

WILLIAMS COLLEGE
WILLIAMSTOWN, MASSACHUSETTS

General Independent, comprehensive, coed **Entrance** Most difficult **Setting** 450-acre small town campus **Total enrollment** 2,069 **Student/faculty ratio** 11:1 **Application deadline** 1/1 **Freshmen** 26% were admitted **Housing** Yes **Expenses** Tuition $22,990; Room & Board $6300 **Undergraduates** 48% women, 1% 25 or older, 0.3% Native American, 7% Hispanic, 6% black, 9% Asian American or Pacific Islander **Most popular recent majors** English; economics; history **Academic program** Advanced placement, accelerated degree program, self-designed majors, tutorials, honors program, internships **Contact** Mr. Thomas H. Parker, Director of Admission, Williams College, PO Box 487, Williamstown, MA 01267. Telephone: 413-597-2211. E-mail: admission@williams.edu. Web site: http://www.williams.edu/.

WORCESTER POLYTECHNIC INSTITUTE
WORCESTER, MASSACHUSETTS

General Independent, university, coed **Entrance** Very difficult **Setting** 80-acre suburban campus **Total enrollment** 3,776 **Student/faculty ratio** 12:1 **Application deadline** 2/15 **Freshmen** 78% were admitted **Housing** Yes **Expenses** Tuition $18,910; Room & Board $6240 **Undergraduates** 22% women, 2% part-time, 3% 25 or older, 0.4% Native American, 3% Hispanic, 2% black, 6% Asian American or Pacific Islander **Most popular recent majors** Mechanical engineering; electrical/electronics engineering; computer science **Academic program** English as a second language, advanced placement, accelerated degree program, self-designed majors, summer session, adult/continuing education programs **Contact** Mr. Robert G. Voss, Executive Director of Admissions and Financial Aid, Worcester Polytechnic Institute, 100 Institute Road, Worcester, MA 01609-2280. Telephone: 508-831-5286. Fax: 508-831-5875. E-mail: rgvoss@wpi.edu. Web site: http://www.wpi.edu/.

WORCESTER STATE COLLEGE
WORCESTER, MASSACHUSETTS

General State-supported, comprehensive, coed **Entrance** Moderately difficult **Setting** 53-acre urban campus **Total enrollment** 5,505 **Student/faculty ratio** 16:1 **Application deadline** Rolling **Freshmen** 59% were admitted **Housing** Yes **Expenses** Tuition $2615; Room & Board $4140 **Undergraduates** 64% women, 28% part-time, 36% 25 or older, 0.5% Native American, 3% Hispanic, 4% black, 3% Asian American or Pacific Islander **Most popular recent majors** Business administration; psychology; occupational therapy **Academic program** Advanced placement, accelerated degree program, honors program, summer session, adult/continuing education programs, internships **Contact** Mr. E. Jay Tierney, Director of Admissions, Worcester State College, 486 Chandler Street, Worcester, MA 01602-2597. Telephone: 508-929-8040. Fax: 508-929-8131. E-mail: admissions@worc.mass.edu. Web site: http://www.worc.mass.edu/.

MICHIGAN

ADRIAN COLLEGE
ADRIAN, MICHIGAN

General Independent, 4-year, coed, affiliated with United Methodist Church **Entrance** Moderately difficult **Setting** 100-acre small town campus **Total enrollment** 1,000 **Student/faculty ratio** 16:1 **Application deadline** 8/15 **Freshmen** 90% were admitted **Housing** Yes **Expenses** Tuition $12,830; Room & Board $4120 **Undergraduates** 47% women, 6% part-time, 6% 25 or older, 0.4% Native American, 1% Hispanic, 7% black, 1% Asian American or Pacific Islander **Most popular recent majors** Business administration; biology **Academic program** Average class size 18, English as a second language, advanced placement, self-designed majors, tutorials, honors program, summer session, adult/continuing education programs, internships **Contact** Ms. Carolyn Quinlan, Associate Director of Admissions, Adrian College, 110 South Madison Street, Adrian, MI 49221-2575. Telephone: 517-265-5161 ext. 4326 or toll-free 800-

Adrian College *(continued)*

877-2246. Fax: 517-265-3331. E-mail: admission@adrian.adrian.edu. Web site: http://www.adrian.edu/.

▶ **For more information, see page 384.**

ALBION COLLEGE
ALBION, MICHIGAN

General Independent Methodist, 4-year, coed **Entrance** Moderately difficult **Setting** 225-acre small town campus **Total enrollment** 1,500 **Student/faculty ratio** 13:1 **Application deadline** Rolling **Freshmen** 91% were admitted **Housing** Yes **Expenses** Tuition $16,806; Room & Board $4980 **Undergraduates** 53% women, 2% part-time, 2% 25 or older, 0.3% Native American, 1% Hispanic, 5% black, 2% Asian American or Pacific Islander **Most popular recent majors** Economics; biology; English **Academic program** Advanced placement, self-designed majors, tutorials, honors program, summer session, internships **Contact** Mr. Daniel L. Meyer, Vice President for Enrollment, Albion College, 611 East Porter Street, Albion, MI 49224-1831. Telephone: 517-629-0600 or toll-free 800-858-6770. Fax: 517-629-0569. E-mail: admissions@albion.edu. Web site: http://www.albion.edu/.

▶ **For more information, see page 385.**

ALMA COLLEGE
ALMA, MICHIGAN

General Independent Presbyterian, 4-year, coed **Entrance** Moderately difficult **Setting** 100-acre small town campus **Total enrollment** 1,407 **Student/faculty ratio** 13:1 **Application deadline** Rolling **Freshmen** 90% were admitted **Housing** Yes **Expenses** Tuition $14,238; Room & Board $5052 **Undergraduates** 57% women, 1% part-time, 3% 25 or older, 0.2% Native American, 1% Hispanic, 2% black, 1% Asian American or Pacific Islander **Most popular recent majors** Business administration; biology; exercise sciences **Academic program** Average class size 23, English as a second language, advanced placement, accelerated degree program, self-designed majors, tutorials, honors program, summer session, adult/continuing education programs, internships **Contact** Mr. Mark Nazario, Director of Admissions, Alma College, 614 West Superior, Alma, MI 48801-1599. Telephone: 517-463-7139 or toll-free 800-321-ALMA. Fax: 517-463-7057. E-mail: admissions@alma.edu. Web site: http://www.alma.edu/.

▶ **For more information, see page 388.**

ANDREWS UNIVERSITY
BERRIEN SPRINGS, MICHIGAN

General Independent Seventh-day Adventist, university, coed **Entrance** Moderately difficult **Setting** 1,650-acre small town campus **Total enrollment** 3,152 **Student/faculty ratio** 14:1 **Application deadline** Rolling **Freshmen** 74% were admitted **Housing** Yes **Expenses** Tuition $11,577; Room & Board $3510 **Undergraduates** 56% women, 13% part-time, 25% 25 or older, 0.2% Native American, 7% Hispanic, 20% black, 9% Asian American or Pacific Islander **Most popular recent majors** Anatomy; nursing; medical technology **Academic program** English as a second language, advanced placement, accelerated degree program, self-designed majors, tutorials, honors program, summer session, adult/continuing education programs, internships **Contact** Dr. Dean Hunt, Vice President for Enrollment Services, Andrews University, Berrien Springs, MI 49104. Telephone: 616-471-7771 or toll-free 800-253-2874. Fax: 616-471-3228. E-mail: enroll@andrews.edu. Web site: http://www.cs.andrews.edu/.

AQUINAS COLLEGE
GRAND RAPIDS, MICHIGAN

General Independent Roman Catholic, comprehensive, coed **Entrance** Moderately difficult **Setting** 107-acre suburban campus **Total enrollment** 2,458 **Student/faculty ratio** 13:1 **Application deadline** Rolling **Freshmen** 92% were admitted **Housing** Yes **Expenses** Tuition $12,950; Room & Board $4324 **Undergraduates** 65% women, 31% part-time, 35% 25 or older, 0.4% Native American, 3% Hispanic, 5% black, 1% Asian American or Pacific Islander **Most popular recent majors** Business administration; English; communications **Academic program** Average class size 18, advanced placement, accelerated degree program, self-designed majors, tutorials, honors program, summer session, adult/continuing education programs, internships **Contact** Ms. Karen Lucas, Applications Secretary, Aquinas College, 1607 Robinson Road, SE, Grand Rapids, MI 49506-1799. Telephone: 616-732-4460 or toll-free 800-678-9593. Fax: 616-459-2563. E-mail: admissions@aquinas.edu. Web site: http://www.aquinas.edu/.

▶ **For more information, see page 391.**

BAKER COLLEGE OF AUBURN HILLS
AUBURN HILLS, MICHIGAN

General Independent, 4-year, coed **Contact** Mr. John Tomaszewski, Admission Advisor, Baker College of Auburn Hills, 1500 University Drive, Auburn Hills, MI 48326-1586. Telephone: 810-340-0600. E-mail: love_j@auburnhills.baker.edu. Web site: http://www.baker.com/.

BAKER COLLEGE OF CADILLAC
CADILLAC, MICHIGAN

General Independent, 4-year, coed **Entrance** Noncompetitive **Setting** 40-acre small town campus **Total enrollment** 799 **Student/faculty ratio** 20:1 **Application deadline** Rolling **Freshmen** 100% were admitted **Housing** No **Expenses** Tuition $6300 **Undergraduates** 56% 25 or older **Most popular recent majors** Accounting; medical assistant; business administration **Academic program** Average class size 18, advanced placement, summer session, internships **Contact** Mr. Eric Runstrom, Director of Admissions, Baker College of Cadillac, 9600 East 13th Street, Cadillac, MI 49601. Telephone: 616-775-8458. Fax: 616-775-8505. E-mail: runstr_e@cadillac.baker.edu. Web site: http://www.baker.edu/.

BAKER COLLEGE OF FLINT

FLINT, MICHIGAN

General Independent, 4-year, coed **Entrance** Noncompetitive **Setting** 30-acre urban campus **Total enrollment** 3,934 **Student/faculty ratio** 25:1 **Application deadline** Rolling **Freshmen** 100% were admitted **Housing** Yes **Expenses** Tuition $6300; Room only $1800 **Undergraduates** 70% women, 44% part-time, 53% 25 or older **Most popular recent majors** Business administration; health services administration; accounting **Academic program** Average class size 25, advanced placement, accelerated degree program, summer session, internships **Contact** Mr. Mark Heaton, Vice President for Admissions, Baker College of Flint, 1050 West Bristol Road, Flint, MI 48507-5508. Telephone: 810-766-4015 or toll-free 800-964-4299. Fax: 810-766-4049. E-mail: heaton_m@flint.baker.edu. Web site: http://www.baker.edu/.

BAKER COLLEGE OF JACKSON

JACKSON, MICHIGAN

General Independent, 4-year, coed **Entrance** Noncompetitive **Setting** 42-acre urban campus **Total enrollment** 848 **Student/faculty ratio** 16:1 **Application deadline** Rolling **Housing** No **Expenses** Tuition $6300 **Undergraduates** 80% women, 45% part-time, 56% 25 or older, 0.2% Native American, 2% Hispanic, 9% black, 1% Asian American or Pacific Islander **Academic program** Average class size 20, advanced placement, summer session, internships **Contact** Mr. Steve Kim, Director of Admissions, Baker College of Jackson, 2800 Springport Road, Jackson, MI 49202. Telephone: 517-788-7800. E-mail: kim_s@jackson.baker.edu. Web site: http://www.baker.edu/.

BAKER COLLEGE OF MOUNT CLEMENS

CLINTON TOWNSHIP, MICHIGAN

General Independent, 4-year, coed **Entrance** Noncompetitive **Setting** Urban campus **Total enrollment** 1,261 **Student/faculty ratio** 16:1 **Application deadline** Rolling **Freshmen** 100% were admitted **Housing** No **Expenses** Tuition $6300 **Undergraduates** 42% 25 or older **Most Popular Recent Major** Business administration **Academic program** Average class size 35, advanced placement, summer session, internships **Contact** Ms. Annette M. Looser, Director of Admissions, Baker College of Mount Clemens, 34950 Little Mack Avenue, Clinton Township, MI 48035-4701. Telephone: 810-791-6610. Fax: 810-791-6611. E-mail: looser_a@mtclemens.baker.edu. Web site: http://www.baker.edu.

BAKER COLLEGE OF MUSKEGON

MUSKEGON, MICHIGAN

General Independent, 4-year, coed **Entrance** Noncompetitive **Setting** 40-acre suburban campus **Total enrollment** 2,234 **Student/faculty ratio** 18:1 **Application deadline** Rolling **Housing** Yes **Expenses** Tuition $6480; Room only $1650 **Undergraduates** 75% women, 44% part-time, 26% 25 or older **Most popular recent majors** Physical therapy assistant; business administration; accounting **Academic program** Average class size 20, advanced placement, accelerated degree program, summer session, adult/continuing education programs, internships **Contact** Ms. Kathy Jacobson, Director of Admissions, Baker College of Muskegon, 1903 Marquette Avenue, Muskegon, MI 49442-3497. Telephone: 616-777-5200 or toll-free 800-937-0337 (in-state). Fax: 616-777-5265. E-mail: jacobs_k@muskegon.baker.edu. Web site: http://www.baker.edu/.

BAKER COLLEGE OF OWOSSO

OWOSSO, MICHIGAN

General Independent, 4-year, coed **Entrance** Noncompetitive **Setting** 32-acre small town campus **Total enrollment** 1,850 **Student/faculty ratio** 20:1 **Application deadline** Rolling **Freshmen** 100% were admitted **Housing** Yes **Expenses** Tuition $6300; Room only $1800 **Undergraduates** 40% 25 or older **Most popular recent majors** Industrial radiologic technology; accounting; secretarial science **Academic program** Advanced placement, accelerated degree program, tutorials, summer session, adult/continuing education programs, internships **Contact** Mr. Bruce A. Lundeen, Vice President for Admissions, Baker College of Owosso, 1020 South Washington Street, Owosso, MI 48867-4400. Telephone: 517-723-5251 ext. 454 or toll-free 800-879-3797. Fax: 517-723-3355. E-mail: lundee_b@owosso.baker.edu. Web site: http://www.baker.edu/.

BAKER COLLEGE OF PORT HURON

PORT HURON, MICHIGAN

General Independent, 4-year, coed **Entrance** Noncompetitive **Setting** 10-acre urban campus **To-**

Baker College of Port Huron *(continued)*

tal enrollment 935 **Student/faculty ratio** 20:1 **Application deadline** Rolling **Freshmen** 100% were admitted **Housing** No **Expenses** Tuition $6300 **Undergraduates** 47% 25 or older **Most popular recent majors** Accounting; medical records administration; secretarial science **Academic program** Average class size 20, advanced placement, accelerated degree program, summer session, internships **Contact** Mr. Dan Kenny, Director of Admissions, Baker College of Port Huron, 3403 Lapeer Road, Port Huron, MI 48060-2597. Telephone: 810-985-7000. Fax: 810-985-7066. E-mail: kenny_d@porthuron.baker.edu. Web site: http://www.baker.edu/.

CALVIN COLLEGE
GRAND RAPIDS, MICHIGAN

General Independent, comprehensive, coed, affiliated with Christian Reformed Church **Entrance** Moderately difficult **Setting** 370-acre suburban campus **Total enrollment** 4,071 **Student/faculty ratio** 17:1 **Application deadline** Rolling **Freshmen** 98% were admitted **Housing** Yes **Expenses** Tuition $12,250; Room & Board $4340 **Undergraduates** 57% women, 3% part-time, 2% 25 or older, 0.2% Native American, 1% Hispanic, 1% black, 2% Asian American or Pacific Islander **Most popular recent majors** Education; business administration; English **Academic program** English as a second language, advanced placement, self-designed majors, tutorials, honors program, summer session, adult/continuing education programs, internships **Contact** Mr. Dale D. Kuiper, Director of Admissions, Calvin College, 3201 Burton Street, SE, Grand Rapids, MI 49546-4388. Telephone: 616-957-6106 or toll-free 800-668-0122. E-mail: admissions@calvin.edu. Web site: http://www.calvin.edu/.

▶ **For more information, see page 401.**

CENTER FOR CREATIVE STUDIES—COLLEGE OF ART AND DESIGN
DETROIT, MICHIGAN

General Independent, 4-year, coed **Entrance** Moderately difficult **Setting** 11-acre urban campus **Total enrollment** 975 **Application deadline** Rolling **Freshmen** 46% were admitted **Housing** Yes **Expenses** Tuition $14,496; Room only $3100 **Undergraduates** 41% women, 16% part-time, 26% 25 or older, 1% Native American, 4% Hispanic, 12% black, 5% Asian American or Pacific Islander **Most popular recent majors** Graphic design/commercial art/illustration; industrial design; art **Academic program** Average class size 30, English as a second language, advanced placement, tutorials, summer session, internships **Contact** Receptionist, Center for Creative Studies—College of Art and Design, 201 East Kirby, Detroit, MI 48202-4034. Telephone: 313-664-7425 or toll-free 800-952-ARTS. Fax: 313-872-2739. Web site: http://www.ccscad.edu/.

CENTRAL MICHIGAN UNIVERSITY
MOUNT PLEASANT, MICHIGAN

General State-supported, university, coed **Entrance** Moderately difficult **Setting** 854-acre small town campus **Total enrollment** 24,747 **Student/faculty ratio** 17:1 **Application deadline** Rolling **Freshmen** 94% were admitted **Housing** Yes **Expenses** Tuition $3546; Room & Board $4320 **Undergraduates** 58% women, 15% part-time, 10% 25 or older, 1% Native American, 1% Hispanic, 4% black, 1% Asian American or Pacific Islander **Most popular recent majors** Psychology; business marketing and marketing management; accounting **Academic program** English as a second language, advanced placement, accelerated degree program, self-designed majors, honors program, summer session, adult/continuing education programs, internships **Contact** Mrs. Betty J. Wagner, Director of Admissions, Central Michigan University, Mount Pleasant, MI 48859. Telephone: 517-774-3076. Fax: 517-774-3537. E-mail: 34inz2k@cmuvm.csv.cmich.edu. Web site: http://www.cmich.edu/.

CLEARY COLLEGE
HOWELL, MICHIGAN

General Independent, 4-year, coed **Entrance** Noncompetitive **Setting** 27-acre small town campus **Total enrollment** 644 **Student/faculty ratio** 15:1 **Application deadline** Rolling **Housing** No **Expenses** Tuition $7665 **Undergraduates** 70% 25 or older, 0% Native American, 1% Hispanic, 7% black, 0% Asian American or Pacific Islander **Most Popular Recent Major** Business administration **Academic program** Average class size 15, accelerated degree program, summer session, adult/continuing education programs **Contact** Mr. Jimm L. Crowder, Director of Admissions, Cleary College, 3750 Cleary College Drive, Howell, MI 48843. Telephone: 517-548-3670 ext. 2213 or toll-free 800-589-1979. Fax: 517-548-2170. Web site: http://www.cleary.edu/.

▶ **For more information, see page 414.**

CONCORDIA COLLEGE
ANN ARBOR, MICHIGAN

General Independent, 4-year, coed, affiliated with Lutheran Church–Missouri Synod **Entrance** Moderately difficult **Setting** 234-acre suburban campus **Total enrollment** 550 **Student/faculty ratio** 10:1 **Application deadline** Rolling **Housing** Yes **Expenses** Tuition $11,850; Room & Board

$4850 **Undergraduates** 61% women, 10% part-time, 39% 25 or older, 0.4% Native American, 1% Hispanic, 9% black, 1% Asian American or Pacific Islander **Academic program** Average class size 25, advanced placement, accelerated degree program, self-designed majors, tutorials, summer session, adult/continuing education programs, internships **Contact** Mr. David Koening, Director of Admissions, Concordia College, 4090 Geddes Road, Ann Arbor, MI 48105-2797. Telephone: 313-995-7322 ext. 7311 or toll-free 800-253-0680. Fax: 734-995-4610. E-mail: admissions@ccaa.edu. Web site: http://www.ccaa.edu/.

CORNERSTONE COLLEGE
GRAND RAPIDS, MICHIGAN

General Independent Baptist, 4-year, coed **Entrance** Moderately difficult **Setting** 132-acre suburban campus **Total enrollment** 1,160 **Student/faculty ratio** 18:1 **Application deadline** Rolling **Freshmen** 87% were admitted **Housing** Yes **Expenses** Tuition $10,026; Room & Board $4392 **Undergraduates** 7% 25 or older, 0.1% Native American, 2% Hispanic, 1% black, 1% Asian American or Pacific Islander **Most popular recent majors** Business administration; biblical studies; psychology **Academic program** Advanced placement, honors program, summer session, adult/continuing education programs, internships **Contact** Mr. Rick Newberry, Executive Director of Enrollment Management, Cornerstone College, 1001 East Beltline Avenue, NE, Grand Rapids, MI 49325-5597. Telephone: 616-222-1426 or toll-free 800-968-4722. Fax: 616-949-0875. E-mail: admissions@cornerstone.edu. Web site: http://www.cornerstone.edu/.

DAVENPORT COLLEGE OF BUSINESS
GRAND RAPIDS, MICHIGAN

General Independent, 4-year, coed **Entrance** Noncompetitive **Setting** 5-acre urban campus **Total enrollment** 2,381 **Student/faculty ratio** 19:1 **Application deadline** Rolling **Freshmen** 100% were admitted **Housing** Yes **Expenses** Tuition $8508; Room only $2325 **Undergraduates** 56% 25 or older, 1% Native American, 3% Hispanic, 8% black, 1% Asian American or Pacific Islander **Most popular recent majors** Business administration; accounting **Academic program** English as a second language, advanced placement, accelerated degree program, tutorials, summer session, adult/continuing education programs, internships **Contact** Ms. Colleen Wolfe, Director of Admissions, Davenport College of Business, 415 East Fulton, Grand Rapids, MI 49503. Telephone: 616-732-1200 or toll-free 800-632-9569 (out-of-state). Web site: http://www.davenport.edu/.

DAVENPORT COLLEGE OF BUSINESS, KALAMAZOO CAMPUS
KALAMAZOO, MICHIGAN

General Independent, 4-year, primarily women **Contact** Ms. Brigid Hansen, Admissions Director, Davenport College of Business, Kalamazoo Campus, 4123 West Main Street, Kalamazoo, MI 49006-2791. Telephone: 616-382-2835 ext. 35 or toll-free 800-632-8928 (in-state). Web site: http://www.davenport.edu/.

DAVENPORT COLLEGE OF BUSINESS, LANSING CAMPUS
LANSING, MICHIGAN

General Independent, 4-year, coed **Entrance** Noncompetitive **Setting** 2-acre suburban campus **Total enrollment** 1,153 **Application deadline** 9/15 **Housing** No **Expenses** Tuition $8418 **Undergraduates** 75% women, 72% part-time, 69% 25 or older, 1% Native American, 6% Hispanic, 7% black, 2% Asian American or Pacific Islander **Most popular recent majors** Business administration; secretarial science **Academic program** Average class size 25, advanced placement, accelerated degree program, self-designed majors, tutorials, summer session, adult/continuing education programs, internships **Contact** Mr. Tom Woods, Enrollment Coordinator, Davenport College of Business, Lansing Campus, 220 East Kalamazoo, Lansing, MI 48933-2197. Telephone: 517-484-2600 ext. 288 or toll-free 800-331-3306 (in-state). Fax: 517-484-9719. E-mail: laadmissions@davenport.edu. Web site: http://www.davenport.edu/.

DETROIT COLLEGE OF BUSINESS
DEARBORN, MICHIGAN

General Independent, comprehensive, coed **Entrance** Noncompetitive **Setting** 17-acre suburban campus **Total enrollment** 3,343 **Application deadline** Rolling **Housing** No **Expenses** Tuition $6264 **Undergraduates** 79% women, 51% part-time, 66% 25 or older, 0.4% Native American, 2% Hispanic, 55% black, 1% Asian American or Pacific Islander **Most popular recent majors** Accounting; business administration **Academic program** Advanced placement, tutorials, summer session, internships **Contact** Ms. Lynda Menard, Vice President of Admissions, Detroit College of Business, 4801 Oakman Boulevard, Dearborn, MI 48126-3799. Telephone: 313-581-4400. Fax: 313-581-1985.

DETROIT COLLEGE OF BUSINESS–FLINT
FLINT, MICHIGAN

General Independent, 4-year, coed **Entrance** Noncompetitive **Setting** 1-acre suburban campus

Detroit College of Business–Flint *(continued)*

Total enrollment 1,015 **Application deadline** Rolling **Freshmen** 100% were admitted **Housing** No **Expenses** Tuition $4644 **Undergraduates** 81% women, 33% part-time, 66% 25 or older, 1% Hispanic, 44% black, 0.4% Asian American or Pacific Islander **Most Popular Recent Major** Business administration **Academic program** Advanced placement, tutorials, summer session **Contact** Ms. Wilma Collins, Director of Admissions, Detroit College of Business-Flint, 3488 North Jennings Road, Flint, MI 48504-1700. Telephone: 810-789-2200 or toll-free 800-727-1443 (in-state). Fax: 810-789-2266.

DETROIT COLLEGE OF BUSINESS, WARREN CAMPUS

WARREN, MICHIGAN

General Independent, 4-year, coed **Entrance** Noncompetitive **Setting** 9-acre suburban campus **Total enrollment** 2,095 **Student/faculty ratio** 20:1 **Application deadline** Rolling **Housing** No **Expenses** Tuition $6264 **Undergraduates** 79% women, 58% part-time, 68% 25 or older, 1% Native American, 1% Hispanic, 34% black, 2% Asian American or Pacific Islander **Most popular recent majors** Accounting; business administration **Academic program** Advanced placement, tutorials, summer session, internships **Contact** Ms. Sandy Hazelton, Director of Admissions, Detroit College of Business, Warren Campus, 27650 Dequindre Road, Warren, MI 48092-5209. Telephone: 810-558-8700. Fax: 810-558-7868.

EASTERN MICHIGAN UNIVERSITY

YPSILANTI, MICHIGAN

General State-supported, comprehensive, coed **Entrance** Moderately difficult **Setting** 460-acre suburban campus **Total enrollment** 22,730 **Student/faculty ratio** 18:1 **Application deadline** 7/31 **Freshmen** 73% were admitted **Housing** Yes **Expenses** Tuition $3529; Room & Board $4528 **Undergraduates** 60% women, 33% part-time, 30% 25 or older, 1% Native American, 2% Hispanic, 14% black, 2% Asian American or Pacific Islander **Most popular recent majors** Elementary education; psychology; social work **Academic program** English as a second language, advanced placement, accelerated degree program, self-designed majors, tutorials, honors program, summer session, adult/continuing education programs, internships **Contact** Ms. Judy Benfield-Tatum, Director of Admissions, Eastern Michigan University, Ypsilanti, MI 48197. Telephone: 734-487-3060 or toll-free 800-GO TO EMU. Fax: 734-487-1484. Web site: http://www.emich.edu/.

FERRIS STATE UNIVERSITY

BIG RAPIDS, MICHIGAN

General State-supported, comprehensive, coed **Entrance** Minimally difficult **Setting** 600-acre small town campus **Total enrollment** 9,468 **Student/faculty ratio** 17:1 **Application deadline** Rolling **Housing** Yes **Expenses** Tuition $3908; Room & Board $4792 **Undergraduates** 43% women, 17% part-time, 23% 25 or older, 1% Native American, 1% Hispanic, 10% black, 2% Asian American or Pacific Islander **Most popular recent majors** Business administration; criminal justice/law enforcement administration; pharmacy **Academic program** English as a second language, advanced placement, accelerated degree program, summer session, adult/continuing education programs, internships **Contact** Mr. Don Mullens, Interim Dean of Enrollment Services, Ferris State University, PRK 110, Big Rapids, MI 49307-2742. Telephone: 616-592-2100. Fax: 616-592-2978. E-mail: admissions@act01.ferris.edu. Web site: http://www.ferris.edu/.

▶ **For more information, see page 433.**

GMI ENGINEERING & MANAGEMENT INSTITUTE

See Kettering University

GRACE BIBLE COLLEGE

GRAND RAPIDS, MICHIGAN

General Independent, 4-year, coed, affiliated with Grace Gospel Fellowship **Entrance** Minimally difficult **Setting** 16-acre suburban campus **Total enrollment** 152 **Student/faculty ratio** 11:1 **Application deadline** 7/15 **Freshmen** 68% were admitted **Housing** Yes **Expenses** Tuition $6500; Room & Board $3700 **Undergraduates** 52% women, 8% part-time, 12% 25 or older, 1% Native American, 0% Hispanic, 2% black, 1% Asian American or Pacific Islander **Most popular recent majors** Liberal arts and studies; human services; business administration **Academic program** English as a second language, advanced placement, internships **Contact** Miss Linda K. Siler, Registrar, Grace Bible College, 1011 Aldon Street SW, PO Box 910, Grand Rapids, MI 49509-1921. Telephone: 616-538-2330 or toll-free 800-968-1887. Fax: 616-538-0599. Web site: http://www.gbcol.edu/.

GRAND VALLEY STATE UNIVERSITY

ALLENDALE, MICHIGAN

General State-supported, comprehensive, coed **Entrance** Moderately difficult **Setting** 900-acre small town campus **Total enrollment** 15,676 **Student/faculty ratio** 22:1 **Application deadline** 7/26 **Freshmen** 84% were admitted **Housing** Yes **Expenses** Tuition $3408; Room & Board $4640

Undergraduates 60% women, 19% part-time, 19% 25 or older, 1% Native American, 2% Hispanic, 5% black, 2% Asian American or Pacific Islander **Most popular recent majors** Health science; business administration; psychology **Academic program** Average class size 30, English as a second language, advanced placement, accelerated degree program, honors program, summer session, adult/continuing education programs, internships **Contact** Mr. William Eilola, Director of Admissions, Grand Valley State University, 1 Campus Drive, Allendale, MI 49401-9403. Telephone: 616-895-2025 or toll-free 800-748-0246. Fax: 616-895-2000. E-mail: go2gvsu@gvsu.edu. Web site: http://www.gvsu.edu/.

GREAT LAKES CHRISTIAN COLLEGE
LANSING, MICHIGAN

General Independent, 4-year, coed, affiliated with Church of Christ **Entrance** Moderately difficult **Setting** 50-acre suburban campus **Total enrollment** 153 **Student/faculty ratio** 10:1 **Application deadline** 8/1 **Housing** Yes **Expenses** Tuition $6018; Room & Board $3450 **Undergraduates** 48% women, 23% part-time, 36% 25 or older, 1% Native American, 0% Hispanic, 3% black, 0% Asian American or Pacific Islander **Most popular recent majors** Divinity/ministry; religious education **Academic program** Advanced placement, adult/continuing education programs, internships **Contact** Mr. Ray Maurer, Director of Admissions, Great Lakes Christian College, 6211 West Willow Highway, Lansing, MI 48917-1299. Telephone: 517-321-0242 or toll-free 800-YES-GLCC. Fax: 517-321-5902. Web site: http://www.glcc.edu/.

HILLSDALE COLLEGE
HILLSDALE, MICHIGAN

General Independent, 4-year, coed **Entrance** Very difficult **Setting** 200-acre small town campus **Total enrollment** 1,197 **Student/faculty ratio** 11:1 **Application deadline** Rolling **Freshmen** 83% were admitted **Housing** Yes **Expenses** Tuition $12,680; Room & Board $5430 **Undergraduates** 1% 25 or older **Most popular recent majors** Business administration; biology; education **Academic program** Average class size 20, advanced placement, accelerated degree program, tutorials, honors program, summer session, internships **Contact** Mr. Jeffrey S. Lantis, Director of Admissions, Hillsdale College, 33 East College Street, Hillsdale, MI 49242-1298. Telephone: 517-437-7341 ext. 2327. Fax: 517-437-0190. E-mail: admissions@ac.hillsdale.edu. Web site: http://www.hillsdale.edu/.

HOPE COLLEGE
HOLLAND, MICHIGAN

General Independent, 4-year, coed, affiliated with Reformed Church in America **Entrance** Moderately difficult **Setting** 45-acre small town campus **Total enrollment** 2,911 **Student/faculty ratio** 13:1 **Application deadline** Rolling **Freshmen** 90% were admitted **Housing** Yes **Expenses** Tuition $14,878; Room & Board $4534 **Undergraduates** 59% women, 3% part-time, 1% 25 or older, 0.4% Native American, 2% Hispanic, 1% black, 2% Asian American or Pacific Islander **Most popular recent majors** Business administration; psychology; biology **Academic program** Average class size 35, English as a second language, advanced placement, self-designed majors, tutorials, summer session, internships **Contact** Office of Admissions, Hope College, 69 East 10th Street, PO Box 9000, Holland, MI 49422-9000. Telephone: 616-395-7850 or toll-free 800-966-7850. Fax: 616-395-7130. E-mail: brockl@hope.edu. Web site: http://www.hope.edu/.

KALAMAZOO COLLEGE
KALAMAZOO, MICHIGAN

General Independent, 4-year, coed **Entrance** Very difficult **Setting** 60-acre suburban campus **Total enrollment** 1,241 **Student/faculty ratio** 12:1 **Application deadline** 2/15 **Freshmen** 88% were admitted **Housing** Yes **Expenses** Tuition $17,976; Room & Board $5565 **Undergraduates** 59% women, 1% 25 or older, 0.2% Native American, 1% Hispanic, 5% black, 5% Asian American or Pacific Islander **Most popular recent majors** Biology; economics; (pre)medicine **Academic program** English as a second language, advanced placement, tutorials, adult/continuing education programs, internships **Contact** Ms. Jennifer Earle, Records Manager, Kalamazoo College, Mandelle Hall, Kalamazoo, MI 49006-3295. Telephone: 616-337-7166 or toll-free 800-253-3602. Fax: 616-337-7390. E-mail: admissions@kzoo.edu. Web site: http://www.kzoo.edu/.

KENDALL COLLEGE OF ART AND DESIGN
GRAND RAPIDS, MICHIGAN

General Independent, 4-year, coed **Entrance** Minimally difficult **Setting** Urban campus **Total enrollment** 560 **Student/faculty ratio** 11:1 **Application deadline** Rolling **Housing** No **Expenses** Tuition $10,700 **Undergraduates** 50% women, 31% part-time, 14% 25 or older, 1% Native American, 2% Hispanic, 4% black, 2% Asian American or Pacific Islander **Most popular recent majors** Graphic design/commercial art/illustration; interior design **Academic program** Average class size 25, advanced placement, tuto-

Kendall College of Art and Design *(continued)*

rials, summer session, adult/continuing education programs, internships **Contact** Ms. Amy Packard, Director of Admissions, Kendall College of Art and Design, 111 Division Avenue North, Grand Rapids, MI 49503-3194. Telephone: 616-451-2787 ext. 109 or toll-free 800-676-2787. Web site: http://www.kcad.edu/.

KETTERING UNIVERSITY
FLINT, MICHIGAN

General Independent, comprehensive, coed **Entrance** Very difficult **Setting** 45-acre suburban campus **Total enrollment** 3,239 **Student/faculty ratio** 12:1 **Application deadline** Rolling **Freshmen** 74% were admitted **Housing** Yes **Expenses** Tuition $14,232; Room & Board $3863 **Undergraduates** 20% women, 3% 25 or older, 0.4% Native American, 2% Hispanic, 5% black, 6% Asian American or Pacific Islander **Most popular recent majors** Mechanical engineering; electrical/electronics engineering; industrial engineering **Academic program** Average class size 25, advanced placement, tutorials, internships **Contact** Ms. Julie A. Ulseth, Director of Admissions, Kettering University, 1700 West Third Avenue, Flint, MI 48504-4898. Telephone: 810-762-7865 or toll-free 800-955-4464. Fax: 810-762-9837. E-mail: admissions@kettering.edu/. Web site: http://www.kettering.edu/.

► **For more information, see page 455.**

LAKE SUPERIOR STATE UNIVERSITY
SAULT SAINTE MARIE, MICHIGAN

General State-supported, comprehensive, coed **Entrance** Moderately difficult **Setting** 121-acre small town campus **Total enrollment** 3,369 **Student/faculty ratio** 22:1 **Application deadline** 8/15 **Freshmen** 87% were admitted **Housing** Yes **Expenses** Tuition $3642; Room & Board $4646 **Undergraduates** 50% women, 23% part-time, 22% 25 or older, 6% Native American, 0.5% Hispanic, 0.4% black, 0.4% Asian American or Pacific Islander **Most popular recent majors** Criminal justice/law enforcement administration; business administration; education **Academic program** Advanced placement, self-designed majors, tutorials, honors program, summer session, adult/continuing education programs, internships **Contact** Mr. Kevin Pollock, Director of Admissions, Lake Superior State University, 650 W Easterday Avenue, Sault Sainte Marie, MI 49783-1699. Telephone: 906-635-2231 or toll-free 888-800-LSSU ext. 2231. Fax: 906-635-6669. E-mail: admissions@lakers.lssu.edu. Web site: http://www.lssu.edu/.

LAWRENCE TECHNOLOGICAL UNIVERSITY
SOUTHFIELD, MICHIGAN

General Independent, comprehensive, coed **Entrance** Moderately difficult **Setting** 110-acre suburban campus **Total enrollment** 3,645 **Student/faculty ratio** 14:1 **Application deadline** 8/11 **Housing** Yes **Expenses** Tuition $9340; Room only $2800 **Undergraduates** 23% women, 56% part-time, 0.5% Native American, 2% Hispanic, 15% black, 3% Asian American or Pacific Islander **Most popular recent majors** Mechanical engineering; architecture; electrical/electronics engineering **Academic program** Average class size 22, advanced placement, self-designed majors, tutorials, summer session, adult/continuing education programs, internships **Contact** Mr. Paul F. Kinder, Interim Director of Admissions, Lawrence Technological University, 21000 West Ten Mile Road, Southfield, MI 48075-1058. Telephone: 248-204-3160 or toll-free 800-225-5588. Fax: 248-204-3727. E-mail: admissions@ltu.edu. Web site: http://www.ltu.edu/.

MADONNA UNIVERSITY
LIVONIA, MICHIGAN

General Independent Roman Catholic, comprehensive, coed **Entrance** Moderately difficult **Setting** 49-acre suburban campus **Total enrollment** 3,905 **Student/faculty ratio** 15:1 **Application deadline** Rolling **Housing** Yes **Expenses** Tuition $6040; Room & Board $4334 **Undergraduates** 77% women, 56% part-time, 58% 25 or older, 1% Native American, 2% Hispanic, 9% black, 3% Asian American or Pacific Islander **Most popular recent majors** Business administration; nursing; criminal justice/law enforcement administration **Academic program** Advanced placement, accelerated degree program, honors program, summer session, adult/continuing education programs, internships **Contact** Mr. Frank Hribar, Director of Enrollment Management, Madonna University, 36600 Schoolcraft Road, Livonia, MI 48150-1173. Telephone: 734-432-5317 or toll-free 800-852-4951. Fax: 734-432-5393. E-mail: muinfo@smtp.munet.edu. Web site: http://www.munet.edu/.

MARYGROVE COLLEGE
DETROIT, MICHIGAN

General Independent Roman Catholic, comprehensive, coed **Entrance** Moderately difficult **Setting** 50-acre urban campus **Total enrollment** 3,603 **Student/faculty ratio** 17:1 **Application deadline** 8/15 **Housing** No **Expenses** Tuition $9410 **Undergraduates** 87% women, 57% part-time, 80% 25 or older, 0.3% Native American, 1% Hispanic, 78% black, 0.4% Asian American or Pacific Islander **Most popular recent majors** Social work; education; business administration **Academic program** Average class size 15, advanced placement, self-designed majors, summer session, internships **Contact** Ms. Carla R. Mathews, Director of Undergraduate Admissions, Marygrove College, 8425 West McNichols Road, Detroit, MI 48221-2599. Telephone: 313-927-1240. Fax: 313-927-1345. Web site: http://www.marygrove.edu/.

MICHIGAN CHRISTIAN COLLEGE

See Rochester College

MICHIGAN STATE UNIVERSITY

EAST LANSING, MICHIGAN

General State-supported, university, coed **Entrance** Moderately difficult **Setting** 5,000-acre suburban campus **Total enrollment** 42,603 **Student/faculty ratio** 12:1 **Application deadline** 7/30 **Freshmen** 81% were admitted **Housing** Yes **Expenses** Tuition $4789; Room & Board $4052 **Undergraduates** 53% women, 13% part-time, 7% 25 or older, 1% Native American, 2% Hispanic, 8% black, 4% Asian American or Pacific Islander **Most popular recent majors** Psychology; accounting; finance **Academic program** English as a second language, advanced placement, accelerated degree program, self-designed majors, tutorials, honors program, summer session, adult/continuing education programs, internships **Contact** Dr. William H. Turner, Director of Admissions, Michigan State University, East Lansing, MI 48824-1020. Telephone: 517-355-8332. E-mail: adm00@msu.edu. Web site: http://www.msu.edu/.

MICHIGAN TECHNOLOGICAL UNIVERSITY

HOUGHTON, MICHIGAN

General State-supported, university, coed **Entrance** Moderately difficult **Setting** 240-acre small town campus **Total enrollment** 6,302 **Student/faculty ratio** 12:1 **Application deadline** Rolling **Freshmen** 95% were admitted **Housing** Yes **Expenses** Tuition $4062; Room & Board $4420 **Undergraduates** 26% women, 7% part-time, 9% 25 or older, 1% Native American, 1% Hispanic, 2% black, 1% Asian American or Pacific Islander **Most popular recent majors** Mechanical engineering; electrical/electronics engineering; civil engineering **Academic program** Average class size 26, English as a second language, advanced placement, self-designed majors, tutorials, summer session, internships **Contact** Ms. Nancy Rehling, Director of Undergraduate Admissions, Michigan Technological University, 1400 Townsend Drive, Houghton, MI 49931-1295. Telephone: 906-487-2335. Fax: 906-487-3343. E-mail: mtu4u@mtu.edu. Web site: http://www.mtu.edu/.

NORTHERN MICHIGAN UNIVERSITY

MARQUETTE, MICHIGAN

General State-supported, comprehensive, coed **Entrance** Minimally difficult **Setting** 300-acre small town campus **Total enrollment** 7,787 **Student/faculty ratio** 20:1 **Application deadline** Rolling **Freshmen** 91% were admitted **Housing** Yes **Expenses** Tuition $2986; Room & Board $4340 **Undergraduates** 53% women, 15% part-time, 23% 25 or older, 2% Native American, 1% Hispanic, 1% black, 0.5% Asian American or Pacific Islander **Most popular recent majors** Education; business administration; nursing **Academic program** Average class size 21, advanced placement, accelerated degree program, self-designed majors, tutorials, summer session, adult/continuing education programs, internships **Contact** Ms. Gerri Daniels, Northern Michigan University, 1401 Presque Isle Avenue, Marquette, MI 49855-5301. Telephone: 906-227-2650 or toll-free 800-682-9797 (in-state). Fax: 906-227-1747. E-mail: admiss@nmu.edu. Web site: http://www.nmu.edu/.

NORTHWOOD UNIVERSITY

MIDLAND, MICHIGAN

General Independent, comprehensive, coed **Entrance** Moderately difficult **Setting** 434-acre small town campus **Total enrollment** 2,903 **Student/faculty ratio** 26:1 **Application deadline** Rolling **Freshmen** 93% were admitted **Housing** Yes **Expenses** Tuition $10,889; Room & Board $4878 **Undergraduates** 45% women, 45% part-time, 5% 25 or older, 0.2% Native American, 1% Hispanic, 6% black, 1% Asian American or Pacific Islander **Most popular recent majors** Business marketing and marketing management; accounting; business administration **Academic program** English as a second language, advanced placement, accelerated degree program, honors program, summer session, adult/continuing education programs, internships **Contact** Dr. David Long, University Dean of Admissions, Northwood University, 3225 Cook Road, Midland, MI 48640-2398. Telephone: 517-837-4273 or toll-free 800-457-7878. Fax: 517-837-4104. E-mail: admissions@northwood.edu. Web site: http://www.northwood.edu/.

▶ **For more information, see page 487.**

OAKLAND UNIVERSITY

ROCHESTER, MICHIGAN

General State-supported, university, coed **Entrance** Moderately difficult **Setting** 1,444-acre suburban campus **Total enrollment** 14,379 **Student/faculty ratio** 19:1 **Application deadline** 8/28 **Freshmen** 86% were admitted **Housing** Yes **Expenses** Tuition $3734; Room & Board $4250 **Un-**

Oakland University *(continued)*

dergraduates 66% women, 35% part-time, 32% 25 or older, 1% Native American, 1% Hispanic, 6% black, 2% Asian American or Pacific Islander **Most popular recent majors** Psychology; biology; nursing **Academic program** Average class size 29, advanced placement, accelerated degree program, self-designed majors, tutorials, honors program, summer session, internships **Contact** Mr. Robert E. Johnson, Associate Vice President for Enrollment Management, Oakland University, 101 North Foundation Hall, Rochester, MI 48309-4401. Telephone: 248-370-3360 or toll-free 800-OAK-UNIV. Fax: 248-370-4462. E-mail: ouinfo@oakland.edu. Web site: http://www.oakland.edu/.

OLIVET COLLEGE
OLIVET, MICHIGAN

General Independent, comprehensive, coed, affiliated with Congregational Christian Church **Entrance** Moderately difficult **Setting** 92-acre small town campus **Total enrollment** 884 **Student/faculty ratio** 13:1 **Application deadline** 8/15 **Housing** Yes **Expenses** Tuition $12,660; Room & Board $4038 **Undergraduates** 41% women, 3% part-time, 13% 25 or older, 1% Native American, 3% Hispanic, 14% black, 0.4% Asian American or Pacific Islander **Most popular recent majors** Business administration; biology; psychology **Academic program** Average class size 20, advanced placement, accelerated degree program, self-designed majors, tutorials, honors program, summer session, internships **Contact** Mr. Bernie McConnell, Director of Admissions, Olivet College, 320 South Main Street, Olivet, MI 49076-9701. Telephone: 616-749-7635 or toll-free 800-456-7189. Fax: 616-749-3821. E-mail: admissions@olivetnet.edu. Web site: http://www.olivetnet.edu/.

REFORMED BIBLE COLLEGE
GRAND RAPIDS, MICHIGAN

General Independent religious, 4-year, coed **Entrance** Moderately difficult **Setting** 27-acre suburban campus **Total enrollment** 213 **Student/faculty ratio** 13:1 **Application deadline** Rolling **Freshmen** 98% were admitted **Housing** Yes **Expenses** Tuition $6892; Room & Board $3500 **Undergraduates** 36% 25 or older **Academic program** Average class size 22, advanced placement, accelerated degree program, tutorials, summer session, adult/continuing education programs, internships **Contact** Mr. David De Boer, Director of Admissions/International Student Advisor, Reformed Bible College, 3333 East Beltline, NE, Grand Rapids, MI 49525-9749. Telephone: 616-222-3000. Fax: 616-222-3045.

ROCHESTER COLLEGE
ROCHESTER HILLS, MICHIGAN

General Independent, 4-year, coed, affiliated with Church of Christ **Entrance** Minimally difficult **Setting** 83-acre suburban campus **Total enrollment** 418 **Student/faculty ratio** 17:1 **Application deadline** Rolling **Freshmen** 87% were admitted **Housing** Yes **Expenses** Tuition $6724; Room & Board $3900 **Undergraduates** 51% women, 16% part-time, 15% 25 or older, 0.5% Native American, 2% Hispanic, 8% black, 0.5% Asian American or Pacific Islander **Most popular recent majors** Business administration; psychology; divinity/ministry **Academic program** Advanced placement, accelerated degree program, tutorials, summer session, adult/continuing education programs, internships **Contact** Mr. Phil Conner, Dean of Enrollment Services, Rochester College, 800 West Avon Road, Rochester Hills, MI 48307-2764. Telephone: 248-218-2030 or toll-free 800-521-6010. Fax: 248-218-2005. E-mail: admissions@rc.edu. Web site: http://www.rc.edu/.

SACRED HEART MAJOR SEMINARY
DETROIT, MICHIGAN

General Independent Roman Catholic, comprehensive, coed **Entrance** Moderately difficult **Setting** 24-acre urban campus **Total enrollment** 296 **Student/faculty ratio** 5:1 **Application deadline** 7/31 **Freshmen** 100% were admitted **Housing** Yes **Expenses** Tuition $5210; Room & Board $4241 **Undergraduates** 66% 25 or older, 4% Hispanic, 10% black **Academic program** Average class size 10, advanced placement, honors program **Contact** Rev. Earl Boyea, Dean of Studies, Sacred Heart Major Seminary, 2701 Chicago Boulevard, Detroit, MI 48206. Telephone: 313-883-8556.

SAGINAW VALLEY STATE UNIVERSITY
UNIVERSITY CENTER, MICHIGAN

General State-supported, comprehensive, coed **Entrance** Moderately difficult **Setting** 782-acre rural campus **Total enrollment** 7,493 **Student/faculty ratio** 34:1 **Application deadline** Rolling **Freshmen** 97% were admitted **Housing** Yes **Expenses** Tuition $3448; Room & Board $4375 **Undergraduates** 59% women, 35% part-time, 29% 25 or older, 1% Native American, 4% Hispanic, 6% black, 1% Asian American or Pacific Islander **Most popular recent majors** Elementary education; criminal justice studies; social work **Academic program** Average class size 30, English as a second language, advanced placement, accelerated degree program, self-designed majors, tutorials, honors program, summer session, internships **Contact** Mr. James P. Dwyer, Director of Admissions,

Saginaw Valley State University, 7400 Bay Road, University Center, MI 48710. Telephone: 517-790-4200 or toll-free 800-968-9500. Fax: 517-790-0180. E-mail: admissions@tardis.svsu.edu. Web site: http://www.svsu.edu/.

SAINT MARY'S COLLEGE
ORCHARD LAKE, MICHIGAN

General Independent Roman Catholic, 4-year, coed **Entrance** Moderately difficult **Setting** 120-acre suburban campus **Total enrollment** 310 **Student/faculty ratio** 11:1 **Application deadline** Rolling **Freshmen** 70% were admitted **Housing** Yes **Expenses** Tuition $6844; Room & Board $4500 **Undergraduates** 49% women, 38% part-time, 40% 25 or older, 0.3% Native American, 2% Hispanic, 14% black, 1% Asian American or Pacific Islander **Most popular recent majors** Mass communications; (pre)medicine; business administration **Academic program** English as a second language, advanced placement, tutorials, adult/continuing education programs, internships **Contact** Mr. David Sichterman, Freshman Coordinator, Saint Mary's College, 3535 Indian Trail, Orchard Lake, MI 48324-1623. Telephone: 248-683-0523.

SIENA HEIGHTS UNIVERSITY
ADRIAN, MICHIGAN

General Independent Roman Catholic, comprehensive, coed **Entrance** Moderately difficult **Setting** 140-acre small town campus **Total enrollment** 1,287 **Student/faculty ratio** 14:1 **Application deadline** Rolling **Freshmen** 89% were admitted **Housing** Yes **Expenses** Tuition $10,700; Room & Board $4330 **Undergraduates** 8% 25 or older **Academic program** Average class size 35, advanced placement, accelerated degree program, self-designed majors, tutorials, summer session, adult/continuing education programs, internships **Contact** Mr. Kevin Kucera, Dean of Admissions and Enrollment Services, Siena Heights University, 1247 East Siena Heights Drive, Adrian, MI 49221-1796. Telephone: 517-264-7180 or toll-free 800-521-0009. Fax: 517-264-7745. E-mail: admissions@sienahts.edu.

SPRING ARBOR COLLEGE
SPRING ARBOR, MICHIGAN

General Independent Free Methodist, comprehensive, coed **Entrance** Moderately difficult **Setting** 70-acre small town campus **Total enrollment** 2,242 **Student/faculty ratio** 17:1 **Application deadline** Rolling **Freshmen** 92% were admitted **Housing** Yes **Expenses** Tuition $10,686; Room & Board $4190 **Undergraduates** 24% 25 or older **Most popular recent majors** Business administration; English; physical education **Academic program** Advanced placement, self-designed majors, honors program, summer session, adult/continuing education programs, internships **Contact** Mrs. Shelley Ashley, Acting Director of Admissions, Spring Arbor College, 106 Main Street, Spring Arbor, MI 49283-9799. Telephone: 517-750-1200 ext. 1470 or toll-free 800-968-0011. Fax: 517-750-1604. E-mail: shellya@admin.arbor.edu.

UNIVERSITY OF DETROIT MERCY
DETROIT, MICHIGAN

General Independent Roman Catholic (Jesuit), university, coed **Entrance** Moderately difficult **Setting** 70-acre urban campus **Total enrollment** 6,929 **Student/faculty ratio** 14:1 **Application deadline** 7/1 **Freshmen** 75% were admitted **Housing** Yes **Expenses** Tuition $12,986; Room & Board $5080 **Undergraduates** 65% women, 47% part-time, 50% 25 or older, 0.5% Native American, 2% Hispanic, 37% black, 2% Asian American or Pacific Islander **Most popular recent majors** Nursing; business administration; engineering **Academic program** English as a second language, advanced placement, accelerated degree program, tutorials, honors program, summer session, adult/continuing education programs, internships **Contact** Ms. Dawn Benson, Admissions Counselor, University of Detroit Mercy, PO Box 19900, Detroit, MI 48219-0900. Telephone: 313-993-1245 or toll-free 800-635-5020 (out-of-state). Fax: 313-993-3326. E-mail: admissions@udmercy.edu. Web site: http://www.udmercy.edu/.

UNIVERSITY OF MICHIGAN
ANN ARBOR, MICHIGAN

General State-supported, university, coed **Entrance** Very difficult **Setting** 2,871-acre suburban campus **Total enrollment** 36,995 **Student/faculty ratio** 8:1 **Application deadline** 2/1 **Freshmen** 69% were admitted **Housing** Yes **Expenses** Tuition $5878; Room & Board $5342 **Undergraduates** 50% women, 6% part-time, 4% 25 or older, 1% Native American, 4% Hispanic, 9% black, 11% Asian American or Pacific Islander **Most popular recent majors** Engineering; psychology; English **Academic program** English as a second language, advanced placement, accelerated degree program, self-designed majors, tutorials, honors program, summer session, adult/continuing education programs, internships **Contact** Mr. Ted Spencer, Director of Undergraduate Admissions, University of Michigan, Ann Arbor, MI 48109-1316. Telephone: 734-764-7433. Fax: 734-936-0740. E-mail: ugadmiss@umich.edu. Web site: http://www.umich.edu/.

UNIVERSITY OF MICHIGAN–DEARBORN
DEARBORN, MICHIGAN

General State-supported, comprehensive, coed **Entrance** Moderately difficult **Setting** 210-acre suburban campus **Total enrollment** 8,179 **Student/faculty ratio** 20:1 **Application deadline** Rolling **Housing** No **Expenses** Tuition $4850 **Undergraduates** 54% women, 41% part-time, 31% 25 or older, 1% Native American, 2% Hispanic, 7% black, 5% Asian American or Pacific Islander **Most popular recent majors** Mechanical engineering; electrical/electronics engineering; psychology **Academic program** Accelerated degree program, self-designed majors, honors program, summer session, adult/continuing education programs, internships **Contact** Ms. Carol S. Mack, Director of Admissions, University of Michigan-Dearborn, 4901 Evergreen Road, Dearborn, MI 48128-1491. Telephone: 313-593-5100. E-mail: umdgoblu@umd.umich.edu. Web site: http://www.umd.umich.edu/.

UNIVERSITY OF MICHIGAN–FLINT
FLINT, MICHIGAN

General State-supported, comprehensive, coed **Entrance** Moderately difficult **Setting** 72-acre urban campus **Total enrollment** 6,488 **Student/faculty ratio** 25:1 **Application deadline** 8/21 **Freshmen** 89% were admitted **Housing** No **Expenses** Tuition $3559 **Undergraduates** 64% women, 43% part-time, 33% 25 or older, 1% Native American, 2% Hispanic, 11% black, 1% Asian American or Pacific Islander **Most popular recent majors** Business administration; education **Academic program** Advanced placement, accelerated degree program, self-designed majors, honors program, summer session, adult/continuing education programs **Contact** Dr. Virginia R. Allen, Vice Chancellor for Student Services and Enrollment, University of Michigan–Flint, 303 Kearsley Street, Flint, MI 48502-2186. Telephone: 810-762-3434. E-mail: davis_m@pavilion.flint.umich.edu. Web site: http://www.flint.umich.edu/.

WALSH COLLEGE OF ACCOUNTANCY AND BUSINESS ADMINISTRATION
TROY, MICHIGAN

General Independent, upper-level, coed **Entrance** Noncompetitive **Setting** 29-acre suburban campus **Total enrollment** 3,335 **Application deadline** Rolling **Freshmen** 93% were admitted **Housing** No **Expenses** Tuition $4758 **Undergraduates** 62% women, 85% part-time, 75% 25 or older, 0.1% Native American, 1% Hispanic, 4% black, 2% Asian American or Pacific Islander **Most popular recent majors** Accounting; finance; business administration **Academic program** Accelerated degree program, summer session, adult/continuing education programs, internships **Contact** Ms. Mary Cay Slecman, Director of Admissions, Walsh College of Accountancy and Business Administration, 3838 Livernois Road, PO Box 7006, Troy, MI 48007-7006. Telephone: 248-689-8282 ext. 215. Fax: 248-524-2520. Web site: http://www.walshcol.edu/.

WAYNE STATE UNIVERSITY
DETROIT, MICHIGAN

General State-supported, university, coed **Entrance** Moderately difficult **Setting** 203-acre urban campus **Total enrollment** 30,729 **Student/faculty ratio** 11:1 **Application deadline** 8/1 **Freshmen** 85% were admitted **Housing** Yes **Expenses** Tuition $3486; Room only $3875 **Undergraduates** 60% women, 47% part-time, 43% 25 or older, 0.4% Native American, 2% Hispanic, 29% black, 5% Asian American or Pacific Islander **Most popular recent majors** Psychology; elementary education; social work **Academic program** English as a second language, advanced placement, accelerated degree program, tutorials, honors program, summer session, adult/continuing education programs, internships **Contact** Mr. Michael Wood, Associate Director, Wayne State University, 3E HNJ, Detroit, MI 48202. Telephone: 313-577-7928. Fax: 313-577-7536. E-mail: john.witter@wayne.edu. Web site: http://www.wayne.edu/.

WESTERN MICHIGAN UNIVERSITY
KALAMAZOO, MICHIGAN

General State-supported, university, coed **Entrance** Moderately difficult **Setting** 451-acre urban campus **Total enrollment** 26,132 **Student/faculty ratio** 16:1 **Application deadline** Rolling **Freshmen** 83% were admitted **Housing** Yes **Expenses** Tuition $3655; Room & Board $4398 **Undergraduates** 54% women, 20% part-time, 14% 25 or older, 0.5% Native American, 2% Hispanic, 7% black, 1% Asian American or Pacific Islander **Most popular recent majors** Business marketing and marketing management; sociology; education **Academic program** Average class size 33, English as a second language, advanced placement, accelerated degree program, self-designed majors, tutorials, honors program, summer session, adult/continuing education programs, internships **Contact** Mr. John Fraire, Dean, Office of Admissions and Orientation, Western Michigan University, Office of Admissions and Orientation, Kalamazoo, MI 49008. Telephone: 616-387-2000. Fax: 616-387-2096. E-mail: ask-wmu@wmich.edu. Web site: http://www.wmich.edu/.

► **For more information, see page 554.**

WILLIAM TYNDALE COLLEGE
FARMINGTON HILLS, MICHIGAN

General Independent religious, 4-year, coed **Entrance** Minimally difficult **Setting** 28-acre suburban campus **Total enrollment** 615 **Student/faculty ratio** 7:1 **Application deadline** Rolling **Housing** Yes **Expenses** Tuition $6300; Room only $1800 **Undergraduates** 53% women, 36% part-time, 69% 25 or older, 0.5% Native American, 0.3% Hispanic, 30% black, 1% Asian American or Pacific Islander **Most popular recent majors** Business administration; biblical studies; psychology **Academic program** Average class size 20, advanced placement, accelerated degree program, tutorials, summer session, adult/continuing education programs, internships **Contact** Mrs. Elmarie Odendaal, Counselor, William Tyndale College, 37500 West Twelve Mile Road, Farmington Hills, MI 48331. Telephone: 248-553-7200 or toll-free 800-483-0707. Fax: 248-553-5963. Web site: http://www.tyndalecollege.edu/.

YESHIVA GEDDOLAH OF GREATER DETROIT RABBINICAL COLLEGE
OAK PARK, MICHIGAN

Contact Mr. Eric Krohner, Executive Director, Yeshiva Geddolah of Greater Detroit Rabbinical College, 24600 Greenfield, Oak Park, MI 48237-1544. Telephone: 810-968-3360.

MINNESOTA

AUGSBURG COLLEGE
MINNEAPOLIS, MINNESOTA

General Independent Lutheran, comprehensive, coed **Entrance** Moderately difficult **Setting** 23-acre urban campus **Total enrollment** 2,817 **Student/faculty ratio** 15:1 **Application deadline** 5/1 **Freshmen** 83% were admitted **Housing** Yes **Expenses** Tuition $14,616; Room & Board $5134 **Undergraduates** 59% women, 18% part-time, 20% 25 or older, 2% Native American, 1% Hispanic, 6% black, 4% Asian American or Pacific Islander **Most popular recent majors** Business administration; education; mass communications **Academic program** Average class size 25, English as a second language, advanced placement, accelerated degree program, self-designed majors, tutorials, honors program, summer session, adult/continuing education programs, internships **Contact** Ms. Sally Daniels, Director of Admission, Augsburg College, 2211 Riverside Avenue, Minneapolis, MN 55454-1351. Telephone: 612-330-1001 or toll-free 800-788-5678. Fax: 612-330-1649. E-mail: admissions@augsburg.edu. Web site: http://www.augsburg.edu/.

BEMIDJI STATE UNIVERSITY
BEMIDJI, MINNESOTA

General State-supported, comprehensive, coed **Entrance** Moderately difficult **Setting** 83-acre small town campus **Total enrollment** 4,650 **Student/faculty ratio** 20:1 **Application deadline** 8/15 **Freshmen** 68% were admitted **Housing** Yes **Expenses** Tuition $3118; Room & Board $3084 **Undergraduates** 53% women, 14% part-time, 23% 25 or older, 5% Native American, 1% Hispanic, 1% black, 2% Asian American or Pacific Islander **Most popular recent majors** Elementary education; business administration; industrial technology **Academic program** English as a second language, advanced placement, accelerated degree program, honors program, summer session, adult/continuing education programs, internships **Contact** Mr. Paul Muller, Associate Director of Admissions, Bemidji State University, 1500 Birchmont Drive, NE, Bemidji, MN 56601-2699. Telephone: 218-755-2040 or toll-free 800-475-2001 (in-state), 800-652-9747 (out-of-state). Fax: 218-755-2074. E-mail: admissions@vax1.bemidji.msus.edu.

BETHEL COLLEGE
ST. PAUL, MINNESOTA

General Independent, comprehensive, coed, affiliated with Baptist General Conference **Entrance** Moderately difficult **Setting** 231-acre suburban campus **Total enrollment** 2,612 **Student/faculty ratio** 16:1 **Application deadline** Rolling **Housing** Yes **Expenses** Tuition $13,840; Room & Board $4950 **Undergraduates** 63% women, 3% part-time, 0.2% Native American, 1% Hispanic, 2% black, 3% Asian American or Pacific Islander **Most popular recent majors** Education; nursing; business administration **Academic program** Average class size 22, advanced placement, self-designed majors, honors program, summer session, adult/continuing education programs, internships **Contact** Mr. John C. Lassen, Director of Admissions, Bethel College, 3900 Bethel Drive, St. Paul, MN 55112-6999. Telephone: 612-638-6436 or toll-free 800-255-8706. E-mail: bcoll-admit@bethel.edu. Web site: http://www.bethel.edu/.

▶ **For more information, see page 396.**

CARLETON COLLEGE
NORTHFIELD, MINNESOTA

General Independent, 4-year, coed **Entrance** Very difficult **Setting** 955-acre small town campus **Total enrollment** 1,880 **Student/faculty ratio** 10:1 **Application deadline** 1/15 **Freshmen** 51% were

Carleton College *(continued)*

admitted **Housing** Yes **Expenses** Tuition $21,885; Room & Board $4440 **Undergraduates** 52% women, 0% 25 or older, 0.4% Native American, 4% Hispanic, 3% black, 8% Asian American or Pacific Islander **Most popular recent majors** Biology; English; political science **Academic program** Advanced placement, accelerated degree program, self-designed majors, tutorials, internships **Contact** Mr. Paul Thiboutot, Dean of Admissions, Carleton College, One North College Street, Northfield, MN 55057-4001. Telephone: 507-646-4190 or toll-free 800-995-2275. Fax: 507-646-4526. E-mail: admissions@acs.carleton.edu. Web site: http://www.carleton.edu/.

COLLEGE OF SAINT BENEDICT

COORDINATE WITH SAINT JOHN'S UNIVERSITY (MN)

SAINT JOSEPH, MINNESOTA

General Independent Roman Catholic, 4-year, women only, coordinate with Saint John's University (MN) **Entrance** Moderately difficult **Setting** 315-acre small town campus **Total enrollment** 1,980 **Student/faculty ratio** 13:1 **Application deadline** Rolling **Freshmen** 92% were admitted **Housing** Yes **Expenses** Tuition $14,758; Room & Board $4706 **Undergraduates** 3% part-time, 4% 25 or older, 0.2% Native American, 1% Hispanic, 0.5% black, 1% Asian American or Pacific Islander **Most popular recent majors** Education; business administration; nursing **Academic program** Average class size 21, advanced placement, self-designed majors, tutorials, honors program, internships **Contact** Ms. Mary Milbert, Dean of Admissions, College of Saint Benedict, 37 South College Avenue, Saint Joseph, MN 56374. Telephone: 320-363-5308 or toll-free 800-544-1489. Fax: 320-363-5010. E-mail: admissions@csbsju.edu. Web site: http://www.csbsju.edu/.

▶ **For more information, see page 417.**

COLLEGE OF ST. CATHERINE

ST. PAUL, MINNESOTA

General Independent Roman Catholic, comprehensive, women only **Entrance** Moderately difficult **Setting** 110-acre urban campus **Total enrollment** 2,897 **Student/faculty ratio** 14:1 **Application deadline** 8/15 **Freshmen** 89% were admitted **Housing** Yes **Expenses** Tuition $14,258; Room & Board $4230 **Undergraduates** 16% part-time, 40% 25 or older, 1% Native American, 2% Hispanic, 2% black, 4% Asian American or Pacific Islander **Most popular recent majors** Business administration; nursing; occupational therapy **Academic program** Average class size 19, advanced placement, accelerated degree program, self-designed majors, honors program, summer session, adult/continuing education programs, internships **Contact** Ms. Cory Piper-Hauswirth, Associate Director of Admission and Financial Aid, College of St. Catherine, 2004 Randolph Avenue, St. Paul, MN 55105-1789. Telephone: 612-690-6047 or toll-free 800-945-4599 (in-state). Fax: 612-690-6042. E-mail: stkate@stkate.edu. Web site: http://www.stkate.edu/.

COLLEGE OF ST. SCHOLASTICA

DULUTH, MINNESOTA

General Independent, comprehensive, coed, affiliated with Roman Catholic Church **Entrance** Moderately difficult **Setting** 160-acre suburban campus **Total enrollment** 2,030 **Student/faculty ratio** 12:1 **Application deadline** Rolling **Freshmen** 91% were admitted **Housing** Yes **Expenses** Tuition $13,995; Room & Board $3957 **Undergraduates** 73% women, 13% part-time, 13% 25 or older, 1% Native American, 0.4% Hispanic, 1% black, 1% Asian American or Pacific Islander **Most popular recent majors** Nursing; health science; education **Academic program** Average class size 17, advanced placement, self-designed majors, tutorials, honors program, summer session, adult/continuing education programs, internships **Contact** Ms. Rebecca Urbanski-Junkert, Vice President for Admissions and Financial Aid, College of St. Scholastica, 1200 Kenwood Avenue, Duluth, MN 55811-4199. Telephone: 218-723-6053 or toll-free 800-447-5444. Fax: 218-723-6290. E-mail: admissions@css.edu. Web site: http://www.css.edu/.

COLLEGE OF VISUAL ARTS

ST. PAUL, MINNESOTA

General Independent, 4-year, coed **Entrance** Minimally difficult **Setting** 2-acre urban campus **Total enrollment** 225 **Application deadline** Rolling **Housing** No **Expenses** Tuition $10,020 **Undergraduates** 53% women, 9% part-time, 17% 25 or older, 1% Native American, 3% Hispanic, 1% black, 4% Asian American or Pacific Islander **Most popular recent majors** Graphic design/commercial art/illustration; art **Academic program** Average class size 18, advanced placement, tutorials, summer session, internships **Contact** Ms. Sherry A. Essen, Director of Admissions and Student Affairs, College of Visual Arts, 344 Summit Avenue, St. Paul, MN 55102-2124. Telephone: 612-224-3416 or toll-free 800-224-1536. Fax: 612-224-8854.

CONCORDIA COLLEGE

MOORHEAD, MINNESOTA

General Independent, 4-year, coed, affiliated with Evangelical Lutheran Church in America **En-**

trance Moderately difficult **Setting** 120-acre suburban campus **Total enrollment** 2,931 **Student/faculty ratio** 15:1 **Application deadline** Rolling **Freshmen** 92% were admitted **Housing** Yes **Expenses** Tuition $12,655; Room & Board $3645 **Undergraduates** 63% women, 2% 25 or older, 0.4% Native American, 1% Hispanic, 0.4% black, 1% Asian American or Pacific Islander **Most popular recent majors** Business administration; biology; communications **Academic program** Average class size 25, English as a second language, advanced placement, tutorials, honors program, summer session, adult/continuing education programs, internships **Contact** Mr. Lee E. Johnson, Director of Admissions, Concordia College, 901 8th Street South, Moorhead, MN 56562. Telephone: 218-299-3004 or toll-free 800-699-9897. Fax: 218-299-3947. E-mail: admissions@cord.edu. Web site: http://www.cord.edu/.

CONCORDIA UNIVERSITY AT ST. PAUL
ST. PAUL, MINNESOTA

General Independent, comprehensive, coed, affiliated with Lutheran Church–Missouri Synod **Entrance** Minimally difficult **Setting** 37-acre urban campus **Total enrollment** 1,347 **Student/faculty ratio** 19:1 **Application deadline** 8/15 **Freshmen** 74% were admitted **Housing** Yes **Expenses** Tuition $11,980; Room & Board $4500 **Most popular recent majors** Education; business administration; early childhood education **Academic program** Average class size 18, English as a second language, advanced placement, accelerated degree program, self-designed majors, tutorials, summer session, adult/continuing education programs, internships **Contact** Mr. Tim Utter, Director of Admissions, Concordia University at St. Paul, 275 Syndicate Drive North, St. Paul, MN 55104-5494. Telephone: 612-641-8230 or toll-free 800-333-4705. Fax: 612-659-0207. E-mail: admiss@luther.csp.edu. Web site: http://www.csp.edu/.

CROWN COLLEGE
ST. BONIFACIUS, MINNESOTA

General Independent, comprehensive, coed, affiliated with The Christian and Missionary Alliance **Entrance** Minimally difficult **Setting** 193-acre suburban campus **Total enrollment** 713 **Student/faculty ratio** 14:1 **Application deadline** Rolling **Freshmen** 67% were admitted **Housing** Yes **Expenses** Tuition $9335; Room & Board $4020 **Undergraduates** 54% women, 7% part-time, 25% 25 or older, 2% Hispanic, 1% black, 4% Asian American or Pacific Islander **Most popular recent majors** Elementary education; divinity/ministry; child care/development **Academic program** Average class size 24, English as a second language, advanced placement, tutorials, summer session, adult/continuing education programs, internships **Contact** Ms. Amy Henning, Senior Admissions Counselor, Crown College, 6425 County Road 30, St. Bonifacius, MN 55375-9001. Telephone: 612-446-4142 or toll-free 800-68-CROWN. Fax: 612-446-4149. E-mail: info@gw.crown.edu. Web site: http://www.crown.edu/.

GUSTAVUS ADOLPHUS COLLEGE
ST. PETER, MINNESOTA

General Independent, 4-year, coed, affiliated with Evangelical Lutheran Church in America **Entrance** Very difficult **Setting** 330-acre small town campus **Total enrollment** 2,418 **Student/faculty ratio** 13:1 **Application deadline** 4/1 **Freshmen** 83% were admitted **Housing** Yes **Expenses** Tuition $16,120; Room & Board $4010 **Undergraduates** 56% women, 2% part-time, 0% 25 or older, 0.2% Native American, 1% Hispanic, 1% black, 3% Asian American or Pacific Islander **Most popular recent majors** Psychology; biology; political science **Academic program** Average class size 20, advanced placement, accelerated degree program, self-designed majors, tutorials, honors program, summer session, internships **Contact** Mr. Owen Sammelson, Vice President of Administration, Gustavus Adolphus College, 800 West College Avenue, St. Peter, MN 56082-1498. Telephone: 507-933-7676 or toll-free 800-GUSTAVU(S). E-mail: admission@gac.edu. Web site: http://www.gac.edu/.

HAMLINE UNIVERSITY
ST. PAUL, MINNESOTA

General Independent, comprehensive, coed, affiliated with United Methodist Church **Entrance** Moderately difficult **Setting** 50-acre urban campus **Total enrollment** 3,071 **Student/faculty ratio** 13:1 **Application deadline** Rolling **Freshmen** 84% were admitted **Housing** Yes **Expenses** Tuition $14,850; Room & Board $4799 **Undergraduates** 60% women, 4% part-time, 9% 25 or older, 1% Native American, 1% Hispanic, 3% black, 3% Asian American or Pacific Islander **Most popular recent majors** Psychology; political science; English **Academic program** Average class size 18, English as a second language, advanced placement, self-designed majors, tutorials, honors program, summer session, adult/continuing education programs, internships **Contact** Dr. Louise Cummings-Simmons, Dean of Undergraduate Admission, Hamline University, 1536 Hewitt Avenue C1930, St. Paul, MN 55104-1284. Telephone: 612-523-2207 or toll-free 800-753-9753. Fax: 612-523-2458. E-mail: admis@seq.hamline.edu. Web site: http://www.hamline.edu/.

MACALESTER COLLEGE
ST. PAUL, MINNESOTA

General Independent Presbyterian, 4-year, coed **Entrance** Very difficult **Setting** 53-acre urban campus **Total enrollment** 1,774 **Student/faculty ratio** 11:1 **Application deadline** 1/15 **Freshmen** 54% were admitted **Housing** Yes **Expenses** Tuition $18,758; Room & Board $5430 **Undergraduates** 55% women, 2% part-time, 1% 25 or older, 0.3% Native American, 3% Hispanic, 3% black, 5% Asian American or Pacific Islander **Most popular recent majors** Psychology; English; economics **Academic program** Advanced placement, self-designed majors, tutorials, honors program, internships **Contact** Dr. William Langdon, Dean of Admissions, Macalester College, 1600 Grand Avenue, St. Paul, MN 55105-1899. Telephone: 651-696-6357 or toll-free 800-231-7974. Fax: 612-696-6500. E-mail: admissions@macalester.edu. Web site: http://www.macalester.edu/.

MANKATO STATE UNIVERSITY
MANKATO, MINNESOTA

General State-supported, comprehensive, coed **Entrance** Moderately difficult **Setting** 303-acre small town campus **Total enrollment** 12,507 **Student/faculty ratio** 19:1 **Application deadline** Rolling **Freshmen** 84% were admitted **Housing** Yes **Expenses** Tuition $2983; Room & Board $2965 **Undergraduates** 52% women, 14% part-time, 21% 25 or older, 0.2% Native American, 1% Hispanic, 1% black, 2% Asian American or Pacific Islander **Most popular recent majors** Business administration; education; accounting **Academic program** Advanced placement, accelerated degree program, self-designed majors, honors program, summer session, adult/continuing education programs, internships **Contact** Mr. Walt Wolff, Director of Admissions, Mankato State University, PO Box 8400, MSU 55, Mankato, MN 56002-8400. Telephone: 507-389-1822 or toll-free 800-722-0544. E-mail: linda_meidl@msl.mankato.msus.edu. Web site: http://www.mankato.msus.edu/.

MARTIN LUTHER COLLEGE
NEW ULM, MINNESOTA

General Independent, 4-year, coed, affiliated with Wisconsin Evangelical Lutheran Synod **Entrance** Moderately difficult **Setting** 50-acre small town campus **Total enrollment** 811 **Student/faculty ratio** 9:1 **Application deadline** 5/1 **Freshmen** 94% were admitted **Housing** Yes **Expenses** Tuition $4605; Room & Board $2285 **Undergraduates** 48% women, 1% part-time, 5% 25 or older, 0.1% Native American, 1% Hispanic, 1% black, 1% Asian American or Pacific Islander **Most popular recent majors** Elementary education; (pre)theology; secondary education **Academic program** Advanced placement, summer session, internships **Contact** Mr. John Sebald, Associate Director of Admissions, Martin Luther College, 1995 Luther Court, New Ulm, MN 56073-3965. Telephone: 507-354-8221 ext. 280. Fax: 507-354-8225. E-mail: sebaldja-fac@mlc-wels.edu.

METROPOLITAN STATE UNIVERSITY
ST. PAUL, MINNESOTA

General State-supported, comprehensive, coed **Contact** Ms. Cindy Olson, Registrar, Metropolitan State University, 700 East 7th Street, St. Paul, MN 55106-5000. Telephone: 612-772-7776. Web site: http://www.metro.msus.edu/.

MINNEAPOLIS COLLEGE OF ART AND DESIGN
MINNEAPOLIS, MINNESOTA

General Independent, comprehensive, coed **Entrance** Moderately difficult **Setting** 7-acre urban campus **Total enrollment** 598 **Student/faculty ratio** 11:1 **Application deadline** Rolling **Freshmen** 79% were admitted **Housing** Yes **Expenses** Tuition $15,810; Room only $2787 **Undergraduates** 40% women, 10% part-time, 25% 25 or older, 1% Native American, 3% Hispanic, 2% black, 6% Asian American or Pacific Islander **Most popular recent majors** Graphic design/commercial art/illustration; fine/studio arts; photography **Academic program** Average class size 20, tutorials, summer session, adult/continuing education programs, internships **Contact** Ms. Rebecca Haas, Director of Admissions, Minneapolis College of Art and Design, 2501 Stevens Avenue South, Minneapolis, MN 55404-4347. Telephone: 612-874-3760 or toll-free 800-874-6223. Fax: 612-874-3704. E-mail: admissions@mn.mcad.edu. Web site: http://www.mcad.edu/.

▶ **For more information, see page 474.**

MINNESOTA BIBLE COLLEGE
ROCHESTER, MINNESOTA

General Independent, 4-year, coed, affiliated with Christian Churches and Churches of Christ **Entrance** Noncompetitive **Setting** 40-acre urban campus **Total enrollment** 120 **Student/faculty ratio** 11:1 **Application deadline** 8/15 **Freshmen** 64% were admitted **Housing** Yes **Expenses** Tuition $5345; Room only $1500 **Undergraduates** 44% women, 13% part-time, 20% 25 or older, 0% Native American, 3% Hispanic, 1% black, 8% Asian American or Pacific Islander **Most popular recent majors** Liberal arts and studies; theology **Academic program** Advanced placement, self-designed majors, tutorials, internships **Contact** Mr. Alan D. Wager, Director of Admissions,

Minnesota Bible College, 920 Mayowood Road, SW, Rochester, MN 55902-2382. Telephone: 507-288-4563 ext. 246 or toll-free 800-456-7651. Fax: 507-288-9046. E-mail: admissions@mnbc.edu.

MOORHEAD STATE UNIVERSITY
MOORHEAD, MINNESOTA

General State-supported, comprehensive, coed **Entrance** Moderately difficult **Setting** 118-acre urban campus **Total enrollment** 6,466 **Student/faculty ratio** 18:1 **Application deadline** 8/7 **Freshmen** 96% were admitted **Housing** Yes **Expenses** Tuition $2908; Room & Board $3256 **Undergraduates** 64% women, 15% part-time, 19% 25 or older, 1% Native American, 1% Hispanic, 1% black, 1% Asian American or Pacific Islander **Most popular recent majors** Business administration; accounting **Academic program** Advanced placement, self-designed majors, tutorials, honors program, summer session, adult/continuing education programs, internships **Contact** Ms. Jean Lange, Director of Admissions, Moorhead State University, Owens Hall, Moorhead, MN 56563-0002. Telephone: 218-236-2548 or toll-free 800-593-7246. Fax: 218-236-2168. Web site: http://www.moorhead.msus.edu/.

NATIONAL AMERICAN UNIVERSITY–ST. PAUL CAMPUS
ST. PAUL, MINNESOTA

General Proprietary, 4-year, coed **Contact** Ms. Collette A. Garrity, Vice President, National American University–St. Paul Campus, 1380 Energy Lane, Suite 13, St. Paul, MN 55108-9952. Telephone: 612-644-1265. Fax: 612-644-0690. E-mail: natcoll@iaxs.net.

NORTH CENTRAL BIBLE COLLEGE
MINNEAPOLIS, MINNESOTA

General Independent, 4-year, coed, affiliated with Assemblies of God **Entrance** Noncompetitive **Setting** 9-acre urban campus **Total enrollment** 965 **Student/faculty ratio** 18:1 **Application deadline** Rolling **Freshmen** 95% were admitted **Housing** Yes **Expenses** Tuition $7480; Room & Board $3640 **Undergraduates** 55% women, 14% part-time, 27% 25 or older, 0.3% Native American, 2% Hispanic, 3% black, 2% Asian American or Pacific Islander **Most popular recent majors** Pastoral counseling; divinity/ministry; elementary education **Academic program** Advanced placement, self-designed majors, summer session, adult/continuing education programs, internships **Contact** Ms. Mary Jo Meier, Admissions Secretary, North Central Bible College, 910 Elliot Avenue South, Minneapolis, MN 55404-1322. Telephone: 612-343-4401 or toll-free 800-289-6222. Fax: 612-343-4778. E-mail: akgoetz@topaz.ncbc.edu. Web site: http://www.ncbc.edu/.

NORTHWESTERN COLLEGE
ST. PAUL, MINNESOTA

General Independent nondenominational, 4-year, coed **Entrance** Moderately difficult **Setting** 100-acre suburban campus **Total enrollment** 1,664 **Student/faculty ratio** 15:1 **Application deadline** 8/15 **Freshmen** 70% were admitted **Housing** Yes **Expenses** Tuition $13,920; Room & Board $4176 **Undergraduates** 60% women, 3% part-time, 20% 25 or older, 0.2% Native American, 2% Hispanic, 2% black, 1% Asian American or Pacific Islander **Most popular recent majors** Business administration; psychology; organizational behavior **Academic program** English as a second language, advanced placement, summer session, adult/continuing education programs, internships **Contact** Mr. Kenneth K. Faffler, Director of Recruitment, Northwestern College, 3003 Snelling Avenue North, St. Paul, MN 55113-1598. Telephone: 612-631-5209 or toll-free 800-827-6827. Fax: 612-631-5680. E-mail: admissions@nwc.edu. Web site: http://www.nwc.edu/.

OAK HILLS BIBLE COLLEGE
BEMIDJI, MINNESOTA

General Independent interdenominational, 4-year, coed **Entrance** Minimally difficult **Setting** 180-acre rural campus **Total enrollment** 160 **Student/faculty ratio** 8:1 **Application deadline** Rolling **Housing** Yes **Expenses** Tuition $7680; Room & Board $2475 **Undergraduates** 54% women, 11% part-time, 20% 25 or older, 1% Native American, 0% Hispanic, 1% black, 1% Asian American or Pacific Islander **Most Popular Recent Major** Biblical studies **Academic program** Advanced placement, tutorials, honors program, internships **Contact** Mrs. Monica Bush, Admissions Director, Oak Hills Bible College, 1600 Oak Hills Road, SW, Bemidji, MN 56601-8832. Telephone: 218-751-8670 ext. 284 or toll-free 800-262-8902. Fax: 218-751-8825. E-mail: ohadmit@northernnet.com. Web site: http://www.digitmaster.com/hp/ohf/ohbc/index.html.

PILLSBURY BAPTIST BIBLE COLLEGE
OWATONNA, MINNESOTA

General Independent Baptist, 4-year, coed **Entrance** Noncompetitive **Setting** 14-acre small town campus **Total enrollment** 139 **Student/faculty ratio** 8:1 **Application deadline** 9/1 **Freshmen** 97% were admitted **Housing** Yes **Expenses** Tuition $5560; Room & Board $3100 **Undergraduates** 50% women, 6% part-time, 1% Native American, 1% Hispanic, 0% black, 1% Asian

Pillsbury Baptist Bible College *(continued)*

American or Pacific Islander **Most popular recent majors** Biblical studies; education; business administration **Academic program** Advanced placement, accelerated degree program, self-designed majors, summer session, adult/continuing education programs, internships **Contact** Mr. Paul Rumsey, Director of Admissions, Pillsbury Baptist Bible College, 315 South Grove, Owatonna, MN 55060-3097. Telephone: 507-451-2710 ext. 279 or toll-free 800-747-4557. Fax: 507-451-6459. Web site: http://www.pillsbury.edu/.

ST. CLOUD STATE UNIVERSITY
ST. CLOUD, MINNESOTA

General State-supported, comprehensive, coed **Entrance** Moderately difficult **Setting** 82-acre suburban campus **Total enrollment** 13,946 **Student/faculty ratio** 21:1 **Application deadline** 5/1 **Freshmen** 76% were admitted **Housing** Yes **Expenses** Tuition $3082; Room & Board $3066 **Undergraduates** 53% women, 17% part-time, 16% 25 or older **Most popular recent majors** Elementary education; psychology; mass communications **Academic program** English as a second language, advanced placement, accelerated degree program, self-designed majors, tutorials, honors program, summer session, adult/continuing education programs, internships **Contact** Mr. Sherwood Reid, Director of Admissions, St. Cloud State University, 720 4th Avenue South, St. Cloud, MN 56301-4498. Telephone: 320-255-2244 or toll-free 800-369-4260. E-mail: scsu4u@tigger.stcloud.msus.edu. Web site: http://www.stcloud.state.edu/.

SAINT JOHN'S UNIVERSITY
COORDINATE WITH COLLEGE OF SAINT BENEDICT

COLLEGEVILLE, MINNESOTA

General Independent Roman Catholic, comprehensive, men only, coordinate with College of Saint Benedict **Entrance** Moderately difficult **Setting** 2,400-acre rural campus **Total enrollment** 1,823 **Student/faculty ratio** 13:1 **Application deadline** Rolling **Freshmen** 87% were admitted **Housing** Yes **Expenses** Tuition $14,758; Room & Board $4574 **Undergraduates** 4% part-time, 3% 25 or older, 0.2% Native American, 1% Hispanic, 1% black, 2% Asian American or Pacific Islander **Most popular recent majors** Business administration; political science; psychology **Academic program** Average class size 21, advanced placement, self-designed majors, tutorials, honors program, internships **Contact** Ms. Mary Milbert, Dean of Admissions, Saint John's University, PO Box 7155, Collegeville, MN 56321-7155. Telephone: 320-363-2196 or toll-free 800-24JOHNS. Fax: 320-363-3206. E-mail: admissions@csbsju.edu. Web site: http://www.csbsju.edu/.

▶ **For more information, see page 417.**

SAINT MARY'S UNIVERSITY OF MINNESOTA
WINONA, MINNESOTA

General Independent Roman Catholic, comprehensive, coed **Entrance** Moderately difficult **Setting** 350-acre small town campus **Total enrollment** 5,134 **Student/faculty ratio** 14:1 **Application deadline** Rolling **Freshmen** 92% were admitted **Housing** Yes **Expenses** Tuition $12,495; Room & Board $4120 **Undergraduates** 52% women, 21% part-time, 6% 25 or older, 0.2% Native American, 1% Hispanic, 1% black, 1% Asian American or Pacific Islander **Most popular recent majors** Biology; psychology; elementary education **Academic program** Average class size 20, English as a second language, advanced placement, accelerated degree program, self-designed majors, tutorials, honors program, summer session, adult/continuing education programs, internships **Contact** Mr. Anthony M. Piscitiello, Vice President for Admission, Saint Mary's University of Minnesota, 700 Terrace Heights, Winona, MN 55987-1399. Telephone: 507-457-1700 or toll-free 800-635-5987. Fax: 507-457-1722. E-mail: admissions@smumn.edu. Web site: http://www.smumn.edu/.

ST. OLAF COLLEGE
NORTHFIELD, MINNESOTA

General Independent Lutheran, 4-year, coed **Entrance** Very difficult **Setting** 350-acre small town campus **Total enrollment** 2,975 **Student/faculty ratio** 11:1 **Application deadline** Rolling **Freshmen** 78% were admitted **Housing** Yes **Expenses** Tuition $16,500; Room & Board $4020 **Undergraduates** 59% women, 1% part-time, 1% 25 or older, 0.3% Native American, 1% Hispanic, 1% black, 3% Asian American or Pacific Islander **Most popular recent majors** Biology; English; psychology **Academic program** English as a second language, advanced placement, accelerated degree program, self-designed majors, tutorials, summer session, adult/continuing education programs, internships **Contact** Ms. Sara Kyle, Interim Director of Admissions, St. Olaf College, 1520 St. Olaf Avenue, Northfield, MN 55057-1098. Telephone: 507-646-3025 or toll-free 800-800-3025 (in-state). Fax: 507-646-3832. E-mail: admiss@stolaf.edu. Web site: http://www.stolaf.edu/.

SOUTHWEST STATE UNIVERSITY
MARSHALL, MINNESOTA

General State-supported, comprehensive, coed **Entrance** Moderately difficult **Setting** 216-acre

small town campus **Total enrollment** 3,123 **Student/faculty ratio** 19:1 **Application deadline** Rolling **Freshmen** 60% were admitted **Housing** Yes **Expenses** Tuition $3056; Room & Board $2957 **Undergraduates** 56% women, 39% part-time, 14% 25 or older **Most popular recent majors** Business administration; education; accounting **Academic program** Advanced placement, accelerated degree program, self-designed majors, honors program, summer session, adult/continuing education programs, internships **Contact** Mr. Richard Shearer, Director of Admissions, Southwest State University, 1501 State Street, Marshall, MN 56258-1598. Telephone: 507-537-6286 or toll-free 800-642-0684. Fax: 507-537-7154. E-mail: 509ras@rickyvs.southwest.msus.edu. Web site: http://www.southwest.msus.edu/.

UNIVERSITY OF MINNESOTA, CROOKSTON

CROOKSTON, MINNESOTA

General State-supported, 4-year, coed **Entrance** Noncompetitive **Setting** 95-acre rural campus **Total enrollment** 2,219 **Application deadline** Rolling **Freshmen** 98% were admitted **Housing** Yes **Expenses** Tuition $4568; Room & Board $3687 **Undergraduates** 41% women, 9% part-time, 27% 25 or older, 2% Native American, 1% Hispanic, 1% black, 1% Asian American or Pacific Islander **Most popular recent majors** Information sciences/systems; business administration; natural resources management **Academic program** Average class size 35, advanced placement, tutorials, summer session, adult/continuing education programs, internships **Contact** Mr. Russ Kreager, Director of Admissions and Enrollment Manager, University of Minnesota, Crookston, 2900 University Avenue, Crookston, MN 56716-5001. Telephone: 218-281-8568 or toll-free 800-232-6466. Fax: 218-281-8050. E-mail: info@mail.crk.umn.edu. Web site: http://www.crk.umn.edu/.

▶ **For more information, see page 538.**

UNIVERSITY OF MINNESOTA, DULUTH

DULUTH, MINNESOTA

General State-supported, comprehensive, coed **Entrance** Moderately difficult **Setting** 250-acre suburban campus **Total enrollment** 9,653 **Student/faculty ratio** 18:1 **Application deadline** 2/1 **Freshmen** 78% were admitted **Housing** Yes **Expenses** Tuition $4316; Room & Board $3912 **Undergraduates** 50% women, 34% part-time, 11% 25 or older, 1% Native American, 1% Hispanic, 1% black, 2% Asian American or Pacific Islander **Most popular recent majors** Business administration; criminology **Academic program** English as a second language, advanced placement, self-designed majors, tutorials, honors program, summer session, adult/continuing education programs, internships **Contact** Mr. Edward A. Kawczynski, Director of Admissions, University of Minnesota, Duluth, 10 University Drive, Duluth, MN 55812-2496. Telephone: 218-726-7171 or toll-free 800-232-1339. Fax: 218-726-6394. E-mail: umdadmis@d.umn.edu. Web site: http://www.d.umn.edu/.

UNIVERSITY OF MINNESOTA, MORRIS

MORRIS, MINNESOTA

General State-supported, 4-year, coed **Entrance** Moderately difficult **Setting** 130-acre small town campus **Total enrollment** 1,947 **Student/faculty ratio** 16:1 **Application deadline** 3/15 **Housing** Yes **Expenses** Tuition $4871; Room & Board $3714 **Undergraduates** 57% women, 4% part-time, 5% 25 or older, 6% Native American, 2% Hispanic, 5% black, 2% Asian American or Pacific Islander **Most popular recent majors** Economics; management science; English **Academic program** English as a second language, advanced placement, accelerated degree program, self-designed majors, tutorials, honors program, summer session, adult/continuing education programs, internships **Contact** Mr. Rodney M. Oto, Director of Admissions and Financial Aid, University of Minnesota, Morris, 600 East 4th Street, Morris, MN 56267-2199. Telephone: 320-589-6035 or toll-free 800-992-8863. Fax: 320-589-6399. E-mail: admissions@caa.mrs.umn.edu. Web site: http://www.mrs.umn.edu/.

UNIVERSITY OF MINNESOTA, TWIN CITIES CAMPUS

MINNEAPOLIS, MINNESOTA

General State-supported, university, coed **Entrance** Moderately difficult **Setting** 2,000-acre urban campus **Total enrollment** 45,410 **Student/faculty ratio** 15:1 **Application deadline** Rolling **Housing** Yes **Expenses** Tuition $4450; Room & Board $4311 **Undergraduates** 51% women, 20% part-time, 15% 25 or older, 1% Native American, 2% Hispanic, 4% black, 8% Asian American or Pacific Islander **Most popular recent majors** Psychology; mechanical engineering; chemical engineering **Academic program** English as a second language, advanced placement, accelerated degree program, self-designed majors, tutorials, honors program, summer session, adult/continuing education programs, internships **Contact** Ms. Patricia Jones Whyte, Associate Director of Admissions, University of Minnesota, Twin Cities Campus, 240 Williamson, Minneapolis, MN 55455-0213. Telephone: 612-625-2008 or toll-free 800-752-1000. Fax: 612-626-1693. E-mail: admissions@tc.umn.edu. Web site: http://www1.umn.edu/tc/.

UNIVERSITY OF ST. THOMAS
ST. PAUL, MINNESOTA

General Independent Roman Catholic, university, coed **Entrance** Moderately difficult **Setting** 78-acre urban campus **Total enrollment** 10,436 **Student/faculty ratio** 17:1 **Application deadline** Rolling **Freshmen** 89% were admitted **Housing** Yes **Expenses** Tuition $14,660; Room & Board $4769 **Undergraduates** 53% women, 12% part-time, 15% 25 or older, 1% Native American, 2% Hispanic, 3% black, 4% Asian American or Pacific Islander **Most popular recent majors** Business administration; sociology; journalism **Academic program** English as a second language, advanced placement, self-designed majors, honors program, summer session, adult/continuing education programs, internships **Contact** Ms. Marla Friederichs, Associate Vice President of Enrollment Management, University of St. Thomas, Mail #32F-1, 2115 Summit Avenue, St. Paul, MN 55105-1096. Telephone: 612-962-6150 or toll-free 800-328-6819. Fax: 612-962-6160. E-mail: admissions@stthomas.edu. Web site: http://www.stthomas.edu/.

WINONA STATE UNIVERSITY
WINONA, MINNESOTA

General State-supported, comprehensive, coed **Entrance** Moderately difficult **Setting** 40-acre small town campus **Total enrollment** 6,739 **Student/faculty ratio** 21:1 **Application deadline** Rolling **Freshmen** 66% were admitted **Housing** Yes **Expenses** Tuition $3019; Room & Board $3150 **Undergraduates** 60% women, 8% part-time, 15% 25 or older, 0.2% Native American, 1% Hispanic, 1% black, 2% Asian American or Pacific Islander **Most popular recent majors** Business administration; liberal arts and studies; nursing **Academic program** Average class size 26, English as a second language, advanced placement, accelerated degree program, self-designed majors, tutorials, honors program, summer session, adult/continuing education programs, internships **Contact** Dr. Jim Mootz, Director of Admissions, Winona State University, PO Box 5838, Winona, MN 55987-5838. Telephone: 507-457-5100 or toll-free 800-DIAL WSU. Fax: 507-457-5620. E-mail: admissions@vax2.winona.msus.edu. Web site: http://www.winona.msus.edu/.

MISSISSIPPI

ALCORN STATE UNIVERSITY
LORMAN, MISSISSIPPI

General State-supported, comprehensive, coed **Entrance** Minimally difficult **Setting** 1,756-acre rural campus **Total enrollment** 2,847 **Student/faculty ratio** 13:1 **Application deadline** 8/15 **Freshmen** 36% were admitted **Housing** Yes **Expenses** Tuition $2429; Room & Board $2324 **Undergraduates** 61% women, 9% part-time, 10% 25 or older, 0.1% Hispanic, 97% black **Most popular recent majors** Business administration; agronomy/crop science; computer science **Academic program** Advanced placement, accelerated degree program, honors program, summer session **Contact** Mr. Emmanuel Barnes, Director of Admissions, Alcorn State University, 1000 ASU Drive, # 300, Lorman, MS 39096-9402. Telephone: 601-877-6147 or toll-free 800-222-6790 (in-state). E-mail: ebarnes@loman.alcorn.edu. Web site: http://www.alcorn.edu/.

BELHAVEN COLLEGE
JACKSON, MISSISSIPPI

General Independent Presbyterian, comprehensive, coed **Entrance** Moderately difficult **Setting** 42-acre urban campus **Total enrollment** 1,317 **Student/faculty ratio** 14:1 **Application deadline** Rolling **Freshmen** 90% were admitted **Housing** Yes **Expenses** Tuition $9370; Room & Board $3380 **Undergraduates** 63% women, 22% part-time, 49% 25 or older, 1% Native American, 1% Hispanic, 20% black, 0.5% Asian American or Pacific Islander **Most popular recent majors** Business administration; biology; accounting **Academic program** Average class size 22, English as a second language, advanced placement, accelerated degree program, tutorials, honors program, summer session, adult/continuing education programs, internships **Contact** Ms. Lisa Greer, Director of Admissions, Belhaven College, 1500 Peachtree Street, Jackson, MS 39202-1789. Telephone: 601-968-5940 or toll-free 800-960-5940. Fax: 601-968-9998.

BLUE MOUNTAIN COLLEGE
BLUE MOUNTAIN, MISSISSIPPI

General Independent Southern Baptist, 4-year, coed **Entrance** Minimally difficult **Setting** 44-acre rural campus **Total enrollment** 478 **Student/faculty ratio** 14:1 **Application deadline** Rolling **Freshmen** 72% were admitted **Housing** Yes **Expenses** Tuition $4640; Room & Board $2350 **Undergraduates** 82% women, 27% part-time, 42% 25 or older, 0% Native American, 0.2% Hispanic, 9% black, 0.2% Asian American or Pacific Islander **Most popular recent majors** Education; divinity/ministry **Academic program** Advanced placement, accelerated degree program, honors program, summer session, internships **Contact** Ms. Charlotte Lewis, Director of Admissions, Blue Mountain College, PO Box 126BMC, Blue Mountain, MS 38610-9509. Telephone: 601-685-4161 or toll-free 800-235-0136.

DELTA STATE UNIVERSITY

CLEVELAND, MISSISSIPPI

General State-supported, comprehensive, coed **Entrance** Minimally difficult **Setting** 274-acre small town campus **Total enrollment** 4,012 **Student/faculty ratio** 14:1 **Application deadline** Rolling **Freshmen** 91% were admitted **Housing** Yes **Expenses** Tuition $2354; Room & Board $2400 **Undergraduates** 62% women, 11% part-time, 23% 25 or older, 0.2% Native American, 0.3% Hispanic, 27% black, 1% Asian American or Pacific Islander **Most popular recent majors** Business administration; elementary education; nursing **Academic program** Advanced placement, accelerated degree program, tutorials, summer session, adult/continuing education programs, internships **Contact** Ms. Debbie Heslep, Coordinator of Admissions, Delta State University, Kethley 107, Cleveland, MS 38733-0001. Telephone: 601-846-4018 or toll-free 800-468-6378 (in-state). Fax: 601-846-4016. E-mail: jdcooper@dsu.deltast.edu. Web site: http://www.deltast.edu/.

JACKSON STATE UNIVERSITY

JACKSON, MISSISSIPPI

General State-supported, university, coed **Entrance** Minimally difficult **Setting** 128-acre urban campus **Total enrollment** 6,333 **Student/faculty ratio** 17:1 **Application deadline** 8/1 **Freshmen** 49% were admitted **Housing** Yes **Expenses** Tuition $2380; Room & Board $3296 **Undergraduates** 58% women, 11% part-time, 18% 25 or older **Most popular recent majors** Business administration; computer science; biology **Academic program** English as a second language, advanced placement, accelerated degree program, tutorials, honors program, summer session, adult/continuing education programs, internships **Contact** Mrs. Linda Rush, Admissions Counselor, Jackson State University, PO Box 17330, 1400 John R. Lynch Street, Jackson, MS 39217. Telephone: 601-968-2911 or toll-free 800-682-5390 (in-state), 800-848-6817 (out-of-state). E-mail: schatman@ccaix.jsums.edu. Web site: http://www.jsums.edu/.

MAGNOLIA BIBLE COLLEGE

KOSCIUSKO, MISSISSIPPI

General Independent, 4-year, primarily men, affiliated with Church of Christ **Entrance** Noncompetitive **Setting** 5-acre small town campus **Total enrollment** 59 **Student/faculty ratio** 5:1 **Application deadline** 8/31 **Housing** Yes **Expenses** Tuition $4020; Room & Board $1470 **Undergraduates** 5% women, 33% part-time, 59% 25 or older **Academic program** Summer session **Contact** Mr. Allen Coker, Admissions Officer, Magnolia Bible College, PO Box 1109, Kosciusko, MS 39090-1109. Telephone: 601-289-2896 or toll-free 800-748-8655 (in-state). Web site: http://www.mbc.org/.

MILLSAPS COLLEGE

JACKSON, MISSISSIPPI

General Independent United Methodist, comprehensive, coed **Entrance** Moderately difficult **Setting** 100-acre urban campus **Total enrollment** 1,362 **Student/faculty ratio** 13:1 **Application deadline** 3/1 **Freshmen** 81% were admitted **Housing** Yes **Expenses** Tuition $13,612; Room & Board $5701 **Undergraduates** 56% women, 7% part-time, 5% 25 or older, 0.5% Native American, 0.5% Hispanic, 6% black, 3% Asian American or Pacific Islander **Most popular recent majors** Biology; business administration; English **Academic program** Average class size 20, English as a second language, advanced placement, tutorials, honors program, summer session, adult/continuing education programs, internships **Contact** Mr. Gary L. Fretwell, Vice President of Enrollment and Student Affairs, Millsaps College, 1701 North State Street, Jackson, MS 39210-0001. Telephone: 601-974-1050 or toll-free 800-352-1050. Fax: 601-974-1059. E-mail: admissions@okra.millsaps.edu. Web site: http://www.millsaps.edu/.

MISSISSIPPI COLLEGE

CLINTON, MISSISSIPPI

General Independent Southern Baptist, comprehensive, coed **Entrance** Moderately difficult **Setting** 320-acre suburban campus **Total enrollment** 3,532 **Student/faculty ratio** 15:1 **Application deadline** Rolling **Freshmen** 76% were admitted **Housing** Yes **Expenses** Tuition $8364; Room & Board $3630 **Undergraduates** 57% women, 18% part-time, 22% 25 or older, 0.2% Native American, 1% Hispanic, 13% black, 1% Asian American or Pacific Islander **Most popular recent majors** Nursing; business administration; elementary education **Academic program** Average class size 25, advanced placement, accelerated degree program, honors program, summer session, adult/continuing education programs, internships **Contact** Dr. Jim Turcotte, Dean of Enrollment Services, Mississippi College, PO Box 4026, Clinton, MS 39058. Telephone: 601-925-3240 or toll-free 800-738-1236. Fax: 601-925-3804. E-mail: admissions@mc.edu. Web site: http://www.mc.edu/.

MISSISSIPPI STATE UNIVERSITY

MISSISSIPPI STATE, MISSISSIPPI

General State-supported, university, coed **Entrance** Moderately difficult **Setting** 4,200-acre

Mississippi State University *(continued)*

small town campus **Total enrollment** 15,628 **Student/faculty ratio** 17:1 **Application deadline** 7/26 **Freshmen** 78% were admitted **Housing** Yes **Expenses** Tuition $2731; Room & Board $4100 **Undergraduates** 44% women, 13% part-time, 20% 25 or older, 1% Native American, 1% Hispanic, 16% black, 1% Asian American or Pacific Islander **Most popular recent majors** Elementary education; business administration; business marketing and marketing management **Academic program** English as a second language, advanced placement, accelerated degree program, self-designed majors, honors program, summer session, adult/continuing education programs, internships **Contact** Mr. Jerry Inmon, Director of Admissions, Mississippi State University, PO Box 5268, Mississippi State, MS 39762. Telephone: 601-325-2224. E-mail: admit@admissions.msstate.edu. Web site: http://www.msstate.edu/.

MISSISSIPPI UNIVERSITY FOR WOMEN
COLUMBUS, MISSISSIPPI

General State-supported, comprehensive, primarily women **Entrance** Moderately difficult **Setting** 110-acre small town campus **Total enrollment** 3,309 **Student/faculty ratio** 17:1 **Application deadline** 9/6 **Freshmen** 75% were admitted **Housing** Yes **Expenses** Tuition $2284; Room & Board $2557 **Undergraduates** 83% women, 38% part-time, 46% 25 or older, 0.2% Native American, 0.5% Hispanic, 28% black, 0.5% Asian American or Pacific Islander **Most popular recent majors** Nursing; business administration; elementary education **Academic program** Average class size 25, English as a second language, advanced placement, accelerated degree program, tutorials, honors program, summer session, adult/continuing education programs, internships **Contact** Ms. Melanie Freeman, Director of Admissions, Mississippi University for Women, PO Box 1613, Columbus, MS 39701-9998. Telephone: 601-329-7106 or toll-free 800-247-0758 (in-state). Fax: 601-241-7481. E-mail: admissions@muw.edu. Web site: http://www.muw.edu/.

MISSISSIPPI VALLEY STATE UNIVERSITY
ITTA BENA, MISSISSIPPI

General State-supported, comprehensive, coed **Entrance** Minimally difficult **Setting** 450-acre small town campus **Total enrollment** 2,234 **Student/faculty ratio** 13:1 **Application deadline** Rolling **Freshmen** 25% were admitted **Housing** Yes **Expenses** Tuition $2353; Room & Board $2350 **Undergraduates** 60% women, 7% part-time, 25% 25 or older, 0.05% Hispanic, 98% black, 0.3% Asian American or Pacific Islander **Most popular recent majors** Social work; criminal justice/law enforcement administration; biology **Academic program** Average class size 35, tutorials, honors program, summer session, adult/continuing education programs, internships **Contact** Mrs. Maxine B. Rush, Director of Admissions and Recruitment, Mississippi Valley State University, 14000 Highway 82 West, Itta Bena, MS 38941-1400. Telephone: 601-254-3344 or toll-free 800-844-6885 (in-state). Fax: 601-254-7900.

RUST COLLEGE
HOLLY SPRINGS, MISSISSIPPI

General Independent United Methodist, 4-year, coed **Contact** Miss Joann Scott, Director of Admissions, Rust College, 150 East Rust Avenue, Holly Springs, MS 38635-2328. Telephone: 601-252-8000 ext. 4068. Fax: 601-252-6107.

SOUTHEASTERN BAPTIST COLLEGE
LAUREL, MISSISSIPPI

General Independent Baptist, 4-year, coed **Contact** Mrs. Emma Bond, Director of Admissions, Southeastern Baptist College, 4229 Highway 15 North, Laurel, MS 39440-1096. Telephone: 601-426-6346.

TOUGALOO COLLEGE
TOUGALOO, MISSISSIPPI

General Independent interdenominational, 4-year, coed **Contact** Ms. Cynthia Hewitt, Data Entry Specialist, Tougaloo College, 500 West County Line Road, Tougaloo, MS 39174. Telephone: 601-977-7768. Fax: 601-977-7739.

UNIVERSITY OF MISSISSIPPI
OXFORD, MISSISSIPPI

General State-supported, university, coed **Entrance** Moderately difficult **Setting** 2,500-acre small town campus **Total enrollment** 11,179 **Application deadline** 7/26 **Freshmen** 75% were admitted **Housing** Yes **Expenses** Tuition $2731; Room & Board $3186 **Undergraduates** 53% women, 7% part-time, 10% 25 or older, 0.3% Native American, 1% Hispanic, 11% black, 1% Asian American or Pacific Islander **Most popular recent majors** Business administration; English; accounting **Academic program** English as a second language, advanced placement, accelerated degree program, honors program, summer session, adult/continuing education programs, internships **Contact** Mr. Beckett Howorth, Director of Admissions and Records, University of Mississippi, University, MS 38677-9702. Telephone: 601-232-7226 or toll-free 800-OLE-MISS (in-state). Fax: 601-232-5869. E-mail: info@olemiss.edu. Web site: http://www.olemiss.edu/.

UNIVERSITY OF MISSISSIPPI MEDICAL CENTER
JACKSON, MISSISSIPPI

General State-supported, upper-level, coed **Entrance** Moderately difficult **Setting** 164-acre urban campus **Total enrollment** 1,366 **Student/faculty ratio** 5:1 **Application deadline** 2/15 **Freshmen** 27% were admitted **Housing** Yes **Expenses** Tuition $2106; Room only $1440 **Undergraduates** 35% 25 or older, 0% Native American, 0.5% Hispanic, 14% black, 1% Asian American or Pacific Islander **Most popular recent majors** Nursing; physical therapy; occupational therapy **Academic program** Summer session, internships **Contact** Dr. Billy M. Bishop, Director of Student Services and Records, University of Mississippi Medical Center, 2500 North State Street, Jackson, MS 39216-4505. Telephone: 601-984-1080. Fax: 601-984-1080.

UNIVERSITY OF SOUTHERN MISSISSIPPI
HATTIESBURG, MISSISSIPPI

General State-supported, university, coed **Entrance** Moderately difficult **Setting** 1,090-acre suburban campus **Total enrollment** 14,599 **Student/faculty ratio** 21:1 **Application deadline** Rolling **Freshmen** 67% were admitted **Housing** Yes **Expenses** Tuition $2590; Room & Board $2565 **Undergraduates** 59% women, 16% part-time, 22% 25 or older, 0.4% Native American, 1% Hispanic, 20% black, 1% Asian American or Pacific Islander **Most popular recent majors** Elementary education; nursing; psychology **Academic program** English as a second language, advanced placement, accelerated degree program, tutorials, honors program, summer session, adult/continuing education programs **Contact** Dr. Homer Wesley, Dean of Admissions, University of Southern Mississippi, Box 5166, Hattiesburg, MS 39406-5166. Telephone: 601-266-5000. Web site: http://www.usm.edu/.

WESLEY COLLEGE
FLORENCE, MISSISSIPPI

General Independent religious, 4-year, coed **Entrance** Noncompetitive **Setting** 40-acre small town campus **Total enrollment** 80 **Application deadline** Rolling **Housing** Yes **Expenses** Tuition $2200; Room & Board $2450 **Undergraduates** 39% women, 23% part-time, 29% 25 or older **Academic program** Advanced placement, adult/continuing education programs, internships **Contact** Rev. Chris Lohrstorfer, Director of Admissions, Wesley College, PO Box 1070, Florence, MS 39073-1070. Telephone: 601-845-2265 ext. 21 or toll-free 800-748-9972 ext. 21. Fax: 601-845-2266. E-mail: wcadmit@aol.com.

WILLIAM CAREY COLLEGE
HATTIESBURG, MISSISSIPPI

General Independent Southern Baptist, comprehensive, coed **Contact** Mr. Scott Hilton, Director of Admissions, William Carey College, 498 Tuscan Avenue, Hattiesburg, MS 39401-5499. Telephone: 601-582-5051 ext. 103 or toll-free 800-962-5991 (in-state). Fax: 601-582-6454. E-mail: admiss@mail.wmcarey.edu. Web site: http://www.wmcarey.edu/.

MISSOURI

AVILA COLLEGE
KANSAS CITY, MISSOURI

General Independent Roman Catholic, comprehensive, coed **Entrance** Moderately difficult **Setting** 50-acre suburban campus **Total enrollment** 1,246 **Student/faculty ratio** 12:1 **Application deadline** Rolling **Freshmen** 88% were admitted **Housing** Yes **Expenses** Tuition $10,860; Room & Board $4400 **Undergraduates** 73% women, 31% part-time, 44% 25 or older, 1% Native American, 3% Hispanic, 11% black, 1% Asian American or Pacific Islander **Most popular recent majors** Elementary education; nursing; radiological science **Academic program** Average class size 19, English as a second language, advanced placement, accelerated degree program, tutorials, summer session, adult/continuing education programs, internships **Contact** Mr. Todd H. Moore, Director of Admissions, Avila College, 11901 Wornall Road, Kansas City, MO 64145-1698. Telephone: 816-942-8400 ext. 3500 or toll-free 800-GO-AVILA. Fax: 816-942-3362. E-mail: admissions@mail.avila.edu. Web site: http://www.avila.edu/.

BAPTIST BIBLE COLLEGE
SPRINGFIELD, MISSOURI

General Independent Baptist, comprehensive, coed **Contact** Dr. Joseph Gleason, Director of Admissions, Baptist Bible College, 628 East Kearney, Springfield, MO 65803-3498. Telephone: 417-268-6000 ext. 2219. Fax: 417-831-8029.

BEREAN UNIVERSITY OF THE ASSEMBLIES OF GOD
SPRINGFIELD, MISSOURI

General Independent, comprehensive, coed, affiliated with Assemblies of God **Entrance** Noncompetitive **Total enrollment** 1,100 **Expenses** Tuition $2208 **Undergraduates** 25% 25 or older

Berean University of the Assemblies of God *(continued)*

Most popular recent majors Biblical studies; theology **Academic program** Advanced placement, accelerated degree program, honors program, internships **Contact** Mr. Craig Froman, Registrar, Berean University of the Assemblies of God, 1445 Boonville Avenue, Springfield, MO 65802-1805. Telephone: 417-862-9533 ext. 2321 or toll-free 800-443-1083. Fax: 417-862-5318. E-mail: berean@ag.org.

CALVARY BIBLE COLLEGE AND THEOLOGICAL SEMINARY
KANSAS CITY, MISSOURI

General Independent religious, comprehensive, coed **Entrance** Minimally difficult **Setting** 55-acre suburban campus **Total enrollment** 613 **Student/faculty ratio** 10:1 **Application deadline** Rolling **Housing** Yes **Expenses** Tuition $4570; Room & Board $2950 **Undergraduates** 34% 25 or older **Most popular recent majors** Elementary education; pastoral counseling; secondary education **Academic program** English as a second language, advanced placement, accelerated degree program, self-designed majors, summer session, adult/continuing education programs, internships **Contact** Mr. John H. Bryden, Director of Admissions, Calvary Bible College and Theological Seminary, 15800 Calvary Road, Kansas City, MO 64147-1341. Telephone: 816-322-0110 ext. 1326. Web site: http://www.calvary.edu/.

CENTRAL BIBLE COLLEGE
SPRINGFIELD, MISSOURI

General Independent, 4-year, coed, affiliated with Assemblies of God **Entrance** Moderately difficult **Setting** 108-acre suburban campus **Total enrollment** 1,014 **Student/faculty ratio** 21:1 **Application deadline** Rolling **Freshmen** 90% were admitted **Housing** Yes **Expenses** Tuition $5020; Room & Board $3250 **Undergraduates** 44% women, 10% part-time, 6% 25 or older, 0.5% Native American, 2% Hispanic, 2% black, 2% Asian American or Pacific Islander **Most popular recent majors** Biblical studies; theology; pastoral counseling **Academic program** English as a second language, advanced placement, summer session, internships **Contact** Mrs. Eunice A. Bruegman, Director of Admissions and Records, Central Bible College, 3000 North Grant Avenue, Springfield, MO 65803-1096. Telephone: 417-833-2551 ext. 1184 or toll-free 800-358-3092 (out-of-state). Fax: 417-833-5141.

CENTRAL CHRISTIAN COLLEGE OF THE BIBLE
MOBERLY, MISSOURI

General Independent, 4-year, coed, affiliated with Christian Churches and Churches of Christ **Entrance** Noncompetitive **Setting** 40-acre small town campus **Total enrollment** 150 **Student/faculty ratio** 10:1 **Application deadline** Rolling **Freshmen** 63% were admitted **Housing** Yes **Expenses** Tuition $4495; Room & Board $2640 **Undergraduates** 14% 25 or older **Academic program** English as a second language, self-designed majors, internships **Contact** Mr. Troy Titus, Director of Admissions, Central Christian College of the Bible, 911 Urbandale Drive East, Moberly, MO 65270-1997. Telephone: 816-263-3900. Fax: 660-263-3936.

CENTRAL METHODIST COLLEGE
FAYETTE, MISSOURI

General Independent Methodist, comprehensive, coed **Entrance** Moderately difficult **Setting** 52-acre small town campus **Total enrollment** 1,292 **Student/faculty ratio** 12:1 **Application deadline** Rolling **Freshmen** 86% were admitted **Housing** Yes **Expenses** Tuition $10,710; Room & Board $4150 **Undergraduates** 60% women, 12% part-time, 21% 25 or older, 0.3% Native American, 0.2% Hispanic, 7% black, 0.1% Asian American or Pacific Islander **Most popular recent majors** Elementary education; nursing; biology **Academic program** Accelerated degree program, self-designed majors, tutorials, honors program, summer session, internships **Contact** Mr. David Heringer, Vice President for Enrollment Management and Student Development, Central Methodist College, 411 Central Methodist Square, Fayette, MO 65248-1198. Telephone: 660-248-6247 or toll-free 888-262-1854 (in-state). Fax: 660-248-1872. E-mail: sdaris@cmc2.cmc.edu. Web site: http://www.cmc.edu/.

CENTRAL MISSOURI STATE UNIVERSITY
WARRENSBURG, MISSOURI

General State-supported, comprehensive, coed **Entrance** Moderately difficult **Setting** 1,240-acre small town campus **Total enrollment** 10,320 **Student/faculty ratio** 17:1 **Application deadline** 8/15 **Freshmen** 93% were admitted **Housing** Yes **Expenses** Tuition $2640; Room & Board $4080 **Undergraduates** 54% women, 17% part-time, 22% 25 or older, 1% Native American, 1% Hispanic, 7% black, 1% Asian American or Pacific Islander **Most popular recent majors** Elementary education; criminal justice/law enforcement administration; business administration **Academic program** Average class size 30, English as a second language, advanced placement, self-designed majors, tutorials, honors program, summer session, adult/continuing education programs, internships **Contact** Mrs. Delores Hudson, Director of Admissions, Central Missouri State University, Warrensburg, MO 64093. Telephone: 660-543-4290 or toll-free 800-956-0177 (in-state). Fax: 660-543-8517. E-mail: admit@cmsuvmb.cmsu.edu. Web site: http://www.cmsu.edu/.

COLLEGE OF THE OZARKS
POINT LOOKOUT, MISSOURI

General Independent Presbyterian, 4-year, coed **Entrance** Moderately difficult **Setting** 1,000-acre small town campus **Total enrollment** 1,563 **Student/faculty ratio** 14:1 **Application deadline** Rolling **Freshmen** 14% were admitted **Housing** Yes **Expenses** Tuition $150; Room & Board $2200 **Undergraduates** 55% women, 15% part-time, 6% 25 or older, 1% Native American, 1% Hispanic, 1% black, 0.4% Asian American or Pacific Islander **Most popular recent majors** Education; business administration; psychology **Academic program** Average class size 35, advanced placement, accelerated degree program, self-designed majors, tutorials, honors program, summer session, internships **Contact** Mrs. Janet Miller, Admissions Secretary, College of the Ozarks, Point Lookout, MO 65726. Telephone: 417-334-6411 ext. 4217 or toll-free 800-222-0525. Fax: 417-335-2618. E-mail: admiss4@cofo.edu. Web site: http://www.cofo.edu/.

COLUMBIA COLLEGE
COLUMBIA, MISSOURI

General Independent, comprehensive, coed, affiliated with Christian Church (Disciples of Christ) **Entrance** Moderately difficult **Setting** 29-acre small town campus **Total enrollment** 7,435 **Student/faculty ratio** 11:1 **Application deadline** Rolling **Housing** Yes **Expenses** Tuition $9244; Room & Board $4144 **Undergraduates** 57% women, 91% part-time, 68% 25 or older, 1% Native American, 4% Hispanic, 13% black, 2% Asian American or Pacific Islander **Most popular recent majors** Business administration; art; education **Academic program** English as a second language, advanced placement, accelerated degree program, self-designed majors, honors program, summer session, adult/continuing education programs, internships **Contact** Ms. Regina Morin, Director of Admissions, Columbia College, 1001 Rogers Street, Columbia, MO 65216-0002. Telephone: 573-875-7352 or toll-free 800-231-2391. Fax: 573-875-7506. E-mail: admissions@ccishpccis.edu. Web site: http://www.ccis.edu/.

CONCEPTION SEMINARY COLLEGE
CONCEPTION, MISSOURI

General Independent Roman Catholic, 4-year, men only **Entrance** Noncompetitive **Setting** 30-acre rural campus **Total enrollment** 69 **Student/faculty ratio** 3:1 **Application deadline** 7/31 **Freshmen** 89% were admitted **Housing** Yes **Expenses** Tuition $7184; Room & Board $4100 **Undergraduates** 35% 25 or older, 1% Hispanic, 28% Asian American or Pacific Islander **Academic program** Advanced placement **Contact** Fr. Daniel Petsche, Director of Admissions, Conception Seminary College, PO Box 502, Conception, MO 64433-0502. Telephone: 816-944-2806. Fax: 816-944-2829. E-mail: 0553004@acad.nwmissouri.edu. Web site: http://www.msc-net.com/~/cabbey/.

CULVER-STOCKTON COLLEGE
CANTON, MISSOURI

General Independent, 4-year, coed, affiliated with Christian Church (Disciples of Christ) **Entrance** Moderately difficult **Setting** 143-acre rural campus **Total enrollment** 994 **Student/faculty ratio** 17:1 **Application deadline** Rolling **Freshmen** 84% were admitted **Housing** Yes **Expenses** Tuition $9200; Room & Board $4230 **Undergraduates** 62% women, 9% part-time, 9% 25 or older, 0% Native American, 2% Hispanic, 3% black, 1% Asian American or Pacific Islander **Most popular recent majors** Nursing; business administration; elementary education **Academic program** Average class size 26, advanced placement, accelerated degree program, self-designed majors, tutorials, honors program, summer session, adult/continuing education programs, internships **Contact** Mr. Mike Mason, Director of Admissions, Culver-Stockton College, One College Hill, Canton, MO 63435-1299. Telephone: 217-231-6465 or toll-free 800-537-1883 (out-of-state). Fax: 217-231-6611. E-mail: admissions@culver.edu. Web site: http://www.culver.edu/.

DEACONESS COLLEGE OF NURSING
ST. LOUIS, MISSOURI

General Proprietary, 4-year, coed **Entrance** Moderately difficult **Setting** 15-acre urban campus **Total enrollment** 305 **Application deadline** Rolling **Freshmen** 86% were admitted **Housing** Yes **Expenses** Tuition $7560; Room & Board $3704 **Undergraduates** 93% women, 36% part-time, 23% 25 or older, 0% Native American, 2% Hispanic, 19% black, 1% Asian American or Pacific Islander **Academic program** English as a second language, advanced placement, summer session **Contact** Ms. June Marlowe, Admissions Coordinator, Deaconess College of Nursing, 6150 Oakland Av-

Deaconess College of Nursing *(continued)*

enue, St. Louis, MO 63139-3215. Telephone: 314-768-3044 or toll-free 800-942-4310. Fax: 314-768-5673.

DEVRY INSTITUTE OF TECHNOLOGY
KANSAS CITY, MISSOURI

General Proprietary, 4-year, coed **Entrance** Minimally difficult **Setting** 12-acre urban campus **Total enrollment** 2,414 **Student/faculty ratio** 26:1 **Application deadline** Rolling **Freshmen** 78% were admitted **Housing** No **Expenses** Tuition $7308 **Undergraduates** 21% women, 26% part-time, 47% 25 or older **Most popular recent majors** Telecommunications; information sciences/systems; electrical/electronic engineering technology **Academic program** Advanced placement, accelerated degree program, summer session, adult/continuing education programs **Contact** Mr. Michael Thompson, Director of Admissions, DeVry Institute of Technology, 11224 Holmes Road, Kansas City, MO 64131-3698. Telephone: 816-941-2810 or toll-free 800-821-3766 (out-of-state). Web site: http://www.devry.edu/kans.htm.

DRURY COLLEGE
SPRINGFIELD, MISSOURI

General Independent, comprehensive, coed **Entrance** Moderately difficult **Setting** 60-acre urban campus **Total enrollment** 1,683 **Student/faculty ratio** 12:1 **Application deadline** Rolling **Freshmen** 95% were admitted **Housing** Yes **Expenses** Tuition $10,070; Room & Board $3856 **Undergraduates** 53% women, 2% part-time, 5% 25 or older, 0.4% Native American, 1% Hispanic, 1% black, 1% Asian American or Pacific Islander **Most popular recent majors** Business administration; mass communications; behavioral sciences **Academic program** English as a second language, advanced placement, accelerated degree program, tutorials, honors program, summer session, adult/continuing education programs, internships **Contact** Mr. Michael Thomas, Director of Admissions, Drury College, 900 North Benton Avenue, Springfield, MO 65802-3791. Telephone: 417-873-7205 or toll-free 800-922-2274 (in-state). Fax: 417-873-7529. E-mail: druryad@lib.drury.edu. Web site: http://www.drury.edu/.

EVANGEL UNIVERSITY
SPRINGFIELD, MISSOURI

General Independent, 4-year, coed, affiliated with Assemblies of God **Entrance** Moderately difficult **Setting** 80-acre urban campus **Total enrollment** 1,616 **Student/faculty ratio** 18:1 **Application deadline** 8/15 **Freshmen** 88% were admitted **Housing** Yes **Expenses** Tuition $8850; Room & Board $3550 **Undergraduates** 56% women, 5% part-time, 3% 25 or older, 0.1% Native American, 0.5% Hispanic, 3% black, 0.5% Asian American or Pacific Islander **Most popular recent majors** Business administration; education; mass communications **Academic program** Advanced placement, summer session **Contact** Mr. David I. Schoolfield, Director of Enrollment Management, Evangel University, 1111 North Glenstone, Springfield, MO 65802-2191. Telephone: 417-865-2811 ext. 7202 or toll-free 800-382-6435 (in-state). Fax: 417-865-9599. E-mail: admissions@mail4.evangel.edu. Web site: http://www.evangel.edu/.

FONTBONNE COLLEGE
ST. LOUIS, MISSOURI

General Independent Roman Catholic, comprehensive, coed **Entrance** Moderately difficult **Setting** 13-acre suburban campus **Total enrollment** 2,054 **Student/faculty ratio** 14:1 **Application deadline** 8/1 **Freshmen** 88% were admitted **Housing** Yes **Expenses** Tuition $10,150; Room & Board $4400 **Undergraduates** 71% women, 17% part-time, 40% 25 or older, 0.3% Native American, 1% Hispanic, 12% black, 1% Asian American or Pacific Islander **Most popular recent majors** Business administration; education **Academic program** English as a second language, advanced placement, self-designed majors, honors program, summer session, adult/continuing education programs, internships **Contact** Ms. Peggy Musen, Associate Dean for Enrollment Management, Fontbonne College, 6800 Wydown Boulevard, St. Louis, MO 63105-3098. Telephone: 314-889-1400. Fax: 314-719-8021. E-mail: pmusen@fontbonne.edu. Web site: http://www.fontbonne.edu/.

HANNIBAL-LAGRANGE COLLEGE
HANNIBAL, MISSOURI

General Independent Southern Baptist, 4-year, coed **Entrance** Moderately difficult **Setting** 110-acre small town campus **Total enrollment** 1,086 **Student/faculty ratio** 14:1 **Application deadline** Rolling **Housing** Yes **Expenses** Tuition $7590; Room & Board $2780 **Undergraduates** 65% women, 43% part-time, 28% 25 or older, 0.1% Native American, 0.2% Hispanic, 2% black, 0.4% Asian American or Pacific Islander **Most popular recent majors** Education; business administration **Academic program** Average class size 24, advanced placement, self-designed majors, honors program, summer session, adult/continuing education programs, internships **Contact** Mr. Raymond Carty, Dean of Enrollment Management, Hannibal-LaGrange College, 2800 Palmyra Road, Hannibal, MO 63401-1940. Telephone: 573-

221-3113 or toll-free 800-HLG-1119. Fax: 573-221-6594. E-mail: admissio@hlg.edu. Web site: http://www.hlg.edu/.

HARRIS-STOWE STATE COLLEGE
ST. LOUIS, MISSOURI

General State-supported, 4-year, coed **Contact** Ms. Valerie A. Beeson, Director of Admissions and Academic Advisement, Harris-Stowe State College, 3026 Laclede Avenue, St. Louis, MO 63103-2136. Telephone: 314-340-3300. Fax: 314-340-3322.

JEWISH HOSPITAL COLLEGE OF NURSING AND ALLIED HEALTH
ST. LOUIS, MISSOURI

General Independent, comprehensive, primarily women **Entrance** Moderately difficult **Setting** Urban campus **Total enrollment** 424 **Student/faculty ratio** 10:1 **Application deadline** Rolling **Freshmen** 71% were admitted **Housing** Yes **Expenses** Tuition $8680; Room only $1856 **Undergraduates** 88% women, 48% part-time, 70% 25 or older, 1% Native American, 1% Hispanic, 11% black, 1% Asian American or Pacific Islander **Most Popular Recent Major** Nursing **Academic program** Average class size 20, advanced placement, tutorials, summer session **Contact** Ms. Constance J. Stohlman, Chief Admissions Officer, Jewish Hospital College of Nursing and Allied Health, 306 South Kingshighway, St. Louis, MO 63110-1091. Telephone: 314-454-7057 or toll-free 800-832-9009 (in-state). Fax: 314-454-5239. E-mail: cal7374@bjcmail.carenet.org.

KANSAS CITY ART INSTITUTE
KANSAS CITY, MISSOURI

General Independent, 4-year, coed **Entrance** Moderately difficult **Setting** 12-acre urban campus **Total enrollment** 607 **Student/faculty ratio** 12:1 **Application deadline** Rolling **Freshmen** 72% were admitted **Housing** Yes **Expenses** Tuition $16,930; Room & Board $4964 **Undergraduates** 45% women, 2% part-time, 13% 25 or older, 1% Native American, 5% Hispanic, 1% black, 3% Asian American or Pacific Islander **Academic program** Average class size 20, English as a second language, advanced placement, summer session, adult/continuing education programs, internships **Contact** Mr. Gerald Valet, Admissions Office Supervisor, Kansas City Art Institute, 4415 Warwick Boulevard, Kansas City, MO 64111-1874. Telephone: 816-931-5224 or toll-free 800-522-5224. Fax: 816-531-6296. E-mail: admiss@kcai.edu. Web site: http://www.kcai.edu/.

LINCOLN UNIVERSITY
JEFFERSON CITY, MISSOURI

General State-supported, comprehensive, coed **Entrance** Noncompetitive **Setting** 152-acre small town campus **Total enrollment** 3,041 **Student/faculty ratio** 15:1 **Application deadline** 8/1 **Freshmen** 90% were admitted **Housing** Yes **Expenses** Tuition $2076; Room & Board $3276 **Undergraduates** 30% 25 or older, 1% Native American, 1% Hispanic, 26% black, 1% Asian American or Pacific Islander **Most popular recent majors** Nursing; elementary education; business administration **Academic program** Advanced placement, accelerated degree program, self-designed majors, tutorials, honors program, summer session, adult/continuing education programs, internships **Contact** Mr. Jimmy Arrington, Executive Director of Enrollment Management, Lincoln University, 820 Chestnut, Jefferson City, MO 65102. Telephone: 573-681-5599 or toll-free 800-521-5052. Web site: http://www.lincolnu.edu/.

LINDENWOOD UNIVERSITY
ST. CHARLES, MISSOURI

General Independent Presbyterian, comprehensive, coed **Entrance** Moderately difficult **Setting** 268-acre suburban campus **Total enrollment** 4,788 **Student/faculty ratio** 17:1 **Application deadline** Rolling **Freshmen** 57% were admitted **Housing** Yes **Expenses** Tuition $10,150; Room & Board $5000 **Undergraduates** 58% women, 4% part-time, 35% 25 or older, 1% Native American, 1% Hispanic, 8% black, 1% Asian American or Pacific Islander **Most popular recent majors** Business administration; mass communications; education **Academic program** Average class size 30, advanced placement, accelerated degree program, self-designed majors, tutorials, honors program, summer session, adult/continuing education programs, internships **Contact** Dr. David R. Williams, Dean of Admissions and Financial Aid, Lindenwood University, 209 South Kingshighway, St. Charles, MO 63301-1695. Telephone: 314-949-4902. Fax: 314-949-4910. E-mail: tbroyles@lindenwood.edu. Web site: http://www.lindenwood.edu/.

LOGAN COLLEGE OF CHIROPRACTIC
CHESTERFIELD, MISSOURI

General Independent, upper-level, coed **Contact** Mr. Melvin Reynolds, Dean of Admissions, Logan College of Chiropractic, 1851 Schoettler Road, Box 1065, Chesterfield, MO 63006-1065. Telephone: 314-227-2100 ext. 156 or toll-free 800-782-3344 (out-of-state). Fax: 314-227-9338. E-mail: loganadm@logan.edu.

MARYVILLE UNIVERSITY OF SAINT LOUIS
ST. LOUIS, MISSOURI

General Independent, comprehensive, coed **Entrance** Moderately difficult **Setting** 130-acre suburban campus **Total enrollment** 3,055 **Student/faculty ratio** 14:1 **Application deadline** Rolling **Freshmen** 80% were admitted **Housing** Yes **Expenses** Tuition $10,910; Room & Board $5000 **Undergraduates** 72% women, 50% part-time, 54% 25 or older, 0.4% Native American, 1% Hispanic, 5% black, 1% Asian American or Pacific Islander **Most popular recent majors** Business administration; nursing; psychology **Academic program** Average class size 16, English as a second language, advanced placement, accelerated degree program, tutorials, honors program, summer session, adult/continuing education programs, internships **Contact** Dr. Martha Wade, Dean of Admissions and Enrollment Management, Maryville University of Saint Louis, 13550 Conway Road, St. Louis, MO 63141-7299. Telephone: 314-529-9350 or toll-free 800-627-9855. Fax: 314-529-9927. E-mail: admissions@maryville.edu. Web site: http://www.maryvillestl.edu/.

► **For more information, see page 470.**

MESSENGER COLLEGE
JOPLIN, MISSOURI

General Independent Pentecostal, 4-year, coed **Entrance** Moderately difficult **Setting** 16-acre small town campus **Total enrollment** 66 **Application deadline** 9/1 **Freshmen** 86% were admitted **Housing** Yes **Expenses** Tuition $2160; Room & Board $5540 **Undergraduates** 53% women, 9% part-time, 12% 25 or older, 3% Native American, 6% Hispanic, 0% black, 0% Asian American or Pacific Islander **Most Popular Recent Major** Divinity/ministry **Academic program** Average class size 30, honors program, internships **Contact** Mrs. Gwendolyn Minor, Vice President of Academic Affairs, Messenger College, PO Box 4050, Joplin, MO 64803. Telephone: 417-624-7070. Fax: 417-624-5070.

MISSOURI BAPTIST COLLEGE
ST. LOUIS, MISSOURI

General Independent Southern Baptist, 4-year, coed **Entrance** Moderately difficult **Setting** 65-acre suburban campus **Total enrollment** 2,395 **Student/faculty ratio** 15:1 **Application deadline** Rolling **Housing** Yes **Expenses** Tuition $8820; Room & Board $4230 **Undergraduates** 62% women, 27% part-time, 38% 25 or older, 0.4% Native American, 1% Hispanic, 6% black, 1% Asian American or Pacific Islander **Most popular recent majors** Elementary education; business administration; religious education **Academic program** Average class size 24, English as a second language, advanced placement, accelerated degree program, self-designed majors, summer session, internships **Contact** Mr. Robert Cornwell, Associate Director of Admissions, Missouri Baptist College, 1 College Park Drive, St. Louis, MO 63141-8698. Telephone: 314-434-1115 ext. 4114. Fax: 314-434-7596. E-mail: admissions@mobap.edu. Web site: http://www.mobap.edu/.

MISSOURI SOUTHERN STATE COLLEGE
JOPLIN, MISSOURI

General State-supported, 4-year, coed **Entrance** Moderately difficult **Setting** 350-acre small town campus **Total enrollment** 5,485 **Student/faculty ratio** 27:1 **Application deadline** 8/16 **Freshmen** 99% were admitted **Housing** Yes **Expenses** Tuition $2384; Room & Board $3240 **Undergraduates** 56% women, 26% part-time, 36% 25 or older **Most popular recent majors** Business administration; education; law enforcement/police science **Academic program** Average class size 27, advanced placement, accelerated degree program, honors program, summer session, adult/continuing education programs, internships **Contact** Mr. Derek Skaggs, Director of Enrollment Services, Missouri Southern State College, 3950 East Newman Road, Joplin, MO 64801-1595. Telephone: 417-625-9537 or toll-free 800-606-MSSC. Fax: 417-659-4429. E-mail: admissions@mail.mssc.edu. Web site: http://www.mssc.edu/.

► **For more information, see page 475.**

MISSOURI TECHNICAL SCHOOL
ST. LOUIS, MISSOURI

General Proprietary, 4-year, coed **Entrance** Moderately difficult **Setting** Suburban campus **Total enrollment** 229 **Application deadline** Rolling **Freshmen** 96% were admitted **Housing** Yes **Expenses** Tuition $6664; Room only $2700 **Academic program** Advanced placement, accelerated degree program, tutorials, internships **Contact** Mr. Phil Eberle, Director of Admissions, Missouri Technical School, 1167 Corporate Lake Drive, St. Louis, MO 63132-1716. Telephone: 314-569-3600 or toll-free 800-230-3600 (out-of-state). Fax: 314-569-1167. E-mail: rhonaber@motech.edu. Web site: http://www.motech.edu/.

MISSOURI VALLEY COLLEGE
MARSHALL, MISSOURI

General Independent, 4-year, coed, affiliated with Presbyterian Church **Entrance** Moderately difficult **Setting** 140-acre small town campus **Total enrollment** 1,404 **Student/faculty ratio** 20:1 **Application deadline** Rolling **Freshmen** 85% were admitted **Housing** Yes **Expenses** Tuition

$10,500; Room & Board $5000 **Undergraduates** 38% women, 3% part-time, 10% 25 or older, 1% Native American, 4% Hispanic, 14% black, 2% Asian American or Pacific Islander **Most popular recent majors** Business administration; education; psychology **Academic program** Average class size 20, English as a second language, advanced placement, tutorials, summer session, adult/continuing education programs, internships **Contact** Ms. Debbie Bultman, Admissions, Missouri Valley College, 500 East College, Marshall, MO 65340-3197. Telephone: 660-831-4114. Fax: 660-886-9818. E-mail: mo-valley@juno.com. Web site: http://www.murlin.com/~webfx/mvc/.

MISSOURI WESTERN STATE COLLEGE
ST. JOSEPH, MISSOURI

General State-supported, 4-year, coed **Entrance** Noncompetitive **Setting** 744-acre suburban campus **Total enrollment** 5,124 **Student/faculty ratio** 18:1 **Application deadline** 7/30 **Freshmen** 100% were admitted **Housing** Yes **Expenses** Tuition $2534; Room & Board $3302 **Undergraduates** 62% women, 23% part-time, 28% 25 or older, 1% Native American, 2% Hispanic, 7% black, 1% Asian American or Pacific Islander **Most popular recent majors** Criminal justice studies; nursing; elementary education **Academic program** Average class size 35, advanced placement, accelerated degree program, honors program, summer session, adult/continuing education programs, internships **Contact** Mr. Howard McCauley, Director of Admissions, Missouri Western State College, 4525 Downs Drive, St. Joseph, MO 64507-2294. Telephone: 816-271-4267 or toll-free 800-662-7041 ext. 60. Fax: 816-271-5833. E-mail: admissn@giffon.mwsc.edu. Web site: http://www.mwsc.edu/.

NATIONAL AMERICAN UNIVERSITY
KANSAS CITY, MISSOURI

General Proprietary, 4-year, coed **Contact** Ms. Tanya Carr, Director of Admissions, National American University, 4200 Blue Ridge Boulevard, Kansas City, MO 64133-1612. Telephone: 816-353-4554. Fax: 816-353-1176.

NORTHWEST MISSOURI STATE UNIVERSITY
MARYVILLE, MISSOURI

General State-supported, comprehensive, coed **Entrance** Moderately difficult **Setting** 240-acre small town campus **Total enrollment** 6,280 **Student/faculty ratio** 27:1 **Application deadline** Rolling **Freshmen** 91% were admitted **Housing** Yes **Expenses** Tuition $2813; Room & Board $3890 **Undergraduates** 55% women, 5% part-time, 7% 25 or older, 0.2% Native American, 1% Hispanic, 2% black, 0.4% Asian American or Pacific Islander **Most popular recent majors** Business economics; education **Academic program** English as a second language, advanced placement, accelerated degree program, tutorials, summer session, internships **Contact** Ms. Beverly Schenkel, Associate Director of Admission, Northwest Missouri State University, 800 University Drive, Maryville, MO 64468-6001. Telephone: 660-562-1149 or toll-free 800-633-1175. Fax: 660-562-1121. E-mail: admissions@acad.nwmissouri.edu.

OZARK CHRISTIAN COLLEGE
JOPLIN, MISSOURI

General Independent Christian, 4-year, coed **Entrance** Noncompetitive **Setting** 110-acre suburban campus **Total enrollment** 663 **Student/faculty ratio** 20:1 **Application deadline** 8/15 **Freshmen** 100% were admitted **Housing** Yes **Expenses** Tuition $4305; Room & Board $3200 **Undergraduates** 30% 25 or older, 2% Native American, 1% Hispanic, 1% black, 0.2% Asian American or Pacific Islander **Academic program** English as a second language, summer session, adult/continuing education programs, internships **Contact** Mr. James Marcum, Director of Admissions, Ozark Christian College, 1111 North Main Street, Joplin, MO 64801-4804. Telephone: 417-624-2518 ext. 2021 or toll-free 800-299-4622. Fax: 417-624-0090. E-mail: occadmin@talleytech.com. Web site: http://www.occ.edu/.

PARK COLLEGE
PARKVILLE, MISSOURI

General Independent, comprehensive, coed, affiliated with Reorganized Church of Jesus Christ of Latter Day Saints **Entrance** Moderately difficult **Setting** 800-acre suburban campus **Total enrollment** 8,395 **Student/faculty ratio** 14:1 **Application deadline** 8/1 **Freshmen** 89% were admitted **Housing** Yes **Expenses** Tuition $4410; Room & Board $4430 **Undergraduates** 45% women, 90% part-time, 28% 25 or older, 1% Native American, 10% Hispanic, 17% black, 2% Asian American or Pacific Islander **Most popular recent majors** Business administration; criminal justice studies; elementary education **Academic program** Average class size 25, English as a second language, advanced placement, self-designed majors, honors program, summer session, adult/continuing education programs, internships **Contact** Dr. Ron Carruth, Director of Student Recruiting and Marketing, Park College, 8700 NW River Park Drive, Parkville, MO 64152-4358. Telephone: 816-741-2000 ext. 6215 or toll-free 800-745-7275. Fax: 816-741-4462. E-mail: admissions@mail.park.edu. Web site: http://www.park.edu/.

RESEARCH COLLEGE OF NURSING
KANSAS CITY, MISSOURI

General Independent, comprehensive, coed **Entrance** Moderately difficult **Setting** 66-acre urban campus **Total enrollment** 216 **Student/faculty ratio** 7:1 **Application deadline** 6/30 **Freshmen** 78% were admitted **Housing** Yes **Expenses** Tuition $12,150; Room & Board $5000 **Undergraduates** 96% women, 8% part-time, 30% 25 or older, 1% Native American, 4% Hispanic, 8% black, 1% Asian American or Pacific Islander **Academic program** Average class size 30, advanced placement, accelerated degree program, honors program, summer session **Contact** Rockhurst College Admission Office, Research College of Nursing, 2316 East Meyer Boulevard, Kansas City, MO 64132. Telephone: 816-501-4012 or toll-free 800-842-6776. Fax: 816-501-4588. E-mail: mendenhall@vax2.rockhurst.edu.

ROCKHURST COLLEGE
KANSAS CITY, MISSOURI

General Independent Roman Catholic (Jesuit), comprehensive, coed **Entrance** Moderately difficult **Setting** 35-acre urban campus **Total enrollment** 2,792 **Student/faculty ratio** 11:1 **Application deadline** Rolling **Freshmen** 89% were admitted **Housing** Yes **Expenses** Tuition $11,850; Room & Board $4760 **Undergraduates** 56% women, 34% part-time, 17% 25 or older, 1% Native American, 4% Hispanic, 5% black, 2% Asian American or Pacific Islander **Most popular recent majors** Nursing; biology; psychology **Academic program** Average class size 19, English as a second language, advanced placement, accelerated degree program, tutorials, honors program, summer session, adult/continuing education programs, internships **Contact** Mr. Keith Jaloma, Director of Admissions, Rockhurst College, 1100 Rockhurst Road, Kansas City, MO 64110-2561. Telephone: 816-501-4100 or toll-free 800-842-6776. Fax: 816-501-4241. E-mail: admission@vax2.rockhurst.edu. Web site: http://www.rockhurst.edu/.

ST. LOUIS CHRISTIAN COLLEGE
FLORISSANT, MISSOURI

General Independent Christian, 4-year, coed **Contact** Ms. Wanda Reed, Registrar, St. Louis Christian College, 1360 Grandview Drive, Florissant, MO 63033-6499. Telephone: 314-837-6777 ext. 1500 or toll-free 800-887-SLCC (in-state). Fax: 314-837-8291.

ST. LOUIS COLLEGE OF PHARMACY
ST. LOUIS, MISSOURI

General Independent, comprehensive, coed **Entrance** Moderately difficult **Setting** 5-acre urban campus **Total enrollment** 866 **Student/faculty ratio** 12:1 **Application deadline** Rolling **Freshmen** 87% were admitted **Housing** Yes **Expenses** Tuition $11,600; Room & Board $4950 **Undergraduates** 64% women, 3% part-time, 15% 25 or older, 0% Native American, 1% Hispanic, 3% black, 11% Asian American or Pacific Islander **Academic program** Average class size 100, advanced placement, tutorials, summer session, adult/continuing education programs, internships **Contact** Ms. Lisa Boeschen, Director of Admissions, St. Louis College of Pharmacy, 4588 Parkview Place, St. Louis, MO 63110-1088. Telephone: 314-367-8700 ext. 1072 or toll-free 800-278-5267 (in-state). Fax: 314-367-2784. E-mail: lboeschen@slcop.st.lcop.edu. Web site: http://www.stlcop.edu/.

SAINT LOUIS UNIVERSITY
ST. LOUIS, MISSOURI

General Independent Roman Catholic (Jesuit), university, coed **Entrance** Moderately difficult **Setting** 279-acre urban campus **Total enrollment** 14,229 **Student/faculty ratio** 16:1 **Application deadline** Rolling **Freshmen** 71% were admitted **Housing** Yes **Expenses** Tuition $15,050; Room & Board $5290 **Undergraduates** 55% women, 9% part-time, 17% 25 or older, 0.3% Native American, 2% Hispanic, 7% black, 4% Asian American or Pacific Islander **Most popular recent majors** Nursing; psychology; biology **Academic program** Average class size 22, English as a second language, advanced placement, accelerated degree program, self-designed majors, tutorials, honors program, summer session, adult/continuing education programs, internships **Contact** Ms. Patsy Brooks, Credential Evaluator for Undergraduate Admissions, Saint Louis University, 221 North Grand Boulevard, St. Louis, MO 63103-2097. Telephone: 314-977-2500 or toll-free 800-758-3678 (out-of-state). Fax: 314-977-7136. E-mail: admitme@sluvca.slu.edu. Web site: http://www.slu.edu/.

SAINT LUKE'S COLLEGE
KANSAS CITY, MISSOURI

General Independent Episcopal, upper-level, coed **Entrance** Very difficult **Setting** 3-acre urban campus **Total enrollment** 108 **Student/faculty ratio** 8:1 **Freshmen** 47% were admitted **Housing** Yes **Expenses** Tuition $7070; Room & Board $2200 **Undergraduates** 92% women, 8% part-time, 80% 25 or older, 0% Native American, 6% Hispanic, 1% black, 4% Asian American or Pacific Islander **Academic program** Average class size 50, tutorials, summer session **Contact** Ms. Marsha Thomas, Director, Admissions and Records, Saint Luke's College, 4426 Wornall Road, Kansas City, MO 64111. Telephone: 816-932-2073. E-mail: mjthomas@saint-lukes.org.

SOUTHEAST MISSOURI STATE UNIVERSITY
CAPE GIRARDEAU, MISSOURI

General State-supported, comprehensive, coed **Entrance** Moderately difficult **Setting** 693-acre small town campus **Total enrollment** 8,231 **Student/faculty ratio** 19:1 **Application deadline** 7/15 **Freshmen** 85% were admitted **Housing** Yes **Expenses** Tuition $3000; Room & Board $6920 **Undergraduates** 60% women, 20% part-time, 19% 25 or older, 0.5% Native American, 1% Hispanic, 4% black, 1% Asian American or Pacific Islander **Most popular recent majors** Business administration; education; mass communications **Academic program** Average class size 25, English as a second language, advanced placement, accelerated degree program, self-designed majors, tutorials, honors program, summer session, adult/continuing education programs, internships **Contact** Mr. Jay Goff, Director of Admissions, Southeast Missouri State University, One University Plaza, Cape Girardeau, MO 63701-4799. Telephone: 573-651-2590. Web site: http://www.semo.edu/.

► **For more information, see page 516.**

SOUTHWEST BAPTIST UNIVERSITY
BOLIVAR, MISSOURI

General Independent Southern Baptist, comprehensive, coed **Entrance** Moderately difficult **Setting** 152-acre small town campus **Total enrollment** 3,593 **Student/faculty ratio** 22:1 **Application deadline** 9/7 **Housing** Yes **Expenses** Tuition $8347; Room & Board $2580 **Undergraduates** 66% women, 30% part-time, 43% 25 or older, 1% Native American, 1% Hispanic, 2% black, 1% Asian American or Pacific Islander **Most popular recent majors** Nursing; elementary education; business administration **Academic program** English as a second language, advanced placement, accelerated degree program, honors program, summer session, adult/continuing education programs, internships **Contact** Mr. Rob Harris, Director of Admissions, Southwest Baptist University, 1600 University Avenue, Bolivar, MO 65613-2597. Telephone: 417-326-1814 or toll-free 800-526-5859. Fax: 417-326-1514. E-mail: admitme@shuniv.edu. Web site: http://www.sbuniv.edu/.

SOUTHWEST MISSOURI STATE UNIVERSITY
SPRINGFIELD, MISSOURI

General State-supported, comprehensive, coed **Entrance** Moderately difficult **Setting** 183-acre suburban campus **Total enrollment** 16,468 **Student/faculty ratio** 19:1 **Application deadline** 8/1 **Freshmen** 87% were admitted **Housing** Yes **Expenses** Tuition $3214; Room & Board $3594 **Undergraduates** 55% women, 17% part-time, 17% 25 or older, 1% Native American, 1% Hispanic, 2% black, 1% Asian American or Pacific Islander **Most popular recent majors** Elementary education; psychology; business marketing and marketing management **Academic program** English as a second language, advanced placement, self-designed majors, tutorials, honors program, summer session, adult/continuing education programs, internships **Contact** Ms. Jill Duncan, Associate Director of Admissions, Southwest Missouri State University, 901 South National, Springfield, MO 65804-0094. Telephone: 417-836-5517 or toll-free 800-492-7900. Fax: 417-836-6334. E-mail: smsuinfo@vma.smsu.edu. Web site: http://www.smsu.edu/.

STEPHENS COLLEGE
COLUMBIA, MISSOURI

General Independent, comprehensive, women only **Entrance** Moderately difficult **Setting** 244-acre urban campus **Total enrollment** 819 **Student/faculty ratio** 10:1 **Application deadline** 7/31 **Freshmen** 86% were admitted **Housing** Yes **Expenses** Tuition $14,830; Room & Board $5700 **Undergraduates** 43% part-time, 8% 25 or older **Most popular recent majors** Fashion merchandising; theater arts/drama; business administration **Academic program** Average class size 15, English as a second language, advanced placement, accelerated degree program, self-designed majors, tutorials, summer session, adult/continuing education programs, internships **Contact** Ms. Margaret Herron, Assistant Director of Admissions, Stephens College, Box 2121, Columbia, MO 65215-0002. Telephone: 573-876-7207 or toll-free 800-876-7207. Fax: 573-876-7237. E-mail: apply@sc.stephens.edu. Web site: http://www.stephens.edu/.

TRUMAN STATE UNIVERSITY
KIRKSVILLE, MISSOURI

General State-supported, comprehensive, coed **Entrance** Moderately difficult **Setting** 140-acre small town campus **Total enrollment** 6,421 **Student/faculty ratio** 16:1 **Application deadline** 3/1 **Freshmen** 81% were admitted **Housing** Yes **Expenses** Tuition $3274; Room & Board $3992 **Undergraduates** 57% women, 2% part-time, 3% 25 or older, 0.2% Native American, 2% Hispanic, 3% black, 2% Asian American or Pacific Islander **Most popular recent majors** Business administration; biology; English **Academic program** Average class size 22, English as a second language, advanced placement, accelerated degree program, honors program, summer session, internships **Contact** Mr. Brad Chambers, Co-Director of Admissions, Truman State University, 205 McClain Hall, Kirksville, MO 63501-4221. Telephone: 660-785-4114 or toll-free 800-892-7792 (in-state). Fax:

Truman State University *(continued)*

660-785-7456. E-mail: admissions@truman.edu. Web site: http://www.truman.edu/.

UNIVERSITY OF MISSOURI–COLUMBIA
COLUMBIA, MISSOURI

General State-supported, university, coed **Entrance** Moderately difficult **Setting** 1,348-acre small town campus **Total enrollment** 22,552 **Student/faculty ratio** 19:1 **Application deadline** 5/1 **Freshmen** 80% were admitted **Housing** Yes **Expenses** Tuition $4280; Room & Board $4290 **Undergraduates** 53% women, 7% part-time, 12% 25 or older, 0.5% Native American, 1% Hispanic, 6% black, 3% Asian American or Pacific Islander **Most popular recent majors** Business administration; journalism; education **Academic program** English as a second language, advanced placement, accelerated degree program, self-designed majors, tutorials, honors program, summer session, adult/continuing education programs, internships **Contact** Ms. Georgeanne Porter, Director of Undergraduate Admissions, University of Missouri-Columbia, 225 Jesse Hall, Columbia, MO 65211. Telephone: 573-882-7786 or toll-free 800-225-6075 (in-state). Fax: 573-882-7887. Web site: http://www.missouri.edu/.

UNIVERSITY OF MISSOURI–KANSAS CITY
KANSAS CITY, MISSOURI

General State-supported, university, coed **Entrance** Moderately difficult **Setting** 191-acre urban campus **Total enrollment** 10,445 **Student/faculty ratio** 10:1 **Application deadline** Rolling **Freshmen** 67% were admitted **Housing** Yes **Expenses** Tuition $4278; Room & Board $4270 **Undergraduates** 57% women, 32% part-time, 38% 25 or older, 1% Native American, 3% Hispanic, 10% black, 5% Asian American or Pacific Islander **Most popular recent majors** Biology; liberal arts and studies; psychology **Academic program** English as a second language, advanced placement, accelerated degree program, self-designed majors, honors program, summer session, adult/continuing education programs, internships **Contact** Mr. Melvin C. Tyler, Director of Admissions, University of Missouri-Kansas City, 5100 Rockhill Road, Kansas City, MO 64110-2499. Telephone: 816-235-1111. Fax: 816-235-1717. E-mail: admit@umkc.edu. Web site: http://www.umkc.edu/.

UNIVERSITY OF MISSOURI–ROLLA
ROLLA, MISSOURI

General State-supported, university, coed **Entrance** Very difficult **Setting** 284-acre small town campus **Total enrollment** 4,976 **Student/faculty ratio** 14:1 **Application deadline** 7/1 **Freshmen** 97% were admitted **Housing** Yes **Expenses** Tuition $4194; Room & Board $4220 **Undergraduates** 25% women, 11% part-time, 9% 25 or older, 1% Native American, 1% Hispanic, 3% black, 3% Asian American or Pacific Islander **Most popular recent majors** Mechanical engineering; electrical/electronics engineering; civil engineering **Academic program** English as a second language, advanced placement, accelerated degree program, tutorials, honors program, summer session, adult/continuing education programs **Contact** Dr. Edward Hornsey, Director of Admissions and Financial Aid, University of Missouri-Rolla, 102 Parker Hall, Rolla, MO 65409. Telephone: 573-341-4164. E-mail: umrolla@umr.edu. Web site: http://www.umr.edu/.

UNIVERSITY OF MISSOURI–ST. LOUIS
ST. LOUIS, MISSOURI

General State-supported, university, coed **Entrance** Moderately difficult **Setting** 250-acre suburban campus **Total enrollment** 15,576 **Student/faculty ratio** 10:1 **Application deadline** Rolling **Freshmen** 66% were admitted **Housing** Yes **Expenses** Tuition $4396; Room & Board $4845 **Undergraduates** 59% women, 46% part-time, 44% 25 or older, 0.1% Native American, 1% Hispanic, 12% black, 2% Asian American or Pacific Islander **Most popular recent majors** Education; business administration; psychology **Academic program** English as a second language, advanced placement, accelerated degree program, self-designed majors, tutorials, honors program, summer session, adult/continuing education programs, internships **Contact** Mr. Curtis C. Coonrod, Director of Admissions, University of Missouri-St. Louis, Woods Hall, St. Louis, MO 63121-4499. Telephone: 314-516-5460. Fax: 314-516-5310. E-mail: curt_coonrod@ccmail.umsl.edu. Web site: http://www.umsl.edu/.

WASHINGTON UNIVERSITY IN ST. LOUIS
ST. LOUIS, MISSOURI

General Independent, university, coed **Entrance** Very difficult **Setting** 169-acre suburban campus **Total enrollment** 11,606 **Student/faculty ratio** 7:1 **Application deadline** 1/15 **Freshmen** 40% were admitted **Housing** Yes **Expenses** Tuition $22,422; Room & Board $6922 **Undergraduates** 49% women, 6% part-time, 2% 25 or older, 0.2% Native American, 1% Hispanic, 6% black, 12% Asian American or Pacific Islander **Most popular recent majors** Engineering; business administration; biology **Academic program** Average class size 18, English as a second language, advanced placement, accelerated degree program, self-designed majors, tutorials, summer session, adult/continuing education programs, internships **Contact** Ms. Nanette Clift, Director of

Recruitment, Washington University in St. Louis, Campus Box 1089, 1 Brookings Drive, St. Louis, MO 63130-4899. Telephone: 314-935-6000 or toll-free 800-638-0700. Fax: 314-935-4290. E-mail: admission@wustl.edu. Web site: http://www.wustl.edu/.

▶ **For more information, see page 547.**

WEBSTER UNIVERSITY
ST. LOUIS, MISSOURI

General Independent, comprehensive, coed **Entrance** Moderately difficult **Setting** 47-acre suburban campus **Total enrollment** 11,756 **Student/faculty ratio** 16:1 **Application deadline** 3/1 **Freshmen** 64% were admitted **Housing** Yes **Expenses** Tuition $10,910; Room & Board $5030 **Undergraduates** 65% women, 41% part-time, 51% 25 or older, 1% Native American, 2% Hispanic, 10% black, 1% Asian American or Pacific Islander **Most popular recent majors** Business administration; nursing; education **Academic program** English as a second language, advanced placement, accelerated degree program, self-designed majors, tutorials, summer session, adult/continuing education programs, internships **Contact** Mr. Niel DeVasto, Director of Admission, Webster University, 470 East Lockwood Avenue, St. Louis, MO 63119-3194. Telephone: 314-968-7000 or toll-free 800-75-ENROL. Fax: 314-968-7115. E-mail: admit@websteruniv.edu. Web site: http://www.websteruniv.edu/.

WESTMINSTER COLLEGE
FULTON, MISSOURI

General Independent, 4-year, coed, affiliated with Presbyterian Church **Entrance** Moderately difficult **Setting** 65-acre small town campus **Total enrollment** 654 **Student/faculty ratio** 12:1 **Application deadline** Rolling **Freshmen** 84% were admitted **Housing** Yes **Expenses** Tuition $12,840; Room & Board $4450 **Undergraduates** 41% women, 2% part-time, 1% 25 or older **Most popular recent majors** Business administration; political science; elementary education **Academic program** Average class size 16, English as a second language, advanced placement, accelerated degree program, self-designed majors, tutorials, summer session, internships **Contact** Mr. Alan Liebrecht, Dean of Enrollment Services, Westminster College, 501 Westminster Avenue, Fulton, MO 65251-1299. Telephone: 573-592-1251 or toll-free 800-475-3361. Fax: 573-592-5227. E-mail: admissions@jaynet.wcmo.edu. Web site: http://www.wcmo.edu/.

WILLIAM JEWELL COLLEGE
LIBERTY, MISSOURI

General Independent Baptist, 4-year, coed **Entrance** Moderately difficult **Setting** 700-acre small town campus **Total enrollment** 1,153 **Student/faculty ratio** 13:1 **Application deadline** 3/15 **Freshmen** 89% were admitted **Housing** Yes **Expenses** Tuition $11,850; Room & Board $3560 **Undergraduates** 59% women, 3% part-time, 8% 25 or older **Most popular recent majors** Business administration; nursing; psychology **Academic program** Advanced placement, accelerated degree program, self-designed majors, tutorials, honors program, summer session, adult/continuing education programs, internships **Contact** Mr. David Maltby, Dean of Enrollment Development, William Jewell College, 500 College Hill, Liberty, MO 64068-1843. Telephone: 816-781-7700 ext. 5137 or toll-free 800-753-7009. Fax: 816-415-5027. E-mail: admission@william.jewell.edu. Web site: http://www.jewell.edu/.

WILLIAM WOODS UNIVERSITY
FULTON, MISSOURI

General Independent, comprehensive, coed, affiliated with Christian Church (Disciples of Christ) **Entrance** Moderately difficult **Setting** 170-acre small town campus **Total enrollment** 1,279 **Student/faculty ratio** 16:1 **Application deadline** Rolling **Housing** Yes **Expenses** Tuition $12,300; Room & Board $5000 **Undergraduates** 84% women, 12% part-time, 40% 25 or older, 0.2% Native American, 1% Hispanic, 2% black, 5% Asian American or Pacific Islander **Most popular recent majors** Business administration; paralegal/legal assistant; equestrian studies **Academic program** English as a second language, advanced placement, accelerated degree program, self-designed majors, tutorials, honors program, summer session, adult/continuing education programs, internships **Contact** Ms. Mary Hawk, Dean of Admission, William Woods University, 200 West Twelfth Street, Fulton, MO 65251-1098. Telephone: 573-592-4221 or toll-free 800-995-3159. Fax: 573-592-1146. E-mail: mhawk@iris.wmwoods.edu.

MONTANA

CARROLL COLLEGE
HELENA, MONTANA

General Independent Roman Catholic, 4-year, coed **Entrance** Moderately difficult **Setting** 64-acre small town campus **Total enrollment** 1,206 **Student/faculty ratio** 12:1 **Application deadline** 6/1 **Freshmen** 96% were admitted **Housing** Yes **Expenses** Tuition $11,490; Room & Board $4540 **Undergraduates** 61% women, 8% part-time, 21% 25 or older, 1% Native American, 2% Hispanic, 0.1% black, 1% Asian American or Pa-

Carroll College *(continued)*

cific Islander **Most popular recent majors** Elementary education; psychology; nursing **Academic program** Average class size 24, English as a second language, advanced placement, accelerated degree program, self-designed majors, tutorials, honors program, summer session, adult/continuing education programs, internships **Contact** Ms. Candace A. Cain, Director of Admission, Carroll College, 1601 North Benton Avenue, Helena, MT 59625-0002. Telephone: 406-447-4384 or toll-free 800-99-ADMIT. Fax: 406-447-4533. E-mail: enroll@carroll.edu. Web site: http://www.carroll.edu/.

▶ **For more information, see page 404.**

COMMONWEALTH INTERNATIONAL UNIVERSITY

BILLINGS, MONTANA

General Independent, 4-year, coed **Entrance** Difficulty N/R **Setting** 4-acre urban campus **Total enrollment** 192 **Housing** No **Expenses** Tuition $7500 **Undergraduates** 8% Native American, 1% Hispanic, 2% black, 1% Asian American or Pacific Islander **Contact** Ms. Misty Ross, Director of Admissions, Commonwealth International University, 2520 Fifth Avenue South, Billings, MT 59101. Telephone: 406-256-1000 or toll-free 800-736-5244. Fax: 406-256-4975.

MONTANA STATE UNIVERSITY–BILLINGS

BILLINGS, MONTANA

General State-supported, comprehensive, coed **Entrance** Moderately difficult **Setting** 92-acre urban campus **Total enrollment** 4,277 **Student/faculty ratio** 20:1 **Application deadline** 7/1 **Freshmen** 88% were admitted **Housing** Yes **Expenses** Tuition $2517; Room & Board $3620 **Undergraduates** 64% women, 21% part-time, 6% Native American, 2% Hispanic, 0.4% black, 1% Asian American or Pacific Islander **Most popular recent majors** Elementary education; secondary education; business administration **Academic program** Average class size 35, advanced placement, accelerated degree program, tutorials, honors program, summer session, adult/continuing education programs, internships **Contact** Ms. Karen Everett, Director, Admissions and Records, Montana State University-Billings, 1500 North 30th Street, Billings, MT 59101-9984. Telephone: 406-657-2158. Fax: 406-657-2302. E-mail: adm_tempo@vicuna.emcmt.edu. Web site: http://www.msubillings.edu/.

MONTANA STATE UNIVERSITY–BOZEMAN

BOZEMAN, MONTANA

General State-supported, university, coed **Entrance** Moderately difficult **Setting** 1,170-acre small town campus **Total enrollment** 11,603 **Student/faculty ratio** 18:1 **Application deadline** 7/1 **Freshmen** 84% were admitted **Housing** Yes **Expenses** Tuition $2677; Room & Board $4025 **Undergraduates** 44% women, 13% part-time, 18% 25 or older, 2% Native American, 1% Hispanic, 0.3% black, 1% Asian American or Pacific Islander **Academic program** Average class size 47, English as a second language, advanced placement, self-designed majors, honors program, summer session, adult/continuing education programs, internships **Contact** Ms. Ronda Russell, Director of New Student Services, Montana State University-Bozeman, PO Box 172190, Bozeman, MT 59717. Telephone: 406-994-5541 or toll-free 888-678-2287. E-mail: admissions@montana.edu. Web site: http://www.montana.edu/.

MONTANA STATE UNIVERSITY–NORTHERN

HAVRE, MONTANA

General State-supported, comprehensive, coed **Entrance** Moderately difficult **Setting** 105-acre small town campus **Total enrollment** 1,704 **Student/faculty ratio** 19:1 **Application deadline** Rolling **Housing** Yes **Expenses** Tuition $2504; Room & Board $3650 **Undergraduates** 53% women, 26% part-time, 47% 25 or older, 7% Native American, 0.4% Hispanic, 0.1% black, 0.4% Asian American or Pacific Islander **Most popular recent majors** Education; business administration; nursing **Academic program** English as a second language, advanced placement, tutorials, honors program, summer session, adult/continuing education programs, internships **Contact** Ms. Rosalie Spinler, Director of Admissions, Montana State University-Northern, PO Box 7751, Havre, MT 59501-7751. Telephone: 406-265-3704 or toll-free 800-662-6132 (in-state). Fax: 406-265-3777. E-mail: msunadmit@nmc1.nmclites.edu. Web site: http://polaris.nmclites.edu/.

MONTANA TECH OF THE UNIVERSITY OF MONTANA

BUTTE, MONTANA

General State-supported, comprehensive, coed **Entrance** Moderately difficult **Setting** 56-acre small town campus **Total enrollment** 1,786 **Student/faculty ratio** 16:1 **Application deadline** 7/1 **Housing** Yes **Expenses** Tuition $2542; Room & Board $3568 **Undergraduates** 34% 25 or older, 2% Native American, 1% Hispanic, 0.2% black, 1% Asian American or Pacific Islander **Most popular recent majors** Environmental engineering; computer science; engineering science **Academic program** Average class size 30, advanced placement, tutorials, summer session, adult/continuing education programs, internships **Contact** Ms. Monica Bruning, Director of Admissions, Montana Tech of The University of Montana, 1300 West Park Street, Butte, MT 59701-8997. Telephone: 406-496-4178 or toll-free 800-445-TECH. Fax: 406-496-4710. E-mail: admissions@p01.mtech.edu. Web site: http://www.mtech.edu/.

ROCKY MOUNTAIN COLLEGE

BILLINGS, MONTANA

General Independent interdenominational, 4-year, coed **Entrance** Moderately difficult **Setting** 60-acre suburban campus **Total enrollment** 777 **Student/faculty ratio** 14:1 **Application deadline** Rolling **Freshmen** 90% were admitted **Housing** Yes **Expenses** Tuition $11,173; Room & Board $3978 **Undergraduates** 56% women, 9% part-time, 35% 25 or older, 7% Native American, 2% Hispanic, 1% black, 1% Asian American or Pacific Islander **Most popular recent majors** Business administration; education **Academic program** Average class size 15, English as a second language, advanced placement, accelerated degree program, self-designed majors, tutorials, honors program, summer session, adult/continuing education programs, internships **Contact** Mr. Craig Gould, Director of Admissions, Rocky Mountain College, 1511 Poly Drive, Billings, MT 59102-1796. Telephone: 406-657-1026 or toll-free 800-877-6259. Fax: 406-259-9751. E-mail: admissions@rocky.edu. Web site: http://www.rocky.edu/.

UNIVERSITY OF GREAT FALLS

GREAT FALLS, MONTANA

General Independent Roman Catholic, comprehensive, coed **Entrance** Noncompetitive **Setting** 40-acre urban campus **Total enrollment** 1,164 **Student/faculty ratio** 12:1 **Application deadline** Rolling **Housing** Yes **Expenses** Tuition $8100; Room & Board $3520 **Undergraduates** 69% women, 38% part-time, 67% 25 or older, 10% Native American, 2% Hispanic, 1% black, 1% Asian American or Pacific Islander **Most popular recent majors** Criminal justice/law enforcement administration; human services; education **Academic program** Average class size 25, advanced placement, accelerated degree program, summer session, adult/continuing education programs, internships **Contact** Mr. Robert Hensley, Vice President for Enrollment Management, University of Great Falls, 1301 Twentieth Street South, Great Falls, MT 59405. Telephone: 406-791-5200 or toll-free 800-856-9544. Fax: 406-791-5209. E-mail: adminrec@ugf.edu. Web site: http://www.ugf.edu/.

THE UNIVERSITY OF MONTANA–MISSOULA

MISSOULA, MONTANA

General State-supported, university, coed **Entrance** Moderately difficult **Setting** 220-acre urban campus **Total enrollment** 12,124 **Student/faculty ratio** 19:1 **Application deadline** 7/1 **Freshmen** 83% were admitted **Housing** Yes **Expenses** Tuition $2630; Room & Board $3917 **Undergraduates** 24% 25 or older **Most popular recent majors** Business administration; education; forestry **Academic program** Average class size 50, English as a second language, advanced placement, tutorials, honors program, summer session, adult/continuing education programs, internships **Contact** Office of New Student Services, The University of Montana–Missoula, Missoula, MT 59812-0002. Telephone: 406-243-6266 or toll-free 800-462-8636. Fax: 406-243-5711. E-mail: admiss@selway.umt.edu. Web site: http://www.umt.edu/.

WESTERN MONTANA COLLEGE OF THE UNIVERSITY OF MONTANA

DILLON, MONTANA

General State-supported, 4-year, coed **Entrance** Moderately difficult **Setting** 36-acre small town campus **Total enrollment** 1,122 **Student/faculty ratio** 20:1 **Application deadline** 7/1 **Freshmen** 85% were admitted **Housing** Yes **Expenses** Tuition $2036; Room & Board $3632 **Undergraduates** 56% women, 18% part-time, 30% 25 or older, 2% Native American, 1% Hispanic, 0.4% black, 0.4% Asian American or Pacific Islander **Most popular recent majors** Elementary education; liberal arts and studies; social sciences **Academic program** Average class size 40, advanced placement, accelerated degree program, self-designed majors, tutorials, honors program, summer session, adult/continuing education programs, internships **Contact** Ms. Kay Leum, Director of Admissions and New Student Services, Western Montana College of The University of Montana, 710 South Atlantic, Dillon, MT 59725-3598. Telephone: 406-683-7331 or toll-free 800-WMC-MONT. Fax: 406-683-7493. E-mail: admissions@wmc.edu. Web site: http://www.wmc.edu/.

NEBRASKA

BELLEVUE UNIVERSITY

BELLEVUE, NEBRASKA

General Independent, comprehensive, coed **Entrance** Minimally difficult **Setting** 19-acre suburban campus **Total enrollment** 2,928 **Student/faculty ratio** 27:1 **Application deadline** Rolling **Housing** No **Expenses** Tuition $3650 **Undergraduates** 47% women, 37% part-time, 80% 25 or older, 1% Native American, 1% Hispanic, 7% black, 2% Asian American or Pacific Islander **Most popular recent majors** Business administration; accounting; management information systems/

Bellevue University *(continued)*

business data processing **Academic program** English as a second language, advanced placement, accelerated degree program, tutorials, summer session, adult/continuing education programs **Contact** Ms. Sharon Thonen, Director of Admissions, Bellevue University, 1000 Galvin Road South, Bellevue, NE 68005-3098. Telephone: 402-293-3767. Fax: 402-293-2020. E-mail: set@scholars.bellevue.edu. Web site: http://www.bellevue.edu/.

CHADRON STATE COLLEGE
CHADRON, NEBRASKA

General State-supported, comprehensive, coed **Entrance** Noncompetitive **Setting** 281-acre small town campus **Total enrollment** 2,931 **Student/faculty ratio** 20:1 **Application deadline** Rolling **Freshmen** 100% were admitted **Housing** Yes **Expenses** Tuition $2148; Room & Board $3060 **Undergraduates** 56% women, 22% part-time, 26% 25 or older, 2% Native American, 2% Hispanic, 1% black, 1% Asian American or Pacific Islander **Most popular recent majors** Business administration; education **Academic program** Advanced placement, self-designed majors, honors program, summer session, adult/continuing education programs, internships **Contact** Ms. Terie Dawson, Director of Enrollment Management, Chadron State College, 1000 Main Street, Chadron, NE 69337. Telephone: 308-432-6263. Fax: 308-432-6229. E-mail: admissions@csc1.csc.edu. Web site: http://www.csc.edu/.

CLARKSON COLLEGE
OMAHA, NEBRASKA

General Independent, comprehensive, coed, affiliated with Episcopal Church **Entrance** Moderately difficult **Setting** 3-acre urban campus **Total enrollment** 598 **Student/faculty ratio** 12:1 **Application deadline** Rolling **Freshmen** 69% were admitted **Housing** Yes **Expenses** Tuition $7291; Room only $2040 **Undergraduates** 89% women, 44% part-time, 56% 25 or older, 0% Native American, 2% Hispanic, 5% black, 1% Asian American or Pacific Islander **Most popular recent majors** Nursing science; nursing **Academic program** Average class size 15, advanced placement, accelerated degree program, self-designed majors, tutorials, summer session, adult/continuing education programs, internships **Contact** Mr. Jeffrey S. Beals, Director of Enrollment Management, Clarkson College, 101 South 42nd Street, Omaha, NE 68131-2739. Telephone: 402-552-2551 or toll-free 800-647-5500. Fax: 402-552-6057. E-mail: admiss@clrkcol.crhsnet.edu. Web site: http://www.clarksoncollege.edu/.

▶ **For more information, see page 413.**

COLLEGE OF SAINT MARY
OMAHA, NEBRASKA

General Independent Roman Catholic, 4-year, women only **Entrance** Moderately difficult **Setting** 25-acre suburban campus **Total enrollment** 1,001 **Student/faculty ratio** 11:1 **Application deadline** Rolling **Freshmen** 77% were admitted **Housing** Yes **Expenses** Tuition $11,814; Room & Board $4290 **Undergraduates** 41% 25 or older, 0% Native American, 1% Hispanic, 2% black, 0.4% Asian American or Pacific Islander **Most popular recent majors** Nursing; occupational therapy; business administration **Academic program** Average class size 25, advanced placement, tutorials, summer session, adult/continuing education programs, internships **Contact** Ms. Sue Kropf, Director of Enrollment Services, College of Saint Mary, 1901 South 72nd Street, Omaha, NE 68124-2377. Telephone: 402-399-2425 or toll-free 800-926-5534. Fax: 402-399-2412. E-mail: enroll@csm.edu. Web site: http://www.csm.edu/.

CONCORDIA UNIVERSITY
SEWARD, NEBRASKA

General Independent, comprehensive, coed, affiliated with Lutheran Church–Missouri Synod **Entrance** Moderately difficult **Setting** 120-acre small town campus **Total enrollment** 1,191 **Student/faculty ratio** 13:1 **Application deadline** 8/1 **Freshmen** 87% were admitted **Housing** Yes **Expenses** Tuition $11,310; Room & Board $3786 **Undergraduates** 55% women, 2% part-time, 10% 25 or older, 0.2% Native American, 1% Hispanic, 1% black, 1% Asian American or Pacific Islander **Most popular recent majors** Education; business administration; graphic design/commercial art/illustration **Academic program** English as a second language, advanced placement, accelerated degree program, self-designed majors, honors program, summer session, adult/continuing education programs, internships **Contact** Mr. Don Vos, Director of Admissions, Concordia University, 800 North Columbia Avenue, Seward, NE 68434-1599. Telephone: 402-643-7233 or toll-free 800-535-5494. Fax: 402-643-4073. E-mail: admiss@seward.ccsn.edu. Web site: http://www.ccsn.edu/.

CREIGHTON UNIVERSITY
OMAHA, NEBRASKA

General Independent Roman Catholic (Jesuit), university, coed **Entrance** Moderately difficult **Setting** 85-acre urban campus **Total enrollment** 6,292 **Student/faculty ratio** 14:1 **Application deadline** Rolling **Freshmen** 92% were admitted **Housing** Yes **Expenses** Tuition $12,756; Room & Board $4940 **Undergraduates** 59% women,

5% part-time, 6% 25 or older, 1% Native American, 3% Hispanic, 4% black, 10% Asian American or Pacific Islander **Most popular recent majors** Nursing; biology; psychology **Academic program** English as a second language, advanced placement, accelerated degree program, tutorials, honors program, summer session, adult/continuing education programs, internships **Contact** Ms. Laurie R. Vinduska, Director of Admissions, Creighton University, 2500 California Plaza, Omaha, NE 68178-0001. Telephone: 402-280-2703 or toll-free 800-282-5835 (in-state). Fax: 402-280-2685. E-mail: admissions@creighton.edu. Web site: http://www.creighton.edu/.

DANA COLLEGE
BLAIR, NEBRASKA

General Independent, 4-year, coed, affiliated with Evangelical Lutheran Church in America **Entrance** Moderately difficult **Setting** 150-acre small town campus **Total enrollment** 594 **Student/faculty ratio** 12:1 **Application deadline** 8/1 **Freshmen** 90% were admitted **Housing** Yes **Expenses** Tuition $11,580; Room & Board $3880 **Undergraduates** 53% women, 4% part-time, 6% 25 or older, 0.2% Native American, 1% Hispanic, 3% black, 1% Asian American or Pacific Islander **Most popular recent majors** Elementary education; business administration; social work **Academic program** Average class size 19, English as a second language, advanced placement, tutorials, honors program, summer session, adult/continuing education programs, internships **Contact** Ms. Debra Balzer, Dean of Enrollment, Dana College, 2848 College Drive, Blair, NE 68008-1099. Telephone: 402-426-7220 or toll-free 800-444-3262. Fax: 402-426-7386. E-mail: admissions@dana.edu. Web site: http://www.dana.edu/.

DOANE COLLEGE
CRETE, NEBRASKA

General Independent, comprehensive, coed, affiliated with United Church of Christ **Entrance** Moderately difficult **Setting** 300-acre small town campus **Total enrollment** 1,809 **Student/faculty ratio** 15:1 **Application deadline** 8/1 **Freshmen** 90% were admitted **Housing** Yes **Expenses** Tuition $11,450; Room & Board $3450 **Undergraduates** 57% women, 28% part-time, 3% 25 or older, 0.3% Native American, 2% Hispanic, 3% black, 0.3% Asian American or Pacific Islander **Most popular recent majors** Elementary education; business administration; biology **Academic program** English as a second language, advanced placement, accelerated degree program, self-designed majors, tutorials, honors program, summer session, adult/continuing education programs, internships **Contact** Mr. Dan Kunzman, Dean of Admissions, Doane College, 1014 Boswell Avenue, Crete, NE 68333-2430. Telephone: 402-826-8222 or toll-free 800-333-6263. Fax: 402-826-8600. E-mail: admissions@doane.edu. Web site: http://www.doane.edu/.

GRACE UNIVERSITY
OMAHA, NEBRASKA

General Independent nondenominational, comprehensive, coed **Entrance** Moderately difficult **Setting** Urban campus **Total enrollment** 519 **Student/faculty ratio** 14:1 **Application deadline** Rolling **Freshmen** 80% were admitted **Housing** Yes **Expenses** Tuition $7484; Room & Board $3230 **Academic program** Advanced placement, accelerated degree program, tutorials, summer session, adult/continuing education programs, internships **Contact** Ms. Terri L. Thomas, Director of Admissions, Grace University, 1311 South Ninth Street, Omaha, NE 68108. Telephone: 402-449-2831 or toll-free 800-383-1422. Fax: 402-341-9587. E-mail: admissions@graceu.edu. Web site: http://www.graceu.edu/.

HASTINGS COLLEGE
HASTINGS, NEBRASKA

General Independent Presbyterian, comprehensive, coed **Entrance** Moderately difficult **Setting** 88-acre small town campus **Total enrollment** 1,059 **Student/faculty ratio** 13:1 **Application deadline** 7/15 **Freshmen** 89% were admitted **Housing** Yes **Expenses** Tuition $11,368; Room & Board $3758 **Undergraduates** 54% women, 2% part-time, 9% 25 or older, 0.1% Native American, 1% Hispanic, 2% black, 0.3% Asian American or Pacific Islander **Most popular recent majors** Business administration; education; psychology **Academic program** Average class size 25, English as a second language, advanced placement, accelerated degree program, self-designed majors, tutorials, honors program, summer session, adult/continuing education programs, internships **Contact** Mr. Michael Karloff, Director of Admissions, Hastings College, 720 North Turner Avenue, Hastings, NE 68902-0269. Telephone: 402-461-7316 or toll-free 800-532-7642 (in-state), 800-461-7480 (out-of-state). Fax: 402-463-3002. E-mail: admissions@hastings.edu. Web site: http://www.hastings.edu/.

MIDLAND LUTHERAN COLLEGE
FREMONT, NEBRASKA

General Independent Lutheran, 4-year, coed **Entrance** Moderately difficult **Setting** 27-acre small town campus **Total enrollment** 1,033 **Student/faculty ratio** 15:1 **Application deadline** Rolling **Freshmen** 93% were admitted **Housing** Yes **Expenses** Tuition $12,800; Room & Board $3450

Midland Lutheran College *(continued)*

Undergraduates 58% women, 10% part-time, 15% 25 or older, 0.1% Native American, 1% Hispanic, 4% black, 0.2% Asian American or Pacific Islander **Most popular recent majors** Business administration; education; nursing **Academic program** Advanced placement, self-designed majors, tutorials, summer session, internships **Contact** Mr. Roland R. Kahnk, Vice President for Enrollment Services, Midland Lutheran College, Admissions Office, Fremont, NE 68025-4200. Telephone: 402-721-5487 ext. 6500 or toll-free 800-642-8382 ext. 6500. Fax: 402-721-0250. E-mail: rkahnk@admin.mlc.edu. Web site: http://www.mlc.edu/.

▶ **For more information, see page 472.**

NEBRASKA CHRISTIAN COLLEGE
NORFOLK, NEBRASKA

General Independent, 4-year, coed, affiliated with Christian Churches and Churches of Christ **Entrance** Minimally difficult **Setting** 85-acre small town campus **Total enrollment** 152 **Student/faculty ratio** 16:1 **Application deadline** Rolling **Freshmen** 70% were admitted **Housing** Yes **Expenses** Tuition $4510; Room & Board $2690 **Undergraduates** 59% women, 12% 25 or older **Academic program** Internships **Contact** Mr. Jerry Hopkins, Director of Admissions, Nebraska Christian College, 1800 Syracuse Avenue, Norfolk, NE 68701-2458. Telephone: 402-379-5000. Web site: http://www.nechristian.edu/.

NEBRASKA METHODIST COLLEGE OF NURSING AND ALLIED HEALTH
OMAHA, NEBRASKA

General Independent, comprehensive, primarily women **Entrance** Moderately difficult **Setting** 5-acre urban campus **Total enrollment** 413 **Student/faculty ratio** 10:1 **Application deadline** 4/1 **Freshmen** 97% were admitted **Housing** Yes **Expenses** Tuition $8100; Room & Board $2000 **Undergraduates** 89% women, 48% part-time, 45% 25 or older, 1% Native American, 2% Hispanic, 2% black, 2% Asian American or Pacific Islander **Most Popular Recent Major** Nursing **Academic program** Advanced placement, accelerated degree program, summer session, internships **Contact** Ms. Deann Sterner, Director of Admissions, Nebraska Methodist College of Nursing and Allied Health, 8501 West Dodge Road, Omaha, NE 68114-3426. Telephone: 402-354-4922 or toll-free 800-335-5510.

NEBRASKA WESLEYAN UNIVERSITY
LINCOLN, NEBRASKA

General Independent United Methodist, 4-year, coed **Entrance** Moderately difficult **Setting** 50-acre suburban campus **Total enrollment** 1,709 **Student/faculty ratio** 13:1 **Application deadline** 3/15 **Freshmen** 98% were admitted **Housing** Yes **Expenses** Tuition $11,220; Room & Board $3614 **Undergraduates** 59% women, 11% part-time, 11% 25 or older, 0.2% Native American, 1% Hispanic, 1% black, 1% Asian American or Pacific Islander **Most popular recent majors** Business administration; biology; psychology **Academic program** Average class size 23, advanced placement, summer session, adult/continuing education programs, internships **Contact** Mr. Ken Sieg, Director of Admissions, Nebraska Wesleyan University, 5000 Saint Paul Avenue, Lincoln, NE 68504-2796. Telephone: 402-465-2218 or toll-free 800-541-3818 (in-state). Fax: 402-465-2179. E-mail: adm@nebrwesleyan.edu. Web site: http://www.nebrwesleyan.edu/.

PERU STATE COLLEGE
PERU, NEBRASKA

General State-supported, comprehensive, coed **Entrance** Noncompetitive **Setting** 103-acre rural campus **Total enrollment** 1,807 **Student/faculty ratio** 16:1 **Application deadline** Rolling **Housing** Yes **Expenses** Tuition $2085; Room & Board $3060 **Undergraduates** 52% women, 38% part-time, 8% 25 or older, 1% Native American, 1% Hispanic, 3% black, 0.4% Asian American or Pacific Islander **Most popular recent majors** Business administration; education; psychology **Academic program** Average class size 25, advanced placement, tutorials, honors program, adult/continuing education programs, internships **Contact** Mr. Louis T. Levy, Director of Admissions, Peru State College, PO Box 10, Peru, NE 68421. Telephone: 402-872-3815 ext. 2221 or toll-free 800-742-4412 (in-state). E-mail: levy@pscvax.peru.edu. Web site: http://www.peru.edu/.

UNION COLLEGE
LINCOLN, NEBRASKA

General Independent Seventh-day Adventist, 4-year, coed **Entrance** Minimally difficult **Setting** 26-acre suburban campus **Total enrollment** 603 **Student/faculty ratio** 12:1 **Application deadline** Rolling **Freshmen** 60% were admitted **Housing** Yes **Expenses** Tuition $9926; Room & Board $3240 **Undergraduates** 59% women, 17% part-time, 18% 25 or older, 0.3% Native American, 7% Hispanic, 2% black, 1% Asian American or Pacific Islander **Most popular recent majors** Nursing; business administration; education **Academic program** Average class size 18, English as a second language, advanced placement, accelerated degree program, self-designed majors, tutorials, honors program, summer session, adult/continuing education programs, internships **Contact** Mr. Gene Edelbach, Director of Enrollment Services, Union College, 3800 South 48th Street, Lincoln, NE

68506-4300. Telephone: 402-486-2504 or toll-free 800-228-4600 (out-of-state). Fax: 402-486-2895. E-mail: ucenrol@ucollege.edu. Web site: http://www.ucollege.edu/.

UNIVERSITY OF NEBRASKA AT KEARNEY
KEARNEY, NEBRASKA

General State-supported, comprehensive, coed **Entrance** Moderately difficult **Setting** 235-acre small town campus **Total enrollment** 7,133 **Student/faculty ratio** 19:1 **Application deadline** 8/1 **Freshmen** 100% were admitted **Housing** Yes **Expenses** Tuition $2269; Room & Board $3034 **Undergraduates** 14% 25 or older, 0.3% Native American, 2% Hispanic, 1% black, 1% Asian American or Pacific Islander **Most popular recent majors** Business administration; elementary education; special education **Academic program** Average class size 32, English as a second language, advanced placement, honors program, summer session, internships **Contact** Ms. Linda Morosic, Freshman Student Application Processor, University of Nebraska at Kearney, 905 West 25th Street, Kearney, NE 68849-0001. Telephone: 308-865-8526 or toll-free 800-445-3434. Fax: 308-865-8987. E-mail: admissionsug@platte.unk.edu.

UNIVERSITY OF NEBRASKA AT OMAHA
OMAHA, NEBRASKA

General State-supported, university, coed **Entrance** Minimally difficult **Setting** 88-acre urban campus **Total enrollment** 13,710 **Student/faculty ratio** 22:1 **Application deadline** Rolling **Freshmen** 90% were admitted **Housing** No **Expenses** Tuition $2356 **Undergraduates** 53% women, 35% part-time, 37% 25 or older, 1% Native American, 3% Hispanic, 6% black, 3% Asian American or Pacific Islander **Most popular recent majors** Business administration; education; psychology **Academic program** English as a second language, advanced placement, self-designed majors, honors program, summer session, adult/continuing education programs, internships **Contact** Ms. Jolene Adams, Associate Director of Admissions, University of Nebraska at Omaha, 6001 Dodge Street, Omaha, NE 68182. Telephone: 402-554-2416 or toll-free 800-858-8648 (in-state). Fax: 402-554-3472.

UNIVERSITY OF NEBRASKA–LINCOLN
LINCOLN, NEBRASKA

General State-supported, university, coed **Entrance** Moderately difficult **Setting** 616-acre urban campus **Total enrollment** 22,827 **Student/faculty ratio** 13:1 **Application deadline** 6/30 **Freshmen** 81% were admitted **Housing** Yes **Expenses** Tuition $2829; Room & Board $3700 **Undergraduates** 47% women, 12% part-time, 12% 25 or older, 0.4% Native American, 2% Hispanic, 2% black, 2% Asian American or Pacific Islander **Most popular recent majors** Political science; biology; finance **Academic program** English as a second language, advanced placement, accelerated degree program, self-designed majors, tutorials, honors program, summer session, adult/continuing education programs, internships **Contact** Ms. Peg Blake, Director of Admissions, University of Nebraska–Lincoln, 1410 Q Street, Lincoln, NE 68588-0417. Telephone: 402-472-2030 or toll-free 800-742-8800. Fax: 402-472-0670. E-mail: nuhusker@unl.edu. Web site: http://www.unl.edu/.

UNIVERSITY OF NEBRASKA MEDICAL CENTER
OMAHA, NEBRASKA

General State-supported, upper-level, coed **Entrance** Moderately difficult **Setting** 51-acre urban campus **Total enrollment** 2,618 **Application deadline** 11/1 **Housing** No **Expenses** Tuition $2732 **Undergraduates** 83% women, 8% part-time, 41% 25 or older, 1% Native American, 2% Hispanic, 2% black, 2% Asian American or Pacific Islander **Academic program** Tutorials, summer session, adult/continuing education programs, internships **Contact** Ms. Jo Wagner, Assistant Director of Academic Records, University of Nebraska Medical Center, 600 South 42nd Street, Omaha, NE 68198-4230. Telephone: 402-559-6468 or toll-free 800-626-8431. Fax: 402-559-6796.

WAYNE STATE COLLEGE
WAYNE, NEBRASKA

General State-supported, comprehensive, coed **Entrance** Noncompetitive **Setting** 128-acre small town campus **Total enrollment** 3,839 **Student/faculty ratio** 23:1 **Application deadline** Rolling **Freshmen** 100% were admitted **Housing** Yes **Expenses** Tuition $2140; Room & Board $2860 **Undergraduates** 57% women, 11% part-time, 15% 25 or older, 3% Native American, 1% Hispanic, 2% black, 0.4% Asian American or Pacific Islander **Most popular recent majors** Business administration; education; criminal justice/law enforcement administration **Academic program** Average class size 28, self-designed majors, honors program, summer session, adult/continuing education programs, internships **Contact** Mr. Robert Zetocha, Director of Admissions, Wayne State College, 1111 Main Street, Wayne, NE 68787. Telephone: 402-375-7234. Fax: 402-375-7204. E-mail: wscadmit@wscgate.wsc.edu. Web site: http://www.wsc.edu/.

YORK COLLEGE
YORK, NEBRASKA

General Independent, 4-year, coed, affiliated with Church of Christ **Entrance** Moderately difficult **Setting** 44-acre small town campus **Total enrollment** 497 **Student/faculty ratio** 10:1 **Application deadline** Rolling **Freshmen** 72% were admitted **Housing** Yes **Expenses** Tuition $7300; Room & Board $3300 **Undergraduates** 54% women, 7% part-time, 12% 25 or older, 1% Native American, 2% Hispanic, 2% black, 0.4% Asian American or Pacific Islander **Most popular recent majors** Elementary education; business administration; English **Academic program** Average class size 15, advanced placement, tutorials, honors program, summer session, adult/continuing education programs, internships **Contact** Mr. Steddon Sikes, Admissions Director, York College, 1125 East 8th Street, York, NE 68467-2699. Telephone: 402-363-5668 or toll-free 800-950-9675. Fax: 402-363-5623. E-mail: enroll@york.edu. Web site: http://www.york.edu.

NEVADA

MORRISON COLLEGE
RENO, NEVADA

General Proprietary, 4-year, coed **Contact** Ms. Rose Hoffert, Director of Admissions, Morrison College, 140 Washington Street, Reno, NV 89503-5600. Telephone: 702-323-4145 or toll-free 800-369-6144. Fax: 702-323-8495.

SIERRA NEVADA COLLEGE
INCLINE VILLAGE, NEVADA

General Independent, comprehensive, coed **Entrance** Moderately difficult **Setting** 20-acre small town campus **Total enrollment** 616 **Student/faculty ratio** 12:1 **Application deadline** Rolling **Freshmen** 97% were admitted **Housing** Yes **Expenses** Tuition $10,800; Room & Board $5200 **Undergraduates** 48% women, 15% part-time, 33% 25 or older, 1% Native American, 2% Hispanic, 1% black, 1% Asian American or Pacific Islander **Most popular recent majors** Business administration; hotel and restaurant management; humanities **Academic program** Advanced placement, accelerated degree program, tutorials, summer session, adult/continuing education programs, internships **Contact** Ms. Lane H. Murray, Director of Admissions, Sierra Nevada College, 800 College Drive, PO Box 4269, Incline Village, NV 89480-4269. Telephone: 702-831-1314 ext. 3105 or toll-free 800-332-8666 ext. 3105 (out-of-state). Fax: 702-831-1347. E-mail: admissions@sierranevada.edu. Web site: http://www.sierranevada.edu/.

UNIVERSITY OF NEVADA, LAS VEGAS
LAS VEGAS, NEVADA

General State-supported, university, coed **Entrance** Moderately difficult **Setting** 335-acre urban campus **Total enrollment** 19,249 **Student/faculty ratio** 21:1 **Application deadline** 8/15 **Housing** Yes **Expenses** Tuition $1642; Room & Board $5300 **Undergraduates** 53% women, 34% part-time, 50% 25 or older, 1% Native American, 8% Hispanic, 7% black, 9% Asian American or Pacific Islander **Academic program** English as a second language, advanced placement, accelerated degree program, self-designed majors, honors program, summer session, adult/continuing education programs, internships **Contact** Ms. Susan Horning, Assistant Director of Admissions, University of Nevada, Las Vegas, 4505 Maryland Parkway, Las Vegas, NV 89154-1021. Telephone: 702-895-3443 or toll-free 800-334-UNLV. Fax: 702-895-1118. E-mail: undrgradadmision@ccmail.nevada.edu. Web site: http://www.unlv.edu/.

UNIVERSITY OF NEVADA, RENO
RENO, NEVADA

General State-supported, university, coed **Entrance** Moderately difficult **Setting** 200-acre urban campus **Total enrollment** 12,442 **Student/faculty ratio** 20:1 **Application deadline** 3/1 **Freshmen** 90% were admitted **Housing** Yes **Expenses** Tuition $2109; Room & Board $5095 **Undergraduates** 53% women, 28% part-time, 26% 25 or older, 1% Native American, 6% Hispanic, 2% black, 6% Asian American or Pacific Islander **Most popular recent majors** Elementary education; general studies; special education **Academic program** English as a second language, advanced placement, tutorials, honors program, summer session, adult/continuing education programs, internships **Contact** Dr. Melissa N. Choroszy, Associate Dean of Records and Enrollment Services, University of Nevada, Reno, Reno, NV 89557. Telephone: 702-784-6865 or toll-free 800-622-4867 (in-state). E-mail: unrug@unr.edu. Web site: http://www.unr.edu/.

NEW HAMPSHIRE

COLBY-SAWYER COLLEGE
NEW LONDON, NEW HAMPSHIRE

General Independent, 4-year, coed **Entrance** Moderately difficult **Setting** 196-acre small town campus **Total enrollment** 775 **Student/faculty ratio** 12:1 **Application deadline** Rolling **Freshmen** 80% were admitted **Housing** Yes **Expenses** Tuition $16,310; Room & Board $6240 **Undergraduates** 5% 25 or older **Most popular recent majors** Athletic training/sports medicine; developmental/child psychology; business administration **Academic program** English as a second language, advanced placement, accelerated degree program, self-designed majors, tutorials, honors program, adult/continuing education programs, internships **Contact** Ms. Wendy Beckemeyer, Vice President for Enrollment Management, Colby-Sawyer College, 100 Main Street, New London, NH 03257-4648. Telephone: 603-526-3700 or toll-free 800-272-1015 (out-of-state). Fax: 603-526-3452. E-mail: csadmiss@colby-sawyer.edu. Web site: http://www.colby-sawyer.edu/.

► **For more information, see page 415.**

COLLEGE FOR LIFELONG LEARNING OF THE UNIVERSITY SYSTEM OF NEW HAMPSHIRE

See University System College for Lifelong Learning

DANIEL WEBSTER COLLEGE
NASHUA, NEW HAMPSHIRE

General Independent, 4-year, coed **Entrance** Moderately difficult **Setting** 50-acre suburban campus **Total enrollment** 1,072 **Student/faculty ratio** 14:1 **Application deadline** Rolling **Freshmen** 81% were admitted **Housing** Yes **Expenses** Tuition $14,310; Room & Board $5662 **Undergraduates** 34% women, 27% part-time, 4% 25 or older, 1% Native American, 2% Hispanic, 3% black, 1% Asian American or Pacific Islander **Most popular recent majors** Aviation management; aircraft pilot (professional); business administration **Academic program** Average class size 20, advanced placement, summer session, adult/continuing education programs, internships **Contact** Mr. Paul D. LaBarre, Director of Admissions, Daniel Webster College, 20 University Drive, Nashua, NH 03063-1300. Telephone: 603-577-6603 or toll-free 800-325-6876 (in-state). Fax: 603-577-6001. E-mail: admissions@dwc.edu. Web site: http://www.dwc.edu/.

DARTMOUTH COLLEGE
HANOVER, NEW HAMPSHIRE

General Independent, university, coed **Entrance** Most difficult **Setting** 265-acre rural campus **Total enrollment** 5,407 **Student/faculty ratio** 12:1 **Application deadline** 1/1 **Freshmen** 22% were admitted **Housing** Yes **Expenses** Tuition $23,012; Room & Board $6495 **Undergraduates** 48% women, 1% 25 or older, 2% Native American, 5% Hispanic, 6% black, 10% Asian American or Pacific Islander **Most popular recent majors** Political science; history; engineering **Academic program** Average class size 28, advanced placement, accelerated degree program, self-designed majors, tutorials, honors program, summer session, internships **Contact** Mr. Karl M. Furstenberg, Dean of Admissions and Financial Aid, Dartmouth College, 6016 McNutt Hall, Hanover, NH 03755. Telephone: 603-646-2875. Fax: 603-646-1216. E-mail: admissions.office@dartmouth.edu. Web site: http://www.dartmouth.edu/.

FRANKLIN PIERCE COLLEGE
RINDGE, NEW HAMPSHIRE

General Independent, comprehensive, coed **Entrance** Moderately difficult **Setting** 1,000-acre rural campus **Total enrollment** 3,265 **Application deadline** Rolling **Housing** Yes **Expenses** Tuition $16,170; Room & Board $5050 **Undergraduates** 57% women, 32% part-time, 4% 25 or older, 0.2% Native American, 2% Hispanic, 2% black, 1% Asian American or Pacific Islander **Most popular recent majors** Elementary education; history; mass communications **Academic program** Average class size 25, English as a second language, advanced placement, accelerated degree program, self-designed majors, tutorials, honors program, summer session, adult/continuing education programs, internships **Contact** Ms. Lucy P. Shonk, Director of Admissions, Franklin Pierce College, College Road, PO Box 60, Rindge, NH 03461-0060. Telephone: 603-899-4050 or toll-free 800-437-0048. Fax: 603-899-4372. E-mail: admissions@rindge.fpc.edu. Web site: http://www.fpc.edu/.

KEENE STATE COLLEGE
KEENE, NEW HAMPSHIRE

General State-supported, comprehensive, coed **Entrance** Moderately difficult **Setting** 160-acre small town campus **Total enrollment** 4,409 **Student/faculty ratio** 20:1 **Application deadline** 3/1 **Freshmen** 77% were admitted **Housing** Yes **Expenses** Tuition $4340; Room & Board $4660 **Undergraduates** 57% women, 8% part-time, 12% 25 or older, 0.3% Native American, 1% Hispanic, 1% black, 0.5% Asian American or Pacific Islander **Most popular recent majors** Elementary education; psychology; business administration **Academic program** Average class size 20, English as a second language, advanced placement, accelerated degree program, self-designed majors, honors program, summer session, adult/continuing education programs, internships **Contact** Mrs. Kathryn Dodge, Director of Admissions, Keene State College, 229 Main Street, Keene, NH 03435. Telephone: 603-358-2276 or toll-free 800-572-1909. Fax: 603-358-2767. E-mail: admissions@keene.edu. Web site: http://www.keene.edu/.

NEW ENGLAND COLLEGE
HENNIKER, NEW HAMPSHIRE

General Independent, comprehensive, coed **Entrance** Moderately difficult **Setting** 225-acre small town campus **Total enrollment** 861 **Student/faculty ratio** 12:1 **Application deadline** Rolling **Freshmen** 85% were admitted **Housing** Yes **Expenses** Tuition $15,784; Room & Board $5920 **Undergraduates** 50% women, 19% part-time, 3% 25 or older, 0.3% Native American, 1% Hispanic, 1% black, 2% Asian American or Pacific Islander **Most popular recent majors** Business administration; education; mass communications **Academic program** English as a second language, advanced placement, self-designed majors, tutorials, honors program, summer session, adult/continuing education programs, internships **Contact** Mr. Donald N. Parker, Dean of Admission, New England College, 7 Main Street, Henniker, NH 03242-3293. Telephone: 603-428-2223 or toll-free 800-521-7642 (out-of-state). E-mail: admis@nec1.nec.edu. Web site: http://www.nec.edu/.

NEW HAMPSHIRE COLLEGE
MANCHESTER, NEW HAMPSHIRE

General Independent, comprehensive, coed **Entrance** Moderately difficult **Setting** 280-acre suburban campus **Total enrollment** 5,765 **Student/faculty ratio** 17:1 **Application deadline** Rolling **Housing** Yes **Expenses** Tuition $13,570; Room & Board $5980 **Undergraduates** 53% women, 67% part-time, 1% 25 or older, 0.1% Native American, 2% Hispanic, 2% black, 1% Asian American or Pacific Islander **Most popular recent majors** Business administration; hotel and restaurant management; accounting **Academic program** Average class size 20, English as a second language, advanced placement, accelerated degree program, tutorials, honors program, summer session, adult/continuing education programs, internships **Contact** Mr. Brad Poznanski, Director of Admission and Financial Aid, New Hampshire College, 2500 North River Road, Manchester, NH 03106-1045. Telephone: 603-645-9611 or toll-free 800-NHC-4YOU. Fax: 603-645-9693. E-mail: admission@nhc.edu. Web site: http://www.nhc.edu/.

NOTRE DAME COLLEGE
MANCHESTER, NEW HAMPSHIRE

General Independent Roman Catholic, comprehensive, coed **Entrance** Moderately difficult **Setting** 8-acre suburban campus **Total enrollment** 1,255 **Student/faculty ratio** 13:1 **Application deadline** Rolling **Freshmen** 91% were admitted **Housing** Yes **Expenses** Tuition $12,396; Room & Board $5560 **Undergraduates** 74% women, 28% part-time, 40% 25 or older, 0.4% Native American, 0.5% Hispanic, 1% black, 0.5% Asian American or Pacific Islander **Most popular recent majors** Education; physical therapy; biology **Academic program** Average class size 20, advanced placement, accelerated degree program, summer session, adult/continuing education programs, internships **Contact** Mr. Bonnie M. Galinski Roth, Dean of Graduate and Undergraduate Enrollment, Notre Dame College, 2321 Elm Street, Manchester, NH 03104-2299. Telephone: 603-669-4298 ext. 163. Fax: 603-644-8316. Web site: http://www.notredame.edu/.

PLYMOUTH STATE COLLEGE OF THE UNIVERSITY SYSTEM OF NEW HAMPSHIRE
PLYMOUTH, NEW HAMPSHIRE

General State-supported, comprehensive, coed **Entrance** Moderately difficult **Setting** 170-acre small town campus **Total enrollment** 4,228 **Student/faculty ratio** 18:1 **Application deadline** 4/1 **Freshmen** 80% were admitted **Housing** Yes **Expenses** Tuition $4342; Room & Board $4564 **Undergraduates** 48% women, 4% part-time, 9% 25 or older, 0.4% Native American, 1% Hispanic, 0.5% black, 1% Asian American or Pacific Islander **Most popular recent majors** Physical education; child care/development; business administration **Academic program** Average class size 25, advanced placement, accelerated degree program, self-designed majors, summer session, internships **Contact** Mr. Eugene Fahey, Director of Admission, Plymouth State College of the University System of New Hampshire, 17 High Street, Plymouth, NH 03264-1595. Telephone: 603-535-2237 or toll-free 800-842-6900. Fax: 603-535-2714. E-mail: pscadmit@psc.plymouth.edu. Web site: http://www.plymouth.edu/.

RIVIER COLLEGE
NASHUA, NEW HAMPSHIRE

General Independent Roman Catholic, comprehensive, coed **Entrance** Moderately difficult **Setting** 60-acre suburban campus **Total enrollment** 2,886 **Student/faculty ratio** 18:1 **Application deadline** Rolling **Housing** Yes **Expenses** Tuition $13,190; Room & Board $5525 **Undergraduates** 82% women, 62% part-time, 43% 25 or older, 0.3% Native American, 2% Hispanic, 1% black, 1% Asian American or Pacific Islander **Most popular recent majors** Business administration; education **Academic program** Average class size 18, English as a second language, advanced placement, self-designed majors, tutorials, honors program, summer session, adult/continuing education programs, internships **Contact** Ms. Lynn A. Petrillo, Director of Admissions, Rivier College, 420 Main Street, Nashua, NH 03060-5086. Telephone: 603-888-1311 ext. 8507 or toll-free 800-

44RIVIER. Fax: 603-891-1799. E-mail: rivadmit@rivier.edu. Web site: http://www.rivier.edu/.

SAINT ANSELM COLLEGE
MANCHESTER, NEW HAMPSHIRE

General Independent Roman Catholic, 4-year, coed **Entrance** Moderately difficult **Setting** 450-acre suburban campus **Total enrollment** 2,007 **Student/faculty ratio** 15:1 **Application deadline** Rolling **Freshmen** 79% were admitted **Housing** Yes **Expenses** Tuition $16,670; Room & Board $6160 **Undergraduates** 56% women, 1% 25 or older, 0.1% Native American, 2% Hispanic, 0.2% black, 1% Asian American or Pacific Islander **Most popular recent majors** Biology; business economics; history **Academic program** Average class size 21, advanced placement, tutorials, honors program, summer session, internships **Contact** Mr. Donald E. Healy, Director of Admissions, Saint Anselm College, 100 Saint Anselm Drive, Manchester, NH 03102-1310. Telephone: 603-641-7500 or toll-free 888-4ANSELM. Fax: 603-641-7550. E-mail: admissions@anselm.edu. Web site: http://www.anselm.edu/.

THOMAS MORE COLLEGE OF LIBERAL ARTS
MERRIMACK, NEW HAMPSHIRE

General Independent, 4-year, coed, affiliated with Roman Catholic Church **Entrance** Moderately difficult **Setting** 14-acre small town campus **Total enrollment** 62 **Student/faculty ratio** 9:1 **Application deadline** Rolling **Freshmen** 78% were admitted **Housing** Yes **Expenses** Tuition $9100; Room & Board $7100 **Undergraduates** 56% women, 4% 25 or older, 0% Native American, 5% Hispanic, 2% black, 0% Asian American or Pacific Islander **Most popular recent majors** Literature; philosophy; political science **Academic program** Average class size 15 **Contact** Mr. Peter O'Connor, Director of Admissions, Thomas More College of Liberal Arts, 6 Manchester Street, Merrimack, NH 03054-4818. Telephone: 603-880-8308. Fax: 603-880-9280. E-mail: p.sampo@genie.geis.com.

UNIVERSITY OF NEW HAMPSHIRE
DURHAM, NEW HAMPSHIRE

General State-supported, university, coed **Entrance** Moderately difficult **Setting** 200-acre small town campus **Total enrollment** 13,960 **Student/faculty ratio** 17:1 **Application deadline** 2/1 **Freshmen** 76% were admitted **Housing** Yes **Expenses** Tuition $5889; Room & Board $4524 **Undergraduates** 7% 25 or older **Most popular recent majors** Business administration; English; biology **Academic program** Average class size 47, English as a second language, advanced placement, accelerated degree program, self-designed majors, tutorials, honors program, summer session, adult/continuing education programs, internships **Contact** Mr. James Washington Jr., Director of Admissions, University of New Hampshire, Grant House, 4 Garrison Avenue, Durham, NH 03824. Telephone: 603-862-1360. E-mail: admissions@unh.edu. Web site: http://www.unh.edu/.

UNIVERSITY OF NEW HAMPSHIRE AT MANCHESTER
MANCHESTER, NEW HAMPSHIRE

General State-supported, 4-year, coed **Entrance** Moderately difficult **Setting** 800-acre urban campus **Total enrollment** 729 **Student/faculty ratio** 6:1 **Application deadline** 6/15 **Freshmen** 69% were admitted **Housing** No **Expenses** Tuition $3966 **Undergraduates** 39% 25 or older **Most popular recent majors** Liberal arts and studies; business administration; psychology **Academic program** Advanced placement, self-designed majors, summer session, adult/continuing education programs, internships **Contact** Ms. Susan Miller, Admissions Secretary, University of New Hampshire at Manchester, 220 Hackett Hill Road, Manchester, NH 03102-8597. Telephone: 603-629-4150. Fax: 603-623-2745. E-mail: unhm@unh.edu.

UNIVERSITY SYSTEM COLLEGE FOR LIFELONG LEARNING
CONCORD, NEW HAMPSHIRE

General State and locally supported, 4-year, coed **Contact** Ms. Teresa McDonnell, Associate Dean of Learner Services, University System College for Lifelong Learning, 125 North State Street, Concord, NH 03301. Telephone: 603-228-3000 ext. 308 or toll-free 800-582-7248 (in-state). Fax: 603-229-0964. E-mail: k_king@unhf.unh.edu.

NEW JERSEY

BETH MEDRASH GOVOHA
LAKEWOOD, NEW JERSEY

Contact Rabbi Yehuda Jacobs, Director of Admissions, Beth Medrash Govoha, 617 Sixth Street, Lakewood, NJ 08701-2797. Telephone: 908-367-1060.

BLOOMFIELD COLLEGE
BLOOMFIELD, NEW JERSEY

General Independent, 4-year, coed, affiliated with Presbyterian Church (U.S.A.) **Entrance** Minimally difficult **Setting** 12-acre suburban campus **Total enrollment** 1,997 **Student/faculty ratio** 24:1 **Application deadline** Rolling **Freshmen** 66% were admitted **Housing** Yes **Expenses** Tuition $9650; Room & Board $4850 **Undergraduates** 69% women, 31% part-time, 45% 25 or older, 0.2% Native American, 15% Hispanic, 49% black, 4% Asian American or Pacific Islander **Most popular recent majors** Business administration; nursing; psychology **Academic program** Average class size 19, English as a second language, advanced placement, accelerated degree program, self-designed majors, tutorials, honors program, summer session, internships **Contact** Office of Admission, Bloomfield College, Park Place, Bloomfield, NJ 07003-9981. Telephone: 973-748-9000 ext. 230 or toll-free 800-848-4555. Fax: 973-748-0916. E-mail: admission@bloomfield.edu. Web site: http://bloomfield.edu/.

CALDWELL COLLEGE
CALDWELL, NEW JERSEY

General Independent Roman Catholic, comprehensive, coed **Entrance** Moderately difficult **Setting** 100-acre suburban campus **Total enrollment** 1,827 **Student/faculty ratio** 13:1 **Application deadline** 4/1 **Housing** Yes **Expenses** Tuition $10,800; Room & Board $5300 **Undergraduates** 69% women, 50% part-time, 6% 25 or older, 0.2% Native American, 7% Hispanic, 11% black, 2% Asian American or Pacific Islander **Most popular recent majors** Business administration; psychology; elementary education **Academic program** English as a second language, advanced placement, accelerated degree program, tutorials, honors program, summer session, adult/continuing education programs, internships **Contact** Mr. Raymond Sheenan, Director of Admissions, Caldwell College, 9 Ryerson Avenue, Caldwell, NJ 07006-6195. Telephone: 973-228-4424 ext. 220 or toll-free 800-831-9178 (out-of-state). Web site: http://www.caldwell.edu/.

CAMDEN COLLEGE OF ARTS AND SCIENCES
See Rutgers, The State University of New Jersey, Camden College of Arts and Sciences

CENTENARY COLLEGE
HACKETTSTOWN, NEW JERSEY

General Independent, comprehensive, coed, affiliated with United Methodist Church **Entrance** Moderately difficult **Setting** 42-acre suburban campus **Total enrollment** 959 **Student/faculty ratio** 13:1 **Application deadline** Rolling **Freshmen** 77% were admitted **Housing** Yes **Expenses** Tuition $13,260; Room & Board $5800 **Undergraduates** 76% women, 45% part-time, 53% 25 or older, 0.1% Native American, 2% Hispanic, 6% black, 1% Asian American or Pacific Islander **Most popular recent majors** Business administration; education; equestrian studies **Academic program** Average class size 20, English as a second language, advanced placement, self-designed majors, tutorials, honors program, summer session, internships **Contact** Mr. Dennis Kelly, Vice President for Enrollment Management, Centenary College, 400 Jefferson Street, Hackettstown, NJ 07840-2100. Telephone: 908-852-4696 or toll-free 800-236-8679. Fax: 908-852-3454. E-mail: rankis@centenarycollege.edu. Web site: http://www.centenarycollege.edu/.

THE COLLEGE OF NEW JERSEY
EWING, NEW JERSEY

General State-supported, comprehensive, coed **Entrance** Very difficult **Setting** 255-acre suburban campus **Total enrollment** 6,780 **Student/faculty ratio** 14:1 **Application deadline** 2/15 **Freshmen** 57% were admitted **Housing** Yes **Expenses** Tuition $4843; Room & Board $5996 **Undergraduates** 61% women, 9% part-time, 13% 25 or older, 0.1% Native American, 5% Hispanic, 6% black, 5% Asian American or Pacific Islander **Most popular recent majors** Elementary education; biology; English **Academic program** Average class size 23, advanced placement, tutorials, honors program, summer session, internships **Contact** Ms. Lisa Angeloni, Director of Admissions, The College of New Jersey, PO Box 7718, Ewing, NJ 08628. Telephone: 609-771-2131 or toll-free 800-624-0967 (in-state), 800-345-7354 (out-of-state). E-mail: admiss@vm.tcnj.edu. Web site: http://www.tcnj.edu/.

COLLEGE OF SAINT ELIZABETH
MORRISTOWN, NEW JERSEY

General Independent Roman Catholic, comprehensive, primarily women **Entrance** Moderately difficult **Setting** 188-acre suburban campus **Total enrollment** 1,791 **Application deadline** 8/15 **Freshmen** 82% were admitted **Housing** Yes **Expenses** Tuition $13,060; Room & Board $5950 **Undergraduates** 95% women, 55% part-time, 61% 25 or older, 0.4% Native American, 11% Hispanic, 9% black, 3% Asian American or Pacific Islander **Most popular recent majors** Business administration; psychology; education **Academic program** Average class size 17, English as a second language, advanced placement, accelerated degree program, self-designed majors, honors program, summer session, adult/continuing education programs, internships **Contact** Ms. Donna Yamanis, Dean of Admissions and Financial Aid, College of Saint Elizabeth, 2 Convent Road, Morristown, NJ 07960-6989. Telephone: 973-290-4700 or toll-free 800-210-7900. Fax: 973-290-4710. E-mail: apply@liza.st-elizabeth.edu. Web site: http://www.st-elizabeth.edu/.

COOK COLLEGE

See Rutgers, The State University of New Jersey, Cook College

DOUGLASS COLLEGE

See Rutgers, The State University of New Jersey, Douglass College

DREW UNIVERSITY

MADISON, NEW JERSEY

General Independent, university, coed, affiliated with United Methodist Church **Entrance** Very difficult **Setting** 186-acre suburban campus **Total enrollment** 2,305 **Student/faculty ratio** 13:1 **Application deadline** 2/15 **Freshmen** 74% were admitted **Housing** Yes **Expenses** Tuition $21,396; Room & Board $6114 **Undergraduates** 58% women, 3% part-time, 4% 25 or older, 0.3% Native American, 5% Hispanic, 4% black, 6% Asian American or Pacific Islander **Most popular recent majors** Political science; psychology; English **Academic program** Advanced placement, self-designed majors, honors program, summer session, adult/continuing education programs, internships **Contact** Mr. Roberto Noya, Dean of Admissions for the College of Liberal Arts, Drew University, 36 Madison Avenue, Madison, NJ 07940-1493. Telephone: 973-408-3739. Fax: 973-408-3939. E-mail: cadm@drew.edu. Web site: http://www.drew.edu/.

FAIRLEIGH DICKINSON UNIVERSITY, FLORHAM-MADISON CAMPUS

MADISON, NEW JERSEY

General Independent, comprehensive, coed **Entrance** Moderately difficult **Setting** 178-acre suburban campus **Total enrollment** 3,400 **Student/faculty ratio** 17:1 **Application deadline** Rolling **Freshmen** 75% were admitted **Housing** Yes **Expenses** Tuition $14,122; Room & Board $6040 **Undergraduates** 56% women, 29% part-time, 34% 25 or older, 0.2% Native American, 4% Hispanic, 4% black, 2% Asian American or Pacific Islander **Most popular recent majors** Business administration; psychology; biology **Academic program** English as a second language, advanced placement, accelerated degree program, self-designed majors, tutorials, honors program, summer session, adult/continuing education programs, internships **Contact** Ms. Dale Herold, Dean of Enrollment Management, Fairleigh Dickinson University, Florham-Madison Campus, 1000 River Road, Teaneck, NJ 07666-1914. Telephone: 201-692-7300 or toll-free 800-338-8803. Web site: http://www.fdu.edu/.

FAIRLEIGH DICKINSON UNIVERSITY, TEANECK–HACKENSACK CAMPUS

TEANECK, NEW JERSEY

General Independent, comprehensive, coed **Entrance** Moderately difficult **Setting** 125-acre suburban campus **Total enrollment** 3,750 **Application deadline** Rolling **Freshmen** 64% were admitted **Housing** Yes **Expenses** Tuition $14,122; Room & Board $6040 **Undergraduates** 55% women, 32% part-time, 34% 25 or older, 0.5% Native American, 9% Hispanic, 14% black, 5% Asian American or Pacific Islander **Most popular recent majors** Business administration; psychology; nursing **Academic program** English as a second language, advanced placement, accelerated degree program, self-designed majors, tutorials, honors program, summer session, adult/continuing education programs, internships **Contact** Ms. Dale Herold, Dean of Enrollment Management, Fairleigh Dickinson University, Teaneck-Hackensack Campus, 1000 River Road, Teaneck, NJ 07666-1914. Telephone: 201-692-7300 or toll-free 800-338-8803. Web site: http://www.fdu.edu/.

FELICIAN COLLEGE

LODI, NEW JERSEY

General Independent Roman Catholic, comprehensive, coed **Entrance** Moderately difficult **Setting** 27-acre suburban campus **Total enrollment** 1,160 **Student/faculty ratio** 15:1 **Application deadline** Rolling **Housing** Yes **Expenses** Tuition $10,012; Room & Board $5400 **Undergraduates** 85% women, 46% part-time, 52% 25 or older, 0.1% Native American, 12% Hispanic, 8% black, 5% Asian American or Pacific Islander **Most popular recent majors** Nursing; education **Academic program** Average class size 21, English as a second language, advanced placement, self-designed majors, tutorials, honors program, summer session, adult/continuing education programs, internships **Contact** Ms. Susan M. Chalfin, Director of Admissions, Felician College, 262 South Main Street, Lodi, NJ 07644. Telephone: 973-778-1029. Fax: 973-778-4111. E-mail: admissions@inet.felician.edu.

GEORGIAN COURT COLLEGE

LAKEWOOD, NEW JERSEY

General Independent Roman Catholic, comprehensive, primarily women **Entrance** Moderately

Georgian Court College *(continued)*

difficult **Setting** 150-acre suburban campus **Total enrollment** 2,350 **Student/faculty ratio** 11:1 **Application deadline** 8/1 **Freshmen** 91% were admitted **Housing** Yes **Expenses** Tuition $11,116; Room & Board $4750 **Undergraduates** 91% women, 28% part-time, 40% 25 or older **Most Popular Recent Majors** Psychology; business administration; accounting **Academic program** Average class size 17, advanced placement, tutorials, summer session, adult/continuing education programs, internships **Contact** Mrs. Nancy Hazelgrove, Director of Admissions, Georgian Court College, 900 Lakewood Avenue, Lakewood, NJ 08701-2697. Telephone: 732-364-2200 ext. 760 or toll-free 800-458-8422. Fax: 732-364-4442. E-mail: admissions-ugrad@georgian.edu. Web site: http://www.georgian.edu/.

KEAN UNIVERSITY
UNION, NEW JERSEY

General State-supported, comprehensive, coed **Entrance** Moderately difficult **Setting** 151-acre urban campus **Total enrollment** 11,537 **Student/faculty ratio** 22:1 **Application deadline** 6/15 **Housing** Yes **Expenses** Tuition $3669; Room only $3920 **Undergraduates** 63% women, 32% part-time, 35% 25 or older, 0.1% Native American, 18% Hispanic, 17% black, 6% Asian American or Pacific Islander **Most popular recent majors** Accounting; business administration **Academic program** English as a second language, accelerated degree program, honors program, summer session, adult/continuing education programs, internships **Contact** Mr. Audley Bridges, Director of Admissions, Kean University, 1000 Morris Avenue, Union, NJ 07083. Telephone: 908-527-2195. Fax: 908-355-5143. E-mail: admitme@turbo.kean.edu. Web site: http://www.kean.edu/.

LIVINGSTON COLLEGE
See Rutgers, The State University of New Jersey, Livingston College

MASON GROSS SCHOOL OF THE ARTS
See Rutgers, The State University of New Jersey, Mason Gross School of the Arts

MONMOUTH UNIVERSITY
WEST LONG BRANCH, NEW JERSEY

General Independent, comprehensive, coed **Entrance** Moderately difficult **Setting** 147-acre suburban campus **Total enrollment** 5,311 **Student/faculty ratio** 19:1 **Application deadline** Rolling **Freshmen** 87% were admitted **Housing** Yes **Expenses** Tuition $15,068; Room & Board $6793 **Undergraduates** 58% women, 15% part-time, 25% 25 or older, 0.3% Native American, 4% Hispanic, 5% black, 2% Asian American or Pacific Islander **Most popular recent majors** Business administration; education; communications **Academic program** Average class size 23, advanced placement, accelerated degree program, self-designed majors, tutorials, honors program, summer session, adult/continuing education programs, internships **Contact** Ms. Christine Benol, Associate Director of Undergraduate Admission, Monmouth University, 400 Cedar Avenue, West Long Branch, NJ 07764-1898. Telephone: 732-571-3456 or toll-free 800-543-9671 (out-of-state). Fax: 732-263-5166. E-mail: cbenol@mondec.monmouth.edu. Web site: http://www.monmouth.edu/.

MONTCLAIR STATE UNIVERSITY
UPPER MONTCLAIR, NEW JERSEY

General State-supported, comprehensive, coed **Entrance** Moderately difficult **Setting** 200-acre suburban campus **Total enrollment** 12,808 **Student/faculty ratio** 15:1 **Application deadline** 3/1 **Freshmen** 46% were admitted **Housing** Yes **Expenses** Tuition $3694; Room & Board $5546 **Undergraduates** 33% 25 or older **Most popular recent majors** Business administration; psychology; home economics **Academic program** English as a second language, advanced placement, accelerated degree program, honors program, summer session, adult/continuing education programs, internships **Contact** Dr. Alan L. Buechler, Director of Admissions, Montclair State University, Valley Road and Normal Avenue, Upper Montclair, NJ 07043-1624. Telephone: 973-655-4444 or toll-free 800-331-9205. Fax: 973-893-5455. E-mail: msuadm@saturn.montclair.edu. Web site: http://www.saturn.montclair.edu/.

► **For more information, see page 476.**

NEWARK COLLEGE OF ARTS AND SCIENCES
See Rutgers, The State University of New Jersey, Newark College of Arts and Sciences

NEW JERSEY CITY UNIVERSITY
JERSEY CITY, NEW JERSEY

General State-supported, comprehensive, coed **Entrance** Moderately difficult **Setting** 17-acre urban campus **Total enrollment** 8,503 **Student/faculty ratio** 16:1 **Application deadline** 4/1 **Freshmen** 49% were admitted **Housing** Yes **Expenses** Tuition $3828; Room & Board $5000 **Undergraduates** 60% women, 37% part-time, 43% 25 or older, 0.2% Native American, 25% Hispanic, 19% black, 10% Asian American or Pacific Islander **Most popular recent majors** Business administration; criminal justice/law enforcement administration; computer science **Academic program**

English as a second language, advanced placement, accelerated degree program, tutorials, honors program, summer session, adult/continuing education programs, internships **Contact** Mr. Samuel T. McGhee, Director of Admissions, New Jersey City University, 2039 Kennedy Boulevard, Jersey City, NJ 07305-1957. Telephone: 201-200-3234 or toll-free 800-441-JCSC. Fax: 201-200-2044. E-mail: admissions@jcs1.jcstate.edu.

▶ **For more information, see page 481.**

NEW JERSEY INSTITUTE OF TECHNOLOGY
NEWARK, NEW JERSEY

General State-supported, university, coed **Entrance** Moderately difficult **Setting** 45-acre urban campus **Total enrollment** 8,133 **Student/faculty ratio** 14:1 **Application deadline** 4/1 **Freshmen** 66% were admitted **Housing** Yes **Expenses** Tuition $5802; Room & Board $6382 **Undergraduates** 18% women, 24% part-time, 35% 25 or older, 0.1% Native American, 14% Hispanic, 12% black, 19% Asian American or Pacific Islander **Most popular recent majors** Engineering technology; electrical/electronics engineering; mechanical engineering **Academic program** Average class size 25, English as a second language, advanced placement, accelerated degree program, tutorials, honors program, summer session, adult/continuing education programs, internships **Contact** Ms. Kathy Kelly, Director of Admissions, New Jersey Institute of Technology, University Heights, Newark, NJ 07102-1982. Telephone: 973-596-3300 or toll-free 800-222-NJIT (in-state). Fax: 973-802-1854. E-mail: admissions@njit.edu. Web site: http://www.njit.edu/.

PRINCETON UNIVERSITY
PRINCETON, NEW JERSEY

General Independent, university, coed **Entrance** Most difficult **Setting** 600-acre suburban campus **Total enrollment** 6,605 **Student/faculty ratio** 5:1 **Application deadline** 1/2 **Freshmen** 13% were admitted **Housing** Yes **Expenses** Tuition $23,820; Room & Board $6711 **Undergraduates** 47% women, 0% 25 or older, 1% Native American, 6% Hispanic, 7% black, 14% Asian American or Pacific Islander **Most popular recent majors** Economics; history; molecular biology **Academic program** Advanced placement, accelerated degree program, self-designed majors, tutorials, adult/continuing education programs **Contact** Mr. Fred A. Hargadon, Dean of Admission, Princeton University, Princeton, NJ 08544-1019. Telephone: 609-258-3060. E-mail: g3516@princeton.edu. Web site: http://www.princeton.edu/.

RABBINICAL COLLEGE OF AMERICA
MORRISTOWN, NEW JERSEY

Contact Rabbi Israel Teitelbaum, Registrar, Rabbinical College of America, Box 1996, Morristown, NJ 07962. Telephone: 201-267-9404. Fax: 973-267-5208.

RAMAPO COLLEGE OF NEW JERSEY
MAHWAH, NEW JERSEY

General State-supported, comprehensive, coed **Entrance** Moderately difficult **Setting** 315-acre suburban campus **Total enrollment** 4,821 **Student/faculty ratio** 17:1 **Application deadline** 3/15 **Freshmen** 49% were admitted **Housing** Yes **Expenses** Tuition $4206; Room & Board $5734 **Undergraduates** 55% women, 32% part-time, 7% 25 or older, 0.2% Native American, 6% Hispanic, 7% black, 4% Asian American or Pacific Islander **Most popular recent majors** Business administration; psychology; mass communications **Academic program** Average class size 22, English as a second language, advanced placement, accelerated degree program, self-designed majors, tutorials, honors program, summer session, adult/continuing education programs, internships **Contact** Ms. Nancy Jaeger, Director of Admissions, Ramapo College of New Jersey, 505 Ramapo Valley Road, Mahwah, NJ 07430-1680. Telephone: 201-529-7600 ext. 7601 or toll-free 800-9RAMAPO (in-state). Fax: 201-529-7508. E-mail: adm@ramapo.edu. Web site: http://www.ramapo.edu/.

THE RICHARD STOCKTON COLLEGE OF NEW JERSEY
POMONA, NEW JERSEY

General State-supported, comprehensive, coed **Entrance** Very difficult **Setting** 1,600-acre suburban campus **Total enrollment** 6,205 **Student/faculty ratio** 18:1 **Application deadline** 5/1 **Freshmen** 51% were admitted **Housing** Yes **Expenses** Tuition $3776; Room & Board $4760 **Undergraduates** 57% women, 16% part-time, 24% 25 or older, 0.2% Native American, 4% Hispanic, 7% black, 4% Asian American or Pacific Islander **Most popular recent majors** Business administration; environmental science; criminal justice/law enforcement administration **Academic program** Average class size 23, advanced placement, accelerated degree program, self-designed majors, tutorials, honors program, summer session, adult/continuing education programs, internships **Contact** Mr. Salvatore Catalfamo, Dean of Enrollment Management, The Richard Stockton College of New Jersey, Jimmie Leeds Road, Pomona, NJ 08240-9988. Telephone: 609-652-

The Richard Stockton College of New Jersey *(continued)*

4261. Fax: 609-748-5541. E-mail: admissions@pollux.stockton.edu. Web site: http://loki.stockton.edu/.

▶ **For more information, see page 498.**

RIDER UNIVERSITY
LAWRENCEVILLE, NEW JERSEY

General Independent, comprehensive, coed **Entrance** Moderately difficult **Setting** 340-acre suburban campus **Total enrollment** 5,078 **Student/faculty ratio** 13:1 **Application deadline** Rolling **Freshmen** 81% were admitted **Housing** Yes **Expenses** Tuition $15,410; Room & Board $6270 **Undergraduates** 59% women, 26% part-time, 25% 25 or older, 0.4% Native American, 4% Hispanic, 7% black, 4% Asian American or Pacific Islander **Most popular recent majors** Accounting; elementary education; business administration **Academic program** Average class size 25, English as a second language, advanced placement, tutorials, honors program, summer session, adult/continuing education programs, internships **Contact** Mrs. Susan C. Christian, Director, Office of Admissions, Rider University, 2083 Lawrenceville Road, Lawrenceville, NJ 08648-3001. Telephone: 609-895-5768 or toll-free 800-257-9026. Fax: 609-895-6645. E-mail: admissions@rider.edu. Web site: http://www.rider.edu/.

▶ **For more information, see page 499.**

ROWAN UNIVERSITY
GLASSBORO, NEW JERSEY

General State-supported, comprehensive, coed **Entrance** Moderately difficult **Setting** 200-acre small town campus **Total enrollment** 9,367 **Student/faculty ratio** 16:1 **Application deadline** 3/15 **Freshmen** 51% were admitted **Housing** Yes **Expenses** Tuition $4241; Room & Board $5326 **Undergraduates** 56% women, 17% part-time, 24% 25 or older, 0.4% Native American, 5% Hispanic, 9% black, 3% Asian American or Pacific Islander **Most popular recent majors** Business administration; elementary education; mass communications **Academic program** Average class size 23, English as a second language, advanced placement, accelerated degree program, tutorials, honors program, summer session, adult/continuing education programs, internships **Contact** Mr. Marvin G. Sills, Director of Admissions, Rowan University, 201 Mullica Hill Road, Glassboro, NJ 08028-1701. Telephone: 609-256-4200 or toll-free 800-447-1165 (in-state). E-mail: admissions@rowan.edu. Web site: http://www.rowan.edu/.

RUTGERS, THE STATE UNIVERSITY OF NEW JERSEY, CAMDEN COLLEGE OF ARTS AND SCIENCES
CAMDEN, NEW JERSEY

General State-supported, 4-year, coed **Entrance** Moderately difficult **Setting** 25-acre urban campus **Total enrollment** 48,341 **Student/faculty ratio** 13:1 **Application deadline** 12/15 **Freshmen** 60% were admitted **Housing** Yes **Expenses** Tuition $5190; Room & Board $5314 **Undergraduates** 59% women, 19% part-time, 29% 25 or older, 0.4% Native American, 8% Hispanic, 15% black, 7% Asian American or Pacific Islander **Most popular recent majors** Psychology; accounting; sociology **Academic program** Average class size 32, advanced placement, self-designed majors, tutorials, honors program, summer session, internships **Contact** Ms. Diane Wms. Harris, Associate Director of University Undergraduate Admissions, Rutgers, The State University of New Jersey, Camden College of Arts and Sciences, 65 Davidson Road, Piscataway, NJ 08854-8097. Telephone: 732-732-4636. Fax: 732-445-0237. E-mail: admissions@asb-ugadm.rutgers.edu. Web site: http://www.rutgers.edu/.

RUTGERS, THE STATE UNIVERSITY OF NEW JERSEY, COLLEGE OF ENGINEERING
PISCATAWAY, NEW JERSEY

General State-supported, 4-year, coed **Entrance** Very difficult **Setting** 2,695-acre small town campus **Total enrollment** 48,341 **Student/faculty ratio** 10:1 **Application deadline** 12/15 **Freshmen** 72% were admitted **Housing** Yes **Expenses** Tuition $5836; Room & Board $5314 **Undergraduates** 22% women, 3% part-time, 6% 25 or older, 0.2% Native American, 7% Hispanic, 8% black, 24% Asian American or Pacific Islander **Most popular recent majors** Mechanical engineering; electrical/electronics engineering; chemical engineering **Academic program** Average class size 45, English as a second language, advanced placement, self-designed majors, tutorials, honors program, summer session, internships **Contact** Ms. Diane Wms. Harris, Associate Director of University Undergraduate Admissions, Rutgers, The State University of New Jersey, College of Engineering, 65 Davidson Road, Piscataway, NJ 08854-8097. Telephone: 732-932-4636. Fax: 732-445-0237. E-mail: admissions@asb-ugadm.rutgers.edu. Web site: http://www.rutgers.edu/.

RUTGERS, THE STATE UNIVERSITY OF NEW JERSEY, COLLEGE OF NURSING
NEWARK, NEW JERSEY

General State-supported, comprehensive, coed **Entrance** Moderately difficult **Setting** 34-acre urban campus **Total enrollment** 48,341 **Student/faculty ratio** 9:1 **Application deadline** 12/15 **Freshmen** 29% were admitted **Housing** Yes **Expenses** Tuition $5130; Room & Board $5314 **Undergraduates** 89% women, 13% part-time, 25% 25 or older, 0% Native American, 10% Hispanic, 18% black, 21% Asian American or Pacific Islander **Academic program** Average class size 30, English as a second language, advanced placement, tutorials, honors program, summer session, internships **Contact** Ms. Diane Wms. Harris, Associate Director of University Undergraduate Admissions, Rutgers, The State University of New Jersey, College of Nursing, 65 Davidson Road, Piscataway, NJ 08854-8097. Telephone: 732-932-4636. Fax: 732-445-0237. E-mail: admissions@asb-ugadm.rutgers.edu. Web site: http://www.rutgers.edu/.

RUTGERS, THE STATE UNIVERSITY OF NEW JERSEY, COLLEGE OF PHARMACY

PISCATAWAY, NEW JERSEY

General State-supported, comprehensive, coed **Entrance** Most difficult **Setting** 2,695-acre small town campus **Total enrollment** 48,341 **Student/faculty ratio** 14:1 **Application deadline** 12/15 **Freshmen** 37% were admitted **Housing** Yes **Expenses** Tuition $5836; Room & Board $5314 **Undergraduates** 62% women, 1% part-time, 6% 25 or older, 0% Native American, 6% Hispanic, 6% black, 44% Asian American or Pacific Islander **Academic program** Average class size 45, English as a second language, advanced placement, tutorials, honors program, summer session, internships **Contact** Ms. Diane Wms. Harris, Associate Director of University Undergraduate Admissions, Rutgers, The State University of New Jersey, College of Pharmacy, 65 Davidson Road, Piscataway, NJ 08854-8097. Telephone: 732-932-4636. Fax: 732-445-0237. E-mail: admissions@asb-ugadm.rutgers.edu. Web site: http://www.rutgers.edu/.

RUTGERS, THE STATE UNIVERSITY OF NEW JERSEY, COOK COLLEGE

NEW BRUNSWICK, NEW JERSEY

General State-supported, 4-year, coed **Entrance** Very difficult **Setting** 2,695-acre small town campus **Total enrollment** 48,341 **Student/faculty ratio** 15:1 **Application deadline** 12/15 **Freshmen** 64% were admitted **Housing** Yes **Expenses** Tuition $5817; Room & Board $5314 **Undergraduates** 51% women, 8% part-time, 10% 25 or older, 0.2% Native American, 6% Hispanic, 6% black, 12% Asian American or Pacific Islander **Most popular recent majors** Environmental science; biology; natural resources management **Academic program** Average class size 45, English as a second language, advanced placement, self-designed majors, tutorials, honors program, summer session, internships **Contact** Ms. Diane Wms. Harris, Associate Director of University Undergraduate Admissions, Rutgers, The State University of New Jersey, Cook College, 65 Davidson Road, Piscataway, NJ 08854-8097. Telephone: 732-932-4636. Fax: 732-445-0237. E-mail: admissions@asb-ugadm.rutgers.edu. Web site: http://www.rutgers.edu/.

RUTGERS, THE STATE UNIVERSITY OF NEW JERSEY, DOUGLASS COLLEGE

NEW BRUNSWICK, NEW JERSEY

General State-supported, 4-year, women only **Entrance** Moderately difficult **Setting** 2,695-acre small town campus **Total enrollment** 48,341 **Student/faculty ratio** 17:1 **Application deadline** 12/15 **Freshmen** 70% were admitted **Housing** Yes **Expenses** Tuition $5349; Room & Board $5314 **Undergraduates** 5% part-time, 7% 25 or older, 0.3% Native American, 7% Hispanic, 12% black, 14% Asian American or Pacific Islander **Most popular recent majors** Psychology; English; political science **Academic program** Average class size 45, English as a second language, advanced placement, self-designed majors, tutorials, honors program, summer session, adult/continuing education programs, internships **Contact** Ms. Diane Wms. Harris, Associate Director of University Undergraduate Admissions, Rutgers, The State University of New Jersey, Douglass College, 65 Davidson Road, Piscataway, NJ 08854-8097. Telephone: 732-932-4636. Fax: 732-445-0237. E-mail: admissions@asb-ugadm.rutgers.edu. Web site: http://www.rutgers.edu/.

RUTGERS, THE STATE UNIVERSITY OF NEW JERSEY, LIVINGSTON COLLEGE

PISCATAWAY, NEW JERSEY

General State-supported, 4-year, coed **Entrance** Moderately difficult **Setting** 2,695-acre small town campus **Total enrollment** 48,341 **Student/faculty ratio** 17:1 **Application deadline** 12/15 **Freshmen** 60% were admitted **Housing** Yes **Expenses** Tuition $5382; Room & Board $5314 **Undergraduates** 39% women, 5% part-time, 5% 25 or older, 0.4% Native American, 8% Hispanic, 12% black, 18% Asian American or Pacific Islander **Most popular recent majors** Psychology; economics; criminal justice/law enforcement administration **Academic program** Average class size 45, English as a second language, advanced placement, self-designed majors, tutorials, honors program, summer session, internships **Contact** Ms. Diane Wms. Harris, Associate Director of University Undergraduate Admissions, Rutgers, The State University of New Jersey, Livingston College, 65 Davidson Road, Piscataway, NJ 08854-8097. Telephone: 732-932-4636. Fax: 732-445-0237. E-mail:

Rutgers, The State University of New Jersey, Livingston College *(continued)*

admissions@asb-ugadm.rutgers.edu. Web site: http://www.rutgers.edu/.

RUTGERS, THE STATE UNIVERSITY OF NEW JERSEY, MASON GROSS SCHOOL OF THE ARTS

NEW BRUNSWICK, NEW JERSEY

General State-supported, comprehensive, coed **Entrance** Very difficult **Setting** 2,695-acre small town campus **Total enrollment** 48,341 **Student/faculty ratio** 12:1 **Application deadline** 12/15 **Freshmen** 23% were admitted **Housing** Yes **Expenses** Tuition $5366; Room & Board $5314 **Undergraduates** 56% women, 5% part-time, 6% 25 or older, 1% Native American, 6% Hispanic, 4% black, 7% Asian American or Pacific Islander **Most popular recent majors** Art; theater arts/drama; music **Academic program** Average class size 45, English as a second language, advanced placement, tutorials, honors program, summer session, internships **Contact** Ms. Diane Wms. Harris, Associate Director of University Undergraduate Admissions, Rutgers, The State University of New Jersey, Mason Gross School of the Arts, 65 Davidson Road, Piscataway, NJ 08854-8097. Telephone: 732-932-4636. Fax: 732-445-0237. E-mail: admissions@asb-ugadm.rutgers.edu. Web site: http://www.rutgers.edu/.

RUTGERS, THE STATE UNIVERSITY OF NEW JERSEY, NEWARK COLLEGE OF ARTS AND SCIENCES

NEWARK, NEW JERSEY

General State-supported, 4-year, coed **Entrance** Moderately difficult **Setting** 34-acre urban campus **Total enrollment** 48,341 **Student/faculty ratio** 15:1 **Application deadline** 12/15 **Freshmen** 57% were admitted **Housing** Yes **Expenses** Tuition $5151; Room & Board $5314 **Undergraduates** 54% women, 15% part-time, 21% 25 or older, 0.3% Native American, 21% Hispanic, 18% black, 17% Asian American or Pacific Islander **Most popular recent majors** Accounting; biology; psychology **Academic program** Average class size 30, English as a second language, advanced placement, accelerated degree program, self-designed majors, tutorials, honors program, summer session, adult/continuing education programs, internships **Contact** Ms. Diane Wms. Harris, Associate Director of University Undergraduate Admissions, Rutgers, The State University of New Jersey, Newark College of Arts and Sciences, 65 Davidson Road, Piscataway, NJ 08854-8097. Telephone: 732-932-4636. Fax: 732-445-0237. E-mail: admissions@asb-ugadm.rutgers.edu. Web site: http://www.rutgers.edu/.

RUTGERS, THE STATE UNIVERSITY OF NEW JERSEY, RUTGERS COLLEGE

NEW BRUNSWICK, NEW JERSEY

General State-supported, comprehensive, coed **Entrance** Very difficult **Setting** 2,695-acre small town campus **Total enrollment** 48,341 **Student/faculty ratio** 17:1 **Application deadline** 12/15 **Freshmen** 48% were admitted **Housing** Yes **Expenses** Tuition $5386; Room & Board $5314 **Undergraduates** 51% women, 3% part-time, 3% 25 or older, 0.3% Native American, 10% Hispanic, 7% black, 19% Asian American or Pacific Islander **Most popular recent majors** Psychology; biology; English **Academic program** Average class size 45, English as a second language, advanced placement, self-designed majors, tutorials, honors program, summer session, internships **Contact** Ms. Diane Wms. Harris, Associate Director of University Undergraduate Admissions, Rutgers, The State University of New Jersey, Rutgers College, 65 Davidson Road, Piscataway, NJ 08854-8097. Telephone: 732-932-4636. Fax: 732-445-0237. E-mail: admissions@asb-ugadm.rutgers.edu. Web site: http://www.rutgers.edu/.

RUTGERS, THE STATE UNIVERSITY OF NEW JERSEY, UNIVERSITY COLLEGE–CAMDEN

CAMDEN, NEW JERSEY

General State-supported, 4-year, coed **Entrance** Moderately difficult **Setting** 25-acre urban campus **Total enrollment** 48,341 **Student/faculty ratio** 13:1 **Application deadline** 12/15 **Freshmen** 78% were admitted **Housing** Yes **Undergraduates** 53% women, 40% part-time, 53% 25 or older, 0.3% Native American, 2% Hispanic, 15% black, 7% Asian American or Pacific Islander **Most popular recent majors** Computer science; psychology; political science **Academic program** Average class size 32, advanced placement, self-designed majors, tutorials, honors program, summer session, internships **Contact** Ms. Diane Wms. Harris, Associate Director of University Undergraduate Admissions, Rutgers, The State University of New Jersey, University College–Camden, 65 Davidson Road, Piscataway, NJ 08854-8097. Telephone: 732-932-4636. Fax: 732-445-0237. E-mail: admissions@asb.ugadm.rutgers.edu. Web site: http://www.rutgers.edu/.

RUTGERS, THE STATE UNIVERSITY OF NEW JERSEY, UNIVERSITY COLLEGE–NEWARK

NEWARK, NEW JERSEY

General State-supported, 4-year, coed **Entrance** Moderately difficult **Setting** 34-acre urban campus **Total enrollment** 48,341 **Student/faculty ratio** 15:1 **Application deadline** 12/15 **Freshmen** 72% were admitted **Housing** Yes **Under-**

graduates 58% women, 53% part-time, 56% 25 or older, 0.2% Native American, 16% Hispanic, 31% black, 11% Asian American or Pacific Islander **Most popular recent majors** Accounting; business marketing and marketing management; English **Academic program** Average class size 30, English as a second language, advanced placement, self-designed majors, tutorials, honors program, summer session, adult/continuing education programs, internships **Contact** Ms. Diane Wms. Harris, Associate Director of University Undergraduate Admissions, Rutgers, The State University of New Jersey, University College-Newark, 65 Davidson Road, Piscataway, NJ 08854-8097. Telephone: 732-932-4636. Fax: 732-445-0237. E-mail: admissions@asb-ugadm.rutgers.edu. Web site: http://www.rutgers.edu/.

RUTGERS, THE STATE UNIVERSITY OF NEW JERSEY, UNIVERSITY COLLEGE–NEW BRUNSWICK

NEW BRUNSWICK, NEW JERSEY

General State-supported, 4-year, coed **Entrance** Moderately difficult **Setting** 2,695-acre small town campus **Total enrollment** 48,341 **Student/faculty ratio** 17:1 **Application deadline** 12/15 **Freshmen** 71% were admitted **Housing** Yes **Undergraduates** 54% women, 73% part-time, 68% 25 or older, 1% Native American, 5% Hispanic, 8% black, 9% Asian American or Pacific Islander **Most popular recent majors** Psychology; communications; economics **Academic program** Average class size 45, English as a second language, advanced placement, self-designed majors, tutorials, honors program, summer session, adult/continuing education programs, internships **Contact** Mr. Raul Barriera, Director of Admissions, Rutgers, The State University of New Jersey, University College-New Brunswick, 14 College Avenue, Miller Hall, New Brunswick, NJ 08903. Telephone: 732-932-7276. Fax: 732-932-8767. E-mail: ucnb@rci.rutgers.edu. Web site: http://www.rutgers.edu/.

SAINT PETER'S COLLEGE

JERSEY CITY, NEW JERSEY

General Independent Roman Catholic (Jesuit), comprehensive, coed **Entrance** Moderately difficult **Setting** 15-acre urban campus **Total enrollment** 3,698 **Student/faculty ratio** 15:1 **Application deadline** Rolling **Freshmen** 79% were admitted **Housing** Yes **Expenses** Tuition $14,366; Room & Board $5060 **Undergraduates** 55% women, 21% part-time, 24% 25 or older, 0.2% Native American, 24% Hispanic, 15% black, 7% Asian American or Pacific Islander **Most popular recent majors** Business administration; accounting; elementary education **Academic program** Average class size 23, advanced placement, accelerated degree program, self-designed majors, tutorials, honors program, summer session, adult/continuing education programs, internships **Contact** Ms. Nancy P. Campbell, Associate Vice President for Enrollment, Saint Peter's College, 2641 Kennedy Boulevard, Jersey City, NJ 07306-5997. Telephone: 201-915-9213 or toll-free 888-SPC-9933. Fax: 201-432-5860. E-mail: admissions@spcvxa.spc.edu. Web site: http://www.spc.edu/.

▶ **For more information, see page 508.**

SETON HALL UNIVERSITY

SOUTH ORANGE, NEW JERSEY

General Independent Roman Catholic, university, coed **Entrance** Moderately difficult **Setting** 58-acre suburban campus **Total enrollment** 10,114 **Student/faculty ratio** 16:1 **Application deadline** 3/1 **Freshmen** 78% were admitted **Housing** Yes **Expenses** Tuition $13,600; Room & Board $7020 **Undergraduates** 56% women, 12% part-time, 11% 25 or older, 0.1% Native American, 9% Hispanic, 11% black, 5% Asian American or Pacific Islander **Most popular recent majors** Communications; nursing; criminal justice studies **Academic program** Average class size 30, English as a second language, advanced placement, accelerated degree program, honors program, summer session, internships **Contact** Mr. Gregg A. Meyer, Director of Admissions, Seton Hall University, 400 South Orange Avenue, South Orange, NJ 07079-2697. Telephone: 973-761-9332 or toll-free 800-THE HALL (out-of-state). Fax: 973-761-9452. E-mail: thehall@shu.edu. Web site: http://www.shu.edu/.

STEVENS INSTITUTE OF TECHNOLOGY

HOBOKEN, NEW JERSEY

General Independent, university, coed **Entrance** Very difficult **Setting** 55-acre urban campus **Total enrollment** 3,248 **Student/faculty ratio** 9:1 **Application deadline** 3/1 **Freshmen** 67% were admitted **Housing** Yes **Expenses** Tuition $19,360; Room & Board $6724 **Undergraduates** 22% women, 2% part-time, 4% 25 or older, 0.3% Native American, 11% Hispanic, 5% black, 20% Asian American or Pacific Islander **Most popular recent majors** Mechanical engineering; chemical engineering; computer engineering **Academic program** Average class size 20, advanced placement, accelerated degree program, tutorials, honors program, summer session, internships **Contact** Mrs. Maureen P. Weatherall, Dean of Undergraduate Admissions and Financial Aid, Stevens Institute of Technology, Castle Point on Hudson, Hoboken, NJ 07030. Telephone: 201-216-5194 or toll-free 800-458-5323. Fax: 201-216-8348. E-mail: admissions@stevens-tech.edu. Web site: http://www.stevens-tech.edu/.

TALMUDICAL ACADEMY OF NEW JERSEY
ADELPHIA, NEW JERSEY

Contact Rabbi G. Finkel, Director of Admissions, Talmudical Academy of New Jersey, Route 524, Adelphia, NJ 07710. Telephone: 201-431-1600.

THOMAS EDISON STATE COLLEGE
TRENTON, NEW JERSEY

General State-supported, comprehensive, coed **Entrance** Noncompetitive **Setting** 2-acre urban campus **Total enrollment** 8,552 **Housing** No **Undergraduates** 97% 25 or older, 1% Native American, 4% Hispanic, 8% black, 2% Asian American or Pacific Islander **Most popular recent majors** Social sciences; natural sciences; nuclear technology **Academic program** Advanced placement, accelerated degree program, self-designed majors, summer session, adult/continuing education programs **Contact** Dr. Gordon Holly, Director of Admissions Services, Thomas Edison State College, 101 West State Street, Trenton, NJ 08608-1176. Telephone: 609-984-1150 or toll-free 888-442-8372. Fax: 609-984-8447. E-mail: admissions@call.tesc.edu. Web site: http://www.tesc.edu/.

TRENTON STATE COLLEGE
See The College of New Jersey

WESTMINSTER CHOIR COLLEGE OF RIDER UNIVERSITY
PRINCETON, NEW JERSEY

General Independent, comprehensive, coed **Entrance** Moderately difficult **Setting** 23-acre small town campus **Total enrollment** 437 **Student/faculty ratio** 7:1 **Application deadline** Rolling **Housing** Yes **Expenses** Tuition $15,430; Room & Board $6610 **Most popular recent majors** Music education; sacred music; music (voice and choral/opera performance) **Academic program** English as a second language, advanced placement, honors program, summer session, adult/continuing education programs, internships **Contact** Mr. Stephen B. Milbauer, Assistant Director of Admissions, Westminster Choir College of Rider University, 101 Walnut Lane, Princeton, NJ 08540-3899. Telephone: 609-921-7144 ext. 103 or toll-free 800-96-CHOIR. Fax: 609-921-2538. E-mail: wccadmission@rider.edu. Web site: http://westminster.rider.edu/.

WILLIAM PATERSON UNIVERSITY OF NEW JERSEY
WAYNE, NEW JERSEY

General State-supported, comprehensive, coed **Entrance** Moderately difficult **Setting** 300-acre suburban campus **Total enrollment** 8,941 **Application deadline** 5/15 **Freshmen** 49% were admitted **Housing** Yes **Expenses** Tuition $3786; Room & Board $5100 **Undergraduates** 26% 25 or older **Most popular recent majors** Business administration; psychology; mass communications **Academic program** English as a second language, advanced placement, accelerated degree program, tutorials, honors program, summer session, adult/continuing education programs, internships **Contact** Mr. Leo DeBartolo, Director of Admissions, William Paterson University of New Jersey, 300 Pompton Road, Wayne, NJ 07470-8420. Telephone: 973-720-2906. Fax: 973-720-2910. E-mail: christensen_@wpc.wilpaterson.edu. Web site: http://www.wilpaterson.edu/.

► **For more information, see page 557.**

NEW MEXICO

COLLEGE OF SANTA FE
SANTA FE, NEW MEXICO

General Independent, comprehensive, coed **Entrance** Moderately difficult **Setting** 100-acre suburban campus **Total enrollment** 1,417 **Student/faculty ratio** 12:1 **Application deadline** 3/15 **Freshmen** 84% were admitted **Housing** Yes **Expenses** Tuition $13,240; Room & Board $4724 **Undergraduates** 63% women, 40% part-time, 15% 25 or older, 2% Native American, 25% Hispanic, 2% black, 1% Asian American or Pacific Islander **Most popular recent majors** Film/video production; education; business administration **Academic program** Average class size 16, advanced placement, self-designed majors, tutorials, summer session, adult/continuing education programs, internships **Contact** Dale H. Reinhart, Director of Admissions and Enrollment Management, College of Santa Fe, 1600 Saint Michael's Drive, Santa Fe, NM 87505-7634. Telephone: 505-473-6133 ext. 6136 or toll-free 800-456-2673. Fax: 505-473-6127 ext. 6133. E-mail: admissio@fogelson.csf.edu. Web site: http://www.csf.edu/.

COLLEGE OF THE SOUTHWEST
HOBBS, NEW MEXICO

General Independent, comprehensive, coed **Entrance** Moderately difficult **Setting** 162-acre small town campus **Total enrollment** 682 **Student/faculty ratio** 8:1 **Application deadline** Rolling **Freshmen** 77% were admitted **Housing** Yes **Expenses** Tuition $4430; Room & Board $3418 **Undergraduates** 74% women, 29% part-time, 61% 25 or older, 1% Native American, 20% Hispanic, 3% black, 0% Asian American or Pacific Islander **Most popular recent majors** Education; business administration; psychology **Academic program** Average class size 20, advanced placement, accelerated degree program, tutorials, summer session, adult/continuing education programs, internships **Contact** Mr. Jamie Hodgins, Director of Student Services, College of the Southwest, 6610 Lovington Highway, Hobbs, NM 88240-9129. Telephone: 505-392-6561 or toll-free 800-530-4400.

EASTERN NEW MEXICO UNIVERSITY
PORTALES, NEW MEXICO

General State-supported, comprehensive, coed **Entrance** Minimally difficult **Setting** 240-acre rural campus **Total enrollment** 3,495 **Application deadline** Rolling **Freshmen** 74% were admitted **Housing** Yes **Expenses** Tuition $1716; Room & Board $2942 **Undergraduates** 60% women, 19% part-time, 28% 25 or older, 3% Native American, 22% Hispanic, 4% black, 1% Asian American or Pacific Islander **Most popular recent majors** Education; sociology; liberal arts and studies **Academic program** English as a second language, advanced placement, accelerated degree program, self-designed majors, honors program, summer session, adult/continuing education programs, internships **Contact** Mr. Larry Brock, Director of Admissions, Eastern New Mexico University, Station #7 ENMU, Portales, NM 88130. Telephone: 505-562-2178 or toll-free 800-367-3668. Fax: 505-562-2118. E-mail: larry.brock@enmu.edu. Web site: http://www.enmu.edu/.

METROPOLITAN COLLEGE OF COURT REPORTING
ALBUQUERQUE, NEW MEXICO

Contact Metropolitan College of Court Reporting, 2201 San Pedro NE, Building 1, # 1300, Albuquerque, NM 87110-4129. Telephone: 505-888-3400.

NATIONAL AMERICAN UNIVERSITY
ALBUQUERQUE, NEW MEXICO

General Proprietary, 4-year, coed **Contact** Ms. Nancy Pointer, Educational Consultant, National American University, 1202 Pennsylvania Avenue, NE, Albuquerque, NM 87110. Telephone: 505-265-7517. Fax: 505-265-7542. Web site: http://www.national@rt66.com/.

NAZARENE INDIAN BIBLE COLLEGE
ALBUQUERQUE, NEW MEXICO

General Independent, 4-year, coed, affiliated with Church of the Nazarene **Contact** Ms. Yolanda Vielle, Acting Registrar, Nazarene Indian Bible College, 2315 Markham Road, SW, Albuquerque, NM 87105. Telephone: 505-877-0240 or toll-free 888-877-NIBC.

NEW MEXICO HIGHLANDS UNIVERSITY
LAS VEGAS, NEW MEXICO

General State-supported, comprehensive, coed **Entrance** Minimally difficult **Setting** 120-acre small town campus **Total enrollment** 2,544 **Student/faculty ratio** 20:1 **Application deadline** Rolling **Freshmen** 84% were admitted **Housing** Yes **Expenses** Tuition $1662; Room & Board $2706 **Undergraduates** 54% women, 13% part-time, 20% 25 or older, 6% Native American, 68% Hispanic, 4% black, 2% Asian American or Pacific Islander **Most popular recent majors** Business administration; elementary education; social work **Academic program** Average class size 30, advanced placement, accelerated degree program, tutorials, honors program, summer session, internships **Contact** Mr. Larry Cruz, Director of Student Recruitment, New Mexico Highlands University, Las Vegas, NM 87701. Telephone: 505-454-3256 or toll-free 800-338-6648 (in-state). Fax: 505-454-3311. E-mail: admission@venus.nmnu.edu. Web site: http://www.nmhu.edu/.

NEW MEXICO INSTITUTE OF MINING AND TECHNOLOGY
SOCORRO, NEW MEXICO

General State-supported, university, coed **Entrance** Moderately difficult **Setting** 320-acre small town campus **Total enrollment** 1,419 **Student/faculty ratio** 11:1 **Application deadline** 8/1 **Freshmen** 76% were admitted **Housing** Yes **Expenses** Tuition $2073; Room & Board $3530 **Undergraduates** 33% women, 6% part-time, 20% 25 or older, 3% Native American, 18% Hispanic, 1% black, 3% Asian American or Pacific Islander **Most popular recent majors** Environmental engineering; biology; mathematics **Academic program** Average class size 24, advanced placement, self-designed majors, tutorials, summer session, adult/continuing education programs, internships **Contact** Ms. Melissa Jaramillo-Fleming, Director of Admissions, New Mexico Institute of Mining and Technology, 801 Leroy Place, Socorro, NM 87801. Telephone: 505-835-5424 or toll-free 800-428-TECH. Fax: 505-835-5989. E-mail: admission@admin.nmt.edu. Web site: http://www.nmt.edu/.

NEW MEXICO STATE UNIVERSITY
LAS CRUCES, NEW MEXICO

General State-supported, university, coed **Entrance** Moderately difficult **Setting** 900-acre suburban campus **Total enrollment** 15,067 **Student/faculty ratio** 18:1 **Application deadline** 8/14

New Mexico State University *(continued)*

Freshmen 70% were admitted **Housing** Yes **Expenses** Tuition $2196; Room & Board $3390 **Undergraduates** 52% women, 19% part-time, 3% Native American, 40% Hispanic, 2% black, 1% Asian American or Pacific Islander **Most popular recent majors** Education; business marketing and marketing management; criminal justice/law enforcement administration **Academic program** Advanced placement, accelerated degree program, self-designed majors, honors program, summer session, adult/continuing education programs, internships **Contact** Ms. Angela Mora, Director of Admissions, New Mexico State University, Box 30001, Department 3A, Las Cruces, NM 88003-8001. Telephone: 505-646-3121 or toll-free 800-662-6678. Fax: 505-646-6330. E-mail: admssions@nmsu.edu. Web site: http://www.nmsu.edu/.

ST. JOHN'S COLLEGE
SANTA FE, NEW MEXICO

General Independent, comprehensive, coed **Entrance** Moderately difficult **Setting** 250-acre small town campus **Total enrollment** 488 **Student/faculty ratio** 8:1 **Application deadline** Rolling **Housing** Yes **Expenses** Tuition $19,700; Room & Board $6116 **Undergraduates** 44% women, 2% part-time, 10% 25 or older, 1% Native American, 7% Hispanic, 0% black, 3% Asian American or Pacific Islander **Academic program** Average class size 17, tutorials **Contact** Mr. Larry Clendenin, Director of Admissions, St. John's College, 1160 Camino Cruz Blanca, Santa Fe, NM 87501-4599. Telephone: 505-984-6060 or toll-free 800-331-5232. E-mail: admissions@shadow.sjcsf.edu. Web site: http://www.sjcsf.edu/.

UNIVERSITY OF NEW MEXICO
ALBUQUERQUE, NEW MEXICO

General State-supported, university, coed **Entrance** Moderately difficult **Setting** 625-acre urban campus **Total enrollment** 23,956 **Application deadline** 7/24 **Freshmen** 79% were admitted **Housing** Yes **Expenses** Tuition $2165; Room & Board $4119 **Undergraduates** 57% women, 25% part-time, 34% 25 or older, 6% Native American, 29% Hispanic, 3% black, 3% Asian American or Pacific Islander **Most popular recent majors** Liberal arts and studies; elementary education; nursing **Academic program** English as a second language, advanced placement, self-designed majors, honors program, summer session, adult/continuing education programs, internships **Contact** Mr. Gary L. Kuykendall, Associate Director of Admissions, University of New Mexico, Albuquerque, NM 87131-2046. Telephone: 505-277-2446 or toll-free 800-CALLUNM (in-state). Fax: 505-277-6686. E-mail: apply@unm.edu. Web site: http://www.unm.edu/.

WESTERN NEW MEXICO UNIVERSITY
SILVER CITY, NEW MEXICO

General State-supported, comprehensive, coed **Entrance** Noncompetitive **Setting** 83-acre rural campus **Total enrollment** 2,580 **Student/faculty ratio** 16:1 **Application deadline** 8/1 **Housing** Yes **Expenses** Tuition $855; Room & Board $2786 **Undergraduates** 61% women, 27% part-time, 46% 25 or older, 1% Native American, 42% Hispanic, 2% black, 0.5% Asian American or Pacific Islander **Most popular recent majors** Education; business administration; social sciences **Academic program** Advanced placement, accelerated degree program, self-designed majors, tutorials, summer session, adult/continuing education programs, internships **Contact** Mr. Michael Alecksen, Director of Admissions, Western New Mexico University, College Avenue, Silver City, NM 88062-0680. Telephone: 505-538-6106 or toll-free 800-872-WNMU (in-state). Fax: 505-538-6155.

NEW YORK

ADELPHI UNIVERSITY
GARDEN CITY, NEW YORK

General Independent, university, coed **Entrance** Moderately difficult **Setting** 75-acre suburban campus **Total enrollment** 5,594 **Student/faculty ratio** 12:1 **Application deadline** Rolling **Freshmen** 78% were admitted **Housing** Yes **Expenses** Tuition $14,720; Room & Board $6600 **Undergraduates** 67% women, 32% part-time, 40% 25 or older, 0.1% Native American, 5% Hispanic, 11% black, 2% Asian American or Pacific Islander **Most popular recent majors** Business administration; nursing; psychology **Academic program** Advanced placement, tutorials, honors program, summer session, internships **Contact** Ms. Esther Goodcuff, Director of Admissions, Adelphi University, South Avenue, Garden City, NY 11530. Telephone: 516-877-3050 or toll-free 800-ADELPHI. Fax: 516-877-3039. E-mail: admissions@adelphi.edu. Web site: http://www.adelphi.edu/.

ALBANY COLLEGE OF PHARMACY OF UNION UNIVERSITY
ALBANY, NEW YORK

General Independent, comprehensive, coed **Entrance** Moderately difficult **Setting** 1-acre urban campus **Total enrollment** 684 **Student/faculty ratio** 19:1 **Application deadline** Rolling **Freshmen** 77% were admitted **Housing** Yes **Expenses** Tuition $10,715; Room & Board $4900 **Undergraduates** 58% women, 3% part-time, 13% 25 or older, 0.5% Native American, 1% Hispanic, 2% black, 11% Asian American or Pacific Islander **Academic program** Advanced placement, tutorials, internships **Contact** Mrs. Janis Fisher, Director of Admissions and Registrar, Albany College of Pharmacy of Union University, 106 New Scotland Avenue, Albany, NY 12208-3425. Telephone: 518-445-7221. Fax: 518-445-7202. E-mail: admissions@panther.acp.edu. Web site: http://panther.acp.edu/.

ALBERT A. LIST COLLEGE OF JEWISH STUDIES

See Jewish Theological Seminary of America

ALFRED UNIVERSITY

ALFRED, NEW YORK

General Independent, university, coed **Entrance** Moderately difficult **Setting** 232-acre rural campus **Total enrollment** 2,329 **Student/faculty ratio** 12:1 **Application deadline** 2/1 **Freshmen** 82% were admitted **Housing** Yes **Expenses** Tuition $19,000; Room & Board $6406 **Undergraduates** 49% women, 2% part-time, 9% 25 or older, 0.5% Native American, 3% Hispanic, 3% black, 2% Asian American or Pacific Islander **Most popular recent majors** Art; business administration; psychology **Academic program** Advanced placement, accelerated degree program, self-designed majors, tutorials, honors program, summer session, adult/continuing education programs, internships **Contact** Ms. Katherine McCarthy, Director of Admissions, Alfred University, Alumni Hall, Alfred, NY 14802-1205. Telephone: 607-871-2115 or toll-free 800-541-9229. Fax: 607-871-2198. E-mail: admssn@bigvax.alfred.edu. Web site: http://www.alfred.edu/.

▶ **For more information, see page 386.**

ARNOLD & MARIE SCHWARTZ COLLEGE OF PHARMACY AND HEALTH SCIENCES

See Long Island University, Brooklyn Campus

AUDREY COHEN COLLEGE

NEW YORK, NEW YORK

General Independent, comprehensive, coed **Entrance** Moderately difficult **Setting** Urban campus **Total enrollment** 1,116 **Student/faculty ratio** 25:1 **Application deadline** 8/15 **Freshmen** 79% were admitted **Housing** No **Expenses** Tuition $8860 **Undergraduates** 79% women, 4% part-time, 58% 25 or older, 1% Native American, 17% Hispanic, 64% black, 1% Asian American or Pacific Islander **Most Popular Recent Major** Human services **Academic program** English as a second language, accelerated degree program, tutorials, summer session, adult/continuing education programs, internships **Contact** Ms. Joan M. Miller, Admissions Counselor, Audrey Cohen College, 75 Varick Street, New York, NY 10013-1919. Telephone: 212-343-1234 ext. 2703 or toll-free 800-33-THINK (in-state). Fax: 212-343-8470. Web site: http://www.audrey-cohen.edu/.

▶ **For more information, see page 392.**

BARD COLLEGE

ANNANDALE-ON-HUDSON, NEW YORK

General Independent, comprehensive, coed **Entrance** Very difficult **Setting** 600-acre rural campus **Total enrollment** 1,201 **Student/faculty ratio** 9:1 **Application deadline** 1/31 **Freshmen** 51% were admitted **Housing** Yes **Expenses** Tuition $22,220; Room & Board $6812 **Undergraduates** 59% women, 7% part-time, 1% 25 or older, 0.1% Native American, 4% Hispanic, 3% black, 3% Asian American or Pacific Islander **Most popular recent majors** Social sciences; art; literature **Academic program** Average class size 15, English as a second language, advanced placement, accelerated degree program, self-designed majors, tutorials, adult/continuing education programs, internships **Contact** Ms. Mary Inga Backlund, Director of Admissions, Bard College, Annandale-on-Hudson, NY 12504. Telephone: 914-758-7472. E-mail: admission@bard.edu. Web site: http://www.bard.edu/.

BARNARD COLLEGE

NEW YORK, NEW YORK

General Independent, 4-year, women only **Entrance** Most difficult **Setting** 4-acre urban campus **Total enrollment** 19,000 **Student/faculty ratio** 12:1 **Application deadline** 1/15 **Freshmen** 40% were admitted **Housing** Yes **Expenses** Tuition $20,976; Room & Board $8736 **Undergraduates** 1% part-time, 0% 25 or older, 0.2% Native American, 5% Hispanic, 4% black, 25% Asian American or Pacific Islander **Most popular recent majors** English; psychology; political science **Academic program** Average class size 24, advanced placement, accelerated degree program, self-designed majors, tutorials, honors program, internships **Contact** Ms. Doris Davis, Dean of Admissions, Barnard College, 3009 Broadway, New York, NY 10027. Telephone: 212-854-2014. Fax: 212-854-6220. E-mail: admissions@barnard.columbia.edu. Web site: http://www.barnard.columbia.edu/.

BARUCH COLLEGE OF THE CITY UNIVERSITY OF NEW YORK
NEW YORK, NEW YORK

General State and locally supported, comprehensive, coed **Entrance** Moderately difficult **Setting** Urban campus **Total enrollment** 15,071 **Student/faculty ratio** 31:1 **Application deadline** 6/15 **Freshmen** 23% were admitted **Housing** No **Expenses** Tuition $3330 **Undergraduates** 57% women, 36% part-time, 38% 25 or older, 0.1% Native American, 21% Hispanic, 23% black, 22% Asian American or Pacific Islander **Most popular recent majors** Accounting; finance; human resources management **Academic program** English as a second language, advanced placement, self-designed majors, tutorials, honors program, summer session, adult/continuing education programs, internships **Contact** Mr. James F. Murphy, Director of Admissions, Baruch College of the City University of New York, Box H-0720, New York, NY 10010-5585. Telephone: 212-802-2300. E-mail: udgbb@cunyvm.edu. Web site: http://www.baruch.cuny.edu/.

BETH HAMEDRASH SHAAREI YOSHER INSTITUTE
BROOKLYN, NEW YORK

Contact Mr. Menachem Steinberg, Director of Admissions, Beth HaMedrash Shaarei Yosher Institute, 4102-10 Sixteenth Avenue, Brooklyn, NY 11204. Telephone: 718-854-2290.

BETH HATALMUD RABBINICAL COLLEGE
BROOKLYN, NEW YORK

Contact Rabbi Osina, Director of Admissions, Beth Hatalmud Rabbinical College, 2127 Eighty-second Street, Brooklyn, NY 11214. Telephone: 718-259-2525.

BORICUA COLLEGE
NEW YORK, NEW YORK

General Independent, comprehensive, coed **Entrance** Moderately difficult **Setting** Urban campus **Total enrollment** 1,190 **Application deadline** Rolling **Freshmen** 47% were admitted **Housing** No **Expenses** Tuition $6300 **Undergraduates** 80% women, 89% 25 or older, 0% Native American, 87% Hispanic, 11% black, 0.1% Asian American or Pacific Islander **Most popular recent majors** Business administration; human services; elementary education **Academic program** Average class size 20, accelerated degree program, honors program, summer session, adult/continuing education programs, internships **Contact** Dr. Alicea Mercedes, Director of Registration and Assessment, Boricua College, 3755 Broadway, New York, NY 10032-1560. Telephone: 212-694-1000 ext. 525.

BROOKLYN COLLEGE OF THE CITY UNIVERSITY OF NEW YORK
BROOKLYN, NEW YORK

General State and locally supported, comprehensive, coed **Entrance** Moderately difficult **Setting** 26-acre urban campus **Total enrollment** 15,007 **Student/faculty ratio** 16:1 **Application deadline** 7/30 **Housing** No **Expenses** Tuition $3413 **Undergraduates** 60% women, 29% part-time, 29% 25 or older, 0.04% Native American, 9% Hispanic, 22% black, 7% Asian American or Pacific Islander **Most popular recent majors** Accounting; elementary education; business administration **Academic program** English as a second language, advanced placement, honors program, summer session, adult/continuing education programs, internships **Contact** Ms. Celia Adams, Admissions Counselor/Recruiter, Brooklyn College of the City University of New York, 1602 James Hall, Brooklyn, NY 11210-2889. Telephone: 718-951-5001. E-mail: admissions@brooklyn.cuny.edu. Web site: http://www.brooklyn.cuny.edu/.

CANISIUS COLLEGE
BUFFALO, NEW YORK

General Independent Roman Catholic (Jesuit), comprehensive, coed **Entrance** Moderately difficult **Setting** 25-acre urban campus **Total enrollment** 4,490 **Student/faculty ratio** 18:1 **Application deadline** Rolling **Freshmen** 88% were admitted **Housing** Yes **Expenses** Tuition $13,882; Room & Board $5950 **Undergraduates** 48% women, 9% part-time, 13% 25 or older, 0.3% Native American, 3% Hispanic, 6% black, 2% Asian American or Pacific Islander **Most popular recent majors** Psychology; English; mass communications **Academic program** Average class size 21, English as a second language, advanced placement, self-designed majors, tutorials, honors program, summer session, adult/continuing education programs, internships **Contact** Miss Penelope H. Lips, Director of Admissions, Canisius College, 2001 Main Street, Buffalo, NY 14208-1098. Telephone: 716-888-2200 or toll-free 800-843-1517. Fax: 716-888-2377. E-mail: inquiry@gort.canisius.edu. Web site: http://www.canisius.edu/.

CAZENOVIA COLLEGE
CAZENOVIA, NEW YORK

General Independent, 4-year, coed **Entrance** Minimally difficult **Setting** 40-acre small town campus **Total enrollment** 897 **Student/faculty ratio** 13:1 **Application deadline** Rolling **Fresh-**

men 79% were admitted **Housing** Yes **Expenses** Tuition $11,990; Room & Board $5928 **Undergraduates** 71% women, 21% part-time, 6% 25 or older, 1% Native American, 3% Hispanic, 8% black, 0.3% Asian American or Pacific Islander **Most popular recent majors** Liberal arts and studies; business administration; graphic design/ commercial art/illustration **Academic program** Average class size 18, advanced placement, self-designed majors, tutorials, honors program, summer session, adult/continuing education programs, internships **Contact** Mr. Tim Williams, Dean of Admission, Financial Aid, and Retention, Cazenovia College, Cazenovia, NY 13035-1084. Telephone: 315-655-7208 or toll-free 800-654-3210. Fax: 315-655-2190. Web site: http://www.cazcollege.edu/.

CENTRAL YESHIVA TOMCHEI TMIMIM-LUBAVITCH
BROOKLYN, NEW YORK

General Independent Jewish, comprehensive, men only **Contact** Rabbi Joseph Wilmowski, Director of Admissions, Central Yeshiva Tomchei Tmimim-Lubavitch, 841-853 Ocean Parkway, Brooklyn, NY 11230. Telephone: 718-859-7600.

CITY COLLEGE OF THE CITY UNIVERSITY OF NEW YORK
NEW YORK, NEW YORK

General State and locally supported, university, coed **Entrance** Moderately difficult **Setting** 35-acre urban campus **Total enrollment** 12,061 **Student/faculty ratio** 15:1 **Application deadline** Rolling **Freshmen** 70% were admitted **Housing** No **Expenses** Tuition $3309 **Undergraduates** 51% women, 31% part-time, 39% 25 or older **Most popular recent majors** Computer science; electrical/electronics engineering **Academic program** English as a second language, advanced placement, self-designed majors, honors program, summer session, adult/continuing education programs, internships **Contact** Ms. Laurie Austin, Director of Admissions, City College of the City University of New York, Convent Avenue at 138th Street, New York, NY 10031-6977. Telephone: 212-650-6977. Fax: 212-650-6417. E-mail: admissions@admin.ccny.cuny.edu. Web site: http://www.ccny.cuny.edu/.

CLARKSON UNIVERSITY
POTSDAM, NEW YORK

General Independent, university, coed **Entrance** Very difficult **Setting** 640-acre small town campus **Total enrollment** 2,745 **Student/faculty ratio** 16:1 **Application deadline** 3/15 **Freshmen** 82% were admitted **Housing** Yes **Expenses** Tuition $18,593; Room & Board $6510 **Undergraduates** 25% women, 2% part-time, 5% 25 or older, 1% Native American, 1% Hispanic, 3% black, 2% Asian American or Pacific Islander **Most popular recent majors** Civil engineering; mechanical engineering; chemical engineering **Academic program** Average class size 25, English as a second language, advanced placement, accelerated degree program, self-designed majors, honors program, summer session **Contact** Ms. Kathryn M. Del Guidice, Director of Enrollment Planning Operations, Clarkson University, Holcroft House, Potsdam, NY 13699. Telephone: 315-268-7646 or toll-free 800-527-6577 (in-state), 800-527-6578 (out-of-state). Fax: 315-268-7647. E-mail: fradmis@agent.clarkson.edu. Web site: http://www.clarkson.edu/.

COLGATE UNIVERSITY
HAMILTON, NEW YORK

General Independent, comprehensive, coed **Entrance** Very difficult **Setting** 515-acre rural campus **Total enrollment** 2,847 **Student/faculty ratio** 11:1 **Application deadline** 1/15 **Freshmen** 42% were admitted **Housing** Yes **Expenses** Tuition $22,765; Room & Board $6110 **Undergraduates** 51% women, 0.1% part-time, 1% 25 or older, 0.5% Native American, 3% Hispanic, 4% black, 4% Asian American or Pacific Islander **Most popular recent majors** Economics; political science; English **Academic program** Average class size 21, advanced placement, self-designed majors, tutorials, honors program **Contact** Ms. Mary F. Hill, Dean of Admission, Colgate University, 13 Oak Drive, Hamilton, NY 13346-1386. Telephone: 315-228-7401. Fax: 315-228-7798. E-mail: admission@mail.colgate.edu. Web site: http://www.colgate.edu/.

COLLEGE OF AERONAUTICS
FLUSHING, NEW YORK

General Independent, 4-year, primarily men **Entrance** Minimally difficult **Setting** 6-acre urban campus **Total enrollment** 1,102 **Student/faculty ratio** 20:1 **Application deadline** Rolling **Freshmen** 91% were admitted **Housing** Yes **Expenses** Tuition $7600; Room only $3365 **Undergraduates** 5% women, 22% part-time, 36% 25 or older, 0.1% Native American, 39% Hispanic, 24% black, 13% Asian American or Pacific Islander **Most popular recent majors** Aircraft mechanic/ airframe; aviation technology **Academic program** Advanced placement, summer session, adult/continuing education programs, internships **Contact** Mr. Vincent J. Montera, Director of Admissions, College of Aeronautics, La Guardia Airport, Flushing, NY 11371. Telephone: 718-429-

College of Aeronautics *(continued)*

6600 ext. 188 or toll-free 800-PRO-AERO (in-state). Fax: 718-429-0256. Web site: http://www.aero.edu/.

▶ **For more information, see page 416.**

COLLEGE OF INSURANCE
NEW YORK, NEW YORK

General Independent, comprehensive, coed **Entrance** Very difficult **Setting** Urban campus **Total enrollment** 402 **Student/faculty ratio** 12:1 **Application deadline** 5/1 **Freshmen** 60% were admitted **Housing** Yes **Expenses** Tuition $13,600; Room & Board $9260 **Undergraduates** 51% women, 69% part-time, 0% Native American, 11% Hispanic, 15% black, 9% Asian American or Pacific Islander **Most Popular Recent Major** Insurance and risk management **Academic program** English as a second language, advanced placement, summer session, adult/continuing education programs **Contact** Ms. Theresa C. Marro, Director of Admissions, College of Insurance, 101 Murray Street, New York, NY 10007-2165. Telephone: 212-815-9232 or toll-free 800-356-5146. Web site: http://www.tci.edu/.

COLLEGE OF MOUNT SAINT VINCENT
RIVERDALE, NEW YORK

General Independent, comprehensive, coed **Entrance** Moderately difficult **Setting** 70-acre suburban campus **Total enrollment** 1,597 **Student/faculty ratio** 12:1 **Application deadline** Rolling **Freshmen** 68% were admitted **Housing** Yes **Expenses** Tuition $13,580; Room & Board $6430 **Undergraduates** 80% women, 23% part-time, 31% 25 or older, 22% Hispanic, 18% black, 8% Asian American or Pacific Islander **Most popular recent majors** Nursing; business administration; psychology **Academic program** Average class size 25, English as a second language, advanced placement, accelerated degree program, self-designed majors, tutorials, honors program, summer session, adult/continuing education programs, internships **Contact** Mrs. Lenore M. Mott, Dean of Admissions and Financial Aid, College of Mount Saint Vincent, 6301 Riverdale Avenue, Riverdale, NY 10471-1093. Telephone: 718-405-3268 or toll-free 800-665-CMSV. Fax: 718-549-7945. E-mail: admissns@cmsv.edu. Web site: http://www.cmsv.edu.

COLLEGE OF NEW ROCHELLE
NEW ROCHELLE, NEW YORK

General Independent, comprehensive, primarily women **Entrance** Moderately difficult **Setting** 20-acre suburban campus **Total enrollment** 7,065 **Application deadline** Rolling **Housing** Yes **Expenses** Tuition $11,100; Room & Board $5700 **Undergraduates** 85% women, 15% part-time, 13% 25 or older, 0.2% Native American, 10% Hispanic, 48% black, 1% Asian American or Pacific Islander **Most popular recent majors** Nursing; psychology; fine/studio arts **Academic program** Advanced placement, accelerated degree program, self-designed majors, tutorials, honors program, summer session, adult/continuing education programs, internships **Contact** Mrs. Kelly Getman-Crowley, Director of Admission, College of New Rochelle, 29 Castle Place, New Rochelle, NY 10805-2339. Telephone: 914-654-5452 or toll-free 800-933-5923. Fax: 914-654-5554. Web site: http://cnr.edu/.

THE COLLEGE OF SAINT ROSE
ALBANY, NEW YORK

General Independent, comprehensive, coed **Entrance** Moderately difficult **Setting** 22-acre urban campus **Total enrollment** 3,973 **Student/faculty ratio** 17:1 **Application deadline** 8/15 **Housing** Yes **Expenses** Tuition $11,719; Room & Board $5966 **Undergraduates** 71% women, 18% part-time, 33% 25 or older, 0.2% Native American, 2% Hispanic, 3% black, 1% Asian American or Pacific Islander **Academic program** Average class size 17, advanced placement, self-designed majors, summer session, adult/continuing education programs, internships **Contact** Ms. Mary Elizabeth Amico, Associate Dean of Admissions and Enrollment Services, The College of Saint Rose, 432 Western Avenue, Albany, NY 12203-1419. Telephone: 518-454-5760 or toll-free 800-637-8556. Fax: 518-451-2013. E-mail: admit@rosnet.strose.edu. Web site: http://www.strose.edu/.

COLLEGE OF STATEN ISLAND OF THE CITY UNIVERSITY OF NEW YORK
STATEN ISLAND, NEW YORK

General State and locally supported, comprehensive, coed **Entrance** Noncompetitive **Setting** 204-acre urban campus **Total enrollment** 12,040 **Student/faculty ratio** 19:1 **Application deadline** Rolling **Housing** No **Expenses** Tuition $3316 **Undergraduates** 58% women, 37% part-time, 41% 25 or older, 0.4% Native American, 8% Hispanic, 11% black, 7% Asian American or Pacific Islander **Most popular recent majors** Business administration; psychology **Academic program** Average class size 28, English as a second language, advanced placement, self-designed majors, honors program, summer session, adult/continuing education programs, internships **Contact** Mr. Earl Teasley, Director of Admissions and Recruitment, College of Staten Island of the City University of New York, 2800 Victory Boulevard, Staten Island, NY 10314-6600. Telephone: 718-982-2011. Fax: 718-982-2500. Web site: http://www.csi.cuny.edu/.

COLUMBIA COLLEGE
NEW YORK, NEW YORK

General Independent, 4-year, coed **Entrance** Most difficult **Setting** 35-acre urban campus **Total enrollment** 19,000 **Student/faculty ratio** 7:1 **Application deadline** 1/1 **Freshmen** 17% were admitted **Housing** Yes **Expenses** Tuition $22,650; Room & Board $7344 **Undergraduates** 50% women, 0% 25 or older **Most popular recent majors** English; history; political science **Academic program** English as a second language, advanced placement, self-designed majors, honors program, summer session, internships **Contact** Mr. Eric Furda, Director of Undergraduate Admissions, Columbia College, 1130 Amsterdam Avenue MC 2807, New York, NY 10027. Telephone: 212-854-2522. Fax: 212-854-1209. E-mail: ugrad-admiss@columbia.edu. Web site: http://www.columbia.edu/.

COLUMBIA UNIVERSITY, BARNARD COLLEGE
See Barnard College

COLUMBIA UNIVERSITY, COLUMBIA COLLEGE
See Columbia College

COLUMBIA UNIVERSITY, SCHOOL OF ENGINEERING AND APPLIED SCIENCE
NEW YORK, NEW YORK

General Independent, university, coed **Entrance** Most difficult **Setting** Urban campus **Total enrollment** 19,000 **Application deadline** 1/1 **Freshmen** 38% were admitted **Housing** Yes **Expenses** Tuition $22,650; Room & Board $7344 **Undergraduates** 26% women, 0% 25 or older **Most popular recent majors** Computer science; electrical/electronics engineering; mechanical engineering **Academic program** English as a second language, advanced placement, accelerated degree program, tutorials, honors program, summer session, adult/continuing education programs, internships **Contact** Mr. Eric Furda, Director of Undergraduate Admissions, Columbia University, School of Engineering and Applied Science, 1130 Amsterdam Avenue MC 2807, New York, NY 10027. Telephone: 212-854-2522. Fax: 212-854-1209. E-mail: ugrad-admiss@columbia.edu. Web site: http://www.columbia.edu/.

COLUMBIA UNIVERSITY, SCHOOL OF GENERAL STUDIES
NEW YORK, NEW YORK

General Independent, 4-year, coed **Entrance** Most difficult **Setting** 36-acre urban campus **Total enrollment** 19,000 **Student/faculty ratio** 25:1 **Application deadline** 7/15 **Housing** Yes **Expenses** Tuition $19,623; Room & Board $7300 **Undergraduates** 75% 25 or older, 0.3% Native American, 9% Hispanic, 9% black, 10% Asian American or Pacific Islander **Most popular recent majors** Literature; English; history **Academic program** English as a second language, advanced placement, accelerated degree program, self-designed majors, summer session, adult/continuing education programs, internships **Contact** Mr. Carlos A. Porro, Assistant Director of Admissions, Columbia University, School of General Studies, 2970 Broadway, New York, NY 10027. Telephone: 212-854-2772. E-mail: gs-admit@columbia.edu. Web site: http://www.columbia.edu/cu/gs/.

▶ **For more information, see page 419.**

COLUMBIA UNIVERSITY, SCHOOL OF NURSING
NEW YORK, NEW YORK

General Independent, upper-level, primarily women **Entrance** Moderately difficult **Setting** Urban campus **Total enrollment** 19,000 **Application deadline** Rolling **Housing** Yes **Expenses** Tuition $20,884; Room only $4183 **Undergraduates** 82% 25 or older **Academic program** English as a second language, advanced placement, summer session, adult/continuing education programs, internships **Contact** Mr. Joseph Tomaino, Assistant Dean of Student Services, Columbia University, School of Nursing, 630 West 168th Street, New York, NY 10032-3702. Telephone: 212-305-5756. E-mail: jt238@columbia.edu.

CONCORDIA COLLEGE
BRONXVILLE, NEW YORK

General Independent Lutheran, 4-year, coed **Entrance** Moderately difficult **Setting** 33-acre suburban campus **Total enrollment** 599 **Student/faculty ratio** 12:1 **Application deadline** 3/15 **Freshmen** 82% were admitted **Housing** Yes **Expenses** Tuition $11,990; Room & Board $5550 **Undergraduates** 57% women, 5% part-time, 18% 25 or older, 0% Native American, 5% Hispanic, 12% black, 1% Asian American or Pacific Islander **Most popular recent majors** Education; business administration **Academic program** Average class size 18, English as a second language, advanced placement, accelerated degree program, self-designed majors, honors program, adult/continuing education programs, internships **Con-**

Concordia College *(continued)*

tact Mr. Tom Weede, Dean of Enrollment Management, Concordia College, 171 White Plains Road, Bronxville, NY 10708-1998. Telephone: 914-337-9300 ext. 2155 or toll-free 800-YES-COLLEGE. Fax: 914-395-4500. E-mail: admission@concordia-ny.edu. Web site: http://www.concordia-ny.edu/.

COOPER UNION FOR THE ADVANCEMENT OF SCIENCE AND ART

NEW YORK, NEW YORK

General Independent, comprehensive, coed **Entrance** Most difficult **Setting** Urban campus **Total enrollment** 883 **Student/faculty ratio** 7:1 **Freshmen** 13% were admitted **Housing** Yes **Expenses** Room only $5600 **Undergraduates** 36% women, 1% part-time, 3% 25 or older, 0.1% Native American, 8% Hispanic, 5% black, 24% Asian American or Pacific Islander **Most popular recent majors** Art; architecture; electrical/electronics engineering **Academic program** Average class size 17, advanced placement, self-designed majors, tutorials, honors program, summer session, internships **Contact** Mr. Richard Bory, Dean of Admissions and Records and Registrar, Cooper Union for the Advancement of Science and Art, 30 Cooper Square, New York, NY 10003-7120. Telephone: 212-353-4120. Fax: 212-353-4343. E-mail: admissions@cooper.edu. Web site: http://www.cooper.edu.

CORNELL UNIVERSITY

ITHACA, NEW YORK

General Independent, university, coed **Entrance** Most difficult **Setting** 745-acre small town campus **Total enrollment** 18,428 **Student/faculty ratio** 9:1 **Application deadline** 1/1 **Freshmen** 34% were admitted **Housing** Yes **Expenses** Tuition $21,914; Room & Board $7110 **Undergraduates** 48% women, 2% 25 or older, 1% Native American, 6% Hispanic, 4% black, 17% Asian American or Pacific Islander **Most popular recent majors** Biology; economics; mechanical engineering **Academic program** English as a second language, advanced placement, accelerated degree program, self-designed majors, tutorials, honors program, summer session, internships **Contact** Ms. Nancy Meislahn, Director of Admissions, Cornell University, 410 Thurston Avenue, Ithaca, NY 14850. Telephone: 607-255-5241. Fax: 607-255-0659. E-mail: admissions_mailbox@cornell.edu. Web site: http://www.cornell.edu/.

C.W. POST CAMPUS OF LONG ISLAND UNIVERSITY

See Long Island University, C.W. Post Campus

DAEMEN COLLEGE

AMHERST, NEW YORK

General Independent, comprehensive, coed **Entrance** Moderately difficult **Setting** 35-acre suburban campus **Total enrollment** 1,914 **Student/faculty ratio** 16:1 **Application deadline** Rolling **Freshmen** 69% were admitted **Housing** Yes **Expenses** Tuition $10,980; Room & Board $5500 **Undergraduates** 72% women, 25% part-time, 30% 25 or older, 0.4% Native American, 2% Hispanic, 5% black, 2% Asian American or Pacific Islander **Most popular recent majors** Physical therapy; nursing administration; elementary education **Academic program** Advanced placement, self-designed majors, tutorials, summer session, adult/continuing education programs, internships **Contact** Ms. Maria P. Dillard, Dean of Admissions and Enrollment Management, Daemen College, 4380 Main Street, Amherst, NY 14226-3592. Telephone: 716-839-8225 or toll-free 800-462-7652 (in-state). Fax: 716-839-8516. E-mail: admissions@daemen.edu.

DARKEI NOAM RABBINICAL COLLEGE

BROOKLYN, NEW YORK

Contact Rabbi Pinchas Horowitz, Director of Admissions, Darkei Noam Rabbinical College, 2822 Avenue J, Brooklyn, NY 11219. Telephone: 718-338-6464.

DOMINICAN COLLEGE OF BLAUVELT

ORANGEBURG, NEW YORK

General Independent, comprehensive, coed **Entrance** Moderately difficult **Setting** 14-acre suburban campus **Total enrollment** 1,811 **Student/faculty ratio** 12:1 **Application deadline** Rolling **Freshmen** 74% were admitted **Housing** Yes **Expenses** Tuition $11,620; Room & Board $6950 **Undergraduates** 72% 25 or older **Most popular recent majors** Occupational therapy; education; nursing **Academic program** Average class size 20, English as a second language, advanced placement, accelerated degree program, honors program, summer session, adult/continuing education programs, internships **Contact** Ms. Colleen M. O'Connor, Director of Admissions, Dominican College of Blauvelt, 470 Western Highway, Orangeburg, NY 10962-1210. Telephone: 914-359-7800 ext. 271. Fax: 914-365-3150. E-mail: colleen.oconnor@dc.edu.

DOWLING COLLEGE

OAKDALE, NEW YORK

General Independent, comprehensive, coed **Entrance** Moderately difficult **Setting** 156-acre suburban campus **Total enrollment** 3,489 **Student/**

faculty ratio 9:1 **Application deadline** Rolling **Housing** Yes **Expenses** Tuition $12,630 **Undergraduates** 59% women, 73% part-time, 34% 25 or older **Most popular recent majors** Business administration; liberal arts and studies; education **Academic program** Average class size 17, English as a second language, advanced placement, accelerated degree program, self-designed majors, tutorials, honors program, summer session, internships **Contact** Mrs. Kate Rowe, Director of Admissions, Dowling College, Idle Hour Boulevard, Oakdale, NY 11769-1999. Telephone: 516-244-3030 or toll-free 800-DOWLING. Fax: 516-563-3827. E-mail: rowek@dowling.edu. Web site: http://www.dowling.edu/.

D'YOUVILLE COLLEGE
BUFFALO, NEW YORK

General Independent, comprehensive, coed **Entrance** Moderately difficult **Setting** 7-acre urban campus **Total enrollment** 1,832 **Student/faculty ratio** 13:1 **Application deadline** Rolling **Freshmen** 66% were admitted **Housing** Yes **Expenses** Tuition $10,040; Room & Board $4760 **Undergraduates** 75% women, 13% part-time, 34% 25 or older **Most popular recent majors** Physical therapy; occupational therapy; nursing **Academic program** Average class size 40, advanced placement, tutorials, honors program, summer session, adult/continuing education programs, internships **Contact** Mr. Ron Dannecker, Director of Admissions and Financial Aid, D'Youville College, 320 Porter Avenue, Buffalo, NY 14201-1084. Telephone: 716-881-7600 or toll-free 800-777-3921. Fax: 716-881-7790. E-mail: admiss@dyc.edu. Web site: http://www.dyc.edu/.

EASTMAN SCHOOL OF MUSIC
See University of Rochester

ELMIRA COLLEGE
ELMIRA, NEW YORK

General Independent, comprehensive, coed **Entrance** Moderately difficult **Setting** 42-acre small town campus **Total enrollment** 1,958 **Student/faculty ratio** 15:1 **Application deadline** 4/15 **Housing** Yes **Expenses** Tuition $20,276; Room & Board $6690 **Undergraduates** 69% women, 27% part-time, 4% 25 or older, 0.2% Native American, 1% Hispanic, 1% black, 0.4% Asian American or Pacific Islander **Most popular recent majors** Psychology; business administration; elementary education **Academic program** Average class size 20, English as a second language, advanced placement, accelerated degree program, self-designed majors, tutorials, summer session, adult/continuing education programs, internships **Contact** Mr. William S. Neal, Dean of Admissions, Elmira College, Office of Admissions, Elmira, NY 14901. Telephone: 607-735-1724 or toll-free 800-935-6472. Fax: 607-735-1718. E-mail: admissions@elmira.edu. Web site: http://www.elmira.edu/.

▶ **For more information, see page 428.**

EUGENE LANG COLLEGE, NEW SCHOOL FOR SOCIAL RESEARCH
NEW YORK, NEW YORK

General Independent, 4-year, coed **Entrance** Moderately difficult **Setting** 5-acre urban campus **Total enrollment** 7,179 **Student/faculty ratio** 9:1 **Application deadline** 2/1 **Freshmen** 72% were admitted **Housing** Yes **Expenses** Tuition $17,900; Room & Board $8555 **Undergraduates** 43% women, 5% 25 or older, 0.5% Native American, 13% Hispanic, 8% black, 3% Asian American or Pacific Islander **Most popular recent majors** Interdisciplinary studies; creative writing; theater arts/drama **Academic program** English as a second language, advanced placement, accelerated degree program, self-designed majors, tutorials, summer session, adult/continuing education programs, internships **Contact** Ms. Jennifer Fondiller, Director of Admissions, Eugene Lang College, New School for Social Research, 65 West 11th Street, New York, NY 10011-8601. Telephone: 212-229-5665. Fax: 212-229-5355. E-mail: lang@newschool.edu. Web site: http://www.newschool.edu/.

FASHION INSTITUTE OF TECHNOLOGY
NEW YORK, NEW YORK

General State and locally supported, comprehensive, coed **Entrance** Moderately difficult **Setting** 5-acre urban campus **Total enrollment** 11,696 **Student/faculty ratio** 14:1 **Application deadline** Rolling **Freshmen** 69% were admitted **Housing** Yes **Expenses** Tuition $2710; Room & Board $5425 **Undergraduates** 82% women, 23% part-time, 34% 25 or older, 0.2% Native American, 11% Hispanic, 9% black, 16% Asian American or Pacific Islander **Most popular recent majors** Fashion merchandising; fashion design/illustration; advertising **Academic program** English as a second language, advanced placement, summer session, adult/continuing education programs, internships **Contact** Mr. Jim Pidgeon, Director of Admissions, Fashion Institute of Technology, Seventh Avenue at 27th Street, New York, NY 10001-5992. Telephone: 212-217-7675 or toll-free 800-GOTOFIT (out-of-state). Fax: 212-217-7481. E-mail: fitinfo@sfitva.cc.fitsuny.edu. Web site: http://www.fitnyc.suny.edu/.

FIVE TOWNS COLLEGE
DIX HILLS, NEW YORK

General Independent, comprehensive, coed **Entrance** Minimally difficult **Setting** 40-acre subur-

Five Towns College *(continued)*

ban campus **Total enrollment** 584 **Student/faculty ratio** 13:1 **Application deadline** Rolling **Freshmen** 85% were admitted **Housing** Yes **Expenses** Tuition $9220; Room & Board $5554 **Undergraduates** 27% women, 3% part-time, 18% 25 or older, 0.2% Native American, 10% Hispanic, 27% black, 1% Asian American or Pacific Islander **Most popular recent majors** Business administration; music; music education **Academic program** Advanced placement, tutorials, summer session, internships **Contact** Ms. Christina Kuhl, Director of Admissions, Five Towns College, 305 North Service Road, Dix Hills, NY 11746-6055. Telephone: 516-424-7000 ext. 110. Fax: 516-424-7006. Web site: http://www.fivetowns.edu/.

► **For more information, see page 436.**

FORDHAM UNIVERSITY
NEW YORK, NEW YORK

General Independent Roman Catholic (Jesuit), university, coed **Entrance** Very difficult **Setting** 85-acre urban campus **Total enrollment** 13,668 **Student/faculty ratio** 11:1 **Application deadline** 2/1 **Freshmen** 69% were admitted **Housing** Yes **Expenses** Tuition $17,014; Room & Board $7810 **Undergraduates** 59% women, 17% part-time, 0.1% Native American, 14% Hispanic, 6% black, 4% Asian American or Pacific Islander **Most popular recent majors** Business administration; mass communications; social sciences **Academic program** Average class size 21, English as a second language, advanced placement, accelerated degree program, self-designed majors, tutorials, honors program, summer session, adult/continuing education programs, internships **Contact** Mr. John W. Buckley, Dean of Admission, Fordham University, East Fordham Road, New York, NY 10458. Telephone: 718-817-4000 or toll-free 800-FORDHAM. Fax: 718-367-9404. E-mail: ad_buckley@lars.fordham.edu. Web site: http://www.fordham.edu/.

► **For more information, see page 438.**

FRIENDS WORLD COLLEGE
See Long Island University, Southampton College, Friends World Program

HAMILTON COLLEGE
CLINTON, NEW YORK

General Independent, 4-year, coed **Entrance** Very difficult **Setting** 1,200-acre rural campus **Total enrollment** 1,716 **Student/faculty ratio** 10:1 **Application deadline** 1/15 **Freshmen** 42% were admitted **Housing** Yes **Expenses** Tuition $22,700; Room & Board $5650 **Undergraduates** 48% women, 0.3% part-time, 1% 25 or older, 0.1% Native American, 3% Hispanic, 2% black, 3% Asian American or Pacific Islander **Most popular recent majors** Economics; English; political science **Academic program** English as a second language, advanced placement, accelerated degree program, self-designed majors, tutorials, adult/continuing education programs, internships **Contact** Mr. Richard M. Fuller, Dean of Admission and Financial Aid, Hamilton College, 198 College Hill Road, Clinton, NY 13323-1296. Telephone: 315-859-4421 or toll-free 800-843-2655. Fax: 315-859-4457. E-mail: admission@hamilton.edu. Web site: http://www.hamilton.edu/.

HARTWICK COLLEGE
ONEONTA, NEW YORK

General Independent, 4-year, coed **Entrance** Moderately difficult **Setting** 425-acre small town campus **Total enrollment** 1,494 **Student/faculty ratio** 13:1 **Application deadline** 2/15 **Freshmen** 90% were admitted **Housing** Yes **Expenses** Tuition $22,235; Room & Board $5850 **Undergraduates** 53% women, 2% 25 or older, 0.3% Native American, 3% Hispanic, 4% black, 2% Asian American or Pacific Islander **Most popular recent majors** Psychology; biology; nursing **Academic program** Advanced placement, accelerated degree program, self-designed majors, tutorials, honors program, internships **Contact** Mrs. Karyl B. Clemens, Dean of Admissions, Hartwick College, Oneonta, NY 13820-4020. Telephone: 607-431-4150 or toll-free 888-HARTWICK (out-of-state). Fax: 607-431-4138. E-mail: admissions@hartwick.edu. Web site: http://www.hartwick.edu/.

HILBERT COLLEGE
HAMBURG, NEW YORK

General Independent, 4-year, coed **Entrance** Minimally difficult **Setting** 40-acre small town campus **Total enrollment** 870 **Student/faculty ratio** 20:1 **Application deadline** 9/1 **Freshmen** 100% were admitted **Housing** Yes **Expenses** Tuition $9500; Room & Board $4450 **Undergraduates** 67% women, 37% part-time, 51% 25 or older, 1% Native American, 2% Hispanic, 4% black, 0.2% Asian American or Pacific Islander **Most popular recent majors** Criminal justice/law enforcement administration; business administration; human services **Academic program** Advanced placement, tutorials, summer session, internships **Contact** Ms. Beatrice Slick, Director of Admissions, Hilbert College, 5200 South Park Avenue, Hamburg, NY 14075-1597. Telephone: 716-649-7900 ext. 244. Fax: 716-649-0702.

HOBART AND WILLIAM SMITH COLLEGES
GENEVA, NEW YORK

General Independent, 4-year, coed **Entrance** Very difficult **Setting** 200-acre small town campus **Total enrollment** 1,843 **Student/faculty ratio** 13:1 **Application deadline** 2/1 **Freshmen** 76% were admitted **Housing** Yes **Expenses** Tuition $22,380; Room & Board $6564 **Undergraduates** 53% women, 0.1% part-time, 0% 25 or older, 0.5% Native American, 4% Hispanic, 6% black, 2% Asian American or Pacific Islander **Most popular recent majors** English; economics; interdisciplinary studies **Academic program** English as a second language, advanced placement, accelerated degree program, self-designed majors, tutorials, honors program, adult/continuing education programs, internships **Contact** Ms. Mara O'Laughlin, Director of Admissions, Hobart and William Smith Colleges, Geneva, NY 14456-3397. Telephone: 315-781-3472 or toll-free 800-245-0100. Fax: 315-781-5471. E-mail: hoadm@hws.edu. Web site: http://www.hws.edu/.

HOFSTRA UNIVERSITY
HEMPSTEAD, NEW YORK

General Independent, university, coed **Entrance** Moderately difficult **Setting** 238-acre suburban campus **Total enrollment** 12,439 **Student/faculty ratio** 13:1 **Application deadline** Rolling **Freshmen** 83% were admitted **Housing** Yes **Expenses** Tuition $13,544; Room & Board $6730 **Undergraduates** 54% women, 14% part-time, 13% 25 or older, 0.3% Native American, 5% Hispanic, 6% black, 4% Asian American or Pacific Islander **Most popular recent majors** Psychology; accounting; business marketing and marketing management **Academic program** English as a second language, advanced placement, accelerated degree program, self-designed majors, tutorials, honors program, summer session, adult/continuing education programs, internships **Contact** Ms. Mary Beth Carey, Executive Dean of Enrollment Management, Hofstra University, 100 Hofstra University, Hempstead, NY 11549. Telephone: 516-463-6700 or toll-free 800-HOFSTRA. Fax: 516-560-7660. E-mail: hofstra@hofstra.edu. Web site: http://www.hofstra.edu/.

▶ **For more information, see page 450.**

HOLY TRINITY ORTHODOX SEMINARY
JORDANVILLE, NEW YORK

General Independent Russian Orthodox, 5-year, men only **Entrance** Noncompetitive **Setting** 900-acre rural campus **Total enrollment** 39 **Application deadline** 5/1 **Freshmen** 66% were admitted **Housing** Yes **Expenses** Tuition $1800; Room & Board $1800 **Undergraduates** 30% 25 or older **Academic program** Average class size 8, English as a second language, accelerated degree program, tutorials **Contact** Fr. Vladimir von Tsurikov, Secretary, Holy Trinity Orthodox Seminary, PO Box 36, Jordanville, NY 13361. Telephone: 315-858-0945. Fax: 315-858-0945. E-mail: seminary@telenet.net.

HOUGHTON COLLEGE
HOUGHTON, NEW YORK

General Independent Wesleyan, 4-year, coed **Entrance** Moderately difficult **Setting** 1,300-acre rural campus **Total enrollment** 1,411 **Student/faculty ratio** 15:1 **Application deadline** 3/1 **Freshmen** 85% were admitted **Housing** Yes **Expenses** Tuition $12,765; Room & Board $4238 **Undergraduates** 62% women, 5% part-time, 13% 25 or older, 1% Native American, 1% Hispanic, 1% black, 1% Asian American or Pacific Islander **Most popular recent majors** Elementary education; biology; psychology **Academic program** Average class size 36, English as a second language, advanced placement, tutorials, honors program, summer session, adult/continuing education programs, internships **Contact** Mr. David Mee, Director of Admissions, Houghton College, PO Box 128, Houghton, NY 14744. Telephone: 716-567-9353 or toll-free 800-777-2556. Fax: 716-567-9522. E-mail: admission@houghton.edu. Web site: http://www.houghton.edu/.

HUNTER COLLEGE OF THE CITY UNIVERSITY OF NEW YORK
NEW YORK, NEW YORK

General State and locally supported, comprehensive, coed **Entrance** Moderately difficult **Setting** Urban campus **Total enrollment** 19,689 **Student/faculty ratio** 18:1 **Application deadline** 1/15 **Freshmen** 55% were admitted **Housing** Yes **Expenses** Tuition $3329; Room only $1700 **Undergraduates** 71% women, 33% part-time, 42% 25 or older, 0.2% Native American, 22% Hispanic, 20% black, 15% Asian American or Pacific Islander **Most popular recent majors** Psychology; English; sociology **Academic program** English as a second language, advanced placement, self-designed majors, tutorials, honors program, summer session, internships **Contact** Office of Admissions, Hunter College of the City University of New York, 695 Park Avenue, New York, NY 10021-5085. Telephone: 212-772-4490. Web site: http://www.hunter.cuny.edu/.

IONA COLLEGE
NEW ROCHELLE, NEW YORK

General Independent, comprehensive, coed **Entrance** Moderately difficult **Setting** 35-acre sub-

Iona College *(continued)*

urban campus **Total enrollment** 4,897 **Student/faculty ratio** 16:1 **Application deadline** 3/15 **Freshmen** 76% were admitted **Housing** Yes **Expenses** Tuition $13,420; Room & Board $7720 **Undergraduates** 56% women, 23% part-time, 27% 25 or older, 0.03% Native American, 12% Hispanic, 16% black, 2% Asian American or Pacific Islander **Most popular recent majors** Mass communications; education; accounting **Academic program** Advanced placement, accelerated degree program, honors program, summer session, adult/continuing education programs, internships **Contact** Mr. Tom Delahunt, Director of Undergraduate Admissions, Iona College, 715 North Avenue, New Rochelle, NY 10801-1890. Telephone: 914-633-2502. Fax: 914-633-2096.

ITHACA COLLEGE
ITHACA, NEW YORK

General Independent, comprehensive, coed **Entrance** Moderately difficult **Setting** 757-acre small town campus **Total enrollment** 5,897 **Student/faculty ratio** 11:1 **Application deadline** 3/1 **Freshmen** 70% were admitted **Housing** Yes **Expenses** Tuition $16,900; Room & Board $7340 **Undergraduates** 55% women, 1% part-time, 2% 25 or older, 0.3% Native American, 3% Hispanic, 2% black, 2% Asian American or Pacific Islander **Most popular recent majors** Physical therapy; radio/television broadcasting; music **Academic program** Advanced placement, accelerated degree program, self-designed majors, tutorials, honors program, summer session, adult/continuing education programs, internships **Contact** Ms. Paula J. Mitchell, Director of Admission, Ithaca College, 100 Job Hall, Ithaca, NY 14850-7020. Telephone: 607-274-3124 or toll-free 800-429-4274. Fax: 607-274-1900. E-mail: admission@ithaca.edu. Web site: http://www.ithaca.edu/.

▶ **For more information, see page 452.**

JEWISH THEOLOGICAL SEMINARY OF AMERICA
NEW YORK, NEW YORK

General Independent Jewish, university, coed **Entrance** Very difficult **Setting** 1-acre urban campus **Total enrollment** 617 **Student/faculty ratio** 5:1 **Application deadline** 2/15 **Freshmen** 74% were admitted **Housing** Yes **Expenses** Tuition $7915; Room only $4750 **Undergraduates** 1% 25 or older, 0% Native American, 0% Hispanic, 0% black, 0% Asian American or Pacific Islander **Most popular recent majors** Biblical studies; history; philosophy **Academic program** English as a second language, advanced placement, self-designed majors, tutorials, honors program, summer session, adult/continuing education programs **Contact** Ms. Marci Harris Blumenthal, Director of Admissions, Jewish Theological Seminary of America, Room 614 Schiff, 3080 Broadway, New York, NY 10027-4649. Telephone: 212-678-8832. Fax: 212-678-8947. E-mail: mablumenthal@jtsa.edu. Web site: http://jtsa.edu/.

JOHN JAY COLLEGE OF CRIMINAL JUSTICE, THE CITY UNIVERSITY OF NEW YORK
NEW YORK, NEW YORK

General State and locally supported, comprehensive, coed **Entrance** Moderately difficult **Setting** Urban campus **Total enrollment** 11,963 **Student/faculty ratio** 18:1 **Application deadline** Rolling **Housing** No **Expenses** Tuition $3309 **Undergraduates** 35% 25 or older **Most popular recent majors** Criminal justice/law enforcement administration; public administration; forensic technology **Academic program** English as a second language, advanced placement, honors program, summer session, internships **Contact** Mr. Richard Saulnier, Acting Dean for Admissions and Registration, John Jay College of Criminal Justice, the City University of New York, 899 Tenth Avenue, New York, NY 10019-1093. Telephone: 212-237-8878.

THE JUILLIARD SCHOOL
NEW YORK, NEW YORK

General Independent, comprehensive, coed **Entrance** Most difficult **Setting** Urban campus **Total enrollment** 782 **Student/faculty ratio** 4:1 **Application deadline** 12/1 **Freshmen** 8% were admitted **Housing** Yes **Expenses** Tuition $15,000; Room & Board $6500 **Undergraduates** 50% women, 7% 25 or older, 0.2% Native American, 5% Hispanic, 12% black, 11% Asian American or Pacific Islander **Most popular recent majors** Music (piano and organ performance); stringed instruments; dance **Academic program** English as a second language, accelerated degree program, self-designed majors, tutorials, adult/continuing education programs **Contact** Ms. Mary K. Gray, Director of Admissions, The Juilliard School, 60 Lincoln Center Plaza, New York, NY 10023-6588. Telephone: 212-799-5000 ext. 223. Fax: 212-724-0263. Web site: http://www.juilliard.edu/.

KEHILATH YAKOV RABBINICAL SEMINARY
BROOKLYN, NEW YORK

General Independent religious, comprehensive, men only **Contact** Rabbi Joseph Weber, Director of Admissions, Kehilath Yakov Rabbinical Seminary, 206 Wilson Street, Brooklyn, NY 11211-7207. Telephone: 718-963-1212. Fax: 718-387-8586.

KEUKA COLLEGE
KEUKA PARK, NEW YORK

General Independent, 4-year, coed, affiliated with American Baptist Churches in the U.S.A. **Entrance** Moderately difficult **Setting** 173-acre rural campus **Total enrollment** 832 **Student/faculty ratio** 11:1 **Application deadline** Rolling **Freshmen** 80% were admitted **Housing** Yes **Expenses** Tuition $11,400; Room & Board $5524 **Undergraduates** 74% women, 5% part-time, 16% 25 or older, 0.5% Native American, 2% Hispanic, 2% black, 1% Asian American or Pacific Islander **Most popular recent majors** Occupational therapy; elementary education; business administration **Academic program** Average class size 22, advanced placement, self-designed majors, tutorials, honors program, summer session, adult/continuing education programs, internships **Contact** Ms. Katherine Waye, Director of Freshman Admissions, Keuka College, Office of Admissions, Keuka Park, NY 14478-0098. Telephone: 315-536-4411 ext. 5254 or toll-free 800-33-KEUKA. Fax: 315-536-5386. E-mail: admissions@mail.keuka.edu. Web site: http://www.keuka.edu/.

KOL YAAKOV TORAH CENTER
MONSEY, NEW YORK

General Independent Jewish, comprehensive, men only **Contact** Mr. Aaron Parry, Assistant Director of Admissions, Kol Yaakov Torah Center, 29 West Maple Avenue, Monsey, NY 10952-2954. Telephone: 914-425-3871. E-mail: horizonss@aol.com.

LABORATORY INSTITUTE OF MERCHANDISING
NEW YORK, NEW YORK

General Proprietary, 4-year, coed **Entrance** Minimally difficult **Setting** Urban campus **Total enrollment** 217 **Student/faculty ratio** 8:1 **Application deadline** Rolling **Freshmen** 82% were admitted **Housing** No **Expenses** Tuition $11,950 **Undergraduates** 95% women, 4% part-time, 1% 25 or older, 2% Native American, 17% Hispanic, 18% black, 6% Asian American or Pacific Islander **Academic program** Average class size 20, advanced placement, summer session, internships **Contact** Mr. Drew Ippolito, Director of Admissions, Laboratory Institute of Merchandising, 12 East 53rd Street, New York, NY 10022-5268. Telephone: 212-752-1530 or toll-free 800-677-1323 (out-of-state). Fax: 212-832-6708. E-mail: limcollege@usa.pipeline.com.

LEHMAN COLLEGE OF THE CITY UNIVERSITY OF NEW YORK
BRONX, NEW YORK

General State and locally supported, comprehensive, coed **Entrance** Moderately difficult **Setting** 37-acre urban campus **Total enrollment** 9,386 **Student/faculty ratio** 17:1 **Application deadline** Rolling **Housing** No **Expenses** Tuition $3320 **Undergraduates** 73% women, 38% part-time, 54% 25 or older **Most popular recent majors** Psychology; accounting; nursing **Academic program** English as a second language, advanced placement, self-designed majors, tutorials, honors program, summer session, adult/continuing education programs, internships **Contact** Ms. Norma Rosado, Coordinator of Freshman Processing, Lehman College of the City University of New York, 250 Bedford Park Boulevard West, Bronx, NY 10468-1589. Telephone: 718-960-8705. Fax: 718-960-8712.

LE MOYNE COLLEGE
SYRACUSE, NEW YORK

General Independent Roman Catholic (Jesuit), comprehensive, coed **Entrance** Moderately difficult **Setting** 151-acre suburban campus **Total enrollment** 3,131 **Student/faculty ratio** 13:1 **Application deadline** 3/1 **Freshmen** 80% were admitted **Housing** Yes **Expenses** Tuition $13,450; Room & Board $5680 **Undergraduates** 61% women, 7% part-time, 13% 25 or older, 1% Native American, 4% Hispanic, 3% black, 2% Asian American or Pacific Islander **Most popular recent majors** Psychology; business administration; English **Academic program** Average class size 21, advanced placement, accelerated degree program, tutorials, honors program, summer session, adult/continuing education programs, internships **Contact** Mr. David M. Pirani, Director of Admission, Le Moyne College, Syracuse, NY 13214-1399. Telephone: 315-445-4300 or toll-free 800-333-4733. Fax: 315-445-4711. E-mail: admsoffc@maple.lemoyne.edu. Web site: http://www.lemoyne.edu/.

▶ **For more information, see page 457.**

LIST COLLEGE OF JEWISH STUDIES
See Jewish Theological Seminary of America

LONG ISLAND UNIVERSITY, BROOKLYN CAMPUS
BROOKLYN, NEW YORK

General Independent, comprehensive, coed **Entrance** Minimally difficult **Setting** 10-acre urban campus **Total enrollment** 8,052 **Student/faculty ratio** 14:1 **Application deadline** Rolling

Long Island University, Brooklyn Campus *(continued)*

Freshmen 81% were admitted **Housing** Yes **Expenses** Tuition $14,496; Room & Board $5500 **Undergraduates** 69% women, 16% part-time, 33% 25 or older, 0.3% Native American, 15% Hispanic, 43% black, 12% Asian American or Pacific Islander **Most popular recent majors** Pharmacy; business administration; nursing **Academic program** English as a second language, advanced placement, accelerated degree program, self-designed majors, honors program, summer session, adult/continuing education programs, internships **Contact** Mr. Alan B. Chaves, Dean of Admissions, Long Island University, Brooklyn Campus, One University Plaza, Brooklyn, NY 11201-8423. Telephone: 718-488-1011 or toll-free 800-LIU-PLAN (in-state). E-mail: adm_sunday@eagle.liu.edu. Web site: http://www.liu.edu/.

LONG ISLAND UNIVERSITY, C.W. POST CAMPUS

BROOKVILLE, NEW YORK

General Independent, comprehensive, coed **Entrance** Moderately difficult **Setting** 308-acre suburban campus **Total enrollment** 8,171 **Student/faculty ratio** 9:1 **Application deadline** Rolling **Freshmen** 76% were admitted **Housing** Yes **Expenses** Tuition $14,530; Room & Board $6025 **Undergraduates** 59% women, 21% part-time, 25% 25 or older, 1% Native American, 9% Hispanic, 10% black, 2% Asian American or Pacific Islander **Most popular recent majors** Liberal arts and studies; business administration; education **Academic program** Average class size 30, English as a second language, advanced placement, accelerated degree program, self-designed majors, honors program, summer session, adult/continuing education programs, internships **Contact** Ms. Christine Natali, Director of Admissions, Long Island University, C.W. Post Campus, 720 Northern Boulevard, Brookville, NY 11548-1300. Telephone: 516-299-2413 or toll-free 800-LIU-PLAN. E-mail: admissions@collegehall.liu.edu. Web site: http://www.liunet.edu/.

LONG ISLAND UNIVERSITY, SOUTHAMPTON COLLEGE

SOUTHAMPTON, NEW YORK

General Independent, comprehensive, coed **Entrance** Moderately difficult **Setting** 110-acre rural campus **Total enrollment** 1,563 **Student/faculty ratio** 11:1 **Application deadline** Rolling **Freshmen** 75% were admitted **Housing** Yes **Expenses** Tuition $14,600; Room & Board $6850 **Undergraduates** 62% women, 8% part-time, 12% 25 or older, 1% Native American, 5% Hispanic, 5% black, 1% Asian American or Pacific Islander **Most popular recent majors** Marine biology; art; business administration **Academic program** Average class size 25, English as a second language, advanced placement, accelerated degree program, self-designed majors, tutorials, honors program, summer session, adult/continuing education programs, internships **Contact** Ms. Carol Gilbert, Director of Admissions, Long Island University, Southampton College, 239 Montauk Highway, Southampton, NY 11968-9822. Telephone: 516-283-4000 ext. 200 or toll-free 800-LIU PLAN (in-state). Fax: 516-283-4081. E-mail: sc_info@sand.liunet.edu. Web site: http://www.southampton.liunet.edu/.

LONG ISLAND UNIVERSITY, SOUTHAMPTON COLLEGE, FRIENDS WORLD PROGRAM

SOUTHAMPTON, NEW YORK

General Independent, 4-year, coed **Entrance** Noncompetitive **Setting** 110-acre rural campus **Total enrollment** 229 **Application deadline** Rolling **Freshmen** 89% were admitted **Housing** Yes **Expenses** Tuition $14,440; Room & Board $7050 **Undergraduates** 64% women, 10% 25 or older **Academic program** Average class size 15, English as a second language, advanced placement, self-designed majors, tutorials, adult/continuing education programs, internships **Contact** Mr. Jamison White, Assistant Director of Enrollment, Long Island University, Southampton College, Friends World Program, 239 Montauk Highway, Southampton, NY 11968. Telephone: 516-287-8465 or toll-free 800-LIU PLAN (out-of-state). Fax: 516-287-8463. E-mail: fw@southampton.liunet.edu. Web site: http://www.southampton.liunet.edu/academic/fr_world/program.htm/.

MACHZIKEI HADATH RABBINICAL COLLEGE

BROOKLYN, NEW YORK

General Independent religious, comprehensive, men only **Contact** Rabbi Abraham M. Lezerowitz, Director of Admissions, Machzikei Hadath Rabbinical College, 5407 Sixteenth Avenue, Brooklyn, NY 11204-1805. Telephone: 718-854-8777.

MANHATTAN COLLEGE

RIVERDALE, NEW YORK

General Independent, comprehensive, coed, affiliated with Roman Catholic Church **Entrance** Moderately difficult **Setting** 31-acre urban campus **Total enrollment** 3,076 **Student/faculty ratio** 14:1 **Application deadline** 3/1 **Freshmen** 77% were admitted **Housing** Yes **Expenses** Tuition $14,555; Room & Board $7250 **Undergraduates** 8% 25 or older **Most popular recent majors** Business marketing and marketing management; civil engineering; finance **Academic program** English as a second language, advanced placement, accelerated degree program, tutorials, honors program, summer session, adult/continuing education programs, internships **Contact** Mr. William J. Bisset Jr., Dean of Admissions and Financial Aid, Manhattan College, 4513 Manhattan College Parkway, Riverdale, NY 10471. Telephone: 718-862-7200 or toll-free 800-622-9235 (instate). Fax: 718-862-8019. E-mail: admit@manhattan.edu. Web site: http://www.manhattan.edu/.

► **For more information, see page 465.**

MANHATTAN SCHOOL OF MUSIC
NEW YORK, NEW YORK

General Independent, comprehensive, coed **Entrance** Very difficult **Setting** 1-acre urban campus **Total enrollment** 835 **Student/faculty ratio** 10:1 **Application deadline** 3/15 **Freshmen** 35% were admitted **Housing** Yes **Expenses** Tuition $17,900; Room & Board $9000 **Undergraduates** 50% women, 3% part-time, 20% 25 or older, 0.5% Native American, 4% Hispanic, 5% black, 11% Asian American or Pacific Islander **Most popular recent majors** Music (voice and choral/opera performance); music (piano and organ performance); jazz **Academic program** Average class size 15, English as a second language, advanced placement, tutorials, summer session **Contact** Ms. Lee Cioppa, Director of Admission, Manhattan School of Music, 120 Claremont Avenue, New York, NY 10027-4698. Telephone: 212-749-2802 ext. 2. Fax: 212-749-5471. E-mail: admission@msnnyc.edu. Web site: http://www.msmnyc.edu/.

MANHATTANVILLE COLLEGE
PURCHASE, NEW YORK

General Independent, comprehensive, coed **Entrance** Moderately difficult **Setting** 100-acre suburban campus **Total enrollment** 1,925 **Student/faculty ratio** 11:1 **Application deadline** 3/1 **Freshmen** 70% were admitted **Housing** Yes **Expenses** Tuition $17,300; Room & Board $8000 **Undergraduates** 69% women, 15% part-time, 4% 25 or older, 0.3% Native American, 14% Hispanic, 8% black, 6% Asian American or Pacific Islander **Most popular recent majors** Economics; business administration; political science **Academic program** English as a second language, advanced placement, accelerated degree program, self-designed majors, tutorials, honors program, summer session, adult/continuing education programs, internships **Contact** Mr. Jose Flores, Director of Admissions, Manhattanville College, 2900 Purchase Street, Purchase, NY 10577-2132. Telephone: 914-323-5124 or toll-free 800-328-4553. Fax: 914-694-1732. E-mail: admission@mville.edu. Web site: http://www.manhattanville.edu/.

MANNES COLLEGE OF MUSIC, NEW SCHOOL FOR SOCIAL RESEARCH
NEW YORK, NEW YORK

General Independent, comprehensive, coed **Entrance** Very difficult **Setting** Urban campus **Total enrollment** 7,179 **Application deadline** 7/15 **Housing** Yes **Expenses** Tuition $15,670; Room only $6500 **Undergraduates** 31% women, 11% part-time, 8% 25 or older, 0.3% Native American, 2% Hispanic, 5% black, 3% Asian American or Pacific Islander **Most popular recent majors** Stringed instruments; music (voice and choral/opera performance); music (piano and organ performance) **Academic program** English as a second language, advanced placement, accelerated degree program, summer session, adult/continuing education programs **Contact** Ms. Lisa Wright, Director of Admissions, Mannes College of Music, New School for Social Research, 150 West 85th Street, New York, NY 10024-4402. Telephone: 212-580-0210 ext. 246 or toll-free 800-292-3040 (out-of-state). Fax: 212-580-1738. Web site: http://www.newschool.edu/.

MARIST COLLEGE
POUGHKEEPSIE, NEW YORK

General Independent, comprehensive, coed **Entrance** Moderately difficult **Setting** 135-acre small town campus **Total enrollment** 4,618 **Student/faculty ratio** 15:1 **Application deadline** 3/1 **Freshmen** 60% were admitted **Housing** Yes **Expenses** Tuition $13,098; Room & Board $6772 **Undergraduates** 58% women, 11% part-time, 15% 25 or older, 0.1% Native American, 4% Hispanic, 6% black, 1% Asian American or Pacific Islander **Most popular recent majors** Mass communications; business administration; psychology **Academic program** Average class size 22, English as a second language, advanced placement, accelerated degree program, tutorials, honors program, summer session, adult/continuing education programs, internships **Contact** Mr. Sean Kaylor, Associate Director of Admissions, Marist College, 290 North Road, Poughkeepsie, NY 12601-1387. Telephone: 914-575-3226 ext. 2441 or toll-free 800-436-5483. E-mail: admissions@marist.edu. Web site: http://www.marist.edu/.

MARYMOUNT COLLEGE
TARRYTOWN, NEW YORK

General Independent, 4-year, primarily women **Entrance** Moderately difficult **Setting** 25-acre suburban campus **Total enrollment** 898 **Student/faculty ratio** 12:1 **Application deadline** 4/15

Marymount College *(continued)*

Freshmen 85% were admitted **Housing** Yes **Expenses** Tuition $13,800; Room & Board $7200 **Undergraduates** 96% women, 24% part-time, 43% 25 or older, 0.1% Native American, 13% Hispanic, 14% black, 4% Asian American or Pacific Islander **Most popular recent majors** Education; business administration; nutrition science **Academic program** English as a second language, advanced placement, self-designed majors, tutorials, honors program, summer session, adult/continuing education programs, internships **Contact** Ms. Christine G. Richard, Dean of Admissions, Marymount College, 100 Marymount Avenue, Tarrytown, NY 10591-3796. Telephone: 914-332-8295 or toll-free 800-724-4312. Fax: 914-332-4956. E-mail: admiss@mmc.marymt.edu. Web site: http://www.marymt.edu/.

▶ **For more information, see page 468.**

MARYMOUNT MANHATTAN COLLEGE
NEW YORK, NEW YORK

General Independent, 4-year, coed **Entrance** Moderately difficult **Setting** 1-acre urban campus **Total enrollment** 2,140 **Student/faculty ratio** 17:1 **Application deadline** Rolling **Freshmen** 88% were admitted **Housing** Yes **Expenses** Tuition $12,290; Room only $3182 **Undergraduates** 81% women, 35% part-time, 48% 25 or older **Most popular recent majors** Theater arts/drama; business administration; mass communications **Academic program** English as a second language, advanced placement, accelerated degree program, tutorials, honors program, summer session, adult/continuing education programs, internships **Contact** Ms. Jocelyn Williams, Associate Director of Admissions, Marymount Manhattan College, 221 East 71st Street, New York, NY 10021. Telephone: 212-517-0555 or toll-free 800-MARYMOUNT (out-of-state). E-mail: admissions@marymou.edu. Web site: http://www.marymount.mmm.edu/.

MEDAILLE COLLEGE
BUFFALO, NEW YORK

General Independent, 4-year, coed **Entrance** Minimally difficult **Setting** 13-acre urban campus **Total enrollment** 935 **Student/faculty ratio** 17:1 **Application deadline** Rolling **Housing** Yes **Expenses** Tuition $10,470; Room & Board $4900 **Undergraduates** 82% women, 23% part-time, 53% 25 or older, 1% Native American, 2% Hispanic, 17% black **Most popular recent majors** Elementary education; veterinary technology; liberal arts and studies **Academic program** Average class size 16, advanced placement, accelerated degree program, self-designed majors, tutorials, summer session, adult/continuing education programs, internships **Contact** Mrs. Jacqueline S. Matheny, Director of Enrollment Management, Medaille College, 18 Agassiz Circle, Buffalo, NY 14214-2695. Telephone: 716-884-3281 ext. 203 or toll-free 800-292-1582 (in-state). Fax: 716-884-0291.

MEDGAR EVERS COLLEGE OF THE CITY UNIVERSITY OF NEW YORK
BROOKLYN, NEW YORK

General State and locally supported, 4-year, coed **Contact** Ms. Jessica Celestine, Director of Admissions, Medgar Evers College of the City University of New York, 1650 Bedford Avenue, Brooklyn, NY 11225-2298. Telephone: 718-270-6021.

MERCY COLLEGE
DOBBS FERRY, NEW YORK

General Independent, comprehensive, coed **Entrance** Noncompetitive **Setting** 60-acre suburban campus **Total enrollment** 7,364 **Student/faculty ratio** 14:1 **Application deadline** Rolling **Housing** Yes **Expenses** Tuition $7600; Room & Board $6600 **Undergraduates** 58% 25 or older **Most popular recent majors** Business administration; computer science; behavioral sciences **Academic program** English as a second language, advanced placement, accelerated degree program, self-designed majors, honors program, summer session, adult/continuing education programs, internships **Contact** Ms. Kathy O'Brien, Assistant Dean for Admissions, Mercy College, 555 Broadway, Dobbs Ferry, NY 10522-1189. Telephone: 914-674-7600 or toll-free 800-MERCY-NY. Fax: 914-674-7382. E-mail: admission@merlin.mercynet.edu. Web site: http://www.mercynet.edu.

MESIVTA OF EASTERN PARKWAY RABBINICAL SEMINARY
BROOKLYN, NEW YORK

Contact Rabbi Joseph Halberstadt, Dean, Mesivta of Eastern Parkway Rabbinical Seminary, 510 Dahill Road, Brooklyn, NY 11218-5559. Telephone: 718-438-1002.

MESIVTA TIFERETH JERUSALEM OF AMERICA
NEW YORK, NEW YORK

Contact Rabbi Fishellis, Director of Admissions, Mesivta Tifereth Jerusalem of America, 141 East Broadway, New York, NY 10002-6301. Telephone: 212-964-2830.

MESIVTA TORAH VODAATH SEMINARY
BROOKLYN, NEW YORK

Contact Rabbi A. Braun, Director of Admissions, Mesivta Torah Vodaath Seminary, 425 East Ninth Street, Brooklyn, NY 11218-5209. Telephone: 718-941-8000.

MIRRER YESHIVA
BROOKLYN, NEW YORK

Contact Director of Admissions, Mirrer Yeshiva, 1795 Ocean Parkway, Brooklyn, NY 11223-2010. Telephone: 718-645-0536.

MOLLOY COLLEGE
ROCKVILLE CENTRE, NEW YORK

General Independent, comprehensive, coed **Entrance** Moderately difficult **Setting** 25-acre suburban campus **Total enrollment** 2,297 **Student/faculty ratio** 10:1 **Application deadline** Rolling **Freshmen** 73% were admitted **Housing** No **Expenses** Tuition $10,400 **Undergraduates** 82% women, 31% part-time, 44% 25 or older, 0.3% Native American, 5% Hispanic, 10% black, 3% Asian American or Pacific Islander **Most popular recent majors** Nursing; psychology; social work **Academic program** Average class size 30, English as a second language, advanced placement, self-designed majors, tutorials, summer session, adult/continuing education programs, internships **Contact** Mrs. Linda Finley Albanese, Director of Admissions, Molloy College, 1000 Hempstead Avenue, Rockville Centre, NY 11571-5002. Telephone: 516-678-5000 ext. 240 or toll-free 888-4MOLLOY.

MOUNT SAINT MARY COLLEGE
NEWBURGH, NEW YORK

General Independent, comprehensive, coed **Entrance** Moderately difficult **Setting** 72-acre suburban campus **Total enrollment** 2,077 **Student/faculty ratio** 16:1 **Application deadline** Rolling **Freshmen** 87% were admitted **Housing** Yes **Expenses** Tuition $10,200; Room & Board $5250 **Undergraduates** 69% women, 25% part-time, 35% 25 or older **Most popular recent majors** Business administration; English; accounting **Academic program** Advanced placement, accelerated degree program, self-designed majors, tutorials, honors program, summer session, adult/continuing education programs, internships **Contact** Mr. J. Randall Ognibene, Director of Admissions, Mount Saint Mary College, 330 Powell Avenue, Newburgh, NY 12550-3494. Telephone: 914-569-3248 or toll-free 888-937-6762. Fax: 914-562-6762. E-mail: ogrady@msmc.edu. Web site: http://www.msmc.edu/.

NAZARETH COLLEGE OF ROCHESTER
ROCHESTER, NEW YORK

General Independent, comprehensive, coed **Entrance** Moderately difficult **Setting** 75-acre suburban campus **Total enrollment** 2,782 **Student/faculty ratio** 13:1 **Application deadline** 3/1 **Freshmen** 73% were admitted **Housing** Yes **Expenses** Tuition $12,985; Room & Board $5985 **Undergraduates** 76% women, 14% part-time, 30% 25 or older, 0.3% Native American, 2% Hispanic, 3% black, 1% Asian American or Pacific Islander **Most popular recent majors** Education; psychology; business administration **Academic program** Advanced placement, accelerated degree program, honors program, summer session, adult/continuing education programs, internships **Contact** Mr. Thomas K. DaRin, Dean of Admissions, Nazareth College of Rochester, 4245 East Avenue, Rochester, NY 14618-3790. Telephone: 716-389-2860 or toll-free 800-462-3944 (in-state). Fax: 716-389-2826. E-mail: admissions@naz.edu. Web site: http://www.naz.edu/.

NEW SCHOOL BACHELOR OF ARTS, NEW SCHOOL FOR SOCIAL RESEARCH
NEW YORK, NEW YORK

General Independent, upper-level, coed **Entrance** Moderately difficult **Setting** Urban campus **Total enrollment** 7,179 **Application deadline** 8/1 **Freshmen** 71% were admitted **Housing** Yes **Expenses** Tuition $14,420; Room only $6035 **Undergraduates** 70% 25 or older, 1% Native American, 7% Hispanic, 10% black, 2% Asian American or Pacific Islander **Academic program** English as a second language, advanced placement, accelerated degree program, self-designed majors, tutorials, summer session, adult/continuing education programs, internships **Contact** Ms. Gerianne Brusati, Director of Educational Advising and Admissions, New School Bachelor of Arts, New School for Social Research, 66 West 12th Street, New York, NY 10011-8603. Telephone: 212-229-5630. E-mail: admissions@dialnsa.edu. Web site: http://www.newschool.edu/.

NEW SCHOOL FOR SOCIAL RESEARCH, EUGENE LANG COLLEGE
See Eugene Lang College, New School for Social Research

NEW SCHOOL FOR SOCIAL RESEARCH, MANNES COLLEGE OF MUSIC
See Mannes College of Music, New School for Social Research

New School Bachelor of Arts, New School for Social Research *(continued)*

NEW SCHOOL FOR SOCIAL RESEARCH, PARSONS SCHOOL OF DESIGN

See Parsons School of Design, New School for Social Research

NEW YORK INSTITUTE OF TECHNOLOGY
OLD WESTBURY, NEW YORK

General Independent, comprehensive, coed **Entrance** Moderately difficult **Setting** 1,050-acre suburban campus **Total enrollment** 8,982 **Student/faculty ratio** 16:1 **Application deadline** Rolling **Housing** Yes **Expenses** Tuition $10,630; Room & Board $6280 **Undergraduates** 35% women, 28% part-time, 40% 25 or older, 0.3% Native American, 9% Hispanic, 16% black, 11% Asian American or Pacific Islander **Most popular recent majors** Architectural engineering technology; business administration; mass communications **Academic program** Average class size 25, English as a second language, advanced placement, accelerated degree program, self-designed majors, tutorials, honors program, summer session, adult/continuing education programs, internships **Contact** Ms. Doreen Meyer, Director of Financial Aid, New York Institute of Technology, PO Box 8000, Old Westbury, NY 11568-8000. Telephone: 516-686-7680 or toll-free 800-345-NYIT. Fax: 516-686-7613. E-mail: admissions@iris.nyit.edu. Web site: http://www.nyit.edu/.

NEW YORK SCHOOL OF INTERIOR DESIGN
NEW YORK, NEW YORK

General Independent, comprehensive, coed **Entrance** Moderately difficult **Setting** Urban campus **Total enrollment** 625 **Student/faculty ratio** 12:1 **Application deadline** Rolling **Freshmen** 71% were admitted **Housing** No **Expenses** Tuition $12,670 **Undergraduates** 62% 25 or older **Academic program** Average class size 15, English as a second language, advanced placement, tutorials, summer session, internships **Contact** Ms. Lara Ellis, Admissions Associate, New York School of Interior Design, 170 East 70th Street, New York, NY 10021-5110. Telephone: 212-472-1500 ext. 23 or toll-free 800-336-9743. Fax: 212-472-1867. E-mail: admissions@nysid.edu. Web site: http://www.nysid.edu/.

NEW YORK STATE COLLEGE OF CERAMICS

See Alfred University

NEW YORK UNIVERSITY
NEW YORK, NEW YORK

General Independent, university, coed **Entrance** Most difficult **Setting** 28-acre urban campus **Total enrollment** 36,684 **Student/faculty ratio** 12:1 **Application deadline** 1/15 **Freshmen** 40% were admitted **Housing** Yes **Expenses** Tuition $21,730; Room & Board $8170 **Undergraduates** 59% women, 14% part-time, 0.2% Native American, 9% Hispanic, 9% black, 20% Asian American or Pacific Islander **Most popular recent majors** Business administration; theater arts/drama; social sciences **Academic program** Average class size 25, English as a second language, advanced placement, self-designed majors, tutorials, honors program, summer session, adult/continuing education programs, internships **Contact** Mr. Richard Avitabile, Director of Admissions, New York University, 22 Washington Square North, New York, NY 10012-1019. Telephone: 212-998-4500. Fax: 212-995-4902. E-mail: nyuadmit@uccvm.nyc.edu. Web site: http://www.nyu.edu/.

▶ **For more information, see page 482.**

NIAGARA UNIVERSITY
NIAGARA FALLS, NEW YORK

General Independent, comprehensive, coed **Entrance** Moderately difficult **Setting** 160-acre suburban campus **Total enrollment** 3,079 **Student/faculty ratio** 16:1 **Application deadline** 8/1 **Freshmen** 86% were admitted **Housing** Yes **Expenses** Tuition $12,890; Room & Board $5658 **Undergraduates** 61% women, 9% part-time, 15% 25 or older, 1% Native American, 2% Hispanic, 4% black, 1% Asian American or Pacific Islander **Most popular recent majors** Business administration; travel-tourism management; social sciences **Academic program** English as a second language, advanced placement, accelerated degree program, tutorials, honors program, summer session, adult/continuing education programs, internships **Contact** Ms. Christine M. McDermott, Associate Director of Admissions, Niagara University, Niagara University, NY 14109. Telephone: 716-286-8700 ext. 8715 or toll-free 800-462-2111. Fax: 716-286-8733. E-mail: admissions@niagara.edu/. Web site: http://www.niagara.edu/.

▶ **For more information, see page 483.**

NYACK COLLEGE
NYACK, NEW YORK

General Independent, comprehensive, coed, affiliated with The Christian and Missionary Alliance **Entrance** Moderately difficult **Setting** 102-acre suburban campus **Total enrollment** 1,433 **Student/faculty ratio** 25:1 **Application deadline** 9/11 **Freshmen** 70% were admitted **Housing** Yes **Expenses** Tuition $11,100; Room & Board $4860 **Undergraduates** 56% women, 6% part-time, 33% 25 or older, 0.2% Native American, 12% Hispanic, 18% black, 8% Asian American or Pacific Islander **Most popular recent majors** Elementary education; psychology; business administration **Academic program** Average class size 45, English as a second language, advanced placement, summer session, adult/continuing education programs, internships **Contact** Mr. Miguel A. Sanchez, Director of Admissions, Nyack College, One South Boulevard, Nyack, NY 10960-3698. Telephone: 914-358-1710 ext. 350 or toll-free 800-33-NYACK. Fax: 914-358-3047. E-mail: enroll@nyack.edu. Web site: http://www.nyackcollege.edu/.

OHR HAMEIR THEOLOGICAL SEMINARY

PEEKSKILL, NEW YORK

Contact Rabbi M. Z. Weisverg, Director of Admissions, Ohr Hameir Theological Seminary, Furnace Woods Road, Peekskill, NY 10566. Telephone: 914-736-1500.

OHR SOMAYACH/JOSEPH TANENBAUM EDUCATIONAL CENTER

MONSEY, NEW YORK

Contact Rabbi Avrohom Braun, Dean of Students, Ohr Somayach/Joseph Tanenbaum Educational Center, PO Box 334, Monsey, NY 10952-0334. Telephone: 914-425-1370 ext. 22.

PACE UNIVERSITY

NEW YORK, NEW YORK

General Independent, university, coed **Entrance** Moderately difficult **Total enrollment** 13,317 **Student/faculty ratio** 11:1 **Application deadline** 8/15 **Housing** Yes **Expenses** Tuition $13,820; Room & Board $6100 **Undergraduates** 61% women, 27% part-time, 27% 25 or older, 0.2% Native American, 11% Hispanic, 14% black, 12% Asian American or Pacific Islander **Most popular recent majors** Accounting; finance; computer science **Academic program** Average class size 22, English as a second language, advanced placement, accelerated degree program, tutorials, honors program, summer session, adult/continuing education programs, internships **Contact** Mr. Richard Alvarez, Director of Admission for New York City Campus, Pace University, Pace Plaza, New York, NY 10038. Telephone: 212-346-1225 or toll-free 800-874-7223. Fax: 212-346-1040. E-mail: infoctr@ny2.pace.edu. Web site: http://www.pace.edu/.

▶ **For more information, see page 491.**

PACE UNIVERSITY, PLEASANTVILLE/BRIARCLIFF CAMPUS

See Pace University

PACE UNIVERSITY, WHITE PLAINS CAMPUS

See Pace University

PARSONS SCHOOL OF DESIGN, NEW SCHOOL FOR SOCIAL RESEARCH

NEW YORK, NEW YORK

General Independent, comprehensive, coed **Entrance** Very difficult **Setting** 2-acre urban campus **Total enrollment** 7,179 **Student/faculty ratio** 14:1 **Application deadline** Rolling **Freshmen** 50% were admitted **Housing** Yes **Expenses** Tuition $18,540; Room & Board $8555 **Undergraduates** 72% women, 6% part-time, 17% 25 or older, 0.2% Native American, 8% Hispanic, 3% black, 17% Asian American or Pacific Islander **Most popular recent majors** Fashion design/illustration; graphic design/commercial art/illustration **Academic program** English as a second language, advanced placement, summer session, adult/continuing education programs, internships **Contact** Ms. Nadine M. Bourgeois, Director of Admissions, Parsons School of Design, New School for Social Research, 66 Fifth Avenue, New York, NY 10011-8878. Telephone: 212-229-8910 or toll-free 800-252-0852. Fax: 212-229-8975. E-mail: parsadm@newschool.edu. Web site: http://www.parsons.edu/.

PLATTSBURGH STATE UNIVERSITY OF NEW YORK

PLATTSBURGH, NEW YORK

General State-supported, comprehensive, coed **Entrance** Moderately difficult **Setting** 265-acre small town campus **Total enrollment** 5,920 **Student/faculty ratio** 18:1 **Application deadline** Rolling **Freshmen** 67% were admitted **Housing** Yes **Expenses** Tuition $3845; Room & Board $4476 **Undergraduates** 57% women, 5% part-time, 10% 25 or older, 1% Native American, 3% Hispanic, 3% black, 1% Asian American or Pacific Islander **Most popular recent majors** Elementary education; business administration; psychology **Academic program** English as a second language, advanced placement, accelerated degree program, self-designed majors, tutorials, honors program, summer session, adult/continuing education programs, internships **Contact** Mr. Richard Higgins, Director of Admissions, Plattsburgh State University of New York, 101 Broad Street, Plattsburgh, NY 12901-2681. Telephone: 518-564-2040 or toll-free 800-388-6473 (in-state). Fax: 518-564-2045. E-mail: admissions@splava.cc.plattsburgh.edu. Web site: http://www.plattsburgh.edu/.

POLYTECHNIC UNIVERSITY, BROOKLYN CAMPUS

BROOKLYN, NEW YORK

General Independent, university, coed **Entrance** Very difficult **Setting** 3-acre urban campus **Total enrollment** 2,333 **Student/faculty ratio** 14:1 **Application deadline** Rolling **Freshmen** 83% were admitted **Housing** Yes **Expenses** Tuition $19,150; Room & Board $4240 **Undergraduates** 19% 25 or older **Most popular recent majors** Electrical/electronics engineering; computer science; civil engineering **Academic program** Average class size 25, English as a second language, advanced placement, accelerated degree program, tutorials, honors program, summer session **Contact** Mr. John Steven Kerge, Dean of Admissions, Polytechnic University, Brooklyn Campus, Six Metrotech Center, Brooklyn, NY 11201-2990. Telephone: 718-260-3100 or toll-free 800-POLYTECH. Fax: 718-260-3136. E-mail: admitme@poly.edu. Web site: http://www.poly.edu/.

POLYTECHNIC UNIVERSITY, FARMINGDALE CAMPUS

FARMINGDALE, NEW YORK

General Independent, university, coed **Entrance** Very difficult **Setting** 25-acre suburban campus **Total enrollment** 649 **Student/faculty ratio** 14:1 **Application deadline** Rolling **Freshmen** 87% were admitted **Housing** Yes **Expenses** Tuition $19,150; Room & Board $4400 **Undergraduates** 10% 25 or older **Most popular recent majors** Electrical/electronics engineering; mechanical engineering; civil engineering **Academic program** Average class size 25, English as a second language, advanced placement, accelerated degree program, tutorials, honors program, summer session **Contact** Mr. John Steven Kerge, Dean of Admissions, Long Island Center, Polytechnic University, Farmingdale Campus, Route 110, Farmingdale, NY 11735-3995. Telephone: 516-755-4200 or toll-free 800-POLYTECH. Fax: 516-755-4404. E-mail: admitme@poly.edu. Web site: http://www.poly.edu/.

PRACTICAL BIBLE COLLEGE

BIBLE SCHOOL PARK, NEW YORK

General Independent religious, 4-year, coed **Entrance** Minimally difficult **Setting** 22-acre suburban campus **Total enrollment** 244 **Student/faculty ratio** 23:1 **Application deadline** Rolling **Freshmen** 99% were admitted **Housing** Yes **Expenses** Tuition $5140; Room & Board $3480 **Undergraduates** 36% women, 14% part-time, 42% 25 or older, 0% Native American, 0.4% Hispanic, 2% black, 0% Asian American or Pacific Islander **Academic program** Average class size 40, advanced placement, tutorials, summer session, adult/continuing education programs, internships **Contact** Ms. Debra Thornton, Admissions Office Assistant, Practical Bible College, PO Box 601, Bible School Park, NY 13737-0601. Telephone: 607-729-1581 ext. 406 or toll-free 800-331-4137. Fax: 607-729-2962. E-mail: debrathornton@juno.com. Web site: http://www.lakenet.org/~pbc.

PRATT INSTITUTE

BROOKLYN, NEW YORK

General Independent, comprehensive, coed **Entrance** Moderately difficult **Setting** 25-acre urban campus **Total enrollment** 3,640 **Student/faculty ratio** 12:1 **Application deadline** Rolling **Freshmen** 56% were admitted **Housing** Yes **Expenses** Tuition $17,151; Room & Board $7153 **Undergraduates** 46% women, 7% part-time, 27% 25 or older, 0.1% Native American, 8% Hispanic, 8% black, 12% Asian American or Pacific Islander **Most popular recent majors** Architecture; art **Academic program** Average class size 17, English as a second language, advanced placement, self-designed majors, summer session, internships **Contact** Ms. Judith Aaron, Vice President for Enrollment, Pratt Institute, DeKalb Hall, 200 Willoughby Avenue, Brooklyn, NY 11205-3899. Telephone: 718-636-3669 or toll-free 800-331-0834. Fax: 718-636-3670. E-mail: info@pratt.edu. Web site: http://www.pratt.edu/.

► **For more information, see page 492.**

PURCHASE COLLEGE, STATE UNIVERSITY OF NEW YORK

PURCHASE, NEW YORK

General State-supported, comprehensive, coed **Entrance** Moderately difficult **Setting** 500-acre small town campus **Total enrollment** 3,297 **Student/faculty ratio** 20:1 **Application deadline** Rolling **Freshmen** 54% were admitted **Housing** Yes **Expenses** Tuition $3879; Room & Board $5264 **Undergraduates** 57% women, 8% part-time, 18% 25 or older, 0.2% Native American, 9% Hispanic, 7% black, 3% Asian American or Pacific Islander **Most popular recent majors** Art; literature; liberal arts and studies **Academic program** Advanced placement, self-designed majors, summer session, adult/continuing education programs, internships **Contact** Ms. Betsy Immergut, Director of Admissions, Purchase College, State University of New York, 735 Anderson Hill Road, Purchase, NY 10577-1400. Telephone: 914-251-6300. E-mail: admissn@brick.purchase.edu. Web site: http://www.purchase.edu/.

QUEENS COLLEGE OF THE CITY UNIVERSITY OF NEW YORK
FLUSHING, NEW YORK

General State and locally supported, comprehensive, coed **Entrance** Moderately difficult **Setting** 76-acre urban campus **Total enrollment** 16,381 **Student/faculty ratio** 19:1 **Application deadline** 1/1 **Freshmen** 67% were admitted **Housing** No **Expenses** Tuition $3393 **Undergraduates** 61% women, 34% part-time, 25% 25 or older, 0.1% Native American, 15% Hispanic, 10% black, 16% Asian American or Pacific Islander **Most popular recent majors** Accounting; psychology; sociology **Academic program** English as a second language, advanced placement, accelerated degree program, self-designed majors, tutorials, honors program, summer session, adult/continuing education programs, internships **Contact** Undergraduate Admissions Office, Queens College of the City University of New York, 65-30 Kissena Boulevard, Flushing, NY 11367-1597. Telephone: 718-997-5600. Fax: 718-997-5617. E-mail: admissions@qc.edu. Web site: http://www.qc.edu/.

RABBINICAL ACADEMY MESIVTA RABBI CHAIM BERLIN
BROOKLYN, NEW YORK

General Independent Jewish, comprehensive, men only **Contact** Mr. Mayer Weinberger, Executive Administrator, Rabbinical Academy Mesivta Rabbi Chaim Berlin, 1605 Coney Island Avenue, Brooklyn, NY 11230-4715. Telephone: 718-377-0777.

RABBINICAL COLLEGE BETH SHRAGA
MONSEY, NEW YORK

Contact Rabbi Schiff, Director of Admissions, Rabbinical College Beth Shraga, 28 Saddle River Road, Monsey, NY 10952-3035. Telephone: 914-356-1980.

RABBINICAL COLLEGE BOBOVER YESHIVA B'NEI ZION
BROOKLYN, NEW YORK

Contact Mr. Israel Licht, Director of Admissions, Rabbinical College Bobover Yeshiva B'nei Zion, 1577 Forty-eighth Street, Brooklyn, NY 11219. Telephone: 718-438-2018.

RABBINICAL COLLEGE CH'SAN SOFER
BROOKLYN, NEW YORK

Contact Mr. William Rosenbaum, Director of Admissions, Rabbinical College Ch'san Sofer, 1876 Fiftieth Street, Brooklyn, NY 11204. Telephone: 718-236-1171.

RABBINICAL COLLEGE OF LONG ISLAND
LONG BEACH, NEW YORK

Contact Rabbi Ozer Kushmer, Director of Admissions, Rabbinical College of Long Island, 201 Magnolia Boulevard, Long Beach, NY 11561-3305. Telephone: 516-431-7414.

RABBINICAL SEMINARY ADAS YEREIM
BROOKLYN, NEW YORK

Contact Mr. Hersch Greenschweig, Director of Admissions, Rabbinical Seminary Adas Yereim, 185 Wilson Street, Brooklyn, NY 11211-7206. Telephone: 718-388-1751.

RABBINICAL SEMINARY M'KOR CHAIM
BROOKLYN, NEW YORK

Contact Rabbi Benjamin Paler, Director of Admissions, Rabbinical Seminary M'kor Chaim, 1571 Fifty-fifth Street, Brooklyn, NY 11219. Telephone: 718-851-0183.

RABBINICAL SEMINARY OF AMERICA
FOREST HILLS, NEW YORK

Contact Rabbi Abraham Semmel, Director of Admissions, Rabbinical Seminary of America, 92-15 Sixty-ninth Avenue, Forest Hills, NY 11375. Telephone: 718-268-4700.

REGENTS COLLEGE
ALBANY, NEW YORK

General Independent, 4-year, coed **Entrance** Noncompetitive **Setting** Urban campus **Total enrollment** 17,358 **Application deadline** Rolling **Housing** No **Undergraduates** 97% 25 or older, 1% Native American, 4% Hispanic, 11% black, 4% Asian American or Pacific Islander **Most popular recent majors** Liberal arts and studies; nursing; business administration **Academic program** Advanced placement, accelerated degree program, self-designed majors, adult/continuing education programs **Contact** Ms. Chari Leader, Dean of Enrollment Management, Regents College, 7 Columbia Circle, Albany, NY 12203-5159. Telephone: 518-464-8500. Fax: 518-464-8777. E-mail: rcinfo@regents.edu. Web site: http://www.regents.edu/.

▶ **For more information, see page 496.**

RENSSELAER POLYTECHNIC INSTITUTE
TROY, NEW YORK

General Independent, university, coed **Entrance** Very difficult **Setting** 260-acre suburban campus **Total enrollment** 6,356 **Student/faculty ratio** 12:1 **Application deadline** 1/1

Rensselaer Polytechnic Institute *(continued)*

Freshmen 83% were admitted **Housing** Yes **Expenses** Tuition $20,604; Room & Board $6786 **Undergraduates** 26% women, 0.3% part-time, 5% 25 or older, 0.3% Native American, 4% Hispanic, 3% black, 12% Asian American or Pacific Islander **Most popular recent majors** Mechanical engineering; electrical/electronics engineering; computer science **Academic program** English as a second language, advanced placement, accelerated degree program, self-designed majors, tutorials, honors program, summer session, adult/continuing education programs, internships **Contact** Ms. Teresa Duffy, Dean of Admissions, Rensselaer Polytechnic Institute, 110 8th Street, Troy, NY 12180-3590. Telephone: 518-276-6216 or toll-free 800-448-6562. Fax: 518-276-4072. E-mail: admissions@rpi.edu. Web site: http://www.rpi.edu/.

▶ **For more information, see page 497.**

ROBERTS WESLEYAN COLLEGE
ROCHESTER, NEW YORK

General Independent, comprehensive, coed, affiliated with Free Methodist Church of North America **Entrance** Moderately difficult **Setting** 75-acre suburban campus **Total enrollment** 1,414 **Student/faculty ratio** 14:1 **Application deadline** 2/1 **Freshmen** 91% were admitted **Housing** Yes **Expenses** Tuition $12,400; Room & Board $4260 **Undergraduates** 62% women, 9% part-time, 27% 25 or older, 1% Native American, 2% Hispanic, 4% black, 1% Asian American or Pacific Islander **Most popular recent majors** Education; nursing; business administration **Academic program** Average class size 45, English as a second language, advanced placement, tutorials, honors program, summer session, adult/continuing education programs, internships **Contact** Ms. Linda Kurtz, Director of Admissions, Roberts Wesleyan College, 2301 Westside Drive, Rochester, NY 14624-1997. Telephone: 716-594-6400 or toll-free 800-777-4RWC. Fax: 716-594-6371. Web site: http://www.roberts.edu/.

ROCHESTER INSTITUTE OF TECHNOLOGY
ROCHESTER, NEW YORK

General Independent, comprehensive, coed **Entrance** Moderately difficult **Setting** 1,300-acre suburban campus **Total enrollment** 12,352 **Student/faculty ratio** 13:1 **Application deadline** 7/1 **Freshmen** 78% were admitted **Housing** Yes **Expenses** Tuition $16,359; Room & Board $6417 **Undergraduates** 34% women, 16% part-time, 29% 25 or older, 0.4% Native American, 3% Hispanic, 4% black, 4% Asian American or Pacific Islander **Most popular recent majors** Engineering; engineering technology; graphic design/commercial art/illustration **Academic program** Average class size 30, English as a second language, advanced placement, accelerated degree program, self-designed majors, tutorials, summer session, adult/continuing education programs, internships **Contact** Mr. Daniel Shelley, Director of Admissions, Rochester Institute of Technology, 60 Lomb Memorial Drive, Rochester, NY 14623-5604. Telephone: 716-475-6631. Fax: 716-475-7424. E-mail: admissons@rit.edu. Web site: http://www.rit.edu/.

▶ **For more information, see page 501.**

RUSSELL SAGE COLLEGE
TROY, NEW YORK

General Independent, 4-year, women only **Entrance** Moderately difficult **Setting** 8-acre urban campus **Total enrollment** 1,021 **Application deadline** 8/1 **Freshmen** 95% were admitted **Housing** Yes **Expenses** Tuition $14,230; Room & Board $5760 **Undergraduates** 9% part-time, 23% 25 or older, 0.4% Native American, 3% Hispanic, 5% black, 2% Asian American or Pacific Islander **Most popular recent majors** Physical therapy; nursing; occupational therapy **Academic program** Average class size 20, English as a second language, advanced placement, accelerated degree program, self-designed majors, honors program, summer session, adult/continuing education programs, internships **Contact** Ms. Lisa Carr, Director of Admissions, Russell Sage College, 45 Ferry Street, Troy, NY 12180-4115. Telephone: 518-244-2217 or toll-free 888-VERY-SAGE (in-state), 888-VERY SAGE (out-of-state). Fax: 518-244-6880. E-mail: rscadmin@sage.edu. Web site: http://www.sage.edu/html/rsc/welcome.html.

ST. BONAVENTURE UNIVERSITY
ST. BONAVENTURE, NEW YORK

General Independent, comprehensive, coed, affiliated with Roman Catholic Church **Entrance** Moderately difficult **Setting** 600-acre small town campus **Total enrollment** 2,822 **Student/faculty ratio** 17:1 **Application deadline** 3/1 **Freshmen** 94% were admitted **Housing** Yes **Expenses** Tuition $13,100; Room & Board $5378 **Undergraduates** 51% women, 1% part-time, 3% 25 or older, 0.4% Native American, 1% Hispanic, 1% black, 1% Asian American or Pacific Islander **Most popular recent majors** Accounting; elementary education; mass communications **Academic program** Advanced placement, accelerated degree program, self-designed majors, tutorials, honors program, summer session, internships **Contact** Mr. Alexander P. Nazemetz, Director of Admissions, St. Bonaventure University, Post Office Box D, St. Bonaventure, NY 14778-2284. Telephone: 716-375-2400 or toll-free 800-462-

5050. Fax: 716-375-2005. E-mail: admissions@sbu.edu. Web site: http://www.sbu.edu/.

ST. FRANCIS COLLEGE
BROOKLYN HEIGHTS, NEW YORK

General Independent Roman Catholic, 4-year, coed **Entrance** Moderately difficult **Setting** 1-acre urban campus **Total enrollment** 2,136 **Student/faculty ratio** 27:1 **Application deadline** Rolling **Freshmen** 90% were admitted **Housing** Yes **Expenses** Tuition $7680; Room & Board $3150 **Undergraduates** 61% women, 24% part-time, 24% 25 or older, 0% Native American, 16% Hispanic, 23% black, 2% Asian American or Pacific Islander **Most popular recent majors** Business administration; liberal arts and studies; psychology **Academic program** Average class size 25, English as a second language, advanced placement, accelerated degree program, tutorials, honors program, summer session, adult/continuing education programs, internships **Contact** Br. George Larkin OSF, Dean of Admissions, St. Francis College, 180 Remsen Street, Brooklyn Heights, NY 11201-4398. Telephone: 718-489-5200. Fax: 718-522-1274. Web site: http://www.stfranciscollege.edu/.

▶ **For more information, see page 505.**

ST. JOHN FISHER COLLEGE
ROCHESTER, NEW YORK

General Independent, comprehensive, coed, affiliated with Roman Catholic Church **Entrance** Moderately difficult **Setting** 125-acre suburban campus **Total enrollment** 1,964 **Student/faculty ratio** 15:1 **Application deadline** Rolling **Freshmen** 77% were admitted **Housing** Yes **Expenses** Tuition $12,500; Room & Board $5700 **Undergraduates** 28% 25 or older **Most popular recent majors** Business administration; psychology; accounting **Academic program** Advanced placement, accelerated degree program, self-designed majors, tutorials, honors program, summer session, adult/continuing education programs, internships **Contact** Mr. Gerard J. Rooney, Dean of Enrollment Management, St. John Fisher College, 3690 East Avenue, Rochester, NY 14618-3597. Telephone: 716-385-8064 or toll-free 800-444-4640. Fax: 716-385-8386. E-mail: admissions@sjfc.edu. Web site: http://www.sjfc.edu/.

ST. JOHN'S UNIVERSITY
JAMAICA, NEW YORK

General Independent, university, coed, affiliated with Roman Catholic Church **Entrance** Moderately difficult **Setting** 100-acre urban campus **Total enrollment** 18,523 **Student/faculty ratio** 18:1 **Application deadline** Rolling **Freshmen** 86% were admitted **Housing** No **Expenses** Tuition $12,230 **Undergraduates** 55% women, 11% part-time, 10% 25 or older, 0.2% Native American, 12% Hispanic, 11% black, 9% Asian American or Pacific Islander **Most popular recent majors** Pharmacy; finance; criminal justice/law enforcement administration **Academic program** English as a second language, advanced placement, accelerated degree program, tutorials, honors program, summer session, adult/continuing education programs, internships **Contact** Mr. Glenn Sklarin, Associate Vice President and Dean, Office of Enrollment Management, St. John's University, 8000 Utopia Parkway, Jamaica, NY 11439. Telephone: 718-990-6240. Web site: http://www.stjohns.edu/.

ST. JOSEPH'S COLLEGE, NEW YORK
BROOKLYN, NEW YORK

General Independent, 4-year, coed **Entrance** Moderately difficult **Setting** Urban campus **Total enrollment** 1,292 **Student/faculty ratio** 12:1 **Application deadline** 8/15 **Freshmen** 66% were admitted **Housing** No **Expenses** Tuition $8326 **Undergraduates** 72% 25 or older **Most popular recent majors** Health services administration; early childhood education **Academic program** Average class size 15, advanced placement, tutorials, honors program, summer session, adult/continuing education programs, internships **Contact** Ms. Elizabeth Hughes, Director of Admissions, St. Joseph's College, New York, 245 Clinton Avenue, Brooklyn, NY 11205-3688. Telephone: 718-636-6868. Web site: http://www.sjcnj.edu/.

ST. JOSEPH'S COLLEGE, SUFFOLK CAMPUS
PATCHOGUE, NEW YORK

General Independent, comprehensive, coed **Entrance** Moderately difficult **Setting** 28-acre small town campus **Total enrollment** 2,781 **Student/faculty ratio** 13:1 **Application deadline** 8/15 **Freshmen** 76% were admitted **Housing** No **Expenses** Tuition $8917 **Undergraduates** 78% women, 32% part-time, 49% 25 or older, 0.1% Native American, 4% Hispanic, 2% black, 1% Asian American or Pacific Islander **Most popular recent majors** Elementary education; business administration; accounting **Academic program** Average class size 25, advanced placement, summer session, adult/continuing education programs, internships **Contact** Mrs. Marion E. Salgado, Director of Admissions, St. Joseph's College, Suffolk Campus, 155 West Roe Boulevard, Patchogue, NY 11772-2399. Telephone: 516-447-3200 ext. 3219. Fax: 516-447-1734. Web site: http://www.sjcny.edu/.

ST. LAWRENCE UNIVERSITY
CANTON, NEW YORK

General Independent, comprehensive, coed **Entrance** Very difficult **Setting** 1,000-acre small town campus **Total enrollment** 2,021 **Student/faculty ratio** 12:1 **Application deadline** 2/15 **Freshmen** 71% were admitted **Housing** Yes **Expenses** Tuition $21,435; Room & Board $6340 **Undergraduates** 49% women, 0.4% part-time, 1% 25 or older, 0.5% Native American, 2% Hispanic, 2% black, 2% Asian American or Pacific Islander **Most popular recent majors** English; psychology; biology **Academic program** Average class size 15, English as a second language, advanced placement, accelerated degree program, self-designed majors, tutorials, summer session, internships **Contact** Ms. Terry Lowdrey, Dean of Admissions and Financial Aid, St. Lawrence University, Canton, NY 13617-1455. Telephone: 315-229-5261 or toll-free 800-285-1856. Fax: 315-229-5502. E-mail: admiss@music.stlawu.edu. Web site: http://www.stlawu.edu/.

ST. THOMAS AQUINAS COLLEGE
SPARKILL, NEW YORK

General Independent, comprehensive, coed **Entrance** Moderately difficult **Setting** 46-acre suburban campus **Total enrollment** 2,215 **Student/faculty ratio** 17:1 **Application deadline** Rolling **Freshmen** 81% were admitted **Housing** Yes **Expenses** Tuition $10,700; Room & Board $6700 **Undergraduates** 60% women, 16% part-time, 19% 25 or older, 0% Native American, 10% Hispanic, 5% black, 4% Asian American or Pacific Islander **Most popular recent majors** Education; business administration; psychology **Academic program** Average class size 30, English as a second language, advanced placement, accelerated degree program, honors program, summer session, adult/continuing education programs, internships **Contact** Mr. Joseph L. Chillo, Executive Director of Enrollment Services, St. Thomas Aquinas College, 125 Route 340, Sparkill, NY 10976. Telephone: 914-398-4100 or toll-free 800-999-STAC. E-mail: joestacenroll@rockland.net. Web site: http://www.stac.edu/.

SARAH LAWRENCE COLLEGE
BRONXVILLE, NEW YORK

General Independent, comprehensive, coed **Entrance** Very difficult **Setting** 40-acre suburban campus **Total enrollment** 1,388 **Student/faculty ratio** 6:1 **Application deadline** 2/1 **Freshmen** 46% were admitted **Housing** Yes **Expenses** Tuition $23,076; Room & Board $7219 **Undergraduates** 1% Native American, 4% Hispanic, 5% black, 5% Asian American or Pacific Islander **Most popular recent majors** Literature; creative writing; theater arts/drama **Academic program** Advanced placement, self-designed majors, tutorials, adult/continuing education programs, internships **Contact** Ms. Thyra L. Briggs, Dean of Admissions, Sarah Lawrence College, 1 Mead Way, Bronxville, NY 10708-5999. Telephone: 914-395-2510 or toll-free 800-888-2858. Fax: 914-395-2668. E-mail: slcadmit@mail.slc.edu. Web site: http://www.slc.edu/.

SCHOOL OF VISUAL ARTS
NEW YORK, NEW YORK

General Proprietary, comprehensive, coed **Entrance** Moderately difficult **Setting** 1-acre urban campus **Total enrollment** 5,195 **Student/faculty ratio** 9:1 **Application deadline** Rolling **Freshmen** 61% were admitted **Housing** Yes **Expenses** Tuition $13,890; Room only $6100 **Undergraduates** 42% women, 11% part-time, 24% 25 or older, 1% Native American, 7% Hispanic, 3% black, 6% Asian American or Pacific Islander **Most popular recent majors** Graphic design/commercial art/illustration; photography; fine/studio arts **Academic program** Average class size 22, English as a second language, tutorials, summer session, adult/continuing education programs, internships **Contact** Mr. Richard M. Longo, Director of Admissions, School of Visual Arts, 209 East 23rd Street, New York, NY 10010-3994. Telephone: 212-592-2100 or toll-free 800-436-4204. Fax: 212-592-2116. E-mail: admissions@adm.schoolofvisualarts.edu. Web site: http://www.schoolofvisualarts.edu/.

SH'OR YOSHUV RABBINICAL COLLEGE
FAR ROCKAWAY, NEW YORK

Contact Rabbi Avrohom Halpern, Executive Director, Sh'or Yoshuv Rabbinical College, 1284 Central Avenue, Far Rockaway, NY 11691-4002. Telephone: 718-327-2048 ext. 6.

SIENA COLLEGE
LOUDONVILLE, NEW YORK

General Independent Roman Catholic, comprehensive, coed **Entrance** Moderately difficult **Setting** 155-acre suburban campus **Total enrollment** 3,011 **Student/faculty ratio** 16:1 **Application deadline** 3/1 **Freshmen** 77% were admitted **Housing** Yes **Expenses** Tuition $12,710; Room & Board $5635 **Undergraduates** 54% women, 10% part-time, 16% 25 or older, 0% Native American, 2% Hispanic, 2% black, 2% Asian American or Pacific Islander **Most popular recent majors** Business marketing and marketing management; accounting; finance **Academic program** Average class size 22, advanced placement, tutorials, honors program, summer session, adult/continuing education programs, internships **Contact** Mr. Edward Jones, Director of Admissions, Siena College, 515 Loudon Road, Loudonville, NY 12211-1462. Telephone: 518-783-2423 or toll-free 800-45SIENA. Fax: 518-783-4293. E-mail: admit@siena.edu. Web site: http://www.siena.edu/.

SKIDMORE COLLEGE
SARATOGA SPRINGS, NEW YORK

General Independent, comprehensive, coed **Entrance** Very difficult **Setting** 800-acre small town campus **Total enrollment** 2,603 **Student/faculty ratio** 11:1 **Application deadline** 2/1 **Freshmen** 48% were admitted **Housing** Yes **Expenses** Tuition $21,988; Room & Board $6354 **Undergraduates** 61% women, 11% part-time, 1% 25 or older, 0.4% Native American, 5% Hispanic, 2% black, 3% Asian American or Pacific Islander **Most popular recent majors** Business administration; English; psychology **Academic program** Average class size 17, advanced placement, accelerated degree program, self-designed majors, tutorials, honors program, summer session, internships **Contact** Ms. Mary Lou W. Bates, Director of Admissions, Skidmore College, 815 North Broadway, Saratoga Springs, NY 12866-1632. Telephone: 518-580-5570 or toll-free 800-867-6007. Fax: 518-581-7462. E-mail: admissions@scott.skidmore.edu. Web site: http://www.skidmore.edu/.

SOUTHAMPTON CAMPUS OF LONG ISLAND UNIVERSITY
See Long Island University, Southampton College

STATE UNIVERSITY OF NEW YORK AT ALBANY
ALBANY, NEW YORK

General State-supported, university, coed **Entrance** Moderately difficult **Setting** 560-acre suburban campus **Total enrollment** 16,051 **Student/faculty ratio** 16:1 **Application deadline** Rolling **Freshmen** 61% were admitted **Housing** Yes **Expenses** Tuition $4173; Room & Board $5241 **Undergraduates** 48% women, 6% part-time, 9% 25 or older, 0.3% Native American, 6% Hispanic, 8% black, 8% Asian American or Pacific Islander **Most popular recent majors** English; psychology; business administration **Academic program** English as a second language, advanced placement, self-designed majors, tutorials, honors program, summer session, internships **Contact** Ms. Sheila Mahan, Assistant Vice President for Academic Affairs, State University of New York at Albany, 1400 Washington Avenue, Albany, NY 12222-0001. Telephone: 518-442-5435. E-mail: ugadmit@safnet.albany.edu. Web site: http://www.albany.edu/.

▶ **For more information, see page 521.**

STATE UNIVERSITY OF NEW YORK AT BINGHAMTON
BINGHAMTON, NEW YORK

General State-supported, university, coed **Entrance** Very difficult **Setting** 606-acre suburban campus **Total enrollment** 12,156 **Student/faculty ratio** 17:1 **Application deadline** 2/15 **Freshmen** 42% were admitted **Housing** Yes **Expenses** Tuition $4110; Room & Board $5114 **Undergraduates** 53% women, 3% part-time, 7% 25 or older, 0.1% Native American, 6% Hispanic, 5% black, 16% Asian American or Pacific Islander **Most popular recent majors** Psychology; biology; English **Academic program** English as a second language, advanced placement, accelerated degree program, self-designed majors, tutorials, honors program, summer session, adult/continuing education programs, internships **Contact** Mr. Geoffrey D. Gould, Director of Admissions, State University of New York at Binghamton, PO Box 6001, Binghamton, NY 13902-6000. Telephone: 607-777-2171. E-mail: admit@binghamton.edu. Web site: http://www.binghamton.edu/.

▶ **For more information, see page 522.**

STATE UNIVERSITY OF NEW YORK AT BUFFALO
BUFFALO, NEW YORK

General State-supported, university, coed **Entrance** Very difficult **Setting** 1,350-acre suburban campus **Total enrollment** 23,429 **Student/faculty ratio** 13:1 **Application deadline** Rolling **Freshmen** 72% were admitted **Housing** Yes **Expenses** Tuition $4340; Room & Board $5604 **Undergraduates** 46% women, 15% part-time, 11% 25 or older, 1% Native American, 3% Hispanic, 8% black, 12% Asian American or Pacific Islander **Most popular recent majors** Business administration; social sciences; psychology **Academic program** Average class size 22, English as a second language, advanced placement, self-designed majors, tutorials, honors program, summer session, adult/continuing education programs, internships **Contact** Ms. Regina Toomey, Director of Admissions, State University of New York at Buffalo, Capen Hall, Room 17, North Campus, Buffalo, NY 14260-1660. Telephone: 716-645-6900. Fax: 716-645-6411. E-mail: ub-admissions@acsu.buffalo.edu. Web site: http://www.buffalo.edu/.

▶ **For more information, see page 523.**

STATE UNIVERSITY OF NEW YORK AT FARMINGDALE
FARMINGDALE, NEW YORK

General State-supported, 4-year, coed **Entrance** Moderately difficult **Setting** 380-acre small town campus **Total enrollment** 5,508 **Student/faculty ratio** 21:1 **Application deadline** Rolling **Freshmen** 77% were admitted **Housing** Yes **Expenses** Tuition $3950; Room & Board $5686 **Undergraduates** 43% women, 31% part-time, 34% 25 or older, 0.2% Native American, 9% Hispanic, 13% black, 4% Asian American or Pacific Islander **Most popular recent majors** Liberal arts and studies; business administration; nursing **Academic program** Average class size 30, advanced placement, summer session **Contact** Mr. Jeffrey Stein, Director of Admissions, State University of New York at Farmingdale, Route 110, Farmingdale, NY 11735. Telephone: 516-420-2200. Fax: 516-420-2633. E-mail: admissions@farmingdale.edu. Web site: http://www.farmingdale.edu/.

STATE UNIVERSITY OF NEW YORK AT NEW PALTZ
NEW PALTZ, NEW YORK

General State-supported, comprehensive, coed **Entrance** Moderately difficult **Setting** 216-acre small town campus **Total enrollment** 7,641 **Student/faculty ratio** 19:1 **Application deadline** 5/1 **Freshmen** 41% were admitted **Housing** Yes **Expenses** Tuition $3885; Room & Board $5020 **Undergraduates** 63% women, 14% part-time, 24% 25 or older, 0.3% Native American, 9% Hispanic, 7% black, 4% Asian American or Pacific Islander **Most popular recent majors** Elementary education; psychology; business administration **Academic program** Average class size 25, English as a second language, advanced placement, accelerated degree program, self-designed majors, tutorials, honors program, summer session, adult/continuing education programs, internships **Contact** Ms. Mary Claire Bauer, Director of Freshman Admissions, State University of New York at New Paltz, 75 South Manheim Boulevard, Suite 1, New Paltz, NY 12561-2499. Telephone: 914-257-3200 or toll-free 888-NEWPLTZ (in-state). Fax: 914-257-3209. E-mail: admiss@npvm.newpaltz.edu. Web site: http://www.newpaltz.edu/.

STATE UNIVERSITY OF NEW YORK AT OSWEGO
OSWEGO, NEW YORK

General State-supported, comprehensive, coed **Entrance** Moderately difficult **Setting** 696-acre small town campus **Total enrollment** 7,802 **Student/faculty ratio** 20:1 **Application deadline** Rolling **Freshmen** 57% were admitted **Housing** Yes **Expenses** Tuition $3945; Room & Board $5728 **Undergraduates** 53% women, 7% part-time, 16% 25 or older, 0.5% Native American, 3% Hispanic, 4% black, 2% Asian American or Pacific Islander **Most popular recent majors** Business administration; elementary education **Academic program** English as a second language, advanced placement, self-designed majors, tutorials, honors program, summer session, adult/continuing education programs, internships **Contact** Mr. Robert Stewart, Senior Associate Director, State University of New York at Oswego, Oswego, NY 13126. Telephone: 315-341-2250. Fax: 315-341-3260. E-mail: admiss@oswego.edu. Web site: http://www.oswego.edu/.

STATE UNIVERSITY OF NEW YORK AT STONY BROOK
STONY BROOK, NEW YORK

General State-supported, university, coed **Entrance** Very difficult **Setting** 1,100-acre small town campus **Total enrollment** 17,831 **Student/faculty ratio** 17:1 **Application deadline** Rolling **Freshmen** 57% were admitted **Housing** Yes **Expenses** Tuition $3932; Room & Board $5758 **Undergraduates** 11% 25 or older, 0.1% Native American, 8% Hispanic, 10% black, 20% Asian American or Pacific Islander **Most popular recent majors** Psychology; biology; business administration **Academic program** English as a second language, advanced placement, self-designed majors, tutorials, honors program, summer session, adult/continuing education programs, internships **Contact** Ms. Gigi Lamens, Director of Admissions, State University of New York at Stony Brook, Stony Brook, NY 11794. Telephone: 516-632-6868. E-mail: admiss@mail.upsa.sunysb.edu. Web site: http://www.sunysb.edu/www/studinfo.html.

STATE UNIVERSITY OF NEW YORK COLLEGE AT BROCKPORT
BROCKPORT, NEW YORK

General State-supported, comprehensive, coed **Entrance** Moderately difficult **Setting** 591-acre small town campus **Total enrollment** 8,492 **Student/faculty ratio** 21:1 **Application deadline** Rolling **Freshmen** 58% were admitted **Housing** Yes **Expenses** Tuition $3915; Room & Board $4960 **Undergraduates** 54% women, 16% part-time, 24% 25 or older **Most popular recent majors** Business administration; psychology; criminal justice/law enforcement administration **Academic program** Advanced placement, accelerated degree program, self-designed majors, honors program, summer session, adult/continuing education programs, internships **Contact** Mr. J. Scott Atkinson, Interim Director of Admissions, State University of New York College at Brockport, 350

New Campus Drive, Brockport, NY 14420-2997. Telephone: 716-395-2751 or toll-free 800-382-8447 (in-state). Fax: 716-395-5452. E-mail: admit@po.brockport.edu. Web site: http://www.brockport.edu/.

▶ **For more information, see page 524.**

STATE UNIVERSITY OF NEW YORK COLLEGE AT BUFFALO

BUFFALO, NEW YORK

General State-supported, comprehensive, coed **Entrance** Moderately difficult **Setting** 115-acre urban campus **Total enrollment** 10,821 **Student/faculty ratio** 12:1 **Application deadline** Rolling **Freshmen** 60% were admitted **Housing** Yes **Expenses** Tuition $3791; Room & Board $4560 **Undergraduates** 56% women, 17% part-time, 28% 25 or older, 1% Native American, 3% Hispanic, 11% black, 1% Asian American or Pacific Islander **Most popular recent majors** Business administration; elementary education; criminal justice/law enforcement administration **Academic program** English as a second language, advanced placement, tutorials, honors program, summer session, adult/continuing education programs, internships **Contact** Ms. Deborah Renzi, Director of Admissions, State University of New York College at Buffalo, 1300 Elmwood Avenue, Buffalo, NY 14222-1095. Telephone: 716-878-5519. Fax: 716-878-6100. E-mail: admissio@buffalostate.edu. Web site: http://www.buffalostate.edu/.

STATE UNIVERSITY OF NEW YORK COLLEGE AT CORTLAND

CORTLAND, NEW YORK

General State-supported, comprehensive, coed **Entrance** Moderately difficult **Setting** 191-acre small town campus **Total enrollment** 6,306 **Student/faculty ratio** 22:1 **Freshmen** 57% were admitted **Housing** Yes **Expenses** Tuition $3974; Room & Board $5300 **Undergraduates** 55% women, 4% part-time, 9% 25 or older, 0.4% Native American, 2% Hispanic, 2% black, 1% Asian American or Pacific Islander **Most popular recent majors** Elementary education; physical education; psychology **Academic program** Advanced placement, self-designed majors, tutorials, honors program, summer session, adult/continuing education programs, internships **Contact** Mr. Gradon Avery, Director of Admission, State University of New York College at Cortland, PO Box 2000, Cortland, NY 13045. Telephone: 607-753-4711. Fax: 607-753-5999. E-mail: admssn_info@snycorua.cortland.edu. Web site: http://www.cortland.edu/.

STATE UNIVERSITY OF NEW YORK COLLEGE AT FREDONIA

FREDONIA, NEW YORK

General State-supported, comprehensive, coed **Entrance** Moderately difficult **Setting** 266-acre small town campus **Total enrollment** 4,593 **Student/faculty ratio** 19:1 **Application deadline** Rolling **Freshmen** 62% were admitted **Housing** Yes **Expenses** Tuition $4075; Room & Board $4650 **Undergraduates** 57% women, 5% part-time, 9% 25 or older, 1% Native American, 2% Hispanic, 1% black, 1% Asian American or Pacific Islander **Most popular recent majors** Business administration; elementary education; music **Academic program** Advanced placement, accelerated degree program, self-designed majors, tutorials, honors program, summer session, adult/continuing education programs, internships **Contact** Mr. J. Denis Bolton, Director of Admissions, State University of New York College at Fredonia, Fredonia, NY 14063. Telephone: 716-673-3251 or toll-free 800-252-1212. Fax: 716-673-3249. E-mail: admissionsinq@fredonia.edu. Web site: http://www.fredonia.edu/.

STATE UNIVERSITY OF NEW YORK COLLEGE AT GENESEO

GENESEO, NEW YORK

General State-supported, comprehensive, coed **Entrance** Very difficult **Setting** 220-acre small town campus **Total enrollment** 5,560 **Student/faculty ratio** 19:1 **Application deadline** 2/15 **Freshmen** 54% were admitted **Housing** Yes **Expenses** Tuition $4016; Room & Board $4700 **Undergraduates** 65% women, 2% part-time, 4% 25 or older, 0.2% Native American, 3% Hispanic, 2% black, 5% Asian American or Pacific Islander **Most popular recent majors** Education; biology; psychology **Academic program** Average class size 35, English as a second language, advanced placement, tutorials, honors program, summer session, internships **Contact** Mr. Scott Hooker, Director of Admissions, State University of New York College at Geneseo, 1 College Circle, Geneseo, NY 14454-1401. Telephone: 716-245-5571. Fax: 716-245-5005. E-mail: admissions@sgenaa.cc.geneseo.edu. Web site: http://www.geneseo.edu/.

STATE UNIVERSITY OF NEW YORK COLLEGE AT OLD WESTBURY

OLD WESTBURY, NEW YORK

General State-supported, 4-year, coed **Entrance** Minimally difficult **Setting** 605-acre suburban campus **Total enrollment** 3,647 **Student/faculty ratio** 15:1 **Application deadline** Rolling **Freshmen** 90% were admitted **Housing** Yes **Expenses** Tuition $3731; Room & Board $5903 **Un-**

State University of New York College at Old Westbury *(continued)*

dergraduates 58% women, 22% part-time, 43% 25 or older, 0.1% Native American, 14% Hispanic, 30% black, 7% Asian American or Pacific Islander **Most popular recent majors** Accounting; elementary education; business administration **Academic program** Average class size 30, English as a second language, advanced placement, tutorials, summer session, internships **Contact** Ms. Olga Dunning, Assistant Director of Admissions, State University of New York College at Old Westbury, PO Box 210, Old Westbury, NY 11568-0210. Telephone: 516-876-3073. Fax: 516-876-3307. Web site: http://www.oldwestbury.edu/.

STATE UNIVERSITY OF NEW YORK COLLEGE AT ONEONTA

ONEONTA, NEW YORK

General State-supported, comprehensive, coed **Entrance** Moderately difficult **Setting** 251-acre small town campus **Total enrollment** 5,406 **Student/faculty ratio** 20:1 **Application deadline** 5/1 **Freshmen** 70% were admitted **Housing** Yes **Expenses** Tuition $3904; Room & Board $5456 **Undergraduates** 60% women, 4% part-time, 11% 25 or older, 0.3% Native American, 4% Hispanic, 2% black, 2% Asian American or Pacific Islander **Most popular recent majors** Education; business economics; psychology **Academic program** English as a second language, advanced placement, tutorials, honors program, summer session, adult/continuing education programs, internships **Contact** Mr. Roger Sullivan, Director of Admissions, State University of New York College at Oneonta, Alumni Hall 116, Oneonta, NY 13820-4015. Telephone: 607-436-2524 ext. 3001 or toll-free 800-SUNY-123. Fax: 607-436-3074. E-mail: admissions@oneonta.edu. Web site: http://www.oneonta.edu/.

STATE UNIVERSITY OF NEW YORK COLLEGE AT POTSDAM

POTSDAM, NEW YORK

General State-supported, comprehensive, coed **Entrance** Moderately difficult **Setting** 240-acre small town campus **Total enrollment** 4,038 **Student/faculty ratio** 19:1 **Application deadline** Rolling **Freshmen** 82% were admitted **Housing** Yes **Expenses** Tuition $3899; Room & Board $4900 **Undergraduates** 57% women, 4% part-time, 14% 25 or older, 2% Native American, 2% Hispanic, 3% black, 1% Asian American or Pacific Islander **Most popular recent majors** Education; music education; psychology **Academic program** Average class size 20, advanced placement, self-designed majors, tutorials, honors program, summer session, adult/continuing education programs, internships **Contact** Ms. Karen O'Brien, Director of Admissions and Financial Aid, State University of New York College at Potsdam, 44 Pierrepont Avenue, Potsdam, NY 13676. Telephone: 315-267-2180. Fax: 315-267-2163. E-mail: admissions@potsdam.edu. Web site: http://www.potsdam.edu/.

STATE UNIVERSITY OF NEW YORK COLLEGE AT PURCHASE

See Purchase College, State University of New York

STATE UNIVERSITY OF NEW YORK COLLEGE OF ENVIRONMENTAL SCIENCE AND FORESTRY

SYRACUSE, NEW YORK

General State-supported, university, coed **Entrance** Very difficult **Setting** 12-acre urban campus **Total enrollment** 1,632 **Application deadline** Rolling **Freshmen** 39% were admitted **Housing** Yes **Expenses** Tuition $3762; Room & Board $7360 **Undergraduates** 38% women, 4% part-time, 17% 25 or older, 0.2% Native American, 2% Hispanic, 3% black, 2% Asian American or Pacific Islander **Most popular recent majors** Environmental biology; environmental engineering; environmental science **Academic program** English as a second language, advanced placement, honors program, adult/continuing education programs, internships **Contact** Ms. Susan Sanford, Director of Admissions, State University of New York College of Environmental Science and Forestry, 1 Forestry Drive, Syracuse, NY 13210-2779. Telephone: 315-470-6600 or toll-free 800-777-7ESF. Fax: 315-470-6933. E-mail: esfinfo@1mailbox.syr.edu. Web site: http://www.esf.edu/.

STATE UNIVERSITY OF NEW YORK EMPIRE STATE COLLEGE

SARATOGA SPRINGS, NEW YORK

General State-supported, comprehensive, coed **Entrance** Minimally difficult **Setting** Small town campus **Total enrollment** 7,542 **Student/faculty ratio** 18:1 **Application deadline** Rolling **Housing** No **Expenses** Tuition $3545 **Undergraduates** 80% 25 or older **Academic program** Advanced placement, self-designed majors, adult/continuing education programs **Contact** Dr. Martin Thorsland, Director of Admissions and Assessment, State University of New York Empire State College, 2 Union Avenue, Saratoga Springs, NY 12866-4397. Telephone: 518-587-2100 ext. 223 or toll-free 800-847-3000 (out-of-state). Fax: 518-587-2100 ext. 326. Web site: http://www.esc.edu.

STATE UNIVERSITY OF NEW YORK HEALTH SCIENCE CENTER AT BROOKLYN
BROOKLYN, NEW YORK

General State-supported, upper-level, coed **Contact** Ms. Liliana Montano, Director of Admissions, State University of New York Health Science Center at Brooklyn, 450 Clarkson Avenue, Brooklyn, NY 11203-2098. Telephone: 718-270-3013. Fax: 718-270-7592.

STATE UNIVERSITY OF NEW YORK HEALTH SCIENCE CENTER AT SYRACUSE
SYRACUSE, NEW YORK

General State-supported, university, coed **Contact** Mrs. Noreen Neitz, Assistant Director of Admissions, State University of New York Health Science Center at Syracuse, 750 East Adams Street, Syracuse, NY 13210-2334. Telephone: 315-464-4570. Fax: 315-464-8823. Web site: http://www.hscsyr.edu/.

STATE UNIVERSITY OF NEW YORK INSTITUTE OF TECHNOLOGY AT UTICA/ROME
UTICA, NEW YORK

General State-supported, upper-level, coed **Entrance** Moderately difficult **Setting** 800-acre suburban campus **Total enrollment** 2,498 **Student/faculty ratio** 19:1 **Application deadline** Rolling **Freshmen** 81% were admitted **Housing** Yes **Expenses** Tuition $3939; Room & Board $5880 **Undergraduates** 65% 25 or older, 0.5% Native American, 3% Hispanic, 4% black, 2% Asian American or Pacific Islander **Most popular recent majors** Business administration; nursing; telecommunications **Academic program** Average class size 30, English as a second language, advanced placement, summer session, adult/continuing education programs, internships **Contact** Ms. Marybeth Lyons, Interim Director of Admissions, State University of New York Institute of Technology at Utica/Rome, PO Box 3050, Utica, NY 13504-3050. Telephone: 315-792-7500 or toll-free 800-SUNYTEC. Fax: 315-792-7837. E-mail: admissions@sunyit.edu. Web site: http://www.sunyit.edu/.

STATE UNIVERSITY OF NEW YORK MARITIME COLLEGE
THROGS NECK, NEW YORK

General State-supported, comprehensive, coed **Entrance** Moderately difficult **Setting** 56-acre suburban campus **Total enrollment** 815 **Student/faculty ratio** 14:1 **Application deadline** Rolling **Freshmen** 67% were admitted **Housing** Yes **Expenses** Tuition $4005; Room & Board $5500 **Undergraduates** 13% women, 2% part-time, 9% 25 or older, 0.2% Native American, 6% Hispanic, 6% black, 4% Asian American or Pacific Islander **Most popular recent majors** Business administration; naval architecture/marine engineering **Academic program** Average class size 25, advanced placement, tutorials, summer session, adult/continuing education programs, internships **Contact** Mr. Peter Cooney, Director of Admissions and Enrollment Management, State University of New York Maritime College, 6 Pennyfield Avenue, Fort Schuyler, Throgs Neck, NY 10465-4198. Telephone: 718-409-7220 or toll-free 800-654-1874 (in-state), 800-642-1874 (out-of-state). Fax: 718-409-7392. E-mail: edmaritime@aol.com. Web site: http://www.sunymaritime.edu/.

STERN COLLEGE FOR WOMEN
See Yeshiva University

SYRACUSE UNIVERSITY
SYRACUSE, NEW YORK

General Independent, university, coed **Entrance** Very difficult **Setting** 200-acre urban campus **Total enrollment** 14,557 **Student/faculty ratio** 12:1 **Application deadline** 1/15 **Freshmen** 60% were admitted **Housing** Yes **Expenses** Tuition $18,056; Room & Board $7760 **Undergraduates** 53% women, 1% part-time, 3% 25 or older, 0.3% Native American, 4% Hispanic, 7% black, 4% Asian American or Pacific Islander **Most popular recent majors** Information sciences/systems; psychology; architecture **Academic program** Average class size 18, English as a second language, advanced placement, accelerated degree program, self-designed majors, tutorials, honors program, summer session, adult/continuing education programs, internships **Contact** Office of Admissions, Syracuse University, 201 Tolley Administration Building, Syracuse, NY 13244-0003. Telephone: 315-443-3611. E-mail: orange@suadmin.syr.edu. Web site: http://www.syr.edu/.

SYRACUSE UNIVERSITY, UTICA COLLEGE
See Utica College of Syracuse University

TALMUDICAL INSTITUTE OF UPSTATE NEW YORK
ROCHESTER, NEW YORK

General Independent Jewish, 4-year, men only **Entrance** Noncompetitive **Setting** 1-acre urban campus **Total enrollment** 40 **Student/faculty ratio** 8:1 **Application deadline** Rolling **Freshmen** 100% were admitted **Housing** Yes **Expenses** Tuition $4250; Room & Board $3300 **Undergraduates** 0% 25 or older **Academic pro-**

Talmudical Institute of Upstate New York *(continued)*

gram Self-designed majors, tutorials **Contact** Rabbi Menachem Davidowitz, Director of Admissions, Talmudical Institute of Upstate New York, 769 Park Avenue, Rochester, NY 14607-3046. Telephone: 716-473-2810.

TALMUDICAL SEMINARY OHOLEI TORAH
BROOKLYN, NEW YORK

Contact Rabbi E. Piekarski, Director of Academic Affairs, Talmudical Seminary Oholei Torah, 667 Eastern Parkway, Brooklyn, NY 11213-3310. Telephone: 718-363-2034.

TORAH TEMIMAH TALMUDICAL SEMINARY
BROOKLYN, NEW YORK

Contact Rabbi I. Hisiger, Principal, Torah Temimah Talmudical Seminary, 555 Ocean Parkway, Brooklyn, NY 11218-5913. Telephone: 718-853-8500.

TOURO COLLEGE
NEW YORK, NEW YORK

General Independent, comprehensive, coed **Contact** Ms. Amy Harrison, Director of Admissions, Touro College, 27-33 West 23rd Street, New York, NY 10010. Telephone: 212-463-0400. Fax: 212-779-2344.

UNION COLLEGE
SCHENECTADY, NEW YORK

General Independent, comprehensive, coed **Entrance** Very difficult **Setting** 100-acre suburban campus **Total enrollment** 2,425 **Student/faculty ratio** 11:1 **Application deadline** 2/1 **Freshmen** 52% were admitted **Housing** Yes **Expenses** Tuition $22,135; Room & Board $6330 **Undergraduates** 48% women, 2% part-time, 1% 25 or older, 0.2% Native American, 3% Hispanic, 4% black, 5% Asian American or Pacific Islander **Most popular recent majors** Economics; psychology; biology **Academic program** English as a second language, advanced placement, accelerated degree program, self-designed majors, tutorials, honors program, summer session, adult/continuing education programs, internships **Contact** Mr. Daniel Lundquist, Vice President for Admissions and Financial Aid, Union College, Schenectady, NY 12308-2311. Telephone: 518-388-6112 or toll-free 888-843-6688 (in-state). Fax: 518-388-6986. E-mail: admissions@union.edu. Web site: http://www.union.edu/.

UNITED STATES MERCHANT MARINE ACADEMY
KINGS POINT, NEW YORK

General Federally supported, 4-year, coed **Entrance** Moderately difficult **Setting** 80-acre suburban campus **Total enrollment** 940 **Student/faculty ratio** 11:1 **Application deadline** 3/1 **Freshmen** 42% were admitted **Housing** Yes **Expenses** Tuition $0 **Undergraduates** 0% 25 or older **Academic program** Tutorials, honors program, internships **Contact** Capt. James M. Skinner, Director of Admissions, United States Merchant Marine Academy, Kings Point, NY 11024-1699. Telephone: 516-773-5391 or toll-free 800-732-6267 (out-of-state). Fax: 516-773-5390. E-mail: admissions@usmma.edu. Web site: http://www.usmma.edu/.

UNITED STATES MILITARY ACADEMY
WEST POINT, NEW YORK

General Federally supported, 4-year, coed **Entrance** Most difficult **Setting** 16,080-acre small town campus **Total enrollment** 4,087 **Student/faculty ratio** 7:1 **Application deadline** 3/21 **Freshmen** 14% were admitted **Housing** Yes **Expenses** Tuition $0 **Undergraduates** 14% women, 0% 25 or older, 1% Native American, 5% Hispanic, 7% black, 5% Asian American or Pacific Islander **Most popular recent majors** Mechanical engineering; geography; civil engineering **Academic program** Average class size 15, advanced placement, tutorials, summer session **Contact** Col. Michael C. Jones, Director of Admissions, United States Military Academy, 600 Thayer Road, West Point, NY 10996. Telephone: 914-938-4041. Fax: 914-938-3021. E-mail: 8dad@sunams.usma.army.mil. Web site: http://www.usma.edu/.

▶ **For more information, see page 531.**

UNITED TALMUDICAL SEMINARY
BROOKLYN, NEW YORK

Contact Mr. Philip Klein, Director of Admissions, United Talmudical Seminary, 82 Lee Avenue, Brooklyn, NY 11211-7900. Telephone: 718-963-9260.

UNIVERSITY AT ALBANY, STATE UNIVERSITY OF NEW YORK
See State University of New York at Albany

UNIVERSITY OF ROCHESTER
ROCHESTER, NEW YORK

General Independent, university, coed **Entrance** Very difficult **Setting** 534-acre suburban campus **Total enrollment** 8,451 **Student/**

faculty ratio 11:1 **Application deadline** 1/31 **Freshmen** 54% were admitted **Housing** Yes **Expenses** Tuition $21,020; Room & Board $7185 **Undergraduates** 49% women, 3% part-time, 0.3% Native American, 5% Hispanic, 7% black, 11% Asian American or Pacific Islander **Most popular recent majors** Psychology; biology; political science **Academic program** English as a second language, advanced placement, self-designed majors, honors program, summer session, internships **Contact** Mr. Wayne A. Locust, Director of Admissions, University of Rochester, PO Box 270251, Rochester, NY 14627-0001. Telephone: 716-275-3221 or toll-free 888-822-2256. Fax: 716-461-4595. E-mail: admit@macmail.cc.rochester.edu. Web site: http://www.rochester.edu/.

UNIVERSITY OF THE STATE OF NEW YORK, REGENTS COLLEGE

See Regents College

UTICA COLLEGE OF SYRACUSE UNIVERSITY

UTICA, NEW YORK

General Independent, 4-year, coed **Entrance** Moderately difficult **Setting** 132-acre suburban campus **Total enrollment** 2,018 **Student/faculty ratio** 18:1 **Application deadline** Rolling **Freshmen** 85% were admitted **Housing** Yes **Expenses** Tuition $14,912; Room & Board $5650 **Undergraduates** 64% women, 23% part-time, 30% 25 or older, 0.2% Native American, 3% Hispanic, 6% black, 2% Asian American or Pacific Islander **Most popular recent majors** Occupational therapy; business administration; criminal justice/law enforcement administration **Academic program** Average class size 25, English as a second language, advanced placement, accelerated degree program, tutorials, honors program, summer session, adult/continuing education programs, internships **Contact** Ms. Leslie North, Director of Admissions, Utica College of Syracuse University, 1600 Burrstone Road, Utica, NY 13502-4892. Telephone: 315-792-3006 or toll-free 800-782-8884. Fax: 315-792-3003. E-mail: admiss@utica.ucsu.edu.

VASSAR COLLEGE

POUGHKEEPSIE, NEW YORK

General Independent, comprehensive, coed **Entrance** Very difficult **Setting** 1,000-acre suburban campus **Total enrollment** 2,361 **Student/faculty ratio** 9:1 **Application deadline** 1/1 **Freshmen** 42% were admitted **Housing** Yes **Expenses** Tuition $22,090; Room & Board $6470 **Undergraduates** 62% women, 3% part-time, 2% 25 or older, 0.3% Native American, 5% Hispanic, 5% black, 10% Asian American or Pacific Islander **Most popular recent majors** English; political science; psychology **Academic program** Advanced placement, accelerated degree program, self-designed majors, internships **Contact** Mr. Lloyd Peterson, Director of Admissions, Vassar College, 124 Raymond Avenue, Poughkeepsie, NY 12604. Telephone: 914-437-7300. Fax: 914-437-7063. E-mail: admissions@vassar.edu. Web site: http://www.vassar.edu/.

WADHAMS HALL SEMINARY-COLLEGE

OGDENSBURG, NEW YORK

General Independent Roman Catholic, 4-year, primarily men **Entrance** Minimally difficult **Setting** 208-acre rural campus **Total enrollment** 24 **Student/faculty ratio** 1:1 **Application deadline** Rolling **Freshmen** 86% were admitted **Housing** Yes **Expenses** Tuition $4900; Room & Board $4410 **Undergraduates** 33% 25 or older, 4% Asian American or Pacific Islander **Academic program** Advanced placement, tutorials, adult/continuing education programs **Contact** Rev. Donald A. Robinson, Director of Admissions and Recruitment, Wadhams Hall Seminary-College, 6866 State Highway 37, Ogdensburg, NY 13669. Telephone: 315-393-4231 ext. 224. Fax: 315-393-4249.

WAGNER COLLEGE

STATEN ISLAND, NEW YORK

General Independent, comprehensive, coed **Entrance** Moderately difficult **Setting** 105-acre urban campus **Total enrollment** 2,036 **Student/faculty ratio** 16:1 **Application deadline** Rolling **Freshmen** 71% were admitted **Housing** Yes **Expenses** Tuition $16,000; Room & Board $6000 **Undergraduates** 59% women, 13% part-time, 9% 25 or older, 0.2% Native American, 5% Hispanic, 5% black, 4% Asian American or Pacific Islander **Most popular recent majors** Business administration; nursing; biology **Academic program** Average class size 24, English as a second language, advanced placement, accelerated degree program, self-designed majors, tutorials, honors program, summer session, internships **Contact** Mr. Angelo Araimo, Director of Admissions, Wagner College, 631 Howard Avenue, Staten Island, NY 10301. Telephone: 718-390-3411 or toll-free 800-221-1010 (out-of-state). Fax: 718-390-3105. E-mail: adm@wagner.edu. Web site: http://www.wagner.edu/.

WEBB INSTITUTE

GLEN COVE, NEW YORK

General Independent, comprehensive, primarily men **Entrance** Most difficult **Setting** 26-acre suburban campus **Total enrollment** 86 **Student/faculty ratio** 8:1 **Application deadline** 2/15 **Freshmen** 49% were admitted **Housing** Yes **Expenses** Tuition $0; Room & Board $6050 **Under-**

Webb Institute *(continued)*

graduates 17% women, 0% 25 or older, 3% Asian American or Pacific Islander **Academic program** Average class size 21, internships **Contact** Mr. William G. Murray, Director of Admissions, Webb Institute, Crescent Beach Road, Glen Cove, NY 11542-1398. Telephone: 516-671-2213. Fax: 516-674-9838. E-mail: admissions@webb-institute.edu. Web site: http://www.webb-institute.edu.

WELLS COLLEGE
AURORA, NEW YORK

General Independent, 4-year, women only **Entrance** Moderately difficult **Setting** 360-acre rural campus **Total enrollment** 322 **Student/faculty ratio** 8:1 **Application deadline** 2/15 **Freshmen** 84% were admitted **Housing** Yes **Expenses** Tuition $17,540; Room & Board $5900 **Undergraduates** 3% part-time, 11% 25 or older, 1% Native American, 4% Hispanic, 6% black, 7% Asian American or Pacific Islander **Most popular recent majors** Psychology; English; biology **Academic program** Average class size 12, advanced placement, accelerated degree program, self-designed majors, tutorials, adult/continuing education programs, internships **Contact** Ms. Susan Raith Sloan, Director of Admissions, Wells College, Aurora, NY 13026. Telephone: 315-364-3264 or toll-free 800-952-9355. Fax: 315-364-3362. E-mail: admissions@wells.edu. Web site: http://www.wells.edu/.

▶ **For more information, see page 549.**

WILLIAM SMITH COLLEGE
See Hobart and William Smith Colleges

YESHIVA COLLEGE
See Yeshiva University

YESHIVA DERECH CHAIM
BROOKLYN, NEW YORK

Contact Mr. Y. Borchardt, Administrator, Yeshiva Derech Chaim, 4907 18th Avenue, Brooklyn, NY 11218. Telephone: 718-435-9285.

YESHIVA KARLIN STOLIN
BROOKLYN, NEW YORK

General Independent Jewish, comprehensive, men only **Entrance** Very difficult **Setting** Urban campus **Total enrollment** 53 **Application deadline** Rolling **Housing** Yes **Expenses** Tuition $4200; Room & Board $2600 **Contact** Mr. Shimon Spira, Director of Admissions, Yeshiva Karlin Stolin, 1818 Fifty-fourth Street, Brooklyn, NY 11204. Telephone: 718-232-7800. Fax: 718-331-4833.

YESHIVA OF NITRA RABBINICAL COLLEGE
MOUNT KISCO, NEW YORK

Contact Mr. Ernest Schwartz, Administrator, Yeshiva of Nitra Rabbinical College, Pines Bridge Road, Mount Kisco, NY 10549. Telephone: 718-384-5460.

YESHIVA SHAAR HATORAH TALMUDIC RESEARCH INSTITUTE
KEW GARDENS, NEW YORK

Contact Rabbi Kalman Epstein, Assistant Dean, Yeshiva Shaar Hatorah Talmudic Research Institute, 83-96 117th Street, Kew Gardens, NY 11418-1469. Telephone: 718-846-1940.

YESHIVATH VIZNITZ
MONSEY, NEW YORK

Contact Rabbi Bernard Rosenfeld, Registrar, Yeshivath Viznitz, Phyllis Terrace, PO Box 446, Monsey, NY 10952. Telephone: 914-356-1010.

YESHIVATH ZICHRON MOSHE
SOUTH FALLSBURG, NEW YORK

Contact Rabbi E. Dorfman, Yeshivath Zichron Moshe, Laurel Park Road, South Fallsburg, NY 12779. Telephone: 914-434-5240.

YESHIVAT MIKDASH MELECH
BROOKLYN, NEW YORK

Contact Rabbi S. Churba, Director of Admissions, Yeshivat Mikdash Melech, 1326 Ocean Parkway, Brooklyn, NY 11230-5601. Telephone: 718-339-1090.

YESHIVA UNIVERSITY
NEW YORK, NEW YORK

General Independent, university, coed **Entrance** Moderately difficult **Setting** Urban campus **Total enrollment** 5,329 **Student/faculty ratio** 9:1 **Application deadline** 2/15 **Housing** Yes **Expenses** Tuition $14,590; Room & Board $4590 **Undergraduates** 43% women, 3% part-time, 1% 25 or older **Most popular recent majors** Psychology; biology; accounting **Academic program** English as a second language, advanced placement, self-designed majors, tutorials, honors program, summer session, internships **Contact** Mr. Michael Kranzler, Director of Undergraduate Admissions, Yeshiva University, 500 West 185th Street, New York, NY 10033-3201. Telephone: 212-960-5400 ext. 277. Fax: 212-960-0086. E-mail: yuadmit@ymail.yu.edu. Web site: http://www.yu.edu/.

YORK COLLEGE OF THE CITY UNIVERSITY OF NEW YORK
JAMAICA, NEW YORK

General State and locally supported, 4-year, coed **Entrance** Noncompetitive **Setting** 50-acre urban campus **Total enrollment** 6,030 **Student/faculty ratio** 18:1 **Application deadline** Rolling **Freshmen** 100% were admitted **Housing** No **Expenses** Tuition $3292 **Undergraduates** 70% women, 39% part-time, 62% 25 or older, 0.2% Native American, 16% Hispanic, 63% black, 10% Asian American or Pacific Islander **Most popular recent majors** Psychology; accounting; business administration **Academic program** English as a second language, advanced placement, self-designed majors, tutorials, honors program, summer session, adult/continuing education programs, internships **Contact** Ms. Sally Nelson, Director of Admissions, York College of the City University of New York, 94-20 Guy R Brewer Boulevard, Jamaica, NY 11451-0001. Telephone: 718-262-2165. Web site: http://www.york.cuny.edu/.

NORTH CAROLINA

APPALACHIAN STATE UNIVERSITY
BOONE, NORTH CAROLINA

General State-supported, comprehensive, coed **Entrance** Moderately difficult **Setting** 255-acre small town campus **Total enrollment** 12,108 **Student/faculty ratio** 15:1 **Application deadline** 4/15 **Freshmen** 72% were admitted **Housing** Yes **Expenses** Tuition $1840; Room & Board $3008 **Undergraduates** 10% 25 or older **Most popular recent majors** Business administration; mass communications; elementary education **Academic program** Average class size 30, English as a second language, advanced placement, accelerated degree program, self-designed majors, honors program, summer session, adult/continuing education programs, internships **Contact** Mr. Joe Watts, Director of Admissions/Enrollment Services, Appalachian State University, Boone, NC 28608. Telephone: 704-262-2120. Fax: 704-262-3296. E-mail: admissions@conrad.appstate.edu.

BARBER-SCOTIA COLLEGE
CONCORD, NORTH CAROLINA

General Independent, 4-year, coed, affiliated with Presbyterian Church (U.S.A.) **Entrance** Noncompetitive **Setting** 23-acre small town campus **Total enrollment** 500 **Student/faculty ratio** 14:1 **Application deadline** Rolling **Housing** Yes **Expenses** Tuition $5594; Room & Board $3220 **Undergraduates** 46% women, 4% part-time **Most popular recent majors** Sociology; business administration; biology **Academic program** Advanced placement, honors program, summer session, internships **Contact** Dr. Alexander Erwin, Acting Director of Admissions, Barber-Scotia College, 145 Cabarrus Avenue, West, Concord, NC 28025-5187. Telephone: 704-789-2900 or toll-free 800-610-0778. Fax: 704-784-3817.

BARTON COLLEGE
WILSON, NORTH CAROLINA

General Independent, 4-year, coed, affiliated with Christian Church (Disciples of Christ) **Entrance** Minimally difficult **Setting** 62-acre small town campus **Total enrollment** 1,303 **Student/faculty ratio** 12:1 **Application deadline** Rolling **Freshmen** 88% were admitted **Housing** Yes **Expenses** Tuition $10,150; Room & Board $3778 **Undergraduates** 68% women, 25% part-time, 32% 25 or older, 1% Native American, 1% Hispanic, 15% black, 1% Asian American or Pacific Islander **Most popular recent majors** Business administration; nursing; education **Academic program** Average class size 20, advanced placement, accelerated degree program, tutorials, honors program, summer session, adult/continuing education programs, internships **Contact** Mr. Anthony Britt, Dean of Enrollment Management, Barton College, College Station, Wilson, NC 27893. Telephone: 919-399-6314 or toll-free 800-345-4973. Fax: 919-237-1620. E-mail: adenton@barton.edu. Web site: http://www.barton.edu.

BELMONT ABBEY COLLEGE
BELMONT, NORTH CAROLINA

General Independent Roman Catholic, comprehensive, coed **Entrance** Moderately difficult **Setting** 650-acre small town campus **Total enrollment** 902 **Student/faculty ratio** 16:1 **Application deadline** 8/15 **Freshmen** 31% were admitted **Housing** Yes **Expenses** Tuition $11,034; Room & Board $5666 **Undergraduates** 55% women, 16% part-time, 26% 25 or older, 1% Native American, 2% Hispanic, 6% black, 1% Asian American or Pacific Islander **Most popular recent majors** Business administration; education; accounting **Academic program** Average class size 18, advanced placement, accelerated degree program, honors program, summer session, adult/continuing education programs, internships **Contact** Mr. Denis Stokes, Vice President of Enrollment Management, Belmont Abbey College, 100 Belmont-Mt. Holly Road, Belmont, NC 28012-1802. Telephone: 704-825-6665 or toll-free 888-BAC-0110. Fax: 704-825-6670. E-mail: admissions@crusador.bac.edu. Web site: http://www.bac.edu/.

BENNETT COLLEGE
GREENSBORO, NORTH CAROLINA

General Independent United Methodist, 4-year, women only **Entrance** Moderately difficult **Setting** 55-acre urban campus **Total enrollment** 617 **Application deadline** Rolling **Freshmen** 71% were admitted **Housing** Yes **Expenses** Tuition $7905; Room & Board $3525 **Undergraduates** 2% part-time, 5% 25 or older, 98% black **Most popular recent majors** Psychology; biology; business administration **Academic program** Self-designed majors, tutorials, honors program, summer session, adult/continuing education programs, internships **Contact** Ms. Linda Torrence, Director of Admissions, Bennett College, 900 East Washington Street, Greensboro, NC 27401-3239. Telephone: 910-370-8624. Web site: http://www.bennett.edu.

BREVARD COLLEGE
BREVARD, NORTH CAROLINA

General Independent United Methodist, 4-year, coed **Entrance** Minimally difficult **Setting** 120-acre small town campus **Total enrollment** 707 **Student/faculty ratio** 9:1 **Application deadline** Rolling **Freshmen** 92% were admitted **Housing** Yes **Expenses** Tuition $9900; Room & Board $4320 **Undergraduates** 41% women, 3% part-time, 5% 25 or older, 0.4% Native American, 1% Hispanic, 10% black, 0% Asian American or Pacific Islander **Most popular recent majors** Music; art; environmental science **Academic program** Average class size 19, English as a second language, advanced placement, accelerated degree program, self-designed majors, tutorials, honors program, summer session, adult/continuing education programs, internships **Contact** Ms. B. Barbara Boerner, Vice President for Admissions, Financial Aid, and Enrollment Planning, Brevard College, 400 North Broad Street, Brevard, NC 28712-3306. Telephone: 704-884-8300 or toll-free 800-527-9090. Fax: 704-884-3790. E-mail: admissions@brevard.edu. Web site: http://www.brevard.edu/.

▶ **For more information, see page 398.**

CAMPBELL UNIVERSITY
BUIES CREEK, NORTH CAROLINA

General Independent Baptist, university, coed **Entrance** Moderately difficult **Setting** 850-acre rural campus **Total enrollment** 3,359 **Student/faculty ratio** 18:1 **Application deadline** Rolling **Freshmen** 62% were admitted **Housing** Yes **Expenses** Tuition $10,003; Room & Board $3610 **Undergraduates** 55% women, 5% part-time, 18% 25 or older, 1% Native American, 3% Hispanic, 9% black, 1% Asian American or Pacific Islander **Most popular recent majors** Business administration; (pre)law; mass communications **Academic program** Average class size 25, advanced placement, accelerated degree program, tutorials, honors program, summer session, adult/continuing education programs, internships **Contact** Mr. Herbert V. Kerner Jr., Dean of Admissions, Financial Aid, and Veterans Affairs, Campbell University, PO Box 546, Buies Creek, NC 27506. Telephone: 910-893-1291 or toll-free 800-334-4111 (out-of-state). Fax: 910-893-1288. E-mail: satterfiel@mailcenter.campbell.edu. Web site: http://www.campbell.edu/.

▶ **For more information, see page 402.**

CATAWBA COLLEGE
SALISBURY, NORTH CAROLINA

General Independent, comprehensive, coed, affiliated with United Church of Christ **Entrance** Moderately difficult **Setting** 210-acre small town campus **Total enrollment** 1,307 **Student/faculty ratio** 17:1 **Application deadline** Rolling **Housing** Yes **Expenses** Tuition $11,352; Room & Board $4500 **Undergraduates** 50% women, 4% part-time, 15% 25 or older, 1% Native American, 1% Hispanic, 10% black, 0.5% Asian American or Pacific Islander **Most popular recent majors** Business administration; education; mass communications **Academic program** Average class size 20, advanced placement, self-designed majors, tutorials, honors program, summer session, adult/continuing education programs, internships **Contact** Mrs. Elaine P. Holden, Director of Admissions, Catawba College, 2300 West Innes Street, Salisbury, NC 28144-2488. Telephone: 704-637-4402 or toll-free 800-CATAWBA (out-of-state). E-mail: epholden@catawba.edu. Web site: http://www.catawba.edu/.

CHOWAN COLLEGE
MURFREESBORO, NORTH CAROLINA

General Independent Baptist, 4-year, coed **Entrance** Minimally difficult **Setting** 300-acre rural campus **Total enrollment** 755 **Student/faculty ratio** 11:1 **Application deadline** Rolling **Freshmen** 76% were admitted **Housing** Yes **Expenses** Tuition $10,760; Room & Board $4170 **Undergraduates** 41% women, 3% part-time, 10% 25 or older, 1% Native American, 3% Hispanic, 18% black, 1% Asian American or Pacific Islander **Most popular recent majors** Business administration; physical education; graphic/printing equipment **Academic program** Average class size 25, advanced placement, self-designed majors, tutorials, summer session, internships **Contact** Mrs. Austine O. Evans, Vice President for Enrollment Management, Chowan College, PO Box 1848, Murfreesboro, NC 27855. Telephone: 919-398-

6314 or toll-free 800-488-4101. Fax: 919-398-1190. E-mail: admissions@micah.chowan.edu. Web site: http://www.chowan.edu/.

▶ **For more information, see page 410.**

DAVIDSON COLLEGE
DAVIDSON, NORTH CAROLINA

General Independent Presbyterian, 4-year, coed **Entrance** Very difficult **Setting** 464-acre small town campus **Total enrollment** 1,623 **Student/faculty ratio** 11:1 **Application deadline** 1/15 **Freshmen** 36% were admitted **Housing** Yes **Expenses** Tuition $20,595; Room & Board $5918 **Undergraduates** 49% women, 0.4% 25 or older, 0.2% Native American, 2% Hispanic, 5% black, 2% Asian American or Pacific Islander **Most popular recent majors** Biology; English; history **Academic program** Advanced placement, self-designed majors, tutorials, honors program **Contact** Dr. Nancy J. Cable, Dean of Admission and Financial Aid, Davidson College, PO Box 1719, Davidson, NC 28036-1719. Telephone: 704-892-2231 or toll-free 800-768-0380. Fax: 704-892-2016. E-mail: admission@davidson.edu. Web site: http://www.davidson.edu.

▶ **For more information, see page 422.**

DUKE UNIVERSITY
DURHAM, NORTH CAROLINA

General Independent, university, coed, affiliated with United Methodist Church **Entrance** Most difficult **Setting** 8,500-acre suburban campus **Total enrollment** 11,581 **Student/faculty ratio** 11:1 **Application deadline** 1/2 **Freshmen** 30% were admitted **Housing** Yes **Expenses** Tuition $22,173; Room & Board $6853 **Undergraduates** 49% women, 0.4% part-time, 1% 25 or older, 0.2% Native American, 4% Hispanic, 8% black, 13% Asian American or Pacific Islander **Most popular recent majors** Biology; psychology; history **Academic program** English as a second language, advanced placement, accelerated degree program, self-designed majors, tutorials, honors program, summer session, adult/continuing education programs, internships **Contact** Mr. Christoph Guttentag, Director of Admissions, Duke University, Durham, NC 27708-0586. Telephone: 919-684-3214. Fax: 919-681-8941. E-mail: askduke@admiss.duke.edu. Web site: http://www.duke.edu/.

EAST CAROLINA UNIVERSITY
GREENVILLE, NORTH CAROLINA

General State-supported, university, coed **Entrance** Moderately difficult **Setting** 465-acre urban campus **Total enrollment** 18,271 **Student/faculty ratio** 19:1 **Application deadline** 3/15 **Freshmen** 77% were admitted **Housing** Yes **Expenses** Tuition $1848; Room & Board $3680 **Undergraduates** 58% women, 11% part-time, 17% 25 or older, 1% Native American, 1% Hispanic, 12% black, 2% Asian American or Pacific Islander **Most popular recent majors** Nursing; elementary education; biology **Academic program** English as a second language, advanced placement, accelerated degree program, self-designed majors, tutorials, honors program, summer session, adult/continuing education programs, internships **Contact** Dr. Thomas Powell Jr., Director of Admissions, East Carolina University, East Fifth Street, Greenville, NC 27858-4353. Telephone: 919-328-6640. Fax: 252-328-6495. Web site: http://www.ecu.edu/.

EAST COAST BIBLE COLLEGE
CHARLOTTE, NORTH CAROLINA

General Independent, 4-year, coed, affiliated with Church of God **Entrance** Minimally difficult **Setting** 100-acre urban campus **Total enrollment** 174 **Student/faculty ratio** 10:1 **Application deadline** Rolling **Freshmen** 61% were admitted **Housing** Yes **Expenses** Tuition $5180; Room & Board $2700 **Undergraduates** 44% women, 24% part-time, 37% 25 or older, 0% Native American, 1% Hispanic, 6% black, 0% Asian American or Pacific Islander **Most popular recent majors** Biblical studies; religious education; education **Academic program** Average class size 20, advanced placement, summer session, internships **Contact** Mr. H. Michael Fleming, Director of Admissions, East Coast Bible College, 6900 Wilkinson Boulevard, Charlotte, NC 28214. Telephone: 704-394-2307 ext. 13. Fax: 704-393-3689.

ELIZABETH CITY STATE UNIVERSITY
ELIZABETH CITY, NORTH CAROLINA

General State-supported, 4-year, coed **Entrance** Moderately difficult **Setting** 125-acre small town campus **Total enrollment** 2,000 **Student/faculty ratio** 16:1 **Application deadline** 8/1 **Housing** Yes **Expenses** Tuition $1720; Room & Board $3232 **Undergraduates** 21% 25 or older **Most popular recent majors** Business administration; computer science; criminal justice/law enforcement administration **Academic program** Advanced placement, honors program, summer session, adult/continuing education programs, internships **Contact** Mr. Jeff King, Director of Admissions, Elizabeth City State University, PO Box 901 ECSU, Elizabeth City, NC 27909-7806. Telephone: 919-335-3305 or toll-free 800-347-3278. Fax: 252-335-3731.

ELON COLLEGE
ELON COLLEGE, NORTH CAROLINA

General Independent, comprehensive, coed, affiliated with United Church of Christ **Entrance** Moderately difficult **Setting** 500-acre suburban campus **Total enrollment** 3,685 **Student/faculty ratio** 17:1 **Application deadline** Rolling **Freshmen** 63% were admitted **Housing** Yes **Expenses** Tuition $11,542; Room & Board $4170 **Undergraduates** 58% women, 3% part-time, 1% 25 or older, 0.1% Native American, 1% Hispanic, 6% black, 1% Asian American or Pacific Islander **Most popular recent majors** Business administration; communications; education **Academic program** Advanced placement, accelerated degree program, self-designed majors, tutorials, honors program, summer session, internships **Contact** Mrs. Nan P. Perkins, Dean of Admissions and Financial Planning, Elon College, 2700 Campus Box, Elon College, NC 27244. Telephone: 336-584-2370 or toll-free 800-334-8448. Fax: 336-538-3986. E-mail: admissns@numen.elon.edu. Web site: http://www.elon.edu/.

FAYETTEVILLE STATE UNIVERSITY
FAYETTEVILLE, NORTH CAROLINA

General State-supported, comprehensive, coed **Contact** Mr. Charles Darlington, Director of Enrollment Management, Fayetteville State University, 1200 Murchison Road, Fayetteville, NC 28301-4298. Telephone: 910-486-1371 or toll-free 800-672-6667 (in-state), 800-222-2594 (out-of-state). Fax: 910-486-6024.

GARDNER-WEBB UNIVERSITY
BOILING SPRINGS, NORTH CAROLINA

General Independent Baptist, comprehensive, coed **Entrance** Moderately difficult **Setting** 200-acre small town campus **Total enrollment** 2,932 **Student/faculty ratio** 17:1 **Application deadline** Rolling **Freshmen** 87% were admitted **Housing** Yes **Expenses** Tuition $9620; Room & Board $4630 **Undergraduates** 65% women, 21% part-time, 36% 25 or older, 0.4% Native American, 1% Hispanic, 10% black, 1% Asian American or Pacific Islander **Most popular recent majors** Business administration; education; biology **Academic program** English as a second language, advanced placement, accelerated degree program, honors program, summer session, adult/continuing education programs, internships **Contact** Mr. Ray McKay Hardee, Dean of Admissions, Gardner-Webb University, PO Box 817, Boiling Springs, NC 28017. Telephone: 704-434-4491 or toll-free 800-222-2311 (in-state). E-mail: admissions@gardner-webb.edu. Web site: http://www.gardner-webb.edu/.

▶ **For more information, see page 439.**

GREENSBORO COLLEGE
GREENSBORO, NORTH CAROLINA

General Independent United Methodist, 4-year, coed **Entrance** Moderately difficult **Setting** 40-acre urban campus **Total enrollment** 1,051 **Student/faculty ratio** 10:1 **Application deadline** Rolling **Freshmen** 75% were admitted **Housing** Yes **Expenses** Tuition $9990; Room & Board $4700 **Undergraduates** 54% women, 18% part-time, 24% 25 or older, 0.5% Native American, 2% Hispanic, 13% black, 1% Asian American or Pacific Islander **Most popular recent majors** Education; biology **Academic program** Average class size 23, advanced placement, accelerated degree program, self-designed majors, tutorials, honors program, summer session, adult/continuing education programs, internships **Contact** Mr. Randy Doss, Dean of Admissions, Greensboro College, 815 West Market Street, Greensboro, NC 27401-1875. Telephone: 910-272-7102 ext. 211 or toll-free 800-346-8226. Fax: 336-271-6634. E-mail: admissions@gborocollege.edu. Web site: http://www.gborocollege.edu/.

GUILFORD COLLEGE
GREENSBORO, NORTH CAROLINA

General Independent, 4-year, coed, affiliated with Society of Friends **Entrance** Moderately difficult **Setting** 340-acre suburban campus **Total enrollment** 1,402 **Student/faculty ratio** 15:1 **Application deadline** 2/1 **Freshmen** 81% were admitted **Housing** Yes **Expenses** Tuition $14,750; Room & Board $5270 **Undergraduates** 56% women, 11% part-time, 1% 25 or older, 1% Native American, 2% Hispanic, 8% black, 1% Asian American or Pacific Islander **Most popular recent majors** Psychology; English; business administration **Academic program** English as a second language, advanced placement, accelerated degree program, self-designed majors, tutorials, honors program, summer session, adult/continuing education programs, internships **Contact** Mr. Alton Newell, Dean of Admission, Guilford College, 5800 West Friendly Avenue, Greensboro, NC 27410-4173. Telephone: 336-316-2100 or toll-free 800-992-7759. Fax: 336-316-2954. E-mail: admission@rascal.guilford.edu. Web site: http://www.guilford.edu/.

HERITAGE BIBLE COLLEGE
DUNN, NORTH CAROLINA

General Independent Pentecostal Free Will Baptist, 4-year, coed **Entrance** Difficulty N/R **Setting** 82-acre small town campus **Total enrollment** 108 **Application deadline** Rolling **Freshmen** 100% were admitted **Housing** Yes **Expenses** Tuition $3740; Room & Board $2036 **Undergraduates**

34% women, 22% part-time, 71% 25 or older, 1% Native American, 2% Hispanic, 31% black, 1% Asian American or Pacific Islander **Academic program** Average class size 25, summer session, adult/continuing education programs, internships **Contact** Mr. Paul Williams, Director of Admissions and Registrar, Heritage Bible College, PO Box 1628, Dunn, NC 28335. Telephone: 910-892-4268. Fax: 910-891-1660.

HIGH POINT UNIVERSITY
HIGH POINT, NORTH CAROLINA

General Independent United Methodist, comprehensive, coed **Entrance** Moderately difficult **Setting** 77-acre suburban campus **Total enrollment** 2,743 **Student/faculty ratio** 17:1 **Application deadline** Rolling **Housing** Yes **Expenses** Tuition $11,120; Room & Board $5300 **Undergraduates** 61% women, 10% part-time, 21% 25 or older, 0.3% Native American, 1% Hispanic, 13% black, 1% Asian American or Pacific Islander **Most popular recent majors** Business administration; accounting; elementary education **Academic program** Average class size 20, English as a second language, advanced placement, accelerated degree program, self-designed majors, tutorials, honors program, summer session, adult/continuing education programs, internships **Contact** Mr. James L. Schlimmer, Dean of Admissions, High Point University, University Station, Montlieu Avenue, High Point, NC 27262-3598. Telephone: 336-841-9216 or toll-free 800-345-6993. Fax: 336-841-5123. E-mail: admiss@acme.highpoint.edu. Web site: http://www.highpoint.edu/.

JOHNSON C. SMITH UNIVERSITY
CHARLOTTE, NORTH CAROLINA

General Independent, 4-year, coed **Entrance** Minimally difficult **Setting** 105-acre urban campus **Total enrollment** 1,357 **Student/faculty ratio** 17:1 **Application deadline** 8/1 **Freshmen** 70% were admitted **Housing** Yes **Expenses** Tuition $8469; Room & Board $3328 **Undergraduates** 6% 25 or older **Most popular recent majors** Business administration; mass communications; computer science **Academic program** English as a second language, advanced placement, accelerated degree program, tutorials, honors program, summer session, internships **Contact** Ms. Treva Norman, Vice President for Student Affairs, Johnson C. Smith University, 100 Beatties Ford Road, Charlotte, NC 28216. Telephone: 704-378-1010 or toll-free 800-782-7303.

JOHN WESLEY COLLEGE
HIGH POINT, NORTH CAROLINA

General Independent interdenominational, 4-year, coed **Contact** Ms. Gwen W. Armstrong, Director of Admissions, John Wesley College, 2314 North Centennial Street, High Point, NC 27265-3197. Telephone: 336-889-2262 ext. 127.

LEES-MCRAE COLLEGE
BANNER ELK, NORTH CAROLINA

General Independent, 4-year, coed, affiliated with Presbyterian Church (U.S.A.) **Entrance** Minimally difficult **Setting** 400-acre rural campus **Total enrollment** 463 **Student/faculty ratio** 14:1 **Application deadline** 8/1 **Freshmen** 72% were admitted **Housing** Yes **Expenses** Tuition $10,160; Room & Board $3670 **Undergraduates** 50% women, 3% part-time, 7% 25 or older **Most popular recent majors** Business administration; education; theater arts/drama **Academic program** Average class size 30, advanced placement, accelerated degree program, self-designed majors, tutorials, honors program, summer session, adult/continuing education programs, internships **Contact** Dr. Tim C. Bailey, Dean of Admissions and Financial Aid, Lees-McRae College, PO Box 128, Banner Elk, NC 28604-0128. Telephone: 828-898-8723 or toll-free 800-280-4652. Fax: 828-898-8814. E-mail: admissions@bobcat.lmc.edu. Web site: http://www.lmc.edu/.

LENOIR-RHYNE COLLEGE
HICKORY, NORTH CAROLINA

General Independent Lutheran, comprehensive, coed **Entrance** Moderately difficult **Setting** 100-acre small town campus **Total enrollment** 1,616 **Student/faculty ratio** 13:1 **Application deadline** Rolling **Freshmen** 85% were admitted **Housing** Yes **Expenses** Tuition $12,386; Room & Board $4500 **Undergraduates** 61% women, 8% part-time, 24% 25 or older, 0.3% Native American, 1% Hispanic, 5% black, 2% Asian American or Pacific Islander **Most popular recent majors** Nursing; education; business administration **Academic program** Average class size 23, English as a second language, advanced placement, accelerated degree program, self-designed majors, honors program, summer session, adult/continuing education programs, internships **Contact** Mr. Timothy L. Jackson, Director of Admissions, Lenoir-Rhyne College, PO Box 7227, Hickory, NC 28603. Telephone: 704-328-7300 ext. 300 or toll-free 800-277-5721. Fax: 704-328-7338. E-mail: admissions@lrc.edu. Web site: http://www.lrc.edu/.

▶ **For more information, see page 458.**

LIVINGSTONE COLLEGE
SALISBURY, NORTH CAROLINA

General Independent, 4-year, coed, affiliated with African Methodist Episcopal Zion Church **Contact** Ms. Diedre Stewart, Assistant Director of Ad-

Livingstone College *(continued)*

missions, Livingstone College, 701 West Monroe Street, Salisbury, NC 28144-5298. Telephone: 704-638-5502 or toll-free 800-835-3435.

MARS HILL COLLEGE
MARS HILL, NORTH CAROLINA

General Independent Baptist, 4-year, coed **Entrance** Moderately difficult **Setting** 194-acre small town campus **Total enrollment** 1,244 **Student/faculty ratio** 13:1 **Application deadline** Rolling **Freshmen** 77% were admitted **Housing** Yes **Expenses** Tuition $8900; Room & Board $3800 **Undergraduates** 56% women, 15% part-time, 23% 25 or older, 0.5% Native American, 1% Hispanic, 8% black, 0% Asian American or Pacific Islander **Most popular recent majors** Recreation and leisure studies; education; business administration **Academic program** Average class size 20, English as a second language, advanced placement, accelerated degree program, self-designed majors, tutorials, honors program, summer session, adult/continuing education programs, internships **Contact** Ms. Kari Kirby Rochez, Director of Admissions, Mars Hill College, PO Box 370, Mars Hill, NC 28754. Telephone: 704-689-1201 or toll-free 800-543-1514. Fax: 704-689-1474. E-mail: admissions@mhc.edu. Web site: http://www.mhc.edu/.

MEREDITH COLLEGE
RALEIGH, NORTH CAROLINA

General Independent, comprehensive, women only, affiliated with Baptist Church **Entrance** Moderately difficult **Setting** 225-acre urban campus **Total enrollment** 2,552 **Student/faculty ratio** 14:1 **Application deadline** 2/15 **Freshmen** 86% were admitted **Housing** Yes **Expenses** Tuition $8490; Room & Board $3750 **Undergraduates** 17% part-time, 21% 25 or older, 0.5% Native American, 1% Hispanic, 5% black, 1% Asian American or Pacific Islander **Most popular recent majors** Business administration; child care/development; psychology **Academic program** Average class size 21, English as a second language, advanced placement, accelerated degree program, self-designed majors, tutorials, honors program, summer session, adult/continuing education programs, internships **Contact** Ms. Carol R. Kercheval, Director of Admissions, Meredith College, 3800 Hillsborough Street, Raleigh, NC 27607-5298. Telephone: 919-829-8581 or toll-free 800-MEREDITH. Fax: 919-829-2348. E-mail: admissions@meredith.edu. Web site: http://www.meredith.edu/.

▶ **For more information, see page 471.**

METHODIST COLLEGE
FAYETTEVILLE, NORTH CAROLINA

General Independent United Methodist, 4-year, coed **Entrance** Moderately difficult **Setting** 600-acre suburban campus **Total enrollment** 1,720 **Student/faculty ratio** 17:1 **Application deadline** Rolling **Freshmen** 91% were admitted **Housing** Yes **Expenses** Tuition $11,900; Room & Board $4580 **Undergraduates** 32% 25 or older, 1% Native American, 4% Hispanic, 17% black, 2% Asian American or Pacific Islander **Most popular recent majors** Business administration; education; sociology **Academic program** English as a second language, advanced placement, accelerated degree program, honors program, summer session, adult/continuing education programs, internships **Contact** Mr. Rick Lowe, Vice President of Enrollment Services, Methodist College, 5400 Ramsey Street, Fayetteville, NC 28311-1420. Telephone: 910-630-7027 or toll-free 800-488-7110. Fax: 910-630-2123.

MONTREAT COLLEGE
MONTREAT, NORTH CAROLINA

General Independent Presbyterian, comprehensive, coed **Entrance** Moderately difficult **Setting** 100-acre small town campus **Total enrollment** 1,021 **Application deadline** 8/20 **Freshmen** 69% were admitted **Housing** Yes **Expenses** Tuition $10,042; Room & Board $3940 **Undergraduates** 54% women, 0.3% part-time, 64% 25 or older, 0.4% Native American, 1% Hispanic, 14% black, 1% Asian American or Pacific Islander **Most popular recent majors** Business administration; environmental science; religious studies **Academic program** Advanced placement, adult/continuing education programs, internships **Contact** Ms. Anita Darby, Director of Admissions, Montreat College, PO Box 1267, Montreat, NC 28757-1267. Telephone: 704-669-8012 ext. 3784 or toll-free 800-622-6968 (in-state). Fax: 704-669-0120. E-mail: admissions@montreat.edu. Web site: http://www.montreat.edu/.

▶ **For more information, see page 477.**

MOUNT OLIVE COLLEGE
MOUNT OLIVE, NORTH CAROLINA

General Independent Free Will Baptist, 4-year, coed **Entrance** Minimally difficult **Setting** 123-acre small town campus **Total enrollment** 1,381 **Student/faculty ratio** 15:1 **Application deadline** Rolling **Freshmen** 96% were admitted **Housing** Yes **Expenses** Tuition $8700; Room & Board $3750 **Undergraduates** 52% women, 13% part-time, 61% 25 or older, 0% Native American, 1% Hispanic, 21% black, 0.1% Asian American or Pacific Islander **Most popular recent majors** Business administration; psychology; recreation and leisure studies **Academic program** Advanced placement, accelerated degree program, tutorials, honors program, summer session, adult/continuing education programs, internships **Contact** Mr. Tim Woodard, Director of Admissions, Mount Olive College, 634 Henderson Street, Mount Olive, NC 28365. Telephone: 919-658-2502 ext. 3009 or toll-free 800-653-0854 (in-state). Fax: 919-658-8934. Web site: http://www.horizon.moc.edu/.

NORTH CAROLINA AGRICULTURAL AND TECHNICAL STATE UNIVERSITY

GREENSBORO, NORTH CAROLINA

General State-supported, university, coed **Entrance** Moderately difficult **Setting** 191-acre urban campus **Total enrollment** 7,468 **Student/faculty ratio** 14:1 **Application deadline** 6/1 **Freshmen** 66% were admitted **Housing** Yes **Expenses** Tuition $1622; Room & Board $3850 **Undergraduates** 51% women, 10% part-time, 10% 25 or older, 0.4% Native American, 0.4% Hispanic, 92% black, 1% Asian American or Pacific Islander **Most popular recent majors** Nursing; electrical/electronics engineering; accounting **Academic program** Average class size 24, advanced placement, tutorials, honors program, summer session, adult/continuing education programs, internships **Contact** Mr. John Smith, Director of Admissions, North Carolina Agricultural and Technical State University, 1601 East Market Street, Greensboro, NC 27411. Telephone: 336-334-7946. Fax: 336-334-7136. Web site: http://www.ncat.edu/.

NORTH CAROLINA CENTRAL UNIVERSITY

DURHAM, NORTH CAROLINA

General State-supported, comprehensive, coed **Entrance** Minimally difficult **Setting** 103-acre urban campus **Total enrollment** 5,664 **Application deadline** 7/1 **Freshmen** 69% were admitted **Housing** Yes **Expenses** Tuition $1944; Room & Board $3384 **Undergraduates** 64% women, 17% part-time, 24% 25 or older, 0.2% Native American, 1% Hispanic, 91% black, 1% Asian American or Pacific Islander **Most popular recent majors** Political science; business administration **Academic program** Advanced placement, tutorials, honors program, summer session, adult/continuing education programs, internships **Contact** Dr. Franklin Carver, Acting Director of Admissions/Assistant to Vice Chancellor Academic Affairs, North Carolina Central University, 1801 Fayetteville Street, Durham, NC 27707-3129. Telephone: 919-560-6326. E-mail: ebridges@wpo.nccu.edu. Web site: http://www.nccu.edu/.

NORTH CAROLINA SCHOOL OF THE ARTS

WINSTON-SALEM, NORTH CAROLINA

General State-supported, comprehensive, coed **Entrance** Very difficult **Setting** 57-acre urban campus **Total enrollment** 773 **Student/faculty ratio** 9:1 **Application deadline** Rolling **Housing** Yes **Expenses** Tuition $2522; Room & Board $3970 **Undergraduates** 10% 25 or older **Most Popular Recent Major** Music **Academic program** Tutorials **Contact** Ms. Carol J. Palm, Director of Admissions, North Carolina School of the Arts, 200 Waughtown Street, PO Box 12189, Winston-Salem, NC 27117-2189. Telephone: 910-770-3291. Fax: 336-770-3370. E-mail: palmc@ncsavx.ncarts.edu.

NORTH CAROLINA STATE UNIVERSITY

RALEIGH, NORTH CAROLINA

General State-supported, university, coed **Entrance** Very difficult **Setting** 1,623-acre suburban campus **Total enrollment** 22,199 **Student/faculty ratio** 14:1 **Application deadline** 2/1 **Freshmen** 75% were admitted **Housing** Yes **Expenses** Tuition $2270; Room & Board $3910 **Undergraduates** 40% women, 11% part-time, 11% 25 or older, 1% Native American, 2% Hispanic, 10% black, 5% Asian American or Pacific Islander **Most popular recent majors** Business administration; electrical/electronics engineering; mechanical engineering **Academic program** Average class size 34, English as a second language, advanced placement, self-designed majors, tutorials, honors program, summer session, adult/continuing education programs, internships **Contact** Dr. George R. Dixon, Vice Provost and Director of Admissions, North Carolina State University, Box 7103, 112 Peele Hall, Raleigh, NC 27695. Telephone: 919-515-2434. Fax: 919-515-5039. E-mail: undergrad_admissions@ncsu.edu. Web site: http://www.ncsu.edu/.

NORTH CAROLINA WESLEYAN COLLEGE

ROCKY MOUNT, NORTH CAROLINA

General Independent, 4-year, coed, affiliated with United Methodist Church **Entrance** Moderately difficult **Setting** 200-acre suburban campus **Total enrollment** 1,582 **Application deadline** Rolling **Freshmen** 81% were admitted **Housing** Yes **Expenses** Tuition $8144; Room & Board $4952 **Undergraduates** 56% women, 56% part-time, 1% Native American, 2% Hispanic, 21% black, 1% Asian American or Pacific Islander **Most popular recent majors** Business administration; information sciences/systems **Academic program** Advanced placement, tutorials, honors program, summer session, adult/continuing education programs, internships **Contact** Mr. John C. Hutchins,

North Carolina Wesleyan College *(continued)*

Vice President for Enrollment Management, North Carolina Wesleyan College, 3400 North Wesleyan Boulevard, Rocky Mount, NC 27804-8677. Telephone: 919-985-5200 or toll-free 800-488-6292. Fax: 919-985-5295. E-mail: adm@ncwc.edu. Web site: http://www.ncwc.edu/.

PEACE COLLEGE

RALEIGH, NORTH CAROLINA

General Independent, 4-year, women only, affiliated with Presbyterian Church (U.S.A.) **Entrance** Moderately difficult **Setting** 16-acre urban campus **Total enrollment** 503 **Student/faculty ratio** 14:1 **Application deadline** Rolling **Freshmen** 92% were admitted **Housing** Yes **Expenses** Tuition $7420; Room & Board $4940 **Undergraduates** 2% part-time, 2% 25 or older, 0.2% Native American, 1% Hispanic, 4% black, 0.4% Asian American or Pacific Islander **Academic program** English as a second language, advanced placement, tutorials, honors program, adult/continuing education programs, internships **Contact** Mrs. Christie Hill, Director of Admissions, Peace College, 15 East Peace Street, Raleigh, NC 27604-1194. Telephone: 919-508-2214 or toll-free 800-PEACE-47. Web site: http://www.peace.edu/.

PEMBROKE STATE UNIVERSITY

See University of North Carolina at Pembroke

PFEIFFER UNIVERSITY

MISENHEIMER, NORTH CAROLINA

General Independent United Methodist, comprehensive, coed **Entrance** Moderately difficult **Setting** 300-acre rural campus **Total enrollment** 1,814 **Student/faculty ratio** 16:1 **Application deadline** Rolling **Freshmen** 85% were admitted **Housing** Yes **Expenses** Tuition $9816; Room & Board $4000 **Undergraduates** 52% women, 14% part-time, 41% 25 or older, 0.1% Native American, 1% Hispanic, 14% black, 1% Asian American or Pacific Islander **Most popular recent majors** Business administration; criminal justice/law enforcement administration; athletic training/sports medicine **Academic program** Average class size 35, English as a second language, advanced placement, accelerated degree program, tutorials, honors program, summer session, internships **Contact** Ms. Elsie Lowder, Director of Admissions, Pfeiffer University, PO Box 960, Misenheimer, NC 28109-0960. Telephone: 704-463-1360 ext. 2067 or toll-free 800-338-2060. Fax: 704-463-1363. E-mail: admiss@jfh.pfeiffer.edu. Web site: http://www.pfeifferuniv.edu/.

PIEDMONT BAPTIST COLLEGE

WINSTON-SALEM, NORTH CAROLINA

General Independent Baptist, comprehensive, coed **Entrance** Noncompetitive **Setting** 12-acre urban campus **Total enrollment** 321 **Student/faculty ratio** 13:1 **Application deadline** Rolling **Freshmen** 100% were admitted **Housing** Yes **Expenses** Tuition $5250; Room & Board $3090 **Undergraduates** 45% women, 24% part-time, 42% 25 or older, 0.3% Native American, 5% black, 1% Asian American or Pacific Islander **Most popular recent majors** Aviation technology; elementary education; biblical studies **Academic program** Advanced placement, summer session, adult/continuing education programs, internships **Contact** Mr. Richard Whiteheart, Director of Admissions, Piedmont Baptist College, 716 Franklin Street, Winston-Salem, NC 27101-5197. Telephone: 336-725-8344 or toll-free 800-937-5097. Fax: 336-725-5522. Web site: http://www.ibnet.org/pbc.htm.

QUEENS COLLEGE

CHARLOTTE, NORTH CAROLINA

General Independent Presbyterian, comprehensive, coed **Entrance** Moderately difficult **Setting** 25-acre suburban campus **Total enrollment** 1,652 **Student/faculty ratio** 13:1 **Application deadline** Rolling **Freshmen** 73% were admitted **Housing** Yes **Expenses** Tuition $9410; Room & Board $5830 **Undergraduates** 81% women, 43% part-time, 42% 25 or older, 1% Native American, 2% Hispanic, 12% black, 1% Asian American or Pacific Islander **Most popular recent majors** Business administration; nursing; mass communications **Academic program** Average class size 18, advanced placement, tutorials, honors program, summer session, adult/continuing education programs, internships **Contact** Mr. John D. Clark, Assistant Director of CAS Admissions, Queens College, 1900 Selwyn Avenue, Charlotte, NC 28274-0002. Telephone: 704-337-2212 ext. 2371 or toll-free 800-849-0202. Fax: 704-337-2403. E-mail: case@rex.queens.edu. Web site: http://www.queens.edu/.

ROANOKE BIBLE COLLEGE

ELIZABETH CITY, NORTH CAROLINA

General Independent Christian, 4-year, coed **Entrance** Minimally difficult **Setting** 19-acre small town campus **Total enrollment** 156 **Student/faculty ratio** 10:1 **Application deadline** 8/1 **Freshmen** 72% were admitted **Housing** Yes **Expenses** Tuition $5200; Room & Board $3280 **Undergraduates** 49% women, 18% part-time, 29% 25 or older, 1% Native American, 0% Hispanic, 8% black, 2% Asian American or Pacific Islander **Aca-**

demic program Advanced placement, internships **Contact** Mr. Garrett Lewis, Vice President for Student Affairs, Roanoke Bible College, 714 First Street, Elizabeth City, NC 27909-3926. Telephone: 252-334-2005 or toll-free 800-RBC-8980. Fax: 252-334-2071. E-mail: admissions@roanokebible.edu. Web site: http://www.geocities.com/Athens/Acropolis/1003/.

ST. ANDREWS PRESBYTERIAN COLLEGE

LAURINBURG, NORTH CAROLINA

General Independent Presbyterian, 4-year, coed **Entrance** Moderately difficult **Setting** 600-acre small town campus **Total enrollment** 578 **Student/faculty ratio** 10:1 **Application deadline** Rolling **Freshmen** 80% were admitted **Housing** Yes **Expenses** Tuition $12,215; Room & Board $5300 **Undergraduates** 60% women, 17% part-time, 8% 25 or older, 1% Native American, 1% Hispanic, 11% black, 1% Asian American or Pacific Islander **Most popular recent majors** Business administration; education; physical education **Academic program** Advanced placement, accelerated degree program, self-designed majors, tutorials, honors program, summer session, adult/continuing education programs, internships **Contact** Ms. Marcia Nance, Dean for Student Affairs and Enrollment, St. Andrews Presbyterian College, 1700 Dogwood Mile, Laurinburg, NC 28352-5598. Telephone: 910-277-5555 or toll-free 800-763-0198. Fax: 910-277-5087. E-mail: admission@sapc.edu. Web site: http://www.sapc.edu/.

▶ **For more information, see page 504.**

SAINT AUGUSTINE'S COLLEGE

RALEIGH, NORTH CAROLINA

General Independent Episcopal, 4-year, coed **Entrance** Minimally difficult **Setting** 110-acre urban campus **Total enrollment** 1,639 **Student/faculty ratio** 16:1 **Application deadline** 7/1 **Freshmen** 49% were admitted **Housing** Yes **Expenses** Tuition $6472; Room & Board $4088 **Undergraduates** 59% women, 4% part-time, 12% 25 or older, 91% black **Most popular recent majors** Criminology; business administration; psychology **Academic program** Average class size 30, honors program, summer session, adult/continuing education programs, internships **Contact** Mr. Keith Powell, Director of Admissions, Saint Augustine's College, 1315 Oakwood Avenue, Raleigh, NC 27610-2298. Telephone: 919-516-4016 or toll-free 800-948-1126. Fax: 919-516-4415. Web site: http://www.st-aug.edu/.

SALEM COLLEGE

WINSTON-SALEM, NORTH CAROLINA

General Independent Moravian, comprehensive, primarily women **Entrance** Moderately difficult **Setting** 57-acre urban campus **Total enrollment** 1,002 **Student/faculty ratio** 12:1 **Application deadline** Rolling **Freshmen** 91% were admitted **Housing** Yes **Expenses** Tuition $12,415; Room & Board $7320 **Undergraduates** 99% women, 20% part-time, 36% 25 or older, 0.5% Native American, 1% Hispanic, 15% black, 2% Asian American or Pacific Islander **Most popular recent majors** Business administration; mass communications; interior design **Academic program** Advanced placement, self-designed majors, honors program, summer session, adult/continuing education programs, internships **Contact** Ms. Katherine Knapp-Watts, Dean of Admissions and Financial Aid, Salem College, PO Box 10548, Winston-Salem, NC 27108-0548. Telephone: 336-721-2621 or toll-free 800-327-2536. Fax: 336-724-7102. E-mail: admissions@salem.edu. Web site: http://www.salem.edu/.

SHAW UNIVERSITY

RALEIGH, NORTH CAROLINA

General Independent Baptist, 4-year, coed **Entrance** Minimally difficult **Setting** 18-acre urban campus **Total enrollment** 2,327 **Student/faculty ratio** 14:1 **Application deadline** 7/30 **Freshmen** 76% were admitted **Housing** Yes **Expenses** Tuition $6304; Room & Board $4052 **Undergraduates** 63% women, 10% part-time, 0.2% Native American, 0.5% Hispanic, 96% black, 0.1% Asian American or Pacific Islander **Most popular recent majors** Business administration; social sciences; criminal justice studies **Academic program** English as a second language, advanced placement, accelerated degree program, self-designed majors, tutorials, summer session, adult/continuing education programs, internships **Contact** Mr. Keith Smith, Director of Admissions and Recruitment, Shaw University, 118 East South Street, Raleigh, NC 27601-2399. Telephone: 919-546-8275 or toll-free 800-214-6683. Fax: 919-546-8271. E-mail: ksmith@shawu.edu.

UNIVERSITY OF NORTH CAROLINA AT ASHEVILLE

ASHEVILLE, NORTH CAROLINA

General State-supported, comprehensive, coed **Entrance** Moderately difficult **Setting** 265-acre suburban campus **Total enrollment** 3,179 **Student/faculty ratio** 12:1 **Application deadline** 4/15 **Freshmen** 60% were admitted **Housing** Yes **Expenses** Tuition $1834; Room & Board $3826 **Undergraduates** 57% women, 19% part-time, 30% 25 or older, 0.4% Native American, 1% Hispanic, 3% black, 1% Asian American or Pacific Islander **Most popular recent majors** Business administration; psychology; biology **Academic program** Average class size 23, advanced placement, accelerated degree program, self-designed majors, tu-

University of North Carolina at Asheville *(continued)*

torials, honors program, summer session, adult/continuing education programs, internships **Contact** Mr. John W. White, Director of Admissions, University of North Carolina at Asheville, 1 University Heights, Asheville, NC 28804-3299. Telephone: 704-251-6481 or toll-free 800-531-9842 (in-state). Fax: 828-251-6385. E-mail: wilson@unca.edu. Web site: http://www.unca.edu/.

THE UNIVERSITY OF NORTH CAROLINA AT CHAPEL HILL

CHAPEL HILL, NORTH CAROLINA

General State-supported, university, coed **Entrance** Very difficult **Setting** 789-acre suburban campus **Total enrollment** 24,231 **Student/faculty ratio** 14:1 **Application deadline** 1/15 **Freshmen** 37% were admitted **Housing** Yes **Expenses** Tuition $2224; Room & Board $4760 **Undergraduates** 60% women, 5% part-time, 4% 25 or older, 1% Native American, 1% Hispanic, 11% black, 5% Asian American or Pacific Islander **Most popular recent majors** Biology; business administration; psychology **Academic program** Average class size 34, advanced placement, accelerated degree program, self-designed majors, honors program, summer session, internships **Contact** Mr. Jerome A. Lucido, Associate Vice Chancellor/Director of Undergraduate Admissions, The University of North Carolina at Chapel Hill, Chapel Hill, NC 27599. Telephone: 919-966-3621. E-mail: uadm@email.unc.edu. Web site: http://www.unc.edu/.

UNIVERSITY OF NORTH CAROLINA AT CHARLOTTE

CHARLOTTE, NORTH CAROLINA

General State-supported, university, coed **Entrance** Moderately difficult **Setting** 1,000-acre urban campus **Total enrollment** 16,511 **Student/faculty ratio** 16:1 **Application deadline** 7/1 **Freshmen** 76% were admitted **Housing** Yes **Expenses** Tuition $1777; Room & Board $3446 **Undergraduates** 53% women, 22% part-time, 22% 25 or older, 1% Native American, 2% Hispanic, 17% black, 4% Asian American or Pacific Islander **Most popular recent majors** Psychology; English; criminal justice/law enforcement administration **Academic program** Average class size 37, English as a second language, advanced placement, tutorials, honors program, summer session, adult/continuing education programs, internships **Contact** Mr. Craig Fulton, Director of Admissions, University of North Carolina at Charlotte, 9201 University City Boulevard, Charlotte, NC 28223-0001. Telephone: 704-547-2213. Fax: 704-510-6483. E-mail: unccadm@email.uncc.edu. Web site: http://www.uncc.edu/.

UNIVERSITY OF NORTH CAROLINA AT GREENSBORO

GREENSBORO, NORTH CAROLINA

General State-supported, university, coed **Entrance** Moderately difficult **Setting** 200-acre urban campus **Total enrollment** 12,308 **Student/faculty ratio** 15:1 **Application deadline** 8/1 **Freshmen** 76% were admitted **Housing** Yes **Expenses** Tuition $2031; Room & Board $3661 **Undergraduates** 67% women, 17% part-time, 24% 25 or older, 0.5% Native American, 1% Hispanic, 16% black, 2% Asian American or Pacific Islander **Most popular recent majors** Business administration; nursing; psychology **Academic program** English as a second language, advanced placement, accelerated degree program, self-designed majors, tutorials, honors program, summer session, adult/continuing education programs, internships **Contact** Mr. Jerry W. Harrelson, Acting Director of Admissions, University of North Carolina at Greensboro, 1000 Spring Garden Street, Greensboro, NC 27412-0001. Telephone: 336-334-5243. Fax: 336-334-4180. E-mail: undergrad_admissions@uncg.edu. Web site: http://www.uncg.edu/.

UNIVERSITY OF NORTH CAROLINA AT PEMBROKE

PEMBROKE, NORTH CAROLINA

General State-supported, comprehensive, coed **Entrance** Moderately difficult **Setting** 108-acre rural campus **Total enrollment** 3,034 **Student/faculty ratio** 18:1 **Application deadline** 7/15 **Freshmen** 91% were admitted **Housing** Yes **Expenses** Tuition $1536; Room & Board $2910 **Undergraduates** 60% women, 16% part-time, 33% 25 or older, 26% Native American, 2% Hispanic, 15% black, 1% Asian American or Pacific Islander **Most popular recent majors** Education; business administration; sociology **Academic program** Average class size 20, English as a second language, advanced placement, accelerated degree program, tutorials, honors program, summer session, adult/continuing education programs, internships **Contact** Ms. Jacqueline Clark, Director of Admissions, University of North Carolina at Pembroke, One University Drive, PO Box 1510, Pembroke, NC 28372-1510. Telephone: 910-521-6262 or toll-free 800-822-2185 (in-state). Web site: http://www.uncp.edu/.

UNIVERSITY OF NORTH CAROLINA AT WILMINGTON

WILMINGTON, NORTH CAROLINA

General State-supported, comprehensive, coed **Entrance** Moderately difficult **Setting** 650-acre

urban campus **Total enrollment** 9,176 **Student/faculty ratio** 16:1 **Application deadline** Rolling **Freshmen** 60% were admitted **Housing** Yes **Expenses** Tuition $1796; Room & Board $4260 **Undergraduates** 60% women, 12% part-time, 18% 25 or older, 1% Native American, 1% Hispanic, 6% black, 1% Asian American or Pacific Islander **Most popular recent majors** Psychology; English; criminal justice/law enforcement administration **Academic program** Average class size 30, advanced placement, accelerated degree program, honors program, summer session, adult/continuing education programs, internships **Contact** Mr. Ronald E. Whittaker, Director of Admissions and Registrar, University of North Carolina at Wilmington, 601 South College Road, Wilmington, NC 28403-3201. Telephone: 910-962-3243 or toll-free 800-228-5571 (out-of-state). Fax: 910-962-3038. E-mail: admissions@uncwil.edu. Web site: http://www.uncwil.edu/.

WAKE FOREST UNIVERSITY
WINSTON-SALEM, NORTH CAROLINA

General Independent, university, coed, affiliated with North Carolina Baptist State Convention **Entrance** Very difficult **Setting** 350-acre suburban campus **Total enrollment** 6,124 **Student/faculty ratio** 12:1 **Application deadline** 1/15 **Freshmen** 44% were admitted **Housing** Yes **Expenses** Tuition $19,450; Room & Board $5450 **Undergraduates** 50% women, 2% part-time, 1% 25 or older, 0.2% Native American, 1% Hispanic, 8% black, 2% Asian American or Pacific Islander **Most popular recent majors** Business administration; biology; psychology **Academic program** Advanced placement, accelerated degree program, self-designed majors, honors program, summer session, internships **Contact** Mr. William G. Starling, Director of Admissions, Wake Forest University, PO Box 7305, Winston-Salem, NC 27109. Telephone: 336-758-5201. Fax: 336-758-6074. E-mail: admissions@wfu.edu. Web site: http://www.wfu.edu/.

WARREN WILSON COLLEGE
ASHEVILLE, NORTH CAROLINA

General Independent, comprehensive, coed, affiliated with Presbyterian Church (U.S.A.) **Entrance** Moderately difficult **Setting** 1,100-acre small town campus **Total enrollment** 730 **Student/faculty ratio** 11:1 **Application deadline** 3/15 **Freshmen** 83% were admitted **Housing** Yes **Expenses** Tuition $12,250; Room & Board $4000 **Undergraduates** 60% women, 1% part-time, 3% 25 or older, 1% Native American, 1% Hispanic, 2% black, 1% Asian American or Pacific Islander **Most popular recent majors** Environmental science; recreation and leisure studies; art **Academic program** Average class size 17, English as a second language, advanced placement, self-designed majors, tutorials, honors program, internships **Contact** Mr. Richard Blomgren, Dean of Admission, Warren Wilson College, PO Box 9000, Asheville, NC 28815-9000. Telephone: 704-298-3325 ext. 240 or toll-free 800-934-3536. Fax: 704-298-1440. E-mail: admit@warren-wilson.edu. Web site: http://www.warren-wilson.edu/.

► **For more information, see page 545.**

WESTERN CAROLINA UNIVERSITY
CULLOWHEE, NORTH CAROLINA

General State-supported, comprehensive, coed **Contact** Mr. Doyle Bickers, Director of Admissions, Western Carolina University, Cullowhee, NC 28723. Telephone: 704-227-7317. E-mail: cauley@wcu.edu. Web site: http://www.wcu.edu/.

WINGATE UNIVERSITY
WINGATE, NORTH CAROLINA

General Independent Baptist, comprehensive, coed **Entrance** Moderately difficult **Setting** 330-acre small town campus **Total enrollment** 1,230 **Student/faculty ratio** 13:1 **Application deadline** 8/1 **Freshmen** 85% were admitted **Housing** Yes **Expenses** Tuition $11,690; Room & Board $4100 **Undergraduates** 9% 25 or older **Most popular recent majors** Business administration; mass communications; education **Academic program** Average class size 20, advanced placement, accelerated degree program, tutorials, honors program, summer session, adult/continuing education programs, internships **Contact** Mr. Walter P. Crutchfield III, Dean of Admissions, Wingate University, Wingate, NC 28174. Telephone: 704-233-8000 or toll-free 800-755-5550. E-mail: admit@wingate.edu. Web site: http://www.wingate.edu/.

WINSTON-SALEM STATE UNIVERSITY
WINSTON-SALEM, NORTH CAROLINA

General State-supported, 4-year, coed **Entrance** Minimally difficult **Setting** 94-acre urban campus **Total enrollment** 2,865 **Student/faculty ratio** 19:1 **Application deadline** Rolling **Freshmen** 80% were admitted **Housing** Yes **Expenses** Tuition $1574; Room & Board $3757 **Undergraduates** 68% women, 18% part-time, 32% 25 or older, 0.2% Native American, 1% Hispanic, 80% black, 1% Asian American or Pacific Islander **Most popular recent majors** Physical therapy; business administration; nursing **Academic program** Advanced placement, accelerated degree program, honors program, summer session, adult/continuing education programs, internships **Contact** Mr. Van C. Wilson, Director of Admissions, Winston-Salem State University, 601 Martin Luther King Jr

Winston-Salem State University *(continued)*

Drive, Winston-Salem, NC 27110-0003. Telephone: 336-750-2070 or toll-free 800-257-4052. Fax: 336-750-2079. E-mail: wilsonv@wssu1adp.wssu.edu. Web site: http://www.wssu.edu.

NORTH DAKOTA

DICKINSON STATE UNIVERSITY
DICKINSON, NORTH DAKOTA

General State-supported, 4-year, coed **Entrance** Noncompetitive **Setting** 100-acre small town campus **Total enrollment** 1,736 **Student/faculty ratio** 16:1 **Application deadline** 8/19 **Housing** Yes **Expenses** Tuition $2131; Room & Board $2618 **Undergraduates** 58% women, 17% part-time, 20% 25 or older, 2% Native American, 1% Hispanic, 0.3% black, 0.2% Asian American or Pacific Islander **Most popular recent majors** Business administration; education; nursing **Academic program** Advanced placement, self-designed majors, honors program, summer session, adult/continuing education programs, internships **Contact** Ms. Deb Hourigan, Interim Coordinator of Student Recruitment, Dickinson State University, Dickinson, ND 58601-4896. Telephone: 701-227-2175 or toll-free 800-279-4295. Fax: 701-227-2006. E-mail: dsuhawk@eagle.dsu.nodak.edu.

JAMESTOWN COLLEGE
JAMESTOWN, NORTH DAKOTA

General Independent Presbyterian, 4-year, coed **Entrance** Minimally difficult **Setting** 107-acre small town campus **Total enrollment** 1,072 **Student/faculty ratio** 19:1 **Application deadline** Rolling **Freshmen** 99% were admitted **Housing** Yes **Expenses** Tuition $6770; Room & Board $3180 **Undergraduates** 55% women, 6% part-time, 1% Native American, 1% Hispanic, 1% black, 1% Asian American or Pacific Islander **Most popular recent majors** Nursing; business administration; elementary education **Academic program** English as a second language, advanced placement, accelerated degree program, self-designed majors, tutorials, honors program, summer session, adult/continuing education programs, internships **Contact** Ms. Judy Erickson, Director of Admissions, Jamestown College, 6081 College Lane, Jamestown, ND 58405. Telephone: 701-252-3467 ext. 2548 or toll-free 800-336-2554 (in-state). Fax: 701-253-4318. E-mail: admissions@jc.edu. Web site: http://www.jc.edu/.

MAYVILLE STATE UNIVERSITY
MAYVILLE, NORTH DAKOTA

General State-supported, 4-year, coed **Entrance** Noncompetitive **Setting** 60-acre rural campus **Total enrollment** 705 **Student/faculty ratio** 20:1 **Application deadline** Rolling **Housing** Yes **Expenses** Tuition $1996; Room & Board $2835 **Undergraduates** 55% women, 14% part-time, 15% 25 or older **Most popular recent majors** Elementary education; business administration; information sciences/systems **Academic program** Advanced placement, accelerated degree program, summer session, adult/continuing education programs, internships **Contact** Mr. Ronald G. Brown, Director of Admissions, Mayville State University, 330 3rd Street, NE, Mayville, ND 58257-1299. Telephone: 701-786-2301 or toll-free 800-437-4104. Fax: 701-786-4748. E-mail: muadmiss@plains.nodak.edu. Web site: http://www.masu.nodak.edu/.

MEDCENTER ONE COLLEGE OF NURSING
BISMARCK, NORTH DAKOTA

General Independent, upper-level, coed **Entrance** Moderately difficult **Setting** 15-acre small town campus **Total enrollment** 80 **Student/faculty ratio** 7:1 **Application deadline** 11/7 **Freshmen** 80% were admitted **Housing** Yes **Expenses** Tuition $2815; Room only $900 **Undergraduates** 93% women, 13% part-time, 25% 25 or older, 1% Native American, 1% Hispanic, 0% black, 1% Asian American or Pacific Islander **Academic program** Honors program, summer session, internships **Contact** Dr. Karen Kristensen, Dean/Provost, Medcenter One College of Nursing, 512 North 7th Street, Bismarck, ND 58501-4494. Telephone: 701-224-6832.

MINOT STATE UNIVERSITY
MINOT, NORTH DAKOTA

General State-supported, comprehensive, coed **Entrance** Minimally difficult **Setting** 103-acre small town campus **Total enrollment** 3,294 **Student/faculty ratio** 19:1 **Application deadline** Rolling **Housing** Yes **Expenses** Tuition $2139; Room & Board $2340 **Undergraduates** 30% 25 or older **Most popular recent majors** Business administration; education; criminal justice/law enforcement administration **Academic program** Advanced placement, self-designed majors, tutorials, honors program, summer session, adult/continuing education programs, internships **Contact** Ms. Ronnie Walker, Administrative Assistant, Records Office, Minot State University, 500 University Avenue West, Minot, ND 58707-0002. Telephone: 701-858-3340 or toll-free 800-777-0750. Fax: 701-

839-6933. E-mail: fields@warp6.cs.misu.nodak.edu. Web site: http://www.misu.nodak.edu/.

NORTH DAKOTA STATE UNIVERSITY
FARGO, NORTH DAKOTA

General State-supported, university, coed **Entrance** Moderately difficult **Setting** 2,100-acre urban campus **Total enrollment** 9,408 **Student/faculty ratio** 19:1 **Application deadline** Rolling **Freshmen** 78% were admitted **Housing** Yes **Expenses** Tuition $2566; Room & Board $3135 **Undergraduates** 42% women, 13% part-time, 14% 25 or older, 1% Native American, 0.4% Hispanic, 1% black, 1% Asian American or Pacific Islander **Most popular recent majors** Civil engineering; business administration; mechanical engineering **Academic program** English as a second language, advanced placement, accelerated degree program, self-designed majors, tutorials, honors program, summer session, adult/continuing education programs, internships **Contact** Dr. Kate Haugen, Director of Admission, North Dakota State University, PO Box 5454, Fargo, ND 58105-5454. Telephone: 701-231-8643 or toll-free 800-488-NDSU. Fax: 701-231-8802. E-mail: nuadmiss@plains.nodak.edu. Web site: http://www.ndsu.nodak.edu/.

TRINITY BIBLE COLLEGE
ELLENDALE, NORTH DAKOTA

General Independent, 4-year, coed, affiliated with Assemblies of God **Entrance** Noncompetitive **Setting** 28-acre rural campus **Total enrollment** 322 **Student/faculty ratio** 14:1 **Application deadline** Rolling **Housing** Yes **Expenses** Tuition $6090; Room & Board $3330 **Undergraduates** 54% women, 11% part-time, 21% 25 or older, 2% Native American, 3% Hispanic, 1% black, 0.3% Asian American or Pacific Islander **Most popular recent majors** Biblical studies; psychology **Academic program** Advanced placement, accelerated degree program, tutorials, summer session, internships **Contact** Rev. Jerry Grimshaw, Director of Admissions, Trinity Bible College, 50 South 6th Avenue, Ellendale, ND 58436-7150. Telephone: 701-349-3621 ext. 2045 or toll-free 800-523-1603. Fax: 701-349-5443.

UNIVERSITY OF MARY
BISMARCK, NORTH DAKOTA

General Independent Roman Catholic, comprehensive, coed **Entrance** Moderately difficult **Setting** 107-acre suburban campus **Total enrollment** 2,148 **Student/faculty ratio** 18:1 **Application deadline** Rolling **Housing** Yes **Expenses** Tuition $8055; Room & Board $3150 **Undergraduates** 63% women, 11% part-time, 20% 25 or older, 2% Native American, 1% Hispanic, 1% black, 0.2% Asian American or Pacific Islander **Most popular recent majors** Business administration; education; nursing **Academic program** Advanced placement, accelerated degree program, tutorials, summer session, adult/continuing education programs, internships **Contact** Mrs. Steph Storey, Director of Admissions, University of Mary, 7500 University Drive, Bismarck, ND 58504-9652. Telephone: 701-255-7500 ext. 429 or toll-free 800-288-6279. Fax: 701-255-7687. E-mail: marauder@umary.edu. Web site: http://www.umary.edu.

UNIVERSITY OF NORTH DAKOTA
GRAND FORKS, NORTH DAKOTA

General State-supported, university, coed **Entrance** Moderately difficult **Setting** 570-acre small town campus **Total enrollment** 10,363 **Application deadline** 7/1 **Freshmen** 68% were admitted **Housing** Yes **Expenses** Tuition $3118; Room & Board $3117 **Undergraduates** 49% women, 11% part-time, 19% 25 or older **Most popular recent majors** Aviation/airway science; nursing; psychology **Academic program** Average class size 32, advanced placement, accelerated degree program, self-designed majors, honors program, summer session, adult/continuing education programs, internships **Contact** Ms. Donna Bruce, Associate Director of Admissions, University of North Dakota, Box 8382, Grand Forks, ND 58202. Telephone: 701-777-3821 or toll-free 800-CALL UND. Fax: 701-777-2696. E-mail: enrolser@sage.und.nodak.edu. Web site: http://www.und.nodak.edu/.

VALLEY CITY STATE UNIVERSITY
VALLEY CITY, NORTH DAKOTA

General State-supported, 4-year, coed **Contact** Mr. LaMonte Johnson, Director of Admissions, Valley City State University, 101 College Street, SW, Valley City, ND 58072. Telephone: 701-845-7101 or toll-free 800-532-8641. Fax: 701-845-7245. E-mail: vcadmiss@plains.nodak.edu. Web site: http://www.vcsu.nodak.edu/.

OHIO

ANTIOCH COLLEGE
YELLOW SPRINGS, OHIO

General Independent, 4-year, coed **Entrance** Moderately difficult **Setting** 100-acre small town campus **Total enrollment** 611 **Student/faculty ratio** 9:1 **Application deadline** 2/1 **Freshmen**

Antioch College *(continued)*

79% were admitted **Housing** Yes **Expenses** Tuition $18,487; Room & Board $3998 **Undergraduates** 66% women, 0.4% part-time, 4% 25 or older, 1% Native American, 4% Hispanic, 5% black, 2% Asian American or Pacific Islander **Academic program** Average class size 15, advanced placement, self-designed majors, tutorials, summer session **Contact** Ms. Cathy Paige, Information Manager, Antioch College, 795 Livermore Street, Yellow Springs, OH 45387-1697. Telephone: 937-767-6400 ext. 6559 or toll-free 800-543-9436 (out-of-state). Fax: 937-767-6473. E-mail: admissions@antioch-college.edu. Web site: http://college.antioch.edu/.

ART ACADEMY OF CINCINNATI
CINCINNATI, OHIO

General Independent, comprehensive, coed **Entrance** Moderately difficult **Setting** 184-acre urban campus **Total enrollment** 185 **Student/faculty ratio** 12:1 **Application deadline** 8/1 **Freshmen** 74% were admitted **Housing** No **Expenses** Tuition $10,925 **Undergraduates** 45% women, 8% part-time, 30% 25 or older, 1% Hispanic, 3% black, 1% Asian American or Pacific Islander **Academic program** Average class size 17, advanced placement, self-designed majors, tutorials, summer session, adult/continuing education programs, internships **Contact** Ms. Sarah Colby, Director of Enrollment Services, Art Academy of Cincinnati, 1125 Saint Gregory Street, Cincinnati, OH 45202-1700. Telephone: 513-562-8754. Fax: 513-562-8778. Web site: http://www.artacademy.edu/.

ASHLAND UNIVERSITY
ASHLAND, OHIO

General Independent, comprehensive, coed, affiliated with Brethren Church **Entrance** Moderately difficult **Setting** 98-acre small town campus **Total enrollment** 5,737 **Student/faculty ratio** 16:1 **Application deadline** Rolling **Freshmen** 92% were admitted **Housing** Yes **Expenses** Tuition $13,601; Room & Board $5116 **Undergraduates** 56% women, 27% part-time, 29% 25 or older, 0.2% Native American, 2% Hispanic, 8% black, 0.4% Asian American or Pacific Islander **Most popular recent majors** Business marketing and marketing management; education **Academic program** Average class size 15, English as a second language, advanced placement, accelerated degree program, honors program, summer session, adult/continuing education programs, internships **Contact** Mr. Tom Mansperger, Director of Admissions, Ashland University, 401 College Avenue, Ashland, OH 44805-3702. Telephone: 419-289-5080 or toll-free 800-882-1548. Fax: 419-289-5999. E-mail: auadmsn@ashland.edu. Web site: http://www.ashland.edu/.

BALDWIN-WALLACE COLLEGE
BEREA, OHIO

General Independent Methodist, comprehensive, coed **Entrance** Moderately difficult **Setting** 56-acre suburban campus **Total enrollment** 4,539 **Student/faculty ratio** 13:1 **Application deadline** Rolling **Freshmen** 80% were admitted **Housing** Yes **Expenses** Tuition $13,275; Room & Board $4881 **Undergraduates** 62% women, 25% part-time, 26% 25 or older, 0.1% Native American, 1% Hispanic, 5% black, 1% Asian American or Pacific Islander **Most popular recent majors** Business administration; education; psychology **Academic program** English as a second language, advanced placement, accelerated degree program, self-designed majors, tutorials, honors program, summer session, adult/continuing education programs, internships **Contact** Mrs. Julie Baker, Director of Undergraduate Admission, Baldwin-Wallace College, 275 Eastland Road, Berea, OH 44017-2088. Telephone: 440-826-2222. Fax: 440-826-3830. E-mail: admission@bw.edu. Web site: http://www.bw.edu/.

BLUFFTON COLLEGE
BLUFFTON, OHIO

General Independent Mennonite, comprehensive, coed **Entrance** Moderately difficult **Setting** 65-acre small town campus **Total enrollment** 1,053 **Student/faculty ratio** 15:1 **Application deadline** 5/31 **Freshmen** 87% were admitted **Housing** Yes **Expenses** Tuition $12,375; Room & Board $5121 **Undergraduates** 60% women, 3% part-time, 10% 25 or older, 0.2% Native American, 1% Hispanic, 5% black, 0.2% Asian American or Pacific Islander **Most popular recent majors** Business administration; education; social sciences **Academic program** English as a second language, advanced placement, accelerated degree program, self-designed majors, tutorials, honors program, summer session, adult/continuing education programs, internships **Contact** Mr. Michael Hieronimus, Dean of Admissions, Bluffton College, 280 West College Avenue, Bluffton, OH 45817-1196. Telephone: 419-358-3254 or toll-free 800-488-3257. Fax: 419-358-3232. E-mail: admissions@bluffton.edu. Web site: http://www.bluffton.edu/.

BOWLING GREEN STATE UNIVERSITY
BOWLING GREEN, OHIO

General State-supported, university, coed **Entrance** Moderately difficult **Setting** 1,338-acre small town campus **Total enrollment** 17,328 **Stu-**

dent/faculty ratio 18:1 **Application deadline** Rolling **Housing** Yes **Expenses** Tuition $4422; Room & Board $4626 **Undergraduates** 57% women, 10% part-time, 7% 25 or older, 0.2% Native American, 2% Hispanic, 3% black, 1% Asian American or Pacific Islander **Most popular recent majors** Elementary education; business marketing and marketing management; biology **Academic program** English as a second language, advanced placement, accelerated degree program, self-designed majors, tutorials, honors program, summer session, adult/continuing education programs, internships **Contact** Mr. Michael D. Walsh, Director of Admissions, Bowling Green State University, Bowling Green, OH 43403. Telephone: 419-372-2086. Web site: http://www.bgsu.edu/.

BRYANT AND STRATTON COLLEGE
CLEVELAND, OHIO

General Proprietary, 4-year, coed **Entrance** Moderately difficult **Setting** Urban campus **Total enrollment** 309 **Application deadline** Rolling **Housing** Yes **Expenses** Tuition $6960; Room only $2700 **Undergraduates** 50% 25 or older, 0% Native American, 1% Hispanic, 46% black, 0.3% Asian American or Pacific Islander **Most Popular Recent Major** Electrical/electronic engineering technology **Academic program** Accelerated degree program, adult/continuing education programs, internships **Contact** Ms. Vanetta McClain, Director of Admissions, Bryant and Stratton College, 1700 East 13th Street, Cleveland, OH 44114-3203. Telephone: 216-771-1700. Fax: 216-771-1700. Web site: http://www.bryantstratton.edu/.

CAPITAL UNIVERSITY
COLUMBUS, OHIO

General Independent, comprehensive, coed, affiliated with Evangelical Lutheran Church in America **Entrance** Moderately difficult **Setting** 48-acre suburban campus **Total enrollment** 3,988 **Student/faculty ratio** 13:1 **Application deadline** Rolling **Freshmen** 82% were admitted **Housing** Yes **Expenses** Tuition $14,760; Room & Board $4200 **Undergraduates** 64% women, 29% part-time, 11% 25 or older, 0.3% Native American, 1% Hispanic, 14% black, 1% Asian American or Pacific Islander **Most popular recent majors** Nursing; elementary education; psychology **Academic program** Average class size 20, English as a second language, advanced placement, self-designed majors, summer session, adult/continuing education programs, internships **Contact** Mrs. Kimberly V. Ebbrecht, Director of Admission, Capital University, 2199 East Main Street, Columbus, OH 43209-2394. Telephone: 614-236-6101 or toll-free 800-289-6289. Fax: 614-236-6820. E-mail: admissions@capital.edu. Web site: http://www.capital.edu/.

CASE WESTERN RESERVE UNIVERSITY
CLEVELAND, OHIO

General Independent, university, coed **Entrance** Very difficult **Setting** 128-acre urban campus **Total enrollment** 9,908 **Student/faculty ratio** 8:1 **Application deadline** 2/1 **Freshmen** 79% were admitted **Housing** Yes **Expenses** Tuition $17,940; Room & Board $5050 **Undergraduates** 40% women, 6% part-time, 7% 25 or older, 0.1% Native American, 2% Hispanic, 6% black, 12% Asian American or Pacific Islander **Most popular recent majors** Biology; psychology; chemical engineering **Academic program** Average class size 40, English as a second language, advanced placement, accelerated degree program, self-designed majors, tutorials, honors program, summer session, adult/continuing education programs, internships **Contact** Mr. William T. Conley, Dean of Undergraduate Admission, Case Western Reserve University, 10900 Euclid Avenue, Cleveland, OH 44106. Telephone: 216-368-4450. Fax: 216-368-5111. E-mail: xx329@po.cwru.edu. Web site: http://www.cwru.edu/.

CEDARVILLE COLLEGE
CEDARVILLE, OHIO

General Independent Baptist, 4-year, coed **Entrance** Moderately difficult **Setting** 300-acre rural campus **Total enrollment** 2,559 **Student/faculty ratio** 16:1 **Application deadline** Rolling **Freshmen** 82% were admitted **Housing** Yes **Expenses** Tuition $9312; Room & Board $4716 **Undergraduates** 54% women, 4% part-time, 2% 25 or older, 0.2% Native American, 1% Hispanic, 1% black, 1% Asian American or Pacific Islander **Most popular recent majors** Elementary education; nursing; biology **Academic program** Advanced placement, accelerated degree program, honors program, summer session, internships **Contact** Mr. Roscoe Smith, Director of Admissions, Cedarville College, PO Box 601, Cedarville, OH 45314-0601. Telephone: 937-766-7700 or toll-free 800-CEDARVILLE. Fax: 937-766-7575. E-mail: admiss@cedarville.edu. Web site: http://www.cedarville.edu/.

CENTRAL STATE UNIVERSITY
WILBERFORCE, OHIO

General State-supported, comprehensive, coed **Entrance** Minimally difficult **Setting** 60-acre rural campus **Total enrollment** 1,051 **Application deadline** 6/15 **Freshmen** 31% were admitted **Housing** Yes **Expenses** Tuition $3318; Room

Central State University *(continued)*

& Board $4695 **Undergraduates** 18% 25 or older **Most popular recent majors** Business administration; computer science; education **Academic program** Self-designed majors, honors program, summer session, adult/continuing education programs, internships **Contact** Ms. Nicole Perry, Acting Director of Admissions and Enrollment Management, Central State University, 1400 Brush Row Road, Wilberforce, OH 45384. Telephone: 937-376-6348 or toll-free 800-388-CSU1 (in-state). Fax: 937-376-6648.

CINCINNATI BIBLE COLLEGE AND SEMINARY

CINCINNATI, OHIO

General Independent, comprehensive, coed, affiliated with Church of Christ **Entrance** Minimally difficult **Setting** 40-acre urban campus **Total enrollment** 915 **Student/faculty ratio** 24:1 **Application deadline** 8/10 **Freshmen** 99% were admitted **Housing** Yes **Expenses** Tuition $6190; Room & Board $3700 **Undergraduates** 45% women, 21% part-time, 21% 25 or older, 0% Native American, 0.3% Hispanic, 5% black, 0.3% Asian American or Pacific Islander **Most popular recent majors** Divinity/ministry; education; sacred music **Academic program** Average class size 20, advanced placement, tutorials, summer session, adult/continuing education programs, internships **Contact** Mr. Dick Hess, Director of Enrollment Services, Cincinnati Bible College and Seminary, 2700 Glenway Avenue, Cincinnati, OH 45204-1799. Telephone: 513-244-8141 ext. 142 or toll-free 800-949-4CBC. Fax: 513-244-8140. E-mail: admissions@cincybible.edu. Web site: http://www.cincybible.edu/.

CIRCLEVILLE BIBLE COLLEGE

CIRCLEVILLE, OHIO

General Independent, 4-year, coed, affiliated with Churches of Christ in Christian Union **Entrance** Minimally difficult **Setting** 40-acre small town campus **Total enrollment** 186 **Student/faculty ratio** 8:1 **Application deadline** Rolling **Housing** Yes **Expenses** Tuition $5892; Room & Board $3914 **Undergraduates** 47% women, 17% part-time, 35% 25 or older, 0% Native American, 2% Hispanic, 3% black, 0% Asian American or Pacific Islander **Most popular recent majors** (pre)theology; counselor education/guidance; education **Academic program** Average class size 18, advanced placement, self-designed majors, tutorials, honors program, summer session, internships **Contact** Rev. Matt Taylor, Director of Enrollment, Circleville Bible College, 1476 Lancaster Pike, PO Box 458, Circleville, OH 43113-9487. Telephone: 740-477-7701 or toll-free 800-701-0222. Fax: 740-477-7755. E-mail: enroll@biblecollege.edu. Web site: http://www.biblecollege.edu/.

CLEVELAND COLLEGE OF JEWISH STUDIES

BEACHWOOD, OHIO

General Independent, comprehensive, coed **Entrance** Noncompetitive **Setting** 2-acre suburban campus **Total enrollment** 56 **Student/faculty ratio** 10:1 **Application deadline** Rolling **Freshmen** 100% were admitted **Housing** No **Expenses** Tuition $5715 **Undergraduates** 100% women, 100% part-time, 99% 25 or older, 0% Native American, 0% Hispanic, 0% black, 0% Asian American or Pacific Islander **Academic program** Average class size 10, summer session, adult/continuing education programs, internships **Contact** Ms. Linda L. Rosen, Registrar, Cleveland College of Jewish Studies, 26500 Shaker Boulevard, Beachwood, OH 44122-7116. Telephone: 216-464-4050 ext. 101 or toll-free 888-336-2257. Fax: 216-464-5827.

CLEVELAND INSTITUTE OF ART

CLEVELAND, OHIO

General Independent, 5-year, coed **Entrance** Moderately difficult **Setting** 488-acre urban campus **Total enrollment** 481 **Student/faculty ratio** 9:1 **Application deadline** Rolling **Freshmen** 71% were admitted **Housing** Yes **Expenses** Tuition $13,170; Room & Board $4930 **Undergraduates** 45% women, 6% part-time, 19% 25 or older, 1% Native American, 2% Hispanic, 6% black, 2% Asian American or Pacific Islander **Most popular recent majors** Industrial design; painting **Academic program** Advanced placement, tutorials, honors program, internships **Contact** Office of Admissions, Cleveland Institute of Art, 11141 East Boulevard, Cleveland, OH 44106-1700. Telephone: 216-421-7418 or toll-free 800-223-4700. Fax: 216-421-7438. Web site: http://www.cia.edu/.

CLEVELAND INSTITUTE OF MUSIC

CLEVELAND, OHIO

General Independent, comprehensive, coed **Entrance** Very difficult **Setting** 488-acre urban campus **Total enrollment** 360 **Student/faculty ratio** 7:1 **Application deadline** 12/1 **Freshmen** 30% were admitted **Housing** Yes **Expenses** Tuition $17,029; Room & Board $5220 **Undergraduates** 50% women, 0.5% part-time, 1% 25 or older, 0% Native American, 3% Hispanic, 2% black, 3% Asian American or Pacific Islander **Academic program** English as a second language, advanced placement, accelerated degree program, summer session, internships **Contact** Mr. William Fay, Director of Admission, Cleveland Institute of Music, 11021 East Boulevard, Cleveland, OH 44106-1776. Telephone: 216-795-3107. Fax: 216-791-1530. E-mail: cimadmission@po.cwru.edu. Web site: http://www.cwru.edu/cim/cimhome.html.

CLEVELAND STATE UNIVERSITY
CLEVELAND, OHIO

General State-supported, university, coed **Entrance** Noncompetitive **Setting** 70-acre urban campus **Total enrollment** 15,655 **Student/faculty ratio** 18:1 **Application deadline** 8/1 **Freshmen** 97% were admitted **Housing** Yes **Expenses** Tuition $3528; Room & Board $4410 **Undergraduates** 55% women, 28% part-time, 38% 25 or older, 0.3% Native American, 3% Hispanic, 18% black, 3% Asian American or Pacific Islander **Most popular recent majors** Accounting; psychology; mass communications **Academic program** English as a second language, advanced placement, accelerated degree program, self-designed majors, tutorials, summer session, adult/continuing education programs, internships **Contact** Mr. Douglas Hartnagel, Director of Admissions, Cleveland State University, East 24th and Euclid Avenue, Cleveland, OH 44115. Telephone: 216-687-3754. Fax: 216-687-9366. Web site: http://www.csuohio.edu/.

COLLEGE OF MOUNT ST. JOSEPH
CINCINNATI, OHIO

General Independent Roman Catholic, comprehensive, coed **Entrance** Moderately difficult **Setting** 75-acre suburban campus **Total enrollment** 2,213 **Student/faculty ratio** 15:1 **Application deadline** 8/15 **Freshmen** 86% were admitted **Housing** Yes **Expenses** Tuition $11,950; Room & Board $5050 **Undergraduates** 72% women, 38% part-time, 38% 25 or older, 0.2% Native American, 1% Hispanic, 7% black, 2% Asian American or Pacific Islander **Most popular recent majors** Business administration; nursing; liberal arts and studies **Academic program** Average class size 22, English as a second language, advanced placement, accelerated degree program, self-designed majors, tutorials, honors program, summer session, adult/continuing education programs, internships **Contact** Mr. Edward C. Eckel, Director of Admission, College of Mount St. Joseph, 5701 Delhi Road, Cincinnati, OH 45233-1672. Telephone: 513-244-4302 or toll-free 800-654-9314. Fax: 513-244-4629. E-mail: edward_eckel@mail.msj.edu. Web site: http://www.msj.edu/.

THE COLLEGE OF WOOSTER
WOOSTER, OHIO

General Independent, 4-year, coed, affiliated with Presbyterian Church (U.S.A.) **Entrance** Moderately difficult **Setting** 320-acre small town campus **Total enrollment** 1,714 **Student/faculty ratio** 11:1 **Application deadline** 2/15 **Freshmen** 86% were admitted **Housing** Yes **Expenses** Tuition $19,230; Room & Board $5070 **Undergraduates** 52% women, 0.5% part-time, 1% 25 or older, 0.1% Native American, 1% Hispanic, 5% black, 2% Asian American or Pacific Islander **Most popular recent majors** English; biology; economics **Academic program** Average class size 22, advanced placement, self-designed majors, tutorials, summer session, internships **Contact** Ms. Carol D. Wheatley, Director of Admissions, The College of Wooster, Wooster, OH 44691. Telephone: 330-263-2270 ext. 2118 or toll-free 800-877-9905. Fax: 330-263-2621. E-mail: admissions@acs.wooster.edu. Web site: http://www.wooster.edu/.

▶ **For more information, see page 418.**

COLUMBUS COLLEGE OF ART AND DESIGN
COLUMBUS, OHIO

General Independent, 4-year, coed **Entrance** Moderately difficult **Setting** 7-acre urban campus **Total enrollment** 1,547 **Student/faculty ratio** 9:1 **Application deadline** Rolling **Freshmen** 77% were admitted **Housing** Yes **Expenses** Tuition $11,880; Room & Board $5800 **Undergraduates** 11% 25 or older **Most popular recent majors** Graphic design/commercial art/illustration; art; advertising **Academic program** Advanced placement, summer session, internships **Contact** Mr. Thomas E. Green, Director of Admissions, Columbus College of Art and Design, 107 North Ninth Street, Columbus, OH 43215-1758. Telephone: 614-224-9101.

DAVID N. MYERS COLLEGE
CLEVELAND, OHIO

General Independent, 4-year, coed **Entrance** Minimally difficult **Setting** 1-acre urban campus **Total enrollment** 1,145 **Student/faculty ratio** 11:1 **Application deadline** 9/1 **Freshmen** 68% were admitted **Housing** No **Expenses** Tuition $7800 **Undergraduates** 73% women, 51% part-time, 65% 25 or older, 0.3% Native American, 3% Hispanic, 41% black, 0.4% Asian American or Pacific Islander **Most popular recent majors** Business administration; accounting **Academic program** Average class size 11, advanced placement, accelerated degree program, tutorials, summer session, adult/continuing education programs, internships **Contact** Mr. Laurence Hice Jr., Director of Admissions, David N. Myers College, 112 Prospect Avenue, Cleveland, OH 44115-1096. Telephone: 216-523-3806 ext. 806 or toll-free 800-424-3953. Fax: 216-696-6430. E-mail: lhice@dnmyers.edu. Web site: http://www.dnmyers.edu/.

DEFIANCE COLLEGE
DEFIANCE, OHIO

General Independent, comprehensive, coed, affiliated with United Church of Christ **Entrance** Moderately difficult **Setting** 150-acre small town campus **Total enrollment** 816 **Student/faculty ratio** 13:1 **Application deadline** 8/15 **Freshmen** 71% were admitted **Housing** Yes **Expenses** Tuition $13,875; Room & Board $4070 **Undergraduates** 55% women, 31% part-time, 40% 25 or older, 0.1% Native American, 4% Hispanic, 4% black, 0.4% Asian American or Pacific Islander **Most popular recent majors** Elementary education; criminal justice/law enforcement administration; business administration **Academic program** Average class size 22, advanced placement, self-designed majors, tutorials, summer session, adult/continuing education programs, internships **Contact** Mr. Eric Stockard, Vice President of Enrollment Management, Defiance College, 701 North Clinton Street, Defiance, OH 43512-1610. Telephone: 419-784-4010 or toll-free 800-520-4632 ext. 2359. Fax: 419-783-2468. E-mail: admissions@defiance.edu. Web site: http://www.defiance.edu/.

DENISON UNIVERSITY
GRANVILLE, OHIO

General Independent, 4-year, coed **Entrance** Moderately difficult **Setting** 1,200-acre small town campus **Total enrollment** 2,025 **Student/faculty ratio** 12:1 **Application deadline** 2/1 **Freshmen** 78% were admitted **Housing** Yes **Expenses** Tuition $20,250; Room & Board $5370 **Undergraduates** 52% women, 1% part-time, 1% 25 or older, 0.1% Native American, 1% Hispanic, 3% black, 2% Asian American or Pacific Islander **Most popular recent majors** Economics; English; history **Academic program** Average class size 18, advanced placement, self-designed majors, tutorials, honors program, internships **Contact** Ms. Pennie Miller, Communications Coordinator, Denison University, Box H, Granville, OH 43023. Telephone: 614-587-6618 or toll-free 800-DENISON. Fax: 740-587-6306. E-mail: admissions@denison.edu. Web site: http://www.denison.edu/.

DEVRY INSTITUTE OF TECHNOLOGY
COLUMBUS, OHIO

General Proprietary, 4-year, coed **Entrance** Minimally difficult **Setting** 21-acre urban campus **Total enrollment** 2,883 **Student/faculty ratio** 29:1 **Application deadline** Rolling **Freshmen** 70% were admitted **Housing** No **Expenses** Tuition $7308 **Undergraduates** 23% women, 30% part-time, 37% 25 or older, 0.3% Native American, 1% Hispanic, 19% black, 2% Asian American or Pacific Islander **Most popular recent majors** Information sciences/systems; electrical/electronic engineering technology **Academic program** Advanced placement, accelerated degree program, summer session, adult/continuing education programs **Contact** Ms. Jody Wasmer, Director of Admissions, DeVry Institute of Technology, 1350 Alum Creek Drive, Columbus, OH 43209-2705. Telephone: 614-253-1525 ext. 700 or toll-free 800-426-3916 (in-state), 800-426-3909 (out-of-state). E-mail: admissions@devrycol5.edu. Web site: http://www.devry.col5.edu/.

FRANCISCAN UNIVERSITY OF STEUBENVILLE
STEUBENVILLE, OHIO

General Independent Roman Catholic, comprehensive, coed **Entrance** Moderately difficult **Setting** 100-acre suburban campus **Total enrollment** 1,997 **Student/faculty ratio** 16:1 **Application deadline** 6/30 **Freshmen** 92% were admitted **Housing** Yes **Expenses** Tuition $11,370; Room & Board $4730 **Undergraduates** 60% women, 10% part-time, 18% 25 or older, 0.3% Native American, 4% Hispanic, 1% black, 2% Asian American or Pacific Islander **Most popular recent majors** Theology; elementary education; business administration **Academic program** Average class size 21, English as a second language, advanced placement, accelerated degree program, tutorials, honors program, summer session, adult/continuing education programs, internships **Contact** Mrs. Margaret Weber, Director of Admissions, Franciscan University of Steubenville, 1235 University Boulevard, Steubenville, OH 43952-6701. Telephone: 740-283-6226 or toll-free 800-783-6220. Fax: 740-284-5456. E-mail: admissions@franuniv.edu. Web site: http://www.franuniv.edu/.

FRANKLIN UNIVERSITY
COLUMBUS, OHIO

General Independent, comprehensive, coed **Entrance** Noncompetitive **Setting** 14-acre urban campus **Total enrollment** 4,092 **Student/faculty ratio** 17:1 **Application deadline** Rolling **Freshmen** 100% were admitted **Housing** No **Expenses** Tuition $5314 **Undergraduates** 58% women, 67% part-time, 74% 25 or older, 0.4% Native American, 1% Hispanic, 13% black, 3% Asian American or Pacific Islander **Most popular recent majors** Business administration; accounting; computer science **Academic program** Average class size 22, English as a second language, advanced placement, accelerated degree program, self-designed majors, tutorials, summer session, adult/continuing education programs, internships **Contact** Ms. Linda M. Steele, Vice President for Students and Alumni, Franklin University, 201 South Grant Avenue, Columbus, OH 43215-5399. Telephone: 614-341-6230 or toll-free 888-341-6237. Fax: 614-224-8027. E-mail: info@franklin.edu. Web site: http://www.franklin.edu/.

GOD'S BIBLE SCHOOL AND COLLEGE

CINCINNATI, OHIO

General Independent interdenominational, 4-year, coed **Entrance** Minimally difficult **Setting** 14-acre urban campus **Total enrollment** 196 **Student/faculty ratio** 11:1 **Application deadline** Rolling **Freshmen** 100% were admitted **Housing** Yes **Expenses** Tuition $3850; Room & Board $2550 **Undergraduates** 56% women, 12% part-time, 18% 25 or older **Most popular recent majors** Biblical studies; religious education; music (voice and choral/opera performance) **Academic program** Average class size 60, advanced placement, summer session, internships **Contact** Mr. Phil Collingsworth, Dean of Enrollment Management, God's Bible School and College, 1810 Young Street, Cincinnati, OH 45210-1599. Telephone: 513-721-7944 ext. 270 or toll-free 800-486-4637. Fax: 513-721-3971. E-mail: admissions@gbs.edu.

HEIDELBERG COLLEGE

TIFFIN, OHIO

General Independent, comprehensive, coed, affiliated with United Church of Christ **Entrance** Moderately difficult **Setting** 110-acre small town campus **Total enrollment** 1,480 **Student/faculty ratio** 12:1 **Application deadline** 8/1 **Freshmen** 86% were admitted **Housing** Yes **Expenses** Tuition $16,260; Room & Board $5135 **Undergraduates** 52% women, 22% part-time, 6% 25 or older, 0.5% Native American, 1% Hispanic, 2% black, 0.5% Asian American or Pacific Islander **Most popular recent majors** Business administration; biology; education **Academic program** Average class size 14, English as a second language, advanced placement, accelerated degree program, honors program, summer session, adult/continuing education programs, internships **Contact** Mr. David Rhodes, Vice President for Enrollment, Heidelberg College, 310 East Market Street, Tiffin, OH 44883-2462. Telephone: 419-448-2330 or toll-free 800-434-3352. Fax: 419-448-2334. E-mail: adminfo@nike.heidelberg.edu. Web site: http://www.heidelberg.edu/.

HIRAM COLLEGE

HIRAM, OHIO

General Independent, 4-year, coed, affiliated with Christian Church (Disciples of Christ) **Entrance** Very difficult **Setting** 110-acre rural campus **Total enrollment** 1,151 **Student/faculty ratio** 11:1 **Application deadline** 3/15 **Freshmen** 88% were admitted **Housing** Yes **Expenses** Tuition $16,514; Room & Board $5092 **Undergraduates** 57% women, 21% part-time, 28% 25 or older, 1% Native American, 1% Hispanic, 8% black, 1% Asian American or Pacific Islander **Most popular recent majors** Biology; elementary education; business administration **Academic program** Average class size 15, English as a second language, advanced placement, accelerated degree program, self-designed majors, tutorials, summer session, adult/continuing education programs, internships **Contact** Mr. Monty L. Curtis, Vice President for Admission and College Relations, Hiram College, Box 96, Hiram, OH 44234-0067. Telephone: 330-569-5169 or toll-free 800-362-5280. Fax: 330-569-5944. E-mail: admission@hiram.edu. Web site: http://admission.hiram.edu/.

▶ **For more information, see page 449.**

JOHN CARROLL UNIVERSITY

UNIVERSITY HEIGHTS, OHIO

General Independent Roman Catholic (Jesuit), comprehensive, coed **Entrance** Moderately difficult **Setting** 60-acre suburban campus **Total enrollment** 4,391 **Student/faculty ratio** 10:1 **Application deadline** Rolling **Freshmen** 90% were admitted **Housing** Yes **Expenses** Tuition $14,620; Room & Board $5804 **Undergraduates** 51% women, 5% part-time, 2% 25 or older, 0.3% Native American, 2% Hispanic, 4% black, 3% Asian American or Pacific Islander **Most popular recent majors** Mass communications; psychology; biology **Academic program** Average class size 22, advanced placement, accelerated degree program, self-designed majors, tutorials, honors program, summer session, adult/continuing education programs, internships **Contact** Mr. Thomas P. Fanning, Director of Admission, John Carroll University, 20700 North Park Boulevard, University Heights, OH 44118-4581. Telephone: 216-397-4294. Fax: 216-397-3098. E-mail: admission@jcvaxa.jcu.edu. Web site: http://www.jcu.edu/.

KENT STATE UNIVERSITY

KENT, OHIO

General State-supported, university, coed **Entrance** Moderately difficult **Setting** 1,200-acre small town campus **Total enrollment** 20,743 **Student/faculty ratio** 17:1 **Application deadline** 3/15 **Freshmen** 91% were admitted **Housing** Yes **Expenses** Tuition $4460; Room & Board $4152 **Undergraduates** 19% 25 or older, 0.2% Native American, 1% Hispanic, 8% black, 1% Asian American or Pacific Islander **Most popular recent majors** Nursing; psychology; criminal justice/law enforcement administration **Academic program** Av-

Kent State University *(continued)*

erage class size 22, English as a second language, advanced placement, self-designed majors, tutorials, honors program, summer session, adult/continuing education programs, internships **Contact** Mr. Christopher Buttenschon, Assistant Director of Admissions, Kent State University, 161 Michael Schwartz Center, Kent, OH 44242-0001. Telephone: 330-672-2444 or toll-free 800-988-KENT. Fax: 330-672-2499. E-mail: kentadm@admissions.kent.edu. Web site: http://www.kent.edu/.

KENYON COLLEGE
GAMBIER, OHIO

General Independent, 4-year, coed **Entrance** Very difficult **Setting** 800-acre rural campus **Total enrollment** 1,551 **Student/faculty ratio** 10:1 **Application deadline** 2/1 **Freshmen** 70% were admitted **Housing** Yes **Expenses** Tuition $22,850; Room & Board $3990 **Undergraduates** 54% women, 0% 25 or older, 0.1% Native American, 3% Hispanic, 4% black, 3% Asian American or Pacific Islander **Most popular recent majors** English; history; psychology **Academic program** Advanced placement, self-designed majors, tutorials, honors program, internships **Contact** Mr. John W. Anderson, Dean of Admissions, Kenyon College, Office of Admissions, Gambier, OH 43022-9623. Telephone: 614-427-5776 or toll-free 800-848-2468. Fax: 740-427-2634. E-mail: admissions@kenyon.edu. Web site: http://www.kenyon.edu/.

LAKE ERIE COLLEGE
PAINESVILLE, OHIO

General Independent, comprehensive, coed **Entrance** Moderately difficult **Setting** 57-acre small town campus **Total enrollment** 701 **Student/faculty ratio** 13:1 **Application deadline** 8/1 **Freshmen** 89% were admitted **Housing** Yes **Expenses** Tuition $13,750; Room & Board $4940 **Undergraduates** 73% women, 27% part-time, 43% 25 or older, 0% Native American, 1% Hispanic, 3% black, 0% Asian American or Pacific Islander **Most popular recent majors** Business administration; elementary education; accounting **Academic program** Average class size 15, advanced placement, accelerated degree program, self-designed majors, tutorials, summer session, adult/continuing education programs, internships **Contact** Ms. Mary Ann Kalbaugh, Vice President and Dean of College Services, Lake Erie College, 391 West Washington Street, Painesville, OH 44077-3389. Telephone: 440-639-7879 or toll-free 800-533-4996. Fax: 440-352-3533. E-mail: lecadmit@lakeerie.edu. Web site: http://www.lakeerie.edu/.

LOURDES COLLEGE
SYLVANIA, OHIO

General Independent Roman Catholic, 4-year, coed **Contact** Ms. Beth Tanesky, Director of Admissions, Lourdes College, 6832 Convent Boulevard, Sylvania, OH 43560-2898. Telephone: 419-885-5291 ext. 299. Fax: 419-882-3987. E-mail: btanesky@lourdes.edu.

MALONE COLLEGE
CANTON, OHIO

General Independent, comprehensive, coed, affiliated with Evangelical Friends Church–Eastern Region **Entrance** Moderately difficult **Setting** 78-acre suburban campus **Total enrollment** 2,242 **Student/faculty ratio** 15:1 **Application deadline** 7/1 **Freshmen** 87% were admitted **Housing** Yes **Expenses** Tuition $11,280; Room & Board $4600 **Undergraduates** 62% women, 10% part-time, 26% 25 or older, 0.2% Native American, 1% Hispanic, 4% black, 0.2% Asian American or Pacific Islander **Most popular recent majors** Elementary education; communications **Academic program** Average class size 27, advanced placement, accelerated degree program, self-designed majors, tutorials, summer session, adult/continuing education programs, internships **Contact** Mr. John Chopka, Dean of Admissions, Malone College, 515 25th Street, NW, Canton, OH 44709-3897. Telephone: 330-471-8145 or toll-free 800-521-1146. Fax: 330-454-6977. E-mail: admissions@malone.edu. Web site: http://www.malone.edu/.

MARIETTA COLLEGE
MARIETTA, OHIO

General Independent, comprehensive, coed **Entrance** Moderately difficult **Setting** 120-acre small town campus **Total enrollment** 1,290 **Student/faculty ratio** 12:1 **Application deadline** 4/15 **Freshmen** 76% were admitted **Housing** Yes **Expenses** Tuition $16,150; Room & Board $4586 **Undergraduates** 51% women, 13% part-time, 4% 25 or older, 0.2% Native American, 1% Hispanic, 2% black, 1% Asian American or Pacific Islander **Most popular recent majors** Business administration; mass communications; education **Academic program** Average class size 20, English as a second language, advanced placement, accelerated degree program, self-designed majors, tutorials, honors program, summer session, adult/continuing education programs, internships **Contact** Ms. Marke M. Vickers, Director of Admission, Marietta College, 215 Fifth Street, Marietta, OH 45750-4000. Telephone: 740-376-4600 or toll-free 800-331-7896. Fax: 740-376-8888. E-mail: admit@mcnet.marietta.edu. Web site: http://www.marietta.edu/.

▶ **For more information, see page 467.**

THE MCGREGOR SCHOOL OF ANTIOCH UNIVERSITY
YELLOW SPRINGS, OHIO

General Independent, upper-level, coed **Contact** Ms. Terri J. Haney, Director of Admissions and Community Relations, The McGregor School of Antioch University, 800 Livermore Street, Yellow Springs, OH 45387-1609. Telephone: 937-767-6325. Fax: 937-767-6461. E-mail: admiss@unibase.antioch.edu.

MIAMI UNIVERSITY
OXFORD, OHIO

General State-related, university, coed **Entrance** Moderately difficult **Setting** 2,000-acre small town campus **Total enrollment** 16,328 **Student/faculty ratio** 18:1 **Application deadline** 1/31 **Freshmen** 77% were admitted **Housing** Yes **Expenses** Tuition $5512; Room & Board $4810 **Undergraduates** 55% women, 5% part-time, 3% 25 or older, 0.3% Native American, 2% Hispanic, 4% black, 2% Asian American or Pacific Islander **Most popular recent majors** Business marketing and marketing management; elementary education; zoology **Academic program** Average class size 25, English as a second language, advanced placement, accelerated degree program, self-designed majors, tutorials, honors program, summer session, adult/continuing education programs, internships **Contact** Dr. James S. McCoy, Associate Vice President for Enrollment Services, Miami University, Oxford, OH 45056. Telephone: 513-529-2531. Fax: 513-529-1550. E-mail: admission@muohio.edu. Web site: http://www.muohio.edu/.

MOUNT CARMEL COLLEGE OF NURSING
COLUMBUS, OHIO

General Independent, 4-year **Contact** Ms. Merschel Menefield, Director of Admissions, Mount Carmel College of Nursing, 127 South Davis Avenue, Columbus, OH 43222. Telephone: 614-234-5800.

MOUNT UNION COLLEGE
ALLIANCE, OHIO

General Independent United Methodist, 4-year, coed **Entrance** Moderately difficult **Setting** 105-acre suburban campus **Total enrollment** 1,935 **Student/faculty ratio** 16:1 **Application deadline** Rolling **Freshmen** 88% were admitted **Housing** Yes **Expenses** Tuition $14,290; Room & Board $3870 **Undergraduates** 53% women, 5% part-time, 1% 25 or older, 0.3% Native American, 1% Hispanic, 3% black, 1% Asian American or Pacific Islander **Most popular recent majors** Business administration; education; biology **Academic program** Average class size 19, English as a second language, advanced placement, accelerated degree program, self-designed majors, tutorials, honors program, summer session, adult/continuing education programs, internships **Contact** Mr. Greg King, Director of Admissions and Enrollment Management, Mount Union College, 1972 Clark Avenue, Alliance, OH 44601-3993. Telephone: 330-823-2590 or toll-free 800-334-6682 (in-state), 800-992-6682 (out-of-state). Fax: 330-821-0425. E-mail: admissn@muc.edu. Web site: http://www.muc.edu/.

MOUNT VERNON NAZARENE COLLEGE
MOUNT VERNON, OHIO

General Independent Nazarene, comprehensive, coed **Contact** Ms. Doris Webb, Director of Admissions and Student Recruitment, Mount Vernon Nazarene College, 800 Martinsburg Road, Mount Vernon, OH 43050-9500. Telephone: 740-397-6862 or toll-free 800-782-2435. E-mail: admissions@mvnc.edu. Web site: http://www.mvnc.edu.

MUSKINGUM COLLEGE
NEW CONCORD, OHIO

General Independent, comprehensive, coed, affiliated with Presbyterian Church (U.S.A.) **Entrance** Moderately difficult **Setting** 215-acre small town campus **Total enrollment** 1,431 **Student/faculty ratio** 15:1 **Application deadline** 6/1 **Freshmen** 81% were admitted **Housing** Yes **Expenses** Tuition $10,785; Room & Board $4500 **Undergraduates** 50% women, 2% part-time, 4% 25 or older **Most popular recent majors** Business administration; elementary education; secondary education **Academic program** Average class size 22, English as a second language, advanced placement, accelerated degree program, self-designed majors, tutorials, summer session, internships **Contact** Mr. Doug Kellar, Director of Admission, Muskingum College, 163 Stormont Street, New Concord, OH 43762. Telephone: 740-826-8137 or toll-free 800-752-6082. Fax: 740-826-8404. E-mail: adminfo@muskingum.edu. Web site: http://www.muskingum.edu/.

NOTRE DAME COLLEGE OF OHIO
SOUTH EUCLID, OHIO

General Independent Roman Catholic, comprehensive, women only **Entrance** Moderately difficult **Setting** 53-acre suburban campus **Total enrollment** 627 **Student/faculty ratio** 13:1 **Application deadline** Rolling **Freshmen** 73% were admitted **Housing** Yes **Expenses** Tuition $12,975; Room & Board $5250 **Undergraduates** 50% part-time, 54% 25 or older, 0% Native American, 3%

Notre Dame College of Ohio *(continued)*

Hispanic, 23% black, 1% Asian American or Pacific Islander **Most popular recent majors** Business administration; elementary education; biology **Academic program** Average class size 17, advanced placement, accelerated degree program, self-designed majors, summer session, adult/continuing education programs, internships **Contact** Mr. Ronald L. Bowman Jr., Director of Admissions and Student Records, Notre Dame College of Ohio, 4545 College Road, South Euclid, OH 44121-4293. Telephone: 216-381-1680 ext. 355 or toll-free 800-NDC-1680 ext. 355. Fax: 216-381-3802. E-mail: admissions@ndc.edu.

OBERLIN COLLEGE
OBERLIN, OHIO

General Independent, 4-year, coed **Entrance** Very difficult **Setting** 440-acre small town campus **Total enrollment** 2,904 **Student/faculty ratio** 12:1 **Application deadline** 1/15 **Freshmen** 62% were admitted **Housing** Yes **Expenses** Tuition $22,438; Room & Board $6358 **Undergraduates** 58% women, 2% part-time, 1% 25 or older, 1% Native American, 4% Hispanic, 8% black, 8% Asian American or Pacific Islander **Most popular recent majors** English; history; biology **Academic program** English as a second language, advanced placement, accelerated degree program, self-designed majors, tutorials, honors program, internships **Contact** Ms. Debra Chermonte, Director of College Admissions, Oberlin College, Admissions Office, Carnegie Building, Oberlin, OH 44074-1090. Telephone: 440-775-8411 or toll-free 800-622-OBIE. Fax: 440-775-6905. E-mail: college.admissions@oberlin.edu. Web site: http://www.oberlin.edu/.

OHIO DOMINICAN COLLEGE
COLUMBUS, OHIO

General Independent Roman Catholic, 4-year, coed **Entrance** Moderately difficult **Setting** 62-acre urban campus **Total enrollment** 1,883 **Student/faculty ratio** 17:1 **Application deadline** Rolling **Housing** Yes **Expenses** Tuition $9350; Room & Board $4720 **Undergraduates** 43% 25 or older **Most popular recent majors** Business administration; elementary education; criminal justice/law enforcement administration **Academic program** English as a second language, advanced placement, self-designed majors, honors program, summer session, adult/continuing education programs, internships **Contact** Ms. Vicki Thompson-Campbell, Director of Admissions, Ohio Dominican College, 1216 Sunbury Road, Columbus, OH 43219-2099. Telephone: 614-251-4500 or toll-free 800-854-2670. Fax: 614-252-0776. E-mail: admissions@odc.edu. Web site: http://www.odc.edu.

OHIO NORTHERN UNIVERSITY
ADA, OHIO

General Independent United Methodist, comprehensive, coed **Entrance** Moderately difficult **Setting** 260-acre small town campus **Total enrollment** 2,927 **Student/faculty ratio** 13:1 **Application deadline** 8/15 **Freshmen** 94% were admitted **Housing** Yes **Expenses** Tuition $19,815; Room & Board $4875 **Undergraduates** 50% women, 2% part-time, 3% 25 or older, 0.04% Native American, 0.5% Hispanic, 3% black, 1% Asian American or Pacific Islander **Most popular recent majors** Pharmacy; mechanical engineering; elementary education **Academic program** English as a second language, advanced placement, tutorials, summer session, internships **Contact** Ms. Karen Condeni, Vice President of Admissions and Financial Aid, Ohio Northern University, 525 South Main, Ada, OH 45810-1599. Telephone: 419-772-2260. Fax: 419-772-2313. E-mail: admissions-ug@onu.edu. Web site: http://www.onu.edu/.

THE OHIO STATE UNIVERSITY
COLUMBUS, OHIO

General State-supported, university, coed **Entrance** Moderately difficult **Setting** 2,905-acre urban campus **Total enrollment** 48,278 **Student/faculty ratio** 12:1 **Application deadline** 2/15 **Freshmen** 79% were admitted **Housing** Yes **Expenses** Tuition $3660; Room & Board $5094 **Undergraduates** 48% women, 15% part-time, 15% 25 or older, 0.4% Native American, 2% Hispanic, 8% black, 5% Asian American or Pacific Islander **Most popular recent majors** Psychology; English; communications **Academic program** English as a second language, advanced placement, accelerated degree program, self-designed majors, tutorials, honors program, summer session, adult/continuing education programs, internships **Contact** Ms. Stephanie Ford, Assistant Director, Admissions Information Center, The Ohio State University, 3rd Floor, Lincoln Tower, Columbus, OH 43210-1200. Telephone: 614-292-3980. Fax: 614-292-4818. E-mail: admissions@osu.edu. Web site: http://www.ohio-state.edu/.

THE OHIO STATE UNIVERSITY AT LIMA
LIMA, OHIO

General State-supported, 4-year, coed **Contact** Ms. Garlene Penn, Director of Admissions, The Ohio State University at Lima, 4240 Campus Drive, Lima, OH 45804-3576. Telephone: 419-221-1641. Web site: http://www.ohio-state.edu/.

THE OHIO STATE UNIVERSITY AT MARION
MARION, OHIO

General State-supported, 4-year, coed **Contact** Ms. Becky Vanderlind, Admissions Counselor and Staff Assistant, The Ohio State University at Marion, 1465 Mount Vernon Avenue, Marion, OH 43302-5695. Telephone: 614-389-6786. Web site: http://www.ohio-state.edu/.

THE OHIO STATE UNIVERSITY–MANSFIELD CAMPUS
MANSFIELD, OHIO

General State-supported, 4-year, coed **Contact** Mr. Henry D. Thomas, Coordinator of Admissions and Financial Aid, The Ohio State University-Mansfield Campus, 1680 University Drive, Mansfield, OH 44906-1599. Telephone: 419-755-4226. Web site: http://www.ohio-state.edu/.

THE OHIO STATE UNIVERSITY–NEWARK CAMPUS
NEWARK, OHIO

General State-supported, 4-year, coed **Contact** Ms. Ann Donahue, Coordinator of Admissions, The Ohio State University-Newark Campus, 1179 University Drive, Newark, OH 43055-1797. Telephone: 614-366-9333. Web site: http://www.ohio-state.edu/.

OHIO UNIVERSITY
ATHENS, OHIO

General State-supported, university, coed **Entrance** Moderately difficult **Setting** 1,700-acre small town campus **Total enrollment** 19,564 **Student/faculty ratio** 19:1 **Application deadline** 2/1 **Freshmen** 75% were admitted **Housing** Yes **Expenses** Tuition $4275; Room & Board $4698 **Undergraduates** 54% women, 7% part-time, 7% 25 or older, 0.2% Native American, 1% Hispanic, 3% black, 1% Asian American or Pacific Islander **Most popular recent majors** Biology; journalism; elementary education **Academic program** Average class size 19, English as a second language, advanced placement, accelerated degree program, self-designed majors, tutorials, honors program, summer session, adult/continuing education programs, internships **Contact** Mr. N. Kip Howard, Director of Admissions, Ohio University, Athens, OH 45701-2979. Telephone: 740-593-4100. Fax: 740-593-0560. E-mail: uadmiss1@ohiou.edu. Web site: http://www.ohiou.edu/.

OHIO UNIVERSITY–CHILLICOTHE
CHILLICOTHE, OHIO

General State-supported, 4-year, coed **Contact** Mr. Richard R. Whitney, Director of Student Services, Ohio University-Chillicothe, 571 West Fifth Street, PO Box 629, Chillicothe, OH 45601-0629. Telephone: 614-774-7242. Fax: 614-774-7214. Web site: http://csc.www.cats.ohiou.edu/.

OHIO UNIVERSITY–EASTERN
ST. CLAIRSVILLE, OHIO

General State-supported, 4-year, coed **Contact** Mr. Barry Hess, Director of Student Services, Ohio University-Eastern, 45425 National Road, St. Clairsville, OH 43950-9724. Telephone: 614-695-1720 ext. 213 or toll-free 800-648-3331 (in-state). E-mail: hess@ouvaxa.cats.ohiou.edu.

OHIO UNIVERSITY–LANCASTER
LANCASTER, OHIO

General State-supported, comprehensive, coed **Contact** Dr. Scott Shepherd, Director of Student Services, Ohio University-Lancaster, 1570 Granville Pike, Lancaster, OH 43130-1097. Telephone: 614-654-6711 ext. 209. E-mail: shepherd@ouvaxa.cats.ohiou.edu.

OHIO UNIVERSITY–ZANESVILLE
ZANESVILLE, OHIO

General State-supported, comprehensive, coed **Entrance** Noncompetitive **Setting** 179-acre rural campus **Total enrollment** 1,222 **Student/faculty ratio** 18:1 **Application deadline** Rolling **Freshmen** 100% were admitted **Housing** No **Expenses** Tuition $3117 **Undergraduates** 67% women, 37% part-time, 33% 25 or older, 0.3% Native American, 0.3% Hispanic, 2% black, 0.3% Asian American or Pacific Islander **Most popular recent majors** Nursing; elementary education; liberal arts and studies **Academic program** Advanced placement, self-designed majors, summer session, adult/continuing education programs **Contact** Director of Admissions, Ohio University-Zanesville, 1425 Newark Road, Zanesville, OH 43701-2695. Telephone: 614-453-0762. Fax: 614-453-6161.

OHIO WESLEYAN UNIVERSITY
DELAWARE, OHIO

General Independent United Methodist, 4-year, coed **Entrance** Very difficult **Setting** 200-acre small town campus **Total enrollment** 1,893 **Student/faculty ratio** 14:1 **Application deadline** 3/1 **Freshmen** 82% were admitted **Housing** Yes **Expenses** Tuition $20,040; Room & Board $6370 **Undergraduates** 52% women, 1% part-time, 1% 25 or older, 0.1% Native American, 1% Hispanic, 4% black, 2% Asian American or Pacific Islander **Most popular recent majors** Zoology; psychology; business administration **Academic pro-**

Ohio Wesleyan University *(continued)*

gram Average class size 18, advanced placement, accelerated degree program, self-designed majors, tutorials, honors program, summer session, internships **Contact** Mr. Douglas C. Thompson, Dean of Admission, Ohio Wesleyan University, 61 South Sandusky Street, Delaware, OH 43015. Telephone: 740-368-3020 or toll-free 800-922-8953. Fax: 740-368-3314. E-mail: owuadmit@cc.owu.edu. Web site: http://www.owu.edu/.

OTTERBEIN COLLEGE
WESTERVILLE, OHIO

General Independent United Methodist, comprehensive, coed **Entrance** Moderately difficult **Setting** 140-acre suburban campus **Total enrollment** 2,697 **Student/faculty ratio** 13:1 **Application deadline** 4/20 **Freshmen** 85% were admitted **Housing** Yes **Expenses** Tuition $14,997; Room & Board $4750 **Undergraduates** 59% women, 33% 25 or older **Most popular recent majors** Business administration; accounting; elementary education **Academic program** English as a second language, advanced placement, accelerated degree program, self-designed majors, honors program, summer session, adult/continuing education programs, internships **Contact** Ms. Cass Johnson, Director of Admissions, Otterbein College, Westerville, OH 43081. Telephone: 614-823-1500 or toll-free 800-488-8144. Fax: 614-823-1200. E-mail: uotterb@otterbein.edu. Web site: http://www.otterbein.edu/.

PONTIFICAL COLLEGE JOSEPHINUM
COLUMBUS, OHIO

General Independent Roman Catholic, comprehensive, primarily men **Contact** Ms. Barbara Couts, Secretary for Admissions, Pontifical College Josephinum, 7625 North High Street, Columbus, OH 43235-1498. Telephone: 614-885-5585 ext. 436.

SHAWNEE STATE UNIVERSITY
PORTSMOUTH, OHIO

General State-supported, 4-year, coed **Entrance** Noncompetitive **Setting** 500-acre small town campus **Total enrollment** 3,223 **Student/faculty ratio** 13:1 **Application deadline** Rolling **Freshmen** 100% were admitted **Housing** Yes **Expenses** Tuition $3090; Room & Board $4500 **Undergraduates** 63% women, 18% part-time, 33% 25 or older, 1% Native American, 1% Hispanic, 2% black, 0.4% Asian American or Pacific Islander **Most popular recent majors** Health science; elementary education; business administration **Academic program** Average class size 20, advanced placement, self-designed majors, tutorials, summer session, adult/continuing education programs, internships **Contact** Ms. Suzanne Shelpman, Director of Admission and Retention, Shawnee State University, 940 Second Street, Portsmouth, OH 45662-4344. Telephone: 614-355-2610 ext. 610 or toll-free 800-959-2SSU. Fax: 614-355-2111. E-mail: admsn@shawnee.edu. Web site: http://www.shawnee.edu/.

TIFFIN UNIVERSITY
TIFFIN, OHIO

General Independent, comprehensive, coed **Entrance** Minimally difficult **Setting** 108-acre small town campus **Total enrollment** 1,277 **Student/faculty ratio** 20:1 **Application deadline** Rolling **Freshmen** 90% were admitted **Housing** Yes **Expenses** Tuition $9210; Room & Board $4400 **Undergraduates** 51% women, 36% part-time, 24% 25 or older, 0% Native American, 1% Hispanic, 7% black, 0.3% Asian American or Pacific Islander **Most popular recent majors** Business administration; accounting; criminal justice/law enforcement administration **Academic program** Advanced placement, accelerated degree program, summer session, adult/continuing education programs, internships **Contact** Mr. Ron Schumacher, Director of Admissions, Tiffin University, 155 Miami Street, Tiffin, OH 44883-2161. Telephone: 419-448-3425 or toll-free 800-968-6446. Fax: 419-447-9605. E-mail: admiss@tiffin.edu. Web site: http://www.tiffin.edu/.

THE UNION INSTITUTE
CINCINNATI, OHIO

General Independent, university, coed **Entrance** Moderately difficult **Setting** 5-acre urban campus **Total enrollment** 2,036 **Student/faculty ratio** 16:1 **Application deadline** 10/9 **Freshmen** 79% were admitted **Housing** No **Expenses** Tuition $5808 **Undergraduates** 58% women, 32% part-time, 97% 25 or older, 1% Native American, 11% Hispanic, 29% black, 1% Asian American or Pacific Islander **Most popular recent majors** Business administration; criminal justice/law enforcement administration; psychology **Academic program** Advanced placement, self-designed majors, tutorials, summer session, adult/continuing education programs **Contact** Mr. Michael Robertson, Associate Registrar, The Union Institute, 440 East McMillan Street, Cincinnati, OH 45206-1925. Telephone: 513-861-6400 or toll-free 800-486-3116. Fax: 513-861-0779. E-mail: mrobertson@tui.edu. Web site: http://www.tui.edu/.

THE UNIVERSITY OF AKRON
AKRON, OHIO

General State-supported, university, coed **Entrance** Noncompetitive **Setting** 170-acre urban campus **Total enrollment** 23,538 **Student/faculty ratio** 20:1 **Application deadline** 8/25 **Freshmen** 100% were admitted **Housing** Yes **Expenses** Tuition $3660; Room & Board $4490 **Undergraduates** 54% women, 39% part-time, 33% 25 or older, 1% Native American, 1% Hispanic, 13% black, 2% Asian American or Pacific Islander **Most popular recent majors** Nursing; elementary education; accounting **Academic program** Average class size 27, English as a second language, advanced placement, accelerated degree program, self-designed majors, tutorials, honors program, summer session, adult/continuing education programs, internships **Contact** Ms. Connie Murray, Senior Associate Director of Admissions, The University of Akron, 381 Buchtel Common, Akron, OH 44325-2001. Telephone: 330-972-6428 or toll-free 800-655-4884. Fax: 330-972-7676. Web site: http://www.uakron.edu/.

UNIVERSITY OF CINCINNATI
CINCINNATI, OHIO

General State-supported, university, coed **Entrance** Moderately difficult **Setting** 137-acre urban campus **Total enrollment** 28,161 **Student/faculty ratio** 14:1 **Application deadline** Rolling **Freshmen** 85% were admitted **Housing** Yes **Expenses** Tuition $4359; Room & Board $5643 **Undergraduates** 47% women, 22% part-time, 16% 25 or older, 0.4% Native American, 1% Hispanic, 14% black, 3% Asian American or Pacific Islander **Most popular recent majors** Business administration; engineering; education **Academic program** English as a second language, accelerated degree program, self-designed majors, honors program, summer session, adult/continuing education programs, internships **Contact** Mr. James Williams, Director of Admissions, University of Cincinnati, Mail Location 91, 100 Edwards Center, Cincinnati, OH 45221-0091. Telephone: 513-556-1100. Web site: http://www.uc.edu/.

UNIVERSITY OF DAYTON
DAYTON, OHIO

General Independent Roman Catholic, university, coed **Entrance** Moderately difficult **Setting** 110-acre suburban campus **Total enrollment** 10,208 **Student/faculty ratio** 14:1 **Application deadline** Rolling **Freshmen** 93% were admitted **Housing** Yes **Expenses** Tuition $14,670; Room & Board $4670 **Undergraduates** 51% women, 6% part-time, 6% 25 or older, 0.2% Native American, 2% Hispanic, 3% black, 1% Asian American or Pacific Islander **Most popular recent majors** Mass communications; elementary education; business marketing and marketing management **Academic program** Average class size 27, English as a second language, advanced placement, accelerated degree program, self-designed majors, tutorials, honors program, summer session, adult/continuing education programs, internships **Contact** Mr. Myron H. Achbach, Director of Admission, University of Dayton, 300 College Park, Dayton, OH 45469-1611. Telephone: 937-229-4411 or toll-free 800-837-7433. Fax: 937-229-4545. E-mail: admission@udayton.edu. Web site: http://www.udayton.edu/.

THE UNIVERSITY OF FINDLAY
FINDLAY, OHIO

General Independent, comprehensive, coed, affiliated with Church of God **Entrance** Moderately difficult **Setting** 160-acre small town campus **Total enrollment** 4,017 **Student/faculty ratio** 19:1 **Application deadline** Rolling **Housing** Yes **Expenses** Tuition $13,878; Room & Board $5360 **Undergraduates** 53% women, 22% part-time, 31% 25 or older, 1% Native American, 3% Hispanic, 7% black, 4% Asian American or Pacific Islander **Most popular recent majors** Business administration; (pre)veterinary studies; environmental science **Academic program** Average class size 35, English as a second language, advanced placement, self-designed majors, tutorials, honors program, summer session, adult/continuing education programs, internships **Contact** Mr. Michael Momany, Director of Admissions, The University of Findlay, 1000 N. Main Street, Findlay, OH 45840-3653. Telephone: 419-424-4502 or toll-free 800-548-0932. Fax: 419-424-4822. Web site: http://www.findlay.edu/.

UNIVERSITY OF RIO GRANDE
RIO GRANDE, OHIO

General Independent, comprehensive, coed **Entrance** Noncompetitive **Setting** 170-acre rural campus **Total enrollment** 2,000 **Student/faculty ratio** 18:1 **Application deadline** Rolling **Freshmen** 100% were admitted **Housing** Yes **Expenses** Tuition $4197; Room & Board $4605 **Undergraduates** 59% women, 16% part-time, 25% 25 or older, 0.4% Native American, 1% black, 0.1% Asian American or Pacific Islander **Most popular recent majors** Education; business administration; nursing **Academic program** Average class size 18, English as a second language, advanced placement, accelerated degree program, self-designed majors, tutorials, honors program, summer session, adult/continuing education programs, internships **Contact** Mr. Mark F. Abell, Executive Director of Admissions, University of Rio Grande, 218 North College Avenue, Rio Grande, OH 45674. Telephone: 740-245-5353 ext. 7206 or toll-free 800-282-7201 (in-state). Fax: 740-245-9220. E-mail: mabell@urgrgcc.edu. Web site: http://www.urgrgcc.edu/.

UNIVERSITY OF TOLEDO
TOLEDO, OHIO

General State-supported, university, coed **Entrance** Noncompetitive **Setting** 407-acre suburban campus **Total enrollment** 20,307 **Student/faculty ratio** 20:1 **Application deadline** Rolling **Freshmen** 95% were admitted **Housing** Yes **Expenses** Tuition $3952; Room & Board $4194 **Undergraduates** 53% women, 28% part-time, 25% 25 or older, 1% Native American, 2% Hispanic, 14% black, 2% Asian American or Pacific Islander **Most popular recent majors** Mass communications; business marketing and marketing management **Academic program** English as a second language, advanced placement, accelerated degree program, self-designed majors, tutorials, honors program, summer session, adult/continuing education programs, internships **Contact** Mr. Kent Hopkins, Director of Admissions, University of Toledo, 2801 West Bancroft, Toledo, OH 43606-3398. Telephone: 419-530-8888 or toll-free 800-5TOLEDO (in-state). Fax: 419-530-4504. E-mail: adm0017@uoft01.utoledo.edu. Web site: http://www.utoledo.edu/.

URBANA UNIVERSITY
URBANA, OHIO

General Independent religious, 4-year, coed **Entrance** Moderately difficult **Setting** 128-acre small town campus **Student/faculty ratio** 16:1 **Application deadline** Rolling **Freshmen** 79% were admitted **Housing** Yes **Expenses** Tuition $10,530; Room & Board $4500 **Undergraduates** 20% 25 or older **Most popular recent majors** Business administration; education; liberal arts and studies **Academic program** Average class size 17, English as a second language, advanced placement, accelerated degree program, self-designed majors, honors program, summer session, adult/continuing education programs, internships **Contact** Mr. M.L. Smith, Director of Admissions, Urbana University, 579 College Way, Urbana, OH 43078-2091. Telephone: 937-484-1356 or toll-free 800-787-2262 (in-state). Fax: 937-484-1389. E-mail: admiss2@urbana.edu. Web site: http://www.urbana.edu/.

URSULINE COLLEGE
PEPPER PIKE, OHIO

General Independent Roman Catholic, comprehensive, primarily women **Entrance** Minimally difficult **Setting** 112-acre suburban campus **Total enrollment** 1,233 **Student/faculty ratio** 14:1 **Application deadline** Rolling **Housing** Yes **Expenses** Tuition $12,128; Room & Board $4460 **Undergraduates** 58% 25 or older **Most popular recent majors** Nursing; psychology; business administration **Academic program** Advanced placement, self-designed majors, summer session, adult/continuing education programs, internships **Contact** Ms. Colleen C. Kearney, Director of Admissions, Ursuline College, 2550 Lander Road, Pepper Pike, OH 44124-4398. Telephone: 440-449-4203. Fax: 440-449-2235. E-mail: dgiaco@en.com. Web site: http://www.ursuline.edu/.

WALSH UNIVERSITY
NORTH CANTON, OHIO

General Independent Roman Catholic, comprehensive, coed **Entrance** Moderately difficult **Setting** 58-acre small town campus **Total enrollment** 1,492 **Student/faculty ratio** 19:1 **Application deadline** Rolling **Freshmen** 83% were admitted **Housing** Yes **Expenses** Tuition $10,680; Room & Board $4990 **Undergraduates** 46% 25 or older **Most popular recent majors** Business administration; nursing; education **Academic program** Average class size 19, English as a second language, advanced placement, accelerated degree program, self-designed majors, tutorials, honors program, summer session, adult/continuing education programs, internships **Contact** Mr. Doug Swartz, Director of Admissions, Walsh University, 2020 Easton Street, NW, North Canton, OH 44720-3396. Telephone: 330-490-7172 or toll-free 800-362-9846 (in-state), 800-362-8846 (out-of-state). Fax: 330-490-7165. E-mail: admissions@alex.walsh.edu. Web site: http://www.walsh.edu/.

WILBERFORCE UNIVERSITY
WILBERFORCE, OHIO

General Independent, 4-year, coed, affiliated with African Methodist Episcopal Church **Entrance** Minimally difficult **Setting** 125-acre rural campus **Total enrollment** 800 **Student/faculty ratio** 12:1 **Application deadline** 7/1 **Housing** Yes **Expenses** Tuition $8060; Room & Board $4260 **Undergraduates** 10% 25 or older **Academic program** Advanced placement, tutorials, honors program **Contact** Mr. Kenneth C. Christmon, Director of Admissions, Wilberforce University, 1055 North Bickett Road, Wilberforce, OH 45384. Telephone: 937-376-2911 ext. 789 or toll-free 800-367-8568. Fax: 937-376-4751. E-mail: admissions@shorter.wilberforce.edu. Web site: http://www.wilberforce.edu/.

WILMINGTON COLLEGE
WILMINGTON, OHIO

General Independent Friends, 4-year, coed **Entrance** Moderately difficult **Setting** 1,465-acre small town campus **Total enrollment** 1,033 **Student/faculty ratio** 17:1 **Application deadline** Rolling **Freshmen** 80% were admitted **Housing**

Yes **Expenses** Tuition $12,500; Room & Board $4590 **Undergraduates** 50% women, 6% part-time, 0.4% Hispanic, 4% black, 0.1% Asian American or Pacific Islander **Most popular recent majors** Education; business administration; agricultural sciences **Academic program** Average class size 22, advanced placement, self-designed majors, tutorials, honors program, summer session, adult/continuing education programs, internships **Contact** Dr. Lawrence T. Lesick, Dean of Admission and Financial Aid, Wilmington College, Pyle Center Box 1185, Wilmington, OH 45177. Telephone: 937-382-6661 ext. 260 or toll-free 800-341-9318. Fax: 937-382-7077. E-mail: admission@wilmington.edu. Web site: http://www.wilmington.edu/.

WITTENBERG UNIVERSITY
SPRINGFIELD, OHIO

General Independent, 4-year, coed, affiliated with Evangelical Lutheran Church **Entrance** Moderately difficult **Setting** 71-acre suburban campus **Total enrollment** 2,088 **Student/faculty ratio** 14:1 **Application deadline** 3/15 **Freshmen** 91% were admitted **Housing** Yes **Expenses** Tuition $19,140; Room & Board $4860 **Undergraduates** 58% women, 4% part-time, 1% 25 or older, 0.3% Native American, 1% Hispanic, 7% black, 1% Asian American or Pacific Islander **Most popular recent majors** Business administration; biology; education **Academic program** English as a second language, advanced placement, accelerated degree program, self-designed majors, tutorials, honors program, summer session, adult/continuing education programs, internships **Contact** Mr. Kenneth G. Benne, Dean of Admissions, Wittenberg University, PO Box 720, Springfield, OH 45501-0720. Telephone: 937-327-6314 ext. 6366 or toll-free 800-677-7558. Fax: 937-327-6379. E-mail: admission@wittenberg.edu. Web site: http://www.wittenberg.edu/.

WRIGHT STATE UNIVERSITY
DAYTON, OHIO

General State-supported, university, coed **Entrance** Minimally difficult **Setting** 557-acre suburban campus **Total enrollment** 15,343 **Student/faculty ratio** 20:1 **Application deadline** 9/1 **Freshmen** 89% were admitted **Housing** Yes **Expenses** Tuition $3708; Room & Board $4500 **Undergraduates** 54% women, 21% part-time, 31% 25 or older, 0.3% Native American, 1% Hispanic, 10% black, 2% Asian American or Pacific Islander **Most popular recent majors** Accounting; nursing; psychology **Academic program** English as a second language, advanced placement, self-designed majors, honors program, summer session, adult/continuing education programs, internships **Contact** Mr. Ken Davenport, Director of Undergraduate Admissions, Wright State University, Colonel Glenn Highway, Dayton, OH 45435. Telephone: 937-775-5700 or toll-free 800-247-1770. Fax: 937-775-5795. E-mail: admissions@wright.edu. Web site: http://www.wright.edu/.

XAVIER UNIVERSITY
CINCINNATI, OHIO

General Independent Roman Catholic, comprehensive, coed **Entrance** Moderately difficult **Setting** 100-acre suburban campus **Total enrollment** 6,504 **Student/faculty ratio** 7:1 **Application deadline** Rolling **Freshmen** 85% were admitted **Housing** Yes **Expenses** Tuition $14,520; Room & Board $5900 **Undergraduates** 60% women, 15% part-time, 17% 25 or older, 0.1% Native American, 1% Hispanic, 9% black, 2% Asian American or Pacific Islander **Most popular recent majors** Business administration; education; liberal arts and studies **Academic program** Average class size 22, English as a second language, advanced placement, accelerated degree program, tutorials, honors program, summer session, adult/continuing education programs, internships **Contact** Ms. Lisa Wendel, Interim Director of Admission, Xavier University, 3800 Victory Parkway, Cincinnati, OH 45207-2111. Telephone: 513-745-2945 or toll-free 800-344-4698. Fax: 513-745-4319. E-mail: xuadmit@admin.xu.edu. Web site: http://www.xu.edu/.

YOUNGSTOWN STATE UNIVERSITY
YOUNGSTOWN, OHIO

General State-supported, comprehensive, coed **Entrance** Noncompetitive **Setting** 150-acre urban campus **Total enrollment** 12,324 **Application deadline** 8/15 **Freshmen** 75% were admitted **Housing** Yes **Expenses** Tuition $3558; Room & Board $4350 **Undergraduates** 55% women, 24% part-time, 29% 25 or older, 0.2% Native American, 1% Hispanic, 8% black, 1% Asian American or Pacific Islander **Most popular recent majors** Elementary education; criminal justice/law enforcement administration; accounting **Academic program** English as a second language, advanced placement, accelerated degree program, self-designed majors, honors program, summer session, adult/continuing education programs, internships **Contact** Dr. Jane Reid, Director of Recruitment and Admissions, Youngstown State University, One University Plaza, Youngstown, OH 44555-0002. Telephone: 330-742-2000. Fax: 330-742-3674. E-mail: nsrysu@ysub.ysu.edu. Web site: http://www.ysu.edu/.

OKLAHOMA

AMERICAN BIBLE COLLEGE AND SEMINARY
BETHANY, OKLAHOMA

General Independent interdenominational, comprehensive, coed **Contact** Mr. Paul Leach, Recruiting Coordinator, American Bible College and Seminary, PO Box 99, 7045 NW 16th Street, Bethany, OK 73008-0099. Telephone: 405-495-2526 or toll-free 800-488-2528. Fax: 405-495-2521.

BARTLESVILLE WESLEYAN COLLEGE
BARTLESVILLE, OKLAHOMA

General Independent, 4-year, coed, affiliated with Wesleyan Church **Entrance** Minimally difficult **Setting** 127-acre small town campus **Total enrollment** 570 **Student/faculty ratio** 14:1 **Application deadline** Rolling **Housing** Yes **Expenses** Tuition $8700; Room & Board $3800 **Undergraduates** 65% women, 35% part-time, 40% 25 or older, 8% Native American, 3% Hispanic, 4% black, 1% Asian American or Pacific Islander **Most popular recent majors** Business administration; education; behavioral sciences **Academic program** English as a second language, advanced placement, self-designed majors, summer session, adult/continuing education programs, internships **Contact** Mr. Marty Carver, Enrollment Services Administrator, Bartlesville Wesleyan College, 2201 Silver Lake Road, Bartlesville, OK 74006-6299. Telephone: 918-335-6219 or toll-free 800-GO-TO-BWC (in-state). Fax: 918-335-6229. E-mail: admissions@bwc.edu. Web site: http://www.bwc.edu/.

CAMERON UNIVERSITY
LAWTON, OKLAHOMA

General State-supported, comprehensive, coed **Entrance** Minimally difficult **Setting** 160-acre suburban campus **Total enrollment** 5,147 **Student/faculty ratio** 13:1 **Application deadline** Rolling **Freshmen** 92% were admitted **Housing** Yes **Expenses** Tuition $2180; Room & Board $2600 **Undergraduates** 55% women, 40% part-time, 48% 25 or older, 5% Native American, 7% Hispanic, 17% black, 3% Asian American or Pacific Islander **Most popular recent majors** Business administration; education; information sciences/systems **Academic program** Average class size 50, advanced placement, accelerated degree program, honors program, summer session, adult/continuing education programs **Contact** Ms. Brenda Dally, Coordinator of Student Recruitment, Cameron University, 2800 West Gore Boulevard, Lawton, OK 73505-6377. Telephone: 580-581-2837 or toll-free 888-454-7600. Fax: 580-581-5514. E-mail: admiss@cua.cameron.edu.

EAST CENTRAL UNIVERSITY
ADA, OKLAHOMA

General State-supported, comprehensive, coed **Entrance** Moderately difficult **Setting** 140-acre small town campus **Total enrollment** 4,087 **Student/faculty ratio** 20:1 **Application deadline** 8/21 **Freshmen** 95% were admitted **Housing** Yes **Expenses** Tuition $1812; Room & Board $2066 **Undergraduates** 39% 25 or older **Most popular recent majors** Elementary education; criminal justice/law enforcement administration; nursing **Academic program** Average class size 25, advanced placement, accelerated degree program, tutorials, honors program, summer session, adult/continuing education programs, internships **Contact** Ms. Pamla Armstrong, Registrar, East Central University, Ada, OK 74820-6899. Telephone: 580-332-8000 ext. 239. Fax: 580-436-5495. E-mail: parmstro@mailclerk.ecok.edu. Web site: http://www.ecok.edu/.

HILLSDALE FREE WILL BAPTIST COLLEGE
MOORE, OKLAHOMA

General Independent Free Will Baptist, 4-year, coed **Entrance** Noncompetitive **Setting** 40-acre suburban campus **Total enrollment** 160 **Student/faculty ratio** 12:1 **Application deadline** Rolling **Freshmen** 96% were admitted **Housing** Yes **Expenses** Tuition $4710; Room & Board $3800 **Undergraduates** 34% women, 11% part-time, 16% 25 or older, 7% Native American, 2% Hispanic, 6% black, 2% Asian American or Pacific Islander **Most popular recent majors** Biblical studies; missionary studies; general studies **Academic program** Average class size 20, English as a second language, advanced placement, accelerated degree program, tutorials, summer session, internships **Contact** Ms. Sue Chaffin, Registrar/Assistant Director of Admissions, Hillsdale Free Will Baptist College, PO Box 7208, Moore, OK 73153-1208. Telephone: 405-912-9005. Fax: 405-912-9050. E-mail: gosaints@flash.net. Web site: http://www.flash.net/~hillsdal/.

LANGSTON UNIVERSITY
LANGSTON, OKLAHOMA

General State-supported, comprehensive, coed **Contact** Ms. La Cressa Trice, Admission Counselor, Langston University, PO Box 838, Langston, OK 73050-0838. Telephone: 405-466-3428. Fax: 405-466-3381.

MID-AMERICA BIBLE COLLEGE
OKLAHOMA CITY, OKLAHOMA

General Independent, 4-year, coed, affiliated with Church of God **Entrance** Noncompetitive **Setting** 145-acre suburban campus **Total enrollment** 555 **Application deadline** Rolling **Housing** Yes **Expenses** Tuition $5292; Room & Board $3098 **Undergraduates** 37% 25 or older, 2% Native American, 2% Hispanic, 7% black, 1% Asian American or Pacific Islander **Most popular recent majors** Religious studies; liberal arts and studies; behavioral sciences **Academic program** Advanced placement, accelerated degree program, summer session, adult/continuing education programs, internships **Contact** Mr. Scott Ethridge, Director of College Relations, Mid-America Bible College, 3500 Southwest 119th Street, Oklahoma City, OK 73170-4504. Telephone: 405-691-3800 ext. 107. E-mail: mbcok@cris.com.

NORTHEASTERN STATE UNIVERSITY
TAHLEQUAH, OKLAHOMA

General State-supported, comprehensive, coed **Entrance** Moderately difficult **Setting** 160-acre small town campus **Total enrollment** 8,503 **Application deadline** 8/5 **Housing** Yes **Expenses** Tuition $1740; Room & Board $2610 **Undergraduates** 43% 25 or older, 23% Native American, 1% Hispanic, 4% black, 0.5% Asian American or Pacific Islander **Most popular recent majors** Education; business administration; criminal justice/law enforcement administration **Academic program** Advanced placement, honors program, summer session, adult/continuing education programs, internships **Contact** Mr. Bill Nowlin, Director of Admissions and Registrar, Northeastern State University, 600 North Grand, Tahlequah, OK 74464-2399. Telephone: 918-456-5511 ext. 2200 or toll-free 800-722-9614 (in-state). Fax: 918-458-2342. E-mail: nsuadmis@cherokee.nsuok.edu. Web site: http://www.nsuok.edu/.

NORTHWESTERN OKLAHOMA STATE UNIVERSITY
ALVA, OKLAHOMA

General State-supported, comprehensive, coed **Entrance** Moderately difficult **Setting** 70-acre small town campus **Total enrollment** 1,871 **Student/faculty ratio** 19:1 **Application deadline** Rolling **Freshmen** 100% were admitted **Housing** Yes **Expenses** Tuition $1802; Room & Board $2316 **Undergraduates** 55% women, 28% part-time, 25% 25 or older, 4% Native American, 1% Hispanic, 4% black, 0.3% Asian American or Pacific Islander **Most Popular Recent Major** Elementary education **Academic program** Advanced placement, tutorials, summer session, adult/continuing education programs **Contact** Mr. Marcus Wallace, Director of Pre-Admissions, Northwestern Oklahoma State University, 709 Oklahoma Boulevard, Alva, OK 73717-2799. Telephone: 580-327-8545. Fax: 580-327-1881. E-mail: krschroc@ranger1.nwalva.edu. Web site: http://www.nwalva.edu.

OKLAHOMA BAPTIST UNIVERSITY
SHAWNEE, OKLAHOMA

General Independent Southern Baptist, comprehensive, coed **Entrance** Moderately difficult **Setting** 125-acre small town campus **Total enrollment** 2,211 **Student/faculty ratio** 14:1 **Application deadline** 8/1 **Freshmen** 97% were admitted **Housing** Yes **Expenses** Tuition $8336; Room & Board $3250 **Undergraduates** 58% women, 7% part-time, 19% 25 or older, 5% Native American, 2% Hispanic, 3% black, 1% Asian American or Pacific Islander **Most popular recent majors** Nursing; biblical studies; psychology **Academic program** Average class size 26, advanced placement, self-designed majors, tutorials, honors program, summer session, internships **Contact** Mr. Michael Cappo, Dean of Admissions, Oklahoma Baptist University, 500 West University, Shawnee, OK 74801-2558. Telephone: 405-878-2033 or toll-free 800-654-3285. Fax: 405-878-2046. E-mail: admissions@mail.okbu.edu. Web site: http://www.okbu.edu/.

OKLAHOMA CHRISTIAN UNIVERSITY OF SCIENCE AND ARTS
OKLAHOMA CITY, OKLAHOMA

General Independent, comprehensive, coed, affiliated with Church of Christ **Contact** Mr. Kyle Ray, Director of Admissions, Oklahoma Christian University of Science and Arts, Box 11000, Oklahoma City, OK 73136-1100. Telephone: 405-425-5050 or toll-free 800-877-5010 (in-state). Fax: 405-425-5208. E-mail: info@oc.edu.

OKLAHOMA CITY UNIVERSITY
OKLAHOMA CITY, OKLAHOMA

General Independent United Methodist, comprehensive, coed **Entrance** Moderately difficult **Setting** 68-acre urban campus **Total enrollment** 4,323 **Student/faculty ratio** 14:1 **Application deadline** Rolling **Freshmen** 52% were admitted **Housing** Yes **Expenses** Tuition $8512; Room & Board $3990 **Undergraduates** 56% women, 28% part-time, 36% 25 or older, 3% Native American, 2% Hispanic, 6% black, 10% Asian American or Pacific Islander **Most popular recent majors** Business administration; dance; mass communications **Academic program** Average class size 20,

Oklahoma City University *(continued)*

English as a second language, advanced placement, self-designed majors, honors program, summer session, adult/continuing education programs, internships **Contact** Dr. Blue Clark, Executive Vice President, Oklahoma City University, 2501 North Blackwelder, Oklahoma City, OK 73106-1402. Telephone: 405-521-5050. E-mail: uadmissions@frodo.okcu.edu. Web site: http://www.okcu.edu/.

OKLAHOMA PANHANDLE STATE UNIVERSITY

GOODWELL, OKLAHOMA

General State-supported, 4-year, coed **Entrance** Noncompetitive **Setting** 40-acre rural campus **Total enrollment** 1,234 **Student/faculty ratio** 16:1 **Application deadline** Rolling **Housing** Yes **Expenses** Tuition $1510; Room & Board $2170 **Undergraduates** 50% women, 18% part-time, 25% 25 or older, 3% Native American, 9% Hispanic, 5% black, 0.3% Asian American or Pacific Islander **Most popular recent majors** Agricultural business; business administration; elementary education **Academic program** English as a second language, advanced placement, accelerated degree program, tutorials, summer session, adult/continuing education programs, internships **Contact** Ms. Melissa Worth, Admissions Counselor, Oklahoma Panhandle State University, PO Box 430, Goodwell, OK 73939-0430. Telephone: 580-349-2611 ext. 311 or toll-free 800-664-6778. Fax: 580-349-2302. E-mail: opsu@opsu.edu. Web site: http://www.opsu.edu/.

OKLAHOMA STATE UNIVERSITY

STILLWATER, OKLAHOMA

General State-supported, university, coed **Entrance** Moderately difficult **Setting** 840-acre small town campus **Total enrollment** 19,350 **Student/faculty ratio** 18:1 **Application deadline** Rolling **Freshmen** 88% were admitted **Housing** Yes **Expenses** Tuition $2357; Room & Board $4344 **Undergraduates** 47% women, 10% part-time, 15% 25 or older, 7% Native American, 2% Hispanic, 3% black, 2% Asian American or Pacific Islander **Most popular recent majors** Education; management information systems/business data processing; business marketing and marketing management **Academic program** Average class size 45, English as a second language, advanced placement, accelerated degree program, self-designed majors, tutorials, honors program, summer session, adult/continuing education programs, internships **Contact** Ms. Paulette Cundiff, Coordinator of Admissions Processing, Oklahoma State University, Undergraduate Admissions, Stillwater, OK 74078. Telephone: 405-744-6860 or toll-free 800-233-5019 (in-state), 800-852-1255 (out-of-state). Fax: 405-744-5285. E-mail: gr16458@okstate.edu. Web site: http://www.okstate.edu/.

ORAL ROBERTS UNIVERSITY

TULSA, OKLAHOMA

General Independent interdenominational, university, coed **Entrance** Moderately difficult **Setting** 500-acre urban campus **Total enrollment** 3,966 **Student/faculty ratio** 16:1 **Application deadline** Rolling **Freshmen** 60% were admitted **Housing** Yes **Expenses** Tuition $10,460; Room & Board $4728 **Undergraduates** 19% 25 or older **Most popular recent majors** Business administration; telecommunications; elementary education **Academic program** English as a second language, advanced placement, accelerated degree program, self-designed majors, honors program, summer session, adult/continuing education programs, internships **Contact** Mrs. LeAnne Langley, Director of Undergraduate Admissions, Oral Roberts University, 7777 South Lewis Avenue, Tulsa, OK 74171-0001. Telephone: 918-495-6518 or toll-free 800-678-8876 (out-of-state). Fax: 918-495-6222. E-mail: admissions@oru.edu. Web site: http://www.oru.edu/.

PHILLIPS UNIVERSITY

ENID, OKLAHOMA

General Independent, comprehensive, coed, affiliated with Christian Church (Disciples of Christ) **Entrance** Moderately difficult **Setting** 35-acre small town campus **Total enrollment** 584 **Student/faculty ratio** 13:1 **Application deadline** Rolling **Freshmen** 68% were admitted **Housing** Yes **Expenses** Tuition $7300; Room & Board $3904 **Undergraduates** 47% women, 13% part-time, 29% 25 or older, 2% Native American, 6% Hispanic, 9% black, 1% Asian American or Pacific Islander **Most popular recent majors** Business administration; education; health science **Academic program** Average class size 16, English as a second language, advanced placement, accelerated degree program, self-designed majors, tutorials, summer session, adult/continuing education programs, internships **Contact** Mr. Bill LaFrance, Associate Vice President for Enrollment Management, Phillips University, 100 South University Avenue, Enid, OK 73701-6439. Telephone: 405-548-2316. Fax: 405-237-1607. E-mail: admissions@phillips.edu. Web site: http://www.phillips.edu/.

SOUTHEASTERN OKLAHOMA STATE UNIVERSITY

DURANT, OKLAHOMA

General State-supported, comprehensive, coed **Entrance** Moderately difficult **Setting** 176-acre

small town campus **Total enrollment** 3,946 **Student/faculty ratio** 20:1 **Application deadline** 8/15 **Freshmen** 99% were admitted **Housing** Yes **Expenses** Tuition $1879; Room & Board $2619 **Undergraduates** 54% women, 17% part-time, 38% 25 or older, 31% Native American, 1% Hispanic, 5% black, 1% Asian American or Pacific Islander **Most popular recent majors** Elementary education; psychology; physical education **Academic program** Advanced placement, accelerated degree program, honors program, summer session, adult/continuing education programs, internships **Contact** Ms. Becky Noah, Director of Admissions, Southeastern Oklahoma State University, Fifth and University, Durant, OK 74701-0609. Telephone: 580-924-0121 ext. 2778. Fax: 580-920-7472.

SOUTHERN NAZARENE UNIVERSITY
BETHANY, OKLAHOMA

General Independent Nazarene, comprehensive, coed **Contact** Mr. Brad Townley, Director of Admissions, Southern Nazarene University, 6729 Northwest 39th Expressway, Bethany, OK 73008-2694. Telephone: 405-491-6324 or toll-free 800-648-9899. Fax: 405-491-6381. E-mail: btownley@snu.edu. Web site: http://www.snu.edu/.

SOUTHWESTERN COLLEGE OF CHRISTIAN MINISTRIES
BETHANY, OKLAHOMA

General Independent, comprehensive, coed, affiliated with Pentecostal Holiness Church **Entrance** Minimally difficult **Setting** 7-acre suburban campus **Total enrollment** 182 **Student/faculty ratio** 10:1 **Application deadline** Rolling **Housing** Yes **Expenses** Tuition $4472; Room & Board $2800 **Undergraduates** 29% women, 8% part-time, 20% 25 or older, 1% Native American, 3% Hispanic, 12% black, 1% Asian American or Pacific Islander **Academic program** Advanced placement, summer session, internships **Contact** Mr. John Wheeler, Director of Admissions, Southwestern College of Christian Ministries, PO Box 340, Bethany, OK 73008-0340. Telephone: 405-789-7661.

SOUTHWESTERN OKLAHOMA STATE UNIVERSITY
WEATHERFORD, OKLAHOMA

General State-supported, comprehensive, coed **Entrance** Moderately difficult **Setting** 73-acre small town campus **Total enrollment** 4,478 **Student/faculty ratio** 19:1 **Application deadline** 8/15 **Housing** Yes **Expenses** Tuition $1798; Room & Board $2320 **Undergraduates** 20% 25 or older, 4% Native American, 2% Hispanic, 3% black, 3% Asian American or Pacific Islander **Most popular recent majors** Pharmacy; elementary education; accounting **Academic program** Average class size 30, advanced placement, accelerated degree program, tutorials, summer session, adult/continuing education programs, internships **Contact** Ms. Connie Phillips, Admission Counselor, Southwestern Oklahoma State University, 100 Campus Drive, Weatherford, OK 73096-3098. Telephone: 580-774-3009. Fax: 580-774-3795. E-mail: ropers@swosu.edu. Web site: http://www.swosu.edu/.

UNIVERSITY OF CENTRAL OKLAHOMA
EDMOND, OKLAHOMA

General State-supported, comprehensive, coed **Entrance** Minimally difficult **Setting** 200-acre suburban campus **Total enrollment** 13,928 **Student/faculty ratio** 21:1 **Application deadline** Rolling **Freshmen** 96% were admitted **Housing** Yes **Expenses** Tuition $1806; Room & Board $2481 **Undergraduates** 57% women, 36% part-time, 36% 25 or older, 4% Native American, 2% Hispanic, 6% black, 3% Asian American or Pacific Islander **Most popular recent majors** Liberal arts and studies; elementary education; nursing **Academic program** Average class size 31, English as a second language, advanced placement, accelerated degree program, honors program, summer session, adult/continuing education programs, internships **Contact** Ms. Evelyn Wilson, Dean of Enrollment Services, University of Central Oklahoma, 100 North University Drive, Edmond, OK 73034-5209. Telephone: 405-341-2980 ext. 2333. Fax: 405-341-4964. Web site: http://www.ucok.edu/.

UNIVERSITY OF OKLAHOMA
NORMAN, OKLAHOMA

General State-supported, university, coed **Entrance** Moderately difficult **Setting** 3,200-acre suburban campus **Total enrollment** 25,975 **Student/faculty ratio** 15:1 **Application deadline** 7/15 **Freshmen** 88% were admitted **Housing** Yes **Expenses** Tuition $2311; Room & Board $3800 **Undergraduates** 48% women, 14% part-time, 15% 25 or older, 7% Native American, 3% Hispanic, 7% black, 6% Asian American or Pacific Islander **Most popular recent majors** Management information systems/business data processing; accounting; psychology **Academic program** English as a second language, advanced placement, accelerated degree program, self-designed majors, tutorials, honors program, summer session, adult/continuing education programs, internships **Contact** Mr. J. P. Audas, Director of Prospective Student Services, University of Oklahoma, 1000 Asp Avenue, Norman, OK 73019-0390. Telephone: 405-

University of Oklahoma *(continued)*

325-2151 or toll-free 800-234-6868. Fax: 405-325-7478. E-mail: admission@ou.edu. Web site: http://www.ou.edu/.

UNIVERSITY OF OKLAHOMA HEALTH SCIENCES CENTER

OKLAHOMA CITY, OKLAHOMA

General State-supported, upper-level, coed **Contact** Dr. Willie V. Bryan, Vice Provost for Educational Services and Registrar, University of Oklahoma Health Sciences Center, PO Box 26901, Oklahoma City, OK 73190. Telephone: 405-271-2655. Fax: 405-271-2480. E-mail: sophie-mack@uokhsc.edu.

UNIVERSITY OF SCIENCE AND ARTS OF OKLAHOMA

CHICKASHA, OKLAHOMA

General State-supported, 4-year, coed **Entrance** Moderately difficult **Setting** 75-acre small town campus **Total enrollment** 1,393 **Student/faculty ratio** 16:1 **Application deadline** Rolling **Housing** Yes **Expenses** Tuition $1368; Room & Board $2670 **Undergraduates** 64% women, 23% part-time, 33% 25 or older, 11% Native American, 1% Hispanic, 4% black, 1% Asian American or Pacific Islander **Most popular recent majors** Elementary education; early childhood education; business administration **Academic program** Average class size 42, English as a second language, advanced placement, accelerated degree program, self-designed majors, tutorials, honors program, summer session, adult/continuing education programs, internships **Contact** Dr. Tim McElroy, Registrar and Director of Admissions and Records, University of Science and Arts of Oklahoma, PO Box 82345, Chickasha, OK 73018-0001. Telephone: 405-224-3140 ext. 205. Fax: 405-521-6244. E-mail: registrar@mercur.usao.edu. Web site: http://www.usao.edu/.

UNIVERSITY OF TULSA

TULSA, OKLAHOMA

General Independent, university, coed, affiliated with Presbyterian Church **Entrance** Moderately difficult **Setting** 100-acre urban campus **Total enrollment** 4,171 **Student/faculty ratio** 11:1 **Application deadline** Rolling **Freshmen** 83% were admitted **Housing** Yes **Expenses** Tuition $12,930; Room & Board $4410 **Undergraduates** 53% women, 8% part-time, 17% 25 or older, 6% Native American, 3% Hispanic, 8% black, 2% Asian American or Pacific Islander **Most popular recent majors** Psychology; chemical engineering; accounting **Academic program** English as a second language, advanced placement, self designed majors, honors program, summer session, adult/continuing education programs, internships **Contact** Mr. John C. Corso, Associate VP for Administration/Dean of Admission, University of Tulsa, 600 South College Avenue, Tulsa, OK 74104-3189. Telephone: 918-631-2307 or toll-free 800-331-3050. Fax: 918-631-2247. E-mail: admission@utulsa.edu. Web site: http://www.utulsa.edu/.

OREGON

THE ART INSTITUTES INTERNATIONAL AT PORTLAND

PORTLAND, OREGON

General Proprietary, 4-year, coed **Entrance** Minimally difficult **Setting** 1-acre urban campus **Total enrollment** 148 **Student/faculty ratio** 7:1 **Application deadline** Rolling **Housing** No **Expenses** Tuition $8900 **Undergraduates** 85% women, 45% part-time, 40% 25 or older, 1% Native American, 5% Hispanic, 5% black, 3% Asian American or Pacific Islander **Most Popular Recent Major** Interior design **Academic program** English as a second language, tutorials, summer session, internships **Contact** Ms. Kelly Alston, Director of Admissions, The Art Institutes International at Portland, 2000 Southwest Fifth Avenue, Portland, OR 97201-4907. Telephone: 503-228-6528 or toll-free 888-228-6528. E-mail: admissions@bassist.edu. Web site: http://www.aii.edu/.

BASSIST COLLEGE

See The Art Institutes International at Portland

CASCADE COLLEGE

PORTLAND, OREGON

General Independent, 4-year, coed, affiliated with Church of Christ **Entrance** Noncompetitive **Setting** 13-acre urban campus **Total enrollment** 292 **Student/faculty ratio** 17:1 **Application deadline** Rolling **Freshmen** 100% were admitted **Housing** Yes **Expenses** Tuition $7550; Room & Board $4300 **Undergraduates** 58% women, 5% part-time, 2% Native American, 3% Hispanic, 5% black, 1% Asian American or Pacific Islander **Most popular recent majors** Liberal arts and studies; biblical studies **Academic program** Average class size 30, advanced placement, accelerated degree program, tutorials, summer session, internships **Contact** Ms. Mary Horton, Director of Admissions, Cascade College, 9101 East Burnside Street,

Portland, OR 97216-1515. Telephone: 503-257-1202 or toll-free 800-550-7678. Web site: http://www.oc.edu/cascade/.

CONCORDIA UNIVERSITY
PORTLAND, OREGON

General Independent, comprehensive, coed, affiliated with Lutheran Church–Missouri Synod **Entrance** Minimally difficult **Setting** 13-acre urban campus **Total enrollment** 977 **Student/faculty ratio** 18:1 **Application deadline** Rolling **Freshmen** 84% were admitted **Housing** Yes **Expenses** Tuition $13,900; Room & Board $3590 **Undergraduates** 60% women, 15% part-time, 50% 25 or older, 1% Native American, 3% Hispanic, 4% black, 1% Asian American or Pacific Islander **Most popular recent majors** Education; business administration; psychology **Academic program** English as a second language, advanced placement, accelerated degree program, self-designed majors, tutorials, summer session, adult/continuing education programs, internships **Contact** Mr. Peter D. Johnson, Director of Admissions, Concordia University, 2811 Northeast Holman, Portland, OR 97211-6099. Telephone: 503-280-8501 or toll-free 800-321-9371. Fax: 503-280-8531. E-mail: cu-admission@cu-portland.edu. Web site: http://www.cu-portland.edu/.

▶ **For more information, see page 421.**

EASTERN OREGON UNIVERSITY
LA GRANDE, OREGON

General State-supported, comprehensive, coed **Entrance** Moderately difficult **Setting** 121-acre rural campus **Total enrollment** 1,945 **Student/faculty ratio** 14:1 **Application deadline** 8/1 **Freshmen** 61% were admitted **Housing** Yes **Expenses** Tuition $3231; Room & Board $4165 **Undergraduates** 55% women, 24% part-time, 24% 25 or older, 2% Native American, 3% Hispanic, 1% black, 2% Asian American or Pacific Islander **Most popular recent majors** Education; business economics; biology **Academic program** Average class size 40, advanced placement, self-designed majors, tutorials, summer session, adult/continuing education programs, internships **Contact** Ms. Terral Schut, Director of Admissions and New Student Programs, Eastern Oregon University, 1410 L Avenue, La Grande, OR 97850-2899. Telephone: 541-962-3393 or toll-free 800-452-8639. Fax: 541-962-3418. E-mail: admissions@eou.edu. Web site: http://www.eou.edu/.

EUGENE BIBLE COLLEGE
EUGENE, OREGON

General Independent, 4-year, coed, affiliated with Open Bible Standard Churches **Entrance** Minimally difficult **Setting** 40-acre suburban campus **Total enrollment** 219 **Student/faculty ratio** 14:1 **Application deadline** 9/1 **Freshmen** 54% were admitted **Housing** Yes **Expenses** Tuition $5549; Room & Board $3436 **Undergraduates** 51% women, 7% part-time, 28% 25 or older, 2% Native American, 3% Hispanic, 0% black, 1% Asian American or Pacific Islander **Academic program** Average class size 30, summer session, internships **Contact** Mr. Trent Combs, Director of Admissions, Eugene Bible College, 2155 Bailey Hill Road, Eugene, OR 97405-1194. Telephone: 541-485-1780 ext. 35 or toll-free 800-322-2638. Fax: 541-343-5801. E-mail: admissions@ebc.edu. Web site: http://www.ebc.edu/.

GEORGE FOX UNIVERSITY
NEWBERG, OREGON

General Independent Friends, university, coed **Entrance** Moderately difficult **Setting** 73-acre small town campus **Total enrollment** 2,235 **Student/faculty ratio** 16:1 **Application deadline** 6/1 **Freshmen** 91% were admitted **Housing** Yes **Expenses** Tuition $15,520; Room & Board $4920 **Undergraduates** 60% women, 21% part-time, 21% 25 or older, 1% Native American, 2% Hispanic, 1% black, 3% Asian American or Pacific Islander **Most popular recent majors** Education; business administration; biology **Academic program** Average class size 19, English as a second language, advanced placement, accelerated degree program, self-designed majors, tutorials, honors program, adult/continuing education programs, internships **Contact** Mr. Jeff Rickey, Dean of Admissions, George Fox University, 414 North Meridian, Newberg, OR 97132-2697. Telephone: 503-538-8383 ext. 2240 or toll-free 800-765-4369. Fax: 503-538-7234. E-mail: admissions@georgefox.edu. Web site: http://www.georgefox.edu/.

▶ **For more information, see page 440.**

LEWIS & CLARK COLLEGE
PORTLAND, OREGON

General Independent, comprehensive, coed **Entrance** Very difficult **Setting** 115-acre suburban campus **Total enrollment** 3,023 **Student/faculty ratio** 14:1 **Application deadline** 2/1 **Freshmen** 66% were admitted **Housing** Yes **Expenses** Tuition $18,530; Room & Board $5770 **Undergraduates** 58% women, 1% part-time, 2% 25 or older, 1% Native American, 2% Hispanic, 1% black, 6% Asian American or Pacific Islander **Most popular recent majors** International relations; psychology; biology **Academic program** Average class size 20, English as a second language, advanced placement, accelerated degree program, self-designed majors, tutorials, honors program, summer session, internships **Contact** Mr.

Lewis & Clark College *(continued)*

Michael Sexton, Dean of Admissions, Lewis & Clark College, 0615 SW Palatine Hill Road, Portland, OR 97219-7899. Telephone: 503-768-7040 or toll-free 800-444-4111. Fax: 503-768-7055. E-mail: admissions@lclark.edu. Web site: http://www.lclark.edu/.

LINFIELD COLLEGE
MCMINNVILLE, OREGON

General Independent American Baptist, 4-year, coed **Entrance** Moderately difficult **Setting** 74-acre small town campus **Total enrollment** 2,709 **Student/faculty ratio** 12:1 **Application deadline** 2/15 **Freshmen** 88% were admitted **Housing** Yes **Expenses** Tuition $16,960; Room & Board $5180 **Undergraduates** 64% women, 35% part-time, 2% 25 or older, 1% Native American, 2% Hispanic, 1% black, 5% Asian American or Pacific Islander **Most popular recent majors** Business administration; elementary education; biology **Academic program** Average class size 20, English as a second language, advanced placement, accelerated degree program, tutorials, honors program, summer session, adult/continuing education programs, internships **Contact** Mr. Ernest Sandlin, Director of Admissions, Linfield College, 900 SE Baker Street, McMinnville, OR 97128-6894. Telephone: 503-434-2489 or toll-free 800-640-2287. Fax: 503-434-2472. E-mail: admissions@linfield.edu. Web site: http://www.linfield.edu/.

MARYLHURST UNIVERSITY
MARYLHURST, OREGON

General Independent Roman Catholic, comprehensive, coed **Contact** Mr. John Rolston, Registrar, Marylhurst University, PO Box 261, Marylhurst, OR 97036-0261. Telephone: 503-636-8141 ext. 3316. Fax: 503-636-9526.

MOUNT ANGEL SEMINARY
SAINT BENEDICT, OREGON

General Independent Roman Catholic, comprehensive, men only **Contact** Fr. Odo Recker, OSB, Registrar/Admissions Officer, Mount Angel Seminary, Saint Benedict, OR 97373. Telephone: 503-845-3951.

MULTNOMAH BIBLE COLLEGE AND BIBLICAL SEMINARY
PORTLAND, OREGON

General Independent interdenominational, comprehensive, coed **Entrance** Moderately difficult **Setting** 17-acre urban campus **Total enrollment** 750 **Student/faculty ratio** 13:1 **Application deadline** 7/15 **Freshmen** 78% were admitted **Housing** Yes **Expenses** Tuition $7590; Room & Board $3500 **Undergraduates** 46% women, 11% part-time, 20% 25 or older, 1% Native American, 3% Hispanic, 0.4% black, 2% Asian American or Pacific Islander **Most popular recent majors** Biblical studies; pastoral counseling; missionary studies **Academic program** Average class size 30, advanced placement, summer session, adult/continuing education programs, internships **Contact** Ms. Nancy Gerecz, Admissions Assistant, Multnomah Bible College and Biblical Seminary, 8435 Northeast Glisan Street, Portland, OR 97220-5898. Telephone: 503-255-0332 ext. 373 or toll-free 800-275-4672. Fax: 503-254-1268. E-mail: admiss@multnomah.edu. Web site: http://www.nultnomah.edu/.

NORTHWEST CHRISTIAN COLLEGE
EUGENE, OREGON

General Independent interdenominational, comprehensive, coed **Entrance** Moderately difficult **Setting** 8-acre urban campus **Total enrollment** 438 **Student/faculty ratio** 17:1 **Application deadline** Rolling **Freshmen** 78% were admitted **Housing** Yes **Expenses** Tuition $11,640; Room & Board $4986 **Undergraduates** 66% women, 4% part-time, 46% 25 or older, 1% Native American, 3% Hispanic, 0.3% black, 3% Asian American or Pacific Islander **Most popular recent majors** Elementary education; business administration; psychology **Academic program** Average class size 25, advanced placement, accelerated degree program, self-designed majors, tutorials, adult/continuing education programs, internships **Contact** Dr. Randy Jones, Vice President for Admissions, Northwest Christian College, 828 East 11th Avenue, Eugene, OR 97401-3727. Telephone: 541-684-7201. Fax: 541-684-7317. Web site: http://www.nwcc.edu/.

OREGON COLLEGE OF ART AND CRAFT
PORTLAND, OREGON

General Independent, 4-year, coed **Entrance** Minimally difficult **Setting** 7-acre urban campus **Total enrollment** 87 **Student/faculty ratio** 5:1 **Application deadline** Rolling **Housing** No **Expenses** Tuition $10,425 **Undergraduates** 69% women, 62% part-time, 46% 25 or older **Academic program** Advanced placement, tutorials **Contact** Ms. Jennifer Green, Director of Admissions, Oregon College of Art and Craft, 8245 Southwest Barnes Road, Portland, OR 97225. Telephone: 503-297-5544 or toll-free 800-390-0632. Fax: 503-297-9651. Web site: http://www.ocac.edu/.

OREGON HEALTH SCIENCES UNIVERSITY
PORTLAND, OREGON

General State-related, upper-level, coed **Contact** Ms. Victoria Souza, Registrar and Director of Financial Aid, Oregon Health Sciences University, 3181 SW Sam Jackson Park Road, Portland, OR 97201-3098. Telephone: 503-494-7800. E-mail: porterts@ohsu.edu.

OREGON INSTITUTE OF TECHNOLOGY
KLAMATH FALLS, OREGON

General State-supported, comprehensive, coed **Entrance** Moderately difficult **Setting** 173-acre small town campus **Total enrollment** 2,462 **Application deadline** 6/1 **Freshmen** 76% were admitted **Housing** Yes **Expenses** Tuition $3309; Room & Board $3910 **Undergraduates** 43% women, 21% part-time, 38% 25 or older **Most popular recent majors** Industrial radiologic technology; civil engineering technology; electrical/electronic engineering technology **Academic program** Average class size 25, English as a second language, advanced placement, tutorials, summer session, adult/continuing education programs, internships **Contact** Mr. John Duarte, Admissions Counselor, Oregon Institute of Technology, 3201 Campus Drive, Klamath Falls, OR 97601-8801. Telephone: 541-885-1150 or toll-free 800-422-2017 (in-state), 800-343-6653 (out-of-state). Fax: 541-885-1115. E-mail: oit@oit.edu. Web site: http://www.oit.edu/.

OREGON STATE UNIVERSITY
CORVALLIS, OREGON

General State-supported, university, coed **Entrance** Moderately difficult **Setting** 530-acre small town campus **Total enrollment** 14,490 **Student/faculty ratio** 8:1 **Application deadline** 3/1 **Freshmen** 89% were admitted **Housing** Yes **Expenses** Tuition $3540; Room & Board $5064 **Undergraduates** 46% women, 8% part-time, 12% 25 or older **Most popular recent majors** Business administration; mechanical engineering; mass communications **Academic program** English as a second language, advanced placement, self-designed majors, tutorials, honors program, summer session, internships **Contact** Ms. Michele Sandlin, Associate Director of Processing, Oregon State University, Corvallis, OR 97331. Telephone: 541-737-4411 or toll-free 800-291-4192 (in-state). Fax: 541-737-6157. E-mail: osuadmit@ccmail.orst.edu. Web site: http://www.orst.edu/.

PACIFIC NORTHWEST COLLEGE OF ART
PORTLAND, OREGON

General Independent, 4-year, coed **Entrance** Moderately difficult **Setting** Urban campus **Total enrollment** 243 **Application deadline** 8/1 **Freshmen** 96% were admitted **Housing** Yes **Expenses** Tuition $11,268; Room only $4250 **Undergraduates** 59% women, 14% part-time, 62% 25 or older, 2% Native American, 2% Hispanic, 1% black, 2% Asian American or Pacific Islander **Most popular recent majors** Painting; graphic design/commercial art/illustration; photography **Academic program** Average class size 18, advanced placement, self-designed majors, adult/continuing education programs, internships **Contact** Mr. Clarence Goodman, Enrollment Counselor, Pacific Northwest College of Art, PO Box 2725, Portland, OR 97208. Telephone: 503-226-0462 ext. 267 or toll-free 800-818-PNCA. Fax: 503-226-3587. E-mail: pncainfo@pnca.edu. Web site: http://www.pnca.edu/.

PACIFIC UNIVERSITY
FOREST GROVE, OREGON

General Independent, comprehensive, coed **Entrance** Moderately difficult **Setting** 55-acre small town campus **Total enrollment** 1,854 **Student/faculty ratio** 11:1 **Application deadline** 2/15 **Freshmen** 84% were admitted **Housing** Yes **Expenses** Tuition $16,695; Room & Board $4564 **Undergraduates** 64% women, 4% part-time, 12% 25 or older, 0.5% Native American, 3% Hispanic, 1% black, 13% Asian American or Pacific Islander **Most popular recent majors** Biology; business administration; psychology **Academic program** Average class size 20, English as a second language, advanced placement, accelerated degree program, self-designed majors, tutorials, honors program, summer session, internships **Contact** Ms. Beth Woodward, Director of Undergraduate Admissions, Pacific University, 2043 College Way, Forest Grove, OR 97116-1797. Telephone: 503-359-2218 or toll-free 800-677-6712. Fax: 503-359-2975. E-mail: admissions@pacificu.edu. Web site: http://www.pacificu.edu/.

PORTLAND STATE UNIVERSITY
PORTLAND, OREGON

General State-supported, university, coed **Entrance** Minimally difficult **Setting** 36-acre urban campus **Total enrollment** 16,997 **Student/faculty ratio** 12:1 **Application deadline** 6/1 **Freshmen** 76% were admitted **Housing** Yes **Expenses** Tuition $3357; Room & Board $5850 **Undergraduates** 53% women, 31% part-time, 38% 25 or older, 1% Native American, 3% Hispanic, 3% black, 10% Asian American or Pacific Islander **Most popular recent majors** Accounting; business administration; psychology **Academic program** Average class size 16, English as a second language, advanced placement, accelerated degree program, self-designed majors, tutorials, honors program, summer session, adult/continuing educa-

Portland State University *(continued)*

tion programs, internships **Contact** Ms. Agnes A. Hoffman, Director of Admissions and Records, Portland State University, PO Box 751, Portland, OR 97207-0751. Telephone: 503-725-3511 or toll-free 800-547-8887. Fax: 503-725-5525. E-mail: askadm@osa.pdx.edu. Web site: http://www.pdx.edu/.

REED COLLEGE
PORTLAND, OREGON

General Independent, comprehensive, coed **Entrance** Very difficult **Setting** 98-acre suburban campus **Total enrollment** 1,338 **Student/faculty ratio** 10:1 **Application deadline** 2/1 **Freshmen** 70% were admitted **Housing** Yes **Expenses** Tuition $22,340; Room & Board $6200 **Undergraduates** 54% women, 2% part-time, 3% 25 or older, 1% Native American, 4% Hispanic, 1% black, 7% Asian American or Pacific Islander **Most popular recent majors** Biology; English; psychology **Academic program** Advanced placement, accelerated degree program, self-designed majors, tutorials **Contact** Dr. Nancy Donehower, Dean of Admission, Reed College, 3203 Southeast Woodstock Boulevard, Portland, OR 97202-8199. Telephone: 503-777-7511 or toll-free 800-547-4750 (out-of-state). Fax: 503-777-7553. E-mail: admission@reed.edu. Web site: http://www.reed.edu/.

▶ **For more information, see page 495.**

SOUTHERN OREGON UNIVERSITY
ASHLAND, OREGON

General State-supported, comprehensive, coed **Entrance** Moderately difficult **Setting** 175-acre small town campus **Total enrollment** 5,426 **Student/faculty ratio** 18:1 **Application deadline** Rolling **Freshmen** 62% were admitted **Housing** Yes **Expenses** Tuition $3204; Room & Board $4380 **Undergraduates** 55% women, 21% part-time, 26% 25 or older, 2% Native American, 3% Hispanic, 1% black, 3% Asian American or Pacific Islander **Academic program** Advanced placement, accelerated degree program, self-designed majors, honors program, summer session, adult/continuing education programs **Contact** Mr. Allen H. Blaszak, Director of Admissions and Records, Southern Oregon University, Siskiyou Boulevard, Ashland, OR 97520. Telephone: 541-552-6411 or toll-free 800-482-SOSC ext. 6411 (in-state). Fax: 541-552-6329. E-mail: admissions@sou.edu.

UNIVERSITY OF OREGON
EUGENE, OREGON

General State-supported, university, coed **Entrance** Moderately difficult **Setting** 250-acre urban campus **Total enrollment** 17,530 **Student/faculty ratio** 16:1 **Application deadline** 3/2 **Freshmen** 90% were admitted **Housing** Yes **Expenses** Tuition $3408; Room & Board $4646 **Undergraduates** 52% women, 8% part-time, 3% 25 or older, 1% Native American, 3% Hispanic, 1% black, 7% Asian American or Pacific Islander **Most popular recent majors** Business administration; psychology; journalism **Academic program** English as a second language, advanced placement, accelerated degree program, self-designed majors, tutorials, honors program, summer session, adult/continuing education programs, internships **Contact** Ms. Martha Pitts, Director of Admissions, University of Oregon, Eugene, OR 97403. Telephone: 541-346-3201 or toll-free 800-232-3825 (in-state). Fax: 541-346-5815. E-mail: uoadmit@oregon.uoregon.edu. Web site: http://www.uoregon.edu/.

UNIVERSITY OF PORTLAND
PORTLAND, OREGON

General Independent Roman Catholic, comprehensive, coed **Entrance** Moderately difficult **Setting** 125-acre suburban campus **Total enrollment** 2,606 **Student/faculty ratio** 14:1 **Application deadline** Rolling **Freshmen** 84% were admitted **Housing** Yes **Expenses** Tuition $15,520; Room & Board $4710 **Undergraduates** 13% 25 or older **Most popular recent majors** Business administration; education; nursing **Academic program** Average class size 25, English as a second language, advanced placement, accelerated degree program, self-designed majors, tutorials, honors program, summer session, adult/continuing education programs, internships **Contact** Mr. Daniel B. Reilly, Director of Admissions, University of Portland, 5000 North Willamette Boulevard, Portland, OR 97203-5798. Telephone: 503-283-7147 or toll-free 800-227-4568 (out-of-state). Fax: 503-283-7399. E-mail: admissio@up.edu. Web site: http://www.uofport.edu/.

WARNER PACIFIC COLLEGE
PORTLAND, OREGON

General Independent, comprehensive, coed, affiliated with Church of God **Entrance** Moderately difficult **Setting** 15-acre urban campus **Total enrollment** 639 **Student/faculty ratio** 16:1 **Application deadline** Rolling **Freshmen** 97% were admitted **Housing** Yes **Expenses** Tuition $11,482; Room & Board $4100 **Undergraduates** 65% women, 13% part-time, 53% 25 or older, 1% Native American, 2% Hispanic, 4% black, 3% Asian American or Pacific Islander **Most popular recent majors** Education; business administration; individual/family development **Academic program** Average class size 25, advanced placement, self-designed majors, tutorials, honors program, summer session, adult/continuing education programs, internships **Contact** Mr. William D. Stenberg, Dean of Admissions, Warner Pacific College, 2219 Southeast 68th Avenue, Portland, OR 97215-4099. Telephone: 503-788-7495 or toll-free 800-582-7885. Fax: 503-788-7425. E-mail: admiss@warnerpacific.edu. Web site: http://www.warnerpacific.edu/.

WESTERN BAPTIST COLLEGE
SALEM, OREGON

General Independent religious, 4-year, coed **Entrance** Moderately difficult **Setting** 107-acre suburban campus **Total enrollment** 701 **Student/faculty ratio** 18:1 **Application deadline** Rolling **Freshmen** 91% were admitted **Housing** Yes **Expenses** Tuition $12,350; Room & Board $4820 **Undergraduates** 60% women, 10% part-time, 28% 25 or older, 1% Native American, 2% Hispanic, 1% black, 1% Asian American or Pacific Islander **Most popular recent majors** Business administration; education; psychology **Academic program** Advanced placement, honors program, summer session, adult/continuing education programs, internships **Contact** Mr. Daren Milionis, Director of Admissions, Western Baptist College, 5000 Deer Park Drive, SE, Salem, OR 97301-9392. Telephone: 503-375-7005. Fax: 503-585-4316. E-mail: dmilionis@wbc.edu. Web site: http://www.wbc.edu/.

WESTERN OREGON UNIVERSITY
MONMOUTH, OREGON

General State-supported, comprehensive, coed **Entrance** Moderately difficult **Setting** 157-acre rural campus **Total enrollment** 4,088 **Student/faculty ratio** 15:1 **Application deadline** Rolling **Freshmen** 66% were admitted **Housing** Yes **Expenses** Tuition $3153; Room & Board $4128 **Undergraduates** 59% women, 6% part-time, 23% 25 or older, 2% Native American, 4% Hispanic, 1% black, 2% Asian American or Pacific Islander **Most popular recent majors** Elementary education; secondary education; psychology **Academic program** English as a second language, advanced placement, accelerated degree program, self-designed majors, tutorials, honors program, summer session, adult/continuing education programs, internships **Contact** Ms. Alison Marshall, Director of Admissions, Western Oregon University, 345 North Monmouth Avenue, Monmouth, OR 97361. Telephone: 503-838-8211. Fax: 503-838-8067. E-mail: wolfgram@fsa.wou.edu. Web site: http://www.wou.edu/.

WESTERN STATES CHIROPRACTIC COLLEGE
PORTLAND, OREGON

General Independent, upper-level, coed **Contact** Mr. Jack Roberts, Dean of Enrollment Services, Western States Chiropractic College, 2900 Northeast 132nd Avenue, Portland, OR 97230-3099. Telephone: 503-251-5734 or toll-free 800-641-5641. Fax: 503-251-5723.

WILLAMETTE UNIVERSITY
SALEM, OREGON

General Independent United Methodist, comprehensive, coed **Entrance** Very difficult **Setting** 72-acre urban campus **Total enrollment** 2,502 **Student/faculty ratio** 12:1 **Application deadline** 2/1 **Freshmen** 82% were admitted **Housing** Yes **Expenses** Tuition $20,290; Room & Board $5280 **Undergraduates** 55% women, 1% part-time, 5% 25 or older, 1% Native American, 3% Hispanic, 1% black, 6% Asian American or Pacific Islander **Most popular recent majors** Economics; political science; psychology **Academic program** Average class size 15, advanced placement, accelerated degree program, self-designed majors, tutorials, internships **Contact** Mr. James M. Sumner, Vice President for Enrollment, Willamette University, 900 State Street, Salem, OR 97301-3931. Telephone: 503-370-6303. Fax: 503-375-5363. E-mail: undergrad-admission@willamette.edu. Web site: http://www.willamette.edu/.

PENNSYLVANIA

ACADEMY OF THE NEW CHURCH COLLEGE
See Bryn Athyn College of the New Church

ALBRIGHT COLLEGE
READING, PENNSYLVANIA

General Independent, 4-year, coed, affiliated with United Methodist Church **Entrance** Moderately difficult **Setting** 110-acre suburban campus **Total enrollment** 1,388 **Student/faculty ratio** 12:1 **Application deadline** 2/15 **Freshmen** 86% were admitted **Housing** Yes **Expenses** Tuition $18,310; Room & Board $5450 **Undergraduates** 52% women, 8% part-time, 2% 25 or older, 0.3% Native American, 2% Hispanic, 5% black, 3% Asian American or Pacific Islander **Most popular recent majors** Business administration; biology; psychology **Academic program** Average class size 25, English as a second language, advanced placement, accelerated degree program, self-designed majors, tutorials, honors program, summer session, internships **Contact** Mr. Gregory E. Eichhorn, Director of Admissions, Albright College, 13th and Bern Sts, PO Box 15234, Reading, PA 19612-5234. Telephone: 610-921-7512 or toll-free 800-252-1856. Fax: 610-921-7530. E-mail: albright@joe.alb.edu. Web site: http://www.albright.edu/.

ALLEGHENY COLLEGE
MEADVILLE, PENNSYLVANIA

General Independent, 4-year, coed, affiliated with United Methodist Church **Entrance** Very difficult **Setting** 254-acre small town campus **Total enrollment** 1,890 **Student/faculty ratio** 12:1 **Application deadline** 2/15 **Freshmen** 81% were admitted **Housing** Yes **Expenses** Tuition $19,360; Room & Board $4720 **Undergraduates** 53% women, 1% part-time, 1% 25 or older, 0.3% Native American, 1% Hispanic, 2% black, 2% Asian American or Pacific Islander **Most popular recent majors** Psychology; biology; environmental science **Academic program** Advanced placement, accelerated degree program, self-designed majors, tutorials, internships **Contact** Mrs. Gayle Pollock, Dean of Admissions, Allegheny College, 520 North Main Street, Meadville, PA 16335. Telephone: 814-332-4351 or toll-free 800-521-5293. Fax: 814-337-0431. E-mail: admiss@admin.alleg.edu. Web site: http://www.alleg.edu/.

► **For more information, see page 387.**

ALLEGHENY UNIVERSITY OF THE HEALTH SCIENCES
PHILADELPHIA, PENNSYLVANIA

General Independent, university, coed **Entrance** Moderately difficult **Setting** Urban campus **Total enrollment** 3,283 **Student/faculty ratio** 12:1 **Application deadline** Rolling **Housing** Yes **Expenses** Tuition $9660; Room only $4800 **Undergraduates** 74% women, 47% part-time, 70% 25 or older, 0.3% Native American, 3% Hispanic, 16% black, 8% Asian American or Pacific Islander **Most popular recent majors** Physician assistant; nursing **Academic program** Advanced placement, tutorials, honors program, summer session, adult/continuing education programs, internships **Contact** Ms. Paula Greenberg, Director of Admissions, School of Health Sciences/Humanities, Allegheny University of the Health Sciences, 201 North 15th Street, Mail Stop 506, Philadelphia, PA 19102-1192. Telephone: 215-762-8388. Web site: http://www.auhs.edu/.

ALLENTOWN COLLEGE OF ST. FRANCIS DE SALES
CENTER VALLEY, PENNSYLVANIA

General Independent Roman Catholic, comprehensive, coed **Entrance** Moderately difficult **Setting** 300-acre suburban campus **Total enrollment** 2,236 **Student/faculty ratio** 15:1 **Application deadline** 8/1 **Freshmen** 76% were admitted **Housing** Yes **Expenses** Tuition $11,750; Room & Board $5470 **Undergraduates** 55% women, 32% part-time, 0.1% Native American, 3% Hispanic, 1% black, 1% Asian American or Pacific Islander **Most popular recent majors** Accounting; theater arts/drama; nursing **Academic program** Average class size 18, advanced placement, accelerated degree program, tutorials, honors program, summer session, adult/continuing education programs, internships **Contact** Mrs. Kathy Link, Dean of Enrollment Management, Allentown College of St. Francis de Sales, 2755 Station Avenue, Center Valley, PA 18034-9568. Telephone: 610-282-1100 ext. 1475 or toll-free 800-228-5114. Fax: 610-282-2254. E-mail: khl0@email.allencol.edu. Web site: http://www.allencol.edu/.

ALVERNIA COLLEGE
READING, PENNSYLVANIA

General Independent Roman Catholic, 4-year, coed **Entrance** Moderately difficult **Setting** 85-acre suburban campus **Total enrollment** 1,214 **Student/faculty ratio** 14:1 **Application deadline** Rolling **Freshmen** 76% were admitted **Housing** Yes **Expenses** Tuition $11,750; Room & Board $5200 **Undergraduates** 66% women, 30% part-time, 42% 25 or older, 0% Native American, 2% Hispanic, 3% black, 1% Asian American or Pacific Islander **Most popular recent majors** Business administration; education; criminal justice/law enforcement administration **Academic program** Advanced placement, accelerated degree program, tutorials, honors program, summer session, adult/continuing education programs, internships **Contact** Mr. John McCloskey, Director of Admissions, Alvernia College, 400 Saint Bernardine Street, Reading, PA 19607-1799. Telephone: 610-796-8220. Fax: 610-796-8336. Web site: http://www.alvernia.edu/.

BAPTIST BIBLE COLLEGE OF PENNSYLVANIA
CLARKS SUMMIT, PENNSYLVANIA

General Independent Baptist, comprehensive, coed **Entrance** Minimally difficult **Setting** 124-acre suburban campus **Total enrollment** 725 **Student/faculty ratio** 20:1 **Application deadline** Rolling **Freshmen** 68% were admitted **Housing** Yes **Expenses** Tuition $7530; Room & Board $4534 **Undergraduates** 56% women, 7% part-time, 7% 25 or older, 0% Native American, 1% Hispanic, 1% black, 1% Asian American or Pacific Islander **Academic program** Advanced placement, summer session, internships **Contact** Mr. Andy Giessman, Applications Coordinator, Baptist Bible College of Pennsylvania, PO Box 800, Clarks Summit, PA 18411-1297. Telephone: 717-586-2400 ext. 9376 or toll-free 800-451-7664. Fax: 717-585-9400. E-mail: gamos@bbc.edu. Web site: http://www.bbc.edu/.

BEAVER COLLEGE
GLENSIDE, PENNSYLVANIA

General Independent, comprehensive, coed, affiliated with Presbyterian Church (U.S.A.) **Entrance** Moderately difficult **Setting** 55-acre suburban campus **Total enrollment** 2,705 **Application deadline** Rolling **Housing** Yes **Expenses** Tuition $15,840; Room & Board $6520 **Undergraduates** 73% women, 26% part-time, 32% 25 or older, 0.2% Native American, 2% Hispanic, 15% black, 7% Asian American or Pacific Islander **Most popular recent majors** Biology; art; psychology **Academic program** English as a second language, advanced placement, accelerated degree program, self-designed majors, tutorials, honors program, summer session, adult/continuing education programs, internships **Contact** Mr. Mark Lapreziosa, Director of Admissions, Beaver College, 450 South Easton Road, Glenside, PA 19038-3295. Telephone: 215-572-2910 or toll-free 888-BEAVER3. Fax: 215-572-4049. E-mail: admiss@beaver.edu. Web site: http://www.beaver.edu/.

BLOOMSBURG UNIVERSITY OF PENNSYLVANIA
BLOOMSBURG, PENNSYLVANIA

General State-supported, comprehensive, coed **Entrance** Moderately difficult **Setting** 282-acre small town campus **Total enrollment** 7,499 **Student/faculty ratio** 17:1 **Application deadline** Rolling **Freshmen** 58% were admitted **Housing** Yes **Expenses** Tuition $4278; Room & Board $3368 **Undergraduates** 63% women, 5% part-time, 10% 25 or older, 0.2% Native American, 1% Hispanic, 3% black, 1% Asian American or Pacific Islander **Most popular recent majors** Elementary education; business administration; accounting **Academic program** English as a second language, advanced placement, tutorials, honors program, summer session, adult/continuing education programs, internships **Contact** Mr. Christopher Keller, Director of Admissions, Bloomsburg University of Pennsylvania, Ben Franklin Building, Room 10, Bloomsburg, PA 17815-1905. Telephone: 717-389-4316. Web site: http://www.bloomu.edu/.

BRYN ATHYN COLLEGE OF THE NEW CHURCH
BRYN ATHYN, PENNSYLVANIA

General Independent Swedenborgian, comprehensive, coed **Entrance** Noncompetitive **Setting** 130-acre small town campus **Total enrollment** 174 **Application deadline** 6/1 **Freshmen** 100% were admitted **Housing** Yes **Expenses** Tuition $4920; Room & Board $4071 **Undergraduates** 48% women, 12% part-time, 1% Hispanic, 3% black, 1% Asian American or Pacific Islander **Academic program** Advanced placement, accelerated degree program, self-designed majors, tutorials, internships **Contact** Dr. Dan Synnestvedt, Director of Admissions, Bryn Athyn College of the New Church, PO Box 717, Bryn Athyn, PA 19009-0717. Telephone: 215-938-2503. Fax: 215-938-2658. Web site: http://www.newchurch.edu/college/.

BRYN MAWR COLLEGE
BRYN MAWR, PENNSYLVANIA

General Independent, university, women only **Entrance** Most difficult **Setting** 135-acre suburban campus **Total enrollment** 1,826 **Student/faculty ratio** 10:1 **Application deadline** 1/15 **Freshmen** 58% were admitted **Housing** Yes **Expenses** Tuition $21,430; Room & Board $7500 **Undergraduates** 5% part-time, 3% 25 or older, 0.2% Native American, 3% Hispanic, 4% black, 18% Asian American or Pacific Islander **Most popular recent majors** Biology; English; psychology **Academic program** Average class size 10, advanced placement, accelerated degree program, self-designed majors, tutorials, honors program, summer session, adult/continuing education programs **Contact** Ms. Nancy Monnich, Director of Admissions and Financial Aid, Bryn Mawr College, 101 North Merion Avenue, Bryn Mawr, PA 19010-2899. Telephone: 610-526-5152 or toll-free 800-BMC-1885 (out-of-state). Fax: 610-526-7471. E-mail: admissions@brynmawr.edu. Web site: http://www.brynmawr.edu/.

BUCKNELL UNIVERSITY
LEWISBURG, PENNSYLVANIA

General Independent, comprehensive, coed **Entrance** Very difficult **Setting** 393-acre small town campus **Total enrollment** 3,543 **Student/faculty ratio** 13:1 **Application deadline** 1/1 **Freshmen** 54% were admitted **Housing** Yes **Expenses** Tuition $21,210; Room & Board $5200 **Undergraduates** 48% women, 0.4% part-time, 1% 25 or older, 0.2% Native American, 2% Hispanic, 3% black, 3% Asian American or Pacific Islander **Most popular recent majors** Biology; economics; business administration **Academic program** Advanced placement, accelerated degree program, self-designed majors, honors program, summer session, internships **Contact** Mr. Mark D. Davies, Director of Admissions, Bucknell University, Lewisburg, PA 17837. Telephone: 717-524-1101. Fax: 717-524-3760. E-mail: admissions@bucknell.edu. Web site: http://www.bucknell.edu/.

CABRINI COLLEGE
RADNOR, PENNSYLVANIA

General Independent Roman Catholic, comprehensive, coed **Entrance** Minimally difficult **Set-**

Cabrini College *(continued)*

ting 112-acre suburban campus **Total enrollment** 2,056 **Student/faculty ratio** 10:1 **Application deadline** Rolling **Freshmen** 87% were admitted **Housing** Yes **Expenses** Tuition $13,200; Room & Board $6830 **Undergraduates** 70% women, 32% part-time, 33% 25 or older, 0.4% Native American, 2% Hispanic, 7% black, 2% Asian American or Pacific Islander **Most popular recent majors** Education; business administration; communications **Academic program** English as a second language, advanced placement, accelerated degree program, self-designed majors, tutorials, honors program, summer session, adult/continuing education programs, internships **Contact** Ms. Joanne Mayberry, Director of Admissions, Cabrini College, 610 King of Prussia Road, Radnor, PA 19087-3698. Telephone: 610-902-8552 or toll-free 800-848-1003 (in-state). Fax: 610-902-8309. E-mail: admit@cabrini.edu. Web site: http://www.cabrini.edu/.

CALIFORNIA UNIVERSITY OF PENNSYLVANIA
CALIFORNIA, PENNSYLVANIA

General State-supported, comprehensive, coed **Entrance** Moderately difficult **Setting** 148-acre small town campus **Total enrollment** 5,783 **Student/faculty ratio** 18:1 **Application deadline** 7/30 **Freshmen** 83% were admitted **Housing** Yes **Expenses** Tuition $4475; Room & Board $4106 **Undergraduates** 52% women, 12% part-time, 20% 25 or older, 0.3% Native American, 0.4% Hispanic, 5% black, 0.4% Asian American or Pacific Islander **Most popular recent majors** Education; business administration; accounting **Academic program** Advanced placement, accelerated degree program, honors program, summer session, adult/continuing education programs, internships **Contact** Mr. Norman Hasbrouck, Dean of Enrollment Management and Academic Services, California University of Pennsylvania, 250 University Avenue, California, PA 15419-1394. Telephone: 724-938-4404. Fax: 724-938-4138. E-mail: inquiry@cup.edu. Web site: http://www.cup.edu/.

CARLOW COLLEGE
PITTSBURGH, PENNSYLVANIA

General Independent Roman Catholic, comprehensive, primarily women **Entrance** Moderately difficult **Setting** 13-acre urban campus **Total enrollment** 2,377 **Student/faculty ratio** 14:1 **Application deadline** Rolling **Freshmen** 81% were admitted **Housing** Yes **Expenses** Tuition $11,708; Room & Board $4692 **Undergraduates** 93% women, 53% part-time, 67% 25 or older, 1% Native American, 0.5% Hispanic, 15% black, 1% Asian American or Pacific Islander **Most popular recent majors** Nursing; communications; business **Academic program** Average class size 20, English as a second language, advanced placement, accelerated degree program, self-designed majors, tutorials, honors program, summer session, adult/continuing education programs, internships **Contact** Ms. Carol Descak, Director of Admissions, Carlow College, 3333 Fifth Avenue, Pittsburgh, PA 15213-3165. Telephone: 412-578-6059 or toll-free 800-333-CARLOW. Fax: 412-578-6668. Web site: http://www.carlow.edu/.

CARNEGIE MELLON UNIVERSITY
PITTSBURGH, PENNSYLVANIA

General Independent, university, coed **Entrance** Very difficult **Setting** 103-acre urban campus **Total enrollment** 7,912 **Student/faculty ratio** 9:1 **Application deadline** 1/15 **Freshmen** 43% were admitted **Housing** Yes **Expenses** Tuition $20,375; Room & Board $6225 **Undergraduates** 34% women, 2% part-time, 1% 25 or older, 0.3% Native American, 5% Hispanic, 5% black, 21% Asian American or Pacific Islander **Most popular recent majors** Electrical/electronics engineering; computer science; business administration **Academic program** English as a second language, advanced placement, accelerated degree program, self-designed majors, honors program, summer session, adult/continuing education programs, internships **Contact** Mr. Michael Steidel, Director of Admissions, Carnegie Mellon University, 5000 Forbes Avenue, Pittsburgh, PA 15213-3891. Telephone: 412-268-2082. Fax: 412-268-7838. E-mail: undergraduate-admissions+@andrew.cmu.edu. Web site: http://www.cmu.edu/.

CEDAR CREST COLLEGE
ALLENTOWN, PENNSYLVANIA

General Independent, 4-year, women only, affiliated with United Church of Christ **Entrance** Moderately difficult **Setting** 84-acre suburban campus **Total enrollment** 1,675 **Student/faculty ratio** 12:1 **Application deadline** Rolling **Freshmen** 75% were admitted **Housing** Yes **Expenses** Tuition $15,820; Room & Board $5745 **Undergraduates** 28% part-time, 37% 25 or older, 0% Native American, 2% Hispanic, 2% black, 2% Asian American or Pacific Islander **Most popular recent majors** Biology; psychology; nursing **Academic program** Average class size 16, English as a second language, advanced placement, accelerated degree program, self-designed majors, tutorials, honors program, summer session, adult/continuing education programs, internships **Contact** Ms. Judith A. Neyhart, Vice President for Enrollment Management, Cedar Crest College, 100 College Drive, Allentown, PA 18104-6196. Telephone: 610-

740-3780. Fax: 610-606-4647. E-mail: cccadmis@cedarcrest.edu. Web site: http://www.cedarcrest.edu/.

► **For more information, see page 407.**

CHATHAM COLLEGE
PITTSBURGH, PENNSYLVANIA

General Independent, comprehensive, primarily women **Entrance** Moderately difficult **Setting** 34-acre urban campus **Total enrollment** 850 **Student/faculty ratio** 9:1 **Application deadline** Rolling **Freshmen** 92% were admitted **Housing** Yes **Expenses** Tuition $15,340; Room & Board $5526 **Undergraduates** 100% women, 12% part-time, 27% 25 or older, 0.4% Native American, 2% Hispanic, 7% black, 1% Asian American or Pacific Islander **Most popular recent majors** Psychology; biology; communications **Academic program** Average class size 20, English as a second language, advanced placement, accelerated degree program, self-designed majors, tutorials, honors program, summer session, adult/continuing education programs, internships **Contact** Acting Dean of Admissions, Chatham College, Woodland Road, Pittsburgh, PA 15232-2826. Telephone: 412-365-1290 or toll-free 800-837-1290. Fax: 412-365-1609. E-mail: admissions@chat.edu. Web site: http://www.chatham.edu/.

CHESTNUT HILL COLLEGE
PHILADELPHIA, PENNSYLVANIA

General Independent Roman Catholic, comprehensive, women only **Entrance** Moderately difficult **Setting** 45-acre suburban campus **Total enrollment** 1,429 **Student/faculty ratio** 9:1 **Application deadline** Rolling **Freshmen** 72% were admitted **Housing** Yes **Expenses** Tuition $14,265; Room & Board $6200 **Undergraduates** 56% part-time, 43% 25 or older, 0.4% Native American, 4% Hispanic, 27% black, 3% Asian American or Pacific Islander **Most popular recent majors** Elementary education; early childhood education; English **Academic program** English as a second language, advanced placement, accelerated degree program, self-designed majors, honors program, summer session, adult/continuing education programs, internships **Contact** Ms. Annabelle Smith, Director of Admissions, Chestnut Hill College, 9601 Germantown Avenue, Philadelphia, PA 19118-2693. Telephone: 215-248-7001. Fax: 215-248-7056.

► **For more information, see page 409.**

CHEYNEY UNIVERSITY OF PENNSYLVANIA
CHEYNEY, PENNSYLVANIA

General State-supported, comprehensive, coed **Entrance** Minimally difficult **Setting** 275-acre suburban campus **Total enrollment** 1,430 **Student/faculty ratio** 12:1 **Application deadline** Rolling **Freshmen** 76% were admitted **Housing** Yes **Expenses** Tuition $4023; Room & Board $4528 **Undergraduates** 50% women, 5% part-time, 15% 25 or older, 0.1% Native American, 1% Hispanic, 97% black, 0.2% Asian American or Pacific Islander **Most popular recent majors** Education; social sciences; business administration **Academic program** Summer session, adult/continuing education programs, internships **Contact** Mr. Eldridge Smith, Interim Director of Admissions, Cheyney University of Pennsylvania, Cheyney, PA 19319. Telephone: 610-399-2275 or toll-free 800-CHEYNEY. Fax: 610-399-2099. Web site: http://www.cheyney.edu/.

CLARION UNIVERSITY OF PENNSYLVANIA
CLARION, PENNSYLVANIA

General State-supported, comprehensive, coed **Entrance** Minimally difficult **Setting** 100-acre rural campus **Total enrollment** 5,948 **Student/faculty ratio** 18:1 **Application deadline** Rolling **Freshmen** 91% were admitted **Housing** Yes **Expenses** Tuition $4419; Room & Board $3330 **Undergraduates** 61% women, 9% part-time, 17% 25 or older, 0.2% Native American, 0.4% Hispanic, 4% black, 0.4% Asian American or Pacific Islander **Most popular recent majors** Elementary education; secondary education; mass communications **Academic program** Advanced placement, accelerated degree program, tutorials, honors program, summer session, adult/continuing education programs, internships **Contact** Mr. John S. Shropshire, Dean of Enrollment Management and Academic Records, Clarion University of Pennsylvania, Clarion, PA 16214. Telephone: 814-226-2306 or toll-free 800-672-7171 (in-state). Fax: 814-226-2030. Web site: http://www.clarion.edu/.

► **For more information, see page 412.**

COLLEGE MISERICORDIA
DALLAS, PENNSYLVANIA

General Independent Roman Catholic, comprehensive, coed **Entrance** Moderately difficult **Setting** 100-acre small town campus **Total enrollment** 1,697 **Student/faculty ratio** 13:1 **Application deadline** Rolling **Housing** Yes **Expenses** Tuition $13,830; Room & Board $6150 **Undergraduates** 74% women, 12% part-time, 20% 25 or older **Most popular recent majors** Physical therapy; occupational therapy; elementary education **Academic program** Average class size 28, advanced placement, accelerated degree program, self-designed majors, honors program, summer session, adult/continuing education programs, internships **Contact** Ms. Jane Dessoye, Executive Director of Admissions and Financial Aid,

College Misericordia *(continued)*

College Misericordia, 301 Lake Street, Dallas, PA 18612-1098. Telephone: 717-675-4449 or toll-free 800-852-7675. Fax: 717-675-2441. Web site: http://www.miseri.edu/.

THE CURTIS INSTITUTE OF MUSIC
PHILADELPHIA, PENNSYLVANIA

General Independent, comprehensive, coed **Entrance** Most difficult **Setting** Urban campus **Total enrollment** 162 **Student/faculty ratio** 2:1 **Application deadline** 1/15 **Housing** No **Expenses** Tuition $695 **Undergraduates** 48% women, 2% Hispanic, 4% black, 6% Asian American or Pacific Islander **Academic program** English as a second language, advanced placement, accelerated degree program **Contact** Mr. Christopher Hodges, Admissions Officer, The Curtis Institute of Music, 1726 Locust Street, Philadelphia, PA 19103-6107. Telephone: 215-893-5262. Fax: 215-893-7900.

DELAWARE VALLEY COLLEGE
DOYLESTOWN, PENNSYLVANIA

General Independent, 4-year, coed **Entrance** Moderately difficult **Setting** 600-acre suburban campus **Total enrollment** 2,089 **Student/faculty ratio** 16:1 **Application deadline** Rolling **Freshmen** 90% were admitted **Housing** Yes **Expenses** Tuition $14,929; Room & Board $5655 **Undergraduates** 49% women, 6% part-time, 27% 25 or older, 0.2% Native American, 1% Hispanic, 4% black, 1% Asian American or Pacific Islander **Most popular recent majors** Business administration; ornamental horticulture; animal sciences **Academic program** Advanced placement, tutorials, honors program, summer session, adult/continuing education programs, internships **Contact** Mr. Stephen Zenko, Director of Admissions, Delaware Valley College, 700 East Butler Avenue, Doylestown, PA 18901-2697. Telephone: 215-345-1500 ext. 2211 or toll-free 800-2DELVAL (in-state). Fax: 215-345-5277. E-mail: admitme@devalcol.edu.

DICKINSON COLLEGE
CARLISLE, PENNSYLVANIA

General Independent, 4-year, coed **Entrance** Very difficult **Setting** 103-acre suburban campus **Total enrollment** 1,842 **Student/faculty ratio** 10:1 **Application deadline** 2/15 **Freshmen** 79% were admitted **Housing** Yes **Expenses** Tuition $21,600; Room & Board $5840 **Undergraduates** 57% women, 0.4% part-time, 0% 25 or older, 0.4% Native American, 2% Hispanic, 1% black, 4% Asian American or Pacific Islander **Most popular recent majors** Political science; English; psychology **Academic program** Average class size 18, advanced placement, accelerated degree program, self-designed majors, tutorials, summer session, adult/continuing education programs, internships **Contact** Mr. R. Russell Shunk, Dean of Admissions, Dickinson College, PO Box 1773, Carlisle, PA 17013-2896. Telephone: 717-245-1231 or toll-free 800-644-1773. Fax: 717-245-1442. E-mail: admit@dickinson.edu. Web site: http://www.dickinson.edu/.

DREXEL UNIVERSITY
PHILADELPHIA, PENNSYLVANIA

General Independent, university, coed **Entrance** Moderately difficult **Setting** 38-acre urban campus **Total enrollment** 10,455 **Student/faculty ratio** 15:1 **Application deadline** 3/1 **Freshmen** 68% were admitted **Housing** Yes **Expenses** Tuition $15,048; Room & Board $7266 **Undergraduates** 35% women, 16% part-time, 21% 25 or older, 0.3% Native American, 2% Hispanic, 10% black, 9% Asian American or Pacific Islander **Most popular recent majors** Electrical/electronics engineering; accounting; finance **Academic program** English as a second language, advanced placement, tutorials, honors program, summer session, adult/continuing education programs, internships **Contact** Mr. Gary Hamme, Dean of Enrollment Management and Career Services, Drexel University, Room 220, Philadelphia, PA 19104-2875. Telephone: 215-895-2400 or toll-free 800-2-DREXEL (in-state). Fax: 215-895-5939. E-mail: undergrad-admissions@post.drexel.edu. Web site: http://www.drexel.edu/.

▶ **For more information, see page 423.**

DUQUESNE UNIVERSITY
PITTSBURGH, PENNSYLVANIA

General Independent Roman Catholic, university, coed **Entrance** Moderately difficult **Setting** 43-acre urban campus **Total enrollment** 9,500 **Student/faculty ratio** 16:1 **Application deadline** 7/1 **Freshmen** 65% were admitted **Housing** Yes **Expenses** Tuition $14,066; Room & Board $5978 **Undergraduates** 57% women, 12% part-time, 17% 25 or older, 0.2% Native American, 1% Hispanic, 5% black, 3% Asian American or Pacific Islander **Most popular recent majors** Health science; business administration; pharmacy **Academic program** Average class size 33, English as a second language, advanced placement, accelerated degree program, self-designed majors, tutorials, honors program, summer session, adult/continuing education programs, internships **Contact** Office of Admissions, Duquesne University, 600 Forbes Avenue, Pittsburgh, PA 15282-0201. Telephone: 412-396-5000 or toll-free 800-456-

0590. Fax: 412-396-5644. E-mail: admissions@duq2.cc.duq.edu. Web site: http://www.duq.edu/.

EASTERN COLLEGE
ST. DAVIDS, PENNSYLVANIA

General Independent American Baptist, comprehensive, coed **Entrance** Moderately difficult **Setting** 107-acre campus **Total enrollment** 2,496 **Student/faculty ratio** 15:1 **Application deadline** Rolling **Freshmen** 51% were admitted **Housing** Yes **Expenses** Tuition $13,200; Room & Board $5654 **Undergraduates** 66% women, 17% part-time, 47% 25 or older, 0.3% Native American, 3% Hispanic, 13% black, 1% Asian American or Pacific Islander **Academic program** English as a second language, advanced placement, accelerated degree program, self-designed majors, tutorials, honors program, summer session, adult/continuing education programs, internships **Contact** Mr. Mark Seymour, Executive Director for Enrollment Management, Eastern College, 1300 Eagle Road, St. Davids, PA 19087-3696. Telephone: 610-341-5967 or toll-free 800-452-0996 (in-state). Fax: 610-341-1723. E-mail: ugadm@eastern.edu. Web site: http://www.eastern.edu/.

► **For more information, see page 425.**

EAST STROUDSBURG UNIVERSITY OF PENNSYLVANIA
EAST STROUDSBURG, PENNSYLVANIA

General State-supported, comprehensive, coed **Entrance** Moderately difficult **Setting** 183-acre small town campus **Total enrollment** 5,687 **Student/faculty ratio** 19:1 **Application deadline** 3/1 **Freshmen** 71% were admitted **Housing** Yes **Expenses** Tuition $4322; Room & Board $3720 **Undergraduates** 58% women, 10% part-time, 18% 25 or older, 0.2% Native American, 3% Hispanic, 3% black, 1% Asian American or Pacific Islander **Most popular recent majors** Elementary education; physical education; biology **Academic program** Average class size 40, advanced placement, self-designed majors, honors program, summer session, adult/continuing education programs, internships **Contact** Mr. Alan T. Chesterton, Director of Admissions, East Stroudsburg University of Pennsylvania, 200 Prospect Street, East Stroudsburg, PA 18301-2999. Telephone: 717-422-3542. Fax: 717-422-3933. E-mail: undergrads@po-box.esu.edu. Web site: http://www.esu.edu/.

EDINBORO UNIVERSITY OF PENNSYLVANIA
EDINBORO, PENNSYLVANIA

General State-supported, comprehensive, coed **Entrance** Moderately difficult **Setting** 585-acre small town campus **Total enrollment** 7,083 **Student/faculty ratio** 18:1 **Application deadline** Rolling **Freshmen** 82% were admitted **Housing** Yes **Expenses** Tuition $4193; Room & Board $3674 **Undergraduates** 57% women, 11% part-time, 20% 25 or older, 0.3% Native American, 1% Hispanic, 5% black, 1% Asian American or Pacific Islander **Most popular recent majors** Elementary education; criminal justice/law enforcement administration; psychology **Academic program** Average class size 30, advanced placement, accelerated degree program, self-designed majors, honors program, summer session, adult/continuing education programs, internships **Contact** Mr. Terrence Carlin, Assistant Vice President for Admissions, Edinboro University of Pennsylvania, Biggers House, Edinboro, PA 16444. Telephone: 814-732-2761 or toll-free 800-626-2203. Fax: 814-732-2420. Web site: http://www.edinboro.edu/.

ELIZABETHTOWN COLLEGE
ELIZABETHTOWN, PENNSYLVANIA

General Independent, 4-year, coed, affiliated with Church of the Brethren **Entrance** Moderately difficult **Setting** 185-acre small town campus **Total enrollment** 1,703 **Student/faculty ratio** 13:1 **Application deadline** Rolling **Freshmen** 75% were admitted **Housing** Yes **Expenses** Tuition $16,930; Room & Board $4900 **Undergraduates** 67% women, 10% part-time **Most popular recent majors** Business administration; education; communications **Academic program** Average class size 23, English as a second language, advanced placement, summer session, adult/continuing education programs, internships **Contact** Mr. Gordon Mck. Bateman, Dean of Admissions and Enrollment Management, Elizabethtown College, 1 Alpha Drive, Elizabethtown, PA 17022-2298. Telephone: 717-361-1400. E-mail: admissions@acad.etown.edu. Web site: http://www.etown.edu/.

FRANKLIN AND MARSHALL COLLEGE
LANCASTER, PENNSYLVANIA

General Independent, 4-year, coed **Entrance** Very difficult **Setting** 125-acre suburban campus **Total enrollment** 1,843 **Student/faculty ratio** 11:1 **Application deadline** 2/1 **Freshmen** 54% were admitted **Housing** Yes **Expenses** Tuition $22,664; Room & Board $4906 **Undergraduates** 49% women, 0.4% part-time, 1% 25 or older, 0.2% Native American, 4% Hispanic, 3% black, 6% Asian American or Pacific Islander **Most popular recent majors** Political science; English; biology **Academic program** Advanced placement, accelerated degree program, self-designed majors, tutorials, honors program, summer session, internships **Contact** Mr. Peter W. VanBuskirk, Dean of Admissions, Franklin and Marshall College, PO Box 3003, Lancaster, PA 17604-3003. Telephone: 717-

Franklin and Marshall College *(continued)*

291-3953. Fax: 717-291-4389. E-mail: admission@fandm.edu. Web site: http://www.fandm.edu/.

GANNON UNIVERSITY

ERIE, PENNSYLVANIA

General Independent Roman Catholic, comprehensive, coed **Entrance** Moderately difficult **Setting** 13-acre urban campus **Total enrollment** 3,227 **Student/faculty ratio** 13:1 **Application deadline** Rolling **Freshmen** 83% were admitted **Housing** Yes **Expenses** Tuition $12,994; Room & Board $4860 **Undergraduates** 57% women, 14% part-time, 23% 25 or older, 1% Native American, 1% Hispanic, 3% black, 2% Asian American or Pacific Islander **Most popular recent majors** Nursing; biology; criminal justice studies **Academic program** Average class size 26, advanced placement, accelerated degree program, tutorials, honors program, summer session, adult/continuing education programs, internships **Contact** Ms. Beth Nemenz, Director of Admissions, Gannon University, University Square, Erie, PA 16541. Telephone: 814-871-7240 or toll-free 800-GANNONU. Fax: 814-871-5803. E-mail: admissions@gannon.edu. Web site: http://www.gannon.edu/.

GENEVA COLLEGE

BEAVER FALLS, PENNSYLVANIA

General Independent, comprehensive, coed, affiliated with Reformed Presbyterian Church of North America **Entrance** Moderately difficult **Setting** 55-acre small town campus **Total enrollment** 1,956 **Student/faculty ratio** 18:1 **Application deadline** Rolling **Freshmen** 54% were admitted **Housing** Yes **Expenses** Tuition $11,534; Room & Board $4750 **Undergraduates** 53% women, 12% part-time, 30% 25 or older, 0.2% Native American, 1% Hispanic, 11% black, 1% Asian American or Pacific Islander **Most popular recent majors** Elementary education; business administration; biology **Academic program** Average class size 35, English as a second language, advanced placement, accelerated degree program, self-designed majors, tutorials, honors program, summer session, adult/continuing education programs, internships **Contact** Mr. David Layton, Director of Admissions, Geneva College, 3200 College Avenue, Beaver Falls, PA 15010-3599. Telephone: 724-847-6500 or toll-free 800-847-8255 (out-of-state). Fax: 724-847-6687. E-mail: admissions@geneva.edu. Web site: http://www.geneva.edu/.

GETTYSBURG COLLEGE

GETTYSBURG, PENNSYLVANIA

General Independent, 4-year, coed **Entrance** Very difficult **Setting** 200-acre small town campus **Total enrollment** 2,111 **Student/faculty ratio** 11:1 **Application deadline** 2/15 **Freshmen** 72% were admitted **Housing** Yes **Expenses** Tuition $22,430; Room & Board $5038 **Undergraduates** 51% women, 0.3% part-time, 1% 25 or older, 0.1% Native American, 1% Hispanic, 1% black, 1% Asian American or Pacific Islander **Most popular recent majors** Business administration; political science; psychology **Academic program** Average class size 20, advanced placement, accelerated degree program, self-designed majors, tutorials, honors program, adult/continuing education programs, internships **Contact** Mr. Delwin K. Gustafson, Dean of Admissions, Gettysburg College, Gettysburg, PA 17325-1411. Telephone: 717-337-6100 or toll-free 800-431-0803. Fax: 717-337-6145. E-mail: admiss@gettysburg.edu. Web site: http://www.gettysburg.edu/.

GRATZ COLLEGE

MELROSE PARK, PENNSYLVANIA

General Independent Jewish, comprehensive, coed **Entrance** Noncompetitive **Setting** 28-acre suburban campus **Total enrollment** 332 **Student/faculty ratio** 3:1 **Application deadline** Rolling **Housing** No **Expenses** Tuition $6900 **Undergraduates** 89% 25 or older **Academic program** Summer session, adult/continuing education programs, internships **Contact** Ms. Evelyn Klein, Director of Admissions, Gratz College, Old York Road and Melrose Avenue, Melrose Park, PA 19027. Telephone: 215-635-7300 or toll-free 800-475-4635. Fax: 215-635-7320. E-mail: gratzinfo@aol.com. Web site: http://www.gratz.edu/.

GROVE CITY COLLEGE

GROVE CITY, PENNSYLVANIA

General Independent Presbyterian, comprehensive, coed **Entrance** Very difficult **Setting** 150-acre small town campus **Total enrollment** 2,292 **Student/faculty ratio** 21:1 **Application deadline** 2/15 **Freshmen** 42% were admitted **Housing** Yes **Expenses** Tuition $6576; Room & Board $3816 **Undergraduates** 50% women, 2% part-time, 1% 25 or older, 0.04% Native American, 0.2% Hispanic, 0.3% black, 1% Asian American or Pacific Islander **Most popular recent majors** Business administration; mechanical engineering; elementary education **Academic program** Average class size 59, advanced placement, self-designed majors, summer session, internships **Contact** Mr. Jeffrey C. Mincey, Director of Admissions, Grove City College, 100 Campus Drive, Grove City, PA 16127-2104. Telephone: 724-458-2100. Fax: 724-458-3395. E-mail: admissions@gcc.edu. Web site: http://www.gcc.edu/.

▶ **For more information, see page 446.**

GWYNEDD-MERCY COLLEGE
GWYNEDD VALLEY, PENNSYLVANIA

General Independent Roman Catholic, comprehensive, coed **Entrance** Moderately difficult **Setting** 170-acre suburban campus **Total enrollment** 1,706 **Student/faculty ratio** 13:1 **Application deadline** 7/1 **Freshmen** 76% were admitted **Housing** Yes **Expenses** Tuition $12,280; Room & Board $5800 **Undergraduates** 67% 25 or older, 1% Hispanic, 8% black, 2% Asian American or Pacific Islander **Most popular recent majors** Nursing; business administration; elementary education **Academic program** English as a second language, advanced placement, accelerated degree program, tutorials, honors program, summer session, adult/continuing education programs, internships **Contact** Ms. Jacqueline Williams, Director of Admissions, Gwynedd-Mercy College, Sumneytown Pike, Gwynedd Valley, PA 19437-0901. Telephone: 215-641-5510 or toll-free 800-DIAL-GMC (in-state). Fax: 215-641-5556. Web site: http://www.gmc.edu/.

HAHNEMANN UNIVERSITY
See Allegheny University of the Health Sciences

HAVERFORD COLLEGE
HAVERFORD, PENNSYLVANIA

General Independent, 4-year, coed **Entrance** Most difficult **Setting** 216-acre suburban campus **Total enrollment** 1,147 **Student/faculty ratio** 10:1 **Application deadline** 1/15 **Freshmen** 34% were admitted **Housing** Yes **Expenses** Tuition $21,740; Room & Board $7720 **Undergraduates** 51% women, 1% 25 or older, 0.3% Native American, 6% Hispanic, 5% black, 7% Asian American or Pacific Islander **Most popular recent majors** Biology; history; English **Academic program** Average class size 17, advanced placement, accelerated degree program, self-designed majors, tutorials **Contact** Ms. Delsie Z. Phillips, Director of Admissions, Haverford College, 370 Lancaster Avenue, Haverford, PA 19041-1392. Telephone: 610-896-1350. Fax: 610-896-1338. E-mail: admitme@haverford.edu. Web site: http://www.haverford.edu/.

► **For more information, see page 447.**

HOLY FAMILY COLLEGE
PHILADELPHIA, PENNSYLVANIA

General Independent Roman Catholic, comprehensive, coed **Entrance** Moderately difficult **Setting** 47-acre suburban campus **Total enrollment** 2,587 **Student/faculty ratio** 12:1 **Application deadline** Rolling **Freshmen** 74% were admitted **Housing** No **Expenses** Tuition $10,620 **Undergraduates** 76% women, 47% part-time, 44% 25 or older, 0.2% Native American, 2% Hispanic, 4% black, 2% Asian American or Pacific Islander **Most popular recent majors** Elementary education; nursing science; business administration **Academic program** Advanced placement, accelerated degree program, tutorials, honors program, summer session, adult/continuing education programs, internships **Contact** Mrs. Roberta Nolan, Director of Admissions, Holy Family College, Grant and Frankford Avenues, Philadelphia, PA 19114-2094. Telephone: 215-637-3050 or toll-free 800-637-1191. Fax: 215-281-1022.

IMMACULATA COLLEGE
IMMACULATA, PENNSYLVANIA

General Independent Roman Catholic, comprehensive, primarily women **Entrance** Moderately difficult **Setting** 400-acre suburban campus **Total enrollment** 2,312 **Student/faculty ratio** 12:1 **Application deadline** Rolling **Freshmen** 87% were admitted **Housing** Yes **Expenses** Tuition $12,115; Room & Board $5856 **Undergraduates** 84% women, 43% part-time, 70% 25 or older, 0.1% Native American, 2% Hispanic, 5% black, 1% Asian American or Pacific Islander **Most popular recent majors** Psychology; business administration **Academic program** Average class size 20, English as a second language, advanced placement, accelerated degree program, self-designed majors, honors program, summer session, adult/continuing education programs, internships **Contact** Mr. Ken R. Rasp, Dean of Enrollment Management, Immaculata College, Immaculata, PA 19345-0500. Telephone: 610-647-4400 ext. 3015 or toll-free 888-777-2780. Fax: 610-251-1668. Web site: http://www.immaculata.edu/.

INDIANA UNIVERSITY OF PENNSYLVANIA
INDIANA, PENNSYLVANIA

General State-supported, university, coed **Entrance** Moderately difficult **Setting** 342-acre small town campus **Total enrollment** 13,736 **Student/faculty ratio** 19:1 **Application deadline** Rolling **Housing** Yes **Expenses** Tuition $4204; Room & Board $3408 **Undergraduates** 55% women, 5% part-time, 10% 25 or older, 0.1% Native American, 1% Hispanic, 5% black, 1% Asian American or Pacific Islander **Most popular recent majors** Criminology; elementary education; accounting **Academic program** Average class size 24, English as a second language, advanced placement, accelerated degree program, honors program, summer session, adult/continuing education programs, internships **Contact** Mr. William Nunn, Dean of Admissions, Indiana University of Pennsylvania, 216 Pratt Hall, Indiana, PA 15705. Telephone: 724-357-

Indiana University of Pennsylvania *(continued)*

2230 or toll-free 800-442-6830. E-mail: admissions_inquiry@grove.iup.edu. Web site: http://www.iup.edu/.

JUNIATA COLLEGE

HUNTINGDON, PENNSYLVANIA

General Independent, 4-year, coed, affiliated with Church of the Brethren **Entrance** Moderately difficult **Setting** 800-acre small town campus **Total enrollment** 1,204 **Student/faculty ratio** 15:1 **Application deadline** 3/15 **Freshmen** 87% were admitted **Housing** Yes **Expenses** Tuition $17,580; Room & Board $5205 **Undergraduates** 55% women, 1% part-time, 3% 25 or older, 0.1% Native American, 0.5% Hispanic, 0.5% black, 1% Asian American or Pacific Islander **Most popular recent majors** Biology; business administration; education **Academic program** English as a second language, advanced placement, accelerated degree program, self-designed majors, tutorials, honors program, summer session, adult/continuing education programs, internships **Contact** Mr. David Hawsey, Associate Vice President for Advancement and Marketing, Juniata College, 1700 Moore Street, Huntingdon, PA 16652-2119. Telephone: 814-641-3420 or toll-free 800-526-1970. Fax: 814-641-3100. E-mail: info@juniata.edu. Web site: http://www.juniata.edu/.

KING'S COLLEGE

WILKES-BARRE, PENNSYLVANIA

General Independent Roman Catholic, comprehensive, coed **Entrance** Moderately difficult **Setting** 48-acre suburban campus **Total enrollment** 2,222 **Student/faculty ratio** 17:1 **Application deadline** Rolling **Freshmen** 83% were admitted **Housing** Yes **Expenses** Tuition $14,000; Room & Board $6120 **Undergraduates** 51% women, 16% part-time, 18% 25 or older, 0% Native American, 1% Hispanic, 2% black, 1% Asian American or Pacific Islander **Most popular recent majors** Accounting; communications; business administration **Academic program** Average class size 21, English as a second language, advanced placement, self-designed majors, tutorials, honors program, summer session, adult/continuing education programs, internships **Contact** Mr. Charles O. Bachman, Dean of Enrollment Management, King's College, 133 North River Street, Wilkes-Barre, PA 18711-0801. Telephone: 717-208-5858 or toll-free 888-KINGSPA. Fax: 717-208-5971. E-mail: admssns@leo.kings.edu. Web site: http://www.kings.edu/.

KUTZTOWN UNIVERSITY OF PENNSYLVANIA

KUTZTOWN, PENNSYLVANIA

General State-supported, comprehensive, coed **Entrance** Moderately difficult **Setting** 326-acre rural campus **Total enrollment** 7,920 **Student/faculty ratio** 16:1 **Application deadline** Rolling **Freshmen** 78% were admitted **Housing** Yes **Expenses** Tuition $4219; Room & Board $3650 **Undergraduates** 57% women, 10% part-time, 12% 25 or older, 0.4% Native American, 2% Hispanic, 3% black, 1% Asian American or Pacific Islander **Most popular recent majors** Psychology; applied art; early childhood education **Academic program** Average class size 30, advanced placement, accelerated degree program, self-designed majors, tutorials, honors program, summer session, adult/continuing education programs, internships **Contact** Dr. Robert McGowan, Director of Admissions, Kutztown University of Pennsylvania, Kutztown, PA 19530. Telephone: 610-683-4060 ext. 4053. Fax: 610-683-1375. Web site: http://www.kutztown.edu/.

LAFAYETTE COLLEGE

EASTON, PENNSYLVANIA

General Independent, 4-year, coed, affiliated with Presbyterian Church (U.S.A.) **Entrance** Very difficult **Setting** 110-acre suburban campus **Total enrollment** 2,185 **Student/faculty ratio** 11:1 **Application deadline** 1/1 **Freshmen** 58% were admitted **Housing** Yes **Expenses** Tuition $21,202; Room & Board $6560 **Undergraduates** 46% women, 4% part-time, 5% 25 or older, 0.05% Native American, 2% Hispanic, 3% black, 2% Asian American or Pacific Islander **Most popular recent majors** Biology; business economics; psychology **Academic program** Advanced placement, accelerated degree program, self-designed majors, tutorials, honors program, summer session, adult/continuing education programs, internships **Contact** Dr. Gary Ripple, Director of Admissions, Lafayette College, Easton, PA 18042-1798. Telephone: 610-250-5100. Fax: 610-250-5355. E-mail: rippleg@lafayette.edu. Web site: http://www.lafayette.edu/.

LANCASTER BIBLE COLLEGE

LANCASTER, PENNSYLVANIA

General Independent nondenominational, comprehensive, coed **Entrance** Minimally difficult **Setting** 100-acre suburban campus **Total enrollment** 711 **Student/faculty ratio** 16:1 **Application deadline** Rolling **Freshmen** 76% were admitted **Housing** Yes **Expenses** Tuition $8550; Room & Board $3850 **Undergraduates** 52% women, 13% part-time, 28% 25 or older, 0% Native American, 1% Hispanic, 3% black, 2% Asian

American or Pacific Islander **Academic program** Average class size 45, advanced placement, summer session, adult/continuing education programs, internships **Contact** Mrs. Joanne M. Roper, Director of Admissions, Lancaster Bible College, 901 Eden Road, Lancaster, PA 17601-5036. Telephone: 717-569-8271 or toll-free 888-CALL LBC. Fax: 717-560-8213. Web site: http://www.lbc.edu/.

LA ROCHE COLLEGE
PITTSBURGH, PENNSYLVANIA

General Independent, comprehensive, coed, affiliated with Roman Catholic Church **Entrance** Minimally difficult **Setting** 80-acre suburban campus **Total enrollment** 1,568 **Application deadline** Rolling **Freshmen** 86% were admitted **Housing** Yes **Expenses** Tuition $10,400; Room & Board $5408 **Undergraduates** 66% women, 41% part-time, 52% 25 or older, 0.2% Native American, 0.5% Hispanic, 4% black, 1% Asian American or Pacific Islander **Most popular recent majors** Nursing; business administration; psychology **Academic program** English as a second language, advanced placement, tutorials, honors program, summer session, adult/continuing education programs, internships **Contact** Mr. Brett Freshour, Director of Enrollment Services, La Roche College, 9000 Babcock Boulevard, Pittsburgh, PA 15237-5898. Telephone: 412-536-1277 or toll-free 800-838-4LRC. Fax: 412-536-1048. E-mail: ad-msns@laroche.edu. Web site: http://www.laroche.edu/.

LA SALLE UNIVERSITY
PHILADELPHIA, PENNSYLVANIA

General Independent Roman Catholic, comprehensive, coed **Entrance** Moderately difficult **Setting** 100-acre urban campus **Total enrollment** 5,452 **Student/faculty ratio** 14:1 **Application deadline** 4/1 **Freshmen** 84% were admitted **Housing** Yes **Expenses** Tuition $14,850; Room & Board $6170 **Undergraduates** 60% women, 28% part-time, 2% 25 or older, 0.1% Native American, 4% Hispanic, 13% black, 3% Asian American or Pacific Islander **Most popular recent majors** Accounting; (pre)medicine; mass communications **Academic program** English as a second language, advanced placement, accelerated degree program, self-designed majors, tutorials, honors program, summer session, adult/continuing education programs, internships **Contact** Ms. Anna Melnyk Allen, Acting Director of Admission and Financial Aid, La Salle University, 1900 West Olney Avenue, Philadelphia, PA 19141-1199. Telephone: 215-951-1500 or toll-free 800-328-1910. Fax: 215-951-1656. E-mail: admiss@lasalle.edu. Web site: http://www.lasalle.edu/.

LEBANON VALLEY COLLEGE
ANNVILLE, PENNSYLVANIA

General Independent United Methodist, comprehensive, coed **Entrance** Moderately difficult **Setting** 200-acre small town campus **Total enrollment** 1,856 **Student/faculty ratio** 16:1 **Application deadline** Rolling **Freshmen** 76% were admitted **Housing** Yes **Expenses** Tuition $15,980; Room & Board $5110 **Undergraduates** 60% women, 23% part-time, 22% 25 or older, 0.2% Native American, 1% Hispanic, 2% black, 1% Asian American or Pacific Islander **Most popular recent majors** Business administration; elementary education; biology **Academic program** Average class size 20, English as a second language, advanced placement, accelerated degree program, self-designed majors, tutorials, honors program, summer session, adult/continuing education programs, internships **Contact** Mr. William J. Brown, Dean of Admission and Financial Aid, Lebanon Valley College, PO Box R, Annville, PA 17003-0501. Telephone: 717-867-6181 or toll-free 800-445-6181. Fax: 717-867-6124. E-mail: admiss@lvc.edu. Web site: http://www.lvc.edu/.

LEHIGH UNIVERSITY
BETHLEHEM, PENNSYLVANIA

General Independent, university, coed **Entrance** Very difficult **Setting** 1,600-acre suburban campus **Total enrollment** 6,316 **Student/faculty ratio** 11:1 **Application deadline** 1/15 **Freshmen** 54% were admitted **Housing** Yes **Expenses** Tuition $21,350; Room & Board $6220 **Undergraduates** 38% women, 1% part-time, 1% 25 or older, 0.1% Native American, 2% Hispanic, 3% black, 5% Asian American or Pacific Islander **Most popular recent majors** Finance; civil engineering; mechanical engineering **Academic program** English as a second language, advanced placement, accelerated degree program, tutorials, honors program, summer session, adult/continuing education programs, internships **Contact** Mrs. Lorna Hunter, Dean of Admissions and Financial Aid, Lehigh University, 27 Memorial Drive West, Bethlehem, PA 18015-3094. Telephone: 610-758-3100. Fax: 610-758-4361. E-mail: inado@lehigh.edu. Web site: http://www.lehigh.edu/.

LINCOLN UNIVERSITY
LINCOLN UNIVERSITY, PENNSYLVANIA

General State-related, comprehensive, coed **Entrance** Moderately difficult **Setting** 442-acre rural campus **Total enrollment** 2,020 **Student/faculty ratio** 16:1 **Application deadline** Rolling **Freshmen** 73% were admitted **Housing** Yes **Expenses** Tuition $4762; Room & Board $4440 **Undergraduates** 56% women, 2% part-time, 6% 25

Lincoln University *(continued)*

or older, 0.1% Native American, 0.3% Hispanic, 96% black, 0.2% Asian American or Pacific Islander **Most popular recent majors** Education; business administration; biology **Academic program** Advanced placement, accelerated degree program, self-designed majors, honors program, summer session, adult/continuing education programs, internships **Contact** Dr. Robert Laney Jr., Director of Admissions, Lincoln University, PO Box 179, Lincoln University, PA 19352. Telephone: 610-932-8300 ext. 306 or toll-free 800-215-4858. E-mail: admiss@lu.lincoln.edu. Web site: http://www.lincoln.edu/.

LOCK HAVEN UNIVERSITY OF PENNSYLVANIA
LOCK HAVEN, PENNSYLVANIA

General State-supported, comprehensive, coed **Entrance** Moderately difficult **Setting** 135-acre small town campus **Total enrollment** 3,538 **Student/faculty ratio** 19:1 **Application deadline** Rolling **Freshmen** 81% were admitted **Housing** Yes **Expenses** Tuition $4062; Room & Board $3880 **Undergraduates** 54% women, 4% part-time, 9% 25 or older, 0.3% Native American, 1% Hispanic, 3% black, 1% Asian American or Pacific Islander **Most popular recent majors** Education; health science; biology **Academic program** Average class size 26, advanced placement, accelerated degree program, self-designed majors, tutorials, honors program, summer session, adult/continuing education programs, internships **Contact** Mr. James Reeser, Director of Admissions, Lock Haven University of Pennsylvania, North Fairview Street, Lock Haven, PA 17745-2390. Telephone: 717-893-2027 or toll-free 800-332-8900 (in-state), 800-233-8978 (out-of-state). Fax: 717-893-2201. E-mail: admissions@eagle.lhup.edu. Web site: http://www.lhup.edu/.

LYCOMING COLLEGE
WILLIAMSPORT, PENNSYLVANIA

General Independent United Methodist, 4-year, coed **Entrance** Moderately difficult **Setting** 35-acre small town campus **Total enrollment** 1,465 **Student/faculty ratio** 13:1 **Application deadline** 4/1 **Freshmen** 80% were admitted **Housing** Yes **Expenses** Tuition $16,930; Room & Board $4770 **Undergraduates** 56% women, 3% part-time, 10% 25 or older, 0.1% Native American, 1% Hispanic, 1% black, 1% Asian American or Pacific Islander **Most popular recent majors** Psychology; biology; business administration **Academic program** Average class size 30, advanced placement, accelerated degree program, self-designed majors, tutorials, honors program, summer session, internships **Contact** Mr. James Spencer, Dean of Admissions and Financial Aid, Lycoming College, 700 College Place, Williamsport, PA 17701-5192. Telephone: 717-321-4026 or toll-free 800-345-3920. Fax: 717-321-4337. E-mail: admissions@lycoming.edu. Web site: http://www.lycoming.edu/.

MANSFIELD UNIVERSITY OF PENNSYLVANIA
MANSFIELD, PENNSYLVANIA

General State-supported, comprehensive, coed **Entrance** Moderately difficult **Setting** 205-acre small town campus **Total enrollment** 2,907 **Student/faculty ratio** 16:1 **Freshmen** 86% were admitted **Housing** Yes **Expenses** Tuition $4404; Room & Board $3704 **Undergraduates** 56% women, 5% part-time, 16% 25 or older, 0.5% Native American, 1% Hispanic, 4% black, 1% Asian American or Pacific Islander **Most popular recent majors** Criminal justice/law enforcement administration; elementary education; business administration **Academic program** Advanced placement, accelerated degree program, self-designed majors, honors program, summer session, adult/continuing education programs, internships **Contact** Mr. Brian D. Barden, Director of Admissions, Mansfield University of Pennsylvania, Alumni Hall, Mansfield, PA 16933. Telephone: 717-662-4813 or toll-free 800-577-6826. Fax: 717-662-4121. E-mail: admissions@mnsfld.edu. Web site: http://www.mnsfld.edu/.

MARYWOOD UNIVERSITY
SCRANTON, PENNSYLVANIA

General Independent Roman Catholic, comprehensive, coed **Entrance** Moderately difficult **Setting** 115-acre suburban campus **Total enrollment** 2,948 **Student/faculty ratio** 10:1 **Application deadline** Rolling **Freshmen** 82% were admitted **Housing** Yes **Expenses** Tuition $14,003; Room & Board $5700 **Undergraduates** 75% women, 13% part-time, 21% 25 or older, 0.1% Native American, 1% Hispanic, 1% black, 1% Asian American or Pacific Islander **Most popular recent majors** Elementary education; psychology; business administration **Academic program** Average class size 25, English as a second language, advanced placement, accelerated degree program, self-designed majors, tutorials, honors program, summer session, adult/continuing education programs, internships **Contact** Mr. Fred R. Brooks Jr., Director of Admissions, Marywood University, 2300 Adams Avenue, Scranton, PA 18509-1598. Telephone: 717-348-6234 or toll-free 800-346-5014. Fax: 717-961-4763. E-mail: ugadm@ac.marywood.edu. Web site: http://www.marywood.edu/.

MEDICAL COLLEGE OF PENNSYLVANIA AND HAHNEMANN UNIVERSITY

See Allegheny University of the Health Sciences

MERCYHURST COLLEGE

ERIE, PENNSYLVANIA

General Independent Roman Catholic, comprehensive, coed **Entrance** Moderately difficult **Setting** 88-acre suburban campus **Total enrollment** 2,689 **Student/faculty ratio** 20:1 **Application deadline** Rolling **Housing** Yes **Expenses** Tuition $12,750; Room & Board $4884 **Undergraduates** 56% women, 17% part-time, 21% 25 or older, 0.2% Native American, 1% Hispanic, 4% black, 0.1% Asian American or Pacific Islander **Most popular recent majors** Business administration; archaeology; music **Academic program** Advanced placement, accelerated degree program, self-designed majors, tutorials, honors program, summer session, adult/continuing education programs, internships **Contact** Mr. Matthew Whelan, Director of Undergraduate Admissions, Mercyhurst College, 501 East 38th Street, Erie, PA 16546. Telephone: 814-824-2202 or toll-free 800-825-1926. Fax: 814-824-2071. E-mail: admug@paradise.mercy.edu. Web site: http://www.mercyhurst.edu/.

MESSIAH COLLEGE

GRANTHAM, PENNSYLVANIA

General Independent interdenominational, 4-year, coed **Entrance** Moderately difficult **Setting** 360-acre small town campus **Total enrollment** 2,616 **Student/faculty ratio** 15:1 **Application deadline** Rolling **Freshmen** 87% were admitted **Housing** Yes **Expenses** Tuition $12,990; Room & Board $5500 **Undergraduates** 61% women, 3% part-time, 5% 25 or older, 0.2% Native American, 2% Hispanic, 1% black, 2% Asian American or Pacific Islander **Most popular recent majors** Elementary education; biology; nursing **Academic program** Average class size 24, advanced placement, accelerated degree program, self-designed majors, tutorials, honors program, summer session, adult/continuing education programs, internships **Contact** Mr. William G. Strausbaugh, Dean for Enrollment Management, Messiah College, 1 College Avenue, Grantham, PA 17027. Telephone: 717-691-6000 or toll-free 800-382-1349 (in-state), 800-233-4220 (out-of-state). Fax: 717-796-5374. E-mail: admiss@messiah.edu. Web site: http://www.messiah.edu/.

MILLERSVILLE UNIVERSITY OF PENNSYLVANIA

MILLERSVILLE, PENNSYLVANIA

General State-supported, comprehensive, coed **Entrance** Moderately difficult **Setting** 250-acre small town campus **Total enrollment** 7,564 **Student/faculty ratio** 17:1 **Application deadline** Rolling **Freshmen** 58% were admitted **Housing** Yes **Expenses** Tuition $4400; Room & Board $4510 **Undergraduates** 57% women, 15% part-time, 16% 25 or older, 0.2% Native American, 2% Hispanic, 6% black, 2% Asian American or Pacific Islander **Most popular recent majors** Elementary education; business administration; biology **Academic program** Average class size 25, English as a second language, advanced placement, tutorials, honors program, summer session, adult/continuing education programs, internships **Contact** Mr. Darrell Davis, Director of Admissions, Millersville University of Pennsylvania, PO Box 1002, Millersville, PA 17551-0302. Telephone: 717-872-3371 or toll-free 800-682-3648 (out-of-state). E-mail: adm_info@mu3.millersv.edu. Web site: http://marauder.millersv.edu/.

MOORE COLLEGE OF ART AND DESIGN

PHILADELPHIA, PENNSYLVANIA

General Independent, 4-year, women only **Entrance** Moderately difficult **Setting** 3-acre urban campus **Total enrollment** 385 **Student/faculty ratio** 8:1 **Application deadline** Rolling **Freshmen** 61% were admitted **Housing** Yes **Expenses** Tuition $15,500; Room & Board $6000 **Undergraduates** 10% 25 or older **Most popular recent majors** Art; fashion design/illustration; graphic design/commercial art/illustration **Academic program** Average class size 20, tutorials, honors program, summer session, adult/continuing education programs, internships **Contact** Ms. Deborah Deery, Director of Admissions, Moore College of Art and Design, 20th and the Parkway, Philadelphia, PA 19103. Telephone: 215-568-4515 ext. 1108 or toll-free 800-523-2025. Fax: 215-568-3547. E-mail: admiss@digex.net. Web site: http://www.moore.edu/.

MORAVIAN COLLEGE

BETHLEHEM, PENNSYLVANIA

General Independent, comprehensive, coed, affiliated with Moravian Church **Entrance** Moderately difficult **Setting** 70-acre suburban campus **Total enrollment** 1,830 **Student/faculty ratio** 14:1 **Application deadline** 3/1 **Freshmen** 82% were admitted **Housing** Yes **Expenses** Tuition $17,276; Room & Board $5580 **Undergraduates** 56% women, 13% part-time, 2% 25 or older, 0.1% Native American, 2% Hispanic, 1% black, 2% Asian American or Pacific Islander **Most popular recent majors** Business administration; psychology; biology **Academic program** Average class size 22, advanced placement, accelerated degree program, self-designed majors, tutorials, honors program, summer session, adult/continuing education programs, internships **Contact** Mr. Bernard

Moravian College *(continued)*

J. Story, Dean of Admissions and Financial Aid, Moravian College, 1200 Main Street, Bethlehem, PA 18018-6650. Telephone: 610-861-1320. Fax: 610-861-3956. E-mail: admissions@moravian.edu. Web site: http://www.moravian.edu/.

MOUNT ALOYSIUS COLLEGE

CRESSON, PENNSYLVANIA

General Independent Roman Catholic, 4-year, coed **Entrance** Minimally difficult **Setting** 125-acre rural campus **Total enrollment** 1,399 **Student/faculty ratio** 13:1 **Application deadline** Rolling **Freshmen** 51% were admitted **Housing** Yes **Expenses** Tuition $9520; Room & Board $4580 **Undergraduates** 74% women, 19% part-time, 40% 25 or older, 0.1% Native American, 0.4% Hispanic, 1% black, 0.2% Asian American or Pacific Islander **Most popular recent majors** Nursing; occupational therapy; business administration **Academic program** Advanced placement, summer session, adult/continuing education programs, internships **Contact** Ms. Sylvia Ghezzi Hirsch, Dean of Enrollment Management/Director of Admissions, Mount Aloysius College, 7373 Admiral Peary Highway, Cresson, PA 16630. Telephone: 814-886-6383 or toll-free 888-823-2220. Fax: 814-886-2978. E-mail: shirsch@mtaloy.edu. Web site: http://www.mtaloy.edu/.

MUHLENBERG COLLEGE

ALLENTOWN, PENNSYLVANIA

General Independent, 4-year, coed, affiliated with Lutheran Church **Entrance** Very difficult **Setting** 75-acre suburban campus **Total enrollment** 2,370 **Student/faculty ratio** 12:1 **Application deadline** 2/15 **Freshmen** 66% were admitted **Housing** Yes **Expenses** Tuition $18,660; Room & Board $5025 **Undergraduates** 56% women, 11% part-time, 4% 25 or older, 0.04% Native American, 2% Hispanic, 1% black, 3% Asian American or Pacific Islander **Most popular recent majors** Biology; psychology; English **Academic program** Average class size 30, advanced placement, accelerated degree program, self-designed majors, tutorials, honors program, summer session, adult/continuing education programs, internships **Contact** Mr. Christopher Hooker-Haring, Dean of Admissions, Muhlenberg College, 2400 Chew Street, Allentown, PA 18104-5586. Telephone: 610-821-3245. Fax: 610-821-3234. E-mail: adm@muhlenberg.edu. Web site: http://www.muhlenberg.edu/.

▶ **For more information, see page 479.**

NEUMANN COLLEGE

ASTON, PENNSYLVANIA

General Independent Roman Catholic, comprehensive, coed **Entrance** Moderately difficult **Setting** 28-acre suburban campus **Total enrollment** 1,239 **Student/faculty ratio** 8:1 **Application deadline** Rolling **Freshmen** 89% were admitted **Housing** Yes **Expenses** Tuition $12,940; Room & Board $6300 **Undergraduates** 72% women, 43% part-time, 36% 25 or older, 0.3% Native American, 3% Hispanic, 12% black, 2% Asian American or Pacific Islander **Most popular recent majors** Nursing; liberal arts and studies; education **Academic program** Average class size 22, advanced placement, tutorials, honors program, summer session, adult/continuing education programs, internships **Contact** Mr. Mark Osborn, Director of Admissions and Financial Aid, Neumann College, One Neumann Drive, Aston, PA 19014-1298. Telephone: 610-361-5215. E-mail: neumann@smtpgate.neumann.edu. Web site: http://www.neumann.edu/.

PENNSYLVANIA COLLEGE OF OPTOMETRY

PHILADELPHIA, PENNSYLVANIA

General Independent, upper-level, coed **Contact** Mr. Robert E. Horne, Director of Admissions, Pennsylvania College of Optometry, 1200 West Godfrey Avenue, Philadelphia, PA 19141-3323. Telephone: 215-276-6200 or toll-free 800-824-6262 (out-of-state).

PENNSYLVANIA STATE UNIVERSITY ABINGTON COLLEGE

ABINGTON, PENNSYLVANIA

General State-related, 4-year, coed **Entrance** Moderately difficult **Setting** 45-acre small town campus **Total enrollment** 3,218 **Student/faculty ratio** 25:1 **Application deadline** Rolling **Freshmen** 84% were admitted **Housing** No **Expenses** Tuition $5682 **Undergraduates** 48% women, 15% part-time, 20% 25 or older, 0.3% Native American, 3% Hispanic, 9% black, 8% Asian American or Pacific Islander **Academic program** Advanced placement, summer session, adult/continuing education programs, internships **Contact** Mr. Robert McCaig, Admissions Officer, Pennsylvania State University Abington College, 1600 Woodland Road, Abington, PA 19001-3918. Telephone: 215-881-7600 ext. 266. E-mail: admissions@psu.edu. Web site: http://www.psu.edu/.

PENNSYLVANIA STATE UNIVERSITY ALTOONA COLLEGE

ALTOONA, PENNSYLVANIA

General State-related, 4-year, coed **Entrance** Moderately difficult **Setting** 81-acre suburban campus

Total enrollment 3,727 **Student/faculty ratio** 28:1 **Application deadline** Rolling **Freshmen** 92% were admitted **Housing** Yes **Expenses** Tuition $5682; Room & Board $4640 **Undergraduates** 47% women, 6% part-time, 13% 25 or older, 0.1% Native American, 2% Hispanic, 3% black, 1% Asian American or Pacific Islander **Academic program** Advanced placement, summer session, adult/continuing education programs, internships **Contact** Ms. Fredina Ingold, Admissions Officer, Pennsylvania State University Altoona College, 3000 Ivyside Park, Altoona, PA 16601-3760. Telephone: 814-949-5466. E-mail: admissions@psu.edu. Web site: http://www.psu.edu/.

PENNSYLVANIA STATE UNIVERSITY AT ERIE, THE BEHREND COLLEGE

ERIE, PENNSYLVANIA

General State-related, comprehensive, coed **Entrance** Very difficult **Setting** 727-acre suburban campus **Total enrollment** 3,327 **Student/faculty ratio** 19:1 **Application deadline** Rolling **Freshmen** 86% were admitted **Housing** Yes **Expenses** Tuition $5832; Room & Board $4640 **Undergraduates** 37% women, 8% part-time, 15% 25 or older **Most popular recent majors** Business administration; engineering; psychology **Academic program** Advanced placement, honors program, summer session, adult/continuing education programs, internships **Contact** Ms. Mary-Ellen Madigan, Admissions Director, Pennsylvania State University at Erie, The Behrend College, Station Road, Erie, PA 16563. Telephone: 814-898-6100. E-mail: admissions@psu.edu. Web site: http://www.psu.edu/.

PENNSYLVANIA STATE UNIVERSITY BERKS CAMPUS OF THE BERKS–LEHIGH VALLEY COLLEGE

READING, PENNSYLVANIA

General State-related, 4-year, coed **Entrance** Moderately difficult **Setting** 241-acre suburban campus **Total enrollment** 1,817 **Student/faculty ratio** 25:1 **Application deadline** Rolling **Freshmen** 89% were admitted **Housing** Yes **Expenses** Tuition $5682; Room & Board $4640 **Undergraduates** 43% women, 10% part-time, 13% 25 or older, 0.1% Native American, 3% Hispanic, 3% black, 3% Asian American or Pacific Islander **Academic program** Advanced placement, summer session, adult/continuing education programs, internships **Contact** Mr. Blaine Steensland, Admissions Officer, Pennsylvania State University Berks Campus of the Berks–Lehigh Valley College, Tulpehocken Road, PO Box 7009, Reading, PA 19610-6009. Telephone: 610-396-6066. E-mail: admissions@psu.edu. Web site: http://www.psu.edu/.

PENNSYLVANIA STATE UNIVERSITY HARRISBURG CAMPUS OF THE CAPITAL COLLEGE

MIDDLETOWN, PENNSYLVANIA

General State-related, comprehensive, coed **Entrance** Moderately difficult **Setting** 218-acre small town campus **Total enrollment** 3,466 **Student/faculty ratio** 14:1 **Housing** Yes **Expenses** Tuition $5832; Room & Board $4640 **Undergraduates** 52% women, 35% part-time, 52% 25 or older, 0.3% Native American, 2% Hispanic, 4% black, 3% Asian American or Pacific Islander **Academic program** Advanced placement, summer session, adult/continuing education programs **Contact** Dr. Thomas Streveler, Director of Enrollment Services, Pennsylvania State University Harrisburg Campus of the Capital College, 777 West Harrisburg Pike, Middletown, PA 17057-4898. Telephone: 717-948-6250. E-mail: admissions@psu.edu. Web site: http://www.psu.edu/.

PENNSYLVANIA STATE UNIVERSITY LEHIGH VALLEY CAMPUS OF THE BERKS-LEHIGH VALLEY COLLEGE

FOGELSVILLE, PENNSYLVANIA

General State-related, 4-year, coed **Entrance** Moderately difficult **Setting** 42-acre small town campus **Total enrollment** 614 **Student/faculty ratio** 21:1 **Application deadline** Rolling **Freshmen** 88% were admitted **Housing** No **Expenses** Tuition $5654 **Undergraduates** 43% women, 9% part-time, 13% 25 or older, 1% Native American, 5% Hispanic, 1% black, 7% Asian American or Pacific Islander **Academic program** Advanced placement, summer session, adult/continuing education programs **Contact** Mrs. Judith A. Cary, Admissions Officer, Pennsylvania State University Lehigh Valley Campus of the Berks-Lehigh Valley College, 8380 Mohr Lane, Fogelsville, PA 18051. Telephone: 610-821-6577. Web site: http://www.psu.edu/.

PENNSYLVANIA STATE UNIVERSITY SCHUYLKILL CAMPUS OF THE CAPITAL COLLEGE

SCHUYLKILL HAVEN, PENNSYLVANIA

General State-related, 4-year, coed **Entrance** Moderately difficult **Setting** 42-acre small town campus **Total enrollment** 981 **Student/faculty ratio** 23:1 **Application deadline** Rolling **Freshmen** 91% were admitted **Housing** Yes **Expenses** Tuition $5654; Room & Board $4640 **Undergraduates** 54% women, 12% part-time, 19% 25 or older, 0.4% Native American, 2% Hispanic, 9% black, 3% Asian American or Pacific Islander **Academic program** Advanced placement, summer session, adult/continuing education pro-

Pennsylvania State University Schuylkill Campus of the Capital College *(continued)*

grams, internships **Contact** Mr. Jerry Bowman, Director of Student Programs and Services, Pennsylvania State University Schuylkill Campus of the Capital College, 200 University Drive, Schuylkill Haven, PA 17972-2208. Telephone: 717-385-6242. E-mail: admissions@psu.edu. Web site: http://www.psu.edu/.

PENNSYLVANIA STATE UNIVERSITY UNIVERSITY PARK CAMPUS

STATE COLLEGE, PENNSYLVANIA

General State-related, university, coed **Entrance** Very difficult **Setting** 5,617-acre small town campus **Total enrollment** 40,538 **Student/faculty ratio** 19:1 **Application deadline** Rolling **Freshmen** 56% were admitted **Housing** Yes **Expenses** Tuition $5832; Room & Board $4640 **Undergraduates** 46% women, 4% part-time, 5% 25 or older, 0.1% Native American, 3% Hispanic, 3% black, 5% Asian American or Pacific Islander **Most popular recent majors** Business administration; engineering; psychology **Academic program** English as a second language, advanced placement, self-designed majors, honors program, summer session, adult/continuing education programs, internships **Contact** Dr. John J. Romano, Vice Provost for Enrollment Management and Administration, Pennsylvania State University University Park Campus, 201 Old Main, University Park, PA 16802-1503. Telephone: 814-865-5471. E-mail: admissions@psu.edu. Web site: http://www.psu.edu/.

PHILADELPHIA COLLEGE OF BIBLE

LANGHORNE, PENNSYLVANIA

General Independent nondenominational, comprehensive, coed **Entrance** Moderately difficult **Setting** 105-acre suburban campus **Total enrollment** 1,280 **Student/faculty ratio** 16:1 **Application deadline** Rolling **Freshmen** 64% were admitted **Housing** Yes **Expenses** Tuition $9520; Room & Board $4890 **Undergraduates** 53% women, 10% part-time, 33% 25 or older, 0.2% Native American, 2% Hispanic, 16% black, 4% Asian American or Pacific Islander **Most popular recent majors** Biblical studies; social work; music **Academic program** Average class size 35, advanced placement, accelerated degree program, summer session, adult/continuing education programs, internships **Contact** Mrs. Fran Emmons, Vice President Admissions and Financial Aid, Philadelphia College of Bible, 200 Manor Avenue, Langhorne, PA 19047-2990. Telephone: 215-702-4239 or toll-free 800-876-5800 (out-of-state). Fax: 215-752-5812. E-mail: admissions@pcb.edu. Web site: http://www.pcb.edu/.

PHILADELPHIA COLLEGE OF PHARMACY AND SCIENCE

See University of the Sciences in Philadelphia

PHILADELPHIA COLLEGE OF TEXTILES AND SCIENCE

PHILADELPHIA, PENNSYLVANIA

General Independent, comprehensive, coed **Entrance** Moderately difficult **Setting** 100-acre suburban campus **Total enrollment** 3,308 **Student/faculty ratio** 21:1 **Application deadline** Rolling **Freshmen** 80% were admitted **Housing** Yes **Expenses** Tuition $13,466; Room & Board $6080 **Undergraduates** 64% women, 26% part-time, 28% 25 or older, 0% Native American, 2% Hispanic, 10% black, 4% Asian American or Pacific Islander **Most popular recent majors** Architecture; fashion design/illustration; fashion merchandising **Academic program** Average class size 22, English as a second language, advanced placement, accelerated degree program, honors program, summer session, adult/continuing education programs, internships **Contact** Ms. Laurie C. Grover, Director of Admissions, Philadelphia College of Textiles and Science, School House Lane and Henry Avenue, Philadelphia, PA 19144-5497. Telephone: 215-951-2800. Fax: 215-951-2907. E-mail: admissions@laurel.texsci.edu. Web site: http://www.philacol.edu/.

POINT PARK COLLEGE

PITTSBURGH, PENNSYLVANIA

General Independent, comprehensive, coed **Entrance** Moderately difficult **Setting** Urban campus **Total enrollment** 2,270 **Student/faculty ratio** 15:1 **Application deadline** Rolling **Freshmen** 90% were admitted **Housing** Yes **Expenses** Tuition $11,406; Room & Board $5174 **Undergraduates** 52% women, 41% part-time, 55% 25 or older, 0.4% Native American, 1% Hispanic, 13% black, 1% Asian American or Pacific Islander **Most popular recent majors** Electrical/electronic engineering technology; business administration; mass communications **Academic program** English as a second language, advanced placement, accelerated degree program, self-designed majors, honors program, summer session, adult/continuing education programs, internships **Contact** Mr. Williams Stahler, Dean of Enrollment, Point Park College, 201 Wood Street, Pittsburgh, PA 15222-1984. Telephone: 412-392-3430 or toll-free 800-321-0129. Fax: 412-391-1980. Web site: http://www.ppc.edu/.

ROBERT MORRIS COLLEGE

MOON TOWNSHIP, PENNSYLVANIA

General Independent, comprehensive, coed **Entrance** Moderately difficult **Setting** 230-acre suburban campus **Total enrollment** 4,846 **Student/faculty ratio** 20:1 **Application deadline** Rolling **Housing** Yes **Expenses** Tuition $8339; Room & Board $4934 **Undergraduates** 50% women, 32% part-time, 43% 25 or older, 0.1% Native American, 1% Hispanic, 7% black, 1% Asian American or Pacific Islander **Most popular recent majors** Accounting; business administration; business marketing and marketing management **Academic program** Average class size 22, advanced placement, accelerated degree program, tutorials, honors program, summer session, adult/continuing education programs, internships **Contact** Mr. James R. Welsh, Dean of Enrollment Management, Robert Morris College, 881 Narrows Run Road, Moon Township, PA 15108-1189. Telephone: 412-262-8265 or toll-free 800-762-0097. Fax: 412-262-8619. E-mail: budzisze@robert-morris.edu.

ROSEMONT COLLEGE
ROSEMONT, PENNSYLVANIA

General Independent Roman Catholic, comprehensive, women only **Entrance** Moderately difficult **Setting** 56-acre suburban campus **Total enrollment** 947 **Student/faculty ratio** 8:1 **Application deadline** Rolling **Freshmen** 87% were admitted **Housing** Yes **Expenses** Tuition $13,340; Room & Board $6500 **Undergraduates** 6% 25 or older, 1% Hispanic, 16% black, 4% Asian American or Pacific Islander **Most popular recent majors** Psychology; English; political science **Academic program** Average class size 15, English as a second language, advanced placement, accelerated degree program, self-designed majors, tutorials, honors program, summer session, adult/continuing education programs, internships **Contact** Admissions Office, Rosemont College, 1400 Montgomery Avenue, Rosemont, PA 19010-1699. Telephone: 610-526-2966 or toll-free 800-331-0708. Fax: 610-527-1041. E-mail: rosecoladmit@rosemont.edu. Web site: http://www.rosemont.edu.

▶ **For more information, see page 502.**

ST. CHARLES BORROMEO SEMINARY, OVERBROOK
WYNNEWOOD, PENNSYLVANIA

General Independent Roman Catholic, comprehensive, men only **Entrance** Moderately difficult **Setting** 77-acre suburban campus **Total enrollment** 446 **Student/faculty ratio** 5:1 **Application deadline** 7/1 **Freshmen** 100% were admitted **Housing** Yes **Expenses** Tuition $7200; Room & Board $4750 **Undergraduates** 26% 25 or older, 0% Native American, 4% Hispanic, 15% black, 5% Asian American or Pacific Islander **Academic program** Average class size 14, advanced placement, accelerated degree program, tutorials, honors program, summer session, adult/continuing education programs **Contact** Rev. Paul V. Dougherty, Director of Vocation Office for Diocean Priesthood, St. Charles Borromeo Seminary, Overbrook, 100 East Wynnewood Road, Wynnewood, PA 19096. Telephone: 610-667-5778.

SAINT FRANCIS COLLEGE
LORETTO, PENNSYLVANIA

General Independent Roman Catholic, comprehensive, coed **Entrance** Moderately difficult **Setting** 600-acre rural campus **Total enrollment** 1,904 **Student/faculty ratio** 17:1 **Application deadline** Rolling **Freshmen** 85% were admitted **Housing** Yes **Expenses** Tuition $14,342; Room & Board $6250 **Undergraduates** 58% women, 13% part-time, 15% 25 or older **Most popular recent majors** Physician assistant; accounting; business administration **Academic program** Advanced placement, accelerated degree program, self-designed majors, honors program, summer session, adult/continuing education programs, internships **Contact** Mr. Evan Lipp, Dean for Enrollment Management, Saint Francis College, PO Box 600, Loretto, PA 15940-0600. Telephone: 814-472-3100 or toll-free 800-457-6300 (in-state), 800-342-5732 (out-of-state). Fax: 814-472-3044. E-mail: admission@sfcpa.edu.

SAINT JOSEPH'S UNIVERSITY
PHILADELPHIA, PENNSYLVANIA

General Independent Roman Catholic (Jesuit), comprehensive, coed **Entrance** Moderately difficult **Setting** 60-acre suburban campus **Total enrollment** 7,027 **Student/faculty ratio** 16:1 **Application deadline** Rolling **Freshmen** 70% were admitted **Housing** Yes **Expenses** Tuition $16,165; Room & Board $6972 **Undergraduates** 57% women, 23% part-time, 0.1% Native American, 3% Hispanic, 9% black, 2% Asian American or Pacific Islander **Most popular recent majors** Food sales operations; psychology; business marketing and marketing management **Academic program** Average class size 22, English as a second language, advanced placement, accelerated degree program, self-designed majors, tutorials, honors program, summer session, adult/continuing education programs, internships **Contact** Mr. David Conway, Assistant Vice President of Enrollment Management, Saint Joseph's University, 5600 City Avenue, Philadelphia, PA 19131-1395. Telephone: 610-660-1300 or toll-free 888-BEAHAWK (in-state). E-mail: admi@sju.edu. Web site: http://www.sju.edu/.

SAINT VINCENT COLLEGE
LATROBE, PENNSYLVANIA

General Independent Roman Catholic, 4-year, coed **Entrance** Moderately difficult **Setting** 200-

Saint Vincent College *(continued)*

acre suburban campus **Total enrollment** 1,238 **Student/faculty ratio** 14:1 **Application deadline** Rolling **Freshmen** 88% were admitted **Housing** Yes **Expenses** Tuition $13,461; Room & Board $4642 **Undergraduates** 49% women, 5% part-time, 10% 25 or older, 0.1% Native American, 1% Hispanic, 1% black, 0.5% Asian American or Pacific Islander **Most popular recent majors** Psychology; biology; accounting **Academic program** Average class size 17, advanced placement, accelerated degree program, tutorials, honors program, summer session, adult/continuing education programs, internships **Contact** Rev. Paul Taylor OSB, Director of Admission and Financial Aid, Saint Vincent College, 300 Fraser Purchase Road, Latrobe, PA 15650. Telephone: 724-537-4540 or toll-free 800-SVC-5549. Fax: 724-537-4554. E-mail: admission@stvincent.edu. Web site: http://www.stvincent.edu/.

SETON HILL COLLEGE
GREENSBURG, PENNSYLVANIA

General Independent Roman Catholic, comprehensive, primarily women **Entrance** Moderately difficult **Setting** 200-acre small town campus **Total enrollment** 1,078 **Student/faculty ratio** 14:1 **Application deadline** 8/1 **Freshmen** 89% were admitted **Housing** Yes **Expenses** Tuition $12,640; Room & Board $4730 **Undergraduates** 89% women, 18% part-time, 12% 25 or older, 1% Native American, 3% Hispanic, 4% black, 0.3% Asian American or Pacific Islander **Most popular recent majors** Psychology; family/consumer studies; English **Academic program** Average class size 16, English as a second language, advanced placement, accelerated degree program, self-designed majors, tutorials, honors program, summer session, adult/continuing education programs, internships **Contact** Ms. Barbara C. Hinkle, Vice President for Enrollment Services, Seton Hill College, Seton Hill Drive, Greensburg, PA 15601. Telephone: 724-838-4218 or toll-free 800-826-6234. Fax: 724-830-1294. E-mail: admit@setonhill.edu. Web site: http://www.setonhill.edu/.

▶ **For more information, see page 511.**

SHIPPENSBURG UNIVERSITY OF PENNSYLVANIA
SHIPPENSBURG, PENNSYLVANIA

General State-supported, comprehensive, coed **Entrance** Moderately difficult **Setting** 200-acre rural campus **Total enrollment** 6,674 **Student/faculty ratio** 16:1 **Application deadline** Rolling **Freshmen** 69% were admitted **Housing** Yes **Expenses** Tuition $4344; Room & Board $3722 **Undergraduates** 54% women, 4% part-time, 6% 25 or older, 0.2% Native American, 1% Hispanic, 4% black, 1% Asian American or Pacific Islander **Most Popular Recent Major** Elementary education **Academic program** Advanced placement, accelerated degree program, tutorials, honors program, summer session, internships **Contact** Mr. Joseph Cretella, Dean of Admissions, Shippensburg University of Pennsylvania, 1871 Old Main Drive, Shippensburg, PA 17257-2299. Telephone: 717-532-1231 or toll-free 800-822-8028 (in-state). E-mail: admiss@ark.ship.edu. Web site: http://www.ship.edu/.

SLIPPERY ROCK UNIVERSITY OF PENNSYLVANIA
SLIPPERY ROCK, PENNSYLVANIA

General State-supported, comprehensive, coed **Entrance** Moderately difficult **Setting** 611-acre rural campus **Total enrollment** 7,038 **Student/faculty ratio** 20:1 **Application deadline** 5/1 **Freshmen** 83% were admitted **Housing** Yes **Expenses** Tuition $4302; Room & Board $3590 **Undergraduates** 57% women, 11% part-time, 14% 25 or older, 0.3% Native American, 1% Hispanic, 3% black, 0.4% Asian American or Pacific Islander **Most popular recent majors** Education; business administration; mass communications **Academic program** Advanced placement, accelerated degree program, tutorials, honors program, summer session, adult/continuing education programs, internships **Contact** Dr. Duncan M. Sargent, Director of Admissions, Slippery Rock University of Pennsylvania, Slippery Rock, PA 16057. Telephone: 724-738-2015 or toll-free 800-662-1102 (in-state). E-mail: apply@sru.edu. Web site: http://www.sru.edu/.

SUSQUEHANNA UNIVERSITY
SELINSGROVE, PENNSYLVANIA

General Independent, 4-year, coed, affiliated with Lutheran Church **Entrance** Moderately difficult **Setting** 210-acre small town campus **Total enrollment** 1,725 **Student/faculty ratio** 14:1 **Application deadline** 3/1 **Freshmen** 75% were admitted **Housing** Yes **Expenses** Tuition $18,350; Room & Board $5230 **Undergraduates** 56% women, 3% part-time, 1% 25 or older, 0.2% Native American, 2% Hispanic, 2% black, 1% Asian American or Pacific Islander **Most popular recent majors** Business administration; communications; psychology **Academic program** Average class size 25, advanced placement, accelerated degree program, self-designed majors, tutorials, honors program, summer session, adult/continuing education programs, internships **Contact** Mr. Richard Ziegler, Director of Admissions, Susquehanna University, 514 University Avenue, Selinsgrove, PA 17870-1040. Telephone: 717-372-4260 or toll-free

800-326-9672. Fax: 717-372-2722. E-mail: suadmiss@susqu.edu. Web site: http://www.susqu.edu/.

SWARTHMORE COLLEGE
SWARTHMORE, PENNSYLVANIA

General Independent, 4-year, coed **Entrance** Most difficult **Setting** 330-acre suburban campus **Total enrollment** 1,370 **Student/faculty ratio** 9:1 **Application deadline** 1/1 **Freshmen** 24% were admitted **Housing** Yes **Expenses** Tuition $22,000; Room & Board $7500 **Undergraduates** 53% women, 0% 25 or older, 0.1% Native American, 8% Hispanic, 8% black, 12% Asian American or Pacific Islander **Most popular recent majors** Economics; biology; political science **Academic program** Average class size 18, advanced placement, self-designed majors, tutorials, honors program, internships **Contact** Office of Admissions, Swarthmore College, 500 College Avenue, Swarthmore, PA 19081-1397. Telephone: 610-328-8300. Fax: 610-328-8673. E-mail: admissions@swarthmore.edu. Web site: http://www.swarthmore.edu/.

TALMUDICAL YESHIVA OF PHILADELPHIA
PHILADELPHIA, PENNSYLVANIA

General Independent religious, 4-year, men only **Entrance** Moderately difficult **Setting** 3-acre urban campus **Total enrollment** 108 **Student/faculty ratio** 15:1 **Application deadline** 7/15 **Freshmen** 78% were admitted **Housing** Yes **Expenses** Tuition $5050; Room & Board $4200 **Undergraduates** 0% 25 or older, 0% Native American, 0% Hispanic, 0% black, 0% Asian American or Pacific Islander **Academic program** Average class size 37, tutorials, honors program, internships **Contact** Rabbi Shmuel Kamenetsky, Co-Dean, Talmudical Yeshiva of Philadelphia, 6063 Drexel Road, Philadelphia, PA 19131-1296. Telephone: 215-473-1212.

TEMPLE UNIVERSITY
PHILADELPHIA, PENNSYLVANIA

General State-related, university, coed **Entrance** Moderately difficult **Setting** 76-acre urban campus **Total enrollment** 27,670 **Student/faculty ratio** 24:1 **Application deadline** 5/1 **Freshmen** 69% were admitted **Housing** Yes **Expenses** Tuition $6150; Room & Board $5772 **Undergraduates** 57% women, 18% part-time, 27% 25 or older, 0.2% Native American, 3% Hispanic, 28% black, 9% Asian American or Pacific Islander **Most popular recent majors** Business administration; education; psychology **Academic program** Average class size 25, English as a second language, advanced placement, accelerated degree program, self-designed majors, honors program, summer session, adult/continuing education programs, internships **Contact** Dr. Timm Rinehart, Acting Director of Admissions, Temple University, 1801 North Broad Street, Philadelphia, PA 19122-6096. Telephone: 215-204-8556 or toll-free 888-267-5870. Fax: 215-204-5694. E-mail: tuadm@vm.temple.edu. Web site: http://www.temple.edu/.

THIEL COLLEGE
GREENVILLE, PENNSYLVANIA

General Independent, 4-year, coed, affiliated with Evangelical Lutheran Church in America **Entrance** Moderately difficult **Setting** 135-acre rural campus **Total enrollment** 1,012 **Student/faculty ratio** 11:1 **Application deadline** 5/1 **Freshmen** 87% were admitted **Housing** Yes **Expenses** Tuition $13,390; Room & Board $5220 **Undergraduates** 52% women, 12% part-time, 12% 25 or older, 0.2% Native American, 1% Hispanic, 9% black, 0.4% Asian American or Pacific Islander **Most popular recent majors** Business administration; nursing; communications **Academic program** Average class size 25, English as a second language, advanced placement, accelerated degree program, tutorials, honors program, summer session, adult/continuing education programs, internships **Contact** Mr. Stephen Eidson, Executive Director of Enrollment Management, Thiel College, 75 College Avenue, Greenville, PA 16125-2181. Telephone: 724-589-2176 or toll-free 800-24THIEL. Fax: 724-589-2013. E-mail: admissions@thiel.edu. Web site: http://www.thiel.edu/.

► **For more information, see page 527.**

THOMAS JEFFERSON UNIVERSITY
PHILADELPHIA, PENNSYLVANIA

General Independent, upper-level, coed **Entrance** Moderately difficult **Setting** 13-acre urban campus **Student/faculty ratio** 7:1 **Application deadline** 2/1 **Freshmen** 34% were admitted **Housing** Yes **Expenses** Tuition $16,140; Room only $2400 **Undergraduates** 65% 25 or older **Most popular recent majors** Nursing; physical therapy; occupational therapy **Academic program** Advanced placement, accelerated degree program, adult/continuing education programs, internships **Contact** Assistant Director of Admissions, Thomas Jefferson University, Edison Building, Suite 1610, 130 South Ninth Street, Philadelphia, PA 19107. Telephone: 215-503-8890 or toll-free 800-522-2644 (in-state), 800-247-6933 (out-of-state). Fax: 215-503-7241. Web site: http://www.tju.edu/.

UNIVERSITY OF PENNSYLVANIA
PHILADELPHIA, PENNSYLVANIA

General Independent, university, coed **Entrance** Most difficult **Setting** 260-acre urban cam-

University of Pennsylvania *(continued)*

pus **Total enrollment** 21,643 **Student/faculty ratio** 6:1 **Application deadline** 1/1 **Freshmen** 31% were admitted **Housing** Yes **Expenses** Tuition $22,250; Room & Board $7430 **Undergraduates** 50% women, 17% part-time, 2% 25 or older, 0.3% Native American, 4% Hispanic, 6% black, 17% Asian American or Pacific Islander **Most popular recent majors** Finance; history; communications **Academic program** English as a second language, advanced placement, accelerated degree program, self-designed majors, tutorials, honors program, summer session, adult/continuing education programs, internships **Contact** Mr. Willis J. Stetson Jr., Dean of Admissions, University of Pennsylvania, 1 College Hall, Levy Park, Philadelphia, PA 19104. Telephone: 215-898-7507. Web site: http://www.upenn.edu/.

UNIVERSITY OF PITTSBURGH
PITTSBURGH, PENNSYLVANIA

General State-related, university, coed **Entrance** Moderately difficult **Setting** 132-acre urban campus **Total enrollment** 25,461 **Student/faculty ratio** 14:1 **Application deadline** Rolling **Freshmen** 78% were admitted **Housing** Yes **Expenses** Tuition $6164; Room & Board $5414 **Undergraduates** 52% women, 15% part-time, 18% 25 or older, 0.2% Native American, 1% Hispanic, 9% black, 4% Asian American or Pacific Islander **Most popular recent majors** Psychology; nursing; speech/rhetorical studies **Academic program** English as a second language, advanced placement, self-designed majors, honors program, summer session, adult/continuing education programs, internships **Contact** Dr. Betsy A. Porter, Director of Admissions and Financial Aid, University of Pittsburgh, 4200 Fifth Avenue, Pittsburgh, PA 15260. Telephone: 412-624-7488. Fax: 412-648-8815. E-mail: oafa@pitt.edu. Web site: http://www.pitt.edu/.

UNIVERSITY OF PITTSBURGH AT BRADFORD
BRADFORD, PENNSYLVANIA

General State-related, 4-year, coed **Contact** Ms. Roxie Vanderpoel, Office Manager, University of Pittsburgh at Bradford, 300 Campus Drive, Bradford, PA 16701-2812. Telephone: 814-362-7555 or toll-free 800-872-1787. Fax: 814-362-7578. Web site: http://www.pitt.edu/ñbradford/.

UNIVERSITY OF PITTSBURGH AT GREENSBURG
GREENSBURG, PENNSYLVANIA

General State-related, 4-year, coed **Entrance** Moderately difficult **Setting** 205-acre small town campus **Total enrollment** 1,501 **Student/faculty ratio** 18:1 **Application deadline** 8/1 **Freshmen** 80% were admitted **Housing** Yes **Expenses** Tuition $6074; Room & Board $4280 **Undergraduates** 30% 25 or older **Most popular recent majors** Business administration; psychology; accounting **Academic program** Advanced placement, accelerated degree program, self-designed majors, tutorials, summer session, adult/continuing education programs, internships **Contact** Mr. John R. Sparks, Director of Admissions and Financial Aid, University of Pittsburgh at Greensburg, 1150 Mount Pleasant Road, Greensburg, PA 15601-5860. Telephone: 724-836-9880. Fax: 724-836-9901. E-mail: upgadmit@pitt.edu. Web site: http://www.pitt.edu/~upg/.

UNIVERSITY OF PITTSBURGH AT JOHNSTOWN
JOHNSTOWN, PENNSYLVANIA

General State-related, 4-year, coed **Entrance** Moderately difficult **Setting** 650-acre suburban campus **Total enrollment** 3,096 **Student/faculty ratio** 20:1 **Application deadline** Rolling **Freshmen** 86% were admitted **Housing** Yes **Expenses** Tuition $6154; Room & Board $4720 **Undergraduates** 54% women, 13% part-time, 1% 25 or older, 0.1% Native American, 0.4% Hispanic, 2% black, 1% Asian American or Pacific Islander **Most popular recent majors** Business economics; elementary education; biology **Academic program** Advanced placement, accelerated degree program, self-designed majors, summer session, adult/continuing education programs, internships **Contact** Mr. James F. Gyure, Director of Admissions, University of Pittsburgh at Johnstown, 157 Blackington Hall, Johnstown, PA 15904-2990. Telephone: 814-269-7050 or toll-free 800-765-4875. Fax: 814-269-7044. Web site: http://info.pitt.edu/~upjweb/.

UNIVERSITY OF SCRANTON
SCRANTON, PENNSYLVANIA

General Independent Roman Catholic (Jesuit), comprehensive, coed **Entrance** Moderately difficult **Setting** 50-acre urban campus **Total enrollment** 4,816 **Student/faculty ratio** 13:1 **Application deadline** 3/1 **Freshmen** 78% were admitted **Housing** Yes **Expenses** Tuition $15,880; Room & Board $7011 **Undergraduates** 58% women, 9% part-time, 10% 25 or older, 0.2% Native American, 3% Hispanic, 1% black, 2% Asian American or Pacific Islander **Most popular recent majors** Biology; communications; elementary education **Academic program** Average class size 22, advanced placement, self-designed majors, tutorials, honors program, summer session, adult/continuing education programs, internships **Contact** Mr. Raul A. Fonts, Director of Admissions, University of Scranton, Scranton, PA 18510-4622. Telephone: 717-941-7540 or toll-free 888-SCRANTON. Fax: 717-941-5928. E-mail: admissions@uofs.edu. Web site: http://www.uofs.edu/.

UNIVERSITY OF THE ARTS

PHILADELPHIA, PENNSYLVANIA

General Independent, comprehensive, coed **Entrance** Moderately difficult **Setting** Urban campus **Total enrollment** 1,624 **Student/faculty ratio** 9:1 **Application deadline** Rolling **Freshmen** 58% were admitted **Housing** Yes **Expenses** Tuition $15,070; Room only $4100 **Undergraduates** 49% women, 2% part-time, 11% 25 or older, 0.4% Native American, 4% Hispanic, 9% black, 3% Asian American or Pacific Islander **Most popular recent majors** Dance; graphic design/commercial art/illustration; art **Academic program** English as a second language, advanced placement, tutorials, summer session, adult/continuing education programs, internships **Contact** Ms. Barbara Elliott, Director of Admission, University of the Arts, 320 South Broad Street, Philadelphia, PA 19102-4944. Telephone: 215-732-4832 or toll-free 800-616-ARTS. Fax: 215-875-5458. Web site: http://www.uarts.edu/.

▶ **For more information, see page 541.**

UNIVERSITY OF THE SCIENCES IN PHILADELPHIA

PHILADELPHIA, PENNSYLVANIA

General Independent, university, coed **Entrance** Moderately difficult **Setting** 35-acre urban campus **Total enrollment** 2,135 **Student/faculty ratio** 13:1 **Application deadline** Rolling **Housing** Yes **Expenses** Tuition $13,290; Room & Board $5985 **Undergraduates** 64% women, 4% part-time, 5% 25 or older, 0.1% Native American, 1% Hispanic, 4% black, 26% Asian American or Pacific Islander **Most popular recent majors** Pharmacy; physical therapy; biology **Academic program** Average class size 35, advanced placement, summer session, adult/continuing education programs, internships **Contact** Mr. Louis L. Hegyes, Director of Admission, University of the Sciences in Philadelphia, 600 South 43rd Street, Philadelphia, PA 19104-4495. Telephone: 215-596-8810. Fax: 215-895-1100. Web site: http://www.usip.edu.

URSINUS COLLEGE

COLLEGEVILLE, PENNSYLVANIA

General Independent, 4-year, coed, affiliated with United Church of Christ **Entrance** Very difficult **Setting** 140-acre suburban campus **Total enrollment** 1,194 **Student/faculty ratio** 12:1 **Application deadline** 2/15 **Freshmen** 71% were admitted **Housing** Yes **Expenses** Tuition $17,380; Room & Board $5690 **Undergraduates** 53% women, 2% part-time, 1% 25 or older, 0.2% Native American, 2% Hispanic, 5% black, 5% Asian American or Pacific Islander **Academic program** Average class size 18, English as a second language, advanced placement, accelerated degree program, self-designed majors, tutorials, honors program, adult/continuing education programs, internships **Contact** Mr. Richard G. Di Feliciantonio, Vice President for Enrollment, Ursinus College, Box 1000, Main Street, Collegeville, PA 19426-1000. Telephone: 610-409-3200. Fax: 610-489-0627. E-mail: admissions@ursinus.edu. Web site: http://www.ursinus.edu/.

VALLEY FORGE CHRISTIAN COLLEGE

PHOENIXVILLE, PENNSYLVANIA

General Independent, 4-year, coed, affiliated with Assemblies of God **Entrance** Minimally difficult **Setting** 77-acre small town campus **Total enrollment** 492 **Student/faculty ratio** 16:1 **Application deadline** 8/15 **Freshmen** 79% were admitted **Housing** Yes **Expenses** Tuition $5960; Room & Board $3480 **Undergraduates** 51% women, 6% part-time, 22% 25 or older, 0.2% Native American, 4% Hispanic, 3% black, 5% Asian American or Pacific Islander **Academic program** English as a second language, advanced placement, summer session, adult/continuing education programs, internships **Contact** Mr. James Barco, Executive Director of Enrollment Management, Valley Forge Christian College, 1401 Charlestown Road, Phoenixville, PA 19460. Telephone: 610-935-0450 ext. 1423. E-mail: admissions@vfcc.edu. Web site: http://www.vfcc.edu/.

VILLANOVA UNIVERSITY

VILLANOVA, PENNSYLVANIA

General Independent Roman Catholic, comprehensive, coed **Entrance** Moderately difficult **Setting** 222-acre suburban campus **Total enrollment** 10,019 **Student/faculty ratio** 13:1 **Application deadline** 1/15 **Freshmen** 61% were admitted **Housing** Yes **Expenses** Tuition $19,133; Room & Board $7400 **Undergraduates** 51% women, 6% part-time, 11% 25 or older, 0.2% Native American, 3% Hispanic, 2% black, 3% Asian American or Pacific Islander **Most popular recent majors** Finance; accounting; nursing **Academic program** English as a second language, advanced placement, accelerated degree program, tutorials, honors program, summer session, adult/continuing education programs, internships **Contact** Mr. Stephen R. Merritt, Associate Dean of Enrollment Management for University Admission, Villanova University, 800 Lancaster Av-

Villanova University *(continued)*

enue, Villanova, PA 19085-1672. Telephone: 610-519-4000 or toll-free 800-338-7927. Fax: 610-519-6450. E-mail: gotovu@ucis.vill.edu. Web site: http://www.vill.edu/.

WASHINGTON AND JEFFERSON COLLEGE
WASHINGTON, PENNSYLVANIA

General Independent, 4-year, coed **Entrance** Moderately difficult **Setting** 40-acre small town campus **Total enrollment** 1,218 **Student/faculty ratio** 11:1 **Application deadline** 2/1 **Freshmen** 83% were admitted **Housing** Yes **Expenses** Tuition $18,000; Room & Board $4350 **Undergraduates** 48% women, 1% part-time, 1% 25 or older, 0.1% Native American, 1% Hispanic, 3% black, 2% Asian American or Pacific Islander **Most popular recent majors** Biology; psychology; business administration **Academic program** Advanced placement, accelerated degree program, self-designed majors, tutorials, honors program, summer session, internships **Contact** Mr. Thomas P. O'Connor, Vice President for Enrollment Management, Washington and Jefferson College, 60 South Lincoln Street, Washington, PA 15301-4601. Telephone: 724-223-6025 or toll-free 888-WANDJAY. Fax: 724-223-5271. E-mail: toconnor@washjeff.edu.

WAYNESBURG COLLEGE
WAYNESBURG, PENNSYLVANIA

General Independent, comprehensive, coed, affiliated with Presbyterian Church (U.S.A.) **Entrance** Moderately difficult **Setting** 30-acre small town campus **Total enrollment** 1,290 **Student/faculty ratio** 16:1 **Application deadline** Rolling **Freshmen** 80% were admitted **Housing** Yes **Expenses** Tuition $10,550; Room & Board $4260 **Undergraduates** 48% women, 5% part-time, 13% 25 or older, 0% Native American, 0.5% Hispanic, 5% black, 0.3% Asian American or Pacific Islander **Most popular recent majors** Business administration; nursing; communications **Academic program** English as a second language, advanced placement, accelerated degree program, tutorials, honors program, summer session, adult/continuing education programs, internships **Contact** Ms. Robin L. Moore, Dean of Admissions, Waynesburg College, 51 West College Street, Waynesburg, PA 15370-1222. Telephone: 412-852-3333 or toll-free 800-225-7393. Fax: 412-627-8124. Web site: http://www.waynesburg.edu/.

WEST CHESTER UNIVERSITY OF PENNSYLVANIA
WEST CHESTER, PENNSYLVANIA

General State-supported, comprehensive, coed **Entrance** Moderately difficult **Setting** 547-acre small town campus **Total enrollment** 11,430 **Student/faculty ratio** 17:1 **Application deadline** Rolling **Freshmen** 58% were admitted **Housing** Yes **Expenses** Tuition $4162; Room & Board $4376 **Undergraduates** 60% women, 12% part-time, 15% 25 or older, 0.3% Native American, 2% Hispanic, 9% black, 2% Asian American or Pacific Islander **Most popular recent majors** Education; business marketing and marketing management; criminal justice/law enforcement administration **Academic program** English as a second language, advanced placement, self-designed majors, tutorials, honors program, summer session, adult/continuing education programs, internships **Contact** Ms. Marsha Haug, Director of Admissions, West Chester University of Pennsylvania, 100 West Rosedale Avenue, West Chester, PA 19383. Telephone: 610-436-3411. E-mail: ugadmiss@wcupa.edu. Web site: http://www.wcupa.edu/.

▶ **For more information, see page 551.**

WESTMINSTER COLLEGE
NEW WILMINGTON, PENNSYLVANIA

General Independent, comprehensive, coed, affiliated with Presbyterian Church (U.S.A.) **Entrance** Moderately difficult **Setting** 300-acre small town campus **Total enrollment** 1,571 **Student/faculty ratio** 16:1 **Application deadline** Rolling **Freshmen** 88% were admitted **Housing** Yes **Expenses** Tuition $15,430; Room & Board $4315 **Undergraduates** 61% women, 5% part-time, 1% 25 or older **Most popular recent majors** Business administration; elementary education; history **Academic program** Advanced placement, accelerated degree program, self-designed majors, honors program, summer session, adult/continuing education programs, internships **Contact** Mr. Robert A. Latta, Director of Admissions, Westminster College, South Market Street, New Wilmington, PA 16172-0001. Telephone: 724-946-7100 or toll-free 800-942-8033 (in-state). Fax: 724-946-7171. E-mail: paulrd@westminster.edu. Web site: http://www.westminster.edu/.

▶ **For more information, see page 556.**

WIDENER UNIVERSITY
CHESTER, PENNSYLVANIA

General Independent, comprehensive, coed **Entrance** Moderately difficult **Setting** 110-acre suburban campus **Total enrollment** 7,305 **Student/faculty ratio** 12:1 **Application deadline** Rolling **Freshmen** 87% were admitted **Housing** Yes **Expenses** Tuition $14,380; Room & Board $6200 **Undergraduates** 56% women, 41% part-time, 16% 25 or older, 0.5% Native American, 1% Hispanic, 13% black, 4% Asian American or Pacific Islander **Most popular recent majors** Nursing; business administration; psychology **Academic program** Average class size 27, English as a second language, advanced placement, accelerated degree program, self-designed majors, tutorials, honors program, summer session, adult/continuing education programs, internships **Contact** Dr. Michael L. Mahoney, Vice President of Admissions and Student Services, Widener University, One University Place, Chester, PA 19013-5792. Telephone: 610-499-4126 or toll-free 800-870-6481 (in-state). Fax: 610-499-4676. E-mail: admissions.office@widener.edu. Web site: http://www.widener.edu/.

WILKES UNIVERSITY
WILKES-BARRE, PENNSYLVANIA

General Independent, comprehensive, coed **Entrance** Moderately difficult **Setting** 25-acre urban campus **Total enrollment** 2,834 **Student/faculty ratio** 13:1 **Application deadline** Rolling **Freshmen** 83% were admitted **Housing** Yes **Expenses** Tuition $15,091; Room & Board $6564 **Undergraduates** 51% women, 24% part-time, 23% 25 or older **Most popular recent majors** Business administration; psychology; engineering **Academic program** English as a second language, advanced placement, accelerated degree program, self-designed majors, honors program, summer session, adult/continuing education programs, internships **Contact** Mr. Jason Langdon, Senior Assistant Dean, Wilkes University, 170 South Franklin St, PO Box 111, Wilkes-Barre, PA 18766-0002. Telephone: 717-831-4407 or toll-free 800-945-5378. Fax: 717-831-4904. Web site: http://www.wilkes.edu/.

WILSON COLLEGE
CHAMBERSBURG, PENNSYLVANIA

General Independent, 4-year, women only, affiliated with Presbyterian Church (U.S.A.) **Entrance** Moderately difficult **Setting** 262-acre small town campus **Total enrollment** 821 **Student/faculty ratio** 10:1 **Application deadline** Rolling **Freshmen** 84% were admitted **Housing** Yes **Expenses** Tuition $13,215; Room & Board $6000 **Undergraduates** 14% 25 or older, 0.2% Native American, 1% Hispanic, 4% black, 0.2% Asian American or Pacific Islander **Most popular recent majors** Veterinary sciences; equestrian studies; behavioral sciences **Academic program** Average class size 15, English as a second language, advanced placement, accelerated degree program, self-designed majors, tutorials, summer session, adult/continuing education programs, internships **Contact** Ms. Karen L. Jewell, Director of Admissions, Wilson College, 1015 Philadelphia Avenue, Chambersburg, PA 17201-1285. Telephone: 717-262-2002 or toll-free 800-421-8402. Fax: 717-264-1578. E-mail: wilson@pa.net. Web site: http://www.wilson.edu/.

YESHIVA BETH MOSHE
SCRANTON, PENNSYLVANIA

Contact Rabbi I. Bressler, Dean, Yeshiva Beth Moshe, 930 Hickory Street, PO Box 1141, Scranton, PA 18505-2124. Telephone: 717-346-1747.

YORK COLLEGE OF PENNSYLVANIA
YORK, PENNSYLVANIA

General Independent, comprehensive, coed **Entrance** Moderately difficult **Setting** 80-acre suburban campus **Total enrollment** 5,117 **Student/faculty ratio** 17:1 **Application deadline** Rolling **Freshmen** 73% were admitted **Housing** Yes **Expenses** Tuition $6100; Room & Board $4390 **Undergraduates** 59% women, 19% part-time, 22% 25 or older, 0.1% Native American, 1% Hispanic, 1% black, 1% Asian American or Pacific Islander **Most popular recent majors** Nursing; elementary education; law enforcement/police science **Academic program** Advanced placement, accelerated degree program, self-designed majors, tutorials, summer session, adult/continuing education programs, internships **Contact** Mrs. Nancy L. Spataro, Director of Admissions, York College of Pennsylvania, York, PA 17405-7199. Telephone: 717-849-1600 or toll-free 800-455-8018. E-mail: admissions@ycp.edu. Web site: http://www.ycp.edu/.

RHODE ISLAND

BROWN UNIVERSITY
PROVIDENCE, RHODE ISLAND

General Independent, university, coed **Entrance** Most difficult **Setting** 140-acre urban campus **Total enrollment** 7,579 **Student/faculty ratio** 8:1 **Application deadline** 1/1 **Freshmen** 18% were admitted **Housing** Yes **Expenses** Tuition $23,124; Room & Board $6776 **Undergraduates** 53% women, 2% part-time, 1% 25 or older, 0.4% Native American, 5% Hispanic, 6% black, 15% Asian American or Pacific Islander **Most popular recent majors** Biology; English; history **Academic program** English as a second language, advanced placement, accelerated degree program, self-designed majors, tutorials, honors program, summer session, adult/continuing education programs, internships **Contact** Mr. Michael Goldberger, Director of Admission, Brown University, Box 1876, Providence, RI 02912. Tele-

Brown University *(continued)*

phone: 401-863-2378. Fax: 401-863-9300. E-mail: admission_undergraduate@brown.edu. Web site: http://www.brown.edu/.

BRYANT COLLEGE

SMITHFIELD, RHODE ISLAND

General Independent, comprehensive, coed **Entrance** Moderately difficult **Setting** 387-acre suburban campus **Total enrollment** 3,266 **Student/faculty ratio** 18:1 **Application deadline** 5/1 **Freshmen** 84% were admitted **Housing** Yes **Expenses** Tuition $14,800; Room & Board $6700 **Undergraduates** 43% women, 16% part-time, 19% 25 or older, 0.2% Native American, 2% Hispanic, 2% black, 3% Asian American or Pacific Islander **Most popular recent majors** Business marketing and marketing management; accounting; finance **Academic program** Average class size 30, English as a second language, advanced placement, accelerated degree program, tutorials, honors program, summer session, adult/continuing education programs, internships **Contact** Ms. Margaret L. Drugovich, Dean of Admission and Financial Aid, Bryant College, 1150 Douglas Pike, Smithfield, RI 02917-1284. Telephone: 401-232-6100 or toll-free 800-622-7001. Fax: 401-232-6741. E-mail: admissions@bryant.edu. Web site: http://www.bryant.edu/.

JOHNSON & WALES UNIVERSITY

PROVIDENCE, RHODE ISLAND

General Independent, comprehensive, coed **Entrance** Minimally difficult **Setting** 47-acre urban campus **Total enrollment** 8,124 **Student/faculty ratio** 30:1 **Application deadline** Rolling **Freshmen** 80% were admitted **Housing** Yes **Expenses** Tuition $12,807; Room & Board $5550 **Undergraduates** 47% women, 15% part-time, 11% 25 or older, 0.2% Native American, 5% Hispanic, 11% black, 2% Asian American or Pacific Islander **Most popular recent majors** Culinary arts; hotel and restaurant management; hospitality management **Academic program** Average class size 30, English as a second language, advanced placement, accelerated degree program, honors program, summer session, adult/continuing education programs, internships **Contact** Mr. Kenneth DiSaia, Dean of Admissions, Johnson & Wales University, 8 Abbott Park Place, Providence, RI 02903-3703. Telephone: 401-598-4664 ext. 2345 or toll-free 800-342-5598 (out-of-state). Fax: 401-598-1835. E-mail: admissions@jwu.edu. Web site: http://www.jwu.edu/.

PROVIDENCE COLLEGE

PROVIDENCE, RHODE ISLAND

General Independent Roman Catholic, comprehensive, coed **Entrance** Very difficult **Setting** 105-acre suburban campus **Total enrollment** 5,507 **Student/faculty ratio** 14:1 **Application deadline** 1/15 **Freshmen** 67% were admitted **Housing** Yes **Expenses** Tuition $16,655; Room & Board $6919 **Undergraduates** 59% women, 10% part-time, 1% 25 or older, 0.2% Native American, 3% Hispanic, 2% black, 1% Asian American or Pacific Islander **Most popular recent majors** Business administration; political science **Academic program** Average class size 25, advanced placement, self-designed majors, tutorials, honors program, summer session, adult/continuing education programs, internships **Contact** Mr. Christopher Lydon, Dean of Enrollment Management, Providence College, River Avenue and Eaton Street, Providence, RI 02918. Telephone: 401-865-2535 or toll-free 800-721-6444. Fax: 401-865-2826. E-mail: pcadmiss@providence.edu. Web site: http://www.providence.edu/.

▶ **For more information, see page 493.**

RHODE ISLAND COLLEGE

PROVIDENCE, RHODE ISLAND

General State-supported, comprehensive, coed **Entrance** Moderately difficult **Setting** 170-acre suburban campus **Total enrollment** 8,622 **Student/faculty ratio** 17:1 **Application deadline** 5/1 **Freshmen** 78% were admitted **Housing** Yes **Expenses** Tuition $3076; Room & Board $5200 **Undergraduates** 67% women, 31% part-time, 30% 25 or older, 0.3% Native American, 4% Hispanic, 4% black, 2% Asian American or Pacific Islander **Most popular recent majors** Education; psychology; nursing **Academic program** English as a second language, advanced placement, accelerated degree program, self-designed majors, tutorials, honors program, summer session, adult/continuing education programs, internships **Contact** Dr. Holly Shadoian, Director of Admissions, Rhode Island College, 600 Mount Pleasant Avenue, Providence, RI 02908-1924. Telephone: 401-456-8234. Web site: http://www.ric.edu/.

RHODE ISLAND SCHOOL OF DESIGN

PROVIDENCE, RHODE ISLAND

General Independent, comprehensive, coed **Entrance** Very difficult **Setting** 13-acre urban campus **Total enrollment** 2,001 **Student/faculty ratio** 11:1 **Application deadline** 2/15 **Housing** Yes **Expenses** Tuition $19,670; Room & Board $6390 **Undergraduates** 60% women, 14% 25 or older, 0.4% Native American, 3% Hispanic, 2% black, 11% Asian American or Pacific Islander **Most popular recent majors** Graphic design/commercial art/illustration; architecture **Academic program** English as a second language, advanced placement, tutorials, adult/continuing education programs, internships **Contact** Mr. Edward

Newhall, Director of Admissions, Rhode Island School of Design, 2 College Street, Providence, RI 02903-2784. Telephone: 401-454-6300 or toll-free 800-364-RISD. Fax: 401-454-6309. E-mail: admissions@risd.edu. Web site: http://www.risd.edu/.

ROGER WILLIAMS UNIVERSITY
BRISTOL, RHODE ISLAND

General Independent, comprehensive, coed **Entrance** Moderately difficult **Setting** 140-acre small town campus **Total enrollment** 3,805 **Student/faculty ratio** 11:1 **Application deadline** Rolling **Housing** Yes **Expenses** Tuition $15,840; Room & Board $7080 **Undergraduates** 46% women, 41% part-time, 43% 25 or older, 0.3% Native American, 1% Hispanic, 2% black, 3% Asian American or Pacific Islander **Most popular recent majors** Architecture; business administration; paralegal/legal assistant **Academic program** Average class size 25, English as a second language, advanced placement, accelerated degree program, self-designed majors, tutorials, honors program, summer session, adult/continuing education programs, internships **Contact** Office of Admissions, Roger Williams University, 1 Old Ferry Road, Bristol, RI 02809. Telephone: 401-254-3500 or toll-free 800-458-7144 (out-of-state). Fax: 401-254-3557. E-mail: admit@alpha.rwu.edu. Web site: http://www.rwu.edu/.

SALVE REGINA UNIVERSITY
NEWPORT, RHODE ISLAND

General Independent Roman Catholic, comprehensive, coed **Entrance** Moderately difficult **Setting** 65-acre suburban campus **Total enrollment** 2,168 **Student/faculty ratio** 14:1 **Application deadline** Rolling **Freshmen** 88% were admitted **Housing** Yes **Expenses** Tuition $16,300; Room & Board $7250 **Undergraduates** 67% women, 6% part-time, 8% 25 or older, 0.3% Native American, 1% Hispanic, 2% black, 1% Asian American or Pacific Islander **Most popular recent majors** Business administration; elementary education; nursing **Academic program** Average class size 27, English as a second language, advanced placement, accelerated degree program, tutorials, honors program, summer session, adult/continuing education programs, internships **Contact** Ms. Laura E. McPhie, Dean of Enrollment Services and Admissions, Salve Regina University, 100 Ochre Point Avenue, Newport, RI 02840-4192. Telephone: 401-847-6650 ext. 2908 or toll-free 888-GO SALVE. Fax: 401-848-2823. E-mail: sruadmis@salve.edu. Web site: http://www.salve.edu/.

UNIVERSITY OF RHODE ISLAND
KINGSTON, RHODE ISLAND

General State-supported, university, coed **Entrance** Moderately difficult **Setting** 1,200-acre small town campus **Total enrollment** 13,437 **Student/faculty ratio** 15:1 **Application deadline** 3/1 **Freshmen** 81% were admitted **Housing** Yes **Expenses** Tuition $4592; Room & Board $5764 **Undergraduates** 56% women, 16% part-time, 17% 25 or older, 0.4% Native American, 3% Hispanic, 3% black, 3% Asian American or Pacific Islander **Most popular recent majors** Psychology; individual/family development; pharmacy **Academic program** Advanced placement, accelerated degree program, tutorials, honors program, summer session, adult/continuing education programs, internships **Contact** Ms. Catherine Zeiser, Assistant Dean of Admissions, University of Rhode Island, Kingston, RI 02881. Telephone: 401-874-7100. Fax: 401-874-5523. E-mail: uriadmit@riacc.uri.edu. Web site: http://www.uri.edu/.

SOUTH CAROLINA

ALLEN UNIVERSITY
COLUMBIA, SOUTH CAROLINA

General Independent African Methodist Episcopal, 4-year, coed **Entrance** Noncompetitive **Setting** Suburban campus **Total enrollment** 358 **Application deadline** Rolling **Housing** Yes **Expenses** Tuition $4750; Room & Board $4210 **Undergraduates** 48% women, 15% part-time, 2% 25 or older **Most popular recent majors** Business administration; social work; education **Academic program** Internships **Contact** Ms. Alison Smith, Director of Admissions, Allen University, 1530 Harden Street, Columbia, SC 29204-1085. Telephone: 803-376-5716. Fax: 803-376-5731. E-mail: auniv@mindspring.com.

ANDERSON COLLEGE
ANDERSON, SOUTH CAROLINA

General Independent Baptist, 4-year, coed **Entrance** Moderately difficult **Setting** 44-acre suburban campus **Total enrollment** 1,012 **Student/faculty ratio** 15:1 **Application deadline** 6/30 **Freshmen** 78% were admitted **Housing** Yes **Expenses** Tuition $9475; Room & Board $4145 **Undergraduates** 25% 25 or older, 0% Native American, 1% Hispanic, 14% black, 2% Asian American or Pacific Islander **Most popular recent majors** Business administration; physical education; art **Academic program** Advanced placement, tutorials, honors program, summer session, adult/continuing education programs, internships **Contact** Ms. Pam Bryant, Director of Admissions, Anderson College, 316 Boulevard, Anderson, SC 29621-4035. Telephone: 864-231-2030 or toll-free

Anderson College *(continued)*

800-542-3594. Fax: 864-231-2004. E-mail: apply@anderson-college.edu. Web site: http://www.anderson-college.edu/.

BENEDICT COLLEGE
COLUMBIA, SOUTH CAROLINA

General Independent Baptist, 4-year, coed **Entrance** Noncompetitive **Setting** 20-acre urban campus **Total enrollment** 2,208 **Student/faculty ratio** 17:1 **Application deadline** Rolling **Freshmen** 79% were admitted **Housing** Yes **Expenses** Tuition $7502; Room & Board $3982 **Undergraduates** 53% women, 7% part-time, 17% 25 or older **Most popular recent majors** Business administration; criminal justice/law enforcement administration; social work **Academic program** Advanced placement, honors program, summer session, adult/continuing education programs, internships **Contact** Dr. Marcia Conston, Associate Vice President, Institutional Effectiveness, Benedict College, PO Box 98, Columbia, SC 29204. Telephone: 803-253-5526 or toll-free 800-868-6598 (in-state). Fax: 803-253-5167. Web site: http://BCHOME.Benedict.edu/.

CHARLESTON SOUTHERN UNIVERSITY
CHARLESTON, SOUTH CAROLINA

General Independent Baptist, comprehensive, coed **Entrance** Moderately difficult **Setting** 350-acre suburban campus **Total enrollment** 2,481 **Student/faculty ratio** 16:1 **Application deadline** Rolling **Freshmen** 86% were admitted **Housing** Yes **Expenses** Tuition $9248; Room & Board $3562 **Undergraduates** 57% women, 18% part-time, 29% 25 or older **Most popular recent majors** Business administration; education; psychology **Academic program** Average class size 25, advanced placement, accelerated degree program, summer session, internships **Contact** Mrs. Debbie Williamson, Director of Enrollment Management, Charleston Southern University, PO Box 118087, Charleston, SC 29423-8087. Telephone: 803-863-7050 or toll-free 800-947-7474. E-mail: enroll@csuniv.edu. Web site: http://www.csuniv.edu/.

THE CITADEL, THE MILITARY COLLEGE OF SOUTH CAROLINA
CHARLESTON, SOUTH CAROLINA

General State-supported, comprehensive, coed **Entrance** Moderately difficult **Setting** 130-acre urban campus **Total enrollment** 3,766 **Student/faculty ratio** 18:1 **Application deadline** 7/1 **Freshmen** 85% were admitted **Housing** Yes **Expenses** Tuition $3499; Room & Board $3950 **Undergraduates** 2% women, 3% part-time, 6% 25 or older, 0.3% Native American, 2% Hispanic, 7% black, 2% Asian American or Pacific Islander **Most popular recent majors** Business administration; political science; civil engineering **Academic program** English as a second language, advanced placement, honors program, summer session, adult/continuing education programs, internships **Contact** Lt. Col. Steven D. Klein, Dean of Enrollment Management, The Citadel, The Military College of South Carolina, 171 Moultrie Street, Charleston, SC 29409. Telephone: 803-953-5230 or toll-free 800-868-1842. Fax: 803-953-7630. E-mail: admissions@citadel.edu. Web site: http://www.citadel.edu/.

CLAFLIN COLLEGE
ORANGEBURG, SOUTH CAROLINA

General Independent United Methodist, 4-year, coed **Entrance** Minimally difficult **Setting** 32-acre small town campus **Total enrollment** 1,005 **Student/faculty ratio** 14:1 **Application deadline** Rolling **Freshmen** 64% were admitted **Housing** Yes **Expenses** Tuition $5580; Room & Board $3044 **Undergraduates** 3% 25 or older, 97% black **Most popular recent majors** Business administration; sociology; elementary education **Academic program** Average class size 25, advanced placement, honors program, summer session, adult/continuing education programs, internships **Contact** Ms. Sadie Jarvis, Director of Admission and Records, Claflin College, 700 College Avenue, NE, Orangeburg, SC 29115. Telephone: 803-534-2710 ext. 339 or toll-free 800-922-1276 (in-state). Fax: 803-531-2860. E-mail: sjarvis@clafl.claflin.edu. Web site: http://www.reusc.org/claflin.edu/.

CLEMSON UNIVERSITY
CLEMSON, SOUTH CAROLINA

General State-supported, university, coed **Entrance** Moderately difficult **Setting** 1,400-acre small town campus **Total enrollment** 16,396 **Student/faculty ratio** 17:1 **Application deadline** 5/1 **Freshmen** 74% were admitted **Housing** Yes **Expenses** Tuition $3392; Room & Board $3888 **Undergraduates** 46% women, 6% part-time, 4% 25 or older, 0.2% Native American, 1% Hispanic, 8% black, 1% Asian American or Pacific Islander **Most popular recent majors** Mechanical engineering; elementary education; nursing **Academic program** Advanced placement, accelerated degree program, honors program, summer session, internships **Contact** Mrs. Audrey Bodell, Assistant Director of Admissions, Clemson University, 105 Sikes Hall, PO Box 345124, Clemson, SC 29634. Telephone: 864-656-2287. Fax: 864-656-2464. E-mail: cuadmissions@clemson.edu. Web site: http://www.clemson.edu/.

COASTAL CAROLINA UNIVERSITY
CONWAY, SOUTH CAROLINA

General State-supported, comprehensive, coed **Entrance** Moderately difficult **Setting** 244-acre suburban campus **Total enrollment** 4,408 **Student/faculty ratio** 18:1 **Application deadline** 8/15 **Freshmen** 81% were admitted **Housing** Yes **Expenses** Tuition $3100; Room & Board $4640 **Undergraduates** 56% women, 11% part-time, 11% 25 or older, 0.4% Native American, 1% Hispanic, 9% black, 1% Asian American or Pacific Islander **Most popular recent majors** Marine science; elementary education; business administration **Academic program** Advanced placement, accelerated degree program, self-designed majors, honors program, summer session, adult/continuing education programs, internships **Contact** Mr. Timothy J. McCormick, Director of Admissions, Coastal Carolina University, PO Box 261954, Conway, SC 29528-6054. Telephone: 803-349-2026 or toll-free 800-277-7000. Fax: 803-349-2127. E-mail: admis@coastal.edu. Web site: http://www.coastal.edu/.

COKER COLLEGE
HARTSVILLE, SOUTH CAROLINA

General Independent, 4-year, coed **Entrance** Moderately difficult **Setting** 30-acre small town campus **Total enrollment** 970 **Student/faculty ratio** 10:1 **Application deadline** Rolling **Freshmen** 63% were admitted **Housing** Yes **Expenses** Tuition $13,400; Room & Board $4516 **Undergraduates** 65% women, 20% part-time, 54% 25 or older, 0.2% Native American, 2% Hispanic, 31% black, 0% Asian American or Pacific Islander **Most popular recent majors** Business administration; elementary education; social sciences **Academic program** English as a second language, advanced placement, accelerated degree program, self-designed majors, tutorials, honors program, summer session, adult/continuing education programs, internships **Contact** Mr. David Anthony, Director of Admissions, Coker College, 300 East College Avenue, Hartsville, SC 29550. Telephone: 803-383-8050 or toll-free 800-950-1908. Fax: 803-383-8056. E-mail: admissions@coker.edu. Web site: http://www.coker.edu/.

COLLEGE OF CHARLESTON
CHARLESTON, SOUTH CAROLINA

General State-supported, 4-year, coed **Entrance** Moderately difficult **Setting** 52-acre urban campus **Total enrollment** 9,252 **Student/faculty ratio** 18:1 **Application deadline** 7/1 **Freshmen** 67% were admitted **Housing** Yes **Expenses** Tuition $3290; Room & Board $3850 **Undergraduates** 63% women, 8% part-time, 12% 25 or older, 0.2% Native American, 1% Hispanic, 8% black, 1% Asian American or Pacific Islander **Most popular recent majors** Business administration; communications; elementary education **Academic program** Average class size 25, English as a second language, advanced placement, accelerated degree program, tutorials, honors program, summer session, adult/continuing education programs, internships **Contact** Mr. Donald Burkard, Dean of Admissions, College of Charleston, 66 George Street, Charleston, SC 29424-0002. Telephone: 843-953-5670. E-mail: admissions@cofc.edu. Web site: http://www.cofc.edu/.

COLUMBIA COLLEGE
COLUMBIA, SOUTH CAROLINA

General Independent United Methodist, comprehensive, women only **Entrance** Moderately difficult **Setting** 33-acre suburban campus **Total enrollment** 1,368 **Student/faculty ratio** 14:1 **Application deadline** Rolling **Freshmen** 82% were admitted **Housing** Yes **Expenses** Tuition $12,150; Room & Board $4300 **Undergraduates** 9% part-time, 27% 25 or older, 0.2% Native American, 1% Hispanic, 36% black, 1% Asian American or Pacific Islander **Most popular recent majors** Education; business administration **Academic program** Average class size 22, advanced placement, accelerated degree program, self-designed majors, honors program, summer session, adult/continuing education programs, internships **Contact** Mr. J. Joseph Mitchell, Dean of Enrollment Management, Columbia College, 1301 Columbia College Drive, Columbia, SC 29203-5998. Telephone: 803-786-3871 or toll-free 800-277-1301. Fax: 803-786-3674. E-mail: admissions@colacoll.edu. Web site: http://www.colacoll.edu/.

COLUMBIA INTERNATIONAL UNIVERSITY
COLUMBIA, SOUTH CAROLINA

General Independent nondenominational, comprehensive, coed **Entrance** Minimally difficult **Setting** 450-acre suburban campus **Total enrollment** 937 **Student/faculty ratio** 15:1 **Application deadline** Rolling **Freshmen** 76% were admitted **Housing** Yes **Expenses** Tuition $7891; Room & Board $4110 **Undergraduates** 52% women, 12% part-time, 28% 25 or older, 0.4% Native American, 0.4% Hispanic, 4% black, 0.2% Asian American or Pacific Islander **Academic program** Average class size 100, advanced placement, accelerated degree program, summer session, internships **Contact** Ms. Yvonne Miranda, Director of College Admissions, Columbia International University, PO Box 3122, Columbia, SC 29230-3122. Telephone: 803-754-4100 ext. 3024 or toll-free 800-777-2227. Fax: 803-786-4209. E-mail: yesciu@ciu.edu. Web site: http://www.ciu.edu/.

CONVERSE COLLEGE
SPARTANBURG, SOUTH CAROLINA

General Independent, comprehensive, women only **Entrance** Moderately difficult **Setting** 70-acre urban campus **Total enrollment** 1,474 **Student/faculty ratio** 9:1 **Application deadline** 8/1 **Freshmen** 85% were admitted **Housing** Yes **Expenses** Tuition $14,445; Room & Board $4080 **Undergraduates** 12% part-time, 20% 25 or older, 1% Native American, 1% Hispanic, 11% black, 1% Asian American or Pacific Islander **Most popular recent majors** Education; art; business administration **Academic program** English as a second language, advanced placement, accelerated degree program, honors program, summer session, adult/continuing education programs, internships **Contact** Mr. C. Ray Tatum, Vice President for Enrollment, Converse College, 580 East Main Street, Spartanburg, SC 29302-0006. Telephone: 864-596-9040 ext. 9041 or toll-free 800-766-1125. Fax: 864-596-9158. Web site: http://www.converse.edu/.

ERSKINE COLLEGE
DUE WEST, SOUTH CAROLINA

General Independent, 4-year, coed, affiliated with Associate Reformed Presbyterian Church **Entrance** Moderately difficult **Setting** 85-acre rural campus **Total enrollment** 477 **Student/faculty ratio** 12:1 **Application deadline** Rolling **Freshmen** 88% were admitted **Housing** Yes **Expenses** Tuition $13,902; Room & Board $4760 **Undergraduates** 58% women, 0.2% part-time, 1% 25 or older, 0% Native American, 0% Hispanic, 5% black, 0.4% Asian American or Pacific Islander **Most popular recent majors** Biology; business administration; chemistry **Academic program** Average class size 20, advanced placement, accelerated degree program, tutorials, summer session, internships **Contact** Mr. Jeff Craft, Director of Admissions, Erskine College, PO Box 176, Due West, SC 29639. Telephone: 864-379-8830 or toll-free 800-241-8721. Fax: 864-379-8759. E-mail: admissions@erskine.edu. Web site: http://www.erskine.edu/.

FRANCIS MARION UNIVERSITY
FLORENCE, SOUTH CAROLINA

General State-supported, comprehensive, coed **Entrance** Moderately difficult **Setting** 309-acre rural campus **Total enrollment** 3,554 **Student/faculty ratio** 18:1 **Application deadline** Rolling **Freshmen** 79% were admitted **Housing** Yes **Expenses** Tuition $3390; Room & Board $3310 **Undergraduates** 18% 25 or older, 0.5% Native American, 1% Hispanic, 28% black, 0.4% Asian American or Pacific Islander **Most popular recent majors** Business administration; biology; elementary education **Academic program** Advanced placement, accelerated degree program, tutorials, honors program, summer session, adult/continuing education programs, internships **Contact** Ms. Drucilla Shelton, Director of Admissions, Francis Marion University, Box 100547, Florence, SC 29501-0547. Telephone: 803-661-1231 or toll-free 800-368-7551. Fax: 803-661-4635. E-mail: admission@fmarion.edu.

FURMAN UNIVERSITY
GREENVILLE, SOUTH CAROLINA

General Independent, comprehensive, coed **Entrance** Very difficult **Setting** 750-acre suburban campus **Total enrollment** 2,840 **Student/faculty ratio** 12:1 **Application deadline** 2/1 **Freshmen** 80% were admitted **Housing** Yes **Expenses** Tuition $16,419; Room & Board $4449 **Undergraduates** 55% women, 5% part-time, 1% 25 or older **Most popular recent majors** Political science; business administration; biology **Academic program** Advanced placement, accelerated degree program, self-designed majors, tutorials, summer session, adult/continuing education programs, internships **Contact** Mr. J. Carey Thompson, Director of Admissions, Furman University, 3300 Poinsett Highway, Greenville, SC 29613. Telephone: 864-294-2034. Fax: 864-294-3127. E-mail: admissions@furman.edu. Web site: http://www.furman.edu/.

JOHNSON & WALES UNIVERSITY
CHARLESTON, SOUTH CAROLINA

General Independent, 4-year, coed **Entrance** Minimally difficult **Setting** Urban campus **Total enrollment** 1,325 **Student/faculty ratio** 27:1 **Application deadline** Rolling **Freshmen** 87% were admitted **Housing** Yes **Expenses** Tuition $13,689; Room only $3738 **Undergraduates** 36% women, 5% part-time, 22% 25 or older, 0.2% Native American, 1% Hispanic, 14% black, 1% Asian American or Pacific Islander **Most Popular Recent Major** Culinary arts **Academic program** Average class size 30, English as a second language, accelerated degree program, summer session, adult/continuing education programs, internships **Contact** Ms. Mary Hovis, Director of Admissions, Johnson & Wales University, PCC Box 1409, 701 East Bay Street, Charleston, SC 29403. Telephone: 803-727-3000 or toll-free 800-868-1522 (out-of-state). Fax: 803-763-0318. E-mail: admissions@jwu.edu. Web site: http://www.jwu.edu/.

LANDER UNIVERSITY
GREENWOOD, SOUTH CAROLINA

General State-supported, comprehensive, coed **Contact** Ms. Whitney T. Marcengill, Associate Director of Admissions, Lander University, 320 Stanley Avenue, Greenwood, SC 29649-2099. Telephone: 864-388-8307. Fax: 864-388-8125. E-mail: wmarceng@lander.edu.

LIMESTONE COLLEGE
GAFFNEY, SOUTH CAROLINA

General Independent, 4-year, coed **Entrance** Minimally difficult **Setting** 115-acre small town campus **Total enrollment** 411 **Student/faculty ratio** 11:1 **Application deadline** Rolling **Freshmen** 96% were admitted **Housing** Yes **Expenses** Tuition $8600; Room & Board $3900 **Undergraduates** 43% women, 2% part-time, 0% 25 or older, 0.2% Native American, 0.2% Hispanic, 13% black, 0.2% Asian American or Pacific Islander **Most popular recent majors** Business administration; education; physical education **Academic program** Average class size 20, English as a second language, advanced placement, accelerated degree program, self-designed majors, tutorials, honors program, summer session, adult/continuing education programs, internships **Contact** Dr. Charles Cunning, Vice President for Academic Affairs, Limestone College, 1115 College Drive, Gaffney, SC 29340-3798. Telephone: 864-489-7151 ext. 540 or toll-free 800-795-7151. Fax: 864-487-8706. Web site: http://www.icusc.org//limestne/lchome.htm.

MEDICAL UNIVERSITY OF SOUTH CAROLINA
CHARLESTON, SOUTH CAROLINA

General State-supported, upper-level, coed **Contact** Ms. Wanda L. Taylor, University Director of Admissions, Medical University of South Carolina, 171 Ashley Avenue, Charleston, SC 29425-0002. Telephone: 803-792-5396. Fax: 803-792-3764. Web site: http://www.musc.edu/.

MORRIS COLLEGE
SUMTER, SOUTH CAROLINA

General Independent, 4-year, coed, affiliated with Baptist Educational and Missionary Convention of South Carolina **Entrance** Minimally difficult **Setting** 34-acre small town campus **Total enrollment** 971 **Student/faculty ratio** 16:1 **Application deadline** Rolling **Freshmen** 71% were admitted **Housing** Yes **Expenses** Tuition $5240; Room & Board $2770 **Undergraduates** 65% women, 4% part-time, 16% 25 or older, 99% black **Most popular recent majors** Business administration; criminal justice/law enforcement administration; biology **Academic program** Average class size 35, accelerated degree program, honors program, summer session, internships **Contact** Mrs. Queen W. Spann, Director of Admissions and Records, Morris College, 100 West College Street, Sumter, SC 29150-3599. Telephone: 803-775-9371 ext. 225 or toll-free 888-775-1345. Fax: 803-773-3687. Web site: http://www.isusc.org/morris/mchome.htm.

NEWBERRY COLLEGE
NEWBERRY, SOUTH CAROLINA

General Independent Lutheran, 4-year, coed **Entrance** Moderately difficult **Setting** 60-acre small town campus **Total enrollment** 716 **Student/faculty ratio** 11:1 **Application deadline** Rolling **Freshmen** 82% were admitted **Housing** Yes **Expenses** Tuition $12,326; Room & Board $3218 **Undergraduates** 46% women, 5% part-time **Most popular recent majors** Business administration; physical education; sociology **Academic program** Average class size 15, advanced placement, accelerated degree program, tutorials, honors program, summer session, internships **Contact** Mr. Stephen Cloniger, Vice President for Enrollment Management, Newberry College, 2100 College Street, Newberry, SC 29108-2197. Telephone: 803-321-5127 or toll-free 800-845-4955 (out-of-state). E-mail: admissions@newberry.edu. Web site: http://www.newberry.edu/.

NORTH GREENVILLE COLLEGE
TIGERVILLE, SOUTH CAROLINA

General Independent Southern Baptist, 4-year, coed **Entrance** Minimally difficult **Setting** 500-acre rural campus **Total enrollment** 1,038 **Student/faculty ratio** 15:1 **Application deadline** 8/27 **Freshmen** 67% were admitted **Housing** Yes **Expenses** Tuition $7400; Room & Board $4280 **Undergraduates** 41% women, 10% part-time, 15% 25 or older, 0.1% Native American, 1% Hispanic, 17% black, 0.1% Asian American or Pacific Islander **Most popular recent majors** Religious studies; business administration; elementary education **Academic program** Average class size 25, English as a second language, advanced placement, accelerated degree program, self-designed majors, tutorials, honors program, summer session, internships **Contact** Mr. Buddy Freeman, Executive Director of Admissions, North Greenville College, PO Box 1892, Tigerville, SC 29688-1892. Telephone: 864-977-7052 or toll-free 800-468-6642. Fax: 864-977-7177. E-mail: bfreeman@ngc.edu. Web site: http://www.ngc.edu/.

PRESBYTERIAN COLLEGE
CLINTON, SOUTH CAROLINA

General Independent Presbyterian, 4-year, coed **Entrance** Very difficult **Setting** 215-acre small town campus **Total enrollment** 1,116 **Student/faculty ratio** 12:1 **Application deadline** 4/1

Presbyterian College *(continued)*

Freshmen 84% were admitted **Housing** Yes **Expenses** Tuition $14,806; Room & Board $4216 **Undergraduates** 50% women, 2% part-time, 1% 25 or older **Most popular recent majors** Business administration; education; biology **Academic program** Average class size 20, advanced placement, accelerated degree program, tutorials, honors program, summer session, internships **Contact** Mr. Eddie G. Rogers, Associate Director of Admissions, Presbyterian College, South Broad Street, Clinton, SC 29325. Telephone: 864-833-8228 or toll-free 800-476-7272. Fax: 864-833-8481. E-mail: mwill@admin.presby.edu. Web site: http://www.presby.edu/.

SOUTH CAROLINA STATE UNIVERSITY
ORANGEBURG, SOUTH CAROLINA

General State-supported, comprehensive, coed **Entrance** Minimally difficult **Setting** 160-acre small town campus **Total enrollment** 4,657 **Application deadline** 7/31 **Freshmen** 55% were admitted **Housing** Yes **Expenses** Tuition $2974; Room & Board $2836 **Undergraduates** 55% women, 6% part-time, 12% 25 or older, 0% Native American, 0.2% Hispanic, 95% black, 0.1% Asian American or Pacific Islander **Most popular recent majors** Business administration; electrical/electronic engineering technology **Academic program** Advanced placement, tutorials, honors program, summer session, adult/continuing education programs, internships **Contact** Ms. Dorothy Brown, Director of Admissions, South Carolina State University, 300 College Street Northeast, Orangeburg, SC 29117-0001. Telephone: 803-536-7185 ext. 8407 or toll-free 800-260-5956. Fax: 803-536-8990. E-mail: carolyn-free@scsu.scsu.edu.

SOUTHERN WESLEYAN UNIVERSITY
CENTRAL, SOUTH CAROLINA

General Independent, comprehensive, coed, affiliated with Wesleyan Church **Entrance** Minimally difficult **Setting** 230-acre small town campus **Total enrollment** 1,337 **Student/faculty ratio** 14:1 **Application deadline** 8/10 **Housing** Yes **Expenses** Tuition $10,180; Room & Board $3540 **Undergraduates** 58% women, 3% part-time, 66% 25 or older **Most popular recent majors** Business administration; education; psychology **Academic program** Advanced placement, accelerated degree program, tutorials, honors program, summer session, adult/continuing education programs, internships **Contact** Mr. Mike Ennis, Director of Admissions, Southern Wesleyan University, 907 Wesleyan Drive, PO Box 1020, Central, SC 29630-1020. Telephone: 864-639-2453 ext. 327 or toll-free 800-CUATSWU. Fax: 864-639-0826 ext. 327. E-mail: admissions@swu.edu. Web site: http://www.swu.edu/.

UNIVERSITY OF SOUTH CAROLINA
COLUMBIA, SOUTH CAROLINA

General State-supported, university, coed **Entrance** Moderately difficult **Setting** 242-acre urban campus **Total enrollment** 25,447 **Student/faculty ratio** 17:1 **Application deadline** Rolling **Freshmen** 77% were admitted **Housing** Yes **Expenses** Tuition $3534; Room & Board $3830 **Undergraduates** 54% women, 13% part-time, 9% 25 or older, 0.3% Native American, 1% Hispanic, 19% black, 3% Asian American or Pacific Islander **Academic program** English as a second language, advanced placement, accelerated degree program, self-designed majors, honors program, summer session, adult/continuing education programs, internships **Contact** Ms. Terry L. Davis, Director of Admissions, University of South Carolina, Columbia, SC 29208. Telephone: 803-777-7700 or toll-free 800-922-9755 (in-state). E-mail: admissions-ugrad@scarolina.edu. Web site: http://www.csd.scarolina.edu/.

UNIVERSITY OF SOUTH CAROLINA–AIKEN
AIKEN, SOUTH CAROLINA

General State-supported, comprehensive, coed **Entrance** Minimally difficult **Setting** 453-acre suburban campus **Total enrollment** 3,004 **Student/faculty ratio** 16:1 **Application deadline** 8/1 **Freshmen** 69% were admitted **Housing** Yes **Expenses** Tuition $3014; Room & Board $3576 **Undergraduates** 34% 25 or older, 0.2% Native American, 1% Hispanic, 19% black, 1% Asian American or Pacific Islander **Most popular recent majors** Business administration; elementary education; nursing **Academic program** English as a second language, advanced placement, accelerated degree program, self-designed majors, tutorials, honors program, summer session, adult/continuing education programs, internships **Contact** Mr. Randy R. Duckett, Director of Admissions, University of South Carolina–Aiken, 171 University Parkway, Aiken, SC 29801-6309. Telephone: 803-648-6851 ext. 3366 or toll-free 888-WOW-USCA. Fax: 803-641-3727. E-mail: admit@sc.edu.

UNIVERSITY OF SOUTH CAROLINA SPARTANBURG
SPARTANBURG, SOUTH CAROLINA

General State-supported, comprehensive, coed **Entrance** Minimally difficult **Setting** 298-acre urban campus **Total enrollment** 3,549 **Student/faculty ratio** 16:1 **Application deadline** 8/15 **Freshmen** 61% were admitted **Housing** Yes **Expenses** Tuition $3014; Room & Board $3200 **Un-**

dergraduates 64% women, 31% part-time, 31% 25 or older **Most popular recent majors** Business administration; psychology; nursing **Academic program** Average class size 22, English as a second language, advanced placement, accelerated degree program, self-designed majors, tutorials, honors program, summer session, adult/continuing education programs, internships **Contact** Ms. Donette Stewart, Director of Admissions, University of South Carolina Spartanburg, 800 University Way, Spartanburg, SC 29303-4932. Telephone: 864-503-5280 or toll-free 800-277-8727 (in-state). Web site: http://www.uscs.edu/.

VOORHEES COLLEGE
DENMARK, SOUTH CAROLINA

General Independent Episcopal, 4-year, coed **Entrance** Minimally difficult **Setting** 350-acre rural campus **Total enrollment** 924 **Student/faculty ratio** 20:1 **Application deadline** Rolling **Freshmen** 80% were admitted **Housing** Yes **Expenses** Tuition $5168; Room & Board $2866 **Undergraduates** 63% women, 5% part-time, 10% 25 or older **Most popular recent majors** Sociology; criminal justice/law enforcement administration; business administration **Academic program** Advanced placement, honors program, summer session, adult/continuing education programs, internships **Contact** Mrs. Roe B. W. Kemp, Director of Admissions, Records, and Registration, Voorhees College, 1411 Voorhees Road, Denmark, SC 29042. Telephone: 803-793-3351 ext. 7302 or toll-free 800-446-6250. Fax: 803-793-4584.

WINTHROP UNIVERSITY
ROCK HILL, SOUTH CAROLINA

General State-supported, comprehensive, coed **Entrance** Moderately difficult **Setting** 418-acre suburban campus **Total enrollment** 5,574 **Student/faculty ratio** 17:1 **Application deadline** 5/1 **Housing** Yes **Expenses** Tuition $3938; Room & Board $3764 **Undergraduates** 68% women, 9% part-time, 15% 25 or older, 0.4% Native American, 1% Hispanic, 23% black, 1% Asian American or Pacific Islander **Most popular recent majors** Business administration; elementary education; biology **Academic program** Advanced placement, tutorials, honors program, summer session, adult/continuing education programs, internships **Contact** Ms. Deborah Barber, Director of Admissions, Winthrop University, 701 Oakland Avenue, Rock Hill, SC 29733. Telephone: 803-323-2191 or toll-free 800-763-0230. Fax: 803-323-2137. E-mail: admissions@winthrop.edu. Web site: http://www.winthrop.edu/.

WOFFORD COLLEGE
SPARTANBURG, SOUTH CAROLINA

General Independent, 4-year, coed, affiliated with United Methodist Church **Entrance** Very difficult **Setting** 140-acre urban campus **Total enrollment** 1,074 **Application deadline** 2/1 **Freshmen** 82% were admitted **Housing** Yes **Expenses** Tuition $15,390; Room & Board $4410 **Undergraduates** 47% women, 2% part-time, 1% 25 or older, 0.3% Native American, 0.4% Hispanic, 8% black, 1% Asian American or Pacific Islander **Most popular recent majors** Biology; English; business economics **Academic program** Average class size 22, English as a second language, advanced placement, accelerated degree program, self-designed majors, tutorials, summer session, internships **Contact** Mr. Brand Stille, Director of Admissions, Wofford College, 429 North Church Street, Spartanburg, SC 29303-3663. Telephone: 864-597-4130. Fax: 864-597-4149. E-mail: admissions@wofford.edu. Web site: http://www.wofford.edu/.

SOUTH DAKOTA

AUGUSTANA COLLEGE
SIOUX FALLS, SOUTH DAKOTA

General Independent, comprehensive, coed, affiliated with Evangelical Lutheran Church in America **Entrance** Moderately difficult **Setting** 100-acre urban campus **Total enrollment** 1,691 **Student/faculty ratio** 12:1 **Application deadline** Rolling **Freshmen** 91% were admitted **Housing** Yes **Expenses** Tuition $13,112; Room & Board $3903 **Undergraduates** 65% women, 9% part-time, 5% 25 or older, 0.5% Native American, 0.2% Hispanic, 0.4% black, 0.5% Asian American or Pacific Islander **Most popular recent majors** Nursing; education; business administration **Academic program** Advanced placement, accelerated degree program, self-designed majors, tutorials, honors program, summer session, adult/continuing education programs, internships **Contact** Mr. Robert A. Preloger, Vice President for Enrollment, Augustana College, 2001 South Summit Avenue, Sioux Falls, SD 57197. Telephone: 605-336-5516 or toll-free 800-727-2844. Fax: 605-336-5518. E-mail: info@inst.augie.edu. Web site: http://www.augie.edu/.

BLACK HILLS STATE UNIVERSITY
SPEARFISH, SOUTH DAKOTA

General State-supported, comprehensive, coed **Entrance** Minimally difficult **Setting** 123-acre small town campus **Total enrollment** 3,445 **Stu-**

Black Hills State University *(continued)*

dent/faculty ratio 21:1 **Application deadline** Rolling **Freshmen** 90% were admitted **Housing** Yes **Expenses** Tuition $2878; Room & Board $2614 **Undergraduates** 59% women, 25% part-time, 3% Native American, 1% Hispanic, 1% black, 1% Asian American or Pacific Islander **Most popular recent majors** Education; business administration **Academic program** Average class size 25, advanced placement, summer session, internships **Contact** Ms. Judy Berry, Assistant Director of Admissions, Black Hills State University, University Station Box 9502, Spearfish, SD 57799-9502. Telephone: 605-642-6343 or toll-free 800-255-2478. E-mail: jberry@mystic.bhsu.edu. Web site: http://www.bhsu.edu/.

COLORADO TECHNICAL UNIVERSITY SIOUX FALLS CAMPUS
SIOUX FALLS, SOUTH DAKOTA

Contact Colorado Technical University Sioux Falls Campus, 2900 East 26th Street, Sioux Falls, SD 57105. Telephone: 605-331-5159. Fax: 605-361-5954.

DAKOTA STATE UNIVERSITY
MADISON, SOUTH DAKOTA

General State-supported, 4-year, coed **Entrance** Minimally difficult **Setting** 40-acre rural campus **Total enrollment** 1,333 **Student/faculty ratio** 15:1 **Application deadline** Rolling **Freshmen** 76% were admitted **Housing** Yes **Expenses** Tuition $3027; Room & Board $2694 **Undergraduates** 56% women, 27% part-time, 12% 25 or older **Most popular recent majors** Business administration; education; information sciences/systems **Academic program** English as a second language, advanced placement, honors program, summer session, internships **Contact** Ms. Katy O'Hara, Admissions Secretary, Dakota State University, 820 North Washington, Madison, SD 57042-1799. Telephone: 605-256-5139 or toll-free 888-DSU-9988. Fax: 605-256-5316. E-mail: dsuinfo@columbia.dsu.edu. Web site: http://www.dsu.edu/.

DAKOTA WESLEYAN UNIVERSITY
MITCHELL, SOUTH DAKOTA

General Independent United Methodist, 4-year, coed **Entrance** Moderately difficult **Setting** 40-acre small town campus **Total enrollment** 721 **Student/faculty ratio** 15:1 **Application deadline** 8/26 **Freshmen** 90% were admitted **Housing** Yes **Expenses** Tuition $8825; Room & Board $3240 **Undergraduates** 16% 25 or older **Most popular recent majors** Nursing; business administration; education **Academic program** Accelerated degree program, self-designed majors, tutorials, honors program, summer session, adult/continuing education programs, internships **Contact** Ms. Laura Miller, Director of Admissions, Dakota Wesleyan University, Office of Admissions, Mitchell, SD 57301-4398. Telephone: 605-995-2650 or toll-free 800-333-8506. Fax: 605-995-2699. E-mail: admissions@cc.dwu.edu. Web site: http://www.dwu.edu/.

HURON UNIVERSITY
HURON, SOUTH DAKOTA

General Proprietary, comprehensive, coed **Contact** Mr. Richard Shelton, Director of Admissions, Huron University, 333 9th Street SW, Huron, SD 57350-2798. Telephone: 605-352-9465 or toll-free 800-710-7159. Fax: 605-352-7421.

MOUNT MARTY COLLEGE
YANKTON, SOUTH DAKOTA

General Independent Roman Catholic, comprehensive, coed **Entrance** Moderately difficult **Setting** 80-acre small town campus **Total enrollment** 954 **Student/faculty ratio** 20:1 **Application deadline** 8/15 **Housing** Yes **Expenses** Tuition $9168; Room & Board $3644 **Undergraduates** 70% women, 26% part-time, 1% Native American, 1% Hispanic, 1% black, 1% Asian American or Pacific Islander **Most popular recent majors** Business administration; nursing; education **Academic program** Average class size 18, advanced placement, accelerated degree program, self-designed majors, tutorials, honors program, summer session, adult/continuing education programs, internships **Contact** Mr. J. C. Crane, Director of Admission, Mount Marty College, 1105 West 8th Street, Yankton, SD 57078-3724. Telephone: 605-668-1545 or toll-free 800-658-4552. Fax: 605-668-1607. E-mail: mmcadmit@rs1.mtmc.edu. Web site: http://www.mtmc.edu/.

NATIONAL AMERICAN UNIVERSITY
RAPID CITY, SOUTH DAKOTA

General Proprietary, 4-year, coed **Entrance** Noncompetitive **Setting** 8-acre urban campus **Total enrollment** 721 **Student/faculty ratio** 20:1 **Application deadline** Rolling **Housing** Yes **Expenses** Tuition $8475; Room & Board $3360 **Undergraduates** 54% women, 27% part-time, 43% 25 or older, 3% Native American, 1% Hispanic, 4% black, 2% Asian American or Pacific Islander **Most popular recent majors** Business administration; accounting; information sciences/systems **Academic program** Average class size 15, English as a second language, advanced placement, accelerated degree program, tutorials, summer session, adult/continuing education programs, internships **Contact** Mr. Blake Faulkner, Vice President of Enrollment Management, National American University, PO Box 1780, Rapid City, SD 57709-1780. Telephone: 605-394-4827 or toll-free 800-843-8892. Fax: 605-394-4871. E-mail: apply@server1.natcol-rcy.edu. Web site: http://www.national.edu/.

NATIONAL AMERICAN UNIVERSITY–SIOUX FALLS BRANCH
SIOUX FALLS, SOUTH DAKOTA

General Proprietary, 4-year, coed **Contact** Ms. Joan Meyer, Director of Admissions, National American University-Sioux Falls Branch, 2801 South Kiwanis Avenue, Suite 100, Sioux Falls, SD 57105-4293. Telephone: 605-334-5430. E-mail: jmeyer@national.edu. Web site: http://server1.national.edu/.

NORTHERN STATE UNIVERSITY
ABERDEEN, SOUTH DAKOTA

General State-supported, comprehensive, coed **Entrance** Minimally difficult **Setting** 52-acre small town campus **Total enrollment** 2,646 **Student/faculty ratio** 18:1 **Application deadline** 9/1 **Freshmen** 100% were admitted **Housing** Yes **Expenses** Tuition $2535; Room & Board $2750 **Undergraduates** 60% women, 15% part-time, 25% 25 or older, 6% Native American, 0.1% Hispanic, 0.3% black, 1% Asian American or Pacific Islander **Most popular recent majors** Business administration; elementary education; sociology **Academic program** Average class size 30, English as a second language, advanced placement, accelerated degree program, self-designed majors, tutorials, honors program, summer session, adult/continuing education programs, internships **Contact** Mr. Gary Björdhal, Director of Admissions, Northern State University, 1200 South Jay Street, Aberdeen, SD 57401-7198. Telephone: 605-626-2544. Fax: 605-626-3022. E-mail: admissionl@wolf.northern.edu. Web site: http://www.northern.edu/.

OGLALA LAKOTA COLLEGE
KYLE, SOUTH DAKOTA

Contact Miss Billi K. Hornbeck, Registrar, Oglala Lakota College, PO Box 490, Kyle, SD 57752-0490. Telephone: 605-455-2321 ext. 236. Fax: 605-455-2787.

PRESENTATION COLLEGE
ABERDEEN, SOUTH DAKOTA

General Independent Roman Catholic, 4-year, coed **Entrance** Noncompetitive **Setting** 100-acre small town campus **Total enrollment** 461 **Student/faculty ratio** 13:1 **Application deadline** Rolling **Housing** Yes **Expenses** Tuition $6968; Room & Board $3100 **Undergraduates** 79% women, 26% part-time, 41% 25 or older, 12% Native American, 0.2% Hispanic, 2% black, 0% Asian American or Pacific Islander **Most popular recent majors** Nursing; social work **Academic program** Average class size 15, advanced placement, tutorials, summer session, internships **Contact** Ms. Brenda Schmitt, Director of Admissions and Financial Aid, Presentation College, 1500 North Main Street, Aberdeen, SD 57401-1299. Telephone: 605-225-8493 ext. 492 or toll-free 800-247-6499 ext. 24 (in-state), 800-437-6060 ext. 24 (out-of-state).

SINTE GLESKA UNIVERSITY
ROSEBUD, SOUTH DAKOTA

General Independent, comprehensive, coed **Entrance** Noncompetitive **Setting** 52-acre rural campus **Total enrollment** 766 **Application deadline** 8/20 **Freshmen** 100% were admitted **Housing** No **Expenses** Tuition $2244 **Undergraduates** 71% women, 54% part-time, 73% 25 or older, 80% Native American, 0% Hispanic, 0% black, 0% Asian American or Pacific Islander **Most popular recent majors** Education; business administration; human services **Academic program** Tutorials, honors program, summer session, adult/continuing education programs **Contact** Mr. Michael Benge, Director of Student Services, Sinte Gleska University, PO Box 490, Rosebud, SD 57570-0490. Telephone: 605-747-2263. Fax: 605-747-2098.

SOUTH DAKOTA SCHOOL OF MINES AND TECHNOLOGY
RAPID CITY, SOUTH DAKOTA

General State-supported, university, coed **Entrance** Moderately difficult **Setting** 120-acre suburban campus **Total enrollment** 2,210 **Student/faculty ratio** 16:1 **Application deadline** Rolling **Freshmen** 75% were admitted **Housing** Yes **Expenses** Tuition $3378; Room & Board $2910 **Most popular recent majors** Mechanical engineering; civil engineering; electrical/electronics engineering **Academic program** Advanced placement, self-designed majors, summer session **Contact** Mr. William Kuba, Director, Enrollment Management, South Dakota School of Mines and Technology, 501 East Saint Joseph, Rapid City, SD 57701-3995. Telephone: 605-394-2400 or toll-free 800-544-8162 ext. 2400. Fax: 605-394-2914. E-mail: undergraduate_admissions@silver.sdsmt.edu. Web site: http://www.sdsmt.edu/.

SOUTH DAKOTA STATE UNIVERSITY
BROOKINGS, SOUTH DAKOTA

General State-supported, university, coed **Entrance** Moderately difficult **Setting** 260-acre small town campus **Total enrollment** 8,867 **Student/faculty ratio** 16:1 **Application deadline** Rolling **Freshmen** 85% were admitted **Housing** Yes **Expenses** Tuition $2912; Room & Board $2482 **Undergraduates** 49% women, 9% part-time, 1% Native American, 0.2% Hispanic, 0.5% black, 1% Asian American or Pacific Islander **Most popular recent majors** Nursing; sociology; economics **Academic program** English as a second language, advanced placement, accelerated degree program, honors program, summer session, adult/continuing education programs, internships **Contact** Ms. Michelle Kuebler, Assistant Director of Admissions, South Dakota State University, PO Box 2201, Brookings, SD 57007. Telephone: 605-688-4121 or toll-free 800-952-3541. Fax: 605-688-6384. E-mail: sdsuadms@adm.sdstate.edu. Web site: http://www.sdstate.edu/.

UNIVERSITY OF SIOUX FALLS
SIOUX FALLS, SOUTH DAKOTA

General Independent American Baptist, comprehensive, coed **Entrance** Moderately difficult **Setting** 22-acre suburban campus **Total enrollment** 979 **Student/faculty ratio** 14:1 **Application deadline** Rolling **Freshmen** 96% were admitted **Housing** Yes **Expenses** Tuition $10,750; Room & Board $3450 **Undergraduates** 58% women, 24% part-time, 40% 25 or older, 1% Native American, 1% Hispanic, 1% black, 0.1% Asian American or Pacific Islander **Most popular recent majors** Business administration; education; behavioral sciences **Academic program** Advanced placement, accelerated degree program, self-designed majors, honors program, summer session, adult/continuing education programs, internships **Contact** Mr. Terry Okken, Director of Admissions, University of Sioux Falls, 1101 West 22nd Street, Sioux Falls, SD 57105-1699. Telephone: 605-331-6600 or toll-free 800-888-1047 (out-of-state). Fax: 605-331-6615. E-mail: terry.okken@thecoo.edu. Web site: http://www.thecoo.edu/.

UNIVERSITY OF SOUTH DAKOTA
VERMILLION, SOUTH DAKOTA

General State-supported, university, coed **Entrance** Moderately difficult **Setting** 216-acre small town campus **Total enrollment** 7,392 **Student/faculty ratio** 15:1 **Application deadline** Rolling **Freshmen** 99% were admitted **Housing** Yes **Expenses** Tuition $3012; Room & Board $2912 **Undergraduates** 57% women, 13% part-time, 17% 25 or older, 3% Native American, 1% Hispanic, 1% black, 1% Asian American or Pacific Islander **Most popular recent majors** Business administration; biology; psychology **Academic program** English as a second language, advanced placement, accelerated degree program, self-designed majors, tutorials, honors program, summer session, internships **Contact** Ms. Paula Tacke, Director of Admissions, University of South Dakota, 414 East Clark Street, Vermillion, SD 57069. Telephone: 605-677-5434 or toll-free 800-329-2453. Fax: 605-677-6753.

TENNESSEE

AMERICAN BAPTIST COLLEGE OF AMERICAN BAPTIST THEOLOGICAL SEMINARY
NASHVILLE, TENNESSEE

General Independent Baptist, 4-year, coed **Entrance** Noncompetitive **Setting** 52-acre urban campus **Student/faculty ratio** 10:1 **Application deadline** 7/1 **Freshmen** 66% were admitted **Housing** Yes **Expenses** Tuition $2530; Room only $752 **Undergraduates** 85% 25 or older **Academic program** English as a second language, accelerated degree program, self-designed majors, summer session, adult/continuing education programs **Contact** Ms. Theresa Chandler, Director of Enrollment Management, American Baptist College of American Baptist Theological Seminary, 1800 Baptist World Center Drive, Nashville, TN 37207. Telephone: 615-228-7877 ext. 35.

AMERICAN TECHNICAL INSTITUTE
MEMPHIS, TENNESSEE

Contact Dr. D. R. Brady, Dean of Admissions and Special Programs, American Technical Institute, PO Box 9, Memphis, TN 38137. Telephone: 901-382-5857. Fax: 901-385-7627. E-mail: deanati@netten.net.

AQUINAS COLLEGE
NASHVILLE, TENNESSEE

General Independent Roman Catholic, 4-year, coed **Entrance** Moderately difficult **Setting** 92-acre urban campus **Total enrollment** 385 **Student/faculty ratio** 15:1 **Application deadline** Rolling **Housing** No **Expenses** Tuition $7720 **Undergraduates** 77% women, 55% part-time, 41% 25 or older, 0.3% Native American, 1% Hispanic, 11% black, 3% Asian American or Pacific Islander **Most Popular Recent Major** Liberal arts and studies **Academic program** Advanced placement, summer session **Contact** Ms. Swapna Chinniah,

Director of Enrollment Management, Aquinas College, 4210 Harding Road, Nashville, TN 37205-2005. Telephone: 615-297-7545. Fax: 615-297-7970. Web site: http://www.aquinas-tn.edu/.

AUSTIN PEAY STATE UNIVERSITY
CLARKSVILLE, TENNESSEE

General State-supported, comprehensive, coed **Contact** Mr. Charles McCorkle, Director of Admissions, Austin Peay State University, PO Box 4548, Clarksville, TN 37044-0001. Telephone: 931-648-7661 or toll-free 800-844-2778 (out-of-state). Fax: 931-648-5994. E-mail: mccorklec@apsu.edu. Web site: http://www.apsu.edu/.

BELMONT UNIVERSITY
NASHVILLE, TENNESSEE

General Independent Baptist, comprehensive, coed **Entrance** Moderately difficult **Setting** 34-acre urban campus **Total enrollment** 2,986 **Student/faculty ratio** 14:1 **Application deadline** 8/1 **Freshmen** 79% were admitted **Housing** Yes **Expenses** Tuition $10,300; Room & Board $3890 **Undergraduates** 61% women, 17% part-time, 22% 25 or older, 0.4% Native American, 1% Hispanic, 3% black, 1% Asian American or Pacific Islander **Most popular recent majors** Music business management and merchandising; business administration; nursing **Academic program** Average class size 15, advanced placement, accelerated degree program, tutorials, honors program, summer session, adult/continuing education programs, internships **Contact** Dr. Kathryn Baugher, Dean of Admissions, Belmont University, 1900 Belmont Boulevard, Nashville, TN 37212-3757. Telephone: 615-460-6785. E-mail: buadmission@belmont.edu. Web site: http://www.belmont.edu/.

▶ **For more information, see page 394.**

BETHEL COLLEGE
MCKENZIE, TENNESSEE

General Independent Cumberland Presbyterian, comprehensive, coed **Entrance** Minimally difficult **Setting** 100-acre small town campus **Total enrollment** 573 **Student/faculty ratio** 14:1 **Application deadline** 8/10 **Freshmen** 65% were admitted **Housing** Yes **Expenses** Tuition $7240; Room & Board $3660 **Undergraduates** 53% women, 7% part-time, 34% 25 or older, 0.2% Native American, 0.2% Hispanic, 9% black, 0.2% Asian American or Pacific Islander **Most popular recent majors** Education; business administration **Academic program** Advanced placement, accelerated degree program, self-designed majors, tutorials, honors program, summer session, adult/continuing education programs, internships **Contact** Mr. Willie Mangum, Director of Recruitment and Retention, Bethel College, 325 Cherry Avenue, McKenzie, TN 38201. Telephone: 901-352-4032. Fax: 901-352-4069. Web site: http://www.bethel-college.edu/.

BRYAN COLLEGE
DAYTON, TENNESSEE

General Independent interdenominational, 4-year, coed **Entrance** Moderately difficult **Setting** 100-acre small town campus **Total enrollment** 500 **Student/faculty ratio** 14:1 **Application deadline** Rolling **Freshmen** 79% were admitted **Housing** Yes **Expenses** Tuition $10,400; Room & Board $3950 **Undergraduates** 56% women, 4% part-time, 4% 25 or older, 0% Native American, 1% Hispanic, 2% black, 1% Asian American or Pacific Islander **Most popular recent majors** Education; business administration; biology **Academic program** Average class size 30, advanced placement, tutorials, honors program, summer session, adult/continuing education programs, internships **Contact** Mr. Ronald D. Petitte, Registrar, Bryan College, PO Box 7000, Dayton, TN 37321-7000. Telephone: 423-775-7237 or toll-free 800-277-9522. Fax: 423-775-7330. E-mail: admiss@bryannet.bryan.edu. Web site: http://www.bryan.edu/.

CARSON-NEWMAN COLLEGE
JEFFERSON CITY, TENNESSEE

General Independent Southern Baptist, comprehensive, coed **Entrance** Moderately difficult **Setting** 90-acre small town campus **Total enrollment** 2,308 **Student/faculty ratio** 13:1 **Application deadline** 8/1 **Freshmen** 89% were admitted **Housing** Yes **Expenses** Tuition $10,610; Room & Board $3830 **Undergraduates** 59% women, 8% part-time, 20% 25 or older, 0.3% Native American, 1% Hispanic, 5% black, 0.3% Asian American or Pacific Islander **Most popular recent majors** Education; biology; business administration **Academic program** Average class size 17, English as a second language, advanced placement, accelerated degree program, self-designed majors, honors program, summer session, adult/continuing education programs, internships **Contact** Mrs. Sheryl M. Gray, Director of Undergraduate Admissions, Carson-Newman College, PO Box 72025, Jefferson City, TN 37760. Telephone: 423-471-3223 or toll-free 800-678-9061. Fax: 423-471-3502. E-mail: cnadmiss@cncacc.cn.edu. Web site: http://www.cn.edu/.

▶ **For more information, see page 405.**

CHRISTIAN BROTHERS UNIVERSITY
MEMPHIS, TENNESSEE

General Independent Roman Catholic, comprehensive, coed **Entrance** Moderately difficult **Set-**

Christian Brothers University *(continued)*

ting 70-acre urban campus **Total enrollment** 1,869 **Student/faculty ratio** 16:1 **Application deadline** 7/1 **Freshmen** 84% were admitted **Housing** Yes **Expenses** Tuition $11,930; Room & Board $3730 **Undergraduates** 7% 25 or older, 0.2% Native American, 2% Hispanic, 18% black, 3% Asian American or Pacific Islander **Most popular recent majors** Accounting; psychology; biology **Academic program** Average class size 25, advanced placement, accelerated degree program, tutorials, honors program, summer session, internships **Contact** Mr. Michael Daush, Dean of Admissions, Christian Brothers University, 650 East Parkway South, Memphis, TN 38104-5581. Telephone: 901-321-3205 or toll-free 800-288-7576. Fax: 901-321-3202. E-mail: admissions@bucs.cbu.edu. Web site: http://www.cbu.edu/.

CRICHTON COLLEGE
MEMPHIS, TENNESSEE

General Independent, 4-year, coed **Contact** Mr. Barry Mooney, Vice President of Enrollment Management, Crichton College, 6655 Winchester Road, PO Box 757830, Memphis, TN 38115. Telephone: 901-367-3888.

CUMBERLAND UNIVERSITY
LEBANON, TENNESSEE

General Independent, comprehensive, coed **Entrance** Moderately difficult **Setting** 44-acre small town campus **Total enrollment** 1,150 **Student/faculty ratio** 12:1 **Application deadline** Rolling **Freshmen** 93% were admitted **Housing** Yes **Expenses** Tuition $8190; Room & Board $3400 **Undergraduates** 52% women, 21% part-time, 40% 25 or older, 1% Native American, 1% Hispanic, 9% black, 0.4% Asian American or Pacific Islander **Most popular recent majors** Business administration; education; nursing **Academic program** Advanced placement, tutorials, honors program, summer session, adult/continuing education programs, internships **Contact** Ms. Stephanie Walker, Director of Admissions, Cumberland University, One Cumberland Square, Lebanon, TN 37087-3554. Telephone: 615-444-2562 ext. 1232 or toll-free 800-467-0562 (out-of-state). Fax: 615-444-2569. E-mail: admissions@cumberland.edu. Web site: http://www.cumberland.edu/.

DAVID LIPSCOMB UNIVERSITY
NASHVILLE, TENNESSEE

General Independent, comprehensive, coed, affiliated with Church of Christ **Entrance** Moderately difficult **Setting** 65-acre urban campus **Total enrollment** 2,546 **Student/faculty ratio** 18:1 **Application deadline** Rolling **Housing** Yes **Expenses** Tuition $8470; Room & Board $3910 **Undergraduates** 55% women, 13% part-time, 12% 25 or older, 0.2% Native American, 1% Hispanic, 4% black, 1% Asian American or Pacific Islander **Most popular recent majors** Business administration; education; history **Academic program** Average class size 30, advanced placement, accelerated degree program, self-designed majors, tutorials, honors program, summer session, adult/continuing education programs, internships **Contact** Dr. Jim White, Associate Vice President for Enrollment Management, David Lipscomb University, 3901 Granny White Pike, Nashville, TN 37204-3951. Telephone: 615-269-1000 ext. 1776 or toll-free 800-333-4358. Fax: 615-269-1804. E-mail: admissions@dlu.edu. Web site: http://www.dlu.edu/.

EAST TENNESSEE STATE UNIVERSITY
JOHNSON CITY, TENNESSEE

General State-supported, university, coed **Entrance** Moderately difficult **Setting** 366-acre small town campus **Total enrollment** 11,596 **Student/faculty ratio** 19:1 **Application deadline** Rolling **Freshmen** 83% were admitted **Housing** Yes **Expenses** Tuition $2100; Room & Board $2520 **Undergraduates** 58% women, 18% part-time, 31% 25 or older, 0.5% Native American, 1% Hispanic, 5% black, 1% Asian American or Pacific Islander **Most popular recent majors** Nursing; criminal justice/law enforcement administration; engineering technology **Academic program** Advanced placement, accelerated degree program, tutorials, honors program, summer session, adult/continuing education programs **Contact** Mr. Mike Pitts, Director of Admissions, East Tennessee State University, PO Box 70731, ETSU, Johnson City, TN 37614-0734. Telephone: 423-439-6861 or toll-free 800-462-3878. Fax: 423-439-7156. E-mail: pitts@etsuvax.etsu-tn.edu. Web site: http://www.etsu.edu/.

FISK UNIVERSITY
NASHVILLE, TENNESSEE

General Independent, comprehensive, coed, affiliated with United Church of Christ **Entrance** Moderately difficult **Setting** 40-acre urban campus **Total enrollment** 765 **Student/faculty ratio** 14:1 **Application deadline** 6/15 **Freshmen** 76% were admitted **Housing** Yes **Expenses** Tuition $7750; Room & Board $4304 **Undergraduates** 71% women, 3% part-time, 5% 25 or older, 100% black **Most popular recent majors** Business administration; chemistry; psychology **Academic program** Average class size 26, advanced placement, self-designed majors, honors program, internships **Contact** Mr. Anthony E. Jones, Director of Admissions, Fisk University, 1000 17th Avenue North, Nashville, TN 37208-3051. Telephone: 615-329-8665 or toll-free 800-443-FISK. E-mail: lcampbel@dubois.fisk.edu. Web site: http://www.fisk.edu/.

▶ **For more information, see page 434.**

FREED-HARDEMAN UNIVERSITY
HENDERSON, TENNESSEE

General Independent, comprehensive, coed, affiliated with Church of Christ **Entrance** Moderately difficult **Setting** 96-acre rural campus **Total enrollment** 1,600 **Student/faculty ratio** 20:1 **Application deadline** Rolling **Freshmen** 64% were admitted **Housing** Yes **Expenses** Tuition $7524; Room & Board $3760 **Undergraduates** 55% women, 5% part-time, 11% 25 or older, 0.2% Native American, 0.3% Hispanic, 4% black, 0.1% Asian American or Pacific Islander **Most popular recent majors** Business administration; education; biblical studies **Academic program** Advanced placement, accelerated degree program, self-designed majors, honors program, summer session, adult/continuing education programs, internships **Contact** Ms. Kimberlie Helton, Director of Admissions, Freed-Hardeman University, 158 East Main Street, Henderson, TN 38340-2399. Telephone: 901-989-6651 or toll-free 800-FHU-FHU1. Fax: 901-989-6047. E-mail: admissions@fhu.edu. Web site: http://www.fhu.edu/.

FREE WILL BAPTIST BIBLE COLLEGE
NASHVILLE, TENNESSEE

General Independent Free Will Baptist, 4-year, coed **Entrance** Noncompetitive **Setting** 10-acre suburban campus **Total enrollment** 342 **Student/faculty ratio** 10:1 **Application deadline** Rolling **Housing** Yes **Expenses** Tuition $5374; Room & Board $3518 **Undergraduates** 44% women, 15% part-time, 7% 25 or older, 1% Native American, 0.3% Hispanic, 0.3% black, 1% Asian American or Pacific Islander **Most popular recent majors** Business administration; education; biblical studies **Academic program** English as a second language, advanced placement, self-designed majors, summer session, internships **Contact** Dr. Charles E. Hampton, Registrar/Chairman of Department of General Education, Free Will Baptist Bible College, 3606 West End Avenue, Nashville, TN 37205-2498. Telephone: 615-383-1340 ext. 5233 or toll-free 800-763-9222. Fax: 615-269-6028.

JOHNSON BIBLE COLLEGE
KNOXVILLE, TENNESSEE

General Independent, comprehensive, coed, affiliated with Christian Churches and Churches of Christ **Entrance** Minimally difficult **Setting** 75-acre rural campus **Total enrollment** 514 **Student/faculty ratio** 16:1 **Application deadline** 8/1 **Freshmen** 77% were admitted **Housing** Yes **Expenses** Tuition $5100; Room & Board $3270 **Undergraduates** 46% women, 7% part-time, 23% 25 or older, 0.5% Native American, 0.5% Hispanic, 1% black, 0% Asian American or Pacific Islander **Academic program** Average class size 45, English as a second language, advanced placement, tutorials, summer session, adult/continuing education programs, internships **Contact** Mr. Larry Green, Director of Admissions, Johnson Bible College, 7900 Johnson Drive, Knoxville, TN 37998-0001. Telephone: 423-573-4517 ext. 2346 or toll-free 800-827-2122 (in-state). Fax: 423-579-2336. E-mail: lgreen@jbc.edu. Web site: http://www.jbc.edu/.

KING COLLEGE
BRISTOL, TENNESSEE

General Independent, 4-year, coed, affiliated with Presbyterian Church (U.S.A.) **Entrance** Moderately difficult **Setting** 135-acre suburban campus **Total enrollment** 516 **Student/faculty ratio** 15:1 **Application deadline** Rolling **Freshmen** 74% were admitted **Housing** Yes **Expenses** Tuition $10,550; Room & Board $3444 **Undergraduates** 56% women, 6% part-time, 6% 25 or older, 0% Native American, 0.4% Hispanic, 2% black, 1% Asian American or Pacific Islander **Most popular recent majors** Behavioral sciences; economics; psychology **Academic program** Average class size 25, English as a second language, advanced placement, summer session, internships **Contact** Ms. Pamela S. Hall, Director of Admissions, King College, 1350 King College Road, Bristol, TN 37620-2699. Telephone: 423-652-4861 or toll-free 800-362-0014. Fax: 423-968-4456. E-mail: admissions@king.edu. Web site: http://www.king.edu/.

KNOXVILLE COLLEGE
KNOXVILLE, TENNESSEE

General Independent Presbyterian, 4-year, coed **Contact** Ms. Carol Scott, Director of Admissions, Knoxville College, 901 College Street, NW, Knoxville, TN 37921-4799. Telephone: 423-524-6525 or toll-free 800-743-5669. Fax: 423-524-6686. Web site: http://falcon.nest.kxcol.edu/.

LAMBUTH UNIVERSITY
JACKSON, TENNESSEE

General Independent United Methodist, 4-year, coed **Entrance** Moderately difficult **Setting** 50-acre urban campus **Total enrollment** 1,012 **Student/faculty ratio** 19:1 **Application deadline** Rolling **Freshmen** 59% were admitted **Housing** Yes **Expenses** Tuition $6194; Room & Board $3950 **Undergraduates** 53% women, 8% part-time, 10% 25 or older, 0.2% Native American, 1%

Lambuth University *(continued)*

Hispanic, 15% black, 0.1% Asian American or Pacific Islander **Most popular recent majors** Business administration; education; mass communications **Academic program** Average class size 25, English as a second language, advanced placement, accelerated degree program, self-designed majors, tutorials, summer session, adult/continuing education programs, internships **Contact** Mrs. Nancy M. Callis, Director of Admissions, Lambuth University, 705 Lambuth Boulevard, Jackson, TN 38301. Telephone: 901-425-3223 or toll-free 800-526-2884. Fax: 901-988-4600. E-mail: admit@lambuth.edu. Web site: http://www.lambuth.edu/.

LANE COLLEGE
JACKSON, TENNESSEE

General Independent, 4-year, coed, affiliated with Christian Methodist Episcopal Church **Entrance** Minimally difficult **Setting** 25-acre suburban campus **Total enrollment** 673 **Student/faculty ratio** 15:1 **Application deadline** Rolling **Freshmen** 83% were admitted **Housing** Yes **Expenses** Tuition $5850; Room & Board $3600 **Undergraduates** 48% women, 3% part-time, 7% 25 or older, 99% black **Most popular recent majors** Business administration; sociology; interdisciplinary studies **Academic program** Advanced placement, tutorials, honors program, summer session, internships **Contact** Ms. E. R. Maddox, Director of Admsisions, Lane College, 545 Lane Avenue, Jackson, TN 38301-4598. Telephone: 901-426-7532 or toll-free 800-960-7533. Fax: 901-426-7559. Web site: http://lc.lane-college.edu/.

LEE UNIVERSITY
CLEVELAND, TENNESSEE

General Independent, comprehensive, coed, affiliated with Church of God **Entrance** Minimally difficult **Setting** 45-acre small town campus **Total enrollment** 2,870 **Student/faculty ratio** 22:1 **Application deadline** Rolling **Freshmen** 63% were admitted **Housing** Yes **Expenses** Tuition $5638; Room & Board $3680 **Undergraduates** 56% women, 7% part-time, 16% 25 or older, 0.1% Native American, 2% Hispanic, 1% black, 0.3% Asian American or Pacific Islander **Most popular recent majors** Individual/family development; biology; psychology **Academic program** English as a second language, advanced placement, honors program, summer session, adult/continuing education programs, internships **Contact** Admissions Coordinator, Lee University, PO Box 3450, Cleveland, TN 37320-3450. Telephone: 423-614-8500 or toll-free 800-LEE-9930. Fax: 423-614-8533. E-mail: admissions@leeuniversity.edu. Web site: http://www.leeuniversity.edu/.

LEMOYNE-OWEN COLLEGE
MEMPHIS, TENNESSEE

General Independent, comprehensive, coed, affiliated with United Church of Christ **Contact** Mr. Alex Dancy, Assistant Director Admissions/Recruitment, LeMoyne-Owen College, 807 Walker Avenue, Memphis, TN 38126-6595. Telephone: 901-942-7302 ext. 214 or toll-free 800-737-7778 (in-state). Fax: 901-942-6272. E-mail: admissions@locness.lemoyne-owen.edu. Web site: http://www.mecca.org/LOC/page/LOC.html.

LINCOLN MEMORIAL UNIVERSITY
HARROGATE, TENNESSEE

General Independent, comprehensive, coed **Entrance** Moderately difficult **Setting** 1,000-acre small town campus **Total enrollment** 1,811 **Student/faculty ratio** 13:1 **Application deadline** Rolling **Freshmen** 69% were admitted **Housing** Yes **Expenses** Tuition $8000; Room & Board $3500 **Undergraduates** 70% women, 20% part-time, 22% 25 or older, 0.1% Native American, 0% Hispanic, 3% black, 1% Asian American or Pacific Islander **Most Popular Recent Major** Elementary education **Academic program** English as a second language, advanced placement, accelerated degree program, tutorials, honors program, summer session, adult/continuing education programs **Contact** Mr. Conrad Daniels, Dean of Admissions and Recruitment, Lincoln Memorial University, Cumberland Gap Parkway, Harrogate, TN 37752-1901. Telephone: 423-869-6280 or toll-free 800-325-0900 (in-state), 800-325-2506 (out-of-state). Web site: http://www.lmunet.edu/.

LIPSCOMB UNIVERSITY
See David Lipscomb University

MARTIN METHODIST COLLEGE
PULASKI, TENNESSEE

General Independent United Methodist, 4-year, coed **Entrance** Minimally difficult **Setting** 6-acre small town campus **Total enrollment** 551 **Student/faculty ratio** 13:1 **Application deadline** 8/30 **Freshmen** 92% were admitted **Housing** Yes **Expenses** Tuition $6900; Room & Board $3050 **Undergraduates** 60% women, 18% part-time, 33% 25 or older, 0.2% Native American, 1% Hispanic, 12% black, 0.2% Asian American or Pacific Islander **Most popular recent majors** Business administration; early childhood education; physical education **Academic program** English as a second language, advanced placement, self-designed majors, summer session, adult/continuing education programs **Contact** Mr. Robby Shelton, Director of Admissions and Enrollment Management, Martin Methodist College, 433 West

Madison Street, Pulaski, TN 38478-2716. Telephone: 931-363-9807 or toll-free 800-467-1273. Fax: 931-363-9818.

MARYVILLE COLLEGE
MARYVILLE, TENNESSEE

General Independent Presbyterian, 4-year, coed **Entrance** Moderately difficult **Setting** 350-acre suburban campus **Total enrollment** 955 **Student/faculty ratio** 13:1 **Application deadline** 3/1 **Freshmen** 82% were admitted **Housing** Yes **Expenses** Tuition $14,425; Room & Board $4720 **Undergraduates** 51% women, 6% part-time, 11% 25 or older, 0.4% Native American, 1% Hispanic, 5% black, 1% Asian American or Pacific Islander **Most popular recent majors** Business administration; psychology; biology **Academic program** Average class size 21, English as a second language, advanced placement, self-designed majors, tutorials, honors program, summer session, adult/continuing education programs, internships **Contact** Ms. Linda L. Moore, Administrative Assistant of Admissions, Maryville College, 502 East Lamar Alexander Parkway, Maryville, TN 37804-5907. Telephone: 423-981-8092 or toll-free 800-597-2687. Fax: 423-983-0581. E-mail: admissions@maryvillecollege.edu. Web site: http://www.maryvillecollege.edu/.

MEMPHIS COLLEGE OF ART
MEMPHIS, TENNESSEE

General Independent, comprehensive, coed **Entrance** Moderately difficult **Setting** 200-acre urban campus **Total enrollment** 260 **Application deadline** Rolling **Freshmen** 80% were admitted **Housing** Yes **Expenses** Tuition $11,500; Room only $3000 **Undergraduates** 19% 25 or older, 0% Native American, 0.4% Hispanic, 20% black, 2% Asian American or Pacific Islander **Academic program** Average class size 25, advanced placement, tutorials, summer session, adult/continuing education programs, internships **Contact** Ms. Susan S. Miller, Director of Admissions, Memphis College of Art, Overton Park, 1930 Poplar Avenue, Memphis, TN 38104-2764. Telephone: 901-726-4085 ext. 30 or toll-free 800-727-1088. Fax: 901-726-9371. E-mail: info@mca.edu. Web site: http://www.mca.edu/.

MIDDLE TENNESSEE STATE UNIVERSITY
MURFREESBORO, TENNESSEE

General State-supported, university, coed **Entrance** Moderately difficult **Setting** 500-acre urban campus **Total enrollment** 18,366 **Student/faculty ratio** 19:1 **Application deadline** Rolling **Freshmen** 74% were admitted **Housing** Yes **Expenses** Tuition $2196; Room & Board $3343 **Undergraduates** 55% women, 18% part-time, 28% 25 or older, 0.5% Native American, 1% Hispanic, 11% black, 1% Asian American or Pacific Islander **Most popular recent majors** Interdisciplinary studies; mass communications; aviation/airway science **Academic program** English as a second language, advanced placement, accelerated degree program, self-designed majors, tutorials, honors program, summer session, adult/continuing education programs, internships **Contact** Ms. Lynn Palmer, Director of Admissions, Middle Tennessee State University, Murfreesboro, TN 37132. Telephone: 615-898-2111. E-mail: admissions@mtsu.edu. Web site: http://www.mtsu.edu/.

MILLIGAN COLLEGE
MILLIGAN COLLEGE, TENNESSEE

General Independent Christian, comprehensive, coed **Entrance** Moderately difficult **Setting** 145-acre suburban campus **Total enrollment** 911 **Student/faculty ratio** 14:1 **Application deadline** Rolling **Freshmen** 81% were admitted **Housing** Yes **Expenses** Tuition $10,260; Room & Board $3670 **Undergraduates** 62% women, 3% part-time, 20% 25 or older, 0.4% Native American, 0.5% Hispanic, 1% black, 0.1% Asian American or Pacific Islander **Most popular recent majors** Education; mass communications; biblical studies **Academic program** English as a second language, advanced placement, accelerated degree program, tutorials, summer session, adult/continuing education programs, internships **Contact** Mr. Michael A. Johnson, Vice President for Enrollment Management, Milligan College, PO Box 210, Milligan College, TN 37682. Telephone: 423-461-8730 or toll-free 800-262-8337 (in-state). Fax: 423-461-8960. Web site: http://www.milligan.edu/.

O'MORE COLLEGE OF DESIGN
FRANKLIN, TENNESSEE

General Independent, 4-year, coed **Entrance** Minimally difficult **Setting** 6-acre small town campus **Total enrollment** 149 **Application deadline** 8/1 **Housing** No **Expenses** Tuition $7955 **Undergraduates** 86% women, 23% part-time, 29% 25 or older, 0% Native American, 3% Hispanic, 5% black, 2% Asian American or Pacific Islander **Most popular recent majors** Interior design; graphic design/commercial art/illustration **Academic program** Summer session, adult/continuing education programs, internships **Contact** Ms. Janice K. Miller, Vice President for Admissions and Records, O'More College of Design, 423 South Margin Street, Franklin, TN 37064-2816. Telephone: 615-794-4254. Fax: 615-790-1662. Web site: http://www.omorecollege.edu/.

RHODES COLLEGE
MEMPHIS, TENNESSEE

General Independent Presbyterian, comprehensive, coed **Entrance** Very difficult **Setting** 100-acre suburban campus **Total enrollment** 1,432 **Student/faculty ratio** 12:1 **Application deadline** 2/1 **Freshmen** 75% were admitted **Housing** Yes **Expenses** Tuition $17,518; Room & Board $5110 **Undergraduates** 55% women, 1% part-time, 2% 25 or older, 0.1% Native American, 1% Hispanic, 3% black, 3% Asian American or Pacific Islander **Most popular recent majors** Biology; English; business administration **Academic program** Average class size 18, advanced placement, accelerated degree program, self-designed majors, tutorials, summer session, internships **Contact** Mr. David J. Wottle, Dean of Admissions and Financial Aid, Rhodes College, 2000 North Parkway, Memphis, TN 38112-1690. Telephone: 901-843-3700 or toll-free 800-844-5969 (out-of-state). Fax: 901-843-3719. E-mail: adminfo@rhodes.edu. Web site: http://www.rhodes.edu/.

SOUTHERN ADVENTIST UNIVERSITY
COLLEGEDALE, TENNESSEE

General Independent Seventh-day Adventist, comprehensive, coed **Entrance** Moderately difficult **Setting** 1,000-acre small town campus **Total enrollment** 1,695 **Student/faculty ratio** 14:1 **Application deadline** Rolling **Freshmen** 90% were admitted **Housing** Yes **Expenses** Tuition $9736; Room & Board $3628 **Undergraduates** 57% women, 18% part-time, 15% 25 or older, 1% Native American, 8% Hispanic, 4% black, 4% Asian American or Pacific Islander **Most popular recent majors** Nursing; business administration; biology **Academic program** Average class size 60, English as a second language, advanced placement, accelerated degree program, tutorials, honors program, summer session, internships **Contact** Dr. Ronald M. Barrow, Vice President for Enrollment Services, Southern Adventist University, PO Box 370, Collegedale, TN 37315-0370. Telephone: 423-238-2843 or toll-free 800-768-8437. Fax: 423-238-3005. E-mail: admissions@southern.edu. Web site: http://www.southern.edu/.

TENNESSEE STATE UNIVERSITY
NASHVILLE, TENNESSEE

General State-supported, comprehensive, coed **Entrance** Minimally difficult **Setting** 450-acre urban campus **Total enrollment** 8,625 **Application deadline** 8/1 **Freshmen** 50% were admitted **Housing** Yes **Expenses** Tuition $3069; Room & Board $3060 **Undergraduates** 63% women, 15% part-time, 39% 25 or older, 0.1% Native American, 0.4% Hispanic, 78% black, 1% Asian American or Pacific Islander **Most popular recent majors** Nursing; elementary education; business administration **Academic program** Average class size 35, accelerated degree program, honors program, summer session, adult/continuing education programs, internships **Contact** Ms. Vernella Smith, Admissions Coordinator, Tennessee State University, 3500 John A Merritt Boulevard, Nashville, TN 37209-1561. Telephone: 615-963-5104. Fax: 615-963-5108. E-mail: jcade@picard.tnstate.edu. Web site: http://www.tnstate.edu/.

TENNESSEE TECHNOLOGICAL UNIVERSITY
COOKEVILLE, TENNESSEE

General State-supported, university, coed **Entrance** Moderately difficult **Setting** 235-acre small town campus **Total enrollment** 8,263 **Student/faculty ratio** 17:1 **Application deadline** Rolling **Freshmen** 57% were admitted **Housing** Yes **Expenses** Tuition $2116; Room & Board $3180 **Undergraduates** 47% women, 13% part-time, 30% 25 or older, 0.2% Native American, 1% Hispanic, 3% black, 2% Asian American or Pacific Islander **Most popular recent majors** Mechanical engineering; business administration; elementary education **Academic program** English as a second language, advanced placement, accelerated degree program, honors program, summer session, adult/continuing education programs **Contact** Mr. Jim Rose, Associate Vice President for Enrollment and Records, Tennessee Technological University, TTU Box 5006, Cookeville, TN 38505. Telephone: 931-372-3888 or toll-free 800-255-8881 (in-state). Fax: 931-372-6250. E-mail: u_admissions@tntech.edu. Web site: http://www.tntech.edu/.

TENNESSEE TEMPLE UNIVERSITY
CHATTANOOGA, TENNESSEE

General Independent Baptist, comprehensive, coed **Entrance** Minimally difficult **Setting** 55-acre urban campus **Total enrollment** 641 **Student/faculty ratio** 11:1 **Application deadline** 8/20 **Freshmen** 100% were admitted **Housing** Yes **Expenses** Tuition $6750; Room & Board $4750 **Undergraduates** 47% women, 3% part-time, 25% 25 or older, 0.2% Native American, 1% Hispanic, 2% black, 1% Asian American or Pacific Islander **Academic program** Advanced placement, tutorials, honors program, summer session, adult/continuing education programs, internships **Contact** Mr. David Dunn, Admission Director, Tennessee Temple University, 1815 Union Avenue, Chattanooga, TN 37404-3587. Telephone: 423-493-4100 or toll-free 800-553-4050. Fax: 423-493-4497. E-mail: ttuinfo@tntemple.edu. Web site: http://www.tntemple.edu/.

TENNESSEE WESLEYAN COLLEGE
ATHENS, TENNESSEE

General Independent United Methodist, 4-year, coed **Entrance** Moderately difficult **Setting** 40-acre small town campus **Total enrollment** 756 **Student/faculty ratio** 16:1 **Application deadline** Rolling **Freshmen** 81% were admitted **Housing** Yes **Expenses** Tuition $7050; Room & Board $4000 **Undergraduates** 67% women, 23% part-time, 39% 25 or older, 0.3% Native American, 0.1% Hispanic, 4% black, 3% Asian American or Pacific Islander **Most popular recent majors** Business administration; education; interdisciplinary studies **Academic program** English as a second language, advanced placement, accelerated degree program, self-designed majors, honors program, summer session, adult/continuing education programs, internships **Contact** Mr. John Head, Director of Admission, Tennessee Wesleyan College, PO Box 40, Athens, TN 37371-0040. Telephone: 423-745-7504 or toll-free 800-PICK-TWC. Fax: 423-744-9968. Web site: http://www.tnwc.edu/.

TREVECCA NAZARENE UNIVERSITY
NASHVILLE, TENNESSEE

General Independent Nazarene, comprehensive, coed **Entrance** Noncompetitive **Setting** 65-acre urban campus **Total enrollment** 1,516 **Student/faculty ratio** 13:1 **Application deadline** Rolling **Freshmen** 100% were admitted **Housing** Yes **Expenses** Tuition $9090; Room & Board $4038 **Undergraduates** 55% women, 19% part-time, 35% 25 or older, 0.2% Native American, 2% Hispanic, 8% black, 1% Asian American or Pacific Islander **Most popular recent majors** Business administration; early childhood education; religious studies **Academic program** Advanced placement, accelerated degree program, summer session, adult/continuing education programs, internships **Contact** Ms. Patricia D. Cook, Director of Admissions, Trevecca Nazarene University, 333 Murfreesboro Road, Nashville, TN 37210-2834. Telephone: 615-248-1320 or toll-free 888-210-4862. Fax: 615-248-7728. E-mail: admissions_und@trevecca.edu. Web site: http://www.trevecca.edu/.

TUSCULUM COLLEGE
GREENEVILLE, TENNESSEE

General Independent Presbyterian, comprehensive, coed **Entrance** Moderately difficult **Setting** 140-acre small town campus **Total enrollment** 1,526 **Student/faculty ratio** 13:1 **Application deadline** Rolling **Freshmen** 76% were admitted **Housing** Yes **Expenses** Tuition $11,800; Room & Board $3900 **Undergraduates** 54% women, 3% part-time, 0.3% Native American, 1% Hispanic, 7% black, 0.4% Asian American or Pacific Islander **Most popular recent majors** Business administration; elementary education; psychology **Academic program** Average class size 14, English as a second language, advanced placement, self-designed majors, tutorials, summer session, adult/continuing education programs, internships **Contact** Mr. Dan Hall, Director of Admissions, Tusculum College, PO Box 5047, Greeneville, TN 37743-9997. Telephone: 423-636-7312 or toll-free 800-729-0256. Fax: 423-638-7166 ext. 312. E-mail: admissions@tusculum.edu. Web site: http://www.tusculum.edu/.

UNION UNIVERSITY
JACKSON, TENNESSEE

General Independent Southern Baptist, comprehensive, coed **Entrance** Moderately difficult **Setting** 290-acre small town campus **Total enrollment** 1,953 **Student/faculty ratio** 13:1 **Application deadline** 2/1 **Freshmen** 85% were admitted **Housing** Yes **Expenses** Tuition $8180; Room & Board $3005 **Undergraduates** 65% women, 14% part-time, 0.2% Native American, 1% Hispanic, 5% black, 1% Asian American or Pacific Islander **Most popular recent majors** Nursing; education; business administration **Academic program** Average class size 23, English as a second language, advanced placement, accelerated degree program, tutorials, honors program, summer session, adult/continuing education programs, internships **Contact** Mr. Carroll Griffin, Director of Admissions, Union University, 1050 Union University Drive, Jackson, TN 38305-3697. Telephone: 901-661-5000 or toll-free 800-33-UNION. Fax: 901-661-5187. E-mail: info@buster.uu.edu. Web site: http://www.uu.edu/.

THE UNIVERSITY OF MEMPHIS
MEMPHIS, TENNESSEE

General State-supported, university, coed **Entrance** Moderately difficult **Setting** 1,100-acre urban campus **Total enrollment** 19,851 **Student/faculty ratio** 20:1 **Application deadline** 8/1 **Freshmen** 55% were admitted **Housing** Yes **Expenses** Tuition $2412; Room & Board $3500 **Undergraduates** 58% women, 27% part-time, 31% 25 or older, 0.3% Native American, 1% Hispanic, 29% black, 2% Asian American or Pacific Islander **Most popular recent majors** Education; nursing; accounting **Academic program** Average class size 25, English as a second language, advanced placement, accelerated degree program, self-designed majors, honors program, summer session, adult/continuing education programs, internships **Contact** Mr. David Wallace, Director of Admissions, The University of Memphis, Memphis, TN 38152. Telephone: 901-678-2101 or toll-free

The University of Memphis *(continued)*

800-678-9027 (in-state). Fax: 901-678-3053. E-mail: dwallace@memphis.edu. Web site: http://www.memphis.edu/.

UNIVERSITY OF TENNESSEE AT CHATTANOOGA

CHATTANOOGA, TENNESSEE

General State-supported, comprehensive, coed **Entrance** Moderately difficult **Setting** 101-acre urban campus **Total enrollment** 8,528 **Student/faculty ratio** 17:1 **Application deadline** Rolling **Freshmen** 55% were admitted **Housing** Yes **Expenses** Tuition $2200; Room only $1900 **Undergraduates** 26% 25 or older, 1% Native American, 1% Hispanic, 15% black, 2% Asian American or Pacific Islander **Most popular recent majors** Business administration; secondary education; nursing **Academic program** Average class size 23, English as a second language, advanced placement, accelerated degree program, honors program, summer session, adult/continuing education programs, internships **Contact** Ms. Patsy Reynolds, Director of Admissions, University of Tennessee at Chattanooga, 615 McCallie Avenue, Chattanooga, TN 37403-2598. Telephone: 423-755-4662 or toll-free 800-UTC-6627 (in-state). Fax: 423-755-4157. E-mail: steve-king@utc.edu. Web site: http://www.utc.edu/.

THE UNIVERSITY OF TENNESSEE AT MARTIN

MARTIN, TENNESSEE

General State-supported, comprehensive, coed **Entrance** Moderately difficult **Setting** 250-acre small town campus **Total enrollment** 5,997 **Student/faculty ratio** 14:1 **Application deadline** Rolling **Freshmen** 97% were admitted **Housing** Yes **Expenses** Tuition $2240; Room & Board $3104 **Undergraduates** 57% women, 9% part-time, 7% 25 or older, 0.3% Native American, 0.5% Hispanic, 14% black, 1% Asian American or Pacific Islander **Most popular recent majors** Elementary education; biology; criminal justice/law enforcement administration **Academic program** English as a second language, advanced placement, accelerated degree program, self-designed majors, tutorials, honors program, summer session, adult/continuing education programs, internships **Contact** Ms. Judy Rayburn, Director of Admission, The University of Tennessee at Martin, Post Office Station, Martin, TN 38238-1000. Telephone: 901-587-7032 or toll-free 800-829-8861. Fax: 901-587-7029. E-mail: jrayburn@utm.edu. Web site: http://www.utm.edu/.

UNIVERSITY OF TENNESSEE, KNOXVILLE

KNOXVILLE, TENNESSEE

General State-supported, university, coed **Entrance** Moderately difficult **Setting** 533-acre urban campus **Total enrollment** 25,397 **Student/faculty ratio** 17:1 **Application deadline** 6/1 **Freshmen** 76% were admitted **Housing** Yes **Expenses** Tuition $2576; Room & Board $3802 **Undergraduates** 50% women, 11% part-time, 17% 25 or older, 0.3% Native American, 1% Hispanic, 5% black, 2% Asian American or Pacific Islander **Most popular recent majors** Psychology; English; accounting **Academic program** English as a second language, advanced placement, accelerated degree program, self-designed majors, tutorials, honors program, summer session, adult/continuing education programs, internships **Contact** Dr. Gordon E. Stanley, Director of Admissions, University of Tennessee, Knoxville, Knoxville, TN 37996. Telephone: 423-974-2184 or toll-free 800-221-8657 (in-state). Web site: http://www.utk.edu/.

UNIVERSITY OF TENNESSEE, MEMPHIS

MEMPHIS, TENNESSEE

General State-supported, upper-level, coed **Contact** Ms. June Peoples, Director of Admissions, University of Tennessee, Memphis, 800 Madison Avenue, Memphis, TN 38163-0002. Telephone: 901-448-5560. Fax: 901-448-7585. E-mail: jpeoples@.utmem.edu.

UNIVERSITY OF THE SOUTH

SEWANEE, TENNESSEE

General Independent Episcopal, comprehensive, coed **Entrance** Very difficult **Setting** 10,000-acre small town campus **Total enrollment** 1,355 **Student/faculty ratio** 10:1 **Application deadline** 2/1 **Freshmen** 64% were admitted **Housing** Yes **Expenses** Tuition $17,730; Room & Board $4660 **Undergraduates** 52% women, 0% 25 or older, 1% Hispanic, 3% black, 1% Asian American or Pacific Islander **Most popular recent majors** English; history; psychology **Academic program** Advanced placement, accelerated degree program, self-designed majors, tutorials, honors program, summer session, internships **Contact** Mr. Robert M. Hedrick, Director of Admission, University of the South, 735 University Avenue, Sewanee, TN 37383-1000. Telephone: 931-598-1238 or toll-free 800-522-2234. Fax: 931-598-1667. E-mail: admiss@sewanee.edu. Web site: http://www.sewanee.edu/.

VANDERBILT UNIVERSITY

NASHVILLE, TENNESSEE

General Independent, university, coed **Entrance** Very difficult **Setting** 330-acre urban campus **Total enrollment** 10,210 **Student/faculty ratio** 8:1 **Application deadline** 1/15 **Freshmen** 58% were admitted **Housing** Yes **Expenses** Tuition $21,478; Room & Board $7430 **Undergraduates** 50% women, 1% part-time, 1% 25 or older, 0.2% Native American, 3% Hispanic, 4% black, 5% Asian American or Pacific Islander **Most popular recent majors** Psychology; individual/family development; economics **Academic program** Average class size 24, English as a second language, advanced placement, accelerated degree program, self-designed majors, tutorials, honors program, summer session, internships **Contact** Mr. Bill Shain, Dean of Undergraduate Admissions, Vanderbilt University, 2305 West End Avenue, Nashville, TN 37203-1727. Telephone: 615-322-2561. Fax: 615-343-7765. E-mail: admissions@vanderbilt.edu. Web site: http://www.vanderbilt.edu/.

TEXAS

ABILENE CHRISTIAN UNIVERSITY

ABILENE, TEXAS

General Independent, comprehensive, coed, affiliated with Church of Christ **Entrance** Moderately difficult **Setting** 208-acre urban campus **Total enrollment** 4,507 **Student/faculty ratio** 18:1 **Application deadline** Rolling **Freshmen** 89% were admitted **Housing** Yes **Expenses** Tuition $9180; Room & Board $3810 **Undergraduates** 54% women, 8% part-time, 10% 25 or older, 1% Native American, 5% Hispanic, 5% black, 1% Asian American or Pacific Islander **Most popular recent majors** Biology; elementary education; accounting **Academic program** Average class size 30, English as a second language, advanced placement, accelerated degree program, self-designed majors, tutorials, honors program, summer session, adult/continuing education programs, internships **Contact** Mr. Tim Johnston, Director of Admissions, Abilene Christian University, ACU Box 29000, Abilene, TX 79699-9000. Telephone: 915-674-2650 or toll-free 800-888-6228. E-mail: info@admissions.acu.edu. Web site: http://www.acu.edu/.

AMBER UNIVERSITY

GARLAND, TEXAS

General Independent nondenominational, upper-level, coed **Entrance** Minimally difficult **Setting** 5-acre suburban campus **Total enrollment** 1,561 **Application deadline** 9/1 **Housing** No **Expenses** Tuition $4025 **Undergraduates** 98% 25 or older, 2% Native American, 5% Hispanic, 26% black, 2% Asian American or Pacific Islander **Most popular recent majors** Management information systems/business data processing; human resources management; individual/family development **Academic program** Self-designed majors, summer session, adult/continuing education programs, internships **Contact** Dr. Algia Allen, Vice President for Academic Services, Amber University, 1700 Eastgate Drive, Garland, TX 75041-5595. Telephone: 972-279-6511 ext. 135. E-mail: www.webteam@amberu.edu. Web site: http://www.amberu.edu/.

ANGELO STATE UNIVERSITY

SAN ANGELO, TEXAS

General State-supported, comprehensive, coed **Entrance** Moderately difficult **Setting** 268-acre urban campus **Total enrollment** 6,234 **Student/faculty ratio** 22:1 **Application deadline** 8/1 **Freshmen** 74% were admitted **Housing** Yes **Expenses** Tuition $2242; Room & Board $3908 **Undergraduates** 55% women, 21% part-time, 24% 25 or older, 1% Native American, 18% Hispanic, 5% black, 1% Asian American or Pacific Islander **Most popular recent majors** Education; nursing; business administration **Academic program** Advanced placement, accelerated degree program, summer session, adult/continuing education programs, internships **Contact** Mrs. Monique Cossich, Director of Admissions, Angelo State University, 2601 West Avenue N, San Angelo, TX 76909. Telephone: 915-942-2041 ext. 239 or toll-free 800-946-8627. Fax: 915-942-2078. E-mail: admissions@angelo.edu. Web site: http://www.angelo.edu/.

ARLINGTON BAPTIST COLLEGE

ARLINGTON, TEXAS

General Independent Baptist, 4-year, coed **Entrance** Minimally difficult **Setting** 32-acre urban campus **Total enrollment** 172 **Student/faculty ratio** 15:1 **Application deadline** Rolling **Freshmen** 100% were admitted **Housing** Yes **Expenses** Tuition $2810; Room only $1700 **Undergraduates** 34% women, 19% part-time, 27% 25 or older, 0% Native American, 3% Hispanic, 3% black, 2% Asian American or Pacific Islander **Most popular recent majors** Liberal arts and studies; biblical studies; education **Academic program** Average class size 30, advanced placement, accelerated degree program, summer session, internships **Contact** Br. Danny Moody, Director of Institutional Advancement, Arlington Baptist College, 3001 West Division, Arlington, TX 76012-3425. Telephone: 817-461-8741 ext. 103. Fax: 817-274-1138.

AUSTIN COLLEGE
SHERMAN, TEXAS

General Independent Presbyterian, comprehensive, coed **Entrance** Very difficult **Setting** 60-acre suburban campus **Total enrollment** 1,202 **Student/faculty ratio** 13:1 **Application deadline** 3/1 **Freshmen** 61% were admitted **Housing** Yes **Expenses** Tuition $14,205; Room & Board $5393 **Undergraduates** 52% women, 1% part-time, 3% 25 or older, 0.4% Native American, 7% Hispanic, 4% black, 8% Asian American or Pacific Islander **Most popular recent majors** Psychology; biology; business administration **Academic program** Average class size 25, advanced placement, accelerated degree program, self-designed majors, tutorials, honors program, summer session, adult/continuing education programs, internships **Contact** Mr. Jonathan Stroud, Vice President for Institutional Enrollment, Austin College, 900 North Grand Avenue, Sherman, TX 75090-4440. Telephone: 903-813-3000 or toll-free 800-442-5363. Fax: 903-813-3198. E-mail: admissions@austinc.edu. Web site: http://www.austinc.edu/.

BAPTIST MISSIONARY ASSOCIATION THEOLOGICAL SEMINARY
JACKSONVILLE, TEXAS

General Independent Baptist, comprehensive, primarily men **Entrance** Noncompetitive **Setting** 17-acre small town campus **Total enrollment** 62 **Student/faculty ratio** 8:1 **Application deadline** 7/17 **Freshmen** 100% were admitted **Housing** Yes **Expenses** Tuition $2040; Room only $3432 **Undergraduates** 5% women, 71% part-time, 81% 25 or older, 3% Native American, 0% Hispanic, 21% black, 0% Asian American or Pacific Islander **Academic program** Summer session, adult/continuing education programs, internships **Contact** Dr. W. K. Benningfield, Dean and Registrar, Baptist Missionary Association Theological Seminary, 1530 East Pine Street, Jacksonville, TX 75766-5407. Telephone: 903-586-2501. Web site: http://www.geocities.com/Athens/Acropolis/3386/.

BAYLOR COLLEGE OF DENTISTRY
DALLAS, TEXAS

General State-supported, upper-level, coed **Entrance** Moderately difficult **Setting** 1-acre urban campus **Total enrollment** 496 **Application deadline** Rolling **Freshmen** 39% were admitted **Housing** No **Expenses** Tuition $2700 **Undergraduates** 36% 25 or older, 0% Native American, 2% Hispanic, 0% black, 5% Asian American or Pacific Islander **Academic program** Summer session **Contact** Dr. Jack L. Long, Director of Admissions and Records, Baylor College of Dentistry, PO Box 660677, Dallas, TX 75266-0677. Telephone: 214-828-8230. Web site: http://www.tambcd.edu/.

BAYLOR UNIVERSITY
WACO, TEXAS

General Independent Baptist, university, coed **Entrance** Moderately difficult **Setting** 432-acre urban campus **Total enrollment** 12,472 **Student/faculty ratio** 17:1 **Application deadline** Rolling **Housing** Yes **Expenses** Tuition $10,266; Room & Board $4566 **Undergraduates** 57% women, 4% part-time, 4% 25 or older, 1% Native American, 8% Hispanic, 6% black, 6% Asian American or Pacific Islander **Most Popular Recent Major** English **Academic program** English as a second language, advanced placement, accelerated degree program, self-designed majors, honors program, summer session, adult/continuing education programs, internships **Contact** Ms. Teri Tippit, Director of Recruitment, Baylor University, PO Box 97056, Waco, TX 76798. Telephone: 254-710-3435 or toll-free 800-BAYLOR U. E-mail: admissions_office@baylor.edu. Web site: http://www.baylor.edu/.

CONCORDIA UNIVERSITY AT AUSTIN
AUSTIN, TEXAS

General Independent, 4-year, coed, affiliated with Lutheran Church–Missouri Synod **Entrance** Moderately difficult **Setting** 20-acre urban campus **Total enrollment** 775 **Student/faculty ratio** 11:1 **Application deadline** 8/15 **Freshmen** 90% were admitted **Housing** Yes **Expenses** Tuition $10,500; Room & Board $5000 **Undergraduates** 58% women, 31% part-time, 35% 25 or older, 0.4% Native American, 13% Hispanic, 7% black, 1% Asian American or Pacific Islander **Most popular recent majors** Business administration; elementary education; mass communications **Academic program** English as a second language, advanced placement, accelerated degree program, tutorials, summer session, adult/continuing education programs, internships **Contact** Ms. Rachel Meissner, Director of Admissions, Concordia University at Austin, 3400 Interstate 35 North, Austin, TX 78705-2799. Telephone: 512-452-7661 or toll-free 800-285-4252. Fax: 512-459-8517. E-mail: ctxadmis@crf.cuis.edu. Web site: http://www.concordia.edu/.

THE CRISWELL COLLEGE
DALLAS, TEXAS

General Independent Baptist, comprehensive, coed **Entrance** Minimally difficult **Setting** 1-acre urban campus **Total enrollment** 502 **Student/faculty ratio** 20:1 **Application deadline** 8/15

Housing No **Expenses** Tuition $3240 **Undergraduates** 1% Native American, 8% Hispanic, 20% black, 4% Asian American or Pacific Islander **Most Popular Recent Major** Biblical studies **Academic program** Advanced placement, summer session, internships **Contact** Mr. Rich Grimm, Vice President for Enrollment Services, The Criswell College, 4010 Gaston Avenue, Dallas, TX 75246-1537. Telephone: 214-821-5433 ext. 1302 or toll-free 800-899-0012. Fax: 214-818-1310. Web site: http://www.criswell.edu/.

DALLAS BAPTIST UNIVERSITY
DALLAS, TEXAS

General Independent Southern Baptist, comprehensive, coed **Entrance** Moderately difficult **Setting** 200-acre urban campus **Total enrollment** 3,493 **Student/faculty ratio** 18:1 **Application deadline** Rolling **Housing** Yes **Expenses** Tuition $7800; Room & Board $3422 **Undergraduates** 60% women, 58% part-time, 63% 25 or older, 2% Native American, 6% Hispanic, 18% black, 5% Asian American or Pacific Islander **Most popular recent majors** Business administration; education; music **Academic program** English as a second language, advanced placement, summer session, adult/continuing education programs, internships **Contact** Mr. Jeremy Dutschke, Director of Admissions, Dallas Baptist University, 3000 Mountain Creek Parkway, Dallas, TX 75211-9299. Telephone: 214-333-5360. Fax: 214-333-5447. E-mail: admiss@dbu.edu. Web site: http://www.dbu.edu/.

DALLAS CHRISTIAN COLLEGE
DALLAS, TEXAS

General Independent, 4-year, coed, affiliated with Christian Churches and Churches of Christ **Entrance** Minimally difficult **Setting** 22-acre urban campus **Total enrollment** 290 **Application deadline** Rolling **Freshmen** 100% were admitted **Housing** Yes **Expenses** Tuition $4390; Room & Board $3000 **Undergraduates** 44% women, 11% part-time, 55% 25 or older, 1% Native American, 11% Hispanic, 12% black, 1% Asian American or Pacific Islander **Academic program** Advanced placement, accelerated degree program, tutorials, summer session, adult/continuing education programs, internships **Contact** Mr. Michael Frisbie, Director of Student Recruitment, Dallas Christian College, 2700 Christian Parkway, Dallas, TX 75234-7299. Telephone: 972-241-3371 ext. 123. Fax: 972-241-8021. Web site: http://www.popi.net/dcc/.

DEVRY INSTITUTE OF TECHNOLOGY
IRVING, TEXAS

General Proprietary, 4-year, coed **Entrance** Minimally difficult **Setting** 13-acre suburban campus **Total enrollment** 2,640 **Student/faculty ratio** 18:1 **Application deadline** Rolling **Freshmen** 72% were admitted **Housing** No **Expenses** Tuition $7308 **Undergraduates** 25% women, 36% part-time, 57% 25 or older, 1% Native American, 13% Hispanic, 25% black, 6% Asian American or Pacific Islander **Most popular recent majors** Information sciences/systems; electrical/electronic engineering technology **Academic program** Advanced placement, accelerated degree program, summer session, adult/continuing education programs **Contact** Mr. Daniel Millan, Director of Admissions, DeVry Institute of Technology, 4801 Regent Boulevard, Irving, TX 75063-2440. Telephone: 972-929-5770 or toll-free 800-443-3879 (in-state), 800-633-3879 (out-of-state). Web site: http://www.dal.devry.edu/.

EAST TEXAS BAPTIST UNIVERSITY
MARSHALL, TEXAS

General Independent Baptist, comprehensive, coed **Entrance** Moderately difficult **Setting** 200-acre small town campus **Total enrollment** 1,292 **Student/faculty ratio** 16:1 **Application deadline** Rolling **Housing** Yes **Expenses** Tuition $6750; Room & Board $3098 **Undergraduates** 58% women, 11% part-time, 16% 25 or older, 0.2% Native American, 4% Hispanic, 5% black, 1% Asian American or Pacific Islander **Academic program** English as a second language, advanced placement, accelerated degree program, tutorials, honors program, summer session, adult/continuing education programs, internships **Contact** Mr. David Howard, Director of Admissions, East Texas Baptist University, 1209 North Grove, Marshall, TX 75670-1498. Telephone: 903-935-7963 ext. 225 or toll-free 800-804-3828. Fax: 903-938-1705. E-mail: mbender@etbu.edu. Web site: http://www.etbu.edu/.

EAST TEXAS STATE UNIVERSITY AT TEXARKANA
See Texas A&M University–Texarkana

HARDIN-SIMMONS UNIVERSITY
ABILENE, TEXAS

General Independent Baptist, comprehensive, coed **Entrance** Moderately difficult **Setting** 40-acre urban campus **Total enrollment** 2,312 **Student/faculty ratio** 12:1 **Application deadline** Rolling **Freshmen** 92% were admitted **Housing** Yes **Expenses** Tuition $8130; Room & Board $3240 **Undergraduates** 52% women, 12% part-time, 10% 25 or older, 1% Native American, 7% Hispanic, 3% black, 1% Asian American or Pacific Islander **Most popular recent majors** Elementary education; biology; music education **Academic program** Average class size 20, English as

Hardin-Simmons University *(continued)*

a second language, advanced placement, accelerated degree program, tutorials, summer session, adult/continuing education programs, internships **Contact** Mrs. Teri Sabade, Enrollment Services Counselor, Hardin-Simmons University, Box 16050, Abilene, TX 79698-0001. Telephone: 915-670-1466 or toll-free 800-568-2692. Fax: 915-670-1527. E-mail: enroll.services@hsutx.edu. Web site: http://www.hsutx.edu/.

HOUSTON BAPTIST UNIVERSITY
HOUSTON, TEXAS

General Independent Baptist, comprehensive, coed **Entrance** Moderately difficult **Setting** 158-acre urban campus **Total enrollment** 2,286 **Student/faculty ratio** 18:1 **Application deadline** Rolling **Freshmen** 74% were admitted **Housing** Yes **Expenses** Tuition $8535; Room & Board $2974 **Undergraduates** 31% 25 or older **Most popular recent majors** (pre)medicine; business administration; nursing **Academic program** English as a second language, advanced placement, summer session, adult/continuing education programs, internships **Contact** Mrs. Judie Smelser, Director of Admissions, Houston Baptist University, 7502 Fondren Road, Houston, TX 77074-3298. Telephone: 281-649-3211 or toll-free 800-969-3210. Fax: 281-649-3217. E-mail: unadm@hbu.edu. Web site: http://www.hbu.edu/.

HOWARD PAYNE UNIVERSITY
BROWNWOOD, TEXAS

General Independent Southern Baptist, 4-year, coed **Entrance** Minimally difficult **Setting** 30-acre small town campus **Total enrollment** 1,489 **Student/faculty ratio** 16:1 **Application deadline** Rolling **Freshmen** 99% were admitted **Housing** Yes **Expenses** Tuition $7620; Room & Board $3630 **Undergraduates** 46% women, 18% part-time, 17% 25 or older, 0.3% Native American, 10% Hispanic, 9% black, 1% Asian American or Pacific Islander **Most popular recent majors** Education; business administration; biology **Academic program** Average class size 20, English as a second language, advanced placement, self-designed majors, tutorials, honors program, summer session, adult/continuing education programs, internships **Contact** Ms. Cheryl Mangrum, Coordinator of Admission Services, Howard Payne University, 1000 Fisk Street, Brownwood, TX 76801-2715. Telephone: 915-649-8027 or toll-free 800-880-4478. Fax: 915-649-8900. E-mail: admissions@hputx.edu. Web site: http://www.hputx.edu/.

HUSTON-TILLOTSON COLLEGE
AUSTIN, TEXAS

General Independent interdenominational, 4-year, coed **Entrance** Moderately difficult **Setting** 23-acre urban campus **Total enrollment** 698 **Student/faculty ratio** 15:1 **Application deadline** 5/1 **Freshmen** 87% were admitted **Housing** Yes **Expenses** Tuition $6030; Room & Board $4232 **Undergraduates** 52% women, 13% part-time, 25% 25 or older, 0.1% Native American, 8% Hispanic, 80% black, 5% Asian American or Pacific Islander **Most popular recent majors** Business administration; accounting; mass communications **Academic program** English as a second language, advanced placement, accelerated degree program, summer session, internships **Contact** Mr. Donnie J. Scott, Director of Admissions, Huston-Tillotson College, 900 Chicon Street, Austin, TX 78702-2795. Telephone: 512-505-3027. Fax: 512-505-3190. Web site: http://www.htc.edu/.

ICI UNIVERSITY
IRVING, TEXAS

General Independent, comprehensive, coed, affiliated with Assemblies of God **Contact** Dr. Mark Barcliff, Associate Dean of Student Services, ICI University, 6300 North Belt Line Road, Irving, TX 75063-2631. Telephone: 972-751-1111 ext. 8211 or toll-free 800-444-0424. Fax: 972-714-8185. E-mail: registrar@ici.edu. Web site: http://www.ici.edu/.

INSTITUTE FOR CHRISTIAN STUDIES
AUSTIN, TEXAS

General Independent, upper-level, coed, affiliated with Church of Christ **Entrance** Minimally difficult **Setting** Urban campus **Total enrollment** 125 **Application deadline** Rolling **Freshmen** 100% were admitted **Housing** Yes **Expenses** Tuition $920; Room only $2016 **Undergraduates** 43% women, 52% part-time, 65% 25 or older, 0% Native American, 7% Hispanic, 34% black, 0% Asian American or Pacific Islander **Academic program** Average class size 12, advanced placement, tutorials, summer session, adult/continuing education programs, internships **Contact** Mrs. Cindy Lippe, Director of Admissions and Registrar, Institute for Christian Studies, 1909 University Avenue, Austin, TX 78705-5610. Telephone: 512-476-2772 or toll-free 800-ICS-AUSTIN (in-state). Fax: 512-476-3919. Web site: http://www.ics.edu/.

JARVIS CHRISTIAN COLLEGE
HAWKINS, TEXAS

General Independent, 4-year, coed, affiliated with Christian Church (Disciples of Christ) **Contact** Ms. Serena Sentell, Admissions Counselor, Jarvis Christian College, PO Drawer G, Hawkins, TX 75765-9989. Telephone: 903-769-5700. Fax: 903-769-4842.

LAMAR UNIVERSITY
BEAUMONT, TEXAS

General State-supported, university, coed **Entrance** Minimally difficult **Setting** 200-acre suburban campus **Total enrollment** 9,677 **Student/faculty ratio** 20:1 **Application deadline** 8/1 **Freshmen** 85% were admitted **Housing** Yes **Expenses** Tuition $1868; Room & Board $3200 **Undergraduates** 53% women, 35% part-time, 39% 25 or older **Most popular recent majors** Interdisciplinary studies; electrical/electronics engineering; criminal justice/law enforcement administration **Academic program** English as a second language, advanced placement, accelerated degree program, self-designed majors, honors program, summer session, adult/continuing education programs, internships **Contact** Ms. Melissa Chesser, Director of Recruitment, Lamar University, 4400 Martin Luther King Parkway, Beaumont, TX 77710. Telephone: 409-880-8888 or toll-free 800-458-7558. Fax: 409-880-8463. E-mail: hunterre@hal.lamar.edu. Web site: http://www.lamar.edu/.

LETOURNEAU UNIVERSITY
LONGVIEW, TEXAS

General Independent nondenominational, comprehensive, coed **Entrance** Moderately difficult **Setting** 162-acre suburban campus **Total enrollment** 2,204 **Student/faculty ratio** 20:1 **Application deadline** 8/1 **Freshmen** 89% were admitted **Housing** Yes **Expenses** Tuition $10,744; Room & Board $4770 **Undergraduates** 40% women, 4% part-time, 56% 25 or older, 0.5% Native American, 4% Hispanic, 8% black, 1% Asian American or Pacific Islander **Most popular recent majors** Aviation technology; mechanical engineering; electrical/electronics engineering **Academic program** Average class size 24, advanced placement, summer session, adult/continuing education programs, internships **Contact** Ms. Linda Fitzhugh, Vice President for Enrollment Services, LeTourneau University, PO Box 7001, Longview, TX 75607-7001. Telephone: 903-233-3472 or toll-free 800-759-8811. Fax: 903-233-3411. E-mail: admissions@james.letu.edu. Web site: http://www.letu.edu/.

LUBBOCK CHRISTIAN UNIVERSITY
LUBBOCK, TEXAS

General Independent, comprehensive, coed, affiliated with Church of Christ **Contact** Office of Admissions, Lubbock Christian University, 5601 19th Street, Lubbock, TX 79407-2099. Telephone: 806-796-8800 ext. 260 or toll-free 800-933-7601. Fax: 806-796-8917.

MCMURRY UNIVERSITY
ABILENE, TEXAS

General Independent United Methodist, 4-year, coed **Entrance** Moderately difficult **Setting** 41-acre urban campus **Total enrollment** 1,410 **Student/faculty ratio** 14:1 **Application deadline** 8/15 **Freshmen** 76% were admitted **Housing** Yes **Expenses** Tuition $9075; Room & Board $3760 **Undergraduates** 45% women, 24% part-time, 28% 25 or older, 1% Native American, 12% Hispanic, 9% black, 1% Asian American or Pacific Islander **Most popular recent majors** Education; nursing; sociology **Academic program** Average class size 26, advanced placement, tutorials, honors program, summer session, internships **Contact** Mr. L. Russell Watjen, Vice President, Enrollment Management and Student Relations, McMurry University, Box 947, Abilene, TX 79697. Telephone: 915-691-6370 or toll-free 800-477-0077. Fax: 915-691-6599. E-mail: rwatjen@mcm.edu. Web site: http://www.mcm.edu/.

MIDWESTERN STATE UNIVERSITY
WICHITA FALLS, TEXAS

General State-supported, comprehensive, coed **Entrance** Minimally difficult **Setting** 172-acre urban campus **Total enrollment** 5,770 **Student/faculty ratio** 20:1 **Application deadline** 8/7 **Housing** Yes **Expenses** Tuition $2091; Room & Board $3633 **Undergraduates** 57% women, 40% part-time, 33% 25 or older, 1% Native American, 7% Hispanic, 6% black, 3% Asian American or Pacific Islander **Most popular recent majors** Business administration; nursing; accounting **Academic program** English as a second language, advanced placement, accelerated degree program, honors program, summer session, adult/continuing education programs, internships **Contact** Ms. Billye Tims, Registrar and Director of Admissions, Midwestern State University, 3410 Taft Boulevard, Wichita Falls, TX 76308-2096. Telephone: 940-397-4321 or toll-free 800-842-1922 (in-state). E-mail: school.relations@nexus.mwsu.edu. Web site: http://www.mwsu.edu/.

NORTHWOOD UNIVERSITY, TEXAS CAMPUS
CEDAR HILL, TEXAS

General Independent, 4-year, coed **Entrance** Minimally difficult **Setting** 360-acre small town campus **Total enrollment** 814 **Student/faculty ratio** 17:1 **Application deadline** 9/1 **Freshmen** 100% were admitted **Housing** Yes **Expenses** Tuition $10,889; Room & Board $4632 **Undergraduates** 48% women, 0.2% part-time, 5% 25 or older, 14% Hispanic, 28% black, 1% Asian American or Pacific Islander **Academic program** Average class size 30, advanced placement, tutorials, honors pro-

Northwood University, Texas Campus *(continued)*

gram, summer session, adult/continuing education programs, internships **Contact** Mr. James R. Hickerson, Director of Admissions, Northwood University, Texas Campus, 1114 W FM 1382, PO Box 58, Cedar Hill, TX 75104-1204. Telephone: 972-293-5400 or toll-free 800-927-9663. Fax: 972-291-3824. E-mail: txadmit@northwood.edu.

OUR LADY OF THE LAKE UNIVERSITY OF SAN ANTONIO
SAN ANTONIO, TEXAS

General Independent Roman Catholic, comprehensive, coed **Entrance** Moderately difficult **Setting** 75-acre urban campus **Total enrollment** 3,666 **Student/faculty ratio** 16:1 **Application deadline** Rolling **Freshmen** 75% were admitted **Housing** Yes **Expenses** Tuition $10,872; Room & Board $4206 **Undergraduates** 77% women, 45% part-time, 54% 25 or older, 0.5% Native American, 58% Hispanic, 8% black, 1% Asian American or Pacific Islander **Most popular recent majors** Business administration; information sciences/systems; psychology **Academic program** English as a second language, advanced placement, accelerated degree program, tutorials, summer session, adult/continuing education programs, internships **Contact** Ms. Debbie Hamilton, Director of Admissions, Our Lady of the Lake University of San Antonio, 411 Southwest 24th Street, San Antonio, TX 78207-4689. Telephone: 210-434-6711 ext. 314. Fax: 210-436-0824. E-mail: hamid@lake.occusa.edu. Web site: http://www.ollusa.edu/.

PAUL QUINN COLLEGE
DALLAS, TEXAS

General Independent African Methodist Episcopal, 4-year, coed **Contact** Mr. Ralph Spencer, Director of Admissions, Paul Quinn College, 3837 Simpson-Stuart Road, Dallas, TX 75241-4331. Telephone: 214-302-3520 or toll-free 800-237-2648. Fax: 214-302-3559.

PRAIRIE VIEW A&M UNIVERSITY
PRAIRIE VIEW, TEXAS

General State-supported, comprehensive, coed **Entrance** Moderately difficult **Setting** 1,440-acre small town campus **Total enrollment** 6,004 **Student/faculty ratio** 20:1 **Application deadline** Rolling **Freshmen** 93% were admitted **Housing** Yes **Expenses** Tuition $2364; Room & Board $3953 **Undergraduates** 55% women, 11% part-time, 16% 25 or older, 0.04% Native American, 1% Hispanic, 91% black, 1% Asian American or Pacific Islander **Most popular recent majors** Electrical/electronics engineering; interdisciplinary studies; mechanical engineering **Academic program** Advanced placement, accelerated degree program, honors program, summer session, internships **Contact** Ms. Deborah Dungey, Director of Admissions and Records, Prairie View A&M University, PO Box 3089, Prairie View, TX 77446-0188. Telephone: 409-857-2626. Fax: 409-857-2699.

RICE UNIVERSITY
HOUSTON, TEXAS

General Independent, university, coed **Entrance** Most difficult **Setting** 300-acre urban campus **Total enrollment** 4,209 **Student/faculty ratio** 6:1 **Application deadline** 1/2 **Freshmen** 27% were admitted **Housing** Yes **Expenses** Tuition $14,306; Room & Board $6200 **Undergraduates** 47% women, 1% part-time, 1% 25 or older, 1% Native American, 10% Hispanic, 6% black, 15% Asian American or Pacific Islander **Most popular recent majors** Political science; English; history **Academic program** Advanced placement, accelerated degree program, self-designed majors, tutorials, honors program, summer session, internships **Contact** Ms. Julie M. Browning, Director of Admissions, Rice University, MS 17, Houston, TX 77005. Telephone: 713-527-4036 or toll-free 800-527-OWLS (out-of-state). E-mail: admission@rice.edu. Web site: http://www.rice.edu/.

ST. EDWARD'S UNIVERSITY
AUSTIN, TEXAS

General Independent Roman Catholic, comprehensive, coed **Entrance** Moderately difficult **Setting** 180-acre urban campus **Total enrollment** 3,101 **Student/faculty ratio** 15:1 **Application deadline** 7/15 **Freshmen** 76% were admitted **Housing** Yes **Expenses** Tuition $10,730; Room & Board $4700 **Undergraduates** 60% women, 31% part-time, 15% 25 or older, 1% Native American, 30% Hispanic, 5% black, 2% Asian American or Pacific Islander **Most popular recent majors** Psychology; mass communications; business administration **Academic program** Average class size 25, advanced placement, accelerated degree program, honors program, summer session, adult/continuing education programs, internships **Contact** Ms. Megan Murphy, Director of Admissions, St. Edward's University, 3001 South Congress Avenue, Austin, TX 78704-6489. Telephone: 512-448-8500. Fax: 512-448-8492. E-mail: seu.admit@admin.stedwards.edu. Web site: http://www.stedwards.edu/.

ST. MARY'S UNIVERSITY OF SAN ANTONIO
SAN ANTONIO, TEXAS

General Independent Roman Catholic, comprehensive, coed **Entrance** Moderately difficult **Set-**

ting 135-acre urban campus **Total enrollment** 4,203 **Student/faculty ratio** 18:1 **Application deadline** Rolling **Freshmen** 87% were admitted **Housing** Yes **Expenses** Tuition $10,608; Room & Board $4768 **Undergraduates** 58% women, 12% part-time, 17% 25 or older, 0.3% Native American, 64% Hispanic, 3% black, 2% Asian American or Pacific Islander **Most popular recent majors** Political science; accounting; international business **Academic program** English as a second language, advanced placement, tutorials, honors program, summer session, adult/continuing education programs, internships **Contact** Mr. Richard Castillo, Director of Admissions, St. Mary's University of San Antonio, 1 Camino Santa Maria, San Antonio, TX 78228-8503. Telephone: 210-436-3126 or toll-free 800-FOR-STMU (out-of-state). Fax: 210-431-6742. E-mail: uadm@stmarytx.edu. Web site: http://www.stmarytx.edu/.

▶ **For more information, see page 507.**

SAM HOUSTON STATE UNIVERSITY
HUNTSVILLE, TEXAS

General State-supported, comprehensive, coed **Entrance** Moderately difficult **Setting** 2,143-acre small town campus **Total enrollment** 12,712 **Student/faculty ratio** 21:1 **Application deadline** Rolling **Freshmen** 80% were admitted **Housing** Yes **Expenses** Tuition $1586; Room & Board $3290 **Undergraduates** 54% women, 20% part-time, 19% 25 or older, 1% Native American, 7% Hispanic, 13% black, 1% Asian American or Pacific Islander **Academic program** English as a second language, advanced placement, accelerated degree program, honors program, summer session, adult/continuing education programs, internships **Contact** Ms. Joey Chandler, Director of Admissions and Recruitment, Sam Houston State University, Huntsville, TX 77341. Telephone: 409-294-1828. Web site: http://www.shsu.edu/.

SCHREINER COLLEGE
KERRVILLE, TEXAS

General Independent Presbyterian, comprehensive, coed **Entrance** Moderately difficult **Setting** 175-acre small town campus **Total enrollment** 668 **Student/faculty ratio** 13:1 **Application deadline** Rolling **Freshmen** 77% were admitted **Housing** Yes **Expenses** Tuition $10,690; Room & Board $6380 **Undergraduates** 57% women, 12% part-time, 24% 25 or older, 1% Native American, 17% Hispanic, 3% black, 2% Asian American or Pacific Islander **Most popular recent majors** Business administration; health/physical education; biology **Academic program** English as a second language, advanced placement, self-designed majors, tutorials, honors program, summer session, internships **Contact** Mr. Michael Paris, Director of Admission, Schreiner College, 2100 Memorial Boulevard, Kerrville, TX 78028-5697. Telephone: 830-792-7217 or toll-free 800-343-4919. Fax: 830-792-7226. Web site: http://www.schreiner.edu/.

SOUTHERN METHODIST UNIVERSITY
DALLAS, TEXAS

General Independent, university, coed, affiliated with United Methodist Church **Entrance** Moderately difficult **Setting** 163-acre suburban campus **Total enrollment** 9,708 **Student/faculty ratio** 12:1 **Application deadline** 4/1 **Freshmen** 88% were admitted **Housing** Yes **Expenses** Tuition $16,790; Room & Board $6454 **Undergraduates** 54% women, 5% part-time, 8% 25 or older, 0.5% Native American, 9% Hispanic, 6% black, 6% Asian American or Pacific Islander **Most popular recent majors** Finance; psychology; accounting **Academic program** English as a second language, advanced placement, accelerated degree program, self-designed majors, tutorials, honors program, summer session, adult/continuing education programs, internships **Contact** Mr. Ron W. Moss, Director of Admission and Enrollment Management, Southern Methodist University, 6425 Boaz, Dallas, TX 75275. Telephone: 214-768-2058 or toll-free 800-323-0672. E-mail: ugadmission@smu.edu. Web site: http://www.smu.edu/.

SOUTHWESTERN ADVENTIST UNIVERSITY
KEENE, TEXAS

General Independent Seventh-day Adventist, comprehensive, coed **Entrance** Noncompetitive **Setting** 150-acre rural campus **Total enrollment** 1,106 **Student/faculty ratio** 14:1 **Application deadline** Rolling **Freshmen** 100% were admitted **Housing** Yes **Expenses** Tuition $8500; Room & Board $4084 **Undergraduates** 54% women, 3% part-time, 36% 25 or older, 1% Native American, 15% Hispanic, 12% black, 5% Asian American or Pacific Islander **Academic program** English as a second language, accelerated degree program, self-designed majors, tutorials, honors program, summer session, internships **Contact** Mrs. Danna Burt, Admissions Counselor, Southwestern Adventist University, PO Box 567, Keene, TX 76059. Telephone: 817-645-3921 or toll-free 800-433-2240. Fax: 817-556-4744. E-mail: burtd@swau.edu. Web site: http://www.swau.edu/.

SOUTHWESTERN ASSEMBLIES OF GOD UNIVERSITY
WAXAHACHIE, TEXAS

General Independent, comprehensive, coed, affiliated with Assemblies of God **Entrance** Noncompetitive **Setting** 70-acre small town campus

Southwestern Assemblies of God University *(continued)*

Total enrollment 1,490 **Student/faculty ratio** 28:1 **Application deadline** Rolling **Freshmen** 99% were admitted **Housing** Yes **Expenses** Tuition $5350; Room & Board $3946 **Undergraduates** 51% women, 12% part-time, 24% 25 or older, 2% Native American, 12% Hispanic, 3% black, 1% Asian American or Pacific Islander **Most popular recent majors** Divinity/ministry; elementary education; business administration **Academic program** Advanced placement, summer session, adult/continuing education programs, internships **Contact** Ms. Janet Blackwell, Admissions Counselor, Southwestern Assemblies of God University, 1200 Sycamore Street, Waxahachie, TX 75165-2397. Telephone: 972-937-4010 ext. 1145 or toll-free 800-262-SAGC.

SOUTHWESTERN CHRISTIAN COLLEGE
TERRELL, TEXAS

General Independent, 4-year, coed, affiliated with Church of Christ **Contact** Admissions Department, Southwestern Christian College, Box 10, Terrell, TX 75160-0010. Telephone: 214-524-3341.

SOUTHWESTERN UNIVERSITY
GEORGETOWN, TEXAS

General Independent Methodist, 4-year, coed **Entrance** Very difficult **Setting** 500-acre suburban campus **Total enrollment** 1,215 **Student/faculty ratio** 11:1 **Application deadline** 2/15 **Freshmen** 73% were admitted **Housing** Yes **Expenses** Tuition $14,000; Room & Board $5270 **Undergraduates** 56% women, 2% part-time, 3% 25 or older, 1% Native American, 10% Hispanic, 3% black, 5% Asian American or Pacific Islander **Most popular recent majors** Psychology; biology; business administration **Academic program** Average class size 18, advanced placement, accelerated degree program, self-designed majors, tutorials, honors program, summer session, internships **Contact** Mr. John W. Lind, Vice President for Enrollment Management, Southwestern University, 1001 East University Avenue, Georgetown, TX 78626. Telephone: 512-863-1200 or toll-free 800-252-3166. Fax: 512-863-9601. E-mail: admission@southwestern.edu. Web site: http://www.southwestern.edu/.

SOUTHWEST TEXAS STATE UNIVERSITY
SAN MARCOS, TEXAS

General State-supported, comprehensive, coed **Entrance** Moderately difficult **Setting** 423-acre small town campus **Total enrollment** 20,652 **Student/faculty ratio** 26:1 **Application deadline** 7/1 **Freshmen** 66% were admitted **Housing** Yes **Expenses** Tuition $2214; Room & Board $3901 **Undergraduates** 54% women, 20% part-time, 22% 25 or older, 1% Native American, 19% Hispanic, 5% black, 2% Asian American or Pacific Islander **Most popular recent majors** Elementary education; health/physical education; business administration **Academic program** Average class size 40, English as a second language, advanced placement, accelerated degree program, tutorials, honors program, summer session, internships **Contact** Mr. Fernando Yarrito, Director of Admissions, Southwest Texas State University, Admissions and Visitors Center, San Marcos, TX 78666. Telephone: 512-245-2364 ext. 2803. Fax: 512-245-8044. E-mail: admissions@swt.edu. Web site: http://www.swt.edu/.

▶ **For more information, see page 519.**

STEPHEN F. AUSTIN STATE UNIVERSITY
NACOGDOCHES, TEXAS

General State-supported, comprehensive, coed **Entrance** Moderately difficult **Setting** 400-acre small town campus **Total enrollment** 12,041 **Student/faculty ratio** 20:1 **Application deadline** Rolling **Freshmen** 73% were admitted **Housing** Yes **Expenses** Tuition $2188; Room & Board $3682 **Undergraduates** 56% women, 11% part-time, 23% 25 or older, 1% Native American, 5% Hispanic, 9% black, 1% Asian American or Pacific Islander **Most popular recent majors** Interdisciplinary studies; business marketing and marketing management; exercise sciences **Academic program** Average class size 28, advanced placement, accelerated degree program, self-designed majors, tutorials, honors program, summer session, adult/continuing education programs, internships **Contact** Mr. Roger Bilow, Director of Admission, Stephen F. Austin State University, 1936 North Street, Nacogdoches, TX 75962. Telephone: 409-468-2504. Fax: 409-468-3849. E-mail: mbsmith@sfasu.edu. Web site: http://www.sfasu.edu/.

SUL ROSS STATE UNIVERSITY
ALPINE, TEXAS

General State-supported, comprehensive, coed **Contact** Mr. Robert Cullins, Dean of Admissions and Records, Sul Ross State University, Box C-2, Alpine, TX 79832. Telephone: 915-837-8052. Fax: 915-837-8046. E-mail: rcullins@sul-ross-1.sulross.edu.

TARLETON STATE UNIVERSITY
STEPHENVILLE, TEXAS

General State-supported, comprehensive, coed **Contact** Ms. Gail Mayfield, Director of Admissions, Tarleton State University, 1333 West Washington Street, Stephenville, TX 76402. Telephone: 817-968-9125. Fax: 254-968-9389. Web site: http://www.tarleton.edu/.

TEXAS A&M INTERNATIONAL UNIVERSITY
LAREDO, TEXAS

General State-supported, comprehensive, coed **Contact** Ms. Betty L. Momayez, Director of Enrollment Management and School Relations, Texas A&M International University, 5201 University Boulevard, Laredo, TX 78041-1900. Telephone: 210-326-2270. Fax: 956-326-2348. E-mail: mchayez@tamiu.edu.

TEXAS A&M UNIVERSITY
COLLEGE STATION, TEXAS

General State-supported, university, coed **Entrance** Moderately difficult **Setting** 5,200-acre suburban campus **Total enrollment** 41,461 **Student/faculty ratio** 24:1 **Application deadline** 3/1 **Freshmen** 73% were admitted **Housing** Yes **Expenses** Tuition $2777; Room & Board $4276 **Undergraduates** 47% women, 7% part-time, 0.4% Native American, 11% Hispanic, 3% black, 3% Asian American or Pacific Islander **Most Popular Recent Majors** Interdisciplinary studies; animal sciences; accounting **Academic program** English as a second language, advanced placement, tutorials, honors program, summer session, internships **Contact** Ms. Stephanie D. Hays, Associate Director of Admissions, Texas A&M University, 217 John J. Koldus Building, College Station, TX 77843-1265. Telephone: 409-845-3741. E-mail: admissions@tamu.edu. Web site: http://www.tamu.edu/.

TEXAS A&M UNIVERSITY AT GALVESTON
GALVESTON, TEXAS

General State-supported, 4-year, coed **Entrance** Moderately difficult **Setting** 100-acre suburban campus **Total enrollment** 1,111 **Student/faculty ratio** 15:1 **Application deadline** Rolling **Freshmen** 74% were admitted **Housing** Yes **Expenses** Tuition $2834; Room & Board $3653 **Undergraduates** 47% women, 12% part-time, 13% 25 or older, 1% Native American, 7% Hispanic, 1% black, 2% Asian American or Pacific Islander **Most popular recent majors** Marine biology; marine science; naval architecture/marine engineering **Academic program** English as a second language, advanced placement, accelerated degree program, summer session **Contact** Ms. Cheryl Moon, Director of Admissions, Texas A&M University at Galveston, PO Box 1675, Galveston, TX 77553-1675. Telephone: 409-740-4415 or toll-free 800-850-6376. Fax: 409-740-4709. E-mail: langd@tamug.tamu.edu.

TEXAS A&M UNIVERSITY–COMMERCE
COMMERCE, TEXAS

General State-supported, university, coed **Entrance** Moderately difficult **Setting** 140-acre small town campus **Total enrollment** 7,693 **Student/faculty ratio** 17:1 **Application deadline** 8/1 **Freshmen** 79% were admitted **Housing** Yes **Expenses** Tuition $2286; Room & Board $3816 **Undergraduates** 56% women, 22% part-time, 18% 25 or older, 1% Native American, 4% Hispanic, 15% black, 1% Asian American or Pacific Islander **Most popular recent majors** Education; business administration; computer science **Academic program** Advanced placement, accelerated degree program, tutorials, honors program, summer session, adult/continuing education programs, internships **Contact** Mr. Randy McDonald, Director of School Relations, Texas A&M University–Commerce, PO Box 3011, Commerce, TX 75429-3011. Telephone: 903-886-5072 or toll-free 800-331-3878. Fax: 903-886-5888. E-mail: cathy_griffin@tamu-commerce.edu. Web site: http://www.tamu-commerce.edu/.

TEXAS A&M UNIVERSITY–CORPUS CHRISTI
CORPUS CHRISTI, TEXAS

General State-supported, comprehensive, coed **Entrance** Moderately difficult **Setting** 240-acre suburban campus **Total enrollment** 6,024 **Student/faculty ratio** 16:1 **Application deadline** 7/1 **Freshmen** 86% were admitted **Housing** Yes **Expenses** Tuition $1954 **Undergraduates** 61% women, 33% part-time, 44% 25 or older, 0.4% Native American, 37% Hispanic, 3% black, 2% Asian American or Pacific Islander **Most popular recent majors** Interdisciplinary studies; psychology; accounting **Academic program** Average class size 250, advanced placement, tutorials, summer session, internships **Contact** Ms. Margaret Dechant, Director of Admissions, Texas A&M University–Corpus Christi, 6300 Ocean Drive, Corpus Christi, TX 78412-5503. Telephone: 512-994-2414 or toll-free 800-482-6822. Fax: 512-994-5887. E-mail: jperales@falcon.tamucc.edu. Web site: http://www.tamucc.edu/.

TEXAS A&M UNIVERSITY–KINGSVILLE
KINGSVILLE, TEXAS

General State-supported, university, coed **Entrance** Moderately difficult **Setting** 255-acre small town campus **Total enrollment** 6,050 **Application deadline** Rolling **Housing** Yes **Expenses** Tuition $2180; Room & Board $3484 **Under-**

Texas A&M University–Kingsville *(continued)*

graduates 32% 25 or older, 0.3% Native American, 67% Hispanic, 5% black, 1% Asian American or Pacific Islander **Most popular recent majors** Education; accounting; business administration **Academic program** English as a second language, advanced placement, accelerated degree program, tutorials, summer session, adult/continuing education programs, internships **Contact** Mr. Ray Broglie, Director, School Relations, Texas A&M University-Kingsville, Campus Box 105, Kingsville, TX 78363. Telephone: 512-593-2315 or toll-free 800-687-6000. Web site: http://www.tamuk.edu/.

TEXAS A&M UNIVERSITY–TEXARKANA
TEXARKANA, TEXAS

General State-supported, upper-level, coed **Entrance** Noncompetitive **Setting** 1-acre small town campus **Total enrollment** 1,046 **Application deadline** Rolling **Housing** No **Expenses** Tuition $1586 **Undergraduates** 71% women, 62% part-time, 1% Native American, 1% Hispanic, 11% black, 0.4% Asian American or Pacific Islander **Academic program** Average class size 24, advanced placement, self-designed majors, summer session, internships **Contact** Mrs. Patricia Black, Director of Admissions and Registrar, Texas A&M University-Texarkana, PO Box 5518, Texarkana, TX 75505-5518. Telephone: 903-223-3068. Fax: 903-832-8890. E-mail: pat.black@tamut.edu.

TEXAS CHIROPRACTIC COLLEGE
PASADENA, TEXAS

General Independent, upper-level, coed **Contact** Mr. Robert Cooper, Director of Admissions, Texas Chiropractic College, 5912 Spencer Highway, Pasadena, TX 77505-1699. Telephone: 713-998-6017 or toll-free 800-468-6839.

TEXAS CHRISTIAN UNIVERSITY
FORT WORTH, TEXAS

General Independent, university, coed, affiliated with Christian Church (Disciples of Christ) **Entrance** Moderately difficult **Setting** 237-acre suburban campus **Total enrollment** 7,273 **Student/faculty ratio** 15:1 **Application deadline** 2/15 **Freshmen** 79% were admitted **Housing** Yes **Expenses** Tuition $11,090; Room & Board $3860 **Undergraduates** 59% women, 9% part-time, 7% 25 or older, 1% Native American, 6% Hispanic, 5% black, 2% Asian American or Pacific Islander **Most popular recent majors** Nursing; psychology; finance **Academic program** Average class size 26, English as a second language, advanced placement, accelerated degree program, self-designed majors, tutorials, honors program, summer session, adult/continuing education programs, internships **Contact** Ms. Sandra J. Ware, Interim Dean of Admissions, Texas Christian University, TCU Box 297013, Fort Worth, TX 76129-0002. Telephone: 817-257-7490 or toll-free 800-828-3764. Fax: 817-257-7268. E-mail: frogmail@tcu.edu. Web site: http://www.tcu.edu/.

TEXAS LUTHERAN UNIVERSITY
SEGUIN, TEXAS

General Independent, 4-year, coed, affiliated with Evangelical Lutheran Church **Entrance** Moderately difficult **Setting** 196-acre suburban campus **Total enrollment** 1,344 **Student/faculty ratio** 13:1 **Application deadline** Rolling **Freshmen** 87% were admitted **Housing** Yes **Expenses** Tuition $10,370; Room & Board $3772 **Undergraduates** 57% women, 24% part-time, 8% 25 or older, 1% Native American, 14% Hispanic, 4% black, 1% Asian American or Pacific Islander **Most popular recent majors** Business administration; biology; education **Academic program** English as a second language, advanced placement, accelerated degree program, tutorials, honors program, summer session, adult/continuing education programs, internships **Contact** Mr. E. Norman Jones, Vice President for Enrollment Services, Texas Lutheran University, 1000 West Court Street, Seguin, TX 78155-5999. Telephone: 830-372-8050 or toll-free 800-771-8521. Fax: 830-372-8091. E-mail: admissions@txlutheran.edu.

TEXAS SOUTHERN UNIVERSITY
HOUSTON, TEXAS

General State-supported, university, coed **Entrance** Noncompetitive **Setting** 147-acre urban campus **Total enrollment** 7,282 **Student/faculty ratio** 16:1 **Application deadline** 8/10 **Housing** Yes **Expenses** Tuition $2064; Room & Board $4000 **Undergraduates** 58% women, 16% part-time, 34% 25 or older **Most popular recent majors** Business administration; law enforcement/police science; criminal justice/law enforcement administration **Academic program** English as a second language, accelerated degree program, honors program, summer session, adult/continuing education programs **Contact** Ms. Georgia Cooley, Coordinator of Recruitment, Texas Southern University, 3100 Cleburne, Houston, TX 77004-4598. Telephone: 713-313-7474. Fax: 713-527-7842. Web site: http://www.tsu.edu/.

TEXAS TECH UNIVERSITY
LUBBOCK, TEXAS

General State-supported, university, coed **Entrance** Moderately difficult **Setting** 1,839-acre urban campus **Total enrollment** 25,022 **Student/**

faculty ratio 18:1 **Application deadline** Rolling **Freshmen** 74% were admitted **Housing** Yes **Expenses** Tuition $2607; Room & Board $4290 **Undergraduates** 46% women, 12% part-time, 10% 25 or older, 0.4% Native American, 10% Hispanic, 3% black, 2% Asian American or Pacific Islander **Most popular recent majors** Education; management information systems/business data processing; finance **Academic program** Average class size 30, English as a second language, advanced placement, accelerated degree program, self-designed majors, tutorials, honors program, summer session, adult/continuing education programs, internships **Contact** Mrs. Marty Grassel, Director of New Student Relations, Texas Tech University, Box 45005, Lubbock, TX 79409-5005. Telephone: 806-742-1482. Fax: 806-742-0980. E-mail: a5adms@ttuvm1.ttu.edu. Web site: http://www.ttu.edu/.

TEXAS WESLEYAN UNIVERSITY
FORT WORTH, TEXAS

General Independent United Methodist, comprehensive, coed **Entrance** Moderately difficult **Setting** 74-acre urban campus **Total enrollment** 3,136 **Student/faculty ratio** 14:1 **Application deadline** Rolling **Freshmen** 81% were admitted **Housing** Yes **Expenses** Tuition $7950; Room & Board $3700 **Undergraduates** 62% women, 29% part-time, 30% 25 or older, 2% Native American, 14% Hispanic, 15% black, 2% Asian American or Pacific Islander **Most popular recent majors** Business administration; education; psychology **Academic program** English as a second language, advanced placement, tutorials, summer session, adult/continuing education programs, internships **Contact** Ms. Stephanie Lewis-Boatner, Director of Freshman Admissions, Texas Wesleyan University, 1201 Wesleyan, Fort Worth, TX 76105-1536. Telephone: 817-531-4422 or toll-free 800-580-8980 (in-state). Fax: 817-531-7515. Web site: http://www.txwesleyan.edu/.

TEXAS WOMAN'S UNIVERSITY
DENTON, TEXAS

General State-supported, university, primarily women **Entrance** Minimally difficult **Setting** 270-acre suburban campus **Total enrollment** 9,378 **Student/faculty ratio** 12:1 **Application deadline** 7/15 **Freshmen** 81% were admitted **Housing** Yes **Expenses** Tuition $1980; Room & Board $3360 **Undergraduates** 94% women, 29% part-time, 44% 25 or older, 1% Native American, 9% Hispanic, 15% black, 5% Asian American or Pacific Islander **Most popular recent majors** Nursing; interdisciplinary studies; occupational therapy **Academic program** Advanced placement, accelerated degree program, self-designed majors, tutorials, honors program, summer session, adult/continuing education programs, internships **Contact** Ms. Cynthia Johnson, Director of Undergraduate Admissions, Texas Woman's University, PO Box 425679, Denton, TX 76201-0909. Telephone: 940-898-3040. Fax: 940-898-3198. Web site: http://www.twu.edu/.

TRINITY UNIVERSITY
SAN ANTONIO, TEXAS

General Independent, comprehensive, coed, affiliated with Presbyterian Church **Entrance** Very difficult **Setting** 113-acre urban campus **Total enrollment** 2,560 **Student/faculty ratio** 11:1 **Application deadline** 2/1 **Freshmen** 77% were admitted **Housing** Yes **Expenses** Tuition $14,724; Room & Board $5970 **Undergraduates** 1% 25 or older **Most popular recent majors** Business administration; biology; English **Academic program** Average class size 20, advanced placement, accelerated degree program, tutorials, honors program, summer session, internships **Contact** Dr. George Boyd, Director of Admissions, Trinity University, 715 Stadium Drive, San Antonio, TX 78212-7200. Telephone: 210-736-7207 or toll-free 800-TRINITY. Web site: http://www.trinity.edu/.

UNIVERSITY OF CENTRAL TEXAS
KILLEEN, TEXAS

General Independent, upper-level, coed **Entrance** Noncompetitive **Setting** 545-acre small town campus **Total enrollment** 1,117 **Application deadline** Rolling **Freshmen** 100% were admitted **Housing** Yes **Expenses** Tuition $3224; Room & Board $4652 **Undergraduates** 58% women, 62% part-time, 85% 25 or older **Most popular recent majors** Business administration; social work **Academic program** Self-designed majors, summer session, internships **Contact** Ms. Pam Asmus, Admissions Advisor, University of Central Texas, PO Box 1416, Killeen, TX 76540-1416. Telephone: 254-526-8262. Fax: 254-526-8403.

UNIVERSITY OF DALLAS
IRVING, TEXAS

General Independent Roman Catholic, university, coed **Entrance** Very difficult **Setting** 750-acre suburban campus **Total enrollment** 2,897 **Student/faculty ratio** 11:1 **Application deadline** 2/15 **Freshmen** 94% were admitted **Housing** Yes **Expenses** Tuition $12,856; Room & Board $4920 **Undergraduates** 56% women, 5% part-time, 9% 25 or older, 1% Native American, 12% Hispanic, 1% black, 8% Asian American or Pacific Islander **Most popular recent majors** Biology; English; political science **Academic program** Average class size 27, English as a second language, advanced placement, accelerated degree pro-

University of Dallas *(continued)*

gram, self-designed majors, tutorials, summer session, adult/continuing education programs, internships **Contact** Mr. Richard Mullin, Director of Admissions, University of Dallas, 1845 East Northgate Drive, Irving, TX 75062-4799. Telephone: 972-721-5266 or toll-free 800-628-6999. Fax: 972-721-5017. E-mail: undadmis@acad.udallas.edu.

UNIVERSITY OF HOUSTON
HOUSTON, TEXAS

General State-supported, university, coed **Entrance** Moderately difficult **Setting** 550-acre urban campus **Total enrollment** 31,602 **Application deadline** 7/1 **Freshmen** 70% were admitted **Housing** Yes **Expenses** Tuition $1993; Room & Board $4405 **Undergraduates** 53% women, 31% part-time, 29% 25 or older, 1% Native American, 17% Hispanic, 13% black, 19% Asian American or Pacific Islander **Most popular recent majors** Business administration; biology; psychology **Academic program** Average class size 59, English as a second language, advanced placement, accelerated degree program, tutorials, honors program, summer session, adult/continuing education programs, internships **Contact** Ms. Tyene Houston, Assistant Director of Admissions, University of Houston, 4800 Calhoun, Houston, TX 77204-2161. Telephone: 713-743-9632 or toll-free 800-741-4449. Fax: 713-743-9633. E-mail: admissions@uh.edu. Web site: http://www.uh.edu/.

UNIVERSITY OF HOUSTON–CLEAR LAKE
HOUSTON, TEXAS

General State-supported, upper-level, coed **Entrance** Minimally difficult **Setting** 487-acre suburban campus **Total enrollment** 6,947 **Student/faculty ratio** 17:1 **Application deadline** Rolling **Housing** No **Expenses** Tuition $2106 **Undergraduates** 66% 25 or older, 0.3% Native American, 12% Hispanic, 6% black, 6% Asian American or Pacific Islander **Most popular recent majors** Business administration; interdisciplinary studies; behavioral sciences **Academic program** Average class size 35, accelerated degree program, self-designed majors, tutorials, summer session, internships **Contact** Ms. Darella L. Banks, Executive Director of Enrollment Services, University of Houston–Clear Lake, 2700 Bay Area Boulevard, Box 13, Houston, TX 77058-1098. Telephone: 281-283-2517. Fax: 281-283-2530. E-mail: admissions@cl.uh.edu. Web site: http://www.cl.uh.edu/.

UNIVERSITY OF HOUSTON–DOWNTOWN
HOUSTON, TEXAS

General State-supported, 4-year, coed **Entrance** Noncompetitive **Setting** 20-acre urban campus **Total enrollment** 8,194 **Application deadline** 8/15 **Housing** No **Expenses** Tuition $2046 **Undergraduates** 56% women, 53% part-time, 52% 25 or older, 0.2% Native American, 32% Hispanic, 26% black, 11% Asian American or Pacific Islander **Most popular recent majors** Criminal justice/law enforcement administration; interdisciplinary studies; accounting **Academic program** English as a second language, advanced placement, accelerated degree program, self-designed majors, tutorials, summer session, adult/continuing education programs, internships **Contact** Ms. Penny Cureton, Director, Admissions and Records, University of Houston–Downtown, One Main Street, Houston, TX 77002-1001. Telephone: 713-221-8530. Fax: 713-221-8157. E-mail: uhdadmit@dt.uh.edu. Web site: http://www.dt.uh.edu/.

UNIVERSITY OF HOUSTON–VICTORIA
VICTORIA, TEXAS

General State-supported, upper-level, coed **Entrance** Minimally difficult **Setting** Small town campus **Total enrollment** 1,491 **Student/faculty ratio** 17:1 **Application deadline** Rolling **Housing** No **Expenses** Tuition $1776 **Undergraduates** 74% women, 60% part-time, 59% 25 or older, 1% Native American, 19% Hispanic, 5% black, 2% Asian American or Pacific Islander **Academic program** Summer session, internships **Contact** Mr. Richard Phillips, Director of Enrollment Management, University of Houston–Victoria, 2506 East Red River, Victoria, TX 77901-4450. Telephone: 512-576-3151 or toll-free 800-687-8648 (in-state). Fax: 512-572-9377. E-mail: alexanderc@jade.vic.uh.edu.

UNIVERSITY OF MARY HARDIN-BAYLOR
BELTON, TEXAS

General Independent Southern Baptist, comprehensive, coed **Entrance** Minimally difficult **Setting** 100-acre small town campus **Total enrollment** 2,313 **Student/faculty ratio** 17:1 **Application deadline** Rolling **Housing** Yes **Expenses** Tuition $6944; Room & Board $3250 **Undergraduates** 69% women, 20% part-time, 38% 25 or older, 1% Native American, 9% Hispanic, 7% black, 2% Asian American or Pacific Islander **Most popular recent majors** Education; business administration; nursing **Academic program** Advanced placement, accelerated degree program, honors program, summer session, adult/continuing education programs **Contact** Ms. Diane Stanford, Associate Director of Admissions, University of Mary Hardin-Baylor, UMBH Station Box 8004, Belton, TX 76513. Telephone: 254-939-8642 or toll-free 800-727-8642. Fax: 254-933-5049. E-mail: admissions@umhb.edu. Web site: http://www.umhb.edu/.

UNIVERSITY OF NORTH TEXAS
DENTON, TEXAS

General State-supported, university, coed **Entrance** Moderately difficult **Setting** 456-acre urban campus **Total enrollment** 25,013 **Student/faculty ratio** 20:1 **Application deadline** 6/15 **Housing** Yes **Expenses** Tuition $2187; Room & Board $3842 **Undergraduates** 14% 25 or older, 1% Native American, 7% Hispanic, 9% black, 4% Asian American or Pacific Islander **Most popular recent majors** Biology; psychology; accounting **Academic program** English as a second language, advanced placement, accelerated degree program, self-designed majors, tutorials, honors program, summer session, internships **Contact** Mr. Joel Daboub, Assistant Director of Admissions and Director of Freshman Orientation, University of North Texas, Box 311277, Denton, TX 76203-9988. Telephone: 940-565-2681 or toll-free 800-868-8211 (in-state). Fax: 940-565-2408. E-mail: undergrad@abn.unt.edu. Web site: http://www.unt.edu/.

UNIVERSITY OF ST. THOMAS
HOUSTON, TEXAS

General Independent Roman Catholic, comprehensive, coed **Entrance** Moderately difficult **Setting** 20-acre urban campus **Total enrollment** 2,506 **Student/faculty ratio** 16:1 **Application deadline** Rolling **Freshmen** 84% were admitted **Housing** Yes **Expenses** Tuition $10,550; Room & Board $4690 **Undergraduates** 66% women, 23% part-time, 30% 25 or older, 0.4% Native American, 23% Hispanic, 7% black, 11% Asian American or Pacific Islander **Most popular recent majors** Biology; business administration; psychology **Academic program** Average class size 18, English as a second language, advanced placement, accelerated degree program, self-designed majors, tutorials, honors program, summer session, adult/continuing education programs, internships **Contact** Mrs. Elsie Biron, Director of Admissions, University of St. Thomas, 3800 Montrose Boulevard, Houston, TX 77006-4696. Telephone: 713-525-3500 or toll-free 800-856-8565. Fax: 713-525-3558. E-mail: admissions@stthom.edu. Web site: http://basil.stthom.edu/home/.

THE UNIVERSITY OF TEXAS AT ARLINGTON
ARLINGTON, TEXAS

General State-supported, university, coed **Entrance** Moderately difficult **Setting** 395-acre suburban campus **Total enrollment** 19,286 **Student/faculty ratio** 16:1 **Application deadline** 6/1 **Freshmen** 83% were admitted **Housing** Yes **Expenses** Tuition $2088; Room only $1600 **Undergraduates** 51% women, 38% part-time, 40% 25 or older, 1% Native American, 10% Hispanic, 10% black, 12% Asian American or Pacific Islander **Most popular recent majors** Nursing; accounting; English **Academic program** English as a second language, advanced placement, honors program, summer session, adult/continuing education programs **Contact** Ms. Norma Coppage, Associate Director of Admissions, The University of Texas at Arlington, PO Box 19111, Arlington, TX 76019-0407. Telephone: 817-272-6287. Fax: 817-272-3435. E-mail: adm@uta.edu. Web site: http://www.uta.edu/.

THE UNIVERSITY OF TEXAS AT AUSTIN
AUSTIN, TEXAS

General State-supported, university, coed **Entrance** Very difficult **Setting** 350-acre urban campus **Total enrollment** 48,857 **Student/faculty ratio** 21:1 **Application deadline** 2/1 **Housing** Yes **Expenses** Tuition $2866; Room & Board $3901 **Undergraduates** 50% women, 11% part-time, 11% 25 or older, 0.5% Native American, 14% Hispanic, 4% black, 13% Asian American or Pacific Islander **Academic program** English as a second language, advanced placement, accelerated degree program, self-designed majors, tutorials, honors program, summer session, adult/continuing education programs, internships **Contact** Freshman Admissions Center, The University of Texas at Austin, John Hargis Hall, Austin, TX 78712. Telephone: 512-475-7440. Fax: 512-475-7475. E-mail: adfre@utxdp.dp.utexas.edu. Web site: http://www.utexas.edu/.

THE UNIVERSITY OF TEXAS AT BROWNSVILLE
BROWNSVILLE, TEXAS

General State-supported, upper-level, coed **Contact** Mr. Ernesto Garcia, Director of Enrollment, The University of Texas at Brownsville, 80 Fort Brown, Brownsville, TX 78520-4991. Telephone: 210-544-8254. Fax: 956-544-8832.

THE UNIVERSITY OF TEXAS AT DALLAS
RICHARDSON, TEXAS

General State-supported, university, coed **Entrance** Very difficult **Setting** 455-acre suburban campus **Total enrollment** 9,330 **Student/faculty ratio** 19:1 **Application deadline** 8/1 **Freshmen** 74% were admitted **Housing** Yes **Expenses** Tuition $2414; Room only $1620 **Undergraduates** 50% women, 42% part-time, 49% 25 or older, 1% Native American, 7% Hispanic, 6% black, 17% Asian American or Pacific Islander **Most popular recent majors** Business administration; computer science; electrical/electronics engineering **Academic program** Advanced placement, ac-

The University of Texas at Dallas *(continued)*

celerated degree program, self-designed majors, tutorials, honors program, summer session, adult/continuing education programs, internships **Contact** Admissions Office, The University of Texas at Dallas, PO Box 830688 Mail Station MC18, Richardson, TX 75083-0688. Telephone: 972-883-2341 or toll-free 800-889-2443. Fax: 972-883-2599. E-mail: ugrad-admissions@utdallas.edu. Web site: http://www.utdallas.edu/.

THE UNIVERSITY OF TEXAS AT EL PASO

EL PASO, TEXAS

General State-supported, university, coed **Entrance** Minimally difficult **Setting** 360-acre urban campus **Total enrollment** 15,176 **Student/faculty ratio** 17:1 **Application deadline** 7/1 **Freshmen** 81% were admitted **Housing** Yes **Expenses** Tuition $2266 **Undergraduates** 53% women, 34% part-time, 29% 25 or older, 0.3% Native American, 70% Hispanic, 3% black, 1% Asian American or Pacific Islander **Most popular recent majors** Interdisciplinary studies; criminal justice/law enforcement administration; psychology **Academic program** English as a second language, advanced placement, accelerated degree program, tutorials, honors program, summer session, adult/continuing education programs, internships **Contact** Ms. Diana Guerrero, Director of Admissions, The University of Texas at El Paso, 500 West University Avenue, El Paso, TX 79968-0001. Telephone: 915-747-5588. Fax: 915-747-5122.

THE UNIVERSITY OF TEXAS AT SAN ANTONIO

SAN ANTONIO, TEXAS

General State-supported, comprehensive, coed **Entrance** Moderately difficult **Setting** 600-acre suburban campus **Total enrollment** 17,494 **Student/faculty ratio** 21:1 **Application deadline** 7/1 **Freshmen** 87% were admitted **Housing** Yes **Expenses** Tuition $2744; Room only $3000 **Undergraduates** 54% women, 32% part-time, 37% 25 or older, 1% Native American, 43% Hispanic, 5% black, 4% Asian American or Pacific Islander **Most popular recent majors** Accounting; business administration; interdisciplinary studies **Academic program** English as a second language, advanced placement, accelerated degree program, tutorials, honors program, summer session, internships **Contact** Ms. Sandy Speed, Associate Director of Admissions, The University of Texas at San Antonio, 6900 North Loop 1604 West, San Antonio, TX 78249-0617. Telephone: 210-458-4530 or toll-free 800-669-0919 (out-of-state). Web site: http://www.utsa.edu/.

THE UNIVERSITY OF TEXAS AT TYLER

TYLER, TEXAS

General State-supported, upper-level, coed **Entrance** Difficulty N/R **Setting** 200-acre urban campus **Total enrollment** 3,393 **Student/faculty ratio** 10:1 **Freshmen** 86% were admitted **Housing** Yes **Expenses** Tuition $2084; Room & Board $6029 **Undergraduates** 67% women, 52% part-time, 59% 25 or older, 1% Native American, 3% Hispanic, 8% black, 1% Asian American or Pacific Islander **Academic program** Self-designed majors, honors program, summer session, adult/continuing education programs **Contact** Ms. Martha Wheat, Director of Admissions and Student Records, The University of Texas at Tyler, 3900 University Boulevard, Tyler, TX 75799-0001. Telephone: 903-566-7439. Fax: 903-566-7068. Web site: http://www.uttyl.edu/.

THE UNIVERSITY OF TEXAS HEALTH SCIENCE CENTER AT SAN ANTONIO

SAN ANTONIO, TEXAS

General State-supported, upper-level, coed **Contact** Mr. James Peak, Registrar, The University of Texas Health Science Center at San Antonio, 7703 Floyd Curl Drive, San Antonio, TX 78284-6200. Telephone: 210-567-2629. Fax: 210-567-2685.

THE UNIVERSITY OF TEXAS–HOUSTON HEALTH SCIENCE CENTER

HOUSTON, TEXAS

General State-supported, upper-level, coed **Entrance** Moderately difficult **Setting** Urban campus **Total enrollment** 3,089 **Application deadline** Rolling **Freshmen** 19% were admitted **Housing** Yes **Expenses** Tuition $2455 **Undergraduates** 92% women, 14% part-time, 51% 25 or older, 0% Native American, 9% Hispanic, 9% black, 13% Asian American or Pacific Islander **Academic program** Adult/continuing education programs **Contact** Mr. Robert Jenkins, Assistant Registrar/Admissions, The University of Texas–Houston Health Science Center, PO Box 20036, Houston, TX 77225-0036. Telephone: 713-500-3333 ext. 2203. Fax: 713-500-3026. E-mail: uthschro@admin4.hsc.uth.tmc.edu. Web site: http://www.uth.tmc.edu/.

THE UNIVERSITY OF TEXAS MEDICAL BRANCH AT GALVESTON

GALVESTON, TEXAS

General State-supported, upper-level, coed **Entrance** Most difficult **Setting** 82-acre small town campus **Total enrollment** 2,127 **Student/faculty ratio** 7:1 **Freshmen** 33% were admitted **Housing** Yes **Expenses** Tuition $1674; Room only

$1755 **Undergraduates** 76% women, 17% part-time, 59% 25 or older, 0.3% Native American, 13% Hispanic, 10% black, 11% Asian American or Pacific Islander **Academic program** Advanced placement, summer session, internships **Contact** Mr. Richard Lewis, Registrar, The University of Texas Medical Branch at Galveston, 1.212 Ashbel Smith, Galveston, TX 77555-1305. Telephone: 409-772-1215. Fax: 409-772-5056. E-mail: ybrewer@utmb.edu. Web site: http://www.utmb.edu/.

THE UNIVERSITY OF TEXAS OF THE PERMIAN BASIN

ODESSA, TEXAS

General State-supported, comprehensive, coed **Contact** Ms. Vicki Gomez, Director of Admissions, The University of Texas of the Permian Basin, 4901 East University, Odessa, TX 79762-0001. Telephone: 915-552-2605. Fax: 915-552-2374. E-mail: gomez-v@gusher.pb.utexas.edu. Web site: http://www.utpb.edu/.

THE UNIVERSITY OF TEXAS–PAN AMERICAN

EDINBURG, TEXAS

General State-supported, comprehensive, coed **Contact** Mr. David Zuniga, Director of Admissions, The University of Texas–Pan American, 1201 West University Drive, Edinburg, TX 78539-2999. Telephone: 210-381-2201.

THE UNIVERSITY OF TEXAS SOUTHWESTERN MEDICAL CENTER AT DALLAS

DALLAS, TEXAS

General State-supported, upper-level, coed **Contact** Ms. Laura Jarnagin, Assistant to the Registrar, The University of Texas Southwestern Medical Center at Dallas, 5323 Harry Hines Boulevard, Dallas, TX 75235-9002. Telephone: 214-648-3606. Fax: 214-648-3289. E-mail: admissions@mednet.swmed.edu. Web site: http://www.swmed.edu/.

UNIVERSITY OF THE INCARNATE WORD

SAN ANTONIO, TEXAS

General Independent Roman Catholic, comprehensive, coed **Entrance** Moderately difficult **Setting** 200-acre urban campus **Total enrollment** 3,312 **Student/faculty ratio** 14:1 **Application deadline** Rolling **Housing** Yes **Expenses** Tuition $10,840; Room & Board $4627 **Undergraduates** 71% women, 30% part-time, 38% 25 or older, 0.2% Native American, 52% Hispanic, 7% black, 2% Asian American or Pacific Islander **Most popular recent majors** Business administration; nursing; education **Academic program** Average class size 16, English as a second language, advanced placement, accelerated degree program, tutorials, summer session, adult/continuing education programs, internships **Contact** Ms. Andrea Cyterski, Director of Admissions, University of the Incarnate Word, 4301 Broadway, San Antonio, TX 78209-6397. Telephone: 210-829-6005 or toll-free 800-749-WORD. Fax: 210-829-3921. E-mail: admis@universe.uiwtx.edu. Web site: http://www.uiwtx.edu/.

► **For more information, see page 542.**

WAYLAND BAPTIST UNIVERSITY

PLAINVIEW, TEXAS

General Independent Baptist, comprehensive, coed **Entrance** Minimally difficult **Setting** 80-acre small town campus **Total enrollment** 4,190 **Student/faculty ratio** 15:1 **Application deadline** Rolling **Freshmen** 100% were admitted **Housing** Yes **Expenses** Tuition $6470; Room & Board $3314 **Undergraduates** 43% women, 76% part-time, 72% 25 or older, 1% Native American, 13% Hispanic, 14% black, 2% Asian American or Pacific Islander **Most popular recent majors** Business administration; education; human services **Academic program** Average class size 25, advanced placement, accelerated degree program, tutorials, honors program, summer session, adult/continuing education programs, internships **Contact** Mr. Claude Lusk, Director of Student Admissions, Wayland Baptist University, 1900 West Seventh Street, Plainview, TX 79072-6998. Telephone: 806-296-4709 or toll-free 800-588-1-WBU. Web site: http://www.wbu.edu/.

WEST TEXAS A&M UNIVERSITY

CANYON, TEXAS

General State-supported, comprehensive, coed **Entrance** Moderately difficult **Setting** 128-acre small town campus **Total enrollment** 6,489 **Student/faculty ratio** 24:1 **Application deadline** 8/16 **Freshmen** 79% were admitted **Housing** Yes **Expenses** Tuition $1744; Room & Board $2969 **Undergraduates** 53% women, 23% part-time, 23% 25 or older, 1% Native American, 10% Hispanic, 3% black, 1% Asian American or Pacific Islander **Most popular recent majors** Interdisciplinary studies; nursing **Academic program** Average class size 25, English as a second language, advanced placement, accelerated degree program, self-designed majors, honors program, summer session, adult/continuing education programs, internships **Contact** Ms. Lila Vars, Director of Admissions, West Texas A&M University, WT Box 60907, Canyon, TX 79016-0001. Telephone: 806-656-2020 or toll-free 800-99-WTAMU (in-state), 800-

West Texas A&M University *(continued)*

99-WTMAU (out-of-state). Fax: 806-656-2017. E-mail: lilav@wtamu.edu. Web site: http://www.wtamu.edu/.

WILEY COLLEGE
MARSHALL, TEXAS

General Independent, 4-year, coed, affiliated with United Methodist Church **Contact** Mr. Frederick Pryor Jr., Director of Admissions, Wiley College, 711 Wiley Avenue, Marshall, TX 75670-5199. Telephone: 903-927-3311 or toll-free 800-658-6889. Fax: 903-938-8100.

UTAH

BRIGHAM YOUNG UNIVERSITY
PROVO, UTAH

General Independent, university, coed, affiliated with Church of Jesus Christ of Latter-day Saints **Entrance** Moderately difficult **Setting** 638-acre suburban campus **Total enrollment** 32,161 **Student/faculty ratio** 29:1 **Application deadline** 2/15 **Freshmen** 71% were admitted **Housing** Yes **Expenses** Tuition $2630; Room & Board $4130 **Undergraduates** 53% women, 15% part-time, 7% 25 or older, 1% Native American, 2% Hispanic, 0.2% black, 2% Asian American or Pacific Islander **Most popular recent majors** Family studies; elementary education; accounting **Academic program** Average class size 43, English as a second language, advanced placement, accelerated degree program, honors program, summer session, adult/continuing education programs, internships **Contact** Mr. Erlend D. Peterson, Dean of Admissions and Records, Brigham Young University, Provo, UT 84602-1001. Telephone: 801-378-2539. E-mail: admissions@byu.edu. Web site: http://www.byu.edu/.

SOUTHERN UTAH UNIVERSITY
CEDAR CITY, UTAH

General State-supported, comprehensive, coed **Entrance** Moderately difficult **Setting** 113-acre small town campus **Total enrollment** 5,852 **Student/faculty ratio** 24:1 **Application deadline** 7/1 **Freshmen** 93% were admitted **Housing** Yes **Expenses** Tuition $1854; Room & Board $2502 **Undergraduates** 55% women, 13% part-time, 14% 25 or older, 1% Native American, 1% Hispanic, 1% black, 1% Asian American or Pacific Islander **Most popular recent majors** Elementary education; business administration; biology **Academic program** English as a second language, advanced placement, accelerated degree program, self-designed majors, summer session, adult/continuing education programs, internships **Contact** Mr. Dale S. Orton, Director of Admissions, Southern Utah University, 351 West Center Street, Cedar City, UT 84720-2498. Telephone: 801-586-7740. E-mail: adminfo@suu.edu. Web site: http://www.suu.edu/.

UNIVERSITY OF UTAH
SALT LAKE CITY, UTAH

General State-supported, university, coed **Entrance** Moderately difficult **Setting** 1,500-acre urban campus **Total enrollment** 25,883 **Student/faculty ratio** 23:1 **Application deadline** 7/1 **Freshmen** 95% were admitted **Housing** Yes **Expenses** Tuition $2601; Room & Board $4620 **Undergraduates** 46% women, 32% part-time, 34% 25 or older, 1% Native American, 3% Hispanic, 1% black, 3% Asian American or Pacific Islander **Most popular recent majors** Sociology; psychology; political science **Academic program** Average class size 61, English as a second language, advanced placement, accelerated degree program, self-designed majors, tutorials, honors program, summer session, adult/continuing education programs, internships **Contact** Ms. Suzanne Espinoza, Director of High School Services, University of Utah, 250 South Student Services Building, Salt Lake City, UT 84112. Telephone: 801-581-8761 or toll-free 800-444-8638. Fax: 801-585-3034. Web site: http://www.utah.edu/.

UTAH STATE UNIVERSITY
LOGAN, UTAH

General State-supported, university, coed **Entrance** Moderately difficult **Setting** 456-acre urban campus **Total enrollment** 21,234 **Student/faculty ratio** 22:1 **Application deadline** 7/1 **Freshmen** 99% were admitted **Housing** Yes **Expenses** Tuition $2175; Room & Board $3510 **Undergraduates** 52% women, 24% part-time, 24% 25 or older, 1% Native American, 2% Hispanic, 0.5% black, 1% Asian American or Pacific Islander **Most popular recent majors** Elementary education; family/community studies; accounting **Academic program** English as a second language, advanced placement, accelerated degree program, self-designed majors, honors program, summer session, adult/continuing education programs, internships **Contact** Ms. Rhea H. Wallentine, Acting Director of Admissions, Utah State University, University Hill, Logan, UT 84322-1600. Telephone: 435-797-1107. Fax: 435-797-3900. E-mail: admit@admissions.usu.edu. Web site: http://www.usu.edu/.

WEBER STATE UNIVERSITY
OGDEN, UTAH

General State-supported, comprehensive, coed **Entrance** Noncompetitive **Setting** 526-acre urban campus **Total enrollment** 14,613 **Student/faculty ratio** 18:1 **Application deadline** Rolling **Freshmen** 100% were admitted **Housing** Yes **Expenses** Tuition $1935; Room & Board $3810 **Undergraduates** 54% women, 38% part-time, 34% 25 or older, 1% Native American, 3% Hispanic, 1% black, 2% Asian American or Pacific Islander **Most popular recent majors** Nursing; education; business administration **Academic program** English as a second language, advanced placement, accelerated degree program, self-designed majors, tutorials, honors program, summer session, adult/continuing education programs, internships **Contact** Ms. Kristen Olsen, Admissions Advisor, Weber State University, 1001 University Circle, Ogden, UT 84408-1001. Telephone: 801-626-6050 or toll-free 800-634-6568 (in-state). Fax: 801-626-6747. E-mail: kolsen4@weber.edu. Web site: http://www.weber.edu/.

WESTMINSTER COLLEGE OF SALT LAKE CITY
SALT LAKE CITY, UTAH

General Independent, comprehensive, coed **Entrance** Moderately difficult **Setting** 27-acre suburban campus **Total enrollment** 2,126 **Student/faculty ratio** 12:1 **Application deadline** Rolling **Freshmen** 93% were admitted **Housing** Yes **Expenses** Tuition $11,246; Room & Board $4358 **Undergraduates** 64% women, 27% part-time, 39% 25 or older, 1% Native American, 5% Hispanic, 0.5% black, 3% Asian American or Pacific Islander **Most popular recent majors** Nursing; business; accounting **Academic program** Average class size 20, English as a second language, advanced placement, self-designed majors, tutorials, honors program, summer session, internships **Contact** Mr. Philip J. Alletto, Vice President of Student Development and Enrollment Management, Westminster College of Salt Lake City, 1840 South 1300 East, Salt Lake City, UT 84105-3697. Telephone: 801-488-4200 or toll-free 800-748-4753. Fax: 801-484-3252. E-mail: admispub@wsclc.edu. Web site: http://www.wcslc.edu/.

VERMONT

BENNINGTON COLLEGE
BENNINGTON, VERMONT

General Independent, comprehensive, coed **Entrance** Very difficult **Setting** 550-acre small town campus **Total enrollment** 451 **Student/faculty ratio** 6:1 **Application deadline** 2/1 **Freshmen** 81% were admitted **Housing** Yes **Expenses** Tuition $26,400 **Undergraduates** 69% women, 0.3% part-time, 0.4% 25 or older, 1% Native American, 1% Hispanic, 1% black, 1% Asian American or Pacific Islander **Most popular recent majors** Interdisciplinary studies; literature; visual/performing arts **Academic program** English as a second language, self-designed majors, tutorials, internships **Contact** Ms. Elena Ruocco Bachrach, Dean of Admissions and the Freshman Year, Bennington College, Bennington, VT 05201-9993. Telephone: 802-440-4312 or toll-free 800-833-6845. E-mail: admissions@bennington.edu. Web site: http://www.bennington.edu/.

BURLINGTON COLLEGE
BURLINGTON, VERMONT

General Independent, 4-year, coed **Entrance** Noncompetitive **Setting** 1-acre urban campus **Total enrollment** 137 **Student/faculty ratio** 8:1 **Application deadline** Rolling **Freshmen** 83% were admitted **Housing** No **Expenses** Tuition $8420 **Undergraduates** 64% women, 58% part-time, 65% 25 or older, 4% Native American, 1% Hispanic, 4% black, 1% Asian American or Pacific Islander **Most Popular Recent Major** Psychology **Academic program** Accelerated degree program, self-designed majors, tutorials, summer session, adult/continuing education programs, internships **Contact** Mr. Tobias Kahan, Assistant Director of Admissions, Burlington College, 95 North Avenue, Burlington, VT 05401-2998. Telephone: 802-862-9616 ext. 24 or toll-free 800-862-9616. Fax: 802-658-0071. E-mail: admissions@burlcol.edu.

CASTLETON STATE COLLEGE
CASTLETON, VERMONT

General State-supported, comprehensive, coed **Entrance** Moderately difficult **Setting** 130-acre rural campus **Total enrollment** 1,840 **Student/faculty ratio** 16:1 **Application deadline** Rolling **Freshmen** 85% were admitted **Housing** Yes **Expenses** Tuition $4506; Room & Board $5086 **Undergraduates** 55% women, 9% part-time, 17% 25 or older, 0.3% Native American, 1% Hispanic, 0.5% black, 1% Asian American or Pacific Islander **Most popular recent majors** Business administration; psychology **Academic program** Average class size 20, advanced placement, self-designed majors, tutorials, honors program, summer session, internships **Contact** Ms. Patricia A. Tencza, Director of Admissions, Castleton State College, Castleton, VT 05735. Telephone: 802-468-1213 or toll-free 800-639-8521. Fax: 802-468-1476. E-mail: tenczap@sparrow.csc.vsc.edu. Web site: http://www.csc.vsc.edu.

COLLEGE OF ST. JOSEPH
RUTLAND, VERMONT

General Independent Roman Catholic, comprehensive, coed **Entrance** Minimally difficult **Setting** 90-acre small town campus **Total enrollment** 513 **Application deadline** Rolling **Housing** Yes **Expenses** Tuition $10,100; Room & Board $5800 **Undergraduates** 64% women, 24% part-time, 40% 25 or older, 0.3% Native American, 2% Hispanic, 3% black, 1% Asian American or Pacific Islander **Academic program** English as a second language, advanced placement, accelerated degree program, self-designed majors, tutorials, summer session, adult/continuing education programs, internships **Contact** Mr. Steven Soba, Director of Admissions, College of St. Joseph, 71 Clement Road, Rutland, VT 05701-3899. Telephone: 802-773-5900 ext. 205.

GODDARD COLLEGE
PLAINFIELD, VERMONT

General Independent, comprehensive, coed **Entrance** Moderately difficult **Setting** 250-acre rural campus **Total enrollment** 534 **Student/faculty ratio** 12:1 **Application deadline** Rolling **Housing** Yes **Expenses** Tuition $15,660; Room & Board $5288 **Undergraduates** 59% women, 20% 25 or older, 1% Native American, 4% Hispanic, 7% black, 4% Asian American or Pacific Islander **Most popular recent majors** Creative writing; education; psychology **Academic program** Advanced placement, self-designed majors, tutorials, adult/continuing education programs, internships **Contact** Ms. Sara L. Barrette, Admissions Counselor, Goddard College, 123 Pitkin Road, Plainfield, VT 05667. Telephone: 802-454-8311 ext. 322 or toll-free 800-468-4888. Fax: 802-454-1029. Web site: http://www.goddard.edu/.

GREEN MOUNTAIN COLLEGE
POULTNEY, VERMONT

General Independent, 4-year, coed, affiliated with United Methodist Church **Entrance** Moderately difficult **Setting** 155-acre small town campus **Total enrollment** 583 **Student/faculty ratio** 14:1 **Application deadline** Rolling **Freshmen** 95% were admitted **Housing** Yes **Expenses** Tuition $15,140; Room & Board $3320 **Undergraduates** 4% 25 or older **Most popular recent majors** Behavioral sciences; business administration **Academic program** English as a second language, advanced placement, accelerated degree program, self-designed majors, honors program, adult/continuing education programs, internships **Contact** Mr. Gregory W. Matthews, Dean of Admissions and Financial Aid, Green Mountain College, One College Circle, Poultney, VT 05764-1199. Telephone: 802-287-8208 or toll-free 800-776-6675 (out-of-state). Fax: 802-287-8099. E-mail: admiss@greenmtn.edu. Web site: http://www.greenmtn.edu/.

JOHNSON STATE COLLEGE
JOHNSON, VERMONT

General State-supported, comprehensive, coed **Entrance** Moderately difficult **Setting** 350-acre rural campus **Total enrollment** 1,622 **Student/faculty ratio** 18:1 **Application deadline** Rolling **Freshmen** 85% were admitted **Housing** Yes **Expenses** Tuition $4641; Room & Board $5086 **Undergraduates** 50% women, 19% part-time, 13% 25 or older, 2% Native American, 0.3% Hispanic, 0.3% black, 1% Asian American or Pacific Islander **Most popular recent majors** Business administration; education; environmental science **Academic program** Average class size 16, English as a second language, advanced placement, accelerated degree program, tutorials, summer session, adult/continuing education programs, internships **Contact** Mr. Jonathan H. Henry, Director of Admissions, Johnson State College, RR 2, Box 75, Johnson, VT 05656-9405. Telephone: 802-635-1219 or toll-free 800-635-2356. Fax: 802-635-1230. E-mail: jscapply@badger.jsc.vsc.edu. Web site: http://www.jsc.vsc.edu/.

LYNDON STATE COLLEGE
LYNDONVILLE, VERMONT

General State-supported, comprehensive, coed **Entrance** Moderately difficult **Setting** 175-acre rural campus **Total enrollment** 1,229 **Student/faculty ratio** 17:1 **Application deadline** Rolling **Freshmen** 90% were admitted **Housing** Yes **Expenses** Tuition $4516; Room & Board $5086 **Undergraduates** 46% women, 7% part-time, 12% 25 or older **Most popular recent majors** Business administration; mass communications; education **Academic program** Average class size 20, advanced placement, self-designed majors, summer session, adult/continuing education programs, internships **Contact** Mr. Joseph Bellavance Jr., Director of Admissions, Lyndon State College, Lyndonville, VT 05851. Telephone: 802-626-6413 or toll-free 800-225-1998 (in-state). E-mail: butlers@king.lsc.vsc.edu. Web site: http://www.lsc.vsc.edu/.

MARLBORO COLLEGE
MARLBORO, VERMONT

General Independent, comprehensive, coed **Entrance** Moderately difficult **Setting** 350-acre rural campus **Total enrollment** 290 **Student/faculty ratio** 8:1 **Application deadline** 3/1 **Freshmen** 75% were admitted **Housing** Yes **Expenses** Tuition $20,345; Room & Board $6590 **Undergraduates** 54% women, 2% part-time, 10% 25 or older, 0% Native American, 4% Hispanic, 1% black, 2% Asian American or Pacific Islander **Most popular recent majors** Literature; sociology; biology **Academic program** Advanced placement, accelerated degree program, self-designed majors, tutorials, internships **Contact** Ms. Vanessa E. Gray, Director of Admissions, Marlboro College, Box A, Marlboro, VT 05344. Telephone: 802-257-4333 ext. 237 or toll-free 800-343-0049 (out-of-state). E-mail: admissions@marlboro.edu. Web site: http://www.marlboro.edu/.

MIDDLEBURY COLLEGE
MIDDLEBURY, VERMONT

General Independent, comprehensive, coed **Entrance** Very difficult **Setting** 350-acre small town campus **Total enrollment** 2,176 **Student/faculty ratio** 11:1 **Application deadline** 12/31 **Freshmen** 31% were admitted **Housing** Yes **Expenses** Tuition $29,340 **Undergraduates** 51% women, 2% part-time, 1% Native American, 5% Hispanic, 2% black, 3% Asian American or Pacific Islander **Most popular recent majors** English; international relations; history **Academic program** Advanced placement, accelerated degree program, self-designed majors, tutorials, honors program, summer session, internships **Contact** Mr. John Hanson, Director of Admissions, Middlebury College, Emma Willard House, Middlebury, VT 05753-6002. Telephone: 802-443-3000. Fax: 802-443-2056. E-mail: admit@midd-unix.middlebury.edu. Web site: http://www.middlebury.edu/.

NORWICH UNIVERSITY
NORTHFIELD, VERMONT

General Independent, comprehensive, coed **Entrance** Moderately difficult **Setting** 1,125-acre small town campus **Total enrollment** 2,791 **Student/faculty ratio** 14:1 **Application deadline** Rolling **Freshmen** 94% were admitted **Housing** Yes **Expenses** Tuition $14,950; Room & Board $5717 **Undergraduates** 42% women, 9% part-time, 10% 25 or older, 1% Native American, 4% Hispanic, 2% black, 2% Asian American or Pacific Islander **Most popular recent majors** Criminal justice/law enforcement administration; mechanical engineering; business administration **Academic program** English as a second language, advanced placement, tutorials, honors program, summer session, adult/continuing education programs, internships **Contact** Mr. Frank Griffis, Dean of Admissions and Marketing, Norwich University, Northfield, VT 05663. Telephone: 802-485-2001 or toll-free 800-468-6679 (in-state). Fax: 802-485-2580. E-mail: nuadm@norwich.edu. Web site: http://www.norwich.edu/.

▶ **For more information, see page 488.**

SAINT MICHAEL'S COLLEGE
COLCHESTER, VERMONT

General Independent Roman Catholic, comprehensive, coed **Entrance** Moderately difficult **Setting** 440-acre small town campus **Total enrollment** 2,729 **Student/faculty ratio** 14:1 **Application deadline** 2/1 **Freshmen** 70% were admitted **Housing** Yes **Expenses** Tuition $15,900; Room & Board $7000 **Undergraduates** 54% women, 5% part-time, 2% 25 or older, 0.05% Native American, 1% Hispanic, 0.5% black, 1% Asian American or Pacific Islander **Most popular recent majors** Psychology; business administration; English **Academic program** Average class size 25, English as a second language, advanced placement, self-designed majors, tutorials, honors program, summer session, adult/continuing education programs, internships **Contact** Ms. Jacqueline Murphy, Director of Admission, Saint Michael's College, Winooski Park, Colchester, VT 05439. Telephone: 802-654-3000 or toll-free 800-762-8000. Fax: 802-654-2591. E-mail: admission@smcvt.edu. Web site: http://www.smcvt.edu/.

SCHOOL FOR INTERNATIONAL TRAINING
BRATTLEBORO, VERMONT

General Independent, upper-level, coed **Contact** Mr. Ed Parker, Undergraduate Admissions Counselor, School for International Training, PO Box 676, Kipling Road, Brattleboro, VT 05302-0676. Telephone: 802-257-7751 or toll-free 800-451-4465 (out-of-state). Fax: 802-258-3500. E-mail: admissions.sit@worldlearning.org. Web site: http://www.worldlearning.org/sit.html/.

SOUTHERN VERMONT COLLEGE
BENNINGTON, VERMONT

General Independent, 4-year, coed **Entrance** Minimally difficult **Setting** 371-acre small town campus **Total enrollment** 606 **Student/faculty ratio** 17:1 **Application deadline** Rolling **Freshmen** 78% were admitted **Housing** Yes **Expenses** Tuition $11,130; Room & Board $5150 **Undergraduates** 61% women, 32% part-time, 38% 25 or older, 0.5% Native American, 2% Hispanic, 3% black, 0.2% Asian American or Pacific Islander **Most popular recent majors** Criminal justice/law enforcement administration; business administration; liberal arts and studies **Academic program** Average class size 20, advanced placement, accelerated degree program, self-designed majors, tutorials, honors program, summer session, adult/continuing education programs, intern-

Southern Vermont College *(continued)*

ships **Contact** Ms. Mary Van Arsdale, Director of Admissions, Southern Vermont College, Monument Avenue, Bennington, VT 05201-2128. Telephone: 802-442-5427 ext. 6304 or toll-free 800-378-2782 (in-state). Fax: 802-447-4695. E-mail: admis@svc.edu. Web site: http://www.svc.edu/.

▶ **For more information, see page 518.**

TRINITY COLLEGE OF VERMONT
BURLINGTON, VERMONT

General Independent Roman Catholic, comprehensive, primarily women **Entrance** Moderately difficult **Setting** 24-acre suburban campus **Total enrollment** 961 **Student/faculty ratio** 11:1 **Application deadline** Rolling **Freshmen** 93% were admitted **Housing** Yes **Expenses** Tuition $13,420; Room & Board $6312 **Undergraduates** 88% women, 48% part-time, 54% 25 or older, 0.1% Native American, 1% Hispanic, 1% black, 1% Asian American or Pacific Islander **Most popular recent majors** Business administration; psychology; elementary education **Academic program** Average class size 25, English as a second language, advanced placement, self-designed majors, tutorials, summer session, adult/continuing education programs, internships **Contact** Ms. Molly MacPherson, Assistant Director of Admissions, Trinity College of Vermont, 208 Colchester Avenue, Burlington, VT 05401-1470. Telephone: 802-658-0337 ext. 218 or toll-free 888-277-5975 (out-of-state). Fax: 802-658-5446. Web site: http://www.trinityvt.edu/.

UNIVERSITY OF VERMONT
BURLINGTON, VERMONT

General State-supported, university, coed **Entrance** Moderately difficult **Setting** 425-acre suburban campus **Total enrollment** 10,368 **Student/faculty ratio** 13:1 **Application deadline** 2/1 **Freshmen** 85% were admitted **Housing** Yes **Expenses** Tuition $7550; Room & Board $5272 **Undergraduates** 54% women, 5% part-time, 6% 25 or older, 0.3% Native American, 1% Hispanic, 1% black, 2% Asian American or Pacific Islander **Most popular recent majors** Business administration; English; political science **Academic program** English as a second language, advanced placement, self-designed majors, honors program, summer session, internships **Contact** Mr. Donald M. Honeman, Director of Admissions, University of Vermont, Office of Admissions, Burlington, VT 05401-3596. Telephone: 802-656-3370. Fax: 802-656-8611. Web site: http://www.uvm.edu/.

VIRGINIA

AMERICAN MILITARY UNIVERSITY
MANASSAS PARK, VIRGINIA

General Proprietary, upper-level, coed **Entrance** Noncompetitive **Total enrollment** 1,115 **Student/faculty ratio** 20:1 **Application deadline** Rolling **Freshmen** 50% were admitted **Housing** No **Expenses** Tuition $4835 **Undergraduates** 100% 25 or older **Contact** Ms. Bonnie Struckholz, Director of Admissions, American Military University, 9104-P Manassas Drive, Manassas Park, VA 20111. Telephone: 703-330-5398 ext. 105. Fax: 703-330-5109. E-mail: amugen@amunet.edu. Web site: http://www.amunet.edu/.

AVERETT COLLEGE
DANVILLE, VIRGINIA

General Independent Baptist, comprehensive, coed **Entrance** Moderately difficult **Setting** 25-acre suburban campus **Total enrollment** 2,361 **Student/faculty ratio** 12:1 **Application deadline** 8/15 **Freshmen** 82% were admitted **Housing** Yes **Expenses** Tuition $12,985; Room & Board $4200 **Undergraduates** 59% women, 49% part-time, 61% 25 or older, 0.4% Native American, 1% Hispanic, 18% black, 3% Asian American or Pacific Islander **Most popular recent majors** Business administration; education **Academic program** Average class size 15, English as a second language, advanced placement, accelerated degree program, self-designed majors, tutorials, honors program, summer session, adult/continuing education programs, internships **Contact** Mr. Gary Sherman, Dean of Enrollment Management, Averett College, 420 West Main Street, Danville, VA 24541-3692. Telephone: 804-791-5660 or toll-free 800-AVERETT. Fax: 804-791-5637. E-mail: admit@averett.edu. Web site: http://www.averett.edu/.

BLUEFIELD COLLEGE
BLUEFIELD, VIRGINIA

General Independent Southern Baptist, 4-year, coed **Entrance** Moderately difficult **Setting** 85-acre small town campus **Total enrollment** 818 **Student/faculty ratio** 16:1 **Application deadline** Rolling **Housing** Yes **Expenses** Tuition $7030; Room & Board $4610 **Undergraduates** 51% women, 5% part-time, 25% 25 or older, 0.5% Native American, 1% Hispanic, 9% black, 1% Asian American or Pacific Islander **Most popular recent majors** Business administration; education; psychology **Academic program** Advanced placement, self-designed majors, tutorials, honors program, summer session, adult/continuing education programs, internships **Contact** Office of Admissions, Bluefield College, 3000 College Drive, Bluefield, VA 24605-1799. Telephone: 540-326-4214 or toll-free 800-872-0175. Fax: 540-326-4288. Web site: http://www.bluefield.edu/.

BRIDGEWATER COLLEGE
BRIDGEWATER, VIRGINIA

General Independent, 4-year, coed, affiliated with Church of the Brethren **Entrance** Moderately difficult **Setting** 190-acre small town campus **Total enrollment** 1,066 **Student/faculty ratio** 14:1 **Application deadline** Rolling **Freshmen** 81% were admitted **Housing** Yes **Expenses** Tuition $14,010; Room & Board $5970 **Undergraduates** 57% women, 1% part-time, 3% 25 or older, 0.1% Native American, 1% Hispanic, 4% black, 0.2% Asian American or Pacific Islander **Most popular recent majors** Business administration; biology; psychology **Academic program** Average class size 19, advanced placement, accelerated degree program, tutorials, summer session, adult/continuing education programs, internships **Contact** Mr. Brian C. Hildebrand, Dean for Enrollment Management, Bridgewater College, 402 East College Street, Bridgewater, VA 22812-1599. Telephone: 540-828-5375 or toll-free 800-759-8328. Fax: 540-828-5481. E-mail: admissions@bridgewater.edu. Web site: http://www.bridgewater.edu/.

CHRISTENDOM COLLEGE
FRONT ROYAL, VIRGINIA

General Independent Roman Catholic, comprehensive, coed **Entrance** Moderately difficult **Setting** 100-acre small town campus **Total enrollment** 285 **Student/faculty ratio** 10:1 **Application deadline** Rolling **Freshmen** 91% were admitted **Housing** Yes **Expenses** Tuition $10,545; Room & Board $3700 **Undergraduates** 52% women, 1% part-time, 6% 25 or older **Most popular recent majors** History; literature; political science **Academic program** Average class size 25, advanced placement, accelerated degree program, summer session, internships **Contact** Mr. Paul Heisler, Director of Admissions, Christendom College, 134 Christendom Drive, Front Royal, VA 22630-5103. Telephone: 540-636-2900 ext. 290 or toll-free 800-877-5456. Fax: 540-636-1655. E-mail: admissions@christendom.edu. Web site: http://www.christendom.edu/.

CHRISTOPHER NEWPORT UNIVERSITY
NEWPORT NEWS, VIRGINIA

General State-supported, comprehensive, coed **Entrance** Moderately difficult **Setting** 113-acre suburban campus **Total enrollment** 4,878 **Student/faculty ratio** 19:1 **Application deadline** 8/1 **Freshmen** 83% were admitted **Housing** Yes **Expenses** Tuition $3466; Room & Board $4650 **Undergraduates** 61% women, 26% part-time, 38% 25 or older, 0.4% Native American, 2% Hispanic, 18% black, 3% Asian American or Pacific Islander **Most popular recent majors** Business administration; political science; accounting **Academic program** Average class size 25, English as a second language, advanced placement, accelerated degree program, self-designed majors, tutorials, honors program, summer session, adult/continuing education programs, internships **Contact** Ms. Cynthia L. Guthrie, Assistant Director of Admissions, Christopher Newport University, 50 Shoe Lane, Newport News, VA 23606-2998. Telephone: 757-594-7045 or toll-free 800-333-4CNU. Fax: 757-594-7333. E-mail: admit@cnu.edu. Web site: http://www.cnu.edu/.

CLINCH VALLEY COLLEGE OF THE UNIVERSITY OF VIRGINIA
WISE, VIRGINIA

General State-supported, 4-year, coed **Entrance** Moderately difficult **Setting** 350-acre small town campus **Total enrollment** 1,515 **Student/faculty ratio** 16:1 **Application deadline** 8/1 **Freshmen** 76% were admitted **Housing** Yes **Expenses** Tuition $3348; Room & Board $4284 **Undergraduates** 55% women, 16% part-time, 27% 25 or older, 0% Native American, 0.3% Hispanic, 3% black, 1% Asian American or Pacific Islander **Most popular recent majors** Business administration; psychology **Academic program** Average class size 24, advanced placement, self-designed majors, tutorials, honors program, summer session, adult/continuing education programs, internships **Contact** Ms. Courtney Kilgore, Director of Enrollment Management, Clinch Valley College of the University of Virginia, 1 College Avenue, Wise, VA 24293. Telephone: 540-328-0102 or toll-free 888-282-9324. Fax: 540-328-0251. E-mail: c-kilgore@clinch.edu. Web site: http://www.clinch.edu/.

COLLEGE OF WILLIAM AND MARY
WILLIAMSBURG, VIRGINIA

General State-supported, university, coed **Entrance** Very difficult **Setting** 1,200-acre small town campus **Total enrollment** 7,572 **Student/faculty ratio** 12:1 **Application deadline** 1/15 **Freshmen** 46% were admitted **Housing** Yes **Expenses** Tuition $5032; Room & Board $4586 **Undergraduates** 60% women, 1% part-time, 2% 25 or older, 0.2% Native American, 3% Hispanic, 5% black, 7% Asian American or Pacific Islander **Most popular recent majors** Business administration; biology; English **Academic program** Average class size 23, advanced placement, accelerated degree program, self-designed majors, tutorials, honors

College of William and Mary *(continued)*

program, summer session **Contact** Ms. Virginia Carey, Dean of Admission, College of William and Mary, PO Box 8795, Williamsburg, VA 23187-8795. Telephone: 757-221-4223. Fax: 757-221-1242. E-mail: admiss@facstaff.wm.edu. Web site: http://www.wm.edu/.

COMMUNITY HOSPITAL OF ROANOKE VALLEY–COLLEGE OF HEALTH SCIENCES

ROANOKE, VIRGINIA

General Independent, 4-year, coed **Entrance** Moderately difficult **Setting** Urban campus **Total enrollment** 585 **Student/faculty ratio** 11:1 **Application deadline** 7/31 **Freshmen** 81% were admitted **Housing** Yes **Expenses** Tuition $11,100; Room & Board $4160 **Undergraduates** 76% women, 36% part-time, 66% 25 or older **Most popular recent majors** Nursing; physical therapy; occupational therapy **Academic program** Average class size 15, advanced placement, summer session, adult/continuing education programs, internships **Contact** Ms. Heather Todd, Admissions Representative, Community Hospital of Roanoke Valley–College of Health Sciences, PO Box 13186, Roanoke, VA 24031-3186. Telephone: 540-985-8449 or toll-free 888-985-8483. Fax: 540-985-9773. E-mail: jbailey@health.chs.edu. Web site: http://www.chs.edu/.

EASTERN MENNONITE UNIVERSITY

HARRISONBURG, VIRGINIA

General Independent Mennonite, comprehensive, coed **Entrance** Moderately difficult **Setting** 92-acre small town campus **Total enrollment** 1,225 **Student/faculty ratio** 13:1 **Application deadline** 8/1 **Freshmen** 91% were admitted **Housing** Yes **Expenses** Tuition $12,600; Room & Board $4700 **Undergraduates** 61% women, 2% part-time, 19% 25 or older, 0.2% Native American, 2% Hispanic, 3% black, 1% Asian American or Pacific Islander **Most popular recent majors** Education; biology; nursing **Academic program** Average class size 38, English as a second language, advanced placement, self-designed majors, honors program, summer session, adult/continuing education programs, internships **Contact** Ms. Ellen B. Miller, Director of Admissions, Eastern Mennonite University, 1200 Park Road, Harrisonburg, VA 22802-2462. Telephone: 540-432-4118 or toll-free 800-368-2665 (out-of-state). Fax: 540-432-4444. E-mail: admiss@emu.edu. Web site: http://www.emu.edu/.

▶ **For more information, see page 427.**

EMORY & HENRY COLLEGE

EMORY, VIRGINIA

General Independent United Methodist, 4-year, coed **Entrance** Moderately difficult **Setting** 150-acre rural campus **Total enrollment** 893 **Student/faculty ratio** 14:1 **Application deadline** Rolling **Freshmen** 85% were admitted **Housing** Yes **Expenses** Tuition $11,572; Room & Board $4800 **Undergraduates** 50% women, 2% part-time, 7% 25 or older **Most popular recent majors** Business administration; English; education **Academic program** Advanced placement, self-designed majors, tutorials, honors program, summer session, internships **Contact** Dr. Jean-Marie Luce, Dean of Admissions and Financial Aid, Emory & Henry College, PO Box 947, Emory, VA 24327-0947. Telephone: 540-944-6133 or toll-free 800-848-5493. Fax: 540-944-6935. E-mail: ehadmiss@ehc.edu. Web site: http://www.ehc.edu/.

▶ **For more information, see page 431.**

FERRUM COLLEGE

FERRUM, VIRGINIA

General Independent United Methodist, 4-year, coed **Entrance** Minimally difficult **Setting** 720-acre rural campus **Total enrollment** 908 **Student/faculty ratio** 12:1 **Application deadline** Rolling **Freshmen** 79% were admitted **Housing** Yes **Expenses** Tuition $10,750; Room & Board $4850 **Undergraduates** 44% women, 4% part-time, 8% 25 or older, 0% Native American, 2% Hispanic, 14% black, 0.3% Asian American or Pacific Islander **Most popular recent majors** Environmental science; business administration; social work **Academic program** Average class size 19, advanced placement, self-designed majors, tutorials, summer session, internships **Contact** Mr. Darren Goode, Director of Admissions, Ferrum College, PO Box 1000, Ferrum, VA 24088-9001. Telephone: 540-365-4290 or toll-free 800-868-9797. Fax: 540-365-4266. E-mail: admissions@ferrum.edu. Web site: http://www.ferrum.edu/.

GEORGE MASON UNIVERSITY

FAIRFAX, VIRGINIA

General State-supported, university, coed **Entrance** Moderately difficult **Setting** 677-acre suburban campus **Total enrollment** 23,826 **Student/faculty ratio** 17:1 **Application deadline** 2/1 **Freshmen** 68% were admitted **Housing** Yes **Expenses** Tuition $4296; Room & Board $5120 **Undergraduates** 56% women, 26% part-time, 29% 25 or older, 0.4% Native American, 6% Hispanic, 9% black, 16% Asian American or Pacific Islander **Most popular recent majors** Business administration; psychology; English **Academic program** Advanced placement, accelerated degree program, self-designed majors, tutorials, summer session, adult/continuing education programs, internships **Contact** Mr. John C. Carter, Associate Director of Admissions, George Mason University, Finley Building, Fairfax, VA 22030-4444. Telephone: 703-993-2421. E-mail: admissions@gmu.edu. Web site: http://www.gmu.edu/.

HAMPDEN-SYDNEY COLLEGE
HAMPDEN-SYDNEY, VIRGINIA

General Independent Presbyterian, 4-year, men only **Entrance** Moderately difficult **Setting** 850-acre rural campus **Total enrollment** 962 **Student/faculty ratio** 13:1 **Application deadline** 3/1 **Freshmen** 85% were admitted **Housing** Yes **Expenses** Tuition $15,074; Room & Board $5557 **Undergraduates** 0% 25 or older, 0.1% Native American, 2% Hispanic, 4% black, 1% Asian American or Pacific Islander **Most popular recent majors** Economics; history; political science **Academic program** Average class size 16, advanced placement, accelerated degree program, tutorials, honors program, summer session, internships **Contact** Ms. Anita H. Garland, Dean of Admissions, Hampden-Sydney College, PO Box 667, Hampden-Sydney, VA 23943-0667. Telephone: 804-223-6120 or toll-free 800-755-0733. Fax: 804-223-6346. E-mail: hsapp@tiger.hsc.edu. Web site: http://www.hsc.edu/.

HAMPTON UNIVERSITY
HAMPTON, VIRGINIA

General Independent, comprehensive, coed **Entrance** Moderately difficult **Setting** 210-acre urban campus **Total enrollment** 5,704 **Student/faculty ratio** 16:1 **Application deadline** 3/15 **Freshmen** 51% were admitted **Housing** Yes **Expenses** Tuition $9596; Room & Board $4150 **Undergraduates** 61% women, 7% part-time, 19% 25 or older, 0.2% Native American, 1% Hispanic, 88% black, 0.4% Asian American or Pacific Islander **Most popular recent majors** Accounting; biology; psychology **Academic program** Advanced placement, tutorials, honors program, summer session, adult/continuing education programs, internships **Contact** Mr. Leonard M. Jones Jr., Director of Admissions, Hampton University, Hampton, VA 23668. Telephone: 757-727-5328 or toll-free 800-624-3328. Fax: 757-727-5084. Web site: http://www.hampton.edu/admin0.html.

HOLLINS UNIVERSITY
ROANOKE, VIRGINIA

General Independent, comprehensive, women only **Entrance** Moderately difficult **Setting** 475-acre suburban campus **Total enrollment** 1,099 **Student/faculty ratio** 9:1 **Application deadline** 2/15 **Freshmen** 85% were admitted **Housing** Yes **Expenses** Tuition $15,320; Room & Board $5975 **Undergraduates** 6% part-time, 12% 25 or older, 0.2% Native American, 2% Hispanic, 6% black, 2% Asian American or Pacific Islander **Most popular recent majors** English; psychology; biology **Academic program** Average class size 15, advanced placement, accelerated degree program, self-designed majors, tutorials, honors program, adult/continuing education programs, internships **Contact** Mrs. Stuart Trinkle, Director of Admissions, Hollins University, PO Box 9707, Roanoke, VA 24020-1707. Telephone: 540-362-6401 or toll-free 800-456-9595. Fax: 540-362-6218. E-mail: hcadm@matty.hollins.edu. Web site: http://www.hollins.edu/.

JAMES MADISON UNIVERSITY
HARRISONBURG, VIRGINIA

General State-supported, comprehensive, coed **Entrance** Very difficult **Setting** 472-acre small town campus **Total enrollment** 14,115 **Student/faculty ratio** 18:1 **Application deadline** 1/15 **Freshmen** 55% were admitted **Housing** Yes **Expenses** Tuition $4148; Room & Board $4846 **Undergraduates** 55% women, 3% part-time, 3% 25 or older, 0.3% Native American, 2% Hispanic, 5% black, 4% Asian American or Pacific Islander **Most popular recent majors** Psychology; communications; English **Academic program** Average class size 36, English as a second language, advanced placement, accelerated degree program, honors program, summer session, adult/continuing education programs, internships **Contact** Ms. Laika Tamny, Associate Director of Admission Administration, James Madison University, Office of Admissions, Harrisonburg, VA 22807. Telephone: 540-568-6147. Fax: 540-568-3332. E-mail: gotojmu@jmu.edu. Web site: http://www.jmu.edu/.

LIBERTY UNIVERSITY
LYNCHBURG, VIRGINIA

General Independent nondenominational, comprehensive, coed **Entrance** Minimally difficult **Setting** 160-acre suburban campus **Total enrollment** 6,646 **Student/faculty ratio** 28:1 **Application deadline** 8/15 **Freshmen** 61% were admitted **Housing** Yes **Expenses** Tuition $8500; Room & Board $4800 **Undergraduates** 49% women, 13% part-time, 7% 25 or older, 1% Native American, 3% Hispanic, 8% black, 2% Asian American or Pacific Islander **Most popular recent majors** Business administration; psychology; education **Academic program** English as a second language, advanced placement, accelerated degree program, self-designed majors, tutorials, honors program, summer session, internships **Contact** Mr. Mark Camper, Director of Admissions, Liberty University, 1971 University Road, Lynchburg, VA

Liberty University *(continued)*

24502. Telephone: 804-582-2778 or toll-free 800-652-2299. Web site: http://www.liberty.edu/.

LONGWOOD COLLEGE
FARMVILLE, VIRGINIA

General State-supported, comprehensive, coed **Entrance** Moderately difficult **Setting** 154-acre small town campus **Total enrollment** 3,352 **Student/faculty ratio** 14:1 **Application deadline** 3/1 **Freshmen** 77% were admitted **Housing** Yes **Expenses** Tuition $4416; Room & Board $4280 **Undergraduates** 66% women, 3% part-time, 11% 25 or older, 0.2% Native American, 1% Hispanic, 10% black, 1% Asian American or Pacific Islander **Most popular recent majors** Business administration; education; psychology **Academic program** Average class size 25, English as a second language, advanced placement, accelerated degree program, tutorials, honors program, summer session, internships **Contact** Mr. Robert J. Chonko, Director of Admissions, Longwood College, 201 High Street, Farmville, VA 23909-1800. Telephone: 804-395-2060 or toll-free 800-281-4677. Fax: 804-395-2332. E-mail: lcadmit@longwood.lwc.edu. Web site: http://www.lwc.edu/.

LYNCHBURG COLLEGE
LYNCHBURG, VIRGINIA

General Independent, comprehensive, coed, affiliated with Christian Church (Disciples of Christ) **Entrance** Moderately difficult **Setting** 214-acre suburban campus **Total enrollment** 1,972 **Student/faculty ratio** 13:1 **Application deadline** Rolling **Freshmen** 87% were admitted **Housing** Yes **Expenses** Tuition $16,415; Room & Board $4400 **Undergraduates** 63% women, 9% part-time, 18% 25 or older, 0.3% Native American, 1% Hispanic, 11% black, 1% Asian American or Pacific Islander **Most popular recent majors** Education; business administration; mass communications **Academic program** Advanced placement, accelerated degree program, honors program, summer session, adult/continuing education programs, internships **Contact** Ms. Sharon Walters-Bower, Director of Recruitment, Lynchburg College, 1501 Lakeside Drive, Lynchburg, VA 24501-3199. Telephone: 804-544-8300 or toll-free 800-426-8101. Fax: 804-544-8653. E-mail: admissions@lynchburg.edu. Web site: http://www.lynchburg.edu/.

MARY BALDWIN COLLEGE
STAUNTON, VIRGINIA

General Independent, comprehensive, primarily women, affiliated with Presbyterian Church (U.S.A.) **Entrance** Moderately difficult **Setting** 54-acre small town campus **Total enrollment** 1,547 **Student/faculty ratio** 12:1 **Application deadline** 4/15 **Freshmen** 88% were admitted **Housing** Yes **Expenses** Tuition $14,415; Room & Board $7000 **Undergraduates** 95% women, 27% part-time, 0.3% Native American, 2% Hispanic, 9% black, 2% Asian American or Pacific Islander **Most popular recent majors** Psychology; sociology; art **Academic program** Average class size 19, English as a second language, advanced placement, accelerated degree program, self-designed majors, tutorials, honors program, adult/continuing education programs, internships **Contact** Ms. Patricia N. LeDonne, Dean of Admissions and Financial Aid, Mary Baldwin College, Staunton, VA 24401. Telephone: 540-887-7019 or toll-free 800-468-2262. Fax: 540-886-6634. E-mail: dcampbel@cit.mbc.edu. Web site: http://www.mbc.edu/.

MARYMOUNT UNIVERSITY
ARLINGTON, VIRGINIA

General Independent, comprehensive, coed, affiliated with Roman Catholic Church **Entrance** Moderately difficult **Setting** 21-acre suburban campus **Total enrollment** 3,512 **Student/faculty ratio** 14:1 **Application deadline** Rolling **Freshmen** 78% were admitted **Housing** Yes **Expenses** Tuition $12,770; Room & Board $5810 **Undergraduates** 74% women, 25% part-time, 40% 25 or older, 0.2% Native American, 6% Hispanic, 13% black, 7% Asian American or Pacific Islander **Most popular recent majors** Nursing; psychology; business administration **Academic program** Average class size 14, English as a second language, advanced placement, accelerated degree program, self-designed majors, summer session, adult/continuing education programs, internships **Contact** Mr. Brandon Diehm, Associate Director of Admissions, Marymount University, 2807 North Glebe Road, Arlington, VA 22207-4299. Telephone: 703-284-1500 or toll-free 800-548-7638. Fax: 703-522-0349. E-mail: admissions@marymount.edu. Web site: http://www.marymount.edu/.

▶ **For more information, see page 469.**

MARY WASHINGTON COLLEGE
FREDERICKSBURG, VIRGINIA

General State-supported, comprehensive, coed **Entrance** Very difficult **Setting** 176-acre small town campus **Total enrollment** 3,840 **Student/faculty ratio** 18:1 **Application deadline** 2/1 **Freshmen** 57% were admitted **Housing** Yes **Expenses** Tuition $3556; Room & Board $5080 **Undergraduates** 66% women, 15% part-time, 19% 25 or older, 0.3% Native American, 2% Hispanic, 4% black, 4% Asian American or Pacific Islander **Most popular recent majors** Business administration; psychology; English **Academic program**

Average class size 25, advanced placement, accelerated degree program, self-designed majors, tutorials, summer session, adult/continuing education programs, internships **Contact** Dr. Martin A. Wilder Jr., Vice President for Admissions and Financial Aid, Mary Washington College, 1301 College Avenue, Fredericksburg, VA 22401-5358. Telephone: 540-654-2000 or toll-free 800-468-5614. E-mail: admit@mwc.edu. Web site: http://www.mwc.edu/.

NORFOLK STATE UNIVERSITY
NORFOLK, VIRGINIA

General State-supported, comprehensive, coed **Entrance** Moderately difficult **Setting** 130-acre urban campus **Total enrollment** 7,659 **Student/faculty ratio** 22:1 **Application deadline** Rolling **Freshmen** 65% were admitted **Housing** Yes **Expenses** Tuition $3000; Room & Board $4166 **Undergraduates** 62% women, 10% part-time, 0.3% Native American, 1% Hispanic, 88% black, 1% Asian American or Pacific Islander **Academic program** Advanced placement, accelerated degree program, honors program, summer session, adult/continuing education programs, internships **Contact** Dr. Frank W. Cool, Director of Admissions, Norfolk State University, 2401 Corprew Avenue, Norfolk, VA 23504-3907. Telephone: 757-683-8396. Fax: 757-683-2078. Web site: http://www.nsu.edu/.

OLD DOMINION UNIVERSITY
NORFOLK, VIRGINIA

General State-supported, university, coed **Entrance** Moderately difficult **Setting** 186-acre urban campus **Total enrollment** 18,557 **Student/faculty ratio** 12:1 **Application deadline** 3/15 **Freshmen** 82% were admitted **Housing** Yes **Expenses** Tuition $3976; Room & Board $4866 **Undergraduates** 57% women, 35% part-time, 38% 25 or older, 1% Native American, 2% Hispanic, 19% black, 6% Asian American or Pacific Islander **Most popular recent majors** Psychology; interdisciplinary studies; nursing **Academic program** English as a second language, advanced placement, accelerated degree program, self-designed majors, tutorials, honors program, summer session, adult/continuing education programs, internships **Contact** Mr. Michael T. O'Connor, Director of Admissions, Old Dominion University, 5215 Hampton Boulevard, Norfolk, VA 23529. Telephone: 757-683-3637 or toll-free 800-348-7926. Fax: 757-683-5357. E-mail: admit@odu.edu. Web site: http://www.odu.edu/.

RADFORD UNIVERSITY
RADFORD, VIRGINIA

General State-supported, comprehensive, coed **Entrance** Moderately difficult **Setting** 177-acre small town campus **Total enrollment** 8,534 **Student/faculty ratio** 16:1 **Application deadline** 4/1 **Freshmen** 80% were admitted **Housing** Yes **Expenses** Tuition $3180; Room & Board $4416 **Undergraduates** 59% women, 8% part-time, 11% 25 or older, 0.2% Native American, 1% Hispanic, 5% black, 2% Asian American or Pacific Islander **Most popular recent majors** Interdisciplinary studies; criminal justice/law enforcement administration; psychology **Academic program** Average class size 22, English as a second language, advanced placement, accelerated degree program, self-designed majors, tutorials, honors program, summer session, adult/continuing education programs, internships **Contact** Dr. David Kraus, Director of Admissions and Records, Radford University, PO Box 6903, Radford, VA 24142. Telephone: 540-831-5371 or toll-free 800-890-4265. Fax: 540-831-5138. E-mail: pwhite@runet.edu. Web site: http://www.runet.edu/.

RANDOLPH-MACON COLLEGE
ASHLAND, VIRGINIA

General Independent United Methodist, 4-year, coed **Entrance** Moderately difficult **Setting** 110-acre suburban campus **Total enrollment** 1,093 **Student/faculty ratio** 11:1 **Application deadline** 3/1 **Freshmen** 83% were admitted **Housing** Yes **Expenses** Tuition $16,240; Room & Board $4175 **Undergraduates** 49% women, 1% part-time, 1% 25 or older, 1% Native American, 1% Hispanic, 4% black, 1% Asian American or Pacific Islander **Most popular recent majors** Business economics; psychology; English **Academic program** Average class size 22, advanced placement, accelerated degree program, tutorials, honors program, summer session, internships **Contact** Mr. John C. Conkright, Dean of Admissions and Financial Aid, Randolph-Macon College, PO Box 5005, Ashland, VA 23005-5505. Telephone: 804-752-7305 or toll-free 800-888-1762. Fax: 804-752-4707. E-mail: admissions_office@rmc.edu. Web site: http://www.rmc.edu/.

RANDOLPH-MACON WOMAN'S COLLEGE
LYNCHBURG, VIRGINIA

General Independent Methodist, 4-year, women only **Entrance** Moderately difficult **Setting** 100-acre suburban campus **Total enrollment** 720 **Student/faculty ratio** 9:1 **Application deadline** 3/1 **Freshmen** 89% were admitted **Housing** Yes **Expenses** Tuition $16,230; Room & Board $6720 **Undergraduates** 3% part-time, 10% 25 or older, 1% Native American, 3% Hispanic, 6% black, 3% Asian American or Pacific Islander **Most popular recent majors** Psychology; English; biology **Academic program** Average class size 17, English as a second language, advanced placement, accelerated degree program, self-designed majors, tuto-

Randolph-Macon Woman's College *(continued)*

rials, honors program, adult/continuing education programs, internships **Contact** Mr. James Duffy, Senior Associate Director of Admissions, Randolph-Macon Woman's College, 2500 Rivermont Avenue, Lynchburg, VA 24503-1526. Telephone: 804-947-8100 or toll-free 800-745-7692. Fax: 804-947-8996. E-mail: admissions@rmwc.edu. Web site: http://www.rmwc.edu/.

▶ **For more information, see page 494.**

ROANOKE COLLEGE
SALEM, VIRGINIA

General Independent, 4-year, coed, affiliated with Evangelical Lutheran Church in America **Entrance** Moderately difficult **Setting** 68-acre suburban campus **Total enrollment** 1,698 **Student/faculty ratio** 14:1 **Application deadline** 3/1 **Freshmen** 81% were admitted **Housing** Yes **Expenses** Tuition $16,410; Room & Board $5250 **Undergraduates** 57% women, 6% part-time, 7% 25 or older, 1% Native American, 1% Hispanic, 3% black, 1% Asian American or Pacific Islander **Most popular recent majors** Business administration; psychology; English **Academic program** Average class size 20, English as a second language, advanced placement, accelerated degree program, honors program, summer session, adult/continuing education programs, internships **Contact** Mr. Michael C. Maxey, Vice President of Admissions, Roanoke College, 221 College Lane, Salem, VA 24153-3794. Telephone: 540-375-2270 or toll-free 800-388-2276. Fax: 540-375-2267. E-mail: admissions@roanoke.edu. Web site: http://www.roanoke.edu/.

SAINT PAUL'S COLLEGE
LAWRENCEVILLE, VIRGINIA

General Independent Episcopal, 4-year, coed **Contact** Mrs. Mary Ransom, Director of Admissions and Recruitment, Saint Paul's College, 115 College Drive, Lawrenceville, VA 23868-1202. Telephone: 804-848-3984 or toll-free 800-678-7071.

SHENANDOAH UNIVERSITY
WINCHESTER, VIRGINIA

General Independent United Methodist, comprehensive, coed **Entrance** Moderately difficult **Setting** 72-acre small town campus **Total enrollment** 1,927 **Student/faculty ratio** 6:1 **Application deadline** Rolling **Housing** Yes **Expenses** Tuition $14,400; Room & Board $5050 **Undergraduates** 65% women, 12% part-time, 27% 25 or older, 0.3% Native American, 2% Hispanic, 5% black, 2% Asian American or Pacific Islander **Most popular recent majors** Nursing; music; psychology **Academic program** English as a second language, advanced placement, accelerated degree program, self-designed majors, summer session, adult/continuing education programs, internships **Contact** Mr. Michael Carpenter, Director of Admissions, Shenandoah University, 1460 University Drive, Winchester, VA 22601-5195. Telephone: 540-665-4581 or toll-free 800-432-2266. Fax: 540-665-4627. E-mail: admit@su.edu. Web site: http://www.su.edu/.

▶ **For more information, see page 512.**

SWEET BRIAR COLLEGE
SWEET BRIAR, VIRGINIA

General Independent, 4-year, women only **Entrance** Moderately difficult **Setting** 3,300-acre rural campus **Total enrollment** 758 **Student/faculty ratio** 7:1 **Application deadline** 2/15 **Freshmen** 94% were admitted **Housing** Yes **Expenses** Tuition $15,795; Room & Board $6510 **Undergraduates** 4% part-time, 4% 25 or older, 1% Native American, 2% Hispanic, 5% black, 3% Asian American or Pacific Islander **Most popular recent majors** Psychology; political science; international relations **Academic program** Advanced placement, accelerated degree program, self-designed majors, tutorials, honors program, adult/continuing education programs, internships **Contact** Ms. Nancy E. Church, Dean of Admissions, Sweet Briar College, PO Box B, Sweet Briar, VA 24595. Telephone: 804-381-6142 or toll-free 800-381-6142. Fax: 804-381-6152. E-mail: admissions@sbc.edu. Web site: http://www.sbc.edu/.

▶ **For more information, see page 526.**

UNIVERSITY OF RICHMOND
RICHMOND, VIRGINIA

General Independent, comprehensive, coed **Entrance** Very difficult **Setting** 350-acre suburban campus **Total enrollment** 4,425 **Student/faculty ratio** 11:1 **Application deadline** 2/1 **Freshmen** 45% were admitted **Housing** Yes **Expenses** Tuition $18,595; Room & Board $4143 **Undergraduates** 52% women, 17% part-time, 0.2% Native American, 2% Hispanic, 6% black, 2% Asian American or Pacific Islander **Most popular recent majors** Business administration; biology; political science **Academic program** Average class size 23, English as a second language, advanced placement, accelerated degree program, self-designed majors, tutorials, honors program, summer session, adult/continuing education programs, internships **Contact** Ms. Pamela Spence, Dean of Admission, University of Richmond, 28 Westhampton Way, University of Richmond, VA 23173. Telephone: 804-289-8640 or toll-free 800-

700-1662. Fax: 804-287-6003. E-mail: admission@richmond.edu. Web site: http://www.richmond.edu/.

UNIVERSITY OF VIRGINIA
CHARLOTTESVILLE, VIRGINIA

General State-supported, university, coed **Entrance** Most difficult **Setting** 1,131-acre suburban campus **Total enrollment** 21,942 **Student/faculty ratio** 13:1 **Application deadline** 1/2 **Freshmen** 36% were admitted **Housing** Yes **Expenses** Tuition $4786; Room & Board $4279 **Undergraduates** 53% women, 0.5% part-time, 2% 25 or older, 0.2% Native American, 2% Hispanic, 10% black, 10% Asian American or Pacific Islander **Most popular recent majors** Business; English; biology **Academic program** Advanced placement, accelerated degree program, self-designed majors, tutorials, honors program, summer session, adult/continuing education programs, internships **Contact** Mr. John A. Blackburn, Dean of Admission, University of Virginia, Charlottesville, VA 22906. Telephone: 804-982-3200. Fax: 804-924-3587. E-mail: undergrad-admission@virginia.edu. Web site: http://www.virginia.edu/.

VIRGINIA COMMONWEALTH UNIVERSITY
RICHMOND, VIRGINIA

General State-supported, university, coed **Entrance** Moderately difficult **Setting** 102-acre urban campus **Total enrollment** 22,702 **Student/faculty ratio** 13:1 **Application deadline** 2/1 **Freshmen** 80% were admitted **Housing** Yes **Expenses** Tuition $4111; Room & Board $4540 **Undergraduates** 60% women, 22% part-time, 25% 25 or older, 1% Native American, 2% Hispanic, 22% black, 8% Asian American or Pacific Islander **Most popular recent majors** Psychology; nursing; criminal justice/law enforcement administration **Academic program** English as a second language, advanced placement, accelerated degree program, self-designed majors, honors program, summer session, adult/continuing education programs, internships **Contact** Counseling Staff, Virginia Commonwealth University, 821 West Franklin Street, Box 842526, Richmond, VA 23284-9005. Telephone: 804-828-1222 or toll-free 800-841-3638. Fax: 804-828-1899. E-mail: vcuinfo@vcu.edu. Web site: http://www.vcu.edu/.

VIRGINIA INTERMONT COLLEGE
BRISTOL, VIRGINIA

General Independent, 4-year, coed, affiliated with Baptist Church **Entrance** Minimally difficult **Setting** 27-acre small town campus **Total enrollment** 848 **Student/faculty ratio** 12:1 **Application deadline** Rolling **Freshmen** 79% were admitted **Housing** Yes **Expenses** Tuition $10,650; Room & Board $4700 **Undergraduates** 76% women, 12% part-time, 52% 25 or older, 0.4% Native American, 0.4% Hispanic, 3% black, 0.4% Asian American or Pacific Islander **Most popular recent majors** Business administration; elementary education; paralegal/legal assistant **Academic program** Average class size 30, advanced placement, summer session, adult/continuing education programs, internships **Contact** Ms. Robin B. Cozart, Director of Admissions, Virginia Intermont College, 1013 Moore Street, Bristol, VA 24201-4298. Telephone: 540-669-6101 ext. 7854 or toll-free 800-451-1842. Fax: 540-669-5763. E-mail: viadmit@vic.edu. Web site: http://www.vic.edu/.

VIRGINIA MILITARY INSTITUTE
LEXINGTON, VIRGINIA

General State-supported, 4-year, coed **Entrance** Moderately difficult **Setting** 140-acre small town campus **Total enrollment** 1,282 **Student/faculty ratio** 12:1 **Application deadline** 4/1 **Freshmen** 76% were admitted **Housing** Yes **Expenses** Tuition $6380; Room & Board $3695 **Undergraduates** 2% women, 0.3% Native American, 2% Hispanic, 7% black, 4% Asian American or Pacific Islander **Most popular recent majors** Economics; history; mechanical engineering **Academic program** Average class size 20, advanced placement, accelerated degree program, tutorials, honors program, summer session, internships **Contact** Lt. Col. Tom Mortenson, Associate Director of Admissions, Virginia Military Institute, Admissions Office, Lexington, VA 24450. Telephone: 540-464-7211 or toll-free 800-767-4207. Fax: 540-464-7746. E-mail: admissions@vmi.edu. Web site: http://www.vmi.edu/.

VIRGINIA POLYTECHNIC INSTITUTE AND STATE UNIVERSITY
BLACKSBURG, VIRGINIA

General State-supported, university, coed **Entrance** Moderately difficult **Setting** 2,600-acre small town campus **Total enrollment** 27,208 **Student/faculty ratio** 17:1 **Application deadline** 2/1 **Freshmen** 73% were admitted **Housing** Yes **Expenses** Tuition $4147; Room & Board $3420 **Undergraduates** 40% women, 3% part-time, 4% 25 or older, 0.3% Native American, 2% Hispanic, 4% black, 7% Asian American or Pacific Islander **Most popular recent majors** Psychology; mechanical engineering; business marketing and marketing management **Academic program** English as a second language, advanced placement, accelerated degree program, tutorials, honors program, summer session, adult/continuing education programs, internships **Contact** Office of Un-

Virginia Polytechnic Institute and State University *(continued)*

dergraduate Admissions, Virginia Polytechnic Institute and State University, 104 Burruss Hall, Blacksburg, VA 24061-0202. Telephone: 540-231-6267. Fax: 540-231-3242. E-mail: vtadmiss@vt.edu. Web site: http://www.vt.edu/.

VIRGINIA STATE UNIVERSITY
PETERSBURG, VIRGINIA

General State-supported, comprehensive, coed **Entrance** Minimally difficult **Setting** 236-acre suburban campus **Total enrollment** 4,200 **Application deadline** Rolling **Freshmen** 86% were admitted **Housing** Yes **Expenses** Tuition $3307; Room & Board $4910 **Undergraduates** 57% women, 7% part-time, 14% 25 or older, 0.1% Native American, 1% Hispanic, 94% black, 0.2% Asian American or Pacific Islander **Most popular recent majors** Sociology; psychology; business administration **Academic program** Advanced placement, accelerated degree program, tutorials, honors program, summer session, adult/continuing education programs, internships **Contact** Ms. Lisa Winn, Director of Admissions, Virginia State University, PO Box 9018, Petersburg, VA 23806-2096. Telephone: 804-524-5902 or toll-free 800-871-7611. Fax: 804-524-5055. E-mail: lwinn@vsu.edu. Web site: http://www.vsu.edu/.

VIRGINIA UNION UNIVERSITY
RICHMOND, VIRGINIA

General Independent Baptist, comprehensive, coed **Entrance** Moderately difficult **Setting** 72-acre urban campus **Total enrollment** 1,700 **Student/faculty ratio** 16:1 **Application deadline** Rolling **Housing** Yes **Expenses** Tuition $8980; Room & Board $3950 **Most popular recent majors** Business administration; criminology; biology **Academic program** Average class size 16, English as a second language, advanced placement, tutorials, honors program, summer session, adult/continuing education programs, internships **Contact** Mr. Gil Powell, Director of Admissions, Virginia Union University, 1500 North Lombardy Street, Richmond, VA 23220-1170. Telephone: 804-257-5881 or toll-free 800-368-3227 (out-of-state).

VIRGINIA WESLEYAN COLLEGE
NORFOLK, VIRGINIA

General Independent United Methodist, 4-year, coed **Entrance** Moderately difficult **Setting** 300-acre urban campus **Total enrollment** 1,436 **Student/faculty ratio** 14:1 **Application deadline** Rolling **Freshmen** 94% were admitted **Housing** Yes **Expenses** Tuition $13,400; Room & Board $5550 **Undergraduates** 65% women, 23% part-time, 36% 25 or older, 1% Native American, 2% Hispanic, 8% black, 2% Asian American or Pacific Islander **Most popular recent majors** Business administration; social sciences; interdisciplinary studies **Academic program** Advanced placement, self-designed majors, tutorials, honors program, summer session, adult/continuing education programs, internships **Contact** Mr. Richard T. Hinshaw, Vice President for Enrollment Management, Dean of Admissions, Virginia Wesleyan College, 1584 Wesleyan Drive, Norfolk, VA 23502-5599. Telephone: 757-455-3208 or toll-free 800-737-8684. Fax: 757-461-5238. E-mail: admissions@vwc.edu. Web site: http://www.vwc.edu/.

▶ **For more information, see page 544.**

WASHINGTON AND LEE UNIVERSITY
LEXINGTON, VIRGINIA

General Independent, comprehensive, coed **Entrance** Most difficult **Setting** 322-acre small town campus **Total enrollment** 2,052 **Student/faculty ratio** 10:1 **Application deadline** 1/15 **Freshmen** 31% were admitted **Housing** Yes **Expenses** Tuition $16,195; Room & Board $5620 **Undergraduates** 43% women, 0.3% 25 or older, 0.1% Native American, 1% Hispanic, 3% black, 1% Asian American or Pacific Islander **Most popular recent majors** History; journalism; biology **Academic program** Advanced placement, accelerated degree program, self-designed majors, tutorials, honors program, internships **Contact** Mr. William M. Hartog, Dean of Admissions and Financial Aid, Washington and Lee University, Lexington, VA 24450. Telephone: 540-463-8710. Fax: 540-463-8062. E-mail: admissions@wlu.edu. Web site: http://www.wlu.edu/.

WORLD COLLEGE
VIRGINIA BEACH, VIRGINIA

General Proprietary, 4-year, primarily men **Contact** Mr. Michael Smith, Director of Operations and Registrar, World College, 5193 Shore Drive, Suite 105, Virginia Beach, VA 23455-2500. Telephone: 757-464-4600.

WASHINGTON

ANTIOCH UNIVERSITY SEATTLE
SEATTLE, WASHINGTON

General Independent, upper-level, coed **Entrance** Noncompetitive **Setting** Urban campus **Total enrollment** 878 **Application deadline** 9/15 **Housing** No **Expenses** Tuition $9345 **Un-**

dergraduates 80% women, 65% part-time, 95% 25 or older, 8% Native American, 3% Hispanic, 7% black, 2% Asian American or Pacific Islander **Academic program** Advanced placement, accelerated degree program, self-designed majors, summer session, adult/continuing education programs **Contact** Ms. Vicki Tolbert, Admissions Officer, Antioch University Seattle, 2326 Sixth Avenue, Seattle, WA 98121-1814. Telephone: 206-441-5352 ext. 5202. E-mail: dawn_rhodes@mist.seattleantioch.edu. Web site: http://www.seattleantioch.edu/.

BASTYR UNIVERSITY
BOTHELL, WASHINGTON

General Independent, upper-level, coed **Entrance** Moderately difficult **Setting** 50-acre suburban campus **Total enrollment** 685 **Student/faculty ratio** 15:1 **Application deadline** 4/1 **Freshmen** 68% were admitted **Housing** Yes **Expenses** Tuition $8130; Room & Board $5070 **Undergraduates** 81% women, 8% part-time, 80% 25 or older **Academic program** Internships **Contact** Ms. Sandra Lane, Associate Director of Admissions, Bastyr University, 14500 Juanita Drive, NE, Bothell, WA 98011. Telephone: 425-602-3102. Fax: 425-823-6222. Web site: http://www.bastyr.edu/.

CENTRAL WASHINGTON UNIVERSITY
ELLENSBURG, WASHINGTON

General State-supported, comprehensive, coed **Entrance** Moderately difficult **Setting** 380-acre small town campus **Total enrollment** 8,438 **Student/faculty ratio** 20:1 **Application deadline** Rolling **Freshmen** 77% were admitted **Housing** Yes **Expenses** Tuition $2826; Room & Board $4269 **Undergraduates** 53% women, 14% part-time, 23% 25 or older, 2% Native American, 4% Hispanic, 2% black, 4% Asian American or Pacific Islander **Most popular recent majors** Business administration; accounting; elementary education **Academic program** English as a second language, advanced placement, accelerated degree program, self-designed majors, tutorials, honors program, summer session, adult/continuing education programs, internships **Contact** Mr. William Swain, Director of Admissions and Academic Advising Services, Central Washington University, Mitchell Hall, Ellensburg, WA 98926-7567. Telephone: 509-963-1200. Fax: 509-963-3022. E-mail: cwuadmis@cwu.edu.

CITY UNIVERSITY
BELLEVUE, WASHINGTON

General Independent, comprehensive, coed **Entrance** Noncompetitive **Setting** Suburban campus **Total enrollment** 11,162 **Application deadline** Rolling **Freshmen** 100% were admitted **Housing** No **Expenses** Tuition $6000 **Undergraduates** 90% 25 or older, 1% Native American, 2% Hispanic, 5% black, 3% Asian American or Pacific Islander **Most popular recent majors** Business administration; accounting **Academic program** English as a second language, advanced placement, accelerated degree program, honors program, summer session, adult/continuing education programs, internships **Contact** Mr. Nabil El-Khatib, Vice President of Admissions and Student Affairs, City University, 919 SW Grady Way, Renton, WA 98055. Telephone: 425-637-1010 or toll-free 800-426-5596. Fax: 425-277-2437. E-mail: info@cityu.edu. Web site: http://www.cityu.edu/.

CORNISH COLLEGE OF THE ARTS
SEATTLE, WASHINGTON

General Independent, 4-year, coed **Entrance** Moderately difficult **Setting** 4-acre urban campus **Total enrollment** 621 **Student/faculty ratio** 4:1 **Application deadline** 8/15 **Freshmen** 76% were admitted **Housing** No **Expenses** Tuition $11,658 **Undergraduates** 60% women, 5% part-time, 24% 25 or older, 2% Native American, 2% Hispanic, 3% black, 5% Asian American or Pacific Islander **Most popular recent majors** Art; music; theater arts/drama **Academic program** Average class size 25, advanced placement, summer session, internships **Contact** Ms. Sharron Starling, Associate Director of Admissions, Cornish College of the Arts, 710 East Roy Street, Seattle, WA 98102-4696. Telephone: 206-726-5017 or toll-free 800-726-ARTS.

DOMINION COLLEGE
SEATTLE, WASHINGTON

General Independent, 4-year, coed **Entrance** Moderately difficult **Setting** Urban campus **Total enrollment** 76 **Application deadline** Rolling **Housing** No **Expenses** Tuition $5200 **Undergraduates** 68% 25 or older, 4% Native American, 9% Hispanic, 14% black, 0% Asian American or Pacific Islander **Academic program** Average class size 10, advanced placement, tutorials, summer session **Contact** Mr. Dan Hope, Director of Recruitment, Dominion College, 20833 International Boulevard, Seattle, WA 98198. Telephone: 206-878-1010. Fax: 206-878-6073. Web site: http://www.dominion.edu/.

EASTERN WASHINGTON UNIVERSITY
CHENEY, WASHINGTON

General State-supported, comprehensive, coed **Entrance** Moderately difficult **Setting** 335-acre small town campus **Total enrollment** 7,537 **Stu-**

Eastern Washington University *(continued)*

dent/faculty ratio 16:1 **Application deadline** 7/1 **Freshmen** 82% were admitted **Housing** Yes **Expenses** Tuition $2622; Room & Board $4294 **Undergraduates** 39% 25 or older **Most popular recent majors** Business administration; reading education; liberal arts and studies **Academic program** English as a second language, advanced placement, accelerated degree program, self-designed majors, tutorials, honors program, summer session, internships **Contact** Ms. Michelle Whittingham, Associate Director of Admissions, Eastern Washington University, EWU MS-148, Cheney, WA 99004-2431. Telephone: 509-359-6582 or toll-free 888-740-1914 (out-of-state). Fax: 509-359-4330. E-mail: admissions@ewu.edu. Web site: http://www.ewu.edu/.

THE EVERGREEN STATE COLLEGE
OLYMPIA, WASHINGTON

General State-supported, comprehensive, coed **Entrance** Moderately difficult **Setting** 1,000-acre small town campus **Total enrollment** 4,084 **Student/faculty ratio** 24:1 **Application deadline** 3/1 **Freshmen** 88% were admitted **Housing** Yes **Expenses** Tuition $2742; Room & Board $4530 **Undergraduates** 59% women, 8% part-time, 38% 25 or older, 4% Native American, 4% Hispanic, 4% black, 4% Asian American or Pacific Islander **Most popular recent majors** Human services; public policy analysis **Academic program** Advanced placement, self-designed majors, tutorials, summer session, internships **Contact** Ms. Christine Licht, Senior Admissions Officer, The Evergreen State College, 2700 Evergreen Parkway, NW, Olympia, WA 98505. Telephone: 360-866-6000 ext. 6170. Fax: 360-866-6680. E-mail: admissions@elwha.evergreen.edu. Web site: http://www.evergreen.edu/.

GONZAGA UNIVERSITY
SPOKANE, WASHINGTON

General Independent Roman Catholic, comprehensive, coed **Entrance** Moderately difficult **Setting** 94-acre urban campus **Total enrollment** 3,950 **Student/faculty ratio** 20:1 **Application deadline** 4/1 **Freshmen** 92% were admitted **Housing** Yes **Expenses** Tuition $16,097; Room & Board $5170 **Undergraduates** 56% women, 7% part-time, 13% 25 or older, 1% Native American, 3% Hispanic, 1% black, 6% Asian American or Pacific Islander **Most popular recent majors** Business administration; engineering; psychology **Academic program** English as a second language, advanced placement, self-designed majors, honors program, summer session, adult/continuing education programs, internships **Contact** Ms. Julie McCulloh, Associate Dean of Admission, Gonzaga University, 502 East Boone Avenue, Spokane, WA 99258-0102. Telephone: 509-328-4220 ext. 3191 or toll-free 800-322-2584. Fax: 509-324-5780. E-mail: ballinger@gu.gonzaga.edu. Web site: http://www.gonzaga.edu/.

▶ **For more information, see page 443.**

HENRY COGSWELL COLLEGE
EVERETT, WASHINGTON

General Independent, 4-year, primarily men **Entrance** Noncompetitive **Setting** 1-acre urban campus **Total enrollment** 193 **Application deadline** 5/1 **Freshmen** 93% were admitted **Housing** No **Expenses** Tuition $9840 **Undergraduates** 13% women, 89% part-time, 93% 25 or older, 1% Native American, 4% Hispanic, 5% black, 15% Asian American or Pacific Islander **Most popular recent majors** Mechanical engineering technology; electrical/electronics engineering; computer science **Academic program** Average class size 16, advanced placement, tutorials, summer session, adult/continuing education programs **Contact** Mrs. Jacqueline B. Juras, Director of Admissions and Registrar, Henry Cogswell College, 2802 Wetmore Avenue, Suite 100, Everett, WA 98201. Telephone: 425-258-3351. E-mail: jbj@henrycogswell.edu.

HERITAGE COLLEGE
TOPPENISH, WASHINGTON

General Independent, comprehensive, coed **Entrance** Noncompetitive **Setting** 10-acre rural campus **Total enrollment** 1,152 **Student/faculty ratio** 11:1 **Application deadline** Rolling **Housing** No **Expenses** Tuition $6450 **Undergraduates** 71% women, 49% part-time, 79% 25 or older **Most popular recent majors** Elementary education; social sciences; business administration **Academic program** English as a second language, advanced placement, self-designed majors, tutorials, summer session, adult/continuing education programs, internships **Contact** Mr. Norberto T. Espindola, Director of Admissions and Recruitment, Heritage College, 3240 Fort Road, Toppenish, WA 98948-9599. Telephone: 509-865-8500 ext. 2002. Fax: 509-865-4469. E-mail: espindola_b@heritage.edu. Web site: http://www.heritage.edu/.

THE LEADERSHIP INSTITUTE OF SEATTLE
BELLEVUE, WASHINGTON

General Independent, upper-level, coed **Contact** Mr. Don Werner, Director of Undergraduate Admissions, The Leadership Institute of Seattle, 1450 114th Avenue SE, Suite 230, Bellevue, WA 98004-6934. Telephone: 206-635-1187 ext. 254 or toll-free 800-789-5467.

LUTHERAN BIBLE INSTITUTE OF SEATTLE
ISSAQUAH, WASHINGTON

General Independent Lutheran, 4-year, coed **Entrance** Minimally difficult **Setting** 46-acre suburban campus **Total enrollment** 158 **Student/faculty ratio** 13:1 **Application deadline** 8/15 **Housing** Yes **Expenses** Tuition $5310; Room & Board $4345 **Undergraduates** 56% women, 6% part-time, 25% 25 or older **Most popular recent majors** Biblical studies; pastoral counseling **Academic program** English as a second language, advanced placement, adult/continuing education programs, internships **Contact** Ms. Sigrid Cutler, Admission Representative, Lutheran Bible Institute of Seattle, 4221 228th Avenue, SE, Issaquah, WA 98029-9299. Telephone: 425-392-0400 ext. 5513 or toll-free 800-843-5659. Fax: 425-392-0404. E-mail: admissn@lbi.edu. Web site: http://www.lbi.edu/.

NORTHWEST COLLEGE OF ART
POULSBO, WASHINGTON

General Proprietary, 4-year, coed **Entrance** Moderately difficult **Setting** 46-acre small town campus **Total enrollment** 75 **Student/faculty ratio** 4:1 **Application deadline** 6/1 **Housing** No **Expenses** Tuition $7900 **Undergraduates** 55% women, 12% part-time **Most Popular Recent Major** Graphic design/commercial art/illustration **Academic program** Summer session, internships **Contact** Mr. Craig Freeman, President, Northwest College of Art, 16464 State Highway 305, Poulsbo, WA 98370. Telephone: 360-779-9993 or toll-free 800-769-ARTS. Fax: 360-779-9933.

NORTHWEST COLLEGE OF THE ASSEMBLIES OF GOD
KIRKLAND, WASHINGTON

General Independent, 4-year, coed, affiliated with Assemblies of God **Entrance** Moderately difficult **Setting** 65-acre suburban campus **Total enrollment** 858 **Student/faculty ratio** 17:1 **Application deadline** 8/1 **Freshmen** 98% were admitted **Housing** Yes **Expenses** Tuition $8940; Room & Board $4310 **Undergraduates** 58% women, 4% part-time, 24% 25 or older, 1% Native American, 4% Hispanic, 2% black, 4% Asian American or Pacific Islander **Most popular recent majors** Behavioral sciences; pastoral counseling; elementary education **Academic program** Average class size 23, English as a second language, advanced placement, accelerated degree program, self-designed majors, summer session, adult/continuing education programs, internships **Contact** Dr. Calvin L. White, Director of Enrollment Services, Northwest College of the Assemblies of God, PO Box 579, Kirkland, WA 98083-0579. Telephone: 425-889-5231 or toll-free 800-669-3781. Fax: 425-425-0148. E-mail: admissions@ncag.edu. Web site: http://www.nwcollege.edu/.

PACIFIC LUTHERAN UNIVERSITY
TACOMA, WASHINGTON

General Independent, comprehensive, coed, affiliated with Evangelical Lutheran Church in America **Entrance** Moderately difficult **Setting** 126-acre suburban campus **Total enrollment** 3,555 **Student/faculty ratio** 13:1 **Application deadline** Rolling **Freshmen** 86% were admitted **Housing** Yes **Expenses** Tuition $15,680; Room & Board $4890 **Undergraduates** 61% women, 9% part-time, 20% 25 or older, 1% Native American, 2% Hispanic, 2% black, 5% Asian American or Pacific Islander **Most popular recent majors** Business administration; education; nursing **Academic program** English as a second language, advanced placement, accelerated degree program, self-designed majors, tutorials, honors program, summer session, adult/continuing education programs, internships **Contact** Dr. Laura J. Polcyn, Vice President for Admissions and Enrollment Services, Pacific Lutheran University, Tacoma, WA 98447. Telephone: 253-535-7151 or toll-free 800-274-6758. Fax: 253-536-5136. E-mail: admissions@plu.edu. Web site: http://www.plu.edu/.

PUGET SOUND CHRISTIAN COLLEGE
EDMONDS, WASHINGTON

General Independent Christian, 4-year, coed **Entrance** Minimally difficult **Setting** 4-acre suburban campus **Total enrollment** 175 **Student/faculty ratio** 15:1 **Application deadline** 8/15 **Housing** Yes **Expenses** Tuition $6250; Room & Board $4050 **Undergraduates** 51% women, 5% part-time, 43% 25 or older, 2% Native American, 3% Hispanic, 2% black, 3% Asian American or Pacific Islander **Most popular recent majors** Divinity/ministry; religious education; social sciences **Academic program** Average class size 25, advanced placement, summer session, adult/continuing education programs, internships **Contact** Mr. Greg Kaler, Recruitment Director, Puget Sound Christian College, 410 4th Avenue North, Edmonds, WA 98020-3171. Telephone: 425-775-8686 ext. 247. Fax: 425-775-8688. E-mail: psccdeve@ricochet.net.

SAINT MARTIN'S COLLEGE
LACEY, WASHINGTON

General Independent Roman Catholic, comprehensive, coed **Entrance** Moderately difficult **Setting** 380-acre suburban campus **Total enrollment** 1,653 **Student/faculty ratio** 12:1 **Appli-**

Saint Martin's College *(continued)*

cation deadline 8/1 **Freshmen** 91% were admitted **Housing** Yes **Expenses** Tuition $13,120; Room & Board $4590 **Undergraduates** 47% 25 or older, 1% Native American, 4% Hispanic, 6% black, 6% Asian American or Pacific Islander **Most popular recent majors** Education; business administration **Academic program** Average class size 18, English as a second language, advanced placement, accelerated degree program, tutorials, summer session, adult/continuing education programs, internships **Contact** Mr. Ronald Noborikawa, Director of Admissions, Saint Martin's College, 5300 Pacific Avenue, SE, Lacey, WA 98503-7500. Telephone: 360-438-4311 or toll-free 800-368-8803. Fax: 360-459-4124. E-mail: admissions@stmartin.edu. Web site: http://www.stmartin.edu/.

SEATTLE PACIFIC UNIVERSITY
SEATTLE, WASHINGTON

General Independent Free Methodist, comprehensive, coed **Entrance** Moderately difficult **Setting** 35-acre urban campus **Total enrollment** 3,321 **Student/faculty ratio** 15:1 **Application deadline** 9/1 **Freshmen** 92% were admitted **Housing** Yes **Expenses** Tuition $14,541; Room & Board $5574 **Undergraduates** 65% women, 16% part-time, 17% 25 or older, 1% Native American, 2% Hispanic, 2% black, 6% Asian American or Pacific Islander **Most popular recent majors** Nursing; business administration; psychology **Academic program** Average class size 21, English as a second language, advanced placement, self-designed majors, tutorials, honors program, summer session, adult/continuing education programs, internships **Contact** Mr. Ken Cornell, Director of Admissions, Seattle Pacific University, 3307 Third Avenue West, Seattle, WA 98119-1997. Telephone: 206-281-2021 or toll-free 800-366-3344. E-mail: admissions@spu.edu. Web site: http://www.spu.edu/.

SEATTLE UNIVERSITY
SEATTLE, WASHINGTON

General Independent Roman Catholic, comprehensive, coed **Entrance** Moderately difficult **Setting** 46-acre urban campus **Total enrollment** 5,739 **Student/faculty ratio** 14:1 **Application deadline** 2/1 **Freshmen** 84% were admitted **Housing** Yes **Expenses** Tuition $14,805; Room & Board $5199 **Undergraduates** 57% women, 14% part-time, 23% 25 or older, 1% Native American, 4% Hispanic, 4% black, 20% Asian American or Pacific Islander **Most popular recent majors** Psychology; accounting; computer science **Academic program** English as a second language, advanced placement, accelerated degree program, tutorials, honors program, summer session, adult/continuing education programs, internships **Contact** Mr. Michael K. McKeon, Dean of Admissions, Seattle University, 900 Broadway, Seattle, WA 98122. Telephone: 206-296-5800 or toll-free 800-542-0833 (in-state), 800-426-7123 (out-of-state). Fax: 206-296-5656. E-mail: admissions@seattleu.edu. Web site: http://www.seattleu.edu/.

UNIVERSITY OF PUGET SOUND
TACOMA, WASHINGTON

General Independent, comprehensive, coed **Entrance** Very difficult **Setting** 97-acre suburban campus **Total enrollment** 3,011 **Student/faculty ratio** 12:1 **Application deadline** 2/1 **Freshmen** 79% were admitted **Housing** Yes **Expenses** Tuition $18,940; Room & Board $4920 **Undergraduates** 60% women, 5% part-time, 6% 25 or older, 1% Native American, 3% Hispanic, 2% black, 11% Asian American or Pacific Islander **Most popular recent majors** Biology; English; political science **Academic program** Average class size 25, advanced placement, self-designed majors, tutorials, honors program, summer session, internships **Contact** Dr. George H. Mills, Vice President for Enrollment, University of Puget Sound, 1500 North Warner Street, Tacoma, WA 98416-0005. Telephone: 253-756-3211 or toll-free 800-396-7191. Fax: 253-756-3500. E-mail: admission@ups.edu. Web site: http://www.ups.edu/.

UNIVERSITY OF WASHINGTON
SEATTLE, WASHINGTON

General State-supported, university, coed **Entrance** Moderately difficult **Setting** 703-acre urban campus **Total enrollment** 35,367 **Student/faculty ratio** 9:1 **Application deadline** 2/1 **Freshmen** 74% were admitted **Housing** Yes **Expenses** Tuition $3366; Room & Board $4671 **Undergraduates** 21% 25 or older, 2% Native American, 4% Hispanic, 3% black, 22% Asian American or Pacific Islander **Academic program** Average class size 31, English as a second language, advanced placement, accelerated degree program, self-designed majors, honors program, summer session, adult/continuing education programs, internships **Contact** Ms. Stephanie Preston, Assistant Director of Admissions, University of Washington, Office of Admissions, Seattle, WA 98195-5840. Telephone: 206-543-9686. E-mail: askuwadm@u.washington.edu. Web site: http://www.washington.edu/.

WALLA WALLA COLLEGE
COLLEGE PLACE, WASHINGTON

General Independent Seventh-day Adventist, comprehensive, coed **Entrance** Moderately difficult

Setting 77-acre small town campus **Total enrollment** 1,653 **Student/faculty ratio** 12:1 **Application deadline** Rolling **Freshmen** 88% were admitted **Housing** Yes **Expenses** Tuition $12,693; Room & Board $3380 **Undergraduates** 45% women, 4% part-time, 1% Native American, 4% Hispanic, 1% black, 4% Asian American or Pacific Islander **Most popular recent majors** Engineering; nursing; business administration **Academic program** Average class size 24, English as a second language, advanced placement, accelerated degree program, self-designed majors, tutorials, honors program, summer session, internships **Contact** Mr. Dallas Weis, Director of Admissions, Walla Walla College, 204 South College Avenue, College Place, WA 99324-1198. Telephone: 509-527-2327 or toll-free 800-541-8900. Fax: 509-527-2397. E-mail: weisda@wwc.edu. Web site: http://www.wwc.edu/.

WASHINGTON STATE UNIVERSITY
PULLMAN, WASHINGTON

General State-supported, university, coed **Entrance** Moderately difficult **Setting** 620-acre rural campus **Total enrollment** 20,243 **Student/faculty ratio** 11:1 **Application deadline** 5/1 **Freshmen** 88% were admitted **Housing** Yes **Expenses** Tuition $3394; Room & Board $4426 **Undergraduates** 50% women, 12% part-time, 18% 25 or older, 2% Native American, 3% Hispanic, 2% black, 5% Asian American or Pacific Islander **Most popular recent majors** Business administration; mass communications; social sciences **Academic program** English as a second language, advanced placement, honors program, summer session, adult/continuing education programs, internships **Contact** Ms. Wendy Peterson, Interim Director of Admissions, Washington State University, PO Box 641067, Pullman, WA 99164-1610. Telephone: 509-335-5586. E-mail: admiss@wsu.edu. Web site: http://www.wsu.edu/.

WESTERN WASHINGTON UNIVERSITY
BELLINGHAM, WASHINGTON

General State-supported, comprehensive, coed **Entrance** Moderately difficult **Setting** 223-acre small town campus **Total enrollment** 11,476 **Student/faculty ratio** 21:1 **Application deadline** 3/1 **Freshmen** 86% were admitted **Housing** Yes **Expenses** Tuition $2772; Room & Board $4635 **Undergraduates** 56% women, 5% part-time, 15% 25 or older, 2% Native American, 3% Hispanic, 2% black, 7% Asian American or Pacific Islander **Most popular recent majors** Business administration; English **Academic program** English as a second language, advanced placement, accelerated degree program, self-designed majors, tutorials, honors program, summer session, adult/continuing education programs, internships **Contact** Ms. Karen Copetas, Director of Admissions, Western Washington University, 516 High Street, Bellingham, WA 98225-9009. Telephone: 360-650-3440 ext. 3443. E-mail: admit@cc.wwu.edu. Web site: http://www.wwu.edu/.

WHITMAN COLLEGE
WALLA WALLA, WASHINGTON

General Independent, 4-year, coed **Entrance** Very difficult **Setting** 55-acre small town campus **Total enrollment** 1,375 **Student/faculty ratio** 10:1 **Application deadline** 2/1 **Freshmen** 51% were admitted **Housing** Yes **Expenses** Tuition $19,756; Room & Board $5640 **Undergraduates** 55% women, 4% part-time, 2% 25 or older, 1% Native American, 2% Hispanic, 1% black, 6% Asian American or Pacific Islander **Most popular recent majors** English; biology; psychology **Academic program** Average class size 18, advanced placement, accelerated degree program, self-designed majors, tutorials, honors program, internships **Contact** Mr. John Bogley, Dean of Admission and Financial Aid, Whitman College, 345 Boyer Avenue, Walla Walla, WA 99362-2046. Telephone: 509-527-5176. Fax: 509-527-4967. E-mail: admission@whitman.edu. Web site: http://www.whitman.edu/.

WHITWORTH COLLEGE
SPOKANE, WASHINGTON

General Independent Presbyterian, comprehensive, coed **Entrance** Very difficult **Setting** 200-acre suburban campus **Total enrollment** 2,043 **Student/faculty ratio** 16:1 **Application deadline** 3/1 **Freshmen** 87% were admitted **Housing** Yes **Expenses** Tuition $15,593; Room & Board $5300 **Undergraduates** 15% 25 or older **Most popular recent majors** Elementary education; business administration; history **Academic program** Average class size 27, English as a second language, advanced placement, self-designed majors, tutorials, summer session, adult/continuing education programs, internships **Contact** Mr. Fred Pfursich, Dean of Enrollment Services, Whitworth College, 300 West Hawthorne Road, Spokane, WA 99251-0001. Telephone: 509-466-3212 or toll-free 800-533-4668 (out-of-state). Fax: 509-777-3773. E-mail: admissions@whiteworth.edu. Web site: http://www.whitworth.edu/.

WEST VIRGINIA

ALDERSON-BROADDUS COLLEGE
PHILIPPI, WEST VIRGINIA

General Independent, comprehensive, coed, affiliated with Baptist Church **Entrance** Moder-

Alderson-Broaddus College *(continued)*

ately difficult **Setting** 170-acre rural campus **Total enrollment** 740 **Application deadline** Rolling **Freshmen** 59% were admitted **Housing** Yes **Expenses** Tuition $12,215; Room & Board $4165 **Undergraduates** 33% 25 or older, 0.1% Native American, 0% Hispanic, 4% black, 2% Asian American or Pacific Islander **Most popular recent majors** Physician assistant; nursing; secondary education **Academic program** Average class size 35, advanced placement, self-designed majors, tutorials, honors program, summer session, internships **Contact** Mrs. Kimberly N. Klaus, Assistant Director of Admissions, Alderson-Broaddus College, Campus Box 216, Philippi, WV 26416. Telephone: 304-457-1700 ext. 6255 or toll-free 800-263-1549. Fax: 304-457-6239. E-mail: admissions@ab.edu. Web site: http://www.ab.edu/.

APPALACHIAN BIBLE COLLEGE
BRADLEY, WEST VIRGINIA

General Independent nondenominational, 4-year, coed **Entrance** Minimally difficult **Setting** 110-acre small town campus **Total enrollment** 301 **Student/faculty ratio** 15:1 **Application deadline** Rolling **Housing** Yes **Expenses** Tuition $5510; Room & Board $3010 **Undergraduates** 45% women, 19% part-time, 21% 25 or older, 1% Native American, 1% Hispanic, 1% black, 3% Asian American or Pacific Islander **Academic program** Advanced placement, adult/continuing education programs, internships **Contact** Ms. Rita K. Pritt, Director of Admissions, Appalachian Bible College, PO Box ABC, Bradley, WV 25818. Telephone: 304-877-6428 ext. 202 or toll-free 800-678-9ABC. E-mail: admissions@appbibco.edu.

BETHANY COLLEGE
BETHANY, WEST VIRGINIA

General Independent, 4-year, coed, affiliated with Christian Church (Disciples of Christ) **Entrance** Moderately difficult **Setting** 1,600-acre rural campus **Total enrollment** 758 **Student/faculty ratio** 13:1 **Application deadline** Rolling **Freshmen** 75% were admitted **Housing** Yes **Expenses** Tuition $17,349; Room & Board $5716 **Undergraduates** 43% women, 1% part-time, 3% 25 or older, 0.3% Native American, 1% Hispanic, 3% black, 1% Asian American or Pacific Islander **Most popular recent majors** Psychology; communications; education **Academic program** English as a second language, advanced placement, self-designed majors, tutorials, internships **Contact** Mr. Gary R. Forney, Vice President for Enrollment Management, Bethany College, Office of Admission, Bethany, WV 26032. Telephone: 304-829-7611 or toll-free 800-922-7611 (out-of-state). Fax: 304-829-7142. E-mail: g.forney@mail.bethanywv.edu. Web site: http://www.bethanywv.edu/.

BLUEFIELD STATE COLLEGE
BLUEFIELD, WEST VIRGINIA

General State-supported, 4-year, coed **Entrance** Noncompetitive **Setting** 45-acre small town campus **Total enrollment** 2,513 **Student/faculty ratio** 22:1 **Application deadline** Rolling **Freshmen** 65% were admitted **Housing** No **Expenses** Tuition $2044 **Undergraduates** 58% women, 36% part-time, 17% 25 or older, 0.2% Native American, 0.4% Hispanic, 7% black, 0.4% Asian American or Pacific Islander **Most popular recent majors** Business administration; nursing; education **Academic program** Average class size 30, English as a second language, advanced placement, summer session, adult/continuing education programs, internships **Contact** Mr. John C. Cardwell, Director of Enrollment Management, Bluefield State College, 219 Rock Street, Bluefield, WV 24701-2198. Telephone: 304-327-4065 or toll-free 800-344-8892 (in-state), 800-654-7798 (out-of-state). Fax: 304-327-7747. E-mail: bscadmit@bscvax.wvnet.edu. Web site: http://www.bluefield.wvnet.edu/.

THE COLLEGE OF WEST VIRGINIA
BECKLEY, WEST VIRGINIA

General Independent, 4-year, coed **Entrance** Noncompetitive **Setting** 4-acre small town campus **Total enrollment** 1,981 **Student/faculty ratio** 18:1 **Application deadline** Rolling **Freshmen** 100% were admitted **Housing** Yes **Expenses** Tuition $3600; Room & Board $3960 **Undergraduates** 68% women, 26% part-time, 43% 25 or older, 0.1% Native American, 0.3% Hispanic, 9% black, 0.3% Asian American or Pacific Islander **Academic program** English as a second language, advanced placement, accelerated degree program, self-designed majors, tutorials, summer session, adult/continuing education programs, internships **Contact** Ms. Terri Williams, Admissions Coordinator, The College of West Virginia, PO Box AG, Beckley, WV 25802-2830. Telephone: 304-253-7351 ext. 334 or toll-free 800-766-6067. Fax: 304-253-5072. Web site: http://www.cwv.edu/.

CONCORD COLLEGE
ATHENS, WEST VIRGINIA

General State-supported, 4-year, coed **Entrance** Minimally difficult **Setting** 100-acre rural campus **Total enrollment** 2,780 **Student/faculty ratio** 22:1 **Application deadline** Rolling **Freshmen** 94% were admitted **Housing** Yes **Expenses** Tuition $2310; Room & Board $3708 **Undergraduates** 11% 25 or older, 0.5% Native American, 0.3%

Hispanic, 4% black, 1% Asian American or Pacific Islander **Most popular recent majors** Education; business administration; social work **Academic program** English as a second language, advanced placement, accelerated degree program, honors program, summer session, internships **Contact** Dr. Richard A. Edwards, Dean of Admissions and Financial Aid, Concord College, Vermillion Street, PO Box 1000, Athens, WV 24712-1000. Telephone: 304-384-5248 or toll-free 888-384-5249. Fax: 304-384-9044. E-mail: addsm@ccvms.wvnet.edu. Web site: http://www.concord.wvnet.edu/.

▶ **For more information, see page 420.**

DAVIS & ELKINS COLLEGE
ELKINS, WEST VIRGINIA

General Independent Presbyterian, 4-year, coed **Entrance** Moderately difficult **Setting** 170-acre small town campus **Total enrollment** 683 **Student/faculty ratio** 11:1 **Application deadline** Rolling **Freshmen** 84% were admitted **Housing** Yes **Expenses** Tuition $11,200; Room & Board $4680 **Undergraduates** 61% women, 12% part-time, 27% 25 or older, 0% Native American, 1% Hispanic, 4% black, 3% Asian American or Pacific Islander **Most popular recent majors** Business administration; psychology; biology **Academic program** Average class size 20, English as a second language, advanced placement, accelerated degree program, self-designed majors, tutorials, honors program, summer session, adult/continuing education programs, internships **Contact** Mr. Kevin Chenoweth, Director of Admissions, Davis & Elkins College, 100 Campus Drive, Elkins, WV 26241-3996. Telephone: 304-637-1301 or toll-free 800-624-3157. Fax: 304-637-1800. E-mail: admiss@dne.wvnet.edu. Web site: http://www.dne.edu/.

FAIRMONT STATE COLLEGE
FAIRMONT, WEST VIRGINIA

General State-supported, 4-year, coed **Entrance** Minimally difficult **Setting** 80-acre small town campus **Total enrollment** 6,623 **Student/faculty ratio** 21:1 **Application deadline** 6/15 **Freshmen** 99% were admitted **Housing** Yes **Expenses** Tuition $2040; Room & Board $3600 **Undergraduates** 55% women, 33% part-time, 28% 25 or older, 0.3% Native American, 0.5% Hispanic, 2% black, 1% Asian American or Pacific Islander **Academic program** Average class size 30, English as a second language, advanced placement, accelerated degree program, honors program, summer session, adult/continuing education programs, internships **Contact** Dr. John G. Conaway, Director of Admissions, Fairmont State College, 1201 Locust Avenue, Fairmont, WV 26554. Telephone: 304-367-4141 or toll-free 800-641-5678. Fax: 304-367-4789. E-mail: admit@fscvax.fairmont.wvnet.edu. Web site: http://www.fairmont.wvnet.edu/.

▶ **For more information, see page 432.**

GLENVILLE STATE COLLEGE
GLENVILLE, WEST VIRGINIA

General State-supported, 4-year, coed **Entrance** Noncompetitive **Setting** 331-acre rural campus **Total enrollment** 2,288 **Student/faculty ratio** 13:1 **Application deadline** 8/1 **Freshmen** 100% were admitted **Housing** Yes **Expenses** Tuition $1956; Room & Board $3480 **Undergraduates** 57% women, 31% part-time, 27% 25 or older, 0.4% Native American, 0.4% Hispanic, 3% black, 0.3% Asian American or Pacific Islander **Most popular recent majors** Business administration; education; behavioral sciences **Academic program** Average class size 27, English as a second language, advanced placement, accelerated degree program, summer session, adult/continuing education programs **Contact** Dr. Phillip Cottrill, Registrar/Director of Enrollment Management, Glenville State College, 200 High Street, Glenville, WV 26351-1200. Telephone: 304-462-7361 ext. 151 or toll-free 800-924-2010 (in-state). Fax: 304-462-8619. E-mail: cottrill@glenville.wvnet.edu. Web site: http://www.glenville.wvnet.edu/.

▶ **For more information, see page 441.**

MARSHALL UNIVERSITY
HUNTINGTON, WEST VIRGINIA

General State-supported, comprehensive, coed **Entrance** Minimally difficult **Setting** 70-acre urban campus **Total enrollment** 13,388 **Student/faculty ratio** 20:1 **Application deadline** Rolling **Freshmen** 91% were admitted **Housing** Yes **Expenses** Tuition $2184; Room & Board $4420 **Undergraduates** 55% women, 18% part-time, 20% 25 or older, 0.4% Native American, 0.4% Hispanic, 4% black, 1% Asian American or Pacific Islander **Most popular recent majors** Elementary education; criminal justice/law enforcement administration; psychology **Academic program** Average class size 24, advanced placement, accelerated degree program, tutorials, honors program, summer session, adult/continuing education programs, internships **Contact** Dr. James W. Harless, Admissions Director, Marshall University, 400 Hal Greer Boulevard, Huntington, WV 25755-2020. Telephone: 304-696-3160 or toll-free 800-642-3499 (in-state). Fax: 304-696-3135. E-mail: admissions@marshall.edu. Web site: http://www.marshall.edu/.

OHIO VALLEY COLLEGE
PARKERSBURG, WEST VIRGINIA

General Independent, 4-year, coed, affiliated with Church of Christ **Entrance** Minimally difficult **Set-**

Ohio Valley College *(continued)*

ting 267-acre small town campus **Total enrollment** 430 **Student/faculty ratio** 13:1 **Application deadline** Rolling **Freshmen** 46% were admitted **Housing** Yes **Expenses** Tuition $6838; Room & Board $3740 **Undergraduates** 48% women, 5% part-time, 24% 25 or older, 0.2% Native American, 1% Hispanic, 10% black, 0.5% Asian American or Pacific Islander **Most popular recent majors** Elementary education; biblical studies; psychology **Academic program** Advanced placement, honors program, summer session, adult/continuing education programs, internships **Contact** Mr. Larry R. Lyons, Director of Admissions, Vice President for Enrollment, Ohio Valley College, 4501 College Parkway, Parkersburg, WV 26101-8100. Telephone: 304-485-7384 ext. 123 or toll-free 800-678-6780 (out-of-state). Fax: 304-485-3106. E-mail: admissions@juno.com. Web site: http://www.ovcollege.edu/.

SALEM-TEIKYO UNIVERSITY
SALEM, WEST VIRGINIA

General Independent, comprehensive, coed **Entrance** Moderately difficult **Setting** 300-acre rural campus **Total enrollment** 810 **Student/faculty ratio** 15:1 **Application deadline** Rolling **Freshmen** 99% were admitted **Housing** Yes **Expenses** Tuition $12,106; Room & Board $4090 **Undergraduates** 41% women, 1% part-time, 6% 25 or older, 0% Native American, 2% Hispanic, 8% black, 3% Asian American or Pacific Islander **Most popular recent majors** Business administration; molecular biology; education **Academic program** English as a second language, advanced placement, accelerated degree program, summer session, internships **Contact** Mrs. Carolyn S. Ritter, Director of Admissions, Salem-Teikyo University, PO Box 500, Salem, WV 26426-0500. Telephone: 304-782-5336 ext. 336 or toll-free 800-283-4562. E-mail: admiss_new@salem.wvnet.edu. Web site: http://stulib.salem.teikyo.wvnet.edu/.

SHEPHERD COLLEGE
SHEPHERDSTOWN, WEST VIRGINIA

General State-supported, 4-year, coed **Entrance** Moderately difficult **Setting** 320-acre small town campus **Total enrollment** 4,025 **Student/faculty ratio** 14:1 **Application deadline** 2/1 **Freshmen** 89% were admitted **Housing** Yes **Expenses** Tuition $2228; Room & Board $4139 **Undergraduates** 59% women, 20% part-time, 28% 25 or older, 1% Native American, 2% Hispanic, 4% black, 1% Asian American or Pacific Islander **Most popular recent majors** Business administration; elementary education; secondary education **Academic program** Average class size 30, advanced placement, accelerated degree program, honors program, summer session, adult/continuing education programs, internships **Contact** Mr. Karl L. Wolf, Director of Admissions, Shepherd College, King Street, PO Box 3210, Shepherdstown, WV 25443-3210. Telephone: 304-876-5212 or toll-free 800-344-5231. Fax: 304-876-5165. E-mail: admoff@shepherd.wunet.edu. Web site: http://www.shepherd.wvnet.edu/.

UNIVERSITY OF CHARLESTON
CHARLESTON, WEST VIRGINIA

General Independent, comprehensive, coed **Entrance** Moderately difficult **Setting** 40-acre urban campus **Total enrollment** 1,418 **Student/faculty ratio** 15:1 **Application deadline** Rolling **Freshmen** 80% were admitted **Housing** Yes **Expenses** Tuition $11,600; Room & Board $4040 **Undergraduates** 34% 25 or older, 1% Native American, 1% Hispanic, 3% black, 1% Asian American or Pacific Islander **Most popular recent majors** Health science; business administration; biology **Academic program** English as a second language, advanced placement, accelerated degree program, self-designed majors, tutorials, summer session, adult/continuing education programs, internships **Contact** Director of Admissions, University of Charleston, 2300 MacCorkle Avenue, SE, Charleston, WV 25304-1099. Telephone: 304-357-4750 or toll-free 800-995-GOUC. Fax: 304-357-4781. E-mail: admissions@uchaswv.edu. Web site: http://www.uchaswv.edu/.

WEST LIBERTY STATE COLLEGE
WEST LIBERTY, WEST VIRGINIA

General State-supported, 4-year, coed **Entrance** Minimally difficult **Setting** 290-acre rural campus **Total enrollment** 2,397 **Student/faculty ratio** 19:1 **Application deadline** 8/1 **Freshmen** 95% were admitted **Housing** Yes **Expenses** Tuition $2200; Room & Board $3200 **Undergraduates** 55% women, 10% part-time, 19% 25 or older, 0.1% Native American, 1% Hispanic, 3% black, 0.1% Asian American or Pacific Islander **Most popular recent majors** Business administration; education; criminal justice/law enforcement administration **Academic program** Advanced placement, accelerated degree program, self-designed majors, honors program, summer session, adult/continuing education programs, internships **Contact** Mr. Paul Milam, Director of Admissions, West Liberty State College, PO Box 295, West Liberty, WV 26074. Telephone: 304-336-8076 or toll-free 800-732-6204. Fax: 304-336-8285. E-mail: wladmsn1@wlsvax.wvnet.edu. Web site: http://www.wlsc.wvnet.edu/.

WEST VIRGINIA STATE COLLEGE
INSTITUTE, WEST VIRGINIA

General State-supported, 4-year, coed **Entrance** Minimally difficult **Setting** 90-acre suburban campus **Total enrollment** 4,603 **Student/faculty ratio** 18:1 **Application deadline** 8/11 **Housing** Yes **Expenses** Tuition $2184; Room & Board $3450 **Undergraduates** 58% women, 38% part-time, 40% 25 or older **Most popular recent majors** Business administration; elementary education; criminal justice/law enforcement administration **Academic program** Advanced placement, accelerated degree program, summer session, adult/continuing education programs, internships **Contact** Mr. L. Robin Green, Associate Director of Admissions, West Virginia State College, WVSC, Campus Box 188, PO Box 1000, Institute, WV 25112-1000. Telephone: 304-766-3221 or toll-free 800-987-2112. Fax: 304-766-4158. E-mail: greenrl@ernie.wvsc.wvnet.edu. Web site: http://www.wvsc.wvnet.edu/wvsc.html.

WEST VIRGINIA UNIVERSITY
MORGANTOWN, WEST VIRGINIA

General State-supported, university, coed **Entrance** Moderately difficult **Setting** 541-acre small town campus **Total enrollment** 22,238 **Student/faculty ratio** 18:1 **Application deadline** Rolling **Housing** Yes **Expenses** Tuition $2336; Room & Board $4832 **Undergraduates** 47% women, 6% part-time, 9% 25 or older, 0.3% Native American, 1% Hispanic, 4% black, 2% Asian American or Pacific Islander **Most popular recent majors** Accounting; journalism **Academic program** English as a second language, advanced placement, accelerated degree program, self-designed majors, tutorials, honors program, summer session, adult/continuing education programs, internships **Contact** Ms. Evie Brantmayer, Interim Director of Admissions and Records, West Virginia University, Box 6009, Morgantown, WV 26506-6009. Telephone: 304-293-2121 ext. 1511 or toll-free 800-344-9881. Fax: 304-293-3080. E-mail: wvuadmissions@arc.wvu.edu. Web site: http://www.wvu.edu/.

WEST VIRGINIA UNIVERSITY INSTITUTE OF TECHNOLOGY
MONTGOMERY, WEST VIRGINIA

General State-supported, comprehensive, coed **Entrance** Noncompetitive **Setting** 200-acre small town campus **Total enrollment** 2,554 **Student/faculty ratio** 18:1 **Application deadline** Rolling **Freshmen** 100% were admitted **Housing** Yes **Expenses** Tuition $2370; Room & Board $3858 **Undergraduates** 39% women, 29% part-time, 21% 25 or older, 0.5% Native American, 0.2% Hispanic, 6% black, 1% Asian American or Pacific Islander **Most popular recent majors** Electrical/electronics engineering; mechanical engineering; accounting **Academic program** English as a second language, advanced placement, accelerated degree program, self-designed majors, tutorials, summer session, adult/continuing education programs, internships **Contact** Ms. Donna Varney, Director of Admissions, West Virginia University Institute of Technology, Montgomery, WV 25136. Telephone: 304-442-3167 or toll-free 888-554-8324. Fax: 304-442-3097. E-mail: wvutech@wvit.wvnet.edu.

WEST VIRGINIA WESLEYAN COLLEGE
BUCKHANNON, WEST VIRGINIA

General Independent, comprehensive, coed, affiliated with United Methodist Church **Entrance** Moderately difficult **Setting** 80-acre small town campus **Total enrollment** 1,686 **Student/faculty ratio** 15:1 **Application deadline** 8/1 **Freshmen** 86% were admitted **Housing** Yes **Expenses** Tuition $16,750; Room & Board $4100 **Undergraduates** 55% women, 7% part-time, 7% 25 or older, 1% Native American, 1% Hispanic, 7% black, 1% Asian American or Pacific Islander **Most popular recent majors** Psychology; education; political science **Academic program** Average class size 25, English as a second language, advanced placement, accelerated degree program, self-designed majors, honors program, summer session, adult/continuing education programs, internships **Contact** Mr. Robert N. Skinner II, Director of Admission, West Virginia Wesleyan College, 59 College Avenue, Buckhannon, WV 26201. Telephone: 304-473-8510 or toll-free 800-722-9933 (out-of-state). Fax: 304-472-2571. E-mail: admissions@academ.wvwc.edu. Web site: http://www.wvwc.edu/.

WHEELING JESUIT UNIVERSITY
WHEELING, WEST VIRGINIA

General Independent Roman Catholic (Jesuit), comprehensive, coed **Entrance** Moderately difficult **Setting** 70-acre suburban campus **Total enrollment** 1,556 **Student/faculty ratio** 14:1 **Application deadline** Rolling **Freshmen** 88% were admitted **Housing** Yes **Expenses** Tuition $14,200; Room & Board $4980 **Undergraduates** 15% 25 or older **Most popular recent majors** Business administration; psychology; biology **Academic program** Average class size 35, English as a second language, advanced placement, self-designed majors, tutorials, honors program, summer session, adult/continuing education programs, internships **Contact** Mr. Thomas M. Pie, Director of Admissions, Wheeling Jesuit University, 316 Washington Avenue, Wheeling, WV 26003-6295. Tele-

Wheeling Jesuit University *(continued)*

phone: 304-243-2359 or toll-free 800-624-6992. Fax: 304-243-2397. E-mail: admis@wju.edu. Web site: http://www.wju.edu/.

WISCONSIN

ALVERNO COLLEGE
MILWAUKEE, WISCONSIN

General Independent Roman Catholic, comprehensive, women only **Entrance** Moderately difficult **Setting** 46-acre suburban campus **Total enrollment** 2,072 **Student/faculty ratio** 13:1 **Application deadline** 8/1 **Housing** Yes **Expenses** Tuition $9722; Room & Board $3890 **Undergraduates** 45% part-time, 63% 25 or older, 1% Native American, 7% Hispanic, 19% black, 2% Asian American or Pacific Islander **Most Popular Recent Major** Nursing **Academic program** Average class size 17, English as a second language, advanced placement, summer session, adult/continuing education programs, internships **Contact** Mr. Owen Smith, Director of Admissions, Alverno College, 3401 South 39th St, PO Box 343922, Milwaukee, WI 53234-3922. Telephone: 414-382-6113 or toll-free 800-933-3401. Fax: 414-382-6354. E-mail: alvadm5h@exepc.com. Web site: http://www.alverno.edu/.

BELLIN COLLEGE OF NURSING
GREEN BAY, WISCONSIN

General Independent, 4-year, primarily women **Entrance** Moderately difficult **Setting** Urban campus **Total enrollment** 183 **Student/faculty ratio** 10:1 **Application deadline** Rolling **Housing** No **Expenses** Tuition $8592 **Undergraduates** 89% women, 13% part-time, 22% 25 or older, 1% Native American, 0% Hispanic, 1% black, 2% Asian American or Pacific Islander **Academic program** Advanced placement, summer session **Contact** Ms. Teresa Halcsik, Vice President for Support Services, Bellin College of Nursing, 725 South Webster Ave, PO Box 23400, Green Bay, WI 54305-3400. Telephone: 920-433-3673 or toll-free 800-236-8707 (in-state).

BELOIT COLLEGE
BELOIT, WISCONSIN

General Independent, 4-year, coed **Entrance** Very difficult **Setting** 65-acre small town campus **Total enrollment** 1,292 **Student/faculty ratio** 11:1 **Application deadline** Rolling **Freshmen** 72% were admitted **Housing** Yes **Expenses** Tuition $19,050; Room & Board $4140 **Undergraduates** 57% women, 1% part-time, 5% 25 or older, 1% Native American, 3% Hispanic, 4% black, 3% Asian American or Pacific Islander **Most popular recent majors** Anthropology; biology; English **Academic program** Average class size 15, English as a second language, advanced placement, self-designed majors, tutorials, summer session, adult/continuing education programs, internships **Contact** Mr. Alan G. McIvor, Vice President of Enrollment Services, Beloit College, 700 College Street, Beloit, WI 53511-5596. Telephone: 608-363-2500 or toll-free 800-356-0751 (out-of-state). Fax: 608-363-2075. E-mail: admiss@beloit.edu. Web site: http://www.beloit.edu/.

CARDINAL STRITCH UNIVERSITY
MILWAUKEE, WISCONSIN

General Independent Roman Catholic, comprehensive, coed **Entrance** Moderately difficult **Setting** 40-acre suburban campus **Total enrollment** 5,316 **Student/faculty ratio** 17:1 **Application deadline** Rolling **Housing** Yes **Expenses** Tuition $10,130; Room & Board $4280 **Undergraduates** 65% women, 8% part-time, 73% 25 or older **Most popular recent majors** Business administration; education; nursing **Academic program** Average class size 17, English as a second language, advanced placement, accelerated degree program, tutorials, summer session, adult/continuing education programs, internships **Contact** Mr. David Wegener, Director of Admissions, Cardinal Stritch University, 6801 North Yates Road, Milwaukee, WI 53217-3985. Telephone: 414-410-4040 or toll-free 800-347-8822. Fax: 414-410-4239. Web site: http://acs.strich.edu/.

CARROLL COLLEGE
WAUKESHA, WISCONSIN

General Independent Presbyterian, comprehensive, coed **Entrance** Moderately difficult **Setting** 52-acre suburban campus **Total enrollment** 2,521 **Student/faculty ratio** 23:1 **Application deadline** Rolling **Freshmen** 88% were admitted **Housing** Yes **Expenses** Tuition $14,420; Room & Board $4440 **Undergraduates** 67% women, 27% part-time, 9% 25 or older, 0.1% Native American, 3% Hispanic, 3% black, 1% Asian American or Pacific Islander **Most popular recent majors** Nursing; business administration; education **Academic program** Average class size 23, advanced placement, accelerated degree program, self-designed majors, tutorials, honors program, summer session, adult/continuing education programs, internships **Contact** Mr. James V. Wiseman III, Vice President of Enrollment, Carroll College, 100 North East Avenue, Waukesha, WI 53186-5593. Telephone: 414-524-7221 or toll-free 800-CARROLL. Fax: 414-524-7139. E-mail: cc.info@ccadmin.cc.edu. Web site: http://www.cc.edu/.

CARTHAGE COLLEGE
KENOSHA, WISCONSIN

General Independent, comprehensive, coed, affiliated with Evangelical Lutheran Church in America **Entrance** Moderately difficult **Setting** 72-acre suburban campus **Total enrollment** 2,104 **Student/faculty ratio** 16:1 **Application deadline** Rolling **Freshmen** 93% were admitted **Housing** Yes **Expenses** Tuition $15,365; Room & Board $4415 **Undergraduates** 58% women, 21% part-time, 7% 25 or older **Most popular recent majors** Business administration; education; social sciences **Academic program** Average class size 25, advanced placement, accelerated degree program, self-designed majors, tutorials, honors program, summer session, adult/continuing education programs, internships **Contact** Mr. Mark S. Kopenski, Assistant Vice President for Enrollment, Carthage College, 2001 Alford Park Drive, Kenosha, WI 53140-1994. Telephone: 414-551-6000 or toll-free 800-351-4058. Fax: 414-551-5762. E-mail: admissions@carthage.edu. Web site: http://www.carthage.edu/.

COLUMBIA COLLEGE OF NURSING
MILWAUKEE, WISCONSIN

General Independent, 4-year, coed **Entrance** Moderately difficult **Setting** Urban campus **Total enrollment** 327 **Application deadline** Rolling **Freshmen** 80% were admitted **Housing** Yes **Expenses** Tuition $14,140; Room & Board $4280 **Undergraduates** 92% women, 46% part-time, 37% 25 or older, 0% Native American, 3% Hispanic, 6% black, 1% Asian American or Pacific Islander **Academic program** Average class size 20, advanced placement, tutorials, honors program, summer session **Contact** Mr. James Wiseman, Dean of Admissions, Columbia College of Nursing, Carroll College, 100 North East Avenue, Milwaukee, WI 53186. Telephone: 414-524-7220. Web site: http://www.cc.edu/.

CONCORDIA UNIVERSITY WISCONSIN
MEQUON, WISCONSIN

General Independent, comprehensive, coed, affiliated with Lutheran Church–Missouri Synod **Contact** Mr. Kenneth Gaschk, Dean of Admissions, Concordia University Wisconsin, 12800 North Lake Shore Drive, Mequon, WI 53097-2402. Telephone: 414-243-5700 ext. 305. Fax: 414-243-4351. E-mail: kgaschk@bach.cuw.edu. Web site: http://www.cuw.edu/.

EDGEWOOD COLLEGE
MADISON, WISCONSIN

General Independent Roman Catholic, comprehensive, coed **Entrance** Moderately difficult **Setting** 55-acre urban campus **Total enrollment** 1,957 **Student/faculty ratio** 15:1 **Application deadline** Rolling **Freshmen** 77% were admitted **Housing** Yes **Expenses** Tuition $10,280; Room & Board $4380 **Undergraduates** 73% women, 26% part-time, 42% 25 or older, 0.3% Native American, 1% Hispanic, 1% black, 1% Asian American or Pacific Islander **Most popular recent majors** Nursing; business administration; education **Academic program** Advanced placement, self-designed majors, tutorials, honors program, summer session, adult/continuing education programs, internships **Contact** Mr. Kevin C. Kucera, Dean of Admissions and Financial Aid, Edgewood College, 855 Woodrow Street, Madison, WI 53711-1998. Telephone: 608-257-4861 or toll-free 800-444-4861. E-mail: admissions@edgewood.edu. Web site: http://www.edgewood.edu/.

LAKELAND COLLEGE
SHEBOYGAN, WISCONSIN

General Independent, comprehensive, coed, affiliated with United Church of Christ **Contact** Mr. Leo Gavrilos, Director of Admissions, Lakeland College, PO Box 359, Sheboygan, WI 53082-0359. Telephone: 414-565-1217 or toll-free 800-242-3347 (in-state). Fax: 414-565-1206. E-mail: admissions@lakeland.edu. Web site: http://www.lakeland.edu/.

LAWRENCE UNIVERSITY
APPLETON, WISCONSIN

General Independent, 4-year, coed **Entrance** Very difficult **Setting** 84-acre small town campus **Total enrollment** 1,179 **Student/faculty ratio** 11:1 **Application deadline** 2/1 **Freshmen** 80% were admitted **Housing** Yes **Expenses** Tuition $19,620; Room & Board $4575 **Undergraduates** 53% women, 3% part-time, 4% 25 or older, 0.3% Native American, 2% Hispanic, 1% black, 4% Asian American or Pacific Islander **Most popular recent majors** Biology; English; psychology **Academic program** Advanced placement, self-designed majors, tutorials, internships **Contact** Mr. Steven T. Syverson, Dean of Admissions and Financial Aid, Lawrence University, PO Box 599, Appleton, WI 54912-0599. Telephone: 920-832-6500 or toll-free 800-227-0982. Fax: 920-832-6782. E-mail: excel@lawrence.edu. Web site: http://www.lawrence.edu/.

MARANATHA BAPTIST BIBLE COLLEGE
WATERTOWN, WISCONSIN

General Independent Baptist, comprehensive, coed **Entrance** Noncompetitive **Setting** 60-acre small town campus **Total enrollment** 680 **Student/faculty ratio** 13:1 **Application deadline**

Maranatha Baptist Bible College *(continued)*

Rolling **Freshmen** 70% were admitted **Housing** Yes **Expenses** Tuition $5976; Room & Board $3400 **Undergraduates** 54% women, 7% part-time, 9% 25 or older, 1% Native American, 2% Hispanic, 1% black, 1% Asian American or Pacific Islander **Most popular recent majors** Education; biblical studies; business administration **Academic program** Average class size 60, tutorials, summer session, internships **Contact** Mr. Jim Harrison, Director of Admissions, Maranatha Baptist Bible College, 745 West Main Street, Watertown, WI 53094. Telephone: 920-261-9300 ext. 308 or toll-free 800-622-2947. Fax: 920-261-9109 ext. 308. E-mail: admissions@mbbc.edu. Web site: http://www.mbbc.edu/.

MARIAN COLLEGE OF FOND DU LAC
FOND DU LAC, WISCONSIN

General Independent Roman Catholic, comprehensive, coed **Entrance** Moderately difficult **Setting** 50-acre small town campus **Total enrollment** 2,276 **Student/faculty ratio** 14:1 **Application deadline** Rolling **Housing** Yes **Expenses** Tuition $11,370; Room & Board $4188 **Undergraduates** 35% 25 or older **Most popular recent majors** Business administration; nursing; education **Academic program** Advanced placement, accelerated degree program, self-designed majors, tutorials, summer session, adult/continuing education programs, internships **Contact** Ms. Carol A. Reichenberger, Vice President for Enrollment Services, Marian College of Fond du Lac, 45 South National Avenue, Fond du Lac, WI 54935-4699. Telephone: 920-923-7666 or toll-free 800-2-MARIAN (in-state). Fax: 920-923-8755. E-mail: admit@mariancoll.edu. Web site: http://www.mariancoll.edu/.

▶ **For more information, see page 466.**

MARQUETTE UNIVERSITY
MILWAUKEE, WISCONSIN

General Independent Roman Catholic (Jesuit), university, coed **Entrance** Moderately difficult **Setting** 80-acre urban campus **Total enrollment** 10,610 **Student/faculty ratio** 14:1 **Application deadline** Rolling **Freshmen** 86% were admitted **Housing** Yes **Expenses** Tuition $15,384; Room & Board $5530 **Undergraduates** 53% women, 7% part-time, 0.3% Native American, 4% Hispanic, 5% black, 5% Asian American or Pacific Islander **Most popular recent majors** Business administration; psychology; nursing **Academic program** English as a second language, advanced placement, accelerated degree program, self-designed majors, tutorials, honors program, summer session, adult/continuing education programs, internships **Contact** Mr. Raymond A. Brown, Dean of Admissions, Marquette University, PO Box 1881, Milwaukee, WI 53201-1881. Telephone: 414-288-7302 or toll-free 800-222-6544. E-mail: go2marquette@marquette.edu. Web site: http://www.marquette.edu/.

MILWAUKEE INSTITUTE OF ART AND DESIGN
MILWAUKEE, WISCONSIN

General Independent, 4-year, coed **Entrance** Moderately difficult **Setting** Urban campus **Total enrollment** 503 **Student/faculty ratio** 15:1 **Application deadline** Rolling **Freshmen** 83% were admitted **Housing** Yes **Expenses** Tuition $14,800; Room & Board $6336 **Undergraduates** 41% women, 11% part-time, 13% 25 or older, 2% Native American, 6% Hispanic, 3% black, 4% Asian American or Pacific Islander **Academic program** Average class size 15, advanced placement, summer session, adult/continuing education programs, internships **Contact** Ms. Mary Schopp, Executive Director of Enrollment Services, Milwaukee Institute of Art and Design, 273 East Erie Street, Milwaukee, WI 53202. Telephone: 414-291-8070. Fax: 414-291-8077.

MILWAUKEE SCHOOL OF ENGINEERING
MILWAUKEE, WISCONSIN

General Independent, comprehensive, coed **Entrance** Moderately difficult **Setting** 12-acre urban campus **Total enrollment** 3,029 **Student/faculty ratio** 13:1 **Application deadline** Rolling **Freshmen** 65% were admitted **Housing** Yes **Expenses** Tuition $14,325; Room & Board $3855 **Undergraduates** 17% women, 30% part-time, 7% 25 or older, 0.3% Native American, 2% Hispanic, 4% black, 3% Asian American or Pacific Islander **Most popular recent majors** Electrical/electronics engineering; mechanical engineering; architectural engineering **Academic program** Average class size 20, advanced placement, accelerated degree program, tutorials, summer session, adult/continuing education programs, internships **Contact** Mr. Tim A. Valley, Dean, Enrollment Management, Milwaukee School of Engineering, 1025 North Broadway, Milwaukee, WI 53202-3109. Telephone: 414-277-6763 or toll-free 800-332-6763. Fax: 414-277-7475. E-mail: explore@msoe.edu. Web site: http://www.msoe.edu/.

MOUNT MARY COLLEGE
MILWAUKEE, WISCONSIN

General Independent Roman Catholic, comprehensive, women only **Entrance** Moderately difficult **Setting** 80-acre suburban campus **Total enrollment** 1,309 **Student/faculty ratio** 10:1 **Application deadline** 8/15 **Freshmen** 83% were admitted **Housing** Yes **Expenses** Tuition $10,740; Room & Board $3784 **Undergraduates** 32% part-time, 49% 25 or older, 0.3% Native American, 3% Hispanic, 9% black, 2% Asian American or Pacific Islander **Most popular recent majors** Occupational therapy; education; business administration **Academic program** Average class size 20, English as a second language, advanced placement, accelerated degree program, self-designed majors, honors program, summer session, adult/continuing education programs, internships **Contact** Mr. Michael Istwan, Director of Admission, Mount Mary College, 2900 North Menomonee River Parkway, Milwaukee, WI 53222-4597. Telephone: 414-258-4810 ext. 360 or toll-free 800-321-6265. Fax: 414-256-1224. E-mail: admiss@mtmary.edu. Web site: http://www.mtmary.edu/.

MOUNT SENARIO COLLEGE
LADYSMITH, WISCONSIN

General Independent, 4-year, coed **Entrance** Minimally difficult **Setting** 110-acre small town campus **Total enrollment** 1,140 **Student/faculty ratio** 12:1 **Application deadline** 8/20 **Housing** Yes **Expenses** Tuition $9500; Room & Board $3400 **Undergraduates** 31% women, 59% part-time, 62% 25 or older, 3% Native American, 2% Hispanic, 11% black, 4% Asian American or Pacific Islander **Most popular recent majors** Criminal justice/law enforcement administration; business administration; education **Academic program** English as a second language, accelerated degree program, self-designed majors, tutorials, summer session, adult/continuing education programs, internships **Contact** Mr. Max M. Waits, Admissions Consultant/Foreign Student Advisor, Mount Senario College, 1500 College Avenue West, Ladysmith, WI 54848-2128. Telephone: 715-532-5511 ext. 110. Fax: 715-532-7690. E-mail: admissions@mscfs.edu. Web site: http://www.mscfs.edu/.

NORTHLAND COLLEGE
ASHLAND, WISCONSIN

General Independent, 4-year, coed, affiliated with United Church of Christ **Entrance** Moderately difficult **Setting** 130-acre small town campus **Total enrollment** 875 **Student/faculty ratio** 16:1 **Application deadline** 8/1 **Freshmen** 94% were admitted **Housing** Yes **Expenses** Tuition $13,090; Room & Board $4385 **Undergraduates** 57% women, 10% part-time, 17% 25 or older, 3% Native American, 2% Hispanic, 1% black, 1% Asian American or Pacific Islander **Most popular recent majors** Biology; education **Academic program** Advanced placement, accelerated degree program, self-designed majors, honors program, summer session, adult/continuing education programs, internships **Contact** Mr. James L. Miller, Dean of Student Development and Enrollment, Northland College, 1411 Ellis Avenue, Ashland, WI 54806-3925. Telephone: 715-682-1224. Fax: 715-682-1258. E-mail: admit@wakefield.northland.edu. Web site: http://www.northland.edu/.

RIPON COLLEGE
RIPON, WISCONSIN

General Independent, 4-year, coed **Entrance** Moderately difficult **Setting** 250-acre small town campus **Total enrollment** 669 **Student/faculty ratio** 10:1 **Application deadline** 3/15 **Freshmen** 89% were admitted **Housing** Yes **Expenses** Tuition $17,580; Room & Board $4400 **Undergraduates** 53% women, 1% part-time, 1% 25 or older, 1% Native American, 3% Hispanic, 1% black, 2% Asian American or Pacific Islander **Most popular recent majors** History; English; biology **Academic program** Average class size 25, advanced placement, accelerated degree program, self-designed majors, tutorials, internships **Contact** Mr. Scott J. Goplin, Vice President and Dean of Admission and Financial Aid, Ripon College, 300 Seward Street, PO Box 248, Ripon, WI 54971. Telephone: 920-748-8185 or toll-free 800-947-4766. Fax: 920-748-7243. E-mail: adminfo@mac.ripon.edu. Web site: http://www.ripon.edu/.

▶ **For more information, see page 500.**

ST. NORBERT COLLEGE
DE PERE, WISCONSIN

General Independent Roman Catholic, comprehensive, coed **Entrance** Moderately difficult **Setting** 86-acre suburban campus **Total enrollment** 2,000 **Student/faculty ratio** 14:1 **Application deadline** Rolling **Freshmen** 92% were admitted **Housing** Yes **Expenses** Tuition $14,434; Room & Board $5120 **Undergraduates** 59% women, 4% part-time, 4% 25 or older, 1% Native American, 1% Hispanic, 0.2% black, 1% Asian American or Pacific Islander **Most popular recent majors** Business administration; elementary education; mass communications **Academic program** Average class size 30, English as a second language, advanced placement, accelerated degree program, self-designed majors, tutorials, honors program, summer session, internships **Contact** Dr. John Sutton, Interim Dean of Admission, St. Norbert College, 100 Grant Street, Office of Admission, De Pere, WI 54115-2099. Telephone: 920-403-3005 or toll-free 800-236-4878. E-mail: admit@sncac.snc.edu. Web site: http://www.snc.edu/.

SILVER LAKE COLLEGE
MANITOWOC, WISCONSIN

General Independent Roman Catholic, comprehensive, coed **Entrance** Minimally difficult **Set-**

Silver Lake College *(continued)*

ting 30-acre rural campus **Total enrollment** 1,050 **Student/faculty ratio** 9:1 **Application deadline** 8/31 **Freshmen** 93% were admitted **Housing** Yes **Expenses** Tuition $9986; Room & Board $4226 **Undergraduates** 67% women, 49% part-time, 70% 25 or older, 0.5% Native American, 2% Hispanic, 0% black, 1% Asian American or Pacific Islander **Most popular recent majors** Business administration; elementary education; accounting **Academic program** Self-designed majors, summer session, adult/continuing education programs, internships **Contact** Ms. Sandra O. Schwartz, Director of Admissions, Silver Lake College, 2406 South Alverno Road, Manitowoc, WI 54220-9319. Telephone: 920-684-5955 ext. 175 or toll-free 800-236-4752 (in-state). Fax: 920-684-7082. E-mail: admslc@sl.edu. Web site: http://www.sl.edu/slc.html.

UNIVERSITY OF WISCONSIN–EAU CLAIRE

EAU CLAIRE, WISCONSIN

General State-supported, comprehensive, coed **Entrance** Moderately difficult **Setting** 333-acre urban campus **Total enrollment** 10,484 **Student/faculty ratio** 19:1 **Application deadline** 3/1 **Freshmen** 82% were admitted **Housing** Yes **Expenses** Tuition $2872; Room & Board $2986 **Undergraduates** 60% women, 10% part-time, 9% 25 or older, 1% Native American, 1% Hispanic, 1% black, 2% Asian American or Pacific Islander **Most popular recent majors** Nursing; biology; psychology **Academic program** Average class size 29, English as a second language, advanced placement, honors program, summer session, adult/continuing education programs, internships **Contact** Mr. Roger GroeneWold, Director of Admissions, University of Wisconsin–Eau Claire, PO Box 4004, Eau Claire, WI 54702-4004. Telephone: 715-836-5415. Fax: 715-836-2380. E-mail: ask-uwec@uwec.edu. Web site: http://www.uwec.edu/.

UNIVERSITY OF WISCONSIN–GREEN BAY

GREEN BAY, WISCONSIN

General State-supported, comprehensive, coed **Entrance** Moderately difficult **Setting** 700-acre suburban campus **Total enrollment** 5,419 **Student/faculty ratio** 18:1 **Application deadline** 2/1 **Freshmen** 88% were admitted **Housing** Yes **Expenses** Tuition $2738; Room only $1835 **Undergraduates** 63% women, 19% part-time, 24% 25 or older, 2% Native American, 1% Hispanic, 1% black, 2% Asian American or Pacific Islander **Most popular recent majors** Business administration; developmental/child psychology; psychology **Academic program** Average class size 50, English as a second language, advanced placement, accelerated degree program, self-designed majors, tutorials, summer session, adult/continuing education programs, internships **Contact** Mr. Myron Van de Ven, Director of Admissions, University of Wisconsin–Green Bay, 2420 Nicolet Drive, Green Bay, WI 54311-7001. Telephone: 920-465-2111. Fax: 920-465-2032. E-mail: admissns@uwgb.edu. Web site: http://www.uwgb.edu/.

UNIVERSITY OF WISCONSIN–LA CROSSE

LA CROSSE, WISCONSIN

General State-supported, comprehensive, coed **Entrance** Moderately difficult **Setting** 119-acre suburban campus **Total enrollment** 9,086 **Student/faculty ratio** 19:1 **Application deadline** Rolling **Freshmen** 78% were admitted **Housing** Yes **Expenses** Tuition $2859; Room & Board $3060 **Undergraduates** 57% women, 6% part-time, 9% 25 or older, 1% Native American, 1% Hispanic, 1% black, 2% Asian American or Pacific Islander **Most popular recent majors** Biology; business administration; elementary education **Academic program** Average class size 35, English as a second language, advanced placement, accelerated degree program, honors program, summer session, adult/continuing education programs, internships **Contact** Mr. Tim Lewis, Director of Admissions, University of Wisconsin–La Crosse, 1725 State Street, La Crosse, WI 54601-3742. Telephone: 608-785-8576. Fax: 608-785-6695. E-mail: admissions@post.uwlax.edu. Web site: http://www.uwlax.edu/.

UNIVERSITY OF WISCONSIN–MADISON

MADISON, WISCONSIN

General State-supported, university, coed **Entrance** Very difficult **Setting** 1,050-acre urban campus **Total enrollment** 40,196 **Student/faculty ratio** 12:1 **Application deadline** 2/1 **Freshmen** 77% were admitted **Housing** Yes **Expenses** Tuition $3242; Room & Board $4880 **Undergraduates** 4% 25 or older, 0.4% Native American, 2% Hispanic, 2% black, 4% Asian American or Pacific Islander **Most popular recent majors** Political science; mechanical engineering; history **Academic program** English as a second language, advanced placement, accelerated degree program, self-designed majors, tutorials, honors program, summer session, adult/continuing education programs, internships **Contact** Office of Admissions, University of Wisconsin–Madison, 140 Peterson Office Building, 750 University Avenue, Madison, WI 53706-1380. Telephone: 608-262-3961. Fax: 608-262-1429. E-mail: on.wisconsion@mail.admin.wisc.edu. Web site: http://www.wisc.edu/.

UNIVERSITY OF WISCONSIN–MILWAUKEE

MILWAUKEE, WISCONSIN

General State-supported, university, coed **Entrance** Moderately difficult **Setting** 90-acre urban campus **Total enrollment** 21,525 **Application deadline** Rolling **Housing** Yes **Expenses** Tuition $3327; Room only $2457 **Undergraduates** 53% women, 25% part-time, 26% 25 or older, 1% Native American, 4% Hispanic, 9% black, 4% Asian American or Pacific Islander **Academic program** English as a second language, advanced placement, self-designed majors, honors program, summer session, adult/continuing education programs, internships **Contact** Ms. Jan Ford, Director, Recruitment and Outreach, University of Wisconsin–Milwaukee, PO Box 413, Milwaukee, WI 53201-0413. Telephone: 414-229-4397. Fax: 414-229-6940. E-mail: uwmlook@des.uwm.edu. Web site: http://www.uwm.edu/.

UNIVERSITY OF WISCONSIN–OSHKOSH

OSHKOSH, WISCONSIN

General State-supported, comprehensive, coed **Entrance** Moderately difficult **Setting** 192-acre suburban campus **Total enrollment** 10,960 **Student/faculty ratio** 19:1 **Application deadline** 8/1 **Freshmen** 89% were admitted **Housing** Yes **Expenses** Tuition $2609; Room & Board $2658 **Undergraduates** 14% 25 or older, 1% Native American, 1% Hispanic, 1% black, 1% Asian American or Pacific Islander **Most popular recent majors** Nursing; business marketing and marketing management; elementary education **Academic program** Average class size 31, English as a second language, advanced placement, accelerated degree program, self-designed majors, tutorials, honors program, summer session, adult/continuing education programs, internships **Contact** Mr. Richard Hillman, Associate Director of Admissions, University of Wisconsin–Oshkosh, 800 Algoma Boulevard, Oshkosh, WI 54901-8602. Telephone: 920-424-0202. Fax: 920-424-1098. E-mail: oshadmuw@uwosh.edu. Web site: http://www.uwosh.edu/.

UNIVERSITY OF WISCONSIN–PARKSIDE

KENOSHA, WISCONSIN

General State-supported, comprehensive, coed **Entrance** Moderately difficult **Setting** 700-acre suburban campus **Total enrollment** 4,696 **Student/faculty ratio** 14:1 **Application deadline** 8/1 **Freshmen** 93% were admitted **Housing** Yes **Expenses** Tuition $2705; Room & Board $4000 **Undergraduates** 59% women, 28% part-time, 32% 25 or older, 1% Native American, 6% Hispanic, 7% black, 2% Asian American or Pacific Islander **Most popular recent majors** Business administration; psychology; biology **Academic program** Advanced placement, accelerated degree program, honors program, summer session, adult/continuing education programs, internships **Contact** Mr. Charles Murphy, Director of Admissions, University of Wisconsin–Parkside, 900 Wood Road, Box 2000, Kenosha, WI 53141-2000. Telephone: 414-595-2355. E-mail: jucha@it.uwp.edu.

UNIVERSITY OF WISCONSIN–PLATTEVILLE

PLATTEVILLE, WISCONSIN

General State-supported, comprehensive, coed **Contact** Dr. Richard Schumacher, Dean of Admissions and Enrollment Management, University of Wisconsin–Platteville, 1 University Plaza, Platteville, WI 53818-3099. Telephone: 608-342-1125 or toll-free 800-362-5515 (in-state). E-mail: admit@uwplatt.edu. Web site: http://www.uwplatt.edu/.

UNIVERSITY OF WISCONSIN–RIVER FALLS

RIVER FALLS, WISCONSIN

General State-supported, comprehensive, coed **Entrance** Moderately difficult **Setting** 225-acre suburban campus **Total enrollment** 5,441 **Student/faculty ratio** 18:1 **Application deadline** 1/1 **Freshmen** 81% were admitted **Housing** Yes **Expenses** Tuition $2750; Room & Board $3036 **Undergraduates** 10% 25 or older, 0.4% Native American, 1% Hispanic, 1% black, 2% Asian American or Pacific Islander **Most popular recent majors** Business administration; animal sciences; elementary education **Academic program** Average class size 30, advanced placement, accelerated degree program, self-designed majors, tutorials, honors program, summer session, adult/continuing education programs, internships **Contact** Mr. Alan Tuchtenhagen, Director of Admissions, University of Wisconsin–River Falls, 410 South Third Street, River Falls, WI 54022-5001. Telephone: 715-425-3500. Fax: 715-425-0678. E-mail: admit@uwrf.edu. Web site: http://www.uwrf.edu/.

UNIVERSITY OF WISCONSIN–STEVENS POINT

STEVENS POINT, WISCONSIN

General State-supported, comprehensive, coed **Entrance** Moderately difficult **Setting** 335-acre small town campus **Total enrollment** 8,446 **Student/faculty ratio** 19:1 **Application deadline** Rolling **Freshmen** 71% were admitted **Housing** Yes **Expenses** Tuition $2790; Room & Board $3188 **Undergraduates** 54% women, 10% part-time, 17% 25 or older, 1% Native American, 1% Hispanic, 0.5% black, 1% Asian American or Pacific Islander **Most popular recent majors** Biology; elementary education; business administration **Academic program** English as a second language, advanced placement, self-designed majors, honors program, summer session, adult/continuing education programs, internships **Contact** Dr. David Eckholm, Director of Admissions, Univer-

University of Wisconsin–Stevens Point *(continued)*

sity of Wisconsin-Stevens Point, Stevens Point, WI 54481-3897. Telephone: 715-346-2441. E-mail: admiss@uwsp.edu. Web site: http://www.uwsp.edu/.

UNIVERSITY OF WISCONSIN–STOUT
MENOMONIE, WISCONSIN

General State-supported, comprehensive, coed **Entrance** Moderately difficult **Setting** 120-acre small town campus **Total enrollment** 7,418 **Student/faculty ratio** 21:1 **Application deadline** Rolling **Freshmen** 87% were admitted **Housing** Yes **Expenses** Tuition $2806; Room & Board $3062 **Undergraduates** 48% women, 8% part-time, 16% 25 or older, 1% Native American, 1% Hispanic, 1% black, 2% Asian American or Pacific Islander **Most popular recent majors** Hotel and restaurant management; industrial technology **Academic program** English as a second language, advanced placement, accelerated degree program, tutorials, honors program, summer session, adult/continuing education programs, internships **Contact** Mr. Richard Lowery, Associate Director of Admissions, University of Wisconsin-Stout, Menomonie, WI 54751. Telephone: 715-232-1411 or toll-free 800-HI-STOUT (in-state). Fax: 715-232-1667. E-mail: admissions@uwstout.edu. Web site: http://www.uwstout.edu/.

UNIVERSITY OF WISCONSIN–SUPERIOR
SUPERIOR, WISCONSIN

General State-supported, comprehensive, coed **Entrance** Moderately difficult **Setting** 230-acre small town campus **Total enrollment** 2,574 **Student/faculty ratio** 12:1 **Application deadline** Rolling **Freshmen** 86% were admitted **Housing** Yes **Expenses** Tuition $2652; Room & Board $3200 **Undergraduates** 21% 25 or older, 3% Native American, 1% Hispanic, 1% black, 1% Asian American or Pacific Islander **Most popular recent majors** Business administration; education; social work **Academic program** English as a second language, advanced placement, accelerated degree program, self-designed majors, tutorials, honors program, summer session, adult/continuing education programs, internships **Contact** Ms. Lorraine Washa, Student Application Contact, University of Wisconsin-Superior, 1800 Grand Avenue, Superior, WI 54880-2873. Telephone: 715-394-8230. Fax: 715-394-8407. E-mail: admissions@uwsuper.edu. Web site: http://www.uwsuper.edu/.

UNIVERSITY OF WISCONSIN–WHITEWATER
WHITEWATER, WISCONSIN

General State-supported, comprehensive, coed **Entrance** Moderately difficult **Setting** 385-acre small town campus **Total enrollment** 10,563 **Student/faculty ratio** 21:1 **Application deadline** Rolling **Freshmen** 84% were admitted **Housing** Yes **Expenses** Tuition $2772; Room & Board $2812 **Undergraduates** 52% women, 12% part-time, 10% 25 or older, 0.3% Native American, 2% Hispanic, 3% black, 1% Asian American or Pacific Islander **Most popular recent majors** Business administration; accounting; business marketing and marketing management **Academic program** Advanced placement, self-designed majors, honors program, summer session, adult/continuing education programs, internships **Contact** Mr. Lon Sherman, Executive Director of Admissions, University of Wisconsin-Whitewater, 800 West Main Street, Whitewater, WI 53190-1790. Telephone: 414-472-1440. Fax: 414-472-1515. E-mail: uwwadmit@uwwvax.uww.edu. Web site: http://www.uww.edu/.

VITERBO COLLEGE
LA CROSSE, WISCONSIN

General Independent Roman Catholic, comprehensive, coed **Entrance** Moderately difficult **Setting** 5-acre urban campus **Total enrollment** 2,622 **Student/faculty ratio** 15:1 **Application deadline** Rolling **Freshmen** 87% were admitted **Housing** Yes **Expenses** Tuition $11,690; Room & Board $4250 **Undergraduates** 32% 25 or older, 0.4% Native American, 1% Hispanic, 1% black, 1% Asian American or Pacific Islander **Most popular recent majors** Nursing; business administration; elementary education **Academic program** Advanced placement, accelerated degree program, self-designed majors, tutorials, summer session, adult/continuing education programs, internships **Contact** Mr. Brent Brigson, Admission Counselor, Viterbo College, 815 South Ninth Street, La Crosse, WI 54601-4797. Telephone: 608-796-3017 or toll-free 800-VIT-ERBO. Fax: 608-796-3020. E-mail: admission@viterbo.edu. Web site: http://www.viterbo.edu/.

WISCONSIN LUTHERAN COLLEGE
MILWAUKEE, WISCONSIN

General Independent, 4-year, coed, affiliated with Wisconsin Evangelical Lutheran Synod **Entrance** Moderately difficult **Setting** 16-acre suburban campus **Total enrollment** 440 **Student/faculty ratio** 13:1 **Application deadline** 9/1 **Freshmen** 93% were admitted **Housing** Yes **Expenses** Tuition $12,080; Room & Board $4500 **Undergraduates** 60% women, 8% part-time, 8% 25 or older, 0.2% Native American, 0.5% Hispanic, 1% black, 1% Asian American or Pacific Islander **Most popular recent majors** Communications; psychology; business administration **Academic program** Advanced placement, self-designed majors, tutorials, summer session, internships **Contact** Mr.

Jeff Weber, Director of Admissions, Wisconsin Lutheran College, 8800 West Bluemound Road, Milwaukee, WI 53226-9942. Telephone: 414-443-8819. Fax: 414-443-8514. E-mail: admissions@wlc.edu. Web site: http://www.wlc.edu/.

WYOMING

UNIVERSITY OF WYOMING

LARAMIE, WYOMING

General State-supported, university, coed **Entrance** Moderately difficult **Setting** 785-acre small town campus **Total enrollment** 11,094 **Student/faculty ratio** 15:1 **Application deadline** 8/10 **Freshmen** 94% were admitted **Housing** Yes **Expenses** Tuition $2330; Room & Board $4278 **Undergraduates** 51% women, 13% part-time, 22% 25 or older, 1% Native American, 5% Hispanic, 1% black, 1% Asian American or Pacific Islander **Most popular recent majors** Elementary education; psychology; social work **Academic program** English as a second language, advanced placement, self-designed majors, tutorials, honors program, summer session, adult/continuing education programs, internships **Contact** Mr. James T. Mansfield, Director of Admissions, University of Wyoming, Box 3435, Laramie, WY 82071. Telephone: 307-766-5160 or toll-free 800-342-5996 (in-state). Fax: 307-766-4042. E-mail: undergraduate.admissions@uwyo.edu. Web site: http://www.uwyo.edu/.

DESCRIPTIONS

The full-page descriptions in this section provide a broad overview of some of the colleges and universities profiled in the previous section. These descriptions are offered to help give students a better sense of the individuality of each institution, in terms that include mission statements, campus environments, and academic programs. The absence from this section of any college or university does not constitute an editorial decision on the part of Peterson's. In essence, this section is an open forum for colleges and universities, on a voluntary basis, to communicate their particular messages to prospective college students. The descriptions are arranged alphabetically by the official name of the institution.

ADRIAN COLLEGE

■ Adrian, Michigan

THE COLLEGE

Adrian College, chartered in 1859, is a private liberal arts college affiliated with the United Methodist Church. Recognized for providing high-quality education by the *New York Times* and *U.S. News & World Report,* Adrian is characterized by teaching excellence and individual treatment of students. The College's mission is to maintain a learning environment that stimulates individual growth and academic excellence. To fulfill this mission, the College is committed to fostering creativity, encouraging ethical values and the pursuit of truth, and helping students develop the necessary skills to lead satisfying lives and careers within a global society. Nearly all of Adrian's students live on campus in one of nine residence halls that provide unique living and learning environments for residents. With more than sixty-five organizations to choose from, students can apply their talents, interests, and skills in extracurricular activities ranging from academic honoraries and religious, cultural, and social organizations to intercollegiate and intramural athletic teams. Adrian College is a member of the NCAA Division III and the Michigan Intercollegiate Athletics Association.

For more information about Adrian College or to schedule a campus visit, students should contact:

Office of Admissions
Adrian College
110 South Madison Street
Adrian, Michigan 49221-2575
Telephone: 517-265-5161
800-877-2246 (toll-free)
E-mail: admission@adrian.adrian.edu
World Wide Web:
http://www.adrian.edu

ACADEMIC PROGRAM

Distribution requirements are designed to emphasize liberal education through a broad understanding of the liberal arts and have been established in several liberal arts areas (arts, humanities, social sciences, natural and physical sciences, and cross-cultural perspective) and in basic skill areas that indicate education proficiency (communication, linguistics, and physical development). All students must complete at least one course in religion or philosophy and at least one 4-hour laboratory science course. Students must also declare their major during their sophomore year. Successful completion of a minimum of 124 semester hours, with at least 30 hours at the most advanced level, is needed to obtain a baccalaureate degree. Up to 60 semester hours may be earned through nontraditional credit programs such as CLEP, PEP, LLE, Advanced Placement, and others. An honors program is open to highly motivated students of proven ability. Successful completion of the honors program is noted on the student's transcript and diploma.

FINANCIAL AID

Adrian College strives to make a high-quality private liberal arts education affordable to its students through various forms of financial assistance. Approximately 85 percent of the student body receives some form of financial aid through scholarships, grants, loans, and campus employment. The College also participates in all applicable Michigan aid programs, as well as the Federal Work-Study, Federal Pell Grant, and Federal Supplemental Educational Opportunity Grant (FSEOG) programs. The Federal Perkins Loan, Federal Stafford Student Loan, TERI Supplemental Loan, and Federal Parent Loan (PLUS) programs are also available. A number of part-time positions are available for those who wish to work on campus while earning applicable financial assistance. For those with a demonstrated record of high academic ability, merit-based scholarship assistance is available.

APPLICATION AND INFORMATION

A nonrefundable fee of $20 must be submitted with an application for admission. Application can be made anytime following the completion of the junior year of high school. Students are usually notified of the admission decision within two weeks after the application file is complete. Campus visits are strongly encouraged but not required.

ALBION COLLEGE

■ Albion, Michigan

THE COLLEGE

Founded in 1835, Albion College is dedicated to offering a challenging education in the liberal arts tradition, along with practical career preparation. The College sets high standards of performance for its students, which, in turn, means that graduate and professional schools and prospective employers have a high regard for Albion alumni. A private college related to the United Methodist Church, Albion is accredited by the North Central Association of Colleges and Schools, and its programs in music and in chemistry are accredited by the National Association of Schools of Music and the American Chemical Society, respectively.

For further information, students should contact:

Albion College
611 East Porter Street
Albion, Michigan 49224
Telephone: 800-858-6770 (toll-free)
Fax: 517-629-0569
E-mail: admissions@albion.edu
World Wide Web:
http://www.Albion.edu

ACADEMIC PROGRAM

To graduate with the Bachelor of Arts degree, students must complete 31 units (124 semester hours); to earn the Bachelor of Fine Arts degree, visual arts majors must complete 34 units (136 semester hours). All students must pass a writing competence examination. To introduce students to important areas of knowledge, Albion has developed a core requirement that consists of study in the natural sciences and mathematics, the social sciences, the humanities, interdisciplinary studies, and the fine arts, as well as additional requirements in gender and ethnicity studies. The core curriculum and the requirements for a major compose about half to two thirds of a student's program at Albion; the remainder can be used for electives or to complete a second major or a 6–8 course concentration in business management, computer science, human services, mass communication, public service, or women's studies.

FINANCIAL AID

In 1997–98, 68 percent of the students had demonstrated financial need and received $11.1 million in assistance. Need is determined from the Free Application for Federal Student Aid (FAFSA); the FAFSA should be received by the College no later than February 15. Financial aid is awarded as a package, utilizing federal grants and loans and College sources. Michigan residents are eligible for state scholarships and grants. More than 50 percent of Albion's students have campus jobs. Students must apply for admission in order to be considered for financial aid. Students who show outstanding achievement are eligible for academic scholarships ranging up to full tuition. The scholarship application deadline is February 1. Students with demonstrated talent in art, music, and theater may qualify for scholarships up to $3000.

APPLICATION AND INFORMATION

Students may submit an application for admission at any time; however, most students apply after September 1 of their senior year. All information, including an application form and $20 fee, test scores, high school transcripts, and recommendations, should be received by the College by April 1. Albion has a rolling admission policy and responds to applications approximately four weeks after all materials have been received. Albion is also a member of the Common Application and will accept applications via computer, as well as computerized versions of College Link and College View. Qualified students who have decided that Albion College is their first choice may apply by December 1 under the Early Decision Program and will receive notification of the decision before December 15. Financial aid applicants will also receive a preliminary financial aid offer.

ALFRED UNIVERSITY

■ Alfred, New York

THE UNIVERSITY

Alfred University is a residential institution of 2,500 graduate and undergraduate students, located 70 miles south of Rochester, between the Finger Lakes region and the Allegheny Mountains in western New York State. Alfred is composed of the privately endowed Colleges of Business, Liberal Arts and Sciences, and Engineering and Professional Studies, as well as the publicly supported New York State College of Ceramics, which comprises the School of Art and Design and the School of Ceramic Engineering and Materials Science. Alfred is noted for its superior academic quality, outstanding faculty, and commitment to student development. The state of New York has identified Alfred University as one of its ten centers for advanced technology research.

Applications and inquiries should be addressed to:

Katherine McCarthy
Director of Admissions
Alumni Hall
Alfred University
Saxon Drive
Alfred, New York 14802
Telephone: 607-871-2115
800-541-9229 (toll-free)
Fax: 607-871-2198
E-mail: admwww@bigvax.alfred.edu

ACADEMIC PROGRAM

Candidates are required to complete 124 semester hours for the B.A. from the College of Liberal Arts and Sciences, 120 for the B.S. from the College of Business, 125 for the B.S. from the College of Engineering and Professional Studies, 137 for the B.S. from the School of Ceramic Engineering and Sciences, and 128 for the B.F.A. from the School of Art and Design. Students must earn a cumulative index of 2.0 or better and are required to satisfy the physical education requirements through courses or proficiency examinations. A 4-hour course in English composition is required for students who test below a minimum standard. To encourage students with strong ability and initiative, the University recognizes the Advanced Placement and International Baccalaureate programs. In addition, the University offers its own challenge examination program for students already enrolled.

FINANCIAL AID

In 1997–98, University-funded aid provided more than $13 million to undergraduate students. For private-sector programs, 95 percent of freshmen received some form of financial assistance, and for the New York State College of Ceramics, 85 percent of freshmen received assistance. Aid administered by the University usually consists of a combination of scholarships or grants-in-aid, loans, and part-time work. Students may be eligible for financial assistance under the Federal Pell Grant, Federal Supplemental Educational Opportunity Grant, Federal Perkins Loan, and Federal Work-Study programs. New York State residents may be eligible for aid under the Tuition Assistance Program. The University sponsors National Merit Scholarships, departmental talent awards, Presidential, Southern Tier, transfer scholarships, and the Johnathan Allen Award for Leadership.

APPLICATION AND INFORMATION

Candidates must submit a completed Alfred University application form or the Common Application form, SAT I or ACT results, a letter of recommendation, and a $40 application fee. Students who bring their completed application and essay with them when they visit campus will receive a $40 application fee waiver. They must also have their high school guidance office send a copy of their transcript. Applicants to the School of Art and Design must submit a portfolio of their work, normally fifteen to twenty slides. The application and portfolio deadline under the early decision plan is December 1, with notification by December 15. The application deadline for regular admission is February 1, with notification by early March. The portfolio deadline for regular admission is February 15. Transfer applicants should file an application by August 1 for September admission or December 1 for January admission.

ALLEGHENY COLLEGE

■ Meadville, Pennsylvania

THE COLLEGE

For more information, students should contact:

Office of Admissions
Allegheny College
Meadville, Pennsylvania 16335-3902
Telephone: 814-332-4351
800-521-5293 (toll-free)
E-mail: admiss@admin.alleg.edu
Web site: http://www.alleg.edu

Founded on America's western frontier in 1815, Allegheny is a classical, selective college of the liberal arts and sciences. Although highly regarded as a preprofessional school, its impact on students goes well beyond preparation for careers. Allegheny not only develops in its students such essential skills as writing, critical thinking, and problem solving, but also fosters a capacity for lifelong learning, the ability to manage everyday affairs, responsible citizenship, social skills, and values. While nonsectarian in outlook and practice, Allegheny has been affiliated with the United Methodist Church since 1833. The 1,800 students come from forty states and fifteen other countries. Five percent are members of minority groups, and three fourths reside on campus. On-campus residence is required of freshmen and sophomores and is optional for other students, but it is guaranteed for all four years for all who seek it. Faculty members describe Allegheny students as active and hardworking. Seventy percent come from the highest fifth of their high school class, 1 in 3 was president of a student organization, and 80 percent were active in volunteer service groups.

ACADEMIC PROGRAM

Allegheny ensures that students develop wholeness across the divisions of knowledge (arts and humanities, social sciences, and natural sciences) as well as expertise in one or more fields. Each student must complete thirty-two semester courses; the major may require eight to twelve courses, including a junior seminar and the distinctive Senior Project, while the remainder are electives and Liberal Studies Program courses. The innovative Liberal Studies Program includes a freshman seminar, with a strong advising component; a sophomore writing course; and some in-depth study in a subject outside the division of the major. Writing proficiency is emphasized throughout the Allegheny years: it is a central objective of the freshman seminar; it is developed further in the sophomore writing course, after students have mastered some college-level material; and it must be demonstrated in all other courses.

FINANCIAL AID

A large number of merit-based scholarships are awarded annually, making the College more affordable even to families who do not qualify for need-based financial aid. Also, scholarships, grants, loans, and campus employment are awarded to students who need assistance to meet College expenses. The Free Application for Federal Student Aid (FAFSA), which establishes an applicant's eligibility for virtually all institutional, state, and federal assistance, must be submitted by February 15. Notices about the receipt of financial aid are sent to students shortly after their acceptance by the College. Nine out of ten students receive some form of financial aid.

APPLICATION AND INFORMATION

The application for admission should be submitted by February 15 (November 15 to January 15 for early decision), and the SAT I or ACT results should be forwarded to the College by each candidate. Applicants for early decision are notified on a rolling basis between December 15 and January 31. Regular applicants are informed of the admission decision by April 1.

ALMA COLLEGE

■ Alma, Michigan

All records and forms should be mailed to:

Admissions Office
Alma College
614 West Superior Street
Alma, Michigan 48801-1599
Telephone: 800-321-ALMA (toll-free)
E-mail: admissions@alma.edu
Web site: http://www.alma.edu

THE COLLEGE

Regarded as one of the nation's best liberal arts colleges, Alma College is in its second century of superior education and professional distinction. Founded by Presbyterians in 1886, Alma remains a private liberal arts institution committed to a values-oriented style of education. In a time when many professionals find that their technical training is already out of date, Alma's graduates are entering the job market with an education that will always serve them. Alma's academic philosophy, rooted in the liberal arts tradition and providing a broad educational base with flexible, innovative course work, has earned Alma a Phi Beta Kappa chapter. Classes are small—the average size is 21—enabling students to do more than just listen. Students enjoy the rigorous academic atmosphere; 89 percent of the faculty members hold the highest degree in their field. In fall 1997, Alma College enrolled a total of 1,407 students (603 men and 804 women), of whom 1,368 were full-time. Alma's students are high achievers from the upper ranks of some of the best high schools in Michigan and its surrounding states. Current students come from twenty states and eight countries. Entering freshmen have an average high school GPA of 3.62; their mean ACT composite score of 25.5 is approximately equivalent to a combined SAT I score of 1140. More than three fourths of the freshmen enrolled in 1997 ranked in the top 25 percent of their high school class; 43 percent ranked in the top 10 percent. Nearly all of Alma's students live on campus.

ACADEMIC PROGRAM

The College operates on a 4-4-1 calendar—two 4-month terms in the fall and winter and one 1-month term in the spring. During the spring term, there are opportunities for international study as well as for on-campus instruction and research. In keeping with Alma's philosophy of educating the whole person, the College requires that all students complete liberal arts courses spanning the humanities, the natural sciences, and the social sciences.

FINANCIAL AID

At Alma, students can achieve scholarship recognition regardless of need on the basis of outstanding scholastic achievement. Several academically competitive scholarship programs provide awards for eligible students, including a full tuition scholarship for National Merit Finalists. The College also offers performance scholarships in recognition of individual talent, as well as grants, loans, and deferred-payment plans. Up to 400 campus and community jobs are filled by Alma students yearly. To apply for aid, students are required only to file the Free Application for Federal Student Aid (FAFSA) in January of the year of prospective enrollment at Alma.

APPLICATION AND INFORMATION

Students may apply at any time after completing their junior year of high school. Freshman applicants should send the completed application for admission along with a $20 nonrefundable application fee, high school transcripts, and ACT or SAT I scores. Students are required to submit a recommendation from their high school guidance counselor. Early decision applications are due by November 1. Transfer students should submit transcripts from all colleges and high schools attended, the completed application for admission, a $20 nonrefundable application fee, a financial aid transcript, and a Transfer Recommendation Form from the last college attended. Applications are handled on a rolling basis; students should hear about admission decisions within three weeks after sending an application and records.

AMHERST COLLEGE

■ Amherst, Massachusetts

Requests for applications and information should be directed to:

Office of Admission
Box 2231
Amherst College
P.O. Box 5000
Amherst, Massachusetts 01002-5000
Telephone: 413-542-2328
E-mail: admissions@amherst.edu
World Wide Web:
http://www.amherst.edu

THE COLLEGE

The essence of education at Amherst lies not so much in the structure of a curriculum—or even in the original research associated with honors work and independent study—as in the styles of thought Amherst professors expect from their students. Undergraduates must know the subject material, but, even more important, they must learn how to deal with new questions—sometimes with questions they have never confronted before—and to form their own conclusions. Amherst, founded in 1821 as a nonsectarian institution for the education of "young men of piety," today draws its students from most of the fifty states and many countries. Students of color make up more than one third of the student body. Extracurricular activities flourish at Amherst College—newspapers and literary magazines, radio, sports, dramatics, musical organizations, and campus government. There are frequent lectures, art exhibitions, concerts, plays, and other cultural events at Amherst and four nearby colleges. Students are also involved in a variety of public service activities—assisting patients in hospitals, tutoring disadvantaged children in nearby urban areas, organizing ecological and public information campaigns, and working for political causes.

ACADEMIC PROGRAM

The Amherst curriculum offers more than 500 courses a year in the academic departments and additional areas for majors listed above. Students may also engage in independent study, fieldwork, and international study programs. While first-year students do not receive credit for Advanced Placement or college-level courses taken before they come to Amherst, new students, if qualified, may enter classes at advanced levels in foreign languages, mathematics, and the natural sciences. Amherst has no distribution or core requirements. A Liberal Studies Curriculum requires that one First-Year Seminar course be taken in the fall of the first year. Each seminar is planned and taught by members of the faculty who adopt an interdisciplinary approach to a particular topic. More than half of the upperclass students undertake honors work in their majors and write theses based on original research. In all advanced work students work closely with their professors and come to understand their disciplines professionally—with the outlook of the practitioner rather than the spectator.

FINANCIAL AID

The College's financial aid program offers a combination of scholarships, loans, and campus employment to ensure that an Amherst education is possible for all students. Every candidate admitted to the College in 1997 with demonstrated financial need received aid. Amherst awards aid on the basis of need only; it has no merit- or talent-based scholarships. More than 40 percent of the students at Amherst receive direct financial assistance from the College. The average scholarship award to first-year students in 1997 was more than $17,000.

APPLICATION AND INFORMATION

Completed early decision applications must be postmarked by November 15; the College notifies applicants of its decision by December 15. Most early decision applicants not initially accepted are reconsidered in the spring along with regular applicants. Regular applications must be postmarked by December 31. The College notifies all regular applicants of the admission and financial aid decisions before April 15; successful applicants must accept or decline by May 1. Amherst now exclusively uses the Common Application. An application form may be obtained from the College directly or through high school guidance offices.

ANDERSON UNIVERSITY

■ ANDERSON, INDIANA

THE UNIVERSITY

Anderson University is a private, liberal arts community established in 1917 and dedicated to the scholarly and spiritual growth of its students. Today, approximately 2,250 students from forty-five states and fifteen countries compose this learning community. The University is accredited by the North Central Association of Colleges and Schools and has specific program accreditations from the National Council for Accreditation of Teacher Education, the National League for Nursing, the National Association of Schools of Music, the Council on Social Work Education, the National Athletic Training Association, and the Association of Collegiate Business Schools and Programs. As part of its commitment to maintain a distinctive life-style as a Christian university, the school prohibits the use of tobacco in any form and the use of alcoholic beverages and illegal drugs. High moral and ethical standards of behavior are expected of members of the campus community.

For applications and financial aid forms or for more information, students should contact:

Jim King
Director of Admissions
Anderson University
Anderson, Indiana 46012
Telephone: 765-641-4080
800-428-6414 (toll-free)
Fax: 765-641-4091
E-mail: info@anderson.edu
Web site: http://www.anderson.edu

ACADEMIC PROGRAM

A specific set of requirements must be satisfied for each major. Students in the bachelor's degree programs must complete a minimum of 124 semester hours and earn 248 credit points to graduate. All students must also complete a specified number of hours in courses from the core curriculum. The core curriculum, which offers students a great degree of flexibility in class selection, assures the student that he or she will be exposed to several key knowledge areas, including arts and humanities, the contemporary world, the environment, individual behavior, and problem solving. Before graduation, all students must demonstrate competence in three skill areas: English (reading, writing, and oral expression), foreign language, and mathematics.

FINANCIAL AID

More than 90 percent of Anderson University students receive financial aid through scholarships, grants, loans, and employment. The University participates in the Federal Work-Study Program and assists students in applying for aid through the Federal Pell and Federal Supplemental Educational Opportunity Grant programs, the Federal Perkins Loan Program, and the Federal Stafford Student Loan Program. A variety of scholarship programs are also available. These include the Matching Church Scholarship; Presidential, Academic Honors, and Distinguished Student (academic) Scholarships; and music and departmental scholarship programs. Students applying for aid must submit the Free Application for Federal Student Aid. A financial aid transcript from each school previously attended is required of all transfer applicants. Aid is awarded on the basis of financial eligibility or outstanding academic achievement.

APPLICATION AND INFORMATION

Anderson University requires each student to submit an application form and a $20 nonrefundable fee, an official high school transcript, SAT I or ACT scores, two references, and a medical form. Transcripts of all college work and a Transfer Student Information form, completed by an official from each college previously attended, are required of all transfer students. The University also requires a personal essay. Applications are accepted throughout the year. New students, including transfers, may enter in either the fall or spring semester. The University follows a rolling admission format, notifying students of the admission decision as soon as their application file is complete.

AQUINAS COLLEGE

■ GRAND RAPIDS, MICHIGAN

THE COLLEGE

Located on the eastern edge of the city of Grand Rapids, Aquinas enjoys all of the advantages of Michigan's second-largest city and is just a 3-hour drive from Detroit or Chicago. Founded by the Dominican Sisters of Grand Rapids in 1886, Aquinas has a Catholic heritage and a Christian tradition. The Dominican tradition of working and serving remains alive at Aquinas. An ability to see the world from different perspectives is the hallmark of an Aquinas-educated student. Aquinas, a coeducational liberal arts college, offers an approach to learning and living that teaches students unlimited ways of seeing the world. That is why every Aquinas student enrolls in the humanities program, a two-semester exploration of the best that has been thought, written, composed, and painted. And as students find their way in the world of thought, the core curriculum in natural science ensures that they discover the workings of the physical world as well. Aquinas sees a liberal arts education as career preparation. The Aquinas general education plan exposes students to the necessary skills that enable them to become critical thinkers, articulate speakers, strong writers, and effective problem solvers. The College's curriculum, with its more than forty majors and cognates, is designed to provide students with both breadth and depth and to foster a thirst for knowledge and truth and a spirit of intellectual dialogue and inquiry. Coupled with nationally recognized co-op and internship programs, it prepares students to both live and work in the rapidly changing world of today and tomorrow.

For further information, interested students should contact:

Paula Meehan
Dean of Admissions
Aquinas College
1607 Robinson Road, SE
Grand Rapids, Michigan 49506
Telephone: 616-732-4460
800-678-9593 (toll-free)
E-mail: admissions@aquinas.edu
Web site: http://www.aquinas.edu

ACADEMIC PROGRAM

In addition to their major and minor fields of study, students take an integrated skills course called Inquiry and Expression. This course spans the entire freshman year and has an emphasis on writing integrated with reading critically, oral communication skills, critical thinking, library/electronic research methods, computer utilization, and basic quantitative reasoning. The thematic content is American Pluralism: The Individual in a Diverse America. Sophomores take a yearlong course in the humanities. As juniors they are required to take 3 hours in Religious Dimensions of Human Existence, with a choice among three categories: Scripture, Catholic/Christian Thought, or Contemporary Religious Experience. The senior year includes a capstone course called Global Perspective. Students are also required to be proficient in a second language through the 201 level. There also is a distribution plan in the general education plan covering The Individual in a Global Community; Myth, Mind, Body, and Spirit; Natural World; Artistic and Creative Studies; and Quantitative Reasoning and Technology.

FINANCIAL AID

Aquinas College awards both merit-based financial assistance and traditional need-based assistance to qualified students. The Spectrum Scholarship Program was developed to recognize students' achievements in academics, leadership, and service. More than 50 percent of entering freshmen receive some form of financial assistance. The College administers the traditional grant and loan programs, including Federal Stafford Student Loans and Federal PLUS loans. Athletic grants are also available. The College participates in the Academic Management Services Plan and provides the Aquinas College Multiple Payment Plan. These plans assist students in paying costs over a period of time. To apply for financial assistance, students must complete the Free Application for Federal Student Aid (FAFSA).

AUDREY COHEN COLLEGE

■ **New York, New York**

THE COLLEGE

Founded in 1964, Audrey Cohen College offers the student a unique Purpose-Centered System of Education, a design developed by the College. (The curriculum and its components are registered with the U.S. Patent Office.) This system examines the global, information- and service-centered economy, which employs more than 80 percent of the American work force. Audrey Cohen College alone has reinvented higher education to reflect the needs of this economy. Its graduates pursue careers in such diverse areas as banking, child welfare, community affairs, corrections, counseling, early childhood education, finance, gerontology, government, health administration, human resources, law, management, marketing, personnel administration, psychology, public administration, public health, social work, and student services. The College has adapted its Purpose-Centered System of Education to the elementary/secondary experience, and this system is being used by schools around the country.

For additional information, students should contact:

Admissions Office
Audrey Cohen College
75 Varick Street
New York, New York 10013
Telephone: 212-343-1234 Ext. 5001
Fax: 212-343-8470
Web site: http://www.audrey-cohen.edu

ACADEMIC PROGRAM

In both the School for Business and the School for Human Services, each semester of study is organized around a major Purpose, which research has shown to be critical for professionals in a global, information- and service-centered economy. There are eight Purposes in each of the programs. One is "Developing Professional Relationships," another is "Effective Supervision," a third is "Managing Human Resources," and so on. Five courses (whose names remain constant) called Dimensions of Learning, Action and Assessment define how each Purpose is viewed holistically. These courses are Values and Ethics, Self and Others, Systems, Skills, and Purpose. Theory presented in each of these classes is specific to the Purpose of the semester and has incorporated the social and behavioral sciences, the humanities, and professional studies. At the College, knowledge becomes the basis for taking action to improve the world. Thus, simultaneous to attending classes, students must show each semester, at their work site or at an internship, how they have taken theory from all five courses and used it to address an organizational need related to their Purpose. The College terms this taking Constructive Action and awards credit upon its successful completion.

FINANCIAL AID

Audrey Cohen College participates in the federally administered Federal Pell Grant, Federal Stafford Student Loan, and Federal PLUS loan programs and in the Tuition Assistance Program (TAP) sponsored and administered by New York State for its state residents. The College also has limited resources under two other federal financial aid programs: the Federal Supplemental Educational Opportunity Grant Program and the Federal Work-Study Program. In addition, the College has its own scholarship program. Applicants may file through the College Scholarship Service or apply for federal funds directly at the College following their admission. State TAP applications are sent directly to the student once the federal applications have been processed.

APPLICATION AND INFORMATION

All applicants must complete and return the application with a $20 application fee, take the Test of Adult Basic Education (TABE) at the College, have a personal interview with an admission counselor, submit two letters of reference, provide official transcripts from each educational institution previously attended, and submit proof of immunization against measles, mumps, and rubella. Each applicant is also required to write an essay during the admission testing process. Applicants are informed of decisions as soon as all application materials have been received and evaluated.

BAY PATH COLLEGE

■ LONGMEADOW, MASSACHUSETTS

THE COLLEGE

Founded in 1897, Bay Path College today offers baccalaureate and associate degrees. As a pioneer in innovative programs for women, the College educates women to become confident and resourceful contributors to an increasingly interdependent world through its focus on leadership, communication, and technology. Students are challenged to accept the responsibilities and to experience the rewards of leadership throughout their college career. The College thoroughly integrates opportunities to build and strengthen technological, analytical, and oral and written communication skills into the curriculum so that students may interact successfully with others, both professionally and personally. Through the College's comprehensive extracurricular program, students have a choice of a wide variety of on-campus clubs, organizations, and athletic activities. Social events and other joint activities are scheduled with neighboring colleges and with such institutions as West Point and the Coast Guard Academy. Although 50 percent of the 621 women enrolled reside on campus, commuting students are fully involved in College life.

For application forms and additional information, students should contact:

Dean of Enrollment Services
Bay Path College
588 Longmeadow Street
Longmeadow, Massachusetts 01106
Telephone: 413-567-0621
800-782-7284 (toll-free outside 413 area code)
Fax: 413-567-0501
E-mail: admiss@baypath.edu

ACADEMIC PROGRAM

Bay Path's programs prepare women either for entry into careers or for continued studies. A minimum of 60 credits must be completed successfully to earn an associate degree, and a minimum of 120 credits are required for a baccalaureate. The general education requirements are intended to provide students with a foundation for learning in the humanities and fine arts, mathematics, and the natural and social sciences, regardless of their choice of major. All of the course offerings incorporate one or more of the three themes of the College's vision statement, Bay Path 2001: leadership, communication, and technology. Internships are an integral part of many programs, and students are placed with professionals in local businesses for on-the-job experience. Bay Path interns work in law firms, hotels, retail stores, travel agencies, decorating firms, insurance companies, airline offices, cruise lines, social service agencies, correctional facilities, schools, and hospitals.

FINANCIAL AID

Bay Path is keenly interested in admitting talented women who are serious about their education, and it encourages such students to apply regardless of their financial means. Scholarships, grants, loans, and employment opportunities are available. The Bay Path Scholar's Program for high-ability students provides almost full tuition assistance that is renewable for four years, based on meeting established criteria. Bay Path has a commitment to continue to aid qualified students who receive aid in their freshman year; every effort is made to maintain or increase the funding level to enable these students to graduate. Approximately 85 percent of current Bay Path students receive some form of financial aid. Financial aid applicants are reviewed beginning on December 15.

APPLICATION AND INFORMATION

The College follows a rolling admissions policy and encourages students to apply early. Notification of decision is generally within two weeks of receiving the completed application and accompanying materials. The candidate reply is due by May 1. For September enrollment, December 1 is the application deadline recommended for early decision consideration, with notification by December 15. The candidate reply is due by May 1. The application, application fee, and all credentials must be received before the admission process can begin. The completed application should be sent to the Office of Admissions, together with a $25 nonrefundable application fee or fee-waiver request.

BELMONT UNIVERSITY

■ Nashville, Tennessee

THE UNIVERSITY

Located in the heart of metropolitan Nashville, Belmont University offers the best of two worlds in many ways. Nationally recognized programs thrive on a historic campus nestled in the midst of the state's capital city, Music City, U.S.A. Belmont's vision is to be a premier teaching university bringing together the best of liberal arts and professional education in a consistently caring Christian environment. Fundamental to the fulfillment of that vision are faculty members who have a passion for teaching and bring immeasurable life experience and knowledge to Belmont. With an enrollment of 3,000 students, Belmont University is the second-largest private college or university in Tennessee. Affiliated with the Tennessee Baptist Convention, it is the largest private college or university with a religious affiliation in the state. In addition to baccalaureate degrees, graduate degrees offered are the Master of Business Administration, the Master of Accountancy, the Master of English, the Master of Music, the Master of Music Education, the Master of Education, the Master of Science in Nursing, the Master of Science in Occupational Therapy, and the Master of Science in Physical Therapy.

Further information and application materials may be obtained by contacting:

Office of Admissions
Belmont University
1900 Belmont Boulevard
Nashville, Tennessee 37212
Telephone: 615-460-6785
800-56ENROLL (toll-free)

ACADEMIC PROGRAM

Uniquely positioned to provide the best of liberal arts and professional education, Belmont University offers celebrated professional programs structured to provide an academically well-rounded education. Belmont University operates on a two-semester schedule with classes beginning in late August and ending in early May. Two summer sessions are also offered. The academic program is arranged by school: the School of Sciences, the School of Humanities/Education, the School of Music, the School of Religion, the School of Nursing, the School of Business, and the Jack C. Massey Graduate School of Business. In addition to the degrees offered through the schools, Belmont University offers an honors program, which was created to provide an enrichment opportunity for students who have potential for superior academic performance and who seek added challenge and breadth to their studies. Students enrolled in the honors program are led by a private tutor, who is an honors faculty member, in designing and working through a flexible, individual curriculum. The University's advancements in undergraduate research are credited to a faculty committed to helping students practice their disciplines. The annual Belmont Undergraduate Research Symposium puts Belmont at the forefront of this national movement by providing a public forum for in-depth research at the undergraduate level.

FINANCIAL AID

The financial aid program at Belmont combines merit-based assistance with need-based assistance to make the University program affordable. Institutional merit awards range from full tuition Presidential Scholarships to performance scholarships. Also included are many levels of academic merit awards. The University also administers traditional state and federal programs, including the Federal Pell Grant, Federal Stafford Student Loan, Federal Perkins Loan, Federal PLUS loan, and Tennessee Student Assistance Grants and Scholarships. Campus employment is available. Parents may arrange monthly tuition payments through an outside vendor. To apply for assistance, the student must complete the Free Application for Federal Student Aid (FAFSA).

BENEDICTINE UNIVERSITY

■ LISLE, ILLINOIS

For further information, students should contact:

Office of Admissions
Benedictine University
5700 College Road
Lisle, Illinois 60532-0900
Telephone: 630-829-6300
E-mail: admissions@ben.edu
Web site: http://www.ben.edu

THE UNIVERSITY

Benedictine University was founded in 1887 as St. Procopius College. One hundred eleven years later, the University remains committed to providing a high-quality, Catholic, liberal education for men and women. The undergraduate enrollment is 1,750 students. The student body comprises students of diverse ages, religions, races, and national origins. Forty-seven percent of the full-time students reside on campus. Benedictine University is situated on a rolling, tree-covered 108-acre campus of ten major buildings with air-conditioned classrooms and modern, well-equipped laboratories. A student athletic center features three full-size basketball courts, a competition-size swimming pool, three tennis courts, and training facilities. All of the residence halls are comfortable and spacious, and have access to the Internet. Renowned faculty members know students by name and care as much about each student's progress as they do about their own research. Acceptance of Benedictine University graduates to medical, dental, and professional schools is significantly above regional and national averages, and the liberal arts curriculum has helped place the University among some of the finest small private schools in the nation. Benedictine University is highly competitive in varsity sports. Men's varsity sports are baseball, basketball, cross-country, football, golf, hockey, soccer, swimming, tennis, and track. Women's varsity sports are basketball, cross-country, golf, soccer, softball, swimming, tennis, track, and volleyball. Student athletes have been selected as all-Americans in baseball, basketball, football, soccer, softball, swimming, track, and volleyball in recent years. Aside from varsity and intramural athletic programs, a variety of organizations exist, including a newspaper, an orchestra, jazz groups, an African-American Student Union, an Indian Student Union, the Coalition of Latin American Students, campus ministry, a drama club, and various other extracurricular and academic organizations.

ACADEMIC PROGRAM

For graduation, a student must earn at least 120 semester hours, at least half of which must be completed at a four-year regionally accredited college and at least the final 45 semester hours must be completed at Benedictine University. The University makes selective exceptions to the normal academic residency requirement of 45 semester hours for adults who are eligible for the Degree Completion Program. The Second Major Program is designed for people who already have a degree in one area and would like to gain expertise in another. This program allows the student to concentrate on courses that will fulfill the requirements of a second major.

FINANCIAL AID

In 1997–98, Benedictine University freshmen received assistance totaling $2.2 million from sources that included loans, scholarships/grants, tuition remission, and employment opportunities. Almost 89 percent of the freshman class participated, receiving an average package of $9338. Benedictine University has dedicated more than $4 million of the annual budget to providing grants and scholarships to students, including scholarships for study in the humanities and a separate scholarship program designed to attract and serve minority students. Students who wish to apply for aid must complete the Free Application for Federal Student Aid (FAFSA), the Benedictine University application for financial aid, and the Benedictine University application for admission.

APPLICATION AND INFORMATION

Applications are reviewed on a rolling basis. Students are encouraged to apply for admission at any time after completing their junior year of high school. Transfer students may apply for admission during their last semester or quarter before anticipated transfer to Benedictine University. Earlier applications are encouraged.

BETHEL COLLEGE

■ ST. PAUL, MINNESOTA

THE COLLEGE

Bethel College began its four-year Christian liberal arts program in 1945 but traces its roots to Bethel Theological Seminary, founded in 1871. Bethel is a ministry of the churches of the Baptist General Conference. The College encourages growth and learning in a distinctly Christian environment, continually striving to help students discover and develop the skills God has given them. Campus lifestyle expectations have been designed to build unity within diversity. All Bethel students, faculty, and staff members are expected to follow those expectations during their time as members of the Bethel community. Bethel's 2,500 students represent a wide range of national and international cultures and more than thirty denominations. Most of Bethel's students are between 18 and 22 years of age, but older and younger students bring a welcome diversity to campus life. Bethel students are involved in a wealth of cocurricular activities, from music to ministry, Bible study to broadcasting, theater to tennis, and art to athletics. Bethel sports teams compete in NCAA Division III and the Minnesota Intercollegiate Athletic Conference. The Sports and Recreation Center is used almost continuously for intercollegiate and intramural sports events and personal recreation, and a newly completed Community Life Center provides a 1700-seat performance hall and chapel.

For further information about specific Bethel programs and campus visit opportunities, students should contact:

Office of Admissions
Bethel College
3900 Bethel Drive
St. Paul, Minnesota 55112
Telephone: 612-638-6242
800-255-8706 Ext. 6242 (toll-free)
Fax: 612-635-1490
E-mail: bcoll-admit@bethel.edu
World Wide Web: http://www.bethel.edu
AOL Keyword: Bethel

ACADEMIC PROGRAM

Bethel was named among the top ten liberal arts colleges in the Midwest by *U.S. News & World Report* in 1997. Bethel's general education curriculum has become a model for many other liberal arts colleges nationwide. Students are required to take classes that will give them a broad view of the world and their role as Christians. General education classes are grouped around the following themes: Bible and theology, Western heritage, world citizenship, self-understanding, science and technology, and health and wholeness. In addition, in order to graduate, all Bethel students must demonstrate competence in mathematics, writing, speaking, and computing.

FINANCIAL AID

Bethel College strives to make it financially possible for every qualified student to attend. Each year, nearly 90 percent of the students receive some kind of financial aid, including scholarships, grants, loans, and assistance in the form of on-campus employment. Students who wish to be considered for financial aid must first be admitted to the College and then submit a Family Financial Statement (FFS). Bethel's priority deadline is April 15 of each year. Students who have completed and mailed all necessary forms by this date receive first consideration.

APPLICATION AND INFORMATION

Students wishing to apply for admission to Bethel must send the following: a completed Bethel application form with a $20 nonrefundable application fee; test scores from the PSAT, SAT I, or ACT; transcripts of all course work completed at the high school and college levels; and references from a pastor and an adult friend or employer. Admission decisions are made on a rolling basis. Although there is no deadline, applicants for fall admission are encouraged to complete their files before May 1.

BOWIE STATE UNIVERSITY

■ BOWIE, MARYLAND

THE UNIVERSITY

For an application form, students should contact:

Office of Enrollment, Recruitment and Registration
Bowie State University
Bowie, Maryland 20715-9465

Telephone: 301-464-6570
410-880-4100 Ext. 6570
(from the Baltimore-Columbia area)

Bowie State University began as a normal school in the city of Baltimore in 1865, and it has evolved over the years into a four-year, coeducational, liberal arts institution. It is currently situated on a beautiful 312-acre campus in Prince George's County, Maryland, and offers both graduate and undergraduate programs of study. Teacher education programs were established in 1925; in 1935, with state authorization, a four-year program for the training of elementary school teachers was begun and the school became the Maryland State Teachers College at Bowie. In 1951, with the approval of the State Board of Education, its governing body at the time, the college established a teacher-preparation curriculum for the training of teachers for the core program in the junior high schools. Ten years later, permission was granted to institute a teacher-training program for secondary education. A liberal arts program was established in 1963, and the institution's name was changed to Bowie State College. In 1988, Bowie State achieved university status. Bowie State University admits students without regard to sex, religion, or nationality, and the University does not discriminate on the basis of race, creed, color, national or ethnic origin, age, sex, or handicap.

ACADEMIC PROGRAM

The University operates on a semester calendar. Academic offerings can be divided into four main areas: humanities, science and mathematics, social sciences, and education. To receive a bachelor's degree, a student must earn a minimum of 120 semester hours with a cumulative grade point average of 2.0 or better. Students who enter through the University College of Excellence (UCE) are provided the opportunity to complete the General Studies Program, acquire lifelong learning skills for a competitive world, and make a successful transition into their junior year. General studies requirements include communication skills, 9 hours; humanities, 9 hours; social sciences, 18 hours; science and mathematics, 9 hours; and physical education, 2 hours. The remaining credit hours can be electives or from major and minor areas of interest. Students must also pass the test of Proficiency in the English Language and must take the national standardized test in their major area.

FINANCIAL AID

Federal Pell Grants, Supplemental Grants, Work-Study, Perkins Loans, and Direct Loans are available. University scholarships, tuition waivers, and diversity grants are awarded. Most awards are based on need. Merit scholarships could be offered to students with cumulative grade point averages of at least 3.0 and minimum recentered SAT I scores of 1100. Full-tuition awards are possible for out-of-state students who have a minimum cumulative grade point average of 3.3 and a minimum recentered SAT I score of 1130. More than 65 percent of all undergraduate students receive some form of financial aid. Scholarships and assistantships are offered through the Model Institutions for Excellence Program for Science, Engineering, and Mathematics. Deadlines are May 1 for the fall semester and November 15 for the spring semester.

APPLICATION AND INFORMATION

The application deadline is April 1 for the fall semester and November 1 for spring.

BREVARD COLLEGE

■ BREVARD, NORTH CAROLINA

THE COLLEGE

Founded in 1853, Brevard is a church-related, coeducational liberal arts college that offers innovative four-year and two-year curriculums, with specialties in music, art, environmental studies, wilderness leadership, and other interdisciplinary majors, on a beautiful mountain campus near Asheville, North Carolina. The College's low student-faculty ratio of 9:1, a covenant that binds faculty and students in a nurturing community of learning, rich cultural offerings, numerous opportunities for student leadership, nationally competitive athletic programs, and incomparable access to national parks, forest, wilderness areas, and white-water recreational rivers make Brevard distinctive.

For more information, students should contact:

Vice President and Dean for Admissions and Financial Aid
Brevard College
400 North Broad Street
Brevard, North Carolina 28712
Telephone: 828-884-8300
800-527-9090 (toll-free)
Fax: 828-884-3790
E-mail: admissions@brevard.edu

ACADEMIC PROGRAM

The core liberal arts curriculum of the College requires each student to build a strong base in languages and literature, religion, humanities, mathematics and analytical reasoning, history, natural and social sciences, fine arts, and environmental studies. Students are exposed to several other cultures and make a significant investment in volunteer work in the community. The curriculum utilizes classroom studies in the Pisgah National Forest, Davidson and French Broad River ecosystems, Great Smoky Mountain National Park, and the Cradle of Forestry in America, which is designated as a National Historic Site. Through the "Voice of the Rivers," Brevard College offers select students the opportunity to make the world their classroom in an experiential program that combines wilderness leadership and environmental studies. Programs in music and art afford talented students excellent educational and performance opportunities at the College as well as in such off-campus settings as the famed Brevard Music Center, the Brevard Chamber Orchestra, and the Asheville Art Museum. Consistent with the philosophy of the College, various courses at Brevard College use service as a learning component to enhance the classroom environment. Coordination of the student's service experience is performed by the Center for Service Learning, which works with students to prepare transcripts detailing their cocurricular accomplishments.

FINANCIAL AID

Opportunities for student financial aid are available to every student who can show financial need, superior academic achievement, or talent in athletics, art, drama, or music. All students desiring financial aid must submit the Free Application for Federal Student Aid (FAFSA). The College annually awards more than $200,000 in merit scholarships to select students who display academic excellence, unselfish character, and leadership potential as Brevard Scholars. These students participate in a variety of enriched intellectual, cultural, and leadership programs and work closely with distinguished professors who serve both as advisers and program directors. The Angier B. Duke Scholarships, awarded only by Brevard College and Duke University, are the premier scholarships among more than eighty Brevard Scholars Awards made each year.

APPLICATION AND INFORMATION

Students must submit an application for admission, a recommendation from the guidance counselor on the form provided by the Office of Admissions, official SAT I or ACT scores, and an official high school transcript. Students are advised of the admission decision as soon as all required application materials are received. In addition, Brevard College requires a medical history and a physical examination of each applicant prior to enrollment to the College.

CALIFORNIA COLLEGE OF ARTS AND CRAFTS

■ OAKLAND AND SAN FRANCISCO, CALIFORNIA

THE COLLEGE

For undergraduate application forms, current College bulletins, or any additional information, students should contact:

Director of Enrollment Services
California College of Arts and Crafts
450 Irwin Street
San Francisco, California 94107
Telephone: 800-447-1ART (toll-free)

The California College of Arts and Crafts (CCAC) was founded in 1907 with a new approach to art education—to offer training in a wide range of disciplines, creating a spirit of collaboration between artists, craftspeople, and designers. In the ensuing years, the College has expanded its commitment by offering an interdisciplinary curriculum that educates students in the full range of fine arts, architecture, and design studies in the context of a small, private four-year college. Today, CCAC's undergraduate enrollment is about 1,100 men and women. The College comprises two campuses, in San Francisco and Oakland. The San Francisco campus houses the architecture and design programs in a spectacular light-filled building located in the heart of the city's design district. The Oakland campus features a blend of Victorian and modern structures in a four-acre garden setting. The Oakland residence hall serves mainly freshmen; off-campus apartments are also available.

ACADEMIC PROGRAM

The Bachelor of Fine Arts degree requires the completion of a minimum of 126 semester units, of which 75 must be in studio work and 51 must be in humanities and sciences. Most undergraduates at CCAC begin in a foundation—or core—program designed to orient them to a variety of two- and three-dimensional art and design media as well as to strengthen their communication skills and refine and develop their knowledge of history. Students select a major after completing this program. The Bachelor of Architecture, a five-year degree program, requires the completion of a minimum of 162 units, including the one-semester core program with an orientation to two-dimensional and three-dimensional media and a nine-semester major program. Upon completion of the core program, a student's portfolio is developed and reviewed for approval for further study in the program.

FINANCIAL AID

Scholarships, grants, loans, and work-study awards are available for students on the basis of merit and financial need. Students applying for aid in 1998–99 should submit the Free Application for Federal Student Aid (FAFSA) to the Federal Student Aid Processing Agency by March 2. Students should also submit all additional documents required by CCAC by March 2 for priority consideration. CCAC continues to fund students after the priority deadline as long as funds remain available. Applications for Federal Pell Grants and Federal Direct Student Loans may be submitted throughout the school year. CCAC is approved for veterans attending under the Veterans Administration Educational Benefits Program. Approximately 60 percent of students attending CCAC during the 1997–98 year received some type of financial aid. CCAC also offers an extended interest-free payment plan.

APPLICATION AND INFORMATION

CCAC has a rolling admissions deadline. Applications received by the priority filing dates of March 2 for fall admission and October 1 for spring will be given first consideration for registration, housing, and financial aid opportunities. The application fee is $30. Persons who wish to take one or more individual classes may register as nondegree students on a space-available basis and receive College credit for courses completed.

CALIFORNIA STATE POLYTECHNIC UNIVERSITY, POMONA

■ POMONA, CALIFORNIA

For further information, students should contact:

Recruitment Services
California State Polytechnic University, Pomona
3801 West Temple Avenue
Pomona, California 91768
Telephone: 909-869-3210

THE UNIVERSITY

California State Polytechnic University, Pomona (Cal Poly Pomona) is nestled among 1,400 acres of rolling hills and is located 35 miles from downtown Los Angeles. Originally, the University's land was the site for the Arabian horse ranch of cereal magnate W. K. Kellogg. Thousands of people from around the world traveled to the ranch for the Sunday horse shows, which began in 1927 and continue today. Now, thousands of students from throughout California, the United States, and the world come to Cal Poly Pomona for its practical education, which places an emphasis on students. Proud of its heritage but keeping a sharp eye on the future, Cal Poly Pomona is uniquely poised to lead the next millennium. Although Cal Poly Pomona's campus is large, it has the feel of a small, private college. Most buildings are situated within easy walking distance of each other. Most classrooms seat fewer than 50 students, and the student-faculty ratio is 18:1. "Learn by doing" is the University's motto, and the curriculum features hands-on education in sixty undergraduate majors in eight schools and colleges. The largest are the Colleges of Business Administration and Engineering; others are the Colleges of Agriculture; Environmental Design; Letters, Arts, and Social Sciences; and Science. The two schools are the School of Hotel and Restaurant Management and the School of Education and Integrative Studies. Cal Poly Pomona is accredited by the Western Association of Schools and Colleges. Several colleges, schools, and programs have also been accredited.

ACADEMIC PROGRAM

Classes are offered in four 11-week quarters. Candidates for Bachelor of Arts degrees must earn at least 186 quarter units. The Bachelor of Science degree requires at least 198 quarter units. A graduation writing requirement exists for all baccalaureate degrees. Currently, the Bachelor of Architecture degree is impacted and open only to California residents. Cal Poly Pomona offers Air Force and Army Reserve Officers Training Corps, a California Pre-Doctoral Program, CSU International Programs and Cal Poly Pomona Study Abroad, an Educational Opportunity Program, the Faculty Student Mentoring Program, a National Student Exchange, a Teacher Aide Path to Teaching, University Equity Programs, and other special programs.

FINANCIAL AID

Though the cost of attending Cal Poly Pomona is less than many of the CSU campuses, the University administers extensive financial aid programs to approximately half of the student body, totaling more than $43 million annually. The priority application period is January 1 through March 2 for the following fall, and students must submit a Free Application for Federal Student Aid (FAFSA). Aid comes through grants, loans, scholarships, and work-study. Merit-based scholarships, which require individual application, are available. Interested students should call 909-869-3700 or e-mail (finaid@csupomona.edu).

APPLICATION AND INFORMATION

Cal Poly Pomona begins accepting applications for the following fall on November 1 of the preceding year. The application fee is $55, but waivers may be granted. The University encourages students to apply on line over the Internet, with no downloading required. Students can visit Cal Poly Pomona's home page (http://www.csupomona.edu).

CALVIN COLLEGE

■ Grand Rapids, Michigan

THE COLLEGE

Calvin College is dedicated to relating the Christian faith to the whole learning process; this view affects every area of campus life from the content of each course to volunteer service and life in the residence halls. Calvin is one of the nation's largest and most respected evangelical Christian colleges. The 1997 fall enrollment was 4,085. Calvin maintains a strong affiliation with the Christian Reformed Church, and students from more than sixty other church denominations across North America and the world also choose Calvin for its extensive curriculum and Christ-centered mission. Calvin is deeply committed to being a genuinely diverse community and is taking deliberate steps to increase opportunities for women, members of minority groups, and the disabled. Students are challenged not only to obtain a fine education and career preparation but also to live examined lives of commitment and service.

For more information about Calvin or about visiting the campus, students should contact:

Admissions Office
Calvin College
3201 Burton Street, SE
Grand Rapids, Michigan 49546
Telephone: 800-688-0122 (toll-free in North America)
Fax: 616-957-8551
E-mail: admissions@calvin.edu
World Wide Web:
http://www.calvin.edu

ACADEMIC PROGRAM

Graduation requires the successful completion of 124 semester hours, including courses taken in three Interims; the designated liberal arts core; at least two writing enriched courses (part of Calvin's Writing Across the Curriculum Program); and an approved program of concentration. Core curriculum requirements include foreign language, history, literature and arts, mathematics, natural sciences, philosophy, physical education, religion, social sciences, and written and spoken rhetoric. Some requirements can be satisfied by advanced high school work in foreign language, literature, mathematics, and natural sciences. Qualified students can earn course exemption and/or credit by completing college-level work in high school or by examination. Satisfactory scores on Advanced Placement (AP), International Baccalaureate (I.B.), and/or CLEP exams are also accepted.

FINANCIAL AID

Sixty percent of the students receive need-based financial aid; demonstrated need is the most important criterion in determining eligibility. Students wishing to be considered for financial aid must be admitted to the College and must submit the Free Application for Federal Student Aid (FAFSA) and Calvin's Supplemental Application for Financial Aid. February 15 is the suggested filing deadline for maximum consideration. Financial awards to eligible applicants consist of state and federal grants, loans, Federal Work-Study funds, and institutional grants and scholarships. Part-time employment is available on campus, and placement preference is given to needy students. The College also helps students to find and maintain off-campus employment and runs a job transportation service that gets them safely to and from their jobs for a minimal fee.

APPLICATION AND INFORMATION

Applicants must submit a completed application form, a high school or college transcript, results of either the ACT or SAT I, and an educational recommendation completed by a teacher or counselor. Admission decisions are made on a rolling basis beginning in mid-October. Applicants for fall admission are urged to complete their file before February 1, although there is no deadline as long as space remains in the entering class. Campus visits are strongly recommended, although not required. Students and parents are welcome to visit at any time that is convenient for them. The "Fridays at Calvin" campus visit program also provides an excellent opportunity to experience life at Calvin firsthand.

CAMPBELL UNIVERSITY

■ Buies Creek, North Carolina

THE UNIVERSITY

Founded in 1887, Campbell University has had the distinction of being North Carolina's second-largest private undergraduate institution. Graduate programs were established, and in 1979 the name of the institution was changed from Campbell College to Campbell University. Its current enrollment is more than 7,800 students. In an average year, the student body comes from about ninety North Carolina counties, fifty states, and forty-six countries. Sixty-six percent of the students come from North Carolina. Although it is owned by the Baptist State Convention of North Carolina, the University is nonsectarian. Approximately 60 percent of its students are Baptist, but young people of twenty-two other faiths complete its student body. It is concerned with maintaining, for living and learning, an environment consistent with Christian ideals. Among the extracurricular activities available at Campbell are band, choir, and drama groups; religious, political, professional, social, and academic groups; and intercollegiate and intramural sports organizations.

Application forms and further information may be requested from:

Office of Admissions
Campbell University
P.O. Box 546
Buies Creek, North Carolina 27506
Telephone: 910-893-1320
910-893-1415 (international)
800-334-4111 (toll-free)
E-mail:
satterfiel@mailcenter.campbell.edu
adm@mailcenter.campbell.edu
World Wide Web:
http://www.campbell.edu/CUIndex.html

ACADEMIC PROGRAM

The curriculum of Campbell University is designed to meet individual needs and interests. During the first two years, students follow a general course of study, the General College Curriculum, to broaden their backgrounds in the basic fields of knowledge. By the end of the sophomore year, they should have selected a major subject for specialized study during the final two years. Campbell offers a complete curriculum of evening courses on its main campus and at its nearby Fort Bragg campus. The Fort Bragg campus is primarily a service for military personnel on active duty, but classes are open to civilian students. Campbell offers the nation's first undergraduate program in trust management and since 1968 has been training prospective trust officers for the banks and trust companies of the region. Campbell also sponsors the Southeastern Trust School, a summer institute for trust officers.

FINANCIAL AID

Campbell University has private and institutional scholarships, federal grants, loans, and Federal Work-Study Program awards. Loans are available through the Federal Stafford Student Loan Program and the Federal Perkins Loan Program. Needs analysis forms (Free Application for Federal Student Aid) are available January 1 and are due in the Financial Aid Office by March 15 if the applicant wishes to be considered for a maximum award. Ninety-one percent of the student body received financial assistance in 1997–98. All assistance is offered without regard to race, creed, or national origin.

APPLICATION AND INFORMATION

An application for admission, accompanied by a $15 nonrefundable application fee, must be filed. When all records are on file, the Admissions Committee notifies the student of its decision.

CAPITOL COLLEGE

■ LAUREL, MARYLAND

THE COLLEGE

Capitol College, a private coeducational college, provides practical educational experiences that enable graduates to advance, manage, and communicate changes in the information age. Chartered in 1964, Capitol College offers degree programs in engineering, engineering technology, communications, and management. Career development is an integral aspect of the College's mission, and graduates are in great demand by business and industry. The College is accredited by the Commission of Higher Education of the Middle States Association of Colleges and Schools. The Bachelor of Science and Associate in Applied Science degree programs in computer engineering technology and electronics engineering technology and the Bachelor of Science degree program in telecommunications engineering technology are accredited by the Technology Accreditation Commission of the Accreditation Board for Engineering and Technology (TAC/ABET). The Bachelor of Science in electrical engineering is accredited by the Engineering Accreditation Commission of the Accreditation Board of Engineering and Technology (EAC/ABET). Capitol College's apartment-style residence facilities for men and women provide individual and double room accommodations. The student body is composed of 519 men and 115 women who come from sixteen states and twenty-one countries. Basketball and soccer are offered on an intercollegiate level, and basketball, bowling, football, soccer, and softball are offered on an intramural level.

For more information, students should contact:

Anthony G. Miller
Director of Admissions
Capitol College
11301 Springfield Road
Laurel, Maryland 20708
Telephone: 301-953-3200 (from Washington, D.C.)
410-792-8800 (from Baltimore)
800-950-1992 (toll-free outside the Baltimore–Washington, D.C., area)
E-mail: admissions@capitol-college.edu
Web site: http://www.capitol-college.edu

ACADEMIC PROGRAM

At Capitol College, learning is centered both in and out of the classroom. Professors are available on a one-on-one basis outside of the classroom, and tutors and lab aides are available for additional assistance. The College's cooperative education program gives students the opportunity to obtain paid education work experience to supplement their academic program. Each department has its own sequence requirements for graduation. To earn a bachelor's degree, students must complete between 123 and 137 semester credit hours. To earn an associate degree, students must complete between 64 and 67 semester credit hours. In each degree program, students must complete a core of courses, including mathematics, sciences, humanities, and social sciences. The average course load is 15 credits per semester.

FINANCIAL AID

Capitol College maintains an extensive program of financial aid to assist students who need help in financing their education. Aid is available in the form of loans, grants, scholarships, and employment programs. Awards are based on financial need and/or academic ability. All students who wish to apply for aid must submit the Free Application for Federal Student Aid (FAFSA). Students are encouraged to contact the director of financial aid at the College for assistance and for information about institutional scholarships.

APPLICATION AND INFORMATION

An application is considered when the student's file is complete, including a $25 application fee, the required test scores, and transcripts from each school attended. Application forms are available from the Office of Admissions. Capitol College maintains a rolling admission policy, and applicants are notified of the admission decision within one month of the completion of their file. To receive full consideration for financial aid and housing, students are encouraged to apply by April 1.

CARROLL COLLEGE

■ HELENA, MONTANA

THE COLLEGE

For an application form or further information about Carroll College's people and programs, financial aid and scholarships, student activities, or residential life, students should contact:

Director of Admission
Carroll College
1601 North Benton Avenue
Helena, Montana 59625-0002
Telephone: 406-447-4384
800-99-ADMIT (toll-free)
E-mail: enroll@carroll.edu
Web site: http://www.carroll.edu

Carroll College was founded in 1909, when Bishop John Patrick Carroll and William Howard Taft, the twenty-seventh president of the United States, laid the cornerstone of St. Charles Hall. Bishop Carroll envisioned a college that would emphasize students' intellectual, spiritual, imaginative, moral, personal, and social development. In September 1910, Mount Saint Charles College opened its doors for classes, and the first college student graduated in 1916. In 1932, the school's name was changed to Carroll College in honor of its founder. Since then, Carroll has progressively expanded its programs, facilities, and reputation for academic excellence. Today, Carroll is known for its nationally recognized programs, an award-winning faculty, and its talented student body. As a Catholic college, Carroll is dedicated to the principles of Christianity and welcomes everyone. Carroll College is built around its people; the faculty, staff, and administration recognize the unique qualities of each person who comes to Carroll to live and learn. This commitment to the individual needs of each student shows in the accomplishments of Carroll's graduates, many of whom have become national leaders in their fields.

ACADEMIC PROGRAM

As a liberal arts college, Carroll emphasizes an education that prepares students for their chosen career and other areas of life. All students attend classes in the arts, sciences, humanities, and social sciences for at least four of their eight semesters at Carroll. This comprehensive learning curriculum gives students a broad educational background for the future in addition to the skills they need for a competitive edge in the job market.

FINANCIAL AID

Carroll's objective is to ensure that every student who is qualified to attend Carroll has access to financial aid resources. "The Carroll Advantage," which will take effect in the fall of 1998, is a new program designed to maintain the cost of education at the cost of living adjustment or below while providing significantly expanded grants. This commitment ensures that a Carroll education is affordable throughout a student's college career. Carroll is also committed to meeting a minimum of 70 percent of a student's demonstrated financial need and up to 100 percent of the cost of attendance with financial assistance. Carroll requires interested students to submit the Free Application for Federal Student Aid (FAFSA), available from a high school counselor, as early as possible. This ensures that students are awarded all of the aid for which they qualify.

APPLICATION AND INFORMATION

All materials must be received by the Office of Admission by March 1 to qualify for scholarships. Carroll College has a rolling admission policy, with a priority admission deadline of March 1. For general admission for the fall semester, students must ensure that all materials are received by the Office of Admission by July 1. Within three weeks of submission of all materials, candidates are notified of acceptance, conditional acceptance, or denial by Carroll's Office of Admission. Students should note that late submission of materials may jeopardize their financial aid awards.

CARSON-NEWMAN COLLEGE

■ Jefferson City, Tennessee

THE COLLEGE

For additional information, students should contact:

Office of Undergraduate Admissions
Carson-Newman College
Jefferson City, Tennessee 37760
Telephone: 423-471-3223
800-678-9061 (toll-free)
E-mail: sgray@cncadm.cn.edu

Founded in 1851, Carson-Newman is a private liberal arts college affiliated with the Tennessee Baptist Convention. The College has an enrollment of 2,050 undergraduate and 250 graduate students. The average class size is 16 students, and the male-female ratio is 1:1. Each fall Carson-Newman enrolls approximately 450 freshmen and 150 transfers. While Carson-Newman students come primarily from the Southeastern states, forty-one states are represented. In addition to its outstanding academics, C-N also provides many opportunities for student involvement in various clubs and organizations, nationally recognized varsity athletics, intramural athletics, music and drama groups, an award-winning forensics team, and many other extracurricular activities. The majority of C-N students live on campus in one of the two men's and three women's dormitories. Graduate programs in education are available leading to the Master of Arts in Teaching, the Master of Arts in Education, the Master of Education in school counseling, and the Master of Arts in Teaching English as a Second Language degrees. A Master of Science in Nursing program is also offered.

ACADEMIC PROGRAM

The College operates on a traditional semester system. Mayterm is a three-week intensive period of study giving students the opportunity to earn 3 credit hours. Summer term is offered as a six-week program of study. All baccalaureate degrees require completion of 128 semester hours. Students must complete 51 semester hours in general education requirements and a total of 36 semester hours at junior/senior level. Specific course requirements vary depending on major and degree program. Honors courses, independent study, and internships are available to students who qualify. Advanced credit is available for students who achieve required scores on AP exams, CLEP tests, and C-N departmental examinations. New students are assigned a faculty adviser who assists with course selection and student concerns. Career planning services are also available. The College's exceptionally high placement rate in professional programs in medicine, law, business, and theological study is testimony to the excellence of its rigorous academic program.

FINANCIAL AID

Carson-Newman allocates thousands of dollars each year to help supplement the resources of families. Financial aid awards are tailored to meet students' economic needs. Carson-Newman participates in all state and federal aid programs and awards aid based on demonstrated need as documented by a need analysis form, such as the Free Application for Federal Student Aid (FAFSA). Carson-Newman also awards academic scholarships based on achievement. Deadline for filing financial aid forms is April 1.

APPLICATION AND INFORMATION

Applicants must submit an application for admission, official transcripts, and a nonrefundable $25 application fee. Admission decisions are made on a rolling basis, and students are notified within two weeks of receipt of all required documents. Application deadline is May 1 for fall semester, December 1 for spring semester. Applicants who wish to be considered for full-tuition scholarships must apply by December 31.

CATHOLIC UNIVERSITY OF AMERICA

■ **Washington, D.C.**

Dean of Admissions and Financial Aid
The Catholic University of America
Washington, D.C. 20064
Telephone: 202-319-5305
800-673-2772 (toll-free)
Fax: 202-319-6533
E-mail: cua-admissions@cua.edu
World Wide Web:
http://www.cua.edu

THE UNIVERSITY

The Catholic University of America offers an outstanding collegiate experience, with challenging undergraduate programs based in the liberal arts. CUA is the national university of the Catholic Church and the only higher education institution established by the U.S. Catholic bishops. Founded as a graduate institution more than a century ago, CUA introduced undergraduate education in 1904. The University today serves 6,000 students, including 2,400 undergraduates, from all 50 states and more than 100 other countries. Students from all religious traditions are welcome. The University's Washington, D.C., location enriches student life. Cultural, scientific, and political resources are minutes away by Metrorail, a modern mass transit system that stops next to campus.

ACADEMIC PROGRAM

Engineering, nursing, music, and architecture students follow study courses that provide professional training integrated with a broad range of academic disciplines. Students in the School of Arts and Sciences undertake a major course of study within a liberal arts curriculum that encompasses the humanities, languages and literature, philosophy, the social sciences, mathematics and natural sciences, and religion. Most majors require the satisfactory completion of forty courses that are 3 credits each for graduation. Certain majors under the Bachelor of Science degree may require additional credits. In addition to the major, students may complete a minor course sequence by utilizing the elective courses included in the undergraduate program.

FINANCIAL AID

CUA administers two separate and distinct financial assistance programs: merit scholarships and need-based financial aid. A number of scholarships, awarded on the basis of academic achievement in secondary school, are available. The University offers financial aid to students based on need as demonstrated by the Free Application for Federal Student Aid (FAFSA) and the Institutional Aid Form, which can be found in the CUA admissions application. The College Scholarship Service's Financial Aid PROFILE is required. Loans, work-study, and University grants are available. Candidates who complete the admission application process before February 15 of their senior year of secondary school are considered for academic scholarships and receive priority for financial aid.

APPLICATION AND INFORMATION

Admissions decisions are made on a rolling basis. Applicants for early action scholarship awards must apply by November 15 and will be notified by December 15. Regular action scholarship awards and financial aid decisions will be made shortly after the February 15 deadline. Candidates for freshman admission must submit CUA's secondary school report, high school transcripts, scores on the SAT I or ACT, and a $50 application fee. CUA accepts transfer applicants each semester. Transfer candidates should request applications for transfer admission from the Office of Admissions and Financial Aid. In addition to the high school records and SAT I or ACT scores, transfer students must furnish transcripts from the school the students are attending (a minimum 2.8 GPA is recommended). Transfer applicants are notified of their status on a rolling basis and at least one month prior to the opening of the semester for which they are applying for admission. Transfer students are guaranteed on-campus housing. Financial aid is awarded on the same basis as for freshman students.

CEDAR CREST COLLEGE

■ Allentown, Pennsylvania

An application form, the College catalog, financial aid forms, and additional information may be obtained by contacting:

Vice President for Enrollment Management
Cedar Crest College
100 College Drive
Allentown, Pennsylvania 18104-6196
Telephone: 800-360-1222 (toll-free)
Fax: 610-606-4647
E-mail: cccadmis@cedarcrest.edu
Web site: http://www.cedarcrest.edu

THE COLLEGE

Since its founding in 1867 as an independent liberal arts college for women, Cedar Crest has educated women for leadership in a changing world. Of the approximately 1,700 students who come to the College annually from twenty-six states and fourteen other countries, 892 are full-time undergraduates. The 13:1 student-faculty ratio provides for small classes, individual advising, and independent work in an environment that emphasizes interdisciplinary, values-oriented education. The Honor Philosophy is the most compelling statement of each student's rights and responsibilities for her own academic and cocurricular performance.

ACADEMIC PROGRAM

Self-designed majors, double majors, minors, independent study programs, and individual and group research projects support serious concentration at the undergraduate level. Working with her adviser, each student designs a program of study that meets the 120-credit College (nursing: 126 credits) and major requirements as well as her personal interests and professional goals. The College's curriculum is structured to provide course work in the areas that define a liberal arts education: a knowledge-based curriculum with Basic Composition and Construction of Knowledge taught in a computer classroom environment, Scientific Knowledge (The Human Agenda, The Environment), a departmentally determined mathematics requirement, and electives constitute the freshman-year program. The Sophomore Seminar integrates applied ethics and service-learning opportunities. Acquisition of Knowledge courses are selected in four categories: The Study of Humankind, The Study of Written Texts, The Study of Creativity and Creativity in Practice, and Global Issues and Distinct Cultures. Many of these courses also meet the requirements of majors and minors. Science majors begin conducting advanced research at the freshman level, opening opportunities that often lead to internships at major research institutions.

FINANCIAL AID

Cedar Crest offers a generous program of financial aid based on academic achievement and financial need, including scholarships, grants, loans, and employment. Federal funds available are Federal Pell Grants, Federal Supplemental Educational Opportunity Grants, Federal Perkins Loans, Federal Work-Study Program awards, and Nursing Student Loans. The size of an award varies with need. More than 80 percent of the students at Cedar Crest receive aid. Students applying for financial aid should file the Free Application for Federal Student Aid (FAFSA). Outstanding international students may also qualify for financial aid. Students can receive an early estimate of aid eligibility by completing a Cedar Crest financial aid application/planner.

APPLICATION AND INFORMATION

Students need to submit the application form, an official transcript of the secondary school record, examination results from the SAT I or ACT, and a personal essay. Cedar Crest has a rolling admission policy; applications are reviewed on a continuing basis. Students are encouraged to apply early in their senior year of high school. Admission is awarded for the fall or spring semester. Transfer students applying to Cedar Crest must fulfill all of the requirements stated above. They must also submit official transcripts and a catalog from each college previously attended. International students must complete the international student application form; students educated in non-English-speaking countries must also submit TOEFL examination scores.

CHAMINADE UNIVERSITY OF HONOLULU

■ Honolulu, Hawaii

THE UNIVERSITY

Chaminade University of Honolulu, a private, coeducational institution, was established in 1955 by the Society of Mary (Marianists). Named after Father William Joseph Chaminade, a French Catholic priest who ministered to his people during the late eighteenth and early nineteenth centuries and who founded the Society in 1817, the University today continues the Marianist mission of educating leaders through faith and reason. To achieve this mission, Chaminade forms a community encompassing people from diverse cultural origins, both traditional and nontraditional, who hold a variety of religious beliefs. The University encourages learning through cooperation, self-discipline, caring, and mutual respect while offering individualized attention that promotes personal and intellectual growth. A major goal of the University is to educate and train students for leadership both within Chaminade and in communities beyond the campus. The University advocates a personal concern for social justice, ethics, responsibility, and service to the community and exerts institutional leadership by promoting Chaminade's ideals outside the University community.

Inquiries and application materials should be sent to:

Admission Office
Chaminade University
3140 Waialae Avenue
Honolulu, Hawaii 96816
Telephone: 808-735-4735
800-735-3733 (toll-free from the mainland; collect from neighboring islands)
Fax: 808-739-4647

ACADEMIC PROGRAM

Undergraduate study is structured into four parts: practice in basic skills, liberal arts course work that provides a general education, intensive study in a chosen field of concentration (the major), and elective courses outside the major field to complement general and specialized knowledge. All baccalaureate degrees require a minimum of 124 credit hours of course work with a minimum of 45 hours in upper-division courses. Within these guidelines, the student selects a program of study appropriate to personal needs and interests. All appropriate courses at Chaminade require writing assignments from students. Upper-division courses in most fields train students to write in the style and format appropriate to the discipline.

FINANCIAL AID

Those with a high school GPA between 3.5 and 4.0 are eligible for a $5000 yearly scholarship; between 3.0 and 3.49, a $4500 yearly scholarship; between 2.5 and 2.99, a $3500 yearly grant; and between 2.25 to 2.49, a $3000 yearly grant. The Hawaii Grant for new full-time day session students from Hawaii is $1500 per semester. Scholarships and grants, available to regular full-time undergraduate students, are renewable for four years and are awarded without regard to financial need. Students may obtain only one of the Chaminade scholarships or grants. A tuition discount of 20 percent is offered to additional family members when one member of the family is paying full-time tuition.

APPLICATION AND INFORMATION

Chaminade University has a rolling admission process. As soon as all required information is received by the Admission Office, the application is reviewed by an application committee. Students are notified of the committee's decision usually within three to four weeks. Applications are accepted throughout the year. A $50 fee is payable upon application. All students desiring housing must file an application along with a $300 deposit applicable to the total cost per semester. Space and placement are not guaranteed without this deposit. A housing damage deposit of $100 is also required. Evidence of health insurance coverage from a U.S. insurer is required of all dormitory residents and international students. To ensure full consideration for scholarships or grants, students are urged to complete the appropriate application by April 1. Award notices are mailed by April 30.

CHESTNET HILL COLLEGE

■ PHILADELPHIA, PENNSYLVANIA

THE COLLEGE

Chestnut Hill College is a four-year Catholic liberal arts college for women. Founded in 1924 by the Sisters of St. Joseph, it is situated on a 45-acre campus overlooking Wissahickon Creek. Conscious of women's roles in society, Chestnut Hill College has chosen to remain a women's college at the traditional-age undergraduate level. It answers a need for well-educated, values-oriented women who can exert a positive influence on the society of the future. Since opportunities for leadership and self-expression are frequent, the Chestnut Hill graduate can enter a competitive world with confidence in herself. Students come from sixteen states, thirteen countries, and every imaginable background. There are 404 full-time undergraduate women in the day programs and 350 part-time undergraduate men and women. In addition to its undergraduate degrees, Chestnut Hill awards the M.Ed., M.A., and M.S. in six fields, including elementary education, counseling psychology and human services, holistic spirituality, and technology in education.

To arrange an interview or to obtain more detailed information about the academic program, students should contact:

Annabell Smith
Director of Admissions
Chestnut Hill College
9601 Germantown Avenue
Philadelphia, Pennsylvania 19118-2695

Telephone: 215-248-7001
800-248-0052 (toll-free)

ACADEMIC PROGRAM

CHC confers a B.S. or B.A. degree to students who earn 120 semester hours of credit and satisfy specific requirements set by the faculty. Distribution requirements are as follows: 11 semester hours in natural sciences (8 hours of which must be in a laboratory science), 9 semester hours in social sciences, and 21 semester hours in the humanities. In addition to these 41 hours of credit, every student must take 6 semester hours of religious studies, 6 hours beyond the elementary level in a classical or modern foreign language, and 3 hours in a writing course (unless exempted by the English department). As many as 45 of the 120 semester hours may be within the major area. The art therapy, communications, environmental studies, gerontology, international studies, and women in management certificate programs expose liberal arts students in any major to current principles and practices in business and management and in communications.

FINANCIAL AID

Financial aid is available in the form of academic scholarships, guaranteed loans, work-study programs, federal grants, and Chestnut Hill College grants. Most of these are based on financial need and are awarded in financial aid packages that combine various forms of aid and are tailored to each student's need. More than 75 percent of CHC students receive financial aid to meet college costs. All applicants for aid should file a copy of the Free Application for Federal Student Aid (FAFSA). Full tuition scholarships are awarded each year strictly on the basis of achievement. Students should submit a completed application, the application essay, SAT I or ACT scores, a high school transcript, and letters of recommendation from a principal or guidance counselor and a teacher before January 15. An interview is also required for those students wishing to be considered for Presidential Scholarships. The interview may be in person or by phone.

APPLICATION AND INFORMATION

Applications are processed on a rolling admission system.

CHOWAN COLLEGE

■ MURFREESBORO, NORTH CAROLINA

For additional information, students are encouraged to contact:

Admissions Office
Chowan College
Murfreesboro, North Carolina 27855
Telephone: 919-398-6500
800-488-4101 (toll-free)
Fax: 919-398-1190
E-mail: admissions@micah.chowan.edu
Web site: http://www.chowan.edu

THE COLLEGE

Chowan College, a four-year, coeducational liberal arts institution, is founded upon and dedicated to Judeo-Christian principles and values. Originally established in 1848 as a four-year Baptist women's college, Chowan later established itself as one of the leading junior colleges in the South. The second-oldest college of the six institutions affiliated with the North Carolina Baptist State Convention, Chowan returned to four-year status in 1992. Set amid 300 acres of woodlands embracing beautiful Lake Vann, Chowan's main entrance leads gracefully around a college green to the antebellum mansion known as McDowell Columns. Sixteen other major buildings of contemporary design provide air-conditioned residence, academic, athletic, and recreational facilities. The small-town College campus attracts students from at least twenty-seven states and several countries each year.

ACADEMIC PROGRAM

Chowan offers a broad range of undergraduate degrees, all of which carefully integrate effective career preparation with a strong liberal arts education. The integration results in a focus on the knowledge, skills, and qualities necessary for both a successful career and a higher quality of life. Chowan requires at least 120 credit hours for graduation in the College's semester calendar. This requirement includes a 51-credit-hour general education core curriculum in which a student chooses from a selected range of courses, a minimum of 30 credit hours in the student's major field of study, and elective courses. Students may receive college credit for Advanced Placement courses taken in high school and for credits received from the College-Level Examination Program. Demonstrating a strong commitment to high-quality education in a personal, caring context, Chowan employs 1 professor for every 12 students enrolled. In addition, the College provides each student with a faculty adviser who assists the student in developing an appropriate academic schedule and plan throughout the student's years of study. Tutors and review courses are readily available, as are staffed assistance labs for writing, math, and accounting.

FINANCIAL AID

Financial aid is available to help pay for direct educational costs, including tuition, fees, and books, as well as personal living expenses, such as food, housing, and transportation. Several types of financial aid are available, including grants or scholarships, loans, and work-study. Students must submit the Free Application for Federal Student Aid (FAFSA), which is available on line through the College Web site. Chowan College announces awards in early spring. Qualification for Chowan's incentive grant and scholarship program is determined by SAT I/ACT scores and the cumulative, unweighted high school GPA. Awards range from $1000 to $6500 per year for four years. Chowan also offers a $1000 regional incentive grant and a program of grants and scholarships that cover the full cost of tuition for students who have served as president of a high school student council organization. Students should contact the Admissions Office with qualifying information for immediate verification of award status.

APPLICATION AND INFORMATION

Students should submit an application (available on line through the College Web site) with the $20 application fee and an official high school transcript. The SAT I or ACT results must be mailed to Chowan or be included on the official transcript.

CLAREMONT MCKENNA COLLEGE

■ Claremont, California

THE COLLEGE

Founded in 1946 as the third undergraduate college in the cluster of the Claremont Colleges, Claremont McKenna College (CMC) occupies a unique place among American colleges. Through a grounding in the traditional liberal arts, CMC's purpose is to educate future leaders in business, the professions, and public affairs. Economics, government, and international relations are the most popular among twenty-one majors offered at CMC. The College is especially appropriate for students seeking to pursue careers in law, politics, government, international relations, business, management, and finance. Claremont McKenna College is one of seven institutions—five undergraduate colleges and two graduate schools—that constitute the Claremont Colleges. The others are Harvey Mudd College, Pitzer College, Pomona College, Scripps College, the Claremont Graduate University, and Keck Graduate Institute of Applied Life Sciences.

Further information is available from:

Richard C. Vos
Dean of Admission and Financial Aid
Claremont McKenna College
890 Columbia Avenue
Claremont, California 91711-6425
Telephone: 909-621-8088

ACADEMIC PROGRAM

Students must satisfactorily complete thirty-two semester courses, including general education and major requirements, in order to graduate. General education requirements include one course in mathematics, one course in English composition and analysis, two courses in the natural sciences, two courses in the humanities, three courses in the social sciences, and a senior thesis. In addition, students must complete a third semester of a foreign language and a Questions of Civilization course. Depending on the department, credit or advanced placement, or both, may be granted for college courses taken while in high school. Also, CMC may grant credit for scores of 4 or 5 on Advanced Placement (AP) examinations and for scores of 6 or 7 on higher level International Baccalaureate (IB) examinations. CMC sponsors a joint science program with two other Claremont Colleges, Pitzer and Scripps. Virtually all students in the joint science program do independent research, and reports on many student-faculty projects have been published in professional journals. By intercollegiate agreement, CMC students may take courses not offered at Claremont McKenna at any of the Claremont Colleges. Up to one third of a student's courses may be taken at the other Claremont Colleges.

FINANCIAL AID

Financial aid is awarded in the form of grants (nonrepayable gift aid), student loans, and part-time employment. Grants range from $1000 to $20,000 per year and average $12,500; loans for entering freshmen average $3000 per year. The total amount of aid a student is awarded is based on need. The College offers twenty-five McKenna Achievement Awards to members of each entering freshman class. These awards are valued at $5000 or $3000 each and are renewable for each of the four years, provided the student earns at least a B average. To be considered for one of these awards, a student usually must rank among the top 5 percent in his or her high school class and earn a score of more than 650 on both the mathematical and verbal portions of the SAT I. Candidates must also have excellent school recommendations and strong extracurricular involvement and must have filed a completed application by January 1.

APPLICATION AND INFORMATION

Application materials must be received by November 15 from applicants seeking early decision, November 1 for midyear entrance, and January 15 for those seeking entrance in the fall.

CLARION UNIVERSITY OF PENNSYLVANIA

■ Clarion, Pennsylvania

THE UNIVERSITY

Clarion University of Pennsylvania is fully accredited by the Middle States Association of Colleges and Schools. It was founded in 1867 and is one of fourteen state-owned institutions of higher education in Pennsylvania. Its programs in education are accredited by the National Council for Accreditation of Teacher Education and the National Academy of Early Childhood Programs, and its chemistry program is approved by the American Chemical Society. The University is a member of AACSB–The International Association for Management Education, the American Association of Colleges for Teacher Education, and the American Association of State Colleges and Universities and is an Educational Associate of the Institute of International Education. The Bachelor and Associate of Science in Nursing degree programs have the accreditation of the National League for Nursing. The legal business studies program at the Venango campus is approved by the American Bar Association. The occupational therapy assistant program, also at the Venango campus, was recently granted certification by the American Occupational Therapy Association.

Application forms and additional information may be obtained by contacting:

Office of Admissions
Clarion University of Pennsylvania
840 Wood Street
Clarion, Pennsylvania 16214
Telephone: 814-226-2306
800-672-7171 (toll-free in Pennsylvania)
E-mail: admissions@clarion.edu
Web site: http://www.clarion.edu/admiss/admiss.htm

ACADEMIC PROGRAM

A philosophy of liberal education at Clarion allows students to become intellectually well rounded while specializing in one field. The flexibility of the academic program also enables students to have dual majors if they so desire. In most cases, students must complete 128 credits to earn a bachelor's degree and 64 credits to earn an associate degree, but requirements vary according to the specific program. An honors program for high-achieving students is offered. In addition to this program, scholastic excellence may also be recognized through awards and admission to honorary societies. The school year is on a semester basis. Entering students may apply for college credit through Advanced Placement programs, by examination, or by courses taught directly in selected high schools by Clarion University faculty members.

FINANCIAL AID

Clarion University participates in three campus-based federal aid programs: the Federal Perkins Loan, Federal Work-Study, and Federal Supplemental Educational Opportunity Grant programs. The institution also participates in the Federal Pell Grant and Federal Stafford Student Loan programs. Students who are residents of Pennsylvania are potentially eligible for grants and loans through the Pennsylvania Higher Education Assistance Agency (PHEAA) program. In addition, numerous academic scholarships are available to qualified students attending Clarion University. All aid applicants must file the Free Application for Federal Student Aid (FAFSA). This form is available in all high school guidance offices and the Clarion University Financial Aid Office. It is from this form that a student's financial need is determined. For further information, applicants should contact the University's financial aid director at 814-226-2315.

APPLICATION AND INFORMATION

Continuous evaluation is the admission policy at Clarion. Students may apply for early admission, regular admission, or admission under the student development and academic support program. Qualified applicants may receive an acceptance offer one year in advance without being required to respond until the spring of their senior year in high school. Campus visits are welcome, and appointments should be arranged between 9 a.m. and 4 p.m., Monday through Friday, and on some Saturdays. On-campus visitation days, which parents and prospective students are encouraged to attend, are conducted throughout the year.

CLARKSON COLLEGE

■ OMAHA, NEBRASKA

THE COLLEGE

For additional information, students should contact:

Enrollment Services
Clarkson College
101 South 42nd Street
Omaha, Nebraska 68131-2739
Telephone: 402-552-3041
800-647-5500 (toll-free)
E-mail: admiss@clrkcol.crhsnet.edu

Clarkson College is a regionally accredited private institution, with exceptional programs for nursing, radiography and medical imaging, occupational therapy assistant and physical therapist assistant studies, business, and health services management. The College offers the personal qualities of a small institution and the technological advantages found within a larger educational environment. Founded in 1888, it was the first school of nursing in Nebraska and the thirty-fifth in the nation and was approved to grant academic degrees in 1984. The baccalaureate and master's programs in nursing and the associate allied health programs have professional accreditation. The current Clarkson enrollment of 600 students consists of individuals of diverse ages and ethnic and cultural backgrounds. Professional staff members in the offices of admissions, financial aid, student services, and housing are readily available to assist students. Both faculty and staff members are committed to providing the support services needed to ensure that students grow and learn to the maximum of their abilities. The Clarkson Student Nurses' Association, Clarkson Radiography Student Association, Clarkson Physical Therapist Assistant Student Association, and Student Occupational Therapy Association are voluntary organizations for students desiring involvement in preprofessional activities.

ACADEMIC PROGRAM

The goal of Clarkson College is to prepare individuals to be competent in the technical aspects of their profession and educated with the intellectual skills developed with liberal arts courses. The curriculum is supported by courses in the liberal arts and sciences and combines knowledge of course content with the development of intellectual and clinical competencies. Each student's curriculum plan reflects the individual's needs and interest. Although degree requirements remain constant, the scheduling of courses within the curriculum may be individualized. The flexibility of the programs permits full-time or part-time enrollment. The academic year begins with the fall semester in August, is followed by the spring semester in January, and ends with the fifteen-week summer semester. Candidates for the baccalaureate degree must complete 128 semester hours of course work, including 60 hours of general education and support courses. Advanced placement into the curriculum beyond the beginning of the freshman year is accomplished through transfer of credits or credit by examination and other means. The associate degree program requirements also include a general education component.

FINANCIAL AID

In 1997–98, the College awarded financial aid to approximately 85 percent of its undergraduate students. Scholarships, grants, loans, and work-study are available to meet the individual financial needs of students who qualify. Scholarships are awarded to outstanding applicants. Students are required to submit the completed Free Application for Federal Student Aid (FAFSA) or the Renewal Application as well as the Clarkson College Financial Aid Information Form for eligibility for all forms of aid.

APPLICATION AND INFORMATION

The enrollment policy of Clarkson College allows potential students to apply anytime during the year. A completed application form, accompanied by the application fee, an official high school transcript or certification of successful completion of the General Educational Development test (GED) (when no high school diploma is available), and ACT or SAT I scores should be submitted when seeking admission. Students with previous postsecondary course work should also submit an official transcript from each institution of higher education attended.

CLEARY COLLEGE

■ HOWELL AND YPSILANTI, MICHIGAN

THE COLLEGE

Cleary College operates from two campuses in Michigan. The Livingston Campus, situated on 27 wooded acres east of Howell, Michigan, is a growing community featuring a historic downtown area. The Washtenaw Campus, located on 21 acres within the Ypsilanti business district, houses the Bonisteel Library and the Knostman Tax Library. In 1998, construction began on a new state-of-the-art campus on the Washtenaw site. Cleary students are focused on a business career, and most students work while completing their degrees—either on their own or as part of an internship or degree program requirement.

Additional information and application materials are available from:

Office of Admissions
Cleary College
Washtenaw Campus
2170 Washtenaw Avenue
Ypsilanti, Michigan 48197
Telephone: 800-686-1883 (toll-free)

Office of Admissions
Cleary College
Livingston Campus
3750 Cleary College Drive
Howell, Michigan 48843
Telephone: 800-589-1979 (toll-free)

ACADEMIC PROGRAM

The B.B.A. programs are offered in three formats so students can select the best schedule to suit their specific needs. Candidates for the B.B.A. degrees must earn a minimum of 180 quarter credit hours and complete all requisite courses with an average of two honor points for each quarter hour of credit. The first format is the PACE Programs. These B.B.A. programs follow the traditional four-year degree schedule. The second format is the Direct Degree Programs. These B.B.A. programs are designed specifically for the busy professional who has previous college and work experience. Students complete their B.B.A. in just twelve months. The third format offered is the 2+2 Programs. The 2+2 Programs allow students with an associate degree to continue on for their B.B.A. at Cleary with no loss of prior college credit. With full-time study, most students in the 2+2 Programs complete their bachelor's degree in just two years. The A.B.A. programs are offered in two formats so students can select the best schedule to suit their specific needs. Candidates for the A.B.A. degrees must earn a minimum of 90 quarter hours of credit and complete all requisite courses with an average of two honor points for each quarter hour of credit. The first format is the PACE Programs. These A.B.A. programs follow the traditional two-year degree schedule. The second format is the Gateway Program. Gateway is an A.B.A. program designed for students interested in the Direct Degree Programs but who do not have the necessary background or sufficient previous college credits for entry. Successful completion of the two-term (six month) Gateway Program qualifies students to enter the twelve-month Direct Degree Program.

FINANCIAL AID

Cleary participates in state and federal financial aid programs and accepts the Free Application for Federal Student Aid (FAFSA). Some of the programs include the Federal Pell Grant, Federal SEOG, Federal College Work-Study program, Federal Stafford Loan, and Michigan Tuition Grant. In addition, a number of Cleary scholarships and grants are available, including the McKenny Scholarship, the PR Cleary Scholarship, the Rosin Canton Community Grant, the President's Scholarship, and the Morse B. Barker Scholarship.

APPLICATION AND INFORMATION

Quarters begin in September, January, March, and June. Applications are accepted all year and must be submitted with a $25 nonrefundable application fee payable to Cleary College in the form of a check or money order. Application to the Direct Degree and Gateway Programs is recommended at least eight weeks prior to the start of the term.

COLBY–SAWYER COLLEGE

■ NEW LONDON, NEW HAMPSHIRE

THE COLLEGE

Colby-Sawyer College, a coeducational, residential, undergraduate college founded in 1837, evolved from the New England academy tradition and has been engaged in higher education since 1928. The College provides programs of study that innovatively integrate the liberal arts and sciences with professional preparation. Through all of its programs, the College encourages students of varied backgrounds and abilities to realize their full intellectual and personal potential so they may gain understanding about themselves, others, and the major forces shaping our rapidly changing and pluralistic world. At present, students come from all over the United States and seven other countries, with 68 percent of the students coming from outside of New Hampshire. There are eight varsity sports for women (NCAA Division III basketball, lacrosse, soccer, tennis, track and field, and volleyball; ECSC Alpine ski racing; and IHSA riding) and seven for men (NCAA Division III baseball, basketball, soccer, tennis, and track and field; ECSC Alpine ski racing; and IHSA riding). The College is accredited by the New England Association of Schools and Colleges, and professional programs also carry the appropriate accreditations.

Application forms and additional information may be obtained by contacting:

Office of Admissions
Colby-Sawyer College
100 Main Street
New London, New Hampshire 03257
Telephone: 603-526-3700
800-272-1015 (toll-free)
Fax: 603-526-3452
E-mail: csadmiss@colby-sawyer.edu
Web site: http://www.colby-sawyer.edu

ACADEMIC PROGRAM

Colby-Sawyer College faculty and staff are excellent at working with students who are undecided on a major and are highly qualified to help students explore their values, talents, and academic and career interests. At Colby-Sawyer College, it is believed that knowledge and experience nurture each other. Therefore, the combination of classroom learning and professional experience is an integral part of each student's education. Through a carefully crafted program offered by the Harrington Center for Career Development, all students are encouraged throughout their four years of study to continue to clarify their interests and goals and to gain practical experiences through student employment, internships, and voluntary service to the community. Colby-Sawyer has an impressive roster of internship opportunities available, and through the internship experience, students often receive their first offer of a permanent position.

FINANCIAL AID

Seventy-five percent of the students currently receive some form of financial assistance, and Colby-Sawyer provides more than $4.2 million a year in grant assistance to its students. Both need-based and merit awards are available, including recently established merit awards for outstanding academic achievement or student leadership. Merit awards are also available for students with special talents in art, music, or creative writing and for those students who have been significantly involved in community service. Applicants who wish to be considered for merit awards must submit all required admissions materials by February 1. Each applicant for need-based aid must submit the Free Application for Federal Student Aid (FAFSA) and the Colby-Sawyer Application for Financial Aid. Priority will be given to students whose completed forms are received before the March 1 deadline.

APPLICATION AND INFORMATION

Colby-Sawyer receives and considers applications throughout the year. Beginning in December, applications are reviewed as soon as they become complete, and candidates are notified as soon as the admissions decision is finalized. A completed application includes a transcript of the candidate's high school work (including first-quarter grades for the senior year), SAT I or ACT scores, two letters of recommendation (one from a teacher and one from a guidance professional), a personal statement, and a $40 nonrefundable application fee.

COLLEGE OF AERONAUTICS

■ Flushing, New York

THE COLLEGE

The College of Aeronautics is a private, independent technical college that is chartered by the Board of Regents of the State of New York and is accredited by the Middle States Association of Colleges and Schools. Undergraduate enrollment is approximately 1,100 students. This includes full-time, part-time, day, and evening students. Founded in 1932, the College has enjoyed much success preparing men and women for careers in the world of aeronautical technologies. The educational experiences offered by the College are designed to develop both a high degree of technical competence and a sense of personal responsibility—essential characteristics of the engineering technician. The College of Aeronautics is exceptional in that it emphasizes hands-on technical courses, which are given through a number of laboratory exercises and projects. The practical education provided by the College makes its graduates highly desirable candidates for employment. The Career Development Office offers access to the aviation/aerospace industry. Many of the College's graduates have made important contributions to aeronautical developments through the years, and many hold prestigious positions in the industry today.

For further details, interested persons should contact:

Office of Admissions
College of Aeronautics
LaGuardia Airport
Flushing, New York 11371
Telephone: 718-429-6600 Ext. 118
[F18]800-776-2376 (toll-free)
E-mail: pro@aero.edu
World Wide Web:
http://www.aero.edu

ACADEMIC PROGRAM

The B.S., B.T., A.A.S., and A.O.S. degree programs in maintenance focus on the technical skills and theoretical knowledge needed to obtain the federal certificates necessary to maintain aircraft. The College's state-of-the-art educational facilities give students the advantage of working with aircraft before entering the professional world. Students are immersed in a combination of theory and practical applications necessary to begin a career as a commercial pilot in the A.A.S. degree in aircraft operations. Through this program, qualified students may also earn eligibility for the Federal Aviation Administration's private/commercial pilot certificate as well as the required instrument rating. Designed to bridge the gap between the technician and the engineer, the A.A.S. in aeronautical engineering technology (pre-engineering) gives students the skills necessary to begin their engineering or related careers. This degree program provides ease of transfer to four-year engineering technology programs. The A.A.S. and B.S. degrees in avionics (aircraft electronics) involves the precise study and practice of complex electronics systems, including navigation, communications, surveillance, and flight control. Understanding technology is no longer a choice in today's computerized world. The College of Aeronautics' A.A.S. and B.S. degrees in computerized design and animated graphics programs teach the latest in animation and 2-D and 3-D graphics imaging techniques. All of these programs utilize the latest hardware and software and allow students to apply their skills to aviation and other career fields as well.

FINANCIAL AID

Approximately 80 percent of the students receive financial aid. The maximum amount of financial aid awarded to a freshman is $7000; the average amount awarded is $3300. Financial aid is available in the form of Federal Pell Grant and New York State TAP (Tuition Assistance Program) awards, the FSEOG (Federal Supplemental Educational Opportunity Grant), Federal Stafford Student Loan, and the Federal Perkins Loan.

APPLICATION AND INFORMATION

The director of admissions and the counseling staff are available to advise applicants and their parents and to provide up-to-date information and materials for high school guidance counselors.

COLLEGE OF SAINT BENEDICT/SAINT JOHN'S UNIVERSITY

■ ST. JOSEPH AND COLLEGEVILLE, MINNESOTA

THE COLLEGE AND THE UNIVERSITY

The College of Saint Benedict (CSB) and Saint John's University (SJU) are private, residential, liberal arts institutions. CSB for women was founded in 1887; SJU for men was founded in 1857. The Carnegie Foundation for the Advancement of Teaching and *U.S.News & World Report* rank CSB and SJU as two of only five Catholic colleges nationwide included in the selective national liberal arts category. The two institutions offer a common curriculum, class schedule, and social and cultural programming. Women and men students attend classes and utilize the services and facilities at both campuses. Each campus, however, addresses the unique needs of the adult development of its students—including gender-specific issues—through residential life programming and activities. The sponsoring communities of Benedictine women and men continue the centuries-old tradition of a balanced education, addressing the developmental needs of mind, body, and spirit. While they are Catholic institutions, CSB and SJU welcome students and faculty members of all faith backgrounds and preferences. The campus ministry staffs provide a wide array of opportunities for spiritual growth.

Application forms and additional information may be obtained by writing or calling:

Admission Office
College of Saint Benedict (for women)
37 South College Avenue
St. Joseph, Minnesota 56374-2099
Telephone: 800-544-1489 (toll-free)
Fax: 320-363-5010
E-mail: admissions@csbsju.edu
Web site: http://www.csbsju.edu

Admission Office
Saint John's University (for men)
P.O. Box 7155
Collegeville, Minnesota 56321-7155
Telephone: 800-245-6467 (toll-free)
Fax: 320-363-3206
E-mail: admissions@csbsju.edu
Web site: http://www.csbsju.edu

ACADEMIC PROGRAM

The faculties of CSB and SJU jointly offer an innovative core curriculum. First-year students participate in a yearlong symposium, limited to 8 men and 8 women, which focuses on the development of oral and written communication skills along with proficiency in a variety of reading styles. Seniors participate in a seminar in which they integrate moral and ethical decision making with contemporary issues. An honors program of challenging interdisciplinary and major course work that approaches topics beyond the general curriculum is available to selected students. The core also requires proficiency in a foreign language, discussion, writing, and mathematics.

FINANCIAL AID

Assistance for financing an education at CSB and SJU is identified as scholarships for students with excellent academic, service, and leadership records and as grants, employment, and loans for students from low- and middle-income families who demonstrate a need for assistance in paying for college. About 91 percent of the students currently attending the colleges receive financial assistance, many under both (nonneed and need) categories. Students interested in applying for grants, employment, and loans should complete the Free Application for Federal Student Aid (FAFSA). The Colleges participate in state and federal financial aid programs such as the Federal Pell Grant, Federal Work-Study, and Federal Stafford Student Loan programs. In addition, the Colleges offer generous financial assistance from their own funds to assist students.

APPLICATION AND INFORMATION

Offers of admission are granted on a rolling basis, and applicants should expect to be notified within three weeks of the receipt of their completed application. CSB and SJU are members of the Common Application and also accept Apply!, College Connector, CollegeLink, and Peterson's Universal applications. Students are encouraged to visit the campuses for a tour and to meet with an admission counselor. Appointments should be made at least five days in advance.

THE COLLEGE OF WOOSTER

■ WOOSTER, OHIO

Director of Admissions
The College of Wooster
Wooster, Ohio 44691
Telephone: 330-263-2000 Ext. 2270
or 2322
800-877-9905 (toll-free)
Fax: 330-263-2621
E-mail: admissions@acs.wooster.edu
Web site: http://www.wooster.edu

THE COLLEGE

One of the first coeducational colleges in the country, the College of Wooster was founded in 1866 by Presbyterians who wanted to do "their proper part in the great work of educating those who are to mold society and give shape to all its institutions." Today it is a fully independent, privately endowed liberal arts college with a rich tradition of academic excellence. That tradition defines student life at Wooster, beginning with the First-Year Seminar in Critical Inquiry and culminating in the Independent Study program.

ACADEMIC PROGRAM

Wooster's academic program is designed to provide a liberal education that prepares undergraduates for a lifetime of intellectual adventure, allows them to develop harmoniously and independently, and helps them meet new situations as they arise. To be eligible for a Bachelor of Arts degree, a student must successfully complete thirty-two courses, including three courses of Independent Study. An overall grade point average of at least 2.0 (on a 4.0 scale) is required for graduation. Students may receive credit for work done at other colleges and for scores of 4 or better on the Advanced Placement tests offered by the College Board. Courses are graded A–D or No Credit unless the student exercises an option to take certain courses on a Satisfactory/No Credit basis. All first-year students participate in first-year seminars. Wooster requires each senior to complete a two-semester Independent Study project.

FINANCIAL AID

Almost all financial assistance is awarded on the basis of need, as determined by the Free Application for Federal Student Aid (FAFSA). Aid is allocated when students are admitted to the College. Financial assistance information and forms should be requested at the time of application. Applications for aid should be submitted by March 1. Merit aid is available on a competitive basis. The College Scholar program offers eight awards of $16,000 each per year, based on a competitive examination. Additional awards of $9000 to $11,000 per year are available. Selected entering students receive academic and achievement awards independent of the College Scholars program. Synod of the Covenant Scholarships for Presbyterian communicants are available, as are Scottish Arts awards. The Clarence B. Allen Scholarship program awards up to five scholarships of $16,000 a year to entering African-American students with a demonstrated record of academic achievement and promise of continued success in college. The Arthur Holly Compton Scholarships are awarded to students who demonstrate unusual aptitude for Wooster's program of Independent Study. Compton Scholarships are awarded for $7000 and $14,000 annually. Music scholarships of $6000 each are awarded to entering first-year students based on auditions in voice or on an instrument. A 15-minute performance of works representing several styles of music is required. Theater scholarships of $6000 each are awarded on a competitive basis. An audition is required. Byron E. Morris Scholarships of up to $6000 are awarded to students who have a demonstrated record of achievement in their school or community in the areas of volunteer/community service or leadership.

COLUMBIA UNIVERSITY SCHOOL OF GENERAL STUDIES

■ New York, New York

THE UNIVERSITY AND THE SCHOOL

For more information, students should contact:

Office of Admissions and Financial Aid
School of General Studies
408 Lewisohn Hall
2970 Broadway
Columbia University, Mail Code 4101
New York, New York 10027
Telephone: 212-854-2772
E-mail: gs-admit@columbia.edu
Web site: http://www.columbia.edu/cu/gs

Called "the best kept secret in American higher education," the School of General Studies at Columbia University has been a pioneer in this country in providing instruction for nontraditional college students. In 1947 the School of General Studies was established as a degree-granting school in its own right; it was granted its own chapter of Phi Beta Kappa in 1952. Today, the School of General Studies is the liberal arts division of Columbia University for individuals whose education after high school has been interrupted or postponed by at least one year. Students may study full- or part-time. The school is dedicated to the belief that highly motivated students who meet its standards should have full access to the fine education offered by the University. The School has more than 1,000 undergraduate degree candidates and about 250 postbaccalaureate premedical students. Most degree candidates hold jobs as well as study, and many have family responsibilities. Between 75 percent and 80 percent of the School's students go on to graduate and professional schools after graduation. The acceptance rate for General Studies postbaccalaureate students applying to U.S. medical schools and law schools is more than 85 percent.

ACADEMIC PROGRAM

The School of General Studies offers a traditional liberal arts education designed to provide students with the broad knowledge and intellectual skills that make possible continued education and growth in the years after college and that constitute the soundest possible foundation on which to build competence for positions of responsibility in the professional world. Requirements for the bachelor's degree comprise three elements: (1) core requirements, intended to develop in students the ability to write and communicate clearly; to understand the modes of thought that characterize the humanities, the social sciences, and the sciences; to gain some familiarity with central cultural ideas through literature, fine arts, and music; and to acquire a working proficiency in a foreign language; (2) major requirements, designed to give students sustained and coherent exposure to a particular discipline in an area of strong intellectual interest; and (3) elective courses, in which students pursue particular interests and skills for their own sake or for their relationship to future professional or personal objectives. Students are required to complete a minimum of 124 points for the bachelor's degree; 64 of these may be in transfer credit, but at least 60 points (including the last 30 points) must be completed at Columbia.

FINANCIAL AID

The School of General Studies awards financial aid based upon need and academic ability. Approximately 60 percent of General Studies degree candidates receive some form of financial aid, including Federal Pell Grants, New York State TAP Grants, Federal Stafford and unsubsidized Stafford Loans, Federal Perkins Loans, General Studies Scholarships, and Federal Work-Study Program awards. Application deadlines are May 30 for the fall 1998 semester and December 15 for the spring 1999 semester.

APPLICATION AND INFORMATION

Application deadlines are July 1 for the fall semester and December 15 for the spring semester. Applicants from countries outside the U.S. are urged to apply by August 15 for the spring semester and April 1 for the fall semester. Applications are reviewed as they are completed, and applicants are notified of decisions shortly thereafter.

CONCORD COLLEGE

■ ATHENS, WEST VIRGINIA

THE COLLEGE

Concord College, a growing state-run college committed exclusively to undergraduate instruction, was founded 123 years ago. Concord features accredited career-oriented education with a strong liberal arts base and has the needs of the individual student as its fundamental concern. The beautiful 95-acre campus stands on a ridge of the Appalachian Mountains. Concord's 2,780 men and women follow courses of study in the arts and sciences, business administration, teacher education, and such fields as travel industry management and social work. Preparation for advanced and professional study is a Concord hallmark. Students participate in special interest organizations, honor societies, five fraternities, four sororities, the campus cable-TV system, the yearbook, the newspaper, and intramural sports. Intercollegiate competition for men is available in baseball, basketball, cross-country, football, golf, and tennis. Women compete in intercollegiate basketball, softball, tennis, and volleyball.

For further information, students may contact:

Richard A. Edwards
Dean of Admissions
Concord College
P.O. Box 1000
Athens, West Virginia 24712
Telephone: 304-384-5248 or 5249
800-344-6679 (toll-free)
E-mail: admissions@ccvms.concord.wvnet.edu
Web site: http://www.concord.wvnet.edu

ACADEMIC PROGRAM

All students must complete a minimum of 128 semester hours with a grade point average of 2.0 (C) or better to receive a degree. A program of general studies, required of all students, includes courses in communications and literature, fine arts, social sciences, natural sciences, mathematics, foreign languages (optional in most majors), and physical education. Credit is awarded for satisfactory scores on the College-Level Examination Program (CLEP) and Advanced Placement (AP) tests. Honors courses and independent study projects are available in most departments. Semesters begin in late August and mid-January; there are summer terms as well.

FINANCIAL AID

Federal Pell Grants, Federal Supplemental Educational Opportunity Grants, Federal Perkins Loans, West Virginia Higher Education Grants, Federal PLUS loans, and Federal Stafford Student Loans are available through the College. Competitive non-need-based academic, athletic, musical, dramatic, and artistic scholarships are also available and require a separate application. The State Student Assistance Program and the Federal Work-Study Program offer opportunities for student employment. Concord offers scholarships to international students. The average scholarship covers 54 percent of the total institutional cost. Incoming freshmen willing to perform community service may apply for the Bonner Scholars Program, which pays up to $2870 per year for four years as long as its criteria are met. Funded by the Corella and Bertram F. Bonner Foundation of Princeton, New Jersey, the award is primarily based on need and prior service. Approximately 65 percent of the students receive some form of financial assistance. The College participates in the financial aid needs analysis program of the Pennsylvania Higher Education Assistance Agency, subscribing to the principle that the amount of financial aid granted a student should be based on financial need, which is established through analysis of the Free Application for Federal Student Aid (FAFSA). To receive priority, the FAFSA needs analysis must be on file by April 15.

APPLICATION AND INFORMATION

Applications should be submitted by August 1 for admission to the fall semester, which begins in late August and ends in December.

CONCORDIA UNIVERSITY

■ Portland, Oregon

THE UNIVERSITY

Concordia University, Portland, is a private, four-year Lutheran university dedicated to the intellectual and professional development of the whole student. Founded in 1905 as an academy, Concordia grew from a junior college to a four-year college in the late 1970s, awarding its first bachelor's degrees in 1980. Concordia attained university status in 1995. The institution's mission statement is, "Concordia University is a Christian University preparing leaders for the transformation of society." The University is composed of four academic colleges: the College of Education, the School of Management, the College of Arts and Sciences, and the College of Theological Studies. Programmatic development through the 1980s and 1990s increased the University's commitment to local and regional needs through several academic additions. These include a nationally recognized health-care administration program, a regionally unique theater major with an emphasis in theater for youth, and a progressive bachelor's degree in environmental management. Relevant professional experience brings the real world into the classroom. The opportunities to investigate professional applications of a chosen field or career are available to all students. CU sponsors study-abroad opportunities in areas such as Oak Hill College, London; Guangxi Teacher's University in Guilin, China; and Kato School, Japan. Corporate internships that lead directly to employment consideration and human services practicums that provide a supervised learning experience in a community agency place the student directly in a career path. Concordia's Lutheran heritage instills within all academic programs an intent to prepare professional leaders with personal attitudes of service and concern. Personal experiences, academic courses, and daily worship opportunities immerse students in a value-centered education grounded in Christian principles.

For further information and application forms for admission and financial aid, prospective students should contact:

Office of Admissions
Concordia University
2811 Northeast Holman Street
Portland, Oregon 97211
Telephone: 503-288-9371
800-321-9371 (toll-free)
Fax: 503-280-8531
E-mail:
cu-admissions@cu-portland.edu
World Wide Web: http://www.cu-portland.edu

ACADEMIC PROGRAM

For a baccalaureate degree, 124 semester hours are required; for the associate degree, 63 hours are required. All degree-seeking students, regardless of their major, must complete the general education requirements, which include courses in communications, fine arts, humanities, physical education, religion, science, math, and social science. In several academic areas, students may earn credit through successful completion of Advanced Placement and College-Level Examination Program (CLEP) tests.

FINANCIAL AID

The Free Application for Federal Student Aid (FAFSA) is used to determine a student's financial need for the awarding of scholarships, grants, work-study programs, and loans. Most awards are made in the spring for the following academic year. Approximately 80 percent of Concordia's students receive some form of financial aid. Merit-based scholarships are awarded based on academic history.

APPLICATION AND INFORMATION

Candidates for admission must complete a formal Concordia application for admission, submit test scores and/or high school/college transcripts, and furnish one reference. Applicants are encouraged to apply as early in the academic year as possible. Concordia follows a rolling admission procedure, and candidates are notified of a decision shortly after all the necessary credentials have been received.

DAVIDSON COLLEGE

■ DAVIDSON, NORTH CAROLINA

THE COLLEGE

Founded in 1837, Davidson College consistently ranks as one of the most competitive liberal arts and sciences colleges in the United States. Davidson's student body is made up of 1,600 students from forty-three states and twenty-four other countries, chosen not only for their academic promise but also for their character. The liberal arts curriculum at Davidson is designed to give students knowledge and skills that they will put to use throughout their lives. Davidson offers more than 850 courses in twenty major fields and in special interdisciplinary programs. Close relationships between faculty and students are a hallmark of the Davidson experience. The Honor System serves as a foundation for life at Davidson. The Honor Code represents a declaration by the entire College community—students, faculty, staff, and alumni—that an honorable course is the most just and, therefore, the best. Davidson students participate in a wide range of organizations of special interest and attend cultural and social events offered on campus. As one of the smallest schools in the nation competing in Division I of the NCAA, Davidson supports true scholar-athletes in twenty-one varsity sports.

For additional information about Davidson, students should contact:

Nancy J. Cable, Ph.D.
Dean of Admission and Financial Aid
Davidson College
P.O. Box 1737
Davidson, North Carolina 28036
Telephone: 704-892-2230
800-768-0380 (toll-free)
Web site: http://www.DAVIDSON.edu

ACADEMIC PROGRAM

The liberal arts curriculum at Davidson gives students a broad-based and rich education, exposing them to many different academic areas. Davidson requires a total of thirty-two courses to graduate. Through the required core curriculum, every Davidson student takes courses in six areas: the fine arts, natural sciences and mathematics, philosophy and religion, literature, history, and the social sciences. Additional courses are taken in composition, foreign language, cultural diversity, and physical education. In addition to the core curriculum, students choose a major by the end of their sophomore year. A major normally requires up to twelve courses, including at least five upper-level courses.

FINANCIAL AID

Through a combination of state, federal, and private sources, Davidson grants in excess of $6.5 million to students who qualify. The instructions for applying for need-based aid are included with Davidson's application for admission. Students with financial need are assisted through a combination of Davidson scholarships, federal and state grants, loans, and work-study. Davidson awards merit scholarships to approximately 15 percent of each entering first-year class. These awards recognize students' academic promise, special talents, and personal qualities. Recipients are selected based on the strength of their admission application. Merit scholarships range from $2500 to the comprehensive fee and include the following top awards: the Thomas S. and Sarah B. Baker Scholarship (two awarded, comprehensive fee), the John Montgomery Belk Scholarship (one awarded to a student from the southeastern U.S., comprehensive fee), the William Holt Terry Scholarship (two awarded to students with exceptional leadership qualities, full tuition), and the Amos Norris Scholarship (one awarded to an outstanding scholar athlete).

APPLICATION AND INFORMATION

Early decision—round one—has an application deadline of November 15 with notification by December 15. Early decision—round two—has an application deadline of January 2 with notification by February 1. Regular decision has an application deadline of January 2 with notification by April 1. Students are encouraged to visit Davidson for a campus tour and an information session with a member of the Admission Office staff.

DREXEL UNIVERSITY

■ PHILADELPHIA, PENNSYLVANIA

Office of Undergraduate Admissions
Drexel University
3141 Chestnut Streets
Philadelphia, Pennsylvania 19104
Telephone: 800-2-DREXEL (toll-free)
Web site: http://www.drexel.edu

THE UNIVERSITY

Drexel is a private, nonsectarian, coeducational university that has maintained a reputation for academic excellence since its founding in 1891. Its academic programs offer students practical preparation for graduate school and a variety of careers. Full-time, paid professional experience through Drexel's cooperative education program is a vital part of a Drexel education. Students gain professional experience in jobs related to their career interests by alternating classroom study with periods of employment in business, industry, and government. More than 1,700 employers from nineteen states and eleven other countries participate in this program. Another distinctive element is the University's microcomputer requirement, through which all undergraduates participate in a computer-enhanced education.

ACADEMIC PROGRAM

Drexel's distinguishing feature is Drexel Co-op: "The Ultimate Internship"™. Combined with rigorous academic programs, this feature provides an education that enables students to bridge the gap between academic studies and the working world. The co-op/internship program generates a two-way educational force: academic knowledge finds concrete form in the workplace, while personal growth and experiential learning on the job enrich the academic experience. All undergraduates are prepared for full-time professional internships through Drexel's cooperative education program. With the new flexible degree programs, studies in engineering, information systems, and commerce and engineering, as well as science programs in the College of Arts and Sciences, are designed to be completed in four or five years, including eighteen months of co-op experience. Design arts programs require four years to complete and include six months of co-op. Business, humanities, and social science programs offer both four-year and five-year co-op/internship options. Each college has its own sequence of graduation requirements, including a common core of subjects and the opportunity for specialization after the core is complete.

FINANCIAL AID

Approximately 87 percent of all freshmen receive financial aid. The aid package may contain academic, athletic, or performing arts scholarships; grants; or loans; or part-time employment. Federal programs are also included. All students applying for aid must submit the Free Application for Federal Student Aid by May 1. Notification of incoming freshmen and transfer students begins about March 1. Drexel offers a unique achievement-based award, the A. J. Drexel Scholarship, to all qualified incoming freshmen and transfer students. With an annual award value of up to $8000, the A. J. Drexel Scholarship is renewable on a yearly basis, provided the student maintains a 3.0 grade point average and full-time status. Criteria include a strong academic record and involvement in extracurricular and community service activities.

APPLICATION AND INFORMATION

Application forms with complete instructions for admission and financial aid and the appropriate college prospectus may be obtained by writing to the address given below. Each application must be accompanied by a nonrefundable application fee of $35; however, the fee may be waived in cases of extreme hardship if requested by the secondary school or if the student visits the campus. Students may access Drexel's online application at the Web site listed above. Applications for regular full-time undergraduate status are accepted throughout the senior year. Drexel subscribes to the College Board's Candidates Reply Date of May 1. Transfer students should apply at least three months before the beginning of the term in which they wish to enroll.

EARLHAM COLLEGE

■ RICHMOND, INDIANA

THE COLLEGE

Earlham College, founded in 1847 by the Society of Friends, is an independent, liberal arts college. Earlham enrolls approximately 1,050 students—550 women and 500 men—representing forty-six states and eighteen countries. Eighty percent of Earlham's students are from outside Indiana, and 50 percent come from at least 500 miles away. Students are of many races, religious backgrounds, economic levels, and ethnic traditions. Earlham believes that a strong liberal arts education is the best intellectual preparation for a satisfying and successful life. Graduates have distinguished themselves in careers in science, medicine, law, business, higher education, and social and humanitarian service. Student activities and groups are as varied as the students themselves. There are numerous extracurricular programs in music, theater, dance, social and political action, ethnic and international awareness, and intramural and varsity athletics. Students are very active in community service and donated more than 20,000 hours worth of time to the Richmond community during the 1996–97 school year. Earlham is a member of Division III of the NCAA and the North Coast Athletic Conference. The College offers seven intercollegiate sports for men (baseball, basketball, cross-country, football, soccer, tennis, and track) and eight intercollegiate sports for women (basketball, cross-country, field hockey, lacrosse, soccer, tennis, track, and volleyball). Club sports available are swimming, ultimate frisbee, and men's lacrosse and volleyball. Earlham is a residential college. Students live in the seven residence halls and in twenty-three College-owned houses near the campus. Five smoke-free residence halls are available.

Students wishing additional information or materials on Earlham College should contact:

Office of Admissions
Earlham College
Richmond, Indiana 47374
Telephone: 765-983-1600
800-EARLHAM (toll-free)
Fax: 765-983-1560
E-mail: admission@earlham.edu
Web site: http://admis.earlham.edu/

ACADEMIC PROGRAM

An interdisciplinary humanities program provides a common intellectual experience for all students in their first year. Students gain an in-depth understanding of one or more disciplines in their major area of academic concentration. An academic major usually consists of eight to ten courses in one department, a senior research project or seminar, and a departmental comprehensive examination.

FINANCIAL AID

Most financial aid is awarded on the basis of demonstrated need; more than 50 percent of Earlham's students receive financial assistance. Earlham usually meets the full need of all accepted students with a combination of Earlham Grants, endowed scholarships, loans, federal and state grants, and campus work. Students must file both the Free Application for Federal Student Aid (FAFSA) and a special Earlham form. Scholarships are awarded without regard to financial need and recognize achievement in all areas of the liberal arts. The Carleton B. Edwards scholarship is available for students planning to major in chemistry. Earlham also offers scholarships through the National Merit Scholarship Corporation. Special scholarships are available to members of the Society of Friends and students who will enhance the diversity of the student body.

APPLICATION AND INFORMATION

Earlham offers several admission options: the early decision deadline is December 1 (notification by December 15); the early action deadline is January 15 (notification on February 1); the regular decision deadline is February 15 (notification by April 1); and the transfer deadline is April 1. International students (non-U.S. citizens) should apply by March 1. Applications are accepted after these deadline dates as long as places remain in the entering class. Students who submit applications after April 1 are notified of the admission decision approximately two weeks after their application is complete.

EASTERN COLLEGE

■ St. Davids, Pennsylvania

THE COLLEGE

Eastern College brings a special purpose to its mission as a Christian institution of higher education. The College wants to produce world Christians, capable of confronting injustice and indifference with the character, competence, and commitment Eastern has helped them develop. First and foremost, Eastern remains true to its biblical heritage. The power of the prophetic Word and the Lordship of Jesus Christ provide the context for the College's theological position. The College is sure of its Christian stand, and this encourages it to strengthen its faith by confronting serious contemporary issues. Neither narrow-minded nor staid, the College affirms and embraces Christians whose doctrinal positions may be broader or more restrictive. As a result, those at the College can actively pursue the full dynamic of an abundant Christian life and take an obedient walk with Him. In addition, the academic process revolves around a curriculum that emphasizes foundational skills as well as the understanding and application of knowledge in an increasingly complex society. Classroom experience is intellectually rigorous. A creative core curriculum builds on basic truths and continually challenges the potential of an expanding mind. Practical experience is generated through an extensive internship program as well as through relationships with established ministries like Young Life, Youth for Christ, foreign missions, and Christian outreach programs. The academic climate is enhanced through the presence of graduate programs. Knowledge, ultimately, is written as indelibly on the heart as it is on the mind. Justice and a will obedient to the Lord result from such an academic experience.

Students should see Eastern's Web site (address below) for more information or contact:

Mark Seymour
Executive Director of Enrollment Management
Eastern College
St. Davids, Pennsylvania 19087-3696
Telephone: 800-452-0996 (toll-free)
E-mail: ugadm@eastern.edu
Web site: http://www.eastern.edu

ACADEMIC PROGRAM

In the core curriculum, students take courses designed to fulfill the basic mission of Eastern: to provide biblical foundations to which all learning and action can be related, to ensure acquisition of certain basic skills, and to broaden the student's view of the world. Courses in the breadth area of the core are planned and taught in such a way that central themes of the Christian faith are integrated into the course content. The Fixed Core includes courses such as justice and diversity in a pluralistic society and science, technology, and values.

FINANCIAL AID

Eastern is committed to providing education to qualified students regardless of their means. The financial aid program offers scholarships, grants, loans, and employment. The College utilizes the Pennsylvania Higher Education Assistance Agency (PHEAA) for needs analysis forms processing. The student is required to complete the Free Application for Federal Student Aid (FAFSA) to determine financial aid eligibility. Overall, the College views financial assistance to students as a cooperative investment. If parents contribute to the maximum of their ability and if the student contributes his or her fair share through earnings and personal savings, the College attempts to complete the partnership. In addition, estimates of financial aid eligibility may be obtained from the Financial Aid Office whether or not the student is an applicant. Non-need academic scholarships ranging from $500 to $6000 are available. These scholarships are awarded on the basis of SAT I or ACT scores and high school class rank information. Music, leadership, and church-matching grants are other college-based grant programs that are available.

APPLICATION AND INFORMATION

Applications are accepted until the beginning of each term. Admission decisions are made within 48 hours of receipt of all materials.

EASTERN ILLINOIS UNIVERSITY

■ CHARLESTON, ILLINOIS

THE UNIVERSITY

Eastern Illinois University, founded in 1895, continues to offer outstanding yet affordable undergraduate and graduate education. The University community strives to create an educational and cultural environment in which students may refine their abilities to reason competently, communicate clearly, and become responsible citizens in a diverse world. Students are encouraged, by a faculty committed to teaching, to learn the methods and outcomes of free inquiry in the arts, sciences, humanities, and professions. Students at Eastern attend classes on an attractive, 320-acre campus with the lowest crime rate of all state universities in Illinois and one of the lowest nationwide. The Martin Luther King, Jr. University Union, the center of campus activities, houses a hair salon, food services, a bookstore, bowling alleys, meeting rooms, and television lounge areas. Men and women have access to well-balanced intercollegiate and intramural athletic programs. A well-equipped Student Recreation Center, tennis and basketball courts, and other athletic venues are available on campus. Music, theater, and art activities are available to all students. Involvement in a variety of publications is open to those interested in journalism and writing. Other opportunities in the student life area include radio and television, student government, the Greek system, and more than 120 clubs and organizations.

To receive an application for admission and additional information, students should contact:

Office of Admissions
Eastern Illinois University
600 Lincoln Avenue
Charleston, Illinois 61920-3099
Telephone: 217-581-2223
800-252-5711 (toll-free)
Fax: 217-581-7060
E-mail: admissns@eiu.edu
Web site: http://www.eiu.edu

ACADEMIC PROGRAM

An early semester system means fall classes are completed by the middle of December and the spring semester ends in mid-May. A four-week intersession preceding five-week and eight-week concurrent sessions constitute the summer term. It is possible to obtain a full semester's credit in the summer term, allowing students to accelerate their degree completion. Credit toward a degree is awarded for acceptable scores on College-Level Examination Program (CLEP) general and subject tests and on the College Board's Advanced Placement examinations. Specific departments may offer proficiency examinations, and comprehensive departmental and University Honors Programs are available to students who demonstrate superior academic achievement. Candidates for the bachelor's degree must complete a minimum of 120 semester hours (dependent upon major requirements) with a cumulative grade point average of at least 2.0 (C) and a minimum 2.0 GPA in their major area. Higher cumulative grade point averages may be required in certain majors. Students must successfully complete at least 40 semester hours in upper division courses.

FINANCIAL AID

Scholarships, grants, loans, and part-time employment are available to those who need financial assistance. During the 1996–97 academic year, 8,838 Eastern students (76 percent) received financial assistance totaling $38,836,647 from state, federal, and University sources. The University participates in aid programs that use information from the Free Application for Federal Student Aid (FAFSA) to determine eligibility. Since the FAFSA must reflect current parental income as reported to the Internal Revenue Service, the form cannot be completed until after January 1 of the student's senior year in high school. Eastern also requires copies of tax returns for its files. Student employment is available campuswide. Talent awards may be acquired in women's and men's athletics, art, journalism, music, speech, and theater. Academic scholarships, which do not require proof of need, are also available.

EASTERN MENNONITE UNIVERSITY

■ Harrisonburg, Virginia

THE UNIVERSITY

Eastern Mennonite, a private Christian university founded in 1917, provides a high-quality liberal arts education that emphasizes spiritual growth and cross-cultural awareness. The nurturing environment of EMU's student-oriented campus not only prepares students for a wide variety of careers but also challenges students to answer Christ's call to a life of nonviolence, witness, service, and peacebuilding. The undergraduate experience is enriched by the recent addition of graduate programs in conflict transformation, counseling, and education. The University also has a seminary. EMU is accredited by the Southern Association of Colleges and Schools. In addition, the nursing, teacher education, and social work programs are accredited by their specialty organizations at the national level. Undergraduate students make up about 1,000 of the 1,300 students on campus. Of the undergraduates, 60 percent are women and 8 percent are American multiethnic students. Five percent come from international settings. Students represent thirty-seven states and twenty-two other countries. Most students are traditional college age. Religious backgrounds vary widely, with 60 percent representing Mennonites.

Inquiries and application materials should be sent to:

Ellen B. Miller
Director of Admissions
Eastern Mennonite University
Harrisonburg, Virginia 22802
Telephone: 800-368-2665 (toll-free)
Fax: 540-432-4444
E-mail: admiss@emu.edu
World Wide Web:
http://www.emu.edu

ACADEMIC PROGRAM

The academic calendar consists of two 15-week semesters from late August to late April. The baccalaureate degree requires 128 semester hours. All students complete a major, the Global Village general education curriculum, and electives. The Global Village curriculum is a sequence of courses consisting of 49 semester hours distributed as follows: faith (11), humanities (9), cross-cultural studies (9), math/natural science (9), social science (3), writing (3), speech (2), physical education (2), and the first-year experience (1). Associate degrees require 64 semester hours of general education requirements, a concentration in a major, and electives. Thirty semester hours are needed to complete a certificate.

FINANCIAL AID

More than 90 percent of EMU students receive financial aid. Scholarships include those given for academic achievement and an award of $1000 given to new first-year students who are children of alumni. Other grant aid, given to meet financial need, includes federal aid, endowed scholarships, foundation grants, and aid from the operating budget. Admission is need-blind. In addition, students with financial need may obtain federal loans or participate in the work-study program. Virginia residents receive the Virginia Tuition Assistance Grant, regardless of need, which amounts to $2500 or more annually. If students receive grants from their churches, EMU matches up to $500 per year. No application is needed for academic scholarships except for honors awards. Students applying for need-based aid must complete the Free Application for Federal Student Aid (FAFSA). Applications should be completed by February 15.

APPLICATION AND INFORMATION

The freshman application priority filing date is March 1. The final filing date is August 1. The application deadline for transfer applicants is thirty days prior to the start of the term for both fall and spring. Notification of admission is sent on a rolling basis.

ELMIRA COLLEGE

■ ELMIRA, NEW YORK

For further information, applicants should contact:
Dean of Admissions
Elmira College
Elmira, New York 14901
Telephone: 800-935-6472 (toll-free)

THE COLLEGE

Elmira College is a small, independent college that is recognized for its emphasis on education of high quality in the liberal arts and preprofessional preparation. One of the oldest colleges in the United States, Elmira was founded in 1855. The College has always produced graduates interested in both community service and successful careers. Friendliness, personal attention, strong college spirit, and support for learning beyond the classroom help to make Elmira a special place. Elmira College is one of only 250 colleges in the nation to be granted a chapter of the prestigious Phi Beta Kappa honor society. The full-time undergraduate enrollment is about 1,150 men and women. The students at Elmira represent more than twenty-seven states, primarily those in the Northeast, with the highest representation coming from New York, New Jersey, Massachusetts, Connecticut, and Pennsylvania. International students from twenty-three countries were enrolled in September 1997. Ninety-five percent of the full-time undergraduates live in College residence halls. The intercollegiate sports program includes men's and women's basketball, soccer, and tennis; men's golf, ice hockey, and lacrosse; and women's softball and volleyball. Club sports include women's field hockey and women's lacrosse. An intramural program is also available. The newly renovated Emerson Hall houses the student fitness center, a pool, and a gym capable of seating 1000, as well as the Gibson Theatre, which has a state-of-the-art sound and lighting system. Professional societies; clubs; music, dance, and drama groups; a student-operated FM radio station; and the student newspaper, yearbook, and literary magazine also provide numerous opportunities for extracurricular activity.

ACADEMIC PROGRAM

The College's calendar is composed of two 12-week terms followed by a 6-week spring term. Students enroll for four subjects during the 12-week terms, completing the first term by mid-December and the second during the first week of April. The 6-week term, from mid-April through May, may be devoted to a particular project involving travel, internship, research, or independent study. Students are required to participate in internships in order to gain practical and meaningful experience related to their program of study. Credit is awarded for these projects. Special opportunities for outstanding students include participation in eight national honorary societies on campus and a chance to assist faculty members in teaching and research. The College also offers an accelerated three-year graduation option for outstanding students. Army and Air Force ROTC are available.

FINANCIAL AID

Financial aid is available for both freshmen and transfer students. Awards are based upon the Free Application for Federal Student Aid (FAFSA) and Financial Aid PROFILE as well as the student's academic potential. Types of aid include grants, scholarships, federal loans, Elmira College loans, and work opportunities. In addition, superior students may qualify for no-need Elmira College Honors Scholarships. For 1997–98, the average freshman aid package (including all types of aid) amounted to more than $16,000. Transfer students applying for financial aid must submit a financial aid transcript from all colleges previously attended, whether or not they received financial aid. About 80 percent of the full-time undergraduates receive financial aid.

EMBRY–RIDDLE AERONAUTICAL UNIVERSITY

■ DAYTONA BEACH, FLORIDA

THE UNIVERSITY

The purpose of Embry-Riddle Aeronautical University is to provide a comprehensive education of such excellence that graduates are responsible citizens and well prepared for productive careers in aviation and aerospace. In addition to its traditional residential campus in Daytona Beach, Florida, Embry-Riddle serves the continuing education needs of the aviation industry through an extensive network of off-campus centers in the United States and Europe and through its division of continuing education's training seminars and management development programs. The total University enrollment (full-time and part-time) is more than 12,000. Approximately 4,500 undergraduate students are currently enrolled at the residential campus, and more than 6,000 students are enrolled in graduate programs University-wide. Students come from all fifty states and more than eighty countries, which makes Embry-Riddle truly an international university. Embry-Riddle provides cocurricular activities that appeal to almost every taste. Students take advantage of the many opportunities for personal growth and development through social and preprofessional fraternities and sororities and cultural and recreational activities. Embry-Riddle's award-winning Precision Flight Demonstration teams offer students the opportunity to compete nationally in air and ground events. Embry-Riddle also has the largest all-volunteer Air Force ROTC detachment in the country and the fastest-growing Army ROTC detachment. Embry-Riddle's Naval Aviation Club furnishes the U.S. Navy with the second-largest number of naval aviation officers, following the U.S. Naval Academy. Embry-Riddle athletes participate in intercollegiate and intramural competitions in many sports, including baseball, basketball, golf, lacrosse, rugby, soccer, tennis, volleyball, and wrestling.

For further information, interested students should contact:

Director of Admissions
Embry-Riddle Aeronautical University
P.O. Box 11767
Daytona Beach, Florida 32120-1767
Telephone: 904-226-6100
800-862-2416 (toll-free nationwide)

ACADEMIC PROGRAM

Even a field as specialized as aviation requires a broad background. General education courses required of all students who are pursuing a baccalaureate program include communication skills, such as English composition, literature, and technical report writing; humanities; social sciences; mathematics; physical science; economics; and computer science. To ensure academic success, Embry-Riddle provides free tutorial services. The calendar year is divided into three semesters of fifteen weeks each, with the summer session divided into two terms. The average course load for each fall or spring semester is 15 credit hours. By attending all three semesters a year, students can complete some bachelor's degree programs in less than four years.

FINANCIAL AID

Applicants for financial aid are required to complete the Department of Education's Free Application for Federal Student Aid (FAFSA) and any other documents requested by the University. Students are encouraged to apply early if they wish to be considered for all types of programs. Florida residents may also apply for several additional programs available through the state.

APPLICATION AND INFORMATION

Embry-Riddle requires each applicant to submit an application form and fee, SAT I or ACT scores, and an official high school/college transcript. Flight students must provide an FAA Class I or Class II medical certificate. When a student is accepted for admission, a tuition deposit is required. A housing deposit is also due at this time for University-managed housing.

EMERSON COLLEGE

■ Boston, Massachusetts

THE COLLEGE

Emerson College is the nation's only four-year college devoted exclusively to the study of communication and performing arts. As an independent, privately supported coeducational college, Emerson engages students as active participants in learning by providing unique opportunities to explore their fields of interest. On a daily basis, theory and experience are linked in the classroom and in applied learning settings such as television and radio studios, stages and performance spaces, digital production labs, editing booths, writing workshops, and observation areas in the Robbins Speech, Learning and Hearing Center—just some of the options on campus. Strong student-faculty interpersonal communication also creates avenues for students to explore career interests. An internship program, with 1,500 positions in Boston, Los Angeles, and other locations across the country and in Europe, is integrated with the academic course work, which enables students to gain professional experience and develop skills in a hands-on environment.

For application information, prospective students should contact:

Director of Admission
Emerson College
100 Beacon Street
Boston, Massachusetts 02116-1596
Telephone: 617-824-8600
Fax: 617-824-8609
E-mail: admission@emerson.edu
international@emerson.edu (international students)
transfer@emerson.edu (transfer students)
World Wide Web:
http://www.emerson.edu/admiss/

ACADEMIC PROGRAM

Emerson College operates on a calendar of two 15-week semesters, plus two 6-week summer sessions. The requirements for graduation combine a liberal arts curriculum with various communications core curricula specific to individual departments. Within the Institute for Liberal Arts and Interdisciplinary Studies, freshman seminars and innovative courses supplement communication specializations. A four-year honors program challenges students through interdisciplinary seminars and independent study. Students are also given the flexibility to design a program of study according to their individual interests.

FINANCIAL AID

All financial aid applicants are required to apply for the Federal Pell Grant, local state scholarships, and various other sources of funding. Students applying for September admission who wish to apply for financial aid should submit all appropriate forms to the College Scholarship Service six weeks prior to the Emerson College financial aid deadline of March 1. Students who seek January admission should submit these forms to the College Scholarship Service six weeks prior to the Emerson College deadline of December 1. All accepted first-year applicants are considered for merit-based aid in recognition of their academic and personal achievements. Students who plan to apply for financial aid should contact the Financial Assistance Office at Emerson College (telephone: 617-824-8600) for complete information.

APPLICATION AND INFORMATION

To apply, an applicant must submit an application and fee, an official high school transcript, results of the SAT I or ACT, two letters of recommendation, and an essay. Emerson also welcomes transfer students, who must submit official college transcripts in addition to the above materials, and international students, who must submit results of the Test of English as a Foreign Language (TOEFL). Acting, musical theater, and dance applicants are required to audition/interview. For the fall semester, Emerson offers first-year applicants both an Early Action Plan (application deadline November 15) and Regular Admission (priority deadline February 1). The priority deadline for transfer applicants and international applicants is March 1. For the spring semester, the priority deadline is November 1 for first-year, transfer, and international applicants.

EMORY & HENRY COLLEGE

■ EMORY, VIRGINIA

THE COLLEGE

Since its founding in 1836, Emory & Henry College has instilled a strong sense of values in students and prepared them for lifelong learning and success. Among the College's alumni have been congressmen, businesspeople, scientists, teachers, artists, ministers, authors, and many public servants. The College's 900 students (almost equally divided between men and women) constitute a diverse group, coming from rural areas of southwestern Virginia as well as from urban centers nationwide. They represent more than twenty states and several countries. The College was named in honor of Bishop John Emory, an outstanding United Methodist churchman, and Patrick Henry, a Revolutionary War patriot from Virginia. The King Health and Physical Education Center enhances the College athletics program. Varsity sports for men are baseball, basketball, football, golf, soccer, and tennis; women compete in basketball, cross-country, tennis, and volleyball. Students have opportunities for involvement in a variety of campus activities: Christian fellowship, fraternities, sororities, sports clubs, honor groups, multicultural groups, and service clubs.

Application forms and other information may be obtained by contacting:

Office of Admissions and
Financial Aid
Emory & Henry College
P.O. Box 947
Emory, Virginia 24327-0947
Telephone: 540-944-6133
800-848-5493 (toll-free)
Fax: 540-944-6935
E-mail: ehadmiss@ehc.edu
Web site: http://www.ehc.edu

ACADEMIC PROGRAM

Emory & Henry offers a liberal arts program with emphasis on writing, reasoning, value inquiry, and knowledge of global concerns, as well as a broad introduction to liberal arts subjects. All students complete a core curriculum, which includes a yearlong, interdisciplinary Western Tradition course and a writing course for all first-year students. Along with the core curriculum, each student completes a major and a minor or a combined program referred to as an area of concentration. Students also have the opportunity to choose elective courses and to participate in international exchange programs.

FINANCIAL AID

Forms of aid include need-based and non-need-based scholarships, loans, and part-time jobs. A Bonner Scholars program provides substantial scholarships for selected students who do volunteer work in the surrounding region. Virginia residents are eligible for a special grant based on residence. Merit scholarships are awarded based on academic performance, and many can be renewed based on continued academic success. Ninety-five percent of fall 1997 undergraduates received financial aid. The average aided first-year student received an aid package worth $12,624, meeting 80 percent of need. The priority application deadline for financial aid is April 1 and the deadline is August 1.

APPLICATION AND INFORMATION

To apply for admission, students should submit the basic application form, an essay, a copy of the high school transcript, scores from either the SAT I or the ACT, and a nonrefundable $25 fee. Transfer applicants must submit a transcript from any college previously attended and a statement of good standing. A rolling admission policy allows notification of the admission decision within two weeks after a file has been completed. To be considered for Early Decision, a student should submit the completed Application for Admission, including the Early Decision Agreement; the secondary school transcript; and a report of either SAT I or ACT test scores by December 1. The College agrees to notify candidates of their admission by December 20. The $200 enrollment deposit deadline for Early Decision is January 20. Under Early Decision, students will either be admitted or deferred to regular admission, for which they will receive full and unbiased consideration.

FAIRMONT STATE COLLEGE

■ FAIRMONT, WEST VIRGINIA

THE COLLEGE

Fairmont State College (FSC) is the largest state-supported four-year college in West Virginia, with an enrollment of 6,627 students. Founded in 1867, the College is located in the north-central portion of the state in the city of Fairmont, West Virginia. In addition to the main campus, which includes thirteen major buildings, classes are also offered at the FSC Robert C. Byrd National Aerospace Education Center in Bridgeport, as well as in Clarksburg, where a new 36,000-square-foot state-of-the-art facility is now under construction. Named for the state's former governor, the Gaston Caperton Center of Fairmont State College is expected to be ready for students in fall 1999. The College also has satellite facilities reaching across the north-central region of West Virginia. Students who live on campus are housed in one of three residence halls and take their meals at a centrally located dining hall or at the food court in the student center. For those students who prefer to live off campus, private accommodations close to the College are available. Parents who are taking classes at the College may find it convenient to enroll their young children in the day-care center located on the main campus. The Newman Center and the Wesley Foundation are available to minister to the spiritual needs of students; both organizations are adjacent to the FSC campus. There are also various student organizations, honor societies, and social fraternities and sororities to enhance extracurricular life at the College.

For more information or to schedule a tour, students should contact:

Office of Student Affairs
Fairmont State College
1201 Locust Avenue
Fairmont, West Virginia 26554
Telephone: 304-367-4216
800-641-5678 (toll-free)
304-367-4141 (admissions and records)
304-367-4213 (financial aid)
304-367-4216 (housing)
304-367-4000 (campus operator)
304-623-5721 (Clarksburg Center)
304-842-8300 (Aviation Center)

ACADEMIC PROGRAM

Fairmont State College offers 127 program areas in the following divisions: business and economics; education/health, physical education, recreation, and safety; fine arts; health careers; language and literature; science and mathematics; social science; and technology and family and consumer sciences. Special degrees such as the Regents Bachelor of Arts degree offer nontraditional approaches for individual career or personal requirements. Certificate programs are designed to provide basic skills or increased proficiency in specific occupational areas. Preprofessional studies are designed to prepare students for a wide variety of professional programs beyond a four-year degree. The first steps toward a Caribbean classroom were taken by the College in 1994, when 2.2 acres of oceanfront land in Costa Rica were donated by a local physician. The College plans to develop a Costa Rican field station for tropical studies in the areas of natural sciences, social sciences, and educational-recreational programs.

FINANCIAL AID

About 53 percent of Fairmont State College students receive some form of financial aid. Guidelines and forms for West Virginia and out-of-state residents are available from high school guidance counselors or FSC's Financial Aid Office.

APPLICATION AND INFORMATION

Campus tours are available Monday through Friday by appointment. Fairmont State College also sponsors a Saturday Campus Visitation Day once each fall and spring semester.

FERRIS STATE UNIVERSITY

■ **Big Rapids, Michigan**

THE UNIVERSITY

Admission applications may be obtained from high school or college counselors or by contacting:
Admissions Office
Ferris State University
420 Oak Street, PRK 101
Big Rapids, Michigan 49307-2020
Telephone: 616-592-2100
800-4FERRIS (toll-free)
E-mail: admissions@ferris.edu

Ferris State University is Michigan's foremost professional and technical university, providing career-oriented education to nearly 10,000 students. Accredited by the North Central Association of Colleges and Schools, the University offers nearly 100 programs through the Colleges of Allied Health Sciences, Arts and Sciences, Business, Education, Pharmacy, Technology, University College, and the Michigan College of Optometry. These offerings lead to bachelor's and associate degrees and certificates, master's degrees in accountancy, computer information systems management, and career and technical education, and doctorates in optometry and pharmacy. One of Michigan's fifteen public universities, Ferris State University is recognized for its career-oriented educational programs that are designed to meet the technology and workforce demands of business and industry, the health-care professions, and society in general through applied research and practical education. Ferris was founded in 1884 by Woodbridge N. Ferris (1853–1928), a distinguished Michigan educator and politician who served two terms as the state's governor and was elected to the United States Senate. Ferris was a private institution until 1950 when it joined the state higher education system. The college obtained university status in 1987.

ACADEMIC PROGRAM

Ferris is dedicated to the ideal of blending career-oriented professional training with a solid base of general education. While major programs of study provide graduates with the skills and knowledge required to enter a chosen career, general education provides graduates with the academic skills, analytic flexibility, and broad base of knowledge required for continued learning, performance, and advancement in their personal and professional lives. Ferris currently is on the semester system, and the minimum requirement for a baccalaureate degree is 120 semester hours. The average program requires between 120 and 130 semester hours. The minimum number of hours required for an associate degree is 60. The University's academic year begins in August and ends in early May.

FINANCIAL AID

Approximately 70 percent of Ferris students receive some type of financial aid through federal, state, and University programs. In 1997–98, student financial aid included more than $40 million in scholarships, grants, loans, work-study, or a combination of these. The Free Application for Federal Student Aid (FAFSA) must be submitted by April 1 to receive priority consideration for need-based financial aid. The University also provides merit-based scholarships in recognition of superior academic performance and residence-based scholarships for students living on campus who maintain high academic grades. The Woodbridge N. Ferris Scholarship Program offers competitive awards ranging from $500 to $6000 per year to those who qualify. The Residential Life Scholarship offers $2000 per year for entering students who live in a residence hall on campus, have a 3.2 or better high school GPA, and have a minimum score of 21 on the ACT. Information and counseling are available from the office of scholarships and financial aid (telephone: 616-592-2110 or 800-940-4-AID, toll-free).

FISK UNIVERSITY

■ Nashville, Tennessee

THE UNIVERSITY

For further information, students should contact:

Director of Admissions
Fisk University
Nashville, Tennessee 37208-3051
Telephone: 615-329-8665

Money magazine recently listed Fisk University as the nineteenth-best bargain for the dollar among 1,011 public and private colleges and universities in America. Founded in 1866, the University is coeducational, private, and one of America's older historically black universities. It serves a national student body, with an enrollment of 760 students for academic year 1997–98. There are two residence halls for men and three for women. The focal point of the 40-acre campus and architectural symbol of the University is Jubilee Hall, the first permanent building for education of blacks in the South. The Victorian-Gothic structure is named for the internationally renowned Fisk Jubilee Singers, who continue their tradition of singing the Negro spiritual. The original Jubilee Singers toured this country and abroad in 1871. Their selflessness is the saga of Fisk. From its earliest days, Fisk has played a leadership role in the education of African Americans. Faculty and alumni have been among America's intellectual, artistic, and civic leaders. Among them are W. E. B. DuBois, the great social critic and cofounder of the NAACP, and the distinguished artist of the Harlem Renaissance, Aaron Douglas, who taught at Fisk. In proportion to its size, Fisk continues to contribute more alumni to the ranks of scholars pursuing doctoral degrees than any other institution in the United States. In addition to the undergraduate degrees listed below, Fisk offers the Master of Arts in biology, chemistry, physics, psychology (general or clinical), social gerontology, and sociology. Fisk also offers a master's degree in business administration in cooperation with Owen School of Management at Vanderbilt University, as well as an early admission program with Meharry Medical College. The mission of the University is to prepare students to be skilled, resourceful, and imaginative leaders who will address effectively the challenges of life in a technological society, a pluralistic nation, and a multicultural world.

ACADEMIC PROGRAM

The academic year comprises two semesters. All undergraduates are required to complete the core curriculum, which provides a common intellectual background for all students. Its purposes include developing a level of skill in written and oral communication and in quantitative thinking that is appropriate to support a lifelong program of study in the liberal arts. Requirements for graduation vary by program but are approximately 120 credit hours. Fisk is accredited by the Southern Association of Colleges and Schools.

FINANCIAL AID

Student financial aid is based on the principle that all qualified and motivated students who earnestly seek an education should be able to attend college, regardless of the economic status of the student's family. Aid is awarded on an individual basis, and the amount to be offered is determined by an examination of the family's financial position. Assistance is offered to the student from grants, loans, or work, or from a combination of funds. Eligibility requirements vary depending on the financial aid source. Applicants are urged to complete financial aid forms by April 20 to receive consideration while funds are available.

APPLICATION AND INFORMATION

Applications are processed on a rolling basis; that is, the application is acted upon when the file is complete. For an early decision, applications should be filed prior to November 15; students are notified by January 17. Early decision applicants must then notify the University of their decision by January 30.

FITCHBURG STATE COLLEGE

■ Fitchburg, Massachusetts

THE COLLEGE

For further information, students should contact:

Director of Admissions
Fitchburg State College
Fitchburg, Massachusetts 01420
Telephone: 508-665-3144
800-705-9692 (toll-free)
Fax: 508-665-4540
E-mail: admissions@fsc.edu

Fitchburg State College, the Leadership College, is a liberal arts institution where career-oriented and professional education programs thrive. Under the leadership of its new president, Dr. Michael Riccards, Fitchburg State has undertaken a number of major initiatives. The College now offers a three-year baccalaureate program, more internship opportunities, a substantially increased Merit Scholarship program, and a guarantee that its graduates will be qualified for jobs in their fields. The College is investing in new technologies in every curriculum to assure that Fitchburg State continues to place more than 85 percent of its graduates in their chosen professions. Fitchburg State's excellent academic reputation and graduate placement can be attributed to a nationally recognized faculty and a commitment to teaching that is unparalleled in Massachusetts. The College serves 3,000 students in its day division and another 4,000 students in its evening and graduate programs. The average class size is 25, and the overall student-teacher ratio remains low at 15:1. Each student is assigned to an academic adviser to assist with the planning of a program of study. In addition, each department has access to state-of-the-art equipment and an internship network that spreads throughout New England. Student life at Fitchburg State is friendly and informal. There are numerous and varied opportunities for student leadership through the Student Government Association, the Athletic Council, the All-College Committee, the Campus Center Advisory Committee, the Residence Hall Councils, publications, and student-faculty-administration committees. Three student publications offer creative opportunities—the *Strobe,* a weekly newspaper; the *Scrimshaw,* a literary magazine; and the *Saxifrage,* the College yearbook. A number of special interest clubs are open to all students. Several sororities and fraternities contribute to the social and recreational life of the campus. Hundreds of popular and well-attended activities take place during the year, including films, lectures, concerts, seminars, coffeehouses, pub entertainment, recreational tournaments, performing arts series, and visual arts exhibits.

ACADEMIC PROGRAM

The curriculum has a strong liberal arts and sciences requirement, providing a strong foundation for either further academic study or a career. Students may obtain practical experience through volunteer placement in social agencies, government offices, and businesses related to their interests. Some major programs require an extensive supervised practicum to complete degree requirements. For education majors, a broad spectrum of student-teaching experiences is available. The four-year honors program, for students with excellent high school records, culminates in a senior thesis or project.

FINANCIAL AID

Many sources of financial aid are available to Fitchburg State students. The College participates in federal and state programs, including the Federal Direct Student Loan Program. Packages consisting of grants, loans, work-study awards, and scholarships are given to students demonstrating financial need. Financial aid applications for the fall semester must be completed by the preceding March 15 to be given priority consideration.

APPLICATION AND INFORMATION

Acceptance of qualified applicants begins in January and proceeds on a rolling basis until all available spaces are taken. Students should apply by April 1 for the fall semester and by December 1 for the spring semester.

FIVE TOWNS COLLEGE

■ DIX HILLS, NEW YORK

THE COLLEGE

Founded in 1972 by a group of educators and community leaders who wished to provide students with an alternative to the large university atmosphere, Five Towns College is a nonsectarian, coeducational institution that places its emphasis on the student as an individual. Many students are drawn to Five Towns College because of its strong programs in music and music-related fields. As an institution of higher learning that offers two-year, four-year, and master's degree programs, the College is the only school on Long Island with the authority to offer the prestigious Bachelor of Music degree (Mus.B.). The College's music programs are contemporary in nature and therefore easily distinguished from classical-oriented programs.

For further information, students should contact:

Coordinator of Admissions
Five Towns College
305 North Service Road
Dix Hills, New York 11746-6055
Telephone: 516-424-7000 Ext. 110

ACADEMIC PROGRAM

The music education program is designed for students interested in a career as a teacher of music in a public or private school (K–12). The program leads to New York State certification and prepares students for both the National Teacher Education (NTE) Core Battery tests and the New York State Examination for Teacher Certification. The course work provides professional training and includes a student-teaching experience in a cooperating public school district under the supervision of the music education coordinator. Music majors are required to complete at least 40 credits with a minimum grade point average of 3.0 before admission to the music education program. The audio recording technology concentration is designed to provide students with the tools needed to succeed as professional engineers and producers in the recording industry. The music business concentration is designed for students interested in a career in music-related business fields such as the recorded music industry. The composition/songwriting concentration provides professional training for students who intend to pursue careers as composers, arrangers, and songwriters. The performance concentration is designed for students planning to pursue careers as professional performers. The video music concentration provides professional training in music scoring and compositional techniques and in the artistic and technical skills required for the creation of video music.

FINANCIAL AID

The annual tuition at Five Towns College is among the lowest of all the private colleges in the region. Approximately 65 percent of all students on campus receive some form of financial aid. Need-based federal, state, and institutional funds are available to qualified students and include grants, loans, and on-campus work-study arrangements. Merit-based scholarships, not based on financial need, are also available in all subject areas. Scholarships are available for transfer students.

APPLICATION AND INFORMATION

Students must apply to either the two-year associate degree programs or the four-year baccalaureate degree programs. While admission into any of the associate degree programs has been classified as minimally difficult, admission into the Bachelor of Music program is contingent upon passing an audition demonstrating skill in performance on a major instrument or vocally. Bachelor of Music degree applicants are also required to take written and aural examinations in harmony, sight-singing, and ear training in order to demonstrate talent, well-developed musicianship, and artistic sensibilities. An interview is required. Students are accepted on a rolling admission basis and are notified shortly after all required documents have been filed with the admissions office. New students may begin their studies at the start of either the fall semester or the spring semester. There is an application fee of $25.

FLORIDA INSTITUTE OF TECHNOLOGY

■ MELBOURNE, FLORIDA

THE INSTITUTE

For further information, students may contact:

Office of Admissions
Florida Institute of Technology
150 West University Boulevard
Melbourne, Florida 32901-6988
Telephone: 407-674-8030
800-888-4348 (toll-free)
E-mail: admissions@fit.edu

Florida Institute of Technology was founded in 1958 for the purpose of offering science and engineering courses to specialists working on the space program at Cape Canaveral. The primary aim of the university has been to keep abreast of current and anticipated needs in the developing fields of high technology. This philosophy is reflected in Florida Tech's response to the nation's growing need for qualified specialists trained in the fields of science and engineering. Other degree programs offered at Florida Tech (aviation, business administration, psychology, and business and technical communication) give the university a well-rounded approach to higher education. There are more than 4,200 graduate and undergraduate students currently enrolled at Florida Tech. On-campus housing is provided for all freshmen. Limited space is available for upperclass and graduate students. On- and off-campus fraternity housing is also available. Approximately 2,100 students at Florida Institute of Technology are pursuing undergraduate studies. Sixty-nine percent are men. The average class size is 30, and the average laboratory size is 15. Although Florida residents comprise a large portion of the population, there are students from every state, many from the Eastern Seaboard of the United States, and international students from more than ninety countries.

ACADEMIC PROGRAM

The university operates on a calendar of two semesters and three summer sessions. Programs in the pure sciences prepare the student for graduate or professional work. Practical aspects of computer science and engineering can be combined with management science for the business minded, and a wide variety of programs are available for the environmentalist. Baccalaureate programs are completely outlined for each discipline; opportunity for diversification is provided by the technical and humanities electives offered during the junior and senior years. Substitutions or specialized programs require the approval of the student's faculty adviser and the appropriate department heads. Science, engineering, and psychology students frequently participate in senior projects; communication seniors may choose an industrial internship. In the School of Aeronautics, the bachelor's programs provide a strong business or science background in the first two years and concentrate on specialized knowledge in the aviation industry during the final two years. Students can select from five accredited aviation bachelor's degrees, including aviation management, aeronautical science, and aviation computer science. The university offers a four-year Army ROTC program, and it rewards ROTC scholarship winners with free room and board. Prospective students should contact an ROTC representative at the university.

FINANCIAL AID

Awards are based on academic promise, need, college costs, and the availability of funds. Approximately 75 percent of the university's students receive grants, scholarships, loans, and employment, either in a single award or in various combinations. Several kinds of monthly installment plans are available for tuition and other expenses. The application deadline for financial aid is February 1 for incoming freshmen and March 15 for all other students. Inquiries should be sent to the director of financial aid. Students eligible for Veterans Administration benefits may contact the VA representative on the Melbourne campus.

APPLICATION AND INFORMATION

The university encourages applicants from every social, ethnic, racial, and religious background. Florida Tech practices a rolling admission policy. The application fee is $35. Completed applications, high school and college transcripts, and standardized test results should be sent to the office below.

FORDHAM UNIVERSITY

■ NEW YORK, NEW YORK

THE UNIVERSITY

With a long tradition of academic excellence in the liberal arts, Fordham University, New York City's Jesuit University, offers a distinctive combination of benefits. Fordham College at Rose Hill and the College of Business Administration, located on the Rose Hill campus, are adjacent to the New York Botanical Garden and the Bronx Zoological Park. The Rose Hill campus is a self-contained 85-acre campus with residence facilities for 2,424 students and ample parking facilities for commuters. It is easily accessible by public and private transportation as well as by an intercampus van and is only minutes away from Manhattan. Fordham College at Lincoln Center is located at Fordham's urban-style campus in midtown Manhattan, overlooking the famous Lincoln Center for the Performing Arts complex. The Lincoln Center campus has a new 850-bed apartment-style residence hall for its students.

Additional details and application forms are available by contacting:

Dean of Admission
Office of Admission
Dealy Hall, Room 115
Fordham University
East Fordham Road
New York, New York 10458
Telephone: 718-817-4000
800-FORDHAM (toll-free)

ACADEMIC PROGRAM

Students in Fordham College at Rose Hill and Fordham College at Lincoln Center pursue a common core curriculum that includes the study of philosophy, literature, history, theology, and English composition. Beyond these areas, students choose additional course work in the life and physical sciences, modern or classical languages, mathematics, social sciences, and fine arts. Finally, they explore the application of the theory studied in the prerequisite courses by means of enrichment offerings designed to provide ethical, religious, literary, and social awareness. Ordinarily, the students begin their major in the sophomore year. Enrichment, major, and free-elective courses generally carry 4 credits. The College of Business Administration offers a core curriculum in a structure parallel to that of the liberal arts colleges: economics, English, fine arts, mathematics, philosophy, social and behavioral sciences, statistics, and theology, as well as business-related course work.

FINANCIAL AID

More than 85 percent of the entering students enroll with aid from Fordham and outside sources. Among the major aid programs are Federal Pell Grants, Federal Supplemental Educational Opportunity Grants, Federal Perkins Loans, work grants sponsored by both the government and the University, and University grants-in-aid. Outside sources of aid include state scholarships (more than 20,000 are awarded to students entering colleges in New York State each year), the New York State Tuition Assistance Program (TAP), privately sponsored scholarships, state government loan programs, and deferred-payment programs. The University also offers academic scholarships ranging from $7500 to the full cost of tuition and room. Applicants for aid must submit the Free Application for Federal Student Aid (FAFSA) and the College Scholarship Service PROFILE. Inquiries should be directed to the Fordham Office of Admission.

APPLICATION AND INFORMATION

Application may be made for either September or January enrollment. The application deadline is February 1 for fall admission. The completed application, the secondary school report, the results of the SAT I or ACT, all financial aid forms, and an application fee of $50 (check or money order made payable to Fordham University) should be submitted by this date. Students are notified beginning March 1. Candidates for early decision should apply by November 1 and receive notification by December 15. Transfer students must apply by December 1 for spring admission or by July 1 for fall admission.

GARDNER–WEBB UNIVERSITY

■ BOILING SPRINGS, NORTH CAROLINA

THE UNIVERSITY

For further information, students should contact:

Director of Admissions
Gardner-Webb University
Boiling Springs, North Carolina 28017
Telephone: 704-434-4GWU
800-253-6472 (toll-free)
Web site: http://www.gardner-webb.edu

Gardner-Webb University was founded in 1905 as a private high school by a group of Baptist associations. It became a junior college in 1928, was renamed Gardner-Webb College in 1942 in honor of former governor O. Max Gardner, and became a fully accredited senior college in 1971. Gardner-Webb moved to University status in 1993. The most outstanding characteristics of the University are its warmth, friendliness, and proven record of academic distinction. Its origins are obviously deep in Christian tradition, which is exemplified in the lives of staff and faculty members. Because the University is small, students can be well known by a large percentage of the faculty and administration. The cosmopolitan student body (more than 3,040 men and women, of whom nearly 2,600 are undergraduates) represents twenty-eight states and twenty-one other countries and gives an added, valuable dimension to a student's educational experience. About 70 percent of the students live on campus. Cars are permitted for all.

ACADEMIC PROGRAM

The total program is marked by flexibility for the student but encourages, through active faculty advisement, choosing a substantial course of study. Elements of the humanities, the social and physical sciences, and mathematics or related disciplines must be taken. A typical bachelor's degree program requires 128 semester hours for graduation: 40 to 52 in the core (humanities and social and physical sciences), 30 in the major, 42 to 58 in supporting subjects, and 12 to 28 in complementary or free electives. Requirements for science curricula vary somewhat. The associate degree requires the completion of 64 semester hours. A cumulative average of C (2.0 on a 4.0 scale) or better is required for graduation.

FINANCIAL AID

Gardner-Webb University makes available to its students a variety of scholarships, loans, grants-in-aid, and work-study awards. Prospective applicants with financial need should contact the financial aid director early in their senior year of high school for a financial need estimate. Applications received after April 1 can be considered only in terms of available funds. An applicant must be accepted for admission before being awarded aid. Students must file the Free Application for Federal Student Aid (FAFSA). Scholarships and other types of aid include academic awards, Christian service awards, endowed scholarships, and annual scholarships. There are several Gardner-Webb loan funds. The University also administers aid from the full range of federal programs: Federal Pell Grants, Federal Work-Study Program awards, Federal Perkins Loans, and federally guaranteed Federal Stafford Student and Federal PLUS loans. North Carolina students have access to state grant funds administered by the University. Scholarships based on academic promise are also granted each year. Of all students, 80 percent receive aid in some form. The two criteria for receiving financial aid are financial need and academic promise.

APPLICATION AND INFORMATION

Applications, together with a nonrefundable $20 application fee, may be submitted for either semester. Early application is advised. Notification of the admission decision is given on a rolling basis upon receipt of all application data. A $150 room deposit for boarding students is due thirty days after acceptance and is refundable until May 1. A $50 deposit is required of commuting students.

GEORGE FOX UNIVERSITY

■ Newberg, Oregon

For additional information, students should contact:

Office of Admissions
George Fox University
Newberg, Oregon 97132-2697
Telephone: 800-765-4369 Ext. 2240 (toll-free)
E-mail: admissions@georgefox.edu

THE UNIVERSITY

George Fox University was founded 108 years ago by the Society of Friends (Quakers) with the purpose of providing students a challenging academic atmosphere and a commitment to Christian faith. From a modest beginning of 15 students in 1891, George Fox has grown to an enrollment of 2,245 students from thirteen countries. Students find George Fox to be a place where the integration of spiritual and intellectual challenge takes place in a friendly, caring environment. This tradition of integration has been recognized by the Templeton Foundation by naming George Fox University to the honor roll of character-building colleges. National recognition for academic reputation has also been given by *U.S. News & World Report.* Seventy-five percent of George Fox students live in campus residence halls, suites, and apartments. Opportunities for extracurricular involvement are available in music, drama, journalism, student government, radio, clubs, and athletics. George Fox is a member of the NAIA (but is moving to NCAA Division III) and competes in six men's sports (baseball, basketball, cross-country, soccer, tennis, and track) and seven women's sports (basketball, cross-country, soccer, softball, tennis, track, and volleyball). A number of intramural sports are also available. Regular chapel services bring the campus community together in worship. Students have the opportunity to put their faith into action on volunteer mission trips and during community outreach activities. In addition to its undergraduate degrees, George Fox confers the Master of Business Administration, Master of Education, Master of Arts in Teaching, and Doctor of Psychology degrees, and seven master's degrees through Western Evangelical Seminary, a graduate school of George Fox University.

ACADEMIC PROGRAM

The academic year at George Fox University is divided into two semesters of fifteen weeks. In addition to the two semesters, the University sponsors a three-week May Term. For graduation, students are required to earn 126 credit hours, including 54 general education and 42 upper-division credits. Students may reduce the number of required courses and add flexibility to their undergraduate years with credit earned through Advanced Placement, the College-Level Examination Program, and credit by examination. An innovative program called "Computers Across the Curriculum" expands the computer literacy of students. The University issues every incoming freshman a computer for school and personal use. The computer becomes the property of the student upon graduation. To meet the needs of this program, the University has a full-service computer store, a campus network, and a CD-ROM computer center on campus. George Fox demonstrates its commitment to freshmen by providing a Freshman Seminar Program to assist students as they integrate themselves into the academic and social life of the University community.

FINANCIAL AID

George Fox maintains that every qualified student should be able to attend the university of his or her choice without letting limited finances stand in the way. To this end, federal, state, and institutional need-based funds are available, as are merit awards in academics, music, and drama. About 87 percent of all students receive financial aid.

GLENVILLE STATE COLLEGE

■ Glenville, West Virginia

THE COLLEGE

Glenville State College was founded in 1872 and is a part of the state college system of West Virginia. Enrollment generally falls within a range of 2,200 to 2,500 students, with slightly more women than men. The College is nestled deep within the colorful Appalachian hills. Surrounded by towering trees and rich foliage, the campus overlooks the rural town of Glenville. Glenville is a community where students and residents come together along the shaded banks of the Little Kanawha River to create an informal, friendly atmosphere that leaves a lasting impression. Although most students are from West Virginia, many out-of-state students are increasingly attracted to this tranquil, rural setting conducive to academic study. Glenville State offers a number of strong athletic programs (football, basketball, track, golf, and volleyball) for men and women and participates in the WVIAC, which is nationally acknowledged as one of the most respected conferences in the nation.

For an application form and additional information, students should contact:

Office of Records and Enrollment Management
Glenville State College
Glenville, West Virginia 26351
Telephone: 304-462-7361
Fax: 304-462-8619
E-mail: boggs@glenville.wvnet.edu
World Wide Web: http://www.glenville.wvnet.edu

ACADEMIC PROGRAM

In accordance with the stated objectives of Glenville State College, candidates for all baccalaureate degrees must complete a program of general studies. The common program for all degrees covers the areas of the humanities, science and mathematics, the social sciences, and physical education. The traditional grading system is used at Glenville, with an optional credit/no-credit system for electives in the upper division. The College operates on the two-semester system and also has two summer terms of 4[AF]1#/2[AF] weeks' duration. The unit of credit is the semester hour, which represents the equivalent of 1 hour of recitation a week during a semester of seventeen weeks. Laboratory courses require additional time.

FINANCIAL AID

Glenville State College provides financial assistance for qualified students in the form of scholarships, workships, and loans. Scholarships and workships are awarded on the basis of achievement and/or need. Usually they will not be given to a student whose high school average is below 3.0, and no student may receive or continue a workship if his or her overall grade point average is below 2.0. The College participates in the Federal Perkins Loan Program, the Federal Stafford Student Loan Program, and the Federal Pell Grant Program and offers funds from other sources. For further information, students should write to the director of financial aid at the College. The deadline for WV Grant applications as well as for other specific institutional funds is March 1.

APPLICATION AND INFORMATION

Candidates applying under the above guidelines must submit a completed application for admission, their ACT or SAT I scores, a copy of their high school transcript, and proof of measles and rubella vaccinations to the Office of Admissions. Transfer students must submit transcripts from all colleges attended. International students must submit a TOEFL score of at least 550. All correspondence concerning admissions and all credentials in support of an application must be on file at least thirty days prior to the opening of a semester. The College uses a rolling admissions procedure, and students are notified of the admission decision soon after their completed application has been received.

GOLDEN GATE UNIVERSITY

■ San Francisco, California

THE UNIVERSITY

Golden Gate University (GGU), whose origins in San Francisco trace to 1853, is a private, nonprofit institution of higher learning accredited by the Western Association of Schools and Colleges. The University has a combined day and evening enrollment of approximately 5,700 students and offers undergraduate and graduate degrees through the doctoral level. GGU students are mature and highly motivated, and many are employed full- or part-time. Many applicants seeking admission on the basis of their high school records have had several years of work or military experience since high school graduation. Approximately 58 percent of the undergraduate students are women.

Application forms and further information may be obtained from:

Enrollment Services
Golden Gate University
536 Mission Street
San Francisco, California 94105-2968
Telephone: 415-442-7800
800-448-4968 (toll-free)
Fax: 415-442-7807
E-mail: info@ggu.edu
Web site: http://www.ggu.edu

ACADEMIC PROGRAM

Golden Gate University is dedicated to the belief that personally and socially useful higher education requires a combination of professional and liberal studies and a balance of theoretical training and responsible participation in society. Class sizes are limited to ensure opportunities for student-faculty interaction and discussion, and class schedules are arranged to serve both full-time day students and those who wish to combine their academic studies with full- or part-time work. For this purpose, the University offers its undergraduate programs in both the day and the evening, enabling students to attend morning classes on a full-time basis and work in the afternoon or to work during the day and attend evening classes. Through the University's Cooperative Education and Internship Program, students may arrange to pursue their degree by alternating terms of full-time study and full-time work or by working part-time concurrently with their studies. The University's undergraduate curricula are sharply focused on various professional specializations within the general areas of management, public administration accounting, and computer information systems. GGU was one of the first colleges or universities in the nation to institute the trimester system, which enables students to make accelerated progress toward attainment of their educational goals. The completion of 123 units is required for a bachelor's degree. Midterm examinations are given in most courses, and final examinations are given in all courses. A student may take one course per term on a credit/no credit basis, provided that the course is not required and not in the major field of study.

FINANCIAL AID

Financial assistance is available for students who could not attend the University without it. Aid is provided through federal, state, and University loan, grant, and work-study programs. A number of scholarships are available for entering students. Students with Veterans Administration education benefits may use them at Golden Gate University.

APPLICATION AND INFORMATION

An undergraduate applicant seeking admission as a degree candidate must file an application with a nonrefundable application fee of $55 ($70 for international applicants) and submit official transcripts of all high school and previous college work. The University has a rolling admissions policy, but international students and all students applying for financial aid must apply by November 1 for spring admission, July 1 for fall admission, and March 1 for the summer.

GONZAGA UNIVERSITY

■ Spokane, Washington

THE UNIVERSITY

All requests for further information or materials should be addressed to:

Dean of Admission and Records
Gonzaga University
Spokane, Washington 99258-0102
Telephone: 800-322-2584 (toll-free)
E-mail: ballinger@gu.gonzaga.edu
Web site: http://www.gonzaga.edu

Gonzaga, founded in 1887, is an independent, comprehensive university with a distinguished background in the Catholic, Jesuit, and humanistic tradition. Gonzaga emphasizes the moral and ethical implications of learning, living, and working in today's global society. Through the University Core Curriculum, each student develops a strong liberal arts foundation, which many alumni cite as a most valuable asset. In addition, students specialize in any of more than fifty academic majors. Because personal growth is as important as intellectual development, Gonzaga places great emphasis on student life outside of class. Ten of the fourteen residence halls house only 25 to 35 students each, providing an intimate atmosphere. Each hall has a chaplain or a resident Jesuit. Since 85 percent of the freshmen and 50 percent of the total undergraduate student body live on campus, campus-based activities ranging from current affairs symposiums to intramural sports keep students informed and entertained. Students in all academic majors integrate with the Spokane community through a variety of activities, such as volunteer opportunities and internships at numerous businesses and agencies. Gonzaga provides both career and counseling centers.

ACADEMIC PROGRAM

Gonzaga University believes that it is necessary for all students, regardless of their chosen major or profession, to attain an education that goes beyond specialization. Therefore, all students attending Gonzaga receive a strong liberal arts background as well as depth in their major. The Core Curriculum is a very important component of the 128 semester units a student must earn for graduation. The Honors Program challenges special achievers with an integrated curriculum compatible with any major and most double majors. The program requires a separate application. Gonzaga also offers a Dual Enrollment Program that gives qualified Spokane-area high school seniors an opportunity to enroll in classes at the University. Credits earned through the Washington State Running Start Program or International Baccalaureate (I.B.) program are accepted on a class-by-class basis. College credit is given for certain test scores in most Advanced Placement (AP) subjects.

FINANCIAL AID

Gonzaga University offers many different types of financial aid to qualified students, including scholarships, Federal Pell Grants, Federal Supplemental Educational Opportunity Grants, work-study jobs, Federal Perkins Loans, Federal Stafford Student Loans, and on- and off-campus employment. In order to apply for financial aid awards, a student must first be accepted by the University and must see that the Free Application for Federal Student Aid (FAFSA) is submitted by February 1. After this date, awards are made on a funds-available basis. Approximately 90 percent of the students at Gonzaga receive some sort of financial assistance.

APPLICATION AND INFORMATION

Gonzaga University's priority deadline for admissions applications is March 1. The final deadline is April 1 for freshmen and July 1 for transfer students. The nonbinding early application deadline is November 15. A need analysis form provided by the Admission Office is required for early action. Applicants are notified of the admission decision within four weeks of receipt of a completed application (application form, transcripts, test scores, letters of recommendation, an essay, and a list of awards and activities). It is recommended that all students applying for financial aid for the fall semester submit their application materials by March 1.

GOUCHER COLLEGE

■ BALTIMORE, MARYLAND

Director of Admissions
Goucher College
1021 Dulaney Valley Road
Baltimore, Maryland 21204-2794
Telephone: 410-337-6100
800-GOUCHER (toll-free)

THE COLLEGE

Since its inception in 1885, Goucher College has maintained a reputation for academic excellence and a tradition of high quality combined with flexibility. The past few decades have seen many changes in academic programs, governance, and social regulations, during which time Goucher has held fast to its commitment to a superior liberal arts education designed to help students achieve their fullest potential. The 1,100 undergraduates enrolled come from all parts of the United States and several other countries; they represent diverse backgrounds, interests, and points of view. Goucher's fieldstone buildings on a 287-acre wooded campus provide an ideal setting. Residence on campus is generally required of all students who do not live at home, although each year 10 percent of the junior class and 15 percent of the senior class may receive permission to live off campus, on a first-come, first-served basis. The residence halls are an important part of the students' educational and social experience. The social center of campus is the Pearlstone Student Center (refurbished in 1997), which houses a cafe, lounge, bookstore, post office, commuter study area, student activities office, and game room. The cultural center is the 1,000-seat Kraushaar Auditorium. Lectures and performances at Kraushaar by leading actors, actresses, dancers, musicians, writers, and political and cultural figures attract audiences from the entire metropolitan area. Goucher confers a Bachelor of Arts degree; a postbaccalaureate, premedical certificate; and postbaccalaureate teaching certification. There is also a B.A./B.S. dual-degree program in science and engineering with Johns Hopkins University. Entrance to the Whiting School of Engineering at Johns Hopkins is guaranteed for students with a minimum 3.2 GPA in Goucher science classes. Goucher belongs to NCAA Division III.

ACADEMIC PROGRAM

The core curriculum is the foundation for a Goucher education. Recently revised, the core retains Goucher's tradition of academic rigor while becoming more relevant to a changing world. There is a strong emphasis on both interdisciplinary study and the development of a global perspective. Requirements include a demonstrated proficiency in a foreign language, English composition, and computer technology, along with courses in the arts, natural sciences, humanities, social sciences, and mathematics. The computer proficiency requirement gives students a basic familiarity with computers, their applications, and their languages—an increasingly important tool both in business and in academe. All freshmen take the semester-long Freshman Colloquium. Taught in small sections, the course integrates humanities and social sciences perspectives. The Goucher degree requires 120 semester hours of credit. The departmental major consists of at least 30 credits (about ten courses); the double major requires 60 credits. The 5-credit off-campus requirement reflects the College's belief in balancing classroom theory with real-world experience and may take the form of an internship, a period of study abroad, or an independent project.

FINANCIAL AID

In an average year, more than half of Goucher's students receive some form of aid; 45 percent are awarded grants, ranging from $400 to the total cost of the education. The average financial aid award is more than $11,000. Goucher participates in the Federal Work-Study Program and helps students benefit from Federal Supplemental Educational Opportunity Grants, Federal Pell Grants, Federal Perkins Loans, Federal Stafford Student Loans, and College loans. Goucher also offers a competitive merit award program.

GRACE COLLEGE

■ WINONA LAKE, INDIANA

THE COLLEGE

Catalogs, application forms, and additional information may be obtained from the address below.

Grace College
200 Seminary Drive
Winona Lake, Indiana 46590
Telephone: 800-54-GRACE (toll-free)
Web site: http://www.grace.edu

Grace College is a Christian undergraduate college of arts and sciences founded in 1948 and affiliated with the Fellowship of Grace Brethren Churches, a conservative evangelical denomination. Grace College attracts students from a variety of conservative evangelical backgrounds and from around the United States and several other countries. The College offers an environment and academic program that are conservative in theology and progressive in spirit and that emphasize three qualities for students as they reach adulthood—mature Christian character, academic and career competence, and a heart for service to mankind. Enrollment at Grace College is 725, providing an ideal atmosphere in which students can learn, grow, and develop lasting friendships. Grace College has a campus of 150 acres. Approximately 70 percent of the College's students live on campus. The majority of students range in age from 18 to 23 years. Slightly more than a third of the students come from Indiana; students also come from thirty-one other states and thirteen countries. Approximately one third of the students are affiliated with the Fellowship of Grace Brethren Churches; the other two thirds are from other conservative Christian denominations, particularly Baptist and independent church backgrounds.

ACADEMIC PROGRAM

The Christian liberal arts philosophy of Grace College pervades each program of study and reflects the College's recognition that a broad common core of course work is central to each student's education. When combined with detailed study in a major field, this core establishes the foundation for successful graduate study and for a career. The requirements for the bachelor's degree include the successful completion of one major (36–56 semester hours) and one minor (20–28 semester hours) area of concentration in addition to the specified program of general education courses. Students are required to complete a total of 124 semester hours of course work. Through the January session (Winterim) offered each year, students have an opportunity to take courses off campus as well as to take courses at Grace that are not generally offered during the regular school year.

FINANCIAL AID

The College offers extensive financial assistance to qualified students. Most students receive some sort of financial assistance—in the form of a scholarship, grant, loan, or campus employment—to help pay college costs. The average amount of financial aid awarded to a Grace College student totals $6500 per year. To be considered for financial assistance at Grace College, students must submit the Free Application for Federal Student Aid (FAFSA). Students may receive Federal Pell Grants, Federal Perkins Loans, and Federal Supplemental Educational Opportunity Grants. In addition, students may be eligible for Federal Work-Study Program awards. The FAFSA should be on file by March 1 for priority consideration. To renew financial aid, students must refile the FAFSA each year.

APPLICATION AND INFORMATION

Students may apply for admission to any semester. Applications are accepted on a rolling basis until January 1 for the spring term and August 1 for the fall term. There is a $20 nonrefundable application fee. Interested students and their parents are encouraged to visit the campus and to arrange for an interview at that time in order to get a clear picture of Grace College. Arrangements can be made for housing and meals for applicants by contacting the Grace Visitor Center.

GROVE CITY COLLEGE

■ GROVE CITY, PENNSYLVANIA

THE COLLEGE

The beautifully landscaped campus of Grove City College stretches over 150 acres and includes twenty-seven neo-Gothic buildings valued at more than $100 million. It is considered one of the loveliest in the nation. While the College has changed to meet the needs of the society it serves, its basic philosophy has remained unchanged since its founding in 1876. It is a Christian liberal arts and sciences institution of ideal size and dedicated to the principle of providing the highest-quality education at the lowest possible cost. Wishing to remain truly independent and to retain its distinctive qualities as a private school governed by private citizens (trustees), it is one of the very few colleges in the country that does not accept any state or federal monies. Affiliated with the Presbyterian Church (U.S.A.) but not narrowly denominational, the College believes that to be well educated a student should be exposed to the central ideas of the Judeo-Christian tradition. A 20-minute chapel program offered Tuesday and Thursday mornings, along with a Sunday evening worship service, challenge students in their faith. Religious organizations and activities exist to provide fellowship and spiritual growth.

Additional information may be obtained from:

Jeffrey C. Mincey
Director of Admissions
Grove City College
100 Campus Drive
Grove City, Pennsylvania 16127-2104
Telephone: 412-458-2100
Fax: 412-458-3395
E-mail: admissions@gcc.edu
Web site: http://www.gcc.edu

ACADEMIC PROGRAM

Grove City College's goal is to assist young men and women in developing as complete individuals—academically, spiritually, and physically. The general education requirements provide all students with a high level of cultural literacy and communication skills. They include 38–50 semester hours of courses with emphases in the humanities, social sciences, and natural sciences and in quantitative and logical reasoning, as well as a language requirement for nonengineering and science majors. Degree candidates must also complete the requirements in their field of concentration, physical education, electives, and convocation. To graduate, a student must have completed 128 semester hours (136 in engineering) plus 4 convocation credits. About 80 percent of those entering as freshmen stay and receive a diploma.

FINANCIAL AID

Because the College's tuition charges are low, every student, in effect, receives significant financial assistance. More than 30 percent of the freshmen receive additional aid from GCC. Students applying for financial assistance must complete the Free Application for Federal Student Aid. Job opportunities are available both on and off campus.

APPLICATION AND INFORMATION

A regular admission applicant should take the SAT I or ACT by October or November of the senior year in high school. The application should include scores on the SAT I (preferred) or the ACT, a high school transcript, references, a recommendation from the student's principal or counselor, and a nonrefundable application fee of $25. An early decision applicant should take the entrance test in the eleventh grade, visit the College for an interview, and submit the application by November 15; notification of the admission decision is mailed on December 15. Approved early decision applicants must accept by January 15 and submit a nonrefundable deposit of $200. Applicants seeking regular decision must submit the completed application and supporting documents by February 15 of their senior year. Notification of the admission decision is mailed on March 15. Students who are offered admission should reply as soon as possible, but no later than May 1, and include a nonrefundable deposit of $150. Applications received after February 15 will be considered as space permits.

HAVERFORD COLLEGE

■ Haverford, Pennsylvania

THE COLLEGE

Haverford is the first college established by members of the Society of Friends (Quakers). Founded in 1833, Haverford has chosen to remain small, undergraduate, and residential to carry out its educational philosophy and to maintain a strong sense of community. An Honor Code is created and directed by students and is an important element of the Haverford community. The Honor Code allows students to directly confront academic and social issues in a spirit of cooperation and mutual respect. Haverford's 1,100 students represent forty-five states, Puerto Rico, the District of Columbia, and twenty countries. Nineteen percent of the students are students of color, while an additional 4 percent are international students. Haverford is a residential campus with 98 percent of the students and 70 percent of the faculty living on campus. Students may also choose to live at nearby Bryn Mawr College. Housing on Haverford's campus is single-sex or coed, and residence halls vary in accommodations from 4-person apartments to suites and singles. Other choices of residence facilities include the Ira De A. Reid House (Black Cultural Center), La Casa Hispanica, and an environmental house.

For more information or to arrange an interview or tour appointment, students should contact:

Office of Admission
Haverford College
370 Lancaster Avenue
Haverford, Pennsylvania 19041-1392
Telephone: 610-896-1350
Fax: 610-896-1338
E-mail: admitme@haverford.edu
World Wide Web:
http://www.haverford.edu

ACADEMIC PROGRAM

Students plan their programs using established guidelines and with the help of faculty advisers. They must have at least three courses in each of the divisions of the College: humanities, social science, and natural science. In addition, they must fulfill requirements in foreign language, social justice, writing, and quantitative course work. Flexibility in the curriculum allows opportunities for independent study, foreign study, and noncollegiate academic study. Majors are selected at the end of the sophomore year. Normally, students take four courses a semester and thirty-two courses over four years. However, scheduling is flexible, and students may arrange programs to meet individual needs, including six-semester, seven-semester, and five-year programs. Credit is given on the basis of AP (Advanced Placement) examinations, A-Level examinations, and International Baccalaureate Higher Level examinations.

FINANCIAL AID

The College has an extensive financial aid program. Approximately 38 percent of Haverford's students receive College grant aid. Candidates for Haverford College funded aid must file the Financial Aid PROFILE with the College Scholarship Service, along with the FAFSA. Applicants may register for the PROFILE by completing a short form, available from their local high school guidance office, and sending it to the College Scholarship Service. Regular decision students should complete the PROFILE registration process by January 2, so the College Scholarship Service can send the form and have students complete it by the January 31 deadline. The FAFSA is also available from high school guidance offices and must also be filed by January 31. Early decision candidates should complete the PROFILE registration process by October 15 and file the PROFILE form with the College Scholarship Service by November 15.

APPLICATION AND INFORMATION

The application deadlines for admission are November 15 for early decision candidates, January 15 for regular decision candidates, and March 31 for transfer candidates. Haverford also accepts the Common Application, which is available in school guidance offices.

HAWAII PACIFIC UNIVERSITY

■ Honolulu, Hawaii

For further information and for application materials, students should contact:

Office of Admissions
Hawaii Pacific University
1164 Bishop Street, Suite 200
Honolulu, Hawaii 96813
Telephone: 808-544-0238
800-669-4724 (toll-free)
Fax: 808-544-1136
E-mail: admissions@hpu.edu
Web site: http://www.hpu.edu/

THE UNIVERSITY

Hawaii Pacific University (HPU) is an independent, coeducational, career-oriented comprehensive university with a foundation in the liberal arts. Undergraduate and graduate degrees are offered in close to fifty different areas. Hawaii Pacific prides itself on maintaining small class size (averaging 25) and individual attention to students. Students at HPU come from every state in the union and more than ninety countries around the world. The diversity of the student body stimulates learning about other cultures firsthand, both in and out of the classroom. There is no majority population at HPU. Students are encouraged to examine the values, customs, traditions, and principles of others to gain a clearer understanding of their own perspectives. HPU students develop friendships with students from throughout the United States and the world, important connections for success in the global economy of the twenty-first century. HPU has a dual affiliation with both NCAA and NAIA intercollegiate sports. Men's athletic programs include baseball, basketball, cheerleading, cross-country, soccer, and tennis. Women's athletics include cheerleading, cross-country, soccer, softball, tennis, and volleyball. The Housing Office at HPU offers many services and options for students. Residence halls with cafeteria service are available on the Windward campus, while University-sponsored apartments are available in the Waikiki area for those seeking more independent living arrangements.

ACADEMIC PROGRAM

The baccalaureate student must complete at least 124 semester hours of credit. Forty-five of these credits provide the student with a strong foundation in the liberal arts, with the remaining credits comprised of appropriate upper-division classes in the student's major and related areas. The academic year operates on a modified 4-1-4 semester system, featuring a five-week winter intersession. The University also offers extensive summer sessions. A student can earn up to 15 semester credits during the summer. By attending these supplemental sessions, a student may complete the baccalaureate degree program in three years. A five-year B.S.B.A./M.B.A. program is also available.

FINANCIAL AID

The University provides financial aid for qualified students through institutional, state, and federal aid programs. Approximately 50 percent of the University's students receive financial aid. Among the forms of aid available are Federal Perkins Loans, Federal Stafford Student Loans, Guaranteed Parental Loans, Federal Pell Grants, and Federal Supplemental Educational Opportunity Grants. To apply for aid, students must submit the Free Application for Federal Student Aid (FAFSA). The FAFSA may be submitted at any time, but the priority deadline is March 1.

APPLICATION AND INFORMATION

Candidates are notified of admission decisions on a rolling basis, usually within two weeks of receipt of application materials. Early entrance and deferred entrance are available. HPU accepts the Common Application form.

HIRAM COLLEGE

■ HIRAM, OHIO

THE COLLEGE

Prospective students should address questions to:

Dean of Admission
Hiram College
Hiram, Ohio 44234
Telephone: 330-569-5169
800-362-5280 (toll-free)
E-mail: admission@hiram.edu
Web site: http://admission.hiram.edu

Founded by the Christian Church (Disciples of Christ) in 1850, Hiram College cherishes its heritage, while remaining free from sectarian doctrine or denominational control. Hiram's 850 students come from twenty-five states and several countries and represent more than twenty-five different religions. Between 50 and 60 percent of the College's graduates go on to graduate school or professional school within five years. Ninety-three percent of Hiram's students live in the eleven residence halls and eat their meals on campus. Student services include a health center, a fitness center, a sports medicine clinic, a career placement office, professional counseling on a wide range of personal and academic concerns, optional religious services and activities, and sports for everyone. There are honorary societies, social clubs, music and drama groups, student publications, religious groups, and student government and political and social-action groups.

ACADEMIC PROGRAM

Hiram's academic calendar, the Hiram Plan, is unique among colleges and universities. Each fifteen-week semester is divided into a twelve-week and a three-week session. During the three-week session, students take only one intensive course. The plan provides two formats for learning, which increases opportunity for small group study with faculty, study in special topics, hands-on learning through field trips and internships, and study abroad. Required courses include the Freshman Colloquium, a small, seminar course on a special topic taught by a student's adviser; First Year Seminar, providing an introduction to Western thought and emphasizing critical thinking, effective writing, and speaking; and a sequence of interdisciplinary courses. The course of study in most areas of major concentration is specified by the departments and divisions. Students generally take ten courses from within a department, as well as two or three courses from related or supporting departments. Alternatively, a student, with the assistance of the adviser, may develop an area of concentration that consists of related courses from different academic areas, crossing departmental lines to focus on particular needs or interests. A student may also submit a proposal for an individually designed program to the Area of Concentration Board.

FINANCIAL AID

More than 75 percent of Hiram's students receive financial aid based on need. All financial aid awards are made on a one-year basis, and each year a new Free Application for Federal Student Aid (FAFSA) and Hiram College Financial Aid Application must be submitted to determine eligibility. Scholarships awarded on the basis of merit are also available and range from $250 to $12,000 per year. Aid includes Federal Pell Grants, Federal Supplemental Educational Opportunity Grants, Federal Perkins Loans, Federal Stafford Student Loans, state grants, Federal Work-Study awards, and veterans' benefits.

APPLICATION AND INFORMATION

Application materials include the completed application form and a nonrefundable $25 application fee; a secondary school report, which must be completed and returned to Hiram directly by the high school guidance counselor; a statement from the guidance counselor, also returned directly to Hiram; the results of the SAT I or ACT; and an essay. Teacher recommendations are also required. The application deadline is March 15. Applicants are encouraged to visit the campus. The Office of Admission, located in Teachout-Price Hall, is open year-round for interviews from 9 a.m. to 4 p.m. on weekdays and from 9 a.m. to noon on Saturday (except during the summer months).

HOFSTRA UNIVERSITY

■ HEMPSTEAD, NEW YORK

THE UNIVERSITY

Hofstra University is traditional, contemporary, and innovative. The University offers the student with ability a good education and unusual opportunities for choice. Hofstra's philosophy is to provide a strong foundation in the liberal arts and sciences. The University's ultimate goal for its students is "the pursuit of knowledge, understanding, and wisdom upon which a good life can be built." The extracurricular program is full and varied. Students attending Hofstra come from forty-five states and sixty-seven countries. The freshman class numbers more than 1,500. The total enrollment at Hofstra is approximately 12,000; there are 7,149 full-time undergraduates and more than 1,200 part-time undergraduates.

For additional information, students should contact:

Dean of Admissions
Hofstra University
Hempstead, New York 11549-1000
Telephone: 516-463-6700
800-HOFSTRA (toll-free)
Fax: 516-463-5100
E-mail: hofstra@hofstra.edu
Web site: http://www.hofstra.edu

ACADEMIC PROGRAM

The requirement for the B.A. degree is 124 semester hours, of which 94 must be in liberal arts and 30 in free electives. Successful completion of at least 124 semester hours with a quality point average of 2.0 or better is required for graduation. For the major, each academic department defines the special pattern of required and suggested study that suits its discipline. Beyond this major requirement, five general requirements in humanities, natural sciences, social sciences, English, and foreign languages must be fulfilled. A candidate for graduation with the degree of B.B.A. must successfully complete at least 125 semester hours with a quality point average of 2.0 or better, completing at least 62 hours in liberal arts subjects (humanities, mathematics, natural sciences, and social sciences), 30 hours in general business courses (accounting, business law, quantitative methods, business writing, finance, and general business), and all major and additional requirements as listed under the department of specialization. Each of the scientific-technical programs leading to the B.S. degree requires a total of 124 to 134 semester hours, of which approximately half must be in liberal arts courses exclusive of those offered by the academic department of major specialization. The School of Education is a professional school to which undergraduate students are admitted only after they have established a broad liberal arts foundation. Candidates for the A.A.S. degree must complete at least 60 semester hours with a grade point average of at least 2.0. The student must complete 40 credits in liberal arts plus all the departmental major requirements and additional requirements for the major in elementary education.

FINANCIAL AID

Financial aid options range from scholarships through assistance grants to loans and part-time jobs. About 84 percent of all students receive financial help, and almost 65 percent work to earn part of their expenses. Scholarships average $3825 per year; loans average $2625 per year. Hofstra subscribes to the principles of the College Scholarship Service in determining the amount of awards. Federal funds include Federal Perkins Loans, Federal Pell and Federal Supplemental Educational Opportunity grants, and Federal Work-Study Program awards. To be considered for financial aid, completed financial aid applications and credentials (including the Free Application for Federal Student Aid) should be received on or before March 1.

APPLICATION AND INFORMATION

Freshman applicants must submit the application, a $40 application fee, the high school transcript, test scores, and a guidance counselor's recommendation. Transfer students must submit an application, the application fee, high school and college transcripts, and test scores (if fewer than 24 semester hours were attempted at the previous college).

IDAHO STATE UNIVERSITY

■ **Pocatello, Idaho**

THE UNIVERSITY

Idaho State University (ISU) has existed as an institution since 1901, when it was first established as the Academy of Idaho. It gained university status in 1963. Offering instruction in nearly every area of the arts and sciences, the University also conducts well-rounded programs of training in vocational and technical fields. Bachelor's and master's degrees in a variety of areas are awarded by the College of Arts and Sciences, the College of Business, the College of Education, the College of Engineering, the College of Health Professions, the College of Pharmacy, and the Graduate School. Doctoral degrees offered at ISU include the Doctor of Philosophy, Doctor of Arts, and Doctor of Education. Certificate programs of varying lengths, an Associate of Technology degree, an Associate of Applied Science degree, and a Bachelor of Applied Technology degree are included in the curricula of the School of Applied Technology. Because of its location and character, the University serves a diverse population that includes traditional-age students, nontraditional students, working professionals, and senior citizens. More than 13,000 students are enrolled at ISU; they represent nearly every state in the Union and forty-seven countries. U.S. and international students attend Idaho State University because of its reputation as an academic and vocational institution of high quality; its relaxed, safe, and rural atmosphere; and its location at the foot of the Rocky Mountains.

For additional information and application materials, students should contact:

Office of Enrollment Planning and Academic Services
Campus Box 8054
Idaho State University
Pocatello, Idaho 83209-0009
Telephone: 208-236-3277
Fax: 208-236-4314
E-mail: isuinfo@isu.edu
Web site: http://www.isu.edu

ACADEMIC PROGRAM

Idaho State University requires a broad liberal arts education of all candidates for the bachelor's degree. Students are required to complete credits in math, English, speech, the physical and natural sciences, the humanities, and the social sciences before concentrating on their major field. All bachelor's degree candidates must complete a minimum of 128 credit hours. Idaho State University operates on the semester system; opportunities are available for receiving credit by examination or tailoring a degree through the Bachelor of University Studies program. Internships are also arranged for students through the Career Development Center and individual departments.

FINANCIAL AID

The goal of Idaho State University's financial assistance program is twofold: to reward those students who demonstrate outstanding academic, leadership, or other talents and to aid those students unable to bear the costs of attending the University. In keeping with these goals, ISU provides financial assistance for some 80 percent of its students through grant, loan, work, and scholarship programs. ISU accepts the Free Application for Federal Student Aid (FAFSA). The priority deadline for mailing the FAFSA is March 1. The scholarship application deadline for new and transfer students is February 20. A limited number of competitive out-of-state-student tuition and reduced fee waivers are also available, as are campus and off-campus job placement programs.

APPLICATION AND INFORMATION

Deadlines for submission of all application materials are August 1 for the fall semester and December 1 for the spring semester. Notification is made within two weeks of application.

ITHACA COLLEGE

■ ITHACA, NEW YORK

THE COLLEGE

Coeducational and nonsectarian since its founding in 1892, Ithaca College enrolls approximately 5,900 students—about 2,600 men and 3,300 women. The College community is a multicultural one; virtually every state is represented in the student population, as are sixty-eight other countries. Students come to Ithaca because of its comprehensive program, a blend of preprofessional training and liberal arts education. The program is offered in five schools: the School of Humanities and Sciences (2,050 students), School of Business (450 students), Roy H. Park School of Communications (1,250 students), School of Health Sciences and Human Performance (1,450 students), and School of Music (450 students). There are approximately 250 graduate students.

For additional information and application forms, students should contact:

Paula J. Mitchell
Director of Admission
Office of Admission
Ithaca College
100 Job Hall
Ithaca, New York 14850-7020
Telephone: 800-429-4274 (toll-free)
607-274-3124
Fax: 607-274-1900
Web site: http://www.ithaca.edu

ACADEMIC PROGRAM

Undergraduate programs of study address two primary issues: the need for rigorous academic preparation in highly specialized professional fields and the need for students to prepare for the complex demands of society by acquiring an intellectual breadth that extends beyond their chosen profession. Each degree offered requires a minimum of 120 credit hours and a specified number of liberal arts credits. Minors, academic concentrations, and numerous teacher certification programs are available. Exceptionally qualified applicants to the School of Humanities and Sciences will be invited to apply to the honors program, an intensive four-year program of interdisciplinary seminars.

FINANCIAL AID

Financial aid, which totals approximately $65 million from all sources, is extended to nearly 80 percent of Ithaca students. To apply for financial aid, students should check the proper space on the College's admission application, and if seeking federal aid, submit the Free Application for Federal Student Aid (FAFSA) by February 1 with the U.S. Department of Education at the address indicated on the form. Early decision and physical therapy candidates should follow the time line outlined under the Application and Information section below. All accepted applicants are considered for merit aid in recognition of their academic and personal achievement. Programs providing grants and loans include the Federal Work-Study, Federal Pell Grant, Federal Perkins Loan, Federal Stafford Student Loan, and Federal Supplemental Educational Opportunity Grant.

APPLICATION AND INFORMATION

Application should be made no later than March 1; applicants are notified by April 15 and must confirm their enrollment by May 1. There is a $45 application fee for applicants seeking admission in fall 1999 or later; spring 1999 candidates pay a $40 fee. All students seeking federal aid should submit the FAFSA by February 1 with the U.S. Department of Education at the address indicated on the form. Early decision candidates should also file the College Scholarship Service PROFILE application by November 1, with all supporting materials received by November 15; applicants are notified by December 15 and must confirm their enrollment by February 1. Admission to the physical therapy program is through the early decision program only, and candidates follow the same time line. Early decision is a binding agreement.

JUDSON COLLEGE

■ ELGIN, ILLINOIS

THE COLLEGE

For further information, students should telephone, write, or e-mail:

Vice President for Enrollment Services
Judson College
1151 North State Street
Elgin, Illinois 60123
Telephone: 847-695-2500 Ext. 2310
800-879-5376 (toll-free)
E-mail: admissions@mail.judson-il.edu

Judson College is an evangelical Christian college of the liberal arts, sciences, and professions. Founded in 1963, Judson College was named for the first missionary from North America, Adoniram Judson, and the spirit of Christian service that he embodied is very evident on Judson's campus. The College offers residential living in an environment that encourages and supports Christian growth. At Judson, it is believed that all truth is God's truth, and that the honest search for truth in any subject area will lead a student to God the Creator. Judson's students have chosen the College for a number of reasons, but two are consistently mentioned: the vibrant Christian community and a liberal arts curriculum that is practical. They expect to be encouraged to grow in their faith, while being prepared to succeed in a career. The College expects students to be actively involved in their education both inside and outside of the classroom. Student activities are coordinated by the Student Association and involve many on- and off-campus opportunities. Concerts, films, dramatic productions, athletic contests, banquets, and outings to Chicago all make for a complete social calendar. Students also may choose to be involved in choir, chamber singing, drama, the newspaper (*Eagle Outlook*), the yearbook (*Lantern*), campus radio station (WJUD), intramurals, Christian ministry groups, academic clubs, service clubs, and the international club (United Cultures of Judson). The current College enrollment is nearly 1,200 students. Sixty percent of the more than 750 traditional students live in residence halls; married student housing is also available. The remaining 400 students are enrolled in the Division of Continuing Education. Twenty states are represented on campus, as are twenty-four countries.

ACADEMIC PROGRAM

The goal of the College's academic program is to integrate faith and learning. Judson College has instituted a unique program for freshmen that combines small group mentoring by faculty members and upperclassmen with their college success course and cohort registration for initial courses in the general education curriculum. The Bachelor of Arts degree requires completion of 126 semester credit hours. The College operates on a 4-1-4-1 calendar. January and May post-terms, lasting approximately three weeks, feature conventional and travel courses. In addition, students may choose to take additional course work offered on an open-entry, open-exit basis through the Customized Learning Center.

FINANCIAL AID

Scholarships, grants, loans, and church matching grants are available for students who need assistance in meeting college expenses. Academic scholarships are available to incoming freshmen and transfer students who meet the necessary standards. Talent scholarships are also available in athletics, art, communications (newspaper, yearbook, radio, video), drama, and music. In addition, on-campus jobs are available and the local community has a high number of well-paying options available to college students. More than 90 percent of Judson's students receive some form of financial aid.

APPLICATION AND INFORMATION

An application packet or information on visiting the College can be obtained from the Admissions Office. Judson uses a rolling admission procedure, which means that decisions are mailed to applicants within a short period of time after all application materials have been received.

KENTUCKY WESLEYAN COLLEGE

■ OWENSBORO, KENTUCKY

To arrange a campus visit or request application materials, students should contact:

Office of Admission
Kentucky Wesleyan College
3000 Frederica Street
Box 1039
Owensboro, Kentucky 42302-1039
Telephone: 502-926-3111
800-999-0592 (toll free)
E-mail: admission@kwc.edu

THE COLLEGE

The tradition of high-quality teaching and a talent for translating a liberal arts education into usable and useful service have long been hallmarks of Kentucky Wesleyan College (KWC). Founded by the United Methodist Church in 1858, the College's mission is to prepare leaders for the twenty-first century through a coordinated and integrated liberal arts education. To fulfill its mission, Kentucky Wesleyan offers Leadership KWC, a nationally recognized leadership program established with an $800,000 grant from the W.K. Kellogg Foundation. Liberal arts course work forms the basis of Leadership KWC and represents the College's belief that a solid liberal arts education provides the communication, problem-solving, and creative-thinking skills necessary for tomorrow's leaders. To specifically explore leadership, students may enroll in special courses with a leadership emphasis, such as Profiles in Leadership, Women in Leadership, or the Psychology of Leadership. Students put theory into practice through internships, community service, and workshops such as the College's summer sailing experience. Students may choose to participate in Leadership XXI, a more extensive cocurricular leadership program that involves leadership courses, community service, leadership workshops, campus activity participation, and a senior thesis or project. Students who successfully complete Leadership XXI receive a leadership citation at graduation.

ACADEMIC PROGRAM

There are three academic divisions in the Kentucky Wesleyan College curriculum: the Natural Sciences, the Humanities and Fine Arts, and the Social Sciences. The requirements for the degrees of Bachelor of Science and Bachelor of Arts are based on the principle of a broad distribution of studies among the representative fields of human culture and a concentration of studies in a specific field. In most cases, 128 semester hours are required to obtain a bachelor's degree.

FINANCIAL AID

Kentucky Wesleyan participates in all federal student aid programs and is committed to helping each student meet his or her demonstrated financial need. No student should hesitate to apply for admission due to financial reasons. Kentucky Wesleyan awards more than $6.2 million each year in financial aid to eligible students. Kentucky residents may qualify for Kentucky Higher Education Assistance Authority Grants. In addition to federal and state financial aid programs, Kentucky Wesleyan invests more than $2.6 million annually in scholarships and grants for its students. Academic scholarships are awarded to students who attend one of several on-campus scholarship days. These scholarships range from 20 percent of tuition to full tuition and are renewable annually. Students who demonstrate a strong record of leadership in their school, church, place of employment, or community are encouraged to apply for Stanley Reed Leadership Awards. These awards range from $2000 to $4000 and are renewable annually (applications are available from the Office of Admission).

APPLICATION AND INFORMATION

Students may apply for admission after completing their junior year. Applications are evaluated on a rolling basis, and students can expect to be notified of a decision within two weeks of completing their application for admission.

KETTERING UNIVERSITY

■ FLINT, MICHIGAN

Admissions Office
Kettering University
1700 West Third Avenue
Flint, Michigan 48504-4898
Telephone: 810-762-7865
800-955-4464 (toll-free in the United States and Canada)
E-mail: admissions@kettering.edu
Web site: http://www.kettering.edu

THE UNIVERSITY

Kettering University (formerly GMI Engineering & Management Institute), "America's premiere co-op university," has a unique partnership that offers students, business, and industry an opportunity found at no other undergraduate college in America. Kettering, a five-year cooperative engineering, management, science, and math university, is the only institution that assists incoming freshmen to be selected by companies for cooperative employment, a process initiated for all accepted students. Kettering University successfully integrates the practical aspects of the workplace into the world of higher education through its more than 550 corporate partners, corporations, and agencies located throughout the United States, Canada, and selected countries. Kettering's corporate partners represent most major industrial groups; many are recognized as worldwide leaders in business innovation and manufacturing technology. These corporations share a commitment to "grow their own" engineers and managers by employing exceptionally talented young men and women in one of the ten baccalaureate degree programs. Kettering's corporate partners invest in students' futures by providing a five-year program of progressive work experience that exposes them to processes, products, corporate culture, and the technology necessary to compete in tomorrow's business environment.

ACADEMIC PROGRAM

Although each program at Kettering University has its own sequence requirements, 180 credit hours are generally required, including thesis credit hours. The five-year program involves nine semesters of cooperative and academic work and a tenth semester of thesis preparation. Students alternate between twelve-week periods of academic study on the campus in Flint and twelve-week periods of related work experience with their corporate employer.

FINANCIAL AID

One of the many advantages of attending Kettering University is the opportunity for students to earn a salary during work terms. This "ultimate scholarship" covers part of the cost of a Kettering education and supplements the family contribution and the standard forms of need-based financial aid. Students who live at home during work experience periods are able to contribute a greater proportion of earnings directly to educational expenses. About 70 percent of students are able to live at home during work terms. The typical range of co-op earnings over the five-year program is $40,000 to $65,000. Kettering University offers all the traditional forms of financial aid, both need- and merit-based. Because of their talents, many students win scholarships from agencies and organizations from their local communities. Michigan residents often are recipients of the Michigan Competitive Scholarship. The primary purpose of financial aid at Kettering University is to supplement a student's unmet financial need after cooperative earnings and parents' contributions. Students who wish to apply for financial aid should complete the Free Application for Federal Student Aid (FAFSA) and request that a copy of the analysis be sent to Kettering University. Aid is given as grants, scholarships, loans, and work-study awards.

APPLICATION AND INFORMATION

Prospective freshmen are encouraged to file their application early in their senior year. Transfer students can apply any time after successful completion of 30 credits. Applications are accepted all year long; however, early application greatly increases visibility for early employment possibilities in the co-op search process. The application fee is $25.

LAGRANGE COLLEGE

■ LaGrange, Georgia

THE COLLEGE

For additional information, students should contact:

Office of Admission
LaGrange College
601 Broad Street
LaGrange, Georgia 30240
Telephone: 706-812-7260
Fax: 706-812-7348
E-mail:
ageeter@mentor.lgc.peachnet.edu
World Wide Web:
http://www.lgc.peachnet.edu

Founded in 1831, LaGrange College is the oldest private college in Georgia. Affiliated with the United Methodist Church, LaGrange College seeks to admit any qualified student. With an enrollment of approximately 1,000 men and women and only 17 students in the average classroom, LaGrange College provides a challenging and supportive academic environment. The College is fully accredited by the Commission on Colleges of the Southern Association of Colleges and Schools as well as the University Senate of the United Methodist Church. Students come from nineteen states and twenty-five other countries. The Master of Education (M.Ed.) degree and the Master of Business Administration (M.B.A.) degree are offered in addition to the Bachelor of Arts (B.A.), Bachelor of Science (B.S.), Bachelor of Science in Nursing (B.S.N.), and Associate of Arts (A.A.) degrees. The College is located in a residential section of LaGrange, Georgia, which has a population of 28,000. The city of LaGrange is 65 miles southwest of Atlanta and 55 miles southwest of Hartsfield Atlanta International Airport.

ACADEMIC PROGRAM

Each program of study contains a substantial general education component and extensive specified course work in the discipline in which the student has selected a major. Ninety-five quarter hours of general education courses are required for all bachelor's degrees. Most majors require an additional 100 quarter hours of credit beyond the general education curriculum. Students may be eligible for credit and/or exemption in certain areas through the Advanced Placement (AP) tests or the College-Level Examination Program (CLEP).

FINANCIAL AID

As a private college, LaGrange is committed to helping meet the difference between the funds any student has available and the cost of attending LaGrange College. More than 80 percent of LaGrange students receive some combination of financial awards. These awards may include grants, loans, scholarships, and employment opportunities. Federal financial aid and institutional funds are available to all students who qualify. The state of Georgia provides additional funding for Georgia residents. All Georgia residents who enroll as full-time students receive the Georgia Tuition Equalization Grant in the amount of $1000 per year. The HOPE Scholarship, which totals $3000 per year, is awarded to all Georgia residents who have graduated from high school since 1996 with a B average and who enter as freshmen. Georgia residents who do not qualify for the HOPE Scholarship as freshmen may be able to obtain the HOPE Scholarship by maintaining a 3.0 grade point average through the freshman and sophomore years. Academic scholarships that range from $1000 to $4500 are also awarded. All accepted students are considered for scholarships; a separate application is not required. In 1996–97, all financial aid applicants were awarded financial aid. The average award totaled $9245 for the year.

APPLICATION AND INFORMATION

Applications for admission are evaluated on a rolling basis and should be submitted at least one month prior to the beginning of the quarter in which entrance is desired. Applicants can expect to receive notification within two to three weeks of the date that all documents are submitted. Weekday campus visits are encouraged, and appointments can be arranged by contacting the Admission Office.

LE MOYNE COLLEGE

■ SYRACUSE, NEW YORK

David M. Pirani
Director of Admission
Le Moyne College
Syracuse, New York 13214-1399
Telephone: 315-445-4300
800-333-4733 Ext. 4300
(toll-free)

THE COLLEGE

Le Moyne College is a four-year Jesuit college of approximately 1,900 undergraduate students that uniquely balances a comprehensive liberal arts education with preparation for specific career paths or graduate study. Founded by the Society of Jesus in 1946, Le Moyne is the second-youngest of the twenty-eight Jesuit colleges and universities in the United States. The campus environment is one of a closely knit community. Le Moyne's personal approach to education is reflected in the quality of contact between students and faculty members. A wide range of student-directed activities, athletics, clubs, and service organizations complement the academic experience. Intramural sports are very popular with Le Moyne students, and approximately 75 percent of the students participate in athletics. Le Moyne also has sixteen NCAA intercollegiate teams (eight for men and eight for women). Approximately 80 percent of students live in residence halls and town houses on campus. The Residence Hall Councils and the Le Moyne Student Programming Board organize many campus activities, including concerts, dances, a weekly film series, student talent programs, and special lectures as well as off-campus trips and skiing excursions.

ACADEMIC PROGRAM

While each major department has its own sequence requirements for the minimum 120 credit hours needed for the Le Moyne degree, the College is convinced that there is a fundamental intellectual discipline that should characterize the graduate of a superior liberal arts college. Le Moyne's core curriculum provides this foundation by including studies of English language and literature, philosophy, history, religious studies, science, mathematics, and social sciences. For exceptional students, Le Moyne offers an integral honors program that includes an interdisciplinary humanities sequence as well as departmental honors courses. Le Moyne also offers a part-time course of study during evening hours through its Center for Continuous Learning.

FINANCIAL AID

Financial aid is offered to 95 percent of Le Moyne's students through scholarships, grants, loans, and work-study assignments. Le Moyne offers a generous program of merit-based academic and athletic scholarships as well as financial aid based on a student's need and academic promise. Federal funds are available through the Federal Pell Grant, Federal Work-Study, Federal Supplemental Educational Opportunity Grant, and Federal Perkins Loan programs. A student's eligibility for need-based financial aid is determined from both the Free Application for Federal Student Aid (FAFSA) and the Le Moyne Financial Aid Application Form. It is recommended that these forms be mailed by February 1.

APPLICATION AND INFORMATION

The Admission Committee reviews applications and mails decisions on a rolling admission cycle beginning January 1. The priority deadline for applications is March 1; all students who wish to be considered for academic non-need scholarships should have a completed application on file in the Office of Admission before this date. Students who wish to be considered under the early decision program must have a completed application submitted by December 1. Early decision applicants will by notified by December 15. Transfer students are encouraged to apply before May 1 for the fall semester and December 1 for the spring semester. A fun-filled two-day orientation program takes place in mid-summer.

LENOIR–RHYNE COLLEGE

■ HICKORY, NORTH CAROLINA

For additional information, students should contact:

Timothy L. Jackson
Director of Admissions
Lenoir-Rhyne College
Hickory, North Carolina 28603
Telephone: 704-328-7300
800-277-5721 (toll-free)
E-mail: admission@lrc.edu

THE COLLEGE

Lenoir-Rhyne College, founded by 4 Lutheran ministers in 1891, is accredited by the Commission on Colleges of the Southern Association of Colleges and Schools. The College's facilities have grown from one building on a small tract of land to more than twenty major structures on a 100-acre campus. The College seeks to liberate mind and spirit, clarify personal faith, foster physical wholeness, build a sense of community, and promote responsible leadership for service in the world. The campus population of 1,616 includes a wide range of ethnic, cultural, and religious backgrounds. An outstanding faculty, student selectivity, reputation for academic excellence, financial resources, and ability to retain and graduate students make Lenoir-Rhyne one of North Carolina's premier small liberal arts colleges. More than forty campus organizations, including academic honoraries, religious organizations, special interest clubs, four fraternities, and four sororities, invite students to participate and develop their leadership potential. There are intercollegiate teams for men in baseball, basketball, cross-country, football, golf, soccer, tennis, and track and for women in basketball, cross-country, soccer, softball, tennis, and volleyball.

ACADEMIC PROGRAM

The College operates on a semester calendar. A two-term summer session is also offered. The core curriculum includes courses in English, science and mathematics, social and behavioral sciences, humanities, computer science, religion, and physical education. A student may choose a variety of courses within these disciplines to fulfill core requirements. There is a formal final examination period at the end of each term. In cooperation with the North Carolina School for the Deaf in nearby Morganton, Lenoir-Rhyne offers a program in which a student may gain certification to teach students in schools for the deaf throughout the United States or to teach hearing-impaired students in public schools. The College accepts a number of hearing-impaired students in its regular undergraduate program. A business internship program offers students hands-on experience while they earn credit toward their degree. The international business major is comparable to many graduate programs in the field.

FINANCIAL AID

Lenoir-Rhyne College makes every effort to assist students through a program of scholarships, loans, and work-study awards. Last year, more than 90 percent of the student body received financial aid through an aid program totaling approximately $12.1 million. The amount of aid awarded to a student is determined by need, as indicated on the Free Application for Federal Student Aid (FAFSA). The priority filing date for the FAFSA and the Lenoir-Rhyne Scholarship Application is March 1. In addition to need-based aid, Lenoir-Rhyne College also offers academic, athletic, honors, and music scholarships.

APPLICATION AND INFORMATION

Application for admission may be made by submitting a high school transcript showing rank in class, the completed application and $25 fee, and SAT I or ACT scores. Candidates are encouraged to apply early in their senior year of high school. The College accepts students on early acceptance or a rolling basis. Deferred enrollment is available.

LOYOLA MARYMOUNT UNIVERSITY

■ **Los Angeles, California**

THE UNIVERSITY

Loyola Marymount University, situated on a picturesque campus, offers competitive students an education of high quality in a friendly and relaxed atmosphere. As successor of the oldest institution of learning in southern California, St. Vincent's College, the University is steeped in a tradition and history of dedication to academic excellence and the total development of its students. Although the emphasis is within the undergraduate school (enrollment 3,961), 1,318 students attend the Graduate Division, primarily in the evening hours, working toward master's degrees in the fields of arts, arts in teaching, business administration, education, and science (including engineering). The School of Law, situated at a separate campus, has both day and evening divisions and offers the Juris Doctor degree. Law school enrollment is 1,321.

For more information about Loyola Marymount University, prospective students should contact:

Matthew X. Fissinger
Director of Admissions
Loyola Marymount University
7900 Loyola Boulevard
Los Angeles, California 90045
Telephone: 310-338-2750
800-LMU-INFO (toll-free)
Fax: 310-338-2797

ACADEMIC PROGRAM

While premajor and major requirements differ with each area of study, a core curriculum is maintained as a degree requirement in the fields of American cultures, communication skills, fine arts, history, literature/psychology, mathematics/science, philosophy, social science, and theology, thus ensuring each student a balanced education. The maximum requirement in each of the core fields is 6 units of academic work. The interdepartmental honors program provides challenges for the exceptional student. The academic calendar consists of two semesters and a six-week optional summer session. The fall semester begins in late August and ends before Christmas. The spring semester begins in mid-January and ends in mid-May. Students may earn credit through Advanced Placement examinations. In addition, it is possible for students to earn credit by examination for any course offered by LMU.

FINANCIAL AID

Approximately 70 percent of the University's undergraduate students receive some type of financial assistance. The total amount of financial aid awarded to students is approximately $50 million. Students applying for aid must file the Free Application for Student Aid (FAFSA) and the CSS PROFILE. All students are expected to apply for the Federal Pell Grant, and California residents must apply for the California grants. Most aid is awarded on the basis of need, but the University does offer merit scholarships (including full-tuition scholarships). The priority date for financial aid is February 15. Aid is awarded after that date on a funds-available basis.

APPLICATION AND INFORMATION

Applicants must submit official transcripts from the last high school attended and from each college attended, arrange for SAT I or ACT scores to be sent to the Office of Admissions, submit a recommendation form from an official of the last school attended, and file an application with the $35 nonrefundable fee. Applications are considered when all necessary documents have been received prior to the deadline of the semester for which application is made. The deadlines are February 1 for the fall semester and December 1 for the spring semester.

LOYOLA UNIVERSITY CHICAGO

■ CHICAGO, ILLINOIS

THE UNIVERSITY

Loyola University Chicago is the most comprehensive Jesuit university in the United States and has one of the largest endowments of all Catholic universities in the country. Founded in 1870 by priests of the Society of Jesus, Loyola continues the Jesuit commitment to education, which is well-grounded in the liberal arts and traditionally based on excellent teaching. Each year, Loyola enrolls 1,200 freshmen and 500 transfer students. These students choose Loyola because of its personal attention, its environment of academic excellence, and its reputation for career preparation. Loyola students take advantage of Chicago as an educational resource, often combining their studies with internships and part-time work experience. The University provides eleven undergraduate residence halls on the Lake Shore Campus.

To obtain an application and further information and to arrange a visit, students should contact:

Undergraduate Admission Office
Loyola University Chicago
820 North Michigan Avenue
Chicago, Illinois 60611
Telephone: 312-915-6500
800-262-2373 (toll-free)
E-mail: admission@luc.edu
Web site: http://www.luc.edu/

ACADEMIC PROGRAM

Jesuit educators believe that a solid foundation in the liberal arts and sciences is essential for students entering all professions. Loyola's Core Curriculum is designed to give students this foundation. The core requirements vary by college but usually include courses in literature, expressive arts, history, social sciences, mathematical and natural sciences, philosophy, and theology. The core allows students who are undecided about their majors to explore all possibilities before deciding upon a field of study. Most majors require 128 semester hours for graduation. Exceptionally well qualified students may apply to the Honors Program. Students may receive credit through the Advanced Placement (AP) Program tests, the International Baccalaureate (I.B.), and certain College-Level Examination Program (CLEP) tests.

FINANCIAL AID

Loyola attempts to meet the financial need of as many students as possible. Seventy-five percent of Loyola students receive some form of aid, including University-funded scholarships and grants, federal and state grants, work-study, and loans. Students are encouraged to file the Free Application for Federal Student Aid (FAFSA) by mid-February in order to receive consideration for all types of aid. Merit scholarships are awarded to entering freshmen who have outstanding academic records. Presidential, Damen, and Loyola scholarships are awarded to students who rank at the top of their high school graduating class and score well on the ACT or SAT I. Scholarship amounts for these programs are $5000–$10,000 per year. These awards are renewable for up to three years. Other scholarships available include competitive awards for students admitted to the Honors Program and students from Jesuit/BVM/Sisters of Christian Charity high schools, theater scholarships (awarded by audition), and debate, leadership, nursing, and public accounting awards. Transfer students who have completed 30 hours of college credit with an outstanding record of academic achievement may receive a Transfer Academic Scholarship. These awards are renewable for up to three years.

APPLICATION AND INFORMATION

Applicants are notified of the admission decision three to four weeks after the application, supporting credentials, secondary school counselor recommendation, and $25 application fee are received. Prospective students are encouraged to visit the campus. The Undergraduate Admission Office encourages students to schedule individual appointments and campus tours or to participate in one of the many campus programs offered throughout the year.

LOYOLA UNIVERSITY NEW ORLEANS

■ NEW ORLEANS, LOUISIANA

THE UNIVERSITY

Interested students are encouraged to contact:

Office of Admissions
Loyola University
6363 St. Charles Avenue, Box 18
New Orleans, Louisiana 70118
Telephone: 504-865-3240
800-4-LOYOLA (toll-free)
Fax: 504-865-3383
E-mail: admit@loyno.edu
Web site: http://www.loyno.edu

Founded by the Jesuits in 1912, Loyola University's more than 35,000 graduates have excelled in innumerable professional fields for more than eighty years. Approximately 3,500 undergraduate students enjoy the individual attention of a caring faculty in a university dedicated to creating community and fostering individualism while educating the whole person, not only intellectually, but spiritually, socially, and athletically. Loyola students represent forty-seven states and fifty-seven countries. This diversity is found in a setting where the average class size is 22 students. More than 46 percent of the students permanently reside outside Louisiana, and 33 percent belong to minority groups. Loyola's 20-acre main campus and 4-acre Broadway campus are located in the historic uptown area of New Orleans and are hubs of student activity. The University's residence halls, equipped with computer labs, kitchen, laundry, and study facilities, are home to almost 1,000 students. The Joseph A. Danna Center, the student center, houses five food venues, including the remodeled Orleans Room, Pizza Hut, Casa Ortega, and a gourmet coffee shop. Also found in the Danna Center are an art gallery, travel agency, microcomputer center, hair salon, concierge desk, post office, and game room. The University Counseling and Career Services Center provides personal, educational, and vocational counseling and testing services for all students. The center coordinates an active employer-recruitment program that helps students find internships, summer jobs, and career employment after graduation. The center brings more than 200 businesses and graduate/professional schools to campus to interview Loyola students. The office also maintains close contact with the New Orleans Chamber of Commerce, which includes more than 500 businesses.

ACADEMIC PROGRAM

Once enrolled at Loyola, students are introduced to the Common Curriculum, designed to give them a well-rounded preparation in their major field of concentration, as well as the ability to understand and reflect on disciplines allied to or outside their major. The curriculum is divided into four categories: major, minor, Common Curriculum, and elective courses. Students must meet the requirements of their degree program as specified by their particular college; the minimum four-year program requires 128 hours. Common Curriculum courses include seven introductory courses in English composition, math, science, philosophy, religion, literature, and history and nine upper-division courses in humanities, social science, and natural science. The College of Arts and Sciences also requires a minimum of one year of study in a modern foreign language. The honors program and independent studies provide special opportunities for qualified students.

FINANCIAL AID

Loyola University's endowment provides money for financial aid in addition to that provided by federal funding. Assistance in the forms of merit- and talent-based scholarships, loans, work-study program awards, and grants is awarded on the basis of academic achievement and need. More than 450 scholarships are awarded annually to students with competitive grades and test scores. To apply for one of the scholarships, students must have a GPA of at least 3.2 and competitive standardized test scores. Offers of financial aid are not made until after admission. Notifications of awards are sent within four weeks of the receipt of completed financial aid applications. Awards of need-based financial aid packages are made on a first-come, first-served basis.

LUTHER COLLEGE

■ DECORAH, IOWA

THE COLLEGE

As an academic community, the students and faculty of Luther College are committed to liberal learning in the arts and sciences. Founded in 1861 by Norwegian immigrants, Luther is a college of the Evangelical Lutheran Church in America. Most students live on campus in the seven residence halls. Eighty-four percent of the 2,400 students come from Iowa, Minnesota, Wisconsin, and Illinois. All together, thirty-eight states and forty-five other nations are represented in the student body. Throughout the year, the College provides a stimulating cultural and educational atmosphere by bringing distinguished public figures, theater groups, musicians, and educators to the campus. Luther has an active Phi Beta Kappa chapter and several departmental honor societies as well. There are seven local social organizations for both men and women, in addition to one national service fraternity. Extracurricular activities are an important part of campus life. A full theater and dance program and thirteen performing music ensembles, including two bands, seven choirs, two orchestras, the Opera Workshop, the Jazz Band, and the Collegium Musicum, are major cocurricular interests.

For more information about Luther, students should contact:

Admissions Office
Luther College
Decorah, Iowa 52101-1042
Telephone: 319-387-1287
800-458-8437 (toll-free)
Fax: 319-387-2159
319-387-1060 (international)
E-mail: admissions@luther.edu (admissions)
lutherfa@luther.edu (financial planning)
lundsony@luther.edu (international)
Web site: http://www.luther.edu

ACADEMIC PROGRAM

Luther operates on a 4-1-4 academic calendar. The first semester runs from September to December, followed by a 3-week January Term and the second semester, which runs from February to May. Two 4-week summer sessions are offered, one in June and the other in July. Each candidate is required to complete satisfactorily a total of 128 semester hours of credit with a C average or better. At least 76 of the required 128 semester hours must be earned outside the major discipline. Each senior writes a research paper in his or her major. Students are required to complete the following number of semester hours of credit in designated areas: 12 of Paideia, an interdisciplinary course; 9 of religion/philosophy; 8 of natural science (4 of which may be in mathematics); 8 of social science; 3–9 of foreign language or culture (proficiency based); 3 of fine arts; and 2 of physical education. Demonstration of competency in mathematics is required. Advanced placement and credit by examination are available. A qualified student may develop an interdisciplinary major in consultation with a faculty adviser.

FINANCIAL AID

More than 85 percent of all Luther students receive some financial aid in the form of grants, such as the Federal Pell Grant; scholarships from Luther and other sources; loans; and jobs on campus. Luther awards Regents and Presidential scholarships to applicants demonstrating superior academic achievement. The amount of aid given is determined by the College's analysis of the Free Application for Federal Student Aid. The priority deadline for a financial aid application is March 1 each year. Students receive notification of financial aid awards after their acceptance for admission.

APPLICATION AND INFORMATION

An application, SAT I or ACT scores, an educator's reference, a transcript of previous academic work, and a $20 application fee are required for admission. On-campus interviews are recommended but not required.

LYNN UNIVERSITY

■ BOCA RATON, FLORIDA

THE UNIVERSITY

Founded in 1962, Lynn University is a private, coeducational institution located in Boca Raton, Florida. The University, small by design, provides an environment within and outside the classroom in which a community of learners can pursue academic excellence. Accredited in 1967 by the Southern Association of Colleges and Schools, Lynn University has steadily grown to become a comprehensive university offering undergraduate and graduate programs in more than thirty disciplines. Lynn leads the country in offering majors in many of the world's fastest-growing professions, thus preparing its students to meet the career demands of the twenty-first century. The 1,500 students who are currently enrolled come from all parts of the United States and nearly seventy nations. Lynn is a residential institution with four air-conditioned dormitory buildings that house 65 percent of the undergraduates. Laundry facilities, mailboxes, the University bookstore, and a variety of athletic facilities are all located on campus. University life is designed to provide a learning situation through which students are guided toward responsible decision-making and leadership. An extensive program of activities complements the academic program at Lynn, ensuring the development of the whole person. As a new member of the NCAA Division II, Lynn brings a proven record of success from NAIA competition. Lynn has won national titles in many sports. The intercollegiate athletic program includes men's and women's basketball, golf, soccer, and tennis; men's baseball; and women's softball and volleyball.

For additional information about admission, to obtain an application packet, or to arrange for an interview and tour of the campus, prospective students should contact:

Office of Admission
Lynn University
3601 North Military Trail
Boca Raton, Florida 33431
Telephone: 561-994-0770
800-544-8035 (toll-free)
Fax: 561-241-3552
E-mail: admission@lynn.edu

ACADEMIC PROGRAM

The University is committed to student-centered learning, where faculty and staff members provide personalized attention to students who have varying levels of academic proficiency with a motivation to excel. A full range of academic and support programs is coordinated to serve the increasingly diverse needs of all students. These are enhanced by the favorable 19:1 student-faculty ratio. The Freshman Seminar is the cornerstone to freshman advising at Lynn and provides an introduction to college life for all new students. The course includes academic success strategies, time management, communication skills, study and test-taking techniques, academic advisement, and career development. Lynn University's approach to the development of academic programs has been one that focuses on the balance of a carefully selected core of liberal arts subjects within the framework of a curriculum that is career-oriented and provides both theoretical and practical preparation. Upon this solid liberal arts foundation, students build special competence in their chosen fields of concentration. The practical application of knowledge is a vital component of Lynn's academic program; therefore, residencies, student teaching, community service projects, and internships are required for many degrees.

FINANCIAL AID

A student's education is not only a commitment of intellect and time, but a substantial financial investment as well. The University has a broad program of student financial aid, including scholarships, grants, work-study, and loans. Academic, athletic, and need-based scholarships are awarded. Inquiries may be made to the Office of Financial Aid.

APPLICATION AND INFORMATION

There is no formal deadline for admission, and applicants are notified on a rolling basis upon receipt of all credentials. The application fee is $25.

MAINE MARITIME ACADEMY

■ CASTINE, MAINE

THE ACADEMY

Maine Maritime Academy (MMA) offers a unique learning experience and a tradition of seafaring education. The hands-on, practical application of classroom instruction is found in all academic areas. Established in 1941 with an inaugural class of 28, the Academy had as its mission the provision of a comprehensive course of instruction and professional training to prepare graduates to become licensed officers in the U.S. Merchant Marines or commissioned officers in the U.S. Navy or Coast Guard. With additional academic offerings and degrees, modern buildings, sophisticated labs and simulators, and assorted training vessels, Maine Maritime has become one of the most progressive maritime training colleges in North America. Experiential learning is a cornerstone of a Maine Maritime education.

For information and applications, students should contact:

Director of Admissions
Maine Maritime Academy
Pleasant Street
Castine, Maine 04420
Telephone: 800-464-6565
(toll-free in Maine)
800-227-8465
(toll-free outside Maine)
E-mail: admissns@bell.mma.edu
Web site: http://www.mainemaritime.edu

ACADEMIC PROGRAM

The academic year is structured in the traditional two-semester academic format, with most students participating in either cruises, co-ops, or internships during the spring or summer months. All marine engineering and nautical science programs lead to qualification for an unlimited U.S. Coast Guard license. For these programs, students are required to do three 60-day at-sea training cruises aboard the college's training ship, *State of Maine,* as well as aboard commercial merchant ships. Students in the international business and logistics, ocean studies, and power engineering technology majors perform summer internships in their field of study as well. Like the other programs, the marina management and small-vessel operations majors provide similar work experiences, but the number required depends on whether a student is enrolled in the associate or bachelor's degree program. Small-vessel operations graduates qualify to take the U.S. Coast Guard license exam for 200- or 500-ton mate, near coastal waters.

FINANCIAL AID

Maine Maritime participates in the Federal Work-Study, Federal Perkins Loan, and Federal Supplemental Educational Opportunity Grant programs and is an eligible institution for the federally insured Federal Stafford Student Loan, Federal Pell Grant, and veterans' programs. The college also has other campus-based loan and scholarship programs available to its students. To apply for financial aid, students must complete the Free Application for Federal Student Aid (FAFSA) and send it in after January 1 (but not later than April 15) of the year of desired entry. In addition to need-based financial aid, qualified students in each entering class receive Federal Student Incentive Payments of $3000 per year. The NROTC Scholarship Program offers the following benefits: all tuition paid, all books furnished, a monthly subsistence allowance during the school year, and a substantial uniform allowance. The NROTC College Program offers students uniform allowances and a subsistence allowance of $150 per month during their junior and senior years.

APPLICATION AND INFORMATION

Application should be made as early as possible in the senior year of secondary school and no later than June 1. The college uses an early decision process if a completed file is received by December 20. Otherwise, a rolling admissions system is used, and decisions are reached when an applicant's materials are received and evaluated.

MANHATTAN COLLEGE

■ RIVERDALE, NEW YORK

William J. Bisset
Dean of Admissions and Financial Aid
Manhattan College
Riverdale, New York 10471
Telephone: 718-862-7200
800-MC2-XCEL (toll-free)
E-mail: admit@manhattan.edu

THE COLLEGE

Manhattan College was founded by the Brothers of the Christian Schools in 1853 and chartered by the state of New York in 1863. Traditionally a private men's college, in 1964 it began a student-faculty exchange program with the College of Mount Saint Vincent. Manhattan became fully coeducational in 1973. The College has an enrollment of more than 3,200, of whom 2,400 are undergraduates.

ACADEMIC PROGRAM

The core curriculum shared by the School of Arts and the School of Science studies some of the vital works of humankind, explores new ideas, examines the meaning of scientific experimentation, and encourages a student to develop his or her thinking and leadership abilities. The major programs offer advanced work in specific humanistic and scientific disciplines and opportunities to work on research projects in collaboration with faculty scholars. In the School of Engineering, all engineering students follow a common core curriculum during the first two years and choose a major at the beginning of the junior year. Each curriculum includes a generous selection of courses in basic sciences, the engineering sciences, humanistic studies, and mathematics. The School of Business prepares students for positions of executive responsibility in business, government, and nonprofit organizations. The business curriculum is based on a strong commitment to liberal education and is well balanced between professional business courses, humanities, sciences, and social sciences. The School of Education prepares students for teaching, counseling, and health professions. Students complete the College's core curriculum in liberal arts and sciences and then complete a major in various programs in the School's three departments: Education, Physical Education & Human Performance, and Radiological & Health Professions. All programs include internships/practicums in schools, hospitals, or other institutions. Graduates of the school's teacher-preparation programs receive New York State provisional teaching certification. The school also offers a five-year B.A./M.S. program in elementary or secondary education and special education.

FINANCIAL AID

Manhattan grants or administers financial assistance in the form of tuition awards to students on the basis of need and/or ability. Need is evaluated through the FAFSA. In addition to a general scholarship fund, Manhattan offers endowed scholarships, special-category scholarships and grants, student athletic grants, Federal Pell Grants, Federal Supplemental Educational Opportunity Grants, student loans, Federal Work-Study Program awards, and New York State financial assistance. A total of 1,650 students receive financial aid from Manhattan College, and approximately 87 percent receive financial aid from government or private agencies.

APPLICATION AND INFORMATION

Application forms are furnished by the Admission Center on request. The Common Application Form, which is available in many high school guidance offices, may also be used. After supplying the information required, students must send the application for admission to the Admission Center at Manhattan College. The high school report and the student evaluation and transcript must be submitted by the high school guidance counselor. This should be done after six terms of high school or right after the seventh term. There is a rolling admissions policy and a February 15 deadline for financial aid applications. A nonrefundable application fee of $25 is required.

MARIAN COLLEGE OF FOND DU LAC

■ Fond du Lac, Wisconsin

THE COLLEGE

Marian College is a Catholic coeducational liberal arts college whose first commitment is to the education of the whole person. Founded in 1936 by the Sisters of Saint Agnes as a school for teacher education, Marian now offers more than thirty major fields of study. The warm and friendly environment of the campus supports faculty, administration, and students. A strong liberal arts foundation gives students the values and ethics that they will need throughout their lives. There are approximately 1,900 undergraduate students at Marian, and an additional 600 are pursuing a Master of Arts in education. Students at Marian can be involved in many social organizations and clubs on campus, including Greek organizations. Marian participates in NCAA Division III athletic programs and offers men's intercollegiate baseball, basketball, golf, hockey, soccer, and tennis. Women's intercollegiate sports are basketball, soccer, softball, tennis, and volleyball. Two modern residence halls and a town house village are available for Marian students on a first-come, first-served basis. With enrollment growing, a complex of apartment-style housing, the Courtyard Village, was constructed, adding an element of style and excitement to Marian's beautiful 50-acre campus. The instructional divisions of Marian are the Division of Arts and Humanities, the Division of Business, the Division of Educational Studies, the Division of Mathematics and Natural Science, the Division of Nursing, and the Division of Social and Behavioral Science. In addition to the undergraduate degrees listed below, master's degrees are awarded in education and in organizational leadership and quality.

For additional information regarding the application process or for other information, students may contact:

Carol Reichenberger
Vice President for Enrollment Services
Marian College of Fond du Lac
45 South National Avenue
Fond du Lac, Wisconsin 54935
Telephone: 414-923-7650
800-2-MARIAN (toll-free)
E-mail: admit@mariancoll.edu
World Wide Web:
http://www.mariancoll.edu

ACADEMIC PROGRAM

All programs are based upon common general requirements. All students, regardless of their specific degree program, must successfully complete 48 credits in liberal arts, complete at least one major program, and have taken at least 128 hours of credit with a minimum average of 2 grade points for each credit hour. The senior year, or at least the last 32 credit hours, must have been completed in residence at Marian College. Credit is awarded for CLEP subject and general examinations according to the current criteria and policies of Marian College. Details may be obtained from the assistant dean of academic affairs. The College conducts traditional academic programs in two semesters, the first from late August to mid-December and the second from mid-January to mid-May. There is also an extensive summer school session.

FINANCIAL AID

The Marian College Financial Aid Office coordinates an active program of financial assistance for students. Aid is based on need and/or academic merit. The principle sources of aid include the Federal Pell Grant Program, the Federal Work-Study Program, and Marian Assistance. Academic scholarships, including the Presidential Scholarship ($5000), the Naber Leadership Award ($3000), and the Trustee and Regional Awards, are available to entering students and are renewable.

MARIETTA COLLEGE

■ MARIETTA, OHIO

THE COLLEGE

Founded in 1835, Marietta College traces its roots to the Muskingum Academy, which was founded in 1797 as the first institution of higher learning in the Northwest Territory. Marietta's chapter of Phi Beta Kappa was the sixteenth in the nation, showing the College's early dedication to scholarship. Women were first admitted in 1897. About half of Marietta's 1,100 students come from a variety of states along the Eastern Seaboard, the South, and the Midwest; the rest come primarily from Ohio, the surrounding states, and nine other countries. More than forty states are represented in the Marietta student body. Situated on 120 acres within a block of downtown Marietta, the College has a number of academic and extracurricular facilities. Recent additions to the campus include the Andrews Student Center (1993); the McDonough Leadership Center, home to the most comprehensive program in leadership studies in the country; the McKinney Media Center, which houses two radio stations, a cable television station, and an award-winning student newspaper; a pedestrian mall that enhances the central campus; a Cardiovascular Fitness Center; sports medicine facilities; and the Chuck McCoy Athletic Facility (1993), which houses lacrosse, football, women's soccer and softball, athletic offices, weight rooms, and meeting rooms.

To receive information about Marietta or to apply for admission, students should contact:

Office of Admission
Marietta College
Marietta, Ohio 45750-4005
Telephone: 800-331-7896 (toll-free)
E-mail: admit@mcnet.marietta.edu
Web site: http://www.marietta.edu

ACADEMIC PROGRAM

Marietta students are known for both their breadth and depth of study. Freshmen take a special first-year program that begins with the College Experience Seminar and includes courses in composition (English 101), oral presentation (Speech 101), and mathematics. Every student also completes a liberal arts core of sequence courses in the humanities, social sciences, science, and the fine arts. Seniors complete a Senior Capstone, the culmination of advanced study in their majors.

FINANCIAL AID

About 70 percent of current Marietta students receive financial aid based on need. A number of merit-based scholarships are available in addition to funds allocated through College grants and federal and state sources. Members of the entering freshman class receive academic merit scholarships for three different levels of achievement. Students with a minimum GPA of 3.75, a minimum score of 30 on the ACT, or a minimum score of 1350 on the SAT I receive a Trustees scholarship valued at $12,000. Students with a GPA of 3.5, a score of 27 on the ACT, or a score of 1200 on the SAT I receive a President's scholarship valued at $7000. Finally, those students with a GPA of 3.25, a score of 25 on the ACT, or a score of 1150 on the SAT I receive a Dean's scholarship valued at $3500. A Fine Arts Scholarship is awarded annually to winners of an art, music, and drama competition. Numerous work-study jobs are available to students in many campus departments. Grants are available for children and grandchildren of alumni.

APPLICATION AND INFORMATION

Students should apply early in their senior year of high school to guarantee a place in the fall. Marietta operates on a rolling admission plan, and students are notified of acceptance within one month after all application materials are complete. Students applying for financial aid should apply before March 1 of their senior year to be considered for merit scholarships.

MARYMOUNT COLLEGE

■ TARRYTOWN, NEW YORK

THE COLLEGE

Founded in 1907, Marymount is an independent, four-year liberal arts college whose mission is to prepare women for work in the twenty-first century. Having been a leader in women's education for ninety years, the College is aware of women's needs and goals, their particular concerns, and their special contributions to the world. Marymount offers a weeklong session for traditional-age and adult women and a special weekend session to serve the needs of working women and men wishing to pursue a bachelor's degree. The College enrolls 700 women in the weeklong session and 550 men and women in the weekend college. Marymount accommodates both commuting and residential students. The College's physical facilities consist of twelve buildings, seven of which have been constructed since 1950. The facilities include a modern library, an athletic center with an Olympic-size pool, and a completely renovated science building with state-of-the-art laboratory equipment. The four dormitories accommodate approximately 650 students. Students come from many parts of the country to take advantage of the academic facilities of the College and the cultural offerings of New York City. Student organizations include numerous special interest clubs, community service programs, and honor societies. The College provides frequent social and cultural activities in which students may participate, as well as dramatic performances, art exhibits, film festival series, and dance concerts. The Teahouse is a popular meeting spot. Marymount has intercollegiate teams and an extensive intramural program.

For further information, prospective students should contact:

Dean of Admissions
Marymount College
100 Marymount Avenue
Tarrytown, New York 10591-3796
Telephone: 914-332-8295
800-724-4312 (toll-free)
Fax: 914-332-4956

ACADEMIC PROGRAM

Marymount students have great flexibility in their course selection, although there is a general education requirement. In consultation with their academic adviser, they may choose from the wide variety of courses offered in some thirty majors. From this broad background, they are guided in their choice of a major field, which comprises ten to twenty-one of their courses. Candidates for a bachelor's degree must complete 120 semester credits and fulfill the requirements of their major program. Students are also encouraged to participate in our internship program for college credit. The College awards credit for successful scores on the College-Level Examination Program (CLEP) general and subject examinations. Students may also earn credit through Advanced Placement (AP) examinations. Credit for life/work experience is also available to adult students on presentation of a portfolio.

FINANCIAL AID

In 1997–98, Marymount students received more than $6.3 million in student financial aid. Of this, $3.5 million came from federal programs, $659,000 from state programs, and more than $2.3 million from Marymount. Trustee grants and scholarships are also available. Financial aid applicants are required to file the FAFSA. It is recommended that the form be submitted by February 1. Early applicants can expect to receive their award notifications beginning April 15.

APPLICATION AND INFORMATION

The application, a $30 fee, the high school record and recommendation, and test scores should be submitted by May 1 for admission to the fall term or by December 1 for the spring term. Notification of the admission decision, which is given on a rolling basis, begins in the late fall. Deferred admission and early admission are available.

MARYMOUNT UNIVERSITY

■ Arlington, Virginia

THE UNIVERSITY

Marymount University is a comprehensive, coeducational Catholic institution, founded in 1950. Marymount emphasizes excellence in teaching, attention to the individual, and values and ethics across the curriculum. The University enrolls approximately 2,000 undergraduate and 1,900 graduate students. Marymount offers thirty-seven undergraduate majors and twenty-three graduate degree programs through the Schools of Arts and Sciences, Business Administration, Education and Human Services, and Health Professions. The University is located in a residential neighborhood of Arlington, Virginia, adjacent to Washington D.C. Marymount University was recently named one of the "best values" in the South for 1998 by *U.S. News & World Report,* which also recognized Marymount for the diversity of its student body. The University has a 25 percent undergraduate minority enrollment. Marymount students represent more than sixty countries.

An application form, a catalog, curriculum brochures, and other information may be obtained by contacting:

Chris Domes, Dean of Admissions
Marymount University
2807 North Glebe Road
Arlington, Virginia 22207-4299
Telephone: 703-284-1500
800-548-7638 (toll-free)
E-mail: admissions@marymount.edu
World Wide Web:
http://www.marymount.edu

ACADEMIC PROGRAM

Marymount University's goal is to help each student achieve his or her full potential. While students study a liberal arts core curriculum plus the required elements of their discipline, they are able to work with their faculty adviser to tailor an academic program that fits their personal and career objectives. Small classes and personal attention help ensure student success and a strong sense of community. An honor system guides academic and social conduct. Cultural and educational resources of the nation's capital add to the curriculum through off-campus activities. The balancing of academics and hands-on, practical experience is a cornerstone of Marymount's commitment to providing students with a well-rounded education. All students complete an internship as part of their program of study. High-quality academics, ethics across the curriculum, and a focus on service complete the solid foundation Marymount provides students.

FINANCIAL AID

Marymount provides an extensive scholarship and grant program and participates in all federal and state aid programs. To be considered for aid, students must file the Free Application for Federal Student Aid (FAFSA) with the College Scholarship Service and Marymount's financial aid application with the University's Financial Aid Office. Approximately 80 percent of full-time undergraduate students receive aid in the form of scholarships, grants, loans, work-study awards, or on-campus employment. Academic scholarships are available for freshmen and are renewable each year.

APPLICATION AND INFORMATION

High school students seeking admission are advised to apply early during their senior year. They should submit an application, a nonrefundable fee of $35, a high school transcript, SAT I or ACT scores, evidence of expected graduation from an accredited high school, and a recommendation from a high school counselor or an appropriate school official. Those who have attended another college or university must submit the application, $35 fee, test scores, evidence of high school graduation, transcripts of college-level study, and a recommendation from the Dean of Students at the previous institution. The University has a rolling admission policy and notifies applicants soon after the application process is completed and the Admissions Committee has acted on the application.

MARYVILLE UNIVERSITY OF SAINT LOUIS

■ ST. LOUIS, MISSOURI

THE UNIVERSITY

Maryville University is an independent coeducational university with an enrollment of 3,400 undergraduate and graduate students. The quality and variety of its curriculum—solid liberal arts studies and professional programs covering more than forty fields—have attracted an increasing number of students in recent years. A special feature is the large measure of personal concern for each student demonstrated by everyone on campus, from the faculty through the administrative staff to the president. The University was founded in 1872 by the Religious of the Sacred Heart, moved to its present site in suburban St. Louis in 1961, became an independent college in 1972, and became a university in 1991.

For further information, students should contact:

Dr. Martha Wade
Dean of Admissions and Enrollment Management
Maryville University of Saint Louis
13550 Conway Road
St. Louis, Missouri 63141-7299
Telephone: 314-529-9350
800-627-9855 (toll-free)
Fax: 314-529-9927
E-mail: admissions@maryville.edu

ACADEMIC PROGRAM

The academic curriculum and programs are based on a semester calendar with a summer session. Professional programs combine education toward a career with a strong liberal arts base to ensure that students in all fields develop a high degree of competence in professional areas closely related to their academic interests. Special programs include a transitional program for high school seniors, an interior design apprenticeship with professional designers, a hospital internship on preparation for certification by the Registry of Medical Technologists of the American Society of Clinical Pathologists (ASCP), and an actuarial program that prepares students for eight professional examinations for actuaries. There are also opportunities for communications internships with local radio and TV stations, newspapers, and advertising or public relations agencies and clinical opportunities at area hospitals for music therapy, occupational therapy, physical therapy, and nursing students. Maryville also offers one of the nation's few weekend programs in nursing. A cooperative education program combines supervised, paid work experience with classroom studies. An intensive English program is offered for international students.

FINANCIAL AID

Financial aid is available in the form of employment, loans, and grants; awards are based on need as determined by the FAFSA and University-administered forms. Scholarships, which are not awarded on a need basis, are also available. Students are free to accept employment or a grant without being obligated to accept a loan, which may be offered as part of a financial aid package. Last year, more than 75 percent of the University's full-time students received financial aid; the average award was $7854. Deferred payment plans are available through arrangements with the University for those who wish to pay their educational expenses in installments.

APPLICATION AND INFORMATION

Freshman applicants must submit an application form with a $20 application fee, an official high school transcript, and ACT or SAT I scores. Under Maryville's rolling admission policy, applications are reviewed immediately upon receipt of all necessary material. Transfer students must submit an application for admission with a $20 application fee and high school and college transcripts. Certain programs require additional credentials. The physical therapy and occupational therapy programs require submission of a letter of recommendation; physical therapy also requires a personal interview. Admission of students to the B.F.A. or B.A. in art program requires a portfolio evaluation by the art and design faculty. Acceptance into the nursing program requires a personal interview.

MEREDITH COLLEGE

■ RALEIGH, NORTH CAROLINA

THE COLLEGE

Meredith College, founded in 1891 by North Carolina Baptists to provide excellence in education for women, is today the largest private women's college in the Southeast. The College emphasizes the liberal arts, career preparation, and personal development. Approximately 2,050 undergraduate degree candidates choose from more than thirty major fields. Students may also complete a teacher licensure program, preprofessional preparation in medicine and law, or experiential learning through internships and cooperative education in such settings as the state legislature or Research Triangle Park.

For additional information and for planning a campus visit, students should contact:

Office of Admissions
Meredith College
3800 Hillsborough Street
Raleigh, North Carolina 27607-5298
Telephone: 919-829-8581
800-MEREDITH (toll-free)
Fax: 919-829-2348
E-mail: admissions@meredith.edu
Web site: http://www.meredith.edu

ACADEMIC PROGRAM

To achieve breadth in her education, each student must fulfill general education requirements in humanities and arts, social and behavioral sciences, mathematics and natural sciences, and health and physical education. By the end of the sophomore year, she declares a major and begins to study her chosen field in depth. She may round out her program by completing a second major, a minor or a concentration, a teacher education program, an experiential learning component (an internship, co-op, or field work), a study-abroad program, or various other options.

FINANCIAL AID

Meredith's financial aid program is designed to meet a high percentage of the analyzed need of the student. Approximately 45 percent of undergraduate students receive need-based assistance; when competitive scholarships and state entitlement grants are added, approximately 88 percent of Meredith students receive some form of financial assistance. The Free Application for Federal Student Aid (FAFSA) and a Meredith financial aid application are used to determine eligibility for need-based federal, state, and institutional funds that include grants and scholarships, loans, and work-study. A freshman candidate may also file special application forms for the competitive scholarships that recognize students for superior academic ability and talent in art, music, or interior design. A North Carolina Teaching Fellow who is selected for Meredith's program may use her scholarship at the College and will have other gift assistance coordinated to match the stipend provided by the state.

APPLICATION AND INFORMATION

An application for admission should be sent to the Office of Admissions along with a nonrefundable $35 processing fee (or acceptable fee-waiver request). The student is responsible for requesting that her official high school transcript, SAT I or ACT scores, and recommendations be sent to the admissions office. A transfer student must file an official transcript from each postsecondary institution attended. Meredith has two freshman admission plans: early decision and rolling admissions. An early decision candidate must apply by October 15; this "first choice" plan means that if accepted under early decision, the student fully expects to enroll and will withdraw any other pending applications. The student is notified by November 1. A candidate under the rolling plan is encouraged to file early in the senior year, with February 15 as the recommended deadline. Notifications under this plan begin in early November. The candidates' reply dates are December 1 for early decision and May 1 for rolling admission candidates. Transfer applicants are encouraged to apply by February 15. Notifications begin in late January, and May 1 is the candidates' reply date. For admission to the spring semester, a freshman or transfer student should apply by December 1.

MIDLAND LUTHERAN COLLEGE

■ FREMONT, NEBRASKA

THE COLLEGE

Midland Lutheran College is committed to providing a value-based education that prepares students for success in a variety of careers. While the College is related to the Evangelical Lutheran Church in America, it actively seeks and celebrates religious diversity. Students represent the full range of the Judeo-Christian tradition. Midland's 1,033 men and women come from twenty-three states and four countries. With a 15:1 student-faculty ratio, the College emphasizes close relationships between teachers and students. Faculty members at Midland make teaching and advising a priority, keeping generous office hours and making themselves available at home during evenings and weekends. Students may choose to live in one of five dormitories on campus. Upperclass students have the option of living off campus in homes or apartments in the community.

For more information, students should contact:

Roland R. Kahnk
Vice President for Enrollment Services
Midland Lutheran College
900 North Clarkson
Fremont, Nebraska 68025
Telephone: 402-721-5480 (call collect)
800-642-8382 (toll-free in Nebraska)

ACADEMIC PROGRAM

Midland seeks to provide every student with the breadth of study important to a liberal arts education. All students are required to take the yearlong interdisciplinary humanities course, Odyssey in the Human Spirit. The award-winning Odyssey is taught by a team of humanities professors who present major themes in Western cultural heritage through the study of individual personalities. Students in the course also learn basic research and writing skills. Students meet general education requirements in seven general education areas. These courses become the foundation for more specialized learning in the student's academic career. Midland operates under the 4-1-4 academic calendar. The fall and spring semesters are separated by the one-month Interterm in January. Interterm provides unusual on-campus and off-campus study opportunities for the faculty and students. Faculty members often teach courses in special areas of interest; students take courses on the Midland campus or elsewhere.

FINANCIAL AID

More than 90 percent of Midland's students receive financial assistance. The deadline for application is May 1, but awards are made on a rolling basis. Applications received prior to the May 1 deadline receive priority examination. Midland requires that students complete the College's own financial aid application along with the Free Application for Federal Student Aid (FAFSA). Students must be accepted for admission before financial aid can be awarded. Scholarships are awarded on the basis of academic achievement and special abilities in athletics, music, art, and drama. Scholarship assistance may range from $500 to $5000 per year. Lutheran students are automatically eligible for a $500 Lutheran Student Award. In addition, funded scholarships ranging from $100 to $1000 provide assistance for students in a variety of areas. Federally funded programs provide assistance to students in the form of Federal Pell Grants, Federal Supplemental Educational Opportunity Grants, Federal Stafford Student Loans, Federal Perkins Loans, and a variety of other kinds of aid. Students may be eligible to receive work-study assignments that provide on-campus employment opportunities often related to their major.

APPLICATION AND INFORMATION

Students are encouraged to apply as early as possible to Midland. Applications are reviewed on a rolling basis, and students are notified of acceptance as soon as possible after all of their application materials are received. Along with a completed Midland application form and a $20 application fee, students should submit ACT scores and a copy of their high school transcript. Transfer students should also submit copies of transcripts from all colleges or universities attended.

MILLS COLLEGE

■ OAKLAND, CALIFORNIA

THE COLLEGE

Mills is the only women's college among the many fine educational institutions in the San Francisco Bay Area. Founded in 1852 as the first women's college west of the Rockies, it is committed to remaining a women's college because it believes that such an environment offers women special advantages in preparing for new roles and responsibilities.

For more information, students should contact:

Avis E. Hinkson
Dean of Admission
Mills College
5000 MacArthur Boulevard
Oakland, California 94613

Telephone: 510-430-2135
800-87-MILLS (toll-free)
Fax: 510-430-3314
E-mail: admission@mills.edu
Web site: http://www.mills.edu

ACADEMIC PROGRAM

To earn a Mills B.A., students must take thirty-four semester courses (usually four courses each semester). First-year students take interdisciplinary seminars on such topics as Science and Pseudoscience, Tribal Cultures in Fact and Fiction, and Music and the Written Word. Students are also expected to choose two courses from each of four areas (natural sciences and mathematics, social sciences, humanities, and fine arts), a one-semester multicultural or cross-cultural course, and one course that heavily stresses writing skills. They also must choose at least half their courses from outside their major field. Students complete their chosen major with a senior project or thesis. A comprehensive program in mathematics and computer science offers basic grounding in mathematics for women who have had insufficient high school preparation but need math skills for their prospective careers.

FINANCIAL AID

Nearly 80 percent of Mills students are awarded a financial aid package that includes a loan, campus work-study, and a scholarship grant from Mills, outside sources, or both. Awards are primarily need-based, although academic merit is also considered for certain awards. Scholarship grants range from \$200 to \$16,000 per year. Mills makes a special effort to provide financial aid to members of minority groups who demonstrate need. Almost 90 percent of Mills undergraduates who apply for financial aid are offered assistance. Financial aid applicants are expected to apply for assistance from appropriate outside sources, such as the National Merit Scholarship, Federal Pell Grant, and California State Grant programs. More than 40 percent of Mills students have some of their determined need offset by such outside awards. Loans may be obtained by most students, and 45 percent of undergraduates are offered campus work opportunities; some students take off-campus jobs. All freshman and transfer candidates who are California residents must file the Free Application for Federal Student Aid (FAFSA) to be considered for all types of government aid and must also file the Cal Grant GPA Verification Form. Students who seek Mills scholarship funds must also file the Mills Financial Aid Form. Priority is given to applicants who meet the published deadlines.

APPLICATION AND INFORMATION

The priority deadline for admission applications is February 15. Applicants are notified by the Admission Committee in late March. All students are encouraged to meet this deadline; however, international students, merit scholarship applicants, and all other financial aid applicants must apply by February 15. Financial aid is awarded on a first-come, first-served basis, starting with those who meet the deadline. Financial aid awards are made after admission decisions. For admission to the spring term, the deadline is November 1, and admission decisions are mailed in late December. Students who want to be considered for a California State Grant for the spring semester must apply by the previous March 2 deadline.

MINNEAPOLIS COLLEGE OF ART AND DESIGN

■ Minneapolis, Minnesota

THE COLLEGE

The 112-year-old Minneapolis College of Art and Design (MCAD), along with the Minneapolis Institute of Arts and the Children's Theatre Company, occupies three square blocks in a residential neighborhood just south of the downtown district. The three institutions constitute one of the largest art centers in the nation. In addition to its regular academic program, the College offers evening, Saturday, and summer school classes and art-related films, lectures, performances, and conferences through the Continuing Studies Office. The MCAD Gallery hosts exhibitions during the academic year, providing students with an excellent opportunity to view the work of important contemporary artists and designers. As part of a visiting artists program, nationally prominent artists, designers, and critics visit the campus for varying periods of time to teach, lecture, and work with students and the faculty. Although there are a variety of campus social events each year, students who apply to the College should be aware that its standards of professionalism and performance demand a significant commitment.

For a College catalog and an application form, students should write to the following address:

Admissions Office
Minneapolis College of Art and Design
2501 Stevens Avenue South
Minneapolis, Minnesota 55404
Telephone: 612-874-3760
800-874-6223 (toll-free)
Fax: 612-874-3701
E-mail: admissions@mcad.edu
Web site: http://www.mcad.edu/

ACADEMIC PROGRAM

In order to be awarded the B.S. degree, students are required to complete 120 semester credits, 36 of which concentrate in courses relating to visualization (e.g., communication theory and marketing: history, strategies, forms and perceptions, media analysis, hypermedia), and 21 credits, which are taken within MCAD's studio offerings. Students are also required to participate in a community-related project, an externship or study-abroad program, and a senior project/exhibit. This degree program offers preprofessional training in visual persuasion and information techniques applicable to the fields of advertising/marketing, science/technology, entertainment, education, and corporate communications. The B.F.A. program requires students to complete 120 semester credits. Twelve of these are in the first-year Foundation Studies program, 39 are in the liberal arts area, and 69 are in the studio. To facilitate the growth of the perception and judgment necessary for meaningful creative endeavor, the College has developed a curriculum that stresses critical thinking, artistic inquiry, professional responsibility, and interdisciplinary dialogue. The goals of the first-year Foundation Studies Program are to develop a student's ability to integrate verbal and visual communication skills and enhance personal expression while preparing for the major areas of study. Course work within the various majors provides students with a solid foundation in craftsmanship and offers both technical and conceptual information. All students are encouraged to expand their interests and technical abilities in other disciplines through elective courses. Complementing work in the studio courses, the Liberal Arts Division offers study in history, criticism, literature, philosophy, religion, and the social and behavioral sciences.

FINANCIAL AID

More than 72 percent of the College student body receive financial aid to meet education costs. Financial aid administered by the College comes from federal, state, and private sources and includes Federal Pell Grants, Federal Stafford Student Loans, Federal Supplemental Educational Opportunity Grants, Federal Perkins Loans, and Minnesota State Scholarships and Grants-in-Aid. College-controlled aid includes a variety of College grants, scholarships, and work-study contracts. Aid from private sources is also available. To qualify, applicants must submit the Free Application for Federal Student Aid (FAFSA).

MISSOURI SOUTHERN STATE COLLEGE

■ Joplin, Missouri

THE COLLEGE

Missouri Southern State College is a four-year institution that specializes in undergraduate university education with an international perspective. The College focuses on classroom teaching, resulting in a tradition of small classes and close, personal interaction between faculty members and approximately 5,500 students. This approach is maintained through a 16:1 student-teacher ratio. Southern's faculty members come from all over the world, with degrees from prestigious universities and professional experience in the disciplines they teach. In 1995, the Missouri General Assembly enhanced the College's mission through House Bill 442, directing the institution to "develop such academic support programs and public service activities it deems necessary and appropriate to establish international or global education as a distinctive theme of its mission." The centerpiece of the global emphasis is the Institute of International Studies, which coordinates all international programs and activities, including a pervasive global dimension in all curricula, study-abroad opportunities for faculty and students, internships abroad for students, and expanded foreign language offerings. The 500 students who live on campus enjoy air-conditioned residence halls. The newly opened Student Life Center offers a cafeteria, an aerobics room, a weight/exercise room, laundry facilities, a computer lab, a video game room, and a lounge with a big-screen television and surround sound.

Information on specific academic areas and other College programs is readily available from the Admission Office and online by contacting:

Admission Office
Missouri Southern State College
3950 East Newman Road
Joplin, Missouri 64801-1595
Telephone: 417-625-9378
800-606-MSSC (6772)
(toll-free)
Fax: 417-659-4429
E-mail: admissions@mail.mssc.edu
Web site: http://www.mssc.edu

ACADEMIC PROGRAM

Because graduates may change occupations and careers several times during their working lives, all students pursuing a degree complete the core curriculum, a series of courses carefully designed to instill certain lifelong thinking and learning skills. Core courses emphasize critical thinking, problem-solving, and communications skills; a general understanding of scientific and artistic aspects of this culture; and the ability to function in a global society through knowledge and understanding of other cultures. In both the core and major studies, writing skills and computer literacy are developed, and an international perspective is stressed in every possible course. The baccalaureate degree requires 51 credit hours of the core with a total of 128 hours; the Associate of Arts degree requires 64 hours, with 42 hours from the core; and the Associate of Science degree requires 64 hours, with 26 hours from the core curriculum. Many broad-based majors offer emphases that allow students a more specialized direction of study. A prestigious Honors Program provides special challenges and opportunities for qualified students who may receive full scholarships for their academic studies.

FINANCIAL AID

A wide variety of financial aid options assist students with college costs. Federal programs include the Federal Pell Grant, Federal Supplemental Educational Opportunity Grant, Federal Work-Study Program, Federal Perkins Loan, and Federal Stafford Loan, among others. Several state programs aid prospective teachers and students with high academic standing. In addition, the College provides a wide range of academic scholarships, performing awards, and student employment. Special scholarships are available for qualified junior college transfer students, and out-of-state tuition waivers are offered to students in a designated surrounding area.

APPLICATION AND INFORMATION

The College has a priority deadline of August 1. Students may apply any time during their senior year of high school. There is a $15 nonrefundable application fee.

MONTCLAIR STATE UNIVERSITY

■ UPPER MONTCLAIR, NEW JERSEY

THE UNIVERSITY

For application forms and additional admission information, students should contact:

Office of Admissions
Montclair State University
Upper Montclair, New Jersey 07043-1624
Telephone: 800-331-9205 (toll-free)

Founded in 1908 as a normal school oriented to the education of future teachers, Montclair State has evolved into a four-year comprehensive public university that offers a broad range of educational and cultural opportunities. Montclair State is composed of the School of Business, the School of the Arts, the College of Humanities and Social Sciences, the College of Science and Mathematics, the College of Education and Human Services, and the Graduate School and confers degrees in forty-four undergraduate majors and thirty-four graduate majors. Through its diverse programs and services, Montclair State seeks to develop educated men and women who are inquiring, creative, and responsible contributors to society. Montclair State has been designated a Center of Excellence in the fine and performing arts in northern New Jersey. It is accredited by the Middle States Association of Colleges and Schools, and its teacher education, administrative, and school service personnel programs are approved by the National Council for Accreditation of Teacher Education. The total enrollment was 12,808 in fall 1997; 5,989 women and 3,728 men were enrolled as undergraduates. The majority of students are from New Jersey, and approximately 80 percent commute. The remainder live in campus residence halls or apartments or in University-approved off-campus housing. Approximately 70 percent belong to student organizations. Some of the organizations that are involved in student life are the College Life Union Board, which is responsible for coordinating all social, cultural, educational, and recreational student programs; the Intercollegiate Athletic Council, which provides men and women of all the schools with the opportunity to participate in many varsity sports; and the Student Intramural and Leisure Council, which runs one of the country's few student-controlled intramural programs.

ACADEMIC PROGRAM

Successful completion of a minimum of 128 semester hours is necessary for graduation. Course requirements include general education (34–58 semester hours), comprising communication, humanities and the arts, pure and applied sciences, social and behavioral sciences, a physical education requirement, and a multicultural awareness requirement; courses in the major field of study in arts and sciences programs (a minimum of 33–82 semester hours); and electives (12–37 semester hours).

FINANCIAL AID

Four major types of financial aid programs are available at Montclair State: loans, grants, scholarships, and employment. Within each of these categories, funding may be available through federal, state, and/or institutional sources. State aid programs include Tuition Aid Grants, Educational Opportunity Fund Grants, Bloustein Distinguished Scholars awards, Public Tuition Benefits awards, and N.J. CLASS loans. Federal sources of aid include Federal Pell Grants, Federal Supplemental Educational Opportunity Grants, Federal Perkins Loans, Federal Work-Study, Federal Stafford Student Loans, Federal PLUS loans, and programs for veterans. Approximately 75 percent of undergraduates receive financial aid. Students should contact the Financial Aid Office regarding application materials and deadline dates.

APPLICATION AND INFORMATION

Applicants must submit a completed application form, a nonrefundable application fee of $40, a copy of their official high school transcript, and copies of their SAT I or ACT scores. Admission decisions are announced on a rolling basis until all spaces are filled.

MONTREAT COLLEGE

■ MONTREAT, NORTH CAROLINA

THE COLLEGE

Montreat is a four-year Christian liberal arts college affiliated with the Presbyterian Church (USA). At Montreat College, a student's experience is enhanced by an education of value, grounded in a strong liberal arts core, taught by outstanding Christian faculty, and prized by today's employers and graduate schools. Students benefit from Montreat's small classes where their opinions matter, and they grow through one-on-one interaction with professors and classmates. Studies challenge them to integrate faith and learning while considering subjects in ways never thought possible. Hands-on experiences in the majors (internships, field studies, mission programs, community service, and independent research) enable students to gain practical career and life preparation. Montreat College enrollment is rapidly growing. Enrollment is more than 1,000 in the traditional Montreat campus program and in the off-campus School of Professional and Adult Studies. The student body typically represents approximately thirty states and ten other countries.

For more information, students should write or call:

Office of Admissions
Montreat College
P.O. Box 1267
Montreat, North Carolina 28757
Telephone: 704-669-8012 Ext. 3781
800-622-6968 (toll-free)
Fax: 704-669-0120
E-mail: admissions@montreat.edu

ACADEMIC PROGRAM

Upon enrollment, students are assigned a faculty adviser to assist them in clarifying their educational objectives and meeting the requirements for graduation. Students and faculty advisers work together in arranging a program of study leading to graduation. Graduation requirements are a minimum of 126 semester hours, cumulative quality point average of at least 2.0, completion of the general education core requirements, 33 semester hours in 300-level or above courses, completion of all major requirements, a grade of C or better in courses needed for the major or minor, and completion of at least 31 semester hours at Montreat College. Students interested in careers in medicine, law, criminology, and other professional areas are reminded that the best preparation, according to graduate school advisers in these areas, is a solid liberal arts degree program such as that found at Montreat College.

FINANCIAL AID

Through generous financial aid and scholarship packages, deserving students receive the quality academics of a private college at a modest cost. Each year, more than 85 percent of Montreat students receive some form of financial aid. Working individually with each student, the College awards financial aid packages that include scholarships, grants, loans, and work-study jobs. Scholarships are also made available to transfer students. All students must submit the Free Application for Federal Student Aid (FAFSA) and the Montreat College Application for Scholarship and Financial Assistance. To drastically reduce processing time, the FAFSA can be electronically submitted by the College to the federal government for students who have applied, been accepted, and submitted a $100 deposit. For more information, students should call the Financial Aid Office at 800-545-4656 (toll-free).

APPLICATION AND INFORMATION

Students are required to submit a formal application accompanied by a $15 application fee. The common application is accepted. An official transcript of high school credits must be submitted directly from the high school to the College Office of Admissions. SAT I/ACT verification is also required. Montreat College's school code is 005423.

MOUNT IDA COLLEGE

■ Newton Centre, Massachusetts

All correspondence should be directed to:

Judith A. Kaufman, Dean of Admissions or
Harold C. Duvall, Dean of Enrollment Management
Mount Ida College
777 Dedham Street
Newton Centre, Massachusetts 02159
Telephone: 617-928-4553
617-928-4535
Fax: 617-928-4760
World Wide Web:
http://www.mountida.edu

THE COLLEGE

Founded in 1899, Mount Ida has become one of the Northeast's most innovative postsecondary institutions. All freshman students begin in Mount Ida's renowned Junior College Division, which features eight schools that offer 37 two- and three-year associate degree programs. After earning an associate degree, students may choose to enter employment or to continue in one of the Mount Ida Senior College Division's two-year bachelor's degree programs. The associate degree guarantees that a student may enter the junior year of at least one Mount Ida bachelor's degree program. This flexible system allows students to exercise educational options one step at a time as they gain knowledge and experience. Approximately 2,000 full-time students are enrolled at Mount Ida. Ninety percent of these students represent New England, New York, New Jersey, and Pennsylvania. Students are encouraged to start new positive groups on campus that will enrich the College community. Campus organizations and clubs reflect the diversity of the student body and afford wonderful opportunities for creative expression and leadership development. A wide variety of social, cultural, and recreational activities are also an important part of student life. These include intercollegiate mixers, Parents Weekend, international dinners, a faculty lecture series, Winter Carnival, a Spring Semi-Formal, the Spring Fling Weekend, the Annual Fashion Show, and Senior Week. Various intercollegiate sports are offered during the school year, including basketball, lacrosse, and soccer for men, and soccer, softball, and volleyball for women. There is also a coed equestrian team. Mount Ida College is a member of the National Junior College Athletic Association (NJCAA). Many of Mount Ida's teams have enjoyed national rank and tournament action.

ACADEMIC PROGRAM

The Senior College Division's bachelor's degree programs are designed for students who have completed associate degree programs at Mount Ida or at other accredited institutions and choose to continue study to earn a baccalaureate degree. The liberal studies program accepts all credits earned by associate degree graduates or 60 credits earned by students during the first two years of college, regardless of course content, provided that a quality point average (QPA) of at least 2.0 has been achieved. The senior-year core curriculum includes interdisciplinary courses covering liberal arts, humanities, and sciences in addition to an independent study project. Students entering any other senior college program must have their transcripts evaluated on a course-by-course basis to determine what they will earn in transfer credit. Every effort is made to allow maximum credit transfer.

FINANCIAL AID

Mount Ida supplements federal, state, and private funding with a substantial commitment of College funds. As a result, about 70 percent of Mount Ida's students received financial assistance during the academic year 1997–98. Grants, scholarships, campus employment, and loans are utilized to enable students to afford the College's opportunities. Mount Ida does not have a financial aid application deadline.

APPLICATION AND INFORMATION

Mount Ida uses a rolling admission policy, so there is no deadline for the submission of applications. Applications are considered as long as there is space in the desired program of study. Applicants are notified within three to four weeks after all credentials have been received.

MUHLENBERG COLLEGE

■ Allentown, Pennsylvania

THE COLLEGE

For further information, interested students should contact:

Christopher Hooker-Haring
Dean of Admission and Financial Aid
Muhlenberg College
Allentown, Pennsylvania 18104–5586
Telephone: 610-821-3200

Founded in 1848 and affiliated with the Lutheran Church, Muhlenberg College has the primary purpose of helping students develop those capacities of imaginative and critical thinking that make possible humane and responsible living within a free society. A secondary, but related, purpose is to provide students with excellent undergraduate preparation for socially useful and fulfilling occupations. Muhlenberg students achieve the College's goals by assuming strong individual responsibility for intense involvement in vigorous academic work and for personal involvement within the College community. The more than ninety student organizations provide outlets for the diversified cultural, athletic, religious, social, leadership, and service interests of the students. The campus is primarily residential; more than 90 percent of the 1,825 students live on campus. A close sense of community develops naturally, one in which their diversified academic and personal interests enable students to contribute positively to the intellectual and personal growth of their peers. Students are aided by an active Career Planning and Placement Service in relating academic and personal knowledge and skills to appropriate career goals and in obtaining positions upon graduation. More than one third of a typical graduating class proceeds immediately to graduate or professional school.

ACADEMIC PROGRAM

The A.B. and B.S. programs emphasize breadth of study in the liberal arts as well as in-depth study of a particular academic major. All students must fulfill requirements in the humanities, social sciences, natural sciences, and physical education and must demonstrate proficiency in one foreign language. Strong achievement on Advanced Placement examinations may enable a student to receive advanced placement, possibly with credit. Scores of 4 or 5 earn automatic credit. Scores of 3 are evaluated by the appropriate department. Students work closely with academic advisers to formulate programs well suited to their individual interests, abilities, needs, and goals. Generally, students are expected to declare their major at the end of the freshman year; however, many students later change their academic major with no difficulty. A double major is possible, and several fields are available as minor programs. These minor fields are accounting, anthropology, business administration, chemistry, computer science, economics, English, French, German, Greek, history, Latin, mathematics, music, philosophy, physics, political science, religion, sociology, Spanish, and women's studies. In addition, independent study and research are available. The College also enriches the freshman-year experience through more than thirty special-focus Freshman Seminars.

FINANCIAL AID

Muhlenberg College endeavors to make its educational opportunities available to all qualified students regardless of their financial circumstances. While most financial aid at Muhlenberg is based on financial need as demonstrated by the College Scholarship Service Financial Aid PROFILE, there is also a limited amount of merit aid available. Typically, about 65 percent of Muhlenberg's students qualify for and receive financial aid.

APPLICATION AND INFORMATION

Students wishing to be considered for admission should submit a completed application form as early as possible during their senior year of secondary school and no later than February 15. Candidates receive notice of admission decisions in late March. Early decision and early admission plans and transfer admission are possible.

NEWBURY COLLEGE

■ BROOKLINE, MASSACHUSETTS

THE COLLEGE

For more information, students should contact:

Admission Center
Newbury College
129 Fisher Avenue
Brookline, Massachusetts 02146

Telephone: 617-730-7007
800-NEWBURY (toll-free)
E-mail: info@newbury.edu
Web site: http://www.newbury.edu

Newbury College is a private coeducational college that offers a four-year degree program in selected areas as well as a host of two-year associate degree programs. Nearly 1,000 men and women are currently enrolled as full-time day students, and the total College enrollment is near 5,400. Approximately 40 percent of the College's day students come from states other than Massachusetts. The College provides housing for men and women on campus. Residence halls differ in age and design, providing a variety of styles. Approximately 35 percent of the day students live in the College's residence halls. Founded in 1962, Newbury College has grown and changed dramatically in the past thirty-five years. However, its educational philosophy remains the same: to prepare graduates to succeed in their chosen career. All of the College's regionally accredited academic programs feature hands-on training to sharpen job skills. The College is accredited by the New England Association of Schools and Colleges. In addition, the American Physical Therapy Association and the American Medical Association Joint Review Committee for Respiratory Therapy Education have granted accreditation to the physical therapist assistant and respiratory care programs. The interior design program is accredited by the Foundation for Interior Design and Education Research (FIDER).

ACADEMIC PROGRAM

Working with an adviser, students plan their course of study around a prescribed major core. Program requirements establish a framework that includes intensive study in the major area where hands-on training is stressed as well as course work in general education. By fulfilling the general education requirements and selecting courses outside the major, students receive a well-rounded education. At least 121 credit hours, usually five courses per semester, are required for graduation in most bachelor degree programs. At least 60 credit hours are required for the associate degree. Clinical affiliations/internships are an integral part of the health professions programs. Students in the culinary arts and in most other programs also participate in internships and affiliations, which provide them with on-the-job experience in their chosen field.

FINANCIAL AID

It is the College's hope that all qualified and motivated students have the opportunity to pursue a college degree. To this end, Newbury endeavors to meet the financial needs of all students. A brochure describing financial planning, scholarships, grant aid, and loan programs may be obtained from the Financial Aid Office. The College also sponsors several academically based scholarship programs. These include the Presidential Scholarships and the Newbury College Recognition Scholarships, which are awarded on the basis of a student's academic record, extracurricular activities, and motivation to succeed. Applications for these programs will be given to interested students together with admission applications.

APPLICATION AND INFORMATION

Applications for admission should be filed well in advance of the proposed entrance date, especially if the applicant intends to seek financial aid. However, students submitting applications as late as August or September may be considered for admission if there is still space available in the entering freshman class. A nonrefundable application fee of $30 must accompany the application for all day-school applicants. In addition, international students should submit an affidavit of financial support.

NEW JERSEY CITY UNIVERSITY

■ JERSEY CITY, NEW JERSEY

THE COLLEGE

For additional information and application forms, students should contact:

Director of Admissions
New Jersey City University
2039 Kennedy Boulevard
Jersey City, New Jersey 07305
Telephone: 800–441–JCSC (toll-free)

At the heart of the University is a strong academic program that is recognized by a host of accrediting institutions. NJCU has an esteemed and caring faculty and extensive student support services. Twenty-four undergraduate degree programs are offered, as are graduate studies and teacher certification programs. NJCU provides unparalleled opportunity for academic and personal growth through such study options as its nationally recognized Cooperative Education Program, which enables undergraduates in all majors to earn income and academic credit while experiencing field study at one of hundreds of participating corporations, agencies, and organizations. The student population includes high school graduates pursuing the four-year degree sequence, part-time and weekend students, nontraditional older students, and students seeking job retraining — all of whom are able to take advantage of the University's flexible class scheduling. While drawn primarily from northern New Jersey and the New York metropolitan area, students from fifteen other states, some as distant as California and Florida, and the Virgin Islands are enrolled. International students, who come to the University from fifty-four countries around the globe, enrich the multicultural nature of the campus. The total undergraduate and graduate enrollment for full- and part-time students at the University is 8,500. An average class size of 16, smaller than that of most colleges, enables students to work closely and directly with faculty members and classmates, encouraging intellectual exchange and fostering successful mentoring relationships.

ACADEMIC PROGRAM

An institution committed to the liberal arts, New Jersey City University requires 12 credits of core courses that prepare students for the required 30 credits of general studies for all degree programs. Students select courses from each of six clusters: natural sciences, social sciences, fine and performing arts, humanities, communications, and the contemporary world. Students must also fulfill an all-University requirement of 12 credits in communications, mathematics, and computers. There are specific major requirements as well as electives in each degree program. In addition, students may use general electives to complete a minor or a second major, strengthen a major, or pursue areas of personal interest. In their junior and senior years of study, students have ample opportunity to engage in fieldwork in their major.

FINANCIAL AID

NJCU strives to offer students maximum opportunities for financial aid. Financial aid available for eligible students includes needs-based grants, merit-based Corporate Scholarships, Federal Perkins Loans, Federal Stafford Student Loans, and jobs provided under the Federal Work-Study Program. Applicants for aid must submit the Free Application for Federal Student Aid (FAFSA). Approximately 65 percent of NJCU full-time undergraduates receive financial aid.

APPLICATION AND INFORMATION

Application for admission may be made by submitting a completed application, a $35 application fee, an official high school transcript, and SAT I or ACT scores. Transfer students must submit all college transcripts. Applications for the fall semester should be received by April 1; applications for the spring semester should be received by November 1. These dates are subject to change. Admission decisions are made on a rolling basis.

NEW YORK UNIVERSITY

■ New York, New York

Office of Undergraduate Admissions
New York University
22 Washington Square North
New York, New York 10011
Telephone: 212-998-4500
Web site: http://www.nyu.edu

THE UNIVERSITY

New York University (NYU) was founded in 1831 by Albert Gallatin, secretary of the treasury under Thomas Jefferson; he believed that the place for a university was not in "the seclusion of cloistered halls but in the throbbing heart of a great city." NYU draws top students from every state and more than 120 countries. The distinguished academic atmosphere attracts the teachers, and the teachers and the atmosphere together attract the students who are capable of benefiting from both. Within three years of graduation, 80 percent of NYU's students go on to postbaccalaureate work. Of those who apply for admission to medical and dental schools, 80 percent are accepted (the national average is 40 percent). The faculty includes world-famous scholars, researchers, and artists, among them Nobel laureates, winners of the Pulitzer Prize, and members of the National Science Foundation. NYU is a member of the prestigious Association of American Universities. A study sponsored by the National Science Foundation placed NYU among the top four universities in the country in the number of "leading intellectuals" on the faculty. Full professors teach on both the graduate and undergraduate levels. Seven undergraduate divisions provide extensive offerings in a wide range of subjects: more than 2,500 courses in 160 major fields are available to NYU's full-time undergraduates. The average class size is under 30, and the faculty-student ratio is 1:12—benefits generally associated with a much smaller institution.

ACADEMIC PROGRAM

Requirements for graduation vary among departments and schools. A liberal arts core curriculum is an integral part of all areas of concentration. The baccalaureate degree requires completion of at least 128 credits. The University calendar is organized on the traditional semester system, including two 6-week summer sessions. Some divisions offer part-time programs during the day and evening and on weekends.

FINANCIAL AID

Financial aid at NYU comes from many sources. All students are encouraged to apply for financial assistance or one of NYU's innovative financing plans. Sixty-six percent of NYU's undergraduates receive financial assistance. Each year more than 1,600 entering freshmen are awarded scholarships based on academic promise and/or financial need. The University may offer a package of aid that includes scholarships or grants, loans, or work-study programs. NYU requires the submission of the Free Application for Federal Student Aid (FAFSA). The deadline for filing this financial aid form is February 15 for the fall semester and November 1 for the spring semester.

APPLICATION AND INFORMATION

For entrance in the fall term, the application for admission—including all supporting credentials—must be received by November 15 (early decision freshman candidates), January 15 (freshmen), or April 1 (transfer students). For entrance in the spring term, the application materials must be received by December 1 for both freshman and transfer candidates. For entrance in the summer, the application materials should be received by April 15 for both freshman and transfer candidates. Applications for admission received after these dates are considered only if space remains. Official notification of fall admission is made on April 1 and on a rolling basis thereafter. A campus tour or an appointment for an information session can be arranged by calling 212-998-4524.

NIAGARA UNIVERSITY

■ NIAGARA UNIVERSITY, NEW YORK

George C. Pachter
Dean of Admissions
639 Bailo Hall
Niagara University
Niagara University, New York
14109-2011
Telephone: 716-286-8700
800-462-2111 (toll-free)
Fax: 716-286-8710
E-mail: admissions@niagara.edu
Web site: http://www.niagara.edu

THE UNIVERSITY

Niagara University (NU), founded in 1856, is a private, independent university rooted in a Catholic and Vincentian tradition. The suburban 160-acre campus combines the old and new; both ivy-covered buildings and modern architectural structures are among its twenty-seven buildings. DeVeaux, a 50-acre satellite campus, is located a mile from the main campus. The DeVeaux Campus provides Niagara students with additional athletic facilities. The University is easily accessible from every major city in the eastern and midwestern United States via the New York State Thruway, Buffalo International Airport, and rail and bus service. Special student services include the Health Center, which provides inpatient and outpatient care during the day; the Learning Center, which provides free tutoring services; and the Career Development Office, which offers professional and career counseling. Other services include counseling, orientation, academic planning, career planning, and job placement. Niagara University houses approximately 1,200 students in five residence halls and a grouping of four small cottages. Both coed and single-gender accommodations are available. The University offers graduate studies in business, counseling, criminal justice, education, and nursing.

ACADEMIC PROGRAM

Niagara University's curricula enable students to pursue their academic preferences and to complete courses that lead to proficiency in other academic areas. Courses that have been conventionally considered upper-division courses are available to all students. This provides students with the opportunity to avoid introductory and survey courses and permits motivated students to take advantage of more challenging courses early in their collegiate career. The honors program provides special academic opportunities that stimulate, encourage, and challenge participants. In addition, an accelerated three-year degree program is offered to qualified students. Students pursuing a bachelor's degree must complete a total of 40 or 42 course units (120 or 126 hours) to meet graduation requirements. Niagara grants credit for successful scores on the Advanced Placement tests, College-Level Examination Program tests, and College Proficiency Examinations. Internships, research, independent study, and cooperative education are available in many academic programs. An Army ROTC program is also offered. NU is fully accredited by the Middle States Association of Colleges and Schools. Its programs in the respective areas are accredited by the National League for Nursing, the National Council for Accreditation of Teacher Education, the Council on Social Work Education, and the American Chemical Society. The travel, hotel, and restaurant administration program is accredited by the Commission for Programs in Hospitality Administration.

FINANCIAL AID

Ninety-seven percent of the enrolled students at NU receive a financial aid package that averages more than $10,600 per year. They receive assistance in the form of merit scholarships, loans, grants, or campus employment. Students seeking financial aid should file the Free Application for Federal Student Aid (FAFSA). New York State residents should also file a Tuition Assistance Program (TAP) application.

APPLICATION AND INFORMATION

Niagara operates on a rolling admission basis and adheres to the College Board Candidates Reply Date. A visit to the campus is encouraged, and overnight accommodations in a residence hall are available. Information on all aspects of the University can be obtained by contacting the Admissions Office.

NORTHEASTERN UNIVERSITY

■ BOSTON, MASSACHUSETTS

THE UNIVERSITY

Located at the center of Boston's thriving educational and cultural life, Northeastern University is dedicated to excellence in research and scholarship and is committed to responding to individual and community educational needs. Since its founding in 1898, Northeastern has pioneered a wide range of educational programs and services for students of all ages. The University is an internationally recognized leader in cooperative education—a unique approach to undergraduate education that joins the challenges of traditional classroom instruction on campus with the adventure of learning in a variety of paid professional employment situations in industry, government, or public service organizations. The current undergraduate enrollment is 11,978 full-time and 7,713 part-time students.

For more information, students should contact:

Office of Undergraduate Admissions
Northeastern University
360 Huntington Avenue
Boston, Massachusetts 02115

Telephone: 617-373-2200 (voice)
617-373-3100 (TTY)

E-mail: undergrad-admissions@neu.edu

ACADEMIC PROGRAM

A University-wide honors program gives students opportunities to participate in enriched educational experiences, such as honors equivalents of required academic courses and interdisciplinary colloquia. These experiences are designed to help students expand special interests and develop an understanding of new fields. Honors students are selected on the basis of demonstrated ability and academic promise. The Cooperative Education Program enables students to gain practical experience in the workplace while helping to finance their education. The program is both national and international in scope. Alternate quarters of work and study (after a traditional freshman year) constitute a five-year program leading to a bachelor's degree. A four-year co-op option is available to engineering, business, and computer science students, and a four-year non–co-op schedule is available in the College of Arts and Sciences.

FINANCIAL AID

The University operates a substantial aid program designed to make attendance at Northeastern feasible for all qualified students. By coordinating the resources of the University and various public and private scholarship programs, the Office of Student Financial Services was able to provide more than $89 million to more than 8,615 students last year. Approximately 71 percent of the freshman class received financial assistance from University-based sources, and another 8 percent received aid through the Federal Stafford Student Loan Program. In addition, the University's cooperative plan enables students to earn income that offsets a portion of their college expenses after their freshman year. Financial aid is based on need and academic promise and may consist of a grant, a loan, part-time employment, or any combination of these three.

APPLICATION AND INFORMATION

Under Northeastern's rolling admission plan, candidates may apply and be accepted at the point in their secondary school careers where there is sufficient evidence that they can profit from University study. Applications completed by March 2 will secure a decision in time for the May 1 Candidates Reply Date (applies to fall quarter freshman applicants only). Junior-year and deferred admissions are available, and students who have successfully completed study at other accredited institutions are eligible for advanced standing. Freshmen may enroll in all programs in September and, depending on the availability of courses, in January, April, and June. Transfer students in most programs may apply for entrance at the beginning of each quarter.

NORTHERN KENTUCKY UNIVERSITY

■ HIGHLAND HEIGHTS, KENTUCKY

For more information, students should contact:

Office of Admissions
Northern Kentucky University
Highland Heights, Kentucky 41099-7010

Telephone: 606-572-5220
800-637-9948 (toll-free)

THE UNIVERSITY

Northern Kentucky University (NKU) was founded in 1968 and is the newest of Kentucky's eight state universities. The atmosphere of the campus is futuristic, emphasizing a high-quality education by supporting the liberal arts. Twelve major buildings are of modern, contemporary architectural design and are set on 300 acres of rolling countryside. NKU has an enrollment of more than 11,500 students from forty-three states and fifty-eight countries and is accredited by the Southern Association of Colleges and Schools. The Salmon P. Chase College of Law is accredited by both the American Bar Association and the Association of American Law Schools. There are more than eighty student organizations. NKU competes in the NCAA Division II Great Lakes Valley Conference. Intercollegiate sports are offered for men and women in basketball, cross-country, and tennis; for men in baseball, golf, and soccer; and for women in fast-pitch softball and volleyball. Intramural activities are archery, badminton, basketball, canoeing, flag football, innertube water polo, racquetball, soccer, softball, track and field, volleyball, water basketball, and water volleyball.

ACADEMIC PROGRAM

NKU operates on a semester calendar. To receive a bachelor's degree, students must complete a minimum of 128 credit hours. At least 64 credit hours are required for the associate degree. The University offers a variety of career planning and placement, internship, independent study, work-study, and cooperative education programs. There is also an Advising, Counseling, and Testing Center available. Other programs include an honors program, a program that allows for the dual enrollment of high school students, a program where students can combine their career interests in the liberal arts and engineering fields, and University 101, an orientation program for freshmen. NKU recognizes credit earned through the Advanced Placement Program and the general, subject, and institutional tests of the College-Level Examination Program. A maximum of 45 credit hours may be applied toward the bachelor's degree from the AP and CLEP examinations. The International Baccalaureate Program allows students to earn credit in science, mathematics, psychology, and languages.

FINANCIAL AID

Last year, 48 percent of undergraduates received some form of financial assistance. To receive financial aid, applicants must complete the Free Application for Federal Student Aid (FAFSA). Academic, athletic, music-drama, and art scholarships and scholarships for members of minority groups are available at Northern Kentucky University. The application deadline for the University's Presidential, Greaves, Excellence, and Minority scholarships is February 1. There is no deadline for the University's financial aid application; however, students who wish to receive institutional aid must apply by April 1 for priority consideration. Applicants are notified of acceptance on a rolling basis.

APPLICATION AND INFORMATION

There is a $25 fee that may be waived for applicants with demonstrated need. The fall semester early action deadline is February 1; the priority application deadline for freshmen and transfer students is May 1. The priority application deadline for the nursing program is January 31. The deadline for the radiologic technology program is February 15.

NORTH GEORGIA COLLEGE & STATE UNIVERSITY, THE MILITARY COLLEGE OF GEORGIA

■ DAHLONEGA, GEORGIA

THE COLLEGE

Director of Admissions
North Georgia College & State University
Dahlonega, Georgia 30597
Telephone: 706-864-1800
800-498-9581 (toll-free)
Fax: 706-864-1478
E-mail: tdavis@nugget.ngc.peachnet.edu
Web site: http://www.ngc.peachnet.edu

Following the Civil War, the abandoned U.S. Mint property was given to the state of Georgia for educational purposes; thus, what is now North Georgia College & State University was born. Originally named North Georgia Agricultural College, the institution was established in 1873 as a land-grant school of agriculture and mechanical arts, particularly mining engineering. As area gold resources were depleted and agricultural education was assumed by the University of Georgia, the mission of the institution evolved into one emphasizing arts and sciences. The school was renamed North Georgia College in summer 1929 and North Georgia College & State University (NGCSU) in fall 1996. NGCSU is a member of the University System of Georgia. North Georgia College & State University's first class of students requested that military training be a part of the curriculum. Today, approximately 20 percent of the student body choose to be in NGCSU's nationally prominent ROTC program, which is administered by the U.S. Army. NGCSU is the senior military college of Georgia and is one of the only four military colleges in the nation. In fact, NGCSU is the only public, coeducational, liberal arts, military school in the country. Among the institution's many distinctions are its firsts for women: NGCSU was first public college in Georgia to award a degree to a woman, the first to grant athletic scholarships to women, and the first military college in the nation to accept women in the Corps of Cadets. Women have been fully qualified members of the Corps of Cadets since 1973. The Corps of Cadets comprises approximately 20 percent of the student body and 40 percent of the resident population. All male resident students are required to be members of the Corps of Cadets. Although military service is not required after graduation, students who participate in the Corps may advance to a commission in the active Army or U.S. Army Reserve. Membership in the Corps is optional for women and commuter students.

ACADEMIC PROGRAM

North Georgia requires all students to complete core curriculum requirements. The core curriculum consists of 9 semester hours of English and mathematics; 4 semester hours institutionally required (ethics, speech, philosophy); 6 semester hours of humanities/fine arts; 11 semester hours of science, mathematics, and technology; 12 semester hours of social science; and 18 semester hours related to the major. The minimum requirement for a degree is 120 semester hours, including 12 hours of military science for members of the Corps of Cadets. All students must complete an additional 3 semester hours of physical education.

FINANCIAL AID

Of those students who apply for financial assistance, more than 80 percent receive financial aid. Aid is available through a combination of scholarships, grants, loans, and campus employment. Among the federal funds available are grants, student loans, Federal Work-Study, and ROTC scholarships. Georgia residents who participate in the Corps of Cadets receive $750 per semester, provided they maintain a cumulative average of 2.0. Nonresidents who participate in the Corps of Cadets may have their out-of-state tuition waived if they maintain a cumulative average of 2.0.

NORTHWOOD UNIVERSITY

■ **Midland, Michigan; Cedar Hill, Texas; and West Palm Beach, Florida**

THE UNIVERSITY

Northwood University was founded in 1959 by Dr. Arthur E. Turner and Dr. R. Gary Stauffer, who had decided that the liberal arts approach to business did not really expose students to the wealth of opportunities the world of work had to offer. Established originally in Alma, Michigan, the school moved to Midland in 1961. The Texas campus was opened in 1966. Other recent expansions include the Florida campus in West Palm Beach and the Northwood University Margaret Chase Smith Library Center in Skowhegan, Maine. The University has extension centers in Mt. Clemens, Michigan; New Orleans, Louisiana; Dallas, Texas; and Washington, D.C. In terms of facilities, the Michigan campus is the most fully developed. The 268-acre campus is heavily wooded, and all of the buildings were designed by Alden B. Dow. About 60 percent of the students live on campus. The Michigan campus has a well-developed athletic program, headquartered in the Bennett Sports Center. The Texas campus is located near the Dallas–Fort Worth metroplex. Students participate in intercollegiate baseball, cross-country, the Student Senate, newspaper and yearbook, Auto Club, DECA, field trips, and the annual ribfest and chili cook-off. Current facilities on the Florida campus comprise more than 26,000 square feet of classroom, office, and library space and include a 38,000-square-foot multipurpose building. On-campus housing for students is also available. Even though Northwood's campuses are in different locations, with students coming from more than forty states and many countries, all have one goal in common: the preservation and promotion of the American free enterprise work ethic.

For more information, students should contact the appropriate campus:

Director of Admissions
Northwood University
3225 Cook Road
Midland, Michigan 48640
Telephone: 800-457-7878 (toll-free)

Director of Admissions
Northwood University
P.O. Box 58
Cedar Hill, Texas 75104
Telephone: 214-291-1541
800-927-9663 (toll-free)

Director of Admissions
Northwood University
2600 North Military Trail
West Palm Beach, Florida 33409
Telephone: 800-458-8325 (toll-free)

ACADEMIC PROGRAM

Northwood University's programs have been designed to prepare men and women for specific career goals. The courses for the major (approximately 30 percent of the total requirements) are reinforced by classes in general business (30 percent) and the humanities (40 percent). Associate degree candidates are required to complete 90 term hours with a minimum GPA of 2.0. Bachelor's degree candidates must complete 180 term hours with a minimum GPA of 2.0. Northwood believes strongly in the free enterprise system and, accordingly, has designed its curriculum to reflect this belief. All students must satisfactorily complete core courses in accounting, business law, economics, management, and marketing. No matter what the ultimate career goal of a student may be, he or she will have acquired a set of basic skills as preparation for the productive world of work. This academic program, however, does not prohibit students from appreciating the arts.

FINANCIAL AID

Students should file the Free Application for Federal Student Aid (FAFSA). Available aid includes Federal Pell Grants, Federal Supplemental Educational Opportunity Grants, state and institutional grants and scholarships, Federal Stafford Student Loans, loans for parents, Federal Perkins Loans, and Federal Work-Study awards. Approximately 70 percent of students receive some type of financial aid.

APPLICATION AND INFORMATION

There is no deadline for submitting applications for freshman-year admission. Transfer students are admitted year-round.

NORWICH UNIVERSITY

■ NORTHFIELD, VERMONT

Director of Admissions
Norwich University
Northfield, Vermont 05663
Telephone: 800-468-NORWICH (toll-free)
E-mail: nuadm@norwich.edu
Web site: http://www.norwich.edu

THE UNIVERSITY

Norwich University is unique among institutions of higher education. No other university combines a military tradition of nearly two centuries, a broad range of traditional undergraduate degree programs, and five of the more innovative low-residency and nonresidency programs in higher education. Students on the Northfield campus may enroll in the Corps of Cadets and follow a disciplined military regime or join civilian students who lead a more traditional collegiate lifestyle. Both groups are coeducational and attend classes and participate in sports and other activities together. There are approximately 1,600 students enrolled on the Northfield campus. Founded in 1819 by Alden Partridge, Norwich University was the first private military college in the United States. Here the idea of the citizen soldier developed, a guiding philosophy that later became the impetus for the creation of the Reserve Officer Training Corps (ROTC). It was the first private school to offer engineering and, in 1974, the first school to offer military training to women, preceding the armed service academies by two years. Norwich students have come from forty-eight states and twenty-nine countries. The University's minority enrollment is consistently the largest representation by percentage of any Vermont college or university. In addition, 800 adult students are served by a number of programs on the Vermont College campus in Montpelier.

ACADEMIC PROGRAM

To qualify for the baccalaureate degree, students must have a final cumulative quality point average of at least 2.0. Teacher licensure candidates reserve the eighth semester for sixteen weeks of student teaching. For military cadets, eight semesters of Army, Air Force, or Naval ROTC are required. Prior to the start of the junior year, a cadet may elect to contract with his or her ROTC program of study for consideration for a commission upon graduation as a second lieutenant in the Army, Air Force, or Marine Corps or as an ensign in the Navy. A cadet not wishing to contract for a commission has no military obligation upon completion of the required four years of ROTC courses. Norwich students entering their junior year may enroll in the nation's first college-based Peace Corps Preparatory Program.

FINANCIAL AID

All applicants for financial aid must submit both the Financial Aid Form and the Free Application for Federal Student Aid (FAFSA). Financial awards are made on the basis of need, but academic and extracurricular activities are taken into consideration. Most awards consist of an aid package of University scholarships, work-study programs, federal grants, and student loans. Winners of three- and four-year Army, Air Force, and Naval ROTC scholarships are strongly encouraged to consider the Norwich program. ROTC scholarship winners attending Norwich University receive full scholarships for room and board as long as they maintain scholarship status each year. ROTC students receive an annual uniform allowance, and students who are working toward a commission through advanced ROTC receive a monthly subsistence allowance during the school year. Eligible students may also apply for three- and two-year Air Force, Army, and Naval ROTC scholarships while attending Norwich. For further ROTC scholarship information, students should write to the Admissions Office.

APPLICATION AND INFORMATION

There is no deadline for applications. The University uses a rolling admission system; an admission decision is announced as soon as all of an applicant's materials have been received, processed, and reviewed.

NOVA SOUTHEASTERN UNIVERSITY

■ FORT LAUDERDALE, FLORIDA

THE UNIVERSITY

Nova Southeastern University (NSU) is the largest independent or non-tax-supported university in the state of Florida. Based upon annual expenditures, it is among the 100 largest independent colleges and universities in this country. Nova Southeastern University is an independent, nonsectarian, nonprofit, and racially nondiscriminatory university. It is accredited by the Southern Association of Colleges and Schools. Unusual among institutions of higher education, NSU is a university for all ages: the University School for children, numerous undergraduate and graduate degree programs in a variety of fields, and nondegree continuing education programs are all available at Nova Southeastern. The traditional population in the undergraduate program is approximately 1,000 students. Since its beginning, the University has been distinguished by its uncommon programs, which provide alternative choices in forms of education, and by its research, which is aimed at finding solutions to problems of immediate concern to mankind. With students from Florida and twenty-two other states, NSU is a university of national scope.

For further information, prospective applicants are invited to contact:

Office of Undergraduate Admissions
Nova Southeastern University
3301 College Avenue
Fort Lauderdale, Florida 33314
Telephone: 954-262-8001
954-262-8002 (for adult programs)
800-338-4723 Ext. 8001 (toll-free)
E-mail: ncsinfo@polaris.nova.edu

ACADEMIC PROGRAM

The undergraduate program for Nova Southeastern's daytime population combines a core curriculum with a set of majors designed to prepare students for work in graduate school or a professional career. The general education program assumes that the most appropriate learning experience is intensive and focused on issues, thinking skills, and communication and computation, rather than focused simply on disciplinary content. General education courses, therefore, are interdisciplinary in their approach to content and integrate lectures, student-based discussions, films, speakers, and research and field experiences into the curriculum. Through a small, intimate classroom setting, NSU's program provides a cooperative form of learning in which students are encouraged to help each other achieve competence while they receive close personal attention and support from individual instructors. The legal studies and other programs may lead to enrollment in the NSU Law School. The academic year is divided into six terms of eight weeks each, permitting students to be enrolled for up to 9 credits of time-intensive course work per term. Each course of study leads to the Bachelor of Science or Bachelor of Arts degree.

FINANCIAL AID

Nova Southeastern University offers a comprehensive program of financial aid to assist students in meeting their educational expenses. Financial aid is available to help cover direct educational costs, such as tuition, fees, books, and supplies, as well as indirect costs, such as food, clothing, and transportation. In addition, many academic scholarships are available. Deferred-payment plans and veterans' benefits are also offered. Applicants for financial aid are required to submit the Free Application for Federal Student Aid (FAFSA) in order to be considered for all campus-based aid programs. Students who apply before April 1 are given priority consideration for funds; however, applications are accepted all year.

APPLICATION AND INFORMATION

The application should be submitted with a nonrefundable $25 application fee. There is no closing date for applications for the fall term. Applicants are notified of the admission decision on a rolling basis. Deferred admission is available.

OTIS COLLEGE OF ART AND DESIGN

■ LOS ANGELES, CALIFORNIA

THE COLLEGE

Throughout the twentieth century, Otis College of Art and Design has evolved as a trend-setting leader in art and design education. In 1918, Harrison Gray Otis, founder and editor of the *Los Angeles Times,* bequeathed his estate, located near Westlake Park, to establish Los Angeles's first art school, Otis Art Institute. After the passing of the California tax initiative Proposition 103, much of the county's funding for art was lost, and Otis was not excluded. In 1979, Otis merged with the New School for Social Research in New York and became part of a three-school consortium with the Parsons School of Design in New York and in Paris. In 1992, Otis College of Art and Design was reborn with the election of its first independent boards of governors and trustees. That same year, the College began to look for new facilities that would better accommodate the needs of students and enhance its educational goals. The Goldsmith campus in Los Angeles' Westchester district has been designed as the realization of the dreams of Otis's working faculty members and dedicated administrators.

For more information about Otis or to schedule an appointment, students should contact:

The Office of Admissions
Otis College of Art and Design
9045 Lincoln Boulevard
Los Angeles, California 90045-9785
Telephone:
310-665-6800 (Los Angeles residents)
800-527-6847 (toll-free)
E-mail: otisart@otisart.edu
Web site: http://www.otisart.edu

ACADEMIC PROGRAM

The Foundation Year helps new students to master a broad spectrum of studio skills and gives a comprehensive introduction to the liberal arts and sciences. The primary goal of both the Fine Art and Design departments is to prepare students in each major for a professional career. While intensive studio classes form the core of the Otis experience, courses in the liberal arts and sciences, art history, and criticism ensure that students acquire the broad-based education the College feels is necessary for a successful life.

FINANCIAL AID

Otis is proud to award more than $2 million in scholarships to its students. In addition, aid from other sources, such as the state and federal governments, provides aid monies to more than 80 percent of the student body. Students must complete the Free Application for Federal Student Aid (FAFSA) and the Otis Financial Aid Application. Applicants for fall admission are encouraged to file on or before the March 2 priority deadline; applicants for January admission should submit all forms before December 1. California residents are encouraged to file the Cal Grant GPA Verification Form and FAFSA before the strict March 2 deadline. All aid is based on artistic and academic merit and a student's financial eligibility as determined by the United States Department of Education.

APPLICATION AND INFORMATION

Applicants must complete the Otis Application for Admission and attach the nonrefundable $45 application fee. Supporting documents may be sent separate from the application itself. High school transcripts should be sent unless the student has received a bachelor's degree. Students with previous college experience should have transcripts from each institution forwarded as well. Applicants currently in high school must submit either SAT I or ACT scores. Letters of recommendation are encouraged, but are not required. Additional requirements include a portfolio and an essay describing the student's decision to become an artist or designer. The priority deadline for applying to Otis College of Art and Design is March 2. Otis maintains a rolling admission policy. Students are encouraged to visit the Otis campus.

PACE UNIVERSITY

■ NEW YORK CITY AND PLEASANTVILLE, NEW YORK

THE UNIVERSITY

Pace University was founded in 1906 by two brothers, Homer and Charles Pace. The vision they had in 1906 is reflected in Pace's motto: "Opportunitas." Pace provides a remarkable array of learning, living, and working opportunities to all students. More than 100 majors and 3,000 courses of study are offered in the following five undergraduate schools: the Dyson College of Arts and Sciences, the Lubin School of Business, the School of Computer Science and Information Systems, the School of Education, and the Lienhard School of Nursing. There are many activities and clubs to choose from, including the Black Students Organization, the Chinese Club, the Caribbean Students Association, student government associations, fraternities, sororities, two campus newspapers, two literary magazines, two yearbooks, two campus radio stations, and intercollegiate baseball, basketball, cross-country running, equestrian sports, football, lacrosse, soccer (women's), softball, tennis, and volleyball. In 1997–98, approximately 9,050 undergraduate students were enrolled at Pace. The student body is diversified, with students coming from across the United States and from more than sixty-one countries.

Requests for application forms and information for both the Pleasantville and New York City campuses should be addressed to the Student Information Center at the following address.

Student Information Center
Pace University
1 Pace Plaza
New York City, New York 10038
Telephone: 800-874-7223 Ext. UPG1
Fax: 212-346-1821
E-mail: infoctr@ny2.pace.edu
World Wide Web:
http://www.pace.edu

ACADEMIC PROGRAM

The pattern of study at Pace University emphasizes the breadth of the core curriculum and involves taking prerequisites in the first two years and major courses plus electives in the junior and senior years. Selective academic programs in the University are preparatory to professional training in dentistry, law, medicine, and veterinary science. The University honors program is designed to foster the intellectual life of outstanding students by enabling them to take greater responsibility and initiative in their academic work. Honors advisers assist students through individual advising. The Open Curriculum privilege permits an honors program member to choose courses in arts and sciences with a greater degree of freedom. The Independent Study Program encourages qualified students to undertake research and study to a depth beyond the normal course requirements. Pace participates in the Advanced Placement Program of the College Board. The Cooperative Education Program offers qualified students the opportunity to gain experience in their field while earning a four-year degree. Students can choose full-time, part-time, or summer schedules, working in an area directly related to their major course of study. It is recommended that admission to the program take place during the first year at the University.

FINANCIAL AID

Financial aid is available through scholarships, institutional grants-in-aid, athletic scholarships, Federal Pell Grants, Federal Supplemental Educational Opportunity Grants, Federal Perkins Loans, Federal Stafford Student Loans, New York State Tuition Assistance Program awards (as well as awards from other states' incentive grant programs), Federal Work-Study awards, federal nursing scholarships and loans, and Law Enforcement Education Program awards. Further information on these programs may be obtained by contacting the Office of Financial Aid at the appropriate campus.

PRATT INSTITUTE

■ BROOKLYN, NEW YORK

THE INSTITUTE

Founded in 1887 on its present site in Brooklyn by industrialist and philanthropist Charles Pratt, the Institute educated on nonbaccalaureate levels for its first half-century. As the educational preparation necessary for various professions expanded, Pratt Institute moved with the times. It granted its first baccalaureate degree in 1938 and started its first graduate program in 1950. Pratt continues to add programs at all educational levels, including new undergraduate and graduate programs in art history and new graduate programs in art education and design management. A short bus or subway ride from the museum, gallery, and design centers of both Manhattan and Brooklyn, Pratt Institute has twenty-four buildings of differing architectural styles spread about a 25-acre campus. Eighteen of the buildings house studios, classrooms, laboratories, administrative offices, auditoria, sports facilities, food services, and student centers. Six buildings are student residences, including the seventeen-floor Willoughby Residence Hall, which houses 850 students in apartments with kitchens. On-campus housing is available for all students who request it, and there are adequate parking facilities for residents and commuters.

For more information about Pratt Institute, students should contact:

Office of Admissions
Pratt Institute
200 Willoughby Avenue
Brooklyn, New York 11205
Telephone: 718-636-3669
800-331-0834 (toll-free)
E-mail: info@pratt.edu
Web site: http://www.pratt.edu

ACADEMIC PROGRAM

Educating professionals for productive careers in artistic and technical fields has been the mission of Pratt Institute since it assembled its first group of students in 1887. Within the structure of that professional education, Pratt students are encouraged to acquire the diverse knowledge that is necessary for them to succeed in their chosen fields. In addition to the professional studies, the curriculum in each of Pratt's schools includes a broad range of liberal arts courses. Students from all schools take these courses together and have the opportunity to examine the interrelationships of art, science, technology, and human need. At the time of graduation, students in the associate degree programs have completed 66 credit hours of course work. In the bachelor's programs, credit-hour requirements range from 132 to 135 credits, depending on the particular program. For the Bachelor of Architecture degree, 175 credits are required.

FINANCIAL AID

Pratt Institute offers a large number of grants, scholarships, loans, and awards on the basis of academic achievement, financial need, or both. More than 75 percent of Pratt students receive aid in one or more of these forms. Through funds from the federal and state governments, contributions from Pratt alumni, and industry scholarships, Pratt is able to maintain an effective aid program in a time of escalating costs. Pratt attempts to ensure that no student is prevented by lack of funds from completing his or her education.

APPLICATION AND INFORMATION

Pratt has three admissions deadlines: January 1, February 1, and May 1 (May 1 applicants may not qualify for merit scholarships). To receive full consideration, students are encouraged to submit applications by February 1 for anticipated entrance in the fall semester and by October 15 for anticipated entrance in the spring semester. All applicants must submit transcripts from high schools and any college attended and letters of recommendation. Additional professional requirements are requested by each department.

PROVIDENCE COLLEGE

■ Providence, Rhode Island

THE COLLEGE

Conducted under the auspices of the Order of Preachers of the Province of St. Joseph, commonly known as the Dominicans, Providence College was established in 1917. Originally a college for men, it became coeducational in 1971. The College's full-time undergraduate enrollment of more than 3,500 is equally divided between men and women. Approximately 1,800 students live in nine residential halls, and an additional 900 upperclass students are housed in one of the five College apartment complexes. The remainder of the students live in apartments directly off campus or commute from home. At the graduate level, the College offers M.A., M.S., M.Ed., M.B.A., and Ph.D. degree programs.

Further information may be obtained by contacting:

Office of Admission
Providence College
549 River Avenue
Providence, Rhode Island 02918-0001
Telephone: 401-865-2535
800-721-6444 (toll-free)
Fax: 401-865-2826
E-mail: pcadmiss@providence.edu
World Wide Web:
http://www.providence.edu

ACADEMIC PROGRAM

The primary objective of Providence College is to further the intellectual development of its students through the disciplines of the sciences and the humanities. The liberal education provided by the College gives students the chance to increase their ability to formulate their thoughts and communicate them to others, evaluate their varied experiences, and achieve insight into the past, present, and future of civilization. The College is concerned about preparing students to become intelligent, productive, and responsible citizens in a democratic society. Students are required to complete a total of 116 credit hours in the core curriculum, in a selected major, and in electives. The core curriculum is built around a broad range of disciplines, and 20 semester hours are allotted to study of the development of Western civilization, 6 to social science, 6 to philosophy, 6 to religion, 6 to natural science, 3 to mathematics, and 3 to the fine arts. Special academic programs offered to enhance the educational experience and allow for a variety of interests, including double majors, individualized programs, nondepartmental courses, liberal arts honors, preprofessional medical and legal programs, the Early Identification Program (offered in cooperation with Brown University Medical School), and Army ROTC.

FINANCIAL AID

Providence College's financial aid is distributed on the basis of demonstrated need and the student's ability to benefit from the educational opportunity the assistance offers. To apply for financial aid, candidates must submit both a College Scholarship Service PROFILE application and the Free Application for Federal Student Aid (FAFSA) by February 1. Upon final determination of students' need, the Office of Financial Aid constructs aid packages consisting of work, loan, and grant assistance in accordance with federal regulations, the availability of funds, and institutional policy as approved by the College's Financial Aid Advisory Committee. Sources of financial aid include Federal Work-Study awards, Federal Perkins Loans, Federal Pell Grants, Federal Supplemental Educational Opportunity Grants (FSEOG), Providence College grants-in-aid, Providence College Achievement Scholarships, and Merit Scholarships.

APPLICATION AND INFORMATION

The deadlines for receiving applications for the September term are January 15 for regular applicants and March 15 for transfer students. Early action applicants must file an application by November 15. The deadlines for receiving applications for the January term are November 1 for regular applicants and December 1 for transfer students.

RANDOLPH–MACON WOMAN'S COLLEGE

■ Lynchburg, Virginia

THE COLLEGE

Randolph-Macon was the first women's college to be accredited by the Southern Association of Colleges and Schools and the first southern women's college to be granted a Phi Beta Kappa charter. Academic excellence through the liberal arts and an emphasis on individual learning continue to be Randolph-Macon's top priorities. The College's enduring commitment to women's education has fostered strong programs in career development and in alumnae networking. To supplement the academic program and student activities, the College brings noted speakers, performers, and artists to the campus, including Boston Globe columnist Ellen Goodman, architect scholar Vincent Scully, and photographer Sally Mann. In addition, various concerts, plays, films, and exhibitions are presented throughout the year.

For more information, students should contact:

Director of Admissions
Randolph-Macon Woman's College
2500 Rivermont Avenue
Lynchburg, Virginia 24503
Telephone: 804-947-8100
800-745-7692 (toll-free)
E-mail: admissions@rmwc.edu
World Wide Web:
http://www.rmwc.edu

ACADEMIC PROGRAM

Randolph-Macon's academic program offers the student both flexibility and choice. Through consultation with her faculty adviser, each student develops a four-year plan to integrate academic interests with career planning, leadership, and volunteer activities. The academic requirements encourage students to pursue a well-rounded curriculum in the liberal arts. A student selects courses from at least four different departments during each of her first two semesters at the College. At least 124 semester hours of credit are required for both the A.B. and B.S. degrees, including a minimum of 24 hours and no more than 62 hours in the major field. Research is encouraged in the various areas of academic concentration, and in the senior year students may pursue honors work involving the presentation and defense of a thesis under the supervision of a faculty member. Sixty-seven percent of all seniors had their education broadened through internships or special summer experiences for academic credit.

FINANCIAL AID

A generous financial assistance program provides 98.62 percent of the student body with some form of assistance, including merit-based scholarships and need-based grants. Applicants for financial aid must file the Free Application for Federal Student Aid (FAFSA) and the R-MWC Application for Financial Aid by March 1. The usual aid package consists of a grant-in-aid, a loan, and campus employment. Funds are available through the Federal Perkins Loan, the Federal Stafford Student Loan, the Federal Pell Grant, the Federal Supplemental Educational Opportunity Grant, and the Federal Work-Study programs, as well as through the College's own endowment. Honor scholarships, based on academic achievement, are awarded to incoming freshmen under the R-MWC Distinguished Scholar Program. No separate application is required, but in order to be considered for top scholarships, students must submit the application for admission by January 15.

APPLICATION AND INFORMATION

Early decision candidates should apply by November 15 of the senior year in secondary school and will receive notification from the College about December 15. Candidates for general admission must apply by March 1 in order to receive preferential consideration; they will receive notification at the time their files are complete, beginning in late January. A $25 application fee must accompany the application for admission, but this fee may be waived in cases of hardship at the request of the student and the recommendation of her high school counselor. Randolph-Macon also participates in the College Board test fee waiver program.

REED COLLEGE

■ Portland, Oregon

THE COLLEGE

For its 1,250 students and 125 faculty members, Reed College is foremost an intellectual community. Since its founding in 1909, Reed has attracted students with a high degree of self-discipline and a genuine enthusiasm for academic work and intellectual challenge. Reed attracts a geographically diversified student body: four fifths of Reed's students come from outside the Northwest, with more than 20 percent from the Northeast and 5 percent from outside the United States. Campus social opportunities are open to all, with no closed clubs or organizations and no sororities or fraternities. Community life is full of activity and variety, with more than fifty student organizations. Club sports are competitive in a number of areas, but Reed is a college where varsity sports have always been viewed with skepticism. Fitness and development of lifelong skills take precedence over competition.

For further information or to arrange a campus tour, overnight stay, information session, or interview, students should call or write:

Office of Admission
Reed College
3203 SE Woodstock Boulevard
Portland, Oregon 97202-8199
Telephone: 503-777-7511
800-547-4750 (toll-free)
Fax: 503-777-7553
E-mail: admission@reed.edu
Web site: http://www.reed.edu

ACADEMIC PROGRAM

Hallmarks of academic life at Reed include the demanding, small group conference method of teaching and its reliance on active student participation, a de-emphasis of grades, a yearlong interdisciplinary humanities program, and an integrated academic program that balances the breadth of traditional course content and distribution requirements with flexibility in designing an in-depth senior thesis. Learning and the development of skills in preparation for a life of learning take precedence over the mere memorization of facts. In addition to fulfilling the requirements for the major, taking the humanities course, and writing the senior thesis, students must satisfy a distributional requirement, consisting of two core classes from each of the following academic divisions: literature, philosophy, and the arts; history, social sciences, and psychology; the natural sciences; and math, foreign language, logic, and linguistics.

FINANCIAL AID

Nearly half of Reed students receive financial assistance from the College. A full need-based financial aid program makes Reed accessible to students from a wide range of economic backgrounds. The College guarantees to meet the full demonstrated need of all continuing students in good academic standing and who file their financial aid applications on time. In addition, during their first two semesters, approximately 50 percent of the freshmen and transfer students receive financial assistance equal to their demonstrated need. Admission decisions are separate from financial aid procedures, and students are admitted regardless of ability to pay. Reed's own funds are the primary source of grants to students. The College budgeted more than $7.5 million for this purpose in 1997–98, with individual awards ranging from $930 to $26,590. Reed also administers federal grants and a variety of other awards. Perkins Loans and other federally subsidized loans are available, along with campus employment and work-study programs. The size of a financial aid award is based upon analysis of the student's need. The financial aid program includes grants, loans, and work opportunities.

APPLICATION AND INFORMATION

The Office of Admission is open from 8:30 a.m. until 5 p.m. (Pacific time) all year, except for major holidays.

REGENTS COLLEGE

■ **ALBANY, NEW YORK**

For information, prospective students should contact:

Regents College
7 Columbia Circle
Albany, New York 12203-5159
Telephone: 518-464-8500
E-mail: rcinfo@regents.edu
Web site: http://www.regents.edu

THE COLLEGE

A recognized leader in the field of nontraditional college education for twenty-five years, Regents College of The University of the State of New York has enabled more than 76,000 individuals—primarily working adults—to earn accredited associate and baccalaureate degrees in liberal arts, business, nursing, and technology. Believing that what individuals know is more important than where or how they learned it, Regents College pioneered the process of knowledge evaluation and assessment. The College has no residency requirement, and its programs are available worldwide. Most Regents College students are returning to college to complete an education begun elsewhere. The College accepts the broadest possible array of prior college-level credit in transfer, including classroom and distance courses from accredited colleges, proficiency examinations, and accredited on-the-job or military training. Although the College itself does not offer courses, Regents College faculty members, drawn from other colleges and universities, design the curriculum and determine how credit can be earned. Professional academic advisers help students design individualized study plans using college courses, examinations, and other sources of credit to complete their degree requirements. Students work at their own pace while maintaining full-time work schedules and family and civic responsibilities. Regents College has approximately 17,000 students currently enrolled. Approximately 5,000 graduate each year, many going directly on to graduate school. Students live in every state in the United States and many other countries. The average student age is 40, but some are as "young" as 80. More than 81 percent are working adults employed full-time. Nearly 23 percent of currently enrolled students belong to groups historically underserved by higher education.

ACADEMIC PROGRAM

Regents College has demanding academic requirements, but its programs are self-paced and highly flexible. Faculty members establish and monitor academic policies and standards and determine degree requirements, including the ways in which credit can be earned. Most students bring prior college credit with them when they enroll. Upon enrollment, students receive an initial evaluation of all prior college-level learning, which includes credit for regionally accredited college course work earned in the classroom or by distance study such as correspondence, video, or computer courses. Students also transfer credit earned through proficiency examinations such as the College-Level Examination Program (CLEP) Subject Examinations, the Graduate Record Examinations (GRE) Subject Tests, DANTES Subject Standardized Tests, and Regents College Examinations. Other credit sources include military and corporate training evaluated by the American Council on Education as college-level and certain certificate and licensure programs. Thousands of people take and pass Regents College Examinations every year, using the results to obtain credit or advanced placement at colleges and universities, to apply credit toward Regents College degree requirements, and for other purposes. Examinations are available in the arts and sciences, business, education, and nursing. Several carry upper-level credit.

FINANCIAL AID

Some financial aid is available, particularly the College's own Chancellor's Scholarships and aid connected with Veterans Affairs benefits. The College participates in the PLATO and TERI supplemental loan programs. Because of the nontraditional nature of Regents College, students seeking financial aid should contact the Regents College Financial Aid Office before enrolling.

APPLICATION AND INFORMATION

Students may apply at any time during the year.

RENSSELAER POLYTECHNIC INSTITUTE

■ **Troy, New York**

THE INSTITUTE

For more information, students should contact:

Dean of Undergraduate Admissions
Rensselaer Polytechnic Institute
Troy, New York 12180
Telephone: 518-276-6216
Fax: 518-276-4072
E-mail: admissions@rpi.edu
World Wide Web:
http://www.rpi.edu/dept/admissions/www

Rensselaer Polytechnic Institute was founded in 1824 by Stephen Van Rensselaer "for the purpose of instructing persons in the application of science to the common purposes of life." Nearly two centuries later, Rensselaer is still pursuing that original mission and has become one of the world's most outstanding technological universities. Today, Rensselaer is composed of five separate but closely aligned schools: the Schools of Architecture, Engineering, Humanities and Social Sciences, and Science and the Lally School of Management and Technology. It offers more than 100 programs at the bachelor's, master's, and doctoral levels and a growing array of on-campus as well as satellite-transmitted courses in continuing education. Rensselaer has long had a tradition of cross-disciplinary, real-world, industry-oriented research and education, which is reflected in its Incubator Center, Technology Park, and its well-known research centers in such fields as microelectronics, simulation-based engineering, and advanced materials. Rensselaer provides leadership in interactive learning and information technology. Rensselaer has strong and deep ties to a broad range of firms, including large multinational companies such as IBM, AT&T, Intel, Lockheed Martin, and GE; fast-growing entrepreneurial companies such as Arrow International Inc. and MapInfo; consumer-oriented companies such as Procter & Gamble, Bugle Boy, and Pepsi-Cola; consulting firms such as Andersen Consulting and Ernst & Young; and a growing array of firms in the financial services sector such as Salomon Brothers and Merrill Lynch. Rensselaer has a total of 6,356 students—4,348 undergraduate and 2,008 graduate students. One of the Institute's strengths is the diversity of its student body. Rensselaer students come from all fifty states as well as the District of Columbia, Puerto Rico, the Virgin Islands, and eighty-three countries around the world.

ACADEMIC PROGRAM

While each school has its own sequence requirements, the following minimums apply to all students: 124 credit hours and a 1.8 quality point average in total courses; 24 credit hours in physical, life, and engineering sciences; 24 in humanities and social sciences; 30 in a selected discipline; and 24 in electives. The Undergraduate Research Program offers hands-on experience to students in hundreds of areas. Any full-time undergraduate, from the first year on, can participate for credit or pay during the academic year or the summer. A cooperative education program with industry provides a study-work experience for students who wish to add practical experience to their academic study. The study-work schedule is such that students graduate in the class with whom they matriculated. A cooperative venture with forty-four liberal arts colleges permits undergraduates at those colleges to transfer to Rensselaer under a number of options and to earn dual degrees—the Bachelor of Arts from the first college and the Bachelor of Science or a master's degree from Rensselaer.

FINANCIAL AID

Nearly all applicants accepted into the freshman class who have financial need are offered assistance. A great many Rensselaer students receive such aid under a comprehensive program of scholarships, loans, and part-time employment that provides assistance ranging from $100 up to full tuition and room and board per year. Among federal funds available are student loans, Federal Work-Study Program awards, and ROTC scholarships.

THE RICHARD STOCKTON COLLEGE

■ Pomona, New Jersey

THE COLLEGE

The Richard Stockton College of New Jersey is an undergraduate college of arts, sciences, and professional studies within the New Jersey System of Higher Education. Named for Richard Stockton, one of the New Jersey signers of the Declaration of Independence, the College was authorized by the passage of the state's 1968 bond referendum for higher education and accepted its charter class in 1971. Approximately 6,000 students are enrolled at the College, which provides distinctive traditional and alternative approaches to education. Stockton seeks to develop the analytic and creative capabilities of its students by encouraging them to undertake individually planned courses of study that promote self-reliance and an acceptance of and responsiveness to change. The College's campus provides an excellent natural setting for a wide range of outdoor recreational activities, including sailing, canoeing, hiking, jogging, and fishing. Students, faculty, and staff take part together in an extensive intramural and club sports program that includes aikido, crew, flag football, golf, soccer, softball, street hockey, swimming, and volleyball. At the intercollegiate level, the College fields teams in men's baseball, basketball, lacrosse, and soccer; women's basketball, crew, soccer, softball, and volleyball; and men's and women's cross-country and track and field. In addition, the College has a gymnasium with fitness facilities, an Olympic-size indoor swimming pool, racquetball courts, weight rooms, and outdoor recreational facilities.

For more information or application forms, students should contact:

Dean of Enrollment Management
The Richard Stockton College of New Jersey
P.O. Box 195
Pomona, New Jersey 08240-0195
Telephone: 609-652-4261
Fax: 609-748-5541
E-mail: admissions@pollux.stockton.edu

ACADEMIC PROGRAM

To earn a baccalaureate degree at Stockton, a student must satisfactorily complete a minimum of 128 semester credits. Degree programs include a combination of general studies and program (major field) studies. The Bachelor of Arts student must earn a total of 64 credits in general studies; the Bachelor of Science student must earn 48. General studies courses are broad cross-disciplinary courses designed to introduce students to all major areas of the curriculum and to the broadly applicable intellectual skills necessary for success in college. Students must select some courses from each major curricular area. The only specifically required courses within general studies are the basic studies courses (up to three), from which students may be exempted on the basis of diagnostic testing. The Bachelor of Arts student must earn a total of 64 credits in program studies; the Bachelor of Science student must earn 80. Program studies (major field) requirements are carefully structured and emphasize sequences of specific courses. Students at Stockton have special opportunities to influence what and how they learn by participating in the major decisions that shape their academic lives. The main avenue of participation is the preceptorial system, which enables students to work, on a personalized basis, with an assigned faculty-staff preceptor in the planning and evaluation of individualized courses of study and in the exploration of various career alternatives. Stockton's academic programs emphasize curricular organization and methods of instruction that promote independent learning and research, cross-disciplinary study, problem solving, and decision making through analysis and synthesis.

FINANCIAL AID

Financial aid is available in the form of scholarships, grants, loans, and jobs. Aid is awarded both on a competitive (merit) basis and according to need. Students seeking financial aid must file the Free Application for Federal Student Aid (FAFSA) by March 1. This form is used by the College in evaluating all applications for financial aid.

RIDER UNIVERSITY

■ LAWRENCEVILLE, NEW JERSEY

THE UNIVERSITY

Founded in 1865, Rider University is an independent, coeducational, nonsectarian institution accredited by the Middle States Association of Colleges and Schools. Rider has two campuses, one in Lawrenceville, New Jersey, and one in Princeton, New Jersey. Rider's four academic units include the College of Business Administration; the College of Liberal Arts, Education, and Sciences; the College of Continuing Studies; and Westminster Choir College, located in Princeton, New Jersey. Rider University is located on a 353-acre campus that contains large open areas and thirty-eight modern buildings constructed within the past twenty-five years. Approximately 70 percent of the 2,650 undergraduates live in University residence halls or in fraternities or sororities on the campus. Entering students and returning students are guaranteed housing on the campus, provided that they meet the stated deadlines for submission of housing applications and deposits.

Interested students are encouraged to contact:

Director of Admissions
Rider University
2083 Lawrenceville Road
Lawrenceville, New Jersey 08648-3099
Telephone: 609-896-5042
800-257-9026 (toll-free)
E-mail: admissions@rider.edu
Web site: http://www.rider.edu

ACADEMIC PROGRAM

Rider University operates on the semester system. Each College requires a minimum of 120 semester hours of credit for graduation; the last 30 semester hours of credit must be earned at Rider University. The College of Business Administration requires that a student earn at least 45 semester hours, including the last 30, at Rider University. Rider University recognizes the Advanced Placement (AP) Program and offers credit and placement for scores of 3, 4, or 5 on most AP tests. Credit is awarded for the College-Level Examination Program (CLEP) tests, provided that the minimum required score is obtained. The minimum score varies according to the specific area covered by the examination.

FINANCIAL AID

Most financial aid is based upon demonstrated financial need. Students and their parents are required to file the Free Application for Federal Student Aid (FAFSA) prior to March 1 to be considered for financial assistance administered by Rider University. The University maintains a need-blind admission policy and attempts to meet the full financial need of all eligible applicants. Entering students are eligible for consideration for Federal Pell Grants, Federal Supplemental Educational Opportunity Grants, Federal Work-Study awards, Federal Perkins Loans, New Jersey Tuition Aid Grants, New Jersey Distinguished Scholar Scholarships, and Rider University grants, Trustee Scholarships, Alumni Scholarships, and other forms of institutional aid. Rider University also offers merit-based scholarship programs for qualified applicants. These scholarships, the Presidential, Diversity, Provost, Dean's, Founders, and Transfer scholarships, are for up to $12,000 and are renewable for up to four years of study if the student maintains the minimum grade point average specified by the Scholarship Committee. Rider also offers two full-tuition actors scholarships.

APPLICATION AND INFORMATION

Rider University works on a rolling admissions basis, but encourages applications for the fall semester to be submitted by February 15 if the student wishes to obtain housing on the campus. Applications for the spring semester should be submitted by December 15. The application fee of $35 should be included with the application. Students will be notified of the admission decision in approximately 3 to 4 weeks, in accordance with the rolling admission policy. Transfer applicants receive the same priority for admission, housing, and financial aid as freshman applicants.

RIPON COLLEGE

■ Ripon, Wisconsin

THE COLLEGE

Founded in 1851, Ripon is a distinctive small college of 800 men and women. With an average class size of 11, students take an active, hands-on leadership role in all aspects of their education. The faculty, 91 percent of whom have a doctorate, are committed to the growth of their students. In all departments, the curriculum emphasizes writing, critical thinking, and analytical skills and encourages students to gain a working familiarity with all the methods of learning that are central to each division of the liberal arts and sciences. Students' out-of-classroom experiences are also significant, and participation in the arts, athletics, publications, and government is open to all regardless of major. Most students are involved in three or more activities; there are more than eighty clubs and organizations to choose from. Housing is guaranteed all four years, and nearly all students live on campus. Both freshman residence halls, as well as the College Union complex and the fine arts building, have been renovated. Ripon's 250-acre campus provides excellent facilities, including twenty-eight academic and residential buildings, most notably Farr Hall of Science. All are equipped to meet the needs of the twenty-first-century student.

For further information, students should contact:

Dean of Admission
Ripon College
300 Seward Street
P.O. Box 248
Ripon, Wisconsin 54971
Telephone: 800-94-RIPON (toll-free)
E-mail: adminfo@mac.ripon.edu
World Wide Web:
http://www.ripon.edu

ACADEMIC PROGRAM

To qualify for a Bachelor of Arts degree, students must earn 124 credit hours, have at least a 2.0 grade point average, complete the required courses with passing grades, and meet the requirements for a major in the field of their choice. Requirements for a major differ with the various departments; the typical major consists of at least 24 credit hours of upperclass work. Ripon permits students to arrange their program for completion in three years. Under this arrangement, students must complete 112 credit hours during six semesters; no summer courses are required. All work must be taken at Ripon.

FINANCIAL AID

Ripon College endeavors to provide financial aid for all eligible students to the extent of their need, as determined from the Free Application for Federal Student Aid (FAFSA). Financial aid is generally given in the form of a package, which may include a scholarship or grant, a work grant, and a loan. Assistance ranges from $100 to full cost; 80 percent of Ripon's students receive some form of aid. Ripon also offers a number of honor scholarships ranging from $500 to $18,000 per year. These awards are given to the most promising high school seniors and transfer students accepted for admission.

APPLICATION AND INFORMATION

Candidates are strongly encouraged to apply by March 15. Applications may be submitted later, but preference is given to students who apply by the suggested deadline. Notices of admission decisions are sent out on a rolling basis.

Application forms, the secondary school transcript, and SAT I or ACT results should be filed as early in the senior year as possible. Ripon's application form is available via the Ripon College Web site below. Students seeking financial aid and scholarships should be sure that all records and the FAFSA are received by the College no later than April 1. Ripon also participates in the Common Application program. Transfer students and international applicants are welcome.

ROCHESTER INSTITUTE OF TECHNOLOGY

■ Rochester, New York

For application forms, students should contact:

Director of Admissions
Rochester Institute of Technology
60 Lomb Memorial Drive
Rochester, New York 14623-5604
Telephone: 716-475-6631
Fax: 716-475-7424
E-mail: admissions@rit.edu
World Wide Web: http://www.rit.edu

THE INSTITUTE

Rochester Institute of Technology was founded in 1829 and has always had a strong orientation toward professional and technological career training. In 1968, RIT moved to a new 1,300-acre campus in a suburban location. Cars are permitted, and many students commute from nearby areas. Unmarried freshmen not living with relatives are required to live in the residence halls or in fraternity or sorority houses and to participate in the board plan. A number of on-campus apartments are available for upperclass students. Besides the social fraternities and sororities, there are professional and honorary societies. A complete program of intercollegiate and intramural sports is offered, as are complementary activities for those with special interests.

ACADEMIC PROGRAM

An integral part of the degree requirements in the Colleges of Business, Engineering, and Science and in the Departments of Computer Science; Information Technology; Engineering Technology; Food, Hotel, and Travel Management; and Printing Management and Sciences is the cooperative education program. In this program, the student alternates quarters of study with quarters of paid work experience in business or industry during the upper-division years. The cooperative program is offered as an option in several other academic departments. Field experience is integrated with academic programs in the areas of criminal justice and social work. A number of RIT's programs are unusual baccalaureate degree offerings. Among these are the programs of the School for American Crafts; programs in biotechnology, imaging science, international business, microelectronic engineering, nuclear medicine technology, packaging, photography, physician assistant studies, printing, software engineering, and telecommunications; and the programs of the National Technical Institute for the Deaf.

FINANCIAL AID

Approximately 70 percent of the full-time undergraduates receive some form of financial aid: Institute scholarships; regional, alumni, or industry-supported scholarships; and state and federal government grants. A variety of loans and part-time work positions are also available. The FAFSA must be submitted by March 15. Giving full recognition to scholarship apart from financial need, RIT awards a number of academic scholarships based on grades, test scores, and activities. Freshmen applying by February 1 and transfers applying as juniors by February 15 are considered for these scholarships.

APPLICATION AND INFORMATION

An application, a nonrefundable processing fee of $40 (payable to Rochester Institute of Technology), official transcripts of all high school or college records, and (for prospective freshmen) SAT I or ACT scores should be forwarded to RIT. Freshman applicants for entry in the fall quarter who provide all required materials by March 1 receive admission notification by March 15. Prospective freshmen who apply after March 1 and all transfer students are notified of the admission decision by mail on a rolling basis four to six weeks after their application is complete. RIT also offers an early decision plan, whereby prospective freshmen must have their completed application with all supporting credentials on file in the Admissions Office by December 15 to receive notification by January 15.

ROSEMONT COLLEGE

■ ROSEMONT, PENNSYLVANIA

THE COLLEGE

Founded in 1921, Rosemont College is a residential liberal arts college for undergraduate women. In addition, it offers a nonresidence undergraduate Accelerated Degree Program for both women and men. The College also provides coeducational graduate degrees and professional studies programs. The M.A., M.Ed., and an accelerated M.S. in management are offered. An M.A. in also offered in English, with tracks in English literature and writing. Founded in the Catholic tradition, Rosemont welcomes individuals of all backgrounds and beliefs. A strong academic program and a commitment to women's education and achievement have long been hallmarks of a Rosemont education. With an enrollment of more than 500 women, Rosemont is a friendly and personal community that both supports and challenges students. Rosemont endeavors to prepare women to be active and responsible members of society. For nine consecutive years, Rosemont College has been ranked by *U.S. News & World Report* as one of the top ten regional liberal arts colleges. Rosemont has also been selected for the *John Templeton Foundation's Honor Roll for Character-Building Colleges,* one of only 134 such colleges nationwide. Life at Rosemont is characterized by attention to the development of the personal, social, moral, cultural, and intellectual strengths that help women meet the challenges of modern life. Rosemont urges women to assess individual strengths and interests to develop the competence and determination necessary to achieve success. The close community atmosphere of the College lends to the development of the individual. For example, the 8:1 student-faculty ratio provides individual attention both in and out of the classroom and promotes lively discussion and conversation.

To arrange for an interview and a tour, or to receive additional information, students should contact:

Sandra L. Zerby
Dean of Admissions and Financial Aid
Rosemont College
1400 Montgomery Avenue
Rosemont, Pennsylvania 19010-1699
Telephone: 610-526-2966
800-331-0708 (toll-free)
Web site: http://www.rosemont.edu

ACADEMIC PROGRAM

To earn a Rosemont degree, each candidate must complete 117 credits (120 credits for the B.F.A. and the B.S. in business). In addition to the requirements of a major concentration, all students must complete the general requirements. The general requirements, or core curriculum, focus on the fields of study closely associated with traditional liberal arts and sciences curricula: writing, literature, foreign language, philosophy, religious studies, history, mathematics, natural science, social science, and art. During their senior year, all students must successfully complete a comprehensive exam exhibiting competency in their declared major. At the end of the freshman year, students exhibiting exceptional independence in their work and interest in serious academic pursuits are nominated by a faculty member to participate in a Special Academic Program, which substitutes for the general core curriculum requirements. Rosemont also has an Honors Society, which, in addition to its academic focus, fosters involvement in both cultural and community service activities.

FINANCIAL AID

More than 70 percent of all Rosemont students receive some form of financial aid. Financial aid includes scholarships, grants, loans, and work-study awards. Most financial packages are a combination of various forms of aid. To apply for aid, students are required to submit the Free Application for Federal Student Aid (FAFSA) by March 1.

APPLICATION AND INFORMATION

Applications are accepted on a rolling basis. Those interested in scholarships should apply no later than February 15.

ST. AMBROSE UNIVERSITY

■ Davenport, Iowa

For more information or to arrange a campus visit, students should contact:

Patrick O'Connor
Dean of Admissions
St. Ambrose University
518 West Locust Street
Davenport, Iowa 52803
Telephone: 319-333-6300
800-383-2627 (toll-free)

THE UNIVERSITY

St. Ambrose offers all the resources needed for a successful college experience as well as a successful future. The student body of 2,900 (57 percent women, 43 percent men) consists of people differing in age and background. Students are encouraged to acquire intellectual awareness for lifelong self-education. St. Ambrose has been providing education of high quality for more than 100 years. Founded in 1882, the University was named for St. Ambrose, the fourth-century saint and bishop of Milan, who was a doctor, scholar, author, orator, and teacher. Classes first met in two rooms of a diocesan school. Today the campus covers nearly fifteen square blocks. There are twenty-six buildings, including historic Ambrose Hall. Extracurricular learning opportunities are available through a student newspaper, a campus radio station, cable TV facilities, athletic programs for men and women, honor societies, professional societies, clubs, and other organizations. A special Student Mentor Program, under the direction of the senior academic vice president, enables students to meet with their faculty advisers at least three times each semester to discuss any aspect of their academic or personal lives. A Student Government Advisory Committee also helps freshmen and transfer students to make the transition to St. Ambrose. Developmental and remedial services and comprehensive counseling are available through the Academic Skills Center. Multicultural advisers are available as is a coordinator for international and minority students.

ACADEMIC PROGRAM

St. Ambrose is committed to combining the liberal arts with career preparation. The liberal arts component in each student's program consists of courses in six major divisions: arts, languages and literature, natural sciences, philosophy and theology, physical education, and social sciences and/or economics. Students are required to study history and literature. Individual courses are chosen by the student in consultation with an academic adviser. A contract degree program is available. Students working toward a bachelor's degree in special studies may develop their own major with the help of a faculty adviser. Such a program must be approved by the Board of Studies. To be eligible for graduation, students must maintain an average grade of at least C (2.0) and must complete a minimum of 120 semester credits (usually forty courses) in the Bachelor of Arts, Bachelor of Science (but 135 semester credits for the Bachelor of Science in Industrial Engineering degree program), Bachelor of Arts in Special Studies, and Bachelor of Elected Studies degree programs or 136 semester credits in the Bachelor of Music and Bachelor of Music Education degree programs.

FINANCIAL AID

Federal, state, and University financial aid programs, scholarships, loans, grants, work-study and cooperative programs, and University employment opportunities are available. Federal programs include the Federal Pell Grant, Federal Supplemental Educational Opportunity Grant, Federal Work-Study, and Federal Perkins Loan programs. State programs are the Iowa Scholarship, Iowa PLUS Loan, and Iowa Tuition Grant programs. Most opportunities for University employment are in the Library and Learning Center, the Division of Arts, and the Physical Education Center. The priority deadline for financial aid applications is March 15 for the following fall semester.

APPLICATION AND INFORMATION

The completed application for admission, a $25 nonrefundable application fee, high school transcripts or equivalent credentials, and test scores should be sent to the dean of admissions.

ST. ANDREWS PRESBYTERIAN COLLEGE

■ LAURINBURG, NORTH CAROLINA

THE COLLEGE

A small private college, St. Andrews is affiliated with the Presbyterian Church (U.S.A.) and welcomes students of all beliefs who are seeking a strong, relevant, and broad liberal arts education grounded in such hands-on, practical experience as internships and study-abroad programs. It is this blending of theory and practice that attracts the 700 students (55 percent women and 45 percent men) and that has allowed graduates to succeed through the changing times since the College was founded in 1958 with the merging of two older institutions with histories dating back to 1896. St. Andrews students come from across the United States and from thirty countries and pursue active community involvement to the same extent as their academic studies. St. Andrews students experience diversity and develop tolerance. They explore responsible living on a global scale, are encouraged to develop individual responsibility, and are challenged to expect the best of themselves and to contribute their best to the world. St. Andrews is committed to providing the full range of programs and services necessary to help students successfully make the transition from college to the world of work. Between 20 and 25 percent of graduates go on for graduate or professional degrees. Ninety-five percent of graduates are either employed or continuing their education within six months of graduation. More than 90 percent of students reside on the award-winning, barrier-free 640-acre campus, which is located on two shores of Lake Ansley C. Moore and joined by a causewalk. The College has eight residence halls, including a residence hall designed especially for students with physical challenges, where 24-hour care is available on a limited basis. St. Andrews' top-ranked equestrian team has won many titles on both the IHSA and the ANRC circuits. St. Andrews also participates in thirteen NCAA Division II sports, including men's and women's basketball, cross-country, equestrian sports, soccer, and tennis; women's softball and volleyball; and men's baseball and lacrosse.

For more information, students should contact:

Dean of Admissions and Student Financial Planning
St. Andrews College
1700 Dogwood Mile
Laurinburg, North Carolina 28352
Telephone: 800-763-0198 (toll-free)
Fax: 910-277-5087
E-mail: admissions@sapc.edu
Web site: http://www.sapc.edu

ACADEMIC PROGRAM

In addition to the twenty majors listed above, St. Andrews students have the opportunity to work closely with their advisers to design a liberal arts thematic major that best fits their academic and career goals. All students take SAGE (St. Andrews General Education), which has been designed not only to impart the essential skills of critical thinking, reading, and writing but also to explore centuries of human accomplishment and to formulate action-based values from their studies. All students are advised by faculty members concerning course selection and postgraduation plans. A total of 120 credits is required for the baccalaureate degree.

FINANCIAL AID

The financial aid program combines merit-based assistance with traditional need-based assistance. Nearly 80 percent of all St. Andrews students receive some type of financial assistance. The College administers traditional federal and state programs, including the Federal Pell Grant, Federal Stafford Student Loan, Federal Perkins Loan, and Federal PLUS Loan, as well as the North Carolina Legislative Tuition Grant for North Carolina students. Campus employment is available. To apply for assistance, students must complete a Free Application for Federal Student Aid (FAFSA).

ST. FRANCIS COLLEGE

■ BROOKLYN HEIGHTS, NEW YORK

Office of Admissions
St. Francis College
180 Remsen Street
Brooklyn Heights, New York 11201
Telephone: 718-489-5200

THE COLLEGE

St. Francis College was established in 1884 by the Franciscan Brothers of Brooklyn. Today St. Francis is an independent Catholic, Franciscan coeducational college that confers degrees in the arts and sciences and preprofessional disciplines. It is chartered by the Board of Regents of the University of the State of New York and accredited by the Middle States Association of Colleges and Schools. Throughout its long history, the College has offered an education of high quality that reflects its willingness to adapt to a constantly changing society and at the same time retain its tradition of liberal education. St. Francis has a full range of extracurricular activities, publications, clubs, fraternities, sororities, and Division I athletic teams. Major activities include student government, the yearbook, the campus newspaper, the literary magazine, and professional societies such as the St. Thomas More Pre-Law Society. There are also many honor societies. Founder's Hall Auditorium was refurbished in 1984, the McArdle Student Center and Gorman Dining Hall were renovated in 1986–87, and the Lee and Peter Callahan Center and adjoining lobbies were completed in 1991–92. McArdle Student Center provides modern and attractive spaces for relaxing, dining, and conversation. The College's facilities for physical education are also modern and comfortable. Sports for men include Division I baseball, basketball, soccer, swimming, tennis, track, and water polo. Sports for women include basketball, softball, swimming, track, volleyball, and water polo. There are coed teams in bowling, cross-country, and tennis. Students also play on intramural teams in basketball, billiards, floor hockey, indoor soccer, softball, table tennis, volleyball, and water basketball.

ACADEMIC PROGRAM

Each candidate for a bachelor's degree must complete a total of 128 credit hours and achieve a cumulative index of at least 2.0. In keeping with its liberal arts framework, the College requires all students to take a core curriculum of 42 credit hours in the humanities, social sciences, and natural sciences. For each major, each department specifies a number of required courses to give depth, unity, and direction to the course of study. After meeting these College and departmental requirements, students may select the remainder of their courses to suit their own needs and special interests. To enhance its degree programs, the College offers minors in a wide variety of subject areas. Independent study, internships, and honors courses are offered for qualified students. Air Force and Army ROTC programs are available.

FINANCIAL AID

Approximately 88 percent of the students at St. Francis receive some form of financial aid. A comprehensive financial aid program enables the College to offer eligible students financial aid packages that consist of combinations of scholarships, grants, loans, and student employment. Students seeking assistance for the academic year are asked to file the appropriate College forms by February 15, 1998, and the Financial Aid Form of the College Scholarship Service by March 1, 1998. A new application is required each year for renewal of any award.

APPLICATION AND INFORMATION

Applications are accepted at any time, and applicants receive notice of the decision regarding their admission as soon as the application and related documents have been received and processed. More information about St. Francis College is available from the Office of Admissions.

ST. MARY'S COLLEGE OF MARYLAND

■ ST. MARY'S CITY, MARYLAND

An application form, financial aid information, and other materials are available by contacting:

Director of Admissions
St. Mary's College of Maryland
St. Mary's City, Maryland 20686
Telephone: 301-862-0200
800-492-7181 (toll-free)
Fax: 301-862-0906
E-mail: admissions@honors.smcm.edu

THE COLLEGE

St. Mary's is a public, state-supported, coeducational college dedicated to providing an excellent liberal arts education. There are 588 men and 765 women enrolled full-time, and 1,030 of these students live on campus. Part-time enrollment is 212 students. St. Mary's combines the educational and personal advantages of a small private college with the affordability of a public institution. Active learning and the development of critical thinking are encouraged in the discussion-oriented format made possible by modest class size. Student leadership in academic, cultural, and social spheres is aided by the community atmosphere; opportunities are greater than at larger schools, and involvement is easier. The College recently received a sizable building grant, which was used for the construction of town house-style residence halls, the renovation of existing dorms, and the construction of a library. A new science building was completed in fall 1993. The renovation of the campus center, Charles Hall, is scheduled for completion in fall 1999, and the expansion of the athletic facilities is scheduled to begin thereafter. The campus covers 275 acres, including riverfront, open space, and woodland. Among the waterfront facilities are a boat house, ocean kayaks, sailboards, and a fleet of sailboats. Other facilities include an Olympic-size indoor pool, lighted tennis courts, and an outdoor track. The College's teams compete in NCAA Division III. Varsity sports for men are baseball, basketball, lacrosse, sailing, soccer, swimming, and tennis; for women, basketball, field hockey, lacrosse, sailing, soccer, swimming, tennis, and volleyball. The College is accredited by the Middle States Association of Colleges and Schools and the National Association of Schools of Music.

ACADEMIC PROGRAM

The course of study at the College provides both diversity and depth, leading to a broad understanding of the liberal arts and a specific competence in at least one major field. All students must complete requirements for one of the majors cited above and the general education requirements. The general education requirements are designed to develop skills in communication and analysis, acquaint students with the heritage of Western civilization, confront students with the forces and insights that are shaping the modern world, and promote the capacity for integration and synthesis of knowledge. Students may receive credit for high scores on the Advanced Placement Program examinations. Independent study for credit is possible in every major, allowing students to investigate subjects not covered in normal course offerings. Also available is the opportunity for students to design their own majors.

FINANCIAL AID

The Office of Financial Aid provides advice and assistance to students in need of financial aid and joins other College offices in awarding scholarships and loans and in offering part-time employment under the work-study program. Several full scholarships are awarded to Maryland residents on a merit basis, and other scholarships, loans, and grants for students are awarded on the basis of ability and need as determined by the federal government's Free Application for Federal Student Aid, which should be filed no later than March 1.

ST. MARY'S UNIVERSITY OF SAN ANTONIO

■ SAN ANTONIO, TEXAS

THE UNIVERSITY

St. Mary's University is a private, coeducational institution administered by the Society of Mary, a teaching order of Catholic priests and brothers. St. Mary's offers small classes and personalized instruction while integrating a value-centered core curriculum into each student's degree plan. Encompassing course work in the arts, humanities, social sciences, natural sciences, and quantitative disciplines, the core helps develop creativity, analytical skills, and an understanding of the human condition.

For application forms and more information, students should contact:

Director of Admissions
St. Mary's University of San Antonio
One Camino Santa Maria
San Antonio, Texas 78228-8503
Telephone: 210-436-3126
800-FOR-STMU (toll-free)
Fax: 210-431-6742
E-mail: uadm@stmarytx.edu
Web site: http://www.stmarytx.edu

ACADEMIC PROGRAM

For the Bachelor of Arts degree, 128 hours of prescribed courses and electives must be completed. Requirements include English, natural science, mathematics, computer science, social science, theology, philosophy, foreign language, public speaking, and fine arts. Forty-five hours of study in residence are required, 12 of which should be in the major. Students seeking a Bachelor of Science degree are required to complete the same residence and core requirements as those for the Bachelor of Arts program, plus additional hours in their field of study. The Bachelor of Business Administration requires completion of 129 hours (132 hours for accounting); 45 hours must be completed in residence, and 12 of these must be in the major. Requirements include philosophy, English, social science, mathematics, natural science, economics, accounting, speech, fine arts, and theology. In addition to a liberal arts core of 66 hours, requirements for the Bachelor of Business Administration include 36 hours of a common body of business knowledge and 18–24 hours of upper-division course work in the major.

FINANCIAL AID

More than 80 percent of all St. Mary's students receive financial aid funds. A number of academic, music, and athletic scholarships are awarded on a non-need basis. All other financial aid awards are based solely on financial need, as determined by an analysis of the Free Application for Federal Student Aid (FAFSA). Presidential Scholarships may be awarded to incoming freshmen who are in the top 10 percent of their high school class and have an ACT composite score of at least 26 or an SAT I combined score of at least 1150. All students who have applied by March 1 are considered for scholarships. Students should mail the FAFSA by February 15 so that the processed document is on file in the Office of Financial Assistance by March 31, the preferred application deadline. St. Mary's undergraduates may qualify for the federally sponsored Federal Pell Grant, Federal Supplemental Educational Opportunity Grant, Federal Perkins Loan, Federal PLUS loan, Federal Stafford Student Loan, and Federal Work-Study programs. At the state level, students can apply for the Tuition Equalization Grant, State Incentive Grant, College Access Loan, and Texas College Work-Study programs. In addition, students may qualify for the St. Mary's University grants and scholarships.

APPLICATION AND INFORMATION

The application deadline is two weeks prior to registration. Students applying for financial aid and/or residence hall space on campus are strongly urged to submit all necessary forms and information prior to April 1. When all records are on file, the Admissions Committee will notify the student of its decision.

SAINT PETER'S COLLEGE

■ JERSEY CITY, NEW JERSEY

THE COLLEGE

Chartered in 1872, Saint Peter's College (SPC) is an independent, coeducational, liberal arts college in the Jesuit tradition. SPC's main campus has an undergraduate enrollment of 2,383 full-time day students and also offers evening and Saturday sessions to undergraduate and graduate adult learners. The College's branch campus in Englewood Cliffs enrolls another 425 undergraduate and 175 graduate adult students. Both campuses offer associate, baccalaureate, and graduate degree programs, as well as certificate programs.

For more information, students should contact:

Office of Admissions
Saint Peter's College
2641 Kennedy Boulevard
Jersey City, New Jersey 07306-5944
Telephone: 201-915-9213
888-SPC-9933 (toll-free)
Fax: 201-432-5860
E-mail: admissions@spcvxa.spc.edu
Web site: http://www.spc.edu

ACADEMIC PROGRAM

All students complete a core curriculum requirement consisting of at least 69 credits, distributed as follows: 3 credits each of composition and fine arts; 6 credits each of literature, a modern language, history, social sciences, philosophy, and theology; 6 to 8 credits of mathematics; 9 credits of natural science; and 12 credits of core electives (including one course in ethical values). The remainder of the academic program is devoted to the major field of specialization. Students must earn 129 credits to graduate.

FINANCIAL AID

Saint Peter's College admits students regardless of financial status. Eighty-seven percent of SPC students receive financial assistance, and the average package is $10,500 for commuting students and $12,500 for resident students. The only form required is the Free Application for Federal Student Aid (FAFSA). It is recommended that students file the FAFSA by April 15 for fullest consideration of all federal, state, and institutional sources available. Federal sources include Federal Pell Grants, Federal Supplemental Educational Opportunity Grants (FSEOG), the Federal Work-Study Program (FWS), Federal Stafford Student Loans, and Parent Loans for Undergraduate Students (PLUS). New Jersey state sources include Tuition Aid Grants (TAG) and the Educational Opportunity Fund (EOF). All applications for admission and FAFSAs are reviewed for academic scholarships, incentive awards, athletic scholarships, and residential and need-based grants. Students should call the Office of Student Financial Aid (201-915-9308 or 9309) for more information.

APPLICATION AND INFORMATION

Students are encouraged to submit their applications in the fall of their senior year of high school. The Admissions Committee prefers that candidates apply before May 1; however, admission is given on a rolling basis. Students who wish to be considered for an academic scholarship must apply by March 1. When a student's complete application and records are on file, they will be reviewed by the committee. Students are ordinarily notified of the admission decision within two weeks of receipt of the complete admission file, which must include the completed application form, including a personal statement, a high school transcript with official SAT I scores, recommendations, and a $30 application fee ($40 for transfer students). Transfer students must submit official copies of all college transcripts and their application fee by December 1 for admission to the spring semester and before August 1 for admission to the fall semester. To complete their admission file, international students should submit the results of the Test of English as a Foreign Language (TOEFL) or the equivalent, all official documents of education, and an affidavit of financial support as well as the completed application form, including a personal statement, and $40 application fee. International students are encouraged to apply before March 1 for the fall term and before October 1 for the spring term.

ST. THOMAS UNIVERSITY

■ MIAMI, FLORIDA

THE UNIVERSITY

Founded in 1961 by the Augustinian Order of Villanova, Pennsylvania, at the invitation of the late Most Reverend Coleman F. Carroll, the Archbishop of Miami, St. Thomas University has grown from an institution with an initial enrollment of 45 students to become one of Florida's most comprehensive Catholic coeducational universities, with more than 2,500 students in all programs of study. Founded originally as Biscayne College, the institution achieved university status in 1984 and changed its name to St. Thomas University. The University is sponsored by the Archdiocese of Miami and is accredited by the Southern Association of Colleges and Schools. Over the past five years, the undergraduate student population has represented twenty-eight states, the District of Columbia, Puerto Rico, the Virgin Islands, and sixty-five countries.

For further information, students should contact:

Office of Admissions
St. Thomas University
16400 Northwest 32nd Avenue
Miami, Florida 33054

Telephone: 305-628-6546
800-367-9006
(toll-free in Florida)
800-367-9010
(toll-free outside Florida)

ACADEMIC PROGRAM

To receive a bachelor's degree, students must complete at least 120 semester credits with a minimum grade point average of 2.0 overall and an average of at least 2.25 in their academic major; 30 of the last 36 semester credit hours must be earned and at least half of a student's academic major courses must be taken at St. Thomas University. All students must fulfill the general core education requirements of 57 semester credits, which include courses in English, humanities/foreign language, history, social science, mathematics/physical science, philosophy, and religious studies. The normal full-time academic load is 15 semester credit hours, but the load may range between 12 and 18 credit hours per semester. To graduate, all students must take an area of concentration or an academic major.

FINANCIAL AID

University scholarships and grants, along with federally funded scholarships, grants, loans, and work-study awards, are allocated in a financial aid package according to a student's financial need. Of all financial aid recipients, 65 percent receive University scholarships and grants. To be eligible for any scholarship or financial aid program, an applicant should complete the University's financial aid application and file a Free Application for Federal Student Aid (FAFSA) with the Department of Education. The filing deadline for University financial aid funds is April 1. The application deadline for need-based state financial aid programs is April 15.

APPLICATION AND INFORMATION

To facilitate the admission and financial aid processes, students should submit applications during the fall or winter of their senior year in high school and have all supporting material forwarded directly to the University's Undergraduate Admissions Office. Application for entrance as a resident student for the fall semester should be filed by May 15; for entrance as a commuting student, by August 1. Application for the spring semester should be made by December 15. The University operates with a policy of rolling admissions; beginning December 15, applicants for the fall semester are notified of the admission decision within a three-week period provided that all appropriate information has been received. The University adheres to the College Board's Candidates Reply Date of May 1 and does not require a tuition deposit or a room reservation deposit until May 1 in order to allow students ample opportunity to select the college or university of their choice. Dormitory space, however, is limited and is assigned in the order that room reservation deposits are received.

SAVANNAH COLLEGE OF ART AND DESIGN

■ Savannah, Georgia

THE COLLEGE

The Savannah College of Art and Design (SCAD), a private coeducational college, is open to both resident and nonresident students. Its philosophy is based on the premise that talent in the visual arts is best nurtured through an education focused on the individual, an education providing that individual with an intellectual diversity that enriches, a learning experience that challenges, and an environment that is creatively centered. The College's mission is to prepare talented students for careers in the visual arts, design, and building arts by emphasizing individual attention in a positively oriented environment. A uniquely balanced curriculum has attracted students from every state and from more than seventy countries to the school, making it the largest art and design college in the United States; its current enrollment is approximately 3,500 students. The College is accredited by the Commission on Colleges of the Southern Association of Colleges and Schools (1866 Southern Lane, Decatur, Georgia 30033-4097; telephone: 404-679-4500) to award bachelor's and master's degrees. The Bachelor of Architecture (B.Arch.) is also accredited by the National Architectural Accrediting Board (NAAB).

For further information on the Savannah College of Art and Design, students should contact:

Admissions Department
Savannah College of Art and Design
342 Bull Street
P.O. Box 3146
Savannah, Georgia 31402-3146
Telephone: 912-238-2483
800-869-SCAD (toll-free)
Fax: 912-238-2456
E-mail: admissions@scad.edu

ACADEMIC PROGRAM

The College operates on the quarter system. Fall, winter, and spring sessions extend from mid-September through May. Summer sessions in Savannah run from mid-June through mid-September and include a two-week session in New York. Three-week sessions abroad through the off-campus program are also offered. Students may accumulate credits during all sessions. The uniquely balanced curriculum prepares students for careers and offers them a well-rounded liberal arts education, the traditional components of a fine arts education, contemporary high-tech skills complemented by state-of-the-art facilities, and a comprehensive curriculum encouraging double majors and multidisciplinary explorations. To enhance the academic programs, the College offers seminars, lectures, and workshops by distinguished artists, scholars, and other professionals during the academic year at no charge. Study trips to major centers of artistic activity are made each quarter and provide further opportunities for enrichment. The College offers supportive academic counseling, with special programs for first-year students and tutors for all students available at no charge.

FINANCIAL AID

Approximately 69 percent of the College's students receive financial assistance. The Savannah College of Art and Design has a number of financial aid programs, which may consist of scholarships, grants, loans, or any combination of these, from federal (including the Federal Direct Loan Program), state, and College sources. Application may be made at any time during the academic year; however, early application is advised. Students may also help finance educational expenses by jobs secured through the Federal Work-Study Program and the College's Student Placement Service. Many employment opportunities exist in the Savannah area, and the College refers interested students to appropriate part-time or free-lance jobs when they are available. A detailed listing of the financial aid programs may be obtained from the financial aid office.

APPLICATION AND INFORMATION

Applicants are encouraged to apply as early as possible. The nonrefundable application fee is $50. Admission decisions are made on a rolling basis.

SETON HILL COLLEGE

■ **GREENSBURG, PENNSYLVANIA**

THE COLLEGE

In 1918, the Sisters of Charity founded Seton Hill College to help women open new doors through the power of education. Since that time, Seton Hill has been recognized as a leader in liberal arts education. Today, Seton Hill College is ranked by *U.S. News & World Report* as one of the top three best buys and one of the top ten for academic reputation among northern liberal arts colleges. Seton Hill College is situated in the Laurel Highlands, an area of southwestern Pennsylvania known for its beautiful scenery and wealth of outdoor activities such as skiing, cycling, hiking, and white-water rafting. Recreational opportunities include an on-campus Internet café, lectures, and theater productions, as well as College-sponsored trips to Pittsburgh for cultural and sports events. Seton Hill has varsity teams in basketball, cross-country, equestrian competition, soccer, softball, tennis, and volleyball, plus a variety of intramural teams. At the graduate level, Seton Hill grants the Master of Arts degree in art therapy, elementary education, and special education.

For more information, students should contact:

Office of Admissions
Seton Hill College
Seton Hill Drive
Greensburg, Pennsylvania 15601-1599
Telephone: 724-838-4255
800-826-6234 (toll-free)
Fax: 724-830-1294
E-mail: admit@setonhill.edu
Web site: http://www.setonhill.edu

ACADEMIC PROGRAM

Seton Hill offers forty-two majors in eighteen departments, with the opportunity to self-design a major, all enhanced by the College's award-winning core curriculum. Special programs are available for students who are undecided about their major. The Seton Hill College Honors Program is available for students who have distinguished themselves academically in high school. Students hoping to one day own a business may be interested in Seton Hill College's National Education Center for Women in Business. The center is the first organization of its kind in the United States to offer courses in business ownership and entrepreneurial activities to students in any major.

FINANCIAL AID

Seton Hill College's Financial Aid Office works with each student to develop an aid package from the wide variety of scholarships, grants, loans, and work-study programs available. Seton Hill offers Presidential Scholarships valued from $3000 to $6200, which are automatically awarded to students who rank in the top 10 percent, 20 percent, or 30 percent of their high school class and meet the admission criteria. In addition, art, music, theater, biology, chemistry, math, and athletic scholarships and the prestigious Bayer Science Scholarships are awarded based on merit.

APPLICATION AND INFORMATION

Seton Hill College has a rolling admissions policy. Decisions of the Admissions Committee are rendered shortly after all application materials have been submitted. The first-time freshman applicant should submit a completed application form, a $30 nonrefundable application fee, an official secondary school transcript that includes the applicant's rank and cumulative grade point average, and official score reports from either the SAT I or ACT.

SHENANDOAH UNIVERSITY

■ Winchester, Virginia

THE UNIVERSITY

Shenandoah University was founded at Dayton, Virginia, in 1875. Although the institution was established to provide "classical" and music studies, by 1877 an unusual blend of educational opportunities had been formulated that included arts, sciences, music, medical arts, and business management. These programs, on a much more sophisticated basis, are found at Shenandoah today. In 1960, Shenandoah moved to a 62-acre campus in Winchester, Virginia. The main campus is now approximately 72 acres with seventeen buildings, including five residence halls. Of these five facilities for boarding students, one is for women and four are coeducational. There are five additional buildings at off-campus locations. Shenandoah's historical relationship with the United Methodist Church does not place sectarian obligations on any student. Shenandoah's students have the distinct advantage of being on a small campus near large metropolitan cultural centers. Such student organizations as academic fraternities, service and honor organizations, and various departmental clubs provide opportunities for leadership and recreation. Students come to Shenandoah because they want an educational experience of superior quality and believe that the facilities of a small campus, with a relaxed and personal atmosphere, are the most conducive to achieving this experience. Fifty-six percent of the 1,933 students are from Virginia; the remaining 44 percent represent thirty-nine states and twenty-nine countries.

An application form, financial aid information, and other materials may be obtained by contacting:

Director of Admissions
Shenandoah University
1460 University Drive
Winchester, Virginia 22601
Telephone: 540-665-4581
800-432-2266 (toll-free)
Fax: 540-665-4627
E-mail: admit@su.edu

ACADEMIC PROGRAM

Shenandoah's academic calendar is divided into fall and spring semesters, and summer terms, ranging in length from two to eleven weeks, are also available. Shenandoah has an excellent conservatory of music, dance, and theater, with 491 undergraduate music students and more than thirty performing ensembles. Many academic programs at Shenandoah are flexible enough to allow the student to develop an individualized educational program. Each academic division (arts and sciences, business, the conservatory, and health professions) offers diversified programs, with specific courses required by the various accreditation agencies.

FINANCIAL AID

Shenandoah makes every effort to assist students in finding resources to finance their education. Approximately 91 percent of the University's students receive some type of financial aid. Shenandoah annually awards more than $3 million in aid to students in the form of grants, loans, scholarships, and employment on the campus. Previous financial aid packages have averaged approximately $9500 per student per year. To qualify for scholarships and financial aid, students must submit the Free Application for Federal Student Aid (FAFSA). Aid is awarded on a first-come, first-served basis, as funds are available. A student must be accepted for admission to a degree program before a financial aid decision is made. Specific information regarding financial aid should be requested from the Director of Financial Aid.

APPLICATION AND INFORMATION

To apply, a student must submit an application with a $30 nonrefundable application fee, SAT I or ACT scores, and an official high school transcript. Transfer students must submit an official college transcript for all postsecondary course work in addition to meeting the freshman score and transcript requirements. Applicants are notified of the admission decision after receipt of all credentials.

SHIMER COLLEGE

■ WAUKEGAN, ILLINOIS

THE COLLEGE

For more information, students should contact:

Office of Admissions
Shimer College
P.O. Box 500
Waukegan, Illinois 60070-0500
Telephone: 847-623-8400
800-215-7173 (toll-free)
E-mail: admiss@shimer.edu
Web site: http://www.shimer.edu/shimer

Shimer College, a distinctive four-year liberal arts institution, is one of a handful of schools with an integrated curriculum based upon the reading of original source materials, sometimes called great books. Shimer's classes are small (fewer than 12 students) and utilize the process of discussion and shared inquiry. It is the mission of the College to teach people how—not what—to think and to develop the skills of clear expression and analytical reasoning. The College believes that education is more than the mere transmittal of knowledge or the imparting of vocational skills. Specifically, Shimer is dedicated to the following principles: that the educational process must be intellectually stimulating and challenging; that the classroom should foster clarity in thought, speech, and writing; that a liberal arts education facilitates the formation of enlightened attitudes, concerns, and values; that the College exists to nurture the critical and creative abilities inherent in each student; and that students must develop skills that will enable them to succeed in whatever profession they choose. Shimer provides an education for life by promoting the classical aim of education—freedom—through an exploration of the relationships among all branches of knowledge. The College is dedicated to the concept of integrative studies, the interweaving of clusters of knowledge. Further, the College is dedicated to the goal of developing its students either intensively in their field of study or practically through the Internship Program.

ACADEMIC PROGRAM

The initial contact a student has with a subject of study is through the writings of the original great thinkers in the humanities, social sciences, and natural sciences. These works have been the basis of formal education for centuries and have been studied by the great scholars of all periods. Students are asked to place these works in their historical context and then to consider their relevance to contemporary life and thought. The Shimer College core curriculum consists of a series of four courses each in humanities, social science, natural science, and integrative studies. All students must complete the 85 semester hours of courses before graduation, although transfer credits and placement examinations may suffice for actual course completion. The student then must pass a Basic Studies Comprehensive Examination. In addition to the Core, students take area studies, advanced general courses, advanced integrative studies, courses in their own concentration, tutorials, field internships, and electives. An Area Comprehensive Examination and a Senior Thesis complete the requirements for graduation. For either the B.A. or B.S. degree, 125 credit hours are required. These hours are as follows for the B.A.: 30 in basic studies, 30 in area studies, 25 in integrative studies, and 40 in the concentration and electives.

FINANCIAL AID

More than 90 percent of the students at Shimer receive some financial assistance in the form of scholarships, grants, loans, or College Work-Study jobs.

APPLICATION AND INFORMATION

Shimer admissions decisions are made on a rolling basis. As soon as all necessary application materials have been received, a decision is made and the candidate is notified. Students are advised to apply as early as possible to secure maximum financial aid.

SHORTER COLLEGE

■ Rome, Georgia

Director of Admissions
Shorter College
315 Shorter Avenue
Box 7
Rome, Georgia 30165-4298
Telephone: 706-233-7319
800-868-6980 Ext. 7319
(toll-free)
Fax: 706-233-7224
E-mail: admissions@shorter.edu
World Wide Web:
http://www.shorter.edu

THE COLLEGE

Since 1873, Shorter College has been combining academic excellence with caring Christian commitment. The College was established through the generosity of a Baptist layman, Alfred Shorter, and the vision of his pastor. Affiliated with the Georgia Baptist Convention, the College carries forth its Christian heritage by holding weekly chapel services. Each year the campus is visited by noted Christian leaders, scholars, and outstanding musical performers. The campus minister works with the director of religious activities to provide a wide range of opportunities for spiritual growth. The largest religious organization on campus is the Baptist Student Union (BSU), which includes Christians of many denominations. Student publications include a newspaper, a yearbook, and a literary magazine. Highly skilled music and drama groups include the Shorter Chorale, the Shorter Classic, the Shorter Mixed Chorus, the Shorter Players, the Opera Workshop, and the Wind Ensemble. The Shorter Chorale was selected to represent the United States in choral festivals held in Yugoslavia, France, and Austria and represented the College in St. Petersburg, Russia. Shorter has also been the home of numerous National Metropolitan Opera Audition winners and finalists.

ACADEMIC PROGRAM

Shorter is accredited by the Southern Association of Colleges and Schools and the National Association of Schools of Music and strives to provide an academic environment of high quality. For any degree, a candidate must have earned a minimum of 126 semester hours; some degrees require a greater number of hours. As part of the orientation program at the beginning of the fall semester, each new student is assigned to one of several small orientation groups that assist the student in adjusting to college life; the student is also assigned to an academic adviser who assists in the selection and scheduling of courses. On-campus evening classes are available in selected disciplines. Shorter offers an honors program that spans all four years and provides students with learning opportunities not generally available to undergraduates.

FINANCIAL AID

Shorter College offers aid through each of the five federal programs: the Federal Pell Grant, Federal Supplemental Educational Opportunity Grant, Federal Work-Study, Federal Perkins Loan, and Federal Stafford Student Loan. Full-time students who are Georgia residents are eligible to receive the Georgia Tuition Equalization Grant and the HOPE Scholarship. Scholarships are offered for achievement in academics, music, art, theater, humanities, and athletics. Awards range from $500 to full tuition. Academic scholarships are renewable each year, provided the student maintains at least the required grade point average. Special grants and scholarships are available to students who plan to enter church-related vocations, who are members of churches in the Georgia Baptist Convention, or who are dependents of employees of a Southern Baptist church, institution, or agency. Small grants are also awarded to students recommended directly by alumni and when 2 or more students from the same family are enrolled at Shorter. Shorter does not award institutional aid toward room and board costs. One hundred percent of all full-time Shorter students receive some form of financial aid.

APPLICATION AND INFORMATION

Shorter accepts students on a rolling basis. Campus visits are highly recommended through a personal campus tour or one of three Open Houses.

SIMPSON COLLEGE

■ INDIANOLA, IOWA

THE COLLEGE

Simpson College was founded in 1860. The institution was named Simpson College to honor Bishop Matthew Simpson (1811–1884), one of the best-known and most influential religious leaders of his day. The College is coeducational; although it is affiliated with the United Methodist Church, it is nonsectarian in spirit and accepts students without regard to race, color, creed, national origin, religion, sex, age, or disability. For more than a century, Simpson has played a vital role in the educational, cultural, intellectual, political, and religious life of the nation. The College has twenty-eight buildings on 63 acres of beautiful campus and enrolls 1,900 students.

For additional information or to obtain application materials, students should contact:

Office of Admissions
Simpson College
701 North "C" Street
Indianola, Iowa 50125
Telephone: 515-961-1624
800-362-2454 (toll-free)
E-mail: admiss@simpson.edu
Web site: http://www.simpson.edu

ACADEMIC PROGRAM

Simpson operates on a 4-4-1 academic calendar. The first semester starts in late August and ends in mid-December; the second semester starts in mid-January and ends in late April. A three-week session takes place during the month of May. During this period, students have the opportunity to take one class that focuses on a single subject, to travel abroad, or to participate in a field experience or internship. New students are assigned faculty advisers who aid them in constructing academically sound majors. Students must participate in one May Term class or program for each year of full-time study or its equivalent at Simpson College. All students must complete the requirements of the Cornerstone Studies in liberal arts and competencies in foreign language, math, and writing. To earn the Bachelor of Arts degree, students may take no more than 42 hours in the major department, excluding May Term programs, and 84 hours in the division of the major, including May Term programs. Also, at least 128 semester hours of course work must be accumulated with a grade point average of C (2.0) or better. For a Bachelor of Music degree, the same requirements apply, except that 84 hours must be earned in the major, excluding May Terms, and the candidate is limited to 12 additional hours in the division of fine arts. Also, at least 132 hours of course work must be completed with a cumulative grade point average of C (2.0) or better.

FINANCIAL AID

Simpson College seeks to make it financially possible for qualified students to experience the advantages of a college education. Generous gifts from alumni, trustees, and friends of the College, in addition to state and federal programs of student aid, make this opportunity possible. Simpson offers financial aid on both a need and no-need basis. Need is determined by filing the Free Application for Federal Student Aid. Financial aid granted on a no-need basis includes academic scholarships, which are awarded on the basis of prior academic records, and talent scholarships, which are available in theater, music, and art. The talent scholarships are determined by audition/portfolio.

APPLICATION AND INFORMATION

Simpson's rolling admission policy allows flexibility; however, early application is recommended. Transfer and international students are welcome. Students are strongly encouraged to visit the campus.

SOUTHEAST MISSOURI STATE UNIVERSITY

■ Cape Girardeau, Missouri

THE UNIVERSITY

Southeast Missouri State University is a comprehensive, Division I, moderately selective, residential, public university with a focus on the professional development of students. The Southeast difference is its student-centered approach. The University has more than 1,000 faculty and staff members who are focused on student success and dedicated to providing students with access to faculty members. More than 95 percent of courses are taught by full-time faculty members. The University maintains a student-faculty ratio of 18:1 and is committed to keeping classes to 30 or fewer students. Southeast has 8,500 students from all fifty states and forty-five countries. The University has more than 150 social and special-interest organizations and many student support services.

Further information and application materials may be obtained by contacting:

Director of Admissions
Southeast Missouri State University
One University Plaza
Cape Girardeau, Missouri 63701-4799
Telephone: 573-651-2590
Web site: http://www.semo.edu

ACADEMIC PROGRAM

Founded in 1873, Southeast has evolved into a university of five colleges and two schools with 120 academic programs. Southeast is fully accredited by the North Central Association of Colleges and Schools. As a comprehensive University, Southeast offers a wide variety of majors. Students can study subjects ranging from business and teacher education to marine biology and historic preservation. The programs in business administration, communication disorders, health management, nursing, social work, and teacher education require separate admission processes. All majors focus on experiential learning, and 90 percent of the programs require internships or clinical experiences. Southeast is nationally known for its general education program, University Studies, which provides a strong foundation for any profession.

FINANCIAL AID

Southeast has an outstanding merit and endowed scholarship program for students who demonstrate high academic and personal achievement. The University offers all of the federal and state aid programs. The first step in applying for need-based financial assistance is to complete the Free Application for Federal Student Aid (FAFSA). Students should complete this form to apply for a Federal Pell Grant, Federal Perkins Loan, Federal Supplemental Educational Opportunity Grants (FSEOG), the Federal Work-Study Program (FWS), the Missouri Grant, and the Federal Family Education Loan Program (subsidized and unsubsidized Federal Stafford Student Loans and the Federal PLUS Program). Scholarships and financial aid are limited and awarded on a priority basis; early application is critical. More information can be obtained through the Admissions Office.

APPLICATION AND INFORMATION

Southeast has a rolling admission policy. Applications are accepted throughout the year. Students must complete the admission application and return it with a nonrefundable $20 processing fee. All applicants must submit complete high school and college transcripts to the Admissions Office. First-year student (freshman) admission is based on the following minimum requirements: high school grade point average, ACT scores, and high school core curriculum. Transfer students from regionally accredited colleges or universities who have completed 24 transferable semester hours with a cumulative grade point average of 2.0 (on a 4.0 scale) are considered for admission. Applicants who have completed fewer than 24 transferable semester hours must also meet first-year student requirements.

SOUTHERN CONNECTICUT STATE UNIVERSITY

■ NEW HAVEN, CONNECTICUT

THE UNIVERSITY

Founded in 1893, Southern Connecticut State University is located on a 168-acre campus in New Haven, a city renowned for its academic and cultural advantages. During its long history, Southern has grown in diversity and excellence. Today, Southern offers bachelor's and master's degrees and sixth-year diplomas in more than 150 areas of study, providing its students with a challenging variety of academic, professional, and personal opportunities. The student body represents the full spectrum of ethnic and socioeconomic groups. Although most students come from Connecticut, Southern students also represent more than thirty states and forty countries. There are approximately 12,000 students enrolled, about 8,000 of whom are undergraduates. Of the 5,500 full-time undergraduates, 2,000 live on campus in twelve modern residence halls and town houses.

To request application forms and further information, students should contact:

Sharon Brennan
Director of Admissions
Admissions House
Southern Connecticut State University
131 Farnham Avenue
New Haven, Connecticut 06515-1355
Telephone: 203-392-5644
800-448-0661 (toll-free)

ACADEMIC PROGRAM

Throughout its history, Southern has held fast to the conviction that the best education stresses the liberal arts and sciences. To ensure all students a chance to acquire such an education, Southern has designed a strong yet flexible program that underscores the basics while encouraging individual choice and self-expression. All baccalaureate degree candidates are required to complete a minimum of 122 hours of credit. Majors consist of at least 30 prescribed hours of credit in one specific, approved field. Degree candidates must also fulfill the All-University Requirements, a common core of courses ranging from 41 to 54 credits in liberal studies. In addition, candidates for the B.A. degree must meet a foreign language requirement and select 28 credits of electives from areas of interest. Candidates for the B.S. degree must also satisfy the foreign language requirement and meet certain distribution requirements. Some of the professional B.S. degree programs enable students to develop a minor or a concentration in addition to the major. Students in these programs are allowed a minimum of 12 credits in electives.

FINANCIAL AID

The Financial Aid Office coordinates a number of programs. These programs, which include grants and scholarships, long-term low-interest loans, and part-time student employment, are based on the demonstrated financial need of students and their families. The University offers the Federal Perkins Loan, the Federal Pell Grant, the Federal Supplemental Educational Opportunity Grant, the Federal Stafford Student Loan, the Federal PLUS loan, and the Federal Work-Study Program. Southern also provides assistance through alumni scholarships. Students interested in applying for assistance must complete the Free Application for Federal Student Aid (FAFSA) and send it to the central processor so that it is received by April 15. The Financial Aid Office also requires students to submit additional forms, including a University financial aid application. All required forms have deadlines and are available at the Financial Aid Office.

APPLICATION AND INFORMATION

Candidates for admission should apply by May of their senior year in high school. The Admissions Office mails its first notice of acceptance on December 1, and early applicants have priority for housing and financial aid. Applicants must submit previous academic records, including a complete transcript of high school grades and rank in class; an admission application; a $40 nonrefundable fee; a written recommendation from the high school principal, a teacher, or a guidance counselor; and an official copy of the SAT I report.

SOUTHERN VERMONT COLLEGE

■ BENNINGTON, VERMONT

THE COLLEGE

Southern Vermont College's philosophy begins with a deep belief in the potential of every individual. Thomas Jefferson's concept of "an aristocracy of achievement arising out of a democracy of opportunity" is attained by keeping Southern Vermont College accessible to motivated students, including those with financial and academic needs, who are serious about improving their lives through higher education. The College is committed to offering a career-oriented liberal arts education to a full spectrum of students from diversified backgrounds who have the innate ability and determination to distinguish themselves.

For more information about SVC, students should contact:

Admissions Office
Southern Vermont College
Monument Avenue
Bennington, Vermont 05201
Telephone: 800-378-2782
(toll-free)
E-mail: admis@svc.edu

ACADEMIC PROGRAM

The academic programs at Southern Vermont College challenge students to think independently and creatively. The blend of career skills and liberal arts provides the depth of learning necessary to succeed in the workplace and throughout life. Southern Vermont College specializes in the development of management skills in some of the bachelor program areas to broaden the career opportunities of its graduates. The management core includes eight courses designed to provide graduates with the expertise to assume entry- and mid-level management positions. Recognizing that some students may prefer greater flexibility in their academic studies, the College permits students to complete 18 credits of course work in one of fifteen minor fields of concentration as an alternative to the management core. A third option of particular benefit to students with special interests or scheduling problems is the individualized degree program, which allows students to create new major and minor degree combinations from existing course offerings or prior learning. The College's newest flexible option is individualized study courses for specific focus within the student's area of interest. Bachelor's degree candidates must successfully complete 120 semester hours of credit in the selected program of study; those studying for the associate degree must complete 60 semester hours of credit.

FINANCIAL AID

Southern Vermont College is committed to meeting the demonstrated financial needs of motivated students who are unable to meet college costs with their own or their families' earnings, savings, or assets. In order to be considered for aid, a student must file the Free Application for Federal Student Aid (FAFSA). The College participates in a variety of federal, state, and local financial aid programs, including the Federal Pell Grant, Federal Supplemental Opportunity Educational Grant, and Federal Work-Study programs; various student loan programs; state grant programs; and the Southern Vermont College scholarship programs. Of first-year students, 86 percent receive some form of financial aid; 73 percent of all students receive aid. Total financial aid for all students is more than $4.2 million, of which 51 percent is from grants. Students are encouraged to research state, community, and private organizations for additional funding sources.

APPLICATION AND INFORMATION

Southern Vermont College follows a rolling admission policy. To be considered for admission, students must submit a completed application form with a $25 fee; an official transcript from their high school and any colleges previously attended; at least two recommendations from teachers, guidance counselors, employers, or civic officials; and a 300-word essay. While a tour and interview are not required at Southern Vermont, students are encouraged to visit the campus and meet with an admissions counselor.

SOUTHWEST TEXAS STATE UNIVERSITY

■ SAN MARCOS, TEXAS

The undergraduate admission application and catalog are available on line at the SWT home page listed below. For additional information, students may also contact SWT by telephone or mail, in person, or via the Internet.

Office of Admission
Southwest Texas State University
429 North Guadalupe
San Marcos, Texas 78666-5709
Telephone: 512-245-2364
E-mail: admissions@swt.edu
Web site: http://www.swt.edu

THE UNIVERSITY

Southwest Texas State University (SWT) is a comprehensive public university committed to providing an intellectually stimulating and socially diverse climate for its graduate and undergraduate students. Serving approximately 21,000 students, SWT is the seventh-largest public university in the state. Chartered in 1899, SWT's original mission was to prepare Texas public school teachers. It became renowned for carrying out this mission, but today it does far more. The school has grown to become a major multipurpose university offering programs in the Schools of Applied Arts and Technology, Business, Fine Arts and Communication, Health Professions, Education, Liberal Arts, and Science and in the Graduate School. Since living on campus is required for most freshmen and sophomores, SWT students can choose from twenty residence halls (thirteen coed) on campus. For students seeking a complete living-learning experience, SWT offers the Residential College—the first of its kind at a Texas public university. Residential College students enroll in the same core courses as other students and interact more directly with faculty members who live in two of the three Residential College halls. An application is required for the Residential College.

ACADEMIC PROGRAM

SWT operates on a two-semester calendar system with the fall semester beginning in late August and the spring semester in mid-January. SWT also offers two 5-week summer sessions. Students may earn college credit hours through the University's credit-by-examination program (AP, CLEP, and departmental exams). The Honors Program offers interdisciplinary courses as part of a five-course requirement, which includes the honors thesis, for graduation in the program. Class size is limited to 17 students. Air Force and Army ROTC programs are also offered. At SWT, all students are required to complete a 52- to 55-hour general studies curriculum that serves as the common foundation for all majors. The requirement for a bachelor's degree is the successful completion of approximately 128 to 136 semester hours, depending on the degree plan.

FINANCIAL AID

Financial aid is provided in the form of grants, loans, work-study, and scholarships. Students should apply early for financial aid. The priority deadline for returning the Free Application for Federal Student Aid (FAFSA) form for the fall semester is April 1. To ensure an early response, students should apply as soon as possible after January 1. For an application or other financial aid materials, students should write to the Office of Student Financial Aid, 601 University Drive, San Marcos, Texas 78666-4602.

APPLICATION AND INFORMATION

To apply for freshman admission, students must submit an official high school transcript verifying class rank, an SAT I or ACT test score, and a $25 application fee. Transfer applicants must submit official college transcripts from all previously attended institutions and a $25 application fee. Deadlines for freshman and transfer candidates are as follows: fall semester, July 1; spring semester, December 1; summer semester I, May 1; and summer semester II, June 15. Fall semester applicants whose files are complete are notified of their admission decision on a rolling basis beginning October 15.

SPRINGFIELD COLLEGE

■ SPRINGFIELD, MASSACHUSETTS

THE COLLEGE

Application forms and further information may be obtained by contacting:

Office of Admissions
Box M
Springfield College
Springfield, Massachusetts 01109
Telephone: 413-748-3136
E-mail: admissions@spfldcol.edu
Web site: http://www.spfldcol.edu

Originally founded as a school for training students for service in the YMCA, Springfield College is in its second century of preparing talented young men and women for careers in the human-helping professions. Just a few years after opening its doors to the first eighteen students in 1885, Springfield College could boast an international reputation as a pioneer in teaching and scholarship related to physical education, wellness, and the training of YMCA executives. Today, with a coed undergraduate and graduate body of 3,871, Springfield College is proud of its reputation in these fields and throughout the human helping professions. Springfield's 34,000 alumni work in more than sixty nations. Alumni have served in various capacities, such as a university president in China, initiators of the Olympic movement in Eastern European countries, and educational leaders in Central and South America. Wherever they work or live, Springfield College alumni become vital links in a human chain that leads to impressive achievements.

ACADEMIC PROGRAM

Humanics, the philosophy that has inspired Springfield College from its beginning, calls for educating the whole person—spirit, mind, and body. Undergraduate education at Springfield College is designed to promote an understanding of how these different aspects of ourselves work together in preparation for a life of leadership in service to others. In the classroom, the humanics approach translates to a careful balance of theory and practice—the daily application of an education that connects people to people. The College has a two-semester academic calendar. In order to successfully complete the Springfield College experience, students are required to accumulate a minimum of 130 credits toward graduation. These credits comprise major requirements, elective courses, and the All-College Requirements (which include studies in English, philosophy, social science, health, and natural science). Qualified students may also earn credit through the Advanced Placement Program and the College-Level Examination Program administered by the College Board.

FINANCIAL AID

Students who feel they do not have sufficient funds to pay for the total cost of their education are encouraged to apply for financial aid in the form of grants, loans, and student employment. All financial aid offered by Springfield College is based on need, intellectual promise, leadership, and character. Students who submit the Free Application for Federal Student Aid (FAFSA) and the College Scholarship Service Financial Aid PROFILE by the following dates are given full consideration for aid: January 30 for early decision candidates, March 15 for first-year students, and May 1 for transfer students. Students not eligible for financial aid may still be considered for institutional employment.

APPLICATION AND INFORMATION

Springfield College's rolling admissions program allows applicants to go into review with the Admissions Committee immediately upon completion of the application process. The deadline for submission of applications for the freshman class is April 1; however, students applying for the programs in physical therapy and athletic training must submit an application prior to December 1. Students applying for the physician assistant program must submit an application prior to January 17. Transfer students must file an application before August 1.

STATE UNIVERSITY OF NEW YORK AT ALBANY

■ ALBANY, NEW YORK

THE UNIVERSITY

A University Center of the State University of New York (SUNY), the University at Albany offers a broad spectrum of academic programs for undergraduate and graduate students while fulfilling the missions of research and service. More than 16,000 students, including 11,000 undergraduates, are enrolled in the University's eight schools and colleges: arts and sciences, business, education, criminal justice, public affairs, information science and policy, social welfare, and public health. Freshmen are invited to participate in Project Renaissance, a distinctive general education program. Project Renaissance offers an integrated introduction to the University through a yearlong 12-credit interdisciplinary course that is team taught by 3 faculty members. Five residential quadrangles uptown and one quad downtown house 6,000 Albany students. Campus life is sustained by the activities of the nearly 200 University-recognized social and professional clubs, which offer numerous opportunities for leadership development. The University, now competing at the NCAA Division II level in the New England Collegiate Conference, is preparing to move to Division I in the 1999–2000 academic year.

For further information, students should contact:

Director of Admissions
State University of New York at Albany
1400 Washington Avenue
Albany, New York 12222
Telephone: 518-442-5435
E-mail: ugadmit@safnet.albany.edu
Web site: http://www.albany.edu/

ACADEMIC PROGRAM

To earn the bachelor's degree, a student must complete a minimum of 120 credits (including general education requirements), satisfy major requirements, and complete a minor or a second major. General education requirements specify that students complete 6 credits of approved course work in each of three categories: humanities and the arts, natural sciences, and social sciences. In addition, students must satisfactorily complete two writing-intensive courses, a 3-credit course in cultural and historical perspectives, and a 3-credit course in human diversity. Students may elect a double major or create their own interdisciplinary major if no existing program suits their particular interests. The University also offers many combined bachelor's/master's degree programs that allow students to complete the requirements of both degrees at an accelerated pace. Albany also offers three special admissions programs for prehealth students: the Early Assurance of Admission to Albany Medical College; the Joint Seven-Year Biology/Optometry Program, in conjunction with the SUNY College of Optometry in New York City; and a seven-year dental program with Boston University's Goldman School of Dental Medicine.

FINANCIAL AID

Merit scholarships are available to Presidential Scholars and other exceptional students. The Office of Financial Aid administers all undergraduate financial assistance, including Federal Work-Study Program employment, Federal Perkins Loans, Federal Supplemental Educational Opportunity Grants, New York Equality of Opportunity Grants, Alumni Scholarships, Federal Pell Grants, Federal Stafford Student Loans, New York Tuition Assistance Program awards, and New York Regents Scholarships. General part-time employment is available both on and off the campus. Aid awarded to students through the Office of Financial Aid is based on demonstrated financial need as determined by the Free Application for Federal Student Aid (FAFSA).

APPLICATION AND INFORMATION

Students may apply for fall, spring, or summer admission. SUNY Common Application forms are available in New York State high schools and all SUNY two- and four-year colleges. To receive full consideration, students should apply by February 15 for the fall term and by November 15 for the spring. Transfer students are encouraged to apply as early as possible and no later than June 15 for fall admission and December 15 for spring admission. Notification is on a rolling basis.

STATE UNIVERSITY OF NEW YORK AT BINGHAMTON

■ Binghamton, New York

For more information, students should contact:

Office of Undergraduate Admissions
Binghamton University
P.O. Box 6001
Binghamton, New York 13902-6001
Telephone: 607-777-2171
E-mail: admit@binghamton.edu
World Wide Web:
http://www.binghamton.edu

THE UNIVERSITY

At Binghamton University, the values of a liberal arts education are central to the college experience. Harpur College of Arts and Sciences, the original component of the University, is well known for its innovative liberal arts program. In 1965, the college was redesignated the State University of New York at Binghamton, one of four university centers in the State University of New York System authorized to award the Ph.D. Harpur retains its identity within the University, serving as the nucleus of an evolving complex of graduate and professional schools. The Thomas J. Watson School of Engineering and Applied Science enrolls undergraduate and graduate students. The School of Management, the Decker School of Nursing, and the School of Education and Human Development offer both undergraduate and graduate programs and have maintained the liberal arts at the core of their programs to ensure students a broad general education.

ACADEMIC PROGRAM

To qualify for a B.A. or B.S. from Harpur, students must complete a minimum of 31½ courses, or 126 credits; fulfill a foreign language requirement; and complete both general education and all college distribution requirements as well as the requirements for the chosen major. The distribution requirement consists of 2 courses in the Division of Humanities (including fine arts), 2 courses in the Division of Science and Mathematics, 2 courses in the Division of Social Sciences, an additional 4 courses taken outside the offerings of the division of the student's major, and 1 half-course (two semesters) in physical education. Students must also fulfill an expository writing requirement and a diversity requirement.

FINANCIAL AID

Aid is available through the Federal Pell Grant, Federal Work-Study, Federal Supplemental Educational Opportunity Grant, Federal Direct Loan, and Federal Perkins Loan programs; Tuition Assistance Program (TAP) awards (for New York State residents only); and the University's own financial aid funds. The Binghamton University Foundation underwrites a merit-based University Scholarship Program and offers other limited need- and merit-based scholarships. More than $34 million in financial aid was disbursed to Binghamton students in 1996–97; 65 percent of undergraduates received some form of financial assistance. The deadlines for submission of the FAFSA is March 1 for fall admission and November 15 for spring admission.

APPLICATION AND INFORMATION

Application forms are available in all New York State schools and community colleges and electronically via the Web site listed below. Nonresidents of the state may obtain an application form from the admission office. Candidates are required to complete and return the Supplementary Admission Form that is mailed to them after the University has received their general SUNY application form. The completed supplementary form provides the admissions office with the personal information it needs to make carefully evaluated admission decisions. It is suggested that students file an application by mid-February for freshman admission and late March for transfers, although deadlines may vary for each undergraduate school. Admission decisions are announced on a rolling basis, starting in January and ending in April, in time for students to adhere to the Candidates' Reply Date of May 1. An early decision plan is available for prospective students who wish to enroll as freshmen in the autumn term. The deadline for filing an application for early decision is November 1; admission decisions are announced by January 1.

STATE UNIVERSITY OF NEW YORK AT BUFFALO

■ Buffalo, New York

THE UNIVERSITY

The University at Buffalo (UB) is a full-spectrum public university where undergraduate education is enriched and intensified by its close association with graduate programs and cutting-edge research. With ninety-four bachelor's degree programs and more than sixty undergraduate minors, 112 master's and 98 doctoral degree programs, and more than 3,000 courses, UB offers more academic choices than any other public university in New York and New England. In addition to its twenty-eight arts and sciences departments, UB has schools of architecture, dental medicine, education (graduate, with a provisional teacher certification program for undergraduates), engineering, health-related professions, library studies, law, management, medicine, nursing, pharmacy, and social work. Because UB is a research-intensive university, undergraduates study and work with faculty members who are leaders in their fields in academic and research facilities that support work at the most advanced levels of knowledge. This environment benefits undergraduates in their preparation for careers or further study by involving them in the discovery process and encouraging them to develop the kind of critical thinking required in the creation of new knowledge. Beyond traditional departmental boundaries, UB undergraduates have an opportunity to combine elements from several fields of knowledge in the University's extensive set of interdisciplinary degree programs or to design their own bachelor's degree programs.

Applications are available in New York State high schools or by contacting:

Office of Admissions
17 Capen Hall
State University of New York at Buffalo
Box 601660
Buffalo, New York 14260-1660
Telephone: 716-645-6900
888-UBADMIT (toll-free)
E-mail: ub-admissions@admissions.buffalo.edu
Web site: http://www.buffalo.edu

ACADEMIC PROGRAM

Candidates for a baccalaureate degree are required to complete a minimum of 120 semester hours, 30 of which must be completed in residence, and earn a minimum grade point average of 2.0. Students have great flexibility in planning their academic programs. All students must fulfill a University general education requirement. They must also complete an academic major, which is selected, with the advice of an academic adviser, usually by the end of the sophomore year and often between the freshman and sophomore years. Students also have ample opportunity for independent study under departmental or faculty auspices. In some cases, independent study may be the focal point in the design of an individual program. In others, it may be used to increase the depth or breadth of a student's formal degree program. Placement and credit are granted on the basis of Advanced Placement or College-Level Examination Program scores. The academic year is composed of two semesters, one beginning in late August, the other in late January. An extensive summer session is also offered.

FINANCIAL AID

The University at Buffalo participates in all New York State and federal financial aid programs, including the Tuition Assistance Program (available only to New York State residents) and the Federal Pell Grant, Federal Work-Study, Federal Direct Student Loan, and Federal Perkins Loan programs. Interested students must complete the Free Application for Federal Student Aid in early March. All inquiries concerning financial aid should be addressed to the Office of Financial Aid, Hayes C, State University of New York at Buffalo.

STATE UNIVERSITY OF NEW YORK COLLEGE AT BROCKPORT

■ BROCKPORT, NEW YORK

For more information, students should contact:

Director of Admissions
State University of New York College at Brockport
350 New Campus Drive
Brockport, New York 14420-2915
Telephone: 716-395-2751
800–382–8447 (toll-free)
Web site: http://www.brockport.edu

THE COLLEGE

SUNY Brockport cherishes its rise to prominence in higher education. Founded in 1835 as the Brockport Collegiate Institute, it became a normal school for teachers in 1867. The comprehensive college of arts and sciences found at Brockport today represents a 131-year tradition of providing education of the highest quality. The College is committed to serving the citizens of New York, including the large, diverse student population, whose varying interests and needs reflect the complex challenges of contemporary society. Most of its 6,600 undergraduate students come from New York State, 11 percent represent minorities, and 1 percent are international students. There are 2,400 students living in various types of campus residence halls, including coed and special option housing for freshmen and transfers. The rest live in private accommodations off campus or commute from their homes. Freshman applicants are guaranteed College housing; there are no triples. Students living on campus are required to sign a housing agreement for the full academic year (September through May).

ACADEMIC PROGRAM

SUNY Brockport's educational programs strengthen, develop, and enrich the intellectual and social abilities of its students, who must complete a minimum of 120 credits in an approved program with a minimum earned academic average of 2.0 (C). Included in the 120 credits are an academic major program and a general education program of courses in composition and quantitative skills, computer literacy, contemporary issues, fine arts, humanities, natural sciences and mathematics, perspectives on women, and social sciences. Freshmen are required to take an Academic Planning Seminar (APS), which introduces them to the academic rigors and opportunities of college life and assists them in planning an individual program of study that relates to their academic, personal, and career goals. APS is taught in small groups by professors who also advise the students.

FINANCIAL AID

Approximately 81 percent of SUNY Brockport's students receive some form of financial aid. The College participates in the Federal Pell Grant, Federal Supplemental Educational Opportunity Grant, Federal Direct Student Loan, Federal Perkins Loan, Nursing Loans, and Federal Work-Study programs. New York State residents may qualify for Tuition Assistance Program awards, State University Supplemental Tuition Assistance, Assistance for Part-time Study, and Educational Opportunity Grants. Special state scholarships are available for veterans and children of deceased or disabled veterans. The Office of Financial Aid assists students in identifying applicable programs and prepares estimated financial aid packages for all newly accepted students prior to the payment of any advance fees. The Student Employment Office arranges part-time work for students on and off the campus. About 3,000 students are taking advantage of these services. Numerous campus-controlled scholarships are also available, including twenty-five Alumni Association Awards and fifty Presidential Scholar in Residence Awards. The Free Application for Federal Student Aid (FAFSA) is required of all aid applicants.

APPLICATION AND INFORMATION

Students may apply for fall or spring on a rolling admission basis. Accepted applicants may also attend summer sessions. Application forms are available from the Admissions Office or from guidance offices in all New York State high schools and all SUNY two-year and four-year colleges. Students should apply by January 15 for the fall semester and by December 1 for the spring semester.

SUFFOLK UNIVERSITY

■ BOSTON, MASSACHUSETTS

THE UNIVERSITY

Application forms and further information may be obtained by contacting:

Admission Office
Suffolk University
8 Ashburton Place
Boston, Massachusetts 02108
Telephone: 617-573-8460
800-6-SUFFOLK (toll-free)
Fax: 617-742-4291
E-mail: admission@admin.suffolk.edu
Web site: http://www.suffolk.edu

Suffolk University, a cosmopolitan university in a cosmopolitan city, attracts students from a wide variety of ethnic, religious, and geographic backgrounds. Many students work at outside jobs and commute to the University via public transportation. In September 1997, Suffolk enrolled 536 freshmen. A survey of that freshman class disclosed that the main reasons they chose to attend Suffolk University were its academic reputation, location, curriculum, reasonable cost, and size. Suffolk University makes a special effort to meet the needs of transfer students, who make up about half of each year's entering class. Of the undergraduate students in September 1997, 20 percent represented minorities. In addition, 14 percent were international students. In the undergraduate schools, students come from twenty-nine states and eighty countries. Suffolk University began as a law school in 1906. Aware of the growing demand for high-quality private higher education in the Boston area, Suffolk opened the College of Liberal Arts and Sciences in 1934 and the School of Management in 1937. The same year, the Law School and the colleges were incorporated as Suffolk University. The Student Activities Office strives to provide extracurricular organizations, activities, and events for both full-time and part-time students.

ACADEMIC PROGRAM

Suffolk University's greatest strength lies in offering educational opportunities that integrate challenging and personal classroom learning with broadening cultural and work experience, taking advantage of the University's dynamic Boston location. Undergraduates are required to complete at least 122 credit hours of course work, including courses both inside and outside their major.

FINANCIAL AID

There are four main sources of financial aid: the federal government, the state government, the University, and private sources. Federal programs include grants, low-interest loans, and a work-study program. The commonwealth of Massachusetts awards grants to state residents who demonstrate financial need. The University and private sources award scholarships based on academic achievement or to offset financial need. Any student enrolled in a degree program of at least 6 semester hours of credit may apply for financial aid. Some awards are limited to full-time students. A student receiving aid must maintain good academic standing. All undergraduate aid applicants are expected to file Federal Pell Grant and state scholarship applications. Awards are usually offered as a package—a combination of grants, loans, and employment. Applications for financial assistance should be submitted to the Office of Financial Aid by March 1 for priority status. November 1 is the priority deadline for spring review and January transfer applications. A complete application includes the Free Application for Federal Student Aid (FAFSA), the Suffolk University Aid Application, and an official statement of income (a copy of the tax return).

APPLICATION AND INFORMATION

Suffolk notifies candidates of the Admission Committee's decision soon after the application is complete. Early decisions are given when there is evidence of three years of highly successful college-preparatory study and above-average junior-year SAT I scores.

International applicants should contact the Admission Office for special requirements and applications.

A campus visit and/or an interview are highly recommended.

SWEET BRIAR COLLEGE

■ Sweet Briar, Virginia

All materials should be sent to the address given below; information may be requested from the same office.

Dean of Admissions
Sweet Briar College
Sweet Briar, Virginia 24595
Telephone: 804-381-6142
800-381-6142 (toll-free)
Fax: 804-381-6152
E-mail: admissions@sbc.edu
World Wide Web:
http://www.sbc.edu

THE COLLEGE

Sweet Briar College, the first women's college to establish a prelaw chapter of Phi Alpha Delta Law Fraternity, is consistently ranked as one of the top colleges for women in the nation. Its academic reputation, beautiful location, and attention to the individual attract smart women who want to excel. The College's focus on women allows students, in full partnership with the faculty, to fulfill their promise as scholars and develop leadership skills. A four-year career planning program capitalizes on the international network of successful Sweet Briar alumnae for worldwide career opportunities and postgraduate education. Students work one-on-one with faculty members and visiting scholars and engage in meaningful research. Classes are small, averaging 12 students. The four-year Honors Program is nationally recognized for its innovative partnering of interdisciplinary academic and cocurricular programs. The College has a wide geographic, ethnic, and socioeconomic representation. About 600 women from more than forty states and twenty countries are enrolled at Sweet Briar's Virginia campus; another 150 students are enrolled in Sweet Briar's coed Junior Year in France and Junior Year in Spain.

ACADEMIC PROGRAM

Sweet Briar's academic program supports its mission to prepare women to be active, responsible members of a world community by integrating the liberal arts and sciences with opportunities for internships, campus and community leadership, and career planning. Students complete courses in English, literature or the arts, science, foreign language, non-Western studies, social sciences, humanities, and physical education. Independent studies, available at all levels, and seminars are included in most majors, and a culminating senior course or exercise is required in all majors. General honors that may be awarded with the degree are cum laude, magna cum laude, or summa cum laude. Sweet Briar has a chapter of Phi Beta Kappa and offers an honors program that provides an opportunity to take special tutorials and seminars and to do a yearlong research project culminating in an honors thesis on an original topic. The Honors Degree may be awarded with honors, high honors, or highest honors.

FINANCIAL AID

A family's financial circumstances do not limit a student's choices at Sweet Briar because of the College's generous financial aid program. About 60 percent of students receive need-based aid, including grants, loans, and work-study awards. Academic merit awards are available, including the Founders', Commonwealth, Betty Bean Black, and Sweet Briar scholarships. Other academic, merit, and leadership awards are also available.

APPLICATION AND INFORMATION

Scholarship candidates should apply by January 15, and regular candidates should apply by February 15 of the senior year. Early decision applications are due by December 1 of the senior year, and notifications are sent December 15; the reservation deposit is due January 15. Transfer applications for the sophomore and junior classes are due by July 1. A completed application includes a transcript of the candidate's school work, scores on the required tests, recommendations from the guidance counselor and a teacher, and essays written by the candidate. Sweet Briar also accepts the Common Application (with an additional essay required) and the CollegeLink application.

THIEL COLLEGE

■ Greenville, Pennsylvania

THE COLLEGE

For inquiries and requests for information, students should contact:

Thiel College Admissions Office
75 College Avenue
Greenville, Pennsylvania 16125
Telephone: 724-589-2345
800-248-4435 (toll-free)
Fax: 724-589-2013
E-mail: admissio@thiel.edu

Thiel College was founded in 1866 as one of the first coeducational institutions of higher education in the United States. Located in Greenville, Pennsylvania, in the northwestern corner of the commonwealth, Thiel has become known for the quality of its educational offerings and its blending of liberal arts cutting-edge technology and experiential learning through extensive cooperative education and internship opportunities. Affiliated with the Evangelical Lutheran Church in America, the College enrolls just over 1,000 women and men. Most students come from Pennsylvania, Ohio, and the Middle Atlantic States. Seven percent of the students are members of minority groups, and 3 percent are from fourteen other countries. Thiel has been ranked in the "top tier" of northern liberal arts colleges by *U.S. News & World Report*, and its sciences and mathematics programs are rated "among the 200 best in the United States" by *Peterson's Guide to the Sciences*.

ACADEMIC PROGRAM

Thiel College provides students with a liberal arts education that increases general and special knowledge of the world, promotes creative and critical thinking, and strengthens communication skills. Each of the majors and degree programs combines liberal arts instruction and values with cutting-edge technology and hands-on learning through internships and co-ops. The Bachelor of Arts degree programs and the Bachelor of Science in Nursing degree program require a minimum of 124 credits for graduation. The Associate of Arts degree programs require a minimum of 64 credits for graduation. All majors must complete liberal arts integrative requirements as well as core and elective courses. Advanced Placement (AP) and CLEP examination scores are welcome from students entering Thiel. Courses taken at other colleges while students are still in high school will be accepted for consideration provided that the grade earned is a C or better (on a 4.0 scale).

FINANCIAL AID

Thiel College participates in all federal financial aid. Students are encouraged to check with state agencies as well as with local, community, civic, industrial, and church-related groups for additional funding sources. Students are encouraged to file the Free Application for Federal Student Aid (FAFSA) as early as possible after January 1 of their senior year. Award notifications are mailed beginning in late January and continue until funding is exhausted. Admission decisions are non-need-based. Thiel College awards its institutional funds after consideration of academic achievement, special talents and skills, and financial need. Thiel maintains an extensive grant, loan, scholarship, and college work program. In 1998–99, $4.6 million will be awarded to students from institutional resources, and 93 percent of students will receive funding through a combination of federal, state, local, and Thiel resources.

APPLICATION AND INFORMATION

Thiel begins to consider applicants in late September each year for the following fall. Decisions are made on a rolling basis, and applicants are notified within ten days of the completion of an application packet. Applications should be received no later than August 1 for the fall term and December 1 for the spring term.

TOWSON UNIVERSITY

■ TOWSON, MARYLAND

Admissions Office
Towson University
Towson, Maryland 21252
Telephone: 410-830-2113
888-4TOWSON (toll-free)
Web site: http://www.towson.edu

THE UNIVERSITY

Founded in 1866, Towson University has undergone a major transition from a traditional teachers college to a highly respected, comprehensive university. Located in Towson, Maryland, just minutes from the heart of downtown Baltimore, the University offers bachelor's degrees in forty fields of study and master's degrees in twenty-five. In addition, special advanced certificates are offered. The University has a long-standing reputation for its teacher education program and a growing reputation in the fields of business administration, mass communication, and fine arts. The total University enrollment is almost 15,000. About 13,000 students are undergraduates. Applications are received from all fifty states. Students come from sixty-five other countries, and about 12 percent of the student body are members of minority groups. The University houses an on-campus population of more than 3,300 students. The University is a Division I member of the National Collegiate Athletic Association (NCAA). Towson, which fields teams in twenty-one sports (ten men's and eleven women's), belongs to America East for intercollegiate athletics. The University competes in nineteen sports in the conference, including basketball, lacrosse, soccer, and tennis. A wide variety of intramural sports are also available to all students. The Towson Center, a 100-acre recreational and special-events center, is used by both the University and the community. Serving as the principal site for indoor athletic events, the center is also used for entertainment and cultural events.

ACADEMIC PROGRAM

The University's first and most important goal is to provide a sound liberal arts and sciences education for all students. To fulfill this goal, the University provides a core program of General Education Requirements to provide a basic introduction to all concepts of the arts and sciences. Students are expected to take at least 60 hours of course work outside their major field of study. To be awarded a bachelor's degree, students must satisfactorily complete a minimum of 120 hours of college credit and attain a grade of C (2.0) or higher in their major and a cumulative average of at least 2.0. In addition to fulfilling the requirements of the major program, all students must complete the General Education Requirements, including a basic composition course and an advanced composition writing course, and 1 credit hour of physical education. A program of academic advising is an essential part of the University's entire mission.

FINANCIAL AID

Approximately 80 percent of the student population at Towson receives financial assistance of some kind. Assistance is available to eligible students through loans, grants, scholarships, and on-campus and off-campus employment. The University participates in the major federal and state programs. In addition, the University offers academic and non-need scholarships for qualified students.

APPLICATION AND INFORMATION

Towson renders admission decisions to qualified candidates on a continuous (rolling admissions) basis. Prospective applicants are encouraged to request and submit all appropriate application materials and required academic credentials as early as possible. The Admissions Office begins mailing application materials in September and begins processing applications for admission on October 1. Priority consideration is given to applicants who have submitted all required forms and credentials by December 1 for spring admission (February) and by May 1 for fall admission (August). A nonrefundable $30 application fee or authorized fee-deferment form is required at the time the application is filed. Application forms are available by calling or writing to the Admissions Office.

TULANE UNIVERSITY

■ New Orleans, Louisiana

THE UNIVERSITY

One of a handful of national independent universities in the South, Tulane was founded in 1834 as the Medical College of Louisiana and reorganized as Tulane in 1884. The University is comprehensive by nature, with more than 11,000 students enrolled in eleven schools and colleges ranging from the liberal arts and sciences through a full spectrum of professional schools: law, medicine, business, engineering, architecture, social work, and public health and tropical medicine. Tulane's 5,174 full-time undergraduates choose from sixty majors in colleges of liberal arts and sciences, engineering, architecture, and business and may opt for joint-degree programs in Tulane's professional schools to earn undergraduate and graduate degrees in a shorter period of time.

For more information, students should contact:

Richard Whiteside
Dean of Admission and Enrollment Management
Tulane University
210 Gibson Hall
6823 St. Charles Avenue
New Orleans, Louisiana 70118-5680
Telephone: 504-865-5731
800-873-9283 (toll-free)
Fax: 504-862-8715
E-mail:
undergrad.admission@tulane.edu
World Wide Web:
http://www.tulane.edu/Admission

ACADEMIC PROGRAM

The School of Engineering emphasizes design, research, and laboratory experimentation for its Bachelor of Science degree programs in biomedical, chemical, civil, computer, electrical, environmental, and mechanical engineering as well as computer science. The School of Architecture takes advantage of its location in New Orleans, a fascinating living architecture laboratory, where about 300 students are enrolled in the five-year Bachelor of Architecture program. Students graduate fully prepared to become licensed architects. The A. B. Freeman School of Business offers majors in accounting, business, finance, management, and marketing, leading to the Bachelor of Science in Management degree. The curriculum emphasizes ethics, entrepreneurship, international business, leadership, and communication skills as well as the major areas.

FINANCIAL AID

The University operates a comprehensive aid program; more than half of the students receive some form of financial aid. The average financial aid package (through scholarships, federal grants, loans, and work-study jobs) was about $20,000 for 1997–98. The University offers assistance to applicants who demonstrate financial need, and 90 percent of freshmen offered aid had their full need met. If financial need continues and the student has an acceptable academic record, aid extends through the normal period of undergraduate study. Notification of the financial aid award follows admission notification. Deans' Honor Scholarships are offered each year to approximately 100 freshmen and cover tuition for the undergraduate career; other merit scholarships, including those for middle-income students, are also available. Tulane also gives at least thirty National Merit Scholarships to National Merit Finalists who have named Tulane as their first-choice college. Tulane offers creative financing options for families that do not qualify for traditional aid but need assistance in meeting costs.

APPLICATION AND INFORMATION

Applications should be submitted by January 15 for admission to the fall semester; admission notification is made no later than April 1. Deans' Honor Scholarship applicants must apply by December 1 and are notified by February 20. Early action candidates should have all credentials on file by November 1 for notification by December 15. Candidates for admission have until May 1 to respond to the University's offer, and housing is required for freshmen. The application fee is $45.

TUSKEGEE UNIVERSITY

■ Tuskegee, Alabama

> **For further information, students should contact:**
>
> Dean of Admissions and Records
> Old Administration Building
> Tuskegee University
> Tuskegee, Alabama 36088
> Telephone: 334-727-8500
> 800-622-6531 (toll-free)
> World Wide Web:
> http://www.tusk.edu

THE UNIVERSITY

Undergraduate instruction at Tuskegee is organized under five major colleges: Agricultural, Environmental, and Natural Sciences; Business, Organization, and Management; Engineering, Architecture and Physical Sciences; Liberal Arts and Education; and Veterinary Medicine, Nursing, and Allied Health. Undergraduate courses are offered leading to the Bachelor of Arts and Bachelor of Science degrees. Graduate instruction leading to the master's degree is offered in four of the five major areas: Agricultural, Environmental, and Natural Sciences; Engineering, Architecture, and Physical Sciences; Liberal Arts and Education; and Veterinary Medicine, Nursing, and Allied Health. The University also offers Master of Science degrees in agricultural economics, animal and poultry sciences, biology, chemistry, counseling, counseling and student development, educational personnel administration, electrical engineering, environmental sciences, extension and technical education, food and nutritional science, general science education, general science nontraditional fifth year, mechanical engineering, school counseling, tropical animal health, and veterinary medicine. Master of Education degrees are offered in counseling and student development, educational personnel administration, extension and technical education, general science education, and school counseling.

ACADEMIC PROGRAM

Tuskegee University's academic year comprises two semesters and one 8-week summer term. In addition to required courses in each academic major, all programs include elective and required courses in the liberal arts. Summer enrichment programs are available in engineering, computer science, veterinary medicine, and the natural sciences. The requirements for a bachelor's degree vary among the colleges, from 124 semester hours in some liberal arts programs to 139 semester hours in engineering. The University is accredited by the Southern Association of Colleges and Schools, while some programs have additional national and specialized accreditation by the appropriate professional associations. These programs include architecture, chemistry, dietetics, engineering, medical technology, nursing, occupational therapy, social work, and veterinary medicine.

FINANCIAL AID

Tuskegee University subscribes to the philosophy that all academically capable high school graduates should be given an opportunity to pursue a postsecondary education. Consequently, every effort is made to assist needy and qualified students through the University's financial aid programs. The amount of aid granted is determined by the availability of funds, the extent of a student's need, and academic performance. Most awards are given for one academic year and are divided equally between the two semesters. Students seeking financial aid must file the Free Application for Federal Student Aid (FAFSA). This form can be obtained from the Financial Aid Office at Tuskegee University.

APPLICATION AND INFORMATION

Students seeking admission to Tuskegee University for the fall semester, which starts in August, should apply by March 15. Those seeking admission for the spring semester, which starts in January, should apply by October 15. Those seeking admission for the summer term should apply by April 1. Tuskegee University does, however, have a rolling admission policy and considers students for admission throughout the year. Early application is always advisable.

UNITED STATES MILITARY ACADEMY

■ West Point, New York

THE ACADEMY

For more information, students should contact:

Director of Admissions
United States Military Academy
606 Thayer Road
West Point, New York 10996-1797
Telephone: 914-938-4041
Web site: http://www.usma.edu/Admissions

The United States Military Academy, the nation's oldest service academy, offers young men and women one of the most highly respected, quality education programs in the nation. West Point advocates the "whole person" concept. The Military Academy has, since its founding in 1802, provided the broad college education demanded by the military profession while maintaining a degree of academic specialization comparable to that of civilian universities. West Point is a college whose mission is to educate, train, and inspire the Corps of Cadets so that each graduate shall have the attributes essential to professional growth throughout a career as a U.S. Army officer and a lifetime of service to the nation. The Military Academy provides its graduates with a solid foundation for intellectual and moral/ethical growth that is essential for successfully handling high-level responsibilities in national service. When students enter West Point, they are also beginning a profession. Upon graduation, cadets are commissioned as second lieutenants in the U.S. Army and are normally required to serve on active duty for at least five years. There are approximately 4,000 men and women enrolled at West Point. Cadets compete annually for Rhodes, Olmsted, Marshall, and Daedalian scholarships and for National Science Foundation, Truman, and Hertz graduate fellowships. West Pointers who remain in the Army are normally selected to attend civilian graduate schools in the United States or abroad between their fourth and tenth years of service.

ACADEMIC PROGRAM

The academic program at the United States Military Academy provides cadets with a broad background in the arts and sciences and prepares them for future graduate study. The total curriculum is designed to develop essential character, competence, and intellectual ability in an officer. The core curriculum is the foundation of the academic program and provides a background in mathematics, physical science, engineering, humanities, behavioral science, and social science. The core curriculum, consisting of thirty-one courses, represents the essential broad base of knowledge necessary for success as a commissioned officer and supports the subsequent choice of an elected area of academic concentration. Courses are required in chemistry, computer science, economics, engineering design, engineering science, English, foreign languages, history, international relations, literature, mathematics, military history, military leadership, philosophy, physics, political science, psychology, and terrain analysis. All cadets study military science and receive classroom instruction in the principles of small-unit tactics and leadership during a two-week intersession between the first and second semesters. Concentrated summer field training provides each cadet with the opportunity to learn and practice individual military skills and to apply the principles of tactics and leadership studied in the classroom.

FINANCIAL AID

There are no financial aid programs because expenses are paid by the U.S. government. Scholarship awards may be used by candidates to offset the cost of the initial deposit.

APPLICATION AND INFORMATION

Prospective candidates should write to Admissions, stating their interest in the Military Academy. Each applicant will be sent a Precandidate Questionnaire and prospectus, which outlines the West Point entrance requirements. All applicants are encouraged to start a candidate file at West Point at the end of their junior year or as soon thereafter as possible. This allows for early completion of all candidate file requirements.

UNIVERSITY OF ARKANSAS

■ Fayetteville, Arkansas

THE UNIVERSITY

Established in 1871, the University of Arkansas (U of A) is the flagship campus of the University of Arkansas System. The University offers more than 200 undergraduate and graduate degrees in more than 150 fields of study in agricultural, food, and life sciences; human environmental sciences; arts and sciences; business; education; engineering; architecture; and law. The University is also recognized as the only comprehensive doctoral degree-granting institution in the state. Fayetteville's 420-acre campus is home to students from all counties in Arkansas, every state in the U.S., and more than eighty-five countries throughout the world. The enrollment for the 1997–98 school year was nearly 14,400 students (more than 11,500 in undergraduate programs) and included a diverse student population, with 627 international students representing ninety-eight countries.

For further information, students should contact:

Ms. M. E. Lynes
Office of Admissions
200 Silas H. Hunt Hall
University of Arkansas
Fayetteville, Arkansas 72701
Telephone: 501-575-5346
800-377-UOFA (toll-free)
Fax: 501-575-7515
E-mail: uafadmis@comp.uark.edu
WWW: http://www.uark.edu/sis/apply/application.html

ACADEMIC PROGRAM

The U of A operates on a traditional two-semester academic year schedule, with two regular summer sessions and some special concurrent summer sessions. Requirements for graduation include a minimum University-wide core along with core requirements in each college. The majority of undergraduate degree offerings follow a four-year plan requiring from 124 to 136 course hours for graduation; there are some exceptions to this requirement, such as the five-year, design-oriented architecture program, which requires 163 hours. A course in English as a second language is offered in five 9-week sessions throughout the year. Classes focus on all language skills: grammar, reading, writing, and listening/speaking.

FINANCIAL AID

Loans, grants, work-study, and scholarships are available to qualifying students. Any need-analysis form recognized by the U.S. Department of Education is acceptable to the Office of Student Financial Services. To receive priority consideration for scholarships, a student enrolling for the fall semester must submit an application by January 15. For other forms of financial aid (student loans, Federal Pell Grants, etc.), the priority application deadline is April 1.

APPLICATION AND INFORMATION

To enroll in the University, students must submit a completed Application for Undergraduate Admission and an application fee. An online admission form can be found at the University's Web site listed below. The application deadline for the fall semester is August 15; the spring deadline is January 1. The student must also request that official transcripts be mailed to the Office of Admissions. A preliminary admission is provided for those high school seniors who have a transcript of six or seven semesters, but a final transcript is needed to certify high school graduation. ACT or SAT I scores no more than four years old must be submitted by all entering freshmen and transfer students with fewer than 24 transferable hours. These scores must be sent directly to the Office of Admissions from the testing agency. International students must submit an application for admission with a $55 application fee. A financial statement, a TOEFL score, and official secondary and postsecondary academic recorded are also required. For the fall term, the application deadline is May 1; the summer term deadline is March 1; and the spring term deadline is October 1.

UNIVERSITY OF BRIDGEPORT

■ BRIDGEPORT, CONNECTICUT

THE UNIVERSITY

Founded in 1927, the University of Bridgeport is a private, nonsectarian, comprehensive, urban university located in Bridgeport, Connecticut. The University has a long-standing partnership with the local community to provide its residents with excellent educational opportunities that lead to degrees and career advancement. Although many of the students are Connecticut residents, the University has a student body representing thirty states and seventy countries. The University is divided into several schools and colleges. The College of Graduate and Undergraduate Studies (CGUS) houses five schools: the Schools of Arts, Humanities, and Social Sciences; Science, Engineering, and Technology; General Studies; Business; and Education and Human Resources. The Division of Health Sciences includes the Nutrition Institute, the Division of Health Technology, Fones School of Dental Hygiene, the College of Chiropractic, and the College of Naturopathic Medicine. Professional accreditations include those from the ABA, NASAD, ABET, CCE, and the ADA. The School of Business is nationally accredited by the Association of Collegiate Business Schools and Programs (ACBSP).

For more information, students should contact:

Office of Admissions
University of Bridgeport
126 Park Avenue
Bridgeport, Connecticut 06601
Telephone: 203-576-4552
800-EXCEL-UB (toll-free)
(800-392-3582)
Fax: 203-576-4941
E-mail: admit@cse.bridgeport.edu
Web site: http://www.bridgeport.edu

ACADEMIC PROGRAM

The University of Bridgeport operates on a two-semester calendar. A minimum of 120 credit hours is required for graduation, and the last 30 of those must be completed at the University. The University also provides one-on-one tutoring and group remedial work in the Academic Resource Center. This Center offers extensive advising, attention to developing essential academic skills, small classes, and the likelihood of increased academic achievement. Credit can be granted for subject area examinations of the College-Level Examination Program (CLEP) on which scores above the 50th percentile have been received. Credit is also granted for Advanced Placement examinations passed with the recommended score.

FINANCIAL AID

The University's financial aid policies are intended to make it possible for students to attend the University who otherwise could not afford a private education. Financial assistance, consisting of grants, scholarships, loans, and employment, is based on the financial need of the student and his or her family. More than 85 percent of all students receive some form of financial assistance from the University and outside sources. Students who are interested in applying for financial aid must file the Free Application for Federal Student Aid (FAFSA). The University of Bridgeport also offers academic scholarships and grants to students on a competitive basis. These awards are renewable for four years based on satisfactory academic achievement and good standing in the University. Qualified students may be eligible to receive financial aid in addition to a scholarship or grant award. Athletic scholarships are also available.

APPLICATION AND INFORMATION

The University admits students for both the fall and the spring semesters on a rolling admission basis, beginning March 1. The priority deadline for freshman applicants is April 1. The application must be completed and returned with a $35 fee. It is the student's responsibility to see that all of the necessary official transcripts and test scores are sent directly from the appropriate institutions to the University. Letters of recommendation are not required but may be submitted as supportive material. Additional requirements may be required by certain programs. Electronic applications are welcome through the University's Web site and Polaris.

UNIVERSITY OF CENTRAL FLORIDA

■ ORLANDO, FLORIDA

THE UNIVERSITY

The University of Central Florida is a comprehensive, metropolitan university with approximately 28,600 students. As one of the nation's fastest-growing universities, UCF enrolls a diverse student body representing forty-eight states and more than 100 countries. The University offers educational and research programs that complement a surging economy, with strong components in aerospace, banking, film, electronics, health, social sciences, and tourism. UCF's programs in communication and the fine arts help to meet the cultural and recreational needs of a growing metropolitan area. The University also offers many graduate programs leading to master's and doctoral degrees. UCF has established extensive partnerships with business and industry in the Central Florida area that provide students with exceptional research and learning experiences. These partnerships bring practical learning environments to UCF students through co-op and internship programs. Joint curriculum development strategies include BE2000, a widely modeled business curriculum incorporating classes taught by local business and industry executives. Students participate in more than 250 organizations, including special interest clubs, multicultural associations, fraternities and sororities, honor societies, and academic and preprofessional organizations. The Offices of Student Life and Student Activities schedule a wide array of extracurricular programs, including concerts, movies, and guest speakers.

For additional information, students should call Undergraduate Admissions at the number below, which also serves as a 24-hour application request line.

Office of Undergraduate Admissions
University of Central Florida
P.O. Box 160111
Orlando, Florida 32816-0111
Telephone: 407-823-3000
E-mail: admissio@pegasus.cc.ucf.edu
Web site: http://www.ucf.edu

ACADEMIC PROGRAM

UCF provides for total education through a core curriculum of 36 hours of general education courses. In addition to fulfilling the general education requirement, each student must complete the necessary major and/or minor requirements to reach the minimum of 120 semester hours necessary for graduation. Several special programs help students reach their academic and leadership potential. The UCF Honors Program and the Honors in the Major program encourage students to achieve academic excellence through small classes and interactive symposiums. The innovative Leadership Enrichment and Academic Development (LEAD) Scholars Program fosters leadership and service commitment through a comprehensive student development program for freshmen. The Academic Exploration Program (AEP) helps entering freshmen define their career goals and develop an academic strategy to reach those goals. The University offers Air Force and Army ROTC programs.

FINANCIAL AID

Financial aid is awarded according to each student's need in relation to college costs and may include grants, loans, scholarships, and/or part-time employment. The priority application deadline is March 15. Programs based on need include the Federal Perkins Loan, Federal Pell Grant, Florida Student Assistance Grant, Federal Work-Study, Florida College Career Work-Study Program, and Federal Stafford Student Loan. To qualify for these programs, students must complete the Free Application for Federal Student Aid. Approximately 66 percent of UCF students receive some form of financial aid.

APPLICATION AND INFORMATION

Students are encouraged to apply several months in advance. Applications are accepted up to a year prior to the start of the term for which entry is desired. Priority application deadlines are July 15 for the fall semester, November 15 for the spring semester, and April 15 for the summer term. Campus tours are given Monday through Friday at 11 a.m. and 2 p.m. (except holidays). Appointments are not required.

UNIVERSITY OF MARYLAND, BALTIMORE COUNTY

■ BALTIMORE, MARYLAND

THE UNIVERSITY

There are few, if any, honors universities like University of Maryland, Baltimore County (UMBC), with its commitment to undergraduate education—and to undergraduate participation in real problem solving, undertaken in locations as different as a hospital in Holland and a rain forest in Australia. UMBC's leadership in technology, friendly campus climate, business and industry partnerships, and ability to place students in exciting internships, leading graduate programs, and promising careers are just a few of the reasons why students who could attend any college are choosing UMBC. The youngest of the eleven-member University System of Maryland, UMBC has grown rapidly since opening its doors in 1966 and now has a population of more than 10,000 students. The 500-acre, contemporary campus on the rolling hills of a former dairy farm overlooks the monuments, steeples, and skyscrapers of the Baltimore skyline.

For further information, students or parents may contact:

Rachel M. Hendrickson
Director of Admissions
University of Maryland, Baltimore County
1000 Hilltop Circle
Baltimore, Maryland 21250
Telephone: 410-455-2291
800-UMBC-4U2 (toll-free)
Fax: 410-455-1094
E-mail: admissions@umbc.edu
Web site: http://www.umbc.edu

ACADEMIC PROGRAM

To receive a UMBC degree, students complete 120 credits plus two physical education courses. In addition to the requirements for the chosen major, a core of courses called the general foundation requirements (GFRs) provides a solid basis for a lifetime of learning. The GFRs encompass four broad areas of human knowledge: humanities and fine arts, mathematics and natural sciences, social sciences, and languages and culture.

FINANCIAL AID

As a member of the state university system, UMBC is able to keep costs relatively low. Fifty percent of all students receive some form of financial aid; the University administers and coordinates a variety of federal, state, and institutional aid programs. UMBC uses the Free Application for Federal Student Aid (FAFSA) to help determine students' financial need. Aid is awarded to qualified applicants on a first-come, first-served basis. In order for the applicant to be considered on time, the FAFSA report and all supporting documents must reach the UMBC Financial Aid Office by March 1. (Since aid is awarded only to admitted students, early application for admission is also important.) A wide range of merit scholarships ranging from $500 to $16,000 per year are awarded to students on the basis of academic or artistic merit. Well-qualified freshmen are automatically considered for general merit scholarships once they are admitted to the University. Special programs, such as the Humanities Scholars program, the Artist Scholars, and the Meyerhoff Scholars, include an extracurricular, travel, or summer-study component. Candidates must be nominated by a high school official and undergo a rigorous selection and interview process.

APPLICATION AND INFORMATION

Prospective freshmen are encouraged to submit applications by December 15 for full consideration for admission, campus housing, financial aid, and scholarships; the final deadline is March 15. Applicants may also be considered for spring admission by applying prior to December 15. The deadline for transfer students is May 31 for fall admission and December 15 for spring admission, although earlier application is recommended for students seeking admission to special programs or wishing to be considered for campus housing, financial aid, or scholarships.

UNIVERSITY OF MARYLAND, COLLEGE PARK

■ College Park, Maryland

THE UNIVERSITY

For further information, students should contact:

Office of Undergraduate Admissions
University of Maryland
College Park, Maryland 20742-5235
Telephone: 301-314-8385
800-422-5867 (toll-free)
E-mail: um-admit@uga.umd.edu
World Wide Web:
http://www.uga.umd.edu

The University of Maryland, College Park dates back to 1856. As the flagship institution of the eleven-campus University System of Maryland, the University serves as the state's premier institution for teaching and research. Located on 1,580 acres of land, Maryland is a coeducational public institution serving 21,224 full-time and 3,230 part-time undergraduates with a full-time faculty of 1,500. About 8,200 students are enrolled in the graduate school. The University encourages diversity in campus activities and sponsors more than 300 clubs, organizations, and religious groups. It provides twenty-five intramural sports for men and women, in addition to Atlantic Coast Conference Division I athletics in fifteen sports for men and women. The University's Stamp Student Union houses several restaurants, a ticket office, a movie theater, a bowling alley, and a bank. About 75 percent of Maryland's undergraduate students are state residents, and 35 percent are students of color. The average freshman is 18 years old; the average full-time undergraduate is 21. The University provides both single-sex (with visiting privileges) and coed housing for about 8,000 of its undergraduates. In addition, nearly 12 percent of the students live in fraternity and sorority houses located next to the campus.

ACADEMIC PROGRAM

The University of Maryland operates on a semester system. Undergraduates must complete a minimum of 46 credit hours of core requirements in addition to course work in their major program and elective courses. Although each major program is unique, generally 30 to 35 credit hours are earned in major fields, and 120 credits are needed to graduate. AP, IB, and CLEP credit is granted. Maryland's honors program includes 1,200 students and consists of small classes and interactive discussions in a wide range of subject matter. College Park Scholars, a living/learning program for academically talented students, offers an innovative mixture of academic and social activities. Many departments offer individual honors programs, and more than forty honor societies have chapters on campus. An Air Force ROTC program exists at College Park.

FINANCIAL AID

Financial aid is available through scholarships, grants, loans, and work-study employment. Merit scholarships include the Banneker/Key and Regents full scholarships as well as President's and Dean's partial scholarships. Eighty percent of students receive some kind of financial aid. The average amount of aid awarded was $8468. Maryland belongs to the College Scholarship Service. The Free Application for Federal Student Aid (FAFSA) should be submitted by February 15 prior to planned fall or spring enrollment.

APPLICATION AND INFORMATION

Applications for the fall semester must be accompanied by a $45 fee and must be received by February 15. Students are encouraged to apply by December 1, however, to be fully considered for early notification, programs for academically talented students, and scholarships. Applications for the spring semester are due by December 15. Freshmen (excluding architecture students) may begin studies during the spring semester.

UNIVERSITY OF MASSACHUSETTS DARTMOUTH

■ North Dartmouth, Massachusetts

THE UNIVERSITY

The University of Massachusetts Dartmouth traces its roots to 1895 when the Massachusetts legislature chartered the New Bedford Textile School and the Bradford Durfee Textile School in Fall River. In 1962 Southeastern Massachusetts Technological Institute (SMTI) was created, and in 1969, out of a need and a clear demand for a comprehensive public university, SMTI became Southeastern Massachusetts University. Then, in 1988, the Swain School of Design was merged with the University's College of Visual and Performing Arts. In 1991, a new University of Massachusetts system was created, which combined the Amherst and Boston campuses with the University of Lowell, Southeastern Massachusetts University, and the Medical Center in Worcester. Today, UMass Dartmouth provides educational programs, research, extension, and continuing education in the liberal and creative arts and sciences and in the professions. A broad range of bachelor's and master's degrees and one program leading to a doctorate are offered. Graduate programs lead to the Master of Arts, Master of Business Administration, Master of Arts in Teaching, Master of Fine Arts, Master of Art Education, and Master of Science. A Ph.D. is offered in electrical engineering.

For application forms and related information, students may call, write, or e-mail the admissions office.

Office of Admissions
UMass Dartmouth
285 Old Westport Road
North Dartmouth, Massachusetts
02747-2300

Telephone: 508-999-8605
Fax: 508-999-8755
E-mail: admissions@umassd.edu
World Wide Web:
http://www.umassd.edu/

ACADEMIC PROGRAMS

Undergraduate students usually enroll in four or five courses each semester, and a typical course earns 3 credits. An undergraduate degree requires a minimum of 120 credits (there are a few majors which require 135 credits); a student can complete degree requirements for a specified major within a department or an approved interdepartmental major (30 credits). Students must also complete requirements according to the degree being sought. UMass Dartmouth is a member of SACHEM (Southeastern Association for Cooperation in Higher Education in Massachusetts), allowing for cross-registration at Bridgewater State College, Bristol Community College, Cape Cod Community College, Dean College, Massachusetts Maritime Academy, Massasoit Community College, Stonehill College, and Wheaton College. The University has formal exchange agreements with the University of Grenoble (France), the Lycée du Grésivaudan at Meylan and the Lycée Aristide Berges, Nottingham Trent University (England), the Baden-Württemburg Universities (Germany), Centro de Arte e Communiçãcao (Portugal), Nova Scotia College of Art and Design, Ben Gurion University of the Negev (Israel), and the École Nationale Superieure des Industries Textiles, Université de Haute Alsace (France). Students may also take initiative in finding other programs in addition to the exchange-agreement institutions. The College of Engineering provides majors in any of the engineering fields to gain work experience through cooperative education or internships.

FINANCIAL AID

Nearly all students are eligible for some type of financial aid. UMass Dartmouth awards financial aid based on federal, state, and institutional guidelines; students must submit the Free Application for Federal Student Aid (FAFSA). In determining need, the Financial Aid Services Office considers the total costs of attending the University (tuition, fees, books, room and board, the cost of commuting, and an allowance for living and personal expenses). The difference between total University cost and the estimate of expected family contribution is the amount that the financial aid staff considers to be financial need.

APPLICATION AND INFORMATION

Admissions is rolling except for early decision (freshman). The early decision deadline is November 15, with notification by December 15. All other decisions are made within three weeks of the completion of an application.

UNIVERSITY OF MINNESOTA, CROOKSTON

■ CROOKSTON, MINNESOTA

THE UNIVERSITY

Nationally recognized as a leader in information technology education, the University of Minnesota, Crookston (UMC), is part of the world-renowned University of Minnesota System. Founded in the late 1800s as a research station and then as a school of agriculture, UMC became a part of the University of Minnesota in 1965. Today, UMC is a four-year, public coeducational institution of 1,650 full- and part-time students with a focus on polytechnic education. UMC is continuing to evolve to meet the educational demands of Minnesota and the world by developing a technology-rich, interactive living and learning community. For example, in 1993, UMC was one of the first campuses in the nation to begin issuing notebook computers to all full-time students. In addition, the entire campus is fully wired to the World Wide Web, with an Internet connection available at every classroom seat and in the library, the cafeteria, every study room, and every residence hall room. Nearly 100 percent of campus classrooms have technologically advanced faculty workstations that feature overhead projection graphics cameras for still, video, and computer displays.

For more information, students should contact:

Office of Admissions and Financial Aid
4 Hill Hall
University of Minnesota, Crookston
2900 University Avenue
Crookston, Minnesota 56716-5001
Telephone: 218-281-8569
800-862-6466 (toll-free)
Web site: http://www.crk.umn.edu

ACADEMIC PROGRAM

Beginning in fall 1999, UMC will operate on the semester system. Students must earn a minimum of 120 semester credits for all bachelor's degree programs. Students benefit from a personalized learning approach that centers on practical, real-world direct applications. The curriculum is learner driven, interactive, and supported with technology and involves collaboration among students, faculty members, and prospective employers.

FINANCIAL AID

Removing financial barriers to students' enrollment and success is the ultimate goal of UMC's financial aid program. UMC wishes to insure that any qualified student who desires to pursue an education at UMC can obtain sufficient resources to do so. Accordingly, the University's Office of Admissions and Financial Aid administers a number of financial aid programs. A number of need-based funding sources are available for new, incoming freshman students as well as for transfer students—whether part-time or full-time. UMC also offers a variety of specialty merit-based scholarships. For the need-based funding sources, a formula is used that factors the difference between UMC's estimate of what it will cost to attend UMC and the amount the federal and state governments expect students and their families to contribute to their education, based on information provided on the Free Application for Federal Student Aid (FAFSA).

APPLICATION AND INFORMATION

Applying for admission to the University of Minnesota, Crookston, involves some important preliminary steps. Students are automatically admitted as freshman students when they do the following: send high school transcripts, submit an application fee and a completed application form, and submit results from the ACT. Transfer students must send college transcripts and submit an application fee and completed application form. The application priority deadline is March 1 of each year. UMC has developed a helpful application guide called *Getting Started At UMC: Admissions Application Guide,* which is available for free by calling UMC's Office of Admissions and Financial Aid. Campus tours are available each weekday at 9 a.m., 10 a.m., and 1 p.m. Students are encouraged to call ahead two days before a planned visit.

UNIVERSITY OF NEW HAVEN

■ West Haven, Connecticut

THE UNIVERSITY

For more information, students should contact:

Dean of Admissions
University of New Haven
300 Orange Avenue
West Haven, Connecticut 06516
Telephone: 203-932-7319
800-DIAL-UNH (toll-free)

The University of New Haven is a private, coeducational university founded as a branch of Northeastern University in 1920. In 1926 it became an independent school and in 1958 expanded its programs to become a four-year college. The acquisition of the present campus in West Haven in 1960 promoted rapid expansion of facilities, faculty, and student body (the current enrollment includes 1,500 full-time undergraduates). The University offers excellent instruction in a great variety of academic disciplines, yet is small enough to accommodate individual programs and needs. Programs are constantly evolving to meet changing academic and career needs and the requirements of business, industry, and professional fields. The University's small class size fosters close student-faculty relationships. The University operates a branch in New London. Off-campus graduate courses are offered in Waterbury, Trumbull, and Stamford. The main campus is located in West Haven on a hillside overlooking Long Island Sound, with a view of downtown New Haven.

ACADEMIC PROGRAM

As a suburban institution, the University of New Haven offers a broad range of programs in both liberal arts and professional areas. Professionalism is emphasized, and there are diverse opportunities for career-oriented internships, cooperative education, independent study, and industrial projects. Certain types of professional experience are required in a number of degree programs. The Center for Learning Resources offers a tutoring service that is open to all students. All tutoring is free, and students are accommodated by appointment or on a walk-in basis. An available option at the University is cooperative education, an academic program that offers students the opportunity to combine career-oriented, paid, full-time work with their education. Students are also eligible to enroll in Air Force Reserve Officer Training Corps courses through a cooperative agreement with the University of Connecticut.

FINANCIAL AID

The University of New Haven offers a comprehensive financial aid program that includes University resources as well as state, federal, and private aid programs. Approximately 70 percent of full-time undergraduate students receive some form of assistance. University students receive federal aid through the Federal Pell Grant, Federal Supplemental Educational Opportunity Grant, Federal Work-Study, Federal Perkins Loan, Federal Stafford Student Loan, and Federal PLUS loan programs. In addition to federal aid programs, the University administers programs sponsored by the state of Connecticut for Connecticut residents attending the University. Some students also qualify for financial aid from other states and from private companies, organizations, and foundations.

APPLICATION AND INFORMATION

To apply to the University, a student must submit the completed application form, a nonrefundable $25 fee, official records of all academic work completed, and results of the SAT I or ACT. International students are required to demonstrate proficiency in English as well as provide documentation of financial support. The University of New Haven does not discriminate on the basis of age, color, sex, religion, race, creed, national origin, or disability in admission or treatment of students, in administration or distribution of financial aid, or in recruitment or treatment of employees. The University is authorized under federal law to enroll nonimmigrant alien students who meet the University's academic and English proficiency standards. The admissions office employs a rolling admissions system.

UNIVERSITY OF TAMPA

■ TAMPA, FLORIDA

THE UNIVERSITY

The University of Tampa is a private comprehensive university that offers challenging learning experiences in two colleges: the College of Liberal Arts and Sciences and the College of Business. Together, they offer hundreds of courses in more than fifty fields of study. In both colleges, students work with experts in their fields, and there is a shared belief in the value of a liberal arts–centered education, practical work experience, and the ability to communicate effectively, all of which are trademarks of a University of Tampa education. The environment outside the classroom is supportive, stimulating, and fun. Students choose from more than eighty student organizations, including service organizations, student government, honor societies, departmental clubs, fraternities, and publications. The University of Tampa has one of the top NCAA Division II sports programs in the nation. Spartan athletes have won three national championships in recent years, two in baseball and one in soccer. Intercollegiate sports for men and women include basketball, cross-country, soccer, and swimming. Men's baseball, golf, and soccer and women's softball, tennis, and volleyball are also offered. All students may have cars on campus.

Requests for application forms, catalogs, and other information should be directed to:

University of Tampa
Office of Admissions
401 West Kennedy Boulevard
Tampa, Florida 33606-1490
Telephone: 813-253-6211
800-733-4773 (toll-free)
Fax: 813-254-4955
E-mail: admissions@alpha.utampa.edu

ACADEMIC PROGRAM

The curriculum is designed to give students a broad academic and cultural background as well as concentrated study in a major. Hundreds of internships are available in many areas of study. The "Baccalaureate Experience" begins with a special freshman seminar program designed to help students assess their skills and research their interests. Students unsure about their major or what they want to do when they graduate may participate in a special Gateways program during the freshman year. During the first two years, students pursue an integrated core program of thirteen courses consisting of two in English, one in math, one in computer science, two in natural sciences, three in social science, and three in humanities. Prior to graduation, students are also required to take three writing-intensive courses, one course that deals with non-Western/Third World concerns, and an international/global awareness course. Transfer students who have an associate degree may be given full junior status. Students receive advanced placement by earning acceptable scores on Advanced Placement exams, the College-Level Examination Program tests, or by completing the International Baccalaureate Diploma. As much as one year's credit may be awarded.

FINANCIAL AID

A high-quality, private education at the University of Tampa is not as difficult to finance as students may think. Each family's situation is evaluated individually for need-based assistance. Academic achievements, leadership potential, athletic skills, and other special talents are recognized, regardless of need. Army and Air Force ROTC scholarships are also available. The Free Application for Federal Student Aid (FAFSA) is required to determine eligibility for need-based funds. Florida residents should complete the FAFSA no later than April 30 for state grants. Early estimates of aid are available October through January.

APPLICATION AND INFORMATION

High school students may request an application after the end of their junior year.

UNIVERSITY OF THE ARTS

■ PHILADELPHIA, PENNSYLVANIA

Office of Admission
University of the Arts
320 South Broad Street
Philadelphia, Pennsylvania 19102
Telephone: 800-616-ARTS (toll-free)
Fax: 215-875-5458
Web site: http://www.uarts.edu

THE UNIVERSITY

Composed of the College of Art and Design, the College of Performing Arts, and the newly formed College of Media and Communication, the University offers intensive concentration within a major field as well as creative, challenging possibilities for multidisciplinary exploration and growth. The Philadelphia College of Performing Arts was founded in 1870 to educate musicians. Since that time, it has expanded to include a School of Dance with rigorous programs in ballet, modern, jazz, and tap dance, as well as a School of Theater Arts with programs in acting and musical theater. In 1996, the University introduced the College of Media and Communication to prepare students for new career opportunities in emerging fields such as multimedia design, CD-ROM development, electronic publishing, computer-generated design and animation, electronic arts and performance, and writing for media.

ACADEMIC PROGRAM

The freshman year in the College of Art and Design is devoted to the Foundation Program and is intended as an exploratory year, allowing students to investigate various disciplines before deciding on a specific major. All students take a set number of liberal arts credits, regardless of their major. A minimum of 123 credits is required for graduation, including 18 credits in Foundation Program courses, 42 credits in the major, 42 credits in the liberal arts, 15 credits in electives (9 credits of which must be taken in a department other than the major), and 6 credits in other areas outside the major. Dual degrees are available, provided that the student has completed the requirements of both departments involved. In the College of Performing Arts, the School of Music program stresses individualized training with a performance emphasis. Students undergo intensive training in theory and musicianship. In the School of Dance, students are required to take two years of ballet, modern, and jazz dance before choosing a major in the junior year. The School of Theater Arts concentrates on developing the student's skill as an actor. A minimum of 130 credits is required for graduation, at least 30 of which must be in the liberal arts. Participation in the 17-credit MATPREP Program enables students to complete bachelor's and master's degrees in teaching music in five years. The College of Media and Communication first opened its doors in 1996 with a four-year undergraduate program in writing for media and performance. In response to emerging digital technologies, multimedia was introduced as an undergraduate major in fall 1997.

FINANCIAL AID

The University funds presidential scholarships based on artistic potential and academic achievement. Financial aid is also available on the basis of the applicant's demonstrated financial need. Applicants must submit the Free Application for Federal Student Aid (FAFSA). The University administers the following federal, campus-based student assistance programs: Federal Perkins Loans, Federal Work-Study Program awards, and Federal Supplemental Educational Opportunity Grants.

APPLICATION AND INFORMATION

In addition to submitting a portfolio or auditioning, applicants should submit their high school transcript, SAT I or ACT scores, one letter of recommendation, and a personal statement of purpose. The University of the Arts follows a system of rolling admission. All students are notified within two weeks of the receipt of all required materials. Students are encouraged to submit applications by March 15 for fall admission and December 1 for spring admission. Students should contact the admission office for additional information.

UNIVERSITY OF THE INCARNATE WORD

■ SAN ANTONIO, TEXAS

THE UNIVERSITY

Consistently rated among the top liberal arts colleges in the Southwest, the University of the Incarnate Word welcomes the interest of prospective students seeking a challenging and diverse small Catholic college atmosphere. The University seeks students who value small classes, interaction with faculty members, and dynamic learning experiences. Founded in 1881 as Incarnate Word College by the Sisters of Charity of the Incarnate Word, the school achieved university status in 1996. The University has a population of 3,312 students, with 2,659 students seeking baccalaureate degrees in forty majors and 653 students seeking master's degrees in fifteen programs. Male students represent 31 percent of the population. The student body at the University of the Incarnate Word reflects the rich cultural diversity of south Texas—49 percent of students are Hispanic American, 36 percent are European American, 6 percent are international, 7 percent are African American, and 2 percent are Asian American and Native American. Students at the University come from twenty-nine states and Puerto Rico as well as twenty-six other countries. Thirty percent of students reside on campus with housing options that include traditional dormitories, suites, and apartments.

Application materials and further information on the University of the Incarnate Word may be obtained by contacting:

Director of Admissions
University of the Incarnate Word
4301 Broadway
San Antonio, Texas 78209
Telephone: 210-829-6005
800-749-WORD (toll-free)
Fax: 210-829-3921

ACADEMIC PROGRAM

To receive any degree from the University of the Incarnate Word, a student must fulfill the requirements of the University's core curriculum in addition to course work specific to the major. The University of the Incarnate Word recognizes the core curriculum as the heart of the institution. The core is composed of 67 hours of course work in rhetoric, literature and arts, foreign language, wellness development, mathematics and natural science, philosophy and religion, history and behavioral sciences, computer literacy, and the integration of knowledge (capstone). Students must complete 30 hours of community service to receive their diploma. The Bachelor of Arts degree entails 128 hours of specified course work; the Bachelor of Business Administration requires 133 hours; the Bachelor of Music specifies 137 hours; the Bachelor of Science in Nursing requires 136 hours; and the Bachelor of Science specifies 133 hours. Individual programs may vary in graduation requirements depending on the minor sought, teacher certification requirements, clinical requirements, and credits transferred.

FINANCIAL AID

Approximately 78 percent of all UIW students receive financial assistance. The University awards Presidential/Academic, Performance/Visual Arts, and Athletic scholarships, none of which are need-based. Presidential/Academic scholarships are awarded based on high school grade point average and SAT/ACT test scores. All other forms of financial assistance are awarded based on financial need as determined by the Free Application for Federal Student Aid (FAFSA). Other federal/state/institutional financial assistance awarded includes the Federal Pell Grant, Federal Supplemental Educational Opportunity Grant, Texas Equalization Grant, UIW Grant, Federal Perkins Loan, Federal Subsidized and Unsubsidized Stafford Loans, Federal Parent Loan, Texas College Access Loan, Federal Work-Study, Texas Work-Study, and Institutional Employment.

APPLICATION AND INFORMATION

Applications for admission are accepted on a rolling basis, although students are advised to submit them before April 1 as this is the priority deadline for financial assistance. A complete application file will be processed within one week.

VALPARAISO UNIVERSITY

■ Valparaiso, Indiana

THE UNIVERSITY

Valparaiso University was founded in 1859 by citizens of Valparaiso, Indiana, but its recent history dates from 1925, when it was purchased by the Lutheran University Association. VU is one of the nation's largest Lutheran-affiliated universities, yet it remains independent and is open to individuals of all faiths. The University's 3,500 students represent most states and more than forty countries; 61 percent come from outside of Indiana. Valparaiso University is a residential community in which activities outside the classroom form an important part of campus life; more than 64 percent of its students live on campus. Approximately 150 extracurricular and cocurricular programs are open to all, including the campus radio station, Pre-Medical Society, International Student Association, and various NCAA Division I intercollegiate and intramural sports teams for men and women. Both in and out of the classroom, students and professors operate under a student-initiated honor code in which integrity is assumed to be the norm.

Information and application forms for admission and financial aid may be obtained from:

Office of Admissions
Valparaiso University
Valparaiso, Indiana 46383-6493
Telephone: 219-464-5011
888-GO-VALPO (toll-free)
Fax: 219-464-6898
E-mail:
undergrad_admissions@valpo.edu
World Wide Web:
http://www.valpo.edu

ACADEMIC PROGRAM

Programs are structured to provide a solid base for exploration in various fields, while offering students the freedom to develop depth in a specific interest. This philosophy is extended through the upper division, where students have three options in completing a degree: an individual plan of study involving the major and complementary courses from related fields of study, the election of a second academic major in addition to the first, or a special minor in connection with the major. Career planning is aided through the professional programs, the Career Track program of the VU Counseling Center, and the University's Career Center. Many students also gain professional work experience in their chosen field before graduation by participating in the cooperative education program.

FINANCIAL AID

Eighty percent of Valparaiso's students receive financial aid totaling more than $38 million. The University attempts to make up the difference between the cost of attending Valparaiso and the amount a family can afford, as determined by the Free Application for Federal Student Aid (FAFSA). VU aid is available in the form of scholarships, grants, loans, and campus employment, and often the aid is a package of these awards. Students are also encouraged to apply for the federal government's Federal Pell Grant, Federal Perkins Loan, and Federal Supplemental Educational Opportunity Grant, state scholarships where applicable, and the various private grants and scholarships that are available. Early application is recommended for VU assistance, since the awarding of aid begins in February of the year of enrollment.

APPLICATION AND INFORMATION

An applicant must complete a formal University admission application or the Common Application to be considered for admission. In addition, VU requires a high school transcript (complete through the junior year), ACT or SAT I scores, and college transcripts (when applicable). Under certain conditions (e.g., when ACT or SAT I scores would not be available early enough for full admission and financial aid action), scores on the PSAT, along with the high school transcript, may be sufficient for preliminary admission consideration. VU's rolling admission procedure means that candidates are notified of a decision shortly after all necessary credentials have been received. For scholarship consideration, May 1 is the deadline for the admission application.

VIRGINIA WESLEYAN COLLEGE

■ NORFOLK, VIRGINIA

Additional information can be obtained by contacting:

Office of Admissions and Financial Aid
Virginia Wesleyan College
1584 Wesleyan Drive
Norfolk/Virginia Beach, Virginia 23502-5599

Telephone: 757-455-3208
800-737-8684 (toll-free)
Fax: 757-461-5238
E-mail: admissions@vwc.edu
Web site: http://www.vwc.edu

THE COLLEGE

Virginia Wesleyan College is a community of scholars who strongly believe that education is the key to achieving life's goals and that the environment in which learning takes place makes all the difference in reaching these goals. The expansive 300-acre campus of this coeducational four-year college of liberal arts and sciences is designed to provide every opportunity to live and learn in an energetic, value-centered academic climate. Affiliated with the United Methodist Church and accredited by the Commission on Colleges of the Southern Association of Colleges and Schools, the College maintains a diverse student body and a low student-faculty ratio. Students come to Virginia Wesleyan from thirty-six states and twenty-three countries and indicate that they are attracted to the College primarily because of its size, the high quality of its academic program, its location, and its friendly atmosphere. Students who desire a strong, individualized academic program, who want the opportunity to study matters of concern to them in a key East Coast area, who have the ability to assume responsibility for their education, and who want to be involved with their colleagues and professors in creating a vital educational experience find a receptive environment.

ACADEMIC PROGRAM

The College offers a liberal arts curriculum that is designed to allow students considerable freedom in planning their own program yet also ensures that they acquire not only the breadth of knowledge traditionally emphasized in a liberal education but also a sound foundation in a specific field. The academic calendar is on the 4-1-4 plan, featuring a one-course term in January when students can take special-topic courses, traditional and interdisciplinary courses, and travel-study courses in the United States and abroad. They can also participate in off-campus internships, field study programs, independent study, and senior projects. The College offers study-abroad programs in a number of countries.

FINANCIAL AID

The College believes that no student who wishes to attend Virginia Wesleyan College should be denied the opportunity because of limited financial resources. The director of financial aid is available to counsel students and their families regarding financial planning. In cases of demonstrated financial need, students may qualify for grants, low-interest loans, and work-study. Financial need is determined by an analysis of the Free Application for Federal Student Aid (FAFSA). March 1 is the mailing deadline for applying for financial assistance. The College also offers merit scholarships, without regard to need, to entering students with outstanding academic records. Scholarships ranging from $4000 to full comprehensive fees (over four years) are awarded to students based on their test scores, academic record, interviews, and essays. Leadership Scholarships from $4000 to $24,000 are available to students with demonstrated leadership abilities as evidenced through community service, extracurricular participation, and volunteerism.

WARREN WILSON COLLEGE

■ Asheville, North Carolina

THE COLLEGE

An application form and further information may be obtained by contacting:

Office of Admission
Warren Wilson College
701 Warren Wilson Road
Asheville, North Carolina 28815-9000

Telephone: 800-934-3536 (toll-free)
E-mail: admit@warren-wilson.edu
World Wide Web: http://www.warren-wilson.edu

Since its founding in 1894, Warren Wilson College has educated students with a unique triad of a strong liberal arts program, work for the College, and service to those in need, which makes Warren Wilson unlike any other college. Its 650 students come from forty-two states and twenty-five countries, creating a diverse and vibrant academic community. The academic program features a first-rate faculty that does all of the teaching and frequently participates in research with students. The average class size is small, and discussion is an important part of teaching. Fifteen majors are offered, with a commitment to quality in each program. Students at Warren Wilson are integral to the day-to-day operation of the College. Each student works 15 hours a week at a job that is essential to running the school. This experience helps build student confidence (students learn that there is no job they cannot learn to do) and a strong sense of community at the College. Many juniors and seniors have work assignments that coincide with their major. Students receive a work fellowship in the amount of $2472 each year for the work they do. Service is also integral to the College's way of thinking. Warren Wilson is one of only a few colleges in the country that require student participation in community service for graduation. Service is offered to a wide range of individuals and agencies, nationally and abroad. Students must provide at least 20 hours of service each year to someone off campus. The 1,100-acre campus includes a 300-acre working farm, 600 acres of forest, 25 miles of hiking trails, and a white-water kayaking course. The campus and the area are havens for outdoor activities, such as white-water sports, hiking, camping, mountain biking, and rock climbing.

ACADEMIC PROGRAM

The goal of the degree program at Warren Wilson College is the completion of three well-designed areas of study. First, students are expected to complete a core of required courses based on the theme "ways of knowing." A student earns 4 credits in each of the ten core areas. Second, students must develop a strength in one or more disciplines. A minimum of 128 semester hours is required for the baccalaureate degree, including the core plus major hours. Finally, a student must demonstrate the ability to work effectively with others by participation in a work-and-service program. There is a required freshman seminar designed to provide new students the opportunity to explore various fields. A senior seminar, designed as a capstone experience, is required, as is a senior letter to evaluate the student's college experiences. All Warren Wilson students must demonstrate competence in writing and mathematics either through testing or by completing core courses.

FINANCIAL AID

Warren Wilson offers a comprehensive financial aid program that seeks to enroll students from all economic backgrounds. This is accomplished through a combination of work, loans, grants, entitlements, and scholarships to students who complete their file prior to May. Students and their families should file the FAFSA and the Warren Wilson Financial Aid Application to be considered for all possible funds.

WASHINGTON COLLEGE

■ CHESTERTOWN, MARYLAND

THE COLLEGE

Founded in 1782, Washington College is the tenth-oldest college in the United States. George Washington, for whom the College was named, was an early benefactor and member of the College's Board of Visitors and Governors. Today, the College is one of the few nationally recognized selective liberal arts institutions with an enrollment of fewer than 1,100 students. The current enrollment is more than 1,000 men and women. Although most students come from the Northeast, international students and students from other regions of the country are enrolled in numbers sufficient to add geographic diversity to the student body. Eighty percent of all students live in residences located on the 120-acre campus; special interest housing is available for students interested in science, foreign languages, international studies, creative arts, and Greek organizations. The College enjoys a high participation rate in intramural sports, in the performing arts, and in student publications, community service clubs, recreational activities, and social organizations. The Division III intercollegiate program offers fifteen varsity sports, including baseball, basketball, lacrosse, rowing, soccer, swimming, and tennis for men and basketball, field hockey, lacrosse, rowing, softball, swimming, tennis, and volleyball for women.

Further information and application forms are available from:

Office of Admissions
Washington College
300 Washington Avenue
Chestertown, Maryland 21620-1197
Telephone: 410-778-7700
800-422-1782 (toll-free)
E-mail: adm.off@washcoll.edu
Web site: http://www.washcoll.edu

ACADEMIC PROGRAM

General education requirements include two freshman seminars, two sophomore seminars, and eight semester courses chosen from the following categories: social science, natural science, the humanities, and formal studies (mathematics, computer science, music theory, logic, and foreign languages). Candidates for a degree must satisfactorily complete thirty-two semester courses and must fulfill the senior obligation (for example, a comprehensive examination or thesis).

FINANCIAL AID

Awards are based on need and academic performance. Financial aid includes scholarships, grants, loans, and jobs. The College participates in the Federal Perkins Loan Program, the Federal Stafford Student Loan Program, and the Federal Work-Study program. Federal Pell Grants and Federal Supplemental Educational Opportunity Grants are applicable to Washington College. In addition, financial assistance from the Maryland scholarship program and other state programs can be applied to expenses at the College. Members of the National Honor Society and Cum Laude Society who are admitted to Washington College are awarded $40,000 academic scholarships ($10,000 annually for four years). Other academic scholarships ranging in value from $2500 to $10,000 are offered without regard to financial need. To be eligible for financial assistance, applicants should file the FAFSA and the CSS PROFILE by February 15. An application for admission, with all supporting credentials, should be received by February 15 to establish eligibility. Students interested in Federal Pell Grant assistance or in-state scholarship programs must apply directly to the program concerned.

APPLICATION AND INFORMATION

The application, a $35 fee, the high school transcript (and college transcript, for transfer applicants), scores on the SAT I or ACT, and two teacher recommendations are required. Applications for early decision must be received by November 15, and candidates are notified of the admission decision by December 15. For regular admission, forms must be submitted prior to February 15. Regular-decision candidates are notified of the admission decision on a rolling basis between January 15 and April 1. Applicants for financial assistance must complete the procedures outlined under Financial Aid.

WASHINGTON UNIVERSITY IN ST. LOUIS

■ ST. LOUIS, MISSOURI

THE UNIVERSITY

Washington University in St. Louis is a nationally ranked independent, coeducational university renowned for academic excellence. Washington comprises the College of Arts and Sciences and professional Schools of Architecture, Art, Business, Engineering and Applied Science, Law, Medicine, and Social Work. A medium-sized major research university with 5,000 full-time undergraduates (plus 5,000 graduate students), the University offers students the complete academic resources and extracurricular opportunities of a larger university plus the friendliness and support of a small community. Students come to Washington because of high-quality academic programs coupled with flexibility, opportunities, and encouragement for students to discover and develop their potential. Eighty-four percent of graduates enter graduate or professional school within seven years of graduation. The students are also diverse; 22 percent of undergraduates are multicultural, and 7 percent are international.

For additional information, students should contact:

Office of Undergraduate Admissions
Washington University in St. Louis
Campus Box 1089
One Brookings Drive
St. Louis, Missouri 63130-4899

Telephone: 314-935-6000
800-638-0700 (toll-free)
Fax: 314-935-4290
E-mail: admission@wustl.edu
Web site: http://www.wustl.edu/

ACADEMIC PROGRAM

Studying across disciplines and taking advantage of myriad courses offered by the five undergraduate schools is a distinguishing feature of a Washington education. Students may pursue minors, double majors, two undergraduate degrees, and joint undergraduate/graduate degrees. Academic advisers work closely with students on course selection, majors, and research and internship opportunities. Some students who receive a grade of 4 or 5 on AP examinations are often able to enter the University with college credits. Although distribution requirements vary, each academic division requires proficiency in English composition. The University's average undergraduate class size is 18. The College of Arts and Sciences offers three programs of small-group classes available exclusively to first-year students. The undergraduate student–faculty ratio is 7:1. The University observes a two-semester academic year calendar.

FINANCIAL AID

Approximately 60 percent of Washington undergraduates receive some form of financial assistance, 90 percent of which comes from University sources. The remaining 10 percent comprises federal and state aid. A typical need-based aid package consists of scholarships; long-term, low-interest loans; and work-study (federally subsidized on-campus employment). Students applying for financial aid should complete the Financial Aid PROFILE provided by the College Scholarship Service and the Free Application for Federal Student Aid (FAFSA). Both the PROFILE registration form and the FAFSA are available in high school guidance offices. The deadline to apply for need-based aid is February 15. Washington is a leader in creating innovative, flexible payment plans. The University also offers academic scholarships and fellowships to a limited number of outstanding students regardless of need. African-American students may also apply for the John B. Ervin Scholarships for Black Americans. High school seniors may compete for four-year Army ROTC scholarship awards.

APPLICATION AND INFORMATION

Freshman application deadlines are as follows: Early Decision I—November 15 with a December 15 notification; Early Decision II—January 1 with a January 15 notification; and regular decision—January 15 with an April 1 notification. Transfer student application deadlines are April 15 for the following fall semester and November 15 for the following spring semester.

WEBBER COLLEGE

■ BABSON PARK, FLORIDA

THE COLLEGE

Webber College was founded in 1927 by Roger Babson, who was an internationally known economist in the early 1900s. The four-year independent coeducational college is located on a beautiful 110-acre campus along the shoreline of Lake Caloosa, 45 minutes from Disney World, Cypress Gardens, and many other attractions. Webber is accredited by the Southern Association of Colleges and Schools. Built on a strong tradition that sets it apart, the College exemplifies integrity, high standards, and achievement. Webber College provides an environment that encourages success through academic excellence and hard work. About 240 men and 200 women are enrolled as undergraduates at Webber. Fifty-five percent of them are from Florida; the other 45 percent represent eleven states and forty-five different countries.

For application forms, catalogs, and additional information, students should contact:

Director of Admissions
Webber College
1201 Alternate 27 South
P.O. Box 96
Babson Park, Florida 33827-9990
Telephone: 941-638-1431
E-mail: webber@hotmail.com
Web site: http://www.webber.edu

ACADEMIC PROGRAM

The school operates on the semester system with two 15-week semesters, a 6-week Summer Term A, and a 6-week Summer Term B. The College requires the completion of 61 credit hours for the Associate of Science degree and 122 credit hours for the Bachelor of Science degree with a minimum grade point average of 2.0. The average course load is 15 hours per semester. Students in the Bachelor of Science degree program are required to complete 30 hours in the area of concentration, 30 hours in the business core, 41 hours in the general education core, and 21 hours of tailored electives. Students in the Associate of Science degree program are required to complete 21 hours in the business core, 19 hours in the general education core, and 21 hours in the area of concentration and tailored electives. All students must complete the last 30 credit hours at Webber College to receive a degree.

FINANCIAL AID

Aid is awarded on the basis of an applicant's need, academic performance, and promise. To demonstrate need, applicants are required to file the Free Application for Federal Student Aid (FAFSA). Various types of aid, such as scholarships, grants, loans, and Federal Work-Study awards, are used to meet student needs. A limited number of no-need scholarships are available; these awards are based on academic performance, on community and college service, or on athletic ability in basketball, tennis, volleyball, golf, soccer, softball, and cross-country. Applicants for aid must reapply each year. Webber College participates in the Federal Perkins Loan, Federal Supplemental Educational Opportunity Grant, and Federal Work-Study programs. All applicants are expected to apply for any entitlement grant for which they are eligible, such as the Federal Pell Grant; Florida residents must apply for a Florida Student Assistance Grant and the Florida Tuition Voucher Program. Federal Stafford Student Loans are also available. Financial aid applicants should submit their requests and forms before April 1 in order to be eligible for certain financial aid programs.

APPLICATION AND INFORMATION

An application is ready for consideration by the Admissions Committee when it has been received with a $35 application fee, the required test scores and references, and transcripts from each school attended. The College uses a system of rolling admissions. It is recommended that applications be submitted as early as possible, since on-campus housing is limited. (Freshmen are required to live in the dormitory unless they reside with a parent, guardian, or spouse.)

WELLS COLLEGE

■ AURORA, NEW YORK

THE COLLEGE

For more information about Wells College or to schedule a campus visit, students should contact:

Admissions Office
Wells College
Aurora, New York 13026
Telephone: 800-952-9355 (toll-free)
E-mail: admissions@wells.edu

Wells College, founded in 1868, is proud to be the second institution in the country to award the baccalaureate degree to women. Its founder, Henry Wells, who built his fortune with the creation of the Wells Fargo Express, believed that women would play a vital role in the future of America. What truly distinguishes Wells from other colleges and universities is that it dares to be small. With an enrollment of 316 students, Wells students do not sit quietly among rows of neatly lined desks; instead, they join their classmates and professors around seminar tables where they are expected to contribute their ideas. Wells faculty members are graduates of many of the country's top universities, and 97 percent hold a Ph.D. or equivalent degree. They are widely published and respected in their fields, but teaching is their first priority. Academic opportunities include independent and interdisciplinary study, internships, and study-abroad programs. In addition, a campus newspaper, several musical and drama groups, a literary magazine and book arts center, environmental and political organizations, and other organizations provide important opportunities for student involvement. A full program of cultural events, symposia, and lectures enhances the academic and social life of the College.

ACADEMIC PROGRAM

The academic philosophy at Wells is firmly rooted in the liberal arts. The College is organized into four academic divisions: the humanities, natural and mathematical sciences, social sciences, and the arts, but faculty members in all divisions work together to produce a curriculum that recognizes connections between subject areas and fits many pieces together, just as they fit together in life. Students at Wells take one course in common during their first and second years. The purpose of the core curriculum is to give every student a shared academic experience. The first-year course, 21st Century Issues, addresses issues that will become increasingly important in the future. Readings and discussions bring these issues into focus through many different lenses: cultural, historical, psychological, sociological, artistic, and scientific. Students become familiar with academic and campus resources through writing assignments and become active participants in College life through required attendance at plays, concerts, and other campus events. Wells students are traditionally required to complete a thesis or project during the senior year. While the core curriculum provides a shared academic experience for students, the senior thesis provides a student with the opportunity to complete a thoughtful, in-depth analysis of a topic of the student's choosing.

FINANCIAL AID

Approximately 80 percent of Wells students receive financial aid packaged in the form of grants, scholarships, and loans.

APPLICATION AND INFORMATION

Applications should be received early in the senior year of high school and not later than February 15 of the year in which entrance is desired. Applications from early decision and early action candidates must be received by December 15. Transfer applications are reviewed on a rolling basis. Transfer students are eligible for merit scholarships and financial aid. A campus visit is highly recommended for prospective students. Typically, the visit includes a guided tour of the Wells College campus and facilities, overnight accommodations in the residence halls, a personal interview, and the option of attending classes. Appointments with faculty and financial aid representatives are also available.

WENTWORTH INSTITUTE OF TECHNOLOGY

■ BOSTON, MASSACHUSETTS

THE INSTITUTE

Wentworth Institute of Technology was founded in 1904 to provide education in the mechanical arts. Today, it is one of the nation's leading technical institutes, offering study in a variety of disciplines. Wentworth has a current undergraduate day enrollment of 2,490 men and women and graduates more engineering technicians and technologists each year than any other college in the United States. The technical education acquired at Wentworth enables graduates to assume creative and responsible careers in business and industry. Wentworth is located on a 35-acre campus on Huntington Avenue in Boston.

An application form, an application fee of $30, transcripts from the secondary school and any colleges previously attended, and SAT I scores should be sent to:

Admissions Office
Wentworth Institute of Technology
550 Huntington Avenue
Boston, Massachusetts 02115
Telephone: 617-989-4000
800-556-0610 (toll-free)
Fax: 617-989-4010
E-mail: admissions@wit.edu
Web site: http://www.wit.edu

ACADEMIC PROGRAM

At Wentworth Institute of Technology, college-level study in technological fundamentals and principles is combined with appropriate laboratory, field, and studio experience. Students apply theory to practical problems, and they acquire skills and techniques by using, operating, and controlling equipment and instruments particular to their area of specialization. In addition, study in the social sciences and humanities provides a balanced understanding of the world in which graduates work. Wentworth's programs of study are more practical than theoretical in approach, and the Institute's academic requirements demand extensive time and effort. While nearly all majors allow continuous study from the freshman through the senior year, the architecture major requires a petition for readmission to the baccalaureate program during the sophomore year. All bachelor's degree programs are conducted as cooperative (co-op) education programs: upon entering their third year, students alternate semesters of academic study at Wentworth with semester-long periods of employment in industry. Two semesters of co-op employment are required; one additional (summer) semester of co-op is optional. Both students and the companies that hire them are enthusiastic about the co-op program and agree that it is a mutually valuable experience.

FINANCIAL AID

Scholarships are available to students who demonstrate need and academic promise. Merit scholarships are also available. Wentworth also provides federal and state financial assistance, such as Federal Pell and Federal Supplemental Educational Opportunity Grants, Federal Perkins Loans, Federal Work-Study awards, Gilbert Matching Grants, and Massachusetts No-Interest Loans to students with financial need in accordance with federal and state guidelines. Wentworth participates in the Federal Direct Lending program. As a result, students are eligible to borrow under the Federal Direct Stafford Loan program and parents may borrow under the Federal Direct PLUS program. Individuals participating in these programs borrow money directly from the federal government rather than through lending institutions. In addition to these need-based programs, Wentworth also participates in the MassPlan loan program sponsored by the Massachusetts Educational Financing Authority. Wentworth offers several payment options through payment plans and alternative loan financing. To apply for financial aid, new students should complete the Free Application for Federal Student Aid (FAFSA) by March 1. Applications received after this date will be considered as funds allow.

APPLICATION AND INFORMATION

Students are admitted to Wentworth for September and January enrollment. The priority application deadline for the fall semester is May 1; for the spring, the deadline is December 1. Notification of admission is made on a rolling basis.

WEST CHESTER UNIVERSITY

■ WEST CHESTER, PENNSYLVANIA

THE UNIVERSITY

West Chester University is the second largest of the fourteen institutions in the Pennsylvania State System of Higher Education and the third-largest university in the Philadelphia metropolitan area. Officially founded in 1871, the University traces its heritage to the West Chester Academy, which existed from 1812 to 1869. The University's 388-acre campus has well-maintained facilities, including eight modern residence halls and garden-style apartments. In keeping with West Chester's rich heritage, the University's Quadrangle buildings, part of the original campus, are on the National Register of Historic Places. While the University attracts the majority of its students from Pennsylvania, New Jersey, and Delaware, it also enrolls many students from other areas across the United States and from more than fifty countries. The undergraduate enrollment is 7,930 men and women full-time and 1,602 part-time. Each year, the University community schedules an impressive series of events, including programs with well-known musicians, authors, political figures, and others. Numerous campus groups in music, theater, athletics, and other activities, as well as clubs, fraternities, sororities, service organizations, and honor societies, provide students with the opportunity to participate in a full range of programs. The University offers twenty-three intercollegiate sports and thirteen club sports for men and women. In addition to the facilities in the health and physical education complex, the University has a field house and a gymnasium for varsity sports.

Additional information and required forms are available from:

Office of Admissions
Emil H. Messikomer Hall
West Chester University of Pennsylvania
100 West Rosedale Avenue
West Chester, Pennsylvania 19383
Telephone: 610-436-3411
E-mail: ugadmiss@wcupa.edu
Web site: http://www.wcupa.edu

ACADEMIC PROGRAM

West Chester University is a comprehensive, multipurpose institution now in its second century. The University comprises the College of Arts and Sciences, the School of Business and Public Affairs, the School of Education, the School of Health Sciences, and the School of Music. It operates on a two-semester basis; summer sessions are available. An honors program is available to qualified students for both upper and lower division study; internships and field experiences, self-designed majors, and independent study are also offered. A variety of credit-by-examination programs are available.

FINANCIAL AID

The financial aid available to students includes work-study programs, grants, loans, special awards, and scholarships. A limited number of Merit Scholarships are awarded based on the student's academic standing and accomplishments in high school. Students who qualify will be invited to apply. About 72 percent of all full-time undergraduate students receive some form of aid.

APPLICATION AND INFORMATION

Students are admitted for the fall or spring semester. Applicants for the fall semester are urged to begin the application procedure at the start of their senior year of secondary school. Applicants for the spring semester should apply by December 1. International students are encouraged to apply by May 1 for the fall semester and August 1 for the spring semester. The University operates on a modified rolling admission policy; applicants with the best qualifications are given priority, and their applications are processed expeditiously. Students are encouraged to visit WCU's campus. To arrange a visit or to attend an information session, students may call the Office of Admissions; for updated information or directions, they may check the University's World Wide Web site.

WESTERN ILLINOIS UNIVERSITY

■ MACOMB, ILLINOIS

THE UNIVERSITY

The campus of Western Illinois University (WIU) extends over 1,050 acres and includes fifty-three buildings. The residence halls on campus provide for a variety of lifestyles and house 4,800 of the approximately 12,100 students at the University. Single and double rooms, study floors, nonsmoking rooms, and academic major areas are just a few examples of residence options. The University Union is the center of campus activities and includes restaurants, a bookstore, bowling alleys, an ice-cream parlor, meeting rooms, an area for billiards, and lounge areas. More than 250 student organizations offer a variety of cocurricular activities to supplement formal classroom education. Cultural programs reflecting both local and national interests are on the calendar several evenings each week.

Application forms and admission materials may be secured by contacting:

Admissions Office
Sherman Hall 115
Western Illinois University
1 University Circle
Macomb, Illinois 61455-1390
Telephone: 309-298-3157

ACADEMIC PROGRAM

It is the philosophy of the University that a broad general education should be an integral part of every degree program. Thus, approximately one third of the degree requirements involve study and the development of fundamental skills in the arts and sciences. The remainder of the program is devoted to either a comprehensive major or a major/minor plus general electives. Credit is awarded for acceptable scores on CLEP general and subject examinations and on the College Board's Advanced Placement examinations in English, foreign languages, history, and mathematics. Proficiency examinations are administered on campus through specific departments. Special educational opportunities for students with high aptitude and superior ability are offered in all colleges at WIU through the honors program. Western offers a four-year and a two-year program in the study of military science through Army ROTC. Successful completion of the program and requirements for the baccalaureate degree leads to a commission as a second lieutenant in the Army.

FINANCIAL AID

During the 1996–97 academic year, approximately 8,700 WIU undergraduate students received financial aid from funds totaling $48.8 million. Prospective students are urged to apply for the Federal Pell Grant and, if they are Illinois residents, the Illinois Student Assistance Commission Grant. Western also participates in the Federal Perkins Loan, Federal Work-Study, and Federal Supplemental Educational Opportunity Grant programs. Loans and grants are made and work-study jobs are assigned on the basis of calculated financial need, which is determined by the Free Application for Federal Student Aid (FAFSA). The information on the FAFSA must reflect the current income of the applicant's parents, as reported to the Internal Revenue Service. The statement should therefore not be completed until after January 1 of the applicant's senior year in high school. Many student jobs are available in such areas as secretarial work, food service, and building and grounds maintenance. WIU awards talent grants and academic scholarships. Talent grants are offered in men's and women's athletics, music, art, theater, and debate. Students who rank in the upper 15 percent of their class and have an ACT composite score of at least 28 are eligible to apply for an academic scholarship, which does not require proof of need. Applications for financial aid may be obtained from the Financial Aid Office after December 1 of the student's senior year in high school.

WESTERN MARYLAND COLLEGE

■ Westminster, Maryland

THE COLLEGE

Western Maryland College (WMC) provides an ideal location for learning that brings together students from twenty-three states and nineteen countries. Its picturesque campus is situated on a hilltop in historic Westminster, just a short drive from two of the nation's major metropolitan centers, Baltimore and Washington, D.C. Western Maryland was one of the first coeducational colleges in the nation and has been both innovative and independent since its founding in 1867. The tradition of liberal arts studies rests comfortably at Western Maryland, which has exemplary teaching, both at the undergraduate and graduate levels, as its central mission. Faculty members are engaged in research and professional writing, are involved at the highest levels of their respective professions, and are sought after as consultants in many spheres, but their primary mission is teaching. The enrollment of 1,500 undergraduates enables WMC to care about students in a personal way, to provide individual guidance, and to be responsive to the needs of students. Graduates leave Western Maryland enriched not just because of their classwork, but also because of their meaningful interactions with one another. A flexible liberal arts curriculum stresses the ability to think critically and creatively, to act humanely and responsibly, and to be expressive. WMC is fully accredited by the Middle States Association of Colleges and Secondary Schools and is listed as one of the selective national liberal arts colleges by the Carnegie Foundation for the Advancement of Teaching.

Complete applications, along with a $30 nonrefundable application fee, should be sent to:

M. Martha O'Connell, Dean of Admissions
Western Maryland College
2 College Hill
Westminster, Maryland 21157-4390
Telephone: 410-857-2230
800-638-5005 (Voice/TDD) (toll-free)
E-mail: admissio@wmdc.edu
World Wide Web: http://www.wmdc.edu

ACADEMIC PROGRAM

WMC's flexible curriculum enables students to acquire a broad base of knowledge in the areas of humanities, natural sciences and mathematics, and social sciences and to pursue in-depth learning in one or more of the sixty fields of study. The program links wide-ranging educational experiences with strong career through an extensive internship program. A total of 128 credit hours is required for graduation. First-year–student seminars provide students with a unique opportunity to become better prepared for many facets of college life. Limited to 15 students, these courses on a variety of topics emphasize important skills—writing, oral presentation, study skills, critical thinking, and time management.

FINANCIAL AID

WMC supports a program of financial aid to eligible students on the basis of both need and merit. Nearly 80 percent of WMC students receive financial assistance. Students who have been accepted by the College and can demonstrate financial need as required by the federal government may be eligible for assistance in the form of scholarships, grants, loans, and opportunities for student employment. Typically an award is a package of these four resources, tailored to the student's needs. Academic scholarships covering partial to full tuition are available for qualified students based on their academic record, SAT I or ACT scores, and extracurricular involvement. First-year students should apply by February 1; transfer scholarships are competitive, and preference is given to students who apply before March 15. The College also offers partial and full ROTC scholarships.

APPLICATION AND INFORMATION

Deadlines for receiving completed applications are December 1 for early action, February 1 for academic scholarship consideration, and March 15 for regular admission. Applications from transfer students are accepted through the summer.

WESTERN MICHIGAN UNIVERSITY

■ KALAMAZOO, MICHIGAN

THE UNIVERSITY

Western Michigan University is one of the nation's leading midsized universities, making a difference in the world through a commitment to academic excellence and public service. WMU is counted among Michigan's top four universities in both size and the complexity and variety of its offerings. Yet WMU ranks seventh among the state's fifteen public universities in tuition and requried fees and is listed in *America's 100 Best College Buys.* Its student-faculty ratio is a comfortable 16:1. With 26,132 students, WMU is the fourth-largest university in Michigan and among the nation's sixty largest universities. About 6,300 students live in twenty-two residence halls that provide a variety of living arrangements. Founded in 1903, WMU has six degree-granting colleges—Arts and Sciences, the Haworth College of Business, Education, Engineering and Applied Sciences, Fine Arts, and Health and Human Services—as well as the Graduate College and Lee Honors College. Major factors in WMU's success include promotion of out-of-class learning and creation of cutting-edge instructional facilities. The University has 400 registered student organizations that enhance the out-of-class experience of its students, including a wide range of Greek-letter, academic, honorary, and professional organizations. Cultural events at Miller Auditorium, acclaimed arts programs, and NCAA Division I-A Mid-American Conference and Central Collegiate Hockey Association sports teams add variety and vitality to campus life.

For an application or additional information, students should contact:

Office of Admissions and Orientation
Western Michigan University
1201 Oliver Street
Kalamazoo, Michigan 49008–5720
Telephone: 616-387–2000
800-400-4WMU (toll-free)
Web site: http://www.wmich.edu

ACADEMIC PROGRAM

WMU offers undergraduate students a rich blend of academic majors and minors, as well as its new general education program. This new program assures that students graduate with proficiencies and perspectives they need to succeed in the next century. Last fall, 1,800 students enrolled in the University Curriculum Program, which won a national award for outstanding academic advising.

FINANCIAL AID

Last year, more than 18,000 students received financial assistance totaling more than $90 million. There are three basic types of financial aid: merit-based programs, need-based programs, and student employment. Merit-based programs include the Medallion Scholarship Program, the University's most honored scholarships for entering freshmen. Awards range from $4800 to $25,000 over four years. Other scholarships and awards include the $16,000 Higher Education Incentive Scholarships (HEIS), the Army ROTC awards, the Award for National Merit Scholarships, and many other sponsored and departmental scholarships for new and currently enrolled students. Merit-based scholarships also are available to community college transfer students, ranging in value from $500 to $6000. Need-based loans, grants, college work-study, and other aid options are provided for students who demonstrate particular financial need. To be considered, students should complete the Free Application for Federal Student Aid. The student employment option reflects research indicating that students who work part-time are more likely to graduate than students who do not work at all. About 40 percent of WMU's students work while in school, and more than 2,000 jobs are offered through the college work-study program. WMU provides a tuition payment plan through Academic Management Services (AMS) and Tuition Management Systems. This allows parents and students to pay college costs in monthly installments. No interest is charged for these services, which may be renewed annually for $45. Students should contact AMS at 800-556-6684 or Tuition Management Systems at 800-722-4867 for more information.

WESTERN NEW ENGLAND COLLEGE

■ SPRINGFIELD, MASSACHUSETTS

THE COLLEGE

For complete admission information, students should contact:

Admissions Office
Western New England College
1215 Wilbraham Road
Springfield, Massachusetts 01119

Telephone: 413-782-1321
800-325-1122 Ext. 1321 (toll-free)
Fax: 413-782-1777
E-mail: ugradmis@wnec.edu
Web site: http://www.wnec.edu

The history of Western New England College dates from 1919; in that year, Northeastern University established a Springfield Division, which in 1951 became known as Western New England College. From its inception, Western New England has sought to provide students with a strong professional and liberal arts education. The College offers thirty undergraduate majors in the Schools of Arts and Sciences, Business, and Engineering. Western New England College offers two unique programs combining undergraduate and graduate courses, as well as seven graduate degrees. A Juris Doctor program is also available. The College also assists many part-time students with an Office of Continuing Education. Students who enroll at Western New England seek a solid liberal education with the goal of entering a profession or graduate school upon completion of their studies at the College. The average age of undergraduate students is 22 years, and 58 percent of the undergraduates are men. There are about 1,850 full-time undergraduates at Western New England, and the total College enrollment is approximately 4,500. Currently, 51 percent of the students come from out of state; 1 percent are from other countries; and approximately 65 percent of students live on campus. The Campus Activities Board has specific responsibility for lecture programs, concerts, the performing arts, and traditional events such as Homecoming, Family Weekend, and Spring Week. There are athletic programs at the varsity and intramural levels. Varsity sports are played at the NCAA Division III level. Men's sports include baseball, basketball, bowling, football, golf, ice hockey, lacrosse, soccer, swimming, tennis, volleyball, and wrestling. Women's sports include basketball, bowling, field hockey, lacrosse, soccer, softball, swimming, and volleyball. Students live in residence halls varying in type from the traditional to a suite-style arrangement. Students may also reside in garden-style apartments located on campus.

ACADEMIC PROGRAM

Five courses are usually taken each semester. Specific departmental degree requirements are stated in the College Catalogue. Western New England College participates in the College Board's Advanced Placement (AP) Program and College-Level Examination Program (CLEP). Successful completion of these programs may result in the earning of academic credit and the waiving of certain courses. The College operates on a two-semester calendar.

FINANCIAL AID

Western New England College offers an extensive financial assistance program in the form of scholarships, loans, grants, and on-campus employment. Applicants for financial aid must submit the Free Application for Federal Student Aid (FAFSA), the Western New England College application for financial aid, and a copy of the federal income tax form 1040. In 1997–98, approximately 81 percent of the students at WNEC received financial assistance; the average award was $10,348.

APPLICATION AND INFORMATION

The College follows a rolling admission policy; there is no specific deadline for application. However, students are encouraged to apply early in order to receive complete consideration for admission, financial aid, and housing. In addition to the application form, the following must be sent: SAT I or ACT scores, a recommendation from the student's counselor or teacher, and an official secondary school transcript. Transfer applicants should include official transcripts of any college work. Notification of acceptance begins in late fall.

WESTMINSTER COLLEGE

■ NEW WILMINGTON, PENNSYLVANIA

THE COLLEGE

For application forms and further information, students should contact:

Dean of Admissions
Westminster College
New Wilmington, Pennsylvania 16172
Telephone: 800-942-8033 (toll-free)
E-mail: admis@westminster.edu

Westminster College, an independent, coeducational liberal arts college related to the Presbyterian Church (U.S.A.), was founded in 1852. Westminster's liberal arts foundation thrives in a caring environment supported by an integrative curriculum featuring state-of-the-art technology and opportunities for involvement to prepare students for a diverse world. Westminster College is annually recognized among the nation's best liberal arts colleges by *U.S. News & World Report* and as one of the nation's best college buys by *Money*. Nearly 1,500 students benefit from individualized attention from dedicated faculty members while choosing from forty majors and nearly 100 campus organizations on the New Wilmington, Pennsylvania, campus. The College provides many programs to augment the academic and social life of the academic community, including lectures, dramatic productions, art exhibitions, concerts, symposia, dances, films, and other activities. Students may choose to participate in a wide variety of groups and activities, such as dramatics, publications, volunteer and social service teams, athletics, religious groups, musical groups, radio and television stations, fraternities and sororities, honoraries, and special interest groups. A full range of intercollegiate and intramural sports for men and women gives each student the opportunity to participate at the level of his or her interest and ability. Westminster students compete in sixteen varsity sports as Division II members of the NCAA.

ACADEMIC PROGRAM

The liberal arts degree offered by Westminster College reflects the diversity and depth of the classical education and the practicality of its application. Good writing and speaking skills are emphasized, and science and philosophy become a part of life at Westminster. Course requirements for graduation vary according to the major fields, but all-College requirements include courses in writing, communication, religion, computer science, foreign language, and physical education as well as courses from categories covering the humanities, fine arts, social sciences, natural sciences, and literature. Double majors, minors, and individual interdisciplinary programs are possible. Every four years since 1936, in conjunction with the Presidential election year, Westminster has held a Mock National Political Convention (for the party out of office) in which more than three fourths of the students have participated, naming their own "candidate."

FINANCIAL AID

About 80 percent of Westminster's students receive some sort of financial aid. Scholarships, Federal Stafford Student Loans, grants, and campus employment are offered to students who have financial need. The student's eligibility for financial aid is determined by the Free Application for Federal Student Aid form. Also, non-need scholarships of up to 50 percent of tuition are awarded to students of high academic ability; these are renewable each year if the student maintains good academic standing. Activity grants in music, theater, and sports are also available. Information is available through the dean of admissions or director of financial aid.

APPLICATION AND INFORMATION

A completed application with the $20 application fee may be submitted anytime after the student's junior year in secondary school. The student should also see that the required SAT I or ACT scores and a high school transcript are sent to the College. The transcript should include grades from the ninth grade through the eleventh grade.

WILLIAM PATERSON UNIVERSITY OF NEW JERSEY

■ **Wayne, New Jersey**

For additional information and application forms for admission or scholarships, students should contact:

Office of Admissions
William Paterson University of New Jersey
Wayne, New Jersey 07470
Telephone: 973-720-2125
888-4WILPAT (toll-free)

THE UNIVERSITY

Since its founding in 1855, William Paterson University has grown into a comprehensive state institution whose programs reflect the area's need for challenging, affordable educational options. Ideally midsized (the total enrollment is 9,207, of whom 7,729 are degree-seeking undergraduates), William Paterson offers a wider variety of academic programs than smaller universities, yet provides students with a more personalized atmosphere than larger institutions. Once the site of the family estate of Garret Hobart, the twenty-fourth vice president of the United States, William Paterson's spacious campus, which has wooded areas and waterfalls, offers an environment in which students may develop both intellectually and socially. Although the majority of the University's students come from the New Jersey and New York vicinity, some international and out-of-state students enroll each year. Twenty-four percent of the undergraduates reside on campus in residence halls or apartment-style facilities, which accommodate 1,987 students. In general, on-campus housing is offered on a first-come, first-served basis.

ACADEMIC PROGRAM

Students must complete a minimum of 128 credits to earn a baccalaureate degree. Degree programs include a 60-credit general education requirement, 30–60 credits in a major, and 20–40 in elective courses. (In specialized degree programs, such as the B.F.A. and the B.M., general education and major course requirements may differ.) Students uncertain of which career path to follow may take advantage of advisement and counseling programs. In addition, the general education requirements enable students to take up to 60 credits before declaring a major, so that they can acquire a basic understanding of all major fields of knowledge before having to choose a specific area. Diagnostic testing and career seminars, provided by the Career Development Office, also ensure that students receive the guidance necessary to make wise course selections and career decisions.

FINANCIAL AID

Financial aid is available through a number of federal and state grant, loan, scholarship, and work-study programs. To apply for need-based aid, students must file the Free Application for Federal Student Aid (FAFSA) with the United States Department of Education by the priority date of April 1. In addition, both the University and the Alumni Association award a number of competitive scholarships, based solely on academic merit, to entering freshmen. They are the Scholarships for Academic Excellence, scholarships for African-American and Hispanic students, and Trustee and Presidential Scholarships. Academic Achievement Scholarships are awarded only on a competitive basis to continuing students.

APPLICATION AND INFORMATION

Application forms and transcripts from candidates for freshman status must be received by May 1 for fall admission and November 1 for spring admission. Transfer students, readmitted students, and students seeking a second bachelor's degree must submit their materials by May 1 and November 1 for fall and spring entry, respectively. However, the University closes the application process earlier when the number of new and continuing students strains its ability to provide effective programs and services. A $35 application fee is required. Applications are reviewed on a rolling basis. Campus tours are available during the fall and spring semesters on Friday afternoon at 1:30 p.m. when classes are in session.

WOODBURY UNIVERSITY

■ BURBANK, CALIFORNIA

Office of Admission
Woodbury University
7500 Glenoaks Boulevard
Burbank, California 91510-7846
Telephone: 818-767-0888, ext. 221
800-784-WOOD (toll-free)
E-mail: admissions@vaxb.woodbury.edu
Web site: http://www.woodburyu.edu

THE UNIVERSITY

Woodbury University offers students practical, applied education; high academic standards; and small classes. The University is an accredited, independent, nonprofit, coeducational, nonsectarian institution. Students attend Woodbury because of its specialization in the areas of architecture, business, computers, professional design, and arts and sciences. Also offered is a Master of Business Administration program. The carefully designed curricula at Woodbury give students hands-on experience in their majors in addition to an effective general education. Woodbury maintains small classes to ensure individual student attention. The University presents a variety of opportunities for all students to join cultural, social, and professional organizations, both on and off campus. The Office of Student Services at Woodbury helps meet students' needs through career planning and job placement workshops; educational, cultural, social, and recreational programs; the sponsorship of various student groups; and special services for international students. The career services office provides Woodbury students and alumni with lifetime employment assistance. Woodbury's 22-acre campus in Burbank provides students with such on-campus amenities as a swimming pool, gymnasium, residence halls, an athletic field, and food services, all situated on beautifully landscaped grounds. Founded in 1884, Woodbury's primary mission is to provide programs requisite for success and leadership and to encourage each person's creativity. The University is accredited by the Senior Commission of the Western Association of Schools and Colleges and is approved by the Postsecondary Commission, California Department of Education. The Interior Design Program is accredited by the Foundation for Interior Design Education Research. The Architecture Program is accredited by the National Architectural Accrediting Board.

ACADEMIC PROGRAM

The academic programs at Woodbury are designed to provide students with the higher education necessary for success and leadership in their chosen fields. The principal emphasis is on relevance of subject matter and personalized instruction, complemented by a strong focus on general education. The academic calendar is based on the semester system. The number of elective units varies depending on the major. To encourage the achievement of academic excellence, Woodbury University recognizes students who demonstrate the initiative and sense of responsibility to excel. Such superior performance is recognized with special awards.

FINANCIAL AID

Assisting students who lack adequate financial resources to attend Woodbury is a primary concern of the University. Various sources of financial aid are available to help meet education costs. Eligible students generally are awarded a financial aid package consisting of a combination of available funds. Financial aid for eligible U.S. citizens and permanent residents includes Federal Pell Grants, California Grants A and B for California residents, Federal Family Educational Loans, veterans' educational benefits, Federal Supplemental Educational Opportunity Grants, Federal Work-Study awards, Federal Perkins Loans, local scholarships, and Woodbury grants. The University offers financial aid and counseling, as well as part-time employment and full-time placement services. Classes are scheduled to permit students to work part-time, usually in the area of their major interest, so that they may not only meet financial needs but also gain excellent experience.

APPLICATION AND INFORMATION

Applications are accepted throughout the year for entrance in the fall, spring, and summer terms. Freshman applicants are encouraged to apply before the priority date, March 1. The priority application deadline for transfer students is April 15. Students should direct all materials and inquiries to the Office of Admission at the address above.

INDEX

of Colleges and Universities

The index lists the colleges and universities in this almanac alphabetically. Page numbers refer to each college's profile; page numbers in **bold-faced** text refer to full-page descriptions.

NOTES